Get a Better Grade!

In MyOBLab you are treated as an individual with specific learning needs.

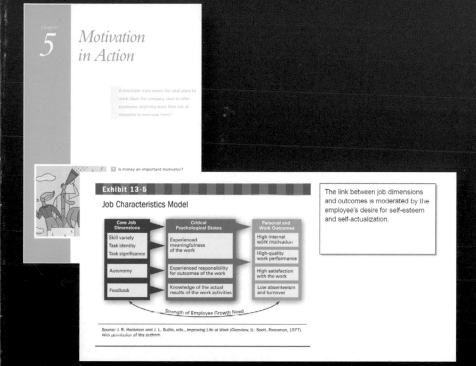

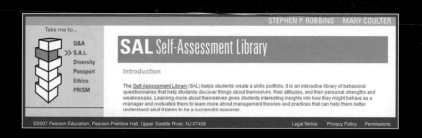

eBook+

Access the eText while you study—witho leaving the online environment! You can highlight passages and make notes right the eText page to help you study.

Annotated Exhibits and Table from the Text

Detailed explanations—in addition to what's in the text—help you understan the concepts.

Robbins Self-Assessment Lib

The Self-Assessment Library is an inte library of 51 behavioural questionnair will help you discover yourself and giv insight into how you might behave as a manager.

Talking OB

Linda Donville and Emily Donville Centennial College developed Talki for students who need help understa the special terminology of Organiza Behaviour. This online primer consi five parts corresponding to the parts textbook. Each part of the primer c interactive grammar and concept ac with audio reinforcements, enabling to understand the learning arc for e part in the textbook and reinforcin understanding of the topics and ter under discussion.

Personalized Learning!

Content and tools to enrich your learning experience and foster interest and mastery of the subject.

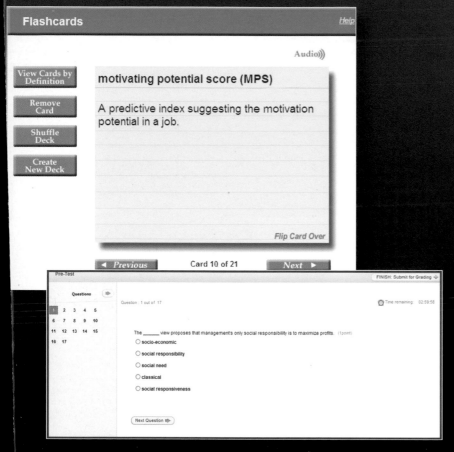

Glossary Flashcards

Use these quick and fun flashcards to study the text's key terms.

Auto-graded Tests and Assignments

MyOBLab comes with two preloaded Sample Tests per chapter (the Pre-Test and the Post-Test). Work through these diagnostic tests to identify areas you haven't fully understood. The Sample Tests generate a personalized Study Plan designed specifically to suit your studying needs. Instructors can assign these Sample Tests or create assignments, quizzes, and tests using a mix of publisher-supplied content and their own custom exercises.

Personalized Study Plan

Because you have limited study time, it's important for you to be as effective as possible during that time. A personalized Study Plan is generated from your results on Sample Tests and instructor assignments. You can clearly see which topics you have mastered and, more importantly, which ones you still need to work on.

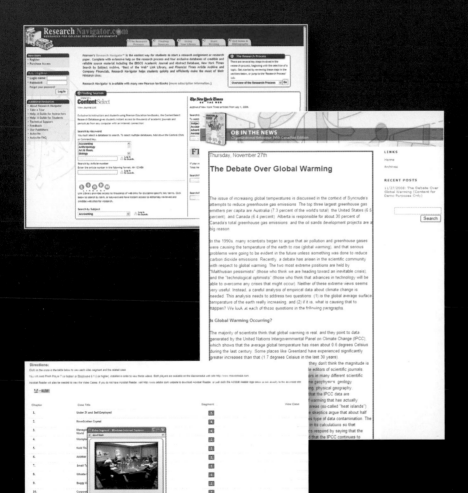

PEARSON myOBlab™

Save Time.

Improve Results.

myOBlab™

| HOME | LEARN ABOUT | TOURS & TRAINING | SUPPORT |

Returning Users

Already registered?

MyOBLab ▶

Need help?

Register or Buy Access

New user? Start here!

Students ▶

Instructors ▶

Need help?

Welcome to MyOBLab. With the help of MyOBLab, you can save time and improve results.

MyOBLab is a state-of-the-art interactive online solution that provides a rich and flexible set of course materials for your Organizational Behaviour courses. MyOBLab can be used to supplement a traditional lecture course, completely administer an online course, or to serve as a study tool. MyOBLab offers many ways to cover textbook material by combining multimedia tutorials, animations, tests, quizzes, and an eText to make learning fun. Learn more!

PEARSON Pearson product. Copyright © 2009 Pearson Education Canada, a division of Pearson Canada Inc.

Terms of Use | Privacy Statement | Permissions | Feedback

Done

MyOBLab includes the following resources:

- Auto-graded Tests and Assignments
- Personalized Study Plan
- Annotated text figures
- Student PowerPoint® Slides
- Glossary Flashcards
- OB in the News
- Links to business news sources
- Multimedia eText (Flash-based)
- Robbins Self-Assessment Library
- Video links
- Research Navigator

MyOBLab is an online learning system for organizational behaviour courses. This fun and easy-to-navigate site enhances *Organizational Behaviour: Concepts, Controversies, Applications*, Fifth Canadian Edition, with a variety of learning resources.

To take advantage of all that MyOBLab has to offer, you will need an access code. If you do not already have an access code, you can buy one online at **www.pearsoned.ca/myoblab**.

PEARSON

ORGANIZATIONAL

CONCEPTS, CONTROVERSIES, APPLICATIONS

BEHAVIOUR

FIFTH CANADIAN EDITION

NANCY LANGTON
University of British Columbia

STEPHEN P. ROBBINS
San Diego State University

TIMOTHY A. JUDGE
University of Florida

Pearson Canada
Toronto

Library and Archives Canada Cataloguing in Publication

Langton, Nancy
    Organizational behaviour: concepts, controversies, applications / Nancy Langton, Stephen P. Robbins, Timothy A. Judge.—5th Canadian ed.

First and 2nd Canadian eds. by Stephen P. Robbins. 3rd Canadian ed. by Stephen P. Robbins and Nancy Langton. 4th ed. by Nancy Langton and Stephen P. Robbins.

Includes bibliographical references and index.
ISBN 978-0-13-503348-7

1. Organizational behavior—Textbooks. 2. Management—Textbooks. I. Robbins, Stephen P., 1943– II. Judge, Tim III. Robbins, Stephen P., 1943–. Organizational behaviour. IV. Title.
HD58.7.L35 2010   658   C2008-908127-7

ISBN-13: 978-0-13-503348-7
ISBN-10: 0-13-503348-9

Vice President, Editorial Director: Gary Bennett
Editor-in-Chief: Ky Pruesse
Acquisitions Editor: Karen Elliott
Executive Marketing Manager: Cas Shields
Developmental Editor: Su Mei Ku
Production Editors: Laura Neves, Richard di Santo
Copy Editor: Claudia Forgas
Proofreader: Sheila Wawanash
Production Coordinators: Patricia Ciardullo, Peggy Brown
Composition: Debbie Kumpf
Photo and Permissions Research: Lisa Brant
Art Director: Julia Hall
Cover and Interior Design: Anthony Leung
Cover Image: GettyImages

3 4 5   13 12 11 10

Printed and bound in the United States of America.

Brief Contents

Contents

PART 3
INTERACTING EFFECTIVELY 264

CHAPTER 12 Decision Making, Creativity, and Ethics. . . 450

OB AT WORK

PART 5
REORGANIZING THE WORKPLACE 500

Preface

Welcome to the fifth Canadian edition of *Organizational Behaviour*. Since its arrival in Canada, *Organizational Behaviour* has enjoyed widespread acclaim across the country for its rich Canadian content and has quickly established itself as the leading textbook in the field.

Organizational Behaviour, Fifth Canadian Edition, is truly a Canadian product. While it draws upon the strongest aspects of its American cousin, it expresses its own vision and voice. It provides the context for understanding organizational behaviour (OB) in the Canadian workplace and highlights the many Canadian contributions to the field. Indeed, it goes a step further than most OB textbooks prepared for the Canadian marketplace.

Specifically, it asks, in many instances:

- How does this theory apply in the Canadian workplace of today?

- What are the implications of the theory for managers and employees working in the twenty-first century?

- What are the implications of the theory for everyday life? OB, after all, is not something that applies only in the workplace.

This textbook is sensitive to important Canadian issues. Subject matter reflects the broad multicultural flavour of Canada, and also highlights the roles of women and visible minorities. Examples reflect the broad range of organizations in Canada: large, small, public and private sector, unionized and non-unionized.

Organizational Behaviour continues to be a vibrant and relevant text because it is a product of the Canadian classroom. It is used in Canada by the first author and her colleagues. Thus, there is a "frontline" approach to considering revisions. We also solicit considerable feedback from OB instructors and students throughout the country. While we have kept the features of the previous edition that adopters continue to say they like, there is also a great deal that is new.

Our Pedagogical Approach in Writing the Textbook

- *Relevance.* The text reminds both teacher and student alike that we have entered the twenty-first century and must contend with a new paradigm of work that may be considerably different from the past. The new paradigm is more globally focused and competitive, relies more heavily on part-time and contract jobs, and places a higher premium on entrepreneurial acumen, either within the traditional workplace structure, as an individual seeking out an alternative job, or as the creator of your own new business.

    When the first Canadian edition appeared, it was the first text to emphasize that OB is for everyone, from the bottom-rung employee to the CEO, as well as to anyone who has to interact with others to accomplish a task. We continue to emphasize this theme. We remind readers of the material's relevance beyond a "9-to-5" job by concluding each chapter with a summary that outlines the implications not only for the workplace, but also for individuals in their daily lives. We also include the feature **OB in the Street**, which further emphasizes how OB applies outside the workplace.

- *Writing style.* We continue to make clarity and readability the hallmarks of this text. Our reviewers find the text "conversational," "interesting," "student-friendly," and "very clear and understandable." Students say they really like the informal style and personal examples.

- *Examples, examples, examples.* From our teaching experience, we know that students may not remember a concept, but they will remember an example. This textbook is packed full of recent real-world examples drawn from a variety of organizations: business and not-for-profit, large and small, and local and international. We also use examples taken from the world at large, to illustrate the broader applicability of OB material.

- *Comprehensive literature coverage.* This textbook is regularly singled out for its comprehensive and up-to-date coverage of OB from both academic journals as well as business periodicals.

- *Skill-building emphasis.* Each chapter's **OB at Work** is full of exercises to help students make the connections between theories and real-world applications. Exercises at the end of each chapter reinforce critical thinking, behavioural analysis, and team building.

Highlights of the Fifth Edition

The fifth edition takes a fresh approach to organizational behaviour coverage through more relevant examples, updated theory coverage, and a continued emphasis on pedagogically sound design. Based on reviews from numerous instructors and students across Canada, we have found that many potential users want chapters that have the right balance of theory, research, and application material, while being relevant to student learning. To accomplish this, we have:

- Continued to focus on shorter opening vignettes and then allow them to unfold throughout the chapter at the start of most major sections.

- Integrated questions (in the form of green notes) throughout the chapters to encourage students to think about how OB applies to their everyday lives and engage students in their reading of the material. These questions first appear in the chapter opener, under the heading OB Is For Everyone, and then appear throughout.

- Added more **OB in Action** features to provide "take-aways" from each chapter, things that readers can put into action right now, based on what they have learned in the chapter.

- Increased the number of **Focus on Research** vignettes and also highlighted research findings with an icon to help instructors identify key research findings. These features provide students with greater awareness of the research base that underlies OB.

- Provided **Snapshot Summary**, a study tool at the end of each chapter, to show how all the concepts are connected.

- Continued to include **OB for You** at the end of each chapter, to highlight the relevance of the chapter to one's everyday life.

- Highlighted the key **Learning About Yourself Exercises** that students will be engaged in at the start of the chapter and throughout their learning of the chapter contents. Some of these exercises appear right in the chapter, while more can be found and completed on MyOBLab at **www.pearsoned.ca/myoblab**.

- Included eight new case studies in **Additional Cases** at the end of the textbook.

- Continued our **OB on the Edge** feature, which highlights what's new and hot in OB. OB on the Edge is unique to the Canadian edition, and unique to any organizational behaviour textbook in the market. The feature provides an opportunity to explore challenging issues, and encourages students to read more about these hot topics. In this edition, we cover four topics in this innovative feature: *Stress; Trust; The Toxic Workplace;* and *Spirituality in the Workplace.*

Chapter-by-Chapter Highlights: What's New

The goal of this revision was to continue the emphasis on providing an up-to-date research base, including the latest topics in OB, and illustrating concepts through a broad array of examples and application material. These changes make this text the strongest application of OB material on the market. Each chapter brings new examples, new research, improved discussions of current issues, and a wide variety of application material. The key *changes* are listed below.

Chapter 1: What Is Organizational Behaviour?

- Added the following new sections:
  - "The Importance of Interpersonal Skills"
  - "Helping Employees with Work–Life Balance"
  - "Creating a Positive Work Environment"
- Completely revised the discussion "OB Looks Beyond Common Sense"
- Provided a new section and exhibit that summarizes the essential points of OB

Chapter 2: Perception, Personality, and Emotions

- Extensively revised the section "Factors Influencing Perception"
- Fully rewrote the discussion of stereotyping
- Considerably reworked the discussion of personality, including:
  - A new "Measuring Personality" section
  - Expanded coverage of heredity
  - Completely revised discussion of the Myers-Briggs Type Indicator
  - Fully reworked and updated research findings on the Big Five Personality Model, including a new exhibit (Exhibit 2-6)
  - New discussions of core self-evaluation and narcissism
  - Significantly revised coverage of risk-taking

- Extensively revised the discussion of emotions, including:
  - Completely rewritten sections on emotional labour and emotions in the workplace
  - A new section called "Emotions in the Workplace in a Global Context"

Chapter 3: Values, Attitudes, and Diversity in the Workplace

- Shortened the discussion "The GLOBE Framework for Assessing Cultures" to add and fully explore Hofstede's framework with an exhibit (Exhibit 3-3)
- Revised the sections "Generation X" and "The Ne(x)t Generation"
- Significantly revised the section "Attitudes," including:
  - Fully rewritten coverage of job satisfaction and productivity
  - All-new sections called "What Causes Job Satisfaction?", "Managers Often 'Don't Get It,'" and "Employee Engagement"

Chapter 4: Theories of Motivation

- Introduced a discussion of "stretch goals" under "Goal-Setting Theory"
- Included a new section "Self-Efficacy Theory" with a new exhibit on the joint effects of goals and self-efficacy on performance (Exhibit 4-9)
- Added a discussion on "organizational justice" under the section "Fair Process and Treatment" with an exhibit to illustrate the model (Exhibit 4-11)
- Fully revised and updated the research findings on cognitive evaluation theory

Chapter 5: Motivation in Action

- Extensively reworked coverage of reward systems, including:
  - A new section on pay structure
  - Revised discussion of variable-pay programs
  - New discussion of flexible benefits and employee recognition
- Significantly revised the section "Can We Just Eliminate Rewards?":
  - Included discussion of performance feedback with a new *OB in Action: Giving More Effective Feedback*
  - Expanded coverage of creating a motivating work environment
- Synthesized the key concepts of Chapters 4 and 5 in a new section, "Putting It All Together," which includes an exhibit that illustrates the drivers that motivate employees (Exhibit 5-9)

Chapter 6: Groups and Teamwork

- Revised the section on virtual teams
- Introduced the concept of "multi-team systems"
- Added a new *OB in Action: Building Trust*

- Created a new exhibit on teamwork competencies (Exhibit 6-6)
- Significantly revised the discussion of personality
- Introduced the term "reflexivity" in the discussion of common purpose
- Included a brief discussion of mental models

Chapter 7: Communication

- Revised and expanded the discussions of "downward" and "upward" communication flow
- Considerably revised and updated the section on e-mail
- Included text messaging in the discussion of instant messaging and fully rewrote this section

Chapter 8: Power and Politics

- Expanded the section "Influence Tactics" and introduced the term "political skill"
- Considerably revised coverage of power abuse and harassment by expanding the sections "Workplace Bullying" and "Sexual Harassment"
- Fully revised the research findings on impression management techniques

Chapter 9: Conflict and Negotiation

- Expanded and updated the section "Resolving Intercultural Conflicts," including a new exhibit on strategies for dealing with intercultural conflict (Exhibit 9-3)
- Extended discussion of distributive bargaining and integrative bargaining
- Updated discussion of Japanese negotiation style

Chapter 10: Organizational Culture

- Added two new sections: "Creating an Ethical Culture" and "Creating a Positive Organizational Culture"

Chapter 11: Leadership

- Significantly rewrote and reorganized the chapter
- Extensively revised the "Leadership as Supervision" section:
  - Introduced a new discussion in "Focus on Research"
  - Rewrote coverage of emotional intelligence and leadership
  - Updated the research findings on path-goal theory
- Considerably rewrote the "Inspirational Leadership" section:
  - Introduced the concept of "framing"
  - Revised discussion of charismatic leadership
  - Revised and expanded coverage of transformational leadership

- Revised the content on self-leadership (or self-management) and online leadership
- Updated "Contemporary Issues in Leadership" by adding discussion of authentic leadership and the concept "socialized charismatic leadership"

Chapter 12: Decision Making, Creativity, and Ethics

- Significantly revised this chapter
- Considerably reworked "How Do Individuals Actually Make Decisions?" including:
  - Completely rewritten discussion of intuition and intuitive decision making
  - A fully revised "Judgment Shortcuts" section with new topics, including overconfidence bias, anchoring bias, confirmation bias, randomness bias, winner's curse, and hindsight bias
- Added a new "Effectiveness and Efficiency" section
- Completely revised "Creativity in Organizational Decision Making" with new discussions of creative potential, the three-component model of creativity, and organizational factors that affect creativity
- Expanded the "Four Ethical Decision Criteria" section

Chapter 13: Organizational Structure

- Added new exhibits:
  - Exhibit 13-4 Departmentalization by Function
  - Exhibit 13-5 Departmentalization by Product
  - Exhibit 13-6 Departmentalization by Geography

Chapter 14: Organizational Change

- Added a new exhibit to the discussion of appreciative inquiry (Exhibit 14-6)
- Significantly revised the "Resistance to Change" section, including:
  - Updated discussion of individual resistance with a new exhibit (Exhibit 14-7)
  - Extensive revision of the "Overcoming Resistance to Change" section

Pedagogical Features

The pedagogical features of *Organizational Behaviour: Concepts, Controversies, Applications,* Fifth Canadian Edition, are designed to complement and reinforce the textual material. This textbook offers the most complete assortment of pedagogy available in any OB book on the market.

- The text is developed in a "story-line" format that emphasizes how the topics fit together. Each chapter opens with a concept map of key questions related to a main example that threads through the chapter. The opening vignette is shorter, and it is carried throughout the chapter to help students apply a story to the concepts they are learning. The questions from the concept map appear in the margin of the text, to indicate where they are addressed. The opening questions are repeated and answered at the end of each chapter to summarize the chapter content.

- NEW! **OB Is for Everyone** in the chapter-opener highlights the integrated questions that students will encounter throughout each chapter (in the form of green notes). Right from the start, these questions encourage students to think of how OB applies to everyday lives.

  - NEW! From the outset, students are introduced to the key self-assessments that they will be engaged in within each chapter.

- Exclusive to the Canadian edition, **OB in the Street**, **OB in the Workplace**, **OB Around the Globe**, **Focus on Ethics**, **Focus on Diversity**, and **Focus on Research** help students see the links between theoretical material and applications.

- **OB in Action** features provide tips for using the concepts of OB in everyday life. For instance, **OB in Action** features include *Managing Virtual Teams*, *Ground Rules for Developing Business Partnerships with Aboriginal People*, *Practices of Successful Organizations*, and *Reducing Biases and Errors in Decision Making*.

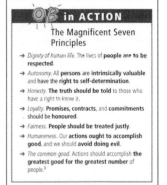

- To help instructors and students readily spot significant discussions of research findings, we have included a research icon to indicate where these discussions appear. This helps emphasize the strong research foundation that underlies OB.

- NEW! **Integrated questions** (in the form of green notes) throughout the chapters encourage students to think about how OB applies to their everyday lives and engage students in their reading of the material. These questions first appear under the heading OB Is for Everyone in the chapter-opener.

- **Summary and Implications** provides responses to the outcomes-based questions at the beginning of each chapter, while the **Snapshot Summary (NEW!)** provides a study tool that helps students to see the overall connections among concepts studied within each chapter.

- Each chapter concludes with **OB at Work**, a set of resources designed to help students apply the lessons of the chapter. Included in **OB at Work** are the following continuing and new features:

  - **For Review** and **For Critical Thinking** provide thought-provoking questions to review the chapter and consider ways to apply the material presented.

  - **OB for You** outlines how OB can be used by individuals in their daily lives.

- **Point/Counterpoint** promotes debate on contentious OB issues. This feature has been shortened to present more focused arguments.

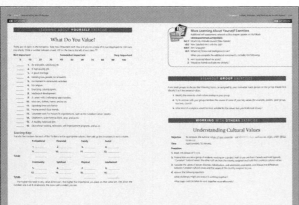

- **Learning About Yourself**, **Breakout Group**, **Working With Others**, and **Ethical Dilemma** exercises are valuable application exercises for the classroom. The many new exercises included here are ones that we have found particularly stimulating in our own classrooms. Our students say they like these exercises *and* they learn from them. Additional exercises can be found on MyOBLab at **www.pearsoned.ca/myoblab**.

- **Case Incidents** (two per chapter) deal with real-world scenarios and require students to exercise their decision-making skills. Each case enables an instructor to quickly generate class discussion on a key theme within the chapter.

- **From Concepts to Skills** provides a wide range of applications for students. The section begins with a practical set of tips on topics such as reading emotions, setting goals, and solving problems creatively, which demonstrate real-world applications of OB theories. These tips are followed by the features *Practising Skills* and *Reinforcing Skills*. *Practising Skills* presents an additional case or group activity to apply the chapter's learning objectives. *Reinforcing Skills* asks students to talk about the material they have learned with others, or to apply it to their own personal experiences.

- **Video Case Incident** presents a video case tied to the material in each chapter. The segments were carefully chosen by Frederick A. Starke (University of Manitoba). The video cases provide instructors with audiovisual material to engage students' attention.

- Exclusive to the Canadian edition, **OB on the Edge** (following each part) takes a close look at some of the hottest topics in the field: work-related stress, trust, behavioural pathologies that can make an organization "toxic," and spirituality in the workplace. Since this is a stand-alone feature, these topics can be introduced at the instructor's discretion.

- Our reviewers have asked for more cases, and more comprehensive and integrated cases. To address this request, we have added a new feature, **Additional Cases**, at the end of the textbook. We include two integrative cases, one on Tech-Depot and the other on the Toledo Zoo, both written by Nancy Langton. In addition, eight new comprehensive cases with discussion questions have been added. All of these cases require students to apply material from a variety of chapters.

Supplements

We have created an outstanding supplements package for *Organizational Behaviour*, Fifth Canadian Edition. In particular, we have introduced MyOBLab, an online study tool for students and an online homework and assessment tool for faculty. An access code to MyOBLab at **www.pearsoned.ca/myoblab** is included with this textbook. MyOBLab provides students with an assortment of tools to help enrich and expedite learning. It lets students assess their understanding through auto-graded tests and assignments, develop a personalized study plan to address areas of weakness, and practise a variety of learning tools to master organizational behaviour principles. Some of these tools are described below:

- *Auto-Graded Tests and Assignments.* MyOBLab comes with two sample tests per chapter. These were prepared by Sandy Findlay (Mount Saint Vincent University). Students can work through these diagnostic tests to identify areas they have not fully understood. These sample tests generate a personalized study plan. Instructors can also assign these sample tests or create assignments, quizzes, or tests using a mix of publisher-supplied content and their own custom exercises.

- *Personalized Study Plan.* In MyOBLab, students are treated as individuals with specific learning needs. Students have limited study time so it is important for them to study as effectively as possible. A personalized study plan is generated from each student's results on sample tests and instructor assignments. Students can clearly see the topics they have mastered—and, more importantly, the concepts they need to work on.

- *PowerPoint Slides.* This tool provides students with highlights and visuals of key concepts.

- *Glossary Flashcards.* This study aid is useful for students' review of key concepts.

- *eBook+.* Students can study without leaving the online environment. They can access the eText online, including animated text figures prepared by Cathy Heyland (Selkirk College).

- *Self-Assessment Library.* The Self-Assessment Library helps students create a skills portfolio. It is an interactive library containing behavioural questionnaires that help students discover things about themselves, their attitudes, and their personal strengths and weaknesses. Learning more about themselves gives students interesting insights into how they might behave in an organizational setting and motivates them to learn more about OB theories and practices that they can apply today and in the future.

- *HR Implications.* This feature spotlights those facets of each chapter topic that are relevant to human resource management.

- *Research Navigator.* Research navigator helps students quickly and efficiently make the most of their research time by providing four exclusive databases of reliable source content including the EBSCO Academic Journal and Abstract Database, New York Times Search by Subject Archive, "Best of the Web" Link Library, and Financial Times Article Archive and Company Financials.

The following materials are available for instructors:

Instructor's Resource CD-ROM (0-13-700547-4). This resource provides all of the following supplements in one convenient package:

- *Instructor's Resource Manual with Video Guide.* The Instructor's Resource Manual includes learning objectives, chapter outlines and synopses, annotated lecture outlines, teaching guides for in-text exercises, a summary and analysis of **Point/Counterpoint** features, and answers to questions found under **OB at Work**'s *For Review* and *For Critical Thinking* sections, **Case Incidents**, and in **Video Case Incidents**. There are additional cases, exercises, and teaching materials as well.

- *Pearson TestGen.* Prepared by Richard Michalski, the Pearson TestGen contains over 1800 items in TestGen format, including multiple choice, true/false, and discussion questions that relate not only to the body of the text but to **From Concepts to Skills**, **Point/Counterpoint**, and case materials. For each question we have provided the correct answer, a reference to the relevant section of the text, a difficulty rating, and a classification (recall/applied). TestGen is a testing software that enables instructors to view and edit the existing questions, add questions, generate tests, and distribute the tests in a variety of formats. Powerful search and sort functions make it easy to locate questions and arrange them in any order desired. TestGen also enables instructors to administer tests on a local area network, have the tests graded electronically and have the results prepared in electronic or printed reports. TestGen is compatible with Windows and Macintosh operating systems, and can be downloaded from the TestGen website located at **www.pearsoned.com/testgen**. Contact your local sales representative for details and access.

- *Electronic Transparencies in PowerPoint.* Prepared by George Dracopoulos (Vanier College), this package includes nearly 700 slides of content and exhibits from the text for electronic presentation.

- *Pearson Education Canada Video Library.* Pearson Education Canada has developed an exciting video package consisting of segments from CBC programs and from Prentice Hall's *Organizational Behavior,* 13th edition Video Library. These segments show students issues of organizational behaviour as they affect real individuals and companies. Teaching notes are provided in the Instructor's Resource Manual with Video Guide. The videos are available in VHS (0-13-700542-3) and DVD (0-13-700541-5) format. These cases were prepared by Frederick A. Starke (University of Manitoba).

- *Image Gallery.* This package provides instructors with images to enhance their teaching.

Most of these instructor supplements are also available for download from a password-protected section of Pearson Education Canada's online catalogue (**vig.pearsoned.ca**). Navigate to your textbook's catalogue page to view a list of those supplements that are available. See your local sales representative for details and access.

Companion Website (**www.pearsoned.ca/langton**). The website for this textbook includes chapter outlines and a glossary.

Innovative Solutions Team. Pearson's Innovative Solutions Team works with faculty and campus course designers to ensure that Pearson technology products, assessment tools, and online course materials are tailored to meet your specific needs. This highly qualified team is dedicated to helping schools take full advantage of a wide range of educational technology, by assisting in the integration of a variety of instructional materials and media formats.

Acknowledgments

A number of people worked hard to give this fifth Canadian edition of *Organizational Behaviour* a new look. Su Mei Ku, who has been the developmental editor on almost all of my projects, again outdid her always excellent performance. Her wit, good humour, helpfulness, support, and organizational skills made working on this textbook immensely easier. Su Mei served as a much-valued sounding board throughout the editorial process.

I received incredible support for this project from a variety of people at Pearson Education Canada. Karen Elliott, Acquisitions Editor, worked hard to keep this project on track. Anthony Leung was responsible for the interior and cover design. Laura Neves and Richard di Santo were the Production Editors for this project and did an admirable job of helping move things along. Steve O'Hearn, President of Higher Education, and Gary Bennett, Vice President, Editorial Director of Higher Education, are extremely supportive on the management side of Pearson Education Canada. This kind of support makes it much easier for an author to get work done and meet dreams and goals. Lisa Brant was very helpful in doing the photo research and made some incredible finds in her search for photos to highlight OB concepts. There are a variety of other people at Pearson who also had their hand in making sure that the manuscript would be transformed into this book and then delivered to your hands. To all of them I extend my thanks for jobs well done. The Pearson sales team is an exceptional group, and I know they will do everything possible to make this book successful. I continue to appreciate and value their support and interaction, particularly that of Cas Shields, Executive Marketing Manager.

Claudia Forgas was copyeditor for the project and continues to amaze for how well she makes sure everything is in place and written clearly. Sheila Wawanash, as the proofreader, was extremely diligent about checking for consistency throughout the text. Both performed a number of helpful fact-checking activities. I enjoyed the opportunity to work with both of them once again. Their keen eyes helped to make these pages as clean as they are.

I also want to acknowledge my divisional secretary, Nancy Tang, who helped to keep the project on track, doing some of the word processing, managing the courier packages and faxes, and always being attentive to detail. I could not ask for a better, more dedicated, or more cheerful assistant. She really helps keep things together.

In our continuing effort to improve the textbook, we conducted many reviews to elicit feedback. Many thanks to several students from the Northern Alberta Institute of Technology (NAIT) who a provided us with suggestions for improving the textbook. The students are Barb Kosak, Prudence Musinguzi, Andres Sarrate, and Robert Tucci

Finally, I want to acknowledge the many reviewers of this textbook for their detailed, helpful comments. I appreciate the time and care that they put into their reviewing: Stan Arnold (Humber College), Gordon Barnard (Durham College), Kelly Beechey (Northern Alberta Institute of Technology), Catherine Connelly (McMaster University), Jane Deighan (Southern Alberta Institute of Technology), Diane Jurkowski (York University), Janina Kon (University of British Columbia), Stoney Kudel (George Brown College), Lesley McCannell (Kwantlen Polytechnic University), and Stephen Rose (University of Ontario Institute of Technology).

Nancy Langton   received her Ph.D. from Stanford University. Since completing her graduate studies, Dr. Langton has taught at the University of Oklahoma and the University of British Columbia. Currently a member of the Organizational Behaviour and Human Resources division in the Sauder School of Business, UBC, she teaches at the undergraduate, MBA and Ph.D. level and conducts executive programs on attracting and retaining employees, time management, family business issues, as well as women and management issues. Dr. Langton has received several major three-year research grants from the Social Sciences and Humanities Research Council of Canada, and her research interests have focused on human resource issues in the workplace, including pay equity, gender equity, and leadership and communication styles. She is currently conducting longitudinal research with entrepreneurs in the Greater Vancouver Region, trying to understand the relationship between their human resource practices and the success of their businesses. Her articles on these and other topics have appeared in such journals as *Administrative Science Quarterly*, *American Sociological Review*, *Sociological Quarterly*, *Journal of Management Education*, and *Gender, Work and Organizations*. She has won Best Paper commendations from both the Academy of Management and the Administrative Sciences Association of Canada.

Dr. Langton routinely wins high marks from her students for teaching. She has been nominated many times for the Commerce Undergraduate Society Awards, and has won several honourable mention plaques. She has also won the Sauder School of Business's most prestigious award for teaching innovation, The Talking Stick. The award was given for Dr. Langton's redesign of the undergraduate organizational behaviour course as well as the many activities that were a spin-off of these efforts. She was also part of the UBC MBA Core design team that won the Alan Blizzard award, a national award that recognizes innovation in teaching.

In Dr. Langton's "other life," she teaches the artistry of quiltmaking, and one day hopes to win first prize at *Visions*, the juried show for quilts as works of art. In the meantime she teaches art quilt courses on colour and design in her spare time. When she is not designing quilts, she is either reading novels (often suggested by a favourite correspondent), or studying cookbooks for new ideas. All of her friends would say that she makes from scratch the best pizza in all of Vancouver.

Stephen P. Robbins

Stephen P. Robbins   received his Ph.D. from the University of Arizona and has taught at the University of Nebraska at Omaha, Concordia University in Montreal, the University of Baltimore, Southern Illinois University at Edwardsville, and San Diego State University. Dr. Robbins' research interests have focused on conflict, power, and politics in organizations, as well as on the development of effective interpersonal skills. His articles on these and other topics have appeared in journals such as *Business Horizons, California Management Review, Business and Economic Perspectives, International Management, Management Review, Canadian Personnel and Industrial Relations,* and *The Journal of Management Education.*

Dr. Robbins is the world's bestselling textbook author in the areas of management and organizational behaviour. His most recent textbooks include *Organizational Behavior,* 13th ed. (Prentice Hall, 2009), *Essentials of Organizational Behavior,* 9th ed. (Prentice Hall, 2008), *Fundamentals of Management,* 6th ed., with David DeCenzo (Prentice Hall, 2008), and *Supervision Today!,* 5th ed., with David DeCenzo (Prentice Hall, 2007). In addition, Dr. Robbins is the author of the global best-sellers *The Truth About Managing People,* 2nd ed. (Financial Times Press, 2008) and *Decide & Conquer* (Financial Times Press, 2004).

An avid participant in masters' track-and-field competition, Dr. Robbins has set numerous indoor and outdoor age-group world sprint records since turning 50 in 1993. He has won more than a dozen indoor and outdoor US national titles at 60, 100, 200, and 400 meters, and has won seven gold medals at the World Masters Championships.

Timothy A. Judge   received his Ph.D. from the University of Illinois at Urbana-Champaign and has taught at the University of Florida in Gainesville, Cornell University in Ithaca, Charles University in the Czech Republic, and Comenius University in Slovakia. Dr. Judge's research interests have focused on personality, moods, and emotions; job attitudes; leadership and influence behaviours; and careers (person–organization fit, career success). His articles on these and other topics have appeared in journals such as *Journal of Organizational Behavior, Personnel Psychology, Academy of Management Journal, Journal of Applied Psychology, European Journal of Personality,* and *European Journal of Work and Organizational Psychology*. He has also co-authored a book with H.G. Heneman III, *Staffing Organizations*, 5th ed. (Mendota House/Irwin, 2006).

In 1995, Dr. Judge received the Earnest J. McCormick Award for Distinguished Early Career Contributions from the Society for Industrial and Organizational Psychology, and in 2001, he received the Larry L. Cummings Award for mid-career contributions from the Organizational Behavior Division of the Academy of Management. In 2007, he received the Professional Practice Award from the Institute of Industrial and Labor Relations, University of Illinois.

Dr. Judge enjoys golf, cooking and baking, literature (he's a particular fan of Thomas Hardy and is a member of the Thomas Hardy Society), and keeping up with his three children.

What Is Organizational Behaviour?

Can you run a successful business without having people skills?

1 What is organizational behaviour?

2 What challenges do managers and employees face in today's workplace?

3 Isn't organizational behaviour common sense? Or just like psychology?

harles Chang started Port Coquitlam, BC-based Sequel Naturals, which makes premium natural health supplements, in April 2001.[1] The nutritional supplement industry was growing rapidly at the time, and six years later his annual revenue was $5.4 million and he had gone from 2 employees to 40.

Despite his strong sales record, by early 2007 the young entrepreneur realized that he had to resolve the people issues facing his company. He had recently hired a controller with "disorganized accounting practices" who caused $400 000 in inventory to be written off. The personality conflicts among his staff made it difficult to get work done. He was having trouble expanding into the United States, and renovations on a new location were behind schedule. All of these problems led Sequel to post a loss of $300 000 at the end of 2006, after a profit of $1.4 million the previous year.

Chang says that one of his problems in running his business was that he was not an "HR guy"—that is, he did not pay much attention to people issues. Instead, he paid far more attention to sales and development issues because that is what he knew. But no one else was paying attention to the people issues either. So there was no real leadership for the employees, which is why the personality conflicts were taking over. The challenges that managers such as Chang face illustrate several concepts you will find as you study the field of organizational behaviour. Let's take a look, then, at what organizational behaviour is.

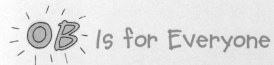 Is for Everyone

- Why do some people do well in organizational settings while others have difficulty?
- Do you know what a "typical" organization looks like?
- Does job satisfaction really make a difference?
- Are you ready to take on more responsibility at work?
- What people-related challenges have you noticed in the workplace?
- Why should you care about understanding other people?

Self-Assessment Library

LEARNING ABOUT YOURSELF

- Your Interpersonal Skills
- Knowledge of OB

Defining Organizational Behaviour

1   What is organizational behaviour?

organizational behaviour A field of study that investigates the impact of individuals, groups, and structure on behaviour within organizations; its purpose is to apply such knowledge toward improving an organization's effectiveness.

Organizational behaviour (often abbreviated as OB) is a field of study that looks at the impact that individuals, groups, and structure have on behaviour within organizations. *Behaviour* refers to what people do in an organization and how they perform. Because the organizations studied are often business organizations, OB is frequently applied to topics such as jobs, absenteeism, turnover, productivity, motivation, working in groups, and job satisfaction. Managers apply the knowledge gained from OB research to help them manage their organizations more effectively.

Why do some people do well in organizational settings while others have difficulty?

However, much of OB is relevant beyond the workplace. The study of OB can cast light on the interactions among family members, students working as a team on a class project, the voluntary group that comes together to do something about reviving the downtown area, the parents who sit on the board of their children's daycare centre, or even the members of a lunchtime pickup basketball team.

What Do We Mean by Organization?

organization   A consciously co-ordinated social unit, composed of a group of people, that functions on a relatively continuous basis to achieve a common goal or set of goals.

An **organization** is a consciously coordinated social unit, composed of a group of people, that functions on a relatively continuous basis to achieve a common goal or set of goals. Manufacturing and service firms are organizations, and so are schools, hospitals, churches, military units, retail stores, police departments, volunteer organizations, start-ups, and local, provincial, and federal government agencies. Thus, when we say "organization" throughout this textbook, we are referring not only to large manufacturing firms but also to small mom-and-pop stores, as well as to the variety

Microsoft understands how organizational behaviour affects an organization's performance. The company maintains good employee relationships by providing a great work environment, generous benefits, and challenging jobs. The two-storey wall painting shown here is one of 4500 pieces of contemporary art displayed at Microsoft's corporate campus for employees' enjoyment. Other benefits, such as valet parking, dry-cleaning and laundry services, free grocery delivery, and take-home meals, help employees focus on their work. At Microsoft, employee loyalty and productivity are high, contributing to the company's growth to over $60 billion in annual revenue since its founding in 1975.

Do you know what a "typical" organization looks like?

of other forms of organization that exist. Businesses that employ no more than 10 people make up 75 percent of the Canadian marketplace. In Canada, small and mid-sized businesses now make up 45 percent of the gross national product, up from 25 percent more than 20 years ago.[2]

The examples in this textbook present various organizations so that you can gain a better understanding of the many types of organizations that exist. Though you might not have considered this before, the college or university you attend is every bit as much a "real" organization as is Hudson's Bay Company or Air Canada or the Toronto Raptors. A small for-profit organization that hires unskilled workers to renovate and build in the inner city of Winnipeg is as much a real organization as is London, Ontario-based EllisDon, one of North America's largest construction companies. Therefore, the theories we cover should be considered in light of the variety of organizations you may encounter. We try to point out instances where the theory may be less applicable (or especially applicable) to a particular type of organization. For the most part, however, you should expect that the discussions in this textbook apply across the broad spectrum of organizations. Throughout, we highlight applications to a variety of organizations in our feature *OB in the Workplace*.

OB Is for Everyone

It might seem natural to think that the study of OB is for leaders and managers of organizations. After all, they often set the agenda for everyone else. However, many organizations also have informal leadership opportunities. As employees are asked to move beyond their traditional function of providing labour and play a more proactive role in achieving organizational success, the roles of managers and employees are becoming blurred in many organizations.[3] Managers are increasingly asking employees to share in their decision-making processes rather than simply follow orders. For instance, employees in some retail operations can make decisions about when to accept returned items, rather than defer the decision to the manager.

OB is not just for managers and employees. Entrepreneurs and self-employed individuals may not act as managers, but they certainly interact with other individuals and organizations as part of their work. OB applies equally well to all situations in which you interact with others: on the basketball court, at the grocery store, in school, or in church. In fact, OB is relevant anywhere that people come together and share experiences, work on goals, or meet to solve problems. To help you understand these broader connections, you will find a feature called *OB in the Street* throughout the textbook.

The Importance of Interpersonal Skills

Although practising managers have long understood the importance of interpersonal (people) skills to organizational effectiveness, business schools have been slower to get the message. Until the late 1980s, business school curricula emphasized the technical aspects of management, specifically focusing on economics, accounting, finance, and quantitative techniques. Course work in human behaviour and people skills received minimal attention relative to the technical aspects of management. Over the past two decades, however, business faculty have come to realize the importance of the role that an understanding of human behaviour plays in determining organizational effectiveness, and required courses on people skills have been added to many curricula. As the director of leadership at MIT's Sloan School of Management recently put it, "M.B.A. students may get by on their technical and quantitative skills the first couple of years out of school. But soon, leadership and communication skills come to the fore in distinguishing those whose careers really take off."[4]

Recognition of the importance of developing interpersonal skills is closely tied to the need for organizations to get and keep high-performing employees. Regardless of labour market conditions, outstanding employees are always in short supply.[5] Companies with reputations as good places to work—such as Toronto-based Environics Group, Regina-based SaskCentral, Vancouver-based Karo Group, Markham, Ontario-based Ceridian Canada, and Toronto-based TD Bank Financial Group—have a big advantage. A recent study found that wages and benefits are not the main reasons people like their jobs or stay with an employer. Far more important is the quality of the employee's job and the supportiveness of the work environment.[6] In addition, creating a pleasant workplace appears to make good economic sense. For instance, companies with reputations as good places to work have been found to generate superior financial performance.[7]

We have come to understand that technical skills are necessary, but they are not enough to succeed in the workplace. In today's increasingly competitive and demanding workplace, individuals need to have good people skills. This textbook has been written to help managers and employees develop those people skills. To learn more about the kinds of people skills needed in the workplace, see the *Working with Others Exercise* on page 29. To find out about the strengths and weaknesses in your people skills, see the *Learning About Yourself Exercise* on page 29.

Learning About Yourself

1. The Competing Values Framework: Identifying Your Interpersonal Skills
(page 28)

Today's Challenges in the Canadian Workplace

Six years after starting Sequel Naturals, Charles Chang was reflecting on the fact that his employees were having daily squabbles because of personality conflicts.[8] His general manager was no better than he was at managing people. He decided he needed to move out of his home office, and spend more time working side by side with his employees at headquarters. He then tackled the people issues.

Chang built a management team to handle operations, sales, marketing, and finances. He took over the human resource role, hired 20 new employees, and fired "five problematic employees." He started holding Monday morning staff meetings where he made everyone aware of the company's performance goals. "I want everyone to know those numbers inside and out," he says. Once his changes were in place, he said, "We went from being unmanaged to extremely managed, and staying on top of our numbers is how we'll stay that way."

Chang is committed to being a good employer, surrounded by a good team. Will keeping them focused on the numbers be enough? What factors affect good teamwork? How can Chang motivate his employees to perform well in their jobs?

2 What challenges do managers and employees face in today's workplace?

OB considers that organizations are made up of individuals, groups, and the entire organizational structure. Each of these units represents a different level within an organization, moving from the smallest unit, the individual, to the largest, the entire organization. Each level contributes to the variety of activities that occur in today's workplace. Exhibit 1-1 presents the three levels of analysis we consider in this textbook, and shows that as we move from the individual level to the organization systems level, we deepen our understanding of behaviour in organizations. The three basic levels are like building blocks: Each level is constructed upon the previous level. Group concepts are built on the foundation we lay out on individual behaviour. We then overlay structural constraints on the individual and group in order to arrive at OB.

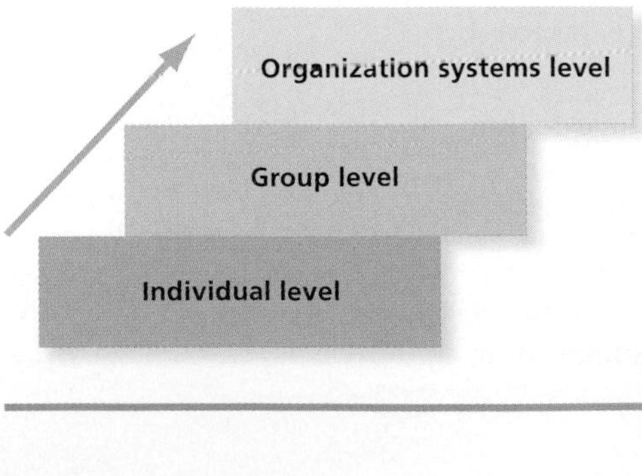

When we look at the different levels in an organization, we recognize that each has challenges that can affect how the levels above and/or below might operate. We consider the challenges at the individual, group, and organizational levels.

EXHIBIT 1-1   Basic OB Model

Organization systems level

Group level

Individual level

Challenges at the Individual Level

At the individual level, managers and employees need to learn how to work with people who may be different from themselves on a variety of dimensions, including personality, perception, values, and attitudes. Individuals also have different levels of job satisfaction and motivation, and these affect how managers manage employees. Perhaps the greatest issue facing individuals (and organizations) is how to behave ethically in the face of competing demands from different stakeholders.

Individual Differences

People enter groups and organizations with certain characteristics that influence their behaviour, the more obvious of these being personality characteristics, perception, values, and attitudes. These characteristics are essentially intact when an individual joins an organization, and for the most part, there is little that those in the organization can do to alter them. Yet they have a very real impact on behaviour. In this light, we look at perception, personality, values, and attitudes, and their impact on individual behaviour in Chapters 2 and 3.

Job Satisfaction

Employees are increasingly demanding satisfaction out of their jobs. As we discuss in Chapter 3, overall job satisfaction in the Canadian workplace is moderately high. The belief that satisfied employees are more productive than dissatisfied employees has been a basic assumption among managers for years. Although some evidence questions that causal relationship,[9] it can be argued that society should be concerned not only with the quantity of life—that is, with concerns such as higher productivity and material acquisitions—but also with its quality. Researchers with strong humanistic values argue that satisfaction is a legitimate objective of an organization. They believe that organizations should be responsible for providing employees with jobs that are challenging and intrinsically rewarding. This chapter's *Ethical Dilemma Exercise* on page 29 questions the extent to which organizations should be responsible for helping individuals achieve balance in their life.

Does job satisfaction really make a difference?

Job satisfaction is also of concern because it is negatively related to absenteeism and turnover, which cost organizations considerable amounts of money annually.

Motivation

A 2004 survey of Canadian employees found that only 24 percent agreed that to a great extent they received recognition for work well done.[10] To address this concern, Chapter 4 discusses the importance of rewards in motivating employees, while Chapter 5 describes specific rewards that can be used in the workplace. You may find the discussion of motivation and rewards particularly interesting in *Case Incident—How a UPS Manager Cut Turnover* on page 30, where a manager faces the challenge of motivating different types of employees to reduce turnover.

Toronto-based Royal Bank of Canada, Canada's largest financial institution in terms of assets, commands the respect of many business leaders. In the 2005 KPMG/Ipsos Reid poll of 250 Canadian CEOs, the company ranked first in five out of the eight categories surveyed: Best Long-Term Investment, Human Resources Management, Financial Performance, Corporate Social Responsibility, and Corporate Governance.

Empowerment

At the same time that managers are being held responsible for employee satisfaction and happiness, they are also being asked to share more of their power with employees.

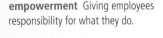

If you read any popular business periodical nowadays, you will find that managers are referred to as *coaches*, *advisers*, *sponsors*, or *facilitators*, rather than *bosses*.[11] In many organizations, employees have become *associates* or *teammates*.[12] The roles of managers and employees have blurred as the responsibilities of employees have grown. Decision making is being pushed down to the operating level, where employees solve work-related problems and are being given the freedom to make choices about schedules and procedures.

In the 1980s, managers were encouraged to involve their employees in work-related decisions.[13] Now, managers are going considerably further by providing employees with full control of their work. Self-managed teams, in which employees operate largely without managers, became the rage in the 1990s.[14] This trend of teamwork and employee responsibility has continued into the twenty-first century. (To help you understand how to perform better as a team player, we discuss the dynamics of teams in Chapter 6.)

What's going on is that managers are empowering employees. **Empowerment** means managers are giving employees more responsibility for what they do. In the process, managers are learning how to give up control, and employees are learning how to take responsibility for their work and make appropriate decisions. The roles for both managers and employees are changing, often without much guidance on how to perform the new functions.

How widespread are these changes in the workplace? While we have no specific Canadian data, a survey by the American Management Association of 1040 executives found that 46 percent of their companies were still operating within a hierarchical structure, but 31 percent defined their companies as empowered.[15] *OB in the Workplace* looks at how WestJet Airlines empowers its employees.

empowerment Giving employees responsibility for what they do.

IN THE WORKPLACE

WestJet Airlines' Employees Work Together

What do empowered employees do? Calgary-based WestJet Airlines employees are given lots of freedom to manage themselves.[16] When the company was started in 1996, Clive Beddoe, the company's founder and chair of the board, was determined to create a company "where people wanted to manage themselves."

At WestJet, employees are asked to be responsible for their tasks, rather than rely on supervisors to tell them what to do. Instead, employees are given guidelines for behaviour. For instance, flight attendants are directed to serve customers in a caring, positive, and cheerful manner. How do they carry that out? It's up to them. Employees also share tasks. When a plane lands, all employees on the flight, even those who are flying off-duty, are expected to prepare the plane for its next takeoff. Beddoe does not excuse himself from helping out when he is on a flight. It's not unusual, he says, for him to "schmooze with the passengers and help our flight attendants pick up garbage."

Sean Durfy, WestJet's president, explains why empowerment is a good business model. "If you empower people to do the right things, then they will. If you align the interests of the people with the interests of the company, it's very powerful. That's what we do." WestJet's empowerment culture is admired by others as well. In 2008, the company placed first on Waterstone Human Capital's "Canada's 10 Most Admired Corporate Cultures" for the third time in a row.

Throughout this textbook, you will find references to empowerment. We discuss it in terms of power in Chapter 8, and how leaders contribute to empowerment in Chapter 11.

Behaving Ethically

In an organizational world characterized by cutbacks, expectations of increasing worker productivity, and tough competition in the marketplace, it's not altogether surprising that many employees feel pressured to cut corners, break rules, and engage in other forms of questionable practices. For example, should they "blow the whistle" if they uncover illegal activities taking place in their company? Should they follow orders with which they don't personally agree? Do they give an inflated performance evaluation to an employee they like, knowing that such an evaluation could save that employee's job? Do they allow themselves to "play politics" in the organization if it will help their career advancement?

Ethics starts at the individual level. **Ethics** is the study of moral values or principles that guide our behaviour and inform us whether actions are right or wrong. Ethical principles help us "do the right thing," such as not padding expense reports, or not phoning in sick to attend the opening of *The Dark Knight*.

ethics The study of moral values or principles that guide our behaviour and inform us whether actions are right or wrong.

As we show in Chapter 12, the study of ethics does not come with black and white answers. Rather, many factors need to be considered in determining the ethical thing to do. Those individuals who strive hard to create their own set of ethical values and those organizations that encourage an ethical climate in the face of financial and other pressures will more often do the right thing.

Throughout this textbook, you will find references to ethical and unethical behaviour. The *Focus on Ethics* feature will provide you with thought-provoking illustrations of how ethics is treated in various organizations.

Challenges at the Group Level

The behaviour of people in a group is more than the sum total of all the individuals acting in their own way. People's behaviour when they are in a group differs from their behaviour when they are alone. Therefore, the next step in developing an understanding of OB is the study of group behaviour.

What people-related challenges have you noticed in the workplace?

Chapter 6 lays the foundation for an understanding of the dynamics of group and team behaviour. That chapter discusses how individuals are influenced by the patterns of behaviour they are expected to exhibit, what the team considers to be acceptable standards of behaviour, and how to make teams more effective.

Chapters 7, 8, and 9 examine some of the more complex issues of interaction, including communication, power and politics, and conflict and negotiation. These chapters give you an opportunity to think about how communication processes sometimes become complicated because of office politicking and interpersonal and group conflict.

Few people work entirely alone, and some organizations make widespread use of teams. Therefore, most individuals interact with others during the workday. This can lead to a need for greater interpersonal skills. The workplace is also made up of people from a variety of different backgrounds. Thus, learning how to work with people from different cultures has become more important. We discuss some of the challenges that occur at the group level below.

Working with Others

Much of the success in any job involves developing good interpersonal, or "people," skills. In fact, the Conference Board of Canada identified the skills that form the

With more than 400 000 employees in 200 countries, United Parcel Service (UPS) embraces the value of diversity. Since 1968, UPS senior managers have participated in a four-week community internship program that deepens their responsiveness to the needs of a diverse workforce and customer base while helping with charitable causes in the community. In this photo, UPS managers from Germany and California help a bicycle-shop owner reorganize his business.

foundation for a high-quality workforce in today's workplace, including the ability to communicate, think, and solve problems, learn continuously, and work with others. The ability to demonstrate positive attitudes and behaviours and take responsibility for one's actions are also key skills.[17] Because many people will work in small and medium-sized firms in the future, Human Resources and Social Development Canada has noted that additional important skills are team building and priority management.[18]

In Canada's increasingly competitive and demanding workplace, neither managers nor employees can succeed on their technical skills alone. Management professor Jin Nam Choi of McGill University reports that research shows 40 percent of managers either leave or stop performing within 18 months of starting at an organization "because they have failed to develop relationships with bosses, colleagues or subordinates."[19] Choi's comment underscores the importance of developing interpersonal skills. This textbook has been written to help you develop those people skills, whether as an employee, manager, or potential manager. It has also been written to help you think about group behaviour from an OB perspective.

To learn more about the interpersonal skills needed in today's workplace, read *From Concepts to Skills* on pages 32–34.

Workforce Diversity

The ability to adapt to many different people is one of the most important and broad-based challenges facing organizations. The term we use to describe this challenge is *workforce diversity*. **Workforce diversity** arises because organizations are becoming more heterogeneous, employing a greater variety of people in terms of gender, race, ethnicity, sexual orientation, and age. A diverse workforce, for instance, includes women, Aboriginal peoples, Asian Canadians, African Canadians, Indo-Canadians, people with disabilities, gays and lesbians, and senior citizens. It also includes people with different demographic characteristics, such as education and socio-economic status. We discuss workforce diversity issues in Chapter 3.

workforce diversity The mix of people in organizations in terms of gender, race, ethnicity, disability, sexual orientation, age, and demographic characteristics, such as education and socio-economic status.

One of the challenges in Canadian workplaces is the mix of generations—members of the Elders, Baby Boomers, Generation X, and Generation Y groups work side by side. Due to their very different life experiences, they bring to the workplace different values and different expectations.

Workforce diversity is an issue in workplaces in many parts of the world. The increase in female employment drives some of that diversity. However, immigration patterns and relatively open national borders in some countries have also led to changes in workforce diversity. For instance, the creation of the European Union, which opened up borders throughout much of Western Europe, has increased workforce diversity in organizations that operate in countries such as Germany, Portugal, Italy, and France.

Why should you care about understanding other people?

Haven't organizations always included members of diverse groups? Yes, but they were a small percentage of the workforce and were, for the most part, ignored by large organizations. For instance, historically the Canadian workforce was predominantly white and male. Now such employees make up far less of the workplace. By 2010, white males will account for even fewer of the new labour-force entrants as visible minorities increase their participation in the workplace.

We used to assume that people in organizations who differed from the stereotypical employee would somehow simply fit in. We now recognize that employees don't set aside their cultural values and lifestyle preferences when they go to work. The challenge for organizations, therefore, is to accommodate diverse groups of people by addressing their different lifestyles, family needs, and work styles.[20] However, what motivates one person may not motivate another. One person may like a straightforward and open style of communication that another finds uncomfortable and threatening. To work effectively with different people, you will need to understand their culture and how it has shaped them, and learn to adapt your interaction style.

The *Focus on Diversity* feature found throughout this textbook highlights diversity issues that arise in organizations. Our first example looks at ways that Regina-based SGI focuses on the diversity of its employees.

FOCUS ON **DIVERSITY**

SGI: Top Diversity Employer

How does an organization accommodate its diverse employees? Regina-based Saskatchewan Government Insurance (SGI) must have some clue.[21] The company was named one of Canada's top diversity employers in 2008. Its workforce demonstrates SGI's commitment to diversity: 10 percent of employees are Aboriginal, 4.4 percent are visible minorities, and 7.5 percent have a disability.

SGI has developed a number of programs to support its workforce. The Aboriginal Network provides an opportunity for First Nation employees to talk about their own issues and also get career counselling. "It works at removing barriers for people," says Jon Schubert, the company's president. "We want to be an employer of choice for Aboriginal Canadians."

The company also hosts a diversity celebration each year with "performances from different cultural groups—from Greek traditional dancing to First Nation dancing." This helps employees learn about each other's heritages.

For its 2009 brokers' calendar, SGI encouraged Canadian artists to submit works of art that reflect the different cultural perspectives found in Canada. Such works might reflect, for instance, "an ethnic glimpse of Oktoberfest in Kitchener, a powwow in Saskatoon."

SGI strives to have a workforce that is as diverse as its customers—a goal, Schubert says, that "just makes good business sense."

Workforce diversity has important implications for management practice. Managers need to shift their philosophy from treating everyone alike to recognizing differences. They need to respond to those differences in ways that will ensure employee retention and greater productivity, while at the same time not discriminating against certain groups. This shift includes, for instance, providing diversity training and revising benefit programs to be more "family-friendly."

Diversity, if positively managed, can increase creativity and innovation in organizations, as well as improve decision making by providing different perspectives on problems.[22] When diversity is not managed properly, there is potential for higher turnover, miscommunication, and more interpersonal conflicts.

Challenges at the Organizational Level

OB becomes more complex when we move to the organizational level of analysis. Just as groups are not just the sum of individuals, organizations are not the sum of individuals and groups. There are many more interacting factors that place constraints on individual and group behaviour. In Chapter 10, we look at organizational culture, which is generally considered the glue that holds organizations together. In Chapter 11, we consider how leadership and management affect employee behaviour. In Chapter 12, we discuss decision making and creativity, and then look at the issues of ethics and corporate social responsibility.

The design of an organization has a big impact on how effective an organization is, and we discuss organizational design in Chapter 13. If the organization is not effective, change may be in order, a topic we consider in Chapter 14. As we have noted already, and as will become clear throughout this textbook, change has become a key issue for organizations.

Canadian businesses face many challenges today. The structure of the workplace is changing. Their ability to be as productive as US businesses is constantly tested. The need to develop effective, committed employees is critical. Meanwhile, Canadian businesses face greater competition because of the global economy. Many companies have expanded their operations overseas, which means they have to learn how to manage people from different cultures.

The Use of Temporary (Contingent) Employees

One of the more comprehensive changes taking place in organizations is the addition of temporary, or contingent, employees. Downsizing has eliminated millions of "permanent" jobs, and the number of openings for nonpermanent workers has increased. Temporary work was responsible for almost 20 percent of the growth in employment between 1997 and 2003, and 18 percent of employees were working part-time in August 2008.[23] These include part-timers, on-call workers, short-term hires, temps, day labourers, independent contractors, and leased workers.

Some contingent employees prefer the freedom of a temporary status that permits them to attend school, care for their children, or have the flexibility to travel or pursue other interests. For instance, 36 percent of those working part-time in 2008 were between the ages of 15 and 24.[24] But many others would prefer to have full-time work if it were available. Because contingent employees lack the security and stability that permanent employees have, they don't always identify with the organization or display the commitment of other employees. Temporary workers typically lack pension plans and have few or no extended health care benefits, such as dental care, prescription plans, and vision care. They are also paid less. For instance, in 2003, temporary workers earned 16 percent less than those who held permanent jobs.[25] Organizations face the challenge of motivating employees who do not feel as connected to the organization as do full-time employees.

Improving Quality and Productivity

Increased competition is forcing managers to reduce costs and, at the same time, improve the quality of the products and services their organization offers, as well as productivity.

An organization or group is productive if it achieves its goals and does so by transferring inputs (employee labour, materials used to produce goods) to outputs (finished goods or services) at the lowest cost. **Productivity** implies a concern for both **effectiveness** and **efficiency**. A hospital, for example, is *effective* when it successfully meets the needs of its clientele. It is efficient when it can do so at a low cost. If a hospital manages to achieve higher output from its present staff—say, by reducing the average number of days a patient is confined to a bed, or by increasing the number of staff-patient contacts per day—we say that the hospital has gained productive *efficiency*. Similarly, a student team is effective when it puts together a group project that gets a high mark. It is efficient when all the members manage their time appropriately and are not at each other's throats.

As you study OB, you will begin to understand those factors that influence the effectiveness and efficiency of individuals, groups, and the overall organization.

productivity A performance measure including effectiveness and efficiency.

effectiveness The achievement of goals.

efficiency The ratio of effective work output to the input required to produce the work.

Developing Effective Employees

One of the major challenges facing organizations today is how to engage employees effectively so that they are committed to the organization. We use the term **organizational citizenship behaviour (OCB)** to describe discretionary behaviour that is not part of an employee's formal job requirements, but that nevertheless promotes the effective functioning of the organization.[26] Recent research has also looked at expanding the work on OCB to team behaviour.[27]

Successful organizations need employees who will go beyond their usual job duties, providing performance that is beyond expectations. In today's dynamic workplace, where tasks are increasingly done in teams and where flexibility is critical, organizations need employees who will engage in "good citizenship" behaviours, such as making constructive statements about their work group and the organization, helping others on their team, volunteering for extra job activities, avoiding unnecessary conflicts, showing care for organizational property, respecting the spirit as well as the letter of rules and regulations, and gracefully tolerating the occasional work-related impositions and nuisances.

Toronto-based BBDO Canada encourages an entrepreneurial spirit as a way of inspiring organizational citizenship behaviour. The ad agency's president and CEO, Gerry Frascione, notes that a team leader on the Campbell Soup account overheard a Campbell's representative musing about a program that would launch Campbell Soup ads when the temperature dipped. "Instead of waiting to get approvals, she acted very entrepreneurially and took it upon herself and made the whole thing happen in one week," says Frascione. "She went back to the client, analyzed the situation, fleshed out the opportunity, came up with an integrated communication plan, came up with a budget, and it was all done within five days."[28]

Organizations want and need employees who will do those things that are not in any job description. And the evidence indicates that organizations that have such employees outperform those that don't.[29] As a result, OB is concerned with organizational citizenship behaviour.

organizational citizenship behaviour (OCB) Discretionary behaviour that is not part of an employee's formal job requirements, but that nevertheless promotes the effective functioning of the organization.

Putting People First

Professor Jeffrey Pfeffer of the Stanford Graduate School of Business advocates that managers should spend more time recognizing the value of the people who work for them. He emphasizes the need to "put people first" in considering organizational objectives and suggests the people-first strategy not only generates a committed workforce, but also significantly affects the bottom line.[30] Pfeffer notes that research shows that

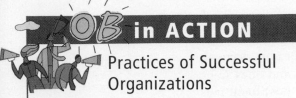

OB in ACTION

Practices of Successful Organizations

According to professor Jeffrey Pfeffer of the Stanford Graduate School of Business, the following practices characterize organizations that manage their employees well:

→ Providing **employment security** so that employees don't fear loss of jobs

→ **Hiring** people who have the **right skills and abilities**

→ Creating **self-managed teams** that have decision-making power

→ **Paying well**, and tying pay to organizational performance

→ Providing **extensive training** for skills, knowledge, and initiative

→ Reducing status differences so that **all employees feel valued**

→ **Sharing information** about organizational performance.[34]

when organizations concern themselves with developing their employees, they are more successful. For instance, a study of 968 US firms found that those that used people-first strategies had significantly less turnover, and significantly greater sales, market value, and profits.[31] Similar results were found in a study of 100 German companies.[32]

Pfeffer explains that people will work harder when they feel they have "more control and say in their work." They work smarter when they are "encouraged to build skills and competence." They work more responsibly when "responsibility is placed in the hands of employees farther down in the organization." *OB in Action—Practices of Successful Organizations* outlines the practices that successful people-first organizations use to encourage their employees to work harder, smarter, and more responsibly. *Case Incident—Great Plains Software: Pursuing a People-First Strategy* on page 31 asks you to consider the impact of "putting people first" in managing an organization.

Helping Employees with Work-Life Balance

Employees are increasingly complaining that the line between work and nonwork time has become blurred, creating personal conflicts and stress.[33] At the same time, however, today's workplace presents opportunities for workers to create and structure their work roles.

A number of forces have contributed to blurring the lines between employees' work life and personal life. First, the creation of global organizations means their world never sleeps. At any time and on any day, for instance, thousands of General Electric employees are working somewhere. The need to consult with colleagues or customers 8 or 10 time zones away means that many employees of global firms are "on call" 24 hours a day. Second, communication technology allows employees to do their work at home, in their cars, or on the ski slopes at Whistler. This lets many people in technical and professional jobs do their work at any time and from any place. Third, organizations are asking employees to put in longer hours.

Employees are increasingly recognizing that work is affecting on their personal lives, and they are not happy about it. For example, recent studies suggest that employees want jobs that give them flexibility in their work schedules so they can better manage work-life conflicts.[35] In fact, evidence indicates that balancing work and life demands now surpasses job security as an employee priority.[36] In addition, the next generation of employees is likely to show similar concerns.[37] A majority of college and university students say that attaining a balance between personal life and work is a primary career goal. They want "a life" as well as a job. Organizations that don't help their people achieve work-life balance will find it increasingly difficult to attract and retain the most capable and motivated employees.

Creating a Positive Work Environment

Although competitive pressures on most organizations are stronger than ever, we have noticed an interesting turn in both OB research and management practice, at least in some organizations. Instead of responding to competitive pressures by "turning up the heat," some organizations are trying to realize a competitive advantage by encouraging a positive work environment. For example, Jeff Immelt and Jim McNerney, both disciples of Jack Welch (former CEO of GE), have tried to maintain high performance expectations (a characteristic of GE's culture) while also encouraging a positive work environment in their organizations (GE and Boeing, respectively). "In this time of turmoil and cynicism about business, you need to be passionate, positive leaders," Immelt recently told his top managers.

At the same time, a real growth area in OB research has been **positive organizational scholarship** (also called *positive organizational behaviour*), which concerns how organizations develop human strengths, foster vitality and resilience, and unlock potential. Researchers in this area argue that too much of OB research and management practice has been targeted toward identifying what is wrong with organizations and their employees. In response, these researchers try to study what is *good* about organizations.[38]

For example, positive organizational scholars have studied a concept called "reflected best-self"—asking employees to think about situations in which they were at their "personal best" to understand how to exploit their strengths. These researchers argue that we all have things at which we are unusually good, yet too often we focus on addressing our limitations and too rarely think about how to exploit our strengths.[39]

Although positive organizational scholarship does not deny the presence (or even the value) of the negative (such as critical feedback), it does challenge researchers to look at OB through a new lens. It also challenges organizations to think about how to exploit their employees' strengths rather than dwell on their limitations. For instance, WestJet makes use of employees' cheerful, outgoing personalities to provide better customer service.

> **positive organizational scholarship** An area of OB research that concerns how organizations develop human strength, foster vitality and resilience, and unlock potential.

Global Competition

In recent years, businesses in Canada have faced tough competition from those in the United States, Europe, Japan, and even China, as well as from other businesses within our borders. To survive, they have had to reduce costs, increase productivity, and improve quality. A number of Canadian companies have found it necessary to merge in order to survive. For instance, Rona, the Boucherville, Quebec-based home improvement store, bought out Lansing, Revy, and Revelstoke in recent years to defend its turf against the

Dallas, Texas-based Pizza Hut is responding to globalization by expanding its restaurants and delivery services worldwide. Pizza Hut introduced pizza to Chinese consumers in 1990. Today, Pizza Hut management targets mainland China as the number one market for new restaurant development because of the country's enormous growth potential. In this photo, a Pizza Hut employee passes out free samples in Nanjing to promote its delivery service. Managers expect delivery to become increasingly important as economic activity continues to expand, placing increased time demands on Chinese families.

Atlanta, Georgia-based Home Depot. That may not be enough to keep it from being swallowed up by the Mooresville, North Carolina-based Lowe's home improvement company, however.

Some employers are starting to outsource jobs to other countries where labour costs are lower. For instance, Toronto-based Dell Canada's technical service lines are handled by technicians working in India. Toronto-based Wall & Associates, a full-service chartered accounting and management consulting firm, outsources document management to Uganda. Employees in Uganda are willing to work for $1 an hour to sort and record receipts. While these wages might seem low, on average, Ugandans make only $1 a day.

These changes in the workplace, and the loss of jobs to international outsourcing, mean that the actual jobs that employees perform, and even those of managers to whom employees report, are in a permanent state of flux. To stay employable under these conditions, employees need to continually update their knowledge and skills to meet new job requirements.[40] Today's managers and employees have to learn to live with flexibility, spontaneity, uncertainty, and unpredictability.

The changing and global competitive environment means that not only do individuals have to become increasingly flexible, but organizations do too. They need to learn how to adjust to shifts in demand, technology, and the economy. For example, Burnaby, BC-based George Third & Son fabricates and installs steel structures in Canada and the United States. The company was founded in 1910 and has since undergone a number of changes, including moving into different manufacturing lines. The family-owned company owes its survival to the ability to shift with the times. "Corporate survival has depended on change, a feisty willingness to leap off a cliff," says Rob Third, grandson of the founder, and the individual responsible for production and purchasing. Adds brother Brett, who is in charge of marketing, sales, and administration, "We need to make changes to keep going in the business."[41]

To make the changes that need to be made, organizations and people must be committed to learning new skills, new ways of thinking, and new ways of doing business.

Managing and Working in a Multicultural World

Twenty or 30 years ago, national borders protected most firms from foreign competitive pressures. This is no longer the case. Trading blocks such as the North American Free Trade Agreement (NAFTA) and the European Union (EU) have significantly reduced tariffs and barriers to trade, and North America and Europe no longer have a monopoly on highly skilled labour. The Internet has also enabled companies to become more globally connected, by opening up international sales and by increasing the opportunities to carry on business. Even small firms can bid on projects in different countries and compete with larger firms via the Internet.

The world has truly become a global village. Hudson's Bay Company, considered a Canadian icon, was bought by NRDC Equity Partners in 2008, and is now American-owned. McDonald's Canada opened the first McDonald's restaurant in Moscow. New employees at Finland-based phone maker Nokia are increasingly being recruited from India, China, and other developing countries—with non-Finns now outnumbering Finns at Nokia's famed research centre in Helsinki. All major automobile manufacturers now build cars outside their borders: Toyota and Honda build cars in Ontario; Ford in Brazil; and both Mercedes and BMW in South Africa. Hitachi Canadian Industries in Saskatoon produces power-generating equipment components for its local market and supplies parts to the parent company in Japan.

The message? As multinational corporations develop operations worldwide, as companies develop joint ventures with foreign partners, and as employees increasingly pursue job opportunities across national borders, managers and employees must become capable of working with people from different cultures. Managing people well and understanding the interpersonal dynamics of the workplace are issues not just for companies operating in Canada.

When individuals travel to other countries to work, they may be confronted with practices different from what they are used to at home. This may present challenges, but it might also offer chances to learn from other cultures. Professor John Eggers of the Richard Ivey School of Business at the University of Western Ontario has commented on how doing business in Asia is different in some ways from doing business in Canada. He notes, "It is important to remember that business is conducted through relationships much more so than it is in Western countries. It takes years to form and develop the relationships a company needs, and to build the trust necessary to do business. Business in Asia is conducted courteously and respectfully, and at a slower pace—foreign managers who do not act in a polite manner will not be well received."[42]

The *OB Around the Globe* feature found throughout this textbook illustrates the similarities and differences of organizations the world over. The first such feature looks at the South African concept of *ubuntu*, or humaneness, and how it guides management activity in that country.

  **AROUND THE GLOBE**

South Africa's *Ubuntu*

What happens when "youngsters" try to manage in South Africa? Values of efficiency, productivity, and increased output may drive North American firms, but they are at odds with the South African notion of *ubuntu*.[43] *Ubuntu* is a concept that emphasizes group well-being and social harmony.

A major industrial company in South Africa failed to consider *ubuntu* when it developed a training program to encourage black employees to become managers. The first men through the program were 20 to 24 years old, and they performed well. However, when they were assigned to management positions, some individuals refused to work for them. After questioning the employees more, senior management found that older men do not work for "youngsters." The company had violated informal norms of the group by not respecting the importance of age for this culture.

Expectations about how management should be carried out are also different. An African manager who was trained in a more characteristic "Western" manner was called before his tribal elders for treating the workers as employees rather than as "brothers and sisters."

The importance of *ubuntu* in South Africa and the absence of an equivalent concept in North America underscores that behaviour and expectations are different across the world. Many of the theories that we present have been developed in North America, particularly in the United States. Therefore, we critically examine their applicability in non-North American settings throughout this textbook.

OB: Making Sense of Behaviour in Organizations

As Charles Chang took more responsibility for managing people at Sequel Naturals, be considered what he could do to make sure his employees felt motivated.[44] He started with a profit-sharing plan and performance bonuses. He looked to create a better organizational culture. He used weekly staff meetings to give recognition rewards, and he regularly holds all-staff retreats. What can Chang learn from organizational behaviour to do an even better job of managing his employees?

3 Isn't organizational behaviour common sense? Or just like psychology?

We have thus far considered how OB can be applied in the workplace. In this next section, we consider the discipline of OB, looking first at the fields of study that have contributed to it. We then discuss the fact that OB is a scientific discipline, with careful research that is conducted to test and evaluate theories.

The Building Blocks of OB

OB emerged as a distinct field in the 1940s in the United States.[45] It is an applied behavioural science that is built upon contributions from a number of behavioural disciplines. The predominant areas are psychology, social psychology, sociology, and anthropology. As we will learn, psychology's contributions have been mainly at the individual, or micro, level of analysis. The other three disciplines have contributed to our understanding of macro concepts, such as group processes and organization. Exhibit 1-2 presents an overview of the major contributions to the study of OB.

EXHIBIT 1-2   Toward an OB Discipline

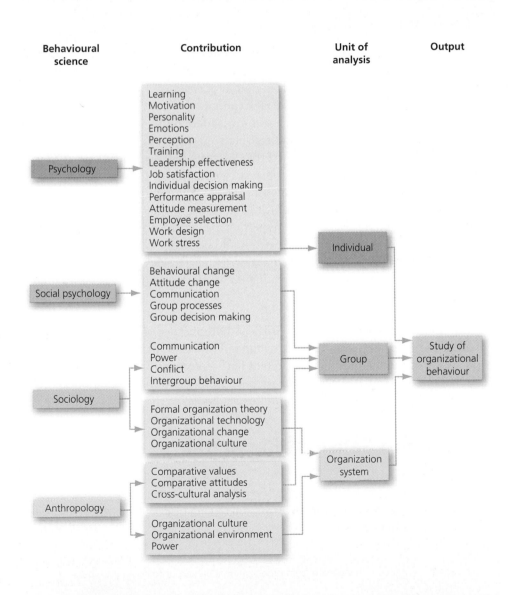

Psychology

Psychology is the science that seeks to measure, explain, and sometimes change the behaviour of humans and other animals. Psychologists concern themselves with studying and attempting to understand individual behaviour. Those who have contributed and continue to add to the knowledge of OB are learning theorists, personality theorists, counselling psychologists, and, most important, industrial and organizational psychologists.

Early industrial and organizational psychologists concerned themselves with problems of fatigue, boredom, and other factors relevant to working conditions that could impede efficient work performance. More recently, their contributions have been expanded to include learning, perception, personality, emotions, training, leadership effectiveness, needs and motivational forces, job satisfaction, decision-making processes, performance appraisals, attitude measurement, employee selection techniques, job design, and work stress.

Social Psychology

Social psychology blends concepts from both psychology and sociology, though it is generally considered a branch of psychology. It focuses on people's influence on one another. One major area that has received considerable attention from social psychologists is *change*—how to implement it and how to reduce barriers to its acceptance. In addition, we find social psychologists making significant contributions in the areas of measuring, understanding, and changing attitudes; communication patterns; and building trust. Finally, social psychologists have made important contributions to our study of group behaviour, power, and conflict.

Sociology

Whereas psychologists focus their attention on the individual, sociologists study the social system in which individuals fill their roles; that is, sociology studies people in relation to their social environment or culture. Specifically, sociologists have made their greatest contribution to OB through their study of group behaviour in organizations, particularly formal and complex organizations. Some of the areas within OB that have received valuable input from sociologists are group dynamics, design of work teams, organizational culture, formal organizational theory and structure, organizational technology, communication, power, and conflict.

Anthropology

Anthropology is the study of societies to learn about human beings and their activities. Anthropologists' work on cultures and environments, for instance, has helped us understand differences in fundamental values, attitudes, and behaviour between people in different countries and within different organizations. Much of our current understanding of organizational culture, organizational environments, and differences between national cultures is the result of the work of anthropologists or those using their methodologies.

The Rigour of OB

Whether you want to respond to the challenges of the Canadian workplace, manage well, or guarantee satisfying and rewarding employment for yourself, it pays to understand organizational behaviour. OB provides a systematic approach to the study of behaviour in organizations. Underlying this systematic approach is the belief that behaviour is not random. It stems from and is directed toward some end that the individual believes, rightly or wrongly, is in his or her best interest. OB is even being adopted by other disciplines, as *OB in the Street* shows.

IN THE STREET

Is OB Just for the Workplace?

Can finance learn anything from OB?   It may surprise you to learn that, increasingly, other business disciplines are employing OB concepts.[46] Marketing has the closest overlap with OB. Trying to predict consumer behaviour is not that different from trying to predict employee behaviour. Both require an understanding of the dynamics and underlying causes of human behaviour, and there is a lot of correspondence between the disciplines.

What is perhaps more surprising is the degree to which the so-called hard disciplines are making use of soft OB concepts. Behavioural finance, behavioural accounting, and behavioural economics (also called *economic psychology*) all have grown in importance and interest in the past several years.

On reflection, the use of OB by these disciplines should not be so surprising. Your common sense will tell you that humans are not perfectly rational creatures, and in many cases, our actions don't conform to a rational model of behaviour. Although some elements of irrationality are incorporated into economic thought, finance, accounting, and economics researchers find it increasingly useful to draw from OB concepts.

For example, investors have a tendency to place more weight on private information (information that only they, or a limited group of people, know) than on public information, even when there is reason to believe that the public information is more accurate. To understand this phenomenon, finance researchers use OB concepts. In addition, behavioural accounting research might study how feedback influences auditors' behaviour, or the functional and dysfunctional implications of earnings warnings on investor behaviour.

The point is that while you take separate courses in various business disciplines, the lines between them are increasingly being blurred as researchers draw from common disciplines to explain behaviour. We think that this is a good thing because it more accurately matches the way managers actually work, think, and behave.

OB Looks at Consistencies

Certainly there are differences among individuals. Placed in similar situations, all people don't act exactly alike. However, there are certain fundamental consistencies underlying the behaviour of most individuals that can be identified and then modified to reflect individual differences.

These fundamental consistencies are very important because they allow predictability. When you get into your car, you make some definite and usually highly accurate predictions about how other people will behave. In North America, for instance, you predict that other drivers will stop at stop signs and red lights, drive on the right side of the road, pass on your left, and not cross the solid double line on mountain roads. Your predictions about the behaviour of people behind the wheels of their cars are almost always correct. Obviously, the rules of driving make predictions about driving behaviour fairly easy.

What may be less obvious is that there are rules (written and unwritten) in almost every setting. Therefore, it can be argued that it's possible to predict behaviour (undoubtedly, not always with 100-percent accuracy) in supermarkets, classrooms, doctors' offices, elevators, and in most structured situations. For instance, do you turn around and face the doors when you get into an elevator? Almost everyone does. Is there a sign inside the elevator that tells you to do this? Probably not! Just as we make predictions about drivers, where there are definite rules of the road, we can make predictions about the behaviour of people in elevators, where there are few written rules. This example supports a major point of this textbook: Behaviour is generally predictable, and the systematic study of behaviour is a means to making reasonably accurate predictions.

OB Looks Beyond Common Sense

Each of us is a student of behaviour. Since our earliest years, we have watched the actions of others and have attempted to interpret what we see. Whether or not you have explicitly thought about it before, you have been "reading" people almost all your life. You watch what others do and try to explain to yourself why they have engaged in their behaviour. In addition, you have attempted to predict what they might do under different sets of conditions. Unfortunately, your casual or commonsensical approach to reading others can often lead to erroneous predictions. However, you can improve your predictive ability by supplementing your intuitive opinions with a more systematic approach.

The systematic approach used in this textbook uncovers important facts and relationships and will provide a base from which more accurate predictions of behaviour can be made. Underlying this systematic approach is the belief that behaviour is not random. Rather, there are certain fundamental consistencies underlying the behaviour of all individuals that can be identified and then modified to reflect individual differences.

These fundamental consistencies are very important. Why? Because they allow predictability. Behaviour is generally predictable, and the *systematic study* of behaviour is a means to making reasonably accurate predictions. When we use the phrase **systematic study**, we mean looking at relationships, attempting to attribute causes and effects, and basing our conclusions on scientific evidence—that is, on data gathered under controlled conditions and measured and interpreted in a reasonably rigorous manner. Exhibit 1-3 illustrates the common methods researchers use to study topics in OB.

systematic study Looking at relationships, attempting to attribute causes and effects, and drawing conclusions based on scientific evidence.

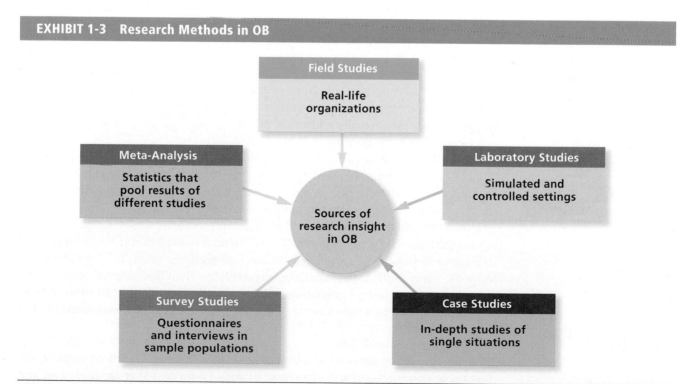

EXHIBIT 1-3   Research Methods in OB

Field Studies
Real-life organizations

Meta-Analysis
Statistics that pool results of different studies

Laboratory Studies
Simulated and controlled settings

Sources of research insight in OB

Survey Studies
Questionnaires and interviews in sample populations

Case Studies
In-depth studies of single situations

Source: J. R. Schermerhorn, J. G. Hunt, and R. N. Osborn, *Organizational Behavior*, 9th Edition, 2005, p. 4. Copyright © 2005 John Wiley & Sons, Inc. Used with permission of John Wiley & Sons, Inc.

evidence-based management (EBM) Basing managerial decisions on the best available scientific evidence.

An approach that complements systematic study is **evidence-based management (EBM)**. EBM involves basing managerial decisions on the best available scientific evidence. We would want doctors to make decisions about patient care based on the latest available evidence, and EBM argues that we want managers to do the same. That means managers must become more scientific in how they think about management problems. For example, a manager might pose a managerial question, search for the best available evidence, and apply the relevant information to the question or case at hand. You might think it's difficult to argue against this (what manager would argue that decisions should not be based on evidence?), but the vast majority of management decisions are still made "on the fly," with little or systematic study of available evidence.[47]

intuition A gut feeling not necessarily supported by research.

Systematic study and EBM add to **intuition**, or those "gut feelings" about "why I do what I do" and "what makes others tick." Of course, a systematic approach does not mean that the things you have come to believe in an unsystematic way are necessarily incorrect. As Jack Welch noted, "The trick, of course, is to know when to go with your gut." If we make all decisions with intuition or gut instinct, we are likely making decisions with incomplete information—sort of like making an investment decision with only half the data. The limits of relying on intuition are made worse by the fact that we tend to overestimate the accuracy of what we think we know. A recent survey revealed that 86 percent of managers thought their organization was treating their employees well. However, only 55 percent of employees thought they were well treated.[48]

We find a similar problem in looking to the business and popular media for management wisdom. The business press tends to be dominated by fads. As a writer for the *New Yorker* put it, "Every few years, new companies succeed, and they are scrutinized for the underlying truths they might reveal. But often there is no underlying truth; the companies just happened to be in the right place at the right time."[49] Although we try to avoid it, we might also fall into this trap. It's not that the business press stories are all wrong; it's that without a systematic approach, it's hard to know the truth.

Some of the conclusions we make in this textbook, based on reasonably substantive research findings, will support what you always knew was true. But you will also be exposed to research evidence that runs counter to what you may have thought was common sense. One of the objectives of this textbook is to encourage you to enhance your intuitive views of behaviour with a systematic analysis, in the belief that such analysis will improve your accuracy in explaining and predicting behaviour.

We are not advising that you throw your intuition, or all the business press, out the window. Nor are we arguing that research is always right. Researchers make mistakes, too. What we are advising is to use evidence as much as possible to inform your intuition and experience. That is the promise of OB.

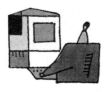

Throughout this textbook, the *Focus on Research* feature will highlight some of the careful studies that form the building blocks of OB. We have also marked major research findings in every chapter with an icon (shown in the margin at right) so that you can easily see what the research says about various concepts we cover.

If understanding behaviour were simply common sense, we would not observe many of the problems that occur in the workplace, because managers and employees would know how to behave. Unfortunately, as you will see from examples throughout the textbook, many individuals and managers exhibit less than desirable behaviour in the workplace. With a stronger grounding in OB, you might be able to avoid some of these mistakes. This chapter's *Point/Counterpoint* on page 27 looks at how systematic OB is.

OB Has Few Absolutes

There are few, if any, simple and universal principles that explain OB. In contrast, the physical sciences—chemistry, astronomy, physics—have laws that are consistent and apply in a wide range of situations. They allow scientists to generalize about the pull of gravity or to confidently send astronauts into space to repair satellites. But as one noted behavioural researcher aptly concluded, "God gave all the easy problems to the physicists."

Social scientists study human problems—and human beings are complex. Because people are not alike, our ability to make simple, accurate, and sweeping generalizations is limited. Two people often act very differently in the same situation, and the same person's behaviour changes in different situations.

OB Takes a Contingency Approach

Just because people can behave differently at different times does not mean, of course, that we cannot offer reasonably accurate explanations of human behaviour or make valid predictions. It does mean, however, that OB must consider behaviour within the context in which it occurs—a strategy known as a **contingency approach**. In other words, OB's answers "depend upon the situation," For example, OB scholars would avoid stating that everyone likes complex and challenging work (the general concept). Why? Because not everyone wants a challenging job. Some people prefer the routine over the varied or the simple over the complex. In other words, a job that is appealing to one person may not be to another, so the appeal of the job is contingent on the person who holds it.

As you proceed through this textbook, you will encounter a wealth of research-based theories about how people behave in organizations. You will also discover descriptions of well-designed research studies. But don't expect to find a lot of straightforward cause-and-effect relationships. There aren't many! OB theories mirror the subject matter with which they deal. People are complex and complicated, and so too must be the theories developed to explain their actions.

Consistent with the contingency approach, *Point/Counterpoint* debates are provided in each chapter. These debates are included to highlight the fact that within OB there are disagreements. Through the *Point/Counterpoint* format, you will gain the opportunity to explore different points of view, discover how diverse perspectives complement and

contingency approach An approach taken by OB that considers behaviour within the context in which it occurs.

EXHIBIT 1-4

"I'm a social scientist, Michael. That means I can't explain electricity or anything like that, but if you ever want to know about people I'm your man."

Source: Drawing by Handelsman in *The New Yorker*, Copyright © 1986 by the New Yorker Magazine. Reprinted by permission.

EXHIBIT 1-5   The Fundamentals of OB
OB considers the multiple levels in an organization: individual, group, and organizational.
OB is built from the wisdom and research of multiple disciplines, including psychology, sociology, social psychology, and anthropology.
OB takes a systematic approach to the study of organizational phenomena. It is research-based.
OB takes a contingency approach to the consideration of organizational phenomena. Recommendations depend on the situation.

oppose each other, and gain insight into some of the debates currently taking place within the OB field.

So in Chapter 5 you will find the argument that money motivates, followed by the argument that there is little evidence to support the claim that money is an important motivator. Similarly, in other chapters you will read both sides of debates on such controversial issues as whether leaders can be successful in any environment and whether open communication is always desirable. These arguments are meant to demonstrate that OB is a lively field and, like many disciplines, has disagreements over specific findings, methods, and theories. Some of the *Point/Counterpoint* arguments are more charged than others, but each makes some valid points that you should find thought-provoking. The key is to be able to decipher under what conditions each argument may be right or wrong.

OB in Summary

We have discussed the meaning of OB throughout this chapter, and revealed different aspects of what OB covers. The essential points of OB that you should keep in mind as you study this topic are illustrated in Exhibit 1-5.

Summary and Implications

1 **What is organizational behaviour?** Organizational behaviour (OB) is a field of study that investigates the impact that individuals, groups, and structure have on behaviour within an organization. It uses that knowledge to make organizations work more effectively. Specifically, OB focuses on how to improve productivity, reduce both absenteeism and turnover, and increase employee job satisfaction. OB also helps us understand how people can work together more effectively in the workplace.

OB recognizes differences, helps us see the value of workforce diversity, and calls attention to practices that may need to be changed when managing and working in different countries. It can help improve quality and employee productivity by showing managers how to empower their people, as well as how to design and implement change programs. It offers specific insights to improve people skills.

2 **What challenges do managers and employees face in today's workplace?** OB considers three levels of analysis—the individual, the group, and the organization—which, combined, help us understand behaviour in organizations. Each level has different challenges.

At the individual level, we encounter employees who have different characteristics, and thus we consider how to better understand and make the most of these differences. Because employees have become more cynical about their employers, job satisfaction and motivation have become important issues in today's organizations. Employees are also confronted with the trend toward an empowered workplace. Perhaps the greatest challenge individuals (and organizations) face is how to behave ethically.

At the group level, individuals are increasingly expected to work in teams, which means that they need to do so more effectively. Employees are expected to have good interpersonal skills. The workplace is now made up of people from many different backgrounds, which requires that we have a greater ability to understand those different from ourselves.

At the organizational level, Canadian businesses face many challenges today. They must continuously improve the quality of products and services as well as productivity. By putting people first, organizations can generate a committed workforce, but taking this approach becomes a challenge for businesses that focus solely on the bottom line. Moreover, employees increasingly are demanding a balance between personal life and work. It has become essential to develop effective employees who are committed to the organization. Canadian businesses also face ongoing competition from US businesses, as well as growing competition from the global marketplace. Organizations also have to learn how to be more sensitive to cultural differences, not only because Canada is a multicultural country, but also because competitive companies often develop global alliances or set up plants in foreign countries, where being aware of other cultures becomes a key to success.

3 **Isn't organizational behaviour common sense? Or just like psychology?** OB is built on contributions from a number of behavioural disciplines, including psychology, sociology, social psychology, and anthropology. We all hold generalizations about the behaviour of people. Some of our generalizations may provide valid insights into human behaviour, but many are wrong. If understanding behaviour were simply common sense, we would see fewer problems in the workplace, because managers and employees would know how to behave. OB provides a more systematic approach to improving predictions of behaviour than would be made from common sense alone.

For Review

1. Define *organizational behaviour*.

2. What is an organization? Is the family unit an organization? Explain.

3. "Behaviour is generally predictable, so there is no need to formally study OB." Do you agree or disagree with this statement? Why?

4. What are some of the challenges and opportunities that managers face in today's workplace?

5. What are the three levels of analysis in our OB model? Are they related? If so, how?

6. Why is job satisfaction an important consideration for OB?

7. What are effectiveness and efficiency, and how are they related to OB?

8. What does it mean to say OB takes a contingency approach in its analysis of behaviour?

For Critical Thinking

1. "OB is for everyone." Build an argument to support this statement.

2. Why do you think the subject of OB might be criticized as being "only common sense," when we would rarely hear such a criticism of a course in physics or statistics? Do you think this criticism of OB is fair?

3. On a scale of 1 to 10 measuring the sophistication of a scientific discipline in predicting phenomena, mathematical physics would probably be a 10. Where do you think OB would fall on the scale? Why?

4. Can empowerment lead to greater job satisfaction?

 **for You**

■ As you journey through this course in OB, bear in mind that the processes we describe are as relevant to you as an individual as they are to organizations, managers, and employees.

■ When you work together with student teams, join a student organization, or volunteer time to a community group, know that your ability to get along with others has an effect on your interactions with the other people in the group and the achievement of the group's goals.

■ If you are aware of how your perceptions and personality affect your interactions with others, you can be more careful in forming your initial impression of others.

■ By knowing how to motivate others who are working with you, how to communicate effectively, and when to negotiate and compromise, you can get along in a variety of situations that are not necessarily work-related.

POINT

COUNTERPOINT

Find the Quick Fix to OB Issues

Walk into your nearest major bookstore. You will undoubtedly find a large section of books devoted to management and managing human behaviour. A close look at the titles will reveal that there is certainly no shortage of popular books on topics related to OB. To illustrate the point, consider the following book titles that are currently available on the topic of leadership:

- *Power Plays: Shakespeare's Lessons on Leadership and Management* (Simon and Schuster, 2001)

- *The Leadership Teachings of Geronimo* (Sterling House, 2002)

- *Catch! A Fishmonger's Guide to Greatness* (Berrett-Koehler, 2003)

- *Leadership the Eleanor Roosevelt Way* (Portfolio Trade, 2003)

- *Leadership Wisdom from the Monk Who Sold His Ferrari* (Hay House, 2003)

- *Tony Soprano on Management: Leadership Lessons Inspired by America's Favorite Mobster* (Berkley, 2004)

- *Beyond Basketball: Coach K's Keywords for Success* (Warner Business Books, 2006)

- *Bhagavad Gita on Effective Leadership* (iUniverse, 2006)

- *If Harry Potter Ran General Electric: Leadership Wisdom from the World of Wizards* (Currency/ Doubleday, 2006)

Organizations are always looking for leaders; and managers and manager-wannabes are continually looking for ways to improve their leadership skills. Publishers respond to this demand by offering hundreds of titles that claim to provide insights into the complex subject of leadership. People hope that there are "shortcuts" to leadership success and that books like these can provide them with the secrets to leadership that others know and that they can quickly learn.

Beware of the Quick Fix!

We all want to find quick and simple solutions to our complex problems. But here is the bad news: On problems related to OB, the quick and simple solutions are often wrong because they fail to consider the diversity among organizations, situations, and individuals. As Einstein said, "Everything should be made as simple as possible, but not simpler."

When it comes to trying to understand people at work, there is no shortage of simplistic ideas that books and consultants promote. And these books are not just on leadership. Consider three books that made it to the bestseller lists. *Our Iceberg Is Melting* looks at change through the eyes of a penguin. *Who Moved My Cheese?* is a fable about two mice that is meant to convey the benefits of accepting change. And *Whale Done!* proposes that managers can learn a lot about motivating people from techniques used by whale trainers at Sea World in San Diego. Are the "insights" from these books generalizable to people working in hundreds of different countries, in a thousand different organizations, and doing a million different jobs? It's very unlikely.

Popular books on OB often have cute titles and are fun to read. But they can be dangerous. They make the job of managing people seem much simpler than it really is. They are also often based on the author's opinions rather than substantive research.

OB is a complex subject. There are few, if any, simple statements about human behaviour that are generalizable to all people in all situations. Should you really try to apply leadership insights you got from a book on Shakespeare or Geronimo to managing software engineers in the twenty-first century?

The capitalist system ensures that when a need exists, opportunistic individuals will surface to fill that need. When it comes to managing people at work, there is clearly a need for valid and reliable insights to guide managers and those aspiring to managerial positions. However, most of the offerings available at your local bookstore tend to be overly simplistic solutions. To the degree that people buy these books and enthusiastically expect them to provide the secrets to effective management, they do a disservice to themselves and those they are trying to manage.

OB *AT WORK*

The Competing Values Framework: Identifying Your Interpersonal Skills

From the list below, identify what you believe to be your strongest skills, and then identify those in which you think your performance is weak. You should identify about 4 strong skills and 4 weak skills.[50]

1. Taking initiative
2. Goal setting
3. Delegating effectively
4. Personal productivity and motivation
5. Motivating others
6. Time and stress management
7. Planning
8. Organizing
9. Controlling

10. Receiving and organizing information
11. Evaluating routine information
12. Responding to routine information
13. Understanding yourself and others
14. Interpersonal communication
15. Developing subordinates
16. Team building

17. Participative decision making
18. Conflict management
19. Living with change
20. Creative thinking
21. Managing change
22. Building and maintaining a power base
23. Negotiating agreement and commitment
24. Negotiating and selling ideas

Scoring Key

These skills are based on the Competing Values Framework (pages 32–35), and they appear in detail in Exhibit 1-7 on page 33. Below, you will see how the individual skills relate to various managerial roles. Using the skills you identified as strongest, identify which roles you feel especially prepared for right now. Then, using the skills you identified as weakest, identify areas in which you might want to gain more skills. You should also use this information to determine whether you are currently more internally or externally focused, or oriented more toward flexibility or control.

Director: 1, 2, 3   Mentor: 13, 14, 15

Producer: 4, 5, 6   Facilitator: 16, 17, 18

Coordinator: 7, 8, 9   Innovator: 19, 20, 21

Monitor: 10, 11, 12   Broker: 22, 23, 24

After reviewing how your strengths and weaknesses relate to the skills that today's managers and leaders need, as illustrated in Exhibit 1-7, you should consider whether you need to develop a broader range of skills.

Self-Assessment Library

More Learning About Yourself Exercises

An additional self-assessment relevant to this chapter appears on MyOBLab (**www.pearsoned.ca/myoblab**).

IV.G.1   How Much Do I Know About OB?

When you complete the additional assessments, consider the following:

1. Am I surprised about my score?
2. Would my friends evaluate me similarly?

BREAKOUT **GROUP** EXERCISES

Form small groups to discuss the following topics, as assigned by your instructor:

1. Consider a group situation in which you have worked. To what extent did the group rely on the technical skills of the group members vs. their interpersonal skills? Which skills seemed most important in helping the group function well?

2. Identify some examples of "worst jobs." What conditions of these jobs made them unpleasant? To what extent were these conditions related to behaviours of individuals?

3. Develop a list of "organizational puzzles," that is, behaviour you have observed in organizations that seemed to make little sense. As the term progresses, see if you can begin to explain these puzzles, using your knowledge of OB.

WORKING WITH **OTHERS** EXERCISE

Interpersonal Skills in the Workplace

This exercise asks you to consider the skills outlined in the Competing Values Framework on pages 32–35 to develop an understanding of managerial expertise. Steps 1–4 can be completed in 15–20 minutes.

1. Using the skills listed in the *Learning About Yourself Exercise*, identify the 4 skills that you think all managers should have.

2. Identify the 4 skills that you think are least important for managers to have.

3. In groups of 5–7, reach a consensus on the most-needed and least-needed skills identified in steps 1 and 2.

4. Using Exhibit 1-7, determine whether your "ideal" managers would have trouble managing in some dimensions of organizational demands.

5. Your instructor will lead a general discussion of your results.

ETHICAL **DILEMMA** EXERCISE

What Is the Right Balance between Work and Personal Life?

When you think of work-life conflicts, you may tend to think of people in lower levels of organizations who might not have as much flexibility in determining their workday.[51] But a survey of 179 CEOs revealed that many of them are struggling with this issue. For instance, 31 percent said that they have a high level of stress in their lives; 47 percent admitted that they would sacrifice some compensation for more personal time; and 16 percent considered changing jobs in the past 6 months to reduce stress or sacrifices made in their personal lives.

Most of these surveyed executives conceded that they had given up, and continue to give up, a lot to get to the top in their organizations. They are often tired from the extensive and exhausting travel their jobs demand, not to mention an average 60-hour workweek. Yet most feel the climb to the CEO position was worth whatever sacrifices they have had to make.

Jean Stone, while not representative of the group, indicates the price that some of these executives have had to pay. As senior VP and chief operating officer of Dukane

Corporation, an Illinois-based manufacturer of electronic communications equipment, Stone describes herself as highly achievement-oriented. She has an intense focus on her job and admits to having lost sight of her personal life. Recently divorced after a 10-year marriage, she acknowledges that "career and work pressures were a factor in that."

How much emphasis on work is too much? What is the right balance between work and personal life? How much would you be willing to give up to be CEO of a major company? And if you were a CEO, what ethical responsibilities, if any, do you think you have to help your employees balance their work-family obligations?

CASE INCIDENTS

How a UPS Manager Cut Turnover

In 1998, Jennifer Shroeger was promoted to district manager for UPS's operation in Buffalo, New York.[52] She was responsible for $225 million in revenue, 2300 employees, and the processing of some 45 000 packages an hour. When she took over in Buffalo, she faced a serious problem: Turnover was out of control. Part-time employees—who load, unload, and sort packages and who account for half of Buffalo's workforce—were leaving at the rate of 50 percent a year. Cutting this turnover rate became her highest priority.

The entire UPS organization relies heavily on part-time employees. In fact, it has historically been the primary route to becoming a full-time employee. Most of UPS's current executives, for instance, began as part-timers while attending college or university, then moved into full-time positions. In addition, UPS has always treated its part-timers well. They are given high pay, flexible work hours, full benefits, and substantial financial aid to go back to school. Yet these pluses did not seem to be enough to keep employees at UPS in Buffalo.

Shroeger developed a comprehensive plan to reduce turnover. It focused on improving hiring, communication, the workplace, and supervisory training.

Shroeger began by modifying the hiring process to screen out people who essentially wanted full-time jobs. She reasoned that unfulfilled expectations were frustrating the hires whose preferences were for full-time work. Given that it typically took new part-timers six years to work up to a full-time job, it made sense to try to identify people who actually preferred part-time work.

Next, Shroeger analyzed the large database of information that UPS had on her district's employees. The data led her to the conclusion that she had five distinct groups working for her—differentiated by age and stages in their careers. And these groups had different needs and interests. In response, Shroeger modified the communication style and motivation techniques she used with each employee to reflect the group to which he or she belonged. For instance, Shroeger found that college students are most interested in

building skills that they can apply later in their careers. As long as these employees saw that they were learning new skills, they were content to keep working at UPS. So Shroeger began offering them Saturday classes for computer-skill development and career-planning discussions.

Many new UPS employees in Buffalo were intimidated by the huge warehouse in which they had to work. To lessen that intimidation, Shroeger improved lighting throughout the building and upgraded break rooms to make them more user-friendly. To further help new employees adjust, she turned some of her best shift supervisors into trainers who provided specific guidance during new hires' first week. She also installed more personal computers on the floor, which gave new employees easier access to training materials and human resource information on UPS's internal network.

Finally, Shroeger expanded training so supervisors had the skills to handle increased empowerment. Because she recognized that her supervisors—most of whom were part-timers themselves—were the ones best equipped to understand the needs of part-time employees, supervisors were taught how to assess difficult management situations, how to communicate in different ways, and how to identify the needs of different people. Supervisors learned to demonstrate interest in their employees as individuals. For instance, they were taught to inquire about employees' hobbies, where they went to school, and the like.

By 2002, Shroeger's program was showing impressive results. Her district's attrition rate had dropped from 50 percent to 6 percent. During the first quarter of 2002, not one part-timer left the night shift. Annual savings attributed to reduced turnover, based largely on lower hiring costs, are estimated to be around $1 million. Additional benefits that the Buffalo district has gained from a more stable workforce include a 20 percent reduction in lost workdays due to work-related injuries and a drop from 4 percent to 1 percent in packages delivered on the wrong day or at the wrong time.

Questions

1. In dollars-and-cents' terms, why did Jennifer Shroeger want to reduce turnover?

2. What are the implications from this case for motivating part-time employees?

3. What are the implications from this case for managing in future years when there may be a severe labour shortage?

4. Is it unethical to teach supervisors "to demonstrate interest in their employees as individuals"? Explain.

5. What facts in this case support the argument that OB should be approached from a contingency perspective?

Great Plains Software: Pursuing a People-First Strategy

Great Plains Software is a success story. It was begun in 1983 and bought in 2000 by Microsoft for $1.5 billion.[53] Management attributes much of its success to the company's people-first strategy.

As the company's CEO, Doug Burgum felt that the company's growth and success could be attributed to three guiding principles. First, make the company such a great place to work that people not only won't want to leave, they'll knock down the door to get in. Second, give employees ownership at every level. Third, let people grow—as professionals and as individuals.

What did Great Plains do to facilitate its people-first culture? Managers point to the company's structure, perks, and its commitment to helping employees develop their skills and leadership. Great Plains had a flat organization structure with a minimal degree of hierarchy. Work was done mostly in teams, and there were no traditional status perks such as executive parking spaces or corner-office suites. There were stock options for everyone, casual dress standards, an on-site daycare centre, and daily extracurricular classes in everything from aerobics to personal finance. But management is most proud of its commitment to the development of its people. The company offered a long list of training and educational opportunities to its employees, run on site and designed to help employees build their skill level. Great Plains' premier training program was called Leadership Is Everywhere. It was designed to ensure that the company had people who could assume new leadership roles in a continuously changing environment. The company reinforced classroom

training by placing its workers in departmental teams. At the helm of these teams were "team leaders," whose job it was to help foster their charges' ideas and projects. They also provided one-on-one job coaching and career-planning advice. Nearly all Great Plains employees were given the opportunity to become team leaders.

Burgum more than just increased revenues to support his belief that his people-first strategy works. He also succeeded in keeping employees content. Turnover, for instance, was a minuscule 5 percent a year—far below the information-technology average of 18 to 25 percent.

Questions

1. Putting people first worked for Great Plains. If the strategy is so effective, why do you think all firms have not adopted these practices?

2. Do you think a people-first approach is more applicable to certain businesses or industries than others? If so, what might they be? Why?

3. What downside, if any, do you see in being an employee at a company like Great Plains?

4. What downside, if any, do you see in managing at a company like Great Plains?

5. Some critics have argued that "People-first policies don't lead to high profits. High profits allow people-first policies." Do you agree? Explain your position.

OB *AT WORK*

From **Concepts**
            to **Skills**

Developing Interpersonal Skills

We note in this chapter that having a broad range of inter-personal skills to draw on makes us more effective organizational participants. So what kinds of interpersonal skills does an individual need in today's workplace? Robert Quinn, Kim Cameron, and their colleagues have developed a model known as the "Competing Values Framework" that can help us identify some of the most useful skills.[54] They note that the range of issues organizations face can be divided along two dimensions: an internal-external and a flexibility-control focus. This is illustrated in Exhibit 1-6. The internal-external dimension refers to the extent that organizations focus on one of two directions: either inwardly, toward employee needs and concerns and/or production processes and internal systems; or outwardly, toward such factors as the marketplace, government regulations, and the changing social, environmental, and technological conditions of the future. The flexibility-control dimension refers

to the competing demands of organizations to stay focused on doing what has been done in the past vs. being more flexible in orientation and outlook.

Because organizations face the competing demands shown in Exhibit 1-6, it becomes obvious that managers and employees need a variety of skills to help them function within the various quadrants at different points in time. For instance, the skills needed to operate an efficient assembly-line process are not the same as those needed to scan the external environment or to create opportunities in anticipation of changes in the environment. Quinn and his colleagues use the term *master manager* to indicate that successful managers learn and apply skills that will help them manage across the range of organizational demands; at some times moving toward flexibility, at others moving toward control, sometimes being more internally focused, sometimes being more externally driven.[55]

EXHIBIT 1-6   Competing Values Framework

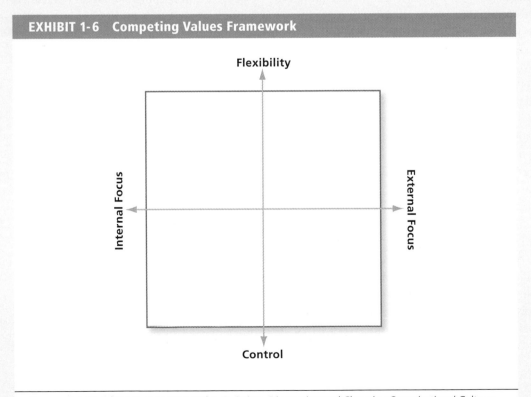

Source: Adapted from K. Cameron and R. E. Quinn, *Diagnosing and Changing Organizational Culture: Based on the Competing Values Framework* (Reading, MA: Addison Wesley Longman, 1999).

As organizations increasingly cut their layers, reducing the number of managers while also relying more on the use of teams in the workplace, the skills of the master manager apply as well to the employee. In other words, considering the Competing Values Framework, we can see that both managers and individual employees need to learn new skills and new ways of interpreting their organizational contexts. Continuing to use traditional skills and practices that worked in the past is not an option. The growth in self-employment also indicates a need to develop more interpersonal skills, particularly for anyone who goes on to build a business that involves hiring and managing employees.

Exhibit 1-7 outlines the many skills required of today's manager. It gives you an indication of the complex roles that managers and employees fill in the changing workplace. The skills are organized in terms of four major roles: maintaining flexibility, maintaining control, maintaining an external focus, and maintaining an internal focus. The *Learning About Yourself Exercise* on page 28 helps you identify your own strengths and weaknesses in these skill areas so that you can have a better sense of how close you

are to becoming a successful manager. For instance, on the flexibility side, organizations want to inspire their employees toward high-performance behaviour. Such behaviour includes looking ahead to the future and imagining possible new directions for the organization. To do these things, employees need to think and act like mentors and facilitators. It is also important to have the skills of innovators and brokers. On the control side, organizations need to set clear goals about productivity expectations, and they have to develop and implement systems to carry out the production process. To be effective on the production side, employees need to have the skills of monitors, coordinators, directors, and producers. The *Working with Others Exercise* on page 29 helps you better understand how closely your views on the ideal skills of managers and leaders match the skills needed to be successful in the broad range of activities that managers and leaders encounter.

At this point, you may wonder whether it is possible for people to learn all of the skills necessary to become a master manager. More important, you may wonder whether we can change our individual style, say from more controlling to

---

EXHIBIT 1-7 Skills for Mastery in the New Workplace

Source: R. E. Quinn, *Beyond Rational Management* (San Francisco: Jossey-Bass, 1988), p. 86.

OB *AT WORK*

more flexible. Here is what Peggy Kent, chair, president, and CEO of Century Mining Corporation (a mid-tier Canadian gold producer), said about how her managerial style changed from controlling to more flexible over time: "I started out being very dictatorial. Everybody in head office reported to me. I had to learn to trust other executives so we could work out problems together."[56] So, while it is probably true that each of us has a preferred style of operating, it is also the case that we can develop new skills if that is something we choose to do.

Practising Skills

As the father of two young children, Marshall Rogers thought that serving on the board of Marysville Daycare would be a good way to stay in touch with those who cared for his children during the day.[57] But he never dreamed that he would become involved in union-management negotiations with daycare-centre workers.

Late one Sunday evening, in his ninth month as president of the daycare centre, Rogers received a phone call from Grace Ng, a union representative of the Provincial Government Employees' Union (PGEU). Ng informed Rogers that the daycare workers would be unionized the following week. Rogers was stunned to hear this news. Early the next morning, he had to present his new marketing plan to senior management at Techtronix Industries, where he was vice-president of marketing. Somehow he made it through the meeting, wondering why he had not been aware of the employees' unhappiness, and how this action would affect his children.

Following his presentation, Rogers received documentation from the Labour Relations Board indicating that the daycare employees had been working to unionize themselves for more than a year. Rogers immediately contacted Xavier Breslin, the board's vice-president, and together they determined that no one on the board had been aware that the daycare workers were unhappy, let alone prepared to join a union.

Hoping that there was some sort of misunderstanding, Rogers called Emma Reynaud, the Marysville supervisor. Reynaud attended most board meetings, but had never mentioned the union-organizing drive. Yet Reynaud now told Rogers that she had actively encouraged the other daycare workers to consider joining the PGEU because the board had not been interested in the employees' concerns, had not increased their wages sufficiently over the past two years, and had not maintained communication channels between the board and the employees.

All of the board members had full-time jobs elsewhere, and many were upper- and middle-level managers in their own companies. They were used to dealing with unhappy employees in their own workplaces, although none had experienced a union-organizing drive. Like Rogers, they had chosen to serve on the board of Marysville to stay informed about the day-to-day events of the centre. They had not really thought of themselves as the centre's employer, although, as board members, they represented all the parents of children enrolled at Marysville. Their main tasks on the daycare-centre board had been setting fees for the children and wages for the daycare employees. The board members usually saw the staff members several times a week, when they picked up their children, yet the unhappiness represented by the union-organizing drive was surprising to all of them. When they met at an emergency board meeting that evening, they tried to evaluate what had gone wrong at Marysville.

Questions

1. If you were either a board member or a parent, how would you know that the employees taking care of your children were unhappy with their jobs?

2. What might you do if you learned about their unhappiness?

3. What might Rogers have done differently as president of the board?

4. In what ways does this case illustrate that knowledge of OB can be applied beyond your own workplace?

Reinforcing Skills

1. Talk to several managers you know and ask them what skills they think are most important in today's workplace. Ask them to specifically consider the use of teams in their workplace, and what skills their team members most need to have but are least likely to have. How might you use this information to develop greater interpersonal skills?

2. Talk to several managers you know and ask them what skills they have found to be most important in doing their jobs. Why did they find these skills most important? What advice would they give a would-be manager about skills worth developing?

VIDEO CASE INCIDENT

CASE 1 Control at TerraCycle

Tom Szaky is a young Canadian who was admitted to prestigious Princeton University in the United States a few years ago. One day he discovered a friend's worm composter. When he learned that worms eat garbage, he got an idea for a business. So he quit Princeton and, together with Jon Beyer, started TerraCycle, a company that makes plant fertilizer from worm droppings. Now he is trying to make a fortune off worms. Each year the size of the company has tripled. It now has 45 full-time employees and annual sales of about $5 million.

Szaky says that things at TerraCycle are never fully under control, and he does not want them to be. He says that when you are frantically doing everything you can to make your business a success, it is almost inevitable that things will be slightly out of control. The company's rapid growth is part of the control problem.

Betsy Cotton, chief financial officer (CFO) of the company, says (with some humour) that she is the most disliked person in the company. She does a wide variety of tasks—cutting cheques, depositing cheques at the bank, running the candy machine, reporting to investors and to the board of directors, providing feedback on how well a product is selling, and providing decision support for things like the advisability of leasing certain office space.

Cotton feels that the company is too reactive and does not have a good planning process. She agrees that it's good when people are excited about new ideas and about the future, but people think about those things in ways that are too abstract, so they don't develop detailed execution plans. She notes that by the time she gets information about an issue, all that can be done is to react to it. She would rather see more proactive planning. Cotton also senses a certain resistance to structure in the company. When people are excited about their work, imposing order seems like it goes against what the company is all about.

Szaky notes that older people and people in the production area want more defined work processes, but developing those is time-consuming. Younger people and people in innovation want less-defined work processes, but that can lead to bad decisions. He realizes that you cannot launch a product without a control process, but you have to walk a fine line between too little and too much process. You also have to dream big and take calculated risks. For example, the least-risky thing would be to package a chemical product in a new bottle, but Szaky says you should not always do the least-risky thing. TerraCycle has a vision to package organic fertilizer in reused bottles, and there are risks associated with that vision.

Questions

1. What is organizational behaviour? How is the concept relevant to a company like TerraCycle?

2. The textbook notes that there are workplace "challenges" at the individual, group, and organizational levels. Explain the extent to which these challenges are evident at TerraCycle. How might TerraCycle address these challenges?

3. What does it mean to take a contingency perspective to organizational behaviour? How does the contingency idea apply to TerraCycle?

4. What is organizational citizenship behaviour? Explain why it might be particularly important at a company like TerraCycle.

Source: Based on "Foundations of Control at TerraCycle," *Organizational Behavior Video Library,* 2008. Copyrighted by Prentice-Hall.

Perception, Personality, and Emotions

Can a company win best employer in Canada awards *and* be regarded as the worst employer in Canada?

1. What is perception?

2. What causes people to have different perceptions of the same situation?

3. Can people be mistaken in their perceptions?

4. Does perception really affect outcomes?

5. What is personality and how does it affect behaviour?

6. Can emotions help or get in the way when we are dealing with others?

Walmart Canada.[1] Just the thought of the retailer being in Canada upsets some people. There was strong resistance when Walmart first announced it was coming to Canada in 1994, and a belief that the retailer would somehow destroy the fabric of Canadian society. Fourteen years after its arrival, Mississauga, Ontario-based Walmart Canada employs more than 77 000 Canadians in 309 stores across Canada.

The company has been ranked as one of Canada's best employers on the Hewitt Associates survey of Canada's Best Employers five times between 2001 and 2007. It has also appeared on KPMG's list of Canada's 25 Most Admired Corporate Cultures. The Retail Council of Canada (RCC) presented former president and CEO Mario Pilozzi with the 2007 Distinguished Canadian Retailer of the Year, noting that Walmart Canada has "one of the lowest staff turnover rates in the Canadian retail industry." In presenting the award, RCC also noted that "more than 100 Canadian communities have lobbied or petitioned to have a Walmart built in their towns" in recent years. With all of these positive statements about Walmart Canada, how can the perception of the company be so negative for some individuals?

All of our behaviour is somewhat shaped by our perceptions, personalities, emotions, and experiences. In this chapter, we consider the role that perception plays in affecting the way we see the world and the people around us. We also consider how personality characteristics affect our attitudes toward people and situations. We then consider how emotions shape many of our work-related behaviours.

Self-Assessment Library

LEARNING ABOUT YOURSELF

- Gender Role Perceptions
- Machiavellianism
- Narcissism
- Self-Monitoring
- Risk-Taking
- Personality Type
- Feelings
- Emotional Intelligence

☼OB Is for Everyone

- Who do you tend to blame when someone makes a mistake? Ever wonder why?
- Have you ever misjudged a person? Do you know why?
- Are people born with their personalities?
- Do you think it is better to be a Type A or a Type B personality?
- Ever wonder why the grocery clerk is always smiling?

Perception Defined

1   What is perception?

perception The process by which individuals organize and interpret their impressions in order to give meaning to their environment.

Perception is the process by which individuals organize and interpret their impressions to give meaning to their environment. However, what we perceive can be substantially different from objective reality. We often disagree about what is real. As we have seen, Walmart Canada has won many awards, but not every Canadian respects the retailer.

Why is perception important in the study of organizational behaviour (OB)? Simply because people's behaviour is based on their perception of what reality is, not on reality itself. *The world as it is perceived is the world that is behaviourally important.* Paul Godfrey, former president and CEO of the Toronto Blue Jays, observes that "a lot of things in life are perception." He backs this up by noting that as chair of Metropolitan Toronto for 11 years, he had little real power, but people believed he could get things done, and so he did.[2]

Factors Influencing Perception

In summer 2005, Walmart Canada faced a vote by the Vancouver City Council on whether the retailer would be allowed to open a store in the southern part of the city.[3] Walmart Canada had bought the property that it was planning to develop in 2001 for $20 million, on advice from the city's planning department. The company proposed an environmentally friendly design, trying to appease the council's "green" views. Nonetheless, the council voted against the proposal, claiming that having a Walmart in the city would lead to more cars, and also harm neighbourhood shops.

Andrew Pelletier, director of corporate affairs for Walmart Canada, expressed dismay at city council's decision. He noted that Walmart Canada had polled more than 4000 Vancouver residents, and "81 per cent were in support of the development." "That's four to one in favour," he said. "There is no question people want this store. I've been talking to seniors and people on fixed incomes who don't have a car and they were looking for discount shopping. I feel very sorry for them." The city council and Vancouver residents appear to have had different perceptions of the same situation. What factors might have influenced these different perceptions?

2   What causes people to have different perceptions of the same situation?

How do we explain that individuals may look at the same thing, yet perceive it differently, and both be right? A number of factors affect perception. These factors can reside in the *perceiver*, in the object, or *target*, being perceived, or in the context of the *situation* in which the perception is made. Exhibit 2-1 summarizes the factors that influence perception. This chapter's *Working with Others Exercise* on page 76 will help you understand how your perceptions affect your evaluation of others.

The Perceiver

When an individual ("the perceiver") looks at a target and attempts to interpret what he or she sees, that interpretation is heavily influenced by the perceiver's personal characteristics. Personal characteristics that affect perception include a person's attitudes, personality, motives, interests, past experiences, and expectations. For instance, if you expect police officers to be authoritative, young people to be lazy, or individuals holding public office to be unscrupulous, you may perceive them as such, regardless of their actual traits. Our attitudes, motives, interests, and past experiences all shape the way we perceive an event.

The Target

A target's characteristics also affect what is perceived. Loud people are more likely to be noticed in a group than are quiet ones. Extremely attractive or unattractive individuals are also more likely to be noticed. Novelty, motion, sounds, size, and other characteristics of a target shape the way we see it.

EXHIBIT 2-1   Factors That Influence Perception

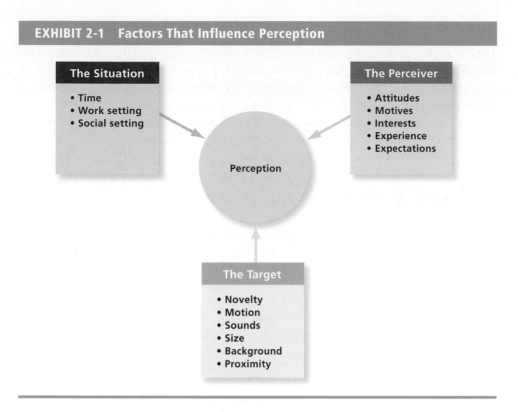

The Situation

- Time
- Work setting
- Social setting

The Perceiver

- Attitudes
- Motives
- Interests
- Experience
- Expectations

Perception

The Target

- Novelty
- Motion
- Sounds
- Size
- Background
- Proximity

Because targets are not looked at in isolation, the relationship of a target to its background influences perception. For instance, people who are female, Aboriginal, or members of any other clearly distinguishable group will tend to be perceived as similar, not only in physical terms but also in other unrelated characteristics.

People's expectations about what employees working for a full-service web development agency should look like often leave them startled when they meet Jason Billingsley (left) and Justin Tilson (foreground), two of the founders of Vancouver-based Ekkon Global. Both men are in wheelchairs after a skiing accident for Billingsley and a mountain bike accident for Tilson. "It's an eye-opener sometimes," says Billingsley. "You've been talking on the phone for two or three weeks before you meet someone and they have no clue, and they kind of walk in and you see a little 'oh.'"

The Situation

The context in which we see objects or events is also important. The time at which we see an object or event can influence attention, as can location, light, heat, or any number of situational factors. For example, at a nightclub on Saturday night, you may not notice a young guest "dressed to the nines." Yet that same person so attired for your Monday morning management class would certainly catch your attention (and that of the rest of the class). Neither the perceiver nor the target changed between Saturday night and Monday morning, but the situation is different.

Perceptual Errors

In their review of whether to allow Walmart Canada to develop a site in south Vancouver, city council decided that having a Walmart in Vancouver was not in the best interest of the city's residents. They noted the increase in the amount of traffic and the potential harm to local businesses as some of the reasons to reject Walmart Canada's application for development. Meanwhile, Walmart Canada felt city residents supported the application, citing their own polling data. These differences in responses might suggest that city council, Vancouver residents, or Walmart Canada were engaged in making perceptual errors, perhaps sticking to their own views rather than honestly listening to the views of those who disagreed with them. What might have caused this to happen?

3 Can people be mistaken in their perceptions?

Perceiving and interpreting why others do what they do takes time. As a result, we develop techniques to make this task more manageable. These techniques are frequently valuable—they allow us to make accurate perceptions rapidly and provide valid data for making predictions. However, they are not foolproof. They can and do get us into trouble. Some of the errors that distort the perception process are attribution theory, selective perception, halo effect, contrast effects, projection, and stereotyping.

Attribution Theory

attribution theory The theory that when we observe what seems like atypical behaviour by an individual, we attempt to determine whether it is internally or externally caused.

Attribution theory explains how we judge people differently, depending on the meaning we attribute to a given behaviour.[4] Basically, the theory suggests that when we observe what seems like atypical behaviour by an individual, we try to make sense of it. We consider whether the individual is responsible for the behaviour (the cause is internal), or whether something outside the individual caused the behaviour (the cause is external). *Internally* caused behaviour is believed to be under the personal control of the individual. *Externally* caused behaviour is believed to result from outside causes; we see the person as having been forced into the behaviour by the situation. For example, if a student is late for class, the instructor might attribute his lateness to partying into the wee hours of the morning and then oversleeping. This would be an internal attribution. But if the instructor assumes a major automobile accident tied up traffic on the student's regular route to school, that is making an external attribution. In trying to determine whether behaviour is internally or externally caused, we rely on three rules about the behaviour: (1) distinctiveness, (2) consensus, and (3) consistency. Let's discuss each of these in turn.

Who do you tend to blame when someone makes a mistake? Ever wonder why?

Distinctiveness

distinctiveness A behavioural rule that considers whether an individual acts similarly across a variety of situations.

Distinctiveness refers to whether an individual acts similarly across a variety of situations. Is the student always underperforming (being late for class, goofing off in team meetings, not answering urgent emails), or is the student's behaviour in one situation uncharacteristic of behaviour usually shown in other situations? If the behaviour is unusual, the observer is likely to make an external attribution. If this action is not unusual, the observer will probably judge it as internally caused.

Consensus

Consensus considers how an individual's behaviour compares with others in the same situation. If everyone who is faced with a similar situation responds in the same way, we can say the behaviour shows consensus. The tardy student's behaviour would meet this criterion if all students who took the same route to school were also late. From an attribution perspective, if consensus is high, you would be expected to give an external attribution to the student's tardiness. But if other students who took the same route made it to class on time, you would conclude the cause of lateness was internal for the student in question.

consensus A behavioural rule that considers if everyone faced with a similar situation responds in the same way.

Consistency

Finally, an observer looks for **consistency** in an action that is repeated over time. If a student is usually on time for class (she has not been late all term), being 10 minutes late will be perceived differently from the way it is when the student is routinely late (almost every class). If a student is almost always late, the observer is likely to attribute lateness to internal causes. If the student is almost never late, then lateness will be attributed to external causes.

consistency A behavioural rule that considers whether the individual has been acting in the same way over time.

Exhibit 2-2 summarizes the key elements in attribution theory. It illustrates, for instance, how to evaluate an employee's behaviour on a new task. To do this, you might note that employee Kim Randolph generally performs at about the same level on other related tasks as she does on her current task (low distinctiveness). You see that other employees frequently perform differently—better or worse—than Kim does on that current task (low consensus). Finally, if Kim's performance on this current task is consistent over time (high consistency), you or anyone else who is judging Kim's work is likely to hold her primarily responsible for her task performance (internal attribution).

How Attributions Get Distorted

One of the more interesting findings from attribution theory is that there are errors or biases that distort attributions. For instance, there is substantial evidence that when we

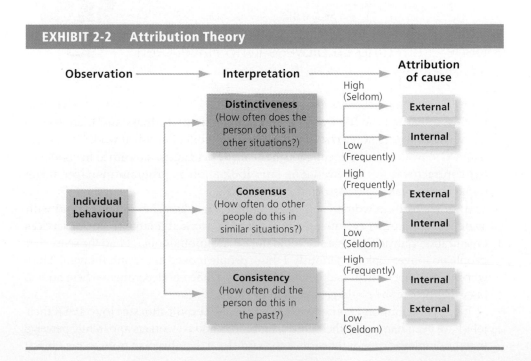

EXHIBIT 2-2   Attribution Theory

fundamental attribution error
The tendency to underestimate the influence of external factors and overestimate the influence of internal factors when making judgments about the behaviour of others.

self-serving bias The tendency for individuals to attribute their own successes to internal factors while putting the blame for failures on external factors.

judge the behaviour of other people, we tend to underestimate the influence of external factors and overestimate the influence of internal, or personal, factors.[5] This is called the **fundamental attribution error**. It can explain why a sales manager attributes the poor performance of his or her sales agents to laziness rather than acknowledging the impact of the innovative product line introduced by a competitor.

Have you ever misjudged a person? Do you know why?

We use **self-serving bias** when we judge ourselves, however. This means that when we are successful, we are more likely to believe it was because of internal factors, such as ability or effort. When we fail, however, we blame external factors, such as luck. In general, people tend to believe that their own behaviour is more positive than the behaviour of those around them. Research suggests, however, that individuals tend to overestimate their own good behaviour, and underestimate the good behaviour of others.[6]

Selective Perception

Because it's impossible for us to see everything, any characteristic that makes a person, object, or event stand out will increase the probability that it will be perceived. This tendency explains why you are more likely to notice cars that look like your own. It also explains why some people may be reprimanded by their manager for doing something that goes unnoticed when other employees do it. Since we cannot observe everything going on about us, we engage in **selective perception**.

selective perception People's selective interpretation of what they see based on their interests, background, experience, and attitudes.

But how does selectivity work as a shortcut in judging other people? Since we cannot take in all that we observe, we take in bits and pieces. But those bits and pieces are not chosen randomly. Rather, they are selectively chosen according to our interests, background, experience, and attitudes. Selective perception allows us to "speed-read" others, but not without the risk of coming to an inaccurate conclusion. Because we see what we want to see, we can draw unwarranted conclusions from an ambiguous situation. Selective perception can make us draw wrong conclusions about co-workers who have suffered serious illnesses, as *Focus on Diversity* shows.

FOCUS ON **DIVERSITY**

Underestimating Employees Who Have Been Seriously Ill

Does having had a serious illness mean that you cannot do your job?   Lynda Davidson learned the hard way that suffering a mental illness and then getting treatment for it does not necessarily give one a clean bill of health at work.[7] When she returned to work after treatment, though she made her targets and earned her bonuses, her contract was not renewed. She later took a job as program manager at the Canadian Mental Health Association in Toronto.

Another Toronto woman suffered a similar fate when she was diagnosed with acute leukemia. After treatment, she returned to work at a large financial services organization only to find that she could not get any promotions. "I had the sense that people no longer took me seriously. I think people looked at me and thought, 'She's going to die,'" the woman said. It took moving to a different department where no one knew her before she could get ahead in her job.

It's not uncommon for employees with critical, chronic illnesses to feel that their jobs have been harmed by their illness. Employers and co-workers apparently perceive that the employee cannot function at the same level that they had prior to the illness.

Describing a recent study done in the United States by the National Coalition for Cancer Survivorship, Dr. Ross Gray, a research psychologist at the Odette Cancer Centre in Toronto, noted: "The study found that employers and co-workers over-estimate the impact of cancer on people's lives. Decisions get made about advancement or capability that are out of line with the realities."

Halo Effect

When we draw a general impression of an individual on the basis of a single characteristic, such as intelligence, likeability, or appearance, a **halo effect** operates.[8] Think about what happens when students evaluate their instructor. Students may give more weight to a single trait, such as enthusiasm, and allow their entire evaluation to be coloured by how they judge the instructor on that one trait. Thus, an instructor may be quiet, assured, knowledgeable, and highly qualified, but if his or her presentation style lacks enthusiasm, those students would probably give the instructor a low rating.

The reality of the halo effect was confirmed in a classic study. Subjects were given a list of traits and asked to evaluate the person to whom those traits applied.[9] When traits such as intelligent, skillful, practical, industrious, determined, and warm were used, the person was judged to be wise, humorous, popular, and imaginative. When cold was substituted for warm, a completely different set of perceptions was obtained, though otherwise the list was identical. Clearly, the subjects were allowing a single trait to influence their overall impression of the person being judged.

> **halo effect** Drawing a general impression of an individual on the basis of a single characteristic.

Contrast Effect

There is an old saying among entertainers who perform in variety shows: Never follow an act that has children or animals in it.

This example demonstrates how **contrast effects** can distort perceptions. We don't evaluate a person in isolation. Our reaction to one person is often influenced by other people we have recently encountered.

> **contrast effects** The concept that our reaction to one person is often influenced by other people we have recently encountered.

Jin, an Asian American rapper, performs at the Garden of Eden in Hollywood, hoping for a hit song in an industry that lacks Asian American pop stars. But Asian North American artists and scholars argue that racial stereotyping inaccurately generalizes Asian North Americans as studious geeks and that someone who looks Asian must be a foreigner. This stereotyping does not fit the "cool" image and born-in-North-America authenticity required for musicians like Jin who aspire to become North American pop stars.

Consider what happens when a manager interviews job candidates from a pool of applicants. The evaluation of a candidate can be distorted as a result of his or her place in the interview schedule. The candidate is likely to receive a more favourable evaluation if preceded by mediocre applicants, and a less favourable evaluation if preceded by strong applicants.

Projection

projection Attributing one's own characteristics to other people.

It's easy to judge others if we assume that they are similar to us. For instance, if you want challenge and responsibility in your job, you assume that others want the same. Or you are honest and trustworthy, so you take it for granted that other people are equally reliable. This tendency to attribute our own characteristics to other people is called **projection**.

People who engage in projection tend to perceive others according to what they themselves are like, rather than perceiving others as they really are. Because they always judge people as being similar to themselves, when they observe someone who is actually like them, their perceptions are naturally correct. But when they observe others who are not like them, their perceptions are not as accurate. Managers who engage in projection compromise their ability to respond to individual differences. They tend to see people as more homogeneous than they really are.

Stereotyping

stereotyping Judging someone on the basis of one's perception of the group to which that person belongs.

heuristics Judgment shortcuts in decision making.

When we judge someone on the basis of our perception of the group to which he or she belongs, we are using the shortcut called **stereotyping**.

We rely on generalizations every day because they help us make decisions quickly. They are a means of simplifying a complex world. It's less difficult to deal with an unmanageable number of stimuli if we use **heuristics** (judgment shortcuts in decision making) or stereotypes. The problem occurs, of course, when we generalize inaccurately

Muslim women in Canada often experience discrimination in being hired, or how their co-workers treat them, when they wear a hijab. Co-workers of nurse Sharon Hoosein, shown here, are surprised that she will be returning from her maternity leave. They assume that because of her religion she would be expected to stay at home to raise children rather than work.

or too much. In organizations, we frequently hear comments that represent stereotypes based on gender, age, race, religion, ethnicity, and even weight:[10] "Women will not relocate for a promotion," "men are not interested in child care," "older workers cannot learn new skills," "Asian immigrants are hard-working and conscientious," "overweight people lack discipline." Stereotypes can be so deeply ingrained and powerful that they influence life-and-death decisions. One study showed that, controlling for a wide array of factors (such as aggravating or mitigating circumstances), the degree to which black defendants in murder trials looked stereotypically black essentially doubled their odds of receiving a death sentence if convicted.[11]

One of the problems of stereotypes is that they *are* widespread and often useful generalizations, despite the fact that they may not contain a shred of truth when applied to a particular person or situation. So we constantly have to check ourselves to make sure we are not unfairly or inaccurately applying a stereotype in our evaluations and decisions. Stereotypes are an example of the warning "The more useful, the more danger from misuse." Stereotypes can lead to strong negative reactions, such as prejudice, which we describe below.

Prejudice

Prejudice is an unfounded dislike of a person or group based on their belonging to a particular stereotyped group. For instance, an individual may dislike people of a particular religion, or state that they do not want to work with someone of a particular ethnicity. Prejudice can lead to negative consequences in the workplace and, in particular, to discrimination. For instance, an individual of a particular ethnic group might be passed over for a management position because of the belief that employees might not see that person as a good manager. In another instance, an individual in his 50s who is looking for work but cannot find a job may be discriminated against because of the belief that younger workers are more appealing than older workers. Prejudice generally starts with stereotypes and then has negative emotional content added.

prejudice An unfounded dislike of a person or group based on their belonging to a particular stereotyped group.

Why Do Perception and Judgment Matter?

Walmart Canada receives mixed reviews from Canadians, who seem to either love the company or hate it.[12] Supporters cite such things as low prices and the increase in jobs that the company has brought. Critics complain about low wages and the loss of local businesses once the company arrives. At least some studies suggest that Walmart benefits communities where it opens stores. For instance, when Walmart arrived in Stettler, Alberta, (near Calgary) in 2004, there was a great deal of apprehension. Subsequently, Boston Pizza and Tim Hortons have come to the town. "It's been very positive, and it's created many more shoppers coming to our community," said Alan Willis of the Stettler and Region Marketing Corporation.

Walmart's management is aware that the company is not universally liked by Canadians. For instance, when Walmart Canada announced in August 2008 that all new stores would be designed to be more energy efficient, and existing stores would be made more environmentally friendly, one might have expected this announcement to be greeted with enthusiasm. But the company anticipated that there would be some who would be cynical about the company's motives. "Some might say we're just another company trying to endear itself to the Canadian public by hopping on the green movement. That perspective misses the point," CEO David Cheesewright said. Can negative perceptions of Walmart by individuals make it impossible to recognize any good that the company does?

People in organizations are always judging each other. For instance, people typically go through an employment interview before being hired. Interviewers make perceptual judgments during the interview that affect whether the individual is hired. Studies show that if negative information is exposed early in the interview, it tends to be more heavily

4 Does perception really affect outcomes?

weighted than if that same information comes out later.[13] If the employment interview is an important factor in the hiring decision—and it usually is—you should recognize that perceptual factors influence who is hired and, eventually, the quality of an organization's labour force. This chapter's *Ethical Dilemma Exercise* on page 77 illustrates how the perception of tattoos affects hiring practices.

It should be pointed out here, though, that an employee's performance appraisal is another example of something in the workplace that depends very much on the perceptual process.[14] An employee's future is closely tied to his or her appraisal—promotions, pay raises, and continuation of employment are among the most obvious outcomes. Although the appraisal can be objective (for example, a salesperson is appraised on how many dollars of sales he or she generates in a given territory), many jobs are evaluated in subjective terms. When managers use subjective measures in appraising employees or choosing whom to promote, what the evaluator perceives to be good or bad employee characteristics or behaviours will significantly influence the outcome of the appraisal. One recent study found that managers in both Hong Kong and the United States were more likely to promote individuals who were more similar to themselves.[15] One's behaviour may also be affected by perceptions. In the next section, we discuss how the self-fulfilling prophecy can lead to people engaging in behaviour that is expected of them.

Hiring and performance appraisals are not the only processes in organizations that are subject to perceptual bias. For instance, we evaluate how much effort our co-workers are putting into their jobs. When a new person joins a work team, he or she is immediately "sized up" by the other team members. Individuals even make judgments about people's virtues based on whether they exercise, as *Focus on Research* shows.

FOCUS ON **RESEARCH**

Exercisers Rule

Can being called an exerciser really make a difference in how others think of you? Stereotypes can strongly affect people's judgments of others, according to a study by McMaster University professor Kathleen Martin Ginis.[16] Students were given descriptions of individuals and then asked to evaluate 12 personality characteristics of "Tom" or "Mary." These characteristics included being afraid or brave, and having or lacking self-control, as well as 8 physical characteristics, including whether they were fit or unfit, sickly or healthy, ugly or good-looking. Some descriptions mentioned whether the individual exercised or not.

Students evaluated nonexercisers more negatively on every personality and physical characteristic they did than those described as exercisers. In fact, those described as nonexercisers were rated more negatively than were those for whom no information about exercise was provided. Martin noted, "When Mary and Tom were described as exercisers, they were considered to be harder workers, more confident, braver, smarter, neater, happier and more sociable than the non-exerciser."

Self-Fulfilling Prophecy

There is an impressive amount of evidence that demonstrates that people will attempt to validate their perceptions of reality, even when those perceptions are faulty.[17] This characteristic is particularly relevant when we consider performance expectations on the job.

The terms **self-fulfilling prophecy** and *Pygmalion effect* have evolved to characterize the fact that people's expectations determine their behaviour. In other words, if a manager

self-fulfilling prophecy A concept that proposes a person will behave in ways consistent with how he or she is perceived by others.

expects big things from his people, they are not likely to let him down. Similarly, if a manager expects people to perform minimally, they will tend to behave so as to meet those low expectations. The result, then, is that the expectations become reality.

   An interesting illustration of the self-fulfilling prophecy is a study undertaken with 105 soldiers in the Israeli Defense Forces who were taking a 15-week combat command course.[18] The four course instructors were told that one-third of the specific incoming trainees had high potential, one-third had normal potential, and the potential of the rest was unknown. In reality, the trainees were randomly placed into those categories by the researchers. The results confirmed the existence of a self-fulfilling prophecy. The trainees whom instructors were told had high potential scored significantly higher on objective achievement tests, exhibited more positive attitudes, and held their leaders in higher regard than did the other two groups. The instructors of the supposedly high-potential trainees got better results from them because the instructors expected them.

As you can see, perception plays a large role in how people are evaluated. Personality, which we review next, is another major factor affecting how people relate and evaluate each other in the workplace.

Personality

Why are some people quiet and passive, while others are loud and aggressive? Are certain personality types better adapted for certain job types? What do we know, from theories of personality, that can help us explain and predict the behaviour of leaders such as Stephen Harper, Stéphane Dion, George W. Bush, or Barack Obama? How do we explain the risk-taking nature of Donald Trump, whose Trump Entertainment Resorts went into bankruptcy protection for part of 2004 and 2005, and yet he still sees himself as the greatest businessman in America? In this section, we will attempt to answer such questions.

5 What is personality and how does it affect behaviour?

What Is Personality?

When we talk of personality, we don't mean that a person has charm, a positive attitude toward life, a smiling face, or is a finalist for "Miss Congeniality." When psychologists talk of personality, they mean a dynamic concept describing the growth and development of a person's whole psychological system. Rather than looking at parts of the person, personality looks at some aggregate whole that is greater than the sum of the parts.

   Gordon Allport produced the most frequently used definition of personality more than 60 years ago. He said personality is "the dynamic organization within the individual of those psychophysical systems that determine his unique adjustments to his environment."[19] For our purposes, you should think of **personality** as the stable patterns of behaviour and consistent internal states that determine how an individual reacts to and interacts with others. It's most often described in terms of measurable traits that a person exhibits.

personality The stable patterns of behaviour and consistent internal states that determine how an individual reacts to and interacts with others.

Measuring Personality

The most important reason managers need to know how to measure personality is that research has shown that personality tests are useful in hiring decisions. Scores on personality tests help managers forecast who is the best fit for a job.[20] And some managers want to know how people score on personality tests to better understand and more effectively manage the people who work for them. Far and away the most common means of measuring personality is through self-report surveys, with which individuals evaluate themselves by rating themselves on a series of factors, such as "I worry a lot about the future." Though self-report measures work well when well constructed, one weakness of these measures is that the respondent might lie or practise impression management—that is, the person could "fake it" on the test to create a good impression. This is especially a concern when the survey is the basis for employment. Another problem is accuracy. In other words, a perfectly good candidate could have just been in a bad mood when the survey was taken.

Observer ratings provide an independent assessment of personality. Instead of a person self-reporting, a co-worker or another observer does the rating (sometimes with the subject's knowledge and sometimes without). Even though the results of self-reports and observer ratings are strongly correlated, research suggests that observer ratings are a better predictor of success on the job.[21] However, each can tell us something unique about an individual's behaviour in the workplace.

Personality Determinants

An early argument in personality research centred on whether an individual's personality was predetermined at birth or the result of the individual's interaction with his or her environment. Clearly, there is no simple answer. Personality appears to be a result of both influences. In addition, today we recognize a third factor—the situation. Thus, an adult's personality is now generally considered to be made up of both hereditary and environmental factors, moderated by situational conditions.

Heredity

Heredity refers to those factors that were determined at conception. Physical stature, facial attractiveness, gender, temperament, muscle composition and reflexes, energy level, and biological rhythms are characteristics that are generally considered to be either completely or substantially influenced by

Are people born with their personalities?

your parents' biological, physiological, and inherent psychological makeup. The heredity approach argues that the ultimate explanation of an individual's personality is a person's genes.

Studies of young children lend strong support to the power of heredity.[22] Evidence demonstrates that traits such as shyness, fear, and distress are most likely caused by inherited genetic characteristics. This finding suggests that some personality traits may be built into the same genetic code that affects factors such as height and hair colour.

If heredity played little or no part in determining personality, you would expect to find few similarities between identical twins who were separated at birth and raised separately. But researchers who looked at more than 100 sets of separated twins found a lot in common.[23] For almost every behavioural trait, a significant part of the variation between the twins turned out to be associated with genetic factors. For instance, one set of twins, who had been separated for 39 years and raised 70 kilometres apart, were found to drive the same model and colour car, chain-smoke the same brand of cigarette, own dogs with the same name, and regularly vacation within three blocks of each other in a beach community 2000 kilometres away.

Researchers have found that genetics can explain about 50 percent of the personality differences and more than 30 percent of the variation in occupational and leisure interests found in individuals. In other words, blood-related siblings are likely to have more similar personalities, occupations, and leisure interests than unrelated people.

Does personality change over one's lifetime? Most research in this area suggests that while some aspects of our personalities do change over time, the rank orderings do not change very much. For example, people's scores on measures of conscientiousness tend to increase as they get older. However, there are still strong individual differences in conscientiousness, and despite the fact that most of us become more responsible over time, people tend to change by about the same amount, so that the rank order stays roughly the same.[24] For instance, if you are more conscientious than your sibling now, that is likely to be true in 20 years, even though you both should become more conscientiousness over time.

Personality Traits

The early work in the structure of personality revolved around attempts to identify and label enduring characteristics that describe an individual's behaviour. Popular characteristics include shy, aggressive, submissive, lazy, ambitious, loyal, and timid. Those characteristics, when they are exhibited in a large number of situations, are called **personality traits**.[25] The more consistent the characteristic and the more frequently it occurs in diverse situations, the more important that trait is in describing the individual.

A number of early research efforts tried to identify the *primary* traits that govern behaviour.[26] However, for the most part, they resulted in long lists of traits that were difficult to generalize from and provided little practical guidance to organizational decision makers. Two exceptions are the Myers-Briggs Type Indicator and the Big Five Personality Model. Over the past 20 years, these two approaches have become the dominant frameworks for identifying and classifying traits.

Keep in mind that each of us reacts differently to personality traits. This is partially a function of how we perceive those traits. In Exhibit 2-3, you will note that Lucy tells Linus a few things about his personality.

The Myers-Briggs Type Indicator

The **Myers-Briggs Type Indicator (MBTI)** is the most widely used personality-assessment instrument in the world.[27] It's a 100-question personality test that asks people how they usually feel or act in particular situations. On the basis of their answers, individuals are classified as extraverted or introverted (E or I), sensing or intuitive (S or N), thinking or feeling (T or F), and judging or perceiving (J or P). These terms are defined as follows:

- *Extraverted/introverted.* Extraverted individuals are outgoing, sociable, and assertive. Introverts are quiet and shy. E/I measures where we direct our energy when dealing with people and things.

- *Sensing/intuitive.* Sensing types are practical and prefer routine and order. They focus on details. Intuitives rely on unconscious processes and look at the "big picture." This dimension looks at how we process information.

- *Thinking/feeling.* Thinking types use reason and logic to handle problems. Feeling types rely on their personal values and emotions.

- *Judging/perceiving.* Judging types want control and prefer their world to be ordered and structured. Perceiving types are flexible and spontaneous.

personality traits Enduring characteristics that describe an individual's behaviour.

Myers-Briggs Type Indicator (MBTI) A personality test that taps four characteristics and classifies people into 1 of 16 personality types.

EXHIBIT 2-3

These classifications together describe 16 personality types. To illustrate, let's look at three examples:

- *INTJs are visionaries.* They usually have original minds and great drive for their own ideas and purposes. They are skeptical, critical, independent, determined, and often stubborn.

- *ESTJs are organizers.* They are realistic, logical, analytical, decisive, and have a natural head for business or mechanics. They like to organize and run activities.

- *ENTPs are conceptualizers.* They are innovative, individualistic, versatile, and attracted to entrepreneurial ideas. They tend to be resourceful in solving challenging problems, but may neglect routine assignments.

A book profiling 13 contemporary businesspeople who created super-successful firms including Apple Computer, FedEx, Honda Motors, Microsoft, and Sony found that all are intuitive thinkers (NTs).[28] This result is particularly interesting because intuitive thinkers represent only about 5 percent of the population.

The MBTI is widely used by organizations including Apple Computer, AT&T, Citigroup, GE, 3M, many hospitals and educational institutions, and even the US Armed Forces. In spite of its popularity, the evidence is mixed as to whether the MBTI is a valid measure of personality—with most of the evidence suggesting that it is not.[29] One problem is that it forces a person into either one type or another (that is, you are either introverted or extraverted). There is no in-between, though people can be both extraverted and introverted to some degree. The best we can say is that the MBTI can be a valuable tool for increasing self-awareness and providing career guidance. But because results tend to be unrelated to job performance, managers probably should not use it as a selection test for job candidates.

The Big Five Personality Model

The MBTI may lack valid supporting evidence, but that cannot be said for the widely accepted five-factor model of personality—more typically called the "Big Five."[30] An impressive body of research supports the notion that five basic personality dimensions underlie all others and encompass most of the significant variation in human personality. The Big Five personality factors are as follows:

- **Extraversion**. This dimension captures a person's comfort level with relationships; it describes the degree to which a person is sociable, talkative, and assertive.

- **Agreeableness**. This dimension refers to a person's propensity to defer to others; it describes the degree to which a person is good-natured, cooperative, and trusting.

- **Conscientiousness**. This dimension is a measure of reliability; it describes the degree to which a person is responsible, dependable, persistent, and achievement-oriented.

- **Emotional stability**. This dimension taps a person's ability to withstand stress; it describes the degree to which a person is calm, self-confident, and secure.

- **Openness to experience**. The final dimension addresses a person's range of interests and fascination with novelty; it describes the degree to which a person is imaginative, artistically sensitive, and intellectual.

Exhibit 2-4 shows the characteristics for the high and low dimensions of each Big Five personality factor.

extraversion A personality factor that describes the degree to which a person is sociable, talkative, and assertive.

agreeableness A personality factor that describes the degree to which a person is good-natured, cooperative, and trusting.

conscientiousness A personality factor that describes the degree to which a person is responsible, dependable, persistent, and achievement-oriented.

emotional stability A personality factor that describes the degree to which a person is calm, self-confident, and secure.

openness to experience A personality factor that describes the degree to which a person is imaginative, artistically sensitive, and intellectual.

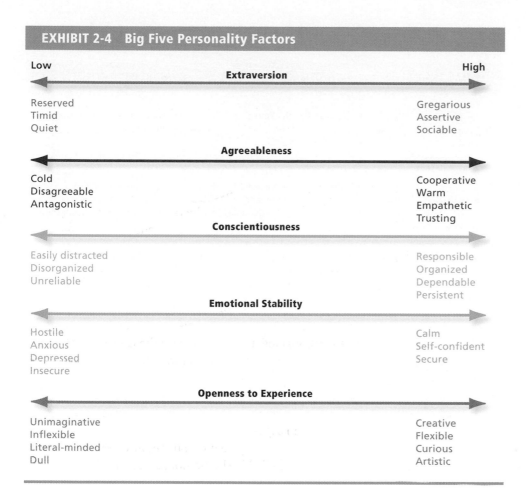

EXHIBIT 2-4 Big Five Personality Factors

Low — **Extraversion** — High

Reserved	Gregarious
Timid	Assertive
Quiet	Sociable

Agreeableness

Cold	Cooperative
Disagreeable	Warm
Antagonistic	Empathetic
	Trusting

Conscientiousness

Easily distracted	Responsible
Disorganized	Organized
Unreliable	Dependable
	Persistent

Emotional Stability

Hostile	Calm
Anxious	Self-confident
Depressed	Secure
Insecure	

Openness to Experience

Unimaginative	Creative
Inflexible	Flexible
Literal-minded	Curious
Dull	Artistic

RESEARCH FINDINGS: THE BIG FIVE

Research on the Big Five has found a relationship between the personality dimensions and job performance.[31] As the authors of the most-cited review put it, "The preponderance of evidence shows that individuals who are dependable, reliable, careful, thorough, able to plan, organized, hardworking, persistent, and achievement-oriented tend to have higher job performance in most if not all occupations."[32] In addition, employees who score higher in conscientiousness develop higher levels of job knowledge, probably because highly conscientious people exert greater levels of effort on their jobs. The higher levels of job knowledge then contribute to higher levels of job performance.[33]

Although conscientiousness is the Big Five trait most consistently related to job performance, the other traits are related to aspects of performance in some situations. All five traits also have other implications for work and for life. Let's look at the implications of these traits one at a time. (Exhibit 2-5 summarizes the discussion.)

Emotional stability. People who score high on emotional stability are happier than those who score low. Of the Big Five traits, emotional stability is most strongly related to life satisfaction, job satisfaction, and low stress levels. This is probably true because high scorers are more likely to be positive and optimistic in their thinking and experience fewer negative emotions. People low on emotional stability are hyper-vigilant (looking for problems or impending signs of

Indra Nooyi, CEO and chair of PepsiCo, scores high on all personality dimensions of the Big Five Model. She is described as sociable, agreeable, conscientious, emotionally stable, and open to experiences. These personality traits have contributed to Nooyi's high job performance and career success at PepsiCo; she joined the company in 1994 as senior vice-president of strategy and development, and she was promoted to president and chief financial officer before moving into the firm's top position.

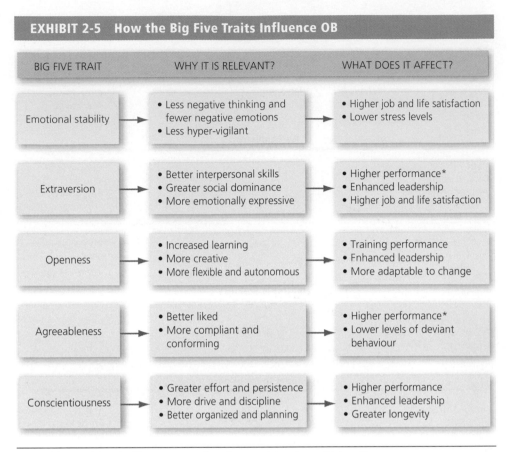

EXHIBIT 2-5   How the Big Five Traits Influence OB

BIG FIVE TRAIT	WHY IT IS RELEVANT?	WHAT DOES IT AFFECT?
Emotional stability	• Less negative thinking and fewer negative emotions • Less hyper-vigilant	• Higher job and life satisfaction • Lower stress levels
Extraversion	• Better interpersonal skills • Greater social dominance • More emotionally expressive	• Higher performance* • Enhanced leadership • Higher job and life satisfaction
Openness	• Increased learning • More creative • More flexible and autonomous	• Training performance • Enhanced leadership • More adaptable to change
Agreeableness	• Better liked • More compliant and conforming	• Higher performance* • Lower levels of deviant behaviour
Conscientiousness	• Greater effort and persistence • More drive and discipline • Better organized and planning	• Higher performance • Enhanced leadership • Greater longevity

*In jobs requiring significant teamwork or frequent interpersonal interactions.

danger), and high scores are associated with fewer health complaints. One upside of low emotional stability, however, is that when in a bad mood, such people make faster and better decisions than emotionally stable people in bad moods.[34]

Extraversion. Compared with introverts, extraverts tend to be happier in their jobs and in their lives as a whole. They experience more positive emotions than do introverts, and they more freely express these feelings. They also tend to perform better in jobs that require significant interpersonal interaction, perhaps because they have more social skills—they usually have more friends and spend more time in social situations than introverts. Finally, extraversion is a relatively strong predictor of leadership emergence in groups; extraverts are more socially dominant, "take charge" sorts of people, and they generally are more assertive than introverts.[35] One downside of extraversion is that extraverts are more impulsive than introverts; they are more likely to be absent from work and engage in risky behaviour such as unprotected sex, drinking, and other impulsive or sensation-seeking acts.[36]

Openness to experience. Individuals who score high on openness to experience are more creative in science and in art than those who score low. Because creativity is important to leadership, open people are more likely to be effective leaders. Also, open individuals are more comfortable with ambiguity and change than are those who score lower on this trait. As a result, open people cope better with organizational change and are more adaptable in changing contexts.[37]

Agreeableness. You might expect agreeable people to be happier than disagreeable people, and they are, but only slightly. When people choose romantic partners, friends, or organizational team members, agreeable individuals are usually their first choice. Thus, agreeable individuals are better liked than disagreeable people, which explains why they tend to do better in interpersonally oriented jobs such as customer service. Agreeable people also are more compliant and rule abiding. Agreeable children do better in school and as adults are less likely to get involved in drugs or excessive drinking.[38] Thus, agreeable individuals are less likely to engage in organizational deviance. One downside of agreeableness is that it is associated with lower levels of career success (especially earnings). This may occur because agreeable individuals are poorer negotiators; they are so concerned with pleasing others that they often don't negotiate as much for themselves as do others.[39]

Conscientiousness. Interestingly, conscientious people live longer than less conscientious people because they tend to take better care of themselves (eat better, exercise more) and engage in fewer risky behaviours (smoking, drinking/drugs, risky sexual or driving behaviour).[40] Still, there are downsides to conscientiousness. It appears that conscientious people, probably because they are so organized and structured, don't adapt as well to changing contexts.

It's not always easy for friends to share top management roles, but Anton Rabie (left), president and CEO, and Ronnen Harary (right), chairman and CEO of Toronto-based Spin Master, like the arrangement. Rabie is an extravert, while Harary is an introvert. The childhood friends feel their personalities complement each other, making an ideal management team.

Conscientious people are generally performance-oriented. They have more trouble than less conscientious people learning complex skills early in the training process because their focus is on performing well rather than on learning. Finally, conscientious people are often less creative than less conscientious people, especially artistically.[41]

Major Personality Attributes Influencing OB

In this section, we evaluate specific personality attributes that have been found to be powerful predictors of behaviour in organizations. The first relates to one's core self-evaluation. The others are Machiavellianism, narcissism, self monitoring, propensity for risk-taking, and Type A and B and proactive personalities. We shall briefly introduce these attributes and summarize what we know about their ability to explain and predict employee behaviour.

If you want to know more about your own personality attributes, this chapter's *Learning About Yourself Exercises* on pages 70–75 present you with a variety of personality measures to explore.

Core Self-Evaluation

People differ in the degree to which they like or dislike themselves and whether they see themselves as capable and effective. This self-perspective is the concept of **core self-evaluation**. People who have positive core self-evaluations like themselves and see themselves as effective, capable, and in control of their environment. Those with negative core self-evaluations tend to dislike themselves, question their capabilities, and view themselves as powerless over their environment.[42]

People with positive core self-evaluations perform better than others because they set more ambitious goals, are more committed to their goals, and persist longer at attempting to reach these goals. For example, one study of life-insurance agents found that core self-evaluations were critical predictors of performance. In life-insurance sales, 90 percent of sales calls end in rejection, so an agent has to believe in him- or herself to persist. In fact, this study showed that the majority of successful salespersons had positive core self-evaluations.[43]

You might wonder whether someone can be too positive. In other words, What happens when someone thinks he is capable, but he is actually incompetent? One study of *Fortune* 500 CEOs, for example, showed that many are overconfident, and their

core self-evaluation The degree to which an individual likes or dislikes himself or herself, whether the person sees himself or herself as capable and effective, and whether the person feels in control of his or her environment or powerless over the environment.

perceived infallibility often causes them to make bad decisions.[44] Teddy Forstmann, chair and CEO of the sports marketing giant IMG, said of himself, "I know God gave me an unusual brain. I can't deny that. I have a God-given talent for seeing potential."[45] One might say that people like Forstmann are overconfident, but very often we humans sell ourselves short and are less happy and effective than we could be because of it. If we decide we cannot do something, for example, we won't try, and not doing it only reinforces our self-doubts.

Machiavellianism

Machiavellianism The degree to which an individual is pragmatic, maintains emotional distance, and believes that ends can justify means.

The personality characteristic of **Machiavellianism** (Mach) is named after Niccolò Machiavelli, who wrote in the sixteenth century on how to gain and use power. An individual high in Machiavellianism is pragmatic, maintains emotional distance, and believes that ends can justify means: "If it works, use it."

A considerable amount of research has been directed toward relating high- and low-Mach personalities to certain behavioural outcomes.[46] High Machs manipulate more, win more, are persuaded less, and persuade others more than do low Machs.[47] Think of Donald Trump interacting with the characters on *The Apprentice*. Yet these high-Mach outcomes are moderated by situational factors. It has been found that high Machs do better (1) when they interact face to face with others rather than indirectly; (2) when the situation has a minimum number of rules and regulations, thus allowing room for improvising; and (3) when emotional involvement with details irrelevant to winning distracts low Machs.[48]

Should we conclude that high Machs make good employees? That answer depends on the type of job and whether you consider ethical implications in evaluating performance. In jobs that require bargaining skills (such as labour negotiation) or that offer substantial rewards for winning (as in commissioned sales), high Machs will be productive. But if the ends cannot justify the means, if there are absolute standards of behaviour, or if the three situational factors noted in the preceding paragraph are not in evidence, our ability to predict a high Mach's performance will be severely limited.

If you are interested in determining your level of Machiavellianism, you might want to complete *Learning About Yourself Exercise #1* on page 70.

Learning About Yourself

1. How Machiavellian Are You? **(page 70)**

Narcissism

Hans likes to be the centre of attention. He likes to look at himself in the mirror a lot. He has extravagant dreams and seems to consider himself a person of many talents. Hans is a narcissist. The term is from the Greek myth of Narcissus, the story of a man so vain and proud that he fell in love with his own image. In psychology, **narcissism** describes a person who has a grandiose sense of self-importance, requires excessive admiration, has a sense of entitlement, and is arrogant.[49] Some research suggests that narcissism can be seen as a combination of the Big Five traits of extraversion and agreeableness; narcissists tend to be disagreeable extraverts.[50]

narcissism The tendency to be arrogant, have a grandiose sense of self-importance, require excessive admiration, and have a sense of entitlement.

A study found that while narcissists thought they were *better* leaders than their colleagues, their supervisors actually rated them as *worse* leaders. For example, an Oracle executive described that company's CEO, Larry Ellison, as follows: "The difference between God and Larry is that God does not believe he is Larry."[51] Because narcissists often want to gain the admiration of others and receive affirmation of their superiority, they tend to "talk down" to those who threaten them, treating others as if they were inferior. Narcissists also tend to be selfish and exploitive, and they often carry the attitude that others exist for their benefit.[52] Studies indicate that narcissists are rated by their bosses as less effective at their jobs than others, particularly when it comes to helping other people.[53]

Self-Monitoring

Some people are better able to pay attention to the external environment and respond accordingly, a characteristic known as self-monitoring.[54] Individuals high in **self-monitoring** show considerable ability to adjust and adapt their behaviour to the situations they are in. They are highly sensitive to external cues and can behave differently in different situations. High self-monitors are capable of presenting striking contradictions between their public personae and their private selves.

Low self-monitors cannot disguise themselves in the same way. They tend to display their true dispositions and attitudes in every situation. There is high behavioural consistency between who they are and what they do.

Research suggests that high self-monitors tend to pay closer attention to the behaviour of others and are more capable of conforming than are low self-monitors.[55] High self-monitoring managers tend to be more mobile in their careers and receive more promotions (both internal and cross-organizational).[56] Recent research found that high self-monitors are more likely to be high performers and more likely to become leaders.[57]

If you are interested in determining whether you are a high or low self-monitor, you might want to complete *Learning About Yourself Exercise #2* on page 71.

> **self-monitoring** A personality trait that measures an individual's ability to adjust behaviour to external, situational factors.

> **Learning About Yourself**
>
> **2.** Are You a High Self-Monitor? **(page 71)**

Risk-Taking

People differ in their willingness to take chances. Matthew Barrett, the former CEO of Bank of Montreal, and Frank Stronach, chair of Magna International, are good examples of high risk-takers. This tendency to assume or avoid risk has been shown to have an impact on how long it takes managers to make a decision and how much information they require before making their choice. In one study, 79 managers worked on simulated exercises that required them to make hiring decisions.[58] High **risk-taking** managers made more rapid decisions and used less information in making their choices than did the low risk-taking managers. Interestingly, the decision accuracy was the same for both groups.

> **risk-taking** A person's willingness to take chances or risks.

Richard Branson's propensity to take risks aligns with his job demands as an entrepreneur. Branson, founder and chairman of London-based Virgin Group, started risky ventures that compete against industry giants. His Virgin Atlantic airline, for example, has taken market share from British Airways and has earned a reputation as one of the financially healthiest airlines in the world. Branson's risk-taking personality extends to his leisure activities of speedboat racing, skydiving, and ballooning.

Although previous studies have shown managers in large organizations to be more risk averse than are growth-oriented entrepreneurs who actively manage small businesses, recent findings suggest that managers in large organizations may actually be more willing to take risks than entrepreneurs.[59] For the work population as a whole, there are also differences in risk propensity.[60] As a result, it makes sense to recognize these differences and even to consider aligning risk-taking propensity with specific job demands. For instance, a high risk-taking propensity may lead to more effective performance for a stock trader in a brokerage firm because that type of job demands rapid decision making. On the other hand, a willingness to take risks might prove a major obstacle to an accountant who performs auditing activities. The latter job might be better filled by someone with a low risk-taking propensity. If you are interested in determining where you stand on risk-taking, you might want to complete *Learning About Yourself Exercise #3* on page 72.

Learning About Yourself

3. Are You a Risk-Taker?
(page 72)

Type A personality A personality with aggressive involvement in a chronic, incessant struggle to achieve more and more in less and less time and, if necessary, against the opposing efforts of other things or other people.

Type A and Type B Personalities

Do you know people who are excessively competitive and always seem to be chronically pushed for time? If you do, it's a good bet that those people have a Type A personality. A person with a **Type A personality** is "aggressively involved in a chronic, incessant struggle to achieve more and more in less and less time, and, if required to do so, against the opposing efforts of other things or other persons."[61] In North American culture, such characteristics tend to be highly prized and positively associated with ambition and the successful acquisition of material goods.

Do you think it is better to be a Type A or a Type B personality?

Type As

- Are always moving, walking, and eating rapidly

- Feel impatient with the rate at which most events take place

- Strive to think or do two or more things at once

- Cannot cope with leisure time

- Are obsessed with numbers, measuring their success in terms of how many or how much of everything they acquire

Type B personality A personality that is described as easy-going, relaxed, and patient.

In contrast to the Type A personality is the **Type B personality**, who is exactly opposite. Research indicates that Type Bs are "rarely harried by the desire to obtain a wildly increasing number of things or participate in an endless growing series of events in an ever-decreasing amount of time."[62]

Type Bs

- Never suffer from a sense of time urgency, with its accompanying impatience

- Feel no need to display or discuss either their achievements or accomplishments unless such exposure is demanded by the situation

- Play for fun and relaxation, rather than to exhibit their superiority at any cost

- Can relax without guilt

Type As are often characterized by impatience, hurriedness, competitiveness, and hostility, but these characteristics tend to emerge when a Type A individual experiences stress or challenge.[63] Type As are fast workers because they emphasize quantity over quality. In managerial positions, Type As demonstrate their competitiveness by working long hours and, not infrequently, making poor decisions because they make them too fast.

Stressed Type As are also rarely creative. Because of their concern with quantity and speed, they rely on past experiences when faced with problems. They will not take the time that is necessary to develop unique solutions to new problems. They rarely vary in their responses to specific challenges in their environment. As a result, their behaviour is easier to predict than that of Type Bs.

Are Type As or Type Bs more successful in organizations? Despite the hard work of Type As, the Type Bs are the ones who appear to make it to the top. Great salespeople are usually Type As; senior executives are usually Type Bs.

Why? The answer lies in the tendency of Type As to trade off quality of effort for quantity. Promotions in corporate and professional organizations "usually go to those who are wise rather than to those who are merely hasty, to those who are tactful rather than to those who are hostile, and to those who are creative rather than to those who are merely agile in competitive strife."[64]

More important than the simple question of promotion is the fact that Type As suffer more serious health consequences when under stress. Stressed Type A individuals tend to exhibit negative health consequences such as higher blood pressure, and their recovery from the stressful situation is slower than that of Type B personalities. These findings suggest why Type A individuals tend to have higher rates of death associated with hypertension, coronary heart disease, and coronary artery disease.[65]

Recent research has looked at the effect of job complexity on the cardiovascular health of both Type A and Type B individuals to see whether Type As always suffered negative health consequences.[66] Type A workers who faced high job complexity had higher death rates from heart-related disorders than Type As who faced lower job complexity. In contrast, Type B individuals did not suffer negative health consequences from jobs with psychological complexity. These findings suggest that, healthwise, Type B workers suffer less when handling complex jobs than do Type As. It also suggests that Type As who face lower job complexity do not face the same health risks as Type As who face higher job complexity.

If you are interested in determining whether you have a Type A or Type B personality, you might want to complete *Learning About Yourself Exercise #4* on page 74.

Learning About Yourself

4. Are You a Type A?
(page 74)

Proactive Personality

Did you ever notice that some people actively take the initiative to improve their current circumstances or create new ones, while others sit by passively reacting to situations? The former individuals have been described as having a proactive personality.[67]

People with a **proactive personality** identify opportunities, show initiative, take action, and persevere until meaningful change occurs. They create positive change in their environment, regardless or even in spite of constraints or obstacles.[68] Not surprisingly, proactives have many behaviours that organizations desire. For instance, the evidence indicates that proactives are more likely to be seen as leaders and more likely to act as change agents within the organization.[69] Other actions of proactives can be positive or negative, depending on the organization and the situation. For example, proactives are more likely to challenge the status quo or voice their displeasure when situations are not to their liking.[70] If an organization requires people with entrepreneurial initiative, proactives make good candidates; however, these are people who are also more likely to leave an organization to start their own business.[71] As individuals, proactives are more likely to achieve career success.[72] This is because they select, create, and influence work situations in their favour. Proactives are more likely to seek out job and organizational information, develop contacts in high places, engage in career planning, and demonstrate persistence in the face of career obstacles.

For an interesting look at how personality can contribute to business success, read this chapter's *Case Incident—A Diamond Personality* on page 79.

proactive personality A person who identifies opportunities, shows initiative, takes action, and perseveres until meaningful change occurs.

Emotions

Former Vancouver city councillor Anne Roberts was a vocal opponent of Walmart Canada opening a store in the city.[73] She was so concerned that a new city council would overturn the views of the previous council, which had denied a permit to Walmart, that she wondered if the retailer was interfering with city elections. "It would be of great concern if a big American corporation was influencing our local election. If they are contributing to the NPA [one of the city's political parties], Walmart is interfering with our political process," said Roberts.

Sam Sullivan, who was running for mayor at the time, was willing to entertain another vote by city council on whether Walmart could open its doors in Vancouver if he was elected. Still, he denied that Walmart was contributing to his campaign. "I usually don't get involved in fundraising, but after I heard her accusations I had to ask. And in fact Walmart has not contributed any money to the NPA. There is no conspiracy theory here," said Sullivan. Could emotions have affected how each individual viewed Walmart's impact on the city?

6   Can emotions help or get in the way when we are dealing with others?

Each of us has a range of personality characteristics, but we also bring with us a range of emotions. Given the obvious role that emotions play in our everyday life, it might surprise you to learn that, until very recently, the topic of emotions was given little or no attention within the field of OB. When emotions were considered, the discussion focused on strong negative emotions—especially anger—that interfered with an employee's ability to do his or her job effectively. Emotions were rarely viewed as being constructive or able to stimulate performance-enhancing behaviours.

Certainly some emotions, particularly when exhibited at the wrong time, can reduce employee performance. But this does not change the reality that employees bring an emotional component with them to work every day, and that no study of OB could be comprehensive without considering the role of emotions in workplace behaviour.

What Are Emotions?

emotions Intense feelings that are directed at someone or something.

moods Feelings that tend to be less intense than emotions and that lack a contextual stimulus.

Emotions are intense feelings that are directed at someone or something.[74] **Moods** are feelings that are less intense than emotions and that lack a contextual stimulus.[75]

Emotions are reactions to an object. You show your emotions when you are "happy about something, angry at someone, afraid of something."[76] Research has identified six universal emotions: anger, fear, sadness, happiness, disgust, and surprise.[77]

Moods, on the other hand, are not directed at an object. Emotions can turn into moods when you stop focusing on the contextual object. So when a colleague criticizes you for the way you spoke to a client, you might become angry at that colleague. That is, you show emotion (anger) toward a specific object (your colleague). But later in the day, you might find yourself just generally dispirited. You cannot attribute this feeling to any single event; you are just not your normal, upbeat self. This state describes a mood.

Choosing Emotions: Emotional Labour

Ever wonder why the grocery clerk is always smiling?

If you have ever had a job working in retail sales or waiting on tables in a restaurant, you know the importance of "being nice." Even though there were days when you did not feel cheerful, you knew management expected you to be upbeat when dealing with customers. So you faked it, and in so doing, you expressed *emotional labour*.

Every employee expends physical and mental labour when they put their bodies and cognitive capabilities, respectively, into their job. But jobs also require emotional labour.

emotional labour When an employee expresses organizationally desired emotions during interpersonal interactions.

Emotional labour is an employee's expression of organizationally desired emotions while at work.[78] For instance, crying may or may not be acceptable in the workplace, as *OB in the Workplace* shows.

Shed Those Tears

Can crying hurt you at work? Kathryn Brady, 34, is a finance manager for a large corporation.[79] Occasionally she has had bosses who have driven her to tears. Brady argues that when she has cried, it has been out of frustration, not weakness. "The misinterpretation that I'm whiny or weak is just not fair," she says.

Although that "old school" wisdom still holds true in many places, it is changing in others. George Merkle, CEO of a San Antonio credit company, does not mind if his employees cry. If someone cries, he says, "No apology needed. I know it's upsetting, and we can work our way through it." When Hillary Clinton was running to be the nominee for US president in 2008, it was said that showing tears had actually made her more likable.

Surveys indicate that women are more likely to cry at work than men, but that may be changing, too. When 6'3" 253-pound football tight end Vernon Davis cried after being selected in the first round of the NFL draft, nobody accused him of being a wimp.

To many, however, these emotional displays are signs of weakness. On the reality TV show *The Apprentice: Martha Stewart*, Stewart warned one of the contestants not to cry. "Cry, and you're out of here," she said. "Women in business don't cry, my dear." ▬▬

The concept of emotional labour emerged from studies of service jobs. Airlines expect their flight attendants, for instance, to be cheerful; we expect funeral directors to be sad; and we expect doctors to be emotionally neutral. But really, emotional labour is relevant to almost every job. Your managers expect you, for example, to be courteous, not hostile, in interactions with co-workers. The true challenge arises when employees have to project one emotion while simultaneously feeling another.[80] This difference is **emotional dissonance**, and it can take a heavy toll on employees. Bottled-up feelings of frustration, anger, and resentment can eventually lead to emotional exhaustion and burnout.[81] It is because of emotional labour's increasing importance in effective job performance that an understanding of emotion has gained heightened relevance within the field of OB.

> **emotional dissonance** Inconsistencies between the emotions people feel and the emotions they show.

Emotional labour creates dilemmas for employees. There are people with whom you have to work that you just don't like. Maybe you consider their personality abrasive. Maybe you know they have said negative things about you behind your back. Regardless, your job requires you to interact with these people on a regular basis. So you are forced to pretend to be friendly.

It can help you, on the job especially, if you separate emotions into *felt* or *displayed* emotions.[82] **Felt emotions** are an individual's actual emotions. In contrast, **displayed emotions** are those that the organization requires employees to show and considers appropriate in a given job. They are not natural; they are learned. "The ritual look of delight on the face of the first runner-up as the [winner] is announced is a product of the display rule that losers should mask their sadness with an expression of joy for the winner."[83] Similarly, most of us know that we are expected to act sad at funerals, regardless of whether we consider the person's death to be a loss, and to pretend to be happy at weddings, even if we don't feel like celebrating.[84]

> **felt emotions** An individual's actual emotions.
>
> **displayed emotions** Emotions that are organizationally required and considered appropriate in a given job.

Effective managers have learned to be serious when giving an employee a negative performance evaluation and to hide their anger when they have been passed over for promotion. And a salesperson who has not learned to smile and appear friendly, regardless of his true feelings at the moment, is not typically going to last long on most sales jobs. How we *experience* an emotion is not always the same as how we *show* it.[85]

surface acting Hiding one's inner feelings to display what is expected.

deep acting Trying to modify one's true inner feelings to match what is expected.

Yet another point is that displaying fake emotions requires us to suppress the emotions we really feel (not showing anger toward a customer, for example). In other words, the individual has to "act" to keep her job. **Surface acting** is hiding one's inner feelings and hiding emotional expressions in response to display rules. For example, when an employee smiles at a customer even when he does not feel like it, he is surface acting. **Deep acting** is trying to modify one's true inner feelings based on display rules. A health care provider trying to genuinely feel more empathy for her patients is deep acting.[86] Surface acting deals with one's *displayed* emotions, and deep acting deals with one's *felt* emotions. Research shows that surface acting is more stressful to employees than deep acting because it entails faking one's true emotions.[87] For further discussion on the costs and benefits of emotional display rules in organizations, read this chapter's *Point/Counterpoint* on page 69 and *Case Incident—Abusive Customers Cause Emotions to Run High* on page 79.

Why Should We Care About Emotions in the Workplace?

There are a number of reasons to be concerned about understanding emotions in the workplace.[88] People who know their own emotions and are good at reading others' emotions may be more effective in their jobs. That, in essence, is the theme underlying contemporary research on emotional intelligence.[89] The entire workplace can be affected by positive or negative workplace emotions, another issue we consider below. Finally, we consider affective events theory, which has increased our understanding of emotions at work.

Emotional Intelligence

emotional intelligence (EI) An assortment of noncognitive skills, capabilities, and competencies that influence a person's ability to succeed in coping with environmental demands and pressures.

Diane Marshall is an office manager. Her awareness of her own and others' emotions is almost zero. She is moody and unable to generate much enthusiasm or interest in her employees. She does not understand why employees get upset with her. She often overreacts to problems and chooses the most ineffectual responses to emotional situations.[90] Diane Marshall has low emotional intelligence. **Emotional intelligence (EI)** is a person's ability to (1) be self-aware (to recognize one's own emotions when one experiences them), (2) detect emotions in others, and (3) manage emotional cues and information. People who know their own emotions and are good at reading emotional cues—for instance, knowing why they are angry and how to express themselves without violating norms—are most likely to be effective.[91]

Several studies suggest that EI plays an important role in job performance. One study looked at the characteristics of engineers at Lucent Technologies (now Alcatel-Lucent) who were rated as stars by their peers. The researchers concluded that stars were better at relating to others. That is, it was EI, not IQ, that characterized high performers. Another illuminating study looked at the successes and failures of 11 American presidents—from Franklin Roosevelt to Bill Clinton. They were evaluated on six qualities—communication, organization, political skill, vision, cognitive style, and emotional intelligence. It was found that the key quality that differentiated the successful (such as Roosevelt, Kennedy, and Reagan) from the unsuccessful (such as Johnson, Carter, and Nixon) was emotional intelligence.[92] Some researchers argue that emotional intelligence is particularly important for leaders.[93]

EI has been a controversial concept in OB. It has supporters and detractors. In the following sections, we review the arguments for and against the effectiveness of EI in OB. If you are interested in determining your EI, you might want to complete *Learning About Yourself Exercise #5* on page 74. This chapter's *From Concepts to Skills* on page 80 gives you some insight into reading the emotions of others.

Learning About Yourself

5. What's Your EI at Work?
   (page 74)

The Case for EI

The arguments in favour of EI include its intuitive appeal, the fact that EI predicts criteria that matter, and the idea that EI is biologically based.

Intuitive Appeal There is a lot of intuitive appeal to the EI concept. Almost everyone would agree that it is good to possess street smarts and social intelligence. People who can detect emotions in others, control their own emotions, and handle social interactions well will have a powerful leg up in the business world, so the thinking goes.[94] As just one example, partners in a multinational consulting firm who scored above the median on an EI measure delivered $1.2 million more in business than did the other partners.[95]

EI Predicts Criteria That Matter More and more evidence is suggesting that a high level of EI means a person will perform well on the job. One study found that EI predicted the performance of employees in a cigarette factory in China.[96] Another study found that being able to recognize emotions in others' facial expressions and to emotionally "eavesdrop" (that is, pick up subtle signals about peoples' emotions) predicted peer ratings of how valuable those people were to their organization.[97] Finally, a review of 59 studies indicated that, overall, EI correlated moderately with job performance.[98]

EI Is Biologically Based One study has shown that people with damage to the part of the brain that governs emotional processing (lesions in an area of the prefrontal cortex) score significantly lower than others on EI tests. Even though these brain-damaged people scored no lower on standard measures of intelligence than people without the same brain damage, they were still impaired in normal decision making. Specifically, when people were playing a card game in which there is a reward (money) for picking certain types of cards and a punishment (a loss of money) for picking other types of cards, the participants with no brain damage learned to succeed in the game, while the performance of the brain-damaged group worsened over time. This study suggests that EI is neurologically based in a way that is unrelated to standard measures of intelligence, and that people who suffer neurological damage score lower on EI and make poorer decisions than people who are healthier in this regard.[99]

Meg Whitman, former CEO and now a director of eBay, is a leader with high emotional intelligence. She is described as self-confident yet humble, trustworthy, culturally sensitive, and expert at building teams and leading change. Shown here, Whitman welcomes Gloria Arroyo, president of the Philippine Islands, to eBay headquarters.

The Case Against EI

For all its supporters, EI has just as many critics. Its critics say that EI is vague and impossible to measure, and they question its validity.

EI Is Too Vague a Concept   To many researchers, it's not clear what EI is. Is it a form of intelligence? Most of us would not think that being self-aware or self-motivated or having empathy is a matter of intellect. Moreover, different researchers often focus on different skills, making it difficult to get a definition of EI. One researcher may study self-discipline. Another may study empathy. Another may look at self-awareness. As one reviewer noted, "The concept of EI has now become so broad and the components so variegated that . . . it is no longer even an intelligible concept."[100]

EI Cannot Be Measured   Many critics have raised questions about measuring EI. Because EI is a form of intelligence, for instance, there must be right and wrong answers about it on tests, they argue. Some tests do have right and wrong answers, although the validity of some of the questions on these measures is questionable. For example, one measure asks you to associate particular feelings with specific colours, as if purple always makes us feel cool and not warm. Other measures are self-reported, meaning that there is no right or wrong answer. For example, an EI test question might ask you to respond to the statement "I'm good at 'reading' other people." In general, the measures of EI are diverse, and researchers have not subjected them to as much rigorous study as they have measures of personality and general intelligence.[101]

The Validity of EI Is Suspect   Some critics argue that because EI is so closely related to intelligence and personality, once you control for these factors, EI has nothing unique to offer. There is some foundation to this argument. EI appears to be highly correlated with measures of personality, especially emotional stability.[102] But there has not been enough research on whether EI adds insight beyond measures of personality and general intelligence in predicting job performance. Still, among consulting firms and in the popular press, EI is wildly popular. For example, one company's promotional materials for an EI measure claimed, "EI accounts for more than 85 percent of star performance in top leaders."[103] To say the least, it's difficult to validate this statement with the research literature.

Weighing the arguments for and against EI, it's still too early to tell whether the concept is useful. It *is* clear, though, that the concept is here to stay.

Negative Workplace Emotions

Negative emotions can lead to a number of deviant workplace behaviours. Anyone who has spent much time in an organization realizes that people often engage in voluntary actions that violate established norms and threaten the organization, its members, or both. These actions are called **employee deviance**.[104] Deviant actions fall into categories such as production (leaving early, intentionally working slowly); property (stealing, sabotage); political (gossiping, blaming co-workers); and personal aggression (sexual harassment, verbal abuse).[105]

   Many of these deviant behaviours can be traced to negative emotions. For instance, envy is an emotion that occurs when you resent someone for having something that you don't, and that you strongly desire—such as a better work assignment, larger office, or higher salary.[106] It can lead to malicious deviant behaviours, such as hostility, "backstabbing," and other forms of political behaviour that negatively distort others' successes and positively distort your own accomplishments.[107] Evidence suggests that people who feel negative emotions, particularly those who feel angry or hostile, are more likely to engage in deviant behavior at work than are people who don't feel negative emotions.[108]

employee deviance Voluntary actions that violate established norms and threaten the organization, its members, or both.

Managing emotions in the workplace becomes important both to ward off negative behaviour and to encourage positive behaviour in those around us. *Focus on Research* looks at the issue of "catching" moods from others. You may be surprised to learn the extent to which your mood can affect the mood of others.

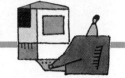

FOCUS ON **RESEARCH**

Moods Affect the Success of Groups

Can you catch moods from those around you? A study of 70 work groups sought to discover whether moods could be spread throughout the group.[109] There were four to eight members in each group. While performing tasks, each group was observed by two people, who tried to judge the mood of the group from posture, facial expression, and vocal expression of group members. To assess the accuracy of the observations, group members filled out questionnaires that asked about their typical behaviour with members of their group, and their mood at the time of the observation.

The researchers found that members of groups do seem to adopt similar moods when the moods are "high-energy" (for example, cheerful enthusiasm, hostile irritability) rather than when they are "low-energy" (for example, serene warmth, depressed sluggishness). The entire group felt unpleasant moods the most strongly. Those who observed the work groups were able to accurately identify many of the moods the groups experienced, just by watching postures and the facial and vocal expressions of group members. The researchers also found that facial and postural cues were more likely to signal the mood of the group than vocal cues. They suggested that group members may feel it's inappropriate to express their moods verbally in some work settings, so that facial gestures become the more likely avenue of mood expression.

Affective Events Theory

Understanding emotions at work has been significantly helped by a model called **affective events theory (AET)**.[110] AET demonstrates that employees react emotionally to things that happen to them at work, and that this emotional reaction influences their job performance and satisfaction.

Exhibit 2-6 summarizes AET. The theory begins by recognizing that emotions are a response to an event in the work environment. The work environment includes everything surrounding the job—characteristics of the job, such as the variety of tasks and degree of autonomy, job demands, and requirements for expressing emotional labour. This environment creates work events that can be hassles, uplifts, or both. Examples of events that employees frequently see as hassles are colleagues who refuse to carry their share of work, conflicting directions by different managers, and excessive time pressures.[111] Examples of uplifting events include meeting a goal, getting support from a colleague, and receiving recognition for an accomplishment.

These work events trigger positive or negative emotional reactions. But the events-reaction relationship is moderated by the employee's personality and mood. Personality predisposes people to respond with greater or lesser intensity to the event. For instance, people who score low on emotional stability are more likely to react strongly to negative events. In addition, a person's emotional response to a given event can change depending on his or her mood. Finally, emotions influence a number of job performance and satisfaction variables, such as organizational citizenship behaviour (OCB), organizational commitment, intentions to quit, and level of effort.

In addition, tests of the theory suggest that (1) an emotional episode is actually a series of emotional experiences precipitated by a single event. It reflects elements of both

affective events theory (AET) The theory that employees react emotionally to things that happen to them at work and that this emotional reaction influences their job performance and satisfaction.

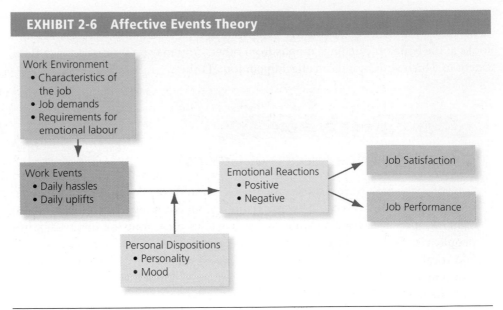

EXHIBIT 2-6   Affective Events Theory

Source: Based on N. M. Ashkanasy and C. S. Daus, "Emotion in the Workplace: The New Challenge for Managers," *Academy of Management Executive*, February 2002, p. 77.

emotions and mood cycles. (2) Job satisfaction is influenced by current emotions at any given time along with the history of emotions surrounding the event. (3) Since moods and emotions fluctuate over time, their effect on performance also fluctuates. (4) Emotion-driven behaviours are typically short in duration and of high variability. (5) Because emotions tend to be incompatible with behaviours required to do a job, they can have a negative influence on job performance (this is the case even for positive emotions like happiness and joy).[112]

An example might help better explain AET.[113] You work as an aeronautical engineer for Bombardier. Because of the downturn in the demand for commercial jets, you have just learned that the company is considering laying off several thousand employees. This could include you. This event is likely to elicit a negative emotional reaction: You are fearful that you might lose your job and primary source of income. Also, because you are prone to worry a lot and obsess about problems, your feelings of insecurity are increased. This event also puts into place a series of subevents that create an episode: You talk with your boss and he assures you that your job is safe; you hear rumours that your department is high on the list to be eliminated; you run into a former colleague who was laid off six months ago and still has not found work. These, in turn, create emotional ups and downs. One day, you are feeling more upbeat and sure that you will survive the cuts. The next day, you might be depressed and anxious, convinced that your department will be eliminated. These swings in your emotions take your attention away from your work and result in reduced job performance and satisfaction. Finally, your response is magnified because this is the fourth large layoff that Bombardier has initiated in the past three years.

In summary, AET offers two important messages.[114] First, emotions provide valuable insights into understanding employee behaviour. The model demonstrates how daily hassles and uplifts influence employee performance and satisfaction. Second, emotions in organizations and the events that cause them should not be ignored, even when they appear to be minor. This is because they accumulate. It's not the intensity of hassles and uplifts that lead to emotional reactions, but more the frequency with which they occur.

Emotions in the Workplace in a Global Context

Does the degree to which people *experience* emotions vary across cultures? Do people's *interpretations* of emotions vary across cultures? Finally, do the norms for the *expression* of emotions differ across cultures? Let's tackle each of these questions.

Does the Degree to Which People Experience Emotions Vary Across Cultures?

Yes. In China, for example, people report experiencing fewer positive and negative emotions than people in other cultures, and the emotions they experience are less intense than what other cultures report. Compared with mainland Chinese, Taiwanese are more like Canadian employees in their experience of emotions: On average, Taiwanese report more positive and fewer negative emotions than their Chinese counterparts.[115] In general, people in most cultures appear to experience certain positive and negative emotions, but the frequency of their experience and their intensity varies to some degree.[116]

Do People's Interpretations of Emotions Vary Across Cultures?

In general, people from all over the world interpret negative and positive emotions the same way. We all view negative emotions, such as hate, terror, and rage, as dangerous and destructive. And we all desire positive emotions, such as joy, love, and happiness. However, some cultures value certain emotions more than others. For example, Americans value enthusiasm, while the Chinese consider negative emotions to be more useful and constructive. In general, pride is seen as a positive emotion in Western, individualistic cultures such as the United States, but Eastern cultures such as China and Japan tend to view pride as undesirable.[117]

Do the Norms for the Expression of Emotions Differ Across Cultures?

Absolutely. For example, some fundamentalist Muslims see smiling as a sign of sexual attraction, so women have learned not to smile at men so as to not be misinterpreted.[118] And research has shown that in collectivist countries, people are more likely to believe that the emotional displays of another have something to do with their own relationship with the person expressing the emotion, while people in individualistic cultures don't think that another's emotional expressions are directed at them. Evidence indicates that in Canada there is a bias against expressing emotions, especially intense negative emotions. French retail clerks, in contrast, are infamous for being surly toward customers. (A report from the French government itself confirmed this.) There are also reports that serious German shoppers have been turned off by Walmart's friendly greeters and helpful personnel.[119]

In general, and not surprisingly, it's easier for people to accurately recognize emotions within their own culture than in other cultures. For example, a Chinese businessperson is more likely to accurately label the emotions underlying the facial expressions of a fellow Chinese colleague than those of a US colleague.[120]

Interestingly, some cultures lack words for standard Canadian emotional terms such as *anxiety*, *depression*, and *guilt*. Tahitians, as a case in point, don't have a word directly equivalent to *sadness*. When Tahitians are sad, their peers attribute their state to a physical illness.[121] Our discussion illustrates the need to consider the fact that cultural factors influence what managers think is emotionally appropriate.[122] What is acceptable in one culture may seem extremely unusual or even dysfunctional in another. Managers need to know the emotional norms in each culture they do business in or with so they don't send unintended signals or misread the reactions of others. For example, a Canadian manager in Japan should know that while Canadian culture tends to view smiling positively, the Japanese attribute frequent smiling to a lack of intelligence.[123]

Summary and Implications

1 **What is perception?** *Perception* is the process by which individuals organize and interpret their impressions to give meaning to their environment. Individuals behave in a given manner based not on the way their environment actually is but, rather, on what they see or believe it to be. An organization may spend millions of dollars to create a pleasant work environment for its employees. However, despite these expenditures, an employee who believes that his or her job is lousy will behave accordingly.

2 **What causes people to have different perceptions of the same situation?** A number of factors operate to shape and sometimes distort perception. These factors can be present in the perceiver, in the object, or target, being perceived, or in the context of the situation in which the perception is made. The perceiver's attitudes, motives, interests, and past experiences all shape the way he or she sees an event. The target's characteristics also affect what is perceived. Novelty, motion, sounds, size, and other characteristics of a target shape the way it is seen. Objects or events that are unrelated are often perceived together because they are close physically or in timing. Persons, objects, or events that are similar to each other also tend to be viewed as a group. The setting in which we see objects or events also affects how they are perceived.

3 **Can people be mistaken in their perceptions?** Perceiving and interpreting what others do is difficult and takes time. As a result, we develop shortcuts to make this task more manageable. These shortcuts, described by attribution theory, selective perception, the halo effect, contrast effect, projection, and stereotyping, are often valuable—they can sometimes allow us to make accurate perceptions quickly and provide valid data for making predictions. However, they are not foolproof. They can and do get us into trouble.

4 **Does perception really affect outcomes?** The evidence suggests that what individuals perceive about their work situation influences their productivity more than the situation does. Whether a job is actually interesting or challenging is irrelevant. Whether a manager actually helps employees to structure their work more efficiently and effectively is far less important than how employees perceive the manager's efforts. Similarly, issues such as fair pay, the validity of performance appraisals, and the adequacy of working conditions are not judged "objectively." Rather, individuals interpret conditions surrounding their jobs based on how they *perceive* their jobs.

5 **What is personality and how does it affect behaviour?** *Personality* is the stable patterns of behaviour and consistent internal states that determine how an individual reacts to and interacts with others. A review of the personality literature offers general guidelines that can lead to effective job performance. As such, it can improve hiring, transfer, and promotion decisions. Personality attributes give us a framework for predicting behaviour. Personality affects how people react to others, and the types of jobs that they may desire. For example, individuals who are shy, introverted, and uncomfortable in social situations would probably make poor salespeople. Individuals who are submissive and conforming might not be effective as advertising "idea" people. Be aware, though, that measuring personality is not an exact science, and as you no doubt learned from the discussion of attribution theory, it's easy to attribute personality characteristics in error.

6 **Can emotions help or get in the way when we are dealing with others?**
Emotions are intense feelings that are directed at someone or something. Positive emotions can be motivating for everyone in the workplace. Negative emotions may make it difficult to get along with others. Can managers control the emotions of their colleagues and employees? No. Emotions are a natural part of an individual's makeup. At the same time, managers err if they ignore the emotional elements in OB and assess individual behaviour as if it were completely rational. Managers who understand the role of emotions will significantly improve their ability to explain and predict individual behaviour.

Do emotions affect job performance? Yes. Emotions, especially negative ones, can hinder performance. That is probably why organizations, for the most part, try to remove emotions from the workplace. But emotions can also enhance performance. How? Two ways.[124] First, emotions can increase arousal levels, thus acting as motivators to higher performance. Second, the concept of emotional labour recognizes that feelings can be part of a job's required behaviour. So, for instance, the ability to effectively manage emotions in leadership and sales positions may be critical to success in those positions. Research also indicates the importance of emotional intelligence, the assortment of noncognitive skills, capabilities, and competencies that influence a person's ability to succeed in coping with environmental demands and pressures.

When working in a global context, it's important to keep in mind that the experience, interpretation, and expression of emotions differs across cultures.

For Review

1. Define *perception*.

2. What is attribution theory? What are its implications for explaining behaviour in organizations?

3. What is stereotyping? Give an example of how stereotyping can create perceptual distortion.

4. Give some positive results of using shortcuts when judging others.

5. Describe the factors in the Big Five Personality Model. Which factor shows the greatest value in predicting behaviour? Why does it?

6. What behavioural predictions might you make if you knew that an employee had (a) a negative core self-evaluation? (b) a low Mach score? (c) low self-monitoring? (d) a Type A personality?

7. To what extent do people's personalities affect how they are perceived?

8. What is emotional labour and why is it important to understanding OB?

9. What is emotional intelligence and why is it important?

10. Explain affective events theory. What are its implications for managing emotions?

For Critical Thinking

1. How might the differences in experience of students and instructors affect their perceptions of classroom behaviour (for example, students' written work and class comments)?

2. An employee does an unsatisfactory job on an assigned project. Explain the attribution process that this person's manager will use to form judgments about this employee's job performance.

3. One day your boss comes in and he is nervous, edgy, and argumentative. The next day he is calm and relaxed. Does this behaviour suggest that personality traits are not consistent from day to day?

4. What, if anything, can managers do to manage employees' emotions? Are there ethical implications in any of these actions? If so, what?

5. Give some examples of situations where expressing emotions might enhance job performance.

 **for You**

- The discussion of perception might get you thinking about how you view the world. When we perceive someone as a troublemaker, for instance, this may be only a perception, and not a real characteristic of that person. It is always good to question your perceptions, just to be sure that you are not reading something into a situation that is not there.

- One important thing to consider when looking for a job is whether your personality will fit the organization to which you are applying. For instance, let's say that you are considering working for a highly structured company. If you, by nature, are much less formal, then that company may not be a good fit for you.

- Sometimes personalities get in the way when working in groups. You may want to see if you can figure out ways to get personality differences to work in favour of group goals.

- Emotions need not always be suppressed when working with others. While emotions can sometimes hinder performance, positive emotions can motivate you and those around you.

POINT

COUNTERPOINT

Display Rules Make Good Business Sense

Organizations today realize that good customer service means good business. After all, who wants to end a shopping trip at the grocery store with a surly cashier? Research clearly shows that organizations that provide good customer service have higher profits than those with poor customer service.[125] An integral part of customer-service training is to set forth display rules to teach employees to interact with customers in a friendly, helpful, professional way—and evidence indicates that such rules work: Having display rules increases the odds that employees will display the emotions expected of them.[126]

As one Starbucks manager says, "What makes Starbucks different is our passion for what we do. We're trying to provide a great experience for people, with a great product. That's what we all care about."[127] Starbucks may have good coffee, but a big part of the company's growth has been the customer experience. For instance, the cashiers are friendly and will get to know you by name if you are a repeat customer.

Asking employees to act friendly is good for them, too. Research shows that employees of organizations that require them to display positive emotions actually feel better as a result.[128] And if someone feels that being asked to smile is bad for him, that person does not belong in the service industry in the first place.

Display Rules Do Not Make Sense

Organizations have no business trying to regulate the emotions of their employees. Companies should not be "the thought police" and force employees to feel and act in ways that serve only organizational needs. Service employees should be professional and courteous, yes, but many companies expect them to take abuse and refrain from defending themselves. That's wrong. As philosopher Jean Paul Sartre wrote, we have a responsibility to be authentic—true to ourselves—and within reasonable limits, organizations have no right to ask us to be otherwise.

Service industries have no business teaching their employees to be smiling punching bags. Most customers might even prefer that employees be themselves. Employees should not be openly nasty or hostile, of course, but who appreciates a fake smile? Think about trying on an outfit in a store and the clerk automatically says it looks "absolutely wonderful" when you know it does not and you sense that the clerk is lying. Most customers would rather talk with a "real" person than someone enslaved to an organization's display rules. Furthermore, if an employee does not feel like slapping on an artificial smile, then it's only going to create friction between her and her employer.[129]

Finally, research shows that forcing display rules on employees takes a heavy emotional toll.[130] It's unnatural to expect someone to smile all the time or to passively take abuse from customers, clients, or fellow employees. Organizations can improve their employees' psychological health by encouraging them to be themselves, within reasonable limits.

How Machiavellian Are You?

For each statement, circle the number that most closely resembles your attitude.[131]

Statement	Disagree			Agree	
	A Lot	A Little	Neutral	A Little	A Lot
1. The best way to handle people is to tell them what they want to hear.	1	2	3	4	5
2. When you ask someone to do something for you, it is best to give the real reason for wanting it rather than giving reasons that might carry more weight.	1	2	3	4	5
3. Anyone who completely trusts anyone else is asking for trouble.	1	2	3	4	5
4. It is hard to get ahead without cutting corners here and there.	1	2	3	4	5
5. It is safest to assume that all people have a vicious streak, and it will come out when they are given a chance.	1	2	3	4	5
6. One should take action only when it is morally right.	1	2	3	4	5
7. Most people are basically good and kind.	1	2	3	4	5
8. There is no excuse for lying to someone else.	1	2	3	4	5
9. Most people more easily forget the death of their father than the loss of their property.	1	2	3	4	5
10. Generally speaking, people won't work hard unless they're forced to do so.	1	2	3	4	5

Scoring Key:

To obtain your Mach score, add the number you have checked on questions 1, 3, 4, 5, 9, and 10. For the other 4 questions (2, 6, 7, and 8), reverse the numbers you have checked: 5 becomes 1, 4 is 2, 2 is 4, and 1 is 5. Total your 10 numbers to find your score. The higher your score, the more Machiavellian you are. Among a random sample of American adults, the national average was 25.

Are You a High Self-Monitor?

Indicate the degree to which you think the following statements are true or false by circling the appropriate number. For example, if a statement is always true, circle the 5 next to that statement.[132]

5	=	**Certainly, always true**
4	=	**Generally true**
3	=	**Somewhat true, but with exceptions**
2	=	**Somewhat false, but with exceptions**
1	=	**Generally false**
0	=	**Certainly, always false**

1. In social situations, I have the ability to alter my behaviour if I feel that something else is called for.   0 1 2 3 ④ 5

2. I am often able to read people's true emotions correctly through their eyes.   0 1 2 3 ④ 5

3. I have the ability to control the way I come across to people, depending on the impression I wish to give them.   0 1 2 ③ 4 5

4. In conversations, I am sensitive to even the slightest change in the facial expression of the person I'm conversing with.   0 1 2 3 ④ 5

5. My powers of intuition are quite good when it comes to understanding others' emotions and motives.   0 1 2 3 ④ 5

6. I can usually tell when others consider a joke in bad taste, even though they may laugh convincingly.   0 1 2 ③ 4 5

7. When I feel that the image I am portraying isn't working, I can readily change it to something that does.   0 1 2 ③ 4 5

8. I can usually tell when I've said something inappropriate by reading the listener's eyes.   0 1 2 3 ④ 5

9. I have trouble changing my behaviour to suit different people and different situations.   0 ① 2 3 4 5   4

10. I have found that I can adjust my behaviour to meet the requirements of any situation I find myself in.   0 1 2 3 ④ 5

11. If someone is lying to me, I usually know it at once from that person's manner of expression.   0 1 2 ③ 4 5

12. Even when it might be to my advantage, I have difficulty putting up a good front.   0 1 ② 3 4 5   3

13. Once I know what the situation calls for, it is easy for me to regulate my actions accordingly.   0 1 2 ③ 4 5

Scoring Key:

To obtain your score, add up the numbers circled, except reverse scores for questions 9 and 12. On those, a circled 5 becomes a 0, 4 becomes a 1, and so forth. High self-monitors are defined as those with scores of 53 or higher.

OB *AT WORK*

Are You a Risk-Taker?

For each of the following situations, indicate the minimum odds of success you would demand before recommending that one alternative be chosen over another.[133] Try to place yourself in the position of the adviser to the central person in each of the situations.

1. Mr. B, a 45-year-old accountant, has recently been informed by his physician that he has developed a severe heart ailment. The disease will be sufficiently serious to force Mr. B to change many of his strongest life habits—reducing his workload, drastically changing his diet, giving up favourite leisure-time pursuits. The physician suggests that a delicate medical operation could be attempted. If successful, the operation would completely relieve the heart condition. But its success cannot be assured, and, in fact, the operation might prove fatal.

   Imagine that you are advising Mr. B. Listed below are several probabilities or odds that the operation will prove successful. Check the *lowest probability* that you would consider acceptable for the operation to be performed.

   _____   Mr. B should not have the operation, no matter what the probabilities.

   _____   The chances are 9 in 10 that the operation will be a success.

   _____   The chances are 7 in 10 that the operation will be a success.

   __√__   The chances are 5 in 10 that the operation will be a success.

   _____   The chances are 3 in 10 that the operation will be a success.

   _____   The chances are 1 in 10 that the operation will be a success.

2. Mr. D is the captain of University X's varsity football team. University X is playing its traditional rival, University Y, in the final game of the season. The game is in its final seconds, and Mr. D's team, University X, is behind in the score. University X has time to make one more play. Mr. D, the captain, must decide on a strategy. Would it be best to try a play that would be almost certain to work and try to settle for a tie score? Or, on the other hand, should he try a more complicated and risky play that would bring victory if it succeeded or defeat if it failed? Imagine that you are advising Mr. D. Listed below are several probabilities or odds that the risky play will work. Check the *lowest probability* that you would consider acceptable for the risky play to be attempted.

   _____   Mr. D should not attempt the risky play, no matter what the probabilities.

   _____   The chances are 9 in 10 that the risky play will work.

   _____   The chances are 7 in 10 that the risky play will work.

   __√__   The chances are 5 in 10 that the risky play will work.

   _____   The chances are 3 in 10 that the risky play will work.

   _____   The chances are 1 in 10 that the risky play will work.

3. Ms. K is a successful businesswoman who has participated in a number of civic activities of considerable value to the community. Ms. K has been approached by the leaders of her political party as a possible candidate in the next provincial election. Ms. K's party is a minority party in the district, though the party has won occasional elections in the past. Ms. K would like to hold political office, but to do so would involve a serious financial sacrifice, since the party has insufficient campaign funds. She would also have to endure the attacks of her political opponents in a hot campaign.

LEARNING ABOUT **YOURSELF** EXERCISE #3 (Continued)

Imagine that you are advising Ms. K. Listed below are several probabilities or odds of Ms. K's winning the election in her district. Check the *lowest probability* that you would consider acceptable to make it worthwhile for Ms. K to run for political office.

_____ Ms. K should not run for political office, no matter what the probabilities.

_____ The chances are 9 in 10 that Ms. K will win the election.

_____ The chances are 7 in 10 that Ms. K will win the election.

___✓___ The chances are 5 in 10 that Ms. K will win the election.

_____ The chances are 3 in 10 that Ms. K will win the election.

_____ The chances are 1 in 10 that Ms. K will win the election.

4. Ms. L, a 30-year-old research physicist, has been given a 5-year appointment by a major university laboratory. As she contemplates the next 5 years, she realizes that she might work on a difficult long-term problem. If a solution to the problem could be found, it would resolve basic scientific issues in the field and bring high scientific honours. If no solution were found, however, Ms. L would have little to show for her 5 years in the laboratory, and it would be hard for her to get a good job afterward. On the other hand, she could, as most of her professional associates are doing, work on a series of short-term problems for which solutions would be easier to find. Those solutions, though, would be of lesser scientific importance.

Imagine that you are advising Ms. L. Listed below are several probabilities or odds that a solution will be found to the difficult long-term problem that Ms. L has in mind. Check the *lowest probability* that you would consider acceptable to make it worthwhile for Ms. L to work on the more difficult long-term problem.

_____ Ms. L should not choose the long-term, difficult problem, no matter what the probabilities.

_____ The chances are 9 in 10 that Ms. L will solve the long-term problem.

___✓___ The chances are 7 in 10 that Ms. L will solve the long-term problem.

_____ The chances are 5 in 10 that Ms. L will solve the long-term problem.

_____ The chances are 3 in 10 that Ms. L will solve the long-term problem.

_____ The chances are 1 in 10 that Ms. L will solve the long-term problem.

Scoring Key:

These situations were based on a longer questionnaire. Your results are an indication of your general orientation toward risk rather than a precise measure. To calculate your risk-taking score, add up the chances you were willing to take and divide by 4. (For any of the situations in which you would not take the risk, regardless of the probabilities, give yourself a 10.) The lower your number, the more risk-taking you are.

LEARNING ABOUT **YOURSELF** EXERCISE #4

Are You a Type A?

Circle the number on the scale below that best characterizes your behaviour for each trait.[134]

1. Casual about appointments	1	2	3	4	5	6	(7)	8	Never late
2. Not competitive	1	2	3	4	(5)	6	7	8	Very competitive
3. Never feel rushed	1	2	3	4	(5)	6	7	8	Always feel rushed
4. Take things one at a time	1	2	3	(4)	5	6	7	8	Try to do many things at once
5. Slow doing things	1	2	3	(4)	5	6	7	8	Fast (eating, walking, etc.)
6. Express feelings	1	(2)	3	4	5	6	7	8	"Sit on" feelings
7. Many interests	1	2	3	4	(5)	6	7	8	Few interests outside work

Scoring Key:

Total your score on the 7 questions. Now multiply the total by 3. A total of 120 or more indicates that you are a hard-core Type A. Scores below 90 indicate that you are a hard-core Type B. The following gives you more specifics:

Points	Personality type
120 or more	A1
106–119	A
100–105	A2
90–99	B1
Less than 90	B

LEARNING ABOUT **YOURSELF** EXERCISE #5

What's Your EI at Work?

Evaluating the following 25 statements will allow you to rate your social skills and self-awareness, the components of emotional intelligence (EI).[135]

EI, the social equivalent of IQ, is complex, in no small part because it depends on some pretty slippery variables—including your innate compatibility, or lack thereof, with the people who happen to be your co-workers. But if you want to get a rough idea of how your EI stacks up, this quiz will help.

As honestly as you can, estimate how you rate in the eyes of peers, bosses, and subordinates on each of the following traits, on a scale of 1–4, with 4 representing strong agreement, and 1 representing strong disagreement.

___3___ I usually stay composed, positive, and unflappable even in trying moments.

___4___ I can think clearly and stay focused on the task at hand under pressure.

___4___ I am able to admit my own mistakes.

___4___ I usually or always meet commitments and keep promises.

___4___ I hold myself accountable for meeting my goals.

___4___ I'm organized and careful in my work.

____3____ I regularly seek out fresh ideas from a wide variety of sources.

____3____ I'm good at generating new ideas.

____3____ I can smoothly handle multiple demands and changing priorities.

____4____ I'm result-oriented, with a strong drive to meet my objectives.

____2____ I like to set challenging goals and take calculated risks to reach them.

____3____ I'm always trying to learn how to improve my performance, including asking advice from people younger than I am.

____2____ I readily make sacrifices to meet an important organizational goal.

____3____ The company's mission is something I understand and can identify with.

____3____ The values of my team—or of our division or department, or the company—influence my decisions and clarify the choices I make.

____2____ I actively seek out opportunities to further the overall goals of the organization and enlist others to help me.

____4____ I pursue goals beyond what's required or expected of me in my current job.

____3____ Obstacles and setbacks may delay me a little, but they don't stop me.

____4____ Cutting through red tape and bending outdated rules are sometimes necessary.

____4____ I seek fresh perspectives, even if that means trying something totally new.

____3____ My impulses or distressing emotions don't often get the best of me at work.

____4____ I can change tactics quickly when circumstances change.

____4____ Pursuing new information is my best bet for cutting down on uncertainty and finding ways to do things better.

____4____ I usually don't attribute setbacks to a personal flaw (mine or someone else's).

____3____ I operate from an expectation of success rather than a fear of failure.

Scoring Key:

Total your score. A score below 70 indicates very low EI. EI is not unimprovable. Says Dan Goleman, author of *Working With Emotional Intelligence,* "Emotional intelligence can be learned, and in fact we are each building it, in varying degrees, throughout life. It's sometimes called maturity. EI is nothing more or less than a collection of tools that we can sharpen to help ensure our own survival."

Self-Assessment Library

More Learning About Yourself Exercises
Additional self-assessments relevant to this chapter appear on MyOBLab (**www.pearsoned.ca/myoblab**).

IV.C.2 What Are My Gender Role Perceptions?
IV.A.I Am I a Narcissist?
IV.D.1 How Are You Feeling Right Now?
I.E.1 What's My Emotional Intelligence Score?

When you complete the additional assessments, consider the following:

1. Am I surprised about my score?
2. Would my friends evaluate me similarly?

OB *AT WORK*

BREAKOUT **GROUP** EXERCISES

Form small groups to discuss the following topics, as assigned by your instructor. Each person in the group should first identify 3–5 key personal values.

1. Think back to your perception of this course and your instructor on the first day of class. What factors might have affected your perceptions of what the rest of the term would be like?

2. Describe a situation where your perception turned out to be wrong. What perceptual errors did you make that might have caused this to happen?

3. Compare your scores on the *Learning About Yourself Exercises* at the end of the chapter. What conclusions could you draw about your group based on these scores?

WORKING WITH OTHERS EXERCISE

Evaluating Your Stereotypes

1. Your instructor will choose 4 volunteers willing to reveal an interesting true-life background fact about themselves. Examples of such background facts are as follows:

   - I can perform various dances, including polka, rumba, bossa nova, and salsa.
   - I am the youngest of four children and I attended Catholic high school.
   - Neither of my parents attended school beyond grade 8.
   - My mother is a homemaker and my father is an author.

2. The instructor will put the 4 facts on the board without revealing to which person each belongs, and the 4 students will remain in the front of the room for the first part of the group discussion below.

3. Students in the class should silently decide which person belongs to which fact.

4. Students should break into groups of about 5 or 6 and try to reach a consensus about which person belongs to which fact. Meanwhile, the 4 students can serve as observers to group discussions, listening in on rationales for how students decide to link the facts with the individuals.

5. After 15 minutes of group discussion, several groups will be asked to present their consensus to the class, with justifications.

6. The classroom discussion will focus on perceptions, assumptions, and stereotyping that led to the decisions made.

7. At the end of the discussion, the instructor will reveal which student belongs to each fact.

ETHICAL **DILEMMA** EXERCISE

Hiring Based on Body Art

When Christine Giacomoni applied for a job at the Sherwood Park (Alberta) location of the Real Canadian Superstore, she was wearing a nose stud.[136] She got the job. Six months later, however, she was told that she could no longer wear her small nose stud at work. The company had just recently decided to apply their policy for front-line workers about no nose studs to employees like Giacomoni, who worked in the deli.

The United Food and Commercial Workers (UFCW), Giacomoni's union, grieved this action for her. The complaint ended up in front of a labour arbitrator. The union argued that this company was out of touch with reality. The company argued that nose studs offended customers. They hired Ipsos Reid to survey shoppers, and the results of the poll indicated that "a significant portion" of shoppers would stop shopping at a store that allowed employee facial piercings.

Ultimately, a judge ruled against Real Canadian Superstore's policy. Meanwhile, Giacomoni left to take a job at TELUS, in part because of the store's policy against her piercing. TELUS does not mind that she has a nose stud.

Many employees are aware that tattoos and body piercings can hurt one's chances of being hired. Consider Russell Parrish, 29, who lives near Orlando, Florida, and has dozens of tattoos on his arms, hands, torso, and neck. In searching for a job, Parrish walked into 100 businesses, and in 60 cases, he was refused an application. "I want a career," Parrish says, "I want the same shot as everybody else."

Employers are mixed in their reactions to employees with tattoos or piercings. At Vancouver-based Whitespot, employees cannot have visible tattoos (or pink or blue hair). They are allowed a small, simple nose stud. BC's Starbucks shops don't allow any pierced tongues or visible tattoos. Staff may not wear more than two reasonably sized earrings per ear. At Victoria-based Arq Salon, nearly everyone has a tattoo. "We work in an artistic field," manager Yasmin Morris explains, then adds that staff cannot wear jeans. "We don't want people to look too casual."

A survey of employers revealed that 58 percent indicated that they would be less likely to hire someone with visible tattoos or body piercings. The career centre at the University of Calgary's Haskayne School of Business advises students to "start out understated" when it comes to piercing. "We coach our students to be conservative, and if they do have any facial piercings, we suggest they remove them for the first interview until they find out what the culture's like in the organization," centre director Voula Cocolakis said. "We don't want them to be taken out of the 'yes' pile because of a facial piercing. We want them to interview and compete in the job market based on their qualifications."

In-house policies toward tattoos vary because, legally, employers can do as they wish. As long as the rule is applied equally to everyone (it would not be permissible to allow tattoos on men but not on women, for example), policies against tattoos are perfectly legal. Though not hiring people with tattoos is discrimination, it is not a form of discrimination that is covered by the Canadian Human Rights Act.

Thirty-six percent of those aged 18 to 25, and 40 percent of those aged 26 to 40, have at least one tattoo, whereas only 15 percent of those over 40 do, according to a fall 2006 survey by the Pew Research Center. One study in *American Demographics* suggested that 57 percent of senior citizens viewed visible tattoos as "freakish."

How does the matter of perception explain why some employers ban tattoos, while others don't mind them? Is it fair for employers to reject applicants who have tattoos? Is it fair to require employees, if hired, to conceal their tattoos? Should it be illegal to allow tattoos to be a factor at all in the hiring process?

CASE INCIDENTS

A Diamond Personality

Oscar Rodriguez, a 38-year-old entrepreneur, owns an Internet business that sells loose diamonds to various buyers.[137] Business is booming. In 2004, Rodriguez had sales of $2.06 million—a 140 percent increase from 2003. Rodriguez's database of almost 60 000 available diamonds is one of the largest in the industry and is valued, according to him, at over $350 million. Needless to say, he is optimistic about his business venture.

The future was not always so bright. In 1985, Rodriguez moved from his native Puerto Rico to Gainesville, Florida, with little ability to speak English. There, he attended community college and worked at a local mall to support himself. After graduation, his roommate's girlfriend suggested that he work at a local jeweller. "I thought she was crazy. I didn't know anything about jewellery," says Rodriguez, but he took her advice. Though he worked hard and received his Diamonds and Diamonds Grading certification from the Gemological Institute of America, he was not satisfied with his progress. "I quickly realized that working there, I was just going to get a salary with a raise here and there. I would never become anything. That drove me to explore other business ventures. I also came to really know diamonds—their pricing and their quality."

In 1997, tired of working for someone else, Rodriguez decided to open his own jewellery store. However, business did not boom. "Some of my customers were telling me they could find diamonds for less on the Internet. It blew my mind." Rodriguez recognized an opportunity and began contacting well-known diamond dealers to see whether they would be interested in selling their gems online. Rodriguez recalls one conversation with a prominent dealer who told him, "You cannot sell diamonds on the Internet. You will not survive." Discouraged, Rodriguez says he then made a mistake. "I stopped working on it. If you have a dream, you have to keep working harder at it."

A year later, Rodriguez did work harder at his dream and found a dealer who agreed to provide him with some diamonds. Says Rodriguez, "Once I had one, I could approach others. Business started to build. The first three months I sold $200,000 worth of diamonds right off the bat. And that was just me. I started to add employees and eventually closed the jewellery store and got out of retail."

Although Rodriquez does have some diamonds in inventory, he primarily acts as a connection point between buyers and suppliers, giving his customers an extraordinary selection from which to choose.

Rodriguez is now a savvy entrepreneur, and his company, Abazias.com, went public in October 2003.

Why is Rodriguez successful? Just ask two people who have known him over the years. Gary Schneider, a realtor who helped build Rodriguez's building, says, "Oscar is a very ambitious young man. I am not surprised at all how successful he is. He is an entrepreneur in the truest sense of the word." One of Rodriguez's former real estate instructors, Howard Freeman, concurs. "I am not surprised at all at his success," says Freeman. "Oscar has always been an extremely motivated individual with a lot of resources. He has a wonderful personality and pays close attention to detail. He also has an ability to stick to things. You could tell from the beginning that he was going to persevere, and I am proud of him."

Rodriguez is keeping his success in perspective, but he also realizes his business's potential: "I take a very small salary, and our overhead is $250,000 a year. I am not in debt, and the business is breaking even. I care about the company. I want to keep everything even until we take off, and then it may be another ball game."

Questions

1. What factors do you think have contributed to Rodriguez's success? Was he merely "in the right place at the right time," or are there characteristics about him that contribute to his success?

2. How do you believe Rodriguez would score on the Big Five dimensions of personality (extraversion, agreeableness, conscientiousness, emotional stability, openness to experience)? Which ones would he score high on? Which ones might he score low on?

3. Do you believe that Rodriguez is high or low on core self-evaluation? On what information did you base your decision?

4. What information about Rodriguez suggests that he has a proactive personality?

Abusive Customers Cause Emotions to Run High

Telephone customer-service representatives have a tough time these days.[138] With automated telephone systems that create a labyrinth for customers, result in long hold times, and make it difficult for them to speak to an actual human being, a customer's frustration often settles in before the representative has had time to say "Hello." Says Donna Earl, an owner of a customer-service consulting firm, "By the time you get to the person you need to talk to, you're mad."

Erin Calabrese knows all too well just how mad customers can get. A customer-service representative at a financial services company, she still vividly recalls one of her worst experiences—with a customer named Jane. Jane called Calabrese over some charges on her credit card and began "ranting and raving." "Your #%#% company, who do you think you are?" yelled Jane. Though Calabrese tried to console the irate customer by offering a refund, Jane only called Calabrese an "idiot." The heated conversation continued for almost 10 minutes before Calabrese, shaking, handed the phone to her supervisor and left her desk.

Sometimes customers can be downright racist. One customer-service representative finally quit her job at a company because she constantly heard racial remarks from customers after, she contends, they heard her Spanish accent. "By the time you leave, your head is spinning with all the complaints," she said.

Unfortunately, these employees have little choice but to take the abuse. Many companies require customer-service employees to display positive emotions at all times to maintain satisfaction in customers. But the result could be an emotional nightmare that does not necessarily end once the calls stop. Calabrese stated that she would frequently take her negative emotions home. The day after she received the abusive call from Jane, Calabrese went home and started a fight with her roommate. It was "an all-out battle," recalls Calabrese, "I just blew up." The former customer-service representative also recalls the effects of the abusive calls on her family. "My children would say, 'Mom, stop talking about your work. You're home.'" she said.

Emma Parsons, who quit her job as a customer-service representative for the travel industry, was frustrated by the inability to do anything about abusive customers and the mood they would put her in. "Sometimes you'd finish a call and you'd want to smash somebody's face. I had no escape, no way of releasing." She said that if she did retaliate toward an abusive customer, her boss would punish her.

Some companies train their representatives to defuse a customer's anger and to avoid taking abuse personally, but the effort is not enough. Liz Aherarn of Radclyffe Group says customer-service employees who work the phones are absent more frequently, are more prone to illness, and are more likely to make stress-related disability claims than other employees. Thus, it is apparent that in the world of customer service, particularly when interactions take place over the phone, emotions can run high, and the effects can be damaging. Although the saying "the customer comes first" has been heard by many, companies should empower employees to decide when it is appropriate to put the customer second. Otherwise, employees are forced to deal with abusive customers, the effects of which can be detrimental to both the individual and the company.

Questions

1. From an emotional labour perspective, how does dealing with an abusive customer lead to stress and burnout?

2. If you were a recruiter for a customer-service call centre, what personality types would you prefer to hire and why? In other words, what individual differences are likely to affect whether an employee can handle customer abuse on a day-to-day basis?

3. Emotional intelligence is one's ability to detect and manage emotional cues and information. How might emotional intelligence play a role in responding to abusive customers? What facets of emotional intelligence might employees who are able to handle abusive customers possess?

4. What steps should companies take to ensure that their employees are not victims of customer abuse? Should companies allow a certain degree of abuse if that abuse results in satisfied customers and perhaps greater profit? What are the ethical implications of this?

From **Concepts**
                to **Skills**

Reading Emotions

Understanding another person's felt emotions is very difficult. But we can learn to read others' displayed emotions.[139] We do this by focusing on verbal, nonverbal, and paralanguage cues.

The easiest way to find out what someone is feeling is to ask them. Saying something as simple as "Are you OK? What's the problem?" can often provide you with the information to assess an individual's emotional state. But relying on a verbal response has two drawbacks. First, almost all of us conceal our emotions to some extent for privacy and to reflect social expectations. So we might be unwilling to share our true feelings. Second, even if we want to verbally convey our feelings, we may be unable to do so. As we noted earlier, some people have difficulty understanding their own emotions and, hence, are unable to express them verbally. So, at best, verbal responses provide only partial information.

Let's say you are talking with a co-worker. Does the fact that his back is rigid, his teeth clenched, and his facial muscles tight tell you something about his emotional state? It probably should. Facial expressions, gestures, body movements, and physical distance are nonverbal cues that can provide additional insights into what a person is feeling. The facial expressions shown in Exhibit 2-7, for instance, are a window into a person's feelings. Notice the difference in facial features: the height of the cheeks, the raising or lowering of the brow, the turn of the mouth, the positioning of the lips, and the configuration of muscles around the eyes. Even something as subtle as the distance someone chooses to position him- or herself from you can convey how much intimacy, aggressiveness, repugnance, or withdrawal that person feels.

When you speak with someone, you may notice a sharp change in the tone of her voice and the speed at which she

EXHIBIT 2-7   Facial Expressions and Emotions

Each picture portrays a different emotion. Try to identify them before looking at the answers.

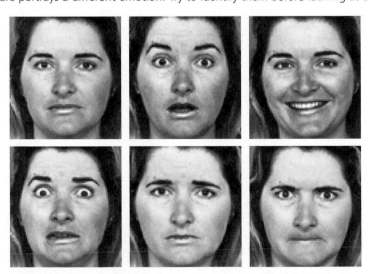

Top, left to right: neutral, surprise, happiness. Bottom: fear, sadness, anger.

Source: S. E. Taylor, L. A. Peplan, and D. O. Sears, *Social Psychology*, 9th ed. (Upper Saddle River, NJ: Prentice Hall, 1997), p. 98; photographs by Paul Ekman, Ph.D. Used with permission.

speaks. You are tapping into the third source of information on a person's emotions—paralanguage. This is communication that goes beyond the specific spoken words. It includes pitch, amplitude, rate, and voice quality of speech. Paralanguage reminds us that people convey their feelings not only in what they say, but also in how they say it.

Practising Skills

Part A. Form groups of 2. Each person is to spend a couple of minutes thinking of a time in the past when he or she was emotional about something. Examples might include being upset with a parent, sibling, or friend; being excited or disappointed about an academic or athletic achievement; being angry with someone over an insult or slight; being disgusted by something someone has said or done; or being happy because of something good that happened. Do not share this event with the other person in your group.

Part B. Now you will conduct 2 role plays. Each will be an interview. In the first, 1 person will play the interviewer and the other will play the job applicant. The job is for a summer management internship with a large retail chain. Each role play will last no longer than 10 minutes. The interviewer is to conduct a normal job interview, except you are to continually rethink the emotional episode you envisioned in part A. Try hard to convey this emotion while, at the same time, being professional in interviewing the job applicant.

Part C. Now reverse positions for the second role play. The interviewer becomes the job applicant and vice versa. The new interviewer will conduct a normal job interview, except that he or she will continually rethink the emotional episode chosen in part A.

Part D. Spend 10 minutes analyzing the interview, with specific attention focused on these questions: What emotion(s) do you think the other person was conveying? What cues did you pick up? How accurate were you in reading those cues?

Reinforcing Skills

1. Rent a video of an emotion-laden film, such as *Death of a Salesman* or *12 Angry Men*. Carefully watch the actors for clues to the emotions they are exhibiting. Try to determine the various emotions projected and explain how you arrived at your conclusion.

2. Spend a day specifically looking for emotional cues in the people with whom you interact. Did this improve communication?

VIDEO CASE INCIDENT

CASE 2 How Bad Is Your Boss?

Everybody has a boss, and it seems that everybody has a "bad boss" story. Here are seven questions that will help you determine if your boss is one of the bad ones. Answer each question with a "yes" or "no."

1. Has your boss ever embarrassed you in front of co-workers?
2. Does your boss have a tough time making decisions or sticking to them once they are made?
3. Does your boss take you for granted?
4. Does your boss hog the limelight when things go well and blame others when things go wrong?
5. Does your boss argue about everything?
6. Is your boss clear about what he or she expects of you?
7. Does your boss pile on the work without any thought as to what you are already doing?

If you answered "yes" to just one or two questions, your boss is probably fine (let's face it, a boss can occasionally slip up). If you answered "yes" to 3–6 questions, you have a boss that is likely to make you feel pretty bad on various occasions. But be careful when confronting your boss. If you are going to complain, you should cite very specific instances of your boss's bad behaviour. You must also realize that if you are not happy with your boss, chances are that your boss is also unhappy with you. If you answered "yes" to all 7 questions, you have a big problem. You probably cannot run fast enough to keep up.

What should you do if you have a bad boss? If you want to better the situation, you might try discussing your concerns with your boss. Be sure to document your experiences and be very specific about the kinds of things that concern you. Jack Welch, the legendary former CEO of General Electric, says that bosses must realize that they are only as good as the people who work for them. If a boss does not develop good people, the boss's unit will underperform and the boss's own career plans will be affected. If the boss behaves badly, Welch thinks employees should not whine and be a victim. Instead, they should just quit.

The practical implications of the seven questions listed above can be profound for employees. For example, for question #3, Shaun Belding, a management consultant, says that the most common complaint from employees is that they are not given any recognition for the work they do. For question #4, this type of boss behaviour sucks the creativity out of an organization because people have no incentive to come up with new ideas if they are not going to get credit for those ideas. For question #7, the fact is that bad bosses are simply not aware of the workloads of their employees. They just expect that all their requests will be met.

Some bosses are taking action to improve their performance. Robert Lemieux, the director of sales at the Delta Chelsea Hotel,

is a young executive moving up the corporate ladder. He would like to be a top manager some day. He currently supervises a staff of 50, and he knows he has to be a great boss if he wants to get to the top. So, he goes to a "boss boot camp" run by Lindsay Sukornyk, a consultant who whips bosses into shape. She first interviews Lemieux's employees to find out what they really think of him. She discovers that his employees think he is professional and intuitive, and that he cares about them. So far so good. But she also hears that he is standoffish, and that he over-promises and under-delivers. He is also seen by employees as too hands-on. Lemieux has to learn to let go and to let employees take ownership of ideas.

At boot camp, Lemieux is owning up to his weaknesses in front of his employees and learning to trust them to do their jobs on their own. From now on, he will be doing less talking and more listening. The employees seem to like the idea, because they want him to coach them, not get involved in all the details and always be the "fixer." As they review his performance, they point out a few areas where he still needs to improve, but Lemieux is on the road to being a better boss.

Questions

1. Think of a boss you have had and answer the seven questions listed above. Was your boss good or bad? Give brief examples of incidents that led you to answer "yes" to any question.

2. Think of a boss you have had and evaluate your boss on the Big 5 personality factors. What impact did the Big 5 have on your boss being a good or bad manager? Give examples to illustrate your reasoning.

3. Think of a boss you have had and give several examples of how the various factors in Exhibit 2-1 influenced your perception of your boss.

4. Think of a specific "bad" behaviour your boss exhibited. Use the model in Exhibit 2-2 to analyze the behaviour and determine whether it had an internal or external cause. Does your conclusion match the attribution you made at the time of the behaviour?

5. Think of a positive experience you had with a boss and use the model in Exhibit 2-6 to analyze how the experience affected your job satisfaction and performance. Think of a negative experience you had with a boss and repeat the analysis.

Source: Based on "How Bad Is Your Boss?" *CBC Venture,* January 15, 2006.

Values, Attitudes, and Diversity in the Workplace

At KPMG Canada, diversity is valued and respected. How does this affect the company's workplace?

1 What are values?

2 How can we understand values across cultures?

3 Are there unique Canadian values?

4 What are attitudes and why are they important?

5 How do we respond to diversity in the workplace?

ichael Bach is the first director of diversity for Toronto-based KPMG Canada, a position he was promoted to in 2006.[1] Bach is a signal that KPMG is committed to an inclusive workplace.

"I'm here to remove barriers. At the core, we want everyone to be able to bring their whole self to work and we want everyone to feel they have the ability to succeed regardless of anything other than their ability to do their job," says Bach.

Generally, we expect that an organization's values, like those of an individual, will be reflected in corresponding behaviour and attitudes. If a company stated that it valued workforce diversity, and yet no behaviour followed from that statement, we would question whether that value was really so important to the company. However, in KPMG's case, the company backs up its value statements with concrete policies and actions to show support for its values. Does having strong values make for a better workplace?

In this chapter, we look more carefully at how values influence behaviour, and consider the relationship between values and attitudes. We then consider two specific issues that arise from our discussion of values and attitudes: job satisfaction and workforce diversity.

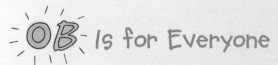

OB Is for Everyone

- How do countries differ in their values?
- Are Gen-Xers really different from their elders?
- What can you learn about OB from Aboriginal culture?
- What would you need to know to set up a business in Asia?

Self-Assessment Library

LEARNING ABOUT YOURSELF

- Values
- Attitudes
- Job Satisfaction
- Engagement

Values

values Basic convictions that a specific mode of conduct or end-state of existence is personally or socially preferable to an opposite or converse mode of conduct or end-state of existence.

Is capital punishment right or wrong? How about racial or gender quotas in hiring—are they right or wrong? If a person likes power, is that good or bad? The answers to these questions are value-laden. Some might argue, for example, that capital punishment is right because it is an appropriate response to crimes such as murder. However, others might argue just as strongly that no government has the right to take anyone's life.

Values represent basic convictions that "a specific mode of conduct or end-state of existence is personally or socially preferable to an opposite or converse mode of conduct or end-state of existence."[2] They contain a judgmental element in that they carry an individual's ideas as to what is right, good, or desirable. Values generally influence attitudes and behaviour.[3]

Values tend to be relatively stable and enduring.[4] Most of our values are formed in our early years—with input from parents, teachers, friends, and others. As children, we were told that certain behaviours or outcomes are always desirable or always undesirable. There were few grey areas. It is this absolute or "black-or-white" learning of values that more or less ensures their stability and endurance.

Below we examine two frameworks for understanding values: Milton Rokeach's terminal and instrumental values, and Kent Hodgson's general moral principles.

Rokeach's Value Survey

terminal values Goals that individuals would like to achieve during their lifetime.

instrumental values Preferable ways of behaving.

Milton Rokeach classified the values that people hold into two sets, with each set containing 18 individual value items.[5] One set, called **terminal values**, refers to desirable end-states of existence. These are the goals that individuals would like to achieve during their lifetime. The other set, called **instrumental values**, refers to preferable ways of behaving. These are the means for achieving the terminal values. Exhibit 3-1 gives common examples for each of these sets.

EXHIBIT 3-1   Terminal and Instrumental Values in Rokeach Value Survey

Terminal Values	Instrumental Values
A comfortable life (a prosperous life)	Ambitious (hard-working, aspiring)
An exciting life (a stimulating, active life)	Broad-minded (open-minded)
A sense of accomplishment (lasting contribution)	Capable (competent, effective)
A world at peace (free of war and conflict)	Cheerful (lighthearted, joyful)
A world of beauty (beauty of nature and the arts)	Clean (neat, tidy)
Equality (brotherhood, equal opportunity for all)	Courageous (standing up for your beliefs)
Family security (taking care of loved ones)	Forgiving (willing to pardon others)
Freedom (independence, free choice)	Helpful (working for the welfare of others)
Happiness (contentedness)	Honest (sincere, truthful)
Inner harmony (freedom from inner conflict)	Imaginative (daring, creative)
Mature love (sexual and spiritual intimacy)	Independent (self-reliant, self-sufficient)
National security (protection from attack)	Intellectual (intelligent, reflective)
Pleasure (an enjoyable, leisurely life)	Logical (consistent, rational)
Salvation (saved, eternal life)	Loving (affectionate, tender)
Self-respect (self-esteem)	Obedient (dutiful, respectful)
Social recognition (respect, admiration)	Polite (courteous, well-mannered)
True friendship (close companionship)	Responsible (dependable, reliable)
Wisdom (a mature understanding of life)	Self-controlled (restrained, self-disciplined)

Source: M. Rokeach, *The Nature of Human Values* (New York: Free Press, 1973), p. 56.

Several studies confirm that these sets of values vary among groups.[6] People in the same occupations or categories (for example, corporate managers, union members, parents, students) tend to hold similar values. For instance, one study compared corporate executives, members of the steelworkers' union, and members of a community activist group. Although a good deal of overlap was found among the three groups,[7] there were also some very significant differences (see Exhibit 3-2). The activists had value preferences that were quite different from those of the other two groups. They ranked "equality" as their most important terminal value; executives and union members ranked this value 12 and 13, respectively. Activists ranked "helpful" as their second-highest instrumental value. The other two groups both ranked it 14. These differences are important, because executives, union members, and activists all have a vested interest in what corporations do. These differences make it difficult when these groups have to negotiate with each other, and can create serious conflicts when they try to reach agreement on the organization's economic and social policies.[8]

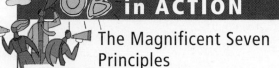

OB in ACTION

The Magnificent Seven Principles

→ *Dignity of human life.* The lives of **people are to be respected**.

→ *Autonomy.* All **persons** are **intrinsically valuable** and have the **right to self-determination**.

→ *Honesty.* **The truth should be told** to those who have a right to know it.

→ *Loyalty.* **Promises, contracts**, and **commitments** should be **honoured**.

→ *Fairness.* **People should be treated justly**.

→ *Humaneness.* Our **actions ought to accomplish good**, and we should **avoid doing evil**.

→ *The common good.* Actions should accomplish **the greatest good for the greatest number** of people.[9]

Hodgson's General Moral Principles

Ethics is the study of moral values or principles that guide our behaviour and inform us whether actions are right or wrong. Thus, ethical values are related to moral judgments about right and wrong.

In recent years, there has been concern that individuals are not grounded in moral values. It is believed that this lack of moral roots has resulted in a number of business scandals, such as those at WorldCom, Enron, Hollinger International, and even in the sponsorship scandal of the Canadian government.

Management consultant Kent Hodgson has identified seven general moral principles that individuals should follow when making decisions about behaviour. He calls these "the Magnificent Seven" and suggests that they are universal values that managers should use to make *principled*, *appropriate*, and *defensible* decisions.[10] They are presented in *OB in Action—The Magnificent Seven Principles*. We discuss the issue of ethics further in Chapter 12.

ethics The study of moral values or principles that guide our behaviour and inform us whether actions are right or wrong.

EXHIBIT 3-2   Value Ranking of Executives, Union Members, and Activists (Top Five Only)

| EXECUTIVES | | UNION MEMBERS | | ACTIVISTS | |
Terminal	Instrumental	Terminal	Instrumental	Terminal	Instrumental
1. Self-respect	1. Honest	1. Family security	1. Responsible	1. Equality	1. Honest
2. Family security	2. Responsible	2. Freedom	2. Honest	2. A world of peace	2. Helpful
3. Freedom	3. Capable	3. Happiness	3. Courageous	3. Family security	3. Courageous
4. A sense of accomplishment	4. Ambitious	4. Self-respect	4. Independent	4. Self-respect	4. Responsible
5. Happiness	5. Independent	5. Mature love	5. Capable	5. Freedom	5. Capable

Source: Based on W. C. Frederick and J. Weber, "The Values of Corporate Managers and Their Critics: An Empirical Description and Normative Implications," in *Business Ethics: Research Issues and Empirical Studies,* ed. W. C. Frederick and L. E. Preston (Greenwich, CT: JAI Press, 1990), pp. 123–144.

Assessing Cultural Values

KPMG Canada's decision to value diversity in its workplace reflects a dominant value of Canada as a multicultural country.[11] The approach to diversity is very different in the United States, which considers itself a melting pot with respect to different cultures. KPMG Canada has other values that guide employees. These include integrity, respect, open and honest communication, and commitment to community. What do we know about the values of other countries? What values make Canada unique?

2 How can we understand values across cultures?

In Chapter 1, we noted that managers have to become capable of working with people from different cultures. Thus it is important to understand how values differ across cultures.

Hofstede's Framework for Assessing Cultures

One of the most widely referenced approaches for analyzing variations among cultures was done in the late 1970s by Geert Hofstede.[12] He surveyed more than 116 000 IBM employees in 40 countries about their work-related values, and found that managers and employees vary on five value dimensions of national culture:

power distance A national culture attribute that describes the extent to which a society accepts that power in institutions and organizations is distributed unequally.

- *Power distance.*   **Power distance** describes the degree to which people in a country accept that power in institutions and organizations is distributed unequally. A high rating on power distance means that large inequalities of power and wealth exist and are tolerated in the culture, as in a class or caste system that discourages upward mobility of its citizens. A low power distance rating characterizes societies that stress equality and opportunity.

Individualism A national culture attribute that describes the degree to which people prefer to act as individuals rather than as members of groups.

- *Individualism vs. collectivism.*   **Individualism** is the degree to which people prefer to act as individuals rather than as members of groups and believe in individual rights above all else. Collectivism emphasizes a tight social framework in which people expect others in groups of which they are a part to look after them and protect them.

masculinity A national culture attribute that describes the extent to which the culture favours traditional masculine work roles of achievement, power, and control. Societal values are characterized by assertiveness and materialism.

- *Masculinity vs. femininity.*   Hofstede's construct of **masculinity** is the degree to which the culture favours traditional masculine roles, such as achievement, power, and control, as opposed to viewing men and women as equals. A high masculinity rating indicates the culture has separate roles for men and women, with men dominating the society. A high **femininity** rating means the culture sees little differentiation between male and female roles and treats women as the equals of men in all respects.

femininity A national culture attribute that sees little differentiation between male and female roles; women are treated as the equals of men in all respects.

uncertainty avoidance A national culture attribute that describes the extent to which a society feels threatened by uncertain and ambiguous situations and tries to avoid them.

- *Uncertainty avoidance.*   The degree to which people in a country prefer structured over unstructured situations defines their uncertainty avoidance. In cultures that score high on uncertainty avoidance, people have an increased level of anxiety about uncertainty and ambiguity, and use laws and controls to reduce uncertainty. Cultures low on **uncertainty avoidance** are more accepting of ambiguity and are less rule-oriented, take more risks, and more readily accept change.

long-term orientation A national culture attribute that emphasizes the future, thrift, and persistence.

short-term orientation A national culture attribute that emphasizes the past and present, respect for tradition, and fulfillment of social obligations.

- *Long-term vs. short-term orientation.*   This is the newest addition to Hofstede's typology. It focuses on the degree of a society's long-term devotion to traditional values. People in a culture with **long-term orientation** value virtues such as thrift and persistence that are oriented to future rewards. In a culture with **short-term orientation**, people value virtues related to the past and present, such as saving "face" and honouring social obligations.

How do different countries score on Hofstede's dimensions? Exhibit 3-3 shows the ratings for the countries for which data are available. For example, power distance is

EXHIBIT 3-3   Hofstede's Cultural Values by Nation

Country	Power Distance		Individualism vs. Collectivism		Masculinity vs. Femininity		Uncertainty Avoidance		Long- vs. Short-Term Orientation	
	Index	Rank	Index	Rank	Index	Rank	Index	Rank	Index	Rank
Argentina	49	35–36	46	22–23	56	20–21	86	10–15		
Australia	36	41	90	2	61	16	51	37	31	22–24
Austria	11	53	55	18	79	2	70	24–25	31	22–24
Belgium	65	20	75	8	54	22	94	5–6	38	18
Brazil	69	14	38	26–27	49	27	76	21–22	65	6
Canada	39	39	80	4–5	52	24	48	41–42	23	30
Chile	63	24–25	23	38	28	46	86	10–15		
Colombia	67	17	13	49	64	11–12	80	20		
Costa Rica	35	42–44	15	46	21	48–49	86	10–15		
Denmark	18	51	74	9	16	50	23	51	46	10
Ecuador	78	8–9	8	52	63	13–14	67	28		
El Salvador	66	18–19	19	42	40	40	94	5–6		
Finland	33	46	63	17	26	47	59	31–32	41	14
France	68	15–16	71	10–11	43	35–36	86	10–15	39	17
Germany	35	42–44	67	15	66	9–10	65	29	31	22–24
Great Britain	35	42–44	89	3	66	9–10	35	47–48	25	28–29
Greece	60	27–28	35	30	57	18–19	112	1		
Guatemala	95	2–3	6	53	37	43	101	3		
Hong Kong	68	15–16	25	37	57	18–19	29	49–50	96	2
India	77	10–11	48	21	56	20–21	40	45	61	7
Indonesia	78	8–9	14	47–48	46	30–31	48	41–42		
Iran	58	29–30	41	24	43	35–36	59	31–32		
Ireland	28	49	70	12	68	7–8	35	47–48	43	13
Israel	13	52	54	19	47	29	81	19		
Italy	50	34	76	7	70	4–5	75	23	34	19
Jamaica	45	37	39	25	68	7–8	13	52		
Japan	54	33	46	22–23	95	1	92	7	80	4
Korea (South)	60	27–28	18	43	39	41	85	16–17	75	5
Malaysia	104	1	26	36	50	25–26	36	46		
Mexico	81	5–6	30	32	69	6	82	18		
The Netherlands	38	40	80	4–5	14	51	53	35	44	11–12
New Zealand	22	50	79	6	58	17	49	39–40	30	25–26
Norway	31	47–48	69	13	8	52	50	38	44	11–12
Pakistan	55	32	14	47–48	50	25–26	70	24–25	0	34
Panama	95	2–3	11	51	44	34	86	10–15		
Peru	64	21–23	16	45	42	37–38	87	9		
Philippines	94	4	32	31	64	11–12	44	44	19	31–32
Portugal	63	24–25	27	33–35	31	45	104	2	30	25–26
Singapore	74	13	20	39–41	48	28	8	53	48	9
South Africa	49	35–36	65	16	63	13–14	49	39–40		
Spain	57	31	51	20	42	37–38	86	10–15	19	31–32
Sweden	31	47–48	71	10–11	5	53	29	49–50	33	20
Switzerland	34	45	68	14	70	4–5	58	33	40	15–16
Taiwan	58	29–30	17	44	45	32–33	69	26	87	3
Thailand	64	21–23	20	39–41	34	44	64	30	56	8
Turkey	66	18–19	37	28	45	32–33	85	16–17		
United States	40	38	91	1	62	15	46	43	29	27
Uruguay	61	26	36	29	38	42	100	4		
Venezuela	81	5–6	12	50	73	3	76	21–22		
Yugoslavia	76	12	27	33–35	21	48–49	88	8		
Regions:										
Arab countries	80	7	38	26–27	53	23	68	27		
East Africa	64	21–23	27	33–35	41	39	52	36	25	28–29
West Africa	77	10–11	20	39–41	46	30–31	54	34	16	33

Scores range from 0 = extremely low on dimension to 100 = extremely high.

Note: 1 = highest rank. LTO ranks: 1 = China; 15-16 = Bangladesh; 21 = Poland; 34 = lowest.

Source: Copyright Geert Hofstede BV, hofstede@bovt.nl. Reprinted with permission.

> How do countries differ in their values?

higher in Malaysia than in any other country. Canada is tied with the Netherlands as one of the top five individualistic countries in the world, falling just behind the United States, Australia, and Great Britain. Canada also tends to be short-term in orientation and is low in power distance (people in Canada tend not to accept built-in class differences between people). Canada is also relatively low on uncertainty avoidance, meaning that most adults are relatively tolerant of uncertainty and ambiguity. Canada scores relatively high on masculinity, meaning that most people emphasize traditional gender roles (at least relative to countries such as Denmark, Finland, Norway, and Sweden).

You will notice regional differences. Western and Northern nations such as Canada and the Netherlands tend to be more individualistic. Compared with other countries, poorer countries such as Mexico and the Philippines tend to be higher on power distance. South American nations tend to be higher than other countries on uncertainty avoidance, and Asian countries tend to have a long-term orientation.

Hofstede's cultural dimensions have been enormously influential on OB researchers and managers. Nevertheless, his research has been criticized. First, although Hofstede's work was updated and reaffirmed by a Canadian researcher at the Chinese University of Hong Kong (Michael Bond), who conducted research on values in 22 countries on 5 continents,[13] the original work is more than 30 years old and was based on a single company (IBM). A lot has happened on the world scene since then. Some of the most obvious changes include the fall of the Soviet Union, the transformation of Central and Eastern Europe, the end of apartheid in South Africa, the spread of Islam throughout the world today, and the rise of China as a global power. Second, few researchers have read the details of Hofstede's methodology closely and are therefore unaware of the many decisions and judgment calls he had to make (for example, reducing the number of cultural values to just five). Some results are unexpected. For example, Japan, which is often considered a highly collectivist nation, is considered only average on collectivism under Hofstede's dimensions.[14] Despite these concerns, many of which Hofstede refutes,[15] he has been one of the most widely cited social scientists ever, and his framework has left a lasting mark on OB.

The GLOBE Framework for Assessing Cultures

Begun in 1993, the Global Leadership and Organizational Behavior Effectiveness (GLOBE) research program is an ongoing cross-cultural investigation of leadership and national culture. Using data from 825 organizations in 62 countries, the GLOBE team identified nine dimensions on which national cultures differ.[16]

The GLOBE dimensions are defined as follows:

- *Assertiveness.* The extent to which a society encourages people to be tough, confrontational, assertive, and competitive vs. modest and tender. This is essentially equivalent to Hofstede's quantity-of-life dimension.

- *Future orientation.* The extent to which a society encourages and rewards future-oriented behaviours such as planning, investing in the future, and delaying gratification. This is essentially equivalent to Hofstede's long-term/short-term orientation.

- *Gender differentiation.* The extent to which a society maximizes gender role differences.

- *Uncertainty avoidance.* As did Hofstede, the GLOBE team defined this term as a society's reliance on social norms and procedures to alleviate the unpredictability of future events.

- *Power distance.* Like Hofstede, the GLOBE team defined this as the extent to which members of a society expect power to be unequally shared.

- *Individualism/collectivism.* Again, this term was defined, as was Hofstede's, as the extent to which individuals are encouraged by societal institutions to be integrated into groups within organizations and society.

- *In-group collectivism.* In contrast to focusing on societal institutions, this dimension encompasses the extent to which members of a society take pride in membership in small groups, such as their family and circle of close friends, and the organizations in which they are employed.

- *Performance orientation.* The extent to which a society encourages and rewards group members for performance improvement and excellence.

- *Humane orientation.* The extent to which a society encourages and rewards individuals for being fair, altruistic, generous, caring, and kind to others. This closely approximates Hofstede's quality-of-life dimension.

The GLOBE study confirms that Hofstede's dimensions are still valid. The main difference between Hofstede's dimensions and the GLOBE framework is that the latter added dimensions, such as humane orientation and performance orientation.

Which framework is better? That is hard to say, and each has its adherents. We give more emphasis to Hofstede's dimensions here because they have stood the test of time and the GLOBE study confirmed them. However, researchers continue to debate the differences between these frameworks, and future studies may, in time, favour the more nuanced perspective of the GLOBE study.[17]

In this chapter's *Working with Others Exercise* on page 115, you have the opportunity to compare the cultural values of two countries and determine how differences might affect group behaviour. The *Ethical Dilemma Exercise* on page 116 asks you to consider when something is a gift and when it is a bribe. Different cultures take different approaches to this question.

Values in the Canadian Workplace

Studies have shown that when individual values align with organizational values, the results are positive. Individuals who have an accurate understanding of the job requirements and the organization's values adjust better to their jobs, and have greater levels of satisfaction and organizational commitment.[18] In addition, shared values between the employee and the organization lead to more positive work attitudes,[19] lower turnover,[20] and greater productivity.[21]

Individual and organizational values do not always align. Moreover, within organizations, individuals can have very different values. Two major factors lead to a potential clash of values in the Canadian workplace: generational differences and cultural differences. Let's look at the implications of both factors.

3 Are there unique Canadian values?

Generational Differences

In his book *Sex in the Snow*, pollster Michael Adams attempted to identify the social values of today's Canadians.[22] He found that within three broad age groups of adult Canadians—the Elders (those over 60), Baby Boomers (born between the mid-1940s and the mid-1960s), and Generation Xers (born between the mid-1960s and the early 1980s)—there are at least 12 distinct "value tribes." We present the age groups and discuss some of their values below. For further information on these different value tribes and an opportunity to see where you might be classified in terms of your social values, visit the Environics Research Group website.

In the discussion of values that follows, bear in mind that we present broad generalizations, and you should certainly avoid stereotyping individuals on the basis of these generalizations. There are individual differences in values. For instance, not every Baby Boomer thinks alike, and neither does every member of Generation X. Thus, the important point about the values discussion is that you should try to understand how others might view things differently from you, even when they are exposed to the same situation.

The Elders

These individuals are characterized as "playing by the rules," and their core values are belief in order, authority, discipline, the Judeo-Christian moral code, and the Golden Rule (do unto others as you would have others do unto you). About 80 percent of the Elders resemble this description of traditional values, although there are variations within that 80 percent in the strength of fit.

Baby Boomers

This cohort was influenced heavily by the civil rights movement, the women's movement, the Beatles, the Vietnam War, and baby-boom competition. The view of Baby Boomers as a somewhat spoiled, hedonistic, rebellious group belies the four categories of Boomers: autonomous rebels (25 percent), anxious communitarians (20 percent), connected enthusiasts (14 percent), and disengaged Darwinists (41 percent). So, unlike the Elders, the Boomers are a bit more fragmented in their views. Yet all but the disengaged Darwinists reflect, to some extent, the stereotypes of this generation: rejection of authority, skepticism regarding the motives of big business and government, a strong concern for the environment, and a strong desire for equality in the workplace and society. Of course, the disengaged Darwinists, the largest single group, do not fit this description well. The Darwinists are characterized as being angry, intimidated by change, and anxious about their professional and financial futures.

Generation X

The lives of Gen-Xers (Generation Xers) have been shaped by globalization, two-career parents, MTV, AIDS, and computers. They value flexibility, life options, and the achievement of job satisfaction. Gen-Xers are skeptical, particularly of authority. They also enjoy team-oriented work. In search of balance in their lives, Gen-Xers are less willing to make personal sacrifices for the sake of their employer than previous generations were. On the Rokeach value survey, they rate high on true friendship, happiness, and pleasure.

Are Gen-Xers really different from their elders?

Despite these common values, Gen-Xers can be divided into five tribes. Thrill-seeking materialists (25 percent) desire money and material possessions, as well as recognition, respect, and admiration. Aimless dependants (27 percent) seek financial independence, security, and stability. Social hedonists (15 percent) are experience-seeking, committed to their own pleasure, and seek immediate gratification. New Aquarians (13 percent) are experience-seeking, and also egalitarian and ecologically minded. Finally, autonomous post-materialists (20 percent) seek personal autonomy and self-fulfillment, and are concerned about human rights.

The Ne(x)t Generation

Since Adams' book appeared, another generation has been identified.

The most recent entrants to the workforce were born between 1977 and 1997. The Nexters (also called Netters, Millennials, Generation Yers, and Generation Nexters) grew up during prosperous times. They have high expectations and seek meaning in their work. Nexters have life goals more oriented toward becoming rich (81 percent) and famous (51 percent) than do Generation Xers (62 percent and 29 percent, respectively). Nexters are at ease with diversity and are the first generation to take technology for granted. They have lived much of their lives with ATMs, DVDs, cellphones, laptops, and the Internet. More than other generations, they tend to be questioning, socially conscious, and entrepreneurial. At the same time, some have described Nexters as needy. One employer said, "This is the most high-maintenance workforce in the history of the world. The good news is they're also going to be the most high-performing."[23]

In this chapter's *Learning About Yourself Exercise* on page 114, you have the opportunity to examine some of the things that you value.

Learning About Yourself

1. What Do You Value?
(page 114)

The Generations Meet in the Workplace

An understanding that individuals' values differ but tend to reflect the societal values of the period in which they grew up can be a valuable aid in explaining and predicting behaviour. Baby Boomers currently dominate the workplace, but their years of being in charge are limited. In 2013, half of them will be at least 55 and 18 percent will be over 60.[24] As Boomers move into head offices, the "play-by-the-rules," "boss-knows-best" Elders are being replaced by somewhat more egalitarian Boomers. They dislike the command-and-control rules that were part of their parents' lives, although the Boomers have also been described as workaholics. Meanwhile, the Generation Xers in the workplace are comfortable in adapting, but also want more experiences. They are not in awe of authority. Most important, they are not interested in copying the workaholic behaviour of their parents. Managing the expectations of each of these very different groups is not an easy task. It requires managers to be flexible, observant, and willing to adjust more to the individual needs of these different employees. Members of the Net Generation will certainly change the face of the workplace in significant ways. They have mastered a communication and information system that many of their parents have yet to understand.

Cultural Differences

Canada is a multicultural country. One in five Canadians is an immigrant, according to the 2006 Census.[25] In 2006, 46 percent of Metropolitan Toronto's population, 40 percent of Vancouver's population, and 21 percent of Montreal's population were made up of immigrants.[26] The 2006 census found that 20.1 percent of Canada's population spoke neither of the country's two official languages as their first language. In Vancouver and Toronto, this rate was 41 percent and 44 percent, respectively, so considerably more than one-third of the population of those two cities does not speak either English or French as a first language.[27] Of those who speak other languages, 16 percent speak Chinese (mainly Mandarin or Cantonese). The other dominant languages in Canada are Italian (in fourth place), followed by German, Punjabi, and Spanish.[28] These figures indicate the very different cultures that are part of the Canadian fabric of life.

Though we live in a multicultural society, there are some tensions among people from different races and ethnic groups. For instance, a Statistics Canada survey on ethnic diversity found that while most Canadians (93 percent) say they have never or rarely experienced unfair treatment because of ethnic or cultural characteristics, 20 percent of visible minorities reported having been unfairly treated sometimes or often.[29]

Canadians often define themselves as "not Americans" and point out differences in the values of the two countries. A recent study, the Pew Global Attitudes Project, identified a number of differences between Canadian and American values.[30] Exhibit 3-4 shows some of the highlights of that study.

In his recent book *Fire and Ice*, Michael Adams finds that there is a growing dissimilarity between Canadian and American values. The two groups differ in 41 of the 56 values that Adams examined. For 24 values the gap has actually widened between 1992 and 2000,

EXHIBIT 3-4 Canadian and American Value Differences		
	Percentage Who Completely Agree with Statement	
Statement	**Canadians**	**Americans**
The impact of globalization on their country can be described as very good.	36	21
People are better off in a free market, despite inequality.	19	28
It is more important that government ensure that nobody is in need than that government stay out of the way.	52	34
It is the responsibility of government to tend to the very poor who cannot take care of themselves.	43	29
Immigrants have a very good influence on how well things are going.	19	8
Religion should be a matter of private faith, kept separate from government policy.	71	55
Homosexuality is a way of life that should be accepted by society.	69	51

Source: The Pew Research Center for the People and the Press, *Views of a Changing World 2003* (Washington, DC: The Pew Research Center for the People and the Press, June 2003).

indicating that Canadians' social values are growing more distinct from those of Americans.[31] Adams suggests that the September 11 attacks have had an impact on the American personality. He finds Americans are more accepting of patriarchy and hierarchy these days, and he concludes that it is "the supposedly bold, individualistic Americans who are the nodding conformists, and the supposedly shy, deferential and law-abiding Canadians who are most likely to assert their personal autonomy and political agency."[32] It will be interesting to see whether Americans value change under President Barack Obama.

In what follows we identify a number of cultural values that influence workplace behaviour in Canada. Be aware that these are generalizations, and it would be a mistake to assume that everyone coming from the same cultural background acts similarly. Rather, these overviews are meant to encourage you to think about cultural differences and similarities so that you can better understand people's behaviour.

Francophone and Anglophone Values

One of the larger issues that has confronted Canada in recent years is the question of Quebec separatism and anglophone-francophone differences. Consequently, it may be of interest to managers and employees in Canadian firms to be aware of some of the potential cultural differences when managing in francophone environments compared with anglophone environments. A number of studies have shown that English-speaking Canadians and French-speaking Canadians have distinctive value priorities. Francophones have been found to be more collectivist, or group-oriented, with a greater need for achievement, and anglophones have been found to be more individualist, or I-centred.[33] Francophones have also been shown to be more concerned about the interpersonal aspects of the workplace than task competence.[34] They have also been found to be more committed to their work organizations.[35] Anglophones have been shown to take more risks.[36] By contrast, a recent study examining work values in French- and English-speaking Canada found that French-speaking Canadians were not risk-takers and had the highest values for "reducing or avoiding ambiguity and uncertainty at work."[37]

Some studies have looked at the difference between francophone and anglophone personality characteristics. One study found that on the Meyers-Briggs personality test, francophones were more likely to be introverted, sensing, thinking, and judging. Anglophones were more likely to be intuitive, feeling, and perceiving.[38] A 2008 study, however, suggests that anglophones and francophones are not very different personality-wise.[39] Other studies have found that anglophone managers tended to value autonomy and intrinsic job values, such as achievement, and thus were more achievement-oriented, while francophone managers tended to value affiliation and extrinsic job values, such as technical supervision.[40] A study conducted at the University of Ottawa and Laval University suggests that some of the differences reported in previous research may be decreasing.[41] Another study indicates that French Canadians have become more like English Canadians in valuing autonomy and self-fulfillment.[42] These studies are consistent with the recent study that suggests there are few differences between francophones and anglophones.[43]

However, there is evidence of some continuing differences in lifestyle values. A recent Canadian Institute for Health Information report noted that Quebecers experience more stress than other Canadians.[44] The study also found that Quebecers smoke more, have the highest workplace absenteeism rate, and are less physically active than people in the rest of the country. Another study found that French-speaking Canadians and English-speaking Canadians have different values regarding cultural activities. For example, francophones are more likely to attend symphonic, classical, or choral music performances than anglophones. Anglophones are more likely to read newspapers, magazines, and books than francophones.[45]

Despite some cultural and lifestyle value differences, both francophone and anglophone managers today would have been exposed to more of the same types of organizational theories during their training in post-secondary school, which might also influence their outlooks as managers. Thus we would not expect to find large differences in the way that firms in francophone Canada are managed, compared with those in the rest of Canada. Throughout the textbook, you will find examples of Quebec-based businesses that support this conclusion.

Asked to define the fundamentals that give National Bank Financial its edge, senior vice-president and company director John Wells said he believes Montreal-based National Bank Financial's edge comes from company management that is largely French Canadian. He argues that French Canadians treat their employees well, and will try to find any means of reducing expenses rather than lay off staff, in sharp contrast to the cost-cutting mechanisms of either English Canadian or American firms.

Aboriginal Values

Entrepreneurial activity among Canada's Aboriginal peoples has been increasing at the same time that there are more partnerships and alliances between Aboriginal and non-Aboriginal businesses. Because of these business interactions, it is important to examine the types of differences we might observe in how each culture manages its businesses. Certainly the opening ceremony for the First Nations Bank of Canada's head office branch in Saskatoon in September 1997 was different from many openings of Western businesses. The ceremony was accompanied by the burning of sweetgrass. "This is a blessing," Blaine Favel, then chief of the Federation of Saskatchewan Indian Nations, said to a large outdoor gathering. "We are celebrating a great accomplishment by our people."[46]

What can you learn about OB from Aboriginal culture?

"Aboriginal values are usually perceived (by non-Aboriginals) as an impediment to economic development and organizational effectiveness."[47] These values include reluctance to compete, a time orientation different from the Western one, and an emphasis on consensus decision making.[48] Aboriginal people do not necessarily agree that these values are business impediments, however.

Specifically, although Canadian businesses and government have historically assumed that "non-Native people must teach Native people how to run their own organizations," the First Nations of Canada are not convinced.[49] They believe that traditional culture, values, and languages do not have to be compromised in the building of a self-sustaining

OB in ACTION

Ground Rules for Developing Business Partnerships with Aboriginal People

→ Modify management operations to **reduce negative impact on wildlife species**.

→ Modify operations to **ensure community access** to lands and resources.

→ **Protect** all those **areas identified by community members** as having biological, cultural, and historical significance.

→ **Recognize and protect Aboriginal and treaty rights** to hunting, fishing, trapping, and gathering activities.

→ **Increase** forest-based **economic opportunities** for community members.

→ **Increase** the **involvement of community members** in decision making.[50]

economy. Moreover, they believe that their cultural values may actually be a positive force in conducting business.[51]

In recent years, Canadian businesses facing Native land claims have met some difficulties in trying to accommodate demands for appropriate land usage. In some cases, accommodation can mean less logging or mining by businesses until land claims are worked out. Cliff Hickey and David Natcher, two anthropologists from the University of Alberta, collaborated with the Little Red River Cree Nation in northern Alberta to develop a new model for forestry operations on First Nations land and achieve better communication between businesses and Native leaders.[52] The anthropologists sought to balance the Native community's traditional lifestyle with the economic concerns of forestry operations. *OB in Action—Ground Rules for Developing Business Partnerships with Aboriginal People* outlines several of Hickey and Natcher's recommended ground rules, which they say could be used in oil and gas developments as well. Johnson Sewepegaham, chief of the Little Red River Cree, said his community will use these recommendations to resolve difficulties on treaty lands for which Vernon, BC-based Tolko Industries and High Level, Alberta-based Footner Forest Products jointly hold forest tenure. The two companies presented their general development plan to the Cree in fall 2008.[53]

Lindsay Redpath of Athabasca University has noted that Aboriginal cultures are more collectivist in orientation than are non-Aboriginal cultures in Canada and the United States.[54] Aboriginal organizations are much more likely to reflect and advance the goals of the community. There is also a greater sense of family within the workplace, with greater affiliation and loyalty. Power distance in Aboriginal cultures is smaller than in non-Aboriginal cultures of Canada and the United States, and there is an emphasis on consensual decision making. Aboriginal cultures are lower on uncertainty avoidance than non-Aboriginal cultures in Canada and the United States. Aboriginal organizations and cultures tend to have fewer rules and regulations. Each of these differences suggests that businesses created by Aboriginal people will differ from non-Aboriginal businesses, and both research and anecdotal evidence support this conjecture.[55] For instance, Richard Prokopanko, director of corporate affairs for Vancouver-based Alcan, says that shifting from handling issues in a generally legalistic, contract-oriented manner to valuing more dialogue and collaboration has helped ease some of the tension that had built up over 48 years between Alcan and First Nations people.[56]

Asian Values

The largest visible minority group in Canada are the Chinese. Over 1 million Chinese live in Canada, representing 26 percent of the country's visible minority population.[57] The Chinese in this country are a diverse group; they come from different countries, speak different languages, and practise different religions. The Chinese are only one part of the entire East and Southeast Asian population that influence Canadian society. It's predicted that by 2017 almost one-half of all visible minorities in Canada will come from two groups, South Asian and Chinese, and that these groups will be represented in almost equal numbers.[58] As well, many Canadian organizations, particularly those in British Columbia, conduct significant

What would you need to know to set up a business in Asia?

business with Asian firms. Asian cultures differ from Canadian culture on many of the GLOBE dimensions discussed earlier. For instance, Asian cultures tend to exhibit greater power distance and greater collectivism. These differences in values can affect individual interactions.

Professor Rosalie Tung of Simon Fraser University and her student Irene Yeung examined the importance of *guanxi* (personal connections with the appropriate authorities or individuals) for a sample of North American, European, and Hong Kong firms doing business with companies in mainland China.[59] They suggest that their findings are also relevant in understanding how to develop relationships with firms from Japan, South Korea, and Hong Kong.

"*Guanxi* refers to the establishment of a connection between two independent individuals to enable a bilateral flow of personal or social transactions. Both parties must derive benefits from the transaction to ensure the continuation of such a relationship."[60] *Guanxi* relations are based on reciprocation, unlike Western networked relationships, which may be characterized more by self-interest. *Guanxi* relationships are meant to be long-term and enduring, in contrast with the immediate gains sometimes expected in Western relationships. *Guanxi* also relies less on institutional law, and more on personal power and authority, than do Western relationships. Finally, *guanxi* relations are governed more by the notion of shame (that is, external pressures on performance), while Western relations often rely on guilt (that is, internal pressures on performance) to maintain agreements. *Guanxi* is seen as extremely important for business success in China—more than such factors as the right location, price, or strategy, or product differentiation and quality. For Western firms wanting to do business with Asian firms, an understanding of *guanxi*, and an effort to build relationships, are important strategic advantages.

Our discussion about differences in cross-cultural values should suggest to you that understanding other cultures matters. When Canadian firms develop operations across Canada, south of the border, or overseas, employees need to understand other cultures to work more effectively and get along with others.

Attitudes

Managers at KPMG Canada consider diversity a competitive advantage.[61] Mario Paron, chief officer of human resources, explains the company's views: "KPMG believes all our initiatives are fundamental business goals about attracting the brightest and best people. This is a real business strategy for us."

To create an attitude of inclusivity among employees, KPMG conducts diversity training for all employees, including a mandatory web-based program that encourages "dialogue about diversity, ethnic and cultural issues." Michael Bach also makes sure that potential hires are representative of the community. "It's about getting everyone to think about diversity in everyday life in everything they do," he says. Thus, KPMG Canada realizes the link between organizational values and employee attitudes. The training is meant to help employees have greater awareness of cultural and style differences. So how do attitudes get formed, and can they really be changed?

Attitudes are evaluative statements—either positive or negative—about objects, people, or events. When I say, "I like my job," I am expressing my attitude to work. Attitudes are thus responses to situations.

Attitudes are not the same as values because values are convictions about what is important, but the two are interrelated. In organizations, attitudes are important because they affect job behaviour. Employees may believe, for example, that supervisors, auditors, managers, and time-and-motion engineers are all conspiring to make them work harder for the same or less money. This may then lead to a negative attitude toward management

4 What are attitudes and why are they important?

attitudes Positive or negative feelings about objects, people, or events.

when an employee is asked to stay late for help on a special project. *Case Incident— Gourmet Foods Works on Employee Attitudes* on page 117 highlights how changes in attitudes can help a company's bottom line.

Employees may be negatively affected by the attitudes of their co-workers or clients. *From Concepts to Skills* on page 118 looks at whether it's possible to change someone's attitude, and how that might happen in the workplace. *OB Around the Globe* looks at how attitudes about appropriate behaviour in the workplace differs for Londoners and Americans.

AROUND THE GLOBE

California Moves to London

Can California "comfortable" take over London "fashion"? Silicon Valley, California, has established an outpost in London.[62] You don't need to know much about Silicon Valley or London to see a culture clash in the making here. London is famous (or notorious, depending on your point of view) for its formality—business suits, formal lunches, conservative offices, and polite, proper communication. California is renowned for just the opposite culture. So which culture wins?

So far, it seems, California. At Google's London offices, the California touches include foosball tables, bean bag chairs, giant games, and catered sandwiches (rather than a three-course meal). The dress code is business casual, even though most of the employees at Google's London headquarters are British. "You can be serious without a suit," says one Google Londoner who has grown accustomed to the California style.

When another Londoner, Nigel Thornton, was hired by Amgen, he was surprised by the number of emails soliciting his opinion and by the different customs. "The funny thing about Americans in our office is that they are always eating or drinking something," said Thornton. "Brits are still used to just breakfast, lunch, and dinner."

When British visit the offices of DVS Shoe Company (based in Torrance, California), they are often surprised by the informal dress and low-key atmosphere. "They'll see us dressed casual," says Erik Ecklund, a DVS manager, "and say, 'Man, you guys should have told us.'"

A person can have thousands of attitudes, but OB focuses our attention on a limited number of job-related attitudes. These job-related attitudes tap positive or negative evaluations that employees hold about aspects of their work environment. Below we consider three important attitudes that affect organizational performance: job satisfaction, organizational commitment, and employee engagement.

Job Satisfaction

job satisfaction An individual's general attitude toward his or her job.

The term **job satisfaction** refers to an individual's general attitude toward his or her job. A person with a high level of job satisfaction holds positive attitudes toward the job; a person who is dissatisfied with his or her job holds negative attitudes toward the job. When people speak of employee attitudes, more often than not they mean job satisfaction. In fact, the terms are frequently used interchangeably.

A recent Canadian Policy Research Networks survey on job satisfaction found that only 40 percent of Canadian employees are very satisfied with their jobs. By comparison, 47 percent of American employees are happy with their work and 54 percent of Danish workers are highly satisfied.[63] Almost 40 percent of Canadian employees would not recommend their company as a good place to work. Forty percent also believe that they never see any of the benefits of their company making money. Almost 40 percent report that red tape and bureaucracy are among the biggest barriers to job satisfaction. A majority of the workforce (55 percent) says that they feel the "pressure of having too much to do."

What Causes Job Satisfaction?

Think about the best job you have ever had. What made it so? Chances are you probably liked the work you did. In fact, of the major job-satisfaction factors (work itself, pay, advancement opportunities, supervision, co-workers), enjoying the work is almost always the one most strongly linked to high levels of overall job satisfaction. Interesting jobs that provide training, variety, independence, and control satisfy most employees.[64] In other words, most people prefer work that is challenging and stimulating over work that is predictable and routine.

You have probably noticed that pay comes up often when people discuss job satisfaction. There is an interesting relationship between salary and job satisfaction. For people who are poor (for example, living below the poverty line) or who live in poor countries, pay does correlate with job satisfaction and with overall happiness. But once an individual reaches a level of comfortable living (in Canada, that occurs at about $40 000 a year, depending on the region and family size), the relationship virtually disappears. In other words, people who earn $80 000 are, on average, no happier with their jobs than those who earn close to $40,000.[65] When we discuss motivation in Chapter 4, this might suggest that money may be less likely to motivate, once people reach a comfortable level of living. This idea would also be consistent with Maslow's hierarchy of needs, also discussed in Chapter 4.

Job satisfaction is not just about job conditions. Personality also plays a role. People who are less positive about themselves are less likely to like their jobs. Research has

When it comes to keeping its employees happy, Google seems to spare no expense. The company provides its workers with a multitude of benefits, including chef-prepared food, a gym with state-of-the-art equipment, a masseuse, on-site car washes, oil changes, haircuts, dry cleaning, free on-site doctor and dentist, child care next door, and free high-tech shuttle buses. According to a recent survey, employees believe that benefits are the most important factor that might increase job satisfaction.

core self-evaluation The degree to which an individual likes or dislikes himself or herself, whether the person sees himself or herself as capable and effective, and whether the person feels in control of his or her environment or powerless over the environment.

shown that people who have positive **core self-evaluations**—who believe in their inner worth and basic competence—are more satisfied with their jobs than those with negative core self-evaluations. Not only do they see their work as more fulfilling and challenging, but they are more likely to gravitate toward challenging jobs in the first place. Those with negative core self-evaluations set less ambitious goals and are more likely to give up when confronting difficulties. Thus, they are more likely to be stuck in boring, repetitive jobs than those with positive core self-evaluations.[66]

So what are the consequences of job satisfaction? We examine this question below.

Job Satisfaction and Productivity

The idea that "happy workers are productive workers" developed in the 1930s and 1940s, largely as a result of findings by researchers conducting the Hawthorne studies at Western Electric. Based on those conclusions, managers worked to make their employees happier by focusing on working conditions and the work environment. Then, in the 1980s, an influential review of the research suggested that the relationship between job satisfaction and job performance was not particularly high. The authors of that review even went so far as to label the relationship as "illusory."[67]

More recently, a review of more than 300 studies corrected some errors in that earlier review. It estimated that the correlation between job satisfaction and job performance is moderately strong. This conclusion also appears to be generalizable across international contexts. The correlation is higher for complex jobs that provide employees with more discretion to act on their attitudes.[68]

We cannot be entirely sure, however, whether satisfaction causes productivity or productivity causes satisfaction.[69] In other words, if you do a good job, you intrinsically feel good about it. In addition, your higher productivity should increase your recognition, your pay level, and your likelihood of promotion. Cumulatively, these rewards, in turn, increase your level of satisfaction with the job. Most likely, satisfaction can lead to high levels of performance for some people, while for others, high performance is satisfying. *Point/Counterpoint* on page 113 further explores the debate on whether job satisfaction is created by the situation or by an individual's characteristics.

As we move from the individual level to that of the organization, we also find support for the satisfaction-performance relationship.[70] When satisfaction and productivity data are gathered for the organization as a whole, we find that organizations with more satisfied employees tend to be more effective than organizations with less satisfied employees.

Job Satisfaction and Organizational Citizenship Behaviour

organizational citizenship behaviour (OCB) Discretionary behaviour that is not part of an employee's formal job requirements, but that nevertheless promotes the effective functioning of the organization.

In Chapter 1, we defined **organizational citizenship behaviour (OCB)** as discretionary behaviour that is not part of an employee's formal job requirements and is not usually rewarded, but that nevertheless promotes the effective functioning of the organization.[71] Individuals who are high in OCB will go beyond their usual job duties, providing performance that is beyond expectations. Examples of such behaviour include helping colleagues with their workloads, taking only limited breaks, and alerting others to work-related problems.[72] More recently OCB has been associated with the following workplace behaviours: "altruism, conscientiousness, loyalty, civic virtue, voice, functional participation, sportsmanship, courtesy, and advocacy participation."[73] Organizational citizenship is important, as it can help the organization function more efficiently and more effectively.[74]

It seems logical to assume that job satisfaction should be a major determinant of an employee's OCB.[75] Satisfied employees would seem more likely to talk positively about an organization, help others, and go beyond the normal expectations in their jobs.[76] Moreover, satisfied employees might be more prone to go beyond the call of duty because they want to reciprocate their positive experiences. Consistent with this thinking, early discussions of OCB assumed that it was closely linked with satisfaction.[77] Some evidence, however, suggests that satisfaction does influence OCB, but through perceptions of fairness.[78]

There is, then, a modest overall relationship between job satisfaction and OCB.[79] But job satisfaction is unrelated to OCB when fairness is considered.[80] What does this mean? Basically, job satisfaction comes down to a belief that there are fair outcomes, treatment, and procedures in the workplace.[81] If you don't feel that your manager, the organization's procedures, or its pay policies are fair, your job satisfaction is likely to suffer significantly. However, when you perceive organizational processes and outcomes to be fair, trust is developed. When you trust your employer, your job satisfaction increases, and you are more willing to voluntarily engage in behaviours that go beyond your formal job requirements.

Job Satisfaction and Customer Satisfaction

Employees in service jobs often interact with customers. Since the management of service organizations should be concerned with pleasing those customers, it is reasonable to ask: Is employee satisfaction related to positive customer outcomes? For front-line employees who have regular contact with customers, the answer is yes.

The evidence indicates that satisfied employees increase customer satisfaction and loyalty.[82] Why? In service organizations, customer retention and defection are highly dependent on how front-line employees deal with customers. Satisfied employees are more likely to be friendly, upbeat, and responsive—which customers appreciate. Because satisfied employees are less prone to turnover, customers are more likely to encounter familiar faces and receive experienced service. These qualities build customer satisfaction and loyalty. In addition, the relationship seems to apply in reverse: Dissatisfied customers can increase an employee's job dissatisfaction. Employees who have regular contact

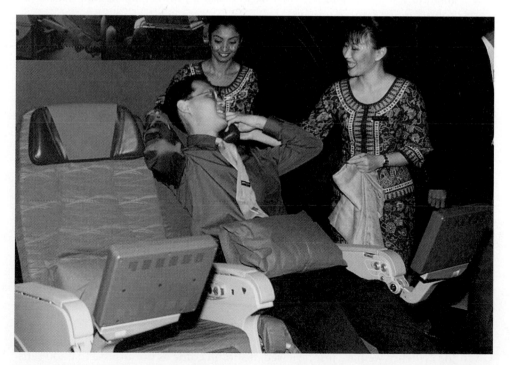

Service organizations know that whether customers are satisfied and loyal depends on how front-line employees deal with customers. Singapore Airlines has earned a reputation among world travellers for outstanding customer service. The airline's "putting people first" philosophy applies to both its employees and customers. In recruiting flight attendants, the airline selects people who are warm, hospitable, and happy to serve others. Through extensive training, Singapore Airlines moulds recruits into attendants focused on complete customer satisfaction.

with customers report that rude, thoughtless, or unreasonably demanding customers adversely affect the employees' job satisfaction.[83]

A number of companies are acting on this evidence. Service-oriented businesses such as FedEx, WestJet Airlines, and Office Depot obsess about pleasing their customers. Toward that end, they also focus on building employee satisfaction—recognizing that employee satisfaction will go a long way toward contributing to their goal of having happy customers. These firms seek to hire upbeat and friendly employees, they train employees in the importance of customer service, they reward customer service, they provide positive employee work climates, and they regularly track employee satisfaction through attitude surveys.

How Employees Can Express Dissatisfaction

The evidence suggests that employees express dissatisfaction in a number of ways.[84] For example, rather than quit, employees can complain, be insubordinate, steal organizational property, or slow down performing their work responsibilities. Researchers argue that these behaviors are indicators of a broader syndrome that we would term *deviant behaviour in the workplace* (or *employee withdrawal*).[85] The key is that if employees don't like their work environment, they will respond somehow.

Exhibit 3-5 presents a model that can be used to examine individual responses to dissatisfaction along two dimensions: whether they are constructive or destructive and whether they are active or passive. Four types of behaviour result:[86]

exit Dissatisfaction expressed by actively attempting to leave the organization.

voice Dissatisfaction expressed by actively and constructively attempting to improve conditions.

loyalty Dissatisfaction expressed by passively waiting for conditions to improve.

neglect Dissatisfaction expressed by passively allowing conditions to worsen.

- **Exit**. Actively attempting to leave the organization, including looking for a new position as well as resigning. This is a destructive action from the point of view of the organization.

- **Voice**. Actively and constructively attempting to improve conditions, including suggesting improvements, discussing problems with superiors, and some forms of union activity.

- **Loyalty**. Passively but optimistically waiting for conditions to improve, including speaking up for the organization in the face of external criticism and trusting the organization and its management to "do the right thing."

- **Neglect**. Passively allowing conditions to worsen, including chronic absenteeism or lateness, reduced effort, and increased error rate. This is a destructive action from the point of view of the organization.

Exit and neglect behaviours reflect employee choices of lowered productivity, absenteeism, and turnover in the face of dissatisfaction. But this model also presents constructive behaviours that allow individuals to tolerate unpleasant situations or to work toward satisfactory working conditions. It helps us understand situations, such as those sometimes found among unionized workers, where low job satisfaction is coupled with low turnover.[87] Union members often express dissatisfaction through the grievance procedure or through formal contract negotiations. These voice mechanisms allow union members to continue in their jobs while convincing themselves that they are acting to improve the situation.

Managers Often "Don't Get It"

Given the evidence we have just reviewed, it should come as no surprise that job satisfaction can affect the bottom line. One study by a management consulting firm separated large organizations into high morale (where more than 70 percent of employees expressed overall job satisfaction) and medium or low morale (lower than 70 percent). The stock prices of companies in the high morale group grew 19.4 percent, compared with 10 percent for the medium or low morale group. Despite these results, many

EXHIBIT 3-5   Responses to Job Dissatisfaction

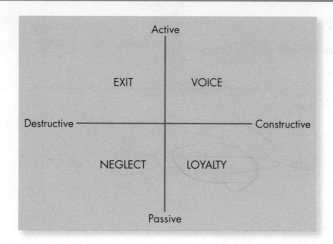

managers are unconcerned about the job satisfaction of their employees. Still others overestimate the degree to which their employees are satisfied with their jobs, so they don't think there's a problem when there is. One study of 262 large employers found that 86 percent of senior managers believed their organization treated its employees well, but only 55 percent of the employees agreed. Another study found 55 percent of managers thought morale was good in their organization, compared with only 38 percent of employees.[88] Managers first need to care about job satisfaction, and then they need to measure it rather than just assume that everything is going well.

Organizational Commitment

Organizational commitment is defined as a state in which an employee identifies with a particular organization and its goals, and wishes to maintain membership in the organization.[89]

Professor John Meyer at the University of Western Ontario and his colleagues have identified and developed measures for three types of commitment:[90]

- **Affective commitment**. An individual's relationship to the organization: his or her emotional attachment to, identification with, and involvement in the organization.

- **Normative commitment**. The obligation an individual feels to staying with the organization.

- **Continuance commitment**. An individual's calculation that it is in his or her best interest to stay with the organization based on the perceived costs of leaving the organization.

A positive relationship appears to exist between organizational commitment and job productivity, but it is a modest one.[91] A review of 27 studies suggested that the relationship between commitment and performance is strongest for new employees, and it is considerably weaker for more experienced employees.[92] And, as with job involvement, the research evidence demonstrates negative relationships between organizational commitment and both absenteeism and turnover.[93]

organizational commitment A state in which an employee identifies with a particular organization and its goals, and wishes to maintain membership in the organization.

affective commitment An individual's emotional attachment to, identification with, and involvement in the organization.

normative commitment The obligation an individual feels to staying with the organization.

continuance commitment An individual's calculation to stay with the organization based on the perceived costs of leaving the organization.

A major focus of Nissan Motor Company's Diversity Development Office in Japan is helping female employees develop their careers. Nissan provides women such as the assembly-line workers shown here with one-on-one counselling services of career advisers and training programs to develop applicable skills. Women can also visit Nissan's corporate intranet to read interviews with "role models," women who have made substantial contributions to the company. Nissan believes that hiring more women and supporting their careers will contribute to the company's competitive edge.

Affective commitment is strongly associated with positive work behaviours such as performance, attendance, and citizenship. Normative commitment is less strongly associated with positive work behaviours. Because continuance commitment reflects an individual's calculation that it is in his or her best interest to stay with the organization (perhaps because it would be difficult to find a job elsewhere), it is often associated with negative work behaviours.[94]

A recent study found that employees who are highly committed to their organization (about 11 percent of the workforce) exert 57 percent more discretionary effort—that is, willingness to go beyond their usual job duties—than employees who lack commitment. Individuals who show very little commitment to their organization (about 13 percent of the workforce) are four times more likely to quit their jobs than the average employee.[95]

How can companies increase organizational commitment? Research on a number of companies known for employees with high organizational commitment identified five reasons why employees commit themselves:[96]

- They are proud of [the company's] aspirations, accomplishments, and legacy; they share its values.

- They know what each person is expected to do, how performance is measured, and why it matters.

- They are in control of their own destinies; they savour the high-risk, high-reward work environment.

- They are recognized mostly for the quality of their individual performance.

- They have fun and enjoy the supportive and highly interactive environment.

These findings suggest a variety of ways for organizations to increase the commitment of employees. Earlier in the chapter, we discussed the role of satisfaction on organizational citizenship behaviour (OCB). We should also note that when individuals have high organizational commitment, they are likely to engage in more OCB. One final question on commitment: Does organizational commitment vary cross-nationally? *OB Around the Globe* explores the matter and offers some answers.

OB AROUND THE GLOBE

Chinese Employees and Organizational Commitment

Are employees from different cultures committed to their organizations in similar ways? A 2003 study explored this question and compared the organizational commitment of Chinese employees with that of Canadian and South Korean employees.[97] Although results revealed that the three types of commitment—normative, affective, and continuance—are present in all three cultures, they differ in importance. In addition, the study found that Canadians and South Koreans are closer to each other in values than either is with the Chinese.

Normative commitment, an obligation to remain with an organization for moral or ethical reasons, was higher in the Chinese sample of employees than in the Canadian and South Korean samples.

Affective commitment, an emotional attachment to the organization and a belief in its values, was also stronger in China than in Canada and South Korea. Chinese culture may explain why. The Chinese emphasize loyalty to one's group, and in this case, one's "group" may be the employer, so employees may feel a certain loyalty from the start and become more emotionally attached as their time with the organization grows. To the extent that the Chinese view their organization as part of their group and become emotionally attached to that group, they will be more committed to their organization. Perhaps as a result of this emphasis on loyalty, the normative commitment of Chinese employees strongly predicted intentions to maintain employment with an organization.

Continuance commitment, the perceived economic value of remaining with an organization compared with leaving it, was lower in the Chinese sample than in the Canadian and South Korean samples. One reason is that Chinese employees value loyalty toward the group more than individual concerns. So, although all three countries experience normative, affective, and continuance commitment, the degree to which each is important differs across countries.

Employee Engagement

A new concept is **employee engagement**, an individual's involvement with, satisfaction with, and enthusiasm for the work he or she does. For example, we might ask employees about the availability of resources and the opportunities to learn new skills, whether they feel their work is important and meaningful, and whether their interactions with co-workers and supervisors are rewarding.[98] Highly engaged employees have a passion for their work and feel a deep connection to their company; disengaged employees have essentially "checked out"—putting time but not energy or attention into their work.

A recent study of nearly 8000 business units in 36 companies found that, compared with other companies, those whose employees had high average levels of engagement had higher levels of customer satisfaction, were more productive, had higher profits, and had lower levels of turnover and accidents.[99] Toronto-based Molson Coors found that engaged employees were five times less likely to have safety incidents, and when one did occur, it was much less serious, and less costly for the engaged employee than for a disengaged one ($63 per incident vs. $392). Engagement becomes a real concern for most organizations because surveys indicate that few employees—between 17 percent and 29 percent—are highly engaged by their work.

employee engagement An individual's involvement with, satisfaction with, and enthusiasm for the work he or she does.

Because of some of these promising findings, employee engagement has attracted quite a following in many business organizations and management consulting firms. However, the concept is relatively new, so we have a lot to learn about how engagement relates to other concepts, such as job satisfaction, organizational commitment, or intrinsic motivation to do one's job well. Engagement may be broad enough that it captures the intersection of these variables. In other words, it may be what these attitudes have in common.

Managing Diversity in the Workplace

KPMG Canada has a strong commitment to diversity in its workplace, exemplified by a workforce that is 23 percent visible minorities.[100] The company's many programs support its commitment to diversity. The company has initiatives to support new Canadians, visible minorities, and "family matters." To help employees deal with aging parents, KPMG reimburses up to 80 hours of care for elderly parents annually. A program called High-Impact Communications in a Diverse Workplace helps managers learn about cross-cultural communication differences. Why does managing diversity well make a difference?

5 How do we respond to diversity in the workplace?

Organizations are increasingly having to face diversity concerns as workplaces become more heterogeneous. Earlier in the chapter, we discussed cultural and generational differences and their implications in the Canadian workplace. Exhibit 3-6 identifies

---

EXHIBIT 3-6   Major Workforce Diversity Categories

GENDER
Nearly half of the Canadian workforce is now made up of women, and women are a growing percentage of the workforce in most countries throughout the world. Organizations need to ensure that hiring and employment policies create equal access and opportunities to individuals regardless of gender.

NATIONAL ORIGIN
A growing percentage of Canadian workers are immigrants or come from homes where English is not the primary language spoken. Because employers in Canada have the right to demand that English be spoken at the workplace on job-related activities except in bilingual parts of the country (i.e., the Ottawa region; all of New Brunswick; parts of northern and eastern Ontario; and within Quebec, the Montreal area and parts of the Eastern Townships, Gaspé, and west Quebec), communication problems can occur when employees' English-language skills are weak.

AGE
The Canadian workforce is aging, and recent polls indicate that an increasing percentage of employees expect to work past the traditional retirement age of 65. Though the rules vary somewhat by province, in general organizations cannot discriminate on the basis of an employee's age until that employee reaches the age of 65, and they are obligated to accommodate the needs of older workers.

DISABILITY
Organizations need to ensure that jobs and workplaces are accessible to people who have mental or physical disabilities, as well as to those who have health challenges.

DOMESTIC PARTNERS
An increasing number of gay and lesbian employees, as well as employees with live-in partners of the opposite sex, are demanding the same rights and benefits for their partners that organizations have provided for traditional married couples.

RELIGION
Organizations need to be sensitive to the customs, rituals, and holidays, as well as the appearance and attire, of individuals of faiths such as Sikhism, Hinduism, Judaism, Islam, and Buddhism, and ensure that these individuals suffer no adverse impact as a result of their appearance or practices.

some of the major categories of workforce diversity and suggests how organizations might accommodate the needs of employees within each category.

Many organizations have attempted to incorporate workforce diversity initiatives into their workplaces to improve relations among co-workers. For example, IBM Canada is one of a number of companies in Canada that have developed diversity polices for their workplace. IBM Canada's policy states the following:

> At IBM we acknowledge, value and respect diversity. . . . At IBM we recognize individual differences and appreciate how these differences provide a powerful competitive advantage and a source of great pride and opportunity in the workplace and marketplace.[101]

The company's statement on diversity is representative of the types of statements that organizations often include in their annual reports and employee information packets. These statements signal corporate values to both employees and other people who might do business with the company. Some corporations choose to signal the value of diversity because they think it is an important strategic goal. Other organizations recognize that the purchasing power of diverse groups is substantial.

When companies design and then publicize statements about the importance of diversity, they are essentially producing value statements. The hope, of course, is that the statements will influence the behaviour of members of the organization. Interestingly enough, however, there is little research showing that values can be changed successfully.[102] Because values tend to be relatively stable, workplaces try to address diversity issues through education aimed at changing attitudes.

Responses to Diversity Initiatives

Michael Adams' *Sex in the Snow* provides some information to help us understand how diversity initiatives might fare in the workplace in light of generational values. First, he notes that Generation Xers "eagerly embrace a number of egalitarian and pluralistic

Ben Barry (left), president of Ben Barry Agency, is trying to change the attitudes toward waif-like models through his modelling agency. Sixty percent of his models are atypical: bigger, shorter, older, or different from what the public usually expects. He has received a number of awards, including "One of the 25 Leaders of Tomorrow" from *Maclean's* magazine.

values."[103] This point might suggest that as Generation Xers move through the workplace, some of the tensions currently surrounding the introduction of diversity initiatives might lessen. On the other hand, Adams also notes that there are 4.3 million Baby Boomers who belong to the disengaged Darwinists group, and many of these tend to be the younger Boomers (that is, closer to their late 40s than their late 50s). This group, together with the rational traditionalists of the Elders group (representing 3.5 million Canadians), tends to be very conservative. As Adams notes, "Among the men in this group are a large number of what have come to be known as 'angry white guys.'" They find that society has changed too much, too quickly, and for the worse. "They do not support the idea of women's equality or alternative family structures. They brand programs of affirmative action or employment equity for women or visible minorities as 'reverse discrimination.'"[104] As a result of these generational differences, it is conceivable that tensions in the workplace over diversity initiatives will remain for some time to come. *Focus on Diversity* encourages you to think about whether changing behaviour without changing attitudes is really enough.

FOCUS ON **DIVERSITY**

Complying with Equity Legislation

What can companies do to change behaviour if not attitude? Nicole Chénier-Cullen is the director-general of the employment equity branch of the Canadian Human Rights Commission.[105] Her job is to see that Canadian organizations follow the laws regarding employment equity. She notes that companies need to be more proactive in the way they recruit visible minority job candidates. Placing an ad in the *Globe and Mail*, for example, often draws applicants who are similar to those placing the ad.

Still, Chénier-Cullen finds that organizations can change the way they recruit more easily than they can change employee attitudes. "That's one of the toughest barriers to admit, and one of the biggest to overcome," she says.

Renée Bazile-Jones is president of Toronto-based Unparalleled, a consulting firm that offers training programs to address discrimination, diversity, and sexual harassment. She encourages companies to go outside their comfort zone when they recruit, to help visible minorities get the message that they will be welcome in the company. Bazile-Jones agrees with Chénier-Cullen that "We can't force people to change their beliefs, but we can force them to change their behaviour."

Individuals or companies may or may not value workforce diversity. A company that values diversity may actively work to increase the diversity of the employees hired. A company that does not value diversity may try to skirt the law, or do the very minimum required by employment equity legislation. However, just because the company's managers may value diversity, this does not mean that all employees will share that value. Consequently, even if they are required to attend diversity training, employees may exhibit negative attitudes toward individuals because of their gender or ethnicity. Additionally, what attitudes are appropriate outside of the workplace may be questioned by some employers, as you will discover in *Case Incident—You Can't Do That* on page 116.

Cultural Intelligence

cultural intelligence The ability to understand someone's unfamiliar and ambiguous gestures in the same way as would people from that person's culture.

Are some individuals better than others at dealing with people from different cultures? Management professors Christopher Earley of the London School of Business and Elaine Mosakowski of the University of Colorado at Boulder have recently introduced the idea of **cultural intelligence**, or CQ, to suggest that people vary in how they deal with other cultures. This term is defined as "the seemingly natural ability to interpret someone's unfamiliar and ambiguous gestures in just the way that person's compatriots and colleagues would, even to mirror them."[106]

Earley and Mosakowski suggest that CQ "picks up where emotional intelligence leaves off." Those with CQ try to figure out whether a person's behaviour is representative of all members of a group, or just of that person. Thus, for example, a person with high CQ who encounters two German engineers would be able to determine which of the engineers' conduct is explained by the fact of being an engineer, by being German, and by behaviour that is simply particular to the individual.

RESEARCH FINDINGS: CULTURAL INTELLIGENCE

According to the researchers, "cultural intelligence resides in the body [the physical] and the heart [the emotional/motivational], as well as the head [the cognitive]." Individuals who have high *cognitive* CQ look for clues to help them identify a culture's shared understandings. Specifically, an individual does this by looking for consistencies in behaviours across a variety of people from the same cultural background. Individuals with high *physical* CQ learn the customs and gestures of those from other cultures and therefore act more like them. This increases understanding, trust, and openness between people of different cultures. One study found that job candidates who used some of the mannerisms of recruiters who had different cultural backgrounds from themselves were more likely to receive job offers than those who did not do so.[107] Those with high *emotional/motivational* CQ believe that they are capable of understanding people from other cultures, and will keep trying to do so, even if they are faced with difficulties in doing so.

Based on their research, Earley and Mosakowski have discovered that most managers fall into the following cultural intelligence profiles:

- *Provincial.* They work best with people of similar background, but have difficulties working with those from different backgrounds.

- *Analyst.* They analyze a foreign culture's rules and expectations to figure out how to interact with others.

- *Natural.* They use intuition rather than systematic study to understand those from other cultural backgrounds.

- *Ambassador.* They communicate convincingly that they fit in, even if they do not know much about the foreign culture.

- *Mimic.* They control actions and behaviours to match others, even if they do not understand the significance of the cultural cues observed.

- *Chameleon.* They have high levels of all three CQ components. They could be mistaken as being from the foreign culture. According to research, only about 5 percent of managers fit this profile.

Exhibit 3-7 can help you assess your own CQ.

EXHIBIT 3-7   Measuring Your Cultural Intelligence

Rate the extent to which you agree with each statement, using the following scale:

>   1 = strongly disagree
>   2 = disagree
>   3 = neutral
>   4 = agree
>   5 = strongly agree

_____ Before I interact with people from a new culture, I ask myself what I hope to achieve.

_____ If I encounter something unexpected while working in a new culture, I use this experience to figure out new ways to approach other cultures in the future.

_____ I plan how I'm going to relate to people from a different culture before I meet them.

_____ When I come into a new cultural situation, I can immediately sense whether something is going well or something is wrong.

Total _____ ÷ 4 = **Cognitive CQ**

_____ It's easy for me to change my body language (for example, eye contact or posture) to suit people from a different culture.

_____ I can alter my expression when a cultural encounter requires it.

_____ I modify my speech style (for example, accent or tone) to suit people from a different culture.

_____ I easily change the way I act when a cross-cultural encounter seems to require it.

Total _____ ÷ 4 = **Physical CQ**

_____ I have confidence that I can deal well with people from a different culture.

_____ I am certain that I can befriend people whose cultural backgrounds are different from mine.

_____ I can adapt to the lifestyle of a different culture with relative ease.

_____ I am confident that I can deal with a cultural situation that is unfamiliar.

Total _____ ÷ 4 = **Emotional/motivational CQ**

Interpretation: Generally, an average of less than 3 would indicate an area calling for improvement, while an average of greater than 4.5 reflects a true CQ strength.

Source: P. C. Earley and E. Mosakowski, "Cultural Intelligence," _Harvard Business Review_ 82, no. 10 (October 2004), pp. 139–146. Reprinted by permission of _Harvard Business Review_.

Summary and Implications

1 **What are values?**   Values guide how we make decisions about and evaluations of behaviours and events. They represent our basic convictions about what is important, right, and good for an individual. Although they do not have a direct impact on behaviour, values strongly influence a person's attitudes. So knowledge of an individual's values can provide insight into his or her attitudes.

2 **How can we understand values across cultures?**   Geert Hofstede found that managers and employees vary on five value dimensions of national culture. These include power distance, individualism vs. collectivism, masculinity vs. femininity, uncertainty avoidance, and long-term vs. short-term orientation. His insights were expanded by the GLOBE research program, an ongoing cross-cultural investigation of leadership and national culture.

3 **Are there unique Canadian values?**   In his recent books, pollster Michael Adams has attempted to identify the social values of today's Canadians. He has found that within three broad age groups of adult Canadians—the Elders (those over 60), Baby Boomers (born between the mid-1940s and mid-1960s), and Generation Xers (born between the mid-1960s and the early 1980s)—there are at least 12 distinct "value tribes." Most recently, discussion has turned to the Net Generation—whose members are now in their early 20s—the newest entrants to the workplace. Canada is a multicultural country, and there are a number of groups that contribute to its diverse values, such as Aboriginal people, French Canadians, and various immigrant groups. Canadian values differ from American values and those of its other trading partners in a variety of ways.

4 **What are attitudes and why are they important?**   *Attitudes* are positive or negative feelings about objects, people, or events. Attitudes affect the way people respond to situations. When I say, "I like my job," I am expressing my attitude to work and I am likely to be more committed in my behaviour than if my attitude was one of not liking my job. A person can have thousands of attitudes, but OB focuses our attention on a limited number of job-related attitudes. These job-related attitudes tap positive or negative evaluations that employees hold about aspects of their work environment. Most of the research in OB has been concerned with three attitudes: job satisfaction, organizational commitment, and employee engagement.

5 **How do we respond to diversity in the workplace?**   Many organizations have attempted to incorporate workforce diversity initiatives into their workplaces to improve relations among co-workers. Organizations have introduced diversity training programs to improve cultural awareness. Recent research suggests that individuals who score high on cultural intelligence have an easier time dealing with people from other cultures.

SNAPSHOT SUMMARY

1 Values
Rokeach Value Survey
General Moral Principles

2 Assessing Cultural Values
Hofstede's Framework for Assessing Cultures
The GLOBE Framework for Assessing Cultures

3 Values in the Canadian Workplace
Generational Differences
Cultural Differences

4 Attitudes
Job Satisfaction
Organizational Commitment
Employee Engagement

5 Managing Diversity in the Workplace
Responses to Diversity Initiatives
Cultural Intelligence

For Review

1. How does ethics relate to values?

2. Describe the five value dimensions of national culture proposed by Geert Hofstede.

3. How might differences in generational values affect the workplace?

4. Compare Aboriginal and non-Aboriginal values.

5. What might explain low levels of employee job satisfaction in recent years?

6. Are satisfied employees productive employees? Explain your answer.

7. Contrast exit, voice, loyalty, and neglect as employee responses to job satisfaction.

8. What is the relationship between job satisfaction and organizational commitment? Job satisfaction and employee engagement? Which is the stronger relationship?

9. How can managers get employees to more readily accept working with colleagues who are different from themselves?

10. What is cultural intelligence? How do its three dimensions relate to understanding people from other cultures?

For Critical Thinking

1. "Thirty-five years ago, young employees we hired were ambitious, conscientious, hard-working, and honest. Today's young workers don't have the same values." Do you agree or disagree with this manager's comments? Support your position.

2. Do you think there might be any relationship between the possession of certain personal values and successful career progression in organizations such as the Toronto Stock Exchange, the Canadian Union of Postal Workers (CUPW), and the City of Regina's police department? Discuss.

3. "Managers should do everything they can to enhance the job satisfaction of their employees." Do you agree or disagree? Support your position.

4. "Organizations should do everything they can to encourage organizational citizenship behaviour." Do you agree or disagree? Support your position.

5. When employees are asked whether they would again choose the same work or whether they would want their children to follow in their footsteps, fewer than half typically answer "yes." What, if anything, do you think this implies about employee job satisfaction?

 **for You**

■ You will encounter many people who have values different from yours in the classroom and in various kinds of activities in which you participate, as well as in the workplace. You should try to understand value differences, and to figure out ways to work positively with people who are different from you.

■ We indicated that a moderate number of Canadians are very satisfied with their jobs, and we mentioned the sources of some of the satisfactions. We also identified some of the reasons people are dissatisfied with their jobs. This information may help you understand your own feelings about whether you are satisfied with your job.

■ You may be able to use some of the information on attitudes to think about how to better work with people from different cultures. An understanding of how cultures differ may provide insight when you observe people doing things differently from the way you do them.

POINT

COUNTERPOINT

Managers Create Job Satisfaction

A review of the evidence has identified four factors conducive to high levels of employee job satisfaction: mentally challenging work, equitable rewards, supportive working conditions, and supportive colleagues.[108] Importantly, each of these factors is controllable by management.

Mentally challenging work. People prefer jobs that give them opportunities to use their skills and abilities and offer a variety of tasks, freedom, and feedback on how well they are doing. These characteristics make work mentally challenging.

Equitable rewards. Employees want pay systems and promotion policies that they perceive as being just, unambiguous, and in line with their expectations. When pay is seen as fair based on job demands, individual skill level, and community pay standards, job satisfaction is likely to result. Similarly, employees seek fair promotion policies and practices. Promotions provide opportunities for personal growth, more responsibilities, and increased social status. Individuals who perceive that promotion decisions are made in a fair and just manner, therefore, are likely to experience satisfaction from their jobs.

Supportive working conditions. Employees want work environments that support personal comfort and doing a good job too. Studies demonstrate that employees prefer physical surroundings that are not dangerous or uncomfortable. Additionally, most employees prefer working relatively close to home, in clean and relatively modern facilities, and with adequate tools and equipment.

Supportive colleagues. People get more out of work than merely money or tangible achievements. For most employees, work also fills the need for social interaction. Not surprisingly, therefore, having friendly and supportive co-workers leads to increased job satisfaction. The behaviour of an employee's boss is also a major determinant of satisfaction. Studies generally find that employee satisfaction increases when the immediate supervisor is understanding and friendly, offers praise for good performance, listens to employees' opinions, and shows a personal interest in them.

Satisfaction Is Individually Determined

The notion that managers and organizations can control the level of employee job satisfaction is inherently attractive. It fits nicely with the view that managers directly influence organizational processes and outcomes. Unfortunately there is a growing body of evidence challenging the notion that managers control the factors that influence employee job satisfaction. The most recent findings indicate that employee job satisfaction is largely genetically determined.[109]

Whether people are happy or not is essentially determined by their gene structure. You either have happy genes or you don't. Approximately 80 percent of people's differences in happiness, or subjective well-being, has been found to be attributable to their different genes.

Analysis of satisfaction data for a selected sample of individuals over a 50-year period found that individual results were consistently stable over time, even when these people changed employers and occupations. This and other research suggests that an individual's disposition toward life—positive or negative—is established by his or her genetic makeup, holds over time, and carries over into his or her disposition toward work.

Given these findings, there is probably little that most managers can do to influence employee satisfaction. In spite of the fact that managers and organizations go to extensive lengths to try to improve employee job satisfaction through actions such as manipulating job characteristics, working conditions, and rewards, these actions are likely to have little effect. The only place where managers will have significant influence is through their control of the selection process. If managers want satisfied employees, they need to make sure their selection process screens out the negative, maladjusted, troublemaking fault-finders who derive little satisfaction in anything about their jobs. This is probably best achieved through personality testing, in-depth interviewing, and careful checking of applicants' previous work records.

OB *AT WORK*

What Do You Value?

There are 16 items in the list below. Rate how important each one is to you on a scale of 0 (not important) to 100 (very important). Write a number between 0 and 100 on the line to the left of each item.[110]

Not Important				Somewhat Important					Very Important		
0	10	20	30	40	50	60	70	80	90	100	

_____   **1.** An enjoyable, satisfying job.

_____   **2.** A high-paying job.

_____   **3.** A good marriage.

_____   **4.** Meeting new people; social events.

_____   **5.** Involvement in community activities.

_____   **6.** My religion.

_____   **7.** Exercising, playing sports.

_____   **8.** Intellectual development.

_____   **9.** A career with challenging opportunities.

_____   **10.** Nice cars, clothes, home, and so on.

_____   **11.** Spending time with family.

_____   **12.** Having several close friends.

_____   **13.** Volunteer work for nonprofit organizations, such as the Canadian Cancer Society.

_____   **14.** Meditation, quiet time to think, pray, and so on.

_____   **15.** A healthy, balanced diet.

_____   **16.** Educational reading, television, self-improvement programs, and so on.

Scoring Key:

Transfer the numbers for each of the 16 items to the appropriate column; then add up the 2 numbers in each column.

	Professional	Financial	Family	Social
	1. _____	2. _____	3. _____	4. _____
	9. _____	10. _____	11. _____	12. _____
Totals	_____	_____	_____	_____

	Community	Spiritual	Physical	Intellectual
	5. _____	6. _____	7. _____	8. _____
	13. _____	14. _____	15. _____	16. _____
Totals	_____	_____	_____	_____

The higher the total in any value dimension, the higher the importance you place on that value set. The closer the numbers are in all 8 dimensions, the more well rounded you are.

More Learning About Yourself Exercises

Additional self-assessments relevant to this chapter appear on MyOBLab (**www.pearsoned.ca/myoblab**).

IV.C.1 What's My Attitude toward Older People?

I.B.3 How Satisfied Am I with My Job?

IV.B.1 Am I Engaged?

I.E.1 What's My Emotional Intelligence Score?

When you complete the additional assessments, consider the following:

1. Am I surprised about my score?
2. Would my friends evaluate me similarly?

BREAKOUT **GROUP** EXERCISES

Form small groups to discuss the following topics, as assigned by your instructor. Each person in the group should first identify 3 to 5 key personal values.

1. Identify the extent to which values overlap in your group.

2. Try to uncover with your group members the source of some of your key values (for example, parents, peer group, teachers, church).

3. What kind of workplace would be most suitable for the values that you hold most closely?

WORKING WITH **OTHERS** EXERCISE

Understanding Cultural Values

Objective   To compare the cultural values of two countries, and determine how differences might affect group behaviour.

Time   Approximately 30 minutes.

Procedure

1. Break into groups of 5 or 6.

2. Pretend that you are a group of students working on a project. Half of you are from Canada and hold typically "Canadian" cultural values; the other half are from the country assigned and hold that country's cultural values.

3. Consider the values of power distance, individualism, and uncertainty avoidance, and discuss the differences between Canadian cultural values and the values of the country assigned to you.

4. Answer the following questions:

What challenges might you expect in working together?

What steps could be taken to work together more effectively?

ETHICAL **DILEMMA** EXERCISE

Is It a Bribe or a Gift?

The Corruption of Foreign Public Officials Act prohibits Canadian firms from making payments to foreign government officials with the aim of gaining or maintaining business.[111] But payments are acceptable if they don't violate local laws. For instance, payments to officers working for foreign corporations are legal. Many countries don't have such legal guidelines.

Bribery is a common way of doing business in many underdeveloped countries. Government jobs there often don't pay very well, so it's tempting for officials to supplement their income with bribes. In addition, in many countries, the penalties for demanding and receiving bribes are few or nonexistent.

You are a Canadian who works for a large European multinational computer manufacturer. You are currently working to sell a $5-million system to a government agency in Nigeria. The Nigerian official who heads up the team that will decide who gets this contract has asked you for a payment of $20 000. He said this payment will not guarantee you get the order, but without it he could not be very encouraging. Your company's policy is very flexible on the issue of "gifts" to facilitate sales. Your boss says that it's OK to pay the $20 000, but only if you can be relatively assured of the order.

You are not sure what you should do. The Nigerian official has told you specifically that any payment to him is not to be mentioned to anyone else on the Nigerian team. You know for certain that three other companies are also negotiating, but it's unconfirmed that two of those companies have turned down the payment request.

What would you do?

CASE INCIDENTS

You Can't Do That

Paul Fromm is a high school teacher employed in one of the most ethnically diverse school districts in Canada.[112] He is an excellent teacher, and receives high ratings from his students.

During weekends and summer holidays, when he is not working, he participates in conferences held by white supremacists and anti-Semitic groups. For instance, he attended a conference at which swastikas were waving, and individuals gave Nazi salutes. Fromm also attended a celebration of Adolf Hitler's birthday.

Though it is known that Fromm attends these conferences, he has never expressed racist views in the classroom or discriminated against any student. "I am here to teach English, not to make a political statement. This is my job, that's what I do. And I do it very well," he says.

The school board and some of the teachers are upset with Fromm's behaviour. They feel that what he does, even though outside of work time, is not consistent with the school board's values of encouraging multicultural diversity. Some suggest he should be fired.

Questions

1. What, if anything, should the school board do in this instance?

2. Should Fromm consider not going to further conferences of this sort?

Gourmet Foods Works on Employee Attitudes

Gourmet Foods is a huge grocery and drug company. It has more than 2400 supermarkets, and its Premier and Polar brands make it the fifth-largest drugstore company in North America.[113] In a typical year, shoppers will make 1.4 billion trips through its stores.

Gourmet Foods competes against tough businesses. Walmart, in particular, has been eating away at its market share. With revenues flat and profits falling, the company hired Larry Johnston to turn the business around.

Johnston came to Gourmet Foods from General Living Medical Systems. It was while he was at General Living that Johnston met a training specialist named Roger Nelson. Nelson endeared himself to Johnston when the latter hired Nelson to help him with a serious problem. At the time, Johnston had been sent to Paris to fix General Living's European division. The division made CT scanners. Over the previous decade, four executives had been brought in to turn the division around and try to make it profitable. All had failed. Johnston responded to the challenge by initiating some important changes—he made a number of acquisitions, he closed down inefficient plants, and he moved factories to Eastern European countries to take advantage of lower labour costs. Then he brought in Nelson to charge up the troops. "After we got Roger in," says Johnston, "people began to live their lives differently. They came to work with a spring in their step." In three years, the division was bringing in annual profits of $100 million. Johnston gives a large part of the credit for this turnaround to Nelson.

What is Nelson's secret? He provides motivation and attitude training. Here is an example of Nelson's primary program—called the Successful Life Course. It lasts three days and begins each morning at 6 a.m. The first day begins with a chapter from an inspirational handout, followed by 12 minutes of yoga-like stretching. Then participants march up a hill, chanting, "I know I can, I know I can." This is followed by breakfast and then a variety of lectures on attitude, diet, and exercise. But the primary focus of the program is on attitude. Says Nelson,

"It's your attitude, not your aptitude, that determines your altitude." Other parts of the program include group hugs, team activities, and mind-control relaxation exercises.

Johnston believes strongly in Nelson's program. "Positive attitude is the single biggest thing that can change a business," says Johnston. He sees Nelson's program as being a critical bridge linking employees with customers: "We're in the business of maintenance and acquisition of customers." With so many shoppers going through his stores, Johnston says there are "a lot of opportunities for customer service. We've got to energize the associates." To prove he is willing to put his money where his mouth is, Johnston has committed $10 million to this training. By the end of 2006, 10 000 managers had taken the course. They, in turn, trained all 190 000 Gourmet Foods "associates," with the help of tapes and books.

Nelson claims his program works. He cites success at companies such as Allstate, Milliken & Co., and Abbott Labs. "The goal is to improve mental, physical, and emotional well-being," he says. "We as individuals determine the success of our lives. Positive thoughts create positive actions."

Questions

1. Explain the logic as to how Nelson's three-day course could positively influence Gourmet Foods' profitability.

2. Johnston says, "Positive attitude is the single biggest thing that can change a business." How valid and generalizable do you think this statement is?

3. If you were Johnston, what could you do to evaluate the effectiveness of your $10-million investment in Nelson's training program?

4. If you were a Gourmet Foods employee, how would you feel about going through Nelson's course? Explain your position.

From **Concepts**
to **Skills**

Changing Attitudes

Can you change unfavourable employee attitudes? Sometimes! It depends on who you are, the strength of the employee's attitude, the magnitude of the change, and the technique you choose to try to change the attitude.

People are most likely to respond to changes suggested by someone who is liked, credible, and convincing. If people like you, they are more apt to identify and adopt your message. Credibility implies trust, expertise, and objectivity. So you are more likely to change someone's attitude if that person views you as believable, knowledgeable about what you are saying, and unbiased in your presentation. Finally, successful attitude change is enhanced when you present your arguments clearly and persuasively.

It's easier to change a person's attitude if he or she is not strongly committed to it. Conversely, the stronger the belief in the attitude, the harder it is to change it. Also, attitudes that have been expressed publicly are more difficult to change because doing so requires admitting having made a mistake.

It's also easier to change attitudes when the change required is not very significant. To get a person to accept a new attitude that varies greatly from his or her current position requires more effort. It may also threaten other deeply held attitudes.

All attitude-change techniques are not equally effective across situations. Oral persuasion techniques are most effective when you use a positive, tactful tone; present strong evidence to support your position; tailor your argument to the listener; use logic; and support your evidence by appealing to the person's fears, frustrations, and other emotions. But people are more likely to embrace change when they can experience it. The use of training sessions where employees share and personalize experiences, and practise new behaviours, can be powerful stimulants for change. Consistent with self-perception theory, changes in behaviour can lead to changes in attitudes.

Practising Skills

Form groups of 2. Person A is to choose any topic that he or she feels strongly about and state his or her position on the topic in 30 words or less. Person B's task will be to try to change Person A's attitude on this topic. Person B will have 10 minutes to make his or her case. When the time is up, the roles are reversed. Person B picks the topic and Person A has 10 minutes to try to change Person B's attitude.

Potential topics (you can choose either side of a topic) include the following: politics; the economy; world events; social practices; or specific management issues, such as that organizations should require all employees to undergo regular drug testing, there is no such thing as organizational loyalty any more, the customer is always right, and layoffs are an indication of management failures.

Questions

1. Were you successful at changing the other person's attitude? Why or why not?

2. Was the other person successful at changing your attitude? Why or why not?

3. What conclusions can you draw about changing the attitudes of yourself and others?

Reinforcing Skills

1. Try to convince a friend or relative to go with you to see a movie or play that you know he or she does not want to see.

2. Try to convince a friend or relative to try a different brand of toothpaste.

VIDEO CASE INCIDENT

CASE 3 Flair Bartending

CBC

Remember *Cocktail*, the movie in which Tom Cruise was a flashy bartender? That style of bartending actually has a name. It's called *flair bartending*. Gavin MacMillan is the top-ranked Canadian flair bartender, and second-ranked in the world. He is also an author and the owner of a bartender-for-hire business called *Movers and Shakers*. Now he is developing a brand-new idea for a bartender school called *Bartender 1*. Eventually, he wants to franchise the idea across Canada, the United States, and the world. He wants to earn enough money to buy a yacht with a helicopter pad on it.

Potential franchisees will like his idea to use an actual bar to teach students flair bartending. MacMillan does not rent space; rather, he borrows a bar for an evening to hold his classes. On one Monday evening, he is at a Toronto bar that is closed, but he has talked the owner into letting him run his class there for free. In return, the bar gets first pick of the graduates of MacMillan's bartending school.

In his first class of 12 students, MacMillan's expenses are $11 000, against $6000 in revenues. He hopes to reduce the cost of running future classes by re-using demonstration equipment. He needs to prove his concept works before he franchises it.

MacMillan discovers there is no problem finding students who want to be bartenders, but there is a problem finding people who can be instructors. There are only about 10 flair bartenders in Toronto and 40 in all of Canada. Finding teachers is not MacMillan's only problem. He is a perfectionist who is always fussing over the little things. Sometimes he focuses so much on the details that he does not see the big picture. He also lacks time to do all the things he wants to do.

MacMillan designed, built, and financed a portable bar to sell to golf courses and hotels. He brings his idea to a business group which runs entrepreneurial self-help sessions. He tells the group that he wants to make 10 of the portable bars in order to be more cost-effective, and he wants the group to help him with ideas to market the bar. But one of the group members questions whether MacMillan should even pursue the idea, noting he already has too many balls in the air. He needs to prioritize.

Two months later, MacMillan is conducting a two-day bartending course at the University of Guelph. His school is now making money, and everything is going well because he listened to the advice about focusing on just a few projects. He has stopped putting energy into his portable bar for the moment, and he has begun delegating duties to others.

Questions

1. What is the difference between terminal and instrumental values? Which of the terminal and instrumental values shown in Exhibit 3-1 apply to Gavin MacMillan?

2. Consider the following statement: "*Individuals who place a great deal of emphasis on the pursuit of money and material possessions are quite narrow in their perspective and are missing out on the really important non-material things in life like friends, family, and helping others. They are also showing a lack of concern for the environment because their desire to acquire things like a yacht leads to environmental damage.*" Do you agree or disagree with the statement? Explain, and be sure to consider the importance of values in your discussion.

3. Explain the difference between "values," "attitudes," and "job satisfaction." How do these ideas apply in practice to Gavin MacMillan? Give examples.

4. What are the three key elements in the definition of motivation? How does Gavin MacMillan score on each of these dimensions? (Review the relevant material in Chapter 4 before answering this question and the one that follows.)

5. What is the difference between extrinsic motivation and intrinsic motivation? Do you think Gavin MacMillan is extrinsically or intrinsically motivated? Explain.

Source: Based on "Flair Bartending," *CBC Venture's Dreamers and Schemers*, November 8, 2006.

Stress at Work

Saint John, New Brunswick-based Moosehead Breweries switched to running its beer production plant 24 hours a day, up from 16 hours, in 2007.[1] The increase in hours had an immediate effect. "Running 24 hours a day has caused significant stresses," said Michael Lee, Moosehead's vice-president of human resources.

The plant's managers are working with employees to deal with the stress. "Our Employment Assistance Program has always been vibrant. But now we are doing more presentations on shift work to help our employees deal with the changes," says Lee.

Moosehead's employees have a good, well-grounded role model in the company's president, Andrew Oland. He regularly attends 6 a.m. spin classes at a local fitness centre. His wife, Leslie, notes that "Andrew is a very involved parent who tries very hard to set aside time for his family."

Being sensitive to workplace stress is putting increased responsibilities on managers. When Janie Toivanen was diagnosed with severe depression in September 2002, she approached her employer, Vancouver-based Electronic Arts Canada, to request indefinite stress leave.[2] Instead, just days later, she was fired. After working there for six years, she "felt like she had been thrown away." Toivanen thought EA cared about its employees, and could not believe it would not do anything to help her as she struggled to overcome her illness. She subsequently filed a complaint with the BC Human Rights Tribunal and in 2006 was awarded, among other things, $20 000 for injury to her dignity, feelings, and self-respect and $19 744 in severance pay.

Are We Overstressed?

Stress appears to be a major factor in the lives of many Canadians. A recent survey conducted by Statistics Canada found that Canadians experience a great deal of stress, with those from Quebec topping the list.[3] The survey also found that women were more stressed than men. The inset *Stress Across the Country, 2005* reports the findings.

The impact of stress on the Canadian economy is huge, costing an estimated $33 billion a year in lost productivity, and considerably more than that in medical costs. To address these costs, Prime Minister Stephen Harper announced the creation of the Mental Health Commission of Canada in 2007. At the launch of the commission, Harper noted that mental health disorders are "now the fastest-growing category of disability insurance claims in Canada."[5]

Shannon Wagner, a clinical psychologist and a specialist in workplace stress research at the University of Northern British Columbia, notes that changes in the nature of jobs may be increasing the levels of stress in the workplace. While many jobs are not as physically demanding, they are often more mentally demanding. "A lot of people now are identifying techno-stress and the 24/7 workday,

which we didn't have even 10 or 15 years ago, this feeling of being constantly plugged in, of checking email 500 times a day."[6]

An additional problem is that employees are increasingly asked to donate labour to their employers, according to Professor Linda Duxbury of Carleton University's Sprott School of Business and Professor Chris Higgins of the Richard Ivey School of Business at the University of Western Ontario. Their survey of 31 571 Canadians found that in the previous month half of them had worked an extra 2.5 days of unpaid overtime, and more than half had donated 3.5 days of working at home to catch up.[7] Canadians are frequently reporting that they want more balance in their work and family lives.[8]

Jobs and Stress Levels

How do jobs rate in terms of stress? The inset *The Most and Least Stressful Jobs* on page 122 shows how selected occupations ranked in an evaluation of 250 jobs. Among the criteria used in the rankings were overtime, quotas, deadlines, competitiveness, physical demands, environmental conditions, hazards encountered, initiative required, stamina required, win-lose situations, and working in the public eye.

Stress is not something that can be ignored in the workplace. A 2005

poll by Ipsos Reid found that 66 percent of the CEOs surveyed said that "stress, burnout or other physical and mental health issues" have a negative effect on productivity.[9] A 2001 study conducted in 15 developed countries found that individuals who report that they are stressed in their jobs are 25 percent more likely to quit and 25 percent more likely to miss days of work.[10] Canadian, French, and Swedish employees reported the highest stress levels. In Canada, 41 percent of employees noted that they "often" or "always" experience stress at work, while only 31 percent of employees in Denmark and Switzerland reported stress levels this high. "In the wake of years of fiscal downsizing, workers across all sectors are working harder and longer than ever while trying to balance family responsibilities," said Scott Morris, former head of the Vancouver-based consulting firm Priority Management Systems.[11] Daniel Ondrack, a professor at the Joseph L. Rotman School of Management at the University of Toronto, notes that "one of the major reasons for absenteeism is the logistical problems workers face in just getting to work, including transporting children to school and finding daycare. Single parents, especially female, have to juggle all the daycare and family responsibilities, and that makes it extremely difficult for people to keep up with work demands."[12]

What Is Stress?

Stress is a dynamic condition in which an individual is confronted with an opportunity, demand, or resource related to what the individual desires and for which the outcome is perceived to be both uncertain and important.[13] This is a

Stress Across the Country, 2005[4]

Region	% with no life stresses	% with quite a lot of stress
Alberta	9.8	22.4
Atlantic Canada	13.1	18.4
British Columbia	13.2	22.7
Ontario	10.6	23.1
The Prairies	9.9	20.5
Quebec	14.4	26.0

The Most and Least Stressful Jobs

How do jobs rate in terms of stress? According to *Health* magazine, the top 10 most and least stressful jobs are as follows.[14]

Ten Most Stressful Jobs
1. Inner-city high school teacher
2. Police officer
3. Miner
4. Air traffic controller
5. Medical intern
6. Stockbroker
7. Journalist
8. Customer-service/complaint worker
9. Secretary
10. Waiter

Ten Least Stressful Jobs
1. Forester
2. Bookbinder
3. Telephone line worker
4. Toolmaker
5. Millwright
6. Repairperson
7. Civil engineer
8. Therapist
9. Natural scientist
10. Sales representative

complicated definition. Let's look at its components more closely.

Stress is not necessarily bad in and of itself. Although stress is typically discussed in a negative context, it also has a positive value.[15] It's an opportunity when it offers potential gain. Consider, for example, the superior performance that an athlete or stage performer gives in "clutch" situations. Such individuals often use stress positively to rise to the occasion and perform at or near their maximum. Similarly, many professionals see the pressures of heavy workloads and deadlines as positive challenges that enhance the quality of their work and the satisfaction they get from their job. In short, some stress can be good, and some can be bad.

Recently, researchers have argued that *challenge stressors*—or stressors associated with workload, pressure to complete tasks, and time urgency—operate quite differently from *hindrance stressors*—or stressors that keep you from reaching your goals (red tape, office politics, confusion over job responsibilities). Although research on challenge and hindrance stress is just starting to accumulate, early evidence suggests that challenge stressors are less harmful (produce less strain) than hindrance stressors.[16]

More typically, stress is associated with *demands* and *resources*. Demands are responsibilities, pressures, obligations, and even uncertainties that individuals face in the workplace. Resources are things within an individual's control that can be used to resolve the demands. For example, when you take a test at school, you feel stress because you confront opportunities and performance pressures. To the extent that you can apply resources to the demands—such as being prepared for the exam—you will feel less stress.

Under the demands and resources perspective on stress, having resources to cope with stress is just as important in offsetting stress as demands are in increasing it.[17] This model has received increasing support in the literature.[18]

Causes of Stress

A variety of changes in the workplace have resulted in additional causes of stress. We identify some of these key changes below:[19]

- *Environmental factors.* Evidence indicates that uncertainty is the biggest reason people have trouble coping with organizational changes.[20] Two types of environmental uncertainty are economic and technological. Changes in the business cycle create *economic uncertainties*. When the economy is contracting, for example, people become increasingly anxious about their job security. *Technological change* is another environmental factor that can cause stress. Because new innovations can make an employee's skills and experience obsolete in a very short time, computers, robotics, automation, and similar forms of technological innovation are a threat to many people and cause them stress.

- *Organizational factors.* There is no shortage of factors within an organization that can cause stress. Pressures to avoid errors or complete tasks in a limited time, work overload, a demanding and insensitive boss, and unpleasant co-workers are a few examples. We have categorized these factors around task, role, and interpersonal demands.[21]

- *Task demands* are factors related to a person's job. They include the design of the individual's job (autonomy, task variety, degree of automation), working conditions, and the physical work layout. Assembly lines, for instance, can put pressure on people when the line's speed is perceived as excessive. Similarly, working in an overcrowded room or in a visible location where noise and interruptions are constant can increase anxiety and stress.[22] Increasingly, as customer service becomes ever more important, emotional labour is a source of stress.[23] Do you think you could put on a happy face when you are having a bad day?

- *Role demands* relate to pressures placed on a person as a function of the particular role he or she plays in the organization.

- *Interpersonal demands* are pressures created by other employees. Lack of social support from colleagues and poor interpersonal relationships can cause stress, especially among employees with a high social need.

- *Personal factors.* The typical individual works about 40 to 50 hours a week. But the experiences and problems that people encounter in the other 120-plus nonwork hours each week can spill over to the job. Our final category, then, encompasses factors in the employee's personal life. Primarily, these factors are family issues, personal economic problems, and inherent personality characteristics.

- National surveys consistently show that people hold *family* and personal relationships dear. Marital difficulties, the breaking off of a relationship, and discipline troubles with children are examples of relationship problems that create stress for employees that are not left at the front door when they arrive at work.[24]

- Furthermore, about one in eight workers was responsible for providing some form of care for

aging parents in 1997, and one survey found that one in three was doing so in 2002.[25] Being a caregiver is an additional stress both at home and at work. Studies indicate that those who have difficulties finding effective child care or elder care have lower work performance and increased absenteeism, decreased satisfaction, and lower physical and psychological well-being.[26]

- *Economic* problems created by individuals overextending their financial resources is another set of personal troubles that can create stress for employees and distract their attention from their work. Regardless of income level—people who make $80 000 per year seem to have as much trouble handling their finances as those who earn $18 000—some people are poor money managers or have wants that always seem to exceed their earning capacity.

- Studies in three diverse organizations found that stress symptoms reported prior to beginning a job accounted for most of the variance in stress symptoms reported nine months later.[27] This led the researchers to conclude that some people may have an inherent tendency to accentuate negative aspects of the world in general. If this is true, then a significant individual factor that influences stress is a person's basic disposition. That is, stress symptoms expressed on the job may actually originate in the person's *personality*.

A fact that tends to be overlooked when stressors are reviewed individually is that stress is an additive

phenomenon.[29] Stress builds up. Each new and persistent stressor adds to an individual's stress level. A single stressor may seem relatively unimportant in and of itself, but if it is added to an already high level of stress, it can be "the straw that breaks the camel's back."

Consequences of Stress

Stress manifests itself in a number of ways. For instance, an individual who is experiencing a high level of stress may develop high blood pressure, ulcers, irritability, difficulty in making routine decisions, loss of appetite, accident proneness, and the like. These symptoms can be placed under three general categories: physiological, psychological, and behavioural symptoms.[30]

- *Physiological symptoms.* Most of the research on stress suggests that it can create changes in metabolism, increase heart and breathing rates, increase blood pressure, cause headaches, and induce heart attacks. An interesting aspect of illness in today's workplace is the considerable change in how stress shows up. In the past, older workers were the ones claiming sick leave, workers' compensation, and short- and long-term disability—most often in cases of catastrophic illness such as heart attacks, cancer, and major back surgeries. These days, however, it is not unusual for long-term disability programs to be filled with employees in their 20s, 30s, and 40s. Employees are claiming illnesses that are either psychiatric (such as depression) or more difficult to diagnose (such as chronic fatigue syndrome or fibromyalgia, a musculoskeletal discomfort). The increase in disability claims may be the result of downsizing taking its toll on the psyches of those in the workforce.[31]

- *Psychological symptoms.* Job dissatisfaction is "the simplest and most obvious psychological effect" of stress.[32] However, stress also shows itself in other psychological states—for instance, tension, anxiety, irritability, boredom, and procrastination.

- The evidence indicates that when people are placed in jobs that make multiple and conflicting demands or in which there is a lack of clarity as to the person's duties, authority, and responsibilities, both stress and dissatisfaction increase.[33]

Similarly, the less control that people have over the pace of their work, the greater the stress and dissatisfaction. More research is needed to clarify the relationship, but the evidence suggests that jobs providing a low level of variety, significance, autonomy, feedback, and identity create stress and reduce satisfaction and involvement in the job.[34]

- *Behavioural symptoms.* Behaviourally related stress symptoms include changes in productivity, absence, and turnover, as well as changes in eating habits, increased smoking or consumption of alcohol, rapid speech, fidgeting, and sleep disorders. More recently, stress has been linked to aggression and violence in the workplace.

Why Do Individuals Differ in Their Experience of Stress?

Some people thrive on stressful situations, while others are overwhelmed by them. What is it that differentiates people in terms of their ability to handle stress? What individual difference variables moderate the relationship between *potential* stressors and *experienced* stress? At least four variables—perception, job experience, social support, and personality—have been found to be relevant moderators.

- *Perception.* Individuals react in response to their *perception* of reality rather than to reality itself. Perception, therefore, moderates the relationship between a potential stress

condition and an employee's reaction to it. For example, one person might fear losing his job because the company is laying off staff, while another might perceive the situation as an opportunity to receive a large severance allowance and start a small business. Similarly, what one employee perceives as a challenging job may be viewed as threatening and demanding by others.[35] So the stress potential in environmental, organizational, and individual factors does not lie in objective conditions. Rather, it lies in an employee's interpretation of those factors.

- *Job experience.* Experience on the job tends to be negatively related to work stress. Two explanations have been offered.[36] First, people who experience more stress on the job when they are first hired may be more likely to quit. Therefore, people who remain with the organization longer are those with more stress-resistant traits or those who are more resistant to the stress characteristics of their organization. Second, people eventually develop coping mechanisms to deal with stress. Because this takes time, senior members of the organization are more likely to be fully adapted and should experience less stress.

- *Social support.* There is increasing evidence that social support—that is, collegial relationships with co-workers or supervisors—can buffer the impact of stress.[37] The logic underlying this moderating variable is that social support helps ease the negative effects of even high-strain jobs.

For individuals whose work associates are unhelpful or even actively hostile, social support may be found outside the job. Involvement with family, friends, and community can provide the support—especially for those with a high social need—that is missing at work, and this can make job stressors more tolerable.

- *Personality.* Personality not only affects the degree to which people experience stress but also how they cope with it. Perhaps the most widely studied personality trait in stress is *Type A personality*, which we discussed in Chapter 2. Type A— particularly that aspect of Type A that manifests itself in hostility and anger—is associated with increased levels of stress and risk for heart disease.[38] More specifically, people who are quick to anger, maintain a persistently hostile outlook, and project a cynical mistrust of others are at increased risk of experiencing stress in situations.

How Do We Manage Stress?

Both the individual and the organization can take steps to help the individual manage stress. Below we discuss ways that individuals can manage stress, and then we examine programs that organizations use to help employees manage stress.

Individual Approaches

An employee can take personal responsibility for reducing his or her stress level. Individual strategies that have proven effective include time

management techniques, physical exercise, relaxation techniques, and a close social support network.

- *Time management.* Many people manage their time poorly. The things we have to accomplish in any given day or week are not necessarily beyond completion if we manage our time properly. The well-organized employee, like the well-organized student, can often accomplish twice as much as the person who is poorly organized. So understanding and using basic time management principles can help individuals cope better with tensions created by job demands.[39] A few of the more well-known time management principles are: (1) making daily lists of activities to be accomplished; (2) prioritizing activities by importance and urgency; (3) scheduling activities according to the priorities set; and (4) knowing your daily cycle and handling the most demanding parts of your job during the high part of your cycle, when you are most alert and productive.[40]

- *Physical activity.* Noncompetitive physical exercise, such as aerobics, walking, jogging, swimming, and riding a bicycle, has long been recommended by physicians as a way to deal with excessive stress levels. These forms of physical exercise increase heart capacity, lower at-rest heart rate, provide a mental diversion from work pressures, and offer a means to "let off steam."[41]

- *Relaxation techniques.* Individuals can teach themselves to reduce tension through relaxation techniques such as meditation,

hypnosis, and biofeedback. The objective is to reach a state of deep relaxation, where you feel physically relaxed, somewhat detached from the immediate environment, and detached from body sensations.[42] Fifteen or 20 minutes a day of deep relaxation releases tension and provides a person with a pronounced sense of peacefulness. Importantly, significant changes in heart rate, blood pressure, and other physiological factors result from achieving the deep relaxation condition.

- *Building social supports.* Having friends, family, or colleagues to talk to provides an outlet when stress levels become excessive. Expanding your social support network, therefore, can be a means for tension reduction. It provides you with someone to listen to your problems and to offer a more objective perspective on the situation.

The inset *Tips for Reducing Stress* on page 126 offers additional ideas for managing stress.

Organizational Approaches

Employees who work at Montreal-based Ericsson Canada, a global telecommunications supplier, have access to a comprehensive wellness program. They can engage in activities that address their intellectual, emotional, social, physical, and spiritual well-being. "The program has really evolved over the years," says Louise Leonhardt, manager of human resources. "We've found it helps people balance their life, just like the on-site daycare does."

Employees who work at Toronto-based BCS Communications, a

publishing, advertising, and public relations agency, receive biweekly shiatsu massages, paid for by the company. The company spends about $700 a month for the massages, equivalent to the amount it used to spend providing coffee to the employees. "It's in my company's best interest to have my employees be healthy," says Caroline Tapp-McDougall, the BCS group publisher.[44]

Most firms that have introduced wellness programs have found significant benefits. Health Canada reports that businesses get back $3.39 for each corporate dollar they invest in wellness initiatives. For individuals with three to five risk factors (such as high cholesterol, being overweight, or smoking) the return was $2.04 for each dollar spent.[45] The savings come about because there is less turnover, greater productivity, and reduced medical claims.[46] About 64 percent of Canadian companies surveyed by Health Canada offered some sort of wellness initiative,

including stop-smoking programs, stress courses, and back-pain management programs; 17.5 percent of companies offered on-site wellness programs.[47]

So what can organizations do to reduce employee stress? In general, strategies to reduce stress include improved processes for choosing employees, placement of employees in appropriate jobs, realistic goal setting, designing jobs with employee needs and skills in mind, increased employee involvement, improved organizational communication, offering employee sabbaticals, and, as mentioned, establishment of corporate wellness programs.

Certain jobs are more stressful than others, but individuals also differ in their response to stress situations. We know, for example, that individuals with little experience or a negative core self-evaluation tend to be more prone to stress. Selection and placement decisions should take these facts into consideration. Although management should not restrict hiring to only experienced individuals with a positive core self-evaluation, such individuals may adapt better to high-stress jobs and perform those jobs more effectively.

Research shows that individuals perform better when they have specific and challenging goals and receive feedback on how well they are progressing toward them.[48] The use of goals can reduce stress as well as provide motivation. Specific goals that are perceived as attainable clarify performance expectations. Additionally, goal feedback reduces uncertainties as to actual job performance. The result is less employee frustration, role ambiguity, and stress.

Creating jobs that give employees more responsibility, more meaningful work, more autonomy, and increased feedback can reduce stress

because these factors give the employee greater control over work activities and lessen dependence on others. Of course, not all employees want jobs with increased responsibility. The right job for employees with a low need for growth might be less responsibility and increased specialization. If individuals prefer structure and routine, more structured jobs should also reduce uncertainties and stress levels.

Increasing formal organizational communication with employees reduces uncertainty by lessening role ambiguity and role conflict. Given the importance that perceptions play in moderating the stress-response relationship, management can also use effective communications as a means to shape employee perceptions. Remember that what employees categorize as demands, threats, or opportunities are merely interpretations, and those interpretations can be affected by the symbols and actions communicated by management.

What some employees need is an occasional escape from the frenetic pace of their work. In recent years, companies such as Charles Schwab, DuPont, L.L.Bean, Nike, and 3Com have begun to provide extended voluntary leaves.[49] These *sabbaticals*— ranging in length from a few weeks to several months—allow employees to travel, relax, or pursue personal projects that consume time beyond normal vacation weeks. Proponents argue that these sabbaticals can revive and rejuvenate workers who might be headed for burnout.

Our final suggestion is to offer organizationally supported wellness programs. These programs focus on the employee's total physical and mental condition.[50] For example, they typically include workshops to help people quit smoking, control

Reducing Stress in the Workplace

- Avoid electronic monitoring of staff. Personal supervision generates considerably less stress.

- Allow employees time to recharge after periods of intense or demanding work.

- Deliver important information that significantly affects employees face to face.

- Encourage positive social interactions between staff to promote problem-solving around work issues and increase emotional support.

- Keep in mind that staff need to balance privacy and social interaction at work. Extremes can generate stress.[51]

alcohol use, lose weight, eat better, and develop a regular exercise program. The assumption underlying most wellness programs is that employees need to take personal responsibility for their physical and mental health. The organization is merely a vehicle to make this happen. The inset *Reducing Stress in the Workplace* offers additional ideas.

Research Exercises

1. Look for data on stress levels in other countries. How do these data compare with the Canadian data presented above? Are the sources of stress the same in different countries? What might you conclude about how stress affects people in different cultures?

2. Find out what three Canadian organizations in three different industries have done to help employees manage stress. Are there common themes in these programs? Did you find any unusual programs? To what extent are these programs tailored to the needs of the employees in those industries?

Your Perspective

1. Think of all of the technological changes that have happened in the workplace in recent years, including email, BlackBerrys, and intranets. What are the positive benefits of this change? What are the downsides? As an employee facing the demand to "stay connected" to your workplace, how would you try to maintain a balance in your life?

2. How much responsibility should individuals take for managing their own stress? To what extent should organizations become involved in the personal lives of their employees when trying to help them manage stress? What are the pros and cons for whether employees or organizations take responsibility for managing stress?

Want to Know More?

If you are wondering how stressed you are, go to **www.heartandstroke.ca** and click on "Risk assessment." The site also offers tips on reducing stress.

FACEOFF

When organizations provide on-site daycare facilities, they are filling a needed role in parents' lives, and making it easier for parents to attend to their job demands rather than worry about child-care arrangements.

When employees expect organizations to provide child care, they are shifting their responsibilities to their employers, rather than keeping their family needs and concerns private. Moreover, it is unfair to give child-care benefits when not all employees have children.

Theories of Motivation

The BC Lions football team ended the 2007 season with a team record of 14 wins last season. How does motivation affect how the team performs?

1 What is motivation?

2 How do needs motivate people?

3 Are there other ways to motivate people?

4 Do equity and fairness matter?

5 What role does reinforcement play in motivation?

6 What are the ethics behind motivation theories?

By most accounts, Vancouver-based BC Lions head coach Wally Buono is not a particularly warm person.[1] Buono is a hard taskmaster with his BC Lions players and coaches, and is not afraid to make tough decisions.

Buono wants to coach winners, not losers. As a coach, Buono has one of the winningest records in the Canadian Football League (CFL), second only to former Lions coach Don Matthews. His teams have been to seven Grey Cups, and the BC Lions have finished first in the West four times, gone to the Grey Cup twice, and won the 2006 CFL championship under his leadership. In 2007, the BC Lions' finished the season with 14 wins (3 losses and 1 tie), setting a franchise record.

Buono seems to motivate by being tough. He's not afraid to criticize his players publicly, and will give them a long list of their faults during contract negotiations. He claims that he gives only two performance reviews to players: "Once when I warn you and once when I cut you."

Buono's players may not like him personally, but they spend hours in training each day because "guys wanna get better," explained slotback Geroy Simon.

In this chapter, we examine the subjects of motivation and rewards. We look at what motivation is, and how needs can be used to motivate individuals. We also present theories of motivation, and then consider the roles that fairness, reinforcement, and ethics play in motivation.

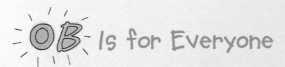 **OB Is for Everyone**

- Are managers manipulating employees when they link rewards to productivity? Is this ethical?
- Why do some managers do a better job of motivating people than others?
- How important is fairness to you?
- What can you do if you think your salary is unfair?

Self-Assessment Library

LEARNING ABOUT YOURSELF

- Motivation
- Goals
- Self-Confidence
- Disciplining Others

1   What is motivation?

motivation The intensity, direction, and persistence of effort a person shows in reaching a goal.

Theory X The assumption that employees dislike work, will attempt to avoid it, and must be coerced, controlled, or threatened with punishment to achieve goals.

Theory Y The assumption that employees like work, are creative, seek responsibility, and will exercise self-direction and self-control if they are committed to the objectives.

intrinsic motivators A person's internal desire to do something, due to such things as interest, challenge, and personal satisfaction.

extrinsic motivators Motivation that comes from outside the person and includes such things as pay, bonuses, and other tangible rewards.

What Is Motivation?

We define **motivation** as the intensity, direction, and persistence of effort a person shows in reaching a goal.[2]

The three key elements in our definition are intensity, direction, and persistence. *Intensity* is concerned with how hard a person tries. This is the element most of us focus on when we talk about motivation. However, high intensity is unlikely to lead to favourable job-performance outcomes unless the effort is channelled in a *direction* that is beneficial. Finally, the effort requires *persistence*. This is a measure of how long a person can maintain his or her effort. Motivated individuals stay with a task long enough to achieve their goal.

Many people incorrectly view motivation as a personal trait—something some people have and others don't. Along these lines, Douglas McGregor proposed two distinct views of human beings. **Theory X**, which is basically negative, suggests that employees dislike work, will attempt to avoid it, and must be coerced, controlled, or threatened with punishment to achieve goals. **Theory Y**, which is basically positive, suggests that employees like work, are creative, seek responsibility, and will exercise self-direction and self-control if they are committed to the objectives.[3]

Our knowledge of motivation tells us that neither theory alone fully accounts for employee behaviour. What we know is that motivation is the result of the interaction of the individual and the situation. Certainly, individuals differ in their basic motivational drive. But the same employee who is quickly bored when pulling the lever on a drill press may enthusiastically pull a slot machine lever in Casino Windsor for hours on end. You may read a thriller at one sitting, yet find it difficult to concentrate on a textbook for more than 20 minutes. It's not necessarily you—it's the situation. So as we analyze the concept of motivation, keep in mind that the level of motivation varies both *among* individuals and *within* individuals at different times.

You should also realize that what motivates individuals will also vary among individuals and situations. Motivation theorists talk about **intrinsic motivators** and **extrinsic motivators**. Extrinsic motivators come from outside the person and include such things as pay, bonuses, and other tangible rewards. Intrinsic motivators come from a person's internal desire to do something, due to such things as interest, challenge, and personal satisfaction. Individuals are intrinsically motivated when they genuinely care about their work, look for better ways to do it, and are energized and fulfilled by doing it well.[4] The rewards the individual gets from intrinsic motivation come from the work itself rather than from external factors such as increases in pay or compliments from the boss.

Are individuals primarily intrinsically or extrinsically motivated? Theory X suggests that people are almost exclusively driven by extrinsic motivators. However, Theory Y suggests that people are more intrinsically motivated. This view is consistent with that of Alfie Kohn, author of *Punished by Rewards*, who suggests that it's only necessary to provide the right environment, and people will be motivated.[5] We discuss his ideas further in Chapter 5.

Intrinsic and extrinsic motivation may reflect the situation, however, rather than individual personalities. For example, suppose your mother has asked you or your brother to take her to a meeting an hour away. You may be willing to drive her, without any thought of compensation, because it will make you feel good to do something for her. That is intrinsic motivation. But if you have a love-hate relationship with your brother, you may insist that he buy you lunch for helping out. Lunch would then be an extrinsic motivator—something that came from outside yourself and motivated you to do the task. Later in the chapter, we review the evidence regarding the significance of extrinsic vs. intrinsic motivators, and also examine how to increase intrinsic motivation. Meanwhile, you might want to consider whether intrinsic and extrinsic motivation vary across countries, as *OB Around the Globe* suggests.

OB AROUND THE GLOBE

Motivation May Vary by Culture

Do managers from different cultures evaluate their employees differently? A recent study found interesting differences in managers' perceptions of employee motivation.[6] The study examined managers from three distinct cultural regions: North America, Asia, and Latin America. The results of the study revealed that North American managers perceive their employees as being motivated more by extrinsic factors (for example, pay) than intrinsic factors (for example, doing meaningful work). Asian managers perceive their employees as being motivated by both extrinsic and intrinsic factors, while Latin American managers perceive their employees as being motivated by intrinsic factors.

Even more interesting, these differences affected evaluations of employee performance. As expected, Asian managers focused on both types of motivation when evaluating their employees' performance, and Latin American managers focused on intrinsic motivation. Oddly, North American managers, though believing that employees are motivated primarily by extrinsic factors, actually focused more on intrinsic factors when evaluating employee performance. Why the paradox? One explanation is that North Americans value uniqueness, so any deviation from the norm—such as being perceived as being unusually high in intrinsic motivation—is rewarded.

Latin American managers' focus on intrinsic motivation when evaluating employees may be related to a cultural norm termed *simpatía*, a tradition that compels employees to display their internal feelings. Consequently, Latin American managers are more sensitized to these displays and can more easily notice their employees' intrinsic motivation.

So, from an employee perspective, the cultural background of your manager can play an important role in how you are evaluated.

Needs Theories of Motivation

Theories of motivation generally fall into two categories: needs theories and process theories. *Needs theories* describe the types of needs that must be met to motivate individuals. *Process theories* help us understand the actual ways in which we and others can be motivated. There are a variety of needs theories, including Maslow's hierarchy of needs, Alderfer's ERG theory, Herzberg's motivation-hygiene theory (sometimes called the two-factor theory), and McClelland's theory of needs. We briefly review these to illustrate the basic properties of needs theories.

Needs theories are widely criticized for not standing up to scientific review, but they are probably still the best-known explanations for employee motivation. Nevertheless, you should know these early theories for at least two reasons: (1) They represent a foundation from which contemporary theories have grown, and (2) practising managers still regularly use these theories and their terminology in explaining employee motivation.

2 How do needs motivate people?

Maslow's Hierarchy of Needs Theory

It's probably safe to say that the most well-known theory of motivation is Abraham Maslow's **hierarchy of needs theory**.[7] Maslow hypothesized that within every human being there exists a hierarchy of five needs:

- *Physiological.* Includes hunger, thirst, shelter, sex, and other bodily needs.

- *Safety.* Includes security and protection from physical and emotional harm.

hierarchy of needs theory
A hierarchy of five needs—physiological, safety, social, esteem, and self-actualization—in which, as each need is substantially satisfied, the next need becomes dominant.

- *Social.* Includes affection, belongingness, acceptance, and friendship.
- *Esteem.* Includes internal esteem factors such as self-respect, autonomy, and achievement; and external esteem factors such as status, recognition, and attention.
- *Self-actualization.* Includes growth, achieving one's potential, and self-fulfillment. This is the drive to become what one is capable of becoming.

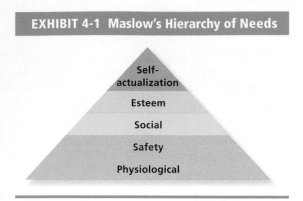

EXHIBIT 4-1 Maslow's Hierarchy of Needs

As each of these needs becomes substantially satisfied, the next need becomes dominant. In terms of Exhibit 4-1, the individual moves up the steps of the hierarchy. From the perspective of motivation, the theory would say that although no need is ever fully met, a substantially satisfied need no longer motivates. So if you want to motivate someone, according to Maslow, you need to understand what level of the hierarchy that person is currently on and focus on satisfying the needs at or above that level.

Maslow separated the five needs into higher and lower orders. Physiological and safety needs were described as lower-order, and social, esteem, and self-actualization as higher-order needs. The differentiation between the two orders was made on the premise that higher-order needs are satisfied internally (within the person), whereas lower-order needs are mainly satisfied externally (by such things as pay, union contracts, and tenure).

Maslow's needs theory continues to receive wide recognition, particularly among practising managers. This can be attributed to the theory's intuitive logic and ease of understanding. Unfortunately, however, research does not generally validate the theory. Maslow himself provided no empirical evidence, and several studies that sought to validate the theory found little support for the prediction that need structures are organized along the dimensions proposed by Maslow, that unsatisfied needs motivate, or that a satisfied need activates movement to a new need level.[8]

ERG Theory

ERG theory A theory that posits three groups of core needs: existence, relatedness, and growth.

Clayton Alderfer reworked Maslow's hierarchy of needs to align it more closely with the empirical research. His revised need hierarchy is called **ERG theory**.[9]

Alderfer argued that there are three groups of core needs—*existence* (similar to Maslow's physiological and safety needs), *relatedness* (similar to Maslow's social and status needs), and *growth* (similar to Maslow's esteem needs and self-actualization). Unlike Maslow, Alderfer did not assume that these needs existed in a rigid hierarchy. An individual could be focusing on all three need categories simultaneously. Despite these differences, empirical research has not been any more supportive of ERG theory than of the needs hierarchy.[10]

Motivation-Hygiene Theory

motivation-hygiene theory A theory that relates intrinsic factors to job satisfaction and associates extrinsic factors with dissatisfaction.

The **motivation-hygiene theory** was proposed by psychologist Frederick Herzberg.[11] In the belief that an individual's relationship to work is a basic one and that an individual's attitude toward this work can very well determine the individual's success or failure, Herzberg investigated the question, "What do people want from their jobs?" He asked people to describe, in detail, situations when they felt exceptionally good and bad about their jobs. These responses were tabulated and categorized. Exhibit 4-2 illustrates factors affecting job attitudes, as reported in 12 investigations conducted by Herzberg.

From the categorized responses, Herzberg concluded that the replies people gave when they felt good about their jobs were significantly different from the replies given when they felt bad. As seen in Exhibit 4-2, certain characteristics tend to be consistently related to job satisfaction (factors on the right side of the figure), and others to job

EXHIBIT 4-2   Comparison of Satisfiers and Dissatisfiers

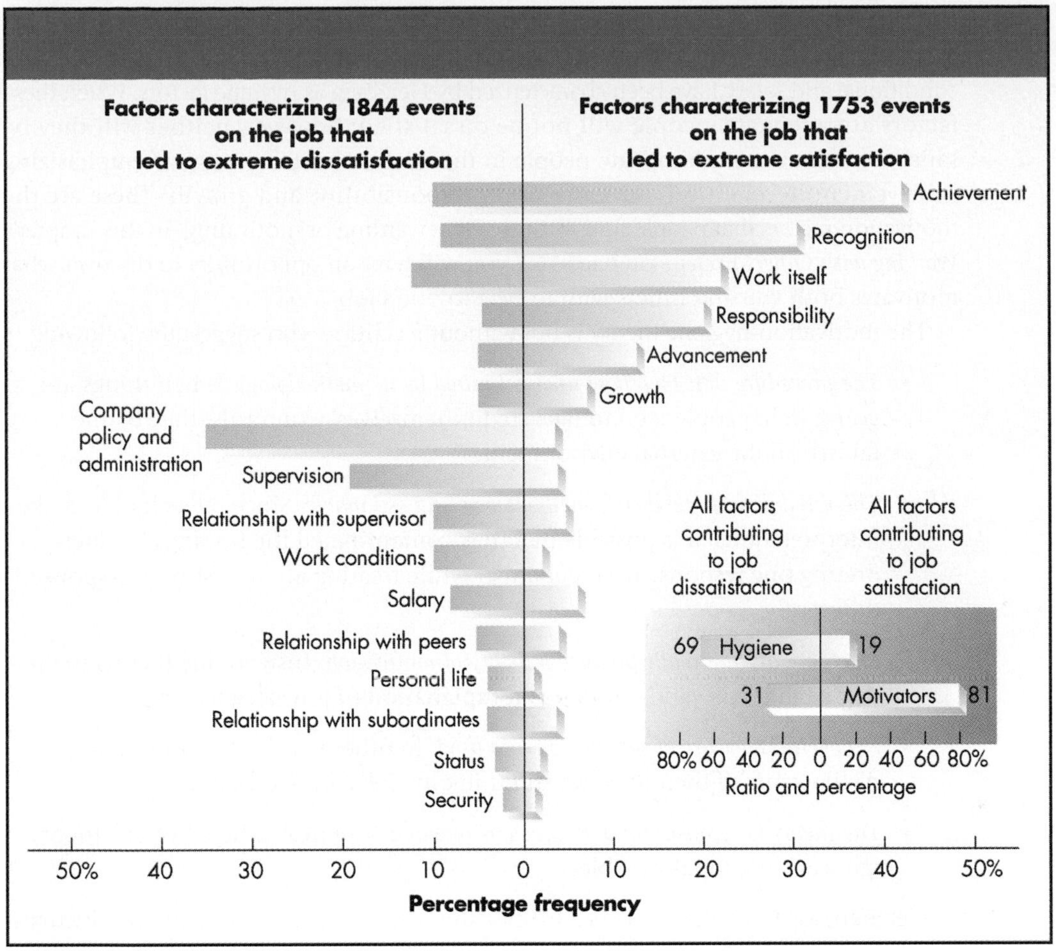

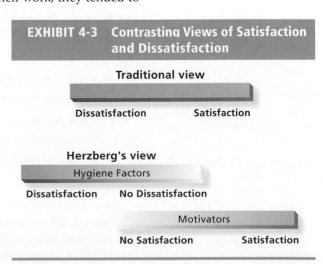

Factors characterizing 1844 events on the job that led to extreme dissatisfaction

Factors characterizing 1753 events on the job that led to extreme satisfaction

Achievement
Recognition
Work itself
Responsibility
Advancement
Growth
Company policy and administration
Supervision
Relationship with supervisor
Work conditions
Salary
Relationship with peers
Personal life
Relationship with subordinates
Status
Security

All factors contributing to job dissatisfaction

All factors contributing to job satisfaction

69 Hygiene 19
31 Motivators 81

80% 60 40 20 0 20 40 60 80%
Ratio and percentage

50% 40 30 20 10 0 10 20 30 40 50%
Percentage frequency

Source: Reprinted by permission of *Harvard Business Review*. An exhibit from Frederick Herzberg, "One More Time: How Do You Motivate Employees?" *Harvard Business Review* 81, no. 1 (January 2003), p. 90. Copyright © 1987 by the President and Fellows of Harvard College; all rights reserved.

dissatisfaction (the left side of the figure). Intrinsic factors, such as achievement, recognition, the work itself, responsibility, advancement, and growth, seem to be related to job satisfaction. When those questioned felt good about their work, they tended to attribute these characteristics to themselves. On the other hand, when they were dissatisfied, they tended to cite extrinsic factors, such as company policy and administration, supervision, interpersonal relations, and work conditions.

According to Herzberg, the data suggest that the opposite of satisfaction is not dissatisfaction, as was traditionally believed. Removing dissatisfying characteristics from a job does not necessarily make the job satisfying. As illustrated in Exhibit 4-3, Herzberg proposes that his findings indicate the existence of a dual continuum: the opposite of "Satisfaction" is "No Satisfaction," and the opposite of "Dissatisfaction" is "No Dissatisfaction."

Herzberg explained that the factors leading to job satisfaction (motivators) are separate and distinct from those that lead to job dissatisfaction (hygiene factors). Therefore,

EXHIBIT 4-3   Contrasting Views of Satisfaction and Dissatisfaction

Traditional view

Dissatisfaction   Satisfaction

Herzberg's view

Hygiene Factors

Dissatisfaction   No Dissatisfaction

Motivators

No Satisfaction   Satisfaction

managers who seek to eliminate factors that create job dissatisfaction can create more pleasant workplaces, but not necessarily more motivated ones. That is, they will be placating employees rather than motivating them. As a result, such characteristics as company policy and administration, supervision, interpersonal relations, work conditions, and salary have been characterized by Herzberg as hygiene factors. When these factors are adequate, people will not be dissatisfied; however, neither will they be satisfied. If we want to motivate people in their jobs, Herzberg suggests emphasizing achievement, recognition, the work itself, responsibility, and growth. These are the motivation factors that people find intrinsically rewarding or motivating. In this chapter's *Working with Others Exercise* on page 162, you will have an opportunity to discover what motivates both you and others with respect to one's job.

The motivation-hygiene theory is not without its critics, who suggest the following:[12]

- *The procedure that Herzberg used is limited by its methodology.* When things are going well, people tend to take credit themselves. Contrarily, they blame failure on the external environment.

- *The reliability of Herzberg's methodology is questionable.* Since raters had to make interpretations, it is possible that they contaminated the findings by interpreting one response in one manner while treating another similar response differently.

- *Herzberg did not really produce a theory of motivation.* Instead, the theory, to the degree that it is valid, provides an explanation of job satisfaction.

- *No overall measure of satisfaction was used.* In other words, individuals may dislike parts of their jobs, yet still think the jobs are acceptable.

- *The theory is inconsistent with previous research.* The motivation-hygiene theory ignores situational variables.

Herzberg assumed that there is a relationship between satisfaction and productivity. But the research methodology he used looked only at satisfaction, not at productivity. To make such research relevant, one must assume a high relationship between satisfaction and productivity.[13]

Regardless of these criticisms, Herzberg's theory has been widely read, and few managers are unfamiliar with his recommendations. The popularity of vertically expanding jobs to allow employees greater responsibility in planning and controlling their work can probably be largely attributed to Herzberg's findings and recommendations.

McClelland's Theory of Needs

McClelland's theory of needs was developed by David McClelland and his associates to help explain motivation.[14] The theory focuses on three needs: achievement, power, and affiliation. They are defined as follows:

- **Need for achievement**. The drive to excel, to achieve in relation to a set of standards, to strive to succeed.

- **Need for power**. The need to make others behave in a way that they would not have behaved otherwise.

- **Need for affiliation**. The desire for friendly and close interpersonal relationships.

Some people have a compelling drive to succeed. They are striving for personal achievement rather than the rewards of success per se. They have a desire to do something better or more efficiently than it has been done before. This drive is the achievement need (*nAch*). From research into the achievement need, McClelland found that high achievers

McClelland's theory of needs Achievement, power, and affiliation are three important needs that help explain motivation.

need for achievement The drive to excel, to achieve in relation to a set of standards, to strive to succeed.

need for power The need to make others behave in a way that they would not have behaved otherwise.

need for affiliation The desire for friendly and close interpersonal relationships.

differentiate themselves from others by their desire to do things better.[15] They seek situations in which they can attain personal responsibility for finding solutions to problems, in which they can receive rapid feedback on their performance so they can determine easily whether they are improving or not, and in which they can set moderately challenging goals. High achievers are not gamblers; they dislike succeeding by chance. They prefer the challenge of working at a problem and accepting the personal responsibility for success or failure rather than leaving the outcome to chance or the actions of others. Importantly, they avoid what they perceive to be very easy or very difficult tasks. They prefer tasks of intermediate difficulty.

The need for power (*nPow*) is the desire to have impact, to be influential, and to control others. Individuals high in nPow enjoy being "in charge," strive for influence over others, prefer to be placed into competitive and status-oriented situations, and tend to be more concerned with prestige and gaining influence over others than with effective performance.

The third need isolated by McClelland is affiliation (*nAff*). This need has received the least attention from researchers. Individuals with a high affiliation motive strive for friendship, prefer cooperative situations rather than competitive ones, and desire relationships that involve a high degree of mutual understanding.

Relying on an extensive amount of research, some reasonably well-supported predictions can be made based on the relationship of these needs to job performance. First, individuals with a high need to achieve prefer and will be motivated by job situations with personal responsibility, feedback, and an intermediate degree of risk. Second, people with a high achievement need are interested in how well they do personally and not in influencing others to do well. Thus, they may not make good managers.[16] Third, the best managers are high in their need for power and low in their need for affiliation.[17]

Anne Sweeney is a high achiever. Since joining the Walt Disney Company in 1996, Sweeney has led the transition of the struggling Disney Channel from a premium cable service to a basic network, quintupling the channel's subscriber base. As co-chair of Disney's Media Networks, Sweeney is trying to achieve a turnaround for Disney's ABC Family channel. In addition, when Sweeney became president of ABC Television in 2004, she accepted the challenging goal of lifting the network from its last-place position.

Summarizing Needs Theories

All needs theories of motivation, including Maslow's hierarchy of needs, Alderfer's ERG (existence, relatedness, growth) theory, Herzberg's motivation-hygiene theory (or the two-factor theory), and McClelland's theory of needs (need for achievement, need for power, need for affiliation), propose a similar idea: Individuals have needs that, when unsatisfied, will result in motivation. For instance, if you have a need to be praised, you may work harder at your task in order to receive recognition from your manager or other co-workers. Similarly, if you need money and you are asked to do something, within reason, that offers money as a reward, you will be motivated to complete the task in order to earn the money.

Where needs theories differ is in the types of needs they consider, and whether they propose a hierarchy of needs (where some needs have to be satisfied before others) or simply a list of needs. Exhibit 4-4 illustrates the relationship among the four needs theories that we discussed. While the theories use different names for the needs, and also have different numbers of needs, we can see that they are somewhat consistent in the types of needs addressed. Exhibit 4-5 indicates whether the theory proposes a hierarchy of needs, and the contribution of and empirical support for each theory.

What can we conclude from the needs theories? We can safely say that individuals do have needs, and that they can be highly motivated to achieve those needs. The types of needs, and their importance, vary by individual, and probably vary over time for the

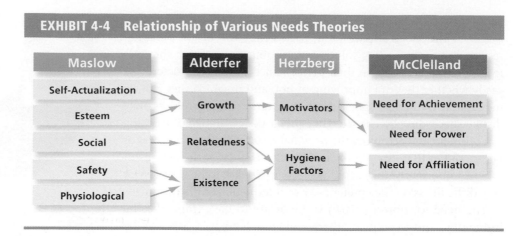

EXHIBIT 4-4   Relationship of Various Needs Theories

Learning About Yourself

1. What Motivates You?
   (page 161)

same individual as well. When rewarding individuals, you should consider their specific needs. Obviously, in a workplace, it would be difficult to design a reward structure that could completely take into account the specific needs of every employee. To better understand what might motivate you in the workplace, look at this chapter's *Learning About Yourself Exercise* on page 161.

EXHIBIT 4-5   Summarizing the Various Needs Theories

Theory	Maslow	Alderfer	Herzberg	McClelland
Is there a hierarchy of needs?	The theory argues that lower-order needs must be satisfied before one progresses to higher-order needs.	More than one need can be important at the same time. If a higher-order need is not being met, the desire to satisfy a lower-level need increases.	Hygiene factors must be met if a person is not to be dissatisfied. They will not lead to satisfaction, however. Motivators lead to satisfaction.	People vary in the types of needs they have. Their motivation and how well they perform in a work situation are related to whether they have a need for achievement, power, or affiliation.
What is the theory's impact/ contribution?	The theory enjoys wide recognition among practising managers. Most managers are familiar with it.	The theory is seen as a more valid version of the need hierarchy. It tells us that achievers will be motivated by jobs that offer personal responsibility, feedback, and moderate risks.	The popularity of giving workers greater responsibility for planning and controlling their work can be attributed to his findings (see, for instance, the job characteristics model in Chapter 5). It shows that more than one need may operate at the same time.	The theory tells us that high-need achievers do not necessarily make good managers, since high achievers are more interested in how they do personally.
What empirical support/ criticisms exist?	Research does not generally validate the theory. In particular, there is little support for the hierarchical nature of needs. The theory is criticized for how data were collected and interpreted.	It ignores situational variables.	It is not really a *theory* of motivation: It assumes a link between satisfaction and productivity that was not measured or demonstrated.	It has mixed empirical support, but the theory is consistent with our knowledge of individual differences among people. Good empirical support exists on needs achievement in particular.

Process Theories of Motivation

> What is the life of a CFL assistant coach like? It's definitely not glamorous.[18] Assistant coaches work long hours, they can be fired readily if the team's owner or the head coach thinks they are responsible for the poor play of the team, and they work long hours without pensions or benefits.
>
> Dan Dorazio, the offensive coordinator with the BC Lions, faced a choice after his team beat the Calgary Stampeders: stay in Calgary overnight or drive home to Abbotsford, BC, and arrive just before midnight. Tired after a long day of coaching, he still was not able to rest. He was expected to have the Calgary game tape analyzed before sunrise so the coaches could plan the post-game practice with the players later in the afternoon. Dorazio chose to drive home, and, after a brief nap, go to his office at 4 a.m. Dorazio is not alone in his dedication to his job. Lions receiver coach Jacques Chapdelaine missed his daughter Kaela's graduation from the University of Oregon because he had training camp commitments.
>
> What would make someone show up for work, day after day, under these conditions?

While needs theories identify the different needs that could be used to motivate individuals, process theories focus on the broader picture of how someone can set about motivating another individual. Process theories include expectancy theory, goal-setting theory (and its application, management by objectives), and self-efficacy theory. By focusing greater attention on these process theories, you will understand how you might motivate either yourself or someone else.

3 Are there other ways to motivate people?

Expectancy Theory

Currently, one of the most widely accepted explanations of motivation is Victor Vroom's **expectancy theory**.[19]

From a practical perspective, expectancy theory says that an employee will be motivated to exert a high level of effort when he or she believes the following:

- That the effort will lead to good performance

- That good performance will lead to organizational rewards, such as a bonus, a salary increase, or a promotion

- That the rewards will satisfy his or her personal goals

The theory, therefore, focuses on the three relationships (expectancy, instrumentality, and valence) illustrated in Exhibit 4-6 and described in the following pages. This exhibit

expectancy theory The theory that individuals act depending upon their evaluation of whether their effort will lead to good performance, whether good performance will be followed by a given outcome, and whether that outcome is attractive to them.

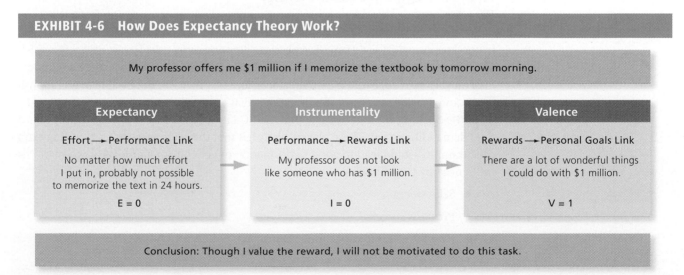

EXHIBIT 4-6   How Does Expectancy Theory Work?

My professor offers me $1 million if I memorize the textbook by tomorrow morning.

Expectancy	Instrumentality	Valence
Effort → Performance Link	Performance → Rewards Link	Rewards → Personal Goals Link
No matter how much effort I put in, probably not possible to memorize the text in 24 hours.	My professor does not look like someone who has $1 million.	There are a lot of wonderful things I could do with $1 million.
E = 0	I = 0	V = 1

Conclusion: Though I value the reward, I will not be motivated to do this task.

Using employee performance software, convenience store retailer 7-Eleven measures the efforts of 2400 store managers and 30 000 employees at company-owned stores in Canada and the United States. The company ties employee compensation to performance outcomes based on 7-Eleven's five fundamental strategic initiatives—product assortment, value, quality, service, and cleanliness—as well as for meeting goals set for new products. The system identifies top performers and rewards them with incentive bonuses.

also provides an example of how you might apply the theory. You might also consider the question asked at the start of this section: Why would offensive line coordinator Dan Dorazio work such long hours for the BC Lions for moderate compensation? Dorazio obviously believes that if he puts effort into coaching, the effort will result in good performance by the team. He must believe that there will be some reward for his efforts, with some of the reward being his compensation, but some of it might be the intrinsic satisfaction of watching the team develop. These rewards then satisfy his personal goals. As he points out "It's really not work. I've never worked a day in my life in football." Dorazio enjoys his work, and that is what keeps him motivated.[20]

Effort-Performance Relationship

expectancy The belief that effort is related to performance.

The effort-performance relationship is commonly called **expectancy**. It refers to the individual's perception of how probable it is that exerting a given amount of effort will lead to good performance. For example, employees are sometimes asked to do things for which they do not have the appropriate skills or training. When that is the case, they will be less motivated to try hard, because they already believe that they will not be able to accomplish the required task. Expectancy can be expressed as a probability, and ranges from 0 to 1.

In the opening vignette, we saw that the BC Lions players were willing to work hard for a demanding coach. These players likely felt that their efforts, such as spending extra time training, would lead to good performance. In general, an employee's expectancy is influenced by the following:

- Self-esteem
- Previous success
- Help from supervisors and subordinates
- Information
- Proper materials and equipment[21]

The *Point/Counterpoint* discussion on page 160 further examines whether failure motivates or demotivates.

Performance-Rewards Relationship

The performance-rewards relationship is commonly called **instrumentality**. It refers to the individual's perception of whether performing at a particular level will lead to the attainment of a desired outcome. In particular, will the performance be acknowledged by those who have the power to allocate rewards? Instrumentality ranges from –1 to +1. A negative instrumentality indicates that high performance reduces the chances of getting the desired outcome. An instrumentality of 0 indicates that there is no relationship between performance and receiving the desired outcome.

> *Are managers manipulating employees when they link rewards to productivity? Is this ethical?*

instrumentality The belief that performance is related to rewards.

In a study by the Angus Reid Group, only 44 percent of employees said that the workplace recognizes employees who excel at their job.[22] Therefore, one possible source of low motivation is employees' belief that no matter how hard they work, the performance won't be recognized. BC Lions offensive coordinator Dan Dorazio works 20-hour days because he feels that his efforts are recognized by the head coach, and by the players on the team.

Rewards–Personal Goals Relationship

The rewards–personal goals relationship is commonly called **valence**. It refers to the degree to which organizational rewards satisfy an individual's personal goals or needs, and the attractiveness of those potential rewards for the individual. Unfortunately, many managers are limited in the rewards they can distribute, which makes it difficult to personalize rewards. Moreover, some managers incorrectly assume that all employees want the same thing. They overlook the motivational effects of differentiating rewards. In either case, employee motivation may be lower because the specific need the employee has is not being met through the reward structure. Valence ranges from –1 (very undesirable reward) to +1 (very desirable reward).

> *Why do some managers do a better job of motivating people than others?*

valence The value or importance an individual places on a reward.

Vancouver-based Radical Entertainment, creator of such digital entertainment as the *Hulk* and *Crash of the Titans*, makes sure the company meets the needs of its employees, because it does not want to lose them to the United States.[23] The company employs a "Radical fun guru" whose job is to make the workplace so much fun no one wants to leave. The company provides free food all day, including catered lunches a few times a week, and there is a log cabin on-site, fitted out with big screens, DVDs, and gaming equipment, where employees can take time out to recharge during their long workdays. Radical Entertainment offers these benefits to meet the needs of its young employees, who find greater motivation from being part of a cool workplace than having a bigger pension plan.

Expectancy Theory in the Workplace

Does expectancy theory work? Although it has its critics,[24] most of the research evidence supports the theory.[25] Research in cross-cultural settings has also indicated support for expectancy theory.[26]

Exhibit 4-7 gives some suggestions for what a manager can do to increase the motivation of employees, using insights from expectancy

Golfers such as Ontario's Alena Sharp illustrate the effectiveness of the expectancy theory of motivation, where rewards are tied to effort and outcome. Players on the LPGA tour are paid strictly according to their performance, unlike members of professional sports teams. Sharp's first LPGA Tour victory came in 2004. As Sharp has put more effort into her play, she has been increasing her earnings each year. In 2007, she earned $223 258, which greatly exceeded her earnings of $97 422 for 2006.

EXHIBIT 4-7   Steps to Increasing Motivation, Using Expectancy Theory

Improving Expectancy	Improving Instrumentality	Improving Valence
Improve the ability of the individual to perform.	Increase the individual's belief that performance will lead to reward.	Make sure that the reward is meaningful to the individual.
• Make sure employees have skills for the task. • Provide training. • Assign reasonable tasks and goals.	• Observe and recognize performance. • Deliver rewards as promised. • Indicate to employees how previous good performance led to greater rewards.	• Ask employees what rewards they value. • Give rewards that are valued.

theory. To appreciate how expectancy theory might apply in the workplace, see this chapter's *Case Incident—Wage Reduction Proposal* on page 165 for an example of what happens when expected rewards are withdrawn. *OB in the Street* demonstrates how expectancy theory works on the golf course.

IN THE STREET

What It's Like to Play Next to Tiger Woods

Are people less motivated if they expect to lose? A recent study by Berkeley professor Jennifer Brown considered whether playing in a tournament with Tiger Woods increased other golfers' performances or decreased them.[27] On the one hand, individuals might be more motivated to try hard when in the presence of a great player. Alternatively, individuals might feel that they were less likely to win, and thus not try as hard.

Brown noted that between 1999 and 2006, players who had to qualify for PGA Tour events averaged 1 to 4 strokes under par. Players who automatically qualified averaged 3 to 6 strokes under par. Woods, by contrast, averaged 10 to 14 strokes under par. In games where Woods played, however, players averaged about a stroke more per tournament.

If money motivated unconditionally, then there should not be any effect on other players if Woods is playing in the tournament. However, if players believe they are less likely to win the top prize, they may be less motivated by the money.

Brown found that the better players tended to play worse than their average when Woods was playing. She also found that when Woods was in his slump period (2003 and 2004), the top competitors' scores were not affected when he played.

Brown's findings suggest that when players are less likely to expect to win, they don't play as well.

Goal-Setting Theory

You have heard the phrase a number of times: "Just do your best. That's all anyone can ask for." But what does "do your best" mean? Do we ever know if we've achieved that vague goal? Might you have done better in your high school English class if your parents had said, "You should strive for 75 percent or higher on all your work in English" instead of "do your best"?

The research on goal setting by Edwin Locke and his colleague, professor Gary Latham at the University of Toronto, shows that intentions to work toward a goal are a major source of work motivation.[28] A **goal** is "what an individual is trying to accomplish; it is

goal What an individual is trying to accomplish.

the object or aim of an action."[29] Goals tell an employee what needs to be done and how much effort will need to be expended.[30]

Goal-setting theory has an impressive base of research support. But as a manager, how do you make it operational? That is often left up to the individual manager or leader. Some managers explicitly set aggressive performance targets—what General Electric called "stretch goals." For example, some CEOs, such as Procter & Gamble's A. G. Laffey and SAP's Hasso Plattner, are known for the demanding performance goals they set. The problem with leaving it up to the individual manager is that, in many cases, managers don't set goals. A recent survey revealed that when asked whether their job had clearly defined goals, only a minority of employees agreed.[31]

A more systematic way to utilize goal setting is with a **management by objectives (MBO)** program.[32] In MBO, managers and employees jointly set performance goals that are tangible, verifiable, and measurable; progress on goals is periodically reviewed, and rewards are allocated on the basis of this progress.

How Does Goal Setting Motivate?

According to Locke, goal setting motivates in four ways (see Exhibit 4-8):[33]

- *Goals direct attention.* Goals indicate where individuals should direct their efforts when they are choosing among things to do. For instance, recognizing that an important assignment is due in a few days, goal setting may encourage you to say no when friends invite you to a movie this evening.

- *Goals regulate effort.* Goals suggest how much effort an individual should put into a given task. For instance, if earning a high mark in accounting is more important to you than earning a high mark in organizational behaviour, you will likely put more effort into studying accounting.

- *Goals increase persistence.* Persistence represents the effort spent on a task over time. When people keep goals in mind, they will work hard on them, even in the face of obstacles.

- *Goals encourage the development of strategies and action plans.* Once goals are set, individuals can develop plans for achieving those goals. For instance, a goal to become more fit may include plans to join a gym, work out with friends, and change eating habits.

In order for goals to be effective, they should be "SMART." SMART stands for

- **S**pecific: Individuals know exactly what is to be achieved.

- **M**easurable: The goals proposed can be tracked and reviewed.

management by objectives (MBO) An approach to goal setting in which specific measurable goals are jointly set by managers and employees; progress on goals is periodically reviewed, and rewards are allocated on the basis of this progress.

EXHIBIT 4-8   Locke's Model of Goal Setting

Source: Adapted from E. A. Locke and G. P. Latham, *A Theory of Goal Setting and Task Performance* (Englewood Cliffs, NJ: Prentice Hall, 1980). Reprinted by permission of Edwin A. Locke.

Hasso Plattner, co-founder of the German software firm SAP, motivates employees by setting stretch goals. Plattner set a shockingly optimistic goal of 15 percent annual growth for SAP's software licence revenues. Employees responded by achieving an even higher growth rate of 18 percent. Plattner set another stretch goal by announcing a bonus plan that would pay $381 million to hundreds of managers and key employees if they could double the company's market capitalization, from a starting point of $57 billion, by the end of 2010. For Plattner, setting stretch goals is a way to inject entrepreneurial energy into the 35-year-old company.

- **Attainable:** The goals, even if difficult, are reasonable and achievable.

- **Results-oriented:** The goals should support the vision of the organization.

- **Time-bound:** The goals are to be achieved within a stated time.

From Concepts to Skills on pages 165–166 presents additional ideas on how to effectively engage in goal setting.

RESEARCH FINDINGS: The Effects of Goal Setting

Locke and his colleagues have spent considerable time studying the effects of goal setting in various situations. The evidence strongly supports the value of goals. More to the point, we can say that

- *Specific goals increase performance, under certain conditions.* In early research, specific goals were linked to better performance.[34] However, more recent research indicates that specific goals can lead to poorer performance in complex tasks. Employees may be too goal-focused on complex tasks, and therefore not consider alternative and better solutions to such tasks.[35]

- *Difficult goals, when accepted, result in higher performance than do easy goals.* Research clearly shows that goal difficulty leads to positive performance.[36] This relationship does not hold when employees view the goals as impossible, rather than just difficult.[37]

- *Feedback leads to higher performance.* Feedback allows individuals to know how they are doing, relative to their goals. Thus, feedback is an important part of goal setting.[38] Feedback encourages individuals to adjust their direction, effort, and action plans if they are falling short of their goals.

- *Goals are equally effective whether participatively set, assigned, or self-set.* Research indicates that how goals are set is not clearly related to performance.[39] Managers may want to consider whether individuals want to participate in goal setting, and whether there is time to do so. Managers should also consider whether individuals need to accept the goals. Employees are more likely to accept goals if they are participatively set.

- *Goal commitment and financial incentives affect whether goals are achieved.* Research suggests that the level of commitment one has to a goal moderates the relationship between goal difficulty and accomplishment.[40] Individuals are more likely to be persistent if they are committed to their goals. Research also indicates that financial incentives can lower commitment to difficult goals. Individuals may fear that they will not achieve difficult goals if these are linked to financial rewards. Financial incentives for difficult goals can also inspire individuals to refuse to help co-workers, or neglect tasks not directly related to goals that will be financially rewarded.[41] For instance, employees may help their own customers, but not help customers who are linked to other co-workers. Quality can also be affected when employees have quantity goals to meet.[42]

One intriguing new approach to looking at how time affects goal setting is the idea that more frequent exposure to challenging goals can "give momentum to new ideas and prevent degradation of skills."[43] While research suggests that frequent exposure to demanding goals can stress people out,[44] some scientists suggest that facing a variety of challenging tasks can lead people to be engrossed and absorbed in what they are doing.[45]

Goal-setting theory is consistent with expectancy theory. The goals can be considered the effort-performance link—in other words, the goals determine what must be done. Feedback can be considered the performance-reward relationship, where the individual's efforts are recognized. Finally, the implication of goal setting is that the achievement of the goals will result in intrinsic satisfaction (and may of course be linked to external rewards).

Self-Efficacy Theory

Self-efficacy (also known as *social cognitive theory* or *social learning theory*) refers to an individual's belief that he or she is capable of performing a task.[46] The higher your self-efficacy, the more confidence you have in your ability to succeed in a task. So, in difficult situations, people with low self-efficacy are more likely to lessen their effort or give up altogether, while those with high self-efficacy will try harder to master the challenge.[47] In addition, individuals high in self-efficacy seem to respond to negative feedback with increased effort and motivation, while those low in self-efficacy are likely to lessen their effort when given negative feedback.[48] How can managers help their employees achieve high levels of self-efficacy? By bringing together goal-setting theory and self-efficacy theory.

Goal-setting theory and self-efficacy theory don't compete with one another; rather, they complement each other. As Exhibit 4-9 on page 144 shows, when a manager sets difficult goals for employees, this leads employees to have a higher level of self-efficacy, and also leads them to set higher goals for their own performance. Why is this the case? Research has shown that setting difficult goals for people communicates confidence. For example, imagine that your boss sets a high goal for you, and you learn it is higher than the goals she has set for your co-workers.

How would you interpret this? As long as you did not feel you were being picked on, you would probably think, "Well, I guess my boss thinks I'm capable of performing better than others." This then sets into motion a psychological process in which you are more confident in yourself (higher self-efficacy) and you set higher personal goals, causing you to perform better both in the workplace and outside it.

EXHIBIT 4-9   Joint Effects of Goals and Self-Efficacy on Performance

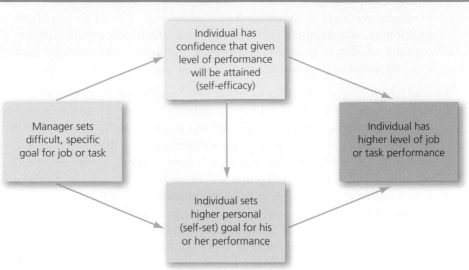

Source: Based on E. A. Locke and G. P. Latham, "Building a Practically Useful Theory of Goal Setting and Task Motivation: A 35-Year Odyssey," *American Psychologist*, September 2002, pp. 705–717.

The researcher who developed self-efficacy theory, Albert Bandura, argues that there are four ways self-efficacy can be increased:[49]

- Enactive mastery

- Vicarious modelling

- Verbal persuasion

- Arousal

According to Bandura, the most important source of increasing self-efficacy is what he calls *enactive mastery*—that is, gaining relevant experience with the task or job. If you have been able to do the job successfully in the past, then you are more confident that you will be able to do it in the future.

The second source is *vicarious modelling*—or becoming more confident because you see someone else doing the task. For example, if your friend loses weight, then it increases your confidence that you can lose weight, too. Vicarious modelling is most effective when you see yourself as similar to the person you are observing. Watching Mike Weir play a difficult golf shot might not increase your confidence in being able to play the shot yourself, but if you watch a golfer with a handicap similar to yours, it's persuasive.

The third source is *verbal persuasion*, which is becoming more confident because someone convinces you that you have the skills necessary to be successful. Motivational speakers use this tactic a lot.

Finally, Bandura argues that *arousal* increases self-efficacy. Arousal leads to an energized state, which drives a person to complete a task. The person gets "psyched up" and performs better. But when arousal is not relevant, then arousal hurts performance. In other words, if the task is something that requires a steady, lower-key perspective (say, carefully editing a manuscript), arousal may in fact hurt performance.

What are the OB implications of self-efficacy theory? Well, it's a matter of applying Bandura's sources of self-efficacy to the work setting. Training programs often make use of enactive mastery by having people practise and build their skills. In fact, one of the reasons training works is because it increases self-efficacy.[50]

The best way for a manager to use verbal persuasion is through the *Pygmalion effect* or the *Galatea effect*. The Pygmalion effect is a form of a self-fulfilling prophecy in which believing something to be true can make it true (also see Chapter 2). In the Pygmalion effect, self-efficacy is increased by communicating to an individual's teacher or supervisor that the person is of high ability. For example, studies were done in which teachers were told their students had very high IQ scores (when in fact they had a range of IQs—some high, some low, and some in between). Consistent with the Pygmalion effect, the teachers spent more time with the students they *thought* were smart, gave them more challenging assignments, and expected more of them—all of which led to higher student self-efficacy and better student grades.[51] This has also been used in the workplace.[52] The Galatea effect occurs when high performance expectations are communicated directly to an employee. For example, sailors who were told, in a convincing manner, that they would not get seasick in fact were much less likely to get seasick.[53]

Note that intelligence and personality are absent from Bandura's list. A lot of research shows that intelligence and personality (especially conscientiousness and emotional stability) can increase self-efficacy.[54] Those individual traits are so strongly related to self-efficacy (people who are intelligent, conscientiousness, and emotionally stable are much more likely to have high self-efficacy than those who score low on these characteristics) that some researchers would argue that self-efficacy does not exist.[55] What this means is that self-efficacy may simply be a by-product in a smart person with a confident personality, and the term *self-efficacy* is superfluous and unnecessary. Although Bandura strongly disagrees with this conclusion, more research on the issue is needed.

Responses to the Reward System

Geroy Simon, a receiver for the BC Lions football team, felt he was in a pretty good position when he negotiated for a contract extension in May 2006.[56] He had the most receptions and most yards of all BC Lions receivers in 2005 and ranked sixth in team history for receptions and touchdowns. But he was not content with just considering how he stood on his team. He also looked to the salary of receivers on other teams, focusing in particular on Edmonton Eskimos receiver Jason Tucker, the CFL's 2005 receiving yards leader.

"I know what I'm worth," said Simon, who knew that Tucker had already signed a contract for close to $200,000 earlier in the year. "I think it'll be a short negotiation once we really get going." Ultimately, Simon signed a four-year extension to his contract with pay similar to Tucker's. He led the league in receiving in 2007 and finished as the second best receiver in 2008. Did the higher salary motivate Simon to be a better player? Did he make the right salary comparison?

To a large extent, motivation theories are about rewards. The theories suggest that individuals have needs and will exert effort in order to have those needs met. The needs theories specifically identify those needs. Goal-setting and expectancy theories portray processes by which individuals act and then receive desirable rewards (intrinsic or extrinsic) for their behaviour.

4 Do equity and fairness matter?

Three additional process theories ask us to consider how individuals respond to rewards. Equity theory suggests that individuals evaluate and interpret rewards. Fair process goes one step further, suggesting that employees are sensitive to a variety of fairness issues in the workplace that extend beyond the reward system but also affect employee motivation. Cognitive evaluation theory examines how individuals respond to the introduction of extrinsic rewards for intrinsically satisfying activities.

Equity Theory

Jane Pearson graduated from university last year with a degree in accounting. After interviews with a number of organizations on campus, she accepted an articling position with one of the nation's largest public accounting firms and was assigned to the company's Edmonton office. Jane was very pleased with the offer she received: challenging work with a prestigious firm, an excellent opportunity to gain valuable experience, and the highest salary any accounting major at her university was offered last year—$5500 a month. But Jane was the top student in her class; she was ambitious and articulate, and fully expected to receive a commensurate salary.

Twelve months have passed since Jane joined her employer. The work has proved to be as challenging and satisfying as she had hoped. Her employer is extremely pleased with her performance; in fact, she recently received a $300-a-month raise. However, Jane's motivational level has dropped dramatically in the past few weeks. Why? Her employer has just hired a new graduate from Jane's university, who lacks the one-year experience Jane has gained, for $5850 a month—$50 more than Jane now makes! It would be an understatement to describe Jane as irate. Jane is even talking about looking for another job.

How important is fairness to you?

Jane's situation illustrates the role that equity plays in motivation. **Equity theory** suggests that individuals compare their job inputs (effort, experience, education, competence, creativity, etc.) and outcomes (salary levels, raises, recognition, challenging assignments, working conditions, etc.) with those of others. We perceive what we get from a job situation (outcomes) in relation to what we put into it (inputs), and then we compare our outcome-input ratio with the outcome-input ratio of relevant others. (This idea is illustrated in Exhibit 4-10.) If we perceive our ratio to be equal to that of the relevant others with whom we compare ourselves, a state of equity is said to exist. We perceive our situation as fair—justice prevails. When we see the ratio as unequal, we experience this as inequity.

For instance, suppose you wrote a case analysis for your marketing professor and spent 18 hours researching and writing it up. Your classmate spent six hours preparing the same analysis. Each of you received a mark of 75 percent. It is likely that you would perceive this as unfair, as you worked considerably harder (that is, exerted more effort) than your classmate. J. Stacy Adams has proposed that those experiencing inequity are motivated to do something to correct it.[57] Thus, you might be inclined to spend considerably less time on your next assignment for your marketing professor.

equity theory Individuals compare their job inputs and outcomes with those of others, and then respond so as to eliminate any inequities.

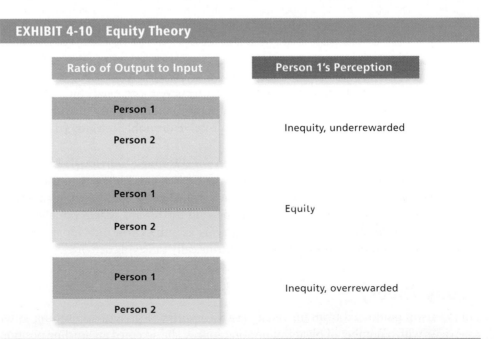

EXHIBIT 4-10　Equity Theory

Ratio of Output to Input	Person 1's Perception
Person 1 / Person 2	Inequity, underrewarded
Person 1 / Person 2	Equity
Person 1 / Person 2	Inequity, overrewarded

To Whom Do We Compare Ourselves?

In the case of the marketing assignment, the obvious referent is your classmate. However, in the workplace, the referent that an employee selects when making comparisons adds to the complexity of equity theory. Recall that Geroy Simon chose a number of people to whom to compare his salary. All were receivers, the same position he played. First he looked at the receivers who played for the same team as he did. Then he considered receivers on other teams, including Jason Tucker, a receiver who played for the Edmonton Eskimos. Evidence indicates that the referent chosen is an important variable in equity theory.[58] There are four referent comparisons that an employee can use:

- *Self-inside.* An employee's experiences in a different position inside his or her current organization.

- *Self-outside.* An employee's experiences in a situation or position outside his or her current organization.

- *Other-inside.* Another individual or group of individuals inside the employee's organization. Simon made this type of comparison when he considered the other Lions receivers' salaries.

- *Other-outside.* Another individual or group of individuals outside the employee's organization. Simon made this type of comparison when he considered the salary of Jason Tucker.

Employees might compare themselves with friends, neighbours, co-workers, colleagues in other organizations, or their own situations in previous jobs. Which referent an employee chooses will be influenced by the information the employee holds about referents, as well as by the attractiveness of the referent. Research has focused on four moderating variables—gender, length of tenure, level in the organization, and amount of education or professionalism.[59]

Gender   Research shows that both men and women often make same-sex comparisons. Research also demonstrates that women are typically paid less than men in comparable jobs and have lower pay expectations than men for the same work. For instance, in 2005 full-time female employees earned, on average, 70.5 cents for every dollar earned by full-time male employees.[60] So a woman who uses another woman as a referent tends to have a lower comparative standard for pay than a woman who uses a man as the referent. If women are to be paid equally to men in comparable jobs, the standard of comparison—as used by both employees and employers—needs to be expanded to include both sexes.

Length of Tenure   Employees with short tenure in their current organizations tend to have little information about others inside the organization, so they rely on their own personal experiences. On the other hand, employees with long tenure rely more heavily on co-workers for comparison.

Level in the Organization and Amount of Education   Upper-level employees, those in the professional ranks, and those with more education tend to be more cosmopolitan and have better information about people in other organizations. Therefore, these types of employees will make more other-outside comparisons.

What Happens When We Feel Treated Inequitably?

Based on equity theory, when employees perceive an inequity, they can be predicted to make one of six choices.[61] We can illustrate these by considering possible responses that BC Lions receiver Geroy Simon can make if he thinks his salary is unfair compared with that of the other receivers in his reference group.

> What can you do if you think your salary is unfair?

- *Change their inputs* (for example, Simon can decide to exert less effort).

- *Change their outcomes* (for example, Simon can work harder than ever to show that he really does deserve higher pay—as he did in the 2006 season, when he won most valuable player).

- *Adjust perceptions of self* (for example, Simon could think to himself, "Maybe I don't really have the same experience as some of the other guys playing receiver").

- *Adjust perceptions of others* (for example, Simon could think, "Jason Tucker of the Eskimos has worked at this job a lot longer, and may deserve greater pay").

- *Choose a different referent* (for example, Simon could consider what other receivers with his same statistics receive).

- *Leave the field* (for example, Simon could start looking at other teams, hoping that he can be picked up by one of them at the end of the season).

One might conclude that Simon felt that his new contract was fair. The Lions won the 2006 Grey Cup, and Simon was named the CFL's most valuable player for the 2006 season.

Bear in mind that being treated equitably is not the same as being treated equally. Equity theory tells us that people who perform better should observe that they are rewarded better than those who do not perform as well. Thus, poor performers should also observe that they are getting smaller rewards than better performers. Paying equally would mean that everyone is paid the same, regardless of performance. Many employees in the nonprofit sector do not feel that they are being paid fairly, compared with people working in other sectors of the economy, as *OB in the Workplace* shows.

IN THE WORKPLACE

Money Matters!

Is intrinsic motivation ever enough? A recent study by the Canadian Policy Research Networks found that employees who work in the nonprofit sector are finding their pay low compared with those in other sectors.[62] Managers in the nonprofit sector (for example, museums, professional associations, food banks, community health clinics, and group homes) make about $8 to $10 less than managers in other fields. The researchers used data collected by Statistics Canada to evaluate wage differences.

The researchers also found that one-third of employees in the nonprofit sector are unhappy with their pay. "One might expect that satisfaction derived from socially valuable or 'morally palatable' work could start to wear thin if juxtaposed against low wages, poor benefits and job insecurity over the longer term," researchers Kathryn McMullen and Grant Schellenberg wrote. The employees are aware that individuals doing similar work in other sectors get paid better.

Unlike for-profit organizations, nonprofit organizations often have very little money to pay their employees. This can cause crises when employees demand better pay. For instance, five group-home workers in Montague, PEI, went on strike for more than eight months to get higher wages and benefits. One employee, Kim MacKenzie, noted that employees were expected to work unpaid overtime so that they could provide round-the-clock care for residents of the home. "Basically we are just determined, we want to take a stand," said Ms MacKenzie. "This may be the profession we have chosen, it's what we want to do. But this does not mean we should work 54 hours a week and only get paid for 44." MacKenzie's complaint underscores that not all employees are expected to work such long hours without pay.

The plight of workers in the nonprofit sector tells us that employees do compare what others around them are making to determine whether they are paid fairly. ▬▬

RESEARCH FINDINGS: Inequitable Pay

Equity theory establishes the following propositions relating to inequitable pay:

- *When paid by time worked, overrewarded employees will produce more than will equitably paid employees.* Hourly and salaried employees will generate high quantity or quality of production in order to increase the input side of the ratio and bring about equity.

- *When paid by number of units produced, overrewarded employees will produce fewer, but higher-quality, units than will equitably paid employees.* Individuals paid on a piece-rate basis will increase their effort to achieve equity, which can result in greater quality or quantity. However, increases in quantity will only increase inequity, since every unit produced results in further overpayment. Therefore, effort is directed toward increasing quality rather than increasing quantity.

- *When paid by time worked, underrewarded employees will produce less or poorer-quality output.* Effort will be decreased, which will bring about lower productivity or poorer-quality output than that of equitably paid subjects.

- *When paid by number of units produced, underrewarded employees will produce a large number of low-quality units in comparison with equitably paid employees.* Employees paid on a piece-rate basis can bring about equity because trading off quality of output for quantity will result in an increase in rewards, with little or no increase in contributions.

These propositions have generally been supported, with a few minor qualifications.[63] First, those who are overrewarded do not seem to change their behaviour. Apparently, people have a great deal more tolerance of overpayment inequities than of underpayment inequities, or are better able to rationalize them. Second, not all people are equity sensitive.[64] For example, some individuals simply do not worry about how their rewards compare with those of others. Predictions from equity theory are unlikely to be accurate with these individuals.

These propositions also suggest that when organizations reward only senior managers after a year of increased profitability and performance, lower-level employees receive a powerful message. They learn that only shareholders and senior management matter. This can lead to employees withholding effort and initiative.

It is important to note that while most research on equity theory has focused on pay, employees also look for equity in the distribution of other organizational rewards. For instance, it's been shown that the use of high-status job titles, as well as large and lavishly furnished offices, may function as desirable outcomes for some employees in their equity equation.[65]

In conclusion, equity theory demonstrates that, for most employees, motivation is influenced significantly by relative

After the 2005 season ended for the BC Lions, Geroy Simon's contract was up for renewal. He wanted a similar salary to Edmonton Eskimo's receiver Jason Tucker, based on his performance during the year. Simon's salary was increased and he led the league in receiving in 2007 and finished as the second best receiver in 2008.

rewards, as well as by absolute rewards. However, some key issues are still unclear.[66] For instance, how do employees handle conflicting equity signals, such as when unions point to other employee groups who are substantially better off, while management argues how much things have improved? How do employees define inputs and outcomes? How do they combine and weigh their inputs and outcomes to arrive at totals? When and how do the factors change over time? Regardless of these problems, equity theory continues to offer some important insights into employee motivation.

Fair Process and Treatment

Recent research has been directed at redefining what is meant by equity, or fairness.[67] Historically, equity theory focused on **distributive justice**, or the perceived fairness of the *amount* and *allocation* of rewards among individuals. But, increasingly, equity is thought of from the standpoint of **organizational justice**, which we define as an overall perception of what is fair in the workplace. In other words, under organizational justice, fairness or equity can be subjective, and it resides in the perception of the person. Thus, people also care about **procedural justice**—the perceived fairness of the *process* used to determine the distribution of rewards. (This includes having a voice in a decision and feeling that the outcome is adequately explained.) They care, too, about **interactional justice**—the quality of the interpersonal treatment received from a manager. (Being treated with dignity, concern, and respect are examples.) Exhibit 4-11 shows a model of organizational justice.

Why does how an employee is treated matter? When people are treated in an unjust manner (at least in their own eyes), they respond by retaliating (for example, badmouthing a supervisor).[68] Because interactional justice or injustice is intimately tied to the person who communicates the information (usually one's supervisor),

distributive justice The perceived fairness of the amount and allocation of rewards among individuals.

organizational justice An overall perception of what is fair in the workplace, composed of distributive, procedural, and interactional justice.

procedural justice The perceived fairness of the process used to determine the distribution of rewards.

interactional justice The quality of the interpersonal treatment received from a manager.

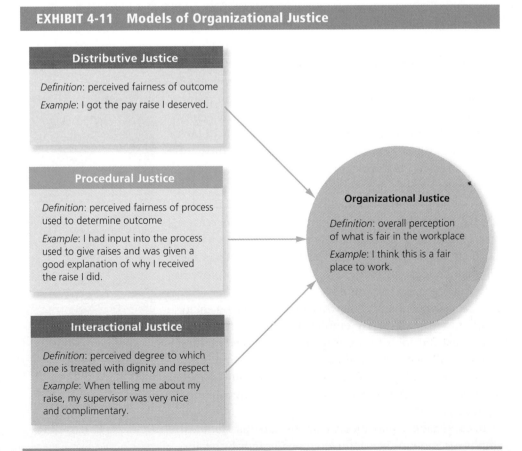

EXHIBIT 4-11   Models of Organizational Justice

Distributive Justice

Definition: perceived fairness of outcome

Example: I got the pay raise I deserved.

Procedural Justice

Definition: perceived fairness of process used to determine outcome

Example: I had input into the process used to give raises and was given a good explanation of why I received the raise I did.

Interactional Justice

Definition: perceived degree to which one is treated with dignity and respect

Example: When telling me about my raise, my supervisor was very nice and complimentary.

Organizational Justice

Definition: overall perception of what is fair in the workplace

Example: I think this is a fair place to work.

whereas procedural injustice often results from impersonal policies, we would expect perceptions of injustice to be more closely related to one's supervisor. Generally, that is what the evidence suggests.[69]

Of these three forms of justice, distributive justice is most strongly related to satisfaction with outcomes (for example, satisfaction with pay) and organizational commitment. Procedural justice relates most strongly to job satisfaction, employee trust, withdrawal from the organization, job performance, and organizational citizenship behaviour. There is less evidence on how interactional justice affects employee behaviour.[70]

Managers can take several steps to foster employees' perceptions of fairness. First, they should realize that employees are especially sensitive to unfairness in procedures when bad news has to be communicated (that is, when distributive justice is low). Thus, when managers have bad news to communicate, it's especially important to openly share information about how allocation decisions are made, follow consistent and unbiased procedures, and engage in similar practices to increase the perception of procedural justice. Second, when addressing perceived injustices, managers need to focus their actions on the source of the problem. Professor Daniel Skarlicki of the Sauder School of Business at the University of British Columbia has found that it is when unfavourable outcomes are combined with unfair procedures or poor interpersonal treatment that resentment and retaliation (for example, theft, badmouthing, sabotage) are most likely.[71] *Case Incident—Bullying Bosses* on page 164 describes what could happen to the motivation and behaviour of employees who have bullies for bosses.

Cognitive Evaluation Theory

Several researchers suggest that the introduction of extrinsic rewards, such as pay, for work effort that was *previously rewarding intrinsically* (that is, that was personally satisfying) will tend to decrease the overall level of a person's motivation.[72] This proposal—which has come to be called **cognitive evaluation theory**—has been extensively researched, and a large number of studies have been supportive of it.[73] Additionally, Alfie Kohn, often cited for his work on rewards, argues that people are actually punished by rewards, and do inferior work when they are enticed by money, grades, or other incentives. His extensive review of incentive studies concluded that "rewards usually improve performance only at extremely simple—indeed, mindless—tasks, and even then they improve only quantitative performance."[74]

> **cognitive evaluation theory** Offering extrinsic rewards (for example, pay) for work effort that was previously rewarding intrinsically will tend to decrease the overall level of a person's motivation.

Extrinsic vs. Intrinsic Rewards

Historically, motivation theorists have generally assumed that intrinsic motivators are independent of extrinsic motivators. That is, the stimulation of one would not affect the other. But cognitive evaluation theory suggests otherwise. It argues that when extrinsic rewards are used by organizations as payoffs for superior performance, the intrinsic rewards, which are derived from individuals doing what they like, are reduced.

In other words, when extrinsic rewards are given to someone for performing an interesting task, it causes intrinsic interest in the task itself to decline. For instance, although a taxi driver expects to be paid for taking your best friend to the airport, you do not expect your friend to pay you if you volunteer to drive her to the airport. In fact, the offer of pay might diminish your pleasure in doing a favour for your friend.

Why would such an outcome occur? The popular explanation is that the individual experiences a loss of control over his or her own behaviour when it is being rewarded by external sources. This causes the previous intrinsic motivation to diminish. Extrinsic rewards can produce a shift—from an internal to an external explanation—in an individual's perception of why he or she works on a task. If you are reading a novel a week because your contemporary literature instructor requires you to, you can attribute your reading behaviour to an external source. If you stop reading novels the moment the course ends, this is more evidence that your behaviour was due to an external source. However, if you find yourself continuing to read a novel a week when the course ends, your natural inclination is to say, "I must enjoy reading novels, because I'm still reading one a week!"

If cognitive evaluation theory is valid, it should have major implications for managerial practices. Compensation specialists argue that motivation comes from extrinsic rewards tied to performance. But cognitive evaluation theorists suggest that introducing extrinsic rewards will tend to decrease the internal satisfaction that the individual receives from doing the job. So, if cognitive evaluation theory is correct, it would make sense to make an individual's pay *noncontingent* on performance in order to avoid decreasing intrinsic motivation. Instead, simply pay fairly, and then allow the individual's intrinsic motivation to guide performance.

RESEARCH FINDINGS: Cognitive Evaluation Theory

We noted earlier that cognitive evaluation theory has been supported in a number of studies. Yet it has also been met with attacks, specifically on the methodology used in these studies[75] and in the interpretation of the findings.[76] But where does this theory stand today? Can we say that when organizations use extrinsic motivators such as pay and promotions and verbal rewards to stimulate employees' performance, they do so at the expense of reducing intrinsic interest and motivation in the work being done? The answer is not a simple "yes" or "no."

Extrinsic rewards that are verbal (for example, receiving praise from a supervisor or co-worker) or tangible (for example, money) can actually have different effects on individuals' intrinsic motivation. That is, verbal rewards increase intrinsic motivation, whereas tangible rewards undermine it. When people are told they will receive a tangible reward, they come to count on it and focus more on the reward than on the task.[77] Verbal rewards, however, seem to keep people focused on the task and encourage them to do it better.

self-concordance The degree to which a person's reasons for pursuing a goal is consistent with the person's interests and core values.

A recent outgrowth of cognitive evaluation research is **self-concordance**, which considers the degree to which people's reasons for pursuing goals are consistent with their interests and core values.[78] For example, if individuals pursue goals because of an intrinsic interest, they are more likely to attain their goals, and are happy even if they do not attain them. Why? Because the process of striving toward them is fun. In contrast, people who pursue goals for extrinsic reasons (money, status, or other benefits) are less likely to attain their goals, and are less happy even when they do achieve them. Why? Because the goals are less meaningful to them. OB research suggests that people who pursue work goals for intrinsic reasons are more satisfied with their jobs, feel like they fit into their organizations better, and may perform better.[79]

Of course, organizations cannot simply ignore financial rewards. When people feel they are being treated unfairly in the workplace, pay often becomes a focal point of their concerns. If tasks are dull or unpleasant, extrinsic rewards will probably increase intrinsic motivation.[80] Even when a job is inherently interesting, there still exists a powerful norm for extrinsic payment.[81] But creating fun, challenging, and empowered workplaces may do more for motivation and performance than focusing simply on the compensation system.

Increasing Intrinsic Motivation

Our discussion of motivation theories and our discussion of how to apply motivation theories in the workplace has focused mainly on improving extrinsic motivation. Professor Kenneth Thomas of the Naval Postgraduate School in Monterey, California, developed a model of intrinsic motivation that draws from the job characteristics model (see Chapter 5) and cognitive evaluation theory.[82] He identified four key rewards that increase an individual's intrinsic motivation:

- *Sense of choice.* The opportunity to select what one will do and perform the way one thinks best. Individuals can use their own judgment to carry out the task.

- *Sense of competence.* The feeling of accomplishment for doing a good job. Individuals are more likely to feel a sense of accomplishment when they carry out challenging tasks.

- *Sense of meaningfulness.* The opportunity to pursue worthwhile tasks. Individuals feel good about what they are doing and believe that what they are doing matters.

- *Sense of progress.* The feeling of accomplishment that one is making progress on a task, and that it is moving forward. Individuals feel that they are spending their time wisely in doing their jobs.

Thomas also identified four sets of behaviours managers can use to build intrinsic rewards for their employees:

- *Leading for choice.* Empowering employees and delegating tasks.

- *Leading for competence.* Supporting and coaching employees.

- *Leading for meaningfulness.* Inspiring employees and modelling desired behaviours.

- *Leading for progress.* Monitoring and rewarding employees.

Exhibit 4-12 describes what managers can do to increase the likelihood that the intrinsic rewards are motivational.

EXHIBIT 4-12   Building Blocks for Intrinsic Rewards

Leading for Choice	Leading for Competence
• Delegated authority	• Knowledge
• Trust in workers	• Positive feedback
• Security (no punishment) for honest mistakes	• Skill recognition
• A clear purpose	• Challenge
• Information	• High, noncomparative standards

Leading for Meaningfulness	Leading for Progress
• A noncynical climate	• A collaborative climate
• Clearly identified passions	• Milestones
• An exciting vision	• Celebrations
• Relevant task purposes	• Access to customers
• Whole tasks	• Measurement of improvement

Source: Reprinted with permission of the publisher. From *Intrinsic Motivation at Work: Building Energy and Commitment.* Copyright © K. Thomas. Berrett-Koehler Publishers Inc., San Francisco, CA. All rights reserved. www.bkconnection.com.

Motivating Employees through Reinforcement

> BC Lions coach Wally Buono does not want his team making costly mistakes on game day and losing yards in penalties.[83] The coach started the 2005 season by illustrating to the players that many of their touchdowns and big plays from the previous year were wiped out by penalties. Then he introduced reinforcement for not making mistakes. If a player receives a penalty during a game, the entire team has to do sprints across the field the next day, for four times as many yards as the penalty received. The players call these runs "gassers," and they don't like doing them.
>
> The players say that Buono's punishment for penalties has paid off: "Guys are making a more conscious decision not to take a stupid penalty," says linebacker Barrin Simpson.
>
> The gassers improved player performance at the start of the season. The team saw a 42 percent drop in penalties in the first nine games of 2005, compared with the first nine games in 2004. Then the team started having morale problems and confusion over who was the team's quarterback. An 11-0 start to the season collapsed into a 12-6 finish. But, the team won the 2006 Grey Cup and had its best regular season in club history in 2007. So how does reinforcement work, and does it motivate?

5 What role does reinforcement play in motivation?

operant conditioning A type of conditioning in which desired voluntary behaviour leads to a reward or prevents a punishment.

The motivation theories we have covered to this point emphasize how people's needs and thought processes can be used to motivate them. As a behaviourist, B. F. Skinner found it "pointless to explain behaviour in terms of unobservable inner states such as needs, drives, attitudes, or thought processes."[84]

Skinner's view of motivation is much simpler. He suggested that people learn how to behave to get something they want or to avoid something they don't want.[85] This idea is known as **operant conditioning**, which means behaviour is influenced by the reinforcement or lack of reinforcement brought about by the consequences of the behaviour. The BC Lions players, for instance, want to avoid doing "gassers," so they avoid getting penalties on game day.

Skinner argued that creating pleasing consequences to follow specific forms of behaviour would increase the frequency of that behaviour. People will most likely engage in desired behaviours if they are positively reinforced for doing so. Rewards are most effective if they immediately follow the desired behaviour. In addition, behaviour that is not rewarded, or is punished, is less likely to be repeated.

You see illustrations of operant conditioning everywhere. For example, any situation where reinforcements are contingent on some action on your part involves the use of operant conditioning. Your instructor says that if you want a high grade in the course, you must supply correct answers on the test. A commissioned salesperson who wants to earn a high income must generate high sales in her territory. Of course, the linkage can also work to teach the individual to engage in behaviours that work against the best interests of the organization. Assume that your boss tells you that if you will work overtime during the next three-week busy season, you will be compensated for it at the next performance appraisal. However, when performance appraisal time comes, you find that you are given no positive reinforcement for your overtime work. The next time your manager asks you to work overtime, you will probably decline! Your behaviour can be explained by operant conditioning: If a behaviour fails to be positively reinforced, the probability that the behaviour will be repeated declines.

Methods of Shaping Behaviour

There are four ways in which to shape behaviour: through positive reinforcement, negative reinforcement, punishment, and extinction.

Following a response with something pleasant is called *positive reinforcement*. Following a response by the termination or withdrawal of something unpleasant is called *negative reinforcement*. *Punishment* is causing an unpleasant condition in an attempt to eliminate

EXHIBIT 4-13 Types of Reinforcement	
Reinforcement Type	**Example**
Positive reinforcement	A manager praises an employee for a job well done.
Negative reinforcement	An instructor asks a question and a student looks through her lecture notes to avoid being called on. She has learned that looking busily through her notes prevents the instructor from calling on her.
Punishment	A manager gives an employee a two-day suspension from work without pay for showing up drunk.
Extinction	An instructor ignores students who raise their hands to ask questions. Hand-raising becomes extinct.

an undesirable behaviour. Eliminating any reinforcement that is maintaining a behaviour is called *extinction*. Exhibit 4-13 gives examples of each type of reinforcement. Negative reinforcement should not be confused with punishment: Negative reinforcement strengthens a behaviour because it takes away an unpleasant situation.

Schedules of Reinforcement

While consequences have an effect on behaviour, the timing of those consequences or reinforcements is also important. The two major types of reinforcement schedules are *continuous* and *intermittent*. A **continuous reinforcement** schedule reinforces the desired behaviour each and every time it is demonstrated. Take, for example, the case of someone who has historically had trouble arriving at work on time. Every time he is not tardy, his manager might compliment him on his desirable behaviour. In an intermittent schedule, on the other hand, not every instance of the desirable behaviour is reinforced, but reinforcement is given often enough to make the behaviour worth repeating. Evidence indicates that the intermittent, or varied, form of reinforcement tends to promote more resistance to extinction than does the continuous form.[86]

An **intermittent reinforcement** schedule can be of a ratio or interval type. Ratio schedules depend on how many responses the subject makes. The individual is reinforced after giving a certain number of specific types of behaviour. Interval schedules depend on how much time has passed since the previous reinforcement. With interval schedules, the individual is reinforced on the first appropriate behaviour after a particular time has elapsed. A reinforcement can also be classified as fixed or variable. When these factors are combined, four types of intermittent schedules of reinforcement result: **fixed-interval schedule**, **variable-interval schedule**, **fixed-ratio schedule**, and **variable-ratio schedule**.

Exhibit 4-14 on page 156 summarizes the five schedules of reinforcement and their effects on behaviour.

Reinforcement in the Workplace

Managers want employees to behave in ways that most benefit the organization. Therefore, they look for ways to reinforce positive behaviour and extinguish negative behaviour. Consider the situation in which an employee's behaviour is significantly different from that sought by management. If management rewarded the individual only when he or she showed desirable responses, there might be very little reinforcement taking place. Instead, managers can reinforce each successive step that moves the individual closer to the desired response. If an employee who usually turns in his work two days late succeeds in turning in his work only one day late, managers can reinforce that improvement. Reinforcement would increase as responses more closely approximated the desired behaviour.

continuous reinforcement A desired behaviour is reinforced each and every time it is demonstrated.

intermittent reinforcement A desired behaviour is reinforced often enough to make the behaviour worth repeating, but not every time it is demonstrated.

fixed-interval schedule The reward is given at fixed time intervals.

variable-interval schedule The reward is given at variable time intervals.

fixed-ratio schedule The reward is given at fixed amounts of output.

variable-ratio schedule The reward is given at variable amounts of output.

EXHIBIT 4-14	Schedules of Reinforcement		
Reinforcement Schedule	**Nature of Reinforcement**	**Effect on Behaviour**	**Example**
Continuous	Reward given after each desired behaviour	Fast learning of new behaviour but rapid extinction	Compliments
Fixed-interval	Reward given at fixed time intervals	Average and irregular performance with rapid extinction	Weekly paycheques
Variable-interval	Reward given at variable time intervals	Moderately high and stable performance with slow extinction	Pop quizzes
Fixed-ratio	Reward given at fixed amounts of output	High and stable performance attained quickly but also with rapid extinction	Piece-rate pay
Variable-ratio	Reward given at variable amounts of output	Very high performance with slow extinction	Commissioned sales

While variable-ratio and variable-interval reinforcement schedules produce the best results for improving behaviour, most work organizations rely on fixed-interval (weekly or monthly) pay or fixed-ratio (piece-rate) pay. In the next chapter, we will discuss the idea of variable pay, as well as reactions to it. We will also look at how rewards in general are used in the workplace.

Motivation for Whom?

6 What are the ethics behind motivation theories?

A current debate among organizational behaviour scholars is, Who benefits from the theories of motivation?[87] Some argue that motivation theories are only intended to help managers get more productivity out of employees, and are little concerned with employees beyond improvements in productivity. Thus, needs theories, process theories, and theories concerned with fairness could be interpreted not as ways to help employees get what they want or need, but rather as means to help managers get what they want from employees. In his review of "meaningful work" literature, professor Christopher Michaelson of the Wharton School at the University of Pennsylvania finds that researchers propose that organizations have a moral obligation to provide employees with "free choice to enter, honest communication, fair and respectful treatment, intellectual challenge, considerable independence to determine work methods, democratic participation in decision making, moral development, due process and justice, nonpaternalism, and fair compensation."[88]

Michaelson suggests that scholars concerned with meaningful work should focus on the conditions of the workplace and improving those conditions. He also suggests that researchers have a moral obligation to make workplaces better for employees. While productivity may be a by-product of better work conditions, the important thing is for employers to treat employees well, and to consider the needs of employees as an end in itself. By contrast, he argues, mainstream motivation theory does not consider the moral obligation of employers to their employees, but it does consider ways to ensure employees are more productive.

While this debate is not easily resolved, and may well guide the elaboration of motivation theories in years to come, it does inspire a provocative analysis of why employers provide the workplace conditions they do. To further provoke your thoughts on this matter, the *Ethical Dilemma Exercise* on page 163 asks you to consider whether motivation is just manipulation.

Putting It All Together

While it's always dangerous to synthesize a large number of complex ideas into a few simple guidelines, the following suggestions summarize the essence of what we know about motivating employees in organizations:

- *Recognize individual differences.* Employees have different needs and should not be treated alike. Managers should spend the time necessary to understand what is important to each employee and then align goals, level of involvement, and rewards with individual needs.

- *Use goals and feedback.* Employees should have challenging, specific goals, as well as feedback on how well they are doing in pursuit of those goals.

- *Allow employees to participate in decisions that affect them.* Employees can contribute to a number of decisions that affect them: setting work goals, choosing their own benefits packages, solving productivity and quality problems, and the like. This can increase employee productivity, commitment to work goals, motivation, and job satisfaction.

- *When giving rewards, be sure that they reward desired performance.* Rewards should be linked to the type of performance expected. It is important that employees perceive a clear linkage. How closely rewards are actually correlated to performance criteria is less important than the perception of this relationship. If individuals perceive this relationship to be low, the results will be low performance, a decrease in job satisfaction, and an increase in turnover and absenteeism.

- *Check the system for equity.* Employees should be able to perceive rewards as equating with the inputs they bring to the job. At a simplistic level, this means that experience, skills, abilities, effort, and other obvious inputs should explain differences in performance and, hence, pay, job assignments, and other obvious rewards.

Summary and Implications

1 **What is motivation?** *Motivation* is the process that accounts for an individual's intensity, direction, and persistence of effort toward reaching a goal. *Intensity* is concerned with how hard a person tries. This is the element most of us focus on when we talk about motivation. However, high intensity is unlikely to lead to good job performance unless the effort is channelled in a useful *direction*. Finally, the effort requires *persistence*.

2 **How do needs motivate people?** All needs theories of motivation, including Maslow's hierarchy of needs, Alderfer's ERG theory, Herzberg's motivation-hygiene theory (sometimes called the two-factor theory), and McClelland's theory of needs, propose a similar idea: Individuals have needs that, when unsatisfied, will result in motivation. Needs theories suggest that motivation will be high to the degree that the rewards individuals receive for high performance satisfy their dominant needs.

3 **Are there other ways to motivate people?** Process theories focus on the broader picture of how someone can set about motivating another individual. Process theories include expectancy theory, goal-setting theory (and its application, management by objectives), and self-efficacy theory. Expectancy theory says that an employee will be motivated to exert a high level of effort when he or she believes (1) that effort will lead to good performance; (2) that good performance will lead to organizational rewards, such as a bonus, a salary increase, or a promotion; and (3) that the rewards will satisfy his or her personal goals. Goal-setting theory suggests that intentions to work toward a goal are a major source of work motivation. That is, goals tell an employee what needs to be done and how much effort will need to be expended. Specific goals increase performance; difficult goals, when accepted, result in higher performance than do easy goals; and feedback leads to higher performance than does nonfeedback. Achieving goals can be affected by one's self-efficacy, which refers to an individual's belief that he or she is capable of performing a task. The higher one's self-efficacy, the more confidence a person has about succeeding in a task.

4 **Do equity and fairness matter?** Individuals look for fairness in the reward system. Rewards should be perceived by employees as related to the inputs they bring to the job. Simply stated, employees expect that experience, skills, abilities, effort, and other job inputs should explain differences in performance and, hence, pay, job assignments, and other obvious rewards.

5 **What role does reinforcement play in motivation?** B. F. Skinner suggested that behaviour is influenced by whether or not it is reinforced. Managers might consider how their actions toward employees reinforce (or do not reinforce) employee behaviour. For example, when an employee goes above and beyond the call of duty, but that action is not recognized (or reinforced), that employee may be reluctant to exert great effort at a later time. Skinner also noted that schedules of reinforcement affect behaviour. For instance, individuals are less likely to perform well when their behaviour is continuously reinforced than when it is randomly reinforced.

6 **What are the ethics behind motivation theories?** A current debate among OB scholars is about who benefits from the theories of motivation. Some argue that motivation theories are only intended to help managers get more productivity out of employees, and are little concerned with employees beyond improvements in productivity. The theories can thus be interpreted as a means to help managers get what they want from employees. Although this debate is certainly controversial, motivation theories can also be applied in nonwork settings, and can just as easily help individuals figure out how to motivate themselves.

For Review

1. Define *motivation*. What are the key elements of motivation?

2. What are the implications of Theories X and Y for motivation practices?

3. Does motivation come from within a person, or is it a result of the situation? Explain.

4. Compare and contrast Maslow's hierarchy theory of needs with Herzberg's motivation-hygiene (two-factor) theory.

5. Explain the difference between hygiene factors and motivators in Herzberg's motivation-hygiene (two-factor) theory.

6. Identify the variables in expectancy theory.

7. What is the role of self-efficacy in goal setting?

8. Contrast distributive and procedural justice. What implications might they have for designing pay systems in different countries?

9. Explain cognitive evaluation theory. What does it assume about the effects of intrinsic and extrinsic rewards on behaviour?

10. Describe the four types of intermittent reinforcers.

For Critical Thinking

1. Identify three activities you really enjoy (for example, playing tennis, reading a novel, going shopping). Next, identify three activities you really dislike (for example, visiting the dentist, cleaning the house, following a low-fat diet). Using the expectancy model, analyze each of your answers to assess why some activities stimulate your effort while others don't.

2. Expectancy theory argues that for people to be motivated, they have to value the rewards that they will receive for their effort. This suggests the need for recognizing individual differences. Does this view contradict the principles of equity theory? Discuss.

3. To what extent will you be motivated to study under the following circumstances:

   a. The instructor gives only one test—a final examination at the end of the course.

   b. The instructor gives four exams during the term, all of which are announced on the first day of class.

   c. The student's grade is based on the results of numerous exams, none of which are announced by the instructor ahead of time.

4. "The cognitive evaluation theory is contradictory to reinforcement and expectancy theories." Do you agree or disagree? Explain.

5. Analyze the application of Maslow's and Herzberg's theories to an African or Caribbean nation where more than a quarter of the population is unemployed.

for You

- Don't think of motivation as something that should be done for you. Think about motivating others and yourself as well. How can you motivate yourself? After finishing a particularly long and dry chapter in a text, you could take a snack break. Or you might buy yourself a new CD once that major accounting assignment is finished.

- Be aware of the kinds of things that motivate you, so you can choose jobs and activities that suit you best.

- When working in a group, keep in mind that you and the other members can think of ways to make sure everyone feels motivated throughout the project.

Failure Motivates

It's sad but true that many of the best lessons we learn in life are from our failures. Often when we are riding on the wings of success, we coast—until we crash to earth. Take the example of Dan Doctoroff. Doctoroff is a successful New York investment banker who spent five years obsessed with bringing the 2012 Olympics to New York. In his efforts, he used $4 million of his own money, travelled half a million miles, worked 100-hour weeks, and staked his reputation on achieving a goal many thought was foolhardy.

What happened? New York was not selected, and all Doctoroff's efforts were in vain. His immediate reaction? He felt "emotionally paralyzed." But Doctoroff is not sorry he made the effort. He said he learned a lot about himself in trying to woo Olympic decision makers in 78 countries. Colleagues had once described him as brash and arrogant. As a result of his efforts, Doctoroff said, he learned to listen more and talk less. He also said that losing made him realize how supportive his wife and three teenage children could be.

Not only does failure bring perspective to people such as Doctoroff, it often provides important feedback on how to improve. The important thing is to learn from the failure and to persist. As Doctoroff says, "The only way to ensure you'll lose is not to try." One of the reasons successful people fail so often is that they set their own bars so high. Harvard's Rosabeth Moss Kanter, who has spent her career studying executives, says, "Many successful people set the bar so high that they don't achieve the distant goal. But they do achieve things that wouldn't have been possible without that bigger goal."[89]

Failure Demotivates

Do people learn from failure? We have seen people who persist in a failed venture just because they think persistence is a virtue or because their ego is involved, even when logic suggests they should move on. One research study found that managers often illogically persist in launching new products, even when the evidence becomes clear that the product is going nowhere. As the authors note, "It sometimes takes more courage to kill a product that's going nowhere than to sustain it." So the thought of learning from failure is a nice ideal, but most people are too defensive to do that.

Moreover, there is ample evidence that when people fail they often rationalize their failures to preserve their self-esteem, and thus don't learn at all. Although the example of Dan Doctoroff is interesting, it's not clear he has done anything but rationalize his failure. It's human nature. Research shows that when we fail, we often engage in external attributions—blaming the failure on bad luck or powerful others—or we devalue what we failed to get ("It wasn't that important to me anyway," we may tell ourselves). These rationalizations may not be correct, but that is not the point. We engage in them not to be right but to preserve our often fragile self-esteem. We need to believe in ourselves to motivate ourselves, and because failing undermines that self-belief, we have to do what we can to recover our self-confidence.[90]

In sum, although it is a nice story that failure is actually good, as one songwriter wrote, "The world is not a song." Failure hurts, and to either protect ourselves or recover from the pain, we often do not learn from failure—we rationalize it away.

LEARNING ABOUT **YOURSELF** EXERCISE

What Motivates You?

Circle the number that most closely agrees with how you feel. Consider your answers in the context of your current job or a past work experience.[91]

		Strongly Disagree				Strongly Agree
1.	I try very hard to improve on my past performance at work.	1	2	(3)	4	5
2.	I enjoy competition and winning.	1	2	(3)	4	5
3.	I often find myself talking to those around me about nonwork matters.	1	2	3	(4)	5
4.	I enjoy a difficult challenge.	1	2	3	(4)	5
5.	I enjoy being in charge.	1	2	3	(4)	5
6.	I want to be liked by others.	1	2	3	(4)	5
7.	I want to know how I am progressing as I complete tasks.	1	2	3	(4)	5
8.	I confront people who do things I disagree with.	1	2	(3)	4	5
9.	I tend to build close relationships with co-workers.	1	2	3	(4)	5
10.	I enjoy setting and achieving realistic goals.	1	2	3	(4)	5
11.	I enjoy influencing other people to get my way.	1	2	3	(4)	5
12.	I enjoy belonging to groups and organizations.	1	2	3	(4)	5
13.	I enjoy the satisfaction of completing a difficult task.	1	2	3	(4)	5
14.	I often work to gain more control over the events around me.	1	2	3	(4)	5
15.	I enjoy working with others more than working alone.	1	2	3	(4)	5

Scoring Key:

To determine your dominant needs—and what motivates you—place the number 1 through 5 that represents your score for each statement next to the number for that statement.

Achievement	Power	Affiliation
1. _3_	**2.** _3_	**3.** _4_
4. _4_	**5.** _4_	**6.** _4_
7. _4_	**8.** _3_	**9.** _4_
10. _4_	**11.** _4_	**12.** _4_
13. _4_	**14.** _4_	**15.** _4_
Totals: _19_	_18_	_20_

Add up the total of each column. The sum of the numbers in each column will be between 5 and 25 points. The column with the highest score tells you your dominant need.

More Learning About Yourself Exercises

Additional self-assessments relevant to this chapter appear on MyOBLab
(**www.pearsoned.ca/myoblab**).

I.C.5 What Are My Course Performance Goals?
IV.A.3 How Confident Am I in My Abilities to Succeed?
II.B.5 How Good Am I at Disciplining Others?

When you complete the additional assessments, consider the following:

1. Am I surprised about my score?
2. Would my friends evaluate me similarly?

BREAKOUT **GROUP** EXERCISES

Form small groups to discuss the following topics, as assigned by your instructor:

1. One of the members of your team continually arrives late for meetings and does not turn drafts of assignments in on time. Choose one of the available theories and indicate how the theory explains the member's current behaviour and how the theory could be used to motivate the group member to perform more responsibly.

2. You are unhappy with the performance of one of your instructors and would like to encourage the instructor to present more lively classes. Choose one of the available theories and indicate how the theory explains the instructor's current behaviour. How could you as a student use the theory to motivate the instructor to present more lively classes?

3. Harvard University recently changed its grading policy to recommend to instructors that the average course mark should be a B. This was the result of a study showing that more than 50 percent of students were receiving an A or A– for coursework. Harvard students are often referred to as "the best and the brightest," and they pay $27 000 (US) for their education, so they expect high grades. Discuss the impact of this change in policy on the motivation of Harvard students to study harder.

WORKING WITH **OTHERS** EXERCISE

Positive Reinforcement vs. Punishment

This 10-step exercise takes approximately 20 minutes.[92]

**Exercise Overview
(Steps 1–4)**

1. Two volunteers are selected to receive reinforcement or punishment from the class while performing a particular task. The volunteers leave the room.

2. The instructor identifies an object for the student volunteers to locate when they return to the room. (The object should be unobstructed but clearly visible to the class. Examples that have worked well include a small triangular piece of paper that was left behind when a notice was torn off a classroom bulletin board, a smudge on the chalkboard, and a chip in the plaster of a classroom wall.)

WORKING WITH **OTHERS** EXERCISE (Continued)

3. The instructor specifies the actions that will be in effect when the volunteers return to the room. For punishment, students should hiss or boo when the first volunteer is moving away from the object. For positive reinforcement, they should cheer and applaud when the second volunteer is getting closer to the object.

4. The instructor should assign a student to keep a record of the time it takes each of the volunteers to locate the object.

Volunteer 1 (Steps 5 and 6)

5. Volunteer 1 is brought back into the room and is told, "Your task is to locate and touch a particular object in the room, and the class has agreed to help you. You cannot use words or ask questions. Begin."

6. Volunteer 1 continues to look for the object until it is found, while the class engages in the punishing behaviour.

Volunteer 2 (Steps 7 and 8)

7. Volunteer 2 is brought back into the room and is told, "Your task is to locate and touch a particular object in the room, and the class has agreed to help you. You cannot use words or ask questions. Begin."

8. Volunteer 2 continues to look for the object until it is found, while the class assists by giving positive reinforcement.

Class Review (Steps 9 and 10)

9. The timekeeper will present the results on how long it took each volunteer to find the object.

10. The class will discuss the following: What was the difference in behaviour of the two volunteers? What are the implications of this exercise for shaping behaviour in organizations?

ETHICAL **DILEMMA** EXERCISE

Is Motivation Manipulation?

Managers are interested in the subject of motivation because they are concerned with learning how to get the most effort from their employees. Is this ethical? For example, when managers link rewards to productivity, aren't they manipulating employees?

"To manipulate" is defined as "(1) to handle, manage, or use, especially with skill, in some process of treatment or performance; (2) to manage or influence by artful skill; (3) to adapt or change to suit one's purpose or advantage." Aren't one or more of these definitions compatible with the notion of managers skillfully seeking to influence employee productivity for the benefit of the manager and the organization?

Do managers have the right to seek control over their employees? Does anyone, for that matter, have the right to control others? Does control imply manipulation? Is there anything wrong with managers manipulating employees?

OB *AT WORK*

CASE INCIDENTS

Bullying Bosses

"It got to where I was twitching, literally, on the way into work," states Carrie Clark, a 52-year-old retired teacher and administrator.[93] After enduring 10 months of repeated insults and mistreatment from her supervisor, she finally quit her job. "I had to take care of my health."

Although many individuals recall bullies from their elementary school days, some are realizing that bullies can exist in the workplace as well. And these bullies do not just pick on the weakest in the group; rather, any subordinate in their path may fall prey to their torment, according to Dr. Gary Namie, director of the Workplace Bullying and Trauma Institute. Dr. Namie further says workplace bullies are not limited to men—women are at least as likely to be bullies. However, gender discrepancies are found in victims of bullying, as women are more likely to be targets.

What motivates a boss to be a bully? Dr. Harvey Hornstein, a retired professor from Teachers College at Columbia University, suggests that supervisors may use bullying as a means to subdue a subordinate who poses a threat to the supervisor's status. In addition, supervisors may bully individuals to vent frustrations. Many times, however, the sheer desire to wield power may be the primary reason for bullying.

What is the impact of bullying on employee motivation and behaviour? Surprisingly, even though victims of workplace bullies may feel less motivated to go to work every day, it does not appear that they discontinue performing their required job duties. However, it does appear that victims of bullies are less motivated to perform extra-role or citizenship behaviours. Helping others, speaking positively about the organization, and going beyond the call of duty are behaviours that are reduced as a result of bullying. According to Dr. Bennett Tepper of the University of North Carolina, fear may be the reason that many employees continue to perform their job duties. And not all individuals reduce their citizenship behaviours. Some continue to engage in extra-role behaviours to make themselves look better than their colleagues.

What should you do if your boss is bullying you? Don't necessarily expect help from co-workers. As Emelise Aleandri, an actress and producer from New York who left her job after being bullied, stated, "Some people were afraid to do anything. But others didn't mind what was happening at all, because they wanted my job." Moreover, according to Dr. Michelle Duffy of the University of Kentucky, co-workers often blame victims of bullying in order to resolve their guilt. "They do this by wondering whether maybe the person deserved the treatment, that he or she has been annoying, or lazy, they did something to earn it," states Dr. Duffy. One example of an employee who observed this phenomenon first-hand is Sherry Hamby, who was frequently verbally abused by her boss and then eventually fired. She stated, "This was a man who insulted me, who insulted my family, who would lay into me while everyone else in the office just sat there and let it happen. The people in my office eventually started blaming me."

What can a bullied employee do? Dr. Hornstein suggests that employees try to ignore the insults and respond only to the substance of the bully's gripe. "Stick with the substance, not the process, and often it won't escalate," he states. Of course, that is easier said than done.

Questions

1. What aspects of motivation might workplace bullying reduce? For example, are there likely to be effects on an employee's self-efficacy? If so, what might those effects be?

2. If you were a victim of workplace bullying, what steps would you take to try to reduce its occurrence? What strategies would be most effective? What strategies might be ineffective? What would you do if one of your colleagues were a victim of an abusive supervisor?

3. What factors do you believe contribute to workplace bullying? Are bullies a product of the situation, or do they have flawed personalities? What situations and what personality factors might contribute to the presence of bullies?

Wage Reduction Proposal

The following proposal was made to employees of Montreal-based Quebecor's Vidéotron cable division:[94]

Employees are asked to increase the number of hours worked per week to 40 from 35, while receiving the same pay as working the shorter work week. In addition, they are asked to accept less paid holiday time.

Quebecor spokesman Luc Lavoie justified the request made to the employees by saying, "They have the richest work contract in the country, including eight weeks of holiday and high absenteeism."

The company made it clear that if this proposal were not accepted, it would sell its cable television and Internet installation and repair operations to Entourage Technology Solutions.

The employees, members of Canadian Union of Public Employees (CUPE) Local 2815, were reluctant to agree to these conditions. If they accepted, 300 to 400 employees were likely to be laid off, and the company could still consider outsourcing the work later.

Questions

1. Analyze this proposal in terms of motivation concepts.

2. As an employee, how would you respond if you received this proposal?

3. If you were the executive vice-president of the company, and a number of your non-unionized employees asked you for a holiday cash gift, would you have responded differently? Why or why not?

From **Concepts** to **Skills**

Setting Goals

You can be more effective at setting goals if you use the following eight suggestions:

1. *Identify your key tasks.* Goal setting begins by defining what it is that you want to accomplish.

2. *Establish specific and challenging goals for each key task.* Identify the level of performance expected. Specify the target toward which you will work.

3. *Specify the deadlines for each goal.* Putting deadlines on each goal reduces ambiguity. Deadlines, however, should not be set arbitrarily. Rather, they need to be realistic, given the tasks to be completed.

4. *Allow the employee to participate actively.* When employees participate in goal setting, they are more likely to accept the goals. However, it must be sincere participation. That is, employees must perceive that you are truly seeking their input, not just going through the motions.

5. *Prioritize goals.* When you have more than one goal, it's important for you to rank the goals in

order of importance. The purpose of prioritizing is to encourage you to take action and expend effort on each goal in proportion to its importance.

6. *Rate goals for difficulty and importance.* Goal setting should not encourage people to choose easy goals. Instead, goals should be rated for their difficulty and importance. When goals are rated, individuals can be given credit for trying difficult goals, even if they don't fully achieve them.

7. *Build in feedback mechanisms to assess goal progress.* Feedback lets you know whether your level of effort is sufficient to attain the goal. Feedback should be frequent and recurring.

8. *Link rewards to goal attainment.* Linking rewards to the achievement of goals will help motivate you.

Practising Skills

You worked your way through college while holding down a part-time job bagging groceries at the Food Town supermarket chain. You liked working in the food industry, and when you graduated, you accepted a position with Food Town as a management trainee. Three years have passed, and you have gained experience in the grocery store industry and in operating a large supermarket. About a year ago, you received a promotion to store manager at one of the chain's locations. One of the things you have liked about Food Town is that it gives store managers a great deal of autonomy in running their stores. The company provides very general guidelines to its managers. Top management is concerned with the bottom line; for the most part, how you get there is up to you. Now that you're finally a store manager, you want to establish an MBO-type program in your store. You like the idea that everyone should have clear goals to work toward and then be evaluated against those goals.

Your store employs 70 people, although except for the managers, most work only 20 to 30 hours per week. You have six people reporting to you: an assistant manager; a weekend manager; and grocery, produce, meat, and bakery managers. The only highly skilled jobs belong to the butchers, who have strict training and regulatory guidelines. Other less-skilled jobs include cashier, shelf stocker, maintenance worker, and grocery bagger.

Specifically describe how you would go about setting goals in your new position. Include examples of goals for the jobs of butcher, cashier, and bakery manager.

Reinforcing Skills

1. Set personal and academic goals you want to achieve by the end of this term. Prioritize and rate them for difficulty.

2. Where do you want to be in five years? Do you have specific five-year goals? Establish three goals you want to achieve in five years. Make sure these goals are specific, challenging, and measurable.

VIDEO CASE INCIDENT

CASE 4 Motivating Employees at KPMG

KPMG International is a Swiss cooperative that provides tax, audit, and advisory services to companies. A few years ago, KPMG realized that turnover was too high and employee motivation was too low. The company knew it had to make some changes because the lack of employee motivation was negatively affecting the business.

Bruce Pfau, vice-president of human resources at KPMG, says that there are many different factors that motivate people at work, but it really boils down to just four things. First, do employees feel that they are working for a winning organization that they are proud of, or do they feel that they are working for a loser? Second, do employees feel that they can get their job done? Frustrations like "my computer doesn't work," or "I don't have the right information to help a customer" are demotivating to employees. Third, do employees feel that they are being treated well in terms of both fairness and in terms of the economic rewards they are receiving for working? Employees want things like competitive pay, a share in the company's annual profits, good earning power, and good career development. Fourth, do employees enjoy the work that they do? Fortunately, most people select occupations they enjoy.

Liz Harper, a senior manager at KPMG, describes how the motivating factors have changed over the years. She started at KPMG in 1992, but back then there was not much emphasis on work-life balance. When she decided to start a family, she left KPMG and went to work part-time for a smaller firm. Twelve years later, she rejoined KPMG and found that much had changed. The firm is much more flexible now and has many initiatives on work-life balance. She places a high priority on work, but the flexibility she is given allows her to achieve a good balance between her job and her personal life.

Employees were interviewed and asked to describe what they liked most about KPMG. Interviewees mentioned the adoption credit, good people to work with, release time to do volunteer work, paternity leave, and being recognized for their hard work. Employees were also asked what motivated them. Answers included career growth, recognition for doing good work, and support from managers when difficult situations arise at work.

Questions

1. What is motivation? When KPMG concluded that employee motivation was low, what did that mean?

2. Bruce Pfau, vice-president of Human Resources at KPMG, identified four important areas that influence employee motivation. Explain how each of these areas relates to the motivation theories discussed in Chapter 4. Be specific.

3. What is the difference between extrinsic and intrinsic motivation? To what extent do the human-resource practices and managerial behaviour at KPMG encourage intrinsic motivation? Explain.

4. When they were asked what motivated them, KPMG employees gave a variety of answers. How well do these answers match with the key ideas of the motivation theories discussed in Chapter 4? Be specific.

5. What is the difference between distributive, procedural, and interactional justice? Which type of justice is the focus of Bruce Pfau's third question? Explain.

Source: Based on "Motivating Employees at KPMG," Organizational Behavior Video Library, 2008. Copyrighted by Prentice-Hall.

Motivation in Action

A chocolate store seems the ideal place to work. Does the company need to offer employees anything more than lots of chocolate to motivate them?

1 Is money an important motivator?

2 What does an effective reward system look like?

3 What kinds of mistakes are made in reward systems?

4 Are rewards overrated?

5 How can jobs be designed to increase motivation?

6 How can flexible workplaces increase motivation?

7 Can we simplify how we think about motivation?

E mployees who work for Vancouver-based Purdy's Chocolates, a chocolate manufacturer and retailer, might not be surprised to hear that some people would envy their jobs.[1] The employees are paid about 20 percent higher than the industry average, and receive medical and dental benefits. They also get a 30 percent discount on any chocolate they buy.

The company was voted by its 800 employees as one of the "50 Best Employers in Canada" in 2002, 2004, and 2008 in surveys conducted by consulting firm Hewitt Associates. Employees report that they love working for the company: Production supervisor Jessie Senghera says, "I wouldn't do anything else, even if anyone asked. It's been a privilege for me." Turnover at the company is low. The average employee has been with the company for nine years, a long time when 58 percent of the employees are retail workers. What makes Purdy's employees so motivated?

In this chapter, we focus on how to apply motivation concepts. We review a number of reward programs and consider whether rewards are overrated. We also discuss how to create more motivating jobs and workplaces, both of which have been shown to be alternatives to rewards in motivating individuals.

OB Is for Everyone

- What is the impact of unions on pay for performance?
- Ever wonder why employees do some strange things?
- When might job redesign be most appropriate?
- Do employers really like flexible arrangements?
- If you want to telecommute, what kind of job should you consider?

Self-Assessment Library

LEARNING ABOUT YOURSELF

- Job Enrichment
- Job Motivating Potential

From Theory to Practice: The Role of Money

1 Is money an
important motivator?

The most commonly used reward in organizations is money. As one author notes, "Money is probably the most emotionally meaningful object in contemporary life: only food and sex are its close competitors as common carriers of such strong and diverse feelings, significance, and strivings."[2]

The motivation theories we have presented only give us vague ideas of how money relates to individual motivation. For instance, Theory X suggests that individuals need to be extrinsically motivated. Money is certainly one such extrinsic motivator. According to Maslow's hierarchy of needs, individuals' basic needs must be met, including food, shelter, and safety. Generally, money can be used to satisfy those needs. Herzberg's motivation-hygiene theory, on the other hand, suggests that money (and other extrinsic motivators) are necessary but not sufficient conditions for individuals to be motivated. Process theories are relatively silent about the role of money specifically, indicating more how rewards motivate, without specifying particular types of rewards. Expectancy theory does note that individuals need to value the reward, or it won't be very motivational.

Despite the importance of money in attracting and retaining employees, and rewarding and recognizing them, little attention has been given to individual differences in people's feelings about money.[3] Some studies indicate that money is not the top priority of employees. Professor Graham Lowe at the University of Alberta and a colleague conducted a survey of 2500 Canadians and discovered that relationships in the workplace mattered more than pay or benefits when it came to employee satisfaction.[4] One respondent explained, "Of course money is important, but that's not what's going to make you jump out of bed in the morning." Another noted, "Everyone here would take more money and more time off—that's a given. But some of the things that really make the job a good or bad one are your relations with your boss."

A number of studies suggest that there are personality traits and demographic factors that correlate with an individual's attitude toward money.[5] People who value money highly score higher on "attributes like sensation seeking, competitiveness, materialism, and control." People who desire money score higher on self-esteem, need for achievement, and Type A personality measures. Men seem to value money more than women.

What these findings suggest is that when organizations develop reward programs, they need to consider very carefully the importance to the individual of the specific rewards offered. You will find a longer discussion of whether money really motivates in *Point/Counterpoint* on page 202. The *Ethical Dilemma Exercise* on page 206 gives you an intriguing look at the amount of money needed to motivate some Canadian CEOs.

Creating Effective Reward Systems

Purdy's Chocolates is a family-owned business.[6] Charles Flavelle bought the company in 1964, and daughter Karen joined the firm in 1994. She became CEO in 1997. The company tries to preserve a family feeling among employees. Karen believes that treating employees well is the key to having a motivated workforce. "We've worked hard to listen to people, respond to people, to treat people with respect—a lot of the things that are the history of the business and that my father did," she notes.

Purdy's pays its employees higher than the industry average, the company has profit-sharing plans, and it promotes people from within. Experienced managers get higher wages if they serve as training managers, helping newer employees learn the culture of the organization.

The company also has a variety of recognition programs. Employees are recognized for birthdays, moving, getting married, or having children. Employees who reach their five-year anniversary with the company are recognized at an annual luncheon, with out-of-town employees flown in for the event. All of these activities signal to employees that they are valued as important contributors to the company's success. What else can a company do to make sure its employees feel valued?

As we saw in Chapter 3, pay is not a primary factor driving job satisfaction. However, it does motivate people, and companies often underestimate the importance of pay in keeping top talent. A 2006 study found that although only 45 percent of employers thought that pay was a key factor in losing top talent, 71 percent of top performers indicated that it was a main reason.[7]

Given that pay is so important, we need to understand what to pay employees and how to pay them. To do that, management must make some strategic decisions. Will the organization lead, match, or lag the market in pay? How will individual contributions be recognized? In this section, we consider four major strategic rewards decisions that need to be made: (1) what to pay employees (which is decided by establishing a pay structure); (2) how to pay individual employees (which is decided through variable-pay plans and skill-based pay plans); (3) what benefits to offer, especially whether to offer employees choice in benefits (flexible benefits); and (4) how to construct employee recognition programs.

2 What does an effective reward system look like?

What to Pay: Establishing a Pay Structure

There are many ways to pay employees. The process of initially setting pay levels can be rather complex and entails balancing *internal equity*—the worth of the job to the organization (usually established through a technical process called job evaluation)—and *external equity*—the external competitiveness of an organization's pay relative to pay elsewhere in its industry (usually established through pay surveys). Obviously, the best pay system pays the job what it is worth (internal equity) while also paying competitively relative to the labour market.

Some organizations prefer to be pay leaders by paying above the market, while some pay below the market because they cannot afford to pay market rates, or they are willing to bear the costs of paying below market (namely, higher turnover as people are lured to better-paying jobs). Walmart, for example, pays less than its competitors and often outsources jobs overseas where pay rates are lower than in North America.

Pay more, and you may get better-qualified, more highly motivated employees who will stay with the organization longer. But pay is often the highest single operating cost for an organization, which means that paying too much can make the organization's products or services too expensive. It's a strategic decision an organization must make, with clear trade-offs.

How to Pay: Rewarding Individuals through Variable-Pay Programs

"Why should I put any extra effort into this job?" asks a frustrated grade 4 teacher. "I can excel or I can do the bare minimum. It makes no difference. I get paid the same. Why do anything above the minimum to get by?" Similar comments have been voiced by schoolteachers for decades because pay increases are tied to seniority.

A number of organizations—business firms as well as school districts and other government agencies—are moving away from paying people based solely on credentials or length of service and toward using variable-pay programs. Piece-rate wages, merit-based pay, bonuses, gainsharing, profit-sharing plans, stock options, and employee stock ownership plans are all forms of **variable-pay programs**. Instead of paying a person only for time on the job or seniority, a variable-pay program bases a portion of an employee's pay on some individual, group, and/or organizational measure of performance. Earnings therefore fluctuate up and down with the measure of performance.[8] Thus, there is no guarantee that just because you made $60 000 last year, you will make the same amount this year.

Burnaby, BC-based TELUS and Hamilton, Ontario-based Dofasco (part of ArcelorMittal) are just a couple of examples of companies that use variable pay with

variable-pay program A reward program in which a portion of an employee's pay is based on some individual and/or organizational measure of performance.

rank-and-file employees. About 10 to 15 percent of the base pay of Dofasco's blue-collar workers is subject to variable compensation, while more than half of the CEO's compensation is based on variable pay.[9]

Variable-pay plans have long been used to compensate salespeople and executives. Recently they have begun to be applied to other employees. The number of employees who have variable-pay programs has been rising in Canada. A 2007 nation-wide survey of Canadian firms by Hewitt Associates found that 80 percent of them have variable-pay programs in place, compared with 43 percent in 1994.[10] These programs are more common among non-unionized companies; only about 8 percent of unionized employees were subject to variable-pay plans in 2004.[11] Today, more than 70 percent of US companies have some form of variable-pay plan, up from only about 5 percent in 1970.[12] Unfortunately, recent survey data indicate that most employees still don't see a strong connection between pay and performance. Only 29 percent say that when they do a good job, their performance is rewarded.[13]

It is precisely the fluctuation in variable pay that has made these programs attractive to management. It turns part of an organization's fixed labour costs into a variable cost, thus reducing expenses when performance declines. So when the economy falters, companies with variable pay are able to reduce their labour costs much faster than companies that maintain non-performance-based compensation systems. In addition, when pay is tied to performance, the employee's earnings recognize contribution rather than become a form of entitlement. Low performers find, over time, that their pay stagnates, while high performers enjoy pay increases commensurate with their contributions.

Despite some reservations by employees, management professor Maria Rotundo of the Joseph L. Rotman School of Management at the University of Toronto noted that merit pay can work. "It all hinges on fair measures" during the performance appraisal. Managers need to explain why people get different amounts of money, or people "get angry, jealous and disenchanted."[14] At Purdy's Chocolates, employees are given written job descriptions that tell them exactly what is expected of them in their job. They also receive a manual that outlines "what they need to learn and by when."[15] Performance reviews are carried out for all staff annually.

Below we describe the different types of variable-pay programs and the level at which they operate: the individual, group, and organization.

Individual-Based Incentives

There are four major forms of individual-based variable-pay programs: piece-rate wages, merit-based pay, bonuses, and skill-based pay.

Piece-Rate Wages Piece-rate wages are one of the earliest forms of individual performance pay. They have long been popular as a means for compensating production employees. In a **piece-rate pay plan**, employees are paid a fixed sum for each unit of production completed. When an employee gets no base salary and is paid only for what he or she produces, this is a pure piece-rate plan. People who work at baseball parks selling peanuts and soft drinks frequently are paid this way. They might get to keep 25 cents for every bag of peanuts they sell. If they sell 200 bags during a game, they make $50. If they sell only 40 bags, their take is a mere $10.

Many organizations use a modified piece-rate plan, where employees earn a base hourly wage plus a piece-rate differential. So a data entry clerk might be paid $8.50 an hour plus 30 cents per page. Such modified plans provide a basic security net while still offering a productivity incentive. Sales associates who are paid commissions based on sales also have a form of individual-based incentive plan.

piece-rate pay plan An individual-based incentive plan in which employees are paid a fixed sum for each unit of production completed.

Merit-Based Pay **Merit-based pay plans** pay for individual performance. However, unlike piece-rate plans, which pay based on objective output, merit-based pay plans are based on performance appraisal ratings. A main advantage of merit pay plans is that they allow employers to differentiate pay based on performance so that those people thought to be high performers are given bigger raises. The plans can be motivating because, if they are designed correctly, individuals perceive a strong relationship between their performance and the rewards they receive. The evidence supports the importance of this linkage.[16]

Most large organizations have merit-based pay plans, especially for salaried employees. IBM Canada's merit pay plan, for example, provides increases to employees' base salary based on their annual performance evaluation. Since the 1990s, when Japan's economy stumbled badly, an increasing number of Japanese companies have abandoned seniority-based pay in favour of merit-based pay. Koichi Yanashita of Takeda Chemical Industries, commented, "The merit-based salary system is an important means to achieve goals set by the company's top management, not just a way to change wages."[17]

In an effort to motivate and retain top performers, more companies are increasing the differential between top and bottom performers. Hewitt Associates found that, in 2006, employers gave their best performers roughly 10 percent raises, compared with 3.6 percent for average performers and 1.3 percent for below-average performers. The consulting firm has also found that these differences have increased over time. Martyn Fisher of Imperial Chemical in the United Kingdom said that his company has widened the merit pay gap between top and average performers because, "as much as we would regret our average performers leaving, we'd regret more an above-target performer leaving."[18]

Despite the intuitive appeal of pay for performance, merit-based pay plans have several limitations. One of them is that, typically, such plans are based on an annual performance appraisal. Thus, the merit pay is as valid or invalid as the performance ratings on which it is based. Another limitation of merit pay is that sometimes the pay raise pool fluctuates based on economic conditions or other factors that have little to do with an individual employee's performance. One year, a colleague at a top university who performed very well in teaching and research was given a pay raise of $300. Why? Because the pay raise pool was very small. Yet that is hardly pay for performance. Finally, unions typically resist merit-based pay plans. Instead, seniority-based pay, where all employees get the same raises, predominates.

Bonuses **Bonuses** are becoming an increasingly popular form of individual incentive in both Canada and the United States.[19] Bonuses are more likely to be viewed as one-time rewards for defined work rather than ongoing entitlements. They are used by such companies as Ontario Hydro Energy, the Bank of Montreal, and Molson Coors Brewing Company. One advantage of bonuses over merit pay is that bonuses reward employees for recent performance rather than historical performance. The incentive effects of performance should be higher because, rather than paying people for performance that may have occurred years ago (and was rolled into their base pay), bonuses reward only recent performance.

Bonuses are not free from organizational politics (which we discuss in Chapter 8), and they can sometimes result in negative behaviour. When using bonuses, managers should be mindful of potential unexpected behaviours that may arise when employees try to ensure they will receive bonuses. *Focus on Ethics* raises the possibility that part of the US financial crisis in September 2008 was due to the way bonuses were awarded to executives.

merit-based pay plan An individual-based incentive plan based on performance appraisal ratings.

bonus An individual-based incentive plan that rewards employees for recent performance rather than historical performance.

Huge Bonuses, Disastrous Results for the United States

Did bonuses help fuel a financial meltdown? During a two-week period in September 2008, the American economy almost looked to be in free fall.[20] The US government bought up the assets of mortgage insurers Freddie Mac and Fannie May. Global financial services firm Merrill Lynch, founded in 1914, agreed to be bought by Bank of America for very little money. Global financial services firm Lehman Brothers, founded in 1850, went into bankruptcy. Morgan Stanley was in merger discussions. Major American insurance corporation AIG received an $85-billion bailout from the US government. Independent investment banks Goldman Sachs, founded in 1869, and Morgan Stanley, founded in 1935, announced that they would become bank holding companies. Investment banks issue and sell securities and provide advice on mergers and acquisitions. By becoming bank holding companies, the two companies will be subjected to greater regulation than they were previously.

There is no simple answer to why all of these corporations faced collapses or near collapses all at once, but the role that bonuses played in the financial meltdown has been raised. The trigger for the economic crisis was the collapse of many subprime mortgages during 2007 and 2008. In the preceding years, numerous Americans had been given mortgages for homes, even though they had no downpayments, and sometimes did not even have jobs. The loan payments were low at the beginning, but eventually many of those given subprime mortgages started to default on their loans.

Why would someone give out a loan to an individual who did not have a job or did not provide clear evidence of earnings? The banking industry rewarded mortgage brokers for making loans, giving out bonus payments based on the size of loans. The loans were then bundled together to make new financial instruments. These resulted in commissions and bonuses for those packaging the instruments. Several Wall Street CEOs who lost their jobs because of the fallout from subprime loans earned "tens of millions in bonuses during the heady days of 2005 and 2006."

The collapse of so many financial institutions at once suggests that rewarding individuals based on financial measures can cause problems.

skill-based pay An individual-based incentive plan that sets pay levels on the basis of how many skills employees have or how many jobs they can do.

Skill-Based Pay **Skill-based pay** is an alternative to job-based pay. Rather than having an individual's job title define his or her pay category, skill-based pay (also called *competency-based* or *knowledge-based pay*) sets pay levels on the basis of how many skills employees have or how many jobs they can do.[21] For instance, Frito-Lay Corporation ties its compensation for front-line operations managers to developing their skills in leadership, workforce development, and functional excellence. For employers, the lure of skill-based pay plans is that they increase the flexibility of the workforce: Filling staffing needs is easier when employee skills are interchangeable. Skill-based pay also facilitates communication across the organization because people gain a better understanding of each others' jobs.

What about the downside of skill-based pay? People can "top out"—that is, they can learn all the skills the program calls for them to learn. This can frustrate employees after they have become challenged by an environment of learning, growth, and continual pay raises. There is also a problem created by paying people for acquiring skills for which there may be no immediate need. As well, skill-based plans don't address the level of performance. They deal only with whether someone can perform the skill.

Finally, not everyone agrees that these rewards are always equitable. *OB in the Street* examines the question of whether athletic scholarships should be given for athletic skills, with little regard for academic merit.

IN THE STREET

Scholarships for Jocks: Skills or Smarts?

Should university athletes be awarded money just for their athletic abilities? Jack Drover, athletic director at Mount Allison University in Sackville, New Brunswick, thinks not.[22] He objects to student-athlete awards that are often offered because of what coaches and teams need, rather than what the individual student needs.

Many university presidents react negatively to schools using financial rewards to recruit athletes. Some high school athletes can get full-tuition scholarships to university, even though they have not achieved high marks in school. While not every university finds this problematic, some feel awarding scholarships that don't recognize academic achievement or financial need is "an affront to the values of higher education."

Schools across the country interpret the rules for scholarships differently, which may affect the quality of school sports teams. Universities in Ontario (which rarely give scholarships to first-year students) have had particular difficulty competing with schools across the country. For example, since 1995, only two football teams in Ontario have won the Vanier Cup: the Ottawa Gee Gees (2000) and the Wilfrid Laurier Golden Hawks (2005); the University of Ottawa is one of the few schools in the province that gives many athletic scholarships. In contrast, the Saint Mary's Huskies of Halifax, Nova Scotia, has been in the Vanier Cup final four times since 1999, winning twice. Rivals claim that a reason for the team's success is its "plentiful" athletic scholarships. Some members of Canadian Interuniversity Sport (CIS) suggest that a level playing field, with no scholarships granted to first-year athletes except in cases of financial need and academic merit, would be fairer to all teams. CIS president Marg MacGregor, however, argues that "we're asking a lot of our students when we say compete every weekend and practise all the time without any support."

Group-Based Incentives

There is one major form of group-based pay-for-performance program: gainsharing.

Gainsharing The variable-pay program that has received the most attention in recent years is undoubtedly **gainsharing**.[23] It is a formula-based group incentive plan. Improvements in group productivity—from one period to another—determine the total amount of money to be shared. For instance, if last month a company produced 1000 items using 10 000 person hours, and this month production of the same number of items was produced with only 9000 person hours, the company experiences a savings of 1000 person hours, at the average cost per hour to hire a person. Productivity savings can be divided between the company and employees in any number of ways, but 50-50 is fairly typical.

Gainsharing differs from profit sharing, discussed below. Gainsharing focuses on productivity gains rather than profits, and so it rewards specific behaviours that are less influenced by external factors. Employees in a gainsharing plan can receive incentive awards even when the organization isn't profitable.

Gainsharing's popularity was initially limited to large unionized manufacturing companies,[24] such as Montreal-based Molson Coors Brewing Company and Montreal-based Hydro-Québec. This has changed in recent years. More than 1500 organizations have now introduced it,[25] including smaller companies, such as Delta, BC-based Avcorp

gainsharing A group-based incentive plan in which improvements in group productivity determine the total amount of money to be shared.

Industries, and governments, such as Ontario's Town of Ajax and Kingston Township. Gainsharing has been found to improve productivity in a majority of cases, and often has a positive impact on employee attitudes.[26]

Organizational-Based Incentives

There are two major forms of organizational-based pay-for-performance programs: profit-sharing and stock option plans, which include employee stock ownership plans.

profit-sharing plan An organization-wide incentive plan in which the employer shares profits with employees based on a predetermined formula.

Profit-Sharing Plans A **profit-sharing plan** is an organization-wide plan in which the employer shares profits with employees based on a predetermined formula. The plan can distribute direct cash outlays or stock options. Though senior executives are most likely to be rewarded through profit-sharing plans, employees at any level can be recipients. IKEA divided every penny rung up in its 152 stores on October 8, 1999, among its 44 000 staffers in 28 countries. This amounted to $2500 for each employee.[27] At Purdy's Chocolates, profit sharing was introduced in 1990 "to have people more conscious of what things cost, and paying attention to not wasting." Profit sharing is provided to all full- and part-time staff who are non-unionized. The practice has been successful. The amount paid is determined by the profits of the company, and is based on a percentage of the employee's salary. In 2003, Purdy's employees received bonuses of about 5.5 percent from profit sharing.[28]

Be aware that profit-sharing plans focus on past financial results. They don't necessarily focus employees on the future, because employees and managers look for ways to cut costs today, without considering longer-term organizational needs. They also tend to ignore factors such as customer service and employee development, which may not be seen as having a direct link to profits. In addition, employees who work in companies in cyclical industries would see inconsistent rewards with such a plan. For example, a financial services company would offer few or no rewards during slumping economic periods, and substantial rewards during times of economic growth. Vancouver-based 1-800-GOT-JUNK? started a profit-sharing program in 2004, which paid out generously to employees. There were no payments in 2007, however. The company's ability to expand in North America was limited, and the profits were to be invested in international expansion. Tania Hall, senior PR manager, acknowledged that the lack of a reward cheque could "test employee staying power. This is an opportunity to grow and be part of shaping the future, and you're either in or not."[29]

From an expectancy theory perspective, employees who have a profit-sharing plan will be less motivated during economic downturns because they know that the likelihood of receiving significant bonuses is low. According to expectancy theory, for employees to be motivated, performance must be directly linked to rewards.

Three Canadian studies by Professor Richard J. Long of the University of Saskatchewan's College of Commerce show that a profit-sharing plan is most effective in workplaces where there is more involvement by employees, more teamwork, and a managerial philosophy that encourages participation.[30]

employee stock ownership plan (ESOP) A company-established benefit plan in which employees acquire stock as part of their benefits.

Stock Options and Employee Stock Ownership Plans Some companies try to encourage employees to adopt the perspective of top management by making them owners of their firms. The idea is that employees will be more likely to think about the consequences of their behaviour on the bottom line if they own part of the company. Employees can become owners of the company either through being granted stock options, or through an **employee stock ownership plan (ESOP)**.[31] Stock options give employees the right to buy stocks in the company at a later date for a guaranteed price. ESOPs are company-established benefit plans in which employees acquire stock as part of their benefits.

Canadian companies lag far behind the United States in the use of ESOPs because Canada's tax environment is less conducive to such plans. More recently, both the dot-com meltdown and the high-tech crash have made employees more reluctant to accept stock options instead of cash. Lisa Slipp, head of executive compensation at Toronto-based consulting firm Mercer Human Resource Consulting, noted that "people are recognizing the reality of stock options, that they are attractive in an up market and less so in a down market."[32] Nevertheless, Edmonton-based PCL Constructors has been owned by its employees since 1977, with 80 percent of employees owning shares. Ross Grieve, the company's president and CEO, says that ownership "elevates [the employees'] commitment to the organization.[33]

RESEARCH FINDINGS: ESOPs

The research on ESOPs indicates that they increase employee satisfaction.[34] But their impact on performance is less clear. A study by the Toronto Stock Exchange found positive results for public companies having ESOPs:[35]

- Five-year profit growth was 123 percent higher.
- Net profit margin was 95 percent higher.
- Productivity, measured by revenue per employee, was 24 percent higher.
- Return on average total equity was 92.3 percent higher.
- Return on capital was 65.5 percent higher.

ESOPs have the potential to increase employee job satisfaction and work motivation. For this potential to be realized, employees need to psychologically experience ownership.[36] So in addition to merely having a financial stake in the company, employees need to be kept regularly informed on the status of the business, and also have the opportunity to exercise influence over the business.

The evidence consistently indicates that it takes ownership and a participative style of management to achieve significant improvements in an organization's performance.[37]

RESEARCH FINDINGS: Variable-Pay Programs

Do variable-pay programs increase motivation and productivity? The answer is a qualified "yes." For example, studies generally support the idea that organizations with profit-sharing plans have higher levels of profitability than those without them.[38] Similarly, gainsharing has been found to improve productivity in a majority of cases, and often has a positive impact on employee attitudes.[39] Another study found that although piece-rate pay-for-performance plans stimulated higher levels of productivity, this positive effect was not observed for risk-averse employees. Thus, in general, what American economist Ed Lazear has said seems generally right: "Workers respond to prices just as economic theory predicts. Claims by sociologists and others that monetizing incentives may actually reduce output are unambiguously refuted by the data." However, that does not mean everyone responds positively to variable-pay programs.[40]

Teamwork, unions, public sector employees, and ethical considerations present distinct challenges to pay-for-performance programs.

Teamwork   Incentive pay, especially when it is awarded to individuals, can have a negative effect on group cohesiveness and productivity, and in some cases it may not offer significant benefits to a company.[41] For example, Montreal-based National Bank of Canada offered a $5 employee bonus for every time employees referred clients for loans, mutual funds, or other bank products. But the bonus so upset employees that the plan was abandoned after just three months.[42] Tellers complained that the bonus caused colleagues to compete against one another. Meanwhile, the bank could not determine whether the referrals actually generated new business.

If an organization wants a group of individuals to function as a "team" (which we define in Chapter 6), emphasis needs to be on team-based rewards, rather than individual rewards. We will discuss the nature of team-based rewards in Chapter 6.

Unions In Canada, there are considerably more unionized workplaces than there are in the United States. Consequently, the unionized context must be considered when motivation theories and practices are examined. Unionized employees are typically paid on the basis of seniority and job categories, with very little range within a category, and few opportunities to receive performance-based pay.

Moreover, organized labour is, in general, cool to the idea of pay for performance. Prem Benimadhu, an analyst at the Conference Board of Canada, notes, "Canadian unions have been very allergic to variable compensation."[43] Andrew Jackson, senior economist for the Canadian Labour Congress in Ottawa, adds

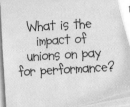

that "it hurts co-operation in the workplace. It can lead to competition between workers, speeding up the pace of work. It's a bad thing if it creates a stressful work environment where older workers can't keep up."[44] Union members are also concerned that factors out of their control might affect whether bonuses are awarded. *OB in the Workplace* illustrates one union's view of rewards that recognize performance.

What is the impact of unions on pay for performance?

IN THE WORKPLACE

No Toronto Hydro Jackets for Union Members

Why would unions oppose rewards for their members? Toronto Hydro discovered that rewarding its unionized employees for a job well done can be a tricky business.[45] A ruling by an arbitrator brought in to settle a dispute between Toronto Hydro and the Canadian Union of Public Employees (CUPE) Local 1 stopped the practice of free lunches, dinners, and such rewards as tickets to events, pen and pencil sets, extra breaks, cellphones, and Toronto Hydro jackets.

Bruno Silano, the local's president, argued that it is demoralizing for employees of some departments to get extra rewards, while other employees do not. Robert Herman, the arbitrator, agreed, stating "the rewards, bestowed at the discretion of management, violated the union's right as exclusive bargaining agent on behalf of its members."

The arbitrator's ruling does not apply to other companies operating with collective agreements, unless the union specifically objects to extra rewards for its members. Toronto labour lawyer Stewart Saxe noted that most unions go along with company reward plans "for obvious political reasons." Toronto Hydro still gives the forbidden perks to non-union employees.

Still, not all unions share similar views to CUPE, and the benefits and drawbacks of incentive plans must be carefully considered before implementing them in a unionized environment. The ability of managers to hand out rewards of any sort may be limited because of the collective agreement. For instance, at Purdy's Chocolates, unionized employees do not participate in the profit-sharing plan. However, collective agreements do not prevent managers from creating better work environments. Showing appreciation in less tangible ways, providing opportunities for training and advancement, and listening to employees' concerns all help create a more positive environment. (Later in the chapter, we consider ways of improving the overall work environment to enhance performance.)

Public Sector Employees   There are special challenges in pay-for-performance programs for public sector employees (those who work for local, provincial, or federal governments). Because public sector work is often of a service nature, it can be hard to measure productivity in the same way manufacturing or retail firms do. One might be able to count how many children an employee places in foster homes, but this might not really address the quality of those placements. Therefore, it becomes more difficult to make a meaningful link between rewards and productivity.

Because pay-for-performance programs can be difficult to administer in the public sector, several researchers have suggested that goal-setting theory be used to improve performance in public sector organizations instead.[46] More recently, another researcher found that goal difficulty and goal specificity, as well as the belief that the goal could be achieved, significantly improved motivation of public sector employees.[47] Because many public sector employees are also unionized, the challenges faced in motivating unionized employees also apply to government employees.

Ethical Considerations   Organizations also need to consider the ethical implications of their performance-based plans. The recent collapse of financial institutions in the United States provides one example of employees manipulating performance results to increase their bonuses. Walmart has been accused by a number of employees of demanding that they work many unpaid hours.[48] According to company policy, Walmart does not allow store managers to schedule employees for overtime, and they are reprimanded if they do so. At the same time, store managers are told to keep payroll costs below fixed targets. They face reprimands and possible demotion or dismissal when they miss their target. To maintain positive evaluations, store managers pressure employees to do work without recording the hours on time sheets. This behaviour, while unethical, is rational from the store managers' perspective, as they are simply following practices to ensure that they will be rewarded for performance by their superiors.

Flexible Benefits: Developing a Benefits Package

Alain Bourdeau and Yasmin Murphy have very different needs in terms of employee benefits. Alain is married and has three young children and a wife who is at home full time. Yasmin, too, is married, but her husband has a high-paying job with the federal government, and they have no children. Alain is concerned about having a good dental plan and enough life insurance to support his family in case it's needed. In contrast, Yasmin's husband already has her dental needs covered on his plan, and life insurance is a low priority for both Yasmin and her husband. Yasmin is more interested in extra vacation time and long-term financial benefits such as a tax-deferred savings plan.

A standardized benefits package for all employees at an organization would be unlikely to satisfactorily meet the needs of both Alain and Yasmin. Some organizations, therefore, cover both sets of needs by offering flexible benefits.

Flexible benefits allow each employee to put together a benefits package individually tailored to his or her own needs and situation. It replaces the traditional "one-benefit-plan-fits-all" programs that dominated organizations for more than 50 years.[49] Consistent with expectancy theory's thesis that organizational rewards should be linked to each individual employee's personal goals, flexible benefits individualize rewards by allowing each employee to choose the compensation package that best satisfies his or her current needs. The average organization provides fringe benefits worth approximately 40 percent of an employee's salary. Traditional benefits programs were designed for the typical employee of the 1950s—a male with a wife and two children at home. Less than 10 percent of employees now fit this stereotype. About 25 percent of today's employees are single, and one-third are part of two-income families with no children. Traditional programs don't meet their diverse needs, but flexible benefits do. Benefits can be uniquely

flexible benefits A benefits plan that allows each employee to put together a benefits package individually tailored to his or her own needs and situation.

tailored to accommodate differences in employee needs based on age, marital status, spouses' benefit status, number and age of dependants, and the like.

The three most popular types of benefits plans are modular plans, core-plus plans, and flexible spending accounts.[50] *Modular plans* are predesigned packages of benefits, with each module put together to meet the needs of a specific group of employees. So a module designed for single employees with no dependants might include only essential benefits. Another, designed for single parents, might have additional life insurance, disability insurance, and expanded health coverage. *Core-plus plans* consist of a core of essential benefits and a menu-like selection of other benefit options from which employees can select and add to the core. Typically, each employee is given "benefit credits," which allow the "purchase" of additional benefits that uniquely meet his or her needs. *Flexible spending accounts* allow employees to set aside up to the dollar amount offered in the plan to pay for particular services. It's a convenient way, for example, for employees to pay for eye care and dental premiums. Flexible spending accounts can increase employee take-home pay because employees don't have to pay taxes on the dollars they spend out of these accounts.

Intrinsic Rewards: Employee Recognition Programs

Expectancy theory tells us that a key component of motivation is the link between performance and rewards (that is, having your behaviour recognized). Employee recognition programs cover a wide spectrum of activities. They range from a spontaneous and private "thank you" on up to widely publicized formal programs in which specific types of behaviour are encouraged and the procedures for attaining recognition are clearly identified.[51]

For instance, Aimia Foods, a British supplier of hot and cold drinks, syrups, and sauces, has a comprehensive recognition program.[52] The central hallway in its production area is lined with "bragging boards," where the accomplishments of various individuals and teams are regularly updated. Monthly awards are presented to people who have been nominated by peers for extraordinary effort on the job. Monthly award winners are eligible for further recognition at an annual off-site meeting for all employees. In contrast, most managers use a far more informal approach. As a case in point, Julia Stewart, former president of Applebee's restaurants, would frequently leave sealed notes on the chairs of employees after everyone had gone home.[53] These notes explained how critical Stewart thought the person's work was or how much she appreciated the completion of a recent project. Stewart also relied heavily on voice mail messages left after office hours to tell employees how appreciative she was for a job well done.

Recognition may not be enough for some jobs, however, as Exhibit 5-1 suggests.

EXHIBIT 5-1

THE WALL STREET JOURNAL

Source: From the *Wall Street Journal*, October 21, 1997. Reprinted by permission of Cartoon Features Syndicate.

Linking Employee Recognition Programs and Reinforcement Theory

A few years ago, 1500 employees were surveyed in a variety of work settings to find out what they considered to be the most powerful workplace motivator. Their response? Recognition, recognition, and more recognition![54]

Consistent with reinforcement theory, rewarding a behaviour with recognition immediately following that behaviour is likely to encourage its repetition.[55] As previously

noted, recognition can take many forms. You can personally congratulate an employee in private for a good job. You
can send a handwritten note or an email message acknowledging something positive that the employee has done. For
employees with a strong need for social acceptance, you can
publicly recognize accomplishments. To enhance group
cohesiveness and motivation, you can celebrate team
successes. For instance, you can throw a team pizza party
to celebrate a team's accomplishments. Or, as illustrated in
Exhibit 5-2, you can follow the example of Phoenix Inn
Suites, a chain of small hotels. They encourage employees to
smile by letting customers identify this desirable behaviour,
then recognize those employees who are identified most
often with rewards and publicity.

Employee Recognition in Practice

In today's highly competitive global economy, most organizations are under severe cost pressures. That makes
recognition programs particularly attractive. Recognizing an
employee's superior performance often costs little or no
money.

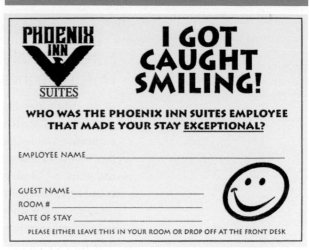

EXHIBIT 5-2

Source: Courtesy of Phoenix Inn Suites. Reprinted with permission of VIP's Industries, Inc.

A survey of Canadian firms in 2004 by Hewitt Associates found that 34 percent of
companies recognized individual or group achievements with cash or merchandise.[56]
Organizations can recognize employees in numerous ways. The *Globe and Mail* awards
the Stephen Godfrey Prize for Newsroom Citizenship. Other ways of recognizing
performance include sending employees personal thank-you notes or emails for good
performance, putting employees on prestigious committees, sending employees for
training, and giving an employee an assistant for a day to help clear backlogs.

Employee recognition may reduce turnover in organizations, particularly that of
good employees. When executives were asked the reasons why employees left for jobs
with other companies, 34 percent said it was due to lack of recognition and praise,
compared with 29 percent who mentioned low compensation, 13 percent who
mentioned limited authority, and 8 percent who cited personality problems.[57]
Recognition and praise, however, need to be meaningful, as *Case Incident—Thanks for
Nothing* on page 207 illustrates.

Caveat Emptor: Apply Motivation Theories Wisely

While motivation theories generally work well in Canada and the United States, they
don't always work successfully in other cultures. Second, applying the theories without
giving performance feedback makes little sense. Finally, when managers are not careful, they
can send the wrong signals with how they use rewards. We examine these issues below.

3 What kinds of
mistakes are made in
reward systems?

Motivation Theories Are Culture-Bound

Motivation theories do not necessarily work equally well throughout the world. Take,
for instance, a study comparing sales representatives at a large electronics company in the
United States with one in Japan. The study found that although Rolex watches, expensive
dinners, and fancy vacations were appropriate rewards for star performers in the United
States, taking the whole sales team bowling was more appreciated in Japan. The study's
authors found that "being a member of a successful team with shared goals and values,
rather than financial rewards, is what drives Japanese sales representatives to succeed."[58]
OB Around the Globe discusses the use of rewards in Russia, China, and Mexico.

AROUND THE GLOBE

Foreign Employees Meet North American Rewards

What motivates employees in other countries? At a cotton mill 140 kilometres northwest of Moscow, a small group of employees was given either highly valued extrinsic rewards (North American T-shirts with logos, children's sweatpants, tapes of North American music, and a variety of other North American articles) or praise and recognition.[59] Both types of rewards significantly increased employee productivity, with more top-grade fabric produced when rewards were delivered.

Interestingly enough, however, the rewards did not increase the productivity very significantly for those who worked the Saturday shift. These findings show that while rewards have some use in Russia, the conditions of work also affect productivity. Because the Russian employees did not want to work the Saturday shift, the rewards had less impact on their productivity. Expectancy theory would tell us that the rewards offered for Saturday work were not valued highly enough by employees to increase their productivity.

In China, the reward structure is undergoing a fundamental shift. During the Cultural Revolution (1966–1976), equal pay for everyone, regardless of productivity, was the rule. Since 1978, however, there has been more openness toward paying for productivity. However, it is still the case that some companies pay everyone a bonus, regardless of individual productivity, and there is debate among Chinese employees about the standards set for performance.

When Dell started producing computers in China, it offered each employee 200 shares of Dell stock, which was then trading at $60. Three months later, with shares trading at $110, each employee had a paper gain of $10 000, roughly a year's salary for the average Xiamen employee. But the Chinese employees had no idea what stock options were. Once these were explained to them, the productivity increased. Nevertheless, Dell has had to deal with the Chinese expectation of employment for life, even though that is no longer a guarantee. Dell executives say that "at first a little 'reeducation' was necessary in Xiamen so that workers understood that their jobs depended on their performance."

A researcher studying an American-owned manufacturing plant in Mexico noted that Mexican employees prefer immediate feedback on their work. Thus a daily incentive system with automatic bonuses for production exceeding quotas is preferable. This is equivalent to piece-rate wages paid daily. Employers often add extra incentives that are meaningful to employees, including weekly food baskets, free meals, bus service, and daycare.

A study that examined how cultural differences affect choice of pay and benefit practices gives us further information about reward practices in different countries.[60] This study linked reward preferences to a country's ratings on GLOBE/Hofstede cultural dimensions, which we discussed in Chapter 3. In Exhibit 5-3, we show the link between a country's rating on particular cultural dimensions, and its preferences for particular types of rewards. Countries that put a high value on uncertainty avoidance prefer pay based on objective measures, such as skill or seniority, because the outcomes are more certain. Countries that put a high value on individualism place more emphasis on an individual's responsibility for performance that leads to rewards. Countries that put a high value on humane orientation offer social benefits and programs that provide work-family balance, such as child care, maternity leave, and sabbaticals. Managers who receive

EXHIBIT 5-3   Reward Preferences in Different Countries

GLOBE/Hofstede Cultural Dimension	Reward Preference	Examples
High uncertainty avoidance	Certainty in compensation systems: • Seniority-based pay • Skill-based pay	Greece, Portugal, Japan
Individualism	Compensation based on individual performance: • Pay for performance • Individual incentives • Stock options	Australia, United Kingdom, United States
Humane orientation (Hofstede's masculinity vs. femininity dimension)	Social benefits and programs: • Flexible benefits • Workplace child-care programs • Career-break schemes • Maternity leave programs	Sweden, Norway, the Netherlands

Source: Based on R. S. Schuler and N. Rogovsky, "Understanding Compensation Practice Variations Across Firms: The Impact of National Culture," *Journal of International Business Studies* 29, no. 1 (First Quarter 1998), pp. 159–177. Reprinted by permission of Palgrave/Macmillan.

overseas assignments should consider a country's cultural orientation when designing and implementing reward practices.

Evaluating Motivation Theories Cross-Culturally

Why do our motivation theories perform less well when we look at their implementation in countries beyond Canada and the United States? Most current motivation theories were developed in the United States, and so take American cultural norms for granted.[61] That may account for why Canada and the United States rely more heavily on extrinsic motivating factors than do some other countries.[62] Japanese and German firms rarely make use of individual-based incentives.[63]

Many of the social-psychological theories of motivation rely heavily on the notion of motivating the individual through individual rewards. Therefore they emphasize, particularly in an organizational context, the meaning of pay, and give little attention to the informal rewards that come from group norms and prestige from peers.[64] In contrast, Japanese organizations do not emphasize motivating each individual one at a time, but rely more heavily on group processes providing motivation to employees.

Motivation theories also assume some consistency in needs across society. For instance, Maslow's hierarchy of needs argues that people start at the physiological level and then move progressively up the hierarchy in this order: physiological, safety, social, esteem, and self-actualization. This hierarchy, if it has any application at all, aligns well with American culture and reasonably well with Canadian culture. However, in countries such as Japan, Greece, and Portugal, where uncertainty avoidance characteristics are strong, security needs would be at the top of the needs hierarchy. Countries that score high on humane orientation characteristics—Denmark, Norway, the Netherlands, and Finland—would have social needs on top.[65] We would predict, for instance, that teamwork will motivate employees more when the country's culture scores high on the humane orientation criterion.

Equity theory has gained a relatively strong following in Canada and the United States. That's not surprising, since North American reward systems assume that employees are highly sensitive to equity in reward allocations, and expect pay to be tied closely to performance. However, recent evidence suggests that in collectivist cultures, especially in the formerly socialist countries of Central and Eastern Europe, employees expect rewards to reflect their individual needs, as well as their performance.[66]

North American firms expanding their operations in China are learning that motivation concepts that succeed in North America don't always apply to Chinese employees. For example, compensation for salespeople in China is based on seniority, not on performance. And most Chinese firms do not offer any nonmonetary motivation, such as employee recognition programs. For the Chinese salesperson shown here assisting a customer interested in GM's Cadillac CTS, motivation may come from satisfying her economic and achievement needs.

Moreover, consistent with a legacy of Communism and centrally planned economies, employees exhibit an entitlement attitude—that is, they expect outcomes to be *greater* than their inputs.[67] These findings suggest that Canadian- and US-style pay practices may need modification, especially in Russia and formerly Communist countries, in order to be perceived as fair by employees.

These cross-cultural findings indicate that it is important to consider the internal norms of a country when developing an incentive plan, rather than simply import a plan that is effective in Canada and the United States.

Provide Performance Feedback

For employees to understand the relationship between rewards and performance, as well as considering whether rewards are equitable, they need to be given performance feedback. For many managers, however, few activities are more unpleasant than providing performance feedback to employees.[68] In fact, unless pressured by organizational policies and controls, managers are likely to ignore this responsibility.[69] Why the reluctance to give performance feedback? There seem to be at least three reasons.

First, managers are often uncomfortable discussing performance weaknesses directly with employees. Even though almost every employee could stand to improve in some areas, managers fear a confrontation when presenting negative feedback.

Second, many employees tend to become defensive when their weaknesses are pointed out. Instead of accepting the feedback as constructive and a basis for improving performance, some employees challenge the evaluation by criticizing the manager or redirecting blame to someone else. A survey of 151 area managers in Philadelphia, for instance, found that 98 percent encountered some type of aggression after giving employees negative appraisals.[70]

Finally, employees tend to have an inflated assessment of their own performance. Statistically speaking, half of all employees must be below-average performers. But the evidence indicates that the average employee's estimate of his or her own performance level generally falls around the 75th percentile.[71] So even when managers are providing good news, employees are likely to perceive it as not good enough.

The solution to the performance feedback problem is not to ignore it, but to train managers to conduct constructive feedback sessions. An effective review—one in which the employee perceives the appraisal as fair, the manager as sincere, and the climate as constructive—can result in the employee's leaving the interview in an upbeat mood, informed about the performance areas needing improvement, and determined to correct the deficiencies.[72] In addition, the performance review should be designed more as a counselling activity than a judgment process. This can best be accomplished by allowing the review to evolve out of the employee's own self-evaluation. For more tips on performance feedback, see *OB in Action— Giving More Effective Feedback*.

OB in ACTION

Giving More Effective Feedback

Managers can use the following tips to give more effective feedback:

→ Relate feedback to existing performance **goals** and clear **expectations**.

→ Give **specific** feedback tied to observable behaviour or measurable results.

→ Channel feedback toward **key result areas**.

→ Give feedback as **soon** as possible.

→ Give positive feedback for **improvement**, not just final results.

→ Focus feedback on **performance**, not personalities.

→ Base feedback on **accurate** and **credible** information.[73]

Beware the Signals That Are Sent by Rewards

Ever wonder why employees do some strange things?

Perhaps more often than we would like, organizations engage in what has been called "the folly of rewarding A, while hoping for B."[74] Organizations do this when they hope that employees will engage in one type of behaviour, but they reward for another type. Hoping for the behaviour you are not rewarding is unlikely to ensure it is carried out. In fact, as expectancy theory suggests, individuals will generally perform in ways that raise the probability of receiving the rewards offered.

Exhibit 5-4 provides further examples of common management reward follies. Research suggests that there are three major obstacles to ending these follies:[75]

1. *Individuals are unable to break out of old ways of thinking about reward and recognition practices.* This approach is demonstrated when management emphasizes quantifiable behaviours to the exclusion of nonquantifiable behaviours; when management is reluctant to change the existing performance system; and when employees have an entitlement mentality (that is, they don't support changing the reward system because they are comfortable with the current behaviours that are rewarded).

2. *Organizations often don't look at the big picture of their performance system.* Consequently, rewards are allocated at subunit levels, with the result that units often compete against each other.

3. *Both management and shareholders often focus on short-term results.* They don't reward employees for longer-range planning.

Organizations would do well to ensure that they do not send the wrong message when offering rewards. When organizations outline an organizational objective of "team performance," for example, but reward each employee according to individual productivity, does this send a message that teams are valued? Or when a retailer tells commissioned employees that they are responsible for monitoring and replacing stock as necessary, are employees more likely to concentrate on making sales or stocking the

EXHIBIT 5-4   Management Reward Follies

We hope for . . .	But we reward . . .
Teamwork and collaboration	The best team members
Innovative thinking and risk-taking	Proven methods and not making mistakes
Development of people skills	Technical achievements and accomplishments
Employee involvement and empowerment	Tight control over operations and resources
High achievement	Another year's effort
Long-term growth; environmental responsibility	Quarterly earnings
Commitment to total quality	Shipping on schedule, even with defects
Candour; surfacing bad news early	Reporting good news, whether it's true or not; agreeing with the manager, whether or not (s)he's right

Sources: Constructed from S. Kerr, "On the Folly of Rewarding A, While Hoping for B," *Academy of Management Executive* 9, no. 1 (1995), pp. 7–14; and "More on the Folly," *Academy of Management Executive* 9, no. 1 (1995), pp. 15–16. Reprinted by permission.

floor? Employees motivated by the promise of rewards will do those things that earn them the rewards they value.

Can We Just Eliminate Rewards?

Karen Flavelle, CEO of Purdy's Chocolates, does not just rely on salary to keep employees involved in the company.[76] New employees are given extensive training so that they will have enough product knowledge to answer any question a customer might ask. Even temporary holiday employees, who typically only work four weeks, receive a full-day's instruction in company policies and product.

Flavelle holds townhall meetings for employees so that she can outline company results and announce company events. Employees receive a company newsletter every two months. Head managers, including Flavelle, visit stores regularly. "It reduces the gap between head office and the stores," says Carmen Grant, Purdy's director of human resources. "In other companies, it can become 'us versus them,' and I don't see that in this company."

Purdy's also relies on a good working environment to motivate employees. Sue Bruzell, retail development coordinator, says, "We want people to come into our organization to work for us and really enjoy the experience, and we obviously have chocolate you can eat all the time . . . It's better than any $500 bonus." What else can companies do, beyond rewards, to create a more motivating workplace?

4 Are rewards overrated?

Alfie Kohn, in his book *Punished by Rewards*, argues that "the desire to do something, much less to do it well, simply cannot be imposed; in this sense, it is a mistake to talk about motivating other people. All we can do is set up certain conditions that will maximize the probability of their developing an interest in what they are doing and remove the conditions that function as constraints."[77]

Employee commitment would benefit many organizations. People will work hard if the job captures their passion and their imagination. They will put in much more energy and devotion than they would if they were simply waiting to be rewarded every step of the way, and they generally do not require a lot of supervision in those situations.

Creating a Motivating Work Environment

Success on a job is helped or hindered by the existence or absence of a supportive work environment. When you attempt to assess why an employee is not performing at the level at which you believe he or she is capable of performing, take a look at the work environment to see if it's supportive. Does the employee have adequate tools, equipment, materials, and supplies? Does the employee have favourable working conditions, helpful co-workers, supportive work rules and procedures, sufficient information to make job-related decisions, adequate time to do a good job, and the like? If not, performance will suffer.

Based on his research and consulting experience, Kohn proposes a number of actions that organizations can take to create a more supportive, motivating work environment.[78]

Abolish Incentive Pay Paying employees generously and fairly makes sure they don't feel exploited, and takes pay off their minds. As a result, employees will be more able to focus on the goals of the organization, rather than have their paycheque as their main goal.

Re-evaluate Evaluation Instead of making performance appraisals look and feel like a punitive effort—who gets raises, who gets promoted, who is told they are performing poorly—the performance evaluation system might be structured more like a two-way conversation to trade ideas and questions, done continuously, not as a competition. The discussion of performance should not be tied to compensation. "Providing feedback that employees can use to do a better job ought never to be confused or combined with controlling them by offering (or withholding) rewards."[79]

Create the Conditions for Authentic Motivation A noted economist summarized the evidence about pay for productivity as follows: "Changing the way workers are *treated* may boost productivity more than changing the way they are *paid*."[80] There is some consensus about what the conditions for authentic motivation might be: helping employees rather than putting them under surveillance; listening to employee concerns and thinking about problems from their viewpoint; and providing plenty of feedback so they know what they have done right and what they need to improve.[81]

Encourage Collaboration People are more likely to perform better in well-functioning groups where they can get feedback and learn from each other.[82] Therefore, it's important to provide the necessary supports to create well-functioning teams.

Enhance Content People are generally the most motivated when their jobs give them an opportunity to learn new skills, provide variety in the tasks that are performed, and enable them to demonstrate competence. Some of this can be fostered by carefully matching people to their jobs, and by giving them the opportunity to try new jobs. It's also possible to increase the meaningfulness of many jobs, as we discuss later in this chapter.

But what about jobs that don't seem inherently interesting? One psychologist suggests that in cases where the jobs are fundamentally unappealing, the manager might acknowledge frankly that the task is not fun, give a meaningful rationale for why it must be done, and then give people as much choice as possible in how the task is completed.[83] One sociologist studying a group of garbage collectors in San Francisco discovered that they were quite satisfied with their work.[84] Their satisfaction came from the way the work and the company were organized: Relationships among the crew were important, the tasks and routes were varied to provide interest, and the company was set up as a cooperative, so that each worker owned a share of the company, and thus felt "pride of ownership."

Provide Choice   "We are most likely to become enthusiastic about what we are doing—and all else being equal, to do it well—when we are free to make decisions about the way we carry out a task."[85] Extrinsic rewards (and punishments too) actually remove choice, because they focus us on rewards, rather than on tasks or goals. Research suggests that burnout, dissatisfaction, absenteeism, stress, and coronary heart disease are related to situations where individuals did not have enough control over their work situations.[86] By *choice* we do not mean lack of management, but rather, involving people in the decisions that are to be made. A number of case studies indicate that participative management, when it includes full participation by everyone, is successful.[87]

These actions represent an alternative to simply providing more and different kinds of incentives to try to induce people to work more effectively. They suggest that providing the proper environment may be more important than the reward structure.

It would be difficult for many organizations to implement these ideas immediately and expect that they would work. Doing so would require managers to be willing to relinquish control and instead take on the job of coaching. It would require employees to truly believe that their participation and input mattered, and that might require breaking down some of the suspicion that employees feel when managers give directives to employees, rather than seek collaborative input. Nevertheless, these actions, when implemented, can lead to quite a different workplace than what we often see. Moreover, Kohn suggests that sometimes it's not the type or amount of rewards that makes a difference as much as whether the work itself is intrinsically interesting.

Below we examine how to create more motivating jobs and workplaces in order to make work itself more intrinsically rewarding for employees.

Job Redesign

> At Purdy's Chocolates, managers emphasize the need to learn about the different jobs required in the organization.[88] CEO Karen Flavelle believes in promoting from within, signalling that employees are valued members of her team. To get employees ready for promotions, she uses job rotation. This helps employees evaluate opportunities for different jobs and gain the skills they might need to be promoted. For example, a warehouse employee was given a temporary job managing a Christmas packaging project. The employee was promoted to the production office later, in recognition of a job well done. What can employers do to make jobs more interesting for employees?

5   How can jobs be designed to increase motivation?

job design How tasks are assigned to form a job.

The writings of Maslow, McGregor, Herzberg, and Kohn all touched on the importance of looking at the work itself as a possible source of motivation. Recent research in **job design** (how tasks are assigned to form a job) provides stronger evidence that the way the elements in a job are organized can increase or decrease effort. This research also offers detailed insights into just what those elements are.

In this section, we look at some of the ways that jobs can be reshaped to make them more motivating. We look at three job redesign options—job rotation, job enlargement, and job enrichment—and show how the job characteristics model can be used to help us understand job enrichment.

Job Rotation

job rotation The periodic shifting of an employee from one task to another.

If employees suffer from overroutinization, one alternative is to use **job rotation** (or what many call *cross-training*). We define this practice as the periodic shifting of an employee from one task to another. When an activity is no longer challenging, the employee is rotated to another job at the same level that has similar skill requirements.[89]

At McDonald's, this approach is used as a way to make sure that the new employees learn all of the tasks associated with making, packaging, and serving hamburgers and other items. Similarly, at Chrysler's Toledo North assembly plant, job rotation helps give employees in different areas a sense of the big picture. Employees are organized in teams of 10, and each learns the jobs of the others. Absenteeism is less of a problem, because team members can fill in for each other. Rotating jobs also decreases the frequency of repetitive stress injuries.[90]

A Statistics Canada survey found that about 19 percent of firms with 10 or more employees engaged in job rotation.[91] Employees in technical trades and clerical and administrative positions were more likely to rotate jobs than managerial and professional employees.

The strengths of job rotation are that it reduces boredom and increases motivation by diversifying the employee's activities. Of course, it can also have indirect benefits for the organization, since employees with a wider range of skills give management more flexibility in scheduling work, adapting to changes, and filling vacancies.

On the other hand, job rotation has drawbacks. Training costs are increased. Productivity is reduced because a worker moves into a new position just when his or her efficiency at the prior job achieves economies for the organization. Job rotation also creates disruptions. Members of the work group must adjust to the new employee. The manager may also have to spend more time answering questions and monitoring the work of the recently rotated employee. Finally, job rotation can demotivate intelligent and ambitious trainees who seek specific responsibilities in their chosen specialty.

Job Enlargement

The idea of expanding jobs horizontally, or what we call **job enlargement**, became popular more than 35 years ago. Increasing the number and variety of tasks that an individual performed resulted in jobs with more diversity. Instead of only sorting the incoming mail by department, for instance, a mail sorter's job could be enlarged to include delivering the mail to the various departments or running outgoing letters through the postage meter.

job enlargement The horizontal expansion of jobs.

Efforts at job enlargement have sometimes met with less than enthusiastic results.[92] As one employee who experienced such a redesign on his job remarked, "Before I had *one* lousy job. Now, through enlargement, I have *three*!"

However, there have been some successful applications of job enlargement. For example, GM Canada's Synchronous Administration through Managerial Excellence (SAME) system ensures that all of the employees in a work unit can perform each of the tasks of any of the individuals in the unit. The system significantly reduces the need for meetings, halves the cost of office equipment, and allows job continuity when workers leave the company or go on holiday.[93] The Candour unit of Montreal-based Bombardier's aerospace group introduced job enlargement to get away from having a large number of highly specialized manufacturing jobs.[94] Serge Perron, vice-president and general manager of operations, notes that the move gave Bombardier more flexibility, with workers installing several types of parts instead of just one, and also led to productivity improvements.

While job enlargement attacks the lack of diversity in overspecialized jobs, it does little to add challenge or meaningfulness to a worker's activities. Job enrichment was developed to deal with the shortcomings of job enlargement.

Job Enrichment and the Job Characteristics Model

OB researchers Richard Hackman from Harvard University and Greg Oldham from the University of Illinois explored the nature of good jobs through their **job characteristics model (JCM)**.[95] The JCM identifies five core job dimensions and their relationship to

job characteristics model (JCM) A model that identifies five core job dimensions and their relationship to personal and work outcomes.

personal and work outcomes. Building on Herzberg's motivation-hygiene theory, the JCM focuses on the content of jobs, rather than the context of jobs, and can be considered as a way of motivating employees and increasing job satisfaction.

Job enrichment, an application of the JCM, refers to the vertical expansion of jobs. It increases the degree to which workers control the planning, execution, and evaluation of their work. An enriched job organizes tasks so that an employee does a complete activity. It expands employees' freedom and independence, increases responsibility, and provides feedback, so individuals will be able to assess and correct their own perform-ance.[96] To find out whether an enriched job matches your own work preferences, see the *Learning About Yourself Exercise* on page 203.

Core Job Dimensions

According to the JCM, any job can be described in terms of five core job dimensions:

- **Skill variety**. The degree to which the job requires a variety of different activities so the employee can use a number of different skills and talents.

- **Task identity**. The degree to which the job requires completion of a whole and identifiable piece of work.

- **Task significance**. The degree to which the job has a substantial impact on the lives or work of other people.

- **Autonomy**. The degree to which the job provides substantial freedom, independence, and discretion to the individual in scheduling the work and determining the procedures to be used in carrying it out.

- **Feedback**. The degree to which carrying out the work activities required by the job results in the individual obtaining direct and clear information about the effectiveness of his or her performance.

Jobs can be rated as high or low on these dimensions. Examples of jobs with high and low ratings appear in Exhibit 5-5.

Critical Psychological States

The JCM, presented in Exhibit 5-5, links the five core job dimensions to three critical psychological states:[97]

- *Experienced meaningfulness*. The model predicts that if an employee's task is meaningful, the employee will view the job as important, valuable, and worthwhile. (Notice how in Exhibit 5-5 skill variety, task identity, and task significance combine to create meaningful work.)

- *Experienced responsibility for outcomes*. Employees feel a sense of personal responsibility for results when their jobs give them greater autonomy.

- *Knowledge of the actual results*. Feedback helps employees know whether they are performing effectively.

The model suggests that the more employees experience meaningfulness, responsibility, and knowledge of the actual results, the greater their motivation, performance, and satisfaction, and the lower their absenteeism and likelihood of leaving the organization.[98] As Exhibit 5-6 on page 192 shows, the links between the job dimensions and the outcomes are moderated or adjusted by the strength of the individual's growth need—in other words, the employee's desire for self-esteem and self-actualization. This means, for example, that not every employee will respond favourably to a job with skill variety, task identity, task significance, autonomy, or feedback. Those with high self-esteem and self-actualization needs will respond more favourably than others with different needs. The desire for

---

job enrichment The vertical expansion of jobs.

Learning About Yourself

1. Is an Enriched Job for You? **(page 203)**

skill variety The degree to which the job requires a variety of different activities.

task identity The degree to which the job requires completion of a whole and identifiable piece of work.

task significance The degree to which the job has a substantial impact on the lives or work of other people.

autonomy The degree to which the job provides substantial freedom, independence, and discretion to the individual in scheduling the work and determining the procedures to be used in carrying it out.

feedback The degree to which carrying out the work activities required by the job results in the individual obtaining direct and clear information about the effectiveness of his or her performance.

EXHIBIT 5-5 Examples of High and Low Job Characteristics

Skill Variety

High variety   The owner-operator of a garage who does electrical repair, rebuilds engines, does body work, and interacts with customers

Low variety   A body shop worker who sprays paint eight hours a day

Task Identity

High identity   A cabinet maker who designs a piece of furniture, selects the wood, builds the object, and finishes it to perfection

Low identity   A worker in a furniture factory who operates a lathe solely to make table legs

Task Significance

High significance   Nursing the sick in a hospital intensive care unit

Low significance   Sweeping hospital floors

Autonomy

High autonomy   A telephone installer who schedules his or her own work for the day, makes visits without supervision, and decides on the most effective techniques for a particular installation

Low autonomy   A telephone operator who must handle calls as they come according to a routine, highly specified procedure

Feedback

High feedback   An electronics factory worker who assembles a radio and then tests it to determine if it operates properly

Low feedback   An electronics factory worker who assembles a radio and then routes it to a quality control inspector who tests it for proper operation and makes needed adjustments

Source: G. Johns, *Organizational Behavior: Understanding and Managing Life at Work,* 4th ed. Copyright © 1997. Adapted by permission of Pearson Education, Inc. Upper Saddle River, NJ.

challenging jobs that are intrinsically motivated may be affected by culture as well, as *OB Around the Globe* illustrates.

AROUND THE GLOBE

Challenging Jobs and Job Satisfaction

How do various factors of one's job contribute to satisfaction in different cultures? A recent study attempted to answer this question in a survey of about 50 countries.[99]

The authors of the study distinguished between intrinsic job characteristics (for example, having a job that allows one to use one's skills, frequently receiving recognition from one's supervisor) and extrinsic job characteristics (for example, receiving pay that is competitive within a given industry, working in an environment that has comfortable physical conditions), and assessed differences between the two in predicting employee job satisfaction.

The study found that, across all countries, *extrinsic* job characteristics were consistently and positively related to satisfaction with one's job. However, wealthier countries, countries with stronger social security, countries that stress individualism rather than collectivism, and countries with a smaller power distance (those that value a more equal distribution of power in organizations and institutions) showed

EXHIBIT 5-6 The Job Characteristics Model

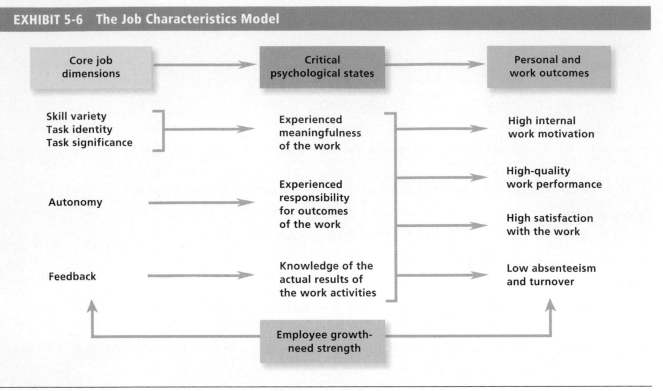

Source: J. R. Hackman, G. R. Oldham, *Work Design* (excerpted from pages 78–80). Copyright ©1980 by Addison-Wesley Publishing Co. Reprinted by permission of Addison-Wesley Longman.

a stronger relationship between the presence of *intrinsic* job characteristics and job satisfaction.

What explains these findings? One explanation is that in countries with greater wealth and social security, concerns over survival are taken for granted, and thus employees have the freedom to place greater importance on intrinsic aspects of the job. Another explanation is that cultural norms that emphasize the individual and have less power asymmetry socialize individuals to focus on the intrinsic aspects of their job. In other words, such norms tell individuals that it is okay to want jobs that are intrinsically rewarding.

A survey of college and university students highlights the underlying theme of the JCM. When the students were asked about what was most important to them as they thought about their careers, their top four answers were as follows:

- Having idealistic and committed co-workers (very important to 68 percent of the respondents)
- Doing work that helps others (very important to 65 percent)
- Doing work that requires creativity (very important to 47 percent)
- Having a lot of responsibility (very important to 39 percent)[100]

Salary and prestige ranked lower in importance than these four job characteristics.

Motivating Potential Score

motivating potential score (MPS) A predictive index suggesting the motivation potential in a job.

The JCM can be viewed as a model of how to increase employee motivation by creating better jobs. The core job dimensions can be combined into a single predictive index, called the **motivating potential score (MPS)**. Its computation is shown in Exhibit 5-7.

EXHIBIT 5-7   Computing a Motivating Potential Score

$$\text{Motivating Potential Score (MPS)} = \left[\frac{\text{Skill variety} + \text{Task identity} + \text{Task significance}}{3} \right] \times \text{Autonomy} \times \text{Feedback}$$

Jobs that are high on motivating potential must be high on at least one of the three factors that lead to experienced meaningfulness, and they must be high on both autonomy and feedback. If jobs score high on motivating potential, the model predicts that motivation, performance, and satisfaction will be positively affected, while the likelihood of absenteeism and turnover will be lessened.

The first part of the *Working with Others Exercise* on page 205 provides an opportunity for you to apply the JCM to a job of your choice. You will also calculate the job's MPS. In the second part of the *Working with Others Exercise*, you can redesign the job to show how you might increase its motivating potential. *From Concepts to Skills* on pages 208–209 provides specific guidelines on the kinds of changes that can help increase the motivating potential of jobs.

RESEARCH FINDINGS: JCM

The JCM has been well researched. Most of the evidence supports the general framework of the theory—that is, there is a multiple set of job characteristics, and these characteristics impact behavioural outcomes.[101] But it appears that the MPS model does not work—that is, we can better derive motivating potential by adding together the characteristics rather than using the complex MPS formula.[102] Beyond employee growth-need strength, other variables, such as the employee's perception of his or her workload compared with that of others, may also moderate the link between the core job dimensions and personal and work outcomes.[103] Overall, though, it appears that jobs that have the intrinsic elements of skill variety, task identity, task significance, autonomy, and feedback are more satisfying and generate higher performance from people than jobs that lack these characteristics.

Working on a fish-processing line requires being comfortable with job specialization. One person cuts off heads, another guts the fish, a third removes the scales. Each person performs the same task repetitively as fish move down the line. Such jobs are low on skill variety, task identity, task significance, autonomy, and feedback.

When might job redesign be most appropriate?

The evidence generally shows that job enrichment reduces absenteeism and turnover costs and increases satisfaction, but on the critical issue of productivity, the evidence is inconclusive.[104] In some situations, job enrichment increases productivity; in others, it decreases productivity. However, even when productivity goes down, there does seem to be consistently more conscientious use of resources and a higher quality of product or service.

Job Redesign in the Canadian Context: The Role of Unions

Until recently, labour unions have been largely resistant to participating in discussions with management over job redesign issues. Redesigns often result in loss of jobs, and labour unions try to prevent job loss. Union head offices, however, can sometimes be at odds with their membership over the acceptance of job redesign. Some members value the opportunity for skill development and more interesting work.

During the 1990s, some of the larger unions became more open to discussions about job redesign. This was reflected, for instance, in the position taken by the Communications, Energy and Paperworkers Union of Canada (CEP).[105] The CEP asserts that unions should be involved in the decisions and share in the benefits of work redesign. It calls for negotiated workplace changes, with greater union input into the conception, development, and implementation of work reorganization initiatives. The CEP also believes that basic wages, negotiated through a collective agreement, must remain the primary form of compensation, although the union is open to other forms of compensation as long as they do not detract from basic wages determined through collective bargaining.

While managers may regard job redesign as more difficult under a collective agreement, the reality is that for change to be effective in the workplace, management must gain employees' acceptance of the plan whether or not they are unionized.

Creating More Flexible Workplaces

6 How can flexible workplaces increase motivation?

The previous section examined how to make jobs more motivating. In this section, we examine practices that workplaces can use to address the needs of their employees, especially the need for work-life balance. Gay Bank, vice-president of human resources at the Royal Bank of Canada, notes that "it is estimated that as many as three in four working Canadians have responsibility for caring for children or aging parents."[106] A recent survey of work arrangements by Hewitt Associates found that almost half of the survey respondents offered flexible work locations or telecommuting, and 64 percent offered some sort of flexible work arrangement.[107] Such arrangements help employees ease the stress of juggling family needs alongside work demands. Below we consider how a compressed workweek, flextime, job sharing, and telecommuting might address the idea that Kohn had for increasing motivation: creating better work environments for people. *Case Incident—Working at Bob's in Rio* on page 208 asks you to look at various possibilities for making the work setting better for employees.

Compressed Workweek

compressed workweek A four-day week, with employees working 10 hours a day; or nine days of work over two weeks.

There are two common forms of a **compressed workweek**:

- The four 10-hour days per week plan (known as the 4–40 program)
- The nine days over two weeks plan (employees get either a Friday or Monday off once every two weeks in exchange for working slightly longer hours the other days)

These compressed workweek programs were conceived to allow employees more leisure and shopping time, and to permit them to travel to and from work outside rush hour. Supporters suggest that such programs can increase employee enthusiasm, morale, and commitment to the organization. Compressed workweek programs should make it easier for the organization to recruit employees. These programs also can provide additional support for employees to manage work and family conflicts.

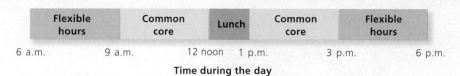

EXHIBIT 5-8   Example of a Flextime Schedule

Flexible hours	Common core	Lunch	Common core	Flexible hours

6 a.m.   9 a.m.   12 noon   1 p.m.   3 p.m.   6 p.m.

Time during the day

Flextime

Do employers really like flexible arrangements?

Flextime is short for flexible work hours. It allows employees some discretion over when they arrive at and leave work. Employees must work a specific number of hours a week, but they are free to vary the hours of work within certain limits. As shown in Exhibit 5-8, each day consists of a common core, usually six hours, with a flexibility band surrounding the core. (For example, exclusive of a one-hour lunch break, the core may be 9 a.m. to 3 p.m., with the office actually opening at 6 a.m. and closing at 6 p.m.) All employees are required to be at their jobs during the common core period, but they are allowed to accumulate their other two hours before and/or after the core time. Some flextime programs allow extra hours to be accumulated and turned into a free day off each month.

Flextime has become an extremely popular scheduling option, although in Canada women are less likely than men to have flexible work schedules.[108] More managers (42.4 percent) enjoy the freedom of flextime than do manufacturing employees (23.3 percent).[109]

Most of the performance evidence looking at the impact of flextime stacks up favourably. Flextime tends to reduce absenteeism and frequently improves employee productivity and satisfaction,[110] probably for several reasons. Employees can schedule their work hours to align with personal demands, thus reducing tardiness and absences, and employees can adjust their work activities to those hours in which they are individually more productive. Other research on the impact of flextime on the Canadian workplace has found that employees have positive attitudes and view it as their most preferred option.[111] Managers are in favour,[112] and women with flextime suffer less stress.[113]

Goodfish Lake, Alberta-based Goodfish Lake Development Corporation (GFLDC) is an Aboriginal business that provides dry-cleaning, clothing manufacturing and repair, protective clothing rentals, and bakery services to Fort McMurray. Many of the company's employees are women who have husbands that work full time in Fort McMurray. This can make it difficult for GFLDC's female employees to care for their children, so the company created flexible schedules to help employees balance work and home life.[114]

Flextime's major drawback is that it is not applicable to every job. It works well with clerical tasks where an employee's interaction with people outside his or her department is limited. It is not a viable option for receptionists, salespeople in retail stores, or similar jobs where people must be at their workstations at fixed times that suit the needs of customers and clients.

Job Sharing

Job sharing is a fairly recent phenomenon in the workplace, and more companies are starting to permit such arrangements. It is the practice of having two or more people split a 40-hour-a-week job. About 48 percent of larger Canadian organizations offer this option.[115]

Job sharing allows the organization to draw upon the talents of more than one individual in a given job. A bank manager who oversees two job sharers describes it as an opportunity to get two heads, but "pay for one."[116] It also opens up the opportunity

flextime An arrangement where employees work during a common core period each day but can form their total workday from a flexible set of hours outside the core.

job sharing The practice of having two or more people split a 40-hour-a-week job.

Jennifer Hong and Beatrice Gauthier share a job at Ceridian Canada. They also share a chair, desk, telephone, and wastebasket! Hong and Gauthier work at the Vancouver office of Manitoba-based Ceridian Canada, a payroll management company. Their arrangement started when Hong half-jokingly asked her friend and colleague Gauthier if she wanted to share a job. Hong was a new mom and wanted to spend time with her young daughter. Gauthier had been looking for such an arrangement for several years.

to acquire skilled workers—for instance, women with young children, retirees, and others desiring flexibility—who might not be available on a full-time basis.[117] Consequently, it can increase motivation and satisfaction for those for whom a 40-hour-a-week job is just not practical. The major difficulty of job sharing is finding compatible pairs of employees who can successfully coordinate the demands of one job.[118]

Job sharing can be a creative solution to some organizational problems. For example, Nunavut has had great difficulty finding doctors willing to commit to serving the territory for more than short periods of time.[119] Dr. Sandy MacDonald, director of Medical Affairs and Telehealth for Nunavut, has tried to increase physician retention by allowing doctors to work for three months at a time. "In the past, the government was trying to get some of them to sign up for two or three years, and most people don't want to do that initially, or they would leave positions unfilled because someone would only come for two or three weeks or a month," he says. Meanwhile, doctors working in Nunavut were overworked because there were not enough doctors on call. MacDonald's approach has changed that—now more doctors are available because of the job-sharing solution.

Telecommuting

It might be close to the ideal job for many people. No commuting, flexible hours, freedom to dress as you please, and few or no interruptions from colleagues. It's called **telecommuting** and refers to employees who do their work at home at least two days a week on a computer that is linked to their office.[120] (A closely related term—*the virtual office*—is increasingly being used to describe employees who work out of their home on a relatively permanent basis).

telecommuting An arrangement where employees do their work at home on a computer that is linked to their office.

> If you want to telecommute, what kind of job should you consider?

About 40 percent of companies offered telecommuting in 2008, up from 25 percent in 2007.[121] Some of the increase may be attributable to the sharp rise in gasoline prices during that period. Longueuil, Quebec-based SICO Paints, Manitoba Hydro, and the Saskatchewan Government are examples of workplaces that encourage telecommuting.

Internationally, too, the concept is catching on. The number of Americans who reported working from home at least one day a year grew from 41.3 million in 2003 to 44.4 million in 2004. Another study found that 8.9 million Americans who were not self-employed worked at home at least three days a month in 2004.[122]

Telecommuting: How and Why It Works

The idea of having a home office appeals to many, but telecommuters do not always work from home. In one TELUS program, for example, employees avoid up to a three-hour-a-day commute to and from downtown Vancouver by reporting for work at a specially established satellite office in suburban Langley, nearer to their homes. Telecommuting employees are more productive than they had previously been because of the reduced commute and fewer disruptions.[123]

Firms must make appropriate arrangements when employees working away from the office need routine administrative support. At North Vancouver, BC-based law firm

Telecommuting is appropriate for the knowledge-based work of employees at KPMG, a global network of professional firms that provides audit, tax, and advisory services. Kelvin Brown, a senior manager in KPMG's research and development tax concession section, works on his laptop at his beef cattle farm near Harden, Australia, a four-hour drive away from the company's office in Sydney. For Brown, working from home increases his productivity and allows him more time to spend with his family.

Ratcliff & Company, one lawyer occasionally works from Bowen Island, while two others work from Vancouver Island. When they need documents typed, they email their dictated audio files to their support staff.[124]

We have been looking at examples from the Vancouver area, but telecommuting does not take place on just a local level, as *OB Around the Globe* indicates.

 AROUND THE GLOBE

Liz Codling Manages Long Distance

Can a manager be effective from five time zones away? Liz Codling, a senior manager at Bank of Montreal in Toronto, manages her staff from the United Kingdom.[125] After running the bank's staff education centre for four years and overseeing a team of eight people, she decided to return home to the United Kingdom with her husband. But Codling's bosses didn't want to lose her, so she became the bank's first transatlantic telecommuter. Although separated from her staff by five time zones and more than 4800 kilometres, Codling, and other communication managers like her, can rely on communication technology such as Skype, Twitter, and Facebook, in addition to email, voice mail, and video conferencing to keep in touch.

Some adjustments were needed. For instance, Codling has had to adjust her workday to align with Toronto hours, and her colleagues now know to schedule meetings in the mornings so she can be included.

What kinds of jobs lend themselves to telecommuting? Three categories have been identified as most appropriate: routine information-handling tasks, mobile activities, and professional and other knowledge-related tasks.[126] Writers, attorneys, analysts, and employees who spend the majority of their time on computers or the phone are natural candidates for telecommuting. Telemarketers, customer-service representatives, reservation agents, and product-support specialists can access information on their computer screens at home as easily as on the company screen in any office.

A recent Ipsos Reid study found that 42 percent of employees reported that they would be more likely to stay with their current employer, or enticed to take a new job, if the employer offered the opportunity to telecommute.[127] Other researchers looking at teleworking in Canada have found that it results in increased productivity,[128] decreased stress,[129] and better service to customers and clients.[130] Telecommuting has been found to reduce turnover[131] and decrease absenteeism.[132]

Telecommuting: The Downside

Not all employees embrace the idea of telecommuting, however. Some workers complain that they miss out on important meetings and informal interactions that lead to new policies and ideas. They also miss the social contact that occurs at work. Teleworking can decrease commitment to the organization,[133] and increase feelings of isolation[134] and burnout.[135] Telecommuters may be less likely or able to function as team players as well.[136] Typically, telecommuters are also remote from their managers.

The long-term future of telecommuting depends on some questions for which we don't yet have definitive answers. For instance, will employees who do their work at home be at a disadvantage in office politics? Might they be less likely to be considered for salary increases and promotions? Is being out of sight equivalent to being out of mind? Will nonwork distractions, such as children, neighbours, and the proximity of the television set and refrigerator, significantly reduce productivity for those without superior willpower and discipline?

We also do not know what the effect of working day after day in somewhat isolated circumstances has on individuals who do most of their work away from the office. Experts agree that home telecommuters in particular should come in to the central office at least once a week. As Ernie Gauvreau, chief operating officer for law firm Ratcliff & Company, explains, it is unlikely that Ratcliff's lawyers will work from home every day. "We need to bounce ideas off each other. And if you're at home, that doesn't exist."[137]

The strategies for work redesign that we have described have already had a profound impact on the ways Canadians perform and think about their jobs. Some even argue that "jobs" as we know them are becoming obsolete—that demands by employers and employees alike for greater flexibility and autonomy will result in the development of a contingent workforce with very little resemblance to job holders of the past.

Motivation: Putting It All Together

7 Can we simplify how we think about motivation?

In Chapter 4, we reviewed basic theories of motivation, considering such factors as how needs affect motivation, the importance of linking performance to rewards, and the need for fair process. In this chapter, we considered various ways to pay and recognize people, and looked at job design and creating more flexible workplaces. Three Harvard University professors recently completed two studies that suggest a way to put all of these ideas together to understand (1) what motivates people, and (2) how to use this knowledge to make sure that organizational processes motivate.[138]

According to the study authors, research suggests that four basic emotional drives (needs) guide individuals.[139] These are the drive to acquire; the drive to bond; the drive to comprehend; and the drive to defend. People want to acquire any number of scarce goods, both tangible and intangible (such as social status). They want to bond with other individuals and groups. They want to understand the world around them. As well, they want to protect against external threats to themselves and others, and want to ensure justice occurs.

EXHIBIT 5-9   How to Fulfill the Drives That Motivate Employees

DRIVE	PRIMARY LEVER	ACTIONS
1 Acquire	Reward System	• Sharply differentiate good performers from average and poor performers • Tie rewards clearly to performance • Pay as well as your competitors
2 Bond	Culture	• Foster mutual reliance and friendship among co-workers • Value collaboration and teamwork • Encourage sharing of best practices
3 Comprehend	Job Design	• Design jobs that have distinct and important roles in the organization • Design jobs that are meaningful and foster a sense of contribution to the organization
4 Defend	Performance Management and Resource Allocation Processes	• Increase the transparency of all processes • Emphasize their fairness • Build trust by being just and transparent in granting rewards, assignments, and other forms of recognition

Source: N. Nohria, B. Groysberg, and L.-E. Lee, "Employee Motivation: A Powerful New Model," *Harvard Business Review* 86, no. 7–8 (July–August 2008), p. 82. Reprinted by permission of *Harvard Business Review*.

Understanding these different drives makes it possible to motivate individuals more effectively. As the study authors point out, "each drive is best met by a distinct organizational lever." The drive to acquire is met through organizational rewards. The drive to bond can be met by "creat[ing] a culture that promotes teamwork, collaboration, openness, and friendship." The drive to comprehend is best met through job design and creating jobs that are "meaningful, interesting, and challenging." The drive to defend can be accomplished through an organization's performance management and resource allocation processes; this includes fair and transparent processes for managing performance and adequate resources to do one's job. Exhibit 5-9 indicates concrete ways that organizational characteristics can address individual drives.

Summary and Implications

1 Is money an important motivator? The most commonly used reward in organizations is money. Despite the importance of money in attracting and retaining employees, and rewarding and recognizing them, little attention has been given to individual differences in people's feelings about money.[140] Some studies indicate that money is not employees' top priority. A number of studies suggest that there are personality traits and demographic factors that correlate with an individual's attitude toward money.[141] People who value money highly score higher on "attributes like sensation seeking, competitiveness, materialism, and control." People who desire money score higher on self-esteem, need for achievement, and Type A personality measures. Men seem to value money more than women do.

2 **What does an effective reward system look like?** In general, an effective reward system links pay to performance, which is consistent with expectancy theory predictions. In variable-pay or pay-for-performance programs, companies operate reward programs at three levels: individual (piece-rate wages, merit-based pay, bonuses, and skill-based pay), group (gainsharing), and organizational (profit-sharing, stock options, and employee stock ownership plans). Under variable-pay programs, individuals should perceive a strong relationship between their performance and the rewards they receive, and thus be more motivated. Research in Canada, which looked at both unionized and non-unionized workplaces, found that variable-pay programs result in "increased productivity, a safer work environment, a better understanding of the business by employees, and little risk of employees losing base pay."[142] Other effective rewards are flexible benefits plans that meet the diverse needs of a workforce and recognition programs that acknowledge individual efforts in concrete ways, such as thank-you notes, employee-of-the-month programs, and public acknowledgments.

3 **What kinds of mistakes are made in reward systems?** Motivation theories and rewards are culture-bound. Individuals respond to rewards in general and specific rewards differently, depending upon what culture they come from. Individuals also need to be given feedback about their performance, something many managers are reluctant to do. Lack of feedback makes it difficult to know how performance and rewards are related. If individuals perceive this relationship to be low, the results will be low performance, a decrease in job satisfaction, and an increase in turnover and absenteeism. Finally, individuals are responsive to the signals sent out by organizations, and if they determine that some activities are not valued, they may not engage in them, even when the firm expects employees to do so. Rewards should be linked to the type of performance expected.

4 **Are rewards overrated?** In the right context, individuals often motivate themselves intrinsically and can achieve quite high levels of performance. We also know that giving rewards for things that were previously done for intrinsic motivation will decrease motivation.

5 **How can jobs be designed to increase motivation?** An understanding of work design can help managers design jobs that affect employee motivation positively. Managers can add more variety to jobs through job rotation and enlargement. They can also enrich jobs, and increase autonomy, following the job characteristics model. The model looks at a job's skill variety, task identity, task significance, autonomy, and feedback. It tells us that jobs in which employees have control over key elements in their work score higher in motivating potential than jobs in which employees don't have such control. Jobs that offer autonomy, feedback, and similar complex task characteristics tend to be more motivating for employees.

6 **How can flexible workplaces increase motivation?** Alternative work schedule options such as the compressed workweek, flextime, job sharing, and telecommuting have grown in popularity in recent years. They have become an important strategic tool as organizations try to increase the flexibility their employees need.

7 **Can we simplify how we think about motivation?** We have covered a lot of material in Chapters 4 and 5 in trying to understand how best to motivate. Recent research suggests that organizational processes should meet the four basic emotional drives of individuals: acquire, bond, comprehend, and defend. In doing so, a greater level of motivation can be achieved.

For Review

1. What role, if any, does money play in employee recognition and job redesign?

2. What are the pros and cons of variable-pay programs from an employee's viewpoint? From management's viewpoint?

3. What is the difference between gainsharing and profit sharing?

4. What is an ESOP? How might it positively influence employee motivation?

5. Why is employee recognition an important reward?

6. What can firms do to create more motivating work environments for their employees?

7. Describe three jobs that score high on the JCM. Describe three jobs that score low.

8. What are the advantages of flextime from an employee's perspective? From management's perspective?

9. What are the advantages of job sharing from an employee's perspective? From management's perspective?

10. From an employee's perspective, what are the pros and cons of telecommuting?

For Critical Thinking

1. "Employee recognition may be motivational for the moment, but it doesn't have any staying power. Why? Because employees can't take recognition to Roots or The Bay!" Do you agree or disagree? Discuss.

2. "Performance cannot be measured, so any effort to link pay with performance is a fantasy. Differences in performance are often caused by the system, which means the organization ends up rewarding the circumstances. It's the same thing as rewarding the weather forecaster for a pleasant day." Do you agree or disagree with this statement? Support your position.

3. "Job redesign is a way of exploiting employees by increasing their responsibilities." Comment on this statement, and explain whether you agree with it or not.

4. What can management do to improve employees' perceptions that their jobs are interesting and challenging?

5. Individuals vary in their emotional drives (or needs). How can we use that information to motivate employees?

 **for You**

- Because the people you interact with appreciate recognition, consider including a brief note on a nice card to show thanks for a job well done. Or you might send a basket of flowers. Sometimes just sending a pleasant, thankful email is enough to make a person feel valued. All of these things are easy enough to do, and appreciated greatly by the recipient.

- If you are working on a team or in a volunteer organization, try to find ways to motivate co-workers using the job characteristics model. For instance, make sure that everyone has some tasks over which they have autonomy, and make sure people get feedback on their work.

- When you are working on a team project, think about whether everyone on the team should get the same reward, or whether rewards should be allocated according to performance. Individual-based performance rewards may decrease team cohesiveness if individuals do not cooperate with each other.

POINT

COUNTERPOINT

Money Motivates!

The importance of money as a motivator has been consistently downplayed by most behavioural scientists. They prefer to point out the value of challenging jobs, goals, participation in decision making, feedback, cohesive work teams, and other nonmonetary factors as stimulants to employee motivation. We argue otherwise here—that money is the crucial incentive to work motivation. As a medium of exchange, it is the vehicle by which employees can purchase the numerous need-satisfying things they desire. Furthermore, money also performs the function of a scorecard, by which employees assess the value that the organization places on their services and by which employees can compare their value to others.[143]

Money's value as a medium of exchange is obvious. People may not work only for money, but remove the money and how many people would come to work? A study of nearly 2500 employees found that while these people disagreed over what their primary motivator was, they unanimously ranked money as their number two.[144] This study reaffirms that for the vast majority of the workforce, a regular paycheque is absolutely necessary in order to meet basic physiological and safety needs.

The best case for money as a motivator is a review of studies done by Ed Locke at the University of Maryland.[145] Locke looked at four methods of motivating employee performance: money, goal setting, participation in decision making, and redesigning jobs to give employees more challenge and responsibility. He found that the average improvement from money was 30 percent; goal setting increased performance 16 percent; participation improved performance by less than 1 percent; and job redesign positively impacted performance by an average of 17 percent. Moreover, every study Locke reviewed that used money as a method of motivation resulted in some improvement in employee performance. Such evidence demonstrates that money may not be the only motivator, but it is difficult to argue that it doesn't motivate!

Money Doesn't Motivate Most Employees Today!

Money can motivate some people under some conditions, so the issue isn't really whether money can motivate. The answer to that is, "It can!" The more relevant question is this: Does money motivate most employees in the workforce today to higher performance? The answer to this question, we will argue, is "no."[146]

For money to motivate an individual's performance, certain conditions must be met. First, money must be important to the individual. Second, money must be perceived by the individual as being a direct reward for performance. Third, the marginal amount of money offered for the performance must be perceived by the individual as being significant. Finally, management must have the discretion to reward high performers with more money. Let's take a look at each of these conditions.

Money is not important to all employees. High achievers, for instance, are intrinsically motivated. Money should have little impact on these people. Similarly, money is relevant to those individuals with strong lower-order needs; but for most of the workforce, lower-order needs are substantially satisfied.

Money would motivate if employees perceived a strong linkage between performance and rewards in organizations. Unfortunately, pay increases are far more often determined by levels of skills and experience, community pay standards, the consumer price index, and the organization's current and future financial prospects than by each employee's level of performance.

For money to motivate, the marginal difference in pay increases between a high performer and an average performer must be significant. In practice, it rarely is. How much motivation is there in knowing that if you work really hard, you are going to end up with $20 a week more than someone who is doing just enough to get by? For a large number of people, not much! Research indicates that merit raises must be at least 7 percent of base pay for employees to perceive them as motivating. Unfortunately, recent surveys find top performers receive, on average, a merit increase of 5.6 percent, with average employees receiving a 3.1 percent increase.[147]

In most organizations, managers have a very small area of discretion within which they can reward their higher-performing employees. So money might be theoretically capable of motivating employees to higher levels of performance, but most managers are not given enough flexibility to do much about it.

Is an Enriched Job for You?

People differ in what they like and dislike in their jobs.[148] Listed below are 12 pairs of jobs. For each pair, indicate which job you would prefer. Assume that everything else about the jobs is the same—pay attention only to the characteristics actually listed for each pair of jobs. If you would prefer the job in Column A, indicate how much you prefer it by putting a checkmark in a blank to the left of the Neutral point. If you prefer the job in Column B, check 1 of the blanks to the right of Neutral. Check the Neutral blank only if you find the 2 jobs equally attractive or unattractive. Try to use the Neutral blank rarely.

Column A		Column B
1. A job that offers little or no challenge.	Strongly prefer A — Neutral — Strongly prefer B	A job that requires you to be completely isolated from co-workers.
2. A job that pays well.	Strongly prefer A — Neutral — Strongly prefer B	A job that allows considerable opportunity to be creative and innovative.
3. A job that often requires you to make important decisions.	Strongly prefer A — Neutral — Strongly prefer B	A job in which there are many pleasant people to work with.
4. A job with little security in a somewhat unstable organization.	Strongly prefer A — Neutral — Strongly prefer B	A job in which you have little or no opportunity to participate in decisions that affect your work.
5. A job in which greater responsibility is given to those who do the best work.	Strongly prefer A — Neutral — Strongly prefer B	A job in which greater responsibility is given to loyal employees who have the most seniority.
6. A job with a manager who sometimes is highly critical.	Strongly prefer A — Neutral — Strongly prefer B	A job that does not require you to use much of your talent.
7. A very routine job.	Strongly prefer A — Neutral — Strongly prefer B	A job in which your co-workers are not very friendly.
8. A job with a manager who respects you and treats you fairly.	Strongly prefer A — Neutral — Strongly prefer B	A job that provides constant opportunities for you to learn new and interesting things.
9. A job that gives you a real chance to develop yourself personally.	Strongly prefer A — Neutral — Strongly prefer B	A job with excellent vacation and fringe benefits.
10. A job in which there is a real chance you could be laid off.	Strongly prefer A — Neutral — Strongly prefer B	A job with very little chance to do challenging work.
11. A job with little freedom and independence to do your work in the way you think best.	Strongly prefer A — Neutral — Strongly prefer B	A job with poor working conditions.
12. A job with very satisfying teamwork.	Strongly prefer A — Neutral — Strongly prefer B	A job that allows you to use your skills and abilities to the fullest extent.

OB *AT WORK*

Scoring Key:

This questionnaire taps the degree to which you have a strong vs. weak desire to obtain growth satisfaction from your work. Each item on the questionnaire yields a score from 1 to 7 (that is, "Strongly prefer A" is scored 1; "Neutral" is scored 4; and "Strongly prefer B" is scored 7). To obtain your individual growth-need strength score, average the 12 items as follows:

Numbers 1, 2, 7, 8, 11, 12 (direct scoring, where "Strongly prefer A" is scored 1)

Numbers 3, 4, 5, 6, 9, 10 (reverse scoring, where "Strongly prefer B" is scored 1)

Average scores for typical respondents are close to the midpoint of 4. Research indicates that if you score high on this measure, you will respond positively to an enriched job. Conversely, if you score low, you will tend not to find enriched jobs satisfying or motivating.

You can use this questionnaire to identify areas where you can improve your interview skills. If you scored 3 or less on any statement, you should consider what you can do to improve that score.

More Learning About Yourself Exercises

An additional self-assessment relevant to this chapter appears on MyOBLab (**www.pearsoned.ca/myoblab**).

I.C.8 What's My Job's Motivating Potential?

When you complete the additional assessments, consider the following:

1. Am I surprised about my score?

2. Would my friends evaluate me similarly?

BREAKOUT **GROUP** EXERCISES

Form small groups to discuss the following topics, as assigned by your instructor:

1. How might the job of student be redesigned to make it more motivating?

2. What is your ideal job? To what extent does it match up with the elements of the JCM?

3. Would you prefer working from home or working at the office? Why?

WORKING WITH OTHERS EXERCISE

Analyzing and Redesigning Jobs

Break into groups of 5 to 7 members each.[149] Each student should describe the worst job he or she has ever had. Use any criteria you want to select 1 of these jobs for analysis by the group.

Members of the group will analyze the job selected by determining how well it scores on the job characteristics model. Use the following scale for your analysis of each job dimension:

7 = **Very high**

6 = **High**

5 = **Somewhat high**

4 = **Moderate**

3 = **Somewhat low**

2 = **Low**

1 = **Very low**

The following sample questions can guide the group in its analysis of the job in question:

- *Skill variety.* Describe the different identifiable skills required to do this job. What is the nature of the oral, written, and/or quantitative skills needed? Physical skills? Does the job holder get the opportunity to use all of his or her skills?

- *Task identity.* What is the product that the job holder creates? Is he or she involved in its production from beginning to end? If not, is he or she involved in a particular phase of its production from beginning to end?

- *Task significance.* How important is the product? How important is the job holder's role in producing it? How important is the job holder's contribution to the people he or she works with? If the job holder's job were eliminated, how inferior would the product be?

- *Autonomy.* How much independence does the job holder have? Does he or she have to follow a strict schedule? How closely is he or she supervised?

- *Feedback.* Does the job holder get regular feedback from his or her manager? From peers? From his or her staff? From customers? How about intrinsic performance feedback when doing the job?

Using the formula in Exhibit 5-7 on page 193, calculate the job's motivating potential score. Discuss whether you think this score accurately reflects your perceptions of the motivating potential of these professions.

Using the suggestions offered in the chapter for redesigning jobs, describe specific actions that management could take to increase this job's motivating potential.

Calculate the costs to management of redesigning the job in question. Do the benefits exceed the costs?

Conclude the exercise by having a representative of each group share his or her group's analysis and redesign suggestions with the entire class. Possible topics for class discussion might include similarities in the jobs chosen, problems in rating job dimensions, and the cost-benefit assessment of design changes.

OB *AT WORK*

ETHICAL **DILEMMA** EXERCISE

Are CEOs Paid Too Much?

Critics have described the astronomical pay packages given to Canadian and American CEOs as "rampant greed."[150] In 2006, the average compensation of Canada's 100 best-paid CEOs was $8 528 304. This was more than 218 times what the average full-time Canadian employee made.[151]

How do you explain such large pay packages for CEOs? Some say this represents a classic economic response to a situation in which the demand is great for high-quality top-executive talent, and the supply is low. Other arguments in favour of paying executives millions a year are the need to compensate people for the tremendous responsibilities and stress that go with such jobs; the motivating potential that seven- and eight-figure annual incomes provide to senior executives and those who might aspire to be; and the influence of senior executives on the company's bottom line.

Critics of executive pay practices in Canada and the United States argue that CEOs choose board members whom they can count on to support ever-increasing pay for top management. If board members fail to "play along," they risk losing their positions, their fees, and the prestige and power inherent in board membership.

In addition, it is not clear that executive compensation is tied to firm performance. For instance, KPMG found in one survey that for 40 percent of the respondents, there was no correlation between the size of the bonus and how poorly or well the company fared. Consider the data in Exhibit 5-10, which illustrates the disconnect that can sometimes happen between CEO compensation and firm performance. *National Post Business* writers calculated that the CEOs noted in that exhibit were overpaid, based on their company's performance in 2007.

Is high compensation of CEOs a problem? If so, does the blame for the problem lie with CEOs or with the shareholders and boards that knowingly allow the practice? Are Canadian and American CEOs greedy? Are these CEOs acting unethically? Should their pay reflect more closely some multiple of their employees' wages? What do you think?

EXHIBIT 5-10   2007 Compensation of Canada's "Most Overpaid" CEOs*

CEO(s)	Was Paid (3-Yr Avg.)	Should Have Been Paid	Amount Overpaid
1. James Balsillie and Michael Lazarides Research in Motion Waterloo, Ontario	$76 871 000	$1 537 000	$75 334 000
2. Jeffrey Orr and Robert Gratton Power Financial Montreal, Quebec	$59 555 000	$11 911 000	$47 644 000
3. Kevin MacArthur, Ian Telfer, and Robert McEwan Goldcorp Vancouver, British Columbia	$8 238 000	$1 730 000	$6 508 000
4. Donald Walker, Siefgried Wolf, and Frank Stronach Magna International Aurora, Ontario	$33 054 000	$7 272 000	$25 782 000
5. Robert Gannicott Harry Winston Diamond Corp. Toronto, Ontario	$2 706 000	$649 000	$2 057 000

*National Post Business calculated a "Bang for the Buck" formula, taking into account CEO performance variables.

Source: D. Dias, "Bang for the Buck," *National Post Business*, November 2007, p. 20. Material reprinted with the express permission of National Post Company, a CanWest Partnership.

CASE INCIDENTS

Thanks for Nothing

Although it may seem fairly obvious that receiving praise and recognition from one's company is a motivating experience, sadly, many companies are failing miserably when it comes to saying thanks to their employees.[152] According to Curt Coffman, global practice leader at Gallup, 71 percent of US workers are "disengaged," essentially meaning that they could not care less about their organization. Coffman states, "We're operating at one-quarter of the capacity in terms of managing human capital. It's alarming." Employee recognition programs, which became more popular as the US economy shifted from industrial to knowledge-based, can be an effective way to motivate employees and make them feel valued. In many cases, however, recognition programs are doing "more harm than good," according to Coffman.

Take Ko, a 50-year-old former employee of a dot-com in California. Her company proudly instituted a rewards program designed to motivate employees. What were the rewards for a job well done? Employees would receive a badge that read "U Done Good" and, each year, would receive a T-shirt as a means of annual recognition. Once an employee received 10 "U Done Good" badges, he or she could trade them in for something bigger and better—a paperweight. Ko states that she would have preferred a raise. "It was patronizing. There wasn't any deep thought involved in any of this." To make matters worse, she says, the badges were handed out arbitrarily and were not tied to performance. And what about those T-shirts? Ko states that the company instilled a strict dress code, so employees could not even wear the shirts if they wanted to. Needless to say, the employee recognition program seemed like an empty gesture rather than a motivator.

Even programs that provide employees with more expensive rewards can backfire, especially if the rewards are given insincerely. Eric Lange, an employee of a trucking company, recalls a time when one of the company's vice-presidents achieved a major financial goal for the company. The vice-president, who worked in an office next to Lange, received a Cadillac Seville as his company car and a new Rolex wristwatch that cost the company $10 000. Both were lavish gifts, but the way they were distributed left a sour taste in the vice-president's mouth. He entered his office to find the Rolex in a cheap cardboard box sitting on his desk, along with a brief letter explaining that he would be receiving a tax form in order to pay taxes on the watch. Lange states of the vice-president, "He came into my office, which was right next door, and said, 'Can you believe this?'" A mere two months later, the vice-president pawned the watch. Lange explains, "It had absolutely no meaning for him."

Such experiences resonate with employees who may find more value in a sincere pat on the back than in gifts from management that either are meaningless or are not conveyed with respect or sincerity. However, sincere pats on the back may be hard to come by. A Gallup poll found that 61 percent of employees stated that they have not received a sincere "thank you" from management in the past year. Findings such as these are troubling, as verbal rewards are not only inexpensive for companies to hand out but also quick and easy to distribute. Of course, verbal rewards do need to be paired sometimes with tangible benefits that employees value—after all, money talks. In addition, when praising employees for a job well done, managers need to ensure that the praise is given in conjunction with the specific accomplishment. In this way, employees may not only feel valued by their organization, but will also know what actions to take to be rewarded in the future.

Questions

1. If praising employees for doing a good job seems to be a fairly easy and obvious motivational tool, why do you think companies and managers don't often do it?

2. As a manager, what steps would you take to motivate your employees after observing them perform well?

3. Are there any downsides to giving employees too much verbal praise? What might these downsides be, and how could you alleviate them as a manager?

4. As a manager, how would you ensure that recognition given to employees is distributed fairly and justly?

OB *AT WORK*

Working at Bob's in Rio

Bob's is one of the largest fast-food chains in Latin America.[153] It's a McDonald's clone, with headquarters in Rio de Janeiro and more than half of its 225 outlets located in Brazil. What's it like to work at Bob's? A day at an outlet in a mall in São Paulo provides some insights.

The most notable characteristic of this fast-food restaurant is the youth of the 12 employees. Silvana, who supervises the training of new hires, has had two promotions in her four years on the job. Yet she is only 21 years old. Levy, the short-order cook, is 20 and has been doing his job for a year. Elisangela is 21 and has been a Bob's employee for two years. The restaurant's manager, who has seven years at Bob's, is 23. Simone is one of the oldest employees at 25.

Bob's employees have another commonality besides their youth. They are all from a humble social background. Middle-class kids want to avoid working in fast-food places.

The jobs at Bob's have a highly structured routine. For instance, if you are working the grill, you need to know that a Big Bob gets two slices of beef, 11 grams of lettuce, and 7 grams of sliced onions on a sesame seed bun; a Bob's Burger is also two slices of beef with special sauce but only a slice of tomato on a plain bun; and a Franburgao

gets a chicken breast, tomato, and curry sauce on a sesame seed bun. If you are working the french-fryer, you need to check the temperature of the oil, make sure it's 174 degrees Celsius, put one package of fries into the bin, push it down slowly into the oil until you hear the click, wait for the machine to bring it back up, shake the bin three times, and pour the fries into the steel container.

Employees seem generally content with their jobs. In spite of having to wear a silly red tie, a blue and red baseball cap, and an apron that says Bob's, these people are glad to have a job in a country where as many as one in five is unemployed. Standard employees earn 500 reals (less than $450 Cdn. a month). The manager's salary is around 1300 reals a month.

Questions

1. Describe an entry-level job at Bob's in JCM terms.

2. What type of employee do you think would fit well at Bob's?

3. Could jobs at Bob's be enriched to make employees more productive?

4. Could flextime work at Bob's? Explain.

From **Concepts** to **Skills**

Designing Enriched Jobs

How does management enrich an employee's job? The following suggestions, based on the JCM, specify the types of changes in jobs that are most likely to lead to improving their motivating potential.[154]

1. *Combine tasks.* Managers should seek to take existing and fractionalized tasks and put them back together to form a new and larger module of work. This increases skill variety and task identity.

2. *Create natural work units.* The creation of natural work units means that the tasks an employee does form an identifiable and meaningful whole. This

increases employee "ownership" of the work and improves the likelihood that employees will view their work as meaningful and important rather than as irrelevant and boring.

3. *Establish client relationships.* The client is the user of the product or service that the employee works on (and may be an "internal customer" as well as someone outside the organization). Wherever possible, managers should try to establish direct relationships between workers and their clients. This increases skill variety, autonomy, and feedback for the employee.

4. *Expand jobs vertically.* Vertical expansion gives employees responsibilities and control that were formerly reserved for management. It seeks to partially close the gap between the "doing" and the "controlling" aspects of the job, and it increases employee autonomy.

5. *Open feedback channels.* By increasing feedback, employees not only learn how well they are performing their jobs, but also whether their performance is improving, deteriorating, or remaining at a constant level. Ideally, this feedback about performance should be received directly as the employee does the job, rather than from management on an occasional basis. For instance, at many restaurants you can find feedback cards on the table to indicate the quality of service received during the meal.

Practising Skills

You own and manage Sunrise Deliveries, a small freight transportation company that makes local deliveries of products for your customers. You have a total of nine employees—an administrative assistant, two warehouse personnel, and six delivery drivers.

The drivers' job is pretty straightforward. Each morning they come in at 7:30 a.m., pick up their daily schedule, and then drive off in their preloaded trucks to make their stops. They occasionally will also pick up packages and return them to the Sunrise warehouse, where they will be unloaded and redirected by the warehouse workers.

You have become very concerned with the high turnover among your drivers. Of your current six drivers, three have been working for you less than two months and only one's tenure exceeds six months. This is frustrating because you are paying your drivers more than many of the larger delivery companies like UPS and FedEx. This turnover is getting expensive because you are constantly having to spend time finding and training replacements. It's also hard to develop a quality customer-service program when customers constantly see new faces. When you have asked departing drivers why they are quitting, common complaints include: "There's no room for advancement," "The job is boring," and "All we do is drive." What should you do to solve this problem?

Reinforcing Skills

1. Think of the worst job you have ever had. Analyze the job according to the five dimensions identified in the JCM. Redesign the job to make it more satisfying and motivating.

2. Spend one to three hours at various times observing employees in your college dining hall. What actions would you recommend to make these jobs more motivating?

VIDEO CASE INCIDENT

CASE 5 Human Resources at KPMG

Bruce Pfau, vice-president of human resources at KPMG, says that the company is dealing with a shortage of qualified people who can take on the many new tasks created by new accounting regulations. The accounting scandals at firms such as Enron and WorldCom and the failure of accounting firm Arthur Andersen have led to a lot of litigation in the industry, which has created a challenging work environment for many accounting firms. In addition to this industry-wide problem, the top management at KPMG determined that "employee engagement" scores were lower than what the company wanted, and only 50 percent of employees felt that KPMG was a great place to work.

Pfau recognizes that KPMG is in a war for talent with other accounting firms. The company needs to attract the best people, and to do that, it needs to have what he calls a "superior employment proposition." Undergraduates are telling KPMG what they want from an ideal employer—great career development, good economic rewards, good benefits, a great work-life balance, and global experience.

To create the desired "superior employment proposition," KPMG makes sure that it is sharing the firm's economic success with its employees. Over 85 percent of employees receive bonuses at the end of the year, and many more employees receive on-the-spot bonuses (called "encore awards" at KPMG) of $100, $200, or $500 for a job well done. The company has also changed the mix of retirement plans, tripled contributions to pension plans, makes sure people have adequate time off, and has a good vacation policy. The #1 priority is career development. People are trained not just in the area of technical skills, but also in leadership and project management skills.

The company has also launched the Employee Career Architecture (ECA) program. As a result of information generated in focus groups, KPMG found that what employees wanted most in their career was to have a close relationship with their performance manager or mentor so they could have in-depth conversations about their career. The company provides resources and tools that help make employee conversations with their performance manager valuable to the employee. For example, Suzanne Barnum, the performance manager for Meredith Ferguson, has regular discussions with Meredith about the behaviours that will make Meredith more successful. Meredith says that people can go on the ECA and determine if there is a domestic or foreign rotation position that is available.

Pfau says that rotations are a win-win proposition because employees learn a lot and come back with more skills that will help the company. Turnover at KPMG is now very low, and the company is hiring people who have high grade point averages from very good schools. There has also been an improvement in engagement scores. These things combined save the company millions of dollars each year.

Questions

1. To what extent are the motivation practices at KPMG consistent with satisfaction of the four employee drives identified in Exhibit 5-9? Explain.

2. Briefly summarize the main points in the debate about the effect of monetary rewards on employee motivation. Do you think that KPMG should continue to give bonuses to employees?

3. KPMG is a multinational firm. What sort of advice would you offer to KPMG management about motivating people across different cultures?

4. To what extent are KPMG's current motivation practices consistent with the recommendations made by Alfie Kohn? Give examples.

5. KPMG spends a significant amount of time getting input from both current and potential employees regarding what they want in a job. Why is this so important to the organization?

Source: Based on "Human Resources at KPMG," Organizational Behavior Video Library, 2008. Copyrighted by Prentice-Hall.

Groups and Teamwork

How can a team go from being at the top of the league to near the bottom in just a few short months?

1 What are teams and groups?

2 Does everyone use teams?

3 What kinds of teams are there?

4 How does one become a team player?

5 Do teams go through stages while they work?

6 How do we create effective teams?

7 Are teams always the answer?

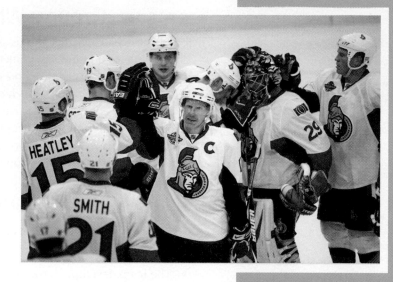

When the Ottawa Senators started the 2007–08 hockey season, they were the runner-up for the 2007 Stanley Cup.[1] They lost to the Anaheim Ducks, who beat them in five games. While disappointed in the outcome, the team had something to be proud of: It was the first time the team had made it to the Cup finals since the Senators became an NHL expansion team in 1992–93. They were 12–3 in playoff games before making it to the final.

They started the season confidently, with thoughts of avenging themselves in the 2008 Stanley Cup playoffs. The team got off to a record 15–2 start, only to become one of the worst teams in the NHL in the second half of the season. The Senators lost to the Pittsburgh Penguins in the first round of the playoffs.

How could the team essentially self-destruct in such a short period of time? There was a lot of finger pointing to go around, but the main answer was that "the team" stopped acting like a team. One of the team's goalies, notable for off-the-field antics, refused to take any responsibility for the team losing in the playoffs. "It was a really bad year for me— the worst year I've had, on and off the ice. It just wasn't enjoyable at all," said Ray Emery.

For teams to excel, a number of conditions need to be met. Effective teams need wise leadership, a variety of resources, and a way to solve problems. Team members need to be dedicated, and they need to build trust. In this chapter, we examine when it's best to have a team, how to create effective teams, and how to deal with diversity on teams.

OB Is for Everyone

- Ever wonder what causes flurries of activity in groups?
- Should individuals be paid for their "teamwork" or their individual performance?
- Why do some teams seem to get along better than others?
- Is building a team just from people who are friends a good idea?
- Why don't some team members pull their weight?

Self-Assessment Library

LEARNING ABOUT YOURSELF

- Building and Leading a Team
- Team Efficacy

Teams vs. Groups: What's the Difference?

1   What are teams and groups?

group Two or more people with a common relationship.

team A small number of people who work closely together toward a common objective and are accountable to one another.

There is some debate whether groups and teams are really separate concepts or the terms can be used interchangeably. We think that there is a subtle difference between the terms. A **group** is two or more people with a common relationship. Thus a group could be co-workers, or people meeting for lunch or standing at the bus stop. Unlike teams, groups do not necessarily engage in collective work that requires interdependent effort.

A **team** is "a small number of people with complementary skills who are committed to a common purpose, performance goals, and approach for which they hold themselves mutually accountable."[2] Groups become teams when they meet the following conditions:[3]

- Team members share *leadership*.

- Both individuals and the team as a whole share *accountability* for the work of the team.

- The team develops its own *purpose* or *mission*.

- The team works on *problem-solving* continuously, rather than just at scheduled meeting times.

- The team's measure of *effectiveness* is the team's outcomes and goals, not individual outcomes and goals.

Thus, while not all groups are teams, all teams can be considered groups. Much of what we discuss in this chapter applies equally well to both. We will offer some suggestions on creating effective teams later in the chapter.

Why Have Teams Become So Popular?

2   Does everyone use teams?

How do we explain the current popularity of teams? As organizations have restructured themselves to compete more effectively and efficiently, they have turned to teams as a better way to use employee talents. Management has found that teams are more flexible and responsive to changing events than are traditional departments or other forms of permanent groupings. Teams have the capability to quickly assemble, deploy, refocus, and disband.

The extensive use of teams creates the potential for an organization to generate greater outputs with no increase in inputs. Notice, however, we said "potential." There is nothing inherently magical in the creation of teams that ensures the achievement of greater output. As we will show later in this chapter, successful, high-performing teams have certain common characteristics. If management hopes to increase organizational performance through the use of teams, it must ensure that its teams possess these characteristics.

Do teams work? The evidence suggests that teams typically outperform individuals when the tasks being done require multiple skills, judgment, and experience.[4] As organizations have restructured to compete more effectively and efficiently, they have turned to teams as a way to better utilize employee talents. Management has found that teams are more flexible and responsive to changing events than traditional departments or other forms of permanent groupings. Teams can quickly assemble, deploy, refocus, and disband. Teams also can be more motivational. Recall from the job characteristics model in Chapter 5 that having greater task identity is one way of increasing motivation. Teams allow for greater task identity, with team members working on tasks together.

Teams are not necessarily appropriate in every situation, however. Read this chapter's *Point/Counterpoint* on page 247 for a debate on whether sports teams are good models for thinking about teams in the workplace.

Types of Teams

Teams can be classified based on their objective. The four most common kinds of teams you are likely to find in an organization are

3 What kinds of teams are there?

- Problem-solving (or process-improvement) teams

- Self-managed (or self-directed) teams

- Cross-functional (or project) teams

- Virtual teams

The types of relationships that members within each team have to one another are shown in Exhibit 6-1.

Problem-Solving Teams

A **problem-solving (or process-improvement) team** is typically made up of 5 to 12 employees from the same department who meet for a few hours each week to discuss ways of improving quality, efficiency, and the work environment.[5] Such teams can also be planning teams, task forces, or committees that are organized to get tasks done. During meetings, members share ideas or offer suggestions on how to improve work processes and methods. Rarely, however, are these teams given the authority to unilaterally implement any of their suggested actions. Montreal-based Clairol Canada is an exception. When a Clairol employee identifies a problem, he or she has the authority to call together an ad hoc group to investigate, and then define and implement solutions. Clairol presents GOC (Group Operating Committee) Awards to teams for their efforts.

problem-solving (or process-improvement) team A group of 5 to 12 employees from the same department who meet for a few hours each week to discuss ways of improving quality, efficiency, and the work environment.

Self-Managed Teams

Problem-solving teams were on the right track, but they did not go far enough in involving employees in work-related decisions and processes. This led to experiments with truly autonomous teams that could not only solve problems but also implement solutions and assume responsibility for outcomes.

A **self-managed (or self-directed) team** is typically made up of 10 to 15 employees. The employees perform highly related or interdependent jobs and take on many of the responsibilities of their former managers.[6] Typically, this includes planning and scheduling of work, assigning tasks to members, collectively controlling the pace of work, making operating decisions, and taking action on problems. Fully self-managed teams even select their own members and leader and have the members evaluate each other's performance. The evidence indicates that self-managed teams often perform better than teams with formally appointed leaders.[7] Under self-managed teams, external managerial positions can take on decreased importance and may even be eliminated.

self-managed (or self-directed) team A group of 10 to 15 employees who take on many of the responsibilities of their former managers.

EXHIBIT 6-1   Four Types of Teams

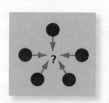
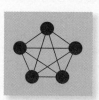
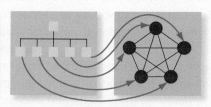
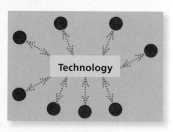

Problem-solving   **Self-managed**   **Cross-functional**   **Virtual**

At the Louis Vuitton factory in Ducey, France, all employees work in problem-solving teams, with each team focusing on one product at a time. Team members are encouraged to suggest improvements in manufacturing work methods and processes, as well as product quality. When a team was asked to make a test run on a prototype of a new handbag, team members discovered that decorative studs were causing the bag's zipper to bunch up. The team alerted managers, who had technicians move the studs away from the zipper, which solved the problem.

Leaders who interfere with self-managed teams can block high performance.[8] At the Deschambault, Quebec-based Alcoa-Aluminerie Lauralco aluminum smelter, employees are organized into self-managed teams that have minimal supervision. Teams have 10 to 15 members who rotate management responsibilities every 12 to 14 months for such tasks as "work organization, training, budgeting, vacation scheduling, performance appraisal and accident prevention." "Their supervisor is a coach, not a boss who tells them what to do," occupational health and safety administrator Lynda Maguire says. "By multi-tasking, we promote employee accountability, as well as a sense of ownership. In fact, we encourage employees to switch to a different sector after a period of time to add even more variety to their work."[9]

A Statistics Canada study found that men were more likely than women to be part of self-directed teams (36 percent vs. 29 percent).[10] This may be explained by a Conference Board of Canada study that found self-directed teams are used more typically in a variety of manufacturing industries (such as the auto industry, chemicals, equipment repair) and service environments (such as hotels, banks, and airlines).[11] It should be noted that some organizations have been disappointed with the results from self-managed teams, because their implementation can be quite challenging.

Business periodicals have been full of articles describing successful applications of self-managed teams. But a word of caution needs to be offered: The overall research on the effectiveness of self-managed work teams has not been uniformly positive.[12] Moreover, although individuals on these teams do tend to report higher levels of job satisfaction compared with other individuals, they also sometimes have higher absenteeism and turnover rates. Inconsistency in findings suggests that the effectiveness of self-managed teams depends on the strength and makeup of team norms, the type of tasks the team undertakes, and the reward structure the team operates under—each of which can significantly influence how well the team performs.

Cross-Functional Teams

Don Swann, vice-president, operations and special projects for Mississauga, Ontario-based Walmart Canada uses a **cross-functional (or project) team** to develop Walmart's Supercentre format for Canada. The team has representatives from all parts of retail business, "including store design, replenishment, systems, merchandising, marketing, operations, HR and finance." He created the cross-functional team because he knew that "we couldn't take a Supercentre from the U.S. and 'drop' it into the Canadian market. We needed to create a Supercentre that was uniquely Canadian."[13]

Cross-functional teams are made up of employees from about the same hierarchical level, but from different work areas, who come together to accomplish a task.[14] For instance, if a business school wanted to design a new integrated curriculum in business for undergraduates, it might bring together a group of faculty members, each of whom represents one discipline (for example, finance, accounting, marketing, and organizational behaviour) to work together to design the new program. Each individual would be expected to contribute knowledge of his or her field, and ways to package together the knowledge in a more integrated fashion.

Many organizations have used groups formed from members of different departments for years. Such groups include **task forces** (temporary cross-functional teams) and **committees** (groups composed of members from different departments). But the popularity of cross-discipline work teams exploded in the late 1980s. All the major automobile manufacturers—including Toyota, Honda, Nissan, BMW, GM, Ford, and Chrysler—use this form of team to coordinate complex projects. Calgary-based Canadian Pacific Railway (CPR) uses cross-functional teams to figure out ways to cut costs. Individuals from all of the functional areas affected by the spending review (such as supply services, operations, and finance) make up the team.[15]

Cross-functional teams are an effective means for allowing people from diverse areas within an organization (or even between organizations) to exchange information, develop new ideas, solve problems, and coordinate complex projects. Of course, cross-functional teams are not easy to manage.[16] Their early stages of development are often time-consuming as members learn to work with diversity and complexity. It takes time to build trust and teamwork, especially among people from different backgrounds, with different experiences and perspectives.

Skunkworks

Skunkworks are cross-functional teams that develop spontaneously to create new products or work on complex problems. Such teams are typically found in the high-tech sector, and are generally sheltered from other organizational members. This gives the team the ability to work on new ideas in isolation, without being watched over by organization members, during creative stages. Skunkworks are thus able to ignore the structure and bureaucratic rules of the organization while they work.

The first skunkworks team appeared in the 1940s, at Lockheed Aerospace Corporation.[17] The team was to create a jet fighter as fast as possible, and avoid bureaucratic delays. In just 43 days, the team of 23 engineers and a group of support personnel put together the first American fighter to fly at more than 800 kilometres an hour.

Not all skunkworks projects are as successful. Many companies, including IBM and Xerox, have had mixed results in using them. Still, skunkworks do offer companies an alternative approach to teamwork when speed is an important factor.

Virtual Teams

Problem-solving, self-managed, and cross-functional teams do their work face to face. **Virtual teams** use computer technology to tie together physically dispersed members in order to achieve a common goal.[18] They allow people to collaborate online—using

cross-functional (or project) team A group of employees at about the same hierarchical level, but from different work areas, who come together to accomplish a task.

task force A temporary cross-functional team.

committee A group composed of members from different departments.

virtual team A team that uses computer technology to tie together physically dispersed members in order to achieve a common goal.

Sheila Goldgrab coaches virtual teams from the comfort of her home in Toronto. She can do that coaching via teleconference, video conference, or email. She gets hired as a consultant to help virtual teams work together more smoothly. As one recipient of her coaching said, "Sheila was the rudder of the planning group. While we were going at high speed in different directions, she ensured there was a link among the group that kept us focused on the task at hand."

communication links such as wide-area networks, video conferencing, and email—whether they are only a room away or continents apart. Virtual teams are so pervasive, and technology has advanced so far, that it's probably a bit of a misnomer to call these teams "virtual." Nearly all teams today do at least some of their work remotely.

Despite their ubiquity, virtual teams face special challenges. They may suffer because there is less social rapport and less direct interaction among members. They are not able to duplicate the normal give-and-take of face-to-face discussion. Especially when members have not personally met, virtual teams tend to be more task oriented and exchange less social-emotional information than face-to-face teams. Not surprisingly, virtual team members report less satisfaction with the group interaction process than do face-to-face teams. An additional concern about virtual teams is whether members are able to build the same kind of trust that face-to-face teams build. *Focus on Research* explores the trust issue.

FOCUS ON **RESEARCH**

If I Can't See You, Can I Trust You?

Can teams build trust if they have never met each other face to face? A study examining how virtual teams work on projects indicates that virtual teams can develop close interaction and trust.[19] These qualities simply evolve differently than in face-to-face groups.

In face-to-face groups, trust comes from direct interaction, over time. In virtual teams, trust is either established at the outset or it generally does not develop. The researchers found that initial electronic messages set the tone for how interactions occurred throughout the project.

OB in ACTION

Managing Virtual Teams

Establishing trust and commitment, encouraging communication, and assessing team members pose tremendous challenges for virtual team managers. Here are a few tips to make the process easier:

→ Establish **regular times** for group interaction.

→ Set up **firm rules** for communication.

→ Use **visual forms of communication** where possible.

→ **Copy the style of face-to-face teams**. For example, allow time for informal chitchat and socializing, and celebrate achievements.

→ **Give and receive feedback** and offer assistance on a regular basis. Be persistent with people who are not communicating with you or each other.

→ Agree on **standard technology** so all team members can work together easily.

→ Consider using **360-degree feedback** to better understand and evaluate team members.

→ Provide a **virtual meeting room** via an intranet, website, or bulletin board.

→ Note which employees **effectively use email** to build team rapport.

→ **Smooth the way for the next assignment** if membership on the team, or the team itself, is not permanent.

→ **Be available** to employees, but don't wait for them to seek you out.

→ Encourage **informal, off-line conversation** between team members.[20]

In one team, for instance, when the appointed leader sent an introductory message that had a distrustful tone, the team suffered low morale and poor performance throughout the project. The researchers suggest that virtual teams should start with an electronic "courtship," where members provide some personal information. Then the teams should assign clear roles to members, helping members to identify with each other.

Finally, the researchers emphasized the importance of a positive outlook. They noted that teams that had the best attitude (eagerness, enthusiasm, and intense action orientation in messages) did considerably better than teams that had one or more pessimists among them.

For virtual teams to be effective, management should ensure that (1) trust is established among team members (research has shown that one inflammatory remark in a team member email can severely undermine team trust); (2) team progress is monitored closely (so the team does not lose sight of its goals and no team member "disappears"); and (3) the efforts and products of the virtual team are publicized throughout the organization (so the team does not become invisible).[21]

Some additional tips for improving the way that virtual teams function include the following: making sure that the team addresses feelings of isolation that members might have; making sure that team members have a mix of interpersonal and technical skills; and paying careful attention to evaluating performance and providing recognition and feedback.[22] For even more tips, see *OB in Action—Managing Virtual Teams*.

From Individual to Team Member

> The start of the 2008–09 hockey season saw some new faces for the Senators.[23] The change started with a new coach, Craig Hartsburg, who is considered a disciplinarian. At team meetings before the first game of the season, Hartsburg emphasized that the players had to remember that they were part of a team, not just a set of individuals. "[We've] had good players here [before], but it's now about being a good team. It's about people doing things that maybe they don't like to do. That's how you become a tight group." How can individual team members actually become a team?

4 How does one become a team player?

For either a group or a team to function, individuals have to achieve some balance between their own needs and the needs of the group. When individuals come together to form groups and teams, they bring with them their personalities and all their previous experiences. They also bring their tendencies to act in different ways at different times, depending on the effects that different situations and different people have on them.

One way to think of these differences is in terms of possible pressures that individual group members put on each other through roles, norms, and status expectations. As we consider the process of how individuals learn to work in groups and teams, we will use the terms interchangeably. Many of the processes that each go through are the same, with the major difference being that teams within the workplace are often set up on a nonpermanent basis, in order to accomplish projects. Becoming a team player is not easy, as *OB in the Street* demonstrates.

OB IN THE STREET

Skeleton Racer Finds Teamwork a Real Challenge

Is being a team player really all that tough? Jeff Pain spent much of the 2000s trying his best not to be a team player, even though he was part of the Canadian men's skeleton team.[24] Much of Pain's negativity toward teamwork was directed at team member Duff Gibson, his rival for over five years.

"When Duff started skeleton [in 1999], I had a difficult time with my team dynamics because I felt that I knew a lot more than the people I was sliding with," says Pain. "I didn't want to share information with them and I carried that mistaken belief right up to [2004]. That was probably my and Duff's worst year."

In summer 2004, Pain, Gibson, and fellow team member Paul Boehm decided to work together to share information about the tracks they are competing on, and then try to help each other out.

Pain and Gibson improved their times and reached the top of international standings. Pain admits that learning how to be more of a team player has helped him improve in a sport that he was thinking of quitting because of his unhappiness related to interactions with other team members. "I really insulated myself, and that didn't create a good environment for me or the team," Pain admits.

The focus on teamwork paid off for Team Canada. Pain finished second in skeleton racing to gold-medaller Gibson at the 2006 Olympics in Turin. Gibson has since retired, but Pain will be trying for another medal in 2010.

As Jeff Pain shows, being a team member requires working together, sharing information, and being willing to take on the role of being a team member. We discuss roles below.

Roles

Shakespeare said, "All the world's a stage, and all the men and women merely players." Using the same metaphor, all group members are actors, each playing a **role**. By this term, we mean a set of expected behaviour patterns of a person in a given position in a social unit. The understanding of role behaviour would be dramatically simplified if each of us chose one role and "played it out" regularly and consistently. Unfortunately, we are required to play a number of diverse roles, both on and off our jobs.

As we will see, one of the tasks in understanding behaviour is grasping the role that a person is currently playing. For example, on the job a person might have the roles of electrical engineer, member of middle management, and primary company spokesperson in the community. Off the job, there are still more roles: spouse, parent, church member, food bank volunteer, and coach of the softball team. Many of these roles are compatible; some create conflicts. For instance, how does one's religious involvement influence managerial decisions regarding meeting with clients on the Sabbath? We address role conflict below.

> **role** A set of expected behaviours of a person in a given position in a social unit.

Role Conflict

Most roles are governed by **role expectations**, that is, how others believe a person should act in a given situation. When an individual is confronted by conflicting role expectations, the result is role conflict. **Role conflict** exists when an individual finds that complying with one role requirement may make it more difficult to comply with another.[25] At the extreme, it can include situations in which two or more role expectations are mutually contradictory!

All of us have faced and will continue to face role conflicts. The critical issue, from our standpoint, is how conflicts imposed by different expectations within the organization affect behaviour. Certainly, they increase internal tension and frustration. There are a number of behavioural responses individuals may engage in. They may, for example, give a formalized bureaucratic response. The conflict is then resolved by relying on the rules, regulations, and procedures that govern organizational activities.

For example, an employee faced with the conflicting requirements imposed by the corporate controller's office and his own plant manager decides in favour of his immediate boss—the plant manager. Other behavioural responses may include withdrawal, stalling, negotiation, or redefining the facts or the situation to make them appear congruent. *Case Incident—Role Conflict among Telephone Service Employees* on page 251 looks at how role conflict can affect one's worklife.

> **role expectations** How others believe a person should act in a given situation.
>
> **role conflict** A situation in which an individual finds that complying with one role requirement may make it more difficult to comply with another.

Role Ambiguity

Role ambiguity exists when a person is unclear about the expectations of his or her role. In teams, role ambiguity can lead to confusion, stress, and even bad feelings. For instance, suppose two group members each think that the other one is responsible for preparing the first draft of a report. At the next group meeting, neither brings a draft report, and both are annoyed that the other person did not do the work.

Groups benefit when individuals know their roles. Roles within groups and teams should be balanced. Edgar Schein suggests that **role overload** occurs when what is expected of a person "far exceeds what he or she is able to do."[26] **Role underload** occurs when too little is expected of someone, and that person feels that he or she is not contributing to the group.

> **role ambiguity** A person is unclear about his or her role.
>
> **role overload** Too much is expected of someone.
>
> **role underload** Too little is expected of someone, and that person feels that he or she is not contributing to the group.

Norms

Have you ever noticed that golfers don't speak while their partners are putting on the green, or that employees don't criticize their bosses in public? Why? The answer is "norms!"

norms Acceptable standards of behaviour within a group that are shared by the group's members.

Norms are acceptable standards of behaviour within a group that are shared by the group's members. All groups have established norms that tell members what they ought and ought not to do under certain circumstances. When agreed to and accepted by the group, norms act as a means of influencing the behaviour of group members, with a minimum of external controls. Norms differ among groups, communities, and societies, but all of these entities have norms.[27]

Formalized norms are written up in organizational manuals that set out rules and procedures for employees to follow. But, by far, most norms in organizations are informal. You don't need someone to tell you that throwing paper airplanes or engaging in prolonged gossip sessions at the water cooler is an unacceptable behaviour when the "big boss from Toronto" is touring the office. Similarly, we all know that when we are in an employment interview discussing what we did not like about our previous job, there are certain things we should not talk about (such as difficulty in getting along with co-workers or our manager). There are other things it's appropriate to talk about (inadequate opportunities for advancement, or unimportant and meaningless work).

Norms for both groups and organizations cover a wide variety of circumstances. Some of the most common norms have to do with issues such as

- *Performance.* How hard to work, what kind of quality, levels of tardiness

- *Appearance.* Personal dress, when to look busy, when to "goof off," how to show loyalty

- *Social arrangement.* How team members interact

- *Allocation of resources.* Pay, assignments, allocation of tools and equipment

OB in Action—Creating a Team Charter presents a way for teams to develop norms when the team first forms.

OB in ACTION
Creating a Team Charter

When you form a new team, you may want to develop a team charter, so that everyone agrees on the basic norms for group performance. Consider including answers to the following in your charter:

→ What are team members' **names and contact information** (e.g., phone, email)?

→ How will **communication** among team members take place (e.g., phone, email)?

→ What will the **team ground rules** be (e.g., where and when to meet, attendance expectations, workload expectations)?

→ How will **decisions** be made (e.g., consensus, majority vote, leader rules)?

→ What **potential conflicts** may arise in the team? Among team members?

→ How will **conflicts be resolved** by the group?[28]

The "How" and "Why" of Norms

How do norms develop? Why are they enforced? A review of the research allows us to answer these questions.[29]

Norms typically develop gradually as group members learn what behaviours are necessary for the team to function effectively. Of course, critical events in the group might short-circuit the process and quickly prompt new norms. Most norms develop in one or more of the following four ways:

- *Explicit statements made by a group member.* Often, instructions from the group's supervisor or a powerful member establish norms. The team leader might specifically say that no personal phone calls are allowed during working hours or that coffee breaks must be no longer than 10 minutes.

- *Critical events in the group's history.* These set important precedents. A bystander is injured while standing too close to a machine and, from that point on, members of the work group regularly monitor each other to ensure that no one other than the operator gets within two metres of any machine.

- *Primacy.* The first behavioural pattern that emerges in a group frequently sets team expectations. Groups of students who are friends often choose seats near each other on the first day of class and become upset if an outsider takes "their" seats in a later class.

- *Carry-over behaviours from past situations.* Group members bring expectations with them from other groups to which they have belonged. Thus, work groups typically prefer to add new members who are similar to current ones in background and experience. This is likely to increase the probability that the expectations they bring are consistent with those already held by the group.

Groups don't establish or enforce norms for every conceivable situation, however. The norms that the groups will enforce tend to be those that are important to them.[30] What makes a norm important?

- *It facilitates the group's survival.* Groups don't like to fail, so they seek to enforce any norm that increases their chances for success. This means that groups try to protect themselves from interference from other groups or individuals.

- *It increases the predictability of group members' behaviours.* Norms that increase predictability enable group members to anticipate each other's actions and to prepare appropriate responses.

- *It reduces embarrassing interpersonal problems for group members.* Norms are important if they ensure the satisfaction of their members and prevent as much interpersonal discomfort as possible.

- *It allows members to express the central values of the group and clarify what is distinctive about the group's identity.* Norms that encourage expression of the group's values and distinctive identity help solidify and maintain the group.

One of the problems that plagued the Ottawa Senators during the 2007–08 season was that one of their goalies, Ray Emery, kept violating team norms about showing up for practice on time and working hard enough during practice. This eventually affected team morale.

Conformity

As a group member, you desire acceptance by the group. Because of your desire for acceptance, you are susceptible to conforming to the group's norms. Considerable evidence shows that the group can place strong pressures on individual members to change their attitudes and behaviours to conform to the group's standard.[31]

The impact that group pressures for **conformity** can have on an individual member's judgment and attitudes was demonstrated in the now classic studies of noted social psychologist Solomon Asch.[32] Asch found that subjects gave answers that they knew were wrong, but that were consistent with the replies of other group members, about 35 percent of the time. The results suggest that group norms can pressure us toward conformity. We desire to be one of the group and avoid being visibly different.

Research by University of British Columbia professor Sandra Robinson and colleague Anne O'Leary-Kelly indicates that conformity may explain why some work groups are more prone to antisocial behaviour than others.[33] Individuals working with others who exhibited antisocial behaviour at work were more likely to engage in antisocial behaviour themselves. Of course, not all conformity leads to negative behaviour. Other research has indicated that work groups can have more positive influences, leading to more prosocial behaviour in the workplace.[34]

Overall, research continues to indicate that conformity to norms is a powerful force in groups and teams.

conformity Adjusting one's behaviour to align with the norms of the group.

Stages of Group and Team Development

> As the Ottawa Senators headed into training camp in July 2008, they faced a number of questions.[35] Would they ever qualify for the playoffs again? What was their new coach, Craig Hartsburg, going to be like? Who would fill some of the key positions, such as defenceman and winger? Could they all work well together again? To rebuild a successful team that makes it to the Stanley Cup finals, the Senators will have to go through several stages. So what stages do teams go through as they develop?

5 Do teams go through stages while they work?

When people get together for the first time with the purpose of achieving some objective, they discover that acting as a team is not something simple, easy, or genetically programmed. Working in a group or team is often difficult, particularly in the initial stages, when people don't necessarily know each other. As time passes, groups and teams go through various stages of development, although the stages are not necessarily exactly the same for each group or team. In this section, we discuss two models of group development. The five-stage model describes the standardized sequence of stages groups pass through. The punctuated-equilibrium model describes the pattern of development specific to temporary groups with deadlines. These models can be applied equally to groups and teams.

The Five-Stage Model

From the mid-1960s, it was believed that groups passed through a standard sequence of five stages.[36] As shown in Exhibit 6-2, these five stages have been labelled forming,

EXHIBIT 6-2   Stages of Group Development and Accompanying Issues

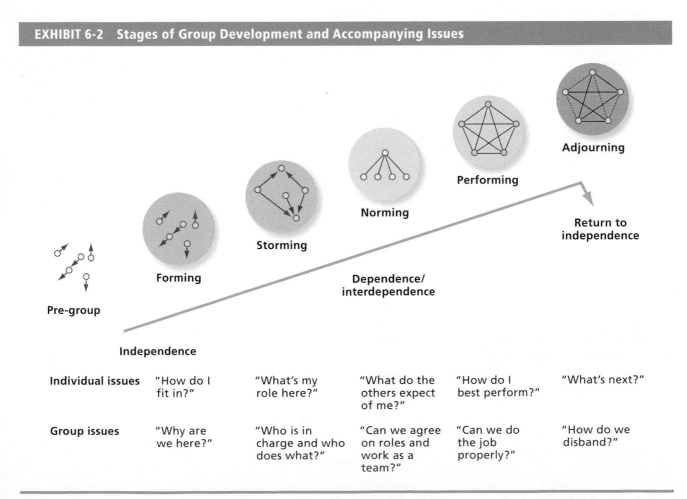

	Forming	Storming	Norming	Performing	Adjourning
Individual issues	"How do I fit in?"	"What's my role here?"	"What do the others expect of me?"	"How do I best perform?"	"What's next?"
Group issues	"Why are we here?"	"Who is in charge and who does what?"	"Can we agree on roles and work as a team?"	"Can we do the job properly?"	"How do we disband?"

storming, norming, performing, and adjourning. Although we now know that not all groups pass through these stages in a linear fashion, the five-stage model of group development can still help in addressing any anxieties you might have about working in groups and teams. The model shows how individuals move from being independent to working interdependently with group members.

- *Stage I: Forming.* Think about the first time you met with a new team. Do you remember how some people seemed silent and others felt confused about the task you were to accomplish? Those feelings arise during the first stage of group development, know as **forming**. Forming is characterized by a great deal of uncertainty about the team's purpose, structure, and leadership. Members are "testing the waters" to determine what types of behaviour are acceptable. This stage is complete when members have begun to think of themselves as part of a team.

  forming The first stage in group development, characterized by much uncertainty.

- *Stage II: Storming.* Do you remember how some people in your team just did not seem to get along, and sometimes power struggles even emerged? These reactions are typical of the **storming** stage, which is one of intragroup conflict. Members accept the existence of the team, but resist the constraints that the team imposes on individuality. Furthermore, there is conflict over who will control the team. When this stage is complete, a relatively clear hierarchy of leadership will emerge within the team.

  storming The second stage in group development, characterized by intragroup conflict.

  Some teams never really emerge from the storming stage, or they move back and forth through storming and the other stages. A team that remains forever planted in the storming stage may have less ability to complete the task because of all the interpersonal problems.

- *Stage III: Norming.* Many teams resolve the interpersonal conflict and reach the third stage, in which close relationships develop and the team demonstrates cohesiveness. There is now a strong sense of team identity and camaraderie. This **norming** stage is complete when the team structure solidifies, and the team has assimilated a common set of expectations of what defines correct member behaviour.

  norming The third stage in group development, characterized by close relationships and cohesiveness.

- *Stage IV: Performing.* Next, and you may have noticed this in some of your own team interactions, some teams just seem to come together well and start to do their work. This fourth stage, when significant task progress is being made, is called **performing**. The structure at this point is fully functional and accepted. Team energy has moved from getting to know and understand each other to performing the task at hand.

  performing The fourth stage in group development, when the group is fully functional.

- *Stage V: Adjourning.* For permanent work groups and teams, performing is the last stage in their development. However, for temporary committees, teams, task forces, and similar groups that have a limited task to perform, there is an **adjourning** stage. In this stage, the group prepares for its disbandment. High task performance is no longer the group's top priority. Instead, attention is directed toward wrapping up activities. Group members' responses vary at this stage. Some members are upbeat, basking in the group's accomplishments. Others may be depressed over the loss of camaraderie and friendships gained during the work group's life.

  adjourning The final stage in group development for temporary groups, where attention is directed toward wrapping up activities rather than task performance.

For some teams, the end of one project may mean the beginning of another. In this case, a team has to transform itself in order to get on with a new project that may need a different focus and different skills, and may need to take on new members. Thus the adjourning stage may lead to renewal of the team to get the next project started.

Having passed through the forming, storming, and norming phases of group development, this group of women at a Delphi Delco Electronics factory in Mexico now functions as a permanent work group in the performing stage. Their structure is functional and accepted, and each day they begin their work with a small shift meeting before performing their tasks.

Putting the Five-Stage Model into Perspective

Many interpreters of the five-stage model have assumed that a group becomes more effective as it progresses through the first four stages. This assumption may be generally true, but what makes a group effective is more complex than this model acknowledges.[37] Under some conditions, high levels of conflict are conducive to high group performance, as long as the conflict is directed toward the task and not toward group members. So we might expect to find situations where groups in Stage II outperform those in Stages III or IV. Similarly, groups do not always proceed clearly from one stage to the next. Sometimes, in fact, several stages go on simultaneously, as when groups are storming and performing at the same time. Teams even occasionally go backwards to previous stages. Therefore, you should not assume that all groups follow the five-stage process precisely, or that Stage IV is always the most preferable.

The five-stage model also ignores organizational context.[38] For instance, a study of a cockpit crew in an airliner found that, within 10 minutes, three strangers assigned to fly together for the first time had become a high-performing team. How could a team come together so quickly? The answer lies in the strong organizational context surrounding the tasks of the cockpit crew. This context provided the rules, task definitions, information, and resources needed for the team to perform. They did not need to develop plans, assign roles, determine and allocate resources, resolve conflicts, and set norms the way the five-stage model predicts.

Within the workplace, some group behaviour takes place within a strong organizational context, and it would appear that the five-stage model has limited applicability for those groups. However, there are a variety of situations in the workplace where groups are assigned to tasks and the individuals do not know each other. They must therefore work out interpersonal differences at the same time as they work through the assigned tasks.

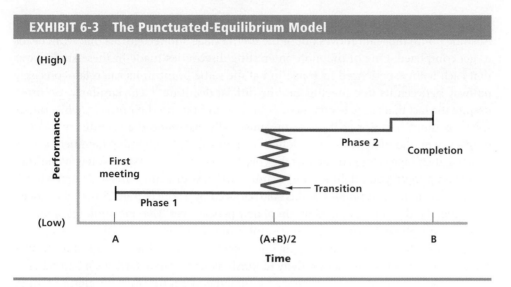

EXHIBIT 6-3   The Punctuated-Equilibrium Model

The Punctuated-Equilibrium Model

Temporary groups with deadlines don't seem to follow the previous model. Studies indicate that temporary groups with deadlines have their own unique sequence of action (or inaction):[39]

- The first meeting sets the group's direction.
- The first phase of group activity is one of inertia.
- A transition takes place at the end of the first phase, which occurs exactly when the group has used up half its allotted time.
- The transition initiates major changes.
- A second phase of inertia follows the transition.
- The group's last meeting is characterized by markedly accelerated activity.

Ever wonder what causes flurries of activity in groups?

This pattern is called the punctuated-equilibrium model, developed by Professor Connie Gersick, a Visiting Scholar at the Yale University School of Management, and is shown in Exhibit 6-3.[40] It is important for you to understand these shifts in group behaviour, if for no other reason than when you are in a group that is not working well or one that has gotten off to a slow start, you can start to think of ways to help the group move to a more productive phase.

Phase 1

As both a team member and possibly a team leader, it's important that you recognize that the first meeting sets the team's direction. A framework of behavioural patterns and assumptions through which the team will approach its project emerges in this first meeting. These lasting patterns can appear as early as the first few seconds of the team's life.

Once set, the team's direction becomes "written in stone" and is unlikely to be re-examined throughout the first half of the team's life. This is a period of inertia—that is, the team tends to stand still or become locked into a fixed course of action. Even if it gains new insights that challenge initial patterns and assumptions, the team is incapable of acting on these new insights in phase 1. You may recognize that in some teams, during the early period of trying to get things accomplished, no one really did his or her assigned tasks. You may also recognize this phase as one where everyone carries out the tasks, but not in a very coordinated fashion. Thus, the team is performing at a relatively low state. This does not necessarily mean that it is doing nothing at all, however.

Phase 2

At some point, the team moves out of the inertia stage and recognizes that work needs to get completed. One of the more interesting discoveries made in these studies was that each team experienced its transition at the same point in its calendar—precisely halfway between its first meeting and its official deadline.[41] The similarity occurred despite the fact that some teams spent as little as an hour on their project, while others spent six months. It was as if the teams universally experienced a midlife crisis at this point. The midpoint appears to work like an alarm clock, heightening members' awareness that their time is limited and that they need to "get moving." When you work on your next team project, you might want to examine when your team starts to "get moving."

This transition ends phase 1 and is characterized by a concentrated burst of changes, dropping of old patterns, and adoption of new perspectives. The transition sets a revised direction for phase 2, which is a new equilibrium or period of inertia. In this phase, the team executes plans created during the transition period. The team's last meeting is characterized by a final burst of activity to finish its work. There have been a number of studies that support the basic premise of punctuated equilibrium, though not all of them found that the transition in the team occurred exactly at the midpoint.[42]

Applying the Punctuated-Equilibrium Model

We can use this model to describe typical experiences of student teams created for doing group term projects. At the first meeting, a basic timetable is established. Members size up one another. They agree they have nine weeks to do their project. The instructor's requirements are discussed and debated. From that point, the group meets regularly to carry out its activities. About four or five weeks into the project, however, problems are confronted. Criticism begins to be taken seriously. Discussion becomes more open. The group reassesses where it has been and aggressively moves to make necessary changes. If the right changes are made, the next four or five weeks find the group developing a first-rate project. The group's last meeting, which will probably occur just before the project is due, lasts longer than the others. In it, all final issues are discussed and details resolved.

In summary, the punctuated-equilibrium model characterizes deadline-oriented teams as exhibiting long periods of inertia, interspersed with brief revolutionary changes triggered primarily by their members' awareness of time and deadlines. To use the terminology of the five-stage model, the team begins by combining the *forming* and *norming* stages, then goes through a period of *low performing*, followed by *storming*, then a period of *high performing*, and, finally, *adjourning*.

Several researchers have suggested that the five-stage and punctuated-equilibrium models are at odds with each other.[43] However, it makes more sense to view the models as complementary: The five-stage model considers the interpersonal process of the group, while the punctuated-equilibrium model considers the time challenges that the group faces.[44]

Creating Effective Teams

When Craig Hartsburg took over as coach for the Ottawa Senators, he was facing a team that did not have a good reputation.[45] They had finished near the bottom of the league, and the team had a reputation as a "party squad." There were concerns that the team lacked discipline, and one reporter asked him if was considering 10 p.m. curfews and giving out alarm clocks. While he laughed at that suggestion, he said, "We have some really good players, star players, and I think we also have a great group of role players here, so the thing is, we've got to get them buying in, all in, to the program." Hartsburg also noted that the team had to work on trust: trust in the team as a whole, in the coaches, and in the individual players. What other factors might contribute to the effectiveness of the Ottawa Senators?

6 How do we create effective teams?

When we consider team effectiveness, we refer to such objective measures as the team's productivity, managers' ratings of the team's performance, and aggregate measures of member satisfaction. Some of the considerations necessary to create effective teams are outlined next. However, we are also interested in team process. Exhibit 6-4 provides a checklist of the characteristics of an effective team.

There is no shortage of efforts that try to identify the factors that lead to team effectiveness.[46] However, studies have taken what was once a "veritable laundry list of characteristics"[47] and organized them into a relatively focused model with four general categories summarized in Exhibit 6-5 on page 230:[48]

- Resources and other contextual influences that make teams effective

- Team composition

- Work design

- Team process (those things that go on in the team that influence how effective the team is)

Kerri Molinaro, president of Burlington, Ontario-based IKEA Canada, believes that teams are the best way to bring employees together. IKEA's leadership style is informal, and the company values people who are humble and trustworthy. This also makes them good team members.

EXHIBIT 6-4   Characteristics of an Effective Team

1.	**Clear purpose**	The vision, mission, goal, or task of the team has been defined and is now accepted by everyone. There is an action plan.
2.	**Informality**	The climate tends to be informal, comfortable, and relaxed. There are no obvious tensions or signs of boredom.
3.	**Participation**	There is much discussion, and everyone is encouraged to participate.
4.	**Listening**	The members use effective listening techniques such as questioning, paraphrasing, and summarizing to get out ideas.
5.	**Civilized disagreement**	There is disagreement, but the team is comfortable with this and shows no signs of avoiding, smoothing over, or suppressing conflict.
6.	**Consensus decisions**	For important decisions, the goal is substantial but not necessarily unanimous agreement through open discussion of everyone's ideas, avoidance of formal voting, or easy compromises.
7.	**Open communication**	Team members feel free to express their feelings on the tasks as well as on the group's operation. There are few hidden agendas. Communication takes place outside of meetings.
8.	**Clear rules and work assignments**	There are clear expectations about the roles played by each team member. When action is taken, clear assignments are made, accepted, and carried out. Work is distributed among team members.
9.	**Shared leadership**	While the team has a formal leader, leadership functions shift from time to time depending on the circumstances, the needs of the group, and the skills of the members. The formal leader models the appropriate behaviour and helps establish positive norms.
10.	**External relations**	The team spends time developing key outside relationships, mobilizing resources, and building credibility with important players in other parts of the organization.
11.	**Style diversity**	The team has a broad spectrum of team-player types including members who emphasize attention to task, goal setting, focus on process, and questions about how the team is functioning.
12.	**Self-assessment**	Periodically, the team stops to examine how well it is functioning and what may be interfering with its effectiveness.

Source: G. M. Parker, *Team Players and Teamwork: The New Competitive Business Strategy* (San Francisco: Jossey-Bass, 1990), Table 2, p. 33. Copyright © 1990 by Jossey-Bass Inc., Publishers. Reprinted by permission of John Wiley & Sons, Inc.

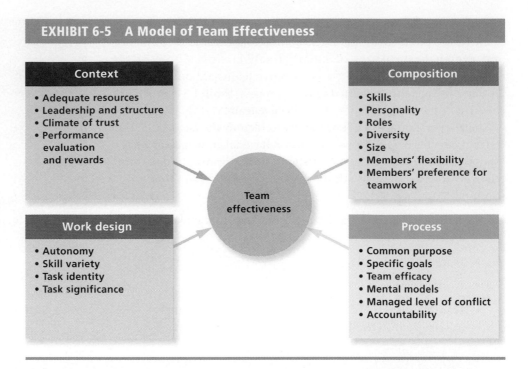

EXHIBIT 6-5   A Model of Team Effectiveness

Context
- Adequate resources
- Leadership and structure
- Climate of trust
- Performance evaluation and rewards

Composition
- Skills
- Personality
- Roles
- Diversity
- Size
- Members' flexibility
- Members' preference for teamwork

Work design
- Autonomy
- Skill variety
- Task identity
- Task significance

Team effectiveness

Process
- Common purpose
- Specific goals
- Team efficacy
- Mental models
- Managed level of conflict
- Accountability

Keep in mind two caveats as you review the issues that lead to effective teams:

- First, teams differ in form and structure. Since the model we present attempts to generalize across all varieties of teams, you need to be careful not to rigidly apply the model's predictions to all teams.[49] The model should be used as a guide, not as an inflexible prescription.

- Second, the model assumes that it's already been determined that teamwork is preferable over individual work. Creating "effective" teams in situations wherein individuals can do the job better is equivalent to solving the wrong problem perfectly.

OB in Action—Harming Your Team presents activities that can make a team ineffective. You might want to evaluate your own team experience against this checklist to give you some idea of how well your team is functioning, or to understand what might be causing problems for your team. Then consider the factors that lead to more effective teams below. For an applied look at the process of building an effective team, see the *Working with Others Exercise* on page 250, which asks you to build a paper tower with teammates and then analyze how the team performed.

Context

Teams can require a great deal of maintenance to function properly. They need management support, as well as an organizational structure that supports teamwork. The four contextual factors that appear to be most significantly related to team performance are the presence of adequate resources, effective leadership, a climate of trust, and a performance evaluation and reward system that reflects team contributions.

Adequate Resources

All work teams rely on resources outside the team to sustain them. A scarcity of resources directly reduces the ability of a team to perform its job effectively. As one set of researchers concluded, after looking at 13 factors potentially related to team performance, "perhaps one of the most important characteristics of an effective work group is the support the group receives from the organization."[50] This includes such support as technology, adequate staffing, administrative assistance, encouragement, and timely information.

Teams must receive the necessary support from management and the larger organization if they are going to succeed in achieving their goals.

Leadership and Structure

Leadership plays a crucial role in the development and success of teams. As the Ottawa Senators started losing more and more games in early 2008, John Paddock, the team's coach, was fired for not doing enough to keep the team together.

Professor Richard Hackman of Harvard University, who is the leading expert on teams, suggests that the role of team leader involves the following:[52]

- Creating a real team rather than a team in name only

- Setting a clear and meaningful direction for the team's work

- Making sure that the team structure will support working effectively

- Ensuring that the team operates within a supportive organizational context

- Providing expert coaching

There are some practical problems that must be resolved when a team first starts working together. Team members must agree on who is to do what, and ensure that all members contribute equally in sharing the workload. The team also needs to determine how schedules will be set, what skills need to be developed, how the team will resolve conflicts, and how the team will make and modify decisions. Agreeing on the specifics of work and how they fit together to integrate individual skills requires team leadership and structure. This, incidentally, can be provided directly by management or by the team members themselves. Although you might think there is no role for leaders in self-managed teams, that could not be further from the truth. It is true that, in self-managed teams, team members absorb many of the duties typically assumed by managers. However, a manager's job becomes managing *outside* (rather than inside) the team.

Leadership is especially important in **multi-team systems**—where different teams need to coordinate their efforts to produce a desired outcome. In such systems, leaders need to empower teams by delegating responsibility to them, and they need to play the role of facilitator, making sure the teams are coordinating their efforts so that they work together rather than against one another.[53] The *Learning About Yourself Exercise* on page 248 will help you evaluate how suited you are to building and leading a team.

Recent research suggests that women may make better team leaders than men, as *Focus on Research* shows.

multi-team systems Systems in which different teams need to coordinate their efforts to produce a desired outcome

Learning About Yourself

1. How Good Am I at Building and Leading a Team? **(page 248)**

OB in ACTION

Harming Your Team

→ **Refuse to share** issues and concerns. Team members refuse to share information and engage in silence, avoidance, and meetings behind closed doors where not all members are included.

→ **Depend** too much **on the leader**. Members rely too much on the leader and do not carry out their responsibilities.

→ **Fail to follow through** on decisions. Teams do not take action after decision making, showing that the needs of the team have low priority, or that members are not committed to the decisions that were made.

→ **Hide conflict**. Team members do not reveal that they have a difference of opinion, and this causes tension.

→ **Fail at conflict resolution**. Infighting, put-downs, and attempts to hurt other members damage the team.

→ **Form subgroups**. The team breaks up into smaller groups that put their needs ahead of the team as a whole.[51]

FOCUS ON **RESEARCH**

Team Leadership Can Affect Grades

How much leadership does a team need? "The more women participating equally in a project, the better the outcome," suggests Professor Jennifer Berdahl of the Joseph

L. Rotman School of Management at the University of Toronto.[54] Berdahl's research looked at 169 students enrolled in her organizational behaviour courses.[55] She found that all of the teams started out with one person taking a leadership role. However, if the groups were predominantly males, the same person stayed in charge the entire time. In predominantly female teams, women shared leadership roles, and were more egalitarian in how they worked. Male-led teams, whether they were predominantly male groups or mixed-gender groups, received poorer grades on their projects than teams where women shared leadership roles.

Berdahl gives this advice to students: "In a creative project team, it's really important to ensure there is equal opportunity for participation."

A leader, of course, is not always needed. For instance, the evidence indicates that self-managed teams often perform better than teams with formally appointed leaders.[56] Leaders can also obstruct high performance when they interfere with self-managed teams.[57] On self-managed teams, team members absorb many of the duties typically assumed by managers.

Climate of Trust

Members of effective teams trust each other. For team members to do this, they must feel that the team is capable of getting the task done, and they must believe that "the team will not harm the individual or his or her interests."[58] Interpersonal trust among team members facilitates cooperation, reduces the need to monitor each others' behaviour, and bonds members around the belief that others on the team won't take advantage of them. Team members are more likely to take risks and expose vulnerabilities when they believe they can trust others on their team. *OB in Action—Building Trust* shows the dimensions that underlie the concept of trust.

Team members must also trust their leaders.[60] Trust in leadership is important in that it allows the team to be willing to accept and commit to their leader's goals and decisions. Mississauga, Ontario-based Flynn Canada management invest in their employees to make sure that they become good team players. The company helps employees build trust in each other, so that they can learn to work effectively. Employees are encouraged to take pride in their work and the outcomes of their work. They are encouraged to be open with one another. "Personally, what attracted me to Flynn is that it's got scale and horsepower but it has a heart and soul; it's not just another corporate entity. We are authentic in our interactions with each other. What you see is what you get," says Gerard Montocchio, vice-president of human resources."[61]

OB in ACTION

Building Trust

The following actions, in order of importance, help build one's trustworthiness.

→ **Integrity**—built through **honesty** and **truthfulness**.

→ **Competence**—demonstrated by technical and interpersonal **knowledge** and **skills**.

→ **Consistency**—shown by **reliability**, **predictability**, and **good judgment** in handling situations.

→ **Loyalty**—one's willingness to **protect** and **stand up** for another person.

→ **Openness**—one's willingness to **share ideas** and **information** freely.[59]

Performance Evaluation and Rewards

Should individuals be paid for their "teamwork" or their individual performance?

How do you get team members to be both individually and jointly accountable? The traditional individually oriented evaluation must be modified to reflect team performance.[62] Individual performance evaluations, fixed hourly wages, individual incentives, and the like are not consistent with the development of high-performance teams. So in addition to evaluating and rewarding employees for their individual contributions, management should consider group-based appraisals, profit sharing, gainsharing, small-group incentives, and other system modifications that will reinforce team effort and commitment.

One additional consideration when deciding whether and how to reward team members is the effect of pay dispersion on team performance. Research by Nancy Langton, your Vancouver-based author, shows that when there is a large discrepancy in wages among group members, collaboration is lowered.[63] A study of baseball player salaries also found that teams where players were paid more similarly often outperformed teams with highly paid "stars" and lowly paid "scrubs."[64]

Composition

This category includes variables that relate to how teams should be staffed. In this section, we will address the skills, personality, and roles of team members, the diversity and size of the team, members' flexibility, and members' preference for teamwork.

Skills

To perform effectively, a team requires three different types of skills:

1. It needs people with *technical expertise*.

2. It needs people with the *problem-solving* and *decision-making skills* to be able to identify problems, generate alternatives, evaluate those alternatives, and make competent choices.

3. It needs people with good listening, feedback, conflict resolution, and other *interpersonal skills*.[65]

No team can achieve its performance potential without developing all three types of skills. The right mix is crucial. Too much of one at the expense of others will result in lower team performance. But teams don't need to have all the complementary skills in place at the beginning. It's not uncommon for one or more members to take responsibility to learn the skills in which the group is deficient, thereby allowing the team to reach its full potential. Exhibit 6-6 identifies some important teamwork skills that help teams function well.

EXHIBIT 6-6 Teamwork Skills	
Orients Team to Problem-Solving Situation	Assists the team in arriving at a common understanding of the situation or problem. Determines the important elements of a problem situation. Seeks out relevant data related to the situation or problem.
Organizes and Manages Team Performance	Helps team establish specific, challenging, and accepted team goals. Monitors, evaluates, and provides feedback on team performance. Identifies alternative strategies or reallocates resources to address feedback on team performance.
Promotes a Positive Team Environment	Assists in creating and reinforcing norms of tolerance, respect, and excellence. Recognizes and praises other team members' efforts. Helps and supports other team members. Models desirable team member behaviour.
Facilitates and Manages Task Conflict	Encourages desirable and discourages undesirable team conflict. Recognizes the type and source of conflict confronting the team and implements an appropriate resolution strategy. Employs "win-win" negotiation strategies to resolve team conflicts.
Appropriately Promotes Perspective	Defends stated preferences, argues for a particular point of view, and withstands pressure to change position for another that is not supported by logical or knowledge-based arguments. Changes or modifies position if a defensible argument is made by another team member. Projects courtesy and friendliness to others while arguing position.

Source: G. Chen, L. M. Donahue, and R. J. Klimoski, "Training Undergraduates to Work in Organizational Teams," *Academy of Management Learning & Education* 3, no. 1 (March 2004), p. 40.

Personality

Teams have different needs, and people should be selected for the team on the basis of their personalities and preferences, as well as the team's needs for diversity and specific roles. We demonstrated in Chapter 2 that personality has a significant influence on individual employee behaviour. This can also be extended to team behaviour.

Why do some teams seem to get along better than others?

Many of the dimensions identified in the Big Five Personality Model have been shown to be relevant to team effectiveness. A recent review of the literature suggests that three of the Big Five traits are especially important for team performance.[66] Specifically, teams that rate higher on mean levels of conscientiousness and openness to experience tend to perform better. Moreover, the minimum level of team member agreeableness also matters: Teams did worse when they had one or more highly disagreeable members. Perhaps one bad apple *can* spoil the whole bunch!

Research has also provided us with a good idea about why these personality traits are important to teams. Conscientious people are valuable in teams because they are good at backing up other team members, and they are also good at sensing when that support is truly needed. Open team members communicate better with one another and throw out more ideas, which leads teams composed of open people to be more creative and innovative.[67]

Even if an organization does a really good job of selecting individuals for team roles, most likely they will find there are not enough, say, conscientious people to go around. Suppose an organization needs to create 20 teams of 4 people each and has 40 highly conscientious people and 40 who score low on conscientiousness. Would the organization be better off (A) putting all the conscientious people together (forming 10 teams with the highly conscientious people and 10 teams of members low on conscientiousness) or (B) "seeding" each team with 2 people who scored high and 2 who scored low on conscientiousness?

Perhaps surprisingly, the evidence tends to suggest that option A is the best choice; performance across the teams will be higher if the organization forms 10 highly conscientious teams and 10 teams low in conscientiousness. "This may be because, in such teams, members who are highly conscientious not only must perform their own tasks but also must perform or re-do the tasks of low-conscientious members. It may also be because such diversity leads to feelings of contribution inequity."[68]

Roles

Earlier in the chapter, we discussed how individuals fill roles within groups. Within almost any group, two sets of role relationships need to be considered: task-oriented roles and maintenance roles. **Task-oriented roles** are performed by group members to ensure that the tasks of the group are accomplished. These roles include initiators, information seekers, information providers, elaborators, summarizers, and consensus makers. **Maintenance roles** are carried out to ensure that group members maintain good relations. These roles include harmonizers, compromisers, gatekeepers, and encouragers.

Effective teams maintain some balance between task orientation and maintenance of relations. Exhibit 6-7 identifies a number of task-oriented and maintenance behaviours in the key roles that you might find in a team.

On many teams, there are individuals who will be flexible enough to play multiple roles and/or complete each other's tasks. This is an obvious plus to a team because it greatly improves its adaptability and makes it less reliant on any single member.[69] Selecting members who themselves value flexibility, and then cross-training them to be able to do each other's jobs, should lead to higher team performance over time.

Occasionally within teams, you will see people take on **individual roles** that are not productive for keeping the team on task. When this happens, the individual is demonstrating more concern for himself or herself than the team as a whole.

task-oriented roles Roles performed by group members to ensure that the tasks of the group are accomplished.

maintenance roles Roles performed by group members to maintain good relations within the group.

individual roles Roles performed by group members that are not productive for keeping the team on task.

EXHIBIT 6-7   Roles Required for Effective Team Functioning

	Function	Description	Example
Roles that build task accomplishment	*Initiating*	Stating the goal or problem, making proposals about how to work on it, setting time limits.	"Let's set up an agenda for discussing each of the problems we have to consider."
	Seeking information and opinions	Asking group members for specific factual information related to the task or problem, or for their opinions about it.	"What do you think would be the best approach to this, Jack?"
	Providing information and opinions	Sharing information or opinions related to the task or problems.	"I worked on a similar problem last year and found . . ."
	Clarifying	Helping one another understand ideas and suggestions that come up in the group.	"What you mean, Sue, is that we could . . .?"
	Elaborating	Building on one another's ideas and suggestions.	"Building on Don's idea, I think we could . . ."
	Summarizing	Reviewing the points covered by the group and the different ideas stated so that decisions can be based on full information.	Appointing a recorder to take notes on a blackboard.
	Consensus testing	Providing periodic testing on whether the group is nearing a decision or needs to continue discussion.	"Is the group ready to decide about this?"
Roles that build and maintain a team	*Harmonizing*	Mediating conflict among other members, reconciling disagreements, relieving tensions.	"Don, I don't think you and Sue really see the question that differently."
	Compromising	Admitting error at times of group conflict.	"Well, I'd be willing to change if you provided some help on . . ."
	Gatekeeping	Making sure all members have a chance to express their ideas and feelings and preventing members from being interrupted.	"Sue, we haven't heard from you on this issue."
	Encouraging	Helping a group member make his or her point. Establishing a climate of acceptance in the group.	"I think what you started to say is important, Jack. Please continue."

Source: "Team Processes," in *Managing for the Future,* ed. D. Ancona, T. Kochan, M. Scully, J. Van Maanen, and D. E. Westney (Cincinnati, OH: South-Western College Publishing, 1996), p. 9.

Diversity

Group diversity refers to the presence of a heterogeneous mix of individuals within a group.[70] Individuals can be different not only in functional characteristics (jobs, positions, or work experiences) but also in demographic or cultural characteristics (age, race, sex, and citizenship). Recent studies have examined the effect of heterogeneous values on

group diversity The presence of a heterogeneous mix of individuals within a group.

performance, and suggested that value differences may have a greater influence than functional, demographic, or cultural differences.[71] *Focus on Research* describes one of those studies.

FOCUS ON **RESEARCH**

Diversity Can Improve or Hurt Teams

How do different types of diversity influence performance? When we talk about team diversity, we often mean demographic differences like race, gender, or age diversity.[72] Professor Margaret Neale of Stanford University's Graduate School of Business has looked at the impact of three types of diversity on group performance: informational, demographic, and value-goal diversity.

Her research did not find a direct effect of diversity on performance. Instead, different forms of diversity generate different types of conflict. The type of conflict and how the team deals with it are what affect the team's performance.

Informational diversity was associated with constructive conflict, with team members debating about the best course of action. Neale considers this positive conflict. Demographic diversity can result in interpersonal conflict. If group members think, "I have a different opinion than you. I don't like what you do or how you do it. I don't like you," Neale says, it can destroy the group.

Groups that have value-goal diversity may face the most damage from the diversity. When team members do not agree on the values and goals, it is hard for them to function. However, if a team works through differences to reach consensus on values and goals, team members then know each other's intentions.

Neale and her colleagues conducted their research through a field study of work teams in a relocation company. They surveyed employees to measure their informational and value-goal diversity. They also collected group performance data and supervisor assessments of the teams' work.

RESEARCH FINDINGS: Team Diversity

Managing diversity on teams is a balancing act (see Exhibit 6-8). On the one hand, a number of researchers have suggested that diversity brings a greater number of ideas, perspectives, knowledge, and skills to the group, which can be used to perform at a higher level.[73] On the other hand, researchers have suggested that diversity can lead people to recall stereotypes and therefore bring bias into their evaluation of people who are different from them.[74] Diversity can thus make it more difficult to unify the team and reach agreements. We consider some of the evidence to help us resolve these opposing views.

In a study examining the effectiveness of teams of strangers and teams of friends on bargaining, researchers found that teams of strangers gained greater profit than teams of friends, when teams reported to a supervisor.[75] However, teams of friends were more cohesive than teams of strangers. Another study of 60 teams found that in effective teams, about 50 percent of the individuals considered themselves friends, which underscores the importance of teams developing friendships.[76] However, the researchers also found that in teams that reported almost 100 percent friendship, performance was much lower. These groups tended to isolate themselves from others, and not seek outside influences. The research on friendships in teams suggests that teams of friends may be less concerned with productivity and more concerned with maintaining their relationship than are teams of strangers.

Is building a team just from people who are friends a good idea?

EXHIBIT 6-8 Advantages and Disadvantages of Diversity	
Advantages	**Disadvantages**
Multiple perspectives	Ambiguity
Greater openness to new ideas	Complexity
Multiple interpretations	Confusion
Increased creativity	Miscommunication
Increased flexibility	Difficulty in reaching a single agreement
Increased problem-solving skills	Difficulty in agreeing on specific actions

Source: Adapted from N. J. Adler, *International Dimensions of Organizational Behavior,* 4th ed., p. 109. © 2002 South-Western, a part of Cengage Learning, Inc. Reproduced by permission. www.cengage.com/permissions.

Overall, studies suggest that the strongest case for diversity on work teams can be made when these teams are engaged in problem-solving and decision-making tasks.[77] Heterogeneous teams may have qualities that lead to creative or unique solutions.[78]

The lack of a common perspective also means diverse teams usually spend more time discussing issues, which decreases the possibility that a weak alternative will be chosen. Although diverse groups have more difficulty working together and solving problems, this goes away with time as the members come to know each other.

Recent research suggests that when team members share a common belief that diversity will positively affect their performance, this sets the foundation for the team to manage the diversity in a positive way. Specifically, if team members set out early to try to learn about one another in order to understand and use their differences, this will have a positive effect on the team.[79] Laurie Milton, at the Haskayne School of Business at the University of Calgary, and several co-authors found that even 10 minutes spent sharing personal information when a group first started working together lowered subsequent group conflict and improved creative performance.[80] When group members did not share personal information at the beginning of their work, they were less likely to do so later.

The research findings, taken as a whole, suggest that diversity can bring increased benefits to the team, but to do so, teams must have some common values, and they need to be willing to share information about themselves early on. Thus, we can expect that diversity begins to provide extra value to the team once team members become more familiar with one another and the team becomes more cohesive. *Focus on Diversity* examines the impact of diversity on learning to work together in teams.

FOCUS ON **DIVERSITY**

Questioning the Impact of Diversity

Do diverse teams really have more difficulty learning how to work together? A study of groups of Caucasian and Chinese men living in Canada examined whether being a token ethnic member in a group (the only Chinese or the only Caucasian) would affect participation and influence levels in groups.[81] Some groups worked face to face, others by computer only.

The study found that for the face-to-face groups, Caucasian males, whether tokens or dominants in their groups, had higher participation levels, on average, than Chinese males. However, in face-to-face groups dominated by Chinese males, the Chinese males also had relatively high participation rates. Only the token Chinese males were low on participation or influence on their groups.

Studies indicate that these employees in Miles, China, collecting harvest grapes for the production of red wine, will perform better in a group than when working alone. In collectivist societies such as China, employees show less propensity to engage in social loafing. Unlike individualistic cultures such as the United States, where people are dominated by self-interest, the Chinese are motivated by in-group goals.

In the computer-only groups, the ethnicity of group members could be determined in some groups, while for others it could not. In those groups where the ethnicity of team members was unknown, there were no differences in participation rates of Chinese and Caucasian men.

This research suggests that participation and influence may be less a cultural issue, and more related to how individuals respond to visible differences when interacting with diverse team members.

Size

Generally speaking, the most effective teams have fewer than 10 members. And experts suggest using the smallest number of people who can do the task. Unfortunately, there is a pervasive tendency for managers to err on the side of making teams too large. While a minimum of four or five may be necessary to develop diversity of views and skills, managers seem to seriously underestimate how coordination problems can dramatically increase as team members are added. When teams have excess members, cohesiveness and mutual accountability decline, social loafing increases, and more and more people do less talking compared with others. So in designing effective teams, managers should try to keep the number of members to less than 10. If a work unit is larger and you want a team effort, consider breaking the unit into subteams. Uneven numbers in teams may help provide a mechanism to break ties and resolve conflicts, while an even number of team members may foster the need to create more consensus.

Size and Social Loafing One of the most important findings related to the size of a team has been labelled **social loafing**. Social loafing is the tendency for individuals to expend less effort when working collectively than when working individually.[82] It directly challenges the logic that the productivity of the team as a whole should at least equal the sum of the productivity of each individual in that team. *Focus on Research* explains how social loafing occurs.

social loafing The tendency for individuals to expend less effort when working collectively than when working individually.

Teams Are Not Always the Sum of Their Parts

Do individuals exert less effort when they are on teams? A common stereotype is that team spirit spurs individual effort and enhances the team's overall productivity. In the late 1920s, German psychologist Max Ringelmann compared the results of individual and team performance on a rope-pulling task.[83] He expected that the team's effort would be equal to the sum of the efforts of individuals within the team. That is, three people pulling together should exert three times as much pull on the rope as one person, and eight people should exert eight times as much pull. Ringelmann's results, however, did not confirm his expectations. One person pulling on a rope alone exerted an average of 63 kilograms of force. In groups of three, per-person force dropped to 53 kilograms. And in groups of eight, it fell to only 31 kilograms per person.

Replications of Ringelmann's research with similar tasks have generally supported his findings.[84] Increases in team size are inversely related to individual performance. More may be better in the sense that the total productivity of a group of four is greater than that of one or two people, but the individual productivity of each group member declines.

What causes this social loafing effect? It may be due to a belief that others in the team are not carrying their fair share. If you view others as lazy or inept, you can re-establish equity by reducing your effort. Another explanation is the dispersion of responsibility. Because the results of the team cannot be attributed to any single person, the relationship between an individual's input and the team's output is clouded. In such situations, individuals may be tempted to become "free riders" and coast on the team's efforts. In other words, there will be a reduction in efficiency when individuals believe that their contribution cannot be measured. To reduce social loafing, teams should not be larger than necessary, and individuals should be held accountable for their actions. You might also consider the ideas presented on dealing with shirkers in this chapter's *Ethical Dilemma Exercise* on page 250.

Why don't some team members pull their weight?

Members' Flexibility

Teams made up of flexible individuals have members who can complete each other's tasks. This is an obvious plus to a team because it greatly improves its adaptability and makes it less reliant on any single member.[85] So selecting members who themselves value flexibility, then cross-training them to be able to do each other's jobs, should lead to higher team performance over time.

Members' Preference for Teamwork

Not every employee is a team player. Given the option, many employees will "select themselves out" of team participation. When people who would prefer to work alone are required to team up, there is a direct threat to the team's morale.[86] This suggests that,

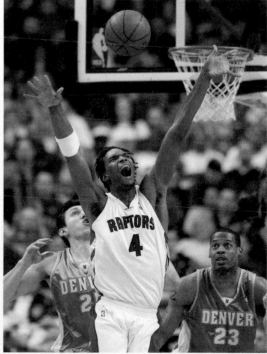

A study of 23 National Basketball Association teams found that "shared experience"—tenure on the team and time on court—tended to improve turnover and boost win-loss performance significantly. Why do you think teams that stay together longer tend to play better?

when selecting team members, individual preferences should be considered, as well as abilities, personalities, and skills. High-performing teams are likely to be composed of people who prefer working as part of a team.

Work Design

Effective teams need to work together and take collective responsibility to complete significant tasks. They must be more than a "team-in-name-only."[87] The work design category includes variables such as freedom and autonomy, the opportunity to utilize different skills and talents, the ability to complete a whole and identifiable task or product, and the participation in a task or project that has a substantial impact on others. The evidence indicates that these characteristics enhance member motivation and increase team effectiveness.[88] These work design characteristics motivate teams because they increase members' sense of responsibility and ownership over the work, and because they make the work more interesting to perform.[89] These recommendations are consistent with the job characteristics model we presented in Chapter 5.

Process

Process variables make up the final component of team effectiveness. The process category includes member commitment to a common purpose, establishment of specific goals, team efficacy, shared mental models, a managed level of conflict, and a system of accountability.

Common Purpose

Effective teams have a common and meaningful purpose that provides direction, momentum, and commitment for members.[90] This purpose is a vision. It's broader than specific goals.

Members of successful teams put a tremendous amount of time and effort into discussing, shaping, and agreeing upon a purpose that belongs to them both collectively and individually. This common purpose, when accepted by the team, becomes the equivalent of what celestial navigation is to a ship captain—it provides direction and guidance under any and all conditions. Like the proverbial ship following the wrong course, teams that don't have good planning skills are doomed; perfectly executing the wrong plan is a lost cause.[91] Effective teams also show **reflexivity**, meaning that they reflect on and adjust their master plan when necessary. A team has to have a good plan, but it also has to be willing and able to adapt when condition call for it.[92]

reflexivity A team characteristic of reflecting on and adjusting the master plan when necessary.

Specific Goals

Successful teams translate their common purpose into specific, measurable, and realistic performance goals. Just as we demonstrated in Chapter 4 how goals lead individuals to higher performance, goals also energize teams. These specific goals facilitate clear communication. They also help teams maintain their focus on achieving results.

Consistent with the research on individual goals, team goals should be challenging. Difficult goals have been found to raise team performance on those criteria for which they are set. So, for instance, goals for quantity tend to raise quantity, goals for speed tend to raise speed, goals for accuracy tend to raise accuracy, and so on.[93]

Teams should also be encouraged to develop milestones—tangible steps toward completion of the project. This allows teams to focus on their goal and evaluate progress toward the goal. The milestones should be sufficiently important and readily accomplished so that teams can celebrate some of their accomplishments along the way.

Team Efficacy

Effective teams have confidence in themselves. They believe they can succeed. We call this *team efficacy*.[94]

Success breeds success. Teams that have been successful raise their beliefs about future success, which, in turn, motivates them to work harder. When the Ottawa Senators started losing multiple games after posting a 15–2 start to the 2007–08 season, they started to lose their confidence. They seemed less sure that they could win another game.

One of the factors that helps teams build their efficacy is **cohesiveness**—the degree to which members are attracted to each other and are motivated to stay on the team.[95] Though teams differ in their cohesiveness, it is important because it has been found to be related to the team's productivity.[96]

Studies consistently show that the relationship of cohesiveness and productivity depends on the performance-related norms established by the group.[97] If performance-related norms are high (for example, high output, quality work, cooperation with individuals outside the group), a cohesive group will be more productive than a less cohesive group. If cohesiveness is high and performance norms are low, productivity will be low. If cohesiveness is low and performance norms are high, productivity increases—but less than in the high cohesiveness–high norms situation. Where cohesiveness and performance-related norms are both low, productivity will tend to fall into the low-to-moderate range. These conclusions are summarized in Exhibit 6-9.

Most studies of cohesiveness focus on socio-emotional cohesiveness, the "sense of togetherness that develops when individuals derive emotional satisfaction from group participation."[98] There is also instrumental cohesiveness: the "sense of togetherness that develops when group members are mutually dependent on one another because they believe they could not achieve the group's goal by acting separately." Teams need to achieve a balance of these two types of cohesiveness to function well. *OB in Action—Increasing Group Cohesiveness* indicates how to increase both socio-emotional and instrumental cohesiveness.

cohesiveness The degree to which team members are attracted to each other and are motivated to stay on the team.

OB in ACTION

Increasing Group Cohesiveness

Increasing socio-emotional cohesiveness

→ Keep the group relatively **small**.

→ Strive for a **favourable public image** to increase the status and prestige of belonging.

→ Encourage **interaction** and **cooperation**.

→ Emphasize members' **common characteristics** and interests.

→ **Point out environmental threats** (e.g., competitors' achievements) to rally the group.

Increasing instrumental cohesiveness

→ Regularly update and **clarify the group's goal(s)**.

→ Give every group member a **vital "piece of the action."**

→ Channel each group member's special talents toward the **common goal(s)**.

→ **Recognize** and equitably reinforce **every member's contributions**.

→ Frequently remind group members they **need one another** to get the job done.[99]

EXHIBIT 6-9   Relationship among Team Cohesiveness, Performance Norms and Productivity

Cohesiveness

Performance Norms	High	Low
High	High productivity	Moderate productivity
Low	Low productivity	Moderate to low productivity

What, if anything, can management do to increase team efficacy? Two possible options are helping the team to achieve small successes and skill training. Small successes build team confidence. As a team develops an increasingly stronger performance record, it also increases the collective belief that future efforts will lead to success. In addition, managers should consider providing training to improve members' technical and interpersonal skills. The greater the abilities of team members, the greater the likelihood that the team will develop confidence and the capability to deliver on that confidence. *OB Around the Globe* explores whether culture affects a group's cohesiveness.

Group Cohesiveness Across Cultures

Does cohesiveness work the same throughout the world? A recent study attempted to determine whether motivating work groups by giving them more complex tasks and greater autonomy resulted in increased group cohesiveness.[100] Researchers studied teams from an international bank with branches in the United States, an individualist culture, and in Hong Kong, a collectivist culture. Teams were entirely composed of individuals from the branch country. The results showed that, regardless of what culture the teams were from, giving teams difficult tasks and more freedom to accomplish those tasks created a more tight-knit group. Consequently, team performance was enhanced.

However, the teams differed in the extent to which increases in task complexity and autonomy resulted in greater group cohesiveness. Teams in individualist cultures responded more strongly than did teams in collectivist cultures, became more united and committed, and, as a result, received higher performance ratings from their supervisors than did teams from collectivist cultures.

Why do these cultural differences exist? One explanation is that individuals from collectivist cultures already have a strong predisposition to work together as a group, so there is less need for increased cohesiveness. What's the lesson? Managers in individualist cultures may need to work harder to increase team cohesiveness. One way to do this is to give teams more challenging assignments and provide them with more independence.

Mental Models

Effective teams have accurate and common mental models—knowledge and beliefs (a "psychological map") about how the work gets done. If team members have the wrong mental models, which is particularly likely to happen with teams under acute stress, their performance suffers.[101] For example, in the Iraq war, many military leaders said they underestimated the power of the insurgency and the infighting among Iraqi religious sects. The similarity of team members' mental models matters, too. If team members have different ideas about how to do things, the teams will fight over how to do things rather than focus on what needs to be done.[102]

Managed Level of Conflict

Conflict on a team is not necessarily bad. Though relationship conflicts—those based on interpersonal incompatibilities, tension, and animosity toward others—are almost always dysfunctional, teams that are completely void of conflict are likely to be less effective, with the members becoming withdrawn and only superficially harmonious. Often, if there is no conflict, the alternative is not agreement, but apathy and disengagement. Teams that avoid conflict also tend to have lower performance levels, forget to consider key issues, or remain unaware of important aspects of their situation.[103] So effective teams are characterized by an appropriate level of conflict.[104]

Kathleen Eisenhardt of the Stanford Graduate School of Business and her colleagues studied top management teams in technology-based companies to understand how they manage conflict.[105] Their research identified six tactics that helped teams successfully manage the interpersonal conflict that can accompany group interactions. These are presented in *OB in Action—Reducing Team Conflict*. By handling the interpersonal conflict well, these groups were able to achieve their goals without letting conflict get in the way.

Groups need mechanisms by which they can manage the conflict, however. From the research reported above, we could conclude that sharing information and goals, and striving to be open and get along, are helpful strategies for negotiating our way through the maze of conflict. A sense of humour, and a willingness to understand the points of others without insisting that everyone agree on all points, are also important. Group members should try to focus on the issues, rather than on personalities, and strive to achieve fairness and equity in the group process.

OB in ACTION

Reducing Team Conflict

→ Work with **more, rather than less, information**, and debate on the basis of facts.

→ Develop **multiple alternatives** to enrich the level of debate.

→ Develop commonly agreed-upon **goals**.

→ Use **humour** when making tough decisions.

→ Maintain a **balanced power** structure.

→ Resolve issues **without forcing consensus**.[106]

Accountability

Successful teams make members individually and jointly accountable for the team's purpose, goals, and approach.[107] They clearly define what they are individually responsible for and what they are jointly responsible for. *From Concepts to Skills* on pages 253–254 discusses how to conduct effective team meetings.

Beware! Teams Aren't Always the Answer

Despite considerable success in the use of teams, they are not necessarily appropriate in all situations, as Exhibit 6-10 on page 244 suggests. Teamwork takes more time and often more resources than individual work. Teams, for instance, have increased communication demands, conflicts to be managed, and meetings to be run. In the excitement to enjoy the benefits of teams, some managers have introduced them into situations where the work is better done by individuals. A 2003 study done by Statistics Canada found that the introduction of teamwork lowered turnover in the service industries, for both high- and low-skilled employees. However, manufacturing companies experienced higher turnover if they introduced teamwork and formal teamwork training, compared with not doing so (15.8 percent vs. 10.7 percent).[108]

How do you know if the work of your group would be better done in teams? It's been suggested that three tests be applied to see if a team fits the situation:[109]

7 Are teams always the answer?

- *Can the work be done better by more than one person?* Simple tasks that don't require diverse input are probably better left to individuals.

- *Does the work create a common purpose or set of goals for the people in the group that is more than the sum of individual goals?* For instance, the service departments of many new-car dealers have introduced teams that link customer service personnel, mechanics, parts specialists, and sales representatives. Such teams can better manage collective responsibility for ensuring that customers' needs are properly met.

- *Are the members of the group interdependent?* Teams make sense where there is interdependence between tasks—where the success of the whole depends on the success of each one, *and* the success of each one depends on the success of the others. Soccer, for instance, is an obvious *team* sport because of the

EXHIBIT 6-10

Source: S. Adams, *Build a Better Life by Stealing Office Supplies* (Kansas City, MO: Andrews and McMeal, 1991), p. 31. Dilbert reprinted with permission of United Features Syndicate.

interdependence of the players. Swim teams, by contrast, rely heavily on individual performance to win a meet.

Others have outlined the conditions under which organizations would find teams more useful: "when work processes cut across functional lines; when speed is important (and complex relationships are involved); when the organization mirrors a complex, differentiated and rapidly changing market environment; when innovation and learning have priority; when the tasks that have to be done require online integration of highly interdependent performers."[110]

Summary and Implications

1 **What are teams and groups?** Groups and teams differ. The outputs of groups are simply the sum of individual efforts. A team, because of the close collaboration among members, produces output that is greater than the sum of individual efforts.

2 **Does everyone use teams?** Teams have become an essential part of the way business is being done these days. In fact, it is more surprising to find an organization that *does not* use teams. As organizations focus on effectiveness and efficiency, they find that teams are a good way to manage talent. Teams are more flexible and responsive to changing events than are traditional departments or other forms of permanent groupings. Teams have the capability to quickly assemble, deploy, refocus, and disband.

3 **What kinds of teams are there?** Teams can be classified based on their objective. The four most common forms of teams you are likely to find in an organization are problem-solving (or process-improvement) teams; self-managed (or self-directed) teams; cross-functional (or project) teams; and virtual teams. A problem-solving team meets for a few hours each week to discuss ways of improving quality, efficiency, and the work environment. A self-managed team consists of members who take on many responsibilities of their former managers and direct themselves. A cross-functional team consists of employees from about the same hierarchical level, but from different work areas, who come together to accomplish a task. A virtual team uses computer technology to tie together physically dispersed members in order to achieve a common goal.

4 **How does one become a team player?** In order for either a group or a team to function, individuals have to achieve some balance between their own needs and the needs of the group. Individuals on the team need to understand their roles, and then work together to create a set of group norms.

5 **Do teams go through stages while they work?** Two different models illustrate how teams develop. The first, the five-stage model, describes the standardized sequence of stages groups pass through: forming, storming, norming, performing, and adjourning. Through these stages, group members learn how to settle conflicts and develop norms, which enable them to perform. The second, the punctuated-equilibrium model, describes the pattern of development specific to temporary groups with deadlines. In this model, the group shows two great periods of activity, first midway through the project, after which it performs at a higher level than it did previously. The second peak in activity takes place right before the project comes due.

6 **How do we create effective teams?** For teams to be effective, careful consideration must be given to resources, the team's composition, work design, and process variables. The four contextual factors that appear to be most significantly related to team performance are the presence of adequate resources, effective leadership and structure, a climate of trust, and a performance evaluation and reward system that reflects team contributions. Effective teams are neither too large nor too small—typically they range in size from 5 to 12 people. They have members who fill role demands, are flexible, and who prefer to be part of a group. Teams will be more effective if members have freedom and opportunity to do their tasks and believe that the task will have a substantial impact on others. Finally, effective teams also have members committed to a common purpose and specific team goals.

7 **Are teams always the answer?** Teams are not necessarily appropriate in every situation. How do you know if the work of your group would be better done in teams? It's been suggested that three tests be applied to see if a team fits the situation: (1) Can the work be done better by more than one person? (2) Does the work create a common purpose or set of goals for the people in the group that is more than the sum of individual goals? and (3) Are the members of the group interdependent? This third test asks whether the success of the whole depends on the success of each one *and* the success of each one depends on the success of the others.

SNAPSHOT SUMMARY

1 Teams vs. Groups: What's the Difference?

2 Why Have Teams Become So Popular?

3 Types of Teams
Problem-Solving Teams
Self-Managed Teams
Cross-Functional Teams
Virtual Teams

4 From Individual to Team Member
Roles
Norms

5 Stages of Group and Team Development
The Five-Stage Model
The Punctuated-Equilibrium Model

6 Creating Effective Teams
Context
Composition
Work Design
Process

7 Beware! Teams Aren't Always the Answer

For Review

1. Contrast self-managed and cross-functional teams.

2. Contrast virtual and face-to-face teams.

3. How do norms develop in a team?

4. Describe the five-stage model of group development.

5. Describe the punctuated-equilibrium model of group development.

6. What are the characteristics of an effective team?

7. What is the difference between task-oriented roles and maintenance roles?

8. Contrast the pros and cons of having diverse teams.

9. What are the effects of team size on performance?

10. How can a team minimize social loafing?

For Critical Thinking

1. Identify five roles you play. What behaviours do they require? Are any of these roles in conflict? If so, in what way? How do you resolve these conflicts?

2. How could you use the punctuated-equilibrium model to better understand team behaviour?

3. Have you experienced social loafing as a team member? What did you do to prevent this problem?

4. Would you prefer to work alone or as part of a team? Why? How do you think your answer compares with that of others in your class?

5. What effect, if any, do you think workforce diversity has on a team's performance and satisfaction?

 **for You**

- Know that you will be asked to work on teams and groups both during your undergraduate years and later on in life, so understanding how teams work is an important skill to have.

- Think about the roles that you play on teams. Teams need task-oriented people to get the job done, but they also need maintenance-oriented people who help keep people working together and feeling committed to the team.

- Help your team set specific, measurable, realistic goals, as this leads to more successful outcomes.

POINT

COUNTERPOINT

Sports Teams Are Good Models for Workplace Teams

Studies from hockey, football, soccer, basketball, and baseball have found a number of elements that successful sports teams have that can be extrapolated to successful work teams:[111]

Successful teams integrate cooperation and competition. Effective team coaches get athletes to help one another, but also push one another to perform at their best. Sports teams with the best win-loss record had coaches who promoted a strong spirit of cooperation and a high level of healthy competition among their players.

Successful teams score early wins. Early successes build teammates' faith in themselves and their capacity as a team. For instance, research on hockey teams of relatively equal ability found that 72 percent of the time the team that was ahead at the end of the first period went on to win the game. So managers should give teams early tasks that are simple, as well as "easy wins."

Successful teams avoid losing streaks. Losing can become a self-fulfilling prophecy. A couple of failures can lead to a downward spiral if a team becomes demoralized and believes it is helpless to end its losing streak. Managers need to instill confidence in team members that they can turn things around when they encounter setbacks.

Practice makes perfect. Successful sports teams execute on game day but learn from their mistakes in practice. A wise manager carves out time and space in which work teams can experiment and learn.

Successful teams use halftime breaks. The best coaches in basketball and football use halftime during a game to reassess what is working and what is not. Managers of work teams should similarly build in assessments at around the halfway point in a team project to evaluate how the team can improve.

Winning teams have a stable membership. Studies of professional basketball teams have found that the more stable a team's membership, the more likely the team is to win. The more time teammates have together, the more able they are to anticipate one another's moves and the clearer they are about one another's roles.

Successful teams debrief after failures and successes. The best sports teams study the game video. Similarly, work teams need to take time to routinely reflect on both their successes and failures and to learn from them.

Sports Teams Are Not the Model for All Teams

There are flaws in using sports as a model for developing effective work teams. Here are just four caveats:[112]

All sport teams are not alike. In baseball, for instance, there is little interaction among teammates. Rarely are more than two or three players directly involved in a play. The performance of the team is largely the sum of the performance of the individual players. In contrast, basketball has much more interdependence among players. Geographic distribution is dense. Usually all players are involved in every play, team members have to be able to switch from offence to defence at a moment's notice, and there is continuous movement by all, not just the player with the ball. The performance of the team is more than the sum of its individual players. So when using sports teams as a model for work teams, you have to make sure you are making the correct comparison.

Work teams are more varied and complex. In an athletic league, teams vary little in their context, their individual design, and the design of the task. But in work teams these variables can differ greatly. As a result, coaching plays a much more significant part in a sports team's performance than a work team's. Performance of work teams is more a function of getting the teams' structural and design variables right. So, in contrast to sports, managers of work teams should focus more on getting the team set up for success than on coaching.

A lot of employees cannot relate to sports metaphors. Not everyone on work teams is conversant with sports. Women are still breaking down barriers for equal treatment in many sports, for example, so individuals may well have very different personal sports experience to draw from. Team members from different cultures also may not know the sports terms you are using. Most Canadians, for instance, know little about the rules of Australian football.

Work team outcomes are not easily defined in terms of wins and losses. Sports teams typically measure success in terms of wins and losses. Such measures of success are rarely as clear for work teams. Managers who try to define success in wins and losses might imply that the workplace is ethically no more complex than the playing field, which is rarely true.

LEARNING ABOUT **YOURSELF** EXERCISE

How Good Am I at Building and Leading a Team?

Use the following rating scale to respond to the 18 questions on building and leading an effective team.[113]

Strongly Disagree	Disagree	Slightly Disagree	Slightly Agree	Agree	Strongly Agree
1	2	3	4	5	6

1. I am knowledgeable about the different stages of development that teams can go through in their life cycles.	1	2	3	4	5	6
2. When a team forms, I make certain that all team members are introduced to one another at the outset.	1	2	3	4	5	6
3. When the team first comes together, I provide directions, answer team members' questions, and clarify goals, expectations, and procedures.	1	2	3	4	5	6
4. I help team members establish a foundation of trust among one another and between themselves and me.	1	2	3	4	5	6
5. I ensure that standards of excellence, not mediocrity or mere acceptability, characterize the team's work.	1	2	3	4	5	6
6. I provide a great deal of feedback to team members regarding their performance.	1	2	3	4	5	6
7. I encourage team members to balance individual autonomy with interdependence among other team members.	1	2	3	4	5	6
8. I help team members become at least as committed to the success of the team as to their own personal success.	1	2	3	4	5	6
9. I help team members learn to play roles that assist the team in accomplishing its tasks, as well as building strong interpersonal relationships.	1	2	3	4	5	6
10. I articulate a clear, exciting, passionate vision of what the team can achieve.	1	2	3	4	5	6
11. I help team members become committed to the team vision.	1	2	3	4	5	6
12. I encourage a win-win philosophy in the team; that is, when one member wins, every member wins.	1	2	3	4	5	6
13. I help the team avoid making the group's survival more important than accomplishing its goal.	1	2	3	4	5	6
14. I use formal process-management procedures to help the group become faster, more efficient, and more productive, and to prevent errors.	1	2	3	4	5	6
15. I encourage team members to represent the team's vision, goals, and accomplishments to outsiders.	1	2	3	4	5	6
16. I diagnose and capitalize on the team's core competence.	1	2	3	4	5	6
17. I encourage the team to achieve dramatic breakthrough innovations, as well as small continuous improvements.	1	2	3	4	5	6
18. I help the team work toward preventing mistakes, not just correcting them after the fact.	1	2	3	4	5	6

Scoring Key:

This instrument assesses team development behaviours in five areas: diagnosing team development (items 1, 16); managing the forming stage (items 2–4); managing the storming stage (items 10–12, 14, 15); managing the norming stage (items 6–9, 13); and managing the performing stage (items 5, 17, 18). Add up your score. Your total score will range between 18 and 108.

Based on a norm group of 500 business students, the following can help estimate where you are relative to others:

95 or above = You're in the top quartile of being able to build and lead a team

72–94 = You're in the second quartile

60–71 = You're in the third quartile

Below 60 = You're in the bottom quartile

Self-
Assessment
Library

More Learning About Yourself Exercises

An additional self-assessment relevant to this chapter appears on MyOBLab (**www.pearsoned.ca/myoblab**).

IV.E.2 What Is My Team Efficacy?

When you complete the additional assessments, consider the following:

1. Am I surprised about my score?
2. Would my friends evaluate me similarly?

Form small groups to discuss the following topics, as assigned by your instructor:

1. One of the members of your team continually arrives late for meetings and does not turn drafts of assignments in on time. In general, this group member is engaging in social loafing. What can the members of your group do to reduce social loafing?

2. Consider a team with which you have worked. Was there more emphasis on task-oriented or maintenance-oriented roles? What impact did this have on the group's performance?

3. Identify 4 or 5 norms that a team could put into place near the beginning of its life that might help the team function better over time.

WORKING WITH OTHERS EXERCISE

The Paper Tower Exercise

Step 1   Each group will receive 20 index cards, 12 paper clips, and 2 marking pens.[114] Groups have 10 minutes to plan a paper tower that will be judged on the basis of 3 criteria: height, stability, and beauty. No physical work (building) is allowed during this planning period.

Step 2   Each group has 15 minutes for the actual construction of the paper tower.

Step 3   Each tower will be identified by a number assigned by your instructor. Each student is to individually examine all the paper towers. Your group is then to come to a consensus as to which tower is the winner (5 minutes). A spokesperson from your group should report its decision and the criteria the group used in reaching it.

Step 4   In your small groups, discuss the following questions (your instructor may choose to have you discuss only a subset of these questions):

    a.   What percentage of the plan did each member of your group contribute, on average?

    b.   Did your group have a leader? Why or why not?

    c.   How did the group generally respond to the ideas that were expressed during the planning period?

    d.   To what extent did your group follow the five-stage model of group development?

    e.   List specific behaviours exhibited during the planning and building sessions that you felt were helpful to the group. Explain why you found them to be helpful.

    f.   List specific behaviours exhibited during the planning and building sessions that you felt were dysfunctional to the group. Explain why you found them dysfunctional.

ETHICAL DILEMMA EXERCISE

Dealing with Shirkers

We have noted that one of the most common problems in groups is social loafing, which means group members contribute less than if they were working on their own. We might call such individuals "shirkers"—those who are contributing far less than other group members.

Most of us have experienced social loafing, or shirking, in groups. And we may even admit to times when we shirked ourselves. We discussed earlier in the chapter some ways of discouraging social loafing, such as limiting group size, holding individuals responsible for their contributions, and setting group goals. While these tactics may be effective, in our experience, many students simply work around shirkers.

"We just did it ourselves—it was easier that way," says one group member.

Consider the following questions for dealing with shirking in groups:

1. If group members end up "working around" shirkers, do you think this information should be communicated to the instructor so that this individual's contribution to the project is judged more fairly? If so, does the group have an ethical responsibility to communicate this to the shirking group member? If not, isn't the shirking group member unfairly reaping the rewards of a "free ride"?

2. Do you think confronting the shirking group member is justified? Does this depend on the skills of the shirker (whether he or she is capable of doing good-quality work)?

3. Social loafing has been found to be higher in Western, more individualist nations than in other countries. Do you think this means we should tolerate shirking on the part of North American workers to a greater degree than if it occurred with someone from Asia?

CASE INCIDENTS

Role Conflict among Telephone Service Employees

All supervisory jobs are not alike. Maggie Beckhard is just learning this fact.[115] After having spent three years as a production-scheduling supervisor at a Procter & Gamble (P&G) manufacturing plant, she recently took a position as manager of telephone services at Halifax Provident Insurance (HPI). In her new job, Maggie supervises 20 telephone service employees. These people have direct contact with customers—providing quotes, answering questions, following up on claims, and the like.

At P&G, Maggie's employees knew they had only one constituency to please. That was management. But Maggie is discovering that her employees at HPI find it more difficult. As service employees, they have to serve two masters—management and the customer. And at least from comments her employees have made, they seem to think there is a discrepancy between what they believe customers want them to do and what they believe management wants them to do. A frequent complaint, for instance, is that customers want the telephone rep's undivided attention and to spend as much time as necessary to solve their problem. But the reps see management as wanting them to handle as many calls as possible per day and to keep each call as short as possible.

This morning, a rep came into Maggie's office complaining of severe headaches. "The more I try to please our customers, the more stress I feel," the rep told Maggie. "I want to do the best job I can for our customers, but I don't feel like I can devote the time that's necessary. You constantly remind us that it's customers that provide our paycheques and how important it is to give reliable, courteous, and responsive service, but then we feel the pressure to handle more calls per hour."

Maggie is well aware of studies that have shown that role conflict is related to reduced job satisfaction, increased turnover and absenteeism, and fewer organizational citizenship behaviours. Severe role conflict is also likely to lead to poor customer service—the antithesis of her department's goals.

After talking with her staff, Maggie concluded that regardless of whether their perceptions were accurate, her people certainly believed them to be. They were reading one set of expectations through their interactions with customers, and another set through what the company conveyed during the selection process, in training sessions, and through the behaviours that management rewarded.

Questions

1. What is the source of role conflict here?

2. Are there functional benefits to management from role conflict? Explain.

3. Should role conflict among these telephone service employees be any greater than it is for a typical employee who works as part of a team and has to meet the expectations of a boss, as well as those of his or her team members? Explain.

4. What can Maggie do to manage this role conflict?

OB *AT WORK*

Team-Building Retreats

Team-building retreats are big business. Companies believe such retreats, where team members participate in activities ranging from mountain climbing, to trust-building exercises (where team members let themselves fall backwards into their colleagues' arms), to Iron Chef–inspired cooking contests (used by UBS, Hewlett-Packard, and Verizon) can foster effective teamwork.[116]

But why do organizations have teammates participate in activities that seem irrelevant to the organization's primary activities? Pat Finelli, vice-president of marketing for Toronto-based Pizza Pizza, believes that corporate retreats aid team building, which in turn improves company performance. Finelli took his staff members to Hockley Valley Resort (which features spa treatments) in Orangeville, Ontario so that his employees could have time for both meetings and relaxation. He explains that the trip "was part thank-you for the previous year's success, but included a lot of brainstorming to come up with ways to surpass the company's goals for next year." He believes that spa treatments motivate employees. "When they're relaxed and feeling good, they give back to you and they're more open to thinking."

Given the level of expense for such retreats, not all companies are keen on providing team-building activities outside the organization. According to Susan Harper, a business psychologist, "team-building has definitely gone down. People are reluctant to spend money on what they think is not an absolute necessity." Atkins believes otherwise: "I know intuitively the payback here is huge. It's a very small investment to make for the payback we are going to get."

Hard drive maker Seagate takes it even further. Every year, Seagate flies roughly 200 managers to New Zealand to participate in "Eco Seagate," its annual team-building exercise. The tab? $9000 (US) per manager. Chief financial officer Charles Pope says it's one of the last things he'd cut from Seagate's budget.

It is clear that companies that invest in team-building retreats think they're worth the investment. Sometimes, though, they have unintended consequences. In 2001, a dozen Burger King employees burned themselves while participating in a "fire walk"—a team-building exercise that requires teammates to walk barefoot across an 8-foot pit of burning-hot coals. The results were injured employees and some very negative publicity for Burger King. In 2006, an employee of security systems company Alarm One was award $1.7 million in damages in a lawsuit in which she claimed she had been spanked on the job as part of a camaraderie-building exercise. One observer of these retreats said, "Most of the time, people asking for these activities are not interested in real teamwork building. What they really want is entertainment."

Some companies are taking team-building exercises in a different direction, having their employees engage in hands-on volunteer work. When the breweries Molson and Coors merged, they wanted to use a team-building exercise to acquaint the executive teams, but they didn't want to go the route of the typical golf outings or a ropes course. So, they helped Habitat for Humanity build a home. UPS has new managers participate in various community projects, such as distributing secondhand medical equipment in developing countries.

It is questionable whether team-building exercises such as mountain climbing, cooking contests, and fire walks result in improved company financial performance, and it may be better to think of such activities as morale boosters. According to Merianne Liteman, a professional corporate retreat organizer, "Where good retreats have a quantifiable effect is on retention, on morale, on productivity." Daryl Jesperson, CEO of RE/MAX International, says, "There is a productivity boost anytime you have one of these. People feel better about themselves, they feel better about the company, and as a result will do a better job."

Questions

1. Do you believe that team-building activities increase productivity? Why or why not? What other factors might be responsible for increases in profitability following a corporate retreat?

2. What are some other ways (besides those described above) to build effective teams and increase teamwork among company employees? How might these alternatives be better or worse than corporate retreats?

3. What should companies do about employees who lack athletic talent but are still pressured to participate in physical activities with their colleagues? How might poor performance by those with low athletic ability affect their status within the organization?

4. How might you increase teamwork when team members are not often in direct contact with one another? Can you think of any "electronic" team-building exercises?

From **Concepts** to **Skills**

Conducting a Team Meeting

Team meetings have a reputation for inefficiency. For instance, noted Canadian-born economist John Kenneth Galbraith has said, "Meetings are indispensable when you don't want to do anything."

When you are responsible for conducting a meeting, what can you do to make it more efficient and effective? Follow these 12 steps:[119]

1. *Prepare a meeting agenda.* An agenda defines what you hope to accomplish at the meeting. It should state the meeting's purpose; who will be in attendance; what, if any, preparation is required of each participant; a detailed list of items to be covered; the specific time and location of the meeting; and a specific finishing time.

2. *Distribute the agenda in advance.* Participants should have the agenda sufficiently in advance so they can adequately prepare for the meeting.

3. *Consult with participants before the meeting.* An unprepared participant cannot contribute to his or her full potential. It is your responsibility to ensure that members are prepared, so check with them ahead of time.

4. *Get participants to go over the agenda.* The first thing to do at the meeting is to have participants review the agenda, make any changes, then approve the final agenda.

5. *Establish specific time parameters.* Meetings should begin on time and have a specific time for completion. It is your responsibility to specify these time parameters and to hold to them.

6. *Maintain focused discussion.* It is your responsibility to give direction to the discussion; to keep it focused on the issues; and to minimize interruptions, disruptions, and irrelevant comments.

7. *Encourage and support participation of all members.* To maximize the effectiveness of problem-oriented meetings, each participant must be encouraged to contribute. Quiet or reserved personalities need to be drawn out so their ideas can be heard.

8. *Maintain a balanced style.* The effective group leader pushes when necessary and is passive when need be.

9. *Encourage the clash of ideas.* You need to encourage different points of view, critical thinking, and constructive disagreement.

10. *Discourage the clash of personalities.* An effective meeting is characterized by the critical assessment of ideas, not attacks on people. When running a meeting, you must quickly intercede to stop personal attacks or other forms of verbal insult.

11. *Be an effective listener.* You need to listen with intensity, empathy, and objectivity, and do whatever is necessary to get the full intended meaning from each participant's comments.

12. *Bring proper closure.* You should close a meeting by summarizing the group's accomplishments. Clarify what actions, if any, need to follow the meeting, and allocate follow-up assignments. If any decisions are made, you also need to determine who will be responsible for communicating and implementing them.

Practising Skills

Jameel Saumur is the leader of a five-member project team that has been assigned the task of moving his engineering firm into the booming area of high-speed intercity rail construction. Saumur and his team members have been researching the field, identifying specific business opportunities, negotiating alliances with equipment vendors, and evaluating high-speed rail experts and consultants from around the world. Throughout the process, Tonya Eckler, a highly qualified and respected engineer, has challenged a number of things Saumur said during team meetings and in the workplace. For example, at a meeting two weeks ago, Saumur presented the team with a list of 10 possible high-speed rail projects and started evaluating the company's ability to compete for them. Eckler contradicted virtually all of Saumur's comments, questioned his statistics, and was quite pessimistic about the possibility of getting contracts on these projects. After this latest display of displeasure, two other group members, Bryan Worth and Maggie Ames, are complaining that Eckler's actions are damaging the team's effectiveness. Eckler was originally assigned to the team for her unique expertise and insight. If you had to advise this team, what suggestions would you make to get the team on the right track to achieve its fullest potential?

Reinforcing Skills

1. Interview three managers at different organizations. Ask them about their experiences in managing teams. Have each describe teams that they thought were effective and why they succeeded. Have each also describe teams that they thought were ineffective and the reasons that might have caused this.

2. Contrast a team you have been in where members trusted each other with another team you have been in where members lacked trust in each other. How did the conditions in each team develop? What were the consequences in terms of interaction patterns and performance?

VIDEO CASE INCIDENT

CASE 6 Teams at Kluster

Kluster is a web-based company that invites individuals and companies to send in ideas for new products so they can get feedback from others. Within the company, teams have been formed to pursue various projects. Peter Wadsworth is an engineer on "the illuminator project" team, which focuses on the web-based, community-driven product development platform that is designed to facilitate good decision making about new product ideas. The team is where all kinds of people and organizations meet to pitch ideas, work on projects, and design products and events. In short, it focuses on anything that requires decision making and deliverables. The team's reward system facilitates teamwork and provides both financial and status rewards to high performers. It does not provide incentives to naysayers or those who simply want to bash ideas. People are allowed to do that, but they won't get very far with that kind of behaviour.

Wadsworth says that Ben Kaufman, Kluster's CEO, comes up with many ideas, but every day the team meets to talk about the website and other important issues. People on the illuminator team have to be disciplined, stay on task, be honest, and exercise self-leadership because Ben does not get involved in everyone's work. But he does want status reports on how things are going. Employees are based in various locations and are also on the road a lot. Each person has milestones that they must achieve week by week, and they all have "to-do" lists to guide their work. They all know that they have a good thing going and enjoy being around talented people.

The website enables the team to accomplish goals and to come up with solutions. Tom Pasley, the project manager, says that everyone has to work together using different skill sets. It is fun to get things done as a group, and it is more rewarding than individual work.

Kaufman believes that everyone wants feedback about what other people think. They may not act on the feedback, but they do want to hear reactions. He also realizes that sometimes people need a break from the team. He says that as long as tasks are being completed on time and employees are communicating well, he does not demand that they come in to the office.

Hitch, a graphic designer, says that all different kinds of people work at Kluster—some are very blunt, some are the calm voice of reason, and some are very creative. But whatever they are like, they focus on bouncing ideas back and forth. No one assumes that they are any better than anyone else.

Questions

1. What are the various types of teams that are found in organizations? Which type of team is the Illuminator team? Explain your reasoning.

2. What are the benefits of a team-based approach? What are the challenges? How have members of the Illuminator project overcome these challenges?

3. This chapter lists twelve characteristics of effective teams. Make a tentative assessment of how the Illuminator team scores on each of the 12 characteristics.

4. What three questions should be asked before the decision is made to form a team? What are the answers to these questions in terms of the Illuminator project? Is a team the best way to proceed?

5. Ben Kaufman says that it is important to make sure that people occasionally get a break from the team. Why do you think he said this?

Source: Based on "Groups and Teams at Kluster," *Organizational Behavior Video Library,* 2008. Copyrighted by Prentice-Hall.

Trust

Joseph Reaume opened Sunnyside Garage (today known as Reaume Chevrolet) in Windsor in 1931, never dreaming how far the company would go.[1] Today, Steve and Rick Reaume carry on the legacy of their great-grandfather, running one of the oldest Chevrolet dealerships in Canada.

Steve Reaume attributes the success of the business to the trust they have built in the community. "Our customers have always come first with us," he says. "They are the reason we have been in business for 76 years."

The brothers are from the fourth generation, and there are fifth-generation family members in the business as well. Sales and leasing consultant Jenn Reaume Natyshak, a member of the fifth generation and Steve's daughter, says, "I'm very proud and committed to 'The Tradition of Trust' banner we display. As part of the 5th generation, I promise to always live up to that tradition." Jenn's twin brother, Jeff, and younger brother Craig work in the business with her.

Trust also plays a part in how the Reaumes treat their employees. Says Dan Nedin, director of parts and service, "A dealership built on honesty was the reason I started my career with the Reaume family. It's resulted in loyalty of employees . . . and customers."

Trust, or lack of trust, is an increasingly important leadership issue in today's organizations.[2] Trust is fragile. It takes a long time to build, can be easily destroyed, and is hard to regain.[3]

Many Canadian and US organizations have created a lack of trust in their employees because of the massive layoffs they embarked on in the 1990s. A survey of Canadian employees concluded that three out of four Canadians do not trust the people they work for.[4] The inset *Why Integrity Is Questioned by Employees* on page 258 shows some of the issues that cause employees to wonder about the integrity of their managers.

Lack of trust in an organization is a serious problem. Professors Linda Duxbury of the Carleton University School of Business and Christopher Higgins of the University of Western Ontario's Richard Ivey School of Business found that employees who work in environments characterized by trust and respect report less stress and greater productivity than those who work in environments where trust is lacking.[5]

What Is Trust?

Trust is a positive expectation (or belief) that another will not—through words, actions, or decisions—act opportunistically.[6] Trust involves making oneself vulnerable, such as when we disclose intimate information or rely on another's promises.[7] By its very nature, trust provides the opportunity for disappointment or to be taken advantage of.[8] When we trust someone, we expect that person will not take advantage of us. The two most important elements of our definition are that it implies familiarity and risk.

The phrase *positive expectation* in our definition assumes knowledge and familiarity about the other party. Trust is a history-dependent process based on relevant but limited samples of experience.[9] It takes time to form, building incrementally and accumulating. Most of us find it hard, if not impossible, to trust someone immediately if we don't know anything about them. At the extreme, in the case of total ignorance, we can gamble, but we cannot trust.[10] But as we get to know someone and the relationship matures, we gain confidence in our ability to form a positive expectation.

The term *opportunistic* refers to the inherent risk and vulnerability in any trusting relationship. Trust involves making oneself vulnerable, as when, for example, we disclose intimate information or rely on another's promises.[11] By its very nature, trust provides the opportunity for disappointment or to be taken advantage of.[12] But trust is not taking risk per se; rather, it is a willingness to take risk.[13] So when I trust someone, I expect that he or she will not take advantage of me. This willingness to take risks is common to all trust situations.[14]

What Determines Trust?
What are the key dimensions of trust? Research has identified five important criteria: integrity, competence, consistency, loyalty, and openness.[15] These dimensions of trust are presented in the illustration on the right and listed in their order of importance in determining one's trustworthiness.

- *Integrity.* Honesty and truthfulness. Of all five dimensions, integrity seems to be most critical when someone assesses another's trustworthiness. For instance, when 570 white-collar employees were recently given a list of 28 attributes related to leadership, honesty was rated the most important by far.[16] "Without a perception of the other's 'moral character' and 'basic honesty,' other dimensions of trust [are] meaningless."[17]

- *Competence.* Technical and interpersonal knowledge and skills. Does the person know what he or she is talking about? You are unlikely to listen to or depend upon someone whose abilities you don't respect. You need to believe that the person has the skills and abilities to carry out what he or she promises to do.

- *Consistency.* Reliability, predictability, and good judgment in handling situations. "Inconsistencies between words and action decrease trust."[18] This dimension is particularly relevant for managers. "Nothing is noticed more quickly . . . than a discrepancy between what executives preach and what they expect their associates to practice."[19]

Why Integrity Is Questioned by Employees

Employees are often distrustful of a manager's integrity for the following reasons:

Sticky labels. It is easy for a manager to get branded a "liar," but difficult to build a reputation as a person who is totally trustworthy. Generally people require far more evidence of positive behaviour than of negative behaviour.

Competing stakeholders. Managers often send different messages to different stakeholders. So they might tell employees that "customers always come first," and yet the staff interpret downsizing as sending the opposite message. Meanwhile, shareholders believe that cuts to staff can increase profitability, and the value of their shares.

Shifting policies. When new managers take the place of old ones, employees can sometimes see changes in behaviour as being inconsistent with the previous management's message. This can cause employees to become cynical.

Changing fashions. Employees often become cynical when managers try out new fads in management techniques. New ways of managing can send a message to employees that management does not really know how to manage.

Unclear priorities. When managers are uncertain about the priorities of the company or their job, this uncertainty can appear to employees to be a lack of integrity.

Blind spots. Sometimes managers are not aware of their own integrity problems. This happens when what a manager says does not match up with what he or she does. For instance, managers might say that employees should be empowered, but then not give up some of their own power so that this happens.[20]

- *Loyalty.* Willingness to protect and save face for another person. Trust requires that you can depend on someone not to act opportunistically.

- *Openness.* Willingness to share ideas and information freely. Can you rely on the person to give you the full truth?

In addition to these factors, a review of the findings for the effects of leadership on building trust indicates that several characteristics of leadership are most likely to build trust. Leaders who engage in procedural justice (ensuring fair procedures and outcomes) and interactional justice (treating people fairly when procedures are carried out), and who encourage participative decision making and use a transformational leadership style, are most successful at building trust.[21]

Three Types of Trust

There are three types of trust in organizational relationships: *deterrence-* based, *knowledge*-based, and *identification*-based.[22]

Deterrence-Based Trust

The most fragile relationships are contained in *deterrence-based trust.* This form of trust is based on fear of reprisal if the trust is violated. Individuals who are in this type of relationship do what they do because they fear the consequences from not following through on their obligations.

Deterrence-based trust will work only to the degree that punishment is possible, consequences are clear, and the punishment is actually imposed if the trust is violated. To be sustained, the potential loss of future interaction with the other party must outweigh the profit potential that comes from violating expectations. Moreover, the potentially harmed party must be willing to introduce harm (for example, "I have no qualms about speaking badly of you if you betray my trust") to the person acting distrustingly.

Most new relationships begin on a base of deterrence. Take, as an illustration, a situation in which you are selling your car to a friend of a friend. You don't know the buyer. You might be motivated to refrain from telling this buyer all the problems with the car that you know about. Such behaviour would increase your chances of selling the car and securing the highest price. But you don't withhold information. You openly share the car's flaws. Why? Probably because of fear of reprisal. If the buyer later thinks you deceived him, he is likely to share this with your mutual friend. If you knew that the buyer would never say anything to the mutual friend, you might be tempted to take advantage of the opportunity. If it's clear that the buyer would tell and that your mutual friend would think considerably less of you for taking advantage of this buyer-friend, your honesty could be explained in deterrence terms.

Knowledge-Based Trust

Most organizational relationships are rooted in *knowledge-based trust*—that is, trust based on the behavioural predictability that comes from a history of interaction. It exists when you have adequate information about someone to understand them well enough to be able to accurately predict his or her behaviour.

Knowledge-based trust relies on information rather than deterrence. Knowledge of the other party and predictability of his or her behaviour replaces the contracts, penalties, and legal arrangements more typical of deterrence-based trust. This knowledge develops over time, largely as a function of experience that builds confidence of trustworthiness and predictability. The better you know someone, the more accurately you can predict what he or she will do. Predictability enhances trust—even if the other is predictably untrustworthy—because the ways that the other will violate the trust can be predicted! The more communication and regular interaction you have with someone else, the more this form of trust can be developed and depended on.

Interestingly, at the knowledge-based level, trust is not necessarily broken by inconsistent behaviour. If you believe you can adequately explain or understand another's apparent violation, you can accept it, forgive the person, and move on in the relationship. However, the same inconsistency at the deterrence level is likely to irrevocably break the trust.

In an organizational context, most manager-employee relationships are knowledge-based. Both parties have enough experience working with each other that they know what to expect. A long history of consistently open and honest interactions, for instance, is not likely to be permanently destroyed by a single violation.

Identification-Based Trust

The highest level of trust is achieved when there is an emotional connection between the parties. It allows one party to act as an agent for the other and substitute for that person in interpersonal transactions. This is called *identification-based trust*. Trust exists because the parties understand each other's intentions and appreciate each other's wants and desires. This mutual understanding is developed to the point that each can effectively act for the other. Controls are minimal at this level. You don't need to monitor the other party because there is unquestioned loyalty.

Basic Principles of Trust

Research offers a few principles that help us better understand how trust and mistrust are created:[23]

- *Mistrust drives out trust.* People who are trusting demonstrate their trust by increasing their openness to others, disclosing relevant information, and expressing their true intentions. People who mistrust conceal information and act opportunistically to take advantage of others. A few mistrusting people can poison an entire organization.

- *Trust begets trust.* Exhibiting trust in others tends to encourage reciprocity.

- *Trust can be regained (sometimes).* Once it is violated, trust can be regained, but only in certain situations. When an individual's trust in another is broken because the other party failed to do what was expected of him, it can be restored when the

individual observes a consistent pattern of trustworthy behaviours by the transgressor. However, when the same untrustworthy behaviour occurs with deception, trust never fully recovers, even when the person deceived is given apologies, promises, or a consistent pattern of trustworthy actions.[25]

- *Mistrusting groups self-destruct.* The corollary to the previous principle is that when group members mistrust each other, they repel and separate. They pursue their own interests rather than the group's. Members of mistrusting groups tend to be suspicious of each other, are constantly on guard against exploitation, and restrict

How Do Companies Destroy Social Capital?

- *Hotelling.* Hotelling takes away employees' individual desks, and assigns space to individuals on the days they show up for work. This decreases the amount of office space needed, but makes it difficult for employees to network, develop trust, and learn organizational culture. Individuals are not able to personalize their workspaces, which would allow others to get to know them better.

- *Re-engineering.* Re-engineering encourages efficiency, often at the expense of the time needed to get to know people better and to form human connections.

- *The leader as superstar.* When some individuals are praised as superstars, it can take away from the trust, collaboration, and perceived fairness that helps to build relationships.

- *Hypocrisy.* When organizations praise teamwork, but promote individuals who act alone, this sends a strong statement about what organizations really value. Whenever an organization says one thing, but does another, it is acting in a hypocritical manner.[28]

communication with others in the group.

- *Trust increases cohesion.* Trust holds people together. If one person needs help or falters, that person knows that the others will be there to fill in.

- *Mistrust generally reduces productivity.* Mistrust focuses attention on the differences in members' interests, making it difficult for people to visualize common goals. People respond by concealing information and secretly pursuing their own interests. When employees encounter problems, they avoid calling on others, fearing that those others will take advantage of them. A climate of mistrust tends to stimulate dysfunctional forms of conflict and make cooperation difficult.

What Can Leaders Do to Increase Trust?

To improve the climate of trust in an organization, it is important to build social capital and build team trust.

Building Social Capital

Maintaining integrity in organizations is a way of building social capital among members of the organization. Scholars use the term *social capital* to refer to strong relationships within organizations that help organizations function smoothly.[26] Social capital is built on trust, and allows deals to move faster, teams to be more productive, and people to perform more creatively.[27]

Some companies seem better able to build social capital than others. The inset *How Do Companies Destroy Social Capital?* indicates ways that

organizations decrease the level of trust available internally.

Building Team Trust

Professor Kurt Dirks of Washington University in St. Louis studied the effect of trust in one's coach on team performance during basketball season for 30 teams in Division I and Division III of the NCAA (National Collegiate Athletic Association).[29] His findings show that basketball players' trust in their coach improves team performance. The two teams with the highest level of trust in their coach had outstanding records for the season he studied. The team with the lowest level of trust won only 10 percent of its games, and the coach was fired at the end of the season.

As these results indicate, team leaders have a significant impact on a team's trust climate. The following points summarize ways to build team trust:[30]

- *Demonstrate that you are working for others' interests, as well as your own.* All of us are concerned with our own self-interest, but if others see you using them, your job, or the organization for your personal goals to the exclusion of your team's, department's, and organization's interests, your credibility will be undermined.

- *Be a team player.* Support your work team both through words and actions. Defend the team and team members when they are attacked by outsiders. This will demonstrate your loyalty to your work group.

- *Practise openness.* Mistrust comes as much from what people don't know as from what they do know. Openness leads to confidence and trust. So keep people informed, explain your

- *Gather data relentlessly.* Gather all the facts, not just the ones that support your hypotheses.

- *Question your interpretations.* Leave room for other interpretations. Don't jump to conclusions; ask trusted advisers for their interpretations of the data.

- *Embrace your enemies.* Do your best to keep your enemies on your side.

- *Trust the shuffler, but cut the deck anyway.* Signal that you trust the other person, but also be sure to protect yourself from being tricked.

- *Be unpredictable.* Unexpected behaviour can lead competitors to question themselves, giving you an edge.

- *Disregard all the rules.* Don't be afraid to go with your instinct, rather than the rules.[34]

decisions, be candid about problems, and fully disclose relevant information.

- *Be fair.* Before making decisions or taking actions, consider how others will perceive them in terms of objectivity and fairness. Give credit where it's due, be objective and impartial in performance evaluations, and pay attention to equity perceptions in reward distributions.

- *Speak your feelings.* Managers and leaders who convey only hard facts come across as cold and distant. By sharing your feelings, you will encourage others to view you as real and human. They will know who you are, and their respect for you will increase.

- *Show consistency in the basic values that guide your decision making.* Mistrust comes from not knowing what to expect. Take the time to think about your values and beliefs. Then let them consistently guide your decisions. When you know your central purpose, your actions will follow accordingly, and you will project a consistency that earns trust.

- *Maintain confidences.* You trust those you can confide in and rely on. So if people tell you something in confidence, they need to feel assured that you won't discuss it with others or betray that confidence. If people perceive you as someone who "leaks" personal confidences, or someone who cannot be depended upon, you won't be perceived as trustworthy.

- *Demonstrate competence.* Develop the admiration and respect of others by demonstrating technical and professional ability and good business sense. Pay particular attention to developing and displaying your communication, team-building, and other interpersonal skills.

- *Work on continuous improvement.* Teams should approach their own development as part of a search for continuous improvement.

High-performance teams are characterized by high mutual trust among members. That is, members believe in the integrity, character, and ability of each other. Since trust begets trust and distrust begets distrust, maintaining trust requires careful attention by leaders and team members. High trust can have a downside, though, if it inspires team members to not pay attention to each other's work. Team members with high trust may not monitor each other, and if the low monitoring is accompanied by high individual autonomy, the team can perform poorly.[31]

Does Distrust Ever Pay Off?

Professor Roderick Kramer of the Graduate School of Business at Stanford University suggests that always being trusting may not be a

Trust in others can be dangerous. If you get too close to someone else, that person could take advantage of you, and possibly hurt your chances to get ahead.

Trust improves relationships among individuals. Through trust, productivity can be increased and more creative ideas are likely to come forward.

desirable strategy. Instead, he offers "prudent paranoia" as a better way for individuals to act. His views are quite contrary to most management literature, which discusses the benefits of trust. Essentially, Kramer argues that distrust can be beneficial.[32]

So what does Kramer mean by *prudent paranoia*? "Prudent paranoia is a form of constructive suspicion regarding the intentions and actions of people and organizations."[33] Kramer argues that such paranoia can be an early warning signal during difficult times. For instance, during times of mergers and acquisitions, employees are naturally distrustful of other departments, and wonder whether they will lose their jobs. Managers may watch out to see who may be threatening their power base. Those with high emotional intelligence are most likely to practise prudent paranoia; after all, one of the signs of emotional intelligence is paying attention to one's environment and responding accordingly.

So how can you demonstrate prudent paranoia? The inset *Making Your Paranoia More Prudent* gives you some tips.

Research Exercises

1. Look for data on the extent to which companies in other countries are trusted by the citizens of those countries. How does this compare with the extent to which Canadians trust companies? Can you draw any inferences about what leads to greater or less trust of corporations?

2. Identify three Canadian organizations that are trying to improve their image to be more trustworthy. What effect is this having on the organizations' bottom lines?

Your Perspective

1. Why might corporations be willing to neglect the importance of trust and instead engage in behaviours such as those that could lead to corporate scandals?

2. What steps can organizations take to make sure that they are seen as trustworthy by the rest of society?

Want to Know More?

If you would like to read more on this topic, see R. F. Hurley, "The Decision to Trust," *Harvard Business Review*, September 2006, pp. 55–62; S. A. Joni, "The Geography of Trust," *Harvard Business Review*, March 2004, pp. 82–88; R. M. Kramer, "When Paranoia Makes Sense," *Harvard Business Review*, July 2002, pp. 62–69; and L. Prusak and D. Cohen, "How to Invest in Social Capital," *Harvard Business Review*, June 2001, pp. 86–93.

Communication

An employer faces employees who feel disconnected from the company they helped make a success. Will communication help reduce tensions?

1   How does communication work?

2   What are the barriers to communication?

3   How does communication flow in organizations?

4   What are other issues in communication?

*I*t is not every day that an oil company reaches a major milestone, so when Fort McMurray, Alberta-based Suncor Energy's oil sands operation did so in 2006 by producing its billionth barrel of oil, it was a time for reflection.[1] The company's workforce had changed significantly in recent years. Only 17 percent of the oil sands employees had worked at the company for more than 10 years. Almost half had been there less than 2 years. Senior executives felt that it was time to bring the workforce together to build a more cohesive culture.

Suncor grew tremendously during the previous 10 years, but employees felt that this was done at their expense. Many were feeling burned out, from long hours and lack of recognition. Senior management decided to address these problems through a coordinated communications program that would bring all the employees together and help them understand where the company was going next, and how employees' concerns would be addressed.

In this chapter, we explore the foundations of communication. By learning how to communicate effectively with others, we can improve our relationships with those around us, and work more effectively on teams.

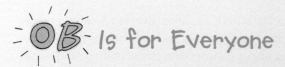 Is for Everyone

- How can you communicate better when you are stressed out?
- Ever notice that communicating via email can lead to misunderstandings?
- Does body language really make a difference?
- How can you improve cross-cultural communication?

Self-Assessment Library

LEARNING ABOUT YOURSELF

- Listening
- Face-to-Face Communication
- Gossiping

The Communication Process

1 How does communication work?

Research indicates that poor communication is probably the most frequently cited source of interpersonal conflict.[2] Individuals spend nearly 70 percent of their waking hours communicating—writing, reading, speaking, listening—which means that they have many opportunities in which to engage in poor communication. A WorkCanada survey of 2039 Canadians in six industrial and service categories explored the state of communication in Canadian businesses.[3] The survey found that 61 percent of senior executives believed that they did a good job of communicating with employees. However, those who worked below the senior executives failed to share this feeling; only 33 percent of the managers and department heads believed that senior executives were effective communicators. Lower-level employees reported that communication was even worse: Only 22 percent of hourly employees, 27 percent of clerical employees, and 22 percent of professional staff reported that senior executives did a good job of communicating with them. Moreover, another study found that Canadians reported less favourable perceptions about their company's communications than did Americans.[4]

The Suncor case and the survey of communication practices in the Canadian workplace point to the same reality: Communication is an important issue and a consideration for organizations and individuals alike. Communication is a foundation for many things that happen among groups and within the workplace—from motivating, to providing information, to controlling behaviour, to expressing emotion. Good communication skills are very important to your career success. A 2007 study of recruiters found that they rated communication skills as *the* most important characteristic of an ideal job candidate.[5]

communication The transfer and understanding of a message between two or more people.

No group can exist without **communication**, which is the *transfer* and *understanding* of a message between two or more people. Communication can be thought of as a process, or flow, as shown in Exhibit 7-1. The model indicates that both the sender and the receiver are part of the communication process, with the sender establishing a message, encoding the message, and choosing the channel to send it, and the receiver decoding the message and providing feedback to the sender. Communication problems occur when something disrupts the flow during encoding, channel selection, decoding, or feedback.

The model indicates that communication is both an interactive and iterative process. The sender has to keep in mind the receiver (or audience), and in finalizing the communication may decide to revisit decisions about the message, the encoding, and/or the feedback. For instance, a manager may want to convey a message face to face, and then is not able to do so for some reason. The message sent by email or voice mail may need to be framed differently than the message that would have been delivered face to face. Similarly, you may decide on a message, and then realize the medium that you have

EXHIBIT 7-1   The Communication Process Model

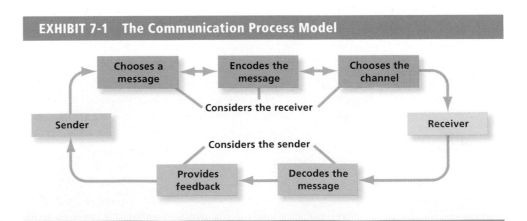

chosen will make the message too complicated. Writing 10 emails to set up a simple lunch appointment may convince you midway through the communication process to pick up the telephone to finalize the details.

We discussed perception in Chapter 2. The communication process is significantly affected by the sender's perception of the receiver and the receiver's perception of the sender. For instance, if the receiver does not trust the sender, he or she may interpret statements intended as positive in a negative manner.

Encoding and Decoding

Messages are **encoded** (converted to symbolic form) by a sender and **decoded** (interpreted) by a receiver. Four factors have been described that affect message encoding and decoding: skill, attitudes, knowledge, and the socio-cultural system. For example, our success in communicating to you depends upon our writing skills and your reading skills. Communicative success also includes speaking, listening, and reasoning skills. As we discussed in Chapter 3, our interactions with others are affected by our attitudes, values, and beliefs. Thus, the attitudes of the sender and receiver toward each other will affect how the message is transmitted and how it is received. As well, the amount of knowledge the source and receiver hold about the subject will affect the clarity of the message that is transferred. Finally, our rank in any hierarchy in which we operate affects our ability to successfully engage in communication. Messages sent and received by people of equal rank are sometimes interpreted differently than messages sent and received by people in very different ranks.

encoding Converting a message to symbolic form.

decoding Interpreting a sender's message.

The Message

The **message** is the actual physical product from the source after it is encoded. "When we speak, the speech is the message. When we write, the writing is the message. When we paint, the picture is the message. When we gesture, the movements of our arms, the expressions on our face are the message."[6] Our message is affected by the code, or group of symbols, we use to transfer meaning; the content of the message itself; and the decisions that we make in selecting and arranging both codes and content. A poor choice of symbols, and confusion in the content of the message, can cause problems.

Messages can also get "lost in translation" when two parties formalize their understanding through contracts. Contracts are meant to be written in legal terms, for lawyers, and may not always capture the underlying meaning of the parties' understandings. Collective agreements written between management and unions sometimes suffer from this problem as well. When either management or union leaders point to the collective agreement for every interaction in the workplace, they are relying on the encoding of their negotiations, but this may not permit some of the flexibility that was intended in some cases.

message What is communicated.

The Channel

The **channel** is the medium through which a message travels. It is selected by the source, who must determine which channel is formal and which is informal. Formal channels are established by the organization and transmit messages that pertain to the job-related activities of members. Traditionally, they follow the authority network within the organization. Other forms of messages, such as personal or social messages, follow the informal channels in the organization. Examples of channels are formal memos, voice mail, email, meetings, and so on. The channel can distort a communication if a poor one is selected or if the noise level is high. Suncor chose to communicate its message of change through formal meetings that all employees attended.

Why do people choose one channel of communication over another; for instance, a phone call instead of a face-to-face talk? One answer might be anxiety! An estimated 5 to 20 percent of the population[7] suffers from debilitating **communication apprehension**, or anxiety, which is undue tension and anxiety about oral communication,

channel The medium through which a message travels.

communication apprehension Undue tension and anxiety about oral communication, written communication, or both.

page 268, Part 3 Interacting Effectively

written communication, or both. We all know people who dread speaking in front of a group, but some people may find it extremely difficult to talk with others face to face or become extremely anxious when they have to use the telephone. As a result, they may rely on memos, letters, or email to convey messages when a phone call would not only be faster but also more appropriate.

But what about the 80 to 95 percent of the population who don't suffer from this problem? Is there any general insight we might be able to provide regarding choice of communication channel? The answer is a qualified "yes." A model of media richness has been developed to explain channel selection among managers.[8]

Research has found that channels differ in their capacity to convey information. Some are rich in that they have the ability to (1) handle multiple cues simultaneously, (2) facilitate rapid feedback, and (3) be very personal. Others are lean in that they score low on these three factors. As Exhibit 7-2 illustrates, face-to-face conversation scores highest in terms of **channel richness** because it provides for the maximum amount of information to be transmitted during a communication episode. That is, it offers multiple information cues (words, postures, facial expressions, gestures, intonations), immediate feedback (both verbal and nonverbal), and the personal touch of "being there." Impersonal written media such as formal reports and bulletins rate lowest in richness. Two students were suspended from class for choosing YouTube, a very rich channel, to distribute their message. Their actions also raised concerns about privacy in the classroom, as *Focus on Ethics* reveals.

channel richness The amount of information that can be transmitted during a communication episode.

FOCUS ON **ETHICS**

YouTube's Darker Side

Is it okay for students to post a teacher's outburst on YouTube?   Two grade 9 students from École Secondaire Mont-Bleu in Gatineau, Quebec, were suspended from school after teachers discovered a video the students had posted on YouTube.[9] One of the students provoked the teacher during class time while the other secretly taped the scene for about 50 minutes with a compact digital camera.

The students, who have academic problems, were in a special-education class. The teacher had 33 years of experience, and specialized in teaching students with learning disabilities. After the incident, the teacher went on sick leave, and his union said, "He is so embarrassed that he may never return to class."

There was no apparent explanation for why the students decided to provoke and then film the teacher. Other students have said that "the teacher was good at helping them improve their grades."

"I think students are just trying to embarrass the teachers they don't like," school board president Jocelyn Blondin said. "In the future, students will have to keep their cellphones in their pockets and use them outside of class," she predicted shortly after the incident.

Teachers and school boards are trying to determine strategies for handling these kinds of events in classrooms. The Gatineau school no longer allows personal electronic devices in the classroom. In Ontario, changes to the Safe Schools Act made in 2007 state that students who engage in online bullying are to be suspended from classes.

The choice of one channel over another depends on whether the message is routine or nonroutine. Routine messages tend to be straightforward and have a minimum of ambiguity. Nonroutine messages are likely to be complicated and have the potential for misunderstanding. Individuals can communicate routine messages efficiently through

EXHIBIT 7-2   Information Richness of Communication Channels

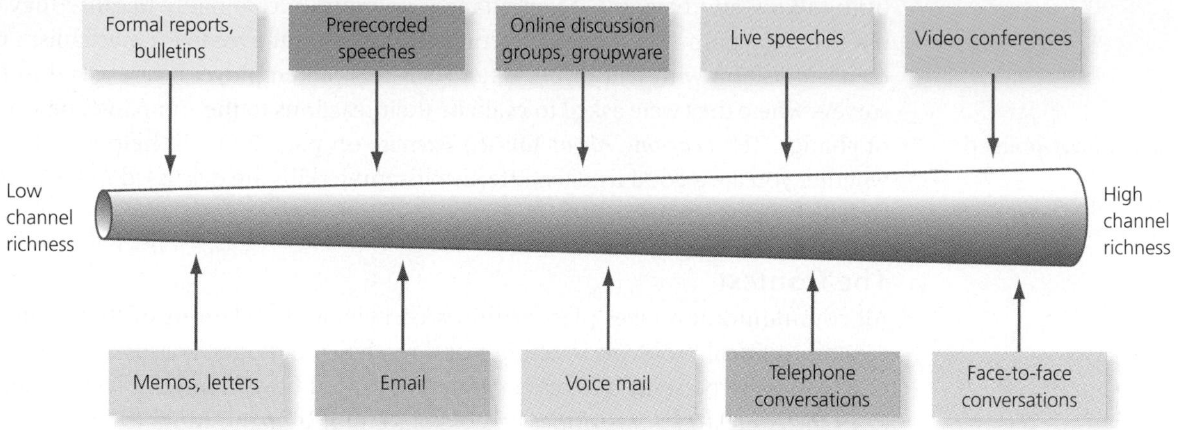

Sources: Based on R. H. Lengel and R. L. Daft, "The Selection of Communication Media as an Executive Skill," *Academy of Management Executive*, August 1988, pp. 225–232; and R. L. Daft and R. H. Lengel, "Organizational Information Requirements, Media Richness, and Structural Design," *Managerial Science*, May 1996, pp. 554–572. Reproduced from R. L. Daft and R. A. Noe, *Organizational Behavior* (Fort Worth, TX: Harcourt, 2001), p. 311.

channels that are lower in richness. However, they communicate nonroutine messages more effectively by selecting rich channels. Evidence indicates that high-performing managers tend to be more media sensitive than low-performing managers.[10] That is, they are better able to match appropriate media richness with the ambiguity involved in the communication.

One study found that managers found it easier to deliver bad news (layoffs, promotion denials, and negative feedback) via email, and that the messages were delivered more accurately this way. This does not mean that sending negative information through email is always recommended. One of the co-authors of the study noted that "offering negative comments face-to-face is often taken as a sign that the news is important and the deliverer cares about the recipient."[11] *Case Incident—Emailing "Lazy" Employees* on page 293 asks you to evaluate one manager's use of email to tell his employees to work harder.

The media richness model is consistent with organizational trends and practices of the past decade. It is not just coincidence that more and more senior managers, like those at Suncor, have been using meetings to facilitate communication and regularly leaving the isolated sanctuary of their executive offices to manage by walking around. These executives are relying on richer channels of communication to transmit the more ambiguous messages they need to convey. The past decade has been characterized by organizations closing facilities, imposing large layoffs, restructuring, merging, consolidating, and introducing new products and services at an accelerated pace—all nonroutine messages high in ambiguity and requiring the use of channels that can convey a large amount of information. It is not surprising, therefore, to see the most effective managers expanding their use of rich channels.

The Feedback Loop

The final link in the communication process is the **feedback loop**. Feedback lets us know whether understanding has been achieved. If the feedback loop is to succeed in preventing miscommunication, the receiver needs to give feedback and the sender needs to check for it. Many receivers forget that there is a responsibility involved in communication: to give feedback. For instance, if you sit in a boring lecture, but never discuss with the instructor ways that the delivery could be improved, you have not engaged in communication with your instructor.

feedback loop The final link in the communication process; it puts the message back into the system as a check against misunderstandings.

When either the sender or the receiver fails to engage in the feedback process, the communication is effectively one-way communication. Two-way communication involves both talking and listening. Many managers communicate badly because they fail to use two-way communication.[12] Suncor deliberately built a feedback mechanism into its communication with employees. After each session, employees were asked to fill out surveys where they were asked to evaluate their reactions to the company's new message of change. The *Learning About Yourself Exercise* on page 290 will help you determine whether you are a good listener. Effective listening skills are discussed in *From Concepts to Skills* on page 294.

Learning About Yourself

1. Listening Self-Inventory
(page 290)

The Context

All communication takes place within a context, and violations of that context may create additional problems in sending and receiving messages. For instance, the context of a workplace presents different expectations about how to interact with people than does the context of a bus stop. The workplace may demand more formal interaction, while communication at a bus stop is generally expected to be informal. In some situations, informal communication can look unprofessional, and thus be viewed negatively. In other situations, formal communication can make others feel awkward, if the formality is out of place. Thus, it is important to consider context in both encoding the message and choosing the channel. One of the greatest communication challenges managers have is providing performance feedback to employees (see *OB in Action—Giving More Effective Feedback* on page 185 in Chapter 5 for some useful tips).

Barriers to Effective Communication

When Suncor Energy decided to approach its employees to discuss plans for the future and their impact, the company faced a significant organizational challenge.[13] Employees had never been asked to attend off-site meetings outside working hours. There were 3000 employees to address, and putting them all in one room at the same time was both logistically impossible and would have prevented the message from being heard. Suncor's communication team decided to work with groups of 500 employees at a time, holding six 90-minute meetings during a two-week period.

With logistics resolved, the communication team still had to consider the best way to deliver the message of change. Hearing from senior management was important, but might not engage the audience very much, causing them to tune out. So the team included humour and interactivity in the meeting agenda. Are there other things the communication team might have considered to make sure everyone was listening at the meetings?

2 **What are the barriers to communication?**

A number of factors have been identified as barriers to communication. The more prominent ones are filtering, selective perception, defensiveness, information overload, and language.

Filtering

filtering A sender's manipulation of information so that it will be seen more favourably by the receiver.

Filtering occurs when a sender manipulates information so that the receiver will view it more favourably. For example, when a manager tells a senior executive what the manager feels the executive wants to hear, the manager is filtering information. Does this happen much in organizations? Sure! As information is passed up to senior executives, employees must condense and synthesize it so that those on top don't become overloaded with information. The personal interests of those doing the synthesizing, as well as their perceptions of what is important, will result in filtering.

The major determinant of filtering is the number of levels in an organization. The more levels there are in an organization's hierarchy, the more opportunities there are for filtering information. The *Ethical Dilemma Exercise* on page 292 asks you to consider whether lying is ever a reasonable strategy.

Selective Perception

Receivers in the communication process selectively see and hear based on their needs, motivations, experience, background, and other personal characteristics. Receivers also project their interests and expectations into communications as they decode them. For example, the employment interviewer who believes that young people are more interested in spending time on leisure and social activities than working extra hours to further their careers is likely to be influenced by that stereotype when interviewing young job applicants. As we discussed in Chapter 2, we don't see reality; rather, we interpret what we see and call it "reality."

Defensiveness

When people feel that they are being threatened, they tend to react in ways that reduce their ability to achieve mutual understanding. That is, they become defensive—engaging in behaviours such as verbally attacking others, making sarcastic remarks, being overly judgmental, and questioning others' motives. So when individuals interpret another's message as threatening, they often respond in ways that hinder effective communication.

Information Overload

Individuals have a finite capacity for processing data. When the information we have to work with exceeds our ability to process it, the result is **information overload**. With emails, phone calls, faxes, meetings, and the need to keep current in one's field, more and more employees are saying that they are suffering from too much information. The information can be distracting as well. A recent study of employees who have tracking software on their computers found that they clicked on their email program more than 50 times in the course of a day, and used instant messaging 77 times. The study also found that, on average, employees visited 40 websites during the workday.[14]

information overload The state of having more information than one can process.

What happens when individuals have more information than they can sort out and use? They tend to select out, ignore, pass over, or forget information. Or they may put off further processing until the overload situation is over. Regardless, the result is lost information and less effective communication.

Call-centre operators at Wipro Spectramind in New Delhi, India, speak English in serving their customers from North America and the United Kingdom. But even though the operators and customers speak a common language, communication barriers exist because of differences in the countries' cultures and language accents. To overcome these barriers, the operators receive training in North American and British pop culture so they can make small talk and are taught to speak with Western accents so they can be more easily understood by the calling clients.

Source: The Far Side by Gary Larson, Copyright © 1994 for Works, Inc. All rights reserved. Used with permission.

Language

Words mean different things to different people. "The meanings of words are not in the words; they are in us."[15] Age, education, and cultural background are three of the obvious variables that influence the language we use and the definitions we give to words. For instance, when Alanis Morissette sang, "Isn't it ironic?" middle-aged English professors complained that she completely misunderstood the meaning of "irony"—but the millions who bought her CD understood what she meant.

In an organization, employees usually come from diverse backgrounds, and therefore have different patterns of speech. Additionally, the grouping of employees into departments creates specialists who develop their own jargon, or technical language. In large organizations, members are also frequently widely dispersed geographically—even operating in different countries—and individuals in each locale will use terms and phrases that are unique to their area. The existence of vertical levels can also cause language problems. The language of senior executives, for instance, can be mystifying to operative employees who are unfamiliar with management jargon.

The point is that even with a common language, such as English, our use of that language is far from uniform. Senders tend to assume that the words and terms they use mean the same to the receiver as they do to them. This, of course, is often incorrect, which creates communication difficulties. The multicultural environment of many of today's workplaces makes communication issues even more complex. In many workplaces, there are people whose first language is something other than English. This means that even more opportunities arise for confusion about meaning. It is therefore important to be aware that your understanding of the particular meaning of a word or phrase may not be shared. Exhibit 7-3 shows individuals who have very different views on what words to use.

Communicating under Stress

How can you communicate better when you are stressed out?

One of the most difficult times to communicate properly is when one is under stress. One consultant has identified several tips for communicating under stress. These tips are also appropriate for less stressful communication.[16]

- *Speak clearly.* Be direct about what you want to say, and avoid hiding behind words. For instance, as difficult as it might be to say, "You did not receive the position," the listener is better able to process the information when it is spoken that directly.

- *Be aware of the nonverbal part of communicating.* Tone, facial expression, and body language send signals that may or may not be consistent with your message. In a stressful situation, it is best to speak in a neutral manner.

- *Think carefully about how you state things.* In many situations, it is better to be restrained so that you do not offend your listener. For instance, when you threaten someone if they do not do exactly what you want ("I insist on speaking to your manager this minute"), you simply escalate the situation. It is better to state what you want calmly, so that you can be heard accurately.

Case Incident—Jeremy W. Caputo Has Communication Problems on page 293 indicates what happens when a person does not communicate effectively.

Organizational Communication

How organizations communicate with their employees plays an important role in whether the employees actually hear the message.[17] Prior to the meetings with the oil sands employees, Suncor Energy had a negative image in the minds of some of its employees. Surveys showed that employees felt disconnected from senior managers, and did not think that management "had their best interests in mind." Less than a third of the employees felt they received enough recognition for their work.

The company developed a multi-pronged approach to getting out its message of change to employees. The company already had a weekly employee newsletter called *Update*. Management used the newsletter to build interest in the upcoming meetings. The meetings were conducted using a variety of forms of communication, including speeches by the management team and video documentaries of the company's history. Other videos showed employees discussing the challenges they faced in their work environment and talking positively about the future. There were question-and-answer sessions to encourage employee involvement. There were also "fun videos," such as a fake newscast from the future and a *Star Trek* parody.

Because there were six meetings scheduled, the Suncor communication team was able to adjust subsequent presentations based on feedback from earlier sessions. After the first meeting, the management team learned that employees thought the answers to their questions were "too long and hard to understand." Answers were shortened and simplified for the later sessions.

The result of all of this attention to how best to communicate? The employees felt more positive about the future of Suncor, and they changed their views about their leaders. More than 50 percent said they felt their contributions were recognized, compared with 32 percent prior to the meetings. So what can managers do to make communication more effective?

In this section, we explore ways that communication occurs in organizations, including the direction of communication, formal small-group networks, the grapevine, and electronic communications.

3 How does communication flow in organizations?

Direction of Communication

Communication can flow downward, upward, and/or laterally in organizations.[18] We will explore each of these directional flows and their implications.

Downward

Communication that flows from one level of a group or organization to a lower level is downward communication. When we think of managers communicating with employees, the downward pattern is the one we usually have in mind. Group leaders and managers use this approach to assign goals, provide job instructions, inform employees of policies and procedures, identify problems that need attention, and offer feedback about performance.

When engaging in downward communication, managers must explain the reasons *why* a decision was made. One study found that employees were twice as likely to be committed to changes when the reasons behind them were fully explained. Although this may seem like common sense, many managers feel they are too busy to explain things, or that explanations will "open up a big can of worms." Evidence clearly indicates, though, that explanations increase employee commitment and support of decision.[19]

Upward

Upward communication flows to a higher level in the group or organization. It's used to provide feedback to higher-ups, inform them of progress toward goals, and relay current problems. Upward communication keeps managers aware of how employees feel about their jobs, co-workers, and the organization in general. Managers also rely on upward communication for ideas on how things can be improved.

Given that job responsibilities of most managers and supervisors have expanded, upward communication is increasingly difficult because managers are overwhelmed and easily distracted. To engage in effective upward communication, try to reduce distractions (meet in a conference room if you can, rather than your boss's office or cubicle), communicate in headlines, not paragraphs (your job is to get your boss's attention, not to engage in a meandering discussion), support your headlines with actionable items (what you believe should happen), and prepare an agenda to make sure you use your boss's attention well.[20]

In general, few Canadian firms rely on upward communication. In their study of 375 Canadian organizations, David Saunders, dean of Queen's School of Business, and Joanne Leck, associate dean (research) at the University of Ottawa School of Management, found that unionized organizations were more likely to use upward communication.[21] The form of upward communication most used was grievance procedures.

Lateral

When communication occurs among members of the same work group, among members of work groups at the same level, among managers at the same level, or among any horizontally equivalent employees, we describe it as lateral (or horizontal) communication.

Horizontal communication is often necessary to save time and to ease coordination. In some cases, lateral relationships are formally sanctioned. Often, they are informally created to short-circuit the vertical hierarchy and speed up action. So lateral communication can, from management's perspective, be good or bad. Because strict adherence to the formal vertical structure for all communications can slow the efficient and accurate transfer of information, lateral communication can be beneficial. In such cases, it occurs with the knowledge and support of managers. But it can create dysfunctional conflicts when the formal vertical channels are breached, when members go above or around their managers to get things done, or when employers find out that actions have been taken or decisions made without their knowledge.

Small-Group Networks

communication networks
Channels by which information flows.

formal networks Task-related communications that follow the authority chain.

Communication networks define the channels by which information flows. These channels are one of two varieties—either formal or informal. **Formal networks** are typically vertical, follow the authority chain, and are limited to task-related communications. Exhibit 7-4 illustrates three common formal small-group networks: the *chain*, *wheel*, and *all-channel*. The chain network rigidly follows the formal chain of command. The wheel network relies on the leader to act as the central conduit for all the

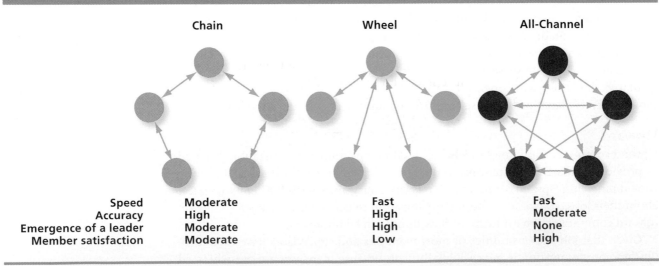

EXHIBIT 7-4   Three Common Small-Group Networks and Their Effectiveness

	Chain	Wheel	All-Channel
Speed	Moderate	Fast	Fast
Accuracy	High	High	Moderate
Emergence of a leader	Moderate	High	None
Member satisfaction	Moderate	Low	High

group's communication. The all-channel network permits all group members to communicate actively with each other. As Exhibit 7-4 illustrates, the effectiveness of each network depends on the dependent variable you are concerned about. For instance, the structure of the wheel network facilitates the emergence of a leader, the all-channel network is best if high member satisfaction is most important, and the chain network is best if accuracy is most important. Thus, we conclude that no single network is appropriate for all occasions.

The Grapevine

The previous discussion of networks emphasized formal communication patterns. In contrast, in **informal networks**, communication flows along social and relational lines. Communication is free to move in any direction, skip authority levels, and is as likely to satisfy group members' social needs as it is to help with task accomplishments.

informal networks
Communications that flow along social and relational lines.

The most common informal network in the organization is the **grapevine**. Research has found that 75 percent of employees hear about matters first through rumours on the grapevine.[22] Thus it is an important source of information for many employees.

grapevine The organization's most common informal network.

Is the information that flows along the grapevine accurate? The evidence indicates that about 75 percent of what is carried is accurate.[23] But what conditions foster an active grapevine? What gets the rumour mill rolling?

It is frequently assumed that rumours start because they make titillating gossip. However, this is rarely the case. Rumours have at least four purposes:

1. To structure and reduce anxiety

2. To make sense of limited or fragmented information

3. To serve as a vehicle to organize group members, and possibly outsiders, into coalitions

4. To signal a sender's status ("I'm an insider and, with respect to this rumour, you're an outsider") or power ("I have the power to make you into an insider")[24]

Research indicates that rumours emerge as a response to situations that are important to us, where there is ambiguity, and under conditions that arouse anxiety.[25] The secrecy and competition that typically prevail in large organizations around such issues as the appointment of new senior managers, the relocation of offices, and the realignment of work assignments create conditions that encourage and sustain rumours on the grapevine. A rumour will persist either until the wants and expectations creating the uncertainty underlying the rumour are fulfilled or until the anxiety is reduced.

This chapter's *Point/Counterpoint* on page 289 examines different perspectives on keeping secrets.

Grapevine Patterns

Communication through grapevines can take several different patterns, as illustrated in Exhibit 7-5 on page 276. In the single strand, each person tells information to just one other person (somewhat like the child's game "Whisper Down the Lane"). In the gossip pattern, one person tells everyone the information. These people are commonly called *gossips*, and make up about 10 percent of organizational members.[26]

The probability and cluster patterns may appear to be similar, but they function quite differently. In the probability pattern, individuals are randomly told information, with no apparent pattern. In the cluster pattern, individuals selectively choose individuals to whom they will relay information. Individuals may strategically select to whom to pass on information, to ensure that it gets spread around. Not everyone passes along information that they hear, but those who consistently do are called *liaison individuals*: "Usually these liaisons are friendly, outgoing people who are in positions that

EXHIBIT 7-5   Grapevine Patterns

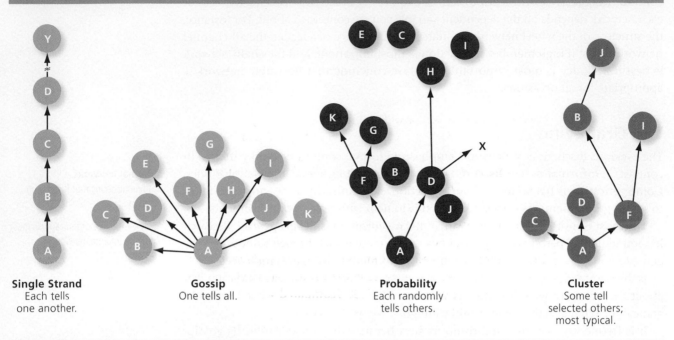

Single Strand
Each tells
one another.

Gossip
One tells all.

Probability
Each randomly
tells others.

Cluster
Some tell
selected others;
most typical.

Source: K. Davis and J. W. Newstrom, *Human Behavior at Work: Organizational Behavior*, 7th ed. (New York: McGraw-Hill, 1985), p. 317. Reprinted by permission.

allow them to cross departmental lines. For example, [administrative assistants] tend to be liaisons because they can communicate with the top executive, the janitor, and everyone in between without raising eyebrows."[27]

The grapevine has three main characteristics.[28] First, it is not controlled by management. Second, it is perceived by most employees as being more believable and reliable than formal communiqués issued by top management. Finally, it is largely used to serve the self-interests of the people within it.

What can we conclude from this discussion? Certainly the grapevine is an important part of any group's or organization's communication network and well worth understanding.[29] It identifies for managers those confusing issues that employees consider important and anxiety-provoking. It acts, therefore, as both a filter and a feedback mechanism, picking up the issues that employees consider relevant. Managers can reduce the negative consequence of rumours by explaining decisions and openly discussing worst-case possibilities.[30]

Electronic Communications

Electronic communications—which include email, instant messaging, text messaging, networking software, blogs, file-transfer websites, and video conferencing—make it possible for you to work, even if you are away from your workstation. These technologies have largely reshaped the way we communicate in organizations.[31] You can be reached when you are in a meeting, having a lunch break, visiting a customer's office across town, watching a movie in a crowded theatre, or playing golf on a Saturday morning. The line between an employee's work and nonwork life is no longer distinct, meaning all employees theoretically can be "on call" 24 hours a day.

Organizational boundaries become less relevant as a result of electronic communications. Why? Because networked computers allow employees to jump vertical levels within the organization, work full time at home or someplace other than "the office," and have ongoing communications with people in other organizations.

Email

Email's growth has been spectacular, and its use is now so pervasive that it's hard to imagine life without it. As a communication tool, email has a long list of benefits. Email messages can be quickly written, edited, and stored. They can be distributed to one person or thousands with a click of a mouse. They can be read, in their entirety, at the convenience of the recipient. And the cost of sending formal email messages to employees is a fraction of the cost of printing, duplicating, and distributing a comparable letter or brochure.

> Ever notice that communicating via email can lead to misunderstandings?

Email, of course, is not without drawbacks. Email has added considerably to the number of hours worked per week, according to a study by Christina Cavanagh, professor of management communications at the Richard Ivey School of Business, University of Western Ontario.[32] One researcher suggests that knowledge workers devote about 28 percent of their day to email.[33] While the increase in the volume of email seems to have slowed, up just 9 percent between 2006 and 2007 (compared with 26 percent between 2005 and 2006), the volume of junk mail shows no let-up.[34] Canadians divert 42 percent of their email directly to "junk mail" folders, according to a 2007 Ipsos Reid study. Over one-third of the survey respondents said they had trouble handling all of their email, and only 43 percent thought that email increased efficiency at work, down from 52 percent in 2006.

The following are some of the most significant limitations of email and what organizations should do to reduce or eliminate these problems:

- *Misinterpreting the message.* It's true that we often misinterpret verbal messages, but the potential for misinterpretation with email is even greater. One research team found that we can accurately decode an email's intent and tone only 50 percent of the time, yet most of us vastly overestimate our ability to send and interpret clear messages. If you are sending an important message, make sure you reread it for clarity. And if you are upset about the presumed tone of someone else's message, keep in mind that you may be misinterpreting it.[35]

- *Communicating negative messages.* When companies have negative information to communicate, managers need to think carefully. Email may not be the best way to communicate the message. When RadioShack decided to lay off 400 employees, it was widely criticized for doing it via email. Employees need to be careful communicating negative messages via email, too. Justen Deal, 22, wrote an email critical of some strategic decisions made by his employer, pharmaceutical giant Kaiser Permanente. In the email, he criticized the "misleadership" of Kaiser CEO George Halvorson and questioned the financing of several information technology projects. Within hours, Deal's computer was seized; he was later fired.[36]

- *Overuse of email.* An estimated 6 trillion emails are sent every year, and someone has to answer all those messages! As people become established in their careers and their responsibilities expand, so do their inboxes. Some people, such as venture capitalist Fred Wilson, have become so overwhelmed by email

David Breda, co-owner of Leader Plumbing and Heating, a mechanical contractor in Woodbridge, Ontario, finds online collaboration a major boon to his business. His employees, mostly plumbers, are able to exchange real-time information, and thus be more efficient in their work.

EXHIBIT 7-6 Showing Emotions in Email

Email need not be emotion-free. Over the years, email users have developed a way of displaying text, as well as a set of symbols (*emoticons*) for expressing emotions. For instance, the use of all caps (as in THIS PROJECT NEEDS YOUR IMMEDIATE ATTENTION!) is the email equivalent of shouting. The following highlights some emoticons:

:)	Smile	:-e	Disappointed
<g>	Grin	:-@	Scream
:(	Frown	:-0	Yell
;)	Wink	:-D	Shock or surprise
:-[	Really sad face	:'(	Crying

that they have declared "email bankruptcy." Recording artist Moby sent an email to all those in his address book announcing that he was taking a break from email for the rest of the year. Although you probably don't want to declare email bankruptcy, or could not get away with it even if you did, you should use email wisely, especially when you are contacting people inside the organization who may already be wading through lots of email messages every day.[37]

- *Email emotions.* We tend to think of email as a sort of sterile, faceless form of communication. But that does not mean it's unemotional. As you no doubt know, emails are often highly emotional. One CEO said, "I've seen people not talk to each other, turf wars break out and people quit their jobs as a result of emails." Email tends to make senders feel free to write things they would never be comfortable saying in person. Facial expressions tend to temper our emotional expressions, but in email, there is no other face to look at, and so many of us fire away. An increasingly common way of communicating emotions in email is with emoticons (see Exhibit 7-6). For example, Yahoo!'s email software allows users to pick from over 60 graphical emoticons. Although emoticons used to be considered for personal use only, adults are increasingly using them in business emails. Still, some see them as too informal for business use.

When others send flaming messages, remain calm and try not to respond in kind. Also, when writing new emails, try to temper your own tendencies to quickly fire off messages.[38]

- *Privacy concerns.* There are two privacy issues with email. First, you need to be aware that your emails may be, and often are, monitored. Also, you cannot always trust that the recipient of your email will keep it confidential. For these reasons, you should not write anything you would not want made public. One survey found that nearly 40 percent of companies have employees whose only job is to read other employees' email. You are being watched—so be careful what you email![39]

Focus on Ethics illustrates that employees cannot assume that their email is private.

FOCUS ON **ETHICS**

Your Email Can Get You Fired

Should your email be safe from your manager's eyes?   A 2008 poll conducted by Environics found that 35 percent of Canadians say they have sent emails from their work-based email address that they worry could come back to hurt them.[40] Even so, about the same percentage of employees believe their employers probably check on email accounts, and 52 percent think their employer has the right to do so. Moreover, 30 percent of Canadians know someone who has been disciplined because of an email sent at work.

While a City of Toronto employee was merely disciplined after sending "inappropriate" pictures using a city computer, Fred Jones (not his real name) was fired from a Canadian company for forwarding dirty jokes to his clients. Until this incident,

Jones had been a high-performing employee who sold network computers for his company. Jones thought that he was only sending the jokes to clients who liked them, and assumed the clients would tell him if they didn't want to receive the jokes. Instead, a client complained to the company about receiving the dirty jokes. After an investigation, the company fired Jones. Jones is still puzzled about being fired. He views his email as private; to him, sending jokes is the same as telling them at the water cooler.

Jones was not aware that under current law, employee information, including email, is not necessarily private. Most federal employees, provincial public sector employees, and employees working for federally regulated industries are covered by the federal Privacy Act and Access to Information Act, in place since 1985. Many private sector employees are not covered by privacy legislation, however.

Ann Cavoukian, Information and Privacy Commissioner of Ontario, notes that "employees deserve to be treated like adults and companies should limit surveillance to rare instances, such as when there is suspicion of criminal activity or harassment."[41] She suggests that employers use respect and courtesy when dealing with employees' email, and she likens email to office phone calls, which generally are not monitored by the employer. It is clearly important, in any event, that employees be aware of their company's policy on email. *OB in the Street* considers employers' responses to blogging, yet another way to keep in touch with friends, family, and co-workers.

IN THE STREET

When a Personal Blog Becomes a Workplace Issue

Should blog entries about work be a concern for employers?   Andrew McDonald landed an internship with the television channel Comedy Central, and on his first day at work, he started a blog.[42] His supervisors asked him to change various things about the blog, essentially removing all specific references to Comedy Central. Kelly Kreth was fired from her job as a marketing director for blogging about her co-workers. So was Jessa Werner, who later said, "I came to the realization that I probably shouldn't have been blogging about work."

Although some companies have policies in place governing the content of blogs, many don't. Many bloggers think their personal blogs are outside their employer's purview, and 39 percent of individual bloggers say they have posted comments that could be construed as harmful to their company's reputation.

If someone else in a company happens to read a blog entry, there is nothing to keep him or her from sharing that information with others, and the employee could be dismissed as a result. Some companies may not fire an employee over any blog entry short of one that broke the law. But most organizations are unlikely to be so forgiving of any blog entry that might cast a negative light on them. In short, if you are going to have a personal blog, maintain a strict work-personal "firewall."

Instant Messaging and Text Messaging

Instant messaging (IM) and text messaging (TM), which have been popular among teens for more than a decade, are now rapidly moving into business.[43]

The growth of IM and TM has been spectacular. In 2002, Canadians sent 174 million text messages, in 2003 they sent 352 million text messages, in 2004 they sent more than 710 million text messages, and in 2006 they sent 4.3 billion text messages, tripling the number sent in 2005.[44] More people use IM than email as their primary communication tool at work.[45]

Facebook founder and CEO Mark Zuckerberg continues to transform communication. He announced a new platform strategy that allows third parties to develop services on the Facebook site, which allows communication opportunities for business entrepreneurs. For Zuckerberg, Facebook is more than a social networking site. He describes it as a communication tool that facilitates the flow of information between users and their friends, family members, and professional connections.

IM and TM represent fast and inexpensive means for managers to stay in touch with employees and for employees to stay in touch with each other. In an increasing number of cases, this is not just a luxury, it is a business imperative.

Despite their advantages, IM and TM are not going to replace email. Email is still probably a better device for conveying long messages that need to be saved. IM is preferable for one- or two-line messages that would just clutter up an email inbox. On the downside, some IM/TM users find the technology intrusive and distracting. Their continual presence can make it hard for employees to concentrate and stay focused. For example, a survey of managers revealed that in 86 percent of meetings, at least some participants checked TM. Finally, because instant messages can be intercepted easily, many organizations are concerned about the security of IM/TM.[46]

One other point: It's important to not let the informality of text messaging ("omg! r u serious? brb") spill over into business emails. Many prefer to keep business communication relatively formal. A survey of employers revealed that 58 percent rate grammar, spelling, and punctuation as "very important" in email messages.[47] By making sure your professional communications are, well, professional, you will show yourself to be mature and serious. That does not mean, of course, that you have to give up TM or IM; you just need to maintain the boundaries between how you communicate with your friends and how you communicate professionally.

Other Issues in Communication

4   What are other issues in communication?

How important is nonverbal communication? What does silence have to do with communicating? Why do men and women often have difficulty communicating with one another? How can individuals improve their cross-cultural communication? We address each of these issues next.

Nonverbal Communication

Anyone who has ever paid a visit to a singles bar or a nightclub is aware that communication need not be verbal to convey a message. A glance, a stare, a smile, a frown, a provocative body movement—they all convey meaning. This example illustrates that no discussion of communication would be complete without a discussion of **nonverbal communication**. This includes body movements, facial expressions, and the physical distance between the sender and receiver.

Does body language really make a difference?

The academic study of body motions has been labelled **kinesics**. It refers to gestures, facial configurations, and other movements of the body. Because it is a relatively new field, there isn't complete agreement on findings. Still, body movement is an important segment of the study of communication.

It has been argued that every body movement has a meaning and that no movement is accidental.[48] Through body language, we can say such things as, "Help me, I'm confused," or "Leave me alone, I'm really angry." Rarely do we send our messages consciously. We act out our state of being with nonverbal body language, even if we are not aware of doing so. We lift one eyebrow for disbelief. We rub our noses for puzzlement. We clasp our arms to isolate ourselves or to protect ourselves. We shrug our shoulders for indifference, wink one eye for intimacy, tap our fingers for impatience, slap our forehead for forgetfulness.[49] Babies and young children provide another good illustration of effective use of nonverbal communication. Although they lack developed language skills, they often use fairly sophisticated body language to communicate their physical and emotional needs. Such use of body language underscores its importance in communicating needs throughout life.

The two most important messages that body language conveys are (1) the extent to which an individual likes another and is interested in his or her views and (2) the relative perceived status between a sender and receiver.[50] For instance, we are more likely to position ourselves closer to people we like and to touch them more often. Similarly, if you feel that you are of higher status than another, you are more likely to display body movements—such as crossed legs or a slouched seated position—that reflect a casual and relaxed manner.[51]

While we may disagree with the specific meaning of certain movements (and different cultures may interpret specific body movements differently), body language adds to and often complicates verbal communication. For instance, if you read the transcript of a meeting, you do not grasp the impact of what was said in the same way you would if you had been there or had seen the meeting on video. Why? There is no record of nonverbal communication. The *intonations*, or emphasis, given to words or phrases is missing.

The *facial expression* of a person also conveys meaning. A snarling face says something different from a smile. Facial expressions, along with intonations, can show arrogance, aggressiveness, fear, shyness, and other characteristics that would never be communicated if you read a transcript of the meeting.

Studies indicate that those who maintain *eye contact* while speaking are viewed with more credibility than those whose eye contact wanders. People who make eye contact are also deemed more competent than those who do not.

The way individuals space themselves in terms of *physical distance*, commonly called **proxemics**, also has meaning. What is considered proper spacing is largely dependent on cultural norms. For instance, studies have shown that those from "contact" cultures (for example, Arabs, Latin Americans, southern Europeans) are more comfortable with body closeness and touch than those from "noncontact" cultures (for example, Asians, North Americans, northern Europeans).[52] These differences can lead to confusion. If someone stands closer to you than expected according to your cultural norms, you may interpret the action as an expression of aggressiveness or sexual interest. However, if the person stands farther away than you expect, you might think he or she is displeased

nonverbal communication Messages conveyed through body movements, facial expressions, and the physical distance between the sender and receiver.

kinesics The study of body motions, such as gestures, facial configurations, and other movements of the body.

proxemics The study of physical space in interpersonal relationships.

with you or uninterested. Someone whose cultural norms differ from yours might be very surprised by your interpretation.

Environmental factors such as seating arrangements or the conditions of the room can also send intended or unintended messages. A person whose desk faces the doorway demonstrates command of his or her physical space, while perhaps also conveying that others should not come too close.

It's important for the receiver to be alert to these nonverbal aspects of communication. You should look for nonverbal cues, as well as listen to the literal meaning of a sender's words. In particular, you should be aware of contradictions between the messages. The manager may say that she is free to talk to you about that raise you have been seeking, but you may see nonverbal signals (such as looking at her watch) that suggest this is not the time to discuss the subject. It's not uncommon for people to express one emotion verbally and another nonverbally. These contradictions often suggest that actions speak louder (and more accurately) than words. The *Working with Others Exercise* on page 291 will help you see the value of nonverbal communication in interpersonal relations.

We should also monitor body language with some care. For instance, while it is often thought that people who cross their arms in front of their chest are showing resistance to a message, individuals might also do this if they're feeling cold, regardless of their reaction to a message.

Silence as Communication

Sherlock Holmes once solved a murder mystery based not on what happened but on what *didn't* happen. Holmes remarked to his assistant, Dr. Watson, about "the curious incident of the dog in the nighttime." Watson, surprised, responds, "But the dog did nothing in the nighttime." To which Holmes replied, "That was the curious incident." Holmes concluded the crime had to be committed by someone with whom the dog was familiar because the watchdog did not bark.

The dog that did not bark in the night is often used as a metaphor for an event that is significant by reason of its absence. That story is also an excellent illustration of the importance of silence in communication.

Professors Craig Pinder of the University of Victoria and Karen Harlos of McGill University have noted that silence—defined here as an absence of speech or noise— generally has been ignored as a form of communication in organizational behaviour because it represents *in*action or *non*behaviour. But silence is not necessarily inaction. Nor is it, as many believe, a failure to communicate. Silence can, in fact, be a powerful form of communication.[53] It can mean someone is thinking or contemplating a response to a question. It can mean a person is anxious and fearful of speaking. It can signal agreement, dissent, frustration, or anger.

In terms of organizational behaviour, we can see several links between silence and work-related behaviour. For instance, silence is a critical element of groupthink, in which it implies agreement with the majority. It can be a way for employees to express dissatisfaction, as when they "suffer in silence." It can be a sign that someone is upset, as when a typically talkative person suddenly says nothing—"What's the matter with him? Is he all right?" It's a powerful tool used by individuals to signal disfavour by shunning or ignoring someone with "silent insults." As well, it's a crucial element of group decision making, allowing individuals to think over and contemplate what others have said.

Failing to pay close attention to the silent portion of a conversation can result in missing a vital part of the message. Astute communicators watch for gaps, pauses, and hesitations. They hear and interpret silence. They treat pauses, for instance, as analogous to a flashing yellow light at an intersection—they pay attention to what comes next. Is the person thinking, deciding how to frame an answer? Is the person suffering from communication apprehension? Sometimes the real message in a communication is buried in the silence.

Communication Barriers between Women and Men

Research by Deborah Tannen provides us with some important insights into the differences between men and women in terms of conversational styles.[54] In particular, Tannen has been able to explain why gender often creates oral communication barriers. Her research does not suggest that all men or all women behave as a gendered class in their communication; rather, she illustrates some important generalizations.

The essence of Tannen's research is that men use talk to emphasize status, while women use it to create connection. According to Tannen, women speak and hear a language of connection and intimacy, while men speak and hear a language of status and independence. So, for many men, conversations are primarily a means to preserve independence and maintain status in a hierarchical social order. For many women, however, conversations are negotiations for closeness in which people try to seek and give confirmation and support. The following examples will illustrate Tannen's thesis.

Men frequently complain that women talk on and on about their problems. Women criticize men for not listening. What is happening is that when men hear a problem, they frequently assert their desire for independence and control by offering solutions. Many women, on the other hand, view telling a problem as a means to promote closeness. The women present the problem to gain support and connection, not to get the male's advice. Mutual understanding, as sought by women, is symmetrical. But giving advice is asymmetrical—it sets up the (male) advice giver as more knowledgeable, more reasonable, and more in control. This contributes to distancing men and women in their efforts to communicate.

In conversation, women and men tend to approach points of conflict in different ways. A woman might say, "Have you looked at the marketing department's research on that point?" (the implication being that the report will show the error). Rather than simply relying on her own knowledge or beliefs, she presents the supporting evidence. A man might say, "I think you're wrong on that point," and not even provide documented evidence. These lead to gendered interpretations of the communication. Men frequently view female indirectness as "covert" or "sneaky," and they also interpret weakness when women won't take definitive stands, whereas women interpret male directness as an assertion of status and one-upmanship. Neither position is correct. It is helpful, though, to begin to understand the ways that females and males sometimes interpret the same dialogue differently.

Finally, men often criticize women for seeming to apologize all the time. Men tend to see the phrase "I'm sorry" as a weakness because they interpret the phrase to mean the woman is accepting blame. However, women typically use "I'm sorry" to express empathy: "I know you must feel bad about this; I probably would too in the same position."

While Tannen has received wide acknowledgment of her work, some suggest that it is anecdotal and/or based on faulty research. Goldsmith and Fulfs argue that men and women have more similarities than differences as communicators, although they acknowledge that when communication difficulties do appear, it is appealing to attribute them to gender.[55] Despite this, Nancy Langton, your Vancouver-based author, has noted, based on evidence from role plays, that men and women make requests for raises differently, and that men are more likely to state that men were more effective at making requests, while women are more likely to indicate that it was women who handled the interaction more favourably.[56]

Cross-Cultural Communication

Effective communication is difficult under the best of conditions. Cross-cultural factors clearly create the potential for increased communication problems.

Cultural Barriers

One author has identified four specific problems related to language difficulties in cross-cultural communication.[57] First, there are *barriers caused by semantics*. As we have noted previously, words mean different things to different people. This is particularly true for people from different national cultures. Some words, for instance, don't translate between cultures. Understanding the word *sisu* will help you communicate with people from Finland, but this word does not have an exact translation in English. It means something akin to "guts" or "dogged persistence." Similarly, the new capitalists in Russia may have difficulty communicating with their English-speaking counterparts because English terms such as *efficiency*, *free market*, and *regulation* cannot be directly translated into Russian.

Second, there are *barriers caused by word connotations*. Words imply different things in different languages. The Japanese word *hai* translates as "yes," but its connotation may be "yes, I'm listening," rather than "yes, I agree." Western executives may be hampered in their negotiations if they don't understand this connotation.

Third are *barriers caused by tone differences*. In some cultures, language is formal; in others, it's informal. In some cultures, the tone changes depending on the context: People speak differently at home, in social situations, and at work. Using a personal, informal style in a situation where a more formal style is expected can be embarrassing and offensive.

Fourth, there are *barriers caused by differences among perceptions*. People who speak different languages actually view the world in different ways. The Inuit perceive snow differently because they have many words for it. They also perceive "no" differently from English speakers because the Inuit have no such word in their vocabulary.

Cultural Context

A better understanding of these cultural barriers and their implications for communicating across cultures can be achieved by considering the concepts of high- and low-context cultures.[58]

Globalization has changed the way Toyota Motor Corporation provides employees with the information they need for decision making. In the past, Toyota transferred employee knowledge on the job from generation to generation through "tacit understanding," a common communication method used in the conformist and subdued Japanese culture. Today, however, as a global organization, Toyota transfers knowledge of its production methods to overseas employees by bringing them to its training centre in Japan, shown here, to teach them production methods by using how-to manuals, practice drills, and lectures.

EXHIBIT 7-7   High- vs. Low-Context Cultures

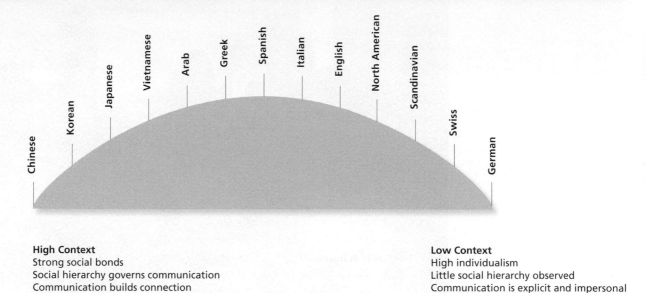

High Context
Strong social bonds
Social hierarchy governs communication
Communication builds connection
Avoidance of direct confrontation

Low Context
High individualism
Little social hierarchy observed
Communication is explicit and impersonal
Comfortable with open confrontation

Source: Based on the work of E. T. Hall. From R. E. Duleck, J.S. Fielden, and J. S. Hill, "International Communication: An Executive Primer," *Business Horizons*, January–February 1991, p. 21.

Cultures tend to differ in the importance of context in influencing the meaning that individuals take from what is actually said or written vs. who the other person is. Countries like China, Vietnam, and Saudi Arabia are **high-context cultures**. Their people rely heavily on nonverbal and subtle situational cues when communicating with others. What is not said may be more significant than what is said. A person's official status, place in society, and reputation carry considerable weight in communications. In contrast, people from Europe and North America reflect their **low-context cultures**. They rely essentially on words to convey meaning. Body language or formal titles are secondary to spoken and written words (see Exhibit 7-7).

What do these contextual differences mean in terms of communication? Actually, quite a lot! Communication in high-context cultures implies considerably more trust by both parties.

What may appear, to an outsider, as a casual and insignificant conversation is important because it reflects the desire to build a relationship and create trust. Oral agreements imply strong commitments in high-context cultures. Also, who you are—your age, seniority, rank in the organization—are highly valued and heavily influence your credibility. But in low-context cultures, enforceable contracts will tend to be in writing, precisely worded, and highly legalistic. Similarly, low-context cultures value directness. Managers are expected to be explicit and precise in conveying intended meaning. It's quite different in high-context cultures, where managers tend to "make suggestions" rather than give orders.

Overcoming Cross-Cultural Difficulties

When communicating with people from a different culture, what can you do to reduce misperceptions, misinterpretations, and misevaluations? Following these four rules can be helpful:[59]

- *Assume differences until similarity is proven.* Most of us assume that others are more similar to us than they actually are. But people from different countries

high-context cultures Cultures that rely heavily on nonverbal and subtle situational cues in communication.

low-context cultures Cultures that rely heavily on words to convey meaning in communication.

Ottawa-based Donna Cona made history when it designed and installed the computer network for the government of Nunavut. Two-thirds of the firm's software engineers are Aboriginal. Peter Baril, Nunavut's director of information technology operations, notes: "Donna Cona's quiet and knowledgeable approach was perhaps the most important skill brought to our project. No other style could have worked in this predominantly Aboriginal environment."

How can you improve cross-cultural communication?

often are very different from us. So you are far less likely to make an error if you assume others are different from you, rather than assuming similarity until difference is proven.

- *Emphasize description rather than interpretation or evaluation.* Interpreting or evaluating what someone has said or done, in contrast with describing, is based more on the observer's culture and background than on the observed situation. As a result, delay judgment until you have had sufficient time to observe and interpret the situation from the differing perspectives of all the cultures involved.

- *Be empathetic.* Before sending a message, put yourself in the recipient's shoes. What are his or her values, experiences, and frames of reference? What do you know about his or her education, upbringing, and background that can give you added insight? Try to see the other person as he or she really is.

- *Treat your interpretations as a working hypothesis.* Once you have developed an explanation for a new situation, or think you empathize with someone from a foreign culture, treat your interpretation as a hypothesis that needs further testing rather than as a certainty. Carefully assess the feedback provided by recipients to see if it confirms your hypothesis. For important decisions or communiqués, you can also check with other foreign and home-country colleagues to ensure that your interpretations are on target.

Summary and Implications

1 **How does communication work?**   Findings in the chapter suggest that the goal of perfect communication is unattainable. Yet there is evidence that demonstrates a positive relationship between effective communication (which includes factors such as perceived trust, perceived accuracy, desire for interaction, top-management receptiveness, and upward information requirements) and employee productivity.[60] Therefore, choosing the correct channel, being an effective listener, and using feedback well may make for more effective communication.

2 **What are the barriers to communication?**   Human beings will always be subject to errors in communication because of filtering, selective perception, defensiveness, information overload, and language. What is said may not be what is heard. Whatever the sender's expectations, the decoded message in the mind of the receiver represents the receiver's reality. This "reality" will determine the individual's reactions, including performance, motivation, and degree of satisfaction in the workplace.

3 **How does communication flow in organizations?**   Communication can flow vertically and laterally, and by formal and informal channels in organizations. We noted that there are three common formal small-group networks: the *chain*, *wheel*, and *all-channel*. The most common informal network in the organization is the *grapevine*. Greater use of informal channels will increase communication flow, reduce uncertainty, and improve group performance and satisfaction. We also noted that email, although pervasive, is causing more stress and can be misused, so it is not always the most effective means of communication. Instant messaging and text messaging are finding their way into the workplace with mixed results.

4 **What are other issues in communication?**   The big topics in communication are the importance of nonverbal communication and silence, gender differences in communication, and cross-cultural differences in communication. As we saw in this chapter, nonverbal cues help provide a clearer picture of what someone is trying to say. Silence can be an important communication clue, and failing to pay attention to silence can result in missing some or all of a message. Good communicators hear and interpret silence. We can make some generalizations about differences in the conversational style of men and women; men are more likely to use talk to emphasize status, while women use talk to create connection. We noted that there are a variety of barriers when communicating with someone from a different culture, and that it's best to assume differences until similarity is proven, emphasize description rather than *interpretation or evaluation*, practise empathy, and treat your interpretation as a working hypothesis.

OB AT WORK

For Review

1. Describe the communication process and identify its key components. Give an example of how this process operates with both oral and written messages.

2. Contrast encoding and decoding.

3. Identify three common formal small-group networks and give the advantages of each.

4. What conditions stimulate the emergence of rumours?

5. What are the advantages and disadvantages of email? Of instant messaging?

6. What is nonverbal communication? Does it aid or hinder verbal communication?

7. What does the expression "sometimes the real message in a communication is buried in the silence" mean?

8. What are the managerial implications from the research contrasting male and female communication styles?

9. List four specific problems related to language difficulties in cross-cultural communication.

10. Contrast high- and low-context cultures. What do the differences mean for communication?

For Critical Thinking

1. "Ineffective communication is the fault of the sender." Do you agree or disagree? Discuss.

2. What can you do to improve the likelihood that your message will be received and understood as you intended?

3. How might managers use the grapevine for their benefit?

4. Using the concept of channel richness, give examples of messages best conveyed by email, in face-to-face communication, and on the company bulletin board.

5. "Most people are poor listeners." Do you agree or disagree? Defend your position.

 **for You**

- If you are having difficulty communicating with someone, you might consider that both you and the other person are contributing something to that breakdown. This tends to be true even if you are inclined to believe that the other person is the party more responsible for the breakdown.

- Often, either selective perception or defensiveness gets in the way of communication. As you work in your groups on student projects, try to observe communication flows more critically to help you understand ways that communication can be improved and dysfunctional conflict avoided.

POINT

COUNTERPOINT

Keeping Secrets Means Keeping One's Word

We are better off keeping more things to ourselves.[61] Workplace gossip is out of control, and very often, we cannot trust people with secrets. Tell a friend never, ever to tell something to someone else, and you have aroused in them an irresistible desire to share the "juicy news" with others. A good rule of thumb is that if you are sure a confidante has told no one else, that probably means he or she has told only three other people. You might think this is a paranoid reaction, but research suggests that so-called confidantes rarely keep secrets, even when they swear they will.

Keeping our own secrets is normal, and most children learn to do it at any early age. People survive by protecting themselves, and when someone is keeping a secret, that person usually has a good reason for doing so.

Even when we feel like confiding in someone else, it's prudent to keep confidential information to ourselves. Research shows that few of us are able to keep secrets, and that if we fear certain negative consequences of telling our secrets (for example, our confidante will think less of us or will tell others), those fears don't stop us from blabbing and are often justified.

Organizational secrets are all the more important to keep quiet. Organizations are rumour mills, and we can permanently damage our careers and the organizations for which we work by disclosing confidential information. Improper disclosure of organizational proprietary information is a huge cost and concern for organizations. Look at the HP debacle when board chair Patricia Dunn lost her job and two other board members resigned. The cause of this disaster? Board members telling reporters secrets they had no business telling.

Keeping Secrets Can Be Unhealthy

The problem with keeping secrets is that they are expensive to maintain.

One social psychologist found that when people are instructed not to disclose certain information, it becomes more distracting and difficult for them to do so. In fact, the more people are instructed to keep something to themselves, the more they see the secret in everything they do. "We don't realize that in keeping it secret we've created an obsession in a jar," he says. So keeping things hidden takes a toll on our psyche—it (usually unnecessarily) adds to the mental burdens we carry with us.

Another psychologist has found that these costs are real. This researcher found that young people who experienced a traumatic experience often had more health problems later in life. As he researched the topic further, he found out why. Generally, these people conceal the event from others. He even did an experiment that showed that when people who have experienced traumatic events shared them, they later had fewer health problems than people who had not shared them. There isn't one identifiable reason why sharing these traumatic events seems to help people, but the result has been found repeatedly.

LEARNING ABOUT **YOURSELF** EXERCISE

Listening Self-Inventory

Go through this 15-item questionnaire twice.[62] The first time, mark yes or no next to each question. Mark as truthfully as you can in light of your behaviour in recent meetings or gatherings you attended. The second time, mark a plus (+) next to your answer if you are satisfied with that answer, or a minus (–) next to the answer if you wish you could have answered that question differently.

		Yes	No	+ or –
1.	I frequently attempt to listen to several conversations at the same time.	____	____	____
2.	I like people to give me only the facts and then let me make my own interpretations.	____	____	____
3.	I sometimes pretend to pay attention to people.	____	____	____
4.	I consider myself a good judge of nonverbal communications.	____	____	____
5.	I usually know what another person is going to say before he or she says it.	____	____	____
6.	I usually end conversations that don't interest me by diverting my attention from the speaker.	____	____	____
7.	I frequently nod, frown, or whatever to let the speaker know how I feel about what he or she is saying.	____	____	____
8.	I usually respond immediately when someone has finished talking.	____	____	____
9.	I evaluate what is being said while it is being said.	____	____	____
10.	I usually formulate a response while the other person is still talking.	____	____	____
11.	The speaker's delivery style frequently keeps me from listening to content.	____	____	____
12.	I usually ask people to clarify what they have said rather than guess at the meaning.	____	____	____
13.	I make a concerted effort to understand other people's point of view.	____	____	____
14.	I frequently hear what I expect to hear rather than what is said.	____	____	____
15.	Most people feel that I have understood their point of view when we disagree.	____	____	____

Scoring Key:

The correct answers to the 15 questions, based on listening theory, are as follows: (1) No; (2) No; (3) No; (4) Yes; (5) No; (6) No; (7) No; (8) No; (9) No; (10) No; (11) No; (12) Yes; (13) Yes; (14) No; (15) Yes. To determine your score, add up the number of incorrect answers, multiply by 7, and subtract that total from 105. If you scored between 91 and 105, you have good listening habits. Scores of 77 to 90 suggest significant room for improvement. Scores below 76 indicate that you are a poor listener and need to work hard on improving this skill.

More Learning About Yourself Exercises

Additional self-assessments relevant to this chapter appear on MyOBLab (**www.pearsoned.ca/myoblab**).

II.A.1 What's My Face-to-Face Communication Style?

IV.E.3 Am I a Gossip?

When you complete the additional assessments, consider the following:

1. Am I surprised about my score?
2. Would my friends evaluate me similarly?

BREAKOUT **GROUP** EXERCISES

Form small groups to discuss the following topics, as assigned by your instructor:

1. What differences have you observed in the ways that men and women communicate?

2. How do you know when a person is listening to you? When someone is ignoring you?

3. Describe a situation in which you ignored someone. What impact did it have on that person's subsequent communication behaviours?

WORKING WITH **OTHERS** EXERCISE

An Absence of Nonverbal Communication

This exercise will help you see the value of nonverbal communication in interpersonal relations.

1. The class is to divide into pairs (Party A and Party B).

2. Party A is to select a topic from the following list:

   a. Managing in the Middle East is significantly different from managing in North America.

   b. Bureaucracies are frustrating to work in.

   c. An employer has a responsibility to provide every employee with an interesting and challenging job.

   d. Organizations should require all employees to undergo regular AIDS testing.

   e. Organizations should require all employees to undergo regular drug testing.

   f. Individuals who have majored in business or economics make better employees than those who have majored in history or English.

   g. The place where you get your college or university degree is more important in determining career success than what you learn while you're there.

   h. Effective managers often have to lie as part of their job.

   i. It's unethical for a manager to purposely distort communications to get a favourable outcome.

3. Party B is to choose his or her position on this topic (for example, arguing *against* the view that "employers have a responsibility to provide every employee with an interesting and challenging job"). Party A now must automatically take the opposite position.

WORKING WITH **OTHERS** EXERCISE (CONTINUED)

4. The 2 parties have 10 minutes in which to debate their topic. The catch is that individuals can only communicate verbally. They may *not* use gestures, facial movements, body movements, or any other nonverbal communication. It may help for both parties to maintain an expressionless look and to sit on their hands to remind them of these restrictions.

5. After the debate is over, the class should discuss the following:

   a. How effective was communication during these debates?

   b. What barriers to communication existed?

   c. What purposes does nonverbal communication serve?

   d. Relate the lessons learned in this exercise to problems that might occur when communicating on the telephone or through email.

ETHICAL **DILEMMA** EXERCISE

Is It Wrong to Tell a Lie?

When we were children, our parents told us, "It's wrong to tell a lie."[63] Yet we all have told lies at one time or another. If most of us agree that telling lies is wrong, how do we justify continuing to do it? The answer is this: Most of us differentiate between "real lies" and "little white lies"—the latter being an acceptable, even necessary, part of social interaction.

A survey of 10 000 people 18 to 50 years old provides some insights into people's attitudes toward lying. Eighty percent described honesty as important, but nearly one-quarter said that they would lie to an employer "if necessary." More than 15 percent admitted to lying on a résumé or job application. And more than 45 percent said they would happily tell you a "little white lie."

Since lying is so closely intertwined with interpersonal communication, let's look at an issue many managers confront: Does a sound purpose justify intentionally distorting information? Consider the following situation:

An employee who works for you asks you about a rumour she has heard that your department and all its employees will be transferred from Calgary to Edmonton. You know the rumour is true, but you would rather not let the information out just yet. You are fearful it could hurt departmental morale and lead to premature resignations. What do you say to your employee? Do you lie, evade the question, distort your answer, or tell the truth?

In a larger context, where do you draw the line between the truth and lying? And if you are in a managerial position, how does your answer to the previous question fit with your desire to be trusted by those who work for you?

CASE INCIDENTS

Emailing "Lazy" Employees

Imagine receiving the following email from your CEO:[64]

We are getting less than 40 hours of work from a large number of our EMPLOYEES. The parking lot is sparsely used at 8 a.m.; likewise at 5 p.m. As managers, you either do not know what your EMPLOYEES are doing or you do not CARE. In either case, you have a problem and you will fix it or I will replace you.

NEVER in my career have I allowed a team which worked for me to think they had a 40-hour job. I have allowed YOU to create a culture which is permitting this. NO LONGER.

The note [paraphrased] continues: "Hell will freeze over before any more employee benefits are given out. I will be watching the parking lot and expect it to be substantially full at 7:30 a.m. and 6:30 p.m. on weekdays and half full on Saturdays. You have two weeks. Tick, tock."

Questions

1. What impact would this message have on you if you received it?

2. Is email the best way to convey such a message?

3. What problems might arise if people outside the organization saw this email?

4. What suggestions, if any, would you make to the CEO to help improve communication effectiveness?

Jeremy W. Caputo Has Communication Problems

Jeremy W. Caputo has only four employees at his public relations firm, Message Out.[65] But he seems to have done a pretty good job of alienating them.

According to his employees, Caputo, 47, is a brilliant guy who has a lot to learn in terms of being a better communicator. His communication style appears to be a regular source of conflict in his firm. Caputo admits he has a problem. "I'm probably not as verbally reinforcing [as I could be] when someone is doing a good job. I'm a very self-confident person. I don't need to be told I'm doing a good job—but there are people who do."

Caputo's employees had no problem listing off things that he does that bother them. He does not meet deadlines; he does a poor job of communicating with clients (which often puts the employees in an uncomfortable position); he does not listen fully to employee ideas before dismissing them; his voice tone is frequently condescending; and he is often quick to criticize employees and is stingy with praise.

Questions

1. A lot of bosses are accused of being "poor communicators." Why do you think this is?

2. What does this case suggest regarding the relationship between reinforcement theory (see Chapter 4, pages 154–156) and communication?

3. What, specifically, do you think Caputo needs to do to improve his communication skills?

4. Assuming Caputo wants to improve, how would you suggest he go about learning to be a better communicator?

From **Concepts** to **Skills**

Effective Listening

Too many people take listening skills for granted.[66] They confuse hearing with listening.

What's the difference? Hearing is merely picking up sound vibrations. Listening is making sense out of what we hear. That is, listening requires paying attention, interpreting, and remembering sound stimuli.

The average person normally speaks at a rate of 125 to 200 words per minute. However, the average listener can comprehend up to 400 words per minute. This leaves a lot of time for idle mind-wandering while listening. For most people, it also means they have acquired a number of bad listening habits to fill in the "idle time."

The following eight behaviours are associated with effective listening skills. If you want to improve your listening skills, look to these behaviours as guides:

1. *Make eye contact.* How do you feel when somebody doesn't look at you when you are speaking? If you are like most people, you are likely to interpret this behaviour as aloofness or lack of interest. We may listen with our ears, but others tend to judge whether we are really listening by looking at our eyes.

2. *Exhibit affirmative head nods and appropriate facial expressions.* The effective listener shows interest in what is being said. How? Through nonverbal signals. Affirmative head nods and appropriate facial expressions, when added to good eye contact, convey to the speaker that you are listening.

3. *Avoid distracting actions or gestures.* The other side of showing interest is avoiding actions that suggest your mind is somewhere else. When listening, don't look at your watch, shuffle papers, play with your pencil, or engage in similar distractions. They make the speaker feel that you are bored or uninterested. Maybe more important, they indicate that you are not fully attentive and may be missing part of the message that the speaker wants to convey.

4. *Ask questions.* The critical listener analyzes what he or she hears and asks questions. This behaviour provides clarification, ensures understanding, and assures the speaker that you are listening.

5. *Paraphrase.* Paraphrasing means restating what the speaker has said in your own words. The effective listener uses phrases such as "What I hear you saying is . . ." or "Do you mean . . .?" Why rephrase what has already been said? Two reasons! First, it's an excellent control device to check on whether you are listening carefully. You cannot paraphrase accurately if your mind is wandering or if you are thinking about what you are going to say next. Second, it's a control for accuracy. By rephrasing what the speaker has said in your own words and feeding it back to the speaker, you verify the accuracy of your understanding.

6. *Avoid interrupting the speaker.* Let the speaker complete his or her thought before you try to respond. Don't try to second-guess where the speaker's thoughts are going. When the speaker is finished, you will know!

7. *Don't overtalk.* Most of us would rather voice our own ideas than listen to what someone else says. Too many of us listen only because it's the price we have to pay to get people to let us talk. While talking may be more fun and silence may be uncomfortable, you cannot talk and listen at the same time. The good listener recognizes this fact and does not overtalk.

8. *Make smooth transitions between the roles of speaker and listener.* When you are a student sitting in a lecture hall, you find it relatively easy to get into an effective listening frame of mind. Why? Because communication is essentially one-way: The teacher talks and you listen. But the teacher-student dyad is not typical. In most work situations, you are continually shifting back and forth between the roles of speaker and listener. The effective listener, therefore, makes transitions smoothly from speaker to listener and back to speaker. From a listening perspective, this means concentrating on what a speaker has to say and practising not thinking about what you are going to say as soon as you get an opportunity.

Practising Skills

Form groups of 2. This exercise is a debate. Person A can choose any contemporary issue. Some examples include business ethics, the value of unions, stiffer grading policies, same-sex marriage, money as a motivator. Person B then selects a position on this issue. Person A must automatically take the counter-position. The debate is to proceed for 8 to 10 minutes, with only one catch. Before each person speaks, he or she must first summarize, in his or her own words and without notes, what the other has said. If the summary does not satisfy the speaker, it must be corrected until it does. What impact do the summaries have on the quality of the debate?

Reinforcing Skills

1. In another class—preferably one with a lecture format—practise active listening. Ask questions, paraphrase, exhibit affirming nonverbal behaviours. Then ask yourself: Was this harder for me than a normal lecture? Did it affect my note taking? Did I ask more questions? Did it improve my understanding of the lecture's content? What was the instructor's response?

2. Spend an entire day fighting your urge to talk. Listen as carefully as you can to everyone you talk to, and respond as appropriately as possible to understand, not to make your own point. What, if anything, did you learn from this exercise?

VIDEO CASE INCIDENT

CASE 7 Communication at Kluster

Kluster is a web-based company that invites individuals and companies to send in ideas for new products so they can get feedback from others. For example, if a company wanted to develop a new logo, it could ask participants to rate various alternative designs using criteria like uniqueness, coolness, colour, and so forth. Kluster promotes collaborative decision making that ". . . turns questions into answers, ideas into opportunities, and analysis into action."

Mat Papprocki, the designer at Kluster, says that everyone has ideas, but they generally keep those ideas to themselves and they don't know how to turn the idea into reality. The whole idea at Kluster is to get people to share their ideas and then have many other people in the web-based community comment on the usefulness of the idea.

Tom Pasley, the project manager at Kluster, says that a lot of companies seem to be afraid of what customers think. But the main goal at Kluster is to get feedback from customers. In each part of the development process, ideas are noted, votes are cast, and decisions are made about the idea. The demographic nature of the voter is taken into account and used to create a "weighted vote" that allows educated decisions to be made about the value of new product ideas. This process helps identify a diverse user base that will actually support decisions that a company makes as a result of feedback it gets.

Papprocki says that the Internet allows people to be anonymous and to say what they really think about new product ideas. CEO Ben Kaufman observes that focus groups—the "old faithful" way of doing product testing—pays people for giving opinions, so they may feel obliged to give an opinion about a product or an idea even if they don't have any really strong views about it. But with Kluster's approach, if people say they like the product, it's probably because they really do like it, not because they are trying to avoid hurting someone's feelings.

The Kluster approach yields three important benefits. First, it provides *respect*. Everyone respects an individual or a company that admits it does not have all the answers and needs help in getting those answers. Second, opening up the process provides *exposure* of the new product or idea to thousands of people. Buzz is created for the new product because there is usually a very interesting story to tell about how the product was developed. Third, the process provides *education*. It gives companies a better idea of where support is coming from, and it helps them understand why certain ideas are better than others.

There are intellectual property issues that arise because of the nature of the Kluster approach, but Kaufman says that if you submit your idea to Kluster, you have a "time and date stamp," and that allows for protection for your idea. As well, when people submit ideas, they control the timing and can stipulate how and where the idea is to be used. If the idea ends up not being used, the person who suggested it retains all rights to the idea. Kaufman recognizes that a big company could steal a good idea from the Kluster website, but if it did so it would incur the wrath of all the people who contributed to assessing the idea. This would create very bad public relations for the big company.

Questions

1. Using Exhibit 7-1, explain how the communication process works in the Illuminator project.

2. What are the benefits of getting customer feedback through the Illuminator project as compared to the traditional focus group? What does this mean for companies?

3. How "rich" is the channel that is used in the Illuminator project? Is the level of richness appropriate for the kind of messages that are being communicated?

4. Briefly describe the barriers to effective communication and indicate which ones might be the most problematic for the Illuminator project.

5. Explain the difference between a high-context culture and a low-context culture. Which type of culture is evident in North America? Are the implications positive or negative for the Illuminator project?

Source: Based on "Communication and IT at Kluster," Organizational Behavior Video Library, 2008. Copyrighted by Prentice-Hall.

Power and Politics

Can three artistic directors reporting to one general director make an efficient team? Power and politics tell much of the story.

1 What is power?

2 How does one get power?

3 How does dependency affect power?

4 What tactics can be used to increase power?

5 What does it mean to be empowered?

6 How are power and harassment related?

7 Why do people engage in politics?

When the Stratford (Ontario) Festival's artistic director, Richard Monette, decided to retire after 14 years in the position, the organization was faced with developing a succession plan.[1] Monette and Antoni Cimolino had worked together for years, with Monette responsible for the creative direction of Stratford, and Cimolino, as executive director, responsible for the financial management. Finding someone to replace Monette proved difficult: the organization "had grown too big for just one individual or artistic vision."

Cimolino made a proposal to the board: he would take on a new title, General Director, and three new artistic directors would report to him, rather than to the board. This would consolidate his power in the organization, giving him more authority and responsibility than when he and Monette reported independently to the board.

The board accepted the proposal and announced the new artistic directors, Marti Maraden, Des McAnuff and Don Shipley, in mid-2006. Less than two years later, however, Maraden and Shipley resigned. Maraden explained her resignation in a long letter to the *Globe and Mail*, indicating that power and politics were at the heart of the discontent. As she explained, "there was no protocol for decision-making, neither written nor spoken" and "a virtually unilateral imposition of [general director Antoni Cimolino's] agenda made it impossible for me to continue."

A major theme throughout this chapter is that power and politics are a natural process in any group or organization. Although you might have heard the saying "Power corrupts, and absolute power corrupts absolutely," power is not always bad. Understanding how to use power and politics effectively makes organizational life more manageable, because it can help you gain the support you need to do your job effectively.

OB Is for Everyone

- Have you ever wondered how you might increase your power?
- What do you need to be truly empowered?
- Why do some people seem to engage in politics more than others?
- In what situations does impression management work best?

Self-Assessment Library

LEARNING ABOUT YOURSELF

- Workplace Politics
- Political Skills

power A capacity that A has to influence the behaviour of B, so that B acts in accordance with A's wishes.

A Definition of Power

Power refers to a capacity that A has to influence the behaviour of B, so that B acts in accordance with A's wishes.[2] This definition implies that there is a *potential* for power if someone is dependent on another. But one can have power and not impose it.

Probably the most important aspect of power is that it is a function of dependency. The more that B depends on A, the more power A has in the relationship. Dependence, in turn, is based on the alternatives that B perceives and the importance that B places on the alternative(s) that A controls. A person can have power over you only if he or she controls something you desire. If you are attending college or university on funds totally provided by your parents, you probably recognize the power that your parents hold over you. You are dependent on them for financial support. But once you are out of school, have a job, and are making a good income, your parents' power is reduced significantly. Who among us, though, has not known or heard of the rich relative who is able to control a large number of family members merely through the implicit or explicit threat of "writing them out of the will"?

Within larger organizations, the information technology (IT) group often has considerable power, because everyone, right up to the CEO, is dependent on this group to keep computers and networks running. Since few people have the technical expertise to do so, IT personnel end up being viewed as irreplaceable. This gives them a lot of power within the organization.

Power should not be considered a bad thing, however. "Power, if used appropriately, should actually be a positive influence in your organization," says Professor Patricia Bradshaw of the Schulich School of Business at York University. "Having more power doesn't necessarily turn you into a Machiavellian monster. It can help your team and your organization achieve its goals and increase its potential."[3]

Bases of Power

> The artistic director of a theatre company often gets more public recognition than the executive director, even though each share management responsibilities. The public can directly see the impact of the artistic director's contribution through the works performed on stage. Antoni Cimolino watched for years as Richard Monette received credit for the growth of the Stratford Festival. When Monette announced his retirement, however, Cimolino did not have the artistic credits to be Monette's replacement. Instead, he suggested that the new artistic directors report to him—making Cimolino the only manager who reported to the board. What bases of power enabled Cimolino to make this proposal to the board?

Where does power come from? What is it that gives an individual or a group influence over others? The answer to these questions was developed by social scientists John French and Bertrand Raven, who first presented a five-category classification scheme of sources or bases of power: coercive, reward, legitimate, expert, and referent.[4] They subsequently added information power to that schema (see Exhibit 8-1).[5]

Coercive Power

coercive power Power that is based on fear.

Coercive power is defined by French and Raven as dependent on fear. One reacts to this power base out of fear of the negative results that might occur if one fails to comply. It rests on the application, or the threat of the application, of physical sanctions such as the infliction of pain, the generation of frustration through restriction of movement, or the controlling by force of basic physiological or safety needs.

Of all the bases of power available, the power to hurt others is possibly the most often used, most often condemned, and most difficult to control: The state relies on its military and legal resources to intimidate nations, or even its own citizens; businesses rely upon the control of economic resources to request tax reductions; and religious

EXHIBIT 8-1 Measuring Bases of Power

Does a person have one or more of the six bases of power? These descriptions help identify the person's power base.

Power Base	Statement
Coercive	The person can make things difficult for people, and you want to avoid getting him or her angry.
Reward	The person is able to give special benefits or rewards to people, and you find it advantageous to trade favours with him or her.
Legitimate	The person has the right, considering his or her position and your job responsibilities, to expect you to comply with legitimate requests.
Expert	The person has the experience and knowledge to earn your respect, and you defer to his or her judgment in some matters.
Referent	You like the person and enjoy doing things for him or her.
Information	The person has data or knowledge that you need.

Source: Adapted from G. Yukl and C. M. Falbe, "Importance of Different Power Sources in Downward and Lateral Relations," *Journal of Applied Psychology,* June 1991, p. 417. With permission.

institutions threaten individuals with dire consequences in the afterlife if they do not conduct themselves properly in this life. At the personal level, individuals exercise coercive power through a reliance upon physical strength, words, or the ability to grant or withhold emotional support from others. These bases provide the individual with the means to physically harm, bully, humiliate, or deny love to others.[6]

At the organizational level, A has coercive power over B if A can dismiss, suspend, or demote B, assuming that B values his or her job. Similarly, if A can assign B work activities that B finds unpleasant or treat B in a manner that B finds embarrassing, A possesses coercive power over B.

Reward Power

The opposite of coercive power is **reward power**. People will go along with the wishes or directives of another if doing so produces positive benefits; therefore, someone who can distribute rewards that others view as valuable will have power over those others. These rewards can be anything that another person values. In an organizational context, we think of money, favourable performance appraisals, promotions, interesting work assignments, friendly colleagues, important information, and preferred work shifts or sales territories.[7] As with coercive power, you don't have to be a manager to be able to exert influence through rewards. Rewards such as friendliness, acceptance, and praise are available to everyone in an organization. To the degree that an individual seeks such rewards, your ability to give or withhold them gives you power over that individual.

Legitimate Power

In formal groups and organizations, probably the most frequent access to one or more of the bases of power is through a person's structural position. This is called **legitimate power**. It represents the power a person receives as a result of his or her position in the formal hierarchy of an organization.

reward power Power that achieves compliance based on the ability to distribute rewards that others view as valuable.

legitimate power Power that a person receives as a result of his or her position in the formal hierarchy of an organization.

In India, Naina Lal Kidwai is a powerful woman in the banking industry. She is the Hongkong and Shanghai Banking Corporation (HSBC) country head for India. Kidwai's formal power is based on her position at the bank.

EXHIBIT 8-2

"I was just going to say 'Well, I don't make the rules.' But, of course, I __do__ make the rules."

Source: Drawing by Leo Cullum in *The New Yorker.* Copyright © 1986 *The New Yorker Magazine.* Reprinted by permission.

Positions of authority include coercive and reward powers. Legitimate power, however, is broader than the power to coerce and reward. Specifically, it includes acceptance by members of an organization of the authority of a position. When school principals, bank presidents, or generals speak (assuming that their directives are viewed to be within the authority of their positions), teachers, tellers, and privates listen and usually comply. You will note in Exhibit 8-2 that one of the men in the meeting identifies himself as the rule maker, which means that he has legitimate power. The Milgram experiment, discussed in *Focus on Research*, looks at the extremes individuals sometimes go to in order to comply with authority figures.

FOCUS ON **RESEARCH**

A Shocking Experiment

Would you shock someone if you were told to do so? A classic experiment conducted by Stanley Milgram studied the extent to which people are willing to obey those in authority.[8] Subjects were recruited for an experiment that asked them to administer electric shocks to a "student" who was supposed to learn a list of words. The experiments were conducted at Yale University, and subjects were assured by the experimenter, who was dressed in a white lab coat, that punishment was an effective way to learn. The subjects were placed in front of an instrument panel that indicated the shocks could go from 15 volts to 450 volts. With each wrong answer, subjects were to administer the next-highest shock level. After the shocks reached a middle level, the "student" started to cry out in pain. The experimenter would instruct the subject to continue administering shocks. What the experimenter was trying to find out was the level at which subjects would stop administering the electric shock. No subject stopped before 300 volts, and 65 percent of the subjects continued to the end of the experiment, even though, at the upper levels, the instrument panel was marked "Danger XXX." It should be noted that subjects were not actually administering shocks, and that the "student" was actually a confederate and was simply acting as if in pain. However, the subjects believed that they were administering electric shocks. This experiment suggests that many people will obey those who appear to have legitimate authority, even in questionable circumstances.

Expert Power

Expert power is influence based on expertise, special skills, or knowledge. Expertise has become one of the most powerful sources of influence as the world has become more technologically oriented. While it is generally acknowledged that physicians have expertise and hence expert power—most of us follow the advice that our doctor gives us— you should also recognize that computer specialists, tax accountants, economists, and other specialists can have power as a result of their expertise. Young people may find they have increased power in the workplace these days because of their technical knowledge and expertise that their Baby Boomer managers may not have.

expert power Influence based on special skills or knowledge.

Expert power relies on trust that all relevant information is given out honestly and completely. Of course, since knowledge is power, the more that information is shared, the less expert power a person has. Thus, some individuals try to protect their power by withholding information.[9] This tactic can result in poor-quality performance by those who need the information.[10] The *Working with Others Exercise* on page 326 gives you the opportunity to explore the effectiveness of different bases of power in changing someone's behaviour.

Referent Power

Referent power develops out of admiration of another and a desire to be like that person. In a sense, it is a lot like charisma. If you admire someone to the point of modelling your behaviour and attitudes after him or her, that person possesses referent power over you. Sometimes teachers and coaches have referent power because of our admiration of them. Referent power explains why celebrities are paid millions of dollars to endorse products in commercials. Advertisers such as Toronto-based Roots Canada use pictures on their website of popular Canadians such as actress Amanda Crew (*15/Love* and *Final Destination 3*) and hip-hop artist Kardinal Offishall to convince people to buy specific products.[11] Similarly, Nike has used sports celebrities such as Ottawa Senators captain Daniel Alfredsson to promote its products.

referent power Influence based on possession by an individual of desirable resources or personal traits.

Information Power

Information power comes from access to and control over information. People in an organization who have data or knowledge that others need can make those others dependent on them. Managers, for instance, because of their access to privileged sales, cost, salary, profit, and similar data, can use this information to control and shape subordinates' behaviour. Similarly, departments that possess information that is critical to a company's performance in times of high uncertainty—for example, the legal department when a firm faces a major lawsuit or the human resource department during critical labour negotiations—will gain increased power in their organization until those uncertainties are resolved.

information power Power that comes from access to and control over information.

Evaluating the Bases of Power

Generally, people will respond in one of three ways when faced with those who use the bases of power described above:

- *Commitment.* The person is enthusiastic about the request, and shows initiative and persistence in carrying it out.

- *Compliance.* The person goes along with the request grudgingly, puts in minimal effort, and takes little initiative in carrying out the request.

- *Resistance.* The person is opposed to the request and tries to avoid it with such tactics as refusing, stalling, or arguing about it.[12]

A review of the research on the effectiveness of these forms of power finds that they differ in their impact on a person's performance.[13] Exhibit 8-3 summarizes some of this research. Coercive power leads to resistance from individuals, decreased satisfaction, and increased mistrust. Reward power results in compliance if the rewards are consistent with what individuals want as rewards, something the *Ethical Dilemma Exercise* on page 327 shows clearly. Legitimate power also results in compliance, but it does not generally result in increased commitment. In other words, legitimate power does not inspire individuals to act beyond the basic level. Expert and referent powers are the most likely to lead to commitment from individuals. Ironically, the least effective bases of power for improving commitment—coercive, reward, and legitimate—are the ones most often used by managers, perhaps because they are the easiest to introduce.[14] Research shows that deadline pressure increases group members' reliance on individuals with expert and information power.[15]

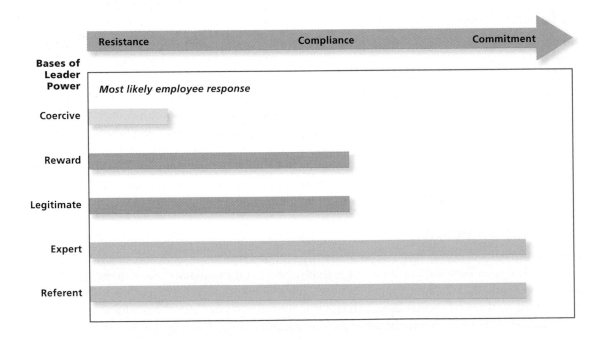

EXHIBIT 8-3   Continuum of Responses to Power

Source: R. M. Steers and J. S. Black, *Organizational Behavior*, 5th ed. (New York: HarperCollins, 1994), p. 487. Reprinted by permission of Pearson Education Inc., Upper Saddle River, New Jersey.

Dependency: The Key to Power

The Canadian arts community was shocked when the General Director of the Shakespeare Festival, Antoni Cimolino, announced in March 2008 that two of his three Artistic Directors, Marti Maraden and Don Shipley, had resigned.[16] There was widespread speculation about what caused the resignations, but lack of decision-making power likely contributed to their departures. When the three directors (including Des McAnuff) were appointed to work as a team, the understanding was that consensus would determine how they would work with each other. "As a group, that's what we'll be striving to do—to find consensus," said Shipley. "It's never going to be easy but certainly we've been skilled at doing that." Over time, however, consensus became more difficult. Maraden and Shipley would side with each other, while McAnuff had a different viewpoint, which meant that Antoni Cimolino had to make decisions. He often chose McAnuff's views over the other two directors. What factors might lead to one person having greater power over another?

In this section, we show how an understanding of dependency is central to furthering your understanding of power itself.

3 How does dependency affect power?

The General Dependency Postulate

Let's begin with a general postulate: *The greater B's dependency on A, the greater the power A has over B.* When you possess anything that others require but that you alone control, you make them dependent upon you and, therefore, you gain power over them.[17] Another way to frame dependency is to think about a relationship in terms of "who needs whom?" The person who has most need is the one most dependent on the relationship.[18]

Dependency is inversely proportional to the alternative sources of supply. If something is plentiful, possession of it will not increase your power. If everyone is intelligent, intelligence gives no special advantage. Similarly, in the circles of the super rich, money does not result in power. But if you can create a monopoly by controlling information, prestige, or anything that others crave, they become dependent on you. Alternatively, the more options you have, the less power you place in the hands of others. This explains, for example, why most organizations develop multiple suppliers rather than give their business to only one.

Because Xerox Corporation has staked its future on development and innovation, Sophie Vandebroek is in a position of power at Xerox. As the company's chief technology officer, she leads the Xerox Innovation Group of 5000 scientists and engineers at the company's global research centres. The group's mission is "to pioneer high-impact technologies that enable us to lead in our core markets and to create future markets for Xerox." Xerox depends on Vandebroek to make that mission a reality.

What Creates Dependency?

Dependency is increased when the resource you control is important, scarce, and cannot be substituted.[19]

Importance

Have you ever wondered how you might increase your power?

If nobody wants what you have, there is no dependency. To create dependency, the thing(s) you control must be perceived as important. In some organizations, people who control the budget have a great deal of importance. In other organizations, those who possess the knowledge to keep technology working smoothly are viewed as important. What is important is situational. It varies among organizations and undoubtedly also varies over time within any given organization.

Scarcity

As noted previously, if something is plentiful, possession of it will not increase your power. A resource must be perceived as scarce to create dependency.

Scarcity can help explain how low-ranking employees gain power if they have important knowledge not available to high-ranking employees. Possession of a scarce resource—in this case, important knowledge—makes those who don't have it dependent on those who do. Thus, an individual might refuse to show others how to do a job, or might refuse to share information, thereby increasing his or her importance.

The scarcity-dependency relationship can further be seen in the power of occupational categories. For example, college and university administrators have no problem finding English instructors to staff classes. There are more individuals who have degrees enabling them to work as English instructors than there are positions available in Canada. The market for corporate finance professors, by contrast, is extremely tight, with the demand high and the supply limited. The result is that the bargaining power of finance faculty allows them to negotiate higher salaries, lighter teaching loads, and other benefits.

Nonsubstitutability

The fewer substitutes there are for a resource, the more power comes from control over that resource. At Apple Computer, for example, most observers, as well as the board, believed that no one other than Steve Jobs could turn the company around when they returned him to the role of CEO in 1997. Thus, the board willingly accepted many of his turnaround suggestions quickly, even though some were controversial. In another example, when a union goes on strike and management is not permitted to replace the striking employees, the union has considerable control over the organization's ability to carry out its tasks.

People are often able to ask for special rewards (higher pay or better assignments) because they have skills that others do not.

Influence Tactics

Looking at the controversy surrounding the resignations of two of the Stratford Festival's general directors, we can find a number of instances where the various people involved in the controversy used influence tactics to get their way. There is some evidence that Antoni Cimolino and Des McAnuff formed a coalition to ensure that McAnuff would have more say over creative direction than Marti Maraden and Don Shipley. Cimolino used assertiveness to resolve disputes when the three directors could not achieve consensus on artistic direction. He also threatened sanctions such as the "unilateral imposition of his agenda," when the directors couldn't reach consensus, according to Maraden. So how and why do influence tactics work?

How do individuals translate their bases of power into specific, desired actions? Research indicates that people use common tactics to influence outcomes.[20] One study identified the nine influence tactics managers and employees use to increase their power:[21]

1. *Rational persuasion.* Using facts and data to make a logical or rational presentation of ideas.

2. *Inspirational appeals.* Appealing to values, ideals, and goals when making a request.

3. *Consultation.* Getting others involved to support one's objectives.

4. *Ingratiation.* Using flattery, creating goodwill, and being friendly prior to making a request.

5. *Personal appeals.* Appealing to loyalty and friendship when asking for something.

6. *Exchange.* Offering favours or benefits in exchange for support.

7. *Coalitions.* Getting the support of other people to provide backing when making a request.

8. *Pressure.* Using demands, threats, and reminders to get someone to do something.

9. *Legitimacy.* Claiming the authority or right to make a request, or showing that it supports organizational goals or policies.

4 What tactics can be used to increase power?

Some tactics are more effective than others. Specifically, evidence indicates that rational persuasion, inspirational appeals, and consultation tend to be the most effective. On the other hand, pressure tends to frequently backfire and is typically the least effective of the nine tactics.[22] You can also increase your chance of success by using more than one type of tactic at the same time or sequentially, as long as your choices are compatible.[23] For instance, using both ingratiation and legitimacy can lessen the negative reactions that might come from the appearance of being "dictated to" by the boss.

The effectiveness of some influence tactics depends on the direction of influence.[24] Studies have found that rational persuasion is the only tactic that is effective across organizational levels. Inspirational appeals work best as a downward-influencing tactic with subordinates. When pressure works, it's generally only to achieve downward influence. And the use of personal appeals and coalitions are most effective with lateral influence attempts. In addition to the direction of influence, a number of other factors have been found to affect which tactics work best. These include the sequencing of tactics, a person's skill in using the tactic, and the culture of the organization.

You are more likely to be effective if you begin with "softer" tactics that rely on personal power such as personal and inspirational appeals, rational persuasion, and consultation. If these fail, you can move to "harder" tactics (which emphasize formal power and involve greater costs and risks), such as exchange, coalitions, and pressure.[25] Interestingly, it has been found that using a single soft tactic is more effective than using a single hard tactic, and that combining two soft tactics or a soft tactic and rational persuasion is more effective than any single tactic or a combination of hard tactics.[26]

Recently, research has shown that people differ in their **political skill**, or the ability to influence others in such a way as to enhance their own objectives. Those who are politically skilled are more effective in their use of influence tactics, regardless of the tactics they are using. Political skill also appears to be more effective when the stakes are high—such as when the individual is accountable for important organizational outcomes. Finally, the politically skilled are able to exert their influence without others detecting it, which is a key element in being effective (it's damaging to be labelled political).[27]

Finally, we know that cultures within organizations differ markedly—for example, some are warm, relaxed, and supportive; others are formal and conservative. The organizational

political skill The ability to influence others in such a way as to enhance one's objectives.

culture in which a person works, therefore, will have a bearing on defining which tactics are considered appropriate. Some cultures encourage the use of participation and consultation, some encourage reason, and still others rely on pressure. So the organization itself will influence which subset of influence tactics is viewed as acceptable for use.

Do influence tactics vary within a country? *OB Around the Globe* looks at three locations in China to answer this question.

AROUND THE GLOBE

Influence Tactics in China

Are the same influence tactics equally effective across a country? Researchers usually examine cross-cultural influences in business by comparing two very different cultures, such as those from Eastern and Western societies.[28] However, it is also important to examine differences within a given culture, because those differences can sometimes be greater than differences between cultures.

For example, although we might view all Chinese people as being alike due to their shared heritage and appearance, China is a big country housing different cultures and traditions. A recent study of mainland Chinese, Taiwanese, and Hong Kong managers explored how the three cultural subgroups differ according to the influence tactics they prefer to use.

Though managers from all three places believe that rational persuasion and exchange are the most effective influence tactics, managers in Taiwan tend to use inspirational appeals and ingratiation more than managers from either mainland China or Hong Kong. The study also found that managers from Hong Kong rate pressure as more effective in influencing others than do managers in Taiwan or mainland China. Such differences have implications for business relationships. For example, Taiwanese or mainland Chinese managers may be taken aback by the use of pressure tactics by a Hong Kong manager. Likewise, managers from Hong Kong may not be persuaded by managers from Taiwan, who tend to use ingratiating tactics. Such differences in influence tactics may make business dealings difficult. Companies should address these issues, perhaps making their managers aware of the differences within cultures.

Managers need to know what variations exist within their local cultures so they can be better prepared to deal with others. Managers who fail to realize these differences may miss out on opportunities to deal effectively with others.

Empowerment: Giving Power to Employees

5 What does it mean to be empowered?

Thus far, our discussion has implied—to some extent, at least—that power is something that is more likely to reside in the hands of managers, to be used as part of their interaction with employees. However, in today's workplace, there is a movement toward sharing more power with employees by putting them in teams and also by making them responsible for some of the decisions regarding their jobs. Organizational specialists refer to this increasing responsibility as *empowerment*. We briefly mention in Chapter 1 that one of the current trends in leadership is empowering employees. Between 1995 and 2005, nearly 50 000 articles about empowerment have appeared in the print media in the United States and Canada, with almost 6000 articles appearing in Canadian newspapers during that time.[29]

Definition of Empowerment

The definition of *empowerment* that we use here refers to the freedom and the ability of employees to make decisions and commitments.[30] Unfortunately, neither managers nor researchers agree on the definition of empowerment. Robert E. Quinn and Gretchen M. Spreitzer, in their consulting work with a *Fortune* 50 manufacturing company, found that executives were split about 50-50 in their definition.[31] One group of executives "believed that empowerment was about delegating decision making within a set of clear boundaries." Empowerment would start at the top, specific goals and tasks would be assigned, responsibility would be delegated, and people would be held accountable for their results. The other group believed that empowerment was "a process of risk-taking and personal growth." This type of empowerment starts at the bottom, with considering the employees' needs, showing them what empowered behaviour looks like, building teams, encouraging risk-taking, and demonstrating trust in employees' ability to perform.

Much of the press on empowerment has been positive, with both executives and employees applauding the ability of front-line workers to make and execute important decisions.[32] However, not all reports are favourable. One management expert noted that much of the talk about empowerment is simply lip service,[33] with organizations telling employees that they have decision-making responsibility, but not giving them the authority to carry out their decisions. For an employee to be fully empowered, he or she needs access to the information required to make decisions; rewards for acting in appropriate, responsible ways; and the authority to make the necessary decisions. Empowerment means that employees understand how their job fits into the organization and are able to make decisions regarding job action guided by the organization's purpose and mission. Managers at Montague, PEI-based Durabelt recognize that to be empowered, employees need to have the appropriate skills to handle their jobs. The company sells customized conveyor belts used to harvest some vegetable and fruit crops. Employees need to be responsive to customer concerns when manufacturing the belts. In order to empower employees to manage customer relations successfully, Durabelt created Duraschool, an ongoing training program that provides employees with the skills they need to be more effective.[34]

Employee empowerment at Good People Company, in Seoul, South Korea, includes a monthly "Pyjamas Day" during which all employees work in the clothing the company designs. Good People managers then hold meetings with employees to solicit their feedback and inspirations about company products, making employees feel that their contributions are important and meaningful.

The concept of empowerment has caused much cynicism in many workplaces. Employees are told that they are empowered, and yet they do not feel that they have the authority to act, or they feel that their manager still micromanages their performance. Some managers are reluctant to empower their employees, because this means sharing or even relinquishing their own power. Other managers worry that empowered employees may decide to work on goals and jobs that are not as closely aligned to organizational goals. Some managers, of course, do not fully understand how to go about empowering their employees. Sometimes empowerment can even make employees ill, as *Focus on Research* shows.

FOCUS ON **RESEARCH**

Empowerment Can Make You Ill

Why would having more power negatively affect an employee? A study carried out by Professor Jia Lin Xie, of the Joseph L. Rotman School of Management at the University of Toronto, and colleagues found that when people are put in charge at work but don't have the confidence to handle their responsibilities, they can become ill.[35] Specifically, people who blame themselves when things go wrong are more likely to suffer colds and infections if they have high levels of control at work.

This finding by Professor Xie and her colleagues was somewhat unexpected, as some have hypothesized that greater control at work would lead to less stress. The study showed, instead, that the impact of empowerment depended on personality and job factors. Those who had control, but did not blame themselves when things went wrong, suffered less stress, even if the job was demanding. The study's findings suggest the importance of choosing carefully which employees to empower when doing so.

The findings are also consistent with the Hackman-Oldham job characteristics model presented in Chapter 5.[36] Empowerment will be positive if a person has high growth-need strengths (see Exhibit 5-6 on page 192), but those with low growth-need strengths may be more likely to experience stress when empowered.

Degrees of Empowerment

job content The tasks and procedures necessary for carrying out a particular job.

job context The reason for doing the job; it reflects the organizational mission, objectives, and setting.

What do you need to be truly empowered?

One study that helps us understand the degrees of empowerment looks at jobs in terms of both their context and their content.[37] The **job content** represents the tasks and procedures necessary for carrying out a particular job. The **job context** is the reason for doing the job and reflects the organizational mission, objectives, and setting. The context of the job would also include the organization's structure, culture, and reward systems.

When employees are empowered, as we noted above, they are given decision-making authority over some aspect of their job.

Exhibit 8-4 indicates three examples of employee power based on job context and content:[38]

- *No discretion* (Point A) is the typical assembly-line job—highly routine and repetitive. The employee is assigned the task, given no discretion, and most likely monitored by a supervisor. When employees have no power, they are less likely to be satisfied with their jobs. They can also be less productive because the lack of discretion may cause a "rule mentality" where the employee chooses to operate strictly by the rules, rather than showing initiative.

EXHIBIT 8-4   Employee Empowerment Grid

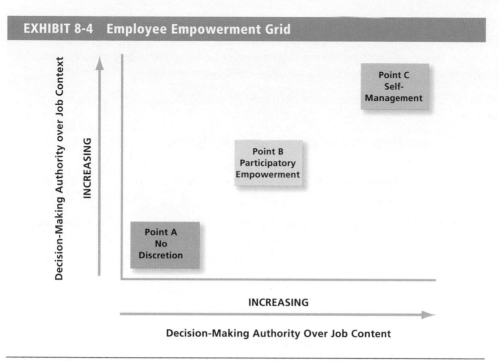

Decision-Making Authority over Job Context

INCREASING

Point A
No
Discretion

Point B
Participatory
Empowerment

Point C
Self-
Management

INCREASING

Decision-Making Authority Over Job Content

Source: Based on R. C. Ford and M. D. Fottler, "Empowerment: A Matter of Degree," *Academy of Management Executive*, August 1995, p. 24. Reprinted by permission.

- *Participatory empowerment* (Point B) represents the situation of autonomous work groups that are given some decision-making authority over both job content and job context. There is some evidence of higher job satisfaction and productivity in such groups.[39]

- *Self-management* (Point C) represents employees who have total decision-making power for both job content and job context. Granting an employee this much power requires considerable faith on the part of management that the employee will carry out the goals and mission of the organization in an

At Vancouver-based Great Little Box Company (GLBC), which designs and manufactures corrugated containers, employees are given the freedom to do whatever they feel is necessary and appropriate to make customers happy. If a customer is dissatisfied with the product, the employee can say, "OK, I'll bring this product back and return it for you," without having to get prior authorization.

EXHIBIT 8-5   Characteristics of Empowered People

Robert E. Quinn and Gretchen M. Spreitzer, in their research on the characteristics of empowered people (through both in-depth interviews and survey analysis), found four characteristics that most empowered people have in common:

- Empowered people have a sense of *self-determination* (this means that they are free to choose how to do their work; they are not micromanaged).

- Empowered people have a sense of *meaning* (they feel that their work is important to them; they care about what they are doing).

- Empowered people have a sense of *competence* (this means that they are confident about their ability to do their work well; they know they can perform).

- Empowered people have a sense of *impact* (this means that people believe they can have influence on their work unit; others listen to their ideas).

Source: R. E. Quinn and G. M. Spreitzer, "The Road to Empowerment: Seven Questions Every Leader Should Consider," *Organizational Dynamics*, Autumn 1997, p. 41.

---

effective manner. Generally this sort of power is reserved for those in top management, although it is also sometimes granted to high-level salespeople. Obviously this kind of power can be very rewarding to those who hold it.

When employees are empowered, it means that they are expected to act, at least in a small way, as owners of the company, rather than just employees. Ownership is not necessary in the financial sense, but in terms of identifying with the goals and mission of the organization. For employees to be empowered, however, and have an ownership mentality, four conditions need to be met, according to Professor Dan Ondrack at the Joseph L. Rotman School of Management at the University of Toronto:[40]

- There must be a clear definition of the values and mission of the company.

- The company must help employees acquire the relevant skills.

- Employees need to be supported in their decision making, and not criticized when they try to do something extraordinary.

- Employees need to be recognized for their efforts.

Exhibit 8-5 outlines what two researchers discovered in studying the characteristics of empowered people.

Effects of Empowerment

Does empowerment work? Researchers have shown that at both the individual level[41] and the team level,[42] empowerment leads to greater productivity. Not all people are affected by empowerment in the same way, however, as we see in *OB Around the Globe*.

 AROUND THE GLOBE

Empowerment in the United States, Mexico, India, and Poland

Does empowerment work the same way around the world? Four US researchers investigated the effects of empowerment on employees of a multinational firm by looking at four of the company's comparable plants: one in the Midwestern US, one in central Mexico, one in west-central India, and one in the south of Poland.[43] These four locations were chosen because they differed on power distance and individualism (concepts we discussed in Chapter 3). India and Mexico are considered high in power distance, and the United States is considered the lowest in power distance. Mexico and India are high in collectivity, the United States is highly individualistic, and Poland is moderately individualistic.

The findings showed that Indian employees gave their supervisors low ratings when empowerment was high, while employees in the other three countries rated their supervisors favourably when empowerment was high. In both the United States and Mexico, empowerment had no effect on satisfaction with co-workers. However, satisfaction with co-workers was higher when employees were empowered in Poland. In India, empowerment led to lower satisfaction with co-workers.

Similar findings in a study comparing empowerment in the United States, Brazil, and Argentina suggest that in hierarchical societies, empowerment may need to be introduced with care.[44] Employees in those countries may be more used to working in teams, but they also expect their manager to be the person with all the answers. ▄

Our discussion of empowerment suggests that a number of problems can arise when organizations decide they want to empower employees. First, some managers do not want empowered employees, because this can take away some of their own base of power. Second, some employees have little or no interest in being empowered, and therefore resist any attempts to be empowered. And finally, empowerment is not something that works well in every workplace throughout the world.

The Abuse of Power: Harassment in the Workplace

People who engage in harassment in the workplace are typically abusing their power position. The manager-employee relationship best characterizes an unequal power relationship, where position power gives the manager the capacity to reward and coerce. Managers give employees their assignments, evaluate their performance, make recommendations for salary adjustments and promotions, and even decide whether employees retain their job. These decisions give a manager power. Since employees want favourable performance reviews, salary increases, and the like, it's clear that managers control the resources that most employees consider important and scarce. It's also worth noting that individuals who occupy high-status roles (such as management positions) sometimes believe that harassing employees is merely an extension of their right to make demands on lower-status individuals.

Although co-workers do not have position power, they can have influence and use it to harass peers. In fact, although co-workers appear to engage in somewhat less severe forms of harassment than do managers, co-workers are the most frequent perpetrators of harassment, particularly sexual harassment, in organizations. How do co-workers exercise power? Most often they provide or withhold information, cooperation, and support. For example, the effective performance of most jobs requires interaction and support from co-workers. This is especially true these days as work is assigned to teams. By threatening to withhold or delay providing information that is necessary for the successful achievement of your work goals, co-workers can exert power over you.

Some categories of harassment have long been illegal in Canada, including those based on race, religion, and national origin, as well as sexual harassment. Unfortunately, some types of harassment that occur in the workplace are not deemed illegal, even if they create problems for employees and managers. We focus here on two types of harassment that have received considerable attention in the press: workplace bullying and sexual harassment.

6 How are power and harassment related?

Workplace Bullying

Many of us are aware, anecdotally if not personally, of managers who harass employees, demanding overtime without pay or excessive work performance. Further, some of the recent stories of workplace violence have reportedly been the result of an employee feeling intimidated at work. In research conducted in the private and public sector in southern Saskatchewan, Céleste Brotheridge, a professor at the Université du Québec à Montréal, found that bullying was rather prevalent in the workplace. Forty percent of the respondents noted that they had experienced one or more forms of bullying weekly in the past six months. Ten percent experienced bullying at a much greater level: five or more incidents a week. Brotheridge notes that bullying has a negative effect on the workplace: "Given bullying's deleterious effects on employee health, it is reason for concern."[45]

There is no clear definition of workplace bullying, and Marilyn Noble, a Fredericton-based adult educator, remarks that in some instances there can be a fine line between managing and bullying. However, Noble, who co-chaired a research team on workplace violence and abuse at the University of New Brunswick, notes that "when it becomes a question of shaming people, embarrassing people, holding them up to ridicule, just constantly being on their case for no apparent reason, then [management] is becoming unreasonable." Moreover, "A bully often acts by isolating an individual. And they may be a serial bully, who always has a victim on the go. They may, in fact, have multiple victims on the go, but their strategy is to isolate them from one another."[46]

The effects of bullying can be devastating. Professors Sandy Hershcovis of the University of Manitoba and Julian Barling of Queen's University found that the consequences of bullying were more harmful to its victims than those who suffered sexual harassment. Bullied employees more often quit their jobs, were less satisfied with their jobs, and had more difficult relationships with their supervisors.[47]

Quebec introduced the first anti-bullying labour legislation in North America on June 1, 2004. The legislation defines psychological harassment as "any vexatious behaviour in the form of repeated and hostile or unwanted conduct, verbal comments, actions or gestures that affect an employee's dignity or psychological or physical integrity and that results in a harmful work environment for the employee."[48] Under the Quebec law, bullying allegations will be sent to mediation, where the accuser and the accused will work with an independent third party to try to resolve the problem. If mediation fails, employers who have allowed psychological harassment can be fined up to $10 000 and ordered to pay financial damages to the victim.

Sexual Harassment

The issue of sexual harassment has received increasing attention from corporations and the media because of the growing ranks of female employees, especially in nontraditional work environments, and because of a number of high-profile cases. For example, in March 2006, it was reported that all four female firefighters in the Richmond, BC, fire department had taken a leave of absence, alleging that they had faced repeated sexual harassment and discrimination from male firefighters in the department. The city has since introduced a code of conduct for its firefighters.[49]

A survey by York University found that 48 percent of working women in Canada reported they had experienced some form of "gender harassment" in the year before they were surveyed.[50] Barbara Orser, a research affiliate with the Conference Board of Canada, notes that "sexual harassment is more likely to occur in workplace environments that tolerate bullying, intimidation, yelling, innuendo and other forms of discourteous behaviour."[51] These behaviours indicate one person trying to use power over another.

The Supreme Court of Canada defines **sexual harassment** as unwelcome behaviour of a sexual nature in the workplace that negatively affects the work environment or leads to adverse job-related consequences for the employee.[52] Despite the legal framework

sexual harassment Unwelcome behaviour of a sexual nature in the workplace that negatively affects the work environment or leads to adverse job-related consequences for the employee.

for defining sexual harassment, there continues to be disagreement as to what *specifically* constitutes sexual harassment. Sexual harassment includes unwanted physical touching, recurring requests for dates when it is made clear the person is not interested, and coercive threats that a person will lose her or his job if she or he refuses a sexual proposition. The problems of interpreting sexual harassment often surface around some of its more subtle forms—unwanted looks or comments, off-colour jokes, sexual artifacts such as nude calendars in the workplace, sexual innuendo, or misinterpretations of where the line between "being friendly" ends and "harassment" begins. *Case Incident— Damned If You Do; Damned If You Don't* on page 328 illustrates how these problems can make people feel uncomfortable in the workplace. Most studies confirm that the concept of power is central to understanding sexual harassment.[53] It's about an individual controlling or threatening another individual. This seems to be true whether the harassment comes from a manager, a co-worker, or an employee.

Because of power inequities, sexual harassment by a manager typically creates great difficulty for an employee being harassed. If there are no witnesses, it's the manager's word against the employee's word. Are there others whom this manager has harassed, and if so, will they come forward? Because of the manager's control over resources, many of those who are harassed are afraid of speaking out for fear of retaliation by the manager.

One of the places where there has been a dramatic increase in the number of sexual harassment complaints is at university campuses across Canada, according to Paddy Stamp, sexual harassment officer at the University of Toronto.[54] However, agreement on what constitutes sexual harassment, and how it should be investigated, is no clearer for universities than for industry.

While nonconsensual sex between professors and students is rape and subject to criminal charges, it's harder to evaluate apparently consensual relationships that occur outside the classroom. There is some argument over whether truly consensual sex is ever possible between students and professors. In an effort to underscore the power discrepancy and potential for abuse of it by professors, in 2003 the University of California, which includes Berkeley, implemented a policy forbidding romantic relationships between professors and their students.[55] Most universities have been unwilling to adopt such an extreme stance. However, this issue is certainly one of concern, as the power difference between professors and students is considerable.

A recent review of the literature shows the damage caused by sexual harassment. As you would expect, individuals who are sexually harassed report more negative job attitudes (lower job satisfaction, diminished organizational commitment) as a result. This review also revealed that sexual harassment undermines the victims' mental and physical health. However, sexual harassment also negatively affects the group in which the victim works, lowering its level of productivity. The authors of this study conclude that sexual harassment "is significantly and substantively associated with a host of harms."[56]

We have seen how sexual harassment can wreak havoc on an organization, not to mention on the victims themselves. But it can be avoided. A manager's role in preventing sexual harassment is critical. Some ways managers can protect themselves and their employees from sexual harassment are as follows:

- Make sure a policy is in place that defines what constitutes sexual harassment, that informs employees that they can be fired for sexually harassing another employee, and that establishes procedures for how complaints can be made.

- Ensure employees that they will not encounter retaliation if they issue a complaint.

- Investigate every complaint and include the legal and human resource departments.

- Make sure that offenders are disciplined or terminated.

- Set up in-house seminars to raise employee awareness about the issues surrounding sexual harassment.

Politics: Power in Action

As the speculation about why Marti Maraden and Don Shipley resigned from the Stratford Festival appeared in the newspapers, Antoni Cimolino tried to control what the public heard about the resignations. His initial statements emphasized that the two had resigned, that they were not asked to quit. However, about a week later, Maraden published a letter in the *Globe and Mail* to give her side of the story. She said that she had urged that the announcement of the resignations wait until later in the season, so as to avoid disruption to the planned performances. Yet in a meeting on March 12, Maraden reports, "Antoni told me that Don's and my resignation would be announced the next day, and that settlement papers had already been drawn up." When Cimolino drew up the papers for Maraden and Shipley to sign, it may have been less about making the "right" decision, and more about making a political decision to silence dissent. So why is politics so prevalent? Is it merely a fact of life?

7 Why do people engage in politics?

Organizational behaviour researchers have learned a lot in recent years about how people gain and use power in organizations. Part of using power in organizations is engaging in organizational politics to influence others to help you achieve your personal objectives. Lobbying others to get them to vote with you on a particular decision is engaging in organizational politics.

When people get together in groups, power will be exerted. People want to carve out a niche from which to exert influence, to earn awards, and to advance their careers.[57] When employees in organizations convert their power into action, we describe them as being engaged in politics. Those with good political skills have the ability to use their bases of power effectively.[58] In this section, we look at political behaviour, the types of political activity people use to try to influence others, and impression management. Political skills are not confined to adults, of course. When your Vancouver author's then six-year-old nephew wanted the latest Game Boy knowing full well his parents did not approve, he waged a careful, deliberate campaign to wear them down, explaining how he would use the toy only at assigned times, etcetera. His politicking paid off: Within six weeks, he succeeded in getting the toy.

Definition of Political Behaviour

There has been no shortage of definitions for organizational politics. One clever definition of politics comes from Tom Jakobek, Toronto's former budget chief, who said, "In politics, you may have to go from A to C to D to E to F to G and then to B."[59]

For our purposes, we will define **political behaviour** in organizations as those activities that are outside one's formal role, and that influence, or attempt to influence, the distribution of advantages and disadvantages within the organization.[60]

This definition encompasses key elements from what most people mean when they talk about organizational politics. Political behaviour is outside one's specified job requirements. The behaviour requires some attempt to use one's bases of power. Our definition also encompasses efforts to influence the goals, criteria, or processes used for decision making when we state that politics is concerned with "the distribution of advantages and disadvantages within the organization." Our definition is broad enough to include such varied political behaviours as withholding key information from decision makers, spreading rumours, leaking confidential information about organizational activities to the media, exchanging favours with others in the organization for mutual benefit, and lobbying on behalf of or against a particular individual or decision alternative. Exhibit 8-6 provides a quick measure to help you assess how political your workplace is.

Now that you have learned a bit about political behaviour, you may want to assess your own political behaviour in the *Learning About Yourself Exercise* on page 325.

Political behaviour is not confined to just individual hopes and goals. Politics might also be used to achieve organizational goals. For instance, if a CEO wants to change

political behaviour Those activities that influence, or attempt to influence, the distribution of advantages and disadvantages within the organization.

Learning About Yourself

How Political Are You, **(page 325)**

EXHIBIT 8-6 A Quick Measure of How Political Your Workplace Is	

How political is your workplace? Answer the 12 questions using the following scale:

SD = Strongly disagree
D = Disagree
U = Uncertain
A = Agree
SA = Strongly agree

1. Managers often use the selection system to hire only people who can help them in their future. _____

2. The rules and policies concerning promotion and pay are fair; it's how managers carry out the policies that is unfair and self-serving. _____

3. The performance ratings people receive from their managers reflect more of the managers' "own agenda" than the actual performance of the employee. _____

4. Although a lot of what my manager does around here appears to be directed at helping employees, it's actually intended to protect my manager. _____

5. There are cliques or "in-groups" that hinder effectiveness around here. _____

6. My co-workers help themselves, not others. _____

7. I have seen people deliberately distort information requested by others for purposes of personal gain, either by withholding it or by selectively reporting it. _____

8. If co-workers offer to lend some assistance, it is because they expect to get something out of it. _____

9. Favouritism rather than merit determines who gets ahead around here. _____

10. You can usually get what you want around here if you know the right person to ask. _____

11. Overall, the rules and policies concerning promotion and pay are specific and well-defined. _____

12. Pay and promotion policies are generally clearly communicated in this organization. _____

This questionnaire taps the three salient dimensions that have been found to be related to perceptions of politics: manager behaviour; co-worker behaviour; and organizational policies and practices. To calculate your score for items 1–10, give yourself 1 point for Strongly disagree; 2 points for Disagree; and so forth (through 5 points for Strongly agree). For items 11 and 12, reverse the score (that is, 1 point for Strongly agree, etc.). Sum up the total: The higher the total score, the greater the degree of perceived organizational politics.

Source: G. R. Ferris, D. D. Frink, D. P. S. Bhawuk, J. Zhou, and D. C. Gilmore, "Reactions of Diverse Groups to Politics in the Workplace," *Journal of Management* 22, no. 1 (1996), pp. 32–33.

the way employees are paid, say from salaries to commissions, this might not be a popular choice for employees. While it might make good organizational sense to make this change (perhaps the CEO believes this will increase productivity), simply imposing the change through the use of power (go along with this or you're fired) might not be very popular. Instead, the CEO may try to pitch the reasons for the change to sympathetic managers and employees, trying to get them to understand the necessity for the change. Burnaby, BC-based TELUS used a direct approach with its employees after four and a half years of unsuccessful bargaining with union leaders. Management became frustrated with the impasse and explained their wage and benefit offer directly to employees in the hopes of getting the employees to side with management rather than their union leaders. The union was outraged by this behaviour, and it took several more months for union members and management to finally complete a new collective agreement in fall 2005.

The Reality of Politics

Why, you may wonder, must politics exist? Isn't it possible for an organization to be politics-free? It's *possible*, but most unlikely. Organizations are made up of individuals and groups with different values, goals, and interests.[61] This sets up the potential for conflict over resources. Organizational members sometimes disagree about the allocation of resources such as departmental budgets, space allocations, project responsibilities, and salary adjustments.

Resources in organizations are also limited, which often turns potential conflict into real conflict. If resources were abundant, all the constituencies within the organization could satisfy their goals. Because they are limited, not everyone's interests can be provided for. Furthermore, whether true or not, gains by one individual or group are often *perceived* as being at the expense of others within the organization. These forces create a competition among members for the organization's limited resources.

Maybe the most important factor behind politics within organizations is the realization that most of the "facts" that are used to allocate the limited resources are open to interpretation. What, for instance, is *good* performance? What is an *adequate* improvement? What constitutes an *unsatisfactory* job? It's in this large and ambiguous middle ground of organizational life—where the facts *don't* speak for themselves—that politics flourish.

Finally, because most decisions must be made in a climate of ambiguity—where facts are rarely fully objective, and thus are open to interpretation—people within organizations will use whatever influence they can to spin the facts to support their goals and interests. That, of course, creates the activities we call *politicking*. For more about how one engages in politicking, see *From Concepts to Skill*s on pages 330–331.

President and CEO Aris Kaplanis of Toronto-based high-tech firm Teranet (shown here at far right with his senior management group) discourages negative office politics among his employees. The company employs the golden rule of "do unto others as you would have others do unto you." He tells his employees, "If you're here to play a game, you're in the wrong business."

Therefore, to answer the earlier question about whether it is possible for an organization to be politics-free, we can say "yes"—but only if all the members of that organization hold the same goals and interests, organizational resources are not scarce, and performance outcomes are completely clear and objective. However, that does not describe the organizational world that most of us live in!

RESEARCH FINDINGS: Politicking

Our earlier discussion focused on the favourable outcomes for individuals who successfully engage in politicking. But for most people—who have modest political skills or are unwilling to play the politics game—outcomes tend to be predominantly negative.[62] There is, for instance, very strong evidence indicating that perceptions of organizational politics are negatively related to job satisfaction.[63] The perception of politics also tends to increase job anxiety and stress. This seems to be because of the perception that, by not engaging in politics, a person may be losing ground to others who are active politickers, or, conversely, because of the additional pressures individuals feel because of having entered into and competing in the political arena.[64] Not surprisingly, when politicking becomes too much to handle, it can lead to employees quitting.[65] Finally, there is preliminary evidence suggesting that politics leads to self-reported declines in employee performance.[66] Perceived organizational politics appears to have a demotivating effect on individuals, and thus leads to decreased performance levels.

Types of Political Activity

Within organizations, we can find a variety of political activities in which people engage. These include the following:[67]

- *Attacking or blaming others.* Used when trying to avoid responsibility for failure.

- *Using information.* Withholding or distorting information, particularly to hide negative information.

- *Managing impressions.* Bringing positive attention to oneself or taking credit for positive accomplishments of others.

- *Building support for ideas.* Making sure that others will support one's ideas before they are presented.

- *Praising others.* Making important people feel good.

- *Building coalitions.* Joining with other people to create a powerful group.

- *Associating with influential people.* Building support networks.

- *Creating obligations.* Doing favours for others so they will owe you favours later.

Individuals will use these political activities for different purposes, as this chapter's *Case Incident—The Politics of Backstabbing* on page 329 illustrates. Some of these activities (such as attacking or blaming others) are more likely to be used to defend one's position, while other activities (such as building support for ideas and managing impressions) are meant to enhance one's image.

Impression Management

The process by which individuals attempt to control the impression others form of them is called **impression management**.[68] Being perceived positively by others should have benefits for people in organizations. It might, for instance, help them initially to get the jobs they want in an organization and, once hired, to get favourable evaluations, superior salary increases, and more rapid promotions. In a political context, it might help bring more advantages their way.

Why do some people seem to engage in politics more than others?

Impression management does not imply that the impressions people convey are necessarily false (although, of course, they sometimes are).[69] Some activities may be done with great sincerity. For instance, you may *actually* believe that ads contribute little to sales in your region or that you are the key to the tripling of your division's sales. However, if the image claimed is false, you may be discredited.[70] The impression manager must be cautious not to be perceived as insincere or manipulative.[71] This chapter's *Point/Counterpoint* on page 324 considers the ethics of managing impressions.

impression management The process by which individuals attempt to control the impression others form of them.

RESEARCH FINDINGS: Impression Management Techniques

Most of the studies undertaken to test the effectiveness of impression management techniques have related it to two criteria: interview success and performance evaluations. Let's consider each of these.

The evidence indicates that most job applicants use impression management techniques in interviews[72] and that, when impression management behaviour is used, it works.[73] In one study, for instance, interviewers felt that applicants for a position as a customer-service representative who used impression management techniques performed better in the interview, and they seemed somewhat more inclined to hire these people.[74] Moreover, when the researchers considered applicants' credentials, they concluded that it was the impression management techniques alone that influenced the interviewers. That is, it did not seem to matter if applicants were well or poorly qualified. If they used impression management techniques, they did better in the interview.

In what situations does impression management work best?

Research indicates that some impression management techniques work better than others in the interview. Researchers have compared applicants who used techniques that focused on promoting one's accomplishments (called *self-promotion*) to applicants who used techniques that focused on complimenting the interviewer and finding areas of agreement (referred to as *ingratiation*). In general, applicants appear to use self-promotion more than ingratiation.[75] What is more, self-promotion tactics may be more important to interviewing success. Applicants who work to create an appearance of competence by enhancing their accomplishments, taking credit for successes, and explaining away failures do better in interviews. These effects reach beyond the interview: Applicants who use more self-promotion tactics also seem to get more follow-up job-site visits, even after adjusting for grade-point average, gender, and job type. Ingratiation also works well in interviews, meaning that applicants who compliment the interviewer, agree with his or her opinions, and emphasize areas of fit do better than those who don't.[76]

In terms of performance ratings, the picture is quite different. Ingratiation is positively related to performance ratings, meaning that those who ingratiate with their supervisors get higher performance evaluations. However, self-promotion appears to backfire: Those who self-promote actually seem to receive *lower* performance evaluations.[77] Another study of 760 boards of directors found that individuals who ingratiate themselves to current board members (express agreement with the director, point out shared attitudes and opinions, compliment the director) increase their chances of landing on a board.[78] What explains these results? If you think about them, they make sense. Ingratiating always works because everyone—both interviewers and supervisors—likes to be treated nicely. However, self-promotion may work only in interviews and backfire on the job because, whereas the interviewer has little idea whether you are blowing smoke about your accomplishments, the supervisor knows because it's his or her job to observe you. Thus, if you are going to self-promote, remember that what works in an interview will not always work once you are on the job.

Making Office Politics Work

One thing to be aware of is that extreme office politics can have a negative effect on employees. Researchers have found that organizational politics is associated with less organizational commitment,[79] lower job satisfaction,[80] and decreased job performance.[81] Individuals who experience greater organizational politics are more likely to report higher levels of job anxiety,[82] and they are more likely to consider leaving the organization.[83]

Is there an effective way to engage in office politics that is less likely to be disruptive or negative? We discuss different negotiation strategies in Chapter 9, including a *win-lose* strategy, which means if I win, you lose, and a *win-win* strategy, which means creating situations where both of us can win. *Fast Company*, a business magazine, identifies several rules that may help improve the climate of the organization while negotiating through the office politics maze:[84]

- *Nobody wins unless everybody wins.* The most successful proposals look for ways to acknowledge, if not include, the interests of others. This requires building support for your ideas across the organization. "Real political skill isn't about campaign tactics," says Lou Di Natale, a veteran political consultant at the University of Massachusetts. "It's about pulling people toward your ideas and then pushing those ideas through to other people." When ideas are packaged to look like they are best for the organization as a whole and will help others, it is harder for others to counteract your proposal.

- *Don't just ask for opinions—change them.* It's helpful to find out what people think and then, if necessary, set out to change their opinions so that they can see what you want to do. It's also important to seek out the opinions of those you don't know well, or who are less likely to agree with you. Gathering together people who always support you is often not enough to build an effective coalition.

- *Everyone expects to be paid back.* In organizations, as in life, we develop personal relationships with those around us. It's those personal relationships that affect much of the behaviour in organizations. By building good relationships with colleagues, supporting them in their endeavours, and showing appreciation for what they accomplish, you are building a foundation of support for your own ideas.

General Electric (GE) wants its managers to share their power with employees. GE is breaking down autocratic barriers between labour and management that "cramp people, inhibit creativity, waste time, restrict visions, smother dreams, and above all, slow things down." GE expects managers to behave more democratically by fostering teamwork and rewarding employees who suggest ideas for improvement. This photo illustrates GE's move toward democracy, as a manager and an employee at the company's plant in Louisville, Kentucky, work together to improve the plant's profitability.

- *Success can create opposition.* As part of the office politics, success can be viewed as a *win-lose* strategy, which we identified above. Some people may feel that your success comes at their expense. So, for instance, your higher profile may mean that a project of theirs will be received less favourably. You have to be prepared to deal with this opposition.

Summary and Implications

1 **What is power?** Power refers to a capacity that A has to influence the behaviour of B, so that B acts in accordance with A's wishes.

2 **How does one get power?** There are six bases or sources of power: coercive, reward, legitimate, expert, referent, and information. These forms of power differ in their ability to improve a person's performance. *Coercive power* tends to result in negative performance responses from individuals; it decreases satisfaction, increases mistrust, and creates fear. *Reward power* may improve performance, but it can also lead to unethical behaviour. *Legitimate power* does not have a negative effect, but does not generally stimulate employees to improve their attitudes or performance, and it does not generally result in increased commitment. Ironically, the least effective bases of power—coercive, legitimate, and reward—are the ones most likely to be used by managers, perhaps because they are the easiest to implement. By contrast, effective leaders use *expert* and/or *referent power*; these forms of power are not derived from the person's position. *Information power* comes from access to and control over information and can be used in both positive (sharing) and negative (withholding) ways in the organization.

3 **How does dependency affect power?** To maximize your power, you will want to increase others' dependence on you. You can, for instance, increase your power in relation to your employer by developing knowledge or a skill that he or she needs and for which there is no ready substitute. However, you will not be alone in attempting to build your bases of power. Others, particularly employees and peers, will seek to make you dependent on them. The result is a continual struggle for power.

4 **What tactics can be used to increase power?** One particular study identified nine tactics, or strategies, that managers and employees use to increase their power: rational persuasion, inspirational appeals, consultation, ingratiation, personal appeals, exchange, coalitions, pressure, and legitimacy.[85]

5 **What does it mean to be empowered?** *Empowerment* refers to the freedom and the ability of employees to make decisions and commitments. There is a lot of positive press on empowerment. However, much of the talk in organizations about empowerment does not result in employees being empowered. Some managers do not fully understand how to go about empowering their employees, and others find it difficult to share their power with employees. As well, some employees have little or no interest in being empowered, and empowerment is not something that works well in every culture.

6 **How are power and harassment related?** People who engage in harassment in the workplace are typically abusing their power position. Harassment can come in many forms, from gross abuse of power toward anyone of lower rank, to abuse of individuals because of their personal characteristics, such as race, religion, national origin, and gender.

7 **Why do people engage in politics?** People use politics to influence others to help them achieve their personal objectives. Whenever people get together in groups, power will be exerted. People also use impression management to influence people. Impression management is the process by which individuals attempt to control the impression others form of them. Though politics is a natural occurrence in organizations, when it is carried to an extreme it can damage relationships among individuals.

AT WORK

For Review

1. What is power? How do you get it?

2. Contrast the bases of power with influence tactics.

3. What are some of the key contingency variables that determine which tactic a power holder is likely to use?

4. Which of the six bases of power lie with the individual? Which are derived from the organization?

5. State the general dependency postulate. What does it mean?

6. What creates dependency? Give an applied example.

7. Identify the range of empowerment that might be available to employees.

8. Define *sexual harassment*. Who is most likely to harass an employee: a boss, a co-worker, or a subordinate? Explain.

9. How are power and politics related?

10. Define *political behaviour*. Why is politics a fact of life in organizations?

For Critical Thinking

1. Based on the information presented in this chapter, what would you do, as a recent graduate entering a new job, to maximize your power and accelerate your career progress?

2. "Politics is not inherently bad. It is merely a way to get things accomplished within organizations." Do you agree or disagree? Defend your position.

3. You are a sales representative for an international software company. After four excellent years, sales in your territory are off 30 percent this year. Describe three impression management techniques you might use to convince your manager that your sales record is better than should be expected under the circumstances.

4. "Sexual harassment should not be tolerated in the workplace." "Workplace romances are a natural occurrence in organizations." Are both of these statements true? Can they be reconciled?

5. Which impression management techniques have you used? What ethical implications, if any, are there in using impression management?

 **for You**

- Power and politics should not simply be viewed as a win-lose situation. Through power and politics, one builds coalitions to work together effectively. It's possible to make sure that everyone is included.

- There are a variety of ways to increase your power in an organization. As an example, you could acquire more knowledge about a situation and then use that information to negotiate a bonus with your employer. Even if you don't get the bonus, the knowledge may help you in other ways.

- To increase your power, consider how dependent others are on you. Dependency is affected by your importance and substitutability and by the scarcity of options. If you have needed skills that no one else has, you will have more power.

- Politics is a reality of most organizations. Being comfortable with politics is important. Politics is often about making deals with other people for mutual gain.

- Political skills can be developed. Remembering to take time to join in an office birthday celebration for someone is part of developing the skill of working with others effectively.

POINT

COUNTERPOINT

Managing Impressions Is Unethical

Managing impressions is wrong for both ethical and practical reasons. First, managing impressions is just another name for lying. Don't we have a responsibility, both to ourselves and to others, to present ourselves as we really are? Australian philosopher Tony Coady wrote, "Dishonesty has always been perceived in our culture, and in all cultures but the most bizarre, as a central human vice." Immanuel Kant's categorical imperative asks us to consider the following: If you want to know whether telling a lie on a particular occasion is justifiable, you must try to imagine what would happen if everyone were to lie. Surely, you would agree that a world in which no one lies is preferable to one in which lying is common, because in such a world we could never trust anyone. Thus, we should try to present the truth as best we can. Impression management goes against this virtue.

Practically speaking, impression management generally backfires in the long run. Remember Sir Walter Scott's quote, "Oh what a tangled web we weave, when first we practise to deceive!" Once we start to distort the facts, where do we stop? When George O'Leary was hired as the football coach for Notre Dame University (in Indiana), he said on his résumé that 30 years before, he had obtained a degree from Stony Brook University, which he never earned. Obviously, this information was unimportant to his football accomplishments, and ironically, he had written it on his résumé 20 years earlier when hired for a job at Syracuse University; he had simply never corrected the inaccuracy. But when the truth came out, O'Leary was out of a job.

People are most satisfied with their jobs when their values match the culture of the organizations. If either side misrepresents itself in the interview process, then odds are, people will not fit in the organizations they choose. What is the benefit in this?

This does not imply that a person should not put his or her best foot forward. But that means exhibiting qualities that are good no matter the context—being friendly, being positive and self-confident, being qualified and competent, while still being honest.

There Is Nothing Wrong with Managing Impressions

Oh, come on. Get off your high horse. Everybody fudges to some degree in the process of applying for a job. If you really told the interviewer what your greatest weakness or worst mistake was, you would never get hired. What if you answered, "I find it hard to get up in the morning and get to work"?

These sorts of "white lies" are expected and act as a kind of social lubricant. If we really knew what people where thinking, we would go crazy. Moreover, you can quote all the philosophy you want, but sometimes it's necessary to lie. You mean you would not lie to save the life of a family member? It's naive to think we can live in a world without lying.

Sometimes a bit of deception is necessary to get a job. I know a gay applicant who was rejected from a job he really wanted because he told the interviewer he had written two articles for gay magazines. What if he had told the interviewer a little lie? Would harm really have been done? At least he would have a job.

As another example, when an interviewer asks you what you earned on your previous job, that information will be used against you, to pay you a salary lower than you deserve. Is it wrong to boost your salary a bit? Or would it be better to disclose your actual salary and be taken advantage of?

The same goes for complimenting interviewers, agreeing with their opinions, and so forth. If an interviewer tells you, "We believe in community involvement," are you supposed to tell the interviewer you have never volunteered for anything?

Of course, you can go too far. We are not advocating that people totally fabricate their backgrounds. What we are talking about here is a reasonable amount of enhancement. If we can help ourselves without doing any real harm, then impression management is not the same as lying and actually is something we should teach others.

How Political Are You?

To determine your political tendencies, please review the following statements.[86] Check the answer that best represents your behaviour or belief, even if that particular behaviour or belief is not present all the time.

		True	False
1.	You should make others feel important through an open appreciation of their ideas and work.	____	____
2.	Because people tend to judge you when they first meet you, always try to make a good first impression.	____	____
3.	Try to let others do most of the talking, be sympathetic to their problems, and resist telling people that they are totally wrong.	____	____
4.	Praise the good traits of the people you meet and always give people an opportunity to save face if they are wrong or make a mistake.	____	____
5.	Spreading false rumours, planting misleading information, and backstabbing are necessary, if somewhat unpleasant, methods to deal with your enemies.	____	____
6.	Sometimes it is necessary to make promises that you know you will not or cannot keep.	____	____
7.	It's important to get along with everybody, even with those who are generally recognized as windbags, abrasive, or constant complainers.	____	____
8.	It's vital to do favours for others so that you can call in these IOUs at times when they will do you the most good.	____	____
9.	Be willing to compromise, particularly on issues that are minor to you but major to others.	____	____
10.	On controversial issues, it's important to delay or avoid your involvement if possible.	____	____

Scoring Key:

According to the author of this instrument, a complete organizational politician will answer "true" to all 10 questions. Organizational politicians with fundamental ethical standards will answer "false" to questions 5 and 6, which deal with deliberate lies and uncharitable behaviour. Individuals who regard manipulation, incomplete disclosure, and self-serving behaviour as unacceptable will answer "false" to all or almost all of the questions.

More Learning About Yourself Exercises

Additional self-assessments relevant to this chapter appear on MyOBLab (**www.pearsoned.ca/myoblab**).

IV.F.1 Is My Workplace Political?

II.C.3 How Good Am I at Playing Politics?

When you complete the additional assessments, consider the following:

1. Am I surprised about my score?

2. Would my friends evaluate me similarly?

BREAKOUT **GROUP** EXERCISES

Form small groups to discuss the following topics, as assigned by your instructor:

1. Describe an incident where you tried to use political behaviour in order to get something you wanted. What influence tactics did you use?

2. In thinking about the incident described above, were your influence tactics effective? Why?

3. Describe an incident where you saw someone engaging in politics. What was your reaction to observing the political behaviour? Under what circumstances do you think political behaviour is appropriate?

WORKING WITH **OTHERS** EXERCISE

Understanding Bases of Power

Step 1:   Your instructor will divide the class into groups of about 5 or 6 (making sure there are at least 5 groups).[87] Each group will be assigned 1 of the following bases of power: (1) coercive, (2) reward, (3) legitimate, (4) expert, and (5) referent. Refer to your text for discussion of these terms.

Step 2:   Each group is to develop a role play that highlights the use of the power assigned. The role play should be developed using the following scenario:

> *You are the leader of a group that is trying to develop a website for a new client. One of your group members, who was assigned the task of researching and analyzing the websites of your client's competition, has twice failed to bring the analysis to scheduled meetings, even though the member knew the assignment was due. Consequently, your group is falling behind in getting the website developed. As leader of the group, you have decided to speak with this team member and to use your specific brand of power to influence the individual's behaviour.*

Step 3:   Each group should select 1 person to play the group leader and another to play the member who has not done the assignment. You have 10 minutes to prepare an influence plan.

Step 4:   Each group will conduct its role play. In the event of multiple groups assigned the same power base, 1 of the groups may be asked to volunteer. While you are watching the other groups' role plays, try to put yourself in the place of the person being influenced, to see whether that type of influence would cause you to change your behaviour.

Immediately after each role play, while the next one is being set up, you should pretend that you were the person being influenced, and then record your reaction using the questionnaire opposite. To do this, take out a sheet of paper and tear it into 5 (or 6) pieces. At the top of each piece of paper, write the type of influence that was used. Then write the letters A, B, C, and D in a column, and indicate which number on the scale (see opposite) reflects the influence attempt.

Reaction to Influence Questionnaire

For each role play, think of yourself as being on the receiving end of the influence attempt described, and record your own reaction.

Type of power used _____

A. As a result of the influence attempt, I will . . .

| **definitely not comply** | 1 | 2 | 3 | 4 | 5 | **definitely comply** |

B. Any change that does come about will be . . .

| **temporary** | 1 | 2 | 3 | 4 | 5 | **long-lasting** |

C. My own personal reaction is . . .

| **resistant** | 1 | 2 | 3 | 4 | 5 | **accepting** |

D. As a result of this influence attempt, my relationship with my group leader will probably be . . .

| **worse** | 1 | 2 | 3 | 4 | 5 | **better** |

Step 5: For each influence type, 1 member of each group will take the pieces of paper from group members and calculate the average group score for each of the 4 questions. For efficiency, this should be done while the role plays are being conducted.

Step 6: Your instructor will collect the summaries from each group, and then lead a discussion based on these results.

Step 7: Discussion.

1. Which kind of influence is most likely to immediately result in the desired behaviour?

2. Which will have the most long-lasting effects?

3. What effect will using a particular base of power have on the ongoing relationship?

4. Which form of power will others find most acceptable? Least acceptable? Why?

5. Are there some situations where a particular type of influence strategy might be more effective than others?

ETHICAL **DILEMMA** EXERCISE

Swapping Personal Favours?

Jack Grubman was a powerful man on Wall Street.[88] As a star analyst of telecom companies for the Salomon Smith Barney unit of Citigroup, his recommendations carried a lot of weight with investors.

For years, Grubman had been negative on the stock of AT&T. But in November 1999, he upgraded his opinion on the stock. Based on email evidence, it appears that Grubman's decision to upgrade AT&T was not based on the stock's fundamentals. There were other factors involved.

At the time, his boss at Citigroup, Sanford Weill, was in the midst of a power struggle with co-CEO John Reed to become the single head of the company. Meanwhile, Salomon was looking for additional business to increase its revenues. Getting investment banking business fees from AT&T would be a big plus toward improving revenues. Salomon's efforts at getting that AT&T business would definitely be improved if Grubman would upgrade his opinion on the stock. Furthermore, Weill sought Grubman's upgrade to win favour with AT&T CEO Michael Armstrong, who sat on Citigroup's board. Weill wanted Armstrong's backing in his efforts to oust Reed.

Grubman had his own concerns. Although he was earning tens of millions a year in his job, he was a man of modest background. He was the son of a city worker in Philadelphia. He wanted the best for his twin daughters, which included entry to an exclusive New York City nursery school—a school that a year earlier had reportedly turned down Madonna's daughter. Weill made a call on Grubman's behalf to the school and pledged a $1-million donation from Citigroup.

At approximately the same time, Weill also asked Grubman to "take a fresh look" at his neutral rating on AT&T. Shortly after being asked to review his rating, Grubman turned positive, raised his rating, and AT&T awarded Salomon an investment-banking job worth nearly $45 million.

Did Sanford Weill do anything unethical? How about Jack Grubman? What do you think?

CASE INCIDENTS

Damned If You Do; Damned If You Don't

Fran Gill has spent 15 years with the Thompson Grocery Company, starting out as a part-time cashier and rising up through the ranks of the grocery store chain.[89] Today, at 34, she is a regional manager, overseeing seven stores and earning nearly $110 000 a year. About five weeks ago, she was contacted by an executive-search firm inquiring about her interest in the position of vice-president and regional manager for a national drugstore chain. The position would be responsible for more than 100 stores in five provinces. After two meetings with top executives at the drugstore chain, she was notified two days ago that she was one of two finalists for the job.

The only person at Thompson who knows this news is Fran's good friend and colleague Ken Hamilton. Ken is director of finance for the grocery chain. "It's a dream job, with a lot more responsibility," Fran told Ken. "The pay is almost double what I earn here, and I'd be their only female vice-president. The job would allow me to be a more visible role model for young women and give me a bigger voice in opening up doors for women and ethnic minorities in retail management."

Since Fran wanted to keep the fact that she was looking at another job secret, she asked Ken, whom she trusted completely, to be one of her references. He promised to write a great recommendation for her. Fran made it very clear to the recruiter that Ken was the only person at Thompson who knew she was considering another job. She knew that if anyone heard she was talking to another company, it might seriously jeopardize her chances for promotion. It's against this backdrop that this morning's incident became more than just a question of sexual harassment. It became a full-blown ethical and political dilemma for Fran.

Jennifer Chung has been a financial analyst in Ken's department for five months. Fran met Jennifer through Ken, and her impression of Jennifer is quite positive. In many ways, Jennifer strikes Fran as a lot like she was 10 years ago. This morning, Jennifer came into Fran's office. It was immediately evident that something was wrong. Jennifer was very nervous and uncomfortable, which was most unlike her. Jennifer said that about a month after she joined Thompson, Ken began making off-colour comments to her when they were alone. From there the behaviour escalated further. Ken would leer at her, put his arm over her shoulder when they were reviewing reports, even pat her bum. Every time one of these occurrences happened, Jennifer would ask him to stop and not do it again, but this fell on deaf ears. Yesterday, Ken reminded Jennifer that her six-month probationary review was coming up. "He told me that if I didn't sleep with him, I couldn't expect a very favourable evaluation."

Jennifer said that she had come to Fran because she did not know what to do or to whom to turn. "I came to you, Fran, because you're a friend of Ken's and the highest-ranking woman here. Will you help me?" Fran had never heard anything like this about Ken before, but neither did she have any reason to suspect that Jennifer was lying.

Questions

1. Analyze Fran's situation in a purely legal sense.

2. Analyze Fran's dilemma in political terms.

3. Analyze Fran's situation in an ethical sense. What is the ethically right thing for her to do? Is that also the politically right thing to do?

4. If you were Fran, what would you do?

The Politics of Backstabbing

Scott Rosen believed that he was making progress as an assistant manager of a financial-services company—until he noticed that his colleague, another assistant manager, was attempting to push him aside.[90] On repeated occasions, Rosen would observe his colleague speaking with their manager behind closed doors. During these conversations, Rosen's colleague would attempt to persuade the supervisor that Rosen was incompetent and mismanaging his job, a practice that Rosen found out after the fact. Rosen recounts one specific instance of his colleague's backstabbing efforts: When a subordinate asked Rosen a question to which Rosen did not know the answer, his colleague would say to their supervisor, "I can't believe he didn't know something like that." On other occasions, after instructing a subordinate to complete a specific task, Rosen's colleague would say, "I wouldn't make you do something like that." What was the end result of such illegitimate political tactics? Rosen was demoted, an action that led him to resign shortly after, while his colleague was promoted. "Whatever I did, I lost," recounts Rosen.

What leads individuals to behave this way? According to Judith Briles, a management consultant who has extensively studied the practice of backstabbing, a tight job market is often a contributing factor. Fred Nader, another management consultant, believes that backstabbing is the result of "some kind of character disorder."

One executive at a technology company admits that blind ambition was responsible for the backstabbing he did. In 1999, he was assigned as an external sales representative, partnered with a colleague who worked internally at their client's office. The executive wanted the internal sales position for himself. To reach this goal, he systematically engaged in backstabbing to shatter his colleague's credibility. Each time he heard a complaint, however small, from the client, he would ask for it in an email and then forward the information to his boss. He would include a short message about his colleague, such as: "I'm powerless to deal with this. She's not being responsive and the customer is beating on me." In addition, he would fail to share important information with her before presentations with their boss, to convey the impression that she did not know what she was talking about. He even went so far as to schedule meetings with

their boss on an electronic calendar, but then altered her version so that she was late. Eventually, he convinced his boss that she was overworked. He was transferred to the client's office, while his colleague was moved back to the main office.

Incidents such as these may not be uncommon in the workplace. Given today's competitive work environment, employees may be using political games to move ahead. To guard against backstabbing, Bob McDonald, a management consultant, recommends telling supervisors and other key personnel that the backstabber is not a friend. He states that this may be effective because backstabbers often claim to be friends of their victims, and then act as if they are hesitant about sharing negative information with others because of this professed friendship. In any event, it is clear that employees in organizations need to be aware of illegitimate political behaviour. Companies may need to adopt formal policies to safeguard employees against such behaviour; however, it may be the case that behaviours such as backstabbing and spreading negative rumours are difficult to detect. Thus, both employees and managers should try to verify information to avoid the negative repercussions that can come from backstabbing and other illegitimate behaviours.

Questions

1. What factors, in addition to those cited here, do you believe lead to illegitimate political behaviours such as backstabbing?

2. Imagine that a colleague is engaging in illegitimate political behaviour toward you. What steps might you take to reduce or eliminate this behaviour? Do you believe that it is ever justifiable to engage in illegitimate political behaviours such as backstabbing? If so, what are some conditions that might justify such behaviour?

4. In addition to the obvious negative effects of illegitimate political behaviour on victims, such as those described in this case, what might be some negative effects on the perpetrators? On the organization as a whole?

From **Concepts** to **Skills**

Politicking

Forget, for a moment, the ethics of politicking and any negative impressions you may have of people who engage in organizational politics.[91] If you wanted to be more politically adept in your organization, what could you do? The following eight suggestions are likely to improve your political effectiveness:

1. *Frame arguments in terms of organizational goals.* Effective politicking requires camouflaging your self-interest. No matter that your objective is self-serving; all the arguments you marshal in support of it must be framed in terms of the benefits that the organization will gain. People whose actions appear to blatantly further their own interests at the expense of the organization's are almost universally denounced, are likely to lose influence, and often suffer the ultimate penalty of being expelled from the organization.

2. *Develop the right image.* If you know your organization's culture, you understand what the organization wants and values from its employees—in terms of dress; associates to cultivate, and those to avoid; whether to appear risk-taking or risk-aversive; the preferred leadership style; the importance placed on getting along well with others; and so forth. Then you are equipped to project the appropriate image. Because the assessment of your performance is not a fully objective process, both style and substance must be addressed.

3. *Gain control of organizational resources.* The control of organizational resources that are scarce and important is a source of power. Knowledge and expertise are particularly effective resources to control. They make you more valuable to the organization and, therefore, more likely to gain security, advancement, and a receptive audience for your ideas.

4. *Make yourself appear indispensable.* Because we are dealing with appearances rather than objective facts, you can enhance your power by appearing to be indispensable. That is, you don't have to really be indispensable as long as key people in the organization believe that you are. If the organization's prime decision makers believe there is

no ready substitute for what you are giving the organization, they are likely to go to great lengths to ensure that your desires are satisfied.

5. *Be visible.* Because performance evaluation has a substantial subjective component, it's important that your manager and those in power in the organization be made aware of your contribution. If you are fortunate enough to have a job that brings your accomplishments to the attention of others, it may not be necessary to take direct measures to increase your visibility. But your job may require you to handle activities that are low in visibility, or your specific contribution may be indistinguishable because you are part of a team endeavour. In such cases, without appearing to be tooting your own horn or creating the image of a braggart, you will want to call attention to yourself by highlighting your successes in routine reports, having satisfied customers relay their appreciation to senior executives in your organization, being seen at social functions, being active in your professional associations, developing powerful allies who speak positively about your accomplishments, and similar tactics. Of course, the skilled politician actively and successfully lobbies to get those projects that will increase his or her visibility.

6. *Develop powerful allies.* It helps to have powerful people in your camp. Cultivate contacts with potentially influential people above you, at your own level, and in the lower ranks. They can provide you with important information that may not be available through normal channels. There will be times, too, when decisions will be made in favour of those with the greatest support. Having powerful allies can provide you with a coalition of support if and when you need it.

7. *Avoid "tainted" members.* In almost every organization, there are fringe members whose status is questionable. Their performance and/or loyalty is suspect. Keep your distance from such individuals. Given the reality that effectiveness has a large subjective component, your own effectiveness might be called into question if you are perceived as being too closely associated with tainted members.

8. *Support your manager.* Your immediate future is in the hands of your current manager. Since he or she evaluates your performance, you will typically want to do whatever is necessary to have your manager on your side. You should make every effort to help your manager succeed, make her look good, and support her if she is under siege, and to spend the time to find out what criteria she will be using to assess your effectiveness. Do not undermine your manager, and do not speak negatively of her to others.

Practising Skills

You used to be the star marketing manager for Hilton Electronics Corporation. But for the past year, you have been outpaced again and again by Sean, a new manager in the design department who has been accomplishing everything expected of him and more. Meanwhile, your best efforts to do your job well have been sabotaged and undercut by Maria—your and Sean's manager. For example, before last year's international consumer electronics show, Maria moved $30 000 from your budget to Sean's. Despite your best efforts, your marketing team could not complete all the marketing materials normally developed to showcase all of your organization's new products at this important industry show. Also, Maria has chipped away at your staff and budget ever since. Although you have been able to meet most of your goals with less staff and budget, Maria has continued to slice away resources from your group. Just last week, she eliminated two positions in your team of eight marketing specialists to make room for a new designer and some extra equipment for Sean. Maria is clearly taking away your resources while giving Sean whatever he wants and more. You think it's time to do something, or soon you will not have any team or resources left. What do you need to do to make sure your division has the resources to survive and grow?

Reinforcing Skills

1. Keep a one-week journal of your behaviour, describing incidents when you tried to influence others around you. Assess each incident by asking: Were you successful at these attempts to influence them? Why or why not? What could you have done differently?

2. Outline a specific action plan, based on concepts in this module, that would improve your career progression in the organization in which you currently work or an organization in which you think you would like to be employed.

VIDEO CASE INCIDENT

CASE 8 Whistle-blowers at the RCMP

CBC

In 2007, four members of the RCMP went public with charges of fraud, misrepresentation, corruption, and nepotism against the leadership of the RCMP. The most senior member of the group was Fraser Macauley, a career Mountie who had worked his way up through the ranks to become a senior human resource officer. He said he had tried to alert his bosses to problems at the RCMP, but that he was lied to, shunned, and eventually pushed out of his job for his whistle-blowing activity.

While it is very unusual to see Mounties talking publicly about fraud, nepotism, and other criminal allegations, the four Mounties testified that a senior group of managers at the RCMP had breached the organization's core values *and* the criminal code. Macauley recognizes that the RCMP is taking a hit in its reputation, but he came forward because he felt that doing so would eventually make the organization a better place.

Many Canadians are wondering how something like this could happen in our national police force. Macauley says that a small group of top managers used the RCMP pension fund to hire people who were related to senior members of the force and who were not even doing pension fund work. The four Mounties who testified said that when they reported this unacceptable activity to senior management, they were stonewalled and punished.

When the allegations first emerged, an internal investigation was launched by the RCMP, but then cancelled by Commissioner Giuliano Zaccardelli. The Ottawa city police then conducted its own investigation, but no formal charges were laid. The Auditor General eventually confirmed much of what Macauley was saying, but by that time he had been transferred to the Department of National Defence (DND). Macauley says the DND was known as the "penalty box." He is certain that he was transferred because he had been looking into pension fund irregularities. He also received a reduced performance bonus from his boss, Assistant Commissioner Barbara George. He was told that happened because he did not support the commissioner.

During his last conversation with Commissioner Zaccardelli, Macauley was told "it was time to go." This was an emotional conversation and Macauley felt terrible. He told Zaccardelli that he (Macauley) had never lied to the commissioner before, so why did Zaccardelli think he would start now? Zaccardelli called the accusations Macauley was making "baseless" and said that the pension fund was not at risk. Macauley points out that he never said that the pension fund was at risk, but that funds were being used in an unacceptable manner and relatives of top managers were being paid for work that was not pension-fund related. Macauley says that now it's about accountability for decisions that top managers made.

After the public investigation, Macauley was reinstated in his former job. His boss, Barbara George, was suspended from her job for allegedly misleading the parliamentary committee that was looking into the allegations. Commissioner Zaccardelli is no longer with the RCMP.

Questions

1. List and briefly describe the bases of power that are available in organizations. Which bases were being used by the top managers at the RCMP?

2. Why were individuals like Macauley dependent on people like Barbara George and Commissioner Zaccardelli?

3. What is political behaviour? To what extent was it evident at the RCMP?

4. Consider the "Magnificent Seven" ethical principles listed in Chapter 3 of the text. Which of these do you think were violated by the top managers at the RCMP? Explain your reasoning.

Source: Based on "Whistleblower," *CBC News: Sunday*, April 1, 2007.

Conflict and Negotiation

York University and CUPE 3903 needed to negotiate a new collective bargaining agreement. What difficulties led them to take so long to reach a deal?

1 What is conflict?

2 How can conflict be resolved?

3 What are the effects of conflict?

4 How does one negotiate effectively?

5 What are the contemporary issues in negotiation?

*I*n July 2008, the contract of CUPE local 3903, the union of almost 3400 contract professors, teaching assistants, and research assistants at York University, was coming up for renewal.[1] Union members gathered together to determine what they wanted to achieve in the next round of collective bargaining with the university. Bargaining did not go well, and each side blamed the other for the stalemate.

"York's bargaining team spent over 40 days in negotiations with CUPE 3903 beginning in July of [2008]," Mamdouh Shoukri, York's President said. "After six months, which included 11 weeks on strike, the union's last offer was still more than double the university's offer for settlement. That is an impasse by any standards."

CUPE members saw the issue somewhat differently. "They are acting more like a private-sector, hard-nosed corporation than a public university that is supposed to be serving the public," said Punam Khosla, a union member and spokeswoman for Local 3903. She also suggested that the university distributed "'confusing information' about the talks."

CUPE 3903 and York University were locked in a conflict that led to the cancellation of classes for three months during the 2008–2009 academic year.

In this chapter, we look at sources of conflict and strategies for resolving conflict, including negotiation.

 **Is for Everyone**

- Is conflict always bad?
- Can someone else be asked to help resolve a conflict?
- Should you try to win at any cost when you bargain?
- Ever wonder if men and women negotiate differently?

 **Self-Assessment Library**

LEARNING ABOUT YOURSELF

- Conflict Handling
- Negotiating

Conflict Defined

1   What is conflict?

conflict A process that begins when one party perceives that another party has negatively affected, or is about to negatively affect, something that the first party cares about.

Several common themes underlie most definitions of conflict.[2] Conflict must be *perceived* by the parties to it; if no one is aware of a conflict, then it is generally agreed that no conflict exists. Conflict also involves opposition or incompatibility, and some form of interaction between the parties.[3] These factors set the conditions that determine the beginning point of the conflict process. We can define **conflict**, then, as a process that begins when one party perceives that another party has negatively affected, or is about to negatively affect, something that the first party cares about.[4]

This definition is deliberately broad. It describes that point in any ongoing activity when an interaction "crosses over" to become an interparty conflict. It encompasses the wide range of conflicts that people experience in groups and organizations—incompatibility of goals, differences over interpretations of facts, disagreements based on behavioural expectations, and the like. Finally, our definition is flexible enough to cover the full range of conflict levels—from subtle forms of disagreement to overt and violent acts.

Conflict has positive sides and negative sides, which we will discuss further when we cover functional and dysfunctional conflict. For more on this debate, refer to the *Point/Counterpoint* discussion on page 360.

Functional vs. Dysfunctional Conflict

functional conflict Conflict that supports the goals of the group and improves its performance.

dysfunctional conflict Conflict that hinders group performance.

Is conflict always bad?

Not all conflict is bad. Some conflicts support the goals of the group and improve its performance; these are **functional**, or constructive, forms of conflict. But there are conflicts that hinder group performance; these are **dysfunctional**, or destructive, forms of conflict. The criterion that differentiates functional from dysfunctional conflict is group performance. If a group is unable to achieve its goals because of conflict, then the conflict is dysfunctional.

Exhibit 9-1 provides a way of visualizing conflict behaviour. All conflicts exist somewhere along this continuum. At the lower part of the continuum, we have conflicts characterized by subtle, indirect, and highly controlled forms of tension. An illustration might be a student politely objecting to a point the instructor has just made in class. Conflict intensities escalate as they move upward along the continuum, until they become highly destructive. Strikes and lockouts, riots, and wars clearly fall in this upper range. For the most part, you should assume that conflicts that reach the upper ranges of the continuum are almost always dysfunctional. Functional conflicts are typically confined to the lower range of the continuum.

RESEARCH FINDINGS: Cognitive and Affective Conflict

cognitive conflict Conflict that is task-oriented and related to differences in perspectives and judgments.

affective conflict Conflict that is emotional and aimed at a person rather than an issue.

Research on conflict has yet to clearly identify those situations where conflict is more likely to be constructive than destructive. However, there is growing evidence that the source of the conflict is a significant factor determining functionality.[5] **Cognitive conflict**, which is task-oriented and occurs because of differences in perspectives and judgments, can often result in identifying potential solutions to problems. Thus it would be regarded as functional conflict. **Affective conflict**, which is emotional and aimed at a person rather than an issue, tends to be dysfunctional conflict.

One study of 53 teams found that cognitive conflict, because it generates more alternatives, led to better decisions, more acceptance of the decisions, and ownership of the decisions. Teams experiencing affective conflict, where members had personality incompatibilities and disputes, had poorer decisions and lower levels of acceptance of the decisions.[6]

Because conflict can involve our emotions in a variety of ways, it can also lead to stress. You may want to refer to the *OB on the Edge—Stress at Work* on pages 120–127 to get some ideas on how to manage the stress that might arise from conflicts you experience.

Sources of Conflict

There are a number of conditions that can give rise to conflict. They *need not* lead directly to conflict, but at least one of these conditions is necessary if conflict is to surface. For simplicity's sake, these conditions (which we can also look at as causes or sources of conflict) have been condensed into three general categories: communication, structure, and personal variables.[7]

Communication

As we saw in Chapter 7, communication can be a source of conflict through semantic difficulties, misunderstandings, and "noise" in the communication channels.

Research has demonstrated a surprising finding: The potential for conflict increases when either too little or too much communication takes place. Apparently, an increase in communication is functional up to a point, whereupon it is possible to overcommunicate, with a resultant increase in the potential for conflict. Furthermore, the channel chosen for communicating can have an influence on stimulating opposition. Poor communication is certainly not the source of all conflicts, however.

Structure

Conflicts between two people can be structural in nature; that is, they can be the consequence of the requirements of the job or the workplace more than personality. For instance, it is not uncommon for the sales department to be in conflict with the production department, if sales perceives that products will be delivered late to customers. The term *structure* in this context includes variables such as size of the group, degree of specialization in the tasks assigned to group members, composition of the group, jurisdictional clarity, reward systems, leadership style, goal compatibility, and the degree of dependence between groups.

A review of structural variables that can lead to conflict in the workplace suggests the following:

- *Size, specialization, and composition* of the group act as forces to stimulate conflict. The larger the group and the more specialized its activities, the greater the likelihood of conflict. The potential for conflict tends to be greatest where group members are younger and where turnover is high.

- *The greater the ambiguity* in precisely defining where responsibility for actions lies, the greater the potential for conflict to emerge. Such jurisdictional ambiguities increase intergroup fighting for control of resources and territory.

- *Reward systems* create conflict when one member's gain is at another's expense. Similarly, the performance evaluation process can create conflict when individuals feel that they are unfairly evaluated, or when managers and employees have differing ideas about the employees' job responsibilities.

- *Leadership style* can create conflict if managers tightly control and oversee the work of employees, allowing employees little discretion in how they carry out tasks.

EXHIBIT 9-1 Conflict Intensity Continuum

Annihilatory conflict	Overt efforts to destroy the other party
	Aggressive physical attacks
	Threats and ultimatums
	Assertive verbal attacks
	Overt questioning or challenging of others
No conflict	Minor disagreements or misunderstandings

Sources: Based on S. P. Robbins, *Managing Organizational Conflict: A Nontraditional Approach* (Upper Saddle River, NJ: Prentice Hall, 1974), pp. 93–97; and F. Glasl, "The Process of Conflict Escalation and the Roles of Third Parties," in *Conflict Management and Industrial Relations*, ed. G. B. J. Bomers and R. Peterson (Boston: Kluwer-Nijhoff, 1982), pp. 119–140.

- *The diversity of goals* among groups is a major source of conflict. When groups within an organization seek diverse ends, some of which are inherently at odds—such as when the sales team promises products that the development team has not yet finalized—opportunities for conflict increase.

- *If one group is dependent on another* (in contrast to the two being mutually independent), or if interdependence allows one group to gain at another's expense, opposing forces are stimulated.

Focus on Diversity illustrates how York University's goal of having all exams marked in the same time period conflicted with the religious needs of some students. Rather than address the different religious needs of students, the university chose to treat everyone equally.

FOCUS ON **DIVERSITY**

Exam-Taking Students Faced with Sabbath Dilemma

Should students with religious needs receive special accommodation? Sabbath-observant Jewish students at York University had a choice to make during their final exam period.[8] They could take exams that were scheduled on the Sabbath, something they would not ordinarily expect to do, or ask for special arrangements to take their exams on another day.

The University of Toronto, McGill University, and York University, which all have significant Jewish faculty and student populations, had not previously scheduled exams on Saturdays. Administrators at York University decided that they could no longer follow this practice, and scheduled final exams for two Saturdays.

York's student population had been growing faster than the capacity of the existing space, which was one reason for scheduling exams on Saturdays, according to Deborah Hobson, York's former vice-president of enrolment and student services. More professors were also giving exams rather than term papers to prevent the use of Internet-purchased papers.

Hobson noted that no special accommodation had been made for Christian or Muslim students regarding exam scheduling. Instead, groups had to ask for accommodation if religious constraints caused a conflict. "In scheduling exams on the Jewish Sabbath, it was felt that all religions would be treated fairly," Hobson said.

The Sabbath does present limitations on exam writing that most other religions do not, but Hobson felt that providing alternative arrangements upon the request of students would pose little difficulty.

Professor Martin Lockshin, director of the Centre for Jewish Studies at York University, worried that Jewish students might not want to ask for special accommodation. Some students fear that asking professors for makeup exams not only burdens professors, but could also harm the students. It means extra work for professors, and the concern is that students' marks might be affected. The students' concerns in this matter reflect power issues that we discussed in Chapter 8. Students recognize that there is a power imbalance in their relationship with professors, which makes them reluctant to ask for special exam accommodation.

Some faculty members also wondered whether "the way to demonstrate tolerance to . . . various multicultural communities is by not giving religious accommodation to anyone."

Personal variables such as personality differences can be the source of conflict among co-workers. To reduce conflict resulting from personality differences, Vertex Pharmaceuticals teaches employees how to identify other people's personality types, and then how to communicate effectively with them. At Vertex, innovation is critical to the company's mission of developing drugs that treat life-threatening diseases. By training employees to work harmoniously in spite of personality differences, Vertex hopes to eliminate unproductive conflict that impedes innovation.

Personal Variables

Have you ever met people to whom you take an immediate dislike? You disagree with most of their opinions. The sound of their voice, their smirk when they smile, and their personality annoy you. We have all met people like that. When you have to work with such individuals, there is often the potential for conflict.

Our last category of potential sources of conflict is personal variables. These variables include the individual value system that each person has, and the personality characteristics that account for individual idiosyncrasies and differences.

The evidence indicates that certain personality types—for example, individuals who are highly authoritarian and dogmatic, and who demonstrate low self-esteem—lead to potential conflict. Most important, and probably the most overlooked variable in the study of social conflict, is differing value systems. For example, value differences are the best explanation of such diverse issues as prejudice, disagreements over an individual's contribution to the group and the rewards the individual deserves, and assessments of whether this particular textbook is any good. That an employee thinks he is worth $60 000 a year but his manager believes him to be worth $55 000 are value judgments. Differences in value systems are important sources for creating the potential for conflict.

Conflict Resolution

For the three months that CUPE 3903 was on strike, prior to being legislated back to work in January 2009, York University and CUPE were both quick to suggest that the other side was to blame for the conflict not being resolved.[9] Christina Rousseau, chair of the union local, acknowledged that the pay for the local's employees was among the highest in Canada, but not enough. "It is one of the best in the country," she said of the pay levels. "If we are the best paid, the pay that we get is still not anywhere near where it should be." York University president Mamdouh Shoukri saw it differently: "We are not going back to the bargaining table . . . York is taking a stand to protect its academic and financial future," he said.

York University and CUPE 3903 may have been unable to resolve their conflict because each party had some interest in maintaining its own position, rather than searching for a way to reach a compromise. What are other ways that the University and CUPE might have tried to resolve their conflict?

2 How can conflict be resolved?

Conflict in the workplace can affect the effectiveness of individuals, teams, and the entire organization.[10] One study found that 20 percent of managers' time is spent managing conflict.[11]

Once conflict arises, what can be done to resolve it? The way a conflict is defined goes a long way toward establishing the sort of outcomes that might settle it. For instance, if I define our salary disagreement as a zero-sum or *win-lose situation*—that is, if you get the increase in pay you want, there will be just that amount less for me—I am going to be far less willing to look for mutual solutions than if I frame the conflict as a potential *win-win situation*. So individual attitudes toward a conflict are important, because attitudes typically define the set of possible settlements.

Conflict Management Strategies

Conflict researchers often use *dual concern theory* to describe people's conflict management strategies.[12] Dual concern theory considers how one's degree of *cooperativeness* (the degree to which one tries to satisfy the other person's concerns) and *assertiveness* (the degree to which one tries to satisfy one's own concerns) determine how a conflict is handled.[13] The five conflict-handling strategies identified by the theory are as follows:

- *Forcing.* Imposing one's will on the other party.

- *Problem solving.* Trying to reach an agreement that satisfies both one's own and the other party's aspirations as much as possible.

- *Avoiding.* Ignoring or minimizing the importance of the issues creating the conflict.

- *Yielding.* Accepting and incorporating the will of the other party.

- *Compromising.* Balancing concern for oneself with concern for the other party in order to reach a solution.

Forcing is a win-lose solution, as is yielding, while problem solving seeks a win-win solution. Avoiding conflict and pretending it does not exist, and compromising, so that neither person gets what they want, can yield lose-lose solutions. Exhibit 9-2 on page 342 illustrates these five strategies, along with specific actions that one might take when using them.

Choosing a particular strategy for resolving conflict depends on a variety of factors. Research shows that while people may choose among the strategies, they have an underlying disposition to handle conflicts in certain ways.[14] In addition, some situations call for particular strategies. For instance, when a small child insists on trying to run into the street, a parent may need a forcing strategy to restrain the child. Co-workers who are having a conflict over setting deadlines to complete a project on time may decide that problem solving is the best strategy to use.

This chapter's *Learning About Yourself Exercise* on page 361 gives you the opportunity to discover your preferred conflict-handling strategy. *OB in Action—Choosing Strategies to Deal with Conflicts* indicates the situations in which each strategy is best used.

Learning About Yourself

What Is Your Primary Conflict-Handling Style?,
(page 361)

OB in ACTION
Choosing Strategies to Deal with Conflicts

Forcing
→ In **emergencies**
→ On **important** but unpopular **issues**
→ On **vital issues** when you know you are right
→ Against **people who take advantage** of noncompetitive behaviour

Problem solving
→ If both sets of concerns are **too important for compromise**
→ To **merge different perspectives**
→ To **gain commitment** through a consensus
→ To **mend a relationship**

Avoiding
→ When an issue is **trivial**
→ When your **concerns won't be met**
→ When potential **disruption outweighs the benefits** of resolution
→ To let people **cool down** and regain perspective

Yielding
→ When you find **you are wrong**
→ To show your **reasonableness**
→ When **issues are more important to others** than yourself
→ To **build social credits** for later issues
→ When **harmony and stability** are especially important

Compromising
→ When **goals are important but not worth more assertive approaches**
→ When opponents are committed to **mutually exclusive goals**
→ To achieve **temporary settlements** to complex issues
→ To arrive at **expedient solutions** under time pressure[15]

What Can Individuals Do to Manage Conflict?

There are a number of conflict resolution techniques that individuals can use to try to defuse conflict inside and outside of the workplace. These include the following:[16]

- *Problem solving.* Requesting a face-to-face meeting to identify the problem and resolve it through open discussion.

- *Developing overarching goals.* Creating a shared goal that requires both parties to work together, and motivates them to do so.

- *Smoothing.* Playing down differences while emphasizing common interests with the other party.

- *Compromising.* Agreeing with the other party that each will give up something of value to reach an accord.

- *Avoidance.* Withdrawing from or suppressing the conflict.

The choice of technique may depend on how serious the issue is to you, whether you take a win-win or a win-lose approach, and your preferred conflict management style.

When the conflict is specifically work-related, there are additional techniques that might be used:

- *Expansion of resources.* The scarcity of a resource—say, money, promotion opportunities, office space—can create conflict. Expansion of the resource can create a win-win solution.

- *Authoritative command.* Management can use its formal authority to resolve the conflict and then communicate its desires to the parties involved.

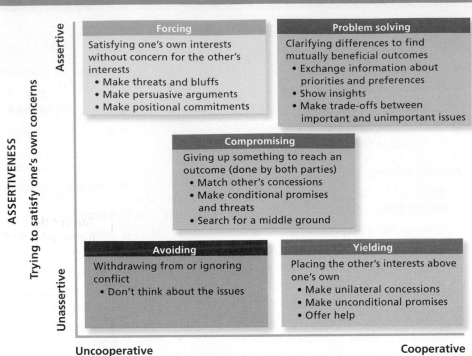

EXHIBIT 9-2   Conflict-Handling Strategies and Accompanying Behaviours

Sources: Based on K. W. Thomas, "Conflict and Negotiation Processes in Organizations," in *Handbook of Industrial and Organizational Psychology*, vol. 3, 2nd ed., ed. M. D. Dunnette and L. M. Hough (Palo Alto, CA: Consulting Psychologists Press, 1992), p. 668; C. K. W. De Dreu, A. Evers, B. Beersma, E. S. Kluwer, and A. Nauta, "A Theory-Based Measure of Conflict Management Strategies in the Workplace," *Journal of Organizational Behavior* 22, no. 6 (September 2001), pp. 645–668; and D. G. Pruitt and J. Rubin, *Social Conflict: Escalation, Stalemate and Settlement* (New York: Random House, 1986).

- *Altering the human variable.* Behavioural change techniques such as human relations training can alter attitudes and behaviours that cause conflict.

- *Altering the structural variables.* The formal organization structure and the interaction patterns of conflicting parties can be changed through job redesign, transfers, creation of coordinating positions, and the like.

Resolving Personality Conflicts

Personality conflicts are an everyday occurrence in the workplace. While there are no available data for Canada, supervisors in the United States spend about 18 percent of their time handling personality conflicts among employees.[17] A variety of factors lead to personality conflicts, including the following:[18]

- Misunderstandings based on age, race, or cultural differences

- Intolerance, prejudice, discrimination, or bigotry

- Perceived inequities

- Misunderstandings, rumours, or falsehoods about an individual or group

- Blaming for mistakes or mishaps (finger-pointing)

Personality conflicts can result in lowered productivity when people find it difficult to work together. The individuals experiencing the conflict may seek sympathy from other members of the work group, causing co-workers to take sides. The ideal solution would be for the two people having a conflict to work it out between themselves, without involving others, but this does not always happen. *OB in Action—Handling Personality Conflicts* suggests ways of dealing with personality conflicts in the workplace.

Resolving Intercultural Conflicts

While personality conflicts may be stimulated by cultural differences, it's important to consider intercultural conflicts as a separate form of conflict. Canada is a multicultural society, and its organizations are increasingly interacting in a global environment, setting up alliances and joint ventures with partners from other parts of the world. Greater contact with people from other cultures can lead to greater understanding, but it can also lead to misunderstanding when individuals ignore the different perspectives that might result from cultural differences.

In Chapter 7, we discussed the idea that people from high- and low-context cultures have different expectations about how to interact with one another. In high-context cultures, communication is based on nonverbal and subtle situational cues. Status and one's place in society are also very important. Low-context cultures, such as those in North America, rely more on words and less on subtle situational cues. In low-context cultures, there is also less formality when communicating with people of different status. As a result of these differences, people from one cultural context may misinterpret the actions of those from another, which could produce conflict.

Professor Rosalie Tung of the Business School at Simon Fraser University studied 409 Canadian and American expatriates who were living in 51 different countries worldwide, to determine the factors that made it easier (or harder) to adjust to living in a foreign culture.[20] As part of that study, she asked expatriates to identify the characteristics that they thought best facilitated interaction with the host country's nationals. The list, presented in Exhibit 9-3 on page 344, provides some guidance for what behaviours individuals might try when dealing with conflict with someone from another culture. The list is ordered from the attribute ranked most important to least important.

OB in ACTION
Handling Personality Conflicts

Tips for employees having a personality conflict

→ **Communicate directly** with the other person to resolve the perceived conflict (emphasize problem solving and common objectives, not personalities).

→ **Avoid dragging** co-workers into the conflict.

→ If dysfunctional conflict persists, **seek help** from direct supervisors or human resource specialists.

Tips for third-party observers of a personality conflict

→ **Do not take sides** in someone else's personality conflict.

→ **Suggest the parties work things out** themselves in a constructive and positive way.

→ If dysfunctional conflict persists, **refer the problem** to parties' direct supervisors.

Tips for managers whose employees are having a personality conflict

→ **Investigate and document** conflict.

→ If appropriate, **take corrective action** (e.g., feedback or behaviour shaping).

→ If necessary, **attempt informal dispute resolution**.

→ **Refer difficult conflicts** to human resource specialists or hired counsellors for formal resolution attempts and other interventions.[19]

RESEARCH FINDINGS: Cultural Views on Conflict

Across cultures, people have different ideas about the appropriateness and effects of conflict. For instance, Mexicans expect conflict to be kept private, while Americans expect conflict to be dealt with directly and openly.[21] We suggest in Exhibit 9-4 on page 344 that there is an optimal level of conflict in the workplace to maximize productivity, but this is decidedly a North American viewpoint. Many Asian cultures believe that conflict almost always has a negative effect on the work unit.[22]

Collectivist cultures value harmony among members more than individualistic cultures do. Consistent with this, research shows that those from Asian cultures show a preference for conflict avoidance, compared with Americans and Britons.[23] Research also shows that Chinese and East Asian managers prefer compromising as a strategy,[24]

EXHIBIT 9-3 Strategies for Dealing with Intercultural Conflict

Behaviour	Rank
Listening rather than talking	1
Being sensitive to others' needs	2 (tie)
Being cooperative rather than competitive	2 (tie)
Being an inclusive leader	4
Compromising rather than domineering	5
Trying to engage in rapport	6
Being compassionate and understanding	7
Emphasizing harmony by avoiding conflict	8
Nurturing people	9

Source: Adapted from R. L. Tung, "American Expatriates Abroad: From Neophytes to Cosmopolitans," *Journal of World Business* 33, no. 2 (Summer 1998), p. 136, Table 6.

even though from a North American perspective, this might be viewed as suboptimal. Compromise may be viewed as a way of saving face, so that each party gets to preserve pride and dignity.[25]

Studies show that North Americans prefer a problem-solving approach to conflicts, because this presents both parties with a win-win solution.[26] Win-win solutions are less likely to be achieved in Asian cultures, however. East Asian managers tend to ignore conflict rather than make it public,[27] and more often than not, Japanese managers tend to choose nonconfrontational styles.[28] Chinese managers prefer compromising and avoiding to manage conflict.[29] These preferences make it difficult to negotiate a win-win solution. In general, Westerners are more comfortable with competition, which may explain why research finds that Westerners are more likely to choose forcing as a strategy than are Asians.[30]

Taken together, these research findings suggest the importance of being aware of cultural preferences with respect to conflict. Using one's own culture's conflict resolution strategies may result in even greater conflict.[31] Some individuals and some cultures prefer harmonious relations over asserting themselves, and may not react well to the con-

EXHIBIT 9-4 Conflict and Unit Performance

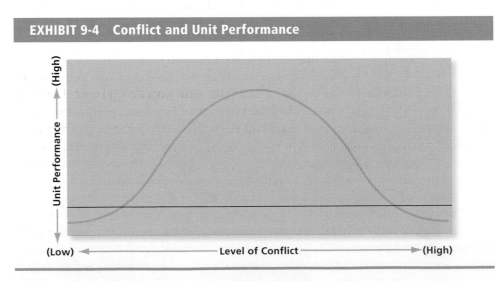

frontational dynamics more common among North Americans. Similarly, North Americans expect that negotiations may lead to a legal contract, whereas Asian cultures rely less on legal contracts and more on relational contracts.

Third-Party Conflict Resolution

Can someone else be asked to help resolve a conflict?

Occasionally, individuals or group representatives reach a stalemate and are unable to resolve their differences. In such cases, they may turn to alternative dispute resolution (ADR), where a third party helps both sides find a solution outside a courtroom. Toronto-based labour lawyers Bernard Morrow and Lauren M. Bernardi note that ADR "uses faster, more user-friendly methods of dispute resolution, instead of traditional, adversarial approaches (such as unilateral decision making or litigation."[32] ADR encompasses a variety of strategies, from more simple to more complex, including facilitation, conciliation, an ombudsperson, peer review, mediation, and arbitration.[33]

Facilitation

A facilitator, generally acquainted with both parties, suggests that the two parties work together to resolve the issue. This is an informal solution that is aimed at getting both parties to talk directly with each other. Can facilitators make a difference? Two managers decided facilitation was a good way to help resolve conflicts before they became serious, as *OB on the Street* shows.

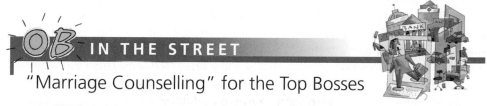

OB IN THE STREET

"Marriage Counselling" for the Top Bosses

Should managers seek help from executive coaches if they cannot reach agreement? That the two top executives of a company were often in conflict with one another is no surprise.[34] What is surprising is what they did about it.

When Watermark, a struggling maker of kayaks and car racks, brought in a new executive team, the top two executives came from very different backgrounds. CEO Jim Clark, 43, was an avid hunter and outdoorsman. COO Thomas Fumarelli, 50, was an urbane professional used to high finance in New York and Paris. Because the organization was struggling, with anxious employees who were playing them off one another, the two executives knew their differences were likely to overwhelm them. So they decided to avoid personality conflicts by engaging a facilitator to conduct two-and-a-half years of joint executive-coaching sessions.

Although such joint coaching sessions are highly unusual, both Clark and Fumarelli (it was his idea) credit the weekly sessions for helping them work through their differences. "It was like marriage counselling," said Clark. "You get all the issues on the table."

Early on, the coaches asked Clark and Fumarelli what they needed from each other. Clark said that he needed Fumarelli to be his eyes and ears for the company and to "cover his back." Fumarelli replied that he needed Clark to support him. "I can check my ego at the door," he recalls saying, "But I need validation and support from you for the role I'm playing to support you."

The two discovered a conflict, though, when the coaches asked them separately how much time they should spend on various corporate activities. Both Clark and Fumarelli claimed the development of the annual budget as their own responsibility. After getting this out in the open, Clark realized the budget should primarily be Fumarelli's responsibility. "Very early on, we knew we were going to be stepping on each other's toes," Clark said.

When a private equity company bought Watermark, both left the company. But even then, the two used coaches to handle what they called their "divorce."

Conciliation

conciliator A trusted third party who provides an informal communication link between the negotiator and the opponent.

A **conciliator** is a trusted third party who provides an informal communication link between the negotiator and the opponent. Conciliation is used extensively in international, labour, family, and community disputes. In practice, conciliators typically act as more than mere communication conduits. They also engage in fact-finding, interpreting messages, and persuading disputants to develop agreements.

The first step in trying to resolve a labour relations dispute can be to bring in a conciliation officer when agreement cannot be reached. This may be a good faith effort to resolve the dispute. Sometimes, however, it is used so that the union can reach a legal strike position or management can engage in a lockout. Provinces vary somewhat in how they set out the ability to engage in a strike after going through a conciliation process. For instance, in Nova Scotia, once the conciliation officer files a report that the dispute cannot be resolved through conciliation, there is a 14-day waiting period before either party can give 48 hours notice of either a strike or a lockout.[35]

Mediators are not always the answer to conflict resolution, however. Two mediators were appointed by the US Federal Mediation and Conciliation Service to help in the hockey dispute. However, they were unable to bring the two sides to an agreement. After meeting a number of times with both parties, "They didn't see how they could assist the process in reaching a resolution," NHL vice-president Bill Daly said.[36]

Ombudsperson

Organizations sometimes create an official role for a person to hear disputes between parties. An ombudsperson is impartial, widely respected, and trusted. He or she investigates the issue confidentially and tries to arrange a solution. The advantage to having an ombudsperson involved in a dispute is that the parties can avoid going through formal organizational channels for a resolution. Going through formal organizational channels can escalate the differences between the parties, leading to greater conflict. The ombudsperson thus acts as a way to resolve differences between two parties in the organization before formal procedures, which might have an impact on one's employment, are initiated.

Peer Review

A panel of peers is put together to hear both sides of the issue from the parties involved and to recommend a solution. The panel is expected to be objective in listening to the issues and in making a recommendation. The peer review panel's decision may or may not be binding on the parties, depending upon what was agreed to at the outset.

Mediation

mediator A neutral third party who facilitates a negotiated solution by using reasoning, persuasion, and suggestions for alternatives.

A **mediator** is a neutral third party who facilitates a negotiated solution by using reasoning and persuasion, suggesting alternatives, and the like. Mediators can be much more aggressive in proposing solutions than conciliators. Mediators are widely used in labour-management negotiations and in civil court disputes. In Vancouver, where there has been a "leaky condo crisis" in recent years, owners and builders can insist upon mediation with the aid of an independent mediator. British Columbia's Motor Vehicle Branch uses mediation to help settle accident claims. In Ontario, all disputes between companies and employees now go to mediation within 100 days. Pilot projects found that more than 60 percent of the disputes were partly or fully resolved within 60 days after the start of the mediation session.[37]

Mediation can also be used directly in the workplace. At Aurora, Ontario-based Magna International, some employees volunteer to be trained in dispute mediation, and are then selected for a "fairness" committee. Grievances are handled by the "fairness" committee, and decisions are generally accepted by management. Decisions have included asking management to remove a written warning from an employee's file, even though the employee had caused considerable damage while operating a lift truck.[38]

The overall effectiveness of mediated negotiations is fairly impressive. The settlement rate is approximately 60 percent, with satisfaction with the mediator at about 75 percent. But the situation is the key to whether mediation will succeed; the conflicting parties must be motivated to bargain and resolve their conflict. Additionally, conflict intensity cannot be too high; mediation is most effective under moderate levels of conflict. Finally, perceptions of the mediator are important; to be effective, the mediator must be perceived as neutral and noncoercive.

Arbitration

An **arbitrator** is a third party with the authority to dictate an agreement. Arbitration can be voluntary (requested by the parties) or compulsory (forced on the parties by law or contract).

arbitrator A third party to a negotiation who has the authority to dictate an agreement.

The authority of the arbitrator varies according to the rules set by the negotiators. For instance, the arbitrator might be limited to choosing one of the negotiating parties' last offers or to suggesting an agreement point that is nonbinding. Or the arbitrator might be free to choose and make any judgment that he or she wishes.

The big advantage of arbitration over mediation is that it always results in a settlement. Whether or not there is a negative side depends on how "heavy-handed" the arbitrator appears. If one party is left feeling overwhelmingly defeated, that party is certain to be dissatisfied and unlikely to accept the arbitrator's decision graciously. Therefore, the conflict may resurface at a later time.

Conflict Outcomes

After enduring a three-month strike, CUPE 3903 members were asked to vote on a "final offer" from the York University administration. Union members resoundingly rejected the university's offer. With no obvious end to the strike in sight, and three months of the academic year lost because of the strike, the Ontario legislature opted to pass back-to-work legislation in late January 2009 so that the 50 000 students, who had been caught in the middle during the conflict between the university and CUPE, could get back to classes.

The back-to-work legislation did not settle the dispute between the university and the union. However, it did order the two parties to agree on a mediator within five days of the legislation, or one would be chosen for them. Thus, the three month strike did not end in a settlement, it resulted in missed classes that had to be made up, and put decision making into the hands of a mediator. While the York University conflict appears to have had a number of negative consequences, is it possible for conflict to have positive outcomes?

As Exhibit 9-4 on page 344 demonstrates, conflict can be functional and improve group performance, or it can be dysfunctional and hinder group performance. As well, we see there is an optimal level of conflict that results in the highest level of unit performance.

Conflict is constructive when it improves the quality of decisions, stimulates creativity and innovation, encourages interest and curiosity among group members, provides the medium through which problems can be aired and tensions released, and fosters an environment of self-evaluation and change. The evidence suggests that conflict can improve the quality of decision making by allowing all points, particularly the ones that are unusual or held by a minority, to be weighed in important decisions.[39] Conflict can prevent groupthink (discussed in Chapter 12). It does not allow the group

3 What are the effects of conflict?

passively to "rubber-stamp" decisions that may be based on weak assumptions, inadequate consideration of relevant alternatives, or other problems. Conflict challenges the status quo and therefore supports the creation of new ideas, promotes reassessment of group goals and activities, and increases the probability that the group will respond to change.

Dean Tjosvold of Lingnan University in Hong Kong suggests three desired outcomes for conflict:[40]

- *Agreement.* Equitable and fair agreements are the best outcome. If agreement means that one party feels exploited or defeated, this will likely lead to further conflict later.

- *Stronger relationships.* When conflict is resolved positively, this can lead to better relationships and greater trust. If the parties trust each other, they are more likely to keep the agreements they make.

- *Learning.* Handling conflict successfully teaches one how to do it better next time. It gives an opportunity to practise the skills one has learned about handling conflict.

Unfortunately, not all conflict results in positive outcomes. A substantial body of literature documents how dysfunctional conflict can reduce group effectiveness.[41] Among the more undesirable outcomes are stopping communication, reducing group cohesiveness, and subordinating group goals due to infighting between members. At the extreme, conflict can bring group functioning to a halt and potentially threaten the group's survival.

Below we examine what research tells us about the constructive effects of conflict. *Case Incident—Managing Conflict at Schneider National* on page 365 describes how functional conflict improves an organization.

RESEARCH FINDINGS: Functional Conflict

Research studies in diverse settings confirm that conflict can be functional and improve productivity. For instance, studies demonstrate that groups composed of members with different interests tend to produce higher-quality solutions to a variety of problems than do homogeneous groups.[42] One study found that high-conflict groups improved their decision-making ability 73 percent more than groups characterized by low-conflict conditions.[43] An investigation of 22 teams of systems analysts found that the more incompatible teams were likely to be more productive.[44] Research and development scientists have been found to be most productive when a certain amount of intellectual conflict exists.[45] These findings suggest that conflict within a group can lead to strength rather than weakness.

Negotiation

When the CUPE 3903 contract with York University ended in the summer of 2008, the university administration and the union members both had decisions to make regarding how they would negotiate a new collective agreement. At first, there were some meetings between the parties to try to address the issues that had been raised by the union. Eventually, the union became frustrated with the university and declared a strike.

Both the university and the union quickly became committed to their positions in the negotiations: The union members were determined to get an agreement that included significant wage and benefit increases, and the university was just as determined that it could not afford the wage increases demanded, nor would it agree to a two-year contract. Because of those positions, it was very difficult to get negotiators from either party to make much progress during talks.

Both the university administration and union members might have been better off focusing on their interests, rather than their positions. Contract faculty members and teaching assistants felt they were underpaid and that they did not have job security. The university administration wanted to keep wage costs as low as possible. So, both sides had to figure out a way to move beyond just talking about salary figures. Because each side focused on salary levels, it is likely that neither side seriously considered other alternatives that might have achieved a similar goal: containing costs for the university while paying reasonable salaries to union members. During the failed negotiations, three months of classes were lost. At the time of publication of this textbook, the final outcome for the union was not known.

The CUPE/York University negotiations could be considered a win-lose situation. Are there other ways to negotiate so that both sides can win?

Earlier in the chapter, we reviewed a number of conflict resolution strategies. One well-developed strategy is to negotiate a resolution. Negotiation permeates the interactions of almost everyone in groups and organizations: Labour bargains with management; managers negotiate with employees, peers, and senior management; salespeople negotiate with customers; purchasing agents negotiate with suppliers; employees agree to answer a colleague's phone for a few minutes in exchange for some past or future benefit. In today's team-based organizations, negotiation skills become critical for teams to work together effectively.

4 How does one negotiate effectively?

We define **negotiation** as a process in which two or more parties try to agree on the exchange rate for goods or services they are trading.[46] Note that we use the terms *negotiation* and *bargaining* interchangeably.

negotiation A process in which two or more parties exchange goods or services and try to agree on the exchange rate for them.

Within a negotiation, be aware that individuals have issues, positions, and interests. *Issues* are items that are specifically placed on the bargaining table for discussion. *Positions* are the individual's stand on the issues. For instance, salary may be an issue for discussion. The salary you hope to receive is your position. Finally, *interests* are the underlying concerns that are affected by the negotiation resolution. For instance, the reason that you might want a six-figure salary is that you are trying to buy a house in Vancouver, and that is your only hope of being able to make mortgage payments.

Negotiators who recognize the underlying interests of themselves and the other party may have more flexibility in achieving a resolution. For instance, in the example just given, an employer who offers you a mortgage at a lower rate than the bank does, or who

Negotiation skills are critical in the buyer-seller relationship. At this open-air cheese market in Alkmaar, Netherlands, two purchasing agents for food buyers taste a sample of Edam cheese before they negotiate prices with the seller of the cheese.

provides you with an interest-free loan that can be used against the mortgage, may be able to address your underlying interests without actually meeting your salary position. You may be satisfied with this alternative, if you understand what your interest is.

Interest-based bargaining enabled Vancouver-based NorskeCanada (now Catalyst Paper Corporation) to sign a mutually beneficial five-year contract with the Communications, Energy and Paperworkers Union of Canada in fall 2002, after just nine days of negotiations.[47] While the union and NorskeCanada had experienced bitter conflict in previous negotiations, in this particular situation both sides agreed to focus more on the interests of the parties, rather than on demands and concessions. Both sides were pleased with the outcome. In the case of the hockey negotiations, neither side engaged in interest-based bargaining. Instead, each side tried to win its position on the salary cap. Even when the players finally agreed to consider a cap, the owners were only willing to consider the cap they wanted, not the cap the players suggested.

Below we discuss bargaining strategies and how to negotiate.

Bargaining Strategies

There are two general approaches to negotiation—*distributive bargaining* and *integrative bargaining*.[48] These are compared in Exhibit 9-5.

Distributive Bargaining

distributive bargaining
Negotiation that seeks to divide up a fixed amount of resources; a win-lose solution.

Distributive bargaining is a negotiating strategy that operates under zero-sum (win-lose) conditions. That is, any gain I make is at your expense, and vice versa. Probably the most widely cited example of distributive bargaining is labour-management negotiations over wages. Typically, labour representatives come to the bargaining table determined to get as much money as possible out of management, while management hopes to keep its labour costs as low as possible. Since every cent more that labour negotiates increases management's costs, each party bargains aggressively and treats the other as an opponent who must be defeated.

Should you try to win at any cost when you bargain?

A party engaged in distributive bargaining focuses on trying to get the opponent to agree to a specific target point, or to get as close to it as possible. Examples of this tactic are persuading your opponent of the impossibility of reaching his or her target point and the advisability of accepting a settlement near yours; arguing that your target is fair, while your opponent's is not; and attempting to get your opponent to feel emotionally generous toward you and thus accept an outcome close to your target point.

When engaged in distributive bargaining, one of the best things you can do is to make the first offer, and to make it an aggressive one. Research consistently shows that

EXHIBIT 9-5   Distributive vs. Integrative Bargaining

Bargaining Characteristic	Distributive Bargaining	Integrative Bargaining
Available resources	Fixed amount of resources to be divided	Variable amount of resources to be divided
Primary motivations	I win, you lose	I win, you win
Primary interests	Opposed to each other	Convergent or congruent with each other
Focus of relationships	Short-term	Long-term

Source: Based on R. J. Lewicki and J. A. Litterer, *Negotiation* (Homewood, IL: Irwin, 1985), p. 280.

the best negotiators are those who make the first offer, and whose initial offer has very favourable terms. Why is this so? One reason is that making the first offer shows power; research shows that individuals in power are much more likely to make initial offers, speak first at meetings, and thereby gain the advantage. Another reason is the anchoring bias (the tendency for people to fixate on initial information). Once that anchoring point is set, people fail to adequately adjust it based on subsequent information. A savvy negotiator sets an anchor with the initial offer, and scores of negotiation studies show that such anchors greatly favour the person who sets it.[49]

For example, say you have a job offer, and your prospective employer asks you what sort of starting salary you would be looking for. You need to realize that you have just been given a great gift—you have a chance to set the anchor, meaning that you should ask for the highest salary that you think the employer could reasonably offer. For most of us, asking for a million dollars is only going to make us look ridiculous, which is why we suggest being on the high end of what you think is *reasonable*. Too often, we err on the side of caution, being afraid of scaring off the employer, and thus settle for too little. It *is* possible to scare off an employer, and it's true that employers do not like candidates to be assertive in salary negotiations, but liking is not the same as respect or doing what it takes to hire or retain someone.[50] You should realize that what happens much more often is that we ask for less than what we could have gotten.

Another distributive bargaining tactic is revealing a deadline. Negotiators who reveal deadlines speed concessions from their negotiating counterparts, making them reconsider their position. And even though negotiators don't *think* this tactic works, in reality, negotiators who reveal deadlines do better.[51]

Integrative Bargaining

In contrast to distributive bargaining, **integrative bargaining** operates under the assumption that there exists one or more settlements that can create a win-win solution. In terms of intraorganizational behaviour, all things being equal, integrative bargaining is preferable to distributive bargaining. Why? Because the former builds long-term relationships and makes working together in the future easier. It bonds negotiators and allows both sides to leave the bargaining table feeling that they have achieved a victory. For instance, in union-management negotiations, both sides might sit down to figure out other ways to reduce costs within an organization, so that it is possible to have greater wage increases. Distributive bargaining, on the other hand, leaves one party a loser. It tends to build animosities and deepen divisions when people must work together on an ongoing basis.

Research shows that over repeated bargaining episodes, when the "losing" party feels positive about the negotiation outcome, the party is much more likely to bargain cooperatively in subsequent negotiations. This points to the important advantage of integrative negotiations: Even when you "win," you want your opponent to feel positively about the negotiation.[52]

Why, then, don't we see more integrative bargaining in organizations? The answer lies in the conditions necessary for this type of negotiation to succeed. These include parties who are open with information and candid about their concerns, sensitivity by both parties to the other's needs, the ability to trust one another, and a willingness by both parties to maintain flexibility.[53] Because these conditions often don't exist in organizations, it isn't surprising that negotiations often take on a win-at-any-cost dynamic.

There are some ways to achieve more integrative outcomes. For example, individuals who bargain in teams reach more integrative agreements than those who bargain individually. This happens because more ideas are generated when more people are at the bargaining table. So try bargaining in teams.[54] Another way to achieve higher joint-gain settlements is to put more issues on the table. The more negotiable issues that are introduced into a negotiation, the more opportunity there is for "logrolling," where

integrative bargaining
Negotiation that seeks one or more settlements that can create a win-win solution.

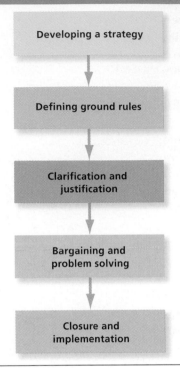

EXHIBIT 9-6   The Negotiation Process

Developing a strategy

↓

Defining ground rules

↓

Clarification and justification

↓

Bargaining and problem solving

↓

Closure and implementation

Source: This model is based on R. J. Lewicki, "Bargaining and Negotiation," *Exchange: The Organizational Behavior Teaching Journal* 6, no. 2 (1981), pp. 39–40.

BATNA The *best alternative to a negotiated agreement*; the outcome an individual faces if negotiations fail.

bargaining zone The zone between each party's resistance point, assuming there is overlap in this range.

issues are traded because of differences in preferences. This approach creates better outcomes for each side than if each issue were negotiated individually.[55]

Finally, you should realize that compromise may be your worst enemy in negotiating a win-win agreement. This is because compromising reduces the pressure to bargain integratively. After all, if you or your opponent caves in easily, it does not require anyone to be creative to reach a settlement. Thus, people end up settling for less than they could have obtained if they had been forced to consider the other party's interests, trade off issues, and be creative.[56] Think of the classic example where two sisters are arguing over who gets an orange. Each sister is unaware of *why* the other wants the orange: One sister wants the orange to drink the juice, whereas the other sister wants the orange peel to bake a cake. If one sister simply gives in and gives the other sister the orange, then they will not be forced to explore their reasons for wanting the orange, and thus they will never find the win-win solution: They could each have the orange because they want different parts of it!

How to Negotiate

Exhibit 9-6 provides a simplified model of the negotiation process. It views negotiation as made up of five steps: (1) developing a strategy; (2) defining ground rules; (3) clarification and justification; (4) bargaining and problem solving; and (5) closure and implementation.

Developing a Strategy

Before you start negotiating, you need to do your homework. What is the nature of the conflict? What is the history leading up to this negotiation? Who is involved, and what are their perceptions of the conflict?

What do you want from the negotiation? What are *your* goals? It often helps to put your goals in writing and develop a range of outcomes—from "most hopeful" to "minimally acceptable"—to keep your attention focused.

You also want to prepare an assessment of what you think the goals of the other party are.[57] What are they likely to ask for? How entrenched are they likely to be in their position? What intangible or hidden interests may be important to them? What might they be willing to settle on? When you can anticipate your opponent's position, you are better equipped to counter his or her arguments with the facts and figures that support your position. You might also be able to anticipate better negotiating options for yourself, as *Case Incident— David Out-Negotiating Goliath: Apotex and Bristol-Myers Squibb* on page 364 shows.

In determining goals, parties are well advised to consider their "target and resistance" points, as well as their *best alternative to a negotiated agreement* (**BATNA**).[58] The buyer and the seller are examples of two negotiators. Each has a *target point* that defines what he or she would like to achieve. Each also has a *resistance point*, which marks the lowest outcome that is acceptable—the point below which each would break off negotiations rather than accept a less favourable settlement. The area between these two points makes up each negotiator's aspiration range. As long as there is some overlap between the buyer's and seller's aspiration ranges, there exists a **bargaining zone** where each side's aspirations can be met. Referring to Exhibit 9-7, if the buyer's resistance point is $450, and the seller's resistance point is $500, then the two may not be able to reach agreement because there is no overlap in their aspiration ranges.

One's BATNA represents the alternative that an individual will face if negotiations fail. For instance, during the winter 2005 hockey negotiations, for both hockey players and owners, the BATNA was the loss of the 2004–2005 season. In the end, both sides must have concluded that they preferred not playing the season to trying to get the conflict resolved.

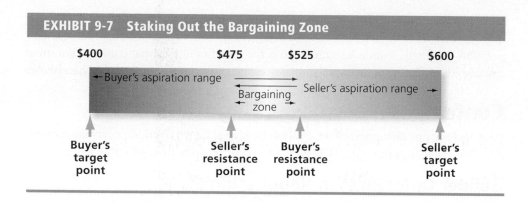

EXHIBIT 9-7   Staking Out the Bargaining Zone

As part of your strategy, you should determine not only your BATNA, but some estimate of the other side's as well.[59] If you go into your negotiation having a good idea of what the other party's BATNA is, even if you are not able to meet theirs, you might be able to get them to change it.

You can practise your negotiating skills in the *Working with Others Exercise* on page 363.

Defining Ground Rules

Once you have done your planning and developed a strategy, you are ready to begin defining the ground rules and procedures with the other party over the negotiation itself. Who will do the negotiating? Where will it take place? What time constraints, if any, will apply? To what issues will negotiation be limited? Will there be a specific procedure to follow if an impasse is reached? During this phase, the parties will also exchange their initial proposals or demands. *From Concepts to Skills* on page 366 directly addresses some of the actions you should take to improve the likelihood that you can achieve a good agreement.

Clarification and Justification

When initial positions have been exchanged, both you and the other party will explain, amplify, clarify, bolster, and justify your original demands. This part of the process need not be confrontational. Rather, it's an opportunity for educating and informing each other on the issues, why they are important, and how each arrived at their initial demands. This is the point at which you might want to provide the other party with any documentation that helps support your position. The *Ethical Dilemma Exercise* on page 364 considers whether it is ever appropriate to lie during negotiations.

Bargaining and Problem Solving

The essence of the negotiation process is the actual give and take in trying to hash out an agreement. It is here that concessions will undoubtedly need to be made by both parties. *OB in Action—Tips for Getting to Yes* gives you further ideas on how to make negotiating work for you, based on the popular book *Getting to Yes*.[61]

Closure and Implementation

The final step in the negotiation process is formalizing the agreement that has been worked out and developing procedures that are necessary for implementation and monitoring. For major negotiations—which would include everything from

OB in ACTION

Tips for Getting to Yes

R. Fisher and W. Ury present four principles for win-win negotiations in their book *Getting to Yes*:[60]

- **Separate** the **people from** the **problem**. Work on the issues at hand, rather than getting involved in personality issues between the parties.

- Focus on **interests, not positions**. Try to identify what each person needs or wants, rather than coming up with an unmovable position.

- Look for ways to achieve **mutual gains**. Rather than focusing on one "right" solution for your position, brainstorm for solutions that will satisfy the needs of both parties.

- Use **objective criteria** to achieve a fair solution. Try to focus on fair standards, such as market value, expert opinion, norms, or laws to help guide decision making.

labour-management negotiations such as in the York University situation, to bargaining over lease terms, to buying real estate, to negotiating a job offer for a senior management position—this will require hammering out the specifics in a formal contract. For most cases, however, closure of the negotiation process is nothing more formal than a handshake.

Contemporary Issues in Negotiation

5 What are the contemporary issues in negotiation?

We conclude our discussion of negotiation by reviewing two contemporary issues: gender differences in negotiating style and cultural differences in negotiating style.

Gender Differences in Negotiating Style

Do men and women negotiate differently? The answer appears to be, "It depends."[62] It is difficult to generalize about gender differences in negotiating style, because the research yields many opinions, but few reliable conclusions. One review of a number of studies found no overall difference in effectiveness of men and women leaders in negotiation, although the study also indicated that men performed better when the negotiations were over male-stereotypical tasks (for example, negotiating for airplanes and turbo-engine parts), whereas women did better when the negotiations were over female-stereotypical tasks (for example, negotiations involving child care and caretaker issues).[63] Moreover, a review of 53 studies suggests that women receive lower gains than men after a negotiation process.[64] Let's look at four basic areas where interesting gender differences in bargaining have been found.[65]

Ever wonder if men and women negotiate differently?

First, women are more inclined to be concerned with feelings and perceptions, and thus take a longer-term view when negotiating. By contrast, men are more inclined to focus on resolving the matter at hand. Bill Forbes, president of Edmonton-based career management firm CDR Associates, observes that women assume they are not going to earn as much as men. They focus "on getting a position that utilizes their skills and gives them some challenge. When presented with the compensation range for their job classification, women generally aren't worried if they end up in the bottom half, whereas males might often be concerned if they're not in the top."[66] Unfortunately, employers may take advantage of these differing expectations to offer women lower wages when they first negotiate salary. This may be changing in recent times. For example, University of Waterloo psychology professor Serge Desmarais found that the narrowest pay gap between men and women existed with those who had graduated from university since 1992. The difference in wages for those men and women was only 6 percent.[67]

Second, men view the bargaining session as a separate event, whereas women view it as part of the overall relationship with the individual. Women therefore put more weight on the importance of maintaining relationships after the bargaining session is over when considering their strategy.

Third, women tend to want all parties in the negotiation to be empowered, whereas men are more likely to use power as part of the bargaining strategy. In other words, women are less likely to negotiate solutions where one person is clearly the winner and the other is clearly the loser.

Finally, the researchers reported differences in dialogue. Men more often used dialogue to persuade other parties in the negotiation, whereas women were more likely to use dialogue to achieve understanding. Desmarais, whose work we noted above, suggests that men are socialized to be more aggressive negotiators, which would account for some of the observed differences in men's and women's styles.[68]

One important thing to note is that even if a difference in style of negotiation exists, one style may not always be preferable to the other. The best style may, in fact, depend

Respected for her intelligence, confident negotiating skills, and successful outcomes, Christine Lagarde was appointed by French president Nicholas Sarkozy to the powerful position of minister for the economy, finance, and employment. Before becoming the first female finance minister of a G8 nation, Lagarde was the trade minister of France, where she used her negotiating skills to boost French exports by 10 percent. Before that, Lagarde was a noted labour and antitrust lawyer for the global law firm Baker & McKenzie. Among her tasks, Lagarde negotiated with France's trade unions to change the country's labour laws, including ending the 35-hour limit on the workweek, to help boost the nation's sluggish economy.

on the situation. For instance, in situations where trust, openness, and long-term relationships are critical, a woman's style may be more useful. However, when conflict, competition, and self-interest are an important part of the agenda, a man's style may be more effective.[69]

There is another thing worth noting: The belief that women are nicer than men in negotiations may well result not from gender, but from the lack of power typically held by women in most large organizations. The research indicates that low-power managers, regardless of gender, attempt to please their opponents and tend to use softly persuasive tactics rather than direct confrontation and threats. Where women and men have similar power bases, there may be less significant differences in their negotiation styles. There is still work to be done in this area, however. A study by two economists found that women were more likely than men to share some of the $10 they were given by researchers (53 percent vs. 40 percent), and women were also more likely than men to give away a larger portion ($1.60 vs. $0.82).[70]

Women's attitudes toward negotiation and toward themselves as negotiators also appear to be quite different from men's. Managerial women demonstrate less confidence in anticipation of negotiating and are less satisfied with their performance after the process is complete, even when their performance and the outcomes they achieve are similar to men's. This latter conclusion suggests that women may unduly penalize themselves by refusing to negotiate with confidence when such action would be in their best interests.

The outcomes of negotiations for women and men also seem to differ. One researcher found that when women negotiated to buy a car, the opening offer by the salesperson was higher than it was for men.[71] In a study of salary offers, researchers found that men were offered higher starting salaries in a negotiating process than were women.[72] While in each of these instances the opening offers were just that, offers to be negotiated, women also fared less well than men at the end of the negotiating process, even when they used the same negotiating tactics as men.

The results of these studies may shed some light on the pay and promotion discrepancies between men and women, which we discuss in Chapter 11. If women negotiate even slightly lower starting salaries, then over time, with raises based on percentages of salaries, the gap between men's and women's salaries can grow quite substantially.

Cultural Differences in Negotiating Style

Although there appears to be no significant direct relationship between an individual's personality and negotiation style, cultural background does seem to be relevant. Negotiating styles clearly do vary across national cultures, as the following examples suggest:[73]

- *France.* The French like conflict. They frequently gain recognition and develop their reputations by thinking and acting against others. As a result, the French tend to take a long time in negotiating agreements, and they are not overly concerned about whether their opponents like or dislike them.[74]

- *China.* The Chinese draw out negotiations because they believe negotiations never end. Just when you think you have pinned down every detail and reached a final solution with a Chinese executive, that executive might smile and start the process all over again. The Chinese negotiate to develop a relationship and a commitment to work together rather than to tie up every loose end.[75]

- *Japan.* The Japanese also negotiate to develop relationships and a commitment to work together. One study compared US and Japanese negotiators and found that the Japanese negotiators tended to communicate indirectly and adapt their behaviours to the situation. A follow-up study showed that whereas among US managers making early offers led to the anchoring effect we noted when discussing distributive negotiation, for Japanese negotiators, early offers led to more information sharing and better integrative outcomes.[76]

- *United States.* Americans are known around the world for their impatience and their desire to be liked. Astute negotiators from other countries often turn these characteristics to their advantage by dragging out negotiations and making friendship conditional on the final settlement.

The cultural context of the negotiation significantly influences the amount and type of preparation for bargaining, the relative emphasis on task vs. interpersonal relationships, the tactics used, and even the place where the negotiation should be conducted. Exhibit 9-8 helps you identify whether countries focus more on win-win or win-lose solutions. These findings are based on research on 300 negotiators in 12 countries. As you

EXHIBIT 9-8   Negotiating Attitude: Win-Win or Win-Lose?

Country	Japan	China	Argentina	France	India	US	UK	Mexico	Germany	Nigeria	Brazil	Spain
Negotiator focuses on win-win solution (%)	100	82	81	80	78	71	59	50	55	47	44	37

Source: J. W. Salacuse, "Ten Ways That Culture Affects Negotiating Style: Some Survey Results," *Negotiation Journal*, July 1998, pp. 221–240.

will note, 100 percent of Japanese negotiators said they focus on finding a win-win solution. By contrast, only 37 percent of Spanish negotiators said the same.[77] *OB Around the Globe* looks at more examples of cross-cultural differences in negotiating style.

OB AROUND THE GLOBE

The Many Styles of Negotiations

How different are bargaining styles cross-culturally? A study comparing North Americans, Arabs, and Russians looked at the groups' negotiating styles, their responses to an opponent's arguments, their approaches to making concessions, and their handling of negotiating deadlines.[78] The researchers found the following:

- North Americans tried to persuade by relying on facts and appealing to logic. They countered opponents' arguments with objective facts. They made small concessions early in the negotiation to establish a relationship, and usually reciprocated opponents' concessions. North Americans treated deadlines as very important.

- Arabs, however, tried to persuade by appealing to emotion. They countered opponents' arguments with subjective feelings. They made concessions throughout the bargaining process, and almost always reciprocated opponents' concessions. The Arabs also approached deadlines very casually.

- Russians based their arguments on asserted ideals. They made few, if any, concessions. Any concession offered by an opponent was viewed as a weakness and almost never reciprocated. Finally, the Russians tended to ignore deadlines.

Another study looked at verbal and nonverbal negotiation tactics exhibited by North Americans, Japanese, and Brazilians during half-hour bargaining sessions.[79] Some of the differences were particularly interesting:

- Brazilians on average said "no" 83 times, compared with 5 times for the Japanese and 9 times for the North Americans.

- Japanese displayed more than 5 periods of silence lasting longer than 10 seconds during the 30-minute sessions. North Americans averaged 3.5 such periods; the Brazilians had none.

- Both Japanese and North Americans interrupted their opponent about the same number of times, but the Brazilians interrupted 2.5 to 3 times more often than the North Americans and the Japanese.

- While Japanese and North Americans had no physical contact with their opponents during negotiations except for handshaking, Brazilians touched each other almost 5 times every half-hour.

Summary and Implications

1 **What is conflict?** Conflict occurs when one party perceives that another party's actions will have a negative effect on something the first party cares about. Many people automatically assume that all conflict is bad. However, conflict can be either functional (constructive) or dysfunctional (destructive) to the performance of a group or unit. An optimal level of conflict encourages communication, prevents stagnation, stimulates creativity, allows tensions to be released, and plants the seeds of change, yet not so much as to be disruptive or to deter activities. For simplicity's sake, the sources of conflict have been condensed into three general categories: communication, structure, and personal variables.

2 **How can conflict be resolved?** The way a conflict is defined goes a long way toward establishing the sort of outcomes that might settle it. One can work toward a *win-lose solution* or a *win-win solution*. Conflict management strategies are determined by the extent to which one wants to cooperate with another party, and the extent to which one asserts his or her own concerns. Occasionally, individuals or group representatives reach a stalemate and are unable to resolve their differences through direct negotiations. In such cases, they may turn to alternative dispute resolution (ADR), where a third party helps both sides find a solution. ADR encompasses a variety of strategies, including facilitation, conciliation, an ombudsperson, peer review, mediation, and arbitration.

3 **What are the effects of conflict?** Conflict can be functional and improve group performance, or it can be dysfunctional and hinder group performance. A substantial body of literature documents how dysfunctional conflict can reduce group effectiveness. Among the more undesirable consequences of conflict are stopping communication, reducing group cohesiveness, and subordinating group goals due to infighting between members. At the extreme, conflict can bring group functioning to a halt and potentially threaten the group's survival.

4 **How does one negotiate effectively?** *Negotiation* is a process in which two or more parties exchange goods or services and try to agree on the exchange rate for them. Negotiation is an ongoing activity in groups and organizations. Distributive bargaining can resolve disputes, but it often negatively affects one or more negotiators' satisfaction because it is focused on the short term and because it is confrontational. Integrative bargaining, by contrast, tends to provide outcomes that satisfy all parties and build lasting relationships.

5 **What are the contemporary issues in negotiation?** Two contemporary issues are gender differences and cultural differences in negotiating style. The evidence suggests that men and women use somewhat different styles in negotiation, and also have somewhat different success rates. Cultural background does seem to be relevant to how negotiations are carried out. Moreover, negotiating styles vary across cultures.

 AT WORK

For Review

1. What are the advantages and disadvantages of conflict?

2. Under what conditions might conflict be beneficial to a group?

3. What is the difference between functional and dysfunctional conflict? What determines functionality?

4. What is dual concern theory?

5. What causes personality conflicts, and how can they be resolved?

6. What is the difference between a conciliator and a mediator?

7. What defines the bargaining zone in distributive bargaining?

8. Why isn't integrative bargaining more widely practised in organizations?

9. How can you improve your negotiating effectiveness?

10. How do men and women differ, if at all, in their approaches to negotiations?

For Critical Thinking

1. Do you think competition and conflict are different? Explain.

2. "Participation is an excellent method for identifying differences and resolving conflicts." Do you agree or disagree? Discuss.

3. From your own experience, describe a situation you were involved in where the conflict was dysfunctional. Describe another example, from your experience, where the conflict was functional. Now analyze how other parties in both conflicts might have interpreted the situation in terms of whether the conflicts were functional or dysfunctional.

4. Assume one of your co-workers had to negotiate a contract with someone from China. What problems might he or she face? If the co-worker asked for advice, what suggestions would you give to help facilitate a settlement?

5. Michael Eisner, former CEO at the Walt Disney Corporation, wanted to stimulate conflict inside his firm. But he wanted to minimize conflict with outside parties—agents, contractors, unions, etcetera. What do Eisner's goals say about conflict levels, functional vs. dysfunctional conflict, and managing conflict?

 for You

- It may seem easier, but avoiding conflict does not necessarily have a more positive outcome than working with someone to resolve the conflict.

- Trying to achieve a win-win solution in a conflict situation tends to lead to better relationships and greater trust.

- It's not always possible to resolve conflict on one's own. There are alternative dispute resolution options, including having someone help mediate the conflict.

- It's better to focus more on interests rather than positions when engaged in a negotiation. Doing so gives you the ability to arrive at more flexible solutions.

POINT

COUNTERPOINT

Conflict Is Good for an Organization

We've made considerable progress in the past 25 years toward overcoming the negative stereotype given to conflict. Most behavioural scientists and an increasing number of practising managers now accept that the goal of effective management is not to eliminate conflict. Rather, it's to create the right intensity of conflict so as to reap its functional benefits.

Let's briefly review how stimulating conflict can provide benefits to the organization:[80]

- *Conflict is a means by which to bring about radical change.* It's an effective device by which management can drastically change the existing power structure, current interaction patterns, and entrenched attitudes.

- *Conflict facilitates group cohesiveness.* While conflict increases hostility between groups, external threats tend to cause a group to pull together as a unit. Intergroup conflicts raise the extent to which members identify with their own group and increase feelings of solidarity, while, at the same time, internal differences and irritations dissolve.

- *Conflict improves group and organizational effectiveness.* The stimulation of conflict initiates the search for new means and goals and clears the way for innovation. The successful solution of a conflict leads to greater effectiveness, to more trust and openness, to greater attraction of members for each other, and to depersonalization of future conflicts. In fact, it has been found that as the number of minor disagreements increases, the number of major clashes decreases.

- *Conflict brings about a slightly higher, more constructive level of tension.* Constructive levels of tension enhance the chances of solving the conflicts in a way satisfactory to all parties concerned. When the level of tension is very low, the parties are not sufficiently motivated to do something about a conflict.

These points are clearly not comprehensive. As noted in the chapter, conflict provides a number of benefits to an organization. However, groups or organizations that lack conflict are likely to suffer from apathy, stagnation, groupthink, and other serious problems. In fact, more organizations probably fail because they have too little conflict rather than too much.

All Conflicts Are Dysfunctional!

It may be true that conflict is an inherent part of any group or organization. It may not be possible to eliminate it completely. However, just because conflicts exist is no reason to glorify them. All conflicts are dysfunctional, and it is one of management's major responsibilities to keep conflict intensity as low as humanly possible. A few points will support this case:

- *The negative consequences from conflict can be devastating.* The list of negatives associated with conflict is awesome. The most obvious are increased turnover, decreased employee satisfaction, inefficiencies between work units, sabotage, labour grievances and strikes, and physical aggression.

- *Effective managers build teamwork.* A good manager builds a coordinated team. Conflict works against such an objective. A successful work group is like a successful sports team: Members all know their roles and support their teammates. When a team works well, the whole becomes greater than the sum of the parts. Management creates teamwork by minimizing internal conflicts and facilitating internal coordination.

- *Competition is good for an organization, but not conflict.* Competition and conflict should not be confused with each other. Conflict is behaviour directed against another party, whereas competition is behaviour aimed at obtaining a goal without interference from another party. Competition is healthy; it's the source of organizational vitality. Conflict, on the other hand, is destructive.

- *Conflict is avoidable.* It may be true that conflict is inevitable when an organization is in a downward spiral, but the goal of good leadership and effective management is to avoid the spiral to begin with.

LEARNING ABOUT **YOURSELF** EXERCISE

What Is Your Primary Conflict-Handling Style?

Indicate how often you rely on each of the following tactics by circling the number you feel is most appropriate.

When I have a conflict at work, I do the following:[81]

		Not at All				Very Much
1.	I give in to the wishes of the other party.	1	2	3	4	5
2.	I try to realize a middle-of-the-road solution.	1	2	3	4	5
3.	I push my own point of view.	1	2	3	4	5
4.	I examine issues until I find a solution that really satisfies me and the other party.	1	2	3	4	5
5.	I avoid a confrontation about our differences.	1	2	3	4	5
6.	I concur with the other party.	1	2	3	4	5
7.	I emphasize that we have to find a compromise solution.	1	2	3	4	5
8.	I search for gains.	1	2	3	4	5
9.	I stand for my own and the other party's goals and interests.	1	2	3	4	5
10.	I avoid differences of opinion as much as possible.	1	2	3	4	5
11.	I try to accommodate the other party.	1	2	3	4	5
12.	I insist we both give in a little.	1	2	3	4	5
13.	I fight for a good outcome for myself.	1	2	3	4	5
14.	I examine ideas from both sides to find a mutually optimal solution.	1	2	3	4	5
15.	I try to make differences loom less large.	1	2	3	4	5
16.	I adapt to the other party's goals and interests.	1	2	3	4	5
17.	I strive whenever possible toward a 50-50 compromise.	1	2	3	4	5
18.	I do everything to win.	1	2	3	4	5
19.	I work out a solution that serves my own, as well as the other party's, interests as well as possible.	1	2	3	4	5
20.	I try to avoid a confrontation with the other party.	1	2	3	4	5

Scoring Key:

To determine your primary conflict-handling strategy, place the number 1 through 5 that represents your score for each statement next to the number for that statement. Then total up the columns.

(See next page.)

LEARNING ABOUT **YOURSELF** EXERCISE (Continued)

Yielding	Compromising	Forcing	Problem-solving	Avoiding
1. _____	2. _____	3. _____	4. _____	5. _____
6. _____	7. _____	8. _____	9. _____	10. _____
11. _____	12. _____	13. _____	14. _____	15. _____
16. _____	17. _____	18. _____	19. _____	20. _____
Totals _____	_____	_____	_____	_____

Your primary conflict-handling style is the category with the highest total. Your fallback intention is the category with the second-highest total.

Source: C. K. W. De Dreu, A. Evers, B. Beersma, E. S. Kluwer, and A. Nauta, "A Theory-Based Measure of Conflict Management Strategies in the Workplace," *Journal of Organizational Behavior* 22, no. 6 (September 2001), pp. 645–668. With permission.

Self-Assessment Library

More Learning About Yourself Exercises

Additional self-assessments relevant to this chapter appear at MyOBLab **(www.pearsoned.ca/myoblab.com)**.

II.C.5 What's My Preferred Conflict-Handling Style?

II.C.6 What's My Negotiating Style?

When you complete the additional assessments, consider the following:

1. Am I surprised about my score?
2. Would my friends evaluate me similarly?

BREAKOUT **GROUP** EXERCISES

Form small groups to discuss the following topics, as assigned by your instructor:

1. You and 2 other students carpool to school every day. The driver has recently taken to playing a new radio station quite loudly. You do not like the music, or the loudness. Using one of the conflict-handling strategies outlined in Exhibit 9-2 on page 342, indicate how you might go about resolving this conflict.

2. Using the example above, identify a number of BATNAs (*best alternative to a negotiated agreement*) available to you, and then decide whether you should continue carpooling.

3. Which conflict-handling strategy is most consistent with how you deal with conflict? Is your strategy effective? Why or why not?

WORKING WITH OTHERS EXERCISE

A Negotiation Role Play

This role play is designed to help you develop your negotiating skills. The class is to break into pairs. One person will play the role of Terry, the department supervisor. The other person will play Dale, Terry's boss.

The Situation: Terry and Dale work for hockey-equipment manufacturer Bauer. Terry supervises a research laboratory. Dale is the manager of R & D. Terry and Dale are former skaters who have worked for Bauer for more than 6 years. Dale has been Terry's boss for 2 years.

One of Terry's employees has greatly impressed Terry. This employee is Lisa Roland. Lisa was hired 11 months ago. She is 24 years old and holds a master's degree in mechanical engineering. Her entry-level salary was $52 500 a year. She was told by Terry that, in accordance with corporation policy, she would receive an initial performance evaluation at 6 months and a comprehensive review after 1 year. Based on her performance record, Lisa was told she could expect a salary adjustment at the time of the 1-year review.

Terry's evaluation of Lisa after 6 months was very positive. Terry commented on the long hours Lisa was working, her cooperative spirit, the fact that others in the lab enjoyed working with her, and her immediate positive impact on the project she had been assigned. Now that Lisa's first anniversary is coming up, Terry has again reviewed Lisa's performance. Terry thinks Lisa may be the best new person the R & D group has ever hired. After only a year, Terry has ranked Lisa as the number three performer in a department of 11.

Salaries in the department vary greatly. Terry, for instance, has a basic salary of $93 800, plus eligibility for a bonus that might add another $7000 to $11 000 a year. The salary range of the 11 department members is $42 500 to $79 000. The lowest salary is a recent hire with a bachelor's degree in physics. The two people that Terry has rated above Lisa earn base salaries of $73 800 and $78 900. They are both 27 years old and have been at Bauer for 3 and 4 years, respectively. The median salary in Terry's department is $65 300.

Terry's Role: You want to give Lisa a big raise. While she's young, she has proven to be an excellent addition to the department. You don't want to lose her. More important, she knows in general what other people in the department are earning, and she thinks she's underpaid. The company typically gives 1-year raises of 5 percent, although 10 percent is not unusual and 20 to 30 percent increases have been approved on occasion. You would like to get Lisa as large an increase as Dale will approve.

Dale's Role: All your supervisors typically try to squeeze you for as much money as they can for their people. You understand this because you did the same thing when you were a supervisor, but your boss wants to keep a lid on costs. He wants you to keep raises for recent hires generally in the range of 5 to 8 percent. In fact, he has sent a memo to all managers and supervisors stating this objective. However, your boss is also very concerned with equity and paying people what they are worth. You feel assured that he will support any salary recommendation you make, as long as it can be justified. Your goal, consistent with cost reduction, is to keep salary increases as low as possible.

The Negotiation: Terry has a meeting scheduled with Dale to discuss Lisa's performance review and salary adjustment. Take a couple of minutes to think through the facts in this exercise and to prepare a strategy. Then you have up to 15 minutes to conduct your negotiation. When your negotiation is complete, the class will compare the various strategies used and the outcomes that resulted.

ETHICAL **DILEMMA** EXERCISE

Is It Unethical to Lie and Deceive during Negotiations?

In Chapter 7, we addressed lying in the context of communication. Here we return to the topic of lying, but specifically as it relates to negotiation.[82] We think this issue is important because, for many people, there is no such thing as lying when it comes to negotiating.

It's been said that the whole notion of negotiation is built on ethical quicksand: To succeed, you must deceive. Is this true? Apparently a lot of people think so. For instance, one study found that 28 percent of negotiators lied about a common-interest issue during negotiations, while another study found that 100 percent of negotiators either failed to reveal a problem or actively lied about it during negotiations if they were not directly asked about the issue.

Is it possible for someone to maintain high ethical standards and, at the same time, deal with the daily need to negotiate with bosses, peers, staff, people from other organizations, friends, and even relatives?

We can probably agree that bald-faced lies during negotiation are wrong. At least most ethicists would probably agree. The universal dilemma surrounds the little lies—the omissions, evasions, and concealments that are often necessary to best an opponent.

During negotiations, when is a lie a lie? Is exaggerating benefits, downplaying negatives, ignoring flaws, or saying "I don't know" when in reality you do considered lying? Is declaring that "this is my final offer and nonnegotiable" (even when you are posturing) a lie? Is pretending to bend over backward to make meaningful concessions lying? Rather than being unethical practices, the use of these "lies" is considered by many as indicators that a negotiator is strong, smart, and savvy.

When is evasiveness and deception out of bounds? Is it naive to be completely honest and bare your soul during negotiations? Or are the rules of negotiations unique: Any tactic that will improve your chance of winning is acceptable?

CASE INCIDENTS

David Out-Negotiating Goliath: Apotex and Bristol-Myers Squibb

Peter Dolan survived many crises in his five-year tenure as CEO of drug giant Bristol-Myers Squibb.[83] There were a corporate accounting scandal, allegations of insider trading, FBI raids of his office, and a stock price that dropped 60 percent during his tenure. But in the end, what may have done Dolan in was his negotiation performance against the head of Apotex, a Canadian drug company founded by Dr. Barry Sherman.

At its peak, Plavix—a drug to prevent heart attacks—was Bristol-Myers's best-selling drug and accounted for a staggering one-third of its profits. So when Apotex developed a generic Plavix knockoff, Dolan sought to negotiate an agreement that would pay Apotex in exchange for a delayed launch of Apotex's generic competitor. Dolan sent one of his closest lieutenants, Andrew Bodnar, to negotiate with Sherman. Bodnar and Sherman developed a good rapport, and at several points in their negotiations asked their attorneys to leave them alone. At one key point

in the negotiations, Bodnar flew to Toronto alone, without Bristol-Myers's attorneys, as a "gesture of goodwill. The thinking was that the negotiations would be more effective this way."

As Dolan, Bodnar, and Bristol-Myers became increasingly concerned with reaching an agreement with Sherman and Apotex, they developed a blind spot. Privately, Sherman was betting that the Federal Trade Commission (FTC) would not approve the noncompete agreement the two parties were negotiating, and his goal in the negotiation was to extract an agreement from Bristol-Myers that would position Apotex favourably should the FTC reject the deal. Indeed, he nonchalantly inserted a clause in the deal that would require Bristol-Myers to pay Apotex $60 million if the FTC rejected the deal. "I thought the FTC would turn it down, but I didn't let on that I did," Sherman said. "They seemed blind to it."

In the meantime, Apotex covertly began shipping its generic equivalent to the United States. Thus, Sherman also managed to launch the generic equivalent without Bristol-Myers even considering the possibility that he would do so while still engaged in negotiations. The company was only able to sell Apotex in the United States for three weeks before a federal judge stopped sales, but in that short period of time, about a six-month supply of the drug had entered the US market. This cost Bristol-Myers about $1 billion in lost sales.

"It looks like a much smaller generic private company completely outmaneuvered two of the giants of the pharmaceutical industry," said Gbola Amusa, European pharmaceutical analyst for Sanford C. Bernstein and Company.

"It's not clear how or why that happened. The reaction from [Bristol-Myers] investors and analysts has ranged from shock to outright anger." Within a few months, Dolan was out at Bristol-Myers. In 2008, Bodnar was indicted for negotiating the agreement with Apotex and not informing US federal regulators of all of its details. Sherman had no obligation to report the deal to US regulators, as Apotex is a Canadian company.

Questions

1. What principles of distributive negotiation did Sherman use to gain his advantage?

2. Do you think Sherman behaved ethically? Why or why not?

3. What does this incident tell you about the role of deception in negotiation?

Managing Conflict at Schneider National

Schneider National is a transportation and logistics firm with locations in Canada, the United States, and Mexico.[84] Begun in 1935, the private company now operates 14 000 trucks and 40 000 trailers that haul freight 8 million kilometres per day. Revenues are approximately $2.4 billion (US) a year.

The company has had only three leaders. The first was the founder; the second was his son, Donald; and in August 2002, the first nonfamily member took the helm when Chris Lofgren was made CEO, replacing Schneider, who was 67 years old. But it was not as if the company was not making preparations for executive leadership. Don Schneider told his board of directors in 1988 that their primary task was finding a successor. Lofgren joined the company in 1994 as a vice-president and became chief operating officer in 2000. After being appointed COO, Lofgren began to lay the framework for the six-person executive group that today shares many of the company's strategic responsibilities.

Everyone who knows Don Schneider concedes that he is a tough act to follow. "Don is an icon," says another top Schneider executive. "He probably commands more respect in transportation and logistics than anybody in the industry." Says Lofgren, "Our approach has been to put together an executive team that has a set of skills, perspectives and experiences that, when you put that team together, is broader and bigger than Don Schneider." The idea, according to Lofgren, is to have individuals with product line or functional focus, while maintaining their oversight of those areas, develop a sense of responsibility for the financial performance of the whole company. "If you have people who aren't taking an enterprise solution, their only role is their function or their business, then ultimately it has to go to someone who's going to referee the points of tension," says Lofgren. And Lofgren has no intention of playing the referee role.

To mediate the points of conflict, the executive group has had to learn how to work together. They have even brought in outside counsel to help them listen and understand one another better, and focus debate on critical issues. "Conflict between people or between groups of people is not positive. Conflict around business issues is the most wonderful, healthy thing," says Lofgren. "Any business without tension will fall to its lowest level of performance."

Questions

1. What view toward conflict does Lofgren support? Explain.

2. Explain why the transition in leadership from Don Schneider to Chris Lofgren was relatively conflict-free.

3. How does the organization of the executive group create conflict? How does it reduce conflict?

4. How does Lofgren manage conflict?

From Concepts to Skills

Negotiating

Once you have taken the time to assess your own goals, to consider the other party's goals and interests, and to develop a strategy, you are ready to begin actual negotiations. The following five suggestions should improve your negotiating skills:[85]

1. *Begin with a positive overture.* Studies on negotiation show that concessions tend to be reciprocated and lead to agreements. As a result, begin bargaining with a positive overture—perhaps a small concession—and then reciprocate your opponent's concessions.

2. *Address problems, not personalities.* Concentrate on the negotiation issues, not on the personal characteristics of your opponent. When negotiations get tough, avoid the tendency to attack your opponent. It's your opponent's ideas or position that you disagree with, not him or her personally. Separate the people from the problem, and don't personalize differences.

3. *Pay little attention to initial offers.* Treat an initial offer as merely a point of departure. Everyone has to have an initial position. These initial offers tend to be extreme and idealistic. Treat them as such.

4. *Emphasize win-win solutions.* Inexperienced negotiators often assume that their gain must come at the expense of the other party. As noted with integrative bargaining, that need not be the case. There are often win-win solutions. But assuming a zero-sum game means missed opportunities for trade-offs that could benefit both sides. So if conditions are supportive, look for an integrative solution. Frame options in terms of your opponent's interests, and look for solutions that can allow your opponent, as well as yourself, to declare a victory.

5. *Create an open and trusting climate.* Skilled negotiators are better listeners, ask more questions, focus their arguments more directly, are less defensive, and have learned to avoid words and phrases that can irritate an opponent (for example, "generous offer," "fair price," "reasonable arrangement"). In other words, they are better at creating the open and trusting climate necessary for reaching an integrative settlement.

Practising Skills

As marketing director for Done Right, a regional home-repair chain, you have come up with a plan you believe has significant potential for future sales. Your plan involves a customer information service designed to help people make their homes more environmentally sensitive. Then, based on homeowners' assessments of their homes' environmental impact, your firm will be prepared to help them deal with problems or concerns they may uncover. You are really excited about the competitive potential of this new service. You envision pamphlets, in-store appearances by environmental experts, as well as contests for consumers and school kids. After several weeks of preparations, you make your pitch to your boss, Nick Castro. You point out how the market for environmentally sensitive products is growing and how this growing demand represents the perfect opportunity for Done Right. Nick seems impressed by your presentation, but he has expressed one major concern: He thinks your workload is already too heavy. He does not see how you are going to have enough time to start this new service and still be able to look after all of your other assigned marketing duties. You really want to start the new service. What strategy will you follow in your negotiation with Nick?

Reinforcing Skills

1. Negotiate with a team member or work colleague to handle a small section of work that you are not going to be able to get done in time for an important deadline.

2. The next time you purchase a relatively expensive item (such as an automobile, apartment lease, appliance, jewellery), attempt to negotiate a better price and gain some concessions such as an extended warranty, smaller down payment, maintenance services, or the like.

CASE 9 Clash of the Co-workers

CBC

Venture conducted a survey to determine workers' perceptions of the causes of conflict at work. The top three vote-getters were (1) people who talk too loudly on the phone, (2) office gossip, and (3) co-workers who waste your time. *Venture* further examined the impact of office gossip, anger about co-workers who don't pull their weight, and clashes between older and younger workers.

Office Gossip

Office gossip can poison a workplace. A tanning-salon owner who had worked hard to build her company encountered big problems when employees started spreading rumours about each other. When the owner became aware of the gossiping, she called all employees into head office and asked them to sign a contract forbidding gossip. One prohibited behaviour is talking about a co-worker when that co-worker is not present. A year after introducing the contract, the salon owner is getting calls from other companies asking about the policy.

Bob Summerhurst, a human resource specialist, says that gossip occurs when bosses play favourites or when they don't communicate properly. Information voids get filled with gossip, which is often negative. His solution is not to ban gossip, but to have regular meetings of managers and employees.

Co-workers Who Don't Pull Their Weight

Jerry Steinberg, a Vancouver teacher, says that employees with children are often treated as "special" and he thinks that this is not fair. He says people like him are asked to work a few extra hours a week to cover for parents who are tending to their children. The problem is worst during the holiday season because people with no children are asked to work holidays so that employees with children can spend time with their kids.

Steinberg is speaking up about his concerns. He has started a website called No Kidding where child-free members can talk about the unfair treatment they receive at work. But Steinberg says it is hard to stand up for yourself: It sounds heartless to be unsympathetic to parents' wishes to spend time with their children. But he also observes that people make a choice to have children, and they should not expect to gain advantages because of that choice. He is also unhappy about the extra employment benefits that parents get. He has a simple solution: Give each employee a certain dollar amount that they can spend on whatever benefits they want.

The Generation Gap

Young people in their 20s have generally grown up in an environment where their Baby Boomer parents gave them a lot of things. Now those young people are entering the workforce, and they want more things: benefits, money, authority, and free time. And they want them right now.

Consider John and Ryan, recent college grads. They feel that they work very hard, but they don't necessarily want to do what their parents did (like wearing a suit and tie to work, or working from 9 to 5). Mike Farrell, who researches attitudes of young people, notes that most young people are plugged in and well informed, and these are qualities that employers crave. Theresa Williams, who hires workers for the *Chronicle-Herald* (Halifax), finds that young people today don't seem grateful to be offered a job like Boomers were. She tries to overcome the difficulties in recruiting young people by emphasizing the good working conditions at the *Chronicle-Herald*.

The way students look for jobs is also changing. One company therefore came up with a gimmick: They posted a job competition on the Internet, with the prize being a job for a year, a free apartment, and a trip home for the holidays. The two winners—John and Ryan—moved to Halifax. A year later, they moved out of their free apartment, but stayed on with the company. Now they are helping to design this year's job competition, and they are on board with "the old guys."

Questions

1. What are the basic causes of conflict in organizations? What caused the conflicts in each of the three situations described above?

2. What is the difference between "cognitive" conflict and "affective" conflict? How are these terms relevant in each of the three situations described above?

3. What conflict resolution strategies could Jerry Steinberg consider as he attempts to resolve his unhappiness about certain people getting "special" treatment in his organization? Which one do you think would be most effective? Explain.

Source: Based on "Clash of the Co-workers," *CBC Venture*, March 26, 2006.

The Toxic Workplace

It's not unusual to find the following employee behaviours in today's workplace:

Answering the phone with a "yeah," neglecting to say thank you or please, using voice mail to screen calls, leaving a half-cup of coffee behind to avoid having to brew the next pot, standing uninvited but impatiently over the desk of someone engaged in a telephone conversation, dropping trash on the floor and leaving it for the maintenance crew to clean up, and talking loudly on the phone about personal matters.[1]

Some employers or managers fit the following descriptions:

In the months since [the new owner of the pharmacy] has been in charge [he] has made it clear that he is at liberty to fire employees at will . . . change their positions, decrease their bonus percentages, and refuse time-off and vacation choices. Furthermore, he has established an authoritarian work structure characterized by distrust, cut-backs on many items deemed essential to work comfort, disrespect, rigidity and poor to no communication.[2]

He walked all over people. He made fun of them; he intimidated them. He criticized work for no reason, and he changed his plans daily.[3]

What Is Happening in Our Workplaces?

Workplaces today are receiving highly critical reviews, being called everything from "uncivil" to "toxic."

Lynne Anderson and Christine Pearson, two management professors from St. Joseph's University and the University of North Carolina, respectively, note that "Historians may view the dawn of the twenty-first century as a time of thoughtless acts and rudeness: We tailgate, even in the slow lane; we dial wrong numbers and then slam the receiver on the innocent respondent; we break appointments with nonchalance."[4] The workplace has often been seen as one of the places where civility still ruled, with co-workers treating each other with a mixture of formality and friendliness, distance and politeness. However, with downsizing, re-engineering, budget cuts, pressures for increased productivity, autocratic work environments, and the use of part-time employees, there has been an increase in "uncivil and aggressive workplace behaviours."[5]

What does civility in the workplace mean? A simple definition of workplace civility is behaviour "involving politeness and regard for others in the workplace, within workplace norms for respect."[6] Workplace incivility, then, "involves acting with disregard for others in the workplace, in violation of workplace norms for respect."[7] Of course, different workplaces will have different norms for what determines mutual respect. For instance, in most restaurants, if the staff were rude to you when you were there for dinner, you would be annoyed, and perhaps even complain to the manager. However, at The Elbow Room in downtown Vancouver, if customers complain they are in a hurry, manager Patrick Savoie might well say, "If you're in a hurry, you should have gone to McDonald's."[8] Such a comeback is acceptable to the diners at The Elbow Room, because rudeness is its trademark.

Most work environments are not expected to be characterized by such rudeness. However, this has been changing in recent years. Robert Warren, a University of Manitoba marketing professor, notes that "simple courtesy has gone by the board."[9]

There is documented evidence of the rise of violence and threats of violence at work.[10] However, several studies have found that there is persistent negative behaviour in the workplace that is not of a violent nature.[11] For instance, a survey of 603 Toronto nurses found that 33 percent had experienced verbal abuse during the five previous days of work.[12]

Another study found that 78 percent of employees interviewed think that workplace incivility has increased in the past 10 years.[13] The researchers found that men are mostly to blame for this change: "Although men and women are targets of disrespect and rudeness in equal numbers . . . men instigate the rudeness 70 percent of the time."[14]

Rude behaviour is not confined to men, however. Professor André Roberge at Laval University suggests that some of the rudeness is generational. He finds that "young clerks often lack both knowledge and civility. Employers are having to train young people in simple manners because that is not being done at home."[15] Professor Warren backs this up: "One of the biggest complaints I hear from businesses when I go to talk about graduates is the lack of interpersonal skills."[16]

Workplace Violence

Recently, researchers have suggested that incivility may be the beginning of more negative behaviours in the workplace, including aggression and violence.[17]

Pierre Lebrun chose a deadly way to exhibit the anger he had stored up from his workplace.[18] He took a hunting rifle to Ottawa-Carleton–based OC Transpo and killed four public transit co-workers on April 6, 1999, before turning the gun on himself. Lebrun felt that he had been the target of harassment by his co-workers for years because of his stuttering. If this sounds like an unusual response for an irate employee, consider the circumstances at OC Transpo. "Quite apart from what's alleged or otherwise with Mr. Lebrun's situation, we know [OC Transpo's] had a very unhappy work environment for a long time," Al Loney, former chair of Ottawa-Carleton's transit commission, noted. A consultant's report produced the year before the shooting found a workplace with "rock-bottom morale and poor management." It was not uncommon for fights to break out in the unit where the four men were killed.

Workplace violence, according to the International Labour Organization (ILO), includes

any incident in which a person is abused, threatened or assaulted in circumstances relating to [his or her] work. These behaviours would originate from customers or co-workers at any level of the organization. This definition would include all forms of harassment, bullying, intimidation, physical threats, assaults, robbery and other intrusive behaviour.[19]

No Canadian statistics on anger at work are available, although

53 percent of women and 47 percent of men reported experiencing workplace violence in 2004.[20] Studies show that anger pervades the US workplace. A 2000 Gallup poll conducted in the United States found that 25 percent of the working adults surveyed felt like screaming or shouting because of job stress, 14 percent had considered hitting a co-worker, and 10 percent worry about colleagues becoming violent. Almost half of America workers experienced yelling and verbal abuse on the job in 2008, and about 2.5 percent report that they have pushed, slapped, or hit someone at work.[21] Twenty employees are murdered each week in the United States.[22]

Canadian workplaces are not murder-free, however. Between 2001 and 2005, an average of 14 workers were killed each year while "on-the-job."[23] Most of these workplace incidents were carried out by male spouses and partners of female employees. Surprisingly, Canada scores higher than the United States on workplace violence. In an ILO study involving 130 000 workers in 32 countries, Argentina was ranked the most violent. Romania was second, France third, and Canada fourth. The United States placed ninth.[24]

Sixty-four percent of union representatives who were surveyed reported an increase in workplace aggression, based on their review of incident reports, grievance files, and other solid evidence.[26] To understand the seriousness of this situation, consider that one-quarter of Nova Scotia teachers surveyed reported that they faced physical violence at work during the 2001–2002 school year.[27]

What Causes Incivility (and Worse) in the Workplace?

If employers and employees are acting with less civility toward each other, what is causing this to happen?

Managers and employees often have different views of the employee's role in the organization. Jeffrey Pfeffer, a professor of organizational behaviour at the Graduate School of Business at Stanford University, notes that many companies don't really value their employees: "Most managers, if they're being honest with themselves, will admit it: When they look at their people, they see costs, they see salaries, they see benefits, they see overhead. Very few companies look at their people and see assets."[28]

Most employees, however, like to think that they are assets to their organization. The realization that they are simply costs and not valued members of an organization can cause frustration for employees.

In addition, "employers' excessive demands and top-down style of management are contributing to the rise of 'work rage,'" claims Gerry Smith, vice-president of organizational health and training at Toronto-based Shepell•fgi and author of *Work Rage*.[29] He cites demands coming from a variety of sources: "overtime, downsizing, rapid technological changes, company restructuring and difficulty balancing the demands of job and home."[30] Smith worries about the consequences of these demands: "If you push people too hard, set unrealistic expectations and cut back their benefits, they're going to strike back."[31]

Smith's work supports the findings of a study that reported the most common cause of anger is the actions of supervisors or managers.[32] Other common causes of anger identified by the researchers include lack of productivity by co-workers and others; tight deadlines; heavy workload; interaction with the public; and bad treatment.

The Psychological Contract

Some researchers have looked at this frustration in terms of a breakdown of the psychological contract formed between employees and employers. Employers and employees begin to develop psychological contracts as they are first introduced to each other in the hiring process.[33] These continue over time as the employer and the employee come to understand each other's expectations about the amounts and quality of work to be performed and the types of rewards to be given. For instance, when an employee is continually asked to work late and/or be available at all hours through pagers

FactBox

- In 2008, 52% of working Canadians reported a strong sense of loyalty to their employer. In 1991, the level of commitment was 62%.

- 72% of Canadian workers would leave their employers if offered a better-paying comparable job..

- Of those who experience rudeness, 12% quit their jobs in response, 22% decrease their work effort, and 52% lose work time worrying about it.

- Employees over the age of 55 express the highest degree of commitment to their employers.[25]

and email, the employee may assume that doing so will result in greater rewards or faster promotion down the line. The employer may have had no such intention, and may even be thinking that the employee should be grateful simply to have a job. Later, when the employee does not get expected (though never promised) rewards, he or she is disappointed.

Sandra Robinson, an organizational behaviour professor at the Sauder School of Business at the University of British Columbia, and her colleagues have found that when a psychological contract is violated (perceptually or actually), the relationship between the employee and the employer is damaged. This can result in the loss of trust.[34] The breakdown in trust can cause employees to be less ready to accept decisions or obey rules.[35] The erosion of trust can also lead employees to take revenge on the employer. So they don't carry out their end of a task. Or they refuse to pass on messages. They engage in any number of subtle and not-so-subtle behaviours that affect the way work gets done—or prevents work from getting done.

The Toxic Organization

Pfeffer suggests that companies have become "toxic places to work.[36] He notes that companies, particularly in Silicon Valley, ask their employees to sign contracts on the first day of work indicating the employee's understanding that the company has the right to fire at will and for any reason. Some employers also ask their employees to choose between having a life and having a career. Pfeffer relates a joke people used to tell about Microsoft: "We offer flexible time—you can work any

Do You Have a Toxic Manager?

Below are some of the toxic behaviours of managers and the workplace cultures that allow these behaviours to thrive.[39]

Managerial Toxic Behaviour

- *Actor behaviour.* These managers act out anger rather than discuss problems. They slam doors, sulk, and make it clear they are angry, but refuse to talk about it.

- *Fragmentor behaviour.* These managers see no connection between what they do and the outcome, and take no responsibility for their behaviour.

- *Me-first behaviour.* These managers make decisions based on their own convenience.

- *Mixed-messenger behaviour.* These managers present themselves one way, but their behaviour does not match what they say.

- *Wooden-stick behaviour.* These managers are extremely rigid and controlling.

- *Escape-artist behaviour.* These managers don't deal with reality; they often lie or, at the extreme, escape through drugs or alcohol.

Workplace Culture That Fosters This Behaviour

- *Macho culture.* People don't discuss problems. The emphasis is to "take it like a man."

- *Specialist culture.* Employees who are technically gifted or great in their fields don't have to consider how their behaviour or work impacts anyone.

- *Elitist culture.* Promotions and rewards are not based on your work but on who your buddies are.

- *Office-politics culture.* Promotions and rewards are based on flattery and positioning.

- *Change-resistant culture.* Upper management struggles to maintain the status quo regardless of the outcome.

- *Workaholic culture.* Employees are forced to spend more time at the office than necessary.

18 hours you want."[37] This kind of attitude can be toxic to employees, though this does not imply that Microsoft is a toxic employer.

What does it mean to be a toxic organization? The late professor Peter Frost of the Sauder School of Business at the University of British Columbia notes that there will always be pain in organizations, but that sometimes it becomes so intense

or prolonged that conditions within the organization begin to break down. In other words, the situation becomes toxic. This is not dissimilar to what the liver or kidneys do when toxins become too intense in a human body.[38]

What causes organizations to be toxic? Like Pfeffer, professors Frost and Robinson identify a number of factors. Downsizing and organizational change are two main factors, particularly in recent years. Sometimes organizations experience unexpected events—such as the sudden death of a key manager, an unwise move by senior management, strong competition from a start-up company—that lead to toxicity. Other organizations are toxic throughout their system due to policies and practices that create distress. Such factors as unreasonable stretch goals or performance targets, or unrelenting internal competition, can create toxicity. There are also toxic managers who lead through insensitivity, vindictiveness, and failure to take responsibility, or they are control freaks or are unethical. The inset *Do You Have a Toxic Manager?* on page 371 lists some types of toxic managers and the workplace culture that fosters their behaviour.

What Are the Effects of Incivility and Toxicity in the Workplace?

In general, researchers have found that the effects of workplace anger are sometimes subtle: a hostile work environment and the tendency to do only enough work to get by.[40]

Those who feel chronic anger in the workplace are more likely to report "feelings of betrayal by the organization, decreased feelings of loyalty, a decreased sense that respondent values and the organization's values are similar, a decreased sense that the employer treated the respondent with dignity and respect, and a decreased sense that employers had fulfilled promises made to respondents."[41] So do these feelings make a difference? Apparently so. Researchers have found that those who felt angry with their employers were less likely to put forth their best effort, more likely to be competitive

toward other employees, and less likely to suggest "a quicker and better way to do their job.[42] All of these actions tend to decrease the productivity possible in the workplace.

It's not just those who work for an organization who are affected by incivility and toxicity. Poor service, from indifference to rudeness to outright hostility, characterizes many transactions in Canadian businesses. "Across the country, better business bureaus, provincial government consumer-help agencies and media ombudsmen report a lengthening litany of complaints about contractors, car dealers, repair shops, moving companies, airlines and department stores."[43] This suggests that customers and clients may well be feeling the impact of internal workplace dynamics.

The Toxin Handler

Employees of toxic organizations suffer pain from their experiences in a toxic environment. In some organizations, mechanisms, often informal, are set up to deal with the results of toxicity.

Frost and Robinson identified a special role that some employees play in trying to relieve the toxicity within an organization: the toxin handler. This person tries to mitigate the pain by softening the blow of downsizing, or change, or the behaviour of the toxic leader. Essentially,

the toxin handler helps others around him or her deal with the strains of the organization by counselling, advising, shielding employees from the wrath of angry managers, reinterpreting the managers' messages to make them less harsh, etcetera.

So who takes on this role? Certainly no organization to date has a line on its organizational chart for "the toxin handler." Often the role emerges as part of an individual's position in an organization; for instance, a manager in the human resource department may take on this role. In many cases, however, handlers are pulled into the role "bit by bit—by their colleagues, who turn to them because they are trustworthy, calm, kind and nonjudgmental."[44]

Frost and Robinson, in profiling these individuals, suggest that toxin handlers are predisposed to say yes, have a high tolerance for pain, a surplus of empathy, and when they notice people in pain, they have a need to make the situation right. But these are not individuals who thrive simply on dealing with the emotional needs of others. Quoting one of the managers in their study, Frost and Robinson cite the full range of activities of most toxin handlers: "These people are usually relentless in their drive to accomplish organizational targets and rarely lose focus on business issues. Managing

How Toxin Handlers Alleviate Organizational Pain

- They listen empathetically.
- They suggest solutions.
- They work behind the scenes to prevent pain.
- They carry the confidences of others.
- They reframe difficult messages.[45]

Manners are an over-romanticized concept. The big issue is not that employees need to be concerned about their manners. Rather, employers should be paying better wages.

The Golden Rule, "Do unto others as you would have others do unto you," should still have a role in today's workplace. Being nice pays off.

emotional pain is one of their means."[46]

The inset *How Toxin Handlers Alleviate Organizational Pain* identifies the many tasks that toxin handlers take on in an organization. Frost and Robinson suggest that these tasks will probably need to be handled forever, and they recommend that organizations take steps to actively support people performing this role.

Research Exercises

1. Look for data on violence and anger in the workplace in other countries. How do these data compare with the Canadian and American data presented here? What might you conclude about

how violence and anger in the workplace are expressed in different cultures?

2. Identify three Canadian organizations that are trying to foster better and/or less toxic environments for their employees. What kind of effect is this having on the organizations' bottom lines?

Your Perspective

1. Is it reasonable to suggest, as some researchers have, that young people today have not learned to be civil to others or do not place a high priority on doing so? Do you see this as one of the causes of incivility in the workplace?

2. What should be done about managers who create toxicity in the workplace while being rewarded because they achieve bottom-line results? Should bottom-line results justify their behaviour?

Want to Know More?

If you would like to read more on this topic, see Peter Frost, *Toxic Emotions at Work* (Cambridge, MA: Harvard Business School Press, 2003); P. Frost and S. Robinson, "The Toxic Handler: Organizational Hero—and Casualty," *Harvard Business Review*, July–August 1999, pp. 96–106 (Reprint 99406); and K. Macklem, "The Toxic Workplace: A Poisoned Work Environment Can Wreak Havoc on a Company's Culture and Its Employees," *Macleans.ca*, January 31, 2005. You can find the latter article at www.macleans.ca/article.jsp?content=20050131_99562_99562&source=srch.

Organizational Culture

How does a pizza franchise business ensure quality control across the country? Developing a strong culture is part of the answer.

1 What is the purpose of organizational culture?

2 How do you read an organization's culture?

3 How do you create and maintain organizational culture?

4 Can organizational culture have a downside?

5 How do you change organizational culture?

When you walk into a Boston Pizza restaurant in BC, Ontario, or Quebec, you will find many similarities, but a few differences too.[1] The Quebec restaurants carry poutine, while the Ontario restaurants have a meatball sub on the menu and use a different type of pepperoni on the pizzas than those made in BC and Quebec.

Despite these menu differences, the similarity that binds the Richmond, BC-based Boston Pizza restaurants throughout Canada and the US is the strong organizational culture created by the company's co-owners, Jim Treliving and George Melville. The two men believe that a strong culture makes for a strong organization, and they emphasize the importance of finding the right people, having good systems in place, training employees, and communicating effectively.

The emphasis on a strong culture seems to be paying off for Boston Pizza. In 2008, it was named one of Canada's 10 Most Admired Corporate Cultures, and its three-year average revenue growth far exceeded industry standards and the TSX 60 Composite index.

In this chapter, we show that every organization has a culture. We examine how that culture reveals itself and the impact it has on the attitudes and behaviours of members of that organization. An understanding of what makes up an organization's culture and how it is created, sustained, and learned enhances our ability to explain and predict the behaviour of people at work.

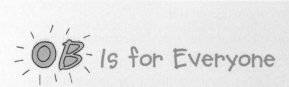 Is for Everyone

- What does organizational culture do?
- What kind of organizational culture would work best for you?
- Is culture the same as rules?

Self-Assessment Library

LEARNING ABOUT YOURSELF

- Organizational Cultural Fit
- Organization Commitment

What Is Organizational Culture?

1 What is the purpose of organizational culture?

When Henry Mintzberg, professor at McGill University and one of the world's leading management experts, was asked to compare organizational structure and corporate culture, he said, "Culture is the soul of the organization—the beliefs and values, and how they are manifested. I think of the structure as the skeleton, and as the flesh and blood. And culture is the soul that holds the thing together and gives it life force."[2]

Mintzberg's culture metaphor provides a clear image of how to think about culture. Culture provides stability to an organization and gives employees a clear understanding of "the way things are done around here." Culture sets the tone for how an organization operates and how individuals within the organization interact. Think of the different impressions you have when a receptionist tells you that "Ms. Dettweiler" will be available in a moment, while at another organization you are told that "Emma" will be with you as soon as she gets off the phone. It's clear that in one organization the rules are more formal than in the other.

As we discuss organizational culture, you may want to remember that organizations differ considerably in the cultures they adopt. Consider the different cultures of Calgary-based WestJet Airlines and Montreal-based Air Canada. WestJet is viewed as having a "young, spunky, can-do environment, where customers will have more fun."[3] Air Canada, by contrast, is considered less helpful and friendly. One analyst even suggested that Air Canada staff "tend to make their customers feel stressed" by their confrontational behaviour.[4] Our discussion of culture should help you understand how these differences across organizations occur.

As you start to think about different organizations where you might work, you will want to research their cultures. An organization that expects employees to work 15 hours a day may not be where you would like to work. To help you think more about culture and its impact on you, you may want to complete the *Learning About Yourself Exercise* on page 401, which assesses whether you would be more comfortable in a formal, rule-oriented culture or a more informal, flexible culture.

Learning About Yourself

1. What Kind of Organizational Culture Fits You Best? **(page 401)**

Definition of Organizational Culture

organizational culture The pattern of shared values, beliefs, and assumptions considered to be the appropriate way to think and act within an organization.

Organizational culture is the pattern of shared values, beliefs, and assumptions considered to be the appropriate way to think and act within an organization. The key features of culture are as follows:

- Culture is shared by the members of the organization.

- Culture helps members of the organization solve and understand the things that it encounters, both internally and externally.

- Because the assumptions, beliefs, and expectations that make up culture have worked over time, the organization's members believe they are valid. Therefore, they are taught to people who join the organization.

- These assumptions, beliefs, and expectations strongly influence how people perceive, think, feel, and behave within the organization.[5]

Not every group develops a culture, although any group that has existed for a while and has shared learnings will likely have a culture. Groups that experience high turnover (so that learnings are not really passed down to new members effectively) and groups that have not experienced any challenging events may not develop cultures.

Levels of Culture

Because organizational culture has multiple levels,[6] the metaphor of an iceberg has often been used to describe it.[7] However, a simmering volcano may better represent the layers

EXHIBIT 10-1   Layers of Culture

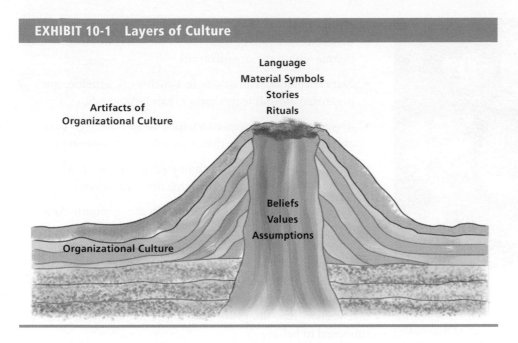

of culture: beliefs, values, assumptions bubble below the surface, producing observable aspects of culture at the surface. Exhibit 10-1 reminds us that culture is very visible at the level of **artifacts**. These are what you see, hear, and feel when you encounter an organization's culture. You may notice, for instance, that employees in two offices have very different dress policies, or one office displays great works of art while another posts company mottos on the wall. These visible artifacts emerge from the organization's culture.

Exhibit 10-1 also shows us that beliefs, values, and assumptions, unlike artifacts, are not always readily observable. Instead, we rely on the visible artifacts (material symbols, special language used, rituals carried out, and stories told to others) to help us uncover the organization's beliefs, values, and assumptions. **Beliefs** are the understandings of how objects and ideas relate to each other. **Values** are the stable, long-lasting beliefs about what is important. For instance, Winnipeg-based Palliser Furniture, a manufacturer of wooden and upholstered furniture, promotes the following corporate values: "demonstrate integrity in all relationships; promote the dignity and value of each other; respect the environment; support our community; and strive for excellence in all we do."[8] **Assumptions** are the taken-for-granted notions of how something should be. When basic assumptions are held by the entire group, members will have difficulty conceiving of another way of doing things. For instance, in Canada, some students hold a basic assumption that universities should not consider costs when setting tuition, and should keep tuition low for greater access by students. Beliefs, values, and assumptions, if we can uncover them, help us understand why organizations do the things that we observe.

artifacts Aspects of an organization's culture that you see, hear, and feel.

beliefs The understandings of how objects and ideas relate to each other.

values The stable, long-lasting beliefs about what is important.

assumptions The taken-for-granted notions of how something should be.

Characteristics of Culture

Research suggests that seven primary characteristics capture the essence of an organization's culture:[9]

- *Innovation and risk-taking.* The degree to which employees are encouraged to be innovative and take risks.

- *Attention to detail.* The degree to which employees are expected to work with precision, analysis, and attention to detail.

- *Outcome orientation.* The degree to which management focuses on results, or outcomes, rather than on the techniques and processes used to achieve these outcomes.

Vancouver-based Playland amusement park hires hundreds of young people each summer to run the rides, sell tickets, and manage the games booths. Managers want to make sure that new employees will fit into the "fun culture" of the environment. Instead of one-on-one interviews, applicants are put into teams where they solve puzzles together while managers watch the group dynamics. Amy Nguyen (left) and Chloe Wong are two of the teens hired after they did well in the group interview.

- *People orientation.* The degree to which management decisions take into consideration the effect of outcomes on people within the organization.

- *Team orientation.* The degree to which work activities are organized around teams rather than individuals.

- *Aggressiveness.* The degree to which people are aggressive and competitive rather than easygoing and supportive.

- *Stability.* The degree to which organizational activities emphasize maintaining the status quo in contrast to growth.

Each of these characteristics exists on a continuum from low to high.

When individuals consider their organization in terms of these seven characteristics, they get a composite picture of the organization's culture. This picture becomes the basis for feelings of shared understanding that members have about the organization, how things are done in it, and the way members are supposed to behave.

Exhibit 10-2 demonstrates how these characteristics can be mixed to create highly diverse organizations. To help you understand some of the characteristics of culture, you may want to look at the *Working with Others Exercise* on page 402, which asks you to rate your classroom culture.

Culture's Functions

Culture performs a number of functions within an organization:

- It has a boundary-defining role because it creates distinction between one organization and others.

- It conveys a sense of identity to organization members.

- It helps create commitment to something larger than an individual's self-interest.

- It enhances stability; it is the social glue that helps hold the organization together by providing appropriate standards for what employees should say and do.

EXHIBIT 10-2   Contrasting Organizational Cultures

Organization A	Organization B
• Managers must fully document all decisions.	• Management encourages and rewards risk-taking and change.
• Creative decisions, change, and risks are not encouraged.	• Employees are encouraged to "run with" ideas, and failures are treated as "learning experiences."
• Extensive rules and regulations exist for all employees.	• Employees have few rules and regulations to follow.
• Productivity is valued over employee morale.	• Productivity is balanced with treating its people right.
• Employees are encouraged to stay within their own department.	• Team members are encouraged to interact with people at all levels and functions.
• Individual effort is encouraged.	• Many rewards are team-based.

- It serves as a control mechanism that guides and shapes the attitudes and behaviour of employees, and helps them make sense of the organization.

This last function is of particular interest to us.[10] As the following quotation makes clear, culture defines the rules of the game:

Culture by definition is elusive, intangible, implicit, and taken for granted. But every organization develops a core set of assumptions, understandings, and implicit rules that govern day-to-day behaviour in the workplace. Until newcomers learn the rules, they are not accepted as full-fledged members of the organization. Transgressions of the rules on the part of high-level executives or front-line employees result in universal disapproval and powerful penalties. Conformity to the rules becomes the primary basis for reward and upward mobility.[11]

The role of culture in influencing employee behaviour appears to be increasingly important in today's workplace.[12] As organizations widen spans of control, flatten

> **What does organizational culture do?**

structures, introduce teams, reduce formalization, and empower employees, the shared meaning provided by a strong culture ensures that everyone is pointed in the same direction. Geoffrey Relph, who was IBM Canada's director of services marketing, compared the culture of his previous company (GE Appliances in Louisville, Kentucky) with that of IBM: "The priorities in GE are: 'Make the financial commitments. Make the financial commitments. Make the financial commitments.' At IBM, the company's attention is divided among customer satisfaction, employee morale, and positive financial results."[13] These two cultures give employees and managers different messages about where they should direct their attention.

Culture can also influence people's ethical behaviour. When lower-level employees see their managers padding expense reports, this sends a signal that the firm tolerates such dishonest behaviour. Firms that emphasize individual sales records may encourage unhealthy competition among sales staff, including "misplacing" phone messages, and not being helpful to someone else's client. Toronto-based GMP Securities, on the other hand, emphasizes the importance of a teamwork culture, so that individuals are not competing against one another and engaging in questionable activities. Founding partner Brad Griffiths notes that "the corporate culture is to make an environment where everybody feels they're involved. We want to be successful, but not at the expense of the individual."[14]

Do Organizations Have Uniform Cultures?

Organizational culture represents a common perception held by the organization's members. This was made explicit when we defined culture as a system of shared meaning. We should expect, therefore, that individuals with different backgrounds or at different levels in the organization will tend to describe the organization's culture in similar terms.[15]

However, the fact that organizational culture has common properties does not mean that there cannot be subcultures within it. Most large organizations have a dominant culture and numerous sets of subcultures.[16]

A **dominant culture** expresses the core values that are shared by a majority of the organization's members. When we talk about an organization's culture, we are referring to its dominant culture. It is this macro view of culture that gives an organization its distinct personality.[17] **Subcultures** tend to develop in large organizations to reflect common problems, situations, or experiences that members face. These subcultures are likely to be defined by department designations and geographical separation.

An organization's purchasing department, for example, can have a subculture that is uniquely shared by members of that department. It will include the **core values**—the primary, or dominant, values in the organization—plus additional values unique to

dominant culture A system of shared meaning that expresses the core values shared by a majority of the organization's members.

subcultures Mini-cultures within an organization, typically defined by department designations and geographical separation.

core values The primary, or dominant, values that are accepted throughout the organization.

Organizational culture guides and shapes the attitudes of employees at New Zealand Air. One of the airline's guiding principles is to champion and promote New Zealand and its national heritage, both within the country and overseas. In this photo, a cabin crew member dressed in traditional Maori clothing and a pilot touch noses to represent the sharing of a single breath following a ceremony for the airline's purchase of a Boeing airplane in Everett, Washington. Such expressions of representing their country with pride create a strong bond among employees.

members of the purchasing department. Similarly, an office or unit of the organization that is physically separated from the organization's main operations may take on a different personality. Again, the core values are essentially retained but modified to reflect the separated unit's distinct situation.

If organizations had no dominant culture and were composed only of numerous subcultures, the value of organizational culture as an explanatory variable for organizational behaviour would be significantly lessened. That is because there would be no uniform interpretation of what represented appropriate and inappropriate behaviour. It is the "shared meaning" aspect of culture that makes it such a potent device for guiding and shaping behaviour. This is what allows us to say that Microsoft's culture values aggressiveness and risk-taking,[18] and then to use that information to better understand the behaviour of Microsoft executives and employees. But we cannot ignore the reality that as well as a dominant culture, many organizations have subcultures that can influence the behaviour of members. Some strong subcultures can even make it difficult for managers to implement organizational change. This can happen in both unionized and non-unionized environments.

Reading an Organization's Culture

Boston Pizza claims to be Canada's number-one casual dining restaurant. It has reached that status by developing a strong organizational culture.[19] The company's reward structure is designed to encourage all employees to meet corporate targets. "We feel strongly that everyone should participate and everyone should be rewarded in company growth and success," says the company's president, Mark Pacinda.

As part of its emphasis on building a strong culture, the company pays careful attention to its hiring strategy. The company also provides long-term incentives for employees to stay at Boston Pizza, so that there is a stable set of individuals in place to help socialize new employees into the culture.

Co-owner George Melville recognizes that when hiring franchisees, business skills and money are not enough. Employees have to fit into the culture as well. He reports that they once hired a person who had money and superb business skills, but who "was basically a jerk." The senior management realized that they had to let him go after six months. "The idea that you can build a team around somebody who isn't a team builder is a mistake," says Melville. Why does culture have such a strong influence on people's behaviour?

Organizations differ in the extent to which they can be characterized as having strong or weak cultures.[20] In a **strong culture**, the organization's core values are both intensely held and widely shared.[21] The more members who accept the core values and the greater their commitment to those values, the stronger the culture is. A strong culture will have a great influence on the behaviour of its members because the high degree of shared experiences and intensity create an internal climate of high behavioural control. For example, American retailer Nordstrom has developed one of the strongest service cultures in the retailing industry. Nordstrom employees know what is expected of them, and these expectations go a long way in shaping their behaviour.

In a weak culture, employees do not feel any great attachment to their organization or their co-workers. They may not take pride in their work. If you think about service and retail experiences you have had, if employees as a whole routinely seem to ignore customers, and the environment is unfriendly or unclean, this may be the result of a weak culture.

A strong culture demonstrates high agreement among members about what the organization stands for. Such unanimity of purpose builds cohesiveness, loyalty, and organizational commitment. These qualities, in turn, lessen employees' tendency to leave the organization.[22]

What kind of organizational culture would work best for you?

As we noted earlier in Exhibit 10-1, the artifacts of culture inform outsiders and employees about the underlying values and beliefs of the organization's culture. These artifacts, or physical manifestations of culture, include stories, rituals, material symbols, and language. The extent to which organizations have artifacts of their culture indicates whether they have strong or weak cultures. *From Concepts to Skills* on pages 406–407 offers additional ideas on how to read an organization's culture.

2 How do you read an organization's culture?

strong culture A culture in which the core values are intensely held and widely shared.

Stories

Nike has a number of senior executives who spend much of their time serving as corporate storytellers. And the stories they tell are meant to convey what Nike is about.[23] When they tell the story of how co-founder (and Oregon track coach) Bill Bowerman went to his workshop and poured rubber into his wife's waffle iron to create a better running shoe, they are talking about Nike's spirit of innovation. When new hires hear tales of Oregon running star Steve Prefontaine's battles to make running a professional sport and to attain better performance equipment, they learn of Nike's commitment to helping athletes. When publisher Hollinger International acquired Canada's Southam Newspapers, the story is that David Radler, Hollinger's former president and COO, interrupted a local Canadian publisher's presentation on the paper's mission statement "and held up a bill from his wallet, pronouncing that 'from now on this is to be the mission.'"[24] This certainly sent the message that financial interests would be the bottom line for Canada's largest chain of newspapers.

Stories such as these circulate through many organizations. They typically tell about the organization's founders, rule breaking, rags-to-riches successes, reductions in the workforce, relocation of employees, reactions to past mistakes, and organizational coping.[25] These stories anchor the present in the past and provide explanations and legitimacy for current practices.[26]

Rituals

Rituals are repetitive sequences of activities that express and reinforce the key values of the organization; what goals are most important; and which people are important, and which ones are expendable.[27]

One well-known corporate ritual is Walmart's company chant. Begun by the company's founder, Sam Walton, as a way to motivate and unite his workforce, "Gimme a W, gimme an A, gimme an L, give me an M, A, R, T!" has become a company ritual that bonds Walmart workers and reinforces Sam Walton's belief in the importance of his employees to the company's success. Similar corporate chants are used by IBM, Ericsson, Novell, Deutsche Bank, and PricewaterhouseCoopers.[28]

Material Symbols

The layout of corporate headquarters, the types of cars given to top executives, and the presence or absence of corporate aircraft are a few examples of material symbols. Others include the size of offices, the elegance of furnishings, executive perks, and dress code, including uniforms.[29] In addition, corporate logos, signs, brochures, and advertisements reveal aspects of the organization's culture.[30] These material symbols convey to employees, customers, and clients who is important, the degree of egalitarianism desired by top management, and the kinds of behaviour (for example, risk-taking, conservative, authoritarian, participative, individualistic, social) that are appropriate. For instance, pictures of all Creo employees hang in the Burnaby, BC-based company's entrance lobby, which visibly conveys Creo's anti-hierarchical culture.

Companies differ in how much separation they make between their executives and employees. This plays out in how material benefits are distributed to executives. Some companies provide their top executives with chauffeur-driven limousines and, when they travel by air, unlimited use of the corporate jet. Other companies might pay for car and air transportation for top executives, only the car is a Chevrolet with no driver, and the jet seat is in the economy section of a commercial airliner. At Bolton, Ontario-

At Walmart, culture is transmitted to employees through the daily ritual of the "Walmart cheer." Shown here is the manager of a Walmart store leading employees in the motivational chant that helps preserve a small-family spirit and work environment within the world's largest retailer.

based Husky Injection Molding Systems, a more egalitarian culture is favoured. Employees and management share the parking lot, dining room, and even washrooms.

Language

Many organizations and units within organizations use language as a way to identify members of a culture or subculture. By learning this language, members show their acceptance of the culture and, in so doing, help to preserve it.

For example, baristas at Starbucks call drinks *short, tall,* or *grande,* not *small, medium,* or *large,* and they know the difference between a half-decaf double tall almond skinny mocha and an iced short schizo skinny hazelnut cappuccino with wings.[31] Students and employees at Grant MacEwan College are informed by the philosophy of the college's namesake. Dr. Grant MacEwan, historian, writer, politician, and environmentalist, was never a formal part of the management of the organization. However, many phrases from his writing and creed have found their way into formal college publications and calendars, as well as informal communications, including his most well known, "I have tried to leave things in the vineyard better than I found them."[32]

Over time, organizations often develop unique terms to describe equipment, offices, key staff, suppliers, customers, or products that relate to their business. New employees are frequently overwhelmed with acronyms and jargon that, after six months on the job, have become fully part of their language. Once assimilated, this terminology acts as a common denominator that unites members of a given culture or subculture.

Creating and Sustaining an Organization's Culture

One of the challenges Boston Pizza co-founders Jim Treliving and George Melville face in managing the 305 restaurants across Canada and more than 28 000 employees is making sure that everyone is on the same page.[33] The individual restaurants in the chain are not owned by the company. Instead, franchisees invest a considerable amount of money in order to gain the right to own a Boston Pizza restaurant. Thus, there could be a conflict between what the co-founders want done, and what a franchisor feels is best for his or her investment.

Treliving and Melville try to prevent this conflict by carefully vetting franchise candidates. Potential franchisees are informed of the initial $60 000 fee and start-up costs that could run between $1.6 and $2.4 million. Despite the size of their investment, franchisees must demonstrate a "willingness to adhere to the Boston Pizza system." Franchisees are given a lot of help in starting out, however.

When Hank Van Poelgeest opened up the first Boston Pizza restaurant in St. John's, Newfoundland in January 2006, he naturally worried. A lot of preparation had gone into the opening, months of planning, careful choice of location, and a team of nine people had been sent from head office to help hire and train staff. The new staff did a dress rehearsal of the grand-opening four times to make sure nothing went wrong.

The preparation was so thorough that the opening exceeded all expectations. "We wanted to use the first couple of weeks as a slow beginning," says Van Poelgeest, "but we've never had a slow beginning." What role does culture play in creating high-performing employees?

An organization's culture does not pop out of thin air. Once established, it rarely fades away. Which forces influence the creation of a culture? What reinforces and sustains these forces once they are in place? Exhibit 10-3 on page 384 summarizes how an organization's culture is established and sustained. The original culture is derived from the philosophy of its founders. This, in turn, strongly influences the selection criteria used in hiring. The actions of the current top management set the general climate of what is

3 How do you create and maintain organizational culture?

EXHIBIT 10-3 How Organizational Cultures Form

acceptable behaviour and what is not. How employees are to be socialized will depend on the degree of success an organization achieves in matching new employees' values to its own in the selection process, and on top management's preference for socialization methods. We describe each part of this process next.

How a Culture Begins

An organization's current customs, traditions, and general way of doing things are largely due to what it has done before and the degree of success it has had with those endeavours. This leads us to the ultimate source of an organization's culture: its founders.[34]

Is culture the same as rules?

The founders of an organization traditionally have a major impact on its early culture. They have a vision of what the organization should be. They are unconstrained by previous customs or ideologies. Because new organizations are typically small, it's possible for the founders to impose their vision on all organizational members.

The process of culture creation occurs in three ways.[35] First, founders only hire and keep employees who think and feel the way they do. Second, they indoctrinate and socialize these employees to their way of thinking and feeling. Finally, the founders' behaviour acts as a role model, encouraging employees to identify with the founders and thereby internalize those beliefs, values, and assumptions. When the organization succeeds, the founders' vision is viewed as a primary determinant of that success. At that point, the founders' personality becomes embedded in the culture of the organization.

The culture at Hyundai, the giant Korean conglomerate, is largely a reflection of its founder, Chung Ju Yung. Hyundai's fierce, competitive style and its disciplined, authoritarian nature are the same characteristics often used to describe Chung. Other contemporary examples of founders who have had an immeasurable impact on their organizations' cultures are Ted Rogers of Toronto-based Rogers Communications, Frank Stronach of Aurora, Ontario-based Magna International, and Richard Branson of UK-based Virgin Group.

Keeping a Culture Alive

Once a culture is in place, there are human resource practices within the organization that act to maintain it by giving employees a set of similar experiences.[36] For example, the selection process, performance evaluation criteria, training and career development activities, and promotion procedures ensure that new employees fit in with the culture, rewarding those who support it and penalizing (even expelling) those who challenge it. Three forces play a particularly important part in sustaining a culture: *selection* criteria, the actions of *top management*, and *socialization* methods. Let's take a closer look at each.

Selection

The explicit goal of the selection process is to identify and hire individuals who have the knowledge, skills, and abilities to perform the jobs within the organization successfully.

The source of Cranium's culture is co-founder and CEO Richard Tait, shown here at a toy fair demonstrating the toys and games his company makes. Tait created a culture of fun and collaboration at Cranium so employees can work in an environment that stimulates creativity and innovation in developing new products. At Cranium, employees choose their own titles. Tait chose Grand Poo Bah, and the chief financial officer selected Professor Profit. The office walls at Cranium are painted in bright primary colours, and music plays everywhere.

Typically, more than one candidate will meet any given job's requirements. The final decision as to who is hired is significantly influenced by the decision maker's judgment of how well each candidate will fit into the organization. This attempt to ensure a proper match, either deliberately or inadvertently, results in the hiring of people who have values essentially consistent with those of the organization, or at least a good portion of those values.[37]

At the same time, the selection process provides information about the organization to applicants. If they perceive a conflict between their values and those of the organization, they can remove themselves from the applicant pool. Selection, therefore, becomes a two-way street, allowing the employer or applicant to look elsewhere if there appears to be a mismatch. In this way, the selection process sustains an organization's culture by "selecting out" those individuals who might attack or undermine its core values. *OB in the Workplace* shows how one company's method of interviewing ensures that applicants are right for the job.

IN THE WORKPLACE

Playland's Interviews Are More Than Fun and Games

How does a company make sure an applicant is right for the job? At Playland, Vancouver's largest amusement park, applicants for a summer job don't do one-on-one interviews with managers or the human resource department.[38] Instead, they are asked to deconstruct a JENGA tower with a group of nine other applicants and answer a variety of "interesting questions." When an applicant removes a block from the tower, they answer a question printed on it.

Amy Nguyen, a 15-year-old high school student applying for her first job, had the following question: "There's a customer who had to line up a long time for food and he was very upset by the time he got to the front of the line. What would you do?"

"I said I would apologize, look cute and tell him, 'Let me see if my manager can do anything for you,'" says Nguyen. This answer got her a second interview, and she eventually got the job.

Jennifer Buensuceso, a PNE gaming manager at Playland, thinks the new way of hiring is much better than when she faced a one-on-one question and answer format when she was hired. She says the new method helps managers learn about the applicant's "team-building and individuality. You get to see them think out of the box."

This format is also good for nervous teens and those whose first language is not English. Getting them to play relaxes them, and helps managers to see "who shows natural leadership skills, who's outgoing, who works well on a team and who's good at problem-solving."[39]

Top Management

The actions of top management also have a major impact on the organization's culture.[40] Through what they say and how they behave, senior executives establish norms that filter down through the organization. These norms establish whether risk-taking is desirable; how much freedom managers should give their employees; what is appropriate dress; what actions will pay off in terms of pay raises, promotions, and other rewards; and the like. Just how much influence top management actions can have is shown in *OB in the Workplace*.

IN THE WORKPLACE

Frugal Board Chair Leads by Example

Can top management help prevent wastefulness in their company? Robert A. Kierlin has been called "the cheapest CEO in America."[41] Kierlin is chairman of Fastenal, the largest specialty retailer of nuts and bolts in the United States, with 6500 employees. He takes a salary of only $60 000 a year. He owns only three suits, each of which he bought used. He clips grocery coupons, drives a Toyota, and stays in low-priced motels when he travels on business. Does Kierlin need to pinch pennies? No. The market value of his stock in Fastenal is worth about $300 million. But the man prefers a modest personal lifestyle. And he prefers the same for his company. Kierlin argues that his behaviour should send a message to all his employees: We don't waste things in this company. Kierlin sees himself as a role model for frugality, and employees at Fastenal have learned to follow his example.

Socialization

No matter how effectively the organization recruits and selects new employees, they are not fully indoctrinated in the organization's culture when they start their job. Because they are unfamiliar with the organization's culture, new employees may disturb the beliefs and customs that are in place. The organization will, therefore, want to help new employees adapt to its culture. This adaptation process is called **socialization**.[42]

socialization The process that adapts new employees to an organization's culture.

New employees at the Japanese electronics company Sanyo are socialized through a particularly long training program. At their intensive five-month course, trainees eat and sleep together in company-subsidized dorms and are required to vacation together at company-owned resorts. They learn the Sanyo way of doing everything—from how to speak to managers to proper grooming and dress.[43] The company considers this program essential for transforming young employees, fresh out of school, into dedicated *kaisha senshi*, or corporate warriors.

Starbucks does not go to the extreme that Sanyo does, but it seeks the same outcome.[44] All new employees go through 24 hours of training. Classes cover everything necessary to transform new employees into brewing consultants. They learn the Starbucks philosophy, the company jargon, and even how to help customers make decisions about beans and grind, as well as about espresso machines. The result is employees who understand Starbucks' culture and who project an enthusiastic and knowledgeable image to customers.

As we discuss socialization, keep in mind that the new employee's entry into the organization is the most critical stage. This is when the organization seeks to mould the outsider into an employee "in good standing." Those employees who fail to learn the essential role behaviours risk being labelled "nonconformists" or "rebels," which often leads to their being fired. The organization continues to socialize every employee, though maybe not as explicitly, throughout his or her career in the organization. This further contributes to sustaining the culture. (Sometimes, however, employees are not fully socialized. For instance, you will note in Exhibit 10-4 that employees had learned they were supposed to wear checkerboard caps to work, but clearly didn't know why.)

Socialization can be conceptualized as a process composed of three stages: prearrival, encounter, and metamorphosis.[45] The first stage, *prearrival*, encompasses all the learning that occurs before a new member joins the organization. In the second stage, *encounter*, the new employee sees what the organization is really like and confronts the possibility that expectations and reality may diverge. In the third stage, *metamorphosis*, the relatively long-lasting changes take place. The new employee masters the skills required for his or her job, successfully performs his or her new roles, and makes the adjustments to his or her work group's values and norms.[46] This three-stage process has an impact on the new employee's work productivity, commitment to the organization's objectives, and eventual decision to stay with the organization. Exhibit 10-5 depicts the socialization process.

The Prearrival Stage The **prearrival stage** explicitly recognizes that each individual arrives with a set of values, attitudes, and expectations. These cover both the work to be done and the organization. For instance, in many jobs, particularly professional work, new members will have undergone a considerable degree of prior socialization in

EXHIBIT 10-4

"I don't know how it started, either. All I know is that it's part of our corporate culture."

Source: Drawing by Mick Stevens in *The New Yorker*, October 3, 1994. Copyright © 1994 by the New Yorker Magazine, Inc. Reprinted by permission.

prearrival stage The period of learning in the socialization process that occurs before a new employee joins the organization.

EXHIBIT 10-5   A Socialization Model

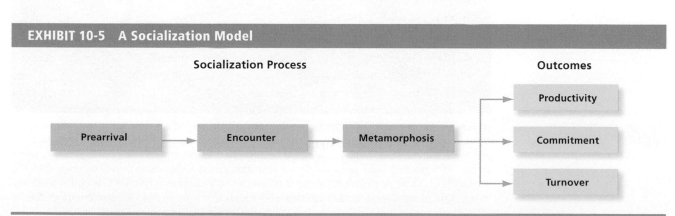

Socialization Process			Outcomes
Prearrival → Encounter → Metamorphosis			Productivity
			Commitment
			Turnover

school and in training. One major purpose of a business school, for example, is to socialize business students to the attitudes and behaviours that business firms want. If business executives believe that successful employees value the profit ethic, are loyal, will work hard, and desire to achieve, they can hire individuals out of business schools who have been premoulded in this pattern.

But prearrival socialization goes beyond the specific job. The selection process is used in most organizations to inform prospective employees about the organization as a whole. In addition, as noted previously, the selection process also ensures the inclusion of the "right type"—those who will fit in. As one study notes, "Indeed, the ability of the individual to present the appropriate face during the selection process determines his or her ability to move into the organization in the first place. Thus, success depends on the degree to which the aspiring member has correctly anticipated the expectations and desires of those in the organization in charge of selection."[47] For a detailed example of how an organization considers its hiring process as a way of maintaining corporate culture, read this chapter's *Case Incident—Wegmans Hires for Passion* on page 404.

The Encounter Stage Upon entering the organization, the new employee begins the **encounter stage**. Here the individual confronts the possible gap between expectations—of the job, co-workers, boss, and the organization in general—and reality. If the employee's expectations are more or less accurate, the encounter stage merely provides a reaffirmation of the perceptions gained earlier.

However, this is often not the case. Where expectations and reality differ, the socialization period for the new employee should be designed to help him or her detach from previous assumptions and replace them with another set that the organization deems desirable. Of course, not all organizations that actively socialize their members

encounter stage The stage in the socialization process in which a new employee sees what the organization is really like and confronts the possibility that expectations and reality may diverge.

New employees at Broad Air Conditioning in Changsha, China, are indoctrinated in the company's military-style culture by going through a 10-day training session of boot camp, where they are divided into platoons and live in barracks. Boot camp prepares new hires for the military formality that prevails at Broad, where employees begin their work week standing in formation during a flag-raising of two company flags and the flag of China. All employees live in dorms on the company campus and receive free food and lodging. To motivate its employees, Broad has scattered throughout the campus 43 life-size bronze statues of inspirational leaders from Confucius to Jack Welch, the former CEO of General Electric.

are so successful that new employees completely adopt the new set of assumptions. At the extreme, new members may become totally disillusioned with the realities of their job and resign. Proper selection should significantly reduce the probability of this happening.

The Metamorphosis Stage Finally, the new employee must work out any problems discovered during the encounter stage. This may mean going through changes to adjust to the values and norms of the job, work group, and organization—hence, we call this the **metamorphosis stage**. The entry socialization options presented in Exhibit 10-6 are designed to bring about the desired metamorphosis. Note, for example, that the more management relies on socialization programs that are formal, collective, fixed, serial, and emphasize divestiture, the greater the likelihood that newcomers' differences and perspectives will be stripped away and replaced by standardized and predictable behaviours. Management's careful selection of socialization experiences for newcomers can—at the extreme—create conformists who maintain traditions and customs, or inventive and creative individualists who consider no organizational practice sacred.

> **metamorphosis stage** The stage in the socialization process in which a new employee adjusts to the values and norms of the job, work group, and organization.

We can say that metamorphosis and the entry socialization process is complete when

- The new employee has become comfortable with the organization and his or her job

- The new employee has internalized the norms of the organization and the work group, and understands and accepts these norms

- The new employee feels accepted by his or her peers as a trusted and valued individual, is self-confident that he or she has the competence to complete the job successfully, and understands the system—not only his or her own tasks, but also the rules, procedures, and informally accepted practices

---

EXHIBIT 10-6 Entry Socialization Options

Formal vs. Informal The more a new employee is segregated from the ongoing work setting and differentiated in some way to make explicit his or her newcomer's role, the more formal socialization is. Specific orientation and training programs are examples. Informal socialization puts the new employee directly into his or her job, with little or no special attention.

Individual vs. Collective New members can be socialized individually. This describes how it's done in many professional offices. They can also be grouped together and processed through an identical set of experiences, as in military boot camp.

Fixed vs. Variable This refers to the time schedule in which newcomers make the transition from outsider to insider. A fixed schedule establishes standardized stages of transition. This characterizes rotational training programs. It also includes probationary periods, such as the 8- to 10-year "associate" status accounting and law firms use before deciding whether to name a candidate as a partner. Variable schedules give no advance notice of their transition timetable. Variable schedules describe the typical promotion system, where individuals are not advanced to the next stage until they are "ready."

Serial vs. Random Serial socialization is characterized by the use of role models who train and encourage the newcomer. Apprenticeship and mentoring programs are examples. In random socialization, role models are deliberately withheld. The new employee is left on his or her own to figure things out.

Investiture vs. Divestiture Investiture socialization assumes that the newcomer's qualities and qualifications are the necessary ingredients for job success, so these qualities and qualifications are confirmed and supported. Divestiture socialization tries to strip away certain characteristics of the recruit. Fraternity and sorority "pledges" go through divestiture socialization to shape them into the proper role.

Sources: Based on J. Van Maanen, "People Processing: Strategies of Organizational Socialization," *Organizational Dynamics,* Summer 1978, pp. 19–36; and E. H. Schein, "Organizational Culture," *American Psychologist,* February 1990, p. 116.

- The new employee understands how he or she will be evaluated and knows what criteria will be used to measure and appraise his or her work; he or she knows what is expected and what constitutes a job "well done"

As Exhibit 10-5 on page 387 shows, successful metamorphosis should have a positive impact on the new employee's productivity and commitment to the organization. It should reduce the tendency to leave the organization.

Some people, of course, do not fit well with the company culture. Doug Hobbes, director of product marketing for Globe Information Services (now Globe Interactive), lasted just four months at Toronto-based GlobeStar Systems.[48] In his words, "It was a culture thing." He did not enjoy going out for hamburgers after work or working late until 9 or 10 p.m. alongside the organization's key people. Because Hobbes's work habits differed from theirs, his co-workers viewed him as unenterprising and aloof. His story serves as a reminder that you should make sure you fit with the organization's culture before you accept a job. For example, would you be comfortable working in an organization whose culture accepts snooping on its employees? This chapter's *Ethical Dilemma Exercise* on page 403 explores this ethical question.

The Liabilities of Organizational Culture

4 Can organizational culture have a downside?

We have treated culture in a nonjudgmental manner thus far. We have not said that it is good or bad, only that it exists. Many of its functions, as outlined, are valuable for both the organization and the employee. Culture enhances organizational commitment and increases the consistency of employee behaviour.[49] These are clearly benefits to an organization. From an employee's standpoint, culture is valuable because it reduces ambiguity. It tells employees how things are done and what is important. However, we should not ignore the potentially dysfunctional aspects of culture, especially of a strong culture, on an organization's effectiveness.

We now consider culture's impact on change, diversity, and mergers and acquisitions.

Culture as a Barrier to Change

Culture is a liability when the shared values are not in agreement with those that will further the organization's effectiveness. Employees are less likely to have shared values when the organization's environment is dynamic. When the environment is undergoing rapid change, the organization's entrenched culture may no longer be appropriate. Consistency of behaviour is an asset to an organization when the company faces a stable environment. However, it may burden the organization and make it difficult to respond to changes in the environment. For many organizations with strong cultures, practices that led to previous successes can lead to failure when those practices no longer match up well with environmental needs.[50]

Culture as a Barrier to Diversity

Hiring new employees who, because of race, gender, disability, or other differences, are not like the majority of the organization's members creates a paradox.[51] Management wants the new employees to accept the organization's core cultural values. Otherwise, these employees are unlikely to fit in or be accepted. But at the same time, management wants to openly acknowledge and demonstrate support for the differences that these employees bring to the workplace.

Strong cultures put considerable pressure on employees to conform. They limit the range of values and styles that are acceptable. It's not a coincidence that employees at Disney theme parks appear to be almost universally attractive, clean, and wholesome-looking, with bright smiles. That is the image Walt Disney Company seeks. It selects employees who will maintain that image. Once the theme-park employees are on the job, a strong culture—supported by formal rules and regulations—ensures that they will act in a relatively uniform and predictable way.

Organizations seek out and hire diverse individuals because of the new strengths these people bring to the workplace. Yet these diverse behaviours and strengths are likely to diminish in strong cultures as people try to fit in. Strong cultures, therefore, can be liabilities when they effectively eliminate the unique strengths that people of different backgrounds bring to the organization. Moreover, strong cultures can also be liabilities when they support institutional bias or become insensitive to people who are different.

Culture as a Barrier to Mergers and Acquisitions

Historically, the key factors that management looked at in making merger or acquisition decisions were related to financial advantages or product synergy. In recent years, cultural compatibility has become the primary concern.[52] While a favourable financial statement or product line may be the initial attraction of a merger or acquisition candidate, whether the merger or acquisition actually works seems to have more to do with how well the two organizations' cultures match up. Daimler-Benz and Chrysler struggled to make their 1998 merger work, as *OB Around the Globe* shows.

Mergers Across National Borders Are Challenging

What happens when two companies with very different cultures merge? When Daimler-Benz and Chrysler merged in 1998 to form DaimlerChrysler, some called it a "marriage made in heaven."[53] The merger was supposed to create a global automaker out of two respected companies. Instead, the merger has been a disaster, with the US-based Chrysler arm becoming a money loser in the years since the merger. In spring 2002, DaimlerChrysler's stock was worth half of what it had been on the day the merger was announced. By 2005, DaimlerChrysler was still not doing as well financially as analysts and shareholders had hoped, although there had been slight improvements in overall profitability.

The Germans and the Americans blame each other for the failure, and the very different cultures of the two organizations no doubt led to many of the problems. Daimler-Benz was extremely hierarchical, while Chrysler, with its "cowboy culture," was more egalitarian. Chrysler's managers were independent, and its middle managers were empowered. While this structure led to a lot of infighting, it also resulted in much creativity—for example, the development of the popular PT Cruiser.

Employees at Chrysler were very slow to trust the German management that took over the company in what was billed as a merger of equals. Jürgen Schrempp, chair of the merged companies until 2005, admitted that he intended for the merger to be a takeover. Thus, to North American employees, it's no surprise that he slashed thousands of jobs in Canada and the United States after the merger.

Distrust went both ways: German management did not trust the American senior managers at Chrysler, and eventually Schrempp let them go. They were viewed as overpaid and lazy, unwilling to work overtime or miss their golf games by flying on weekends. These images of one another did not make it easy for managers from the two companies to work together and created much uncertainty for the employees at Chrysler. In 2007, this "marriage made in heaven" came to an end. Daimler sold Chrysler to a private equity firm, enabling both car manufacturers to get back to basics without the challenges created by conflicting cultures.

As the Daimler-Benz and Chrysler merger and divorce suggests, bringing employees from two different companies together is likely to cause friction. However, the experience did not prevent Chrysler from exploring Fiat as a new merger partner in 2009.

Strategies for Merging Cultures

Organizations can use several strategies when considering how to merge the cultures of two organizations:[54]

- *Assimilation.* The entire new organization is determined to take on the culture of one of the merging organizations. This strategy works best when one of the organizations has a relatively weak culture. However, if a culture is simply imposed on an organization, it rarely works.

- *Separation.* The organizations remain separate and keep their individual cultures. This strategy works best when the organizations have little overlap in the industries in which they operate.

- *Integration.* A new culture is formed by merging parts of each of the organizations. This strategy works best when aspects of each organization's culture need to be improved.

While an integration strategy may take a lot of work, it can pay off, as *OB in the Workplace* shows.

IN THE WORKPLACE

Agrium Creates Its Own Culture through Blending

Can an organization successfully merge many companies together? Calgary-based Agrium, a fertilizer producer and the world's third-largest nitrogen producer with facilities in Canada, the United States, Argentina, and Chile, has a strategy of growth through mergers and acquisitions.[55] Agrium grew out of the fertilizer division of Cominco (now Teck Cominco), and then absorbed fertilizer divisions and spin-off companies from the mining and oil and gas industries, including Esso, Sherritt, and Unocal.

Because Agrium is the result of multiple mergers of companies, employees created a rule that if anyone mentions their former employer, they must contribute money to a fund. The fund is used for a "team-building event" where employees go out together for lunch or dinner.

CEO Michael Wilson's explanation of the company's approach to merging cultures suggests that Agrium has used an integration strategy. "We take the best of the mining culture, which is very proactive, decisive, willing to act, willing to take appropriate risks . . . We blend it with the oil and gas culture [which is] very thorough in its analysis, in dotting of the *i*'s and crossing of the *t*'s, in making sure everyone's marching at the same pace." Wilson adds the culture of Dow Chemicals to the mix, where he worked for 18 years and learned "how to build collaboration across very strong business units, how to get results when you don't have full accountability."

Agrium has performed well in recent years, and Wilson sees this as a measure of a successful organizational culture, which he has built through a combination of a hands-on approach and team building. This enables employees to work toward "a common purpose and long-term goals."

Potential merger partners might do well to conduct a **bicultural audit** before concluding that a merger should occur. Through questionnaires, interviews, and/or focus groups, potential merger partners should examine differences in the "vision, values, structure, management practices and behaviours" of the merging parties.[56] This examination should indicate whether there are commonalities from which to build a successful merger, or differences that could cause extreme difficulties in merging the two organizations. If the decision after a bicultural audit is to merge, the management team should bridge any existing culture gaps by[57]

> **bicultural audit** An examination of the differences between two potential merger partners prior to a merger to determine whether the cultures will be able to work together.

- Defining a structure that is appropriate for both organizations, along with a reorganization plan

- Identifying and implementing a management style that is appropriate for both organizations

- Reinforcing internal communication to make sure that employees are kept aware of changes that will occur

- Getting agreement on what will be considered in performance evaluations, including expected behaviours and performance criteria

Merging two very different cultures can sometimes be successful, as illustrated in this chapter's *Case Incident—Mergers Don't Always Lead to Culture Clashes*, on page 405.

Changing Organizational Culture

Boston Pizza co-owners Jim Treliving and George Melville did not actually found the company.[58] It was started in Edmonton in 1964 by Greek immigrant Gus Agioritis. Treliving was an RCMP officer who became excited about the Boston Pizza concept, and opened his first franchise restaurant in Penticton, BC. In 1973, Melville became Treliving's business partner, after being his accountant for four years. By 1983, the two men owned 16 of the Boston Pizza restaurants, and decided to buy the entire Western-Canada–based chain of 46 restaurants. They hoped to expand the chain across the country.

To achieve a successful expansion, Treliving and Melville recognized the importance of introducing a number of systems and operating standards that would apply to all of the restaurants. They developed the Three Pillar Success Strategy, "which emphasizes continually improving guest experience, franchise profitability and building the brand, to promote expansion." The strategy is continuously communicated to all members of the organization. As Mark Pacinda, president says: "We make sure we're constantly communicating and being very consistent with our message, our goals and our objectives." Why have Treliving and Melville been so successful in creating an organizational culture that enabled a small franchise to expand across the country?

Trying to change the culture of an organization is quite difficult, and requires that many aspects of the organization change at the same time, especially the reward structure. Culture is such a challenge to change because it often represents the established mindset of employees and managers.

> **5** How do you change organizational culture?

The explosion of the space shuttle *Columbia* in February 2003 highlights how difficult changing culture has been for NASA. When the report on the investigation came out that summer, the reasons given for the failure were alarmingly similar to the reasons given for the *Challenger* disaster 20 years before.[59] Even though foam striking the shuttle was the technical cause of the explosion, the problem was rooted in NASA's organizational culture. NASA again promised to change its culture, and create an atmosphere where employees are "encouraged to raise our hand and speak out when there are life-threatening hazards," said then NASA administrator Sean O'Keefe. A NASA engineer was less certain about the possibility of cultural change: "The NASA culture does not accept being wrong." The culture does not accept that "there's no such thing as a stupid question." Instead, "the humiliation factor always runs high."[60]

John Kotter, professor of leadership at Harvard Business School, has created a detailed approach to implementing change.[61] Kotter began by listing common failures that occur when managers try to initiate change. These include the inability to create a sense of urgency about the need for change; failure to create a coalition for managing the change process; the absence of a vision for change; not effectively communicating that vision; not removing obstacles that could impede the achievement of the vision; failure to provide short-term and achievable goals; the tendency to declare victory too soon; and not anchoring the changes in the organization's culture.

See Exhibit 14-5 on page 545 for Kotter's eight-step plan for implementing change. This chapter's *Point/Counterpoint* on page 400 outlines the conditions under which cultural change is most likely to occur.

Efforts directed at changing organizational culture do not usually yield immediate or dramatic results. Cultural change is actually a lengthy process—measured in years, not months. But we can ask the question, "Can culture be changed?" And the answer is, "Yes!"

Below we consider two particular kinds of changes organizations might want to make to their culture: creating an ethical culture and creating a positive organizational culture.

Creating an Ethical Culture

The content and strength of a culture influence an organization's ethical climate and the ethical behaviour of its members.[62] An organizational culture most likely to shape high ethical standards is one that is high in risk tolerance, low to moderate in aggressiveness, and focuses on means, as well as outcomes. Managers in such a culture are supported for taking risks and innovating, are discouraged from engaging in unbridled competition, and will pay attention to *how* goals are achieved as well as to *what* goals are achieved.

A strong organizational culture will exert more influence on employees than a weak one. If the culture is strong and supports high ethical standards, it should have a very powerful and positive influence on employee behaviour. Johnson & Johnson, for example, has a strong culture that has long stressed corporate obligations to customers, employees, the community, and shareholders, in that order. When poisoned Tylenol (a Johnson & Johnson product) was found on store shelves, employees at Johnson & Johnson across the United States independently pulled the product from these stores before management had even issued a statement concerning the tamperings. No one had to tell these individuals what was morally right; they knew what Johnson & Johnson would expect them to do.

What can management do to create a more ethical culture? We suggest a combination of the following practices:

- *Be a visible role model.* Employees will look to top-management behaviour as a benchmark for defining appropriate behaviour. When senior managers are seen to be taking the ethical high road, they provide a positive message for all employees.

- *Communicate ethical expectations.* Ethical ambiguities can be minimized by creating and disseminating an organizational code of ethics. It should state the organization's primary values and the ethical rules that employees are expected to follow.

- *Provide ethics training.* Set up seminars, workshops, and similar ethics training programs. Use these training sessions to reinforce the organization's standards of conduct, to clarify what practices are and are not permissible, and to address possible ethical dilemmas.

- *Visibly reward ethical acts and punish unethical ones.* Performance appraisals of managers should include a point-by-point evaluation of how their decisions measured against the organization's code of ethics. Appraisals must include the means taken to achieve goals, as well as the ends themselves. People who act ethically should be visibly rewarded for their behaviour. Just as importantly, unethical acts should be conspicuously punished.

- *Provide protective mechanisms.* The organization needs to provide formal mechanisms so that employees can discuss ethical dilemmas and report unethical behaviour without fear of reprimand. This might include appointing an ethics counsellor, an ombudsperson, or an ethics officer.

Creating a Positive Organizational Culture

It's often difficult to separate management fads from lasting changes in management thinking, especially when they first come out. In this textbook, we try to keep current while staying away from fads. There is one early trend, though, that we think is here to stay: creating a positive organizational culture. At first blush, creating a positive culture may sound hopelessly naive, or like a Dilbert-style conspiracy. The one thing that makes us believe this trend is here to stay is that there are signs that management practice and OB research are converging.

A **positive organizational culture** is defined as a culture that emphasizes building on employee strengths, rewards more often than it punishes, and emphasizes individual vitality and growth.[63] Let's consider each of these areas.

positive organizational culture
A culture that emphasizes building on employee strengths, rewards more than punishes, and emphasizes individual vitality and growth.

Building on Employee Strengths

A lot of OB, and management practice, is concerned with how to fix employee problems. Although a positive organizational culture does not ignore problems, it does emphasize showing employees how they can capitalize on their strengths. As management guru Peter Drucker said, "Most [employees] do not know what their strengths are. When you ask them, they look at you with a blank stare, or they respond in terms of subject knowledge, which is the wrong answer." Do you know what your strengths are? Wouldn't it be better to be in an organizational culture that helped you discover those, and learn ways to make the most of them?

Larry Hammond used this approach—finding and exploiting employee strengths—at a time when you would least expect it: during the darkest days of his business. Hammond is CEO of Auglaize Provico, an agribusiness company. The company was in the midst of its worst financial struggles and had to lay off one-quarter of its workforce. At that low point, Hammond decided to try a different approach. Rather than dwell on what was wrong, he decided to take advantage of what was right. "If you really want to [excel], you have to know yourself—you have to know what you're good at, and you have to know what you're not so good at," says Hammond. With the help of Gallup consultant Barry Conchie, Auglaize Provico focused on discovering and using employee strengths. Hammond and Auglaize Provico turned the company around. "You ask Larry [Hammond] what the difference is, and he'll say that it's individuals using their natural talents," says Conchie.[64]

Rewarding More Often Than Punishing

There is, of course, a time and place for punishment, but there is also a time and place for rewards. Although most organizations are sufficiently focused on extrinsic rewards like pay and promotions, they often forget about the power of smaller (and cheaper) rewards like praise. Creating a positive organizational culture means that managers "catch employees doing something right." Part of creating a positive culture is articulating praise. Many managers withhold praise either because they are afraid employees will coast, or because they think praise is not valued. Failing to praise can become a "silent killer" like escalating blood pressure. Because employees generally don't ask for praise, managers usually don't realize the costs of failing to do it.

Take the example of Elzbieta Górska-Kolodziejczyk, a plant manager for International Paper's facility in Kwidzyn, Poland. The job environment at the plant is bleak and difficult. Employees work in a windowless basement. Staffing is only roughly one-third of its prior level, while production has tripled. These challenges had done in the previous three managers. So when Górska-Kolodziejczyk took over, she knew she had her work cut out for her. Although she had many items on her list of ways to transform the organization, at the top of her list was recognition and praise. She initially found it difficult to give praise to those who were not used to it, especially men, but she found over time that they valued it, too. "They were like cement at the beginning," she said. "Like cement." Górska-Kolodziejczyk has found that giving praise is often reciprocated. One day a department supervisor pulled her over to tell her she was doing a good job. "This I do remember, yes," she said.[65]

Employees at Genentech, a biotechnology pioneer, work within a positive organizational culture that promotes individuals' vitality and growth. Genentech provides training opportunities and the resources and equipment needed to get work done, and offers courses to help each employee develop the skills they need for their future work. To discover talent within the company, Genentech allows employees to grow their careers both within departments and across them. An internal transfer program encourages employees to apply for jobs that can help them advance their careers. Scientists and engineers are also allowed to spend 20 percent of each workweek pursuing their favourite projects.

Emphasizing Vitality and Growth

A positive organizational culture emphasizes not only organizational effectiveness, but individuals' growth as well. No organization will get the best out of employees if the employees see themselves as mere tools or parts of the organization. A positive culture realizes the difference between a job and a career, and shows an interest not only in what the employee does to contribute to organizational effectiveness, but in what the organization does to contribute to employee growth. Fully one-third of employees feel they are not learning and growing on their job. The figure is even higher in some industries, such as banking, manufacturing, communications, and utilities. Although it may take more creativity to encourage employee growth in some types of industries, it can happen in the fast-paced food service industry. Consider the case of Philippe Lescornez and Didier Brynaert.

Philippe Lescornez leads a team of employees at Masterfoods in Belgium. One of his team members is Didier Brynaert, who works in Luxembourg, about 240 kilometres from Masterfoods' Belgian headquarters. Brynaert was considered a good sales promoter who was meeting expectations. Lescornez decided that Brynaert's job could be made more important if he were seen less as just another sales promoter and more as an expert on the unique features of the Luxembourg market. So Lescornez asked Brynaert for information he could share with the home office. He hoped that by raising Brynaert's profile in Brussels, he could create in him a greater sense of ownership for his remote sales territory. "I started to communicate much more what he did to other people [within the company], because there's quite some distance between the Brussels office and the section he's working in. So I started to communicate, communicate, communicate. The more I communicated, the more he started to provide material," says Lescornez. As a result, "Now he's recognized as the specialist for Luxembourg—the guy who is able to build a strong relationship with the Luxembourg clients," says Lescornez. What is good for Brynaert, of course, is also good for Lescornez, who gets credit for helping Brynaert grow and develop.[66]

Limits of Positive Culture

Is a positive culture the answer to all organizational problems? Cynics (or should we say realists?) may be skeptical about the benefits of positive organizational culture. To be sure, even though some companies such as WestJet, GE, Xerox, Boeing, and 3M have embraced aspects of a positive organizational culture, it is a new enough area that there is some uncertainty about how and when it works best. Moreover, any OB scholar or manager needs to make sure to be objective about the benefits—and risks—of cultivating a positive organizational culture.

Not all cultures value being positive as much as Canadian and US cultures do, and, even within these countries, there surely are limits to how far we should go to preserve a positive culture. When does the pursuit of a positive culture start to seem coercive or even Orwellian? As one critic notes, "Promoting a social orthodoxy of positiveness focuses on a particular constellation of desirable states and traits but, in so doing, can stigmatize those who fail to fit the template."[67]

Our point is that there may be benefits to establishing a positive culture, but an organization also needs to be careful to be objective and not pursue it past the point of effectiveness.

Summary and Implications

1 **What is the purpose of organizational culture?** *Organizational culture* is the pattern of shared values, beliefs, and assumptions considered to be the appropriate way to think and act within an organization. Culture provides stability to an organization and gives employees a clear understanding of "the way things are done around here." Culture performs a number of functions within an organization. First, it creates distinctions between one organization and others. Second, it conveys a sense of identity to organization members. Third, it helps create commitment to the organization. Fourth, it's the social glue that helps hold the organization together. Finally, it helps employees make sense of the organization. Organizations can have subcultures, with individual groups or teams creating their own cultures that may not completely reflect the overall organizational culture.

2 **How do you read an organization's culture?** Organizations differ in the extent to which they can be characterized as having strong or weak cultures. In a strong culture, the organization's core values are both intensely held and widely shared. In a weak culture, employees do not feel any great attachment to their organization or their co-workers. The artifacts of culture inform outsiders and employees about the underlying values and beliefs of the organization's culture. These artifacts— or aspects of an organization's culture that you see, hear, and feel—include stories, rituals, material symbols, and language, and can be used to help people read the organization's culture.

3 **How do you create and maintain organizational culture?** The original culture of an organization is derived from the philosophy of its founders. That philosophy then influences what types of employees are hired. The culture of the organization is then reinforced by top management, who signal what is acceptable behaviour and what is not. Employees are socialized into the culture, and will be more easily socialized to the extent that the employee's values match those of the organization.

4 **Can organizational culture have a downside?** Many of culture's functions are valuable for both the organization and the employee. Culture enhances organizational commitment and increases the consistency of employee behaviour. Culture also reduces ambiguity for employees by telling them what is important and how things are done. However, a strong culture can have a negative effect. Culture can act as a barrier to change, it can make it difficult to create an inclusive environment, and it can hinder the success of mergers and acquisitions.

5 **How do you change organizational culture?** Changing organizational culture is not easy. It is not unusual for managers to try changing the structure, the technology, or the people, but this often is not enough. Because culture is the shared beliefs within the organizations, it influences all of the activities in which people engage. Thus, it's important to change the reward structure, and to work carefully to change employee beliefs, in order to get real culture change. Organizations may want to create either an ethical culture or a positive organizational culture. An ethical culture signals that a company values an ethical climate and the ethical behaviour of its members. A positive organizational culture emphasizes employee strengths, rewards more often than it punishes, and emphasizes individuals' vitality and growth.

For Review

1. What are the levels of organizational culture?

2. What defines an organization's subcultures?

3. Can an employee survive in an organization if he or she rejects its core values? Explain.

4. How can an outsider assess an organization's culture?

5. How is language related to organizational culture?

6. What benefits can socialization provide for the organization? For the new employee?

7. How does a strong culture affect an organization's efforts to improve diversity?

8. Identify the steps a manager can take to implement cultural change in an organization.

9. What is a positive organizational culture?

For Critical Thinking

1. Is socialization brainwashing? Explain.

2. If management sought a culture characterized as innovative and autonomous, what might its socialization program look like?

3. Can you identify a set of characteristics that describe your college's or university's culture? Compare them with what several of your peers have noted. How closely do they agree?

4. "We should be opposed to the manipulation of individuals for organizational purposes, but a degree of social uniformity enables organizations to work better." Do you agree or disagree with this statement? What are its implications for organizational culture? Discuss.

5. Today's workforce is increasingly made up of part-time or contingent employees. Is organizational culture really important if the workforce is mostly temporary employees?

 **for You**

- Increase your understanding of culture by looking for similarities and differences across groups and organizations. For instance, do you have two courses where the classroom environment differs considerably? What does this suggest about the underlying assumptions in teaching students? Similarly, compare customer service at two local coffee shops or sandwich shops. What does the employee behaviour suggest about each organization's culture?

- Carefully consider the culture of any organization at which you are thinking of being employed. You will feel more comfortable in cultures that share your values and expectations. You may find yourself reacting very negatively if an organization's culture (and values) do not match your own.

- Keep in mind that groups create mini-cultures of their own. When you work in a group on a student project, be aware of the values and norms that are being supported early on in the group's life. These will greatly influence the group's culture.

 *POINT*

 *COUNTERPOINT*

Organizational Culture Does Not Change

An organization's culture develops over many years and is rooted in deeply held values to which employees are strongly committed. In addition, there are a number of forces continually operating to maintain a given culture. These would include written statements about the organization's mission and philosophy; the design of physical spaces and buildings; the dominant leadership style; hiring criteria; past promotion practices; entrenched rituals; popular stories about key people and events; the organization's historical performance evaluation criteria; and the organization's formal structure.

Selection and promotion policies are particularly important devices that work against cultural change. Employees chose the organization because they perceived their values to be a "good fit" with those of the organization. They become comfortable with that fit and will strongly resist efforts to disturb the equilibrium.

Those in control in organizations will also select senior managers who will continue the current culture. Even attempts to change a culture by going outside the organization to hire a new chief executive are unlikely to be effective. The evidence indicates that the culture is more likely to change the executive than the other way around. Why? It's too entrenched, and change becomes a potential threat to member self-interest. In fact, a more pragmatic view of the relationship between an organization's culture and its chief executive would be to note that the practice of filling senior-level management positions from the ranks of current managerial employees ensures that those who run the organization have been fully indoctrinated in the organization's culture. Promoting from within provides stability and lessens uncertainty. When a company's board of directors selects as a new chief executive officer an individual who has spent 30 years in the company, it virtually guarantees that the culture will continue unchanged.

Our argument, however, should not be viewed as saying that culture can never be changed. In the unusual case when an organization confronts a survival-threatening crisis—a crisis that is universally acknowledged as a true life-or-death situation—members of the organization will be responsive to efforts at cultural change. However, anything less than a crisis is unlikely to be effective in bringing about cultural change.

How to Change an Organization's Culture

Changing an organization's culture is extremely difficult, but cultures can be changed. The evidence suggests that cultural change is most likely to occur when most or all of the following conditions exist:

- *A dramatic crisis.* This is the shock that undermines the status quo and calls into question the relevance of the current culture. Examples of these crises might be a surprising financial setback, the loss of a major customer, or a dramatic technological breakthrough by a competitor. The *Columbia* disaster was a dramatic crisis for NASA.

- *Turnover in leadership.* New top leadership, which can provide an alternative set of key values, may be perceived as more capable of responding to the crisis. Top leadership definitely refers to the organization's chief executive, but also might need to include all senior management positions. The rush to hire outside CEOs after the Citibank and AIG scandals illustrates attempts to create more ethical climates through the introduction of new leadership. At NASA, some of the top leadership was moved to other positions after the *Columbia* disaster.

- *Young and small organization.* The younger the organization is, the less entrenched its culture will be. Similarly, it's easier for management to communicate its new values when the organization is small. This point helps explain the difficulty that multibillion-dollar corporations have in changing their cultures.

- *Weak culture.* The more widely held a culture is, and the higher the agreement among members on its values, the more difficult it will be to change. A strong culture has been one of the problems facing NASA. Conversely, weak cultures are more open to change than strong ones.

What Kind of Organizational Culture Fits You Best?

For each of the following statements, circle the level of agreement or disagreement that you personally feel:

SA	=	**Strongly Agree**
A	=	**Agree**
U	=	**Uncertain**
D	=	**Disagree**
SD	=	**Strongly disagree**

1. I like being part of a team and having my performance assessed in terms of my contribution to the team.	SA	A	U	D	SD
2. No person's needs should be compromised in order for a department to achieve its goals.	SA	A	U	D	SD
3. I like the thrill and excitement from taking risks.	SA	A	U	D	SD
4. If a person's job performance is inadequate, it's irrelevant how much effort he or she made.	SA	A	U	D	SD
5. I like things to be stable and predictable.	SA	A	U	D	SD
6. I prefer managers who provide detailed and rational explanations for their decisions.	SA	A	U	D	SD
7. I like to work where there isn't a great deal of pressure and where people are essentially easygoing.	SA	A	U	D	SD

Scoring Key:

For items 1, 2, 3, 4, and 7, score as follows: Strongly agree = +2 Agree = +1 Uncertain = 0 Disagree = –1 Strongly disagree = –2

For items 5 and 6, reverse the score (Strongly agree = –2, and so on). Add up your total. Your score will fall somewhere between +14 and –14.

What does your score mean? The lower your score, the more comfortable you will be in a formal, mechanistic, rule-oriented, and structured culture. This is often associated with large corporations and government agencies. Positive scores indicate a preference for informal, humanistic, flexible, and innovative cultures, which are more likely to be found in research units, advertising firms, high-tech companies, and small businesses.

Self-
Assessment
Library

More Learning About Yourself Exercises

An additional self-assessment relevant to this chapter appears on MyOBLab (**www.pearsoned.ca/myoblab**).

III.B.2 How Committed Am I to My Organization?

When you complete the additional assessments, consider the following:

1. Am I surprised about my score?

2. Would my friends evaluate me similarly?

OB *AT WORK*

BREAKOUT **GROUP** EXERCISES

Form small groups to discuss the following topics, as assigned by your instructor:

1. Choose two courses that you are taking this term, ideally in different faculties, and describe the culture of the classroom in each. What are the similarities and differences? What values about learning might you infer from your observations of culture?

2. Identify artifacts of culture in your current or previous workplace. From these artifacts, would you conclude that the organization had a strong or weak culture?

3. Have you or someone you know worked somewhere where the culture was strong? What was your reaction to that strong culture? Did you like that environment, or would you prefer to work where there is a weaker culture? Why?

WORKING WITH **OTHERS** EXERCISE

Rate Your Classroom Culture

Listed here are 14 statements. Using the 5-item scale (from Strongly Agree to Strongly Disagree), respond to each statement by circling the number that best represents your opinion.

	Strongly Agree	Agree	Neutral	Disagree	Strongly Disagree
1. I feel comfortable challenging statements made by my instructor.	5	4	3	2	1
2. My instructor heavily penalizes assignments that are not turned in on time.	1	2	3	4	5
3. My instructor believes that "it's final results that count."	1	2	3	4	5
4. My instructor is sensitive to my personal needs and problems.	5	4	3	2	1
5. A large portion of my grade depends on how well I work with others in the class.	5	4	3	2	1
6. I often feel nervous and tense when I come to class.	1	2	3	4	5
7. My instructor seems to prefer stability over change.	1	2	3	4	5
8. My instructor encourages me to develop new and different ideas.	5	4	3	2	1
9. My instructor has little tolerance for sloppy thinking.	1	2	3	4	5
10. My instructor is more concerned with how I came to a conclusion than with the conclusion itself.	5	4	3	2	1
11. My instructor treats all students alike.	1	2	3	4	5
12. My instructor frowns on class members helping each other with assignments.	1	2	3	4	5
13. Aggressive and competitive people have a distinct advantage in this class.	1	2	3	4	5
14. My instructor encourages me to see the world differently.	5	4	3	2	1

Scoring Key:

Calculate your total score by adding up the numbers you circled. Your score will fall between 14 and 70.

A high score (49 or above) describes an open, risk-taking, supportive, humanistic, team-oriented, easy-going, growth-oriented culture. A low score (35 or below) describes a closed, structured, task-oriented, individualistic, tense, and stability-oriented culture. Note that differences count, so a score of 60 is a more open culture than one that scores 50. Also, realize that one culture isn't preferable over another. The "right" culture depends on you and your preferences for a learning environment.

Form teams of 5 to 7 members each. Compare your scores. How closely do they align? Discuss and resolve any discrepancies. Based on your team's analysis, what type of student do you think would perform best in this class?

ETHICAL **DILEMMA** EXERCISE

Is There Room for Snooping in an Organization's Culture?

Although some of the spying Hewlett-Packard performed on some members of its board of directors appeared to violate California law, much of it was legal. Moreover, many companies spy on their employees—sometimes with and sometimes without their knowledge or consent. Organizations differ in their culture of surveillance. Some differences are due to the type of business. A US Department of Defense contractor has more reason—perhaps even an obligation—to spy on its employees than does an orange juice producer.

However, surveillance in most industries is on the upswing. There are several reasons for this, including the huge growth of two sectors with theft and security problems (services and information technology, respectively) and the increased availability of surveillance technology.

Consider the following surveillance actions and, for each action, decide whether it would never be ethical (mark N), would sometimes be ethical (mark S), or would always be ethical (mark A). For those you mark S, indicate what factors your judgment would depend on.

1. Sifting through an employee's trash for evidence of wrongdoing

2. Periodically reading email messages for disclosure of confidential information or inappropriate use

3. Conducting video surveillance of workspace

4. Monitoring websites visited by employees and determining the appropriateness and work-relatedness of those visited

5. Taping phone conversations

6. Posing as a job candidate, an investor, a customer, or a colleague (when the real purpose is to solicit information)

Would you be less likely to work for an employer that engaged in some of these methods? Why or why not? Do you think use of surveillance says something about an organization's culture?

CASE INCIDENTS

Wegmans Hires for Passion

Typically, grocery stores are not thought of as great places to work.[68] Hours are anything but 9 to 5, and the pay is low compared with other occupations. The result is an industry that sees high annual turnover rates. However, employees at Wegmans, an American chain, view working for a grocer a bit differently. Instead of viewing their job as a temporary setback on the way to a more illustrious career, many employees at Wegmans' view working for the grocer as their career. And given Wegmans' high profitability, it looks like the grocer will be around long enough to make such careers a reality for those who pursue them.

Why is Wegmans so effective? One reason is its culture. The chain began in 1930 when brothers John and Walter Wegman opened their first grocery store. One of its distinguishing features was a café that seated 300 customers. The store's immediate focus on fine foods quickly separated it from other grocers—a focus that is maintained by the company's employees, many of whom are hired based on their interest in food.

In 1950, Walter's son, Robert, became president and immediately added a generous number of employee benefits, such as profit sharing and medical coverage, completely paid for by the company. What was Robert's reason for offering such great benefits? "I was no different from them," he said, referring to the company's employees.

Now, Robert's son, Danny, is president of the company, and he has continued the Wegmans tradition of taking care of its employees. To date, Wegmans has paid for college and university scholarships for a number of its employees, both full time and part time. In addition to benefits, employees receive pay that is well above the market average. As a result, annual turnover at Wegmans for full-time employees is a mere 6 percent, compared with an industry average of 24 percent.

The culture that has developed at Wegmans is an important part of the company's success. Employees are proud to say they work at Wegmans. For example, Sara Goggins, a 19-year-old college student who works part time at Wegmans, recalls when Danny Wegman personally complimented her on a store display that she helped set up. "I love this place," she says. "If teaching doesn't work out, I would so totally work at Wegmans." And Kelly Schoeneck, a store manager, recounts that a few years ago, her supervisor asked her to analyze a frequent-shopper program that a competitor had recently adopted. Though she assumed that her supervisor would take credit for her findings, Schoeneck's supervisor had her present her findings directly to Robert Wegman.

Maintaining a culture of driven, happy, and loyal employees who are eager to help one another is not easy. Wegmans carefully selects each employee, and growth is often slow and meticulous, with only two new stores opened each year. When a new store is opened, employees from existing stores are brought in to the new store to maintain the culture. The existing employees are then able to transmit their knowledge and the store's values to new employees.

Managers especially are ingrained in the Wegmans culture. More than half started working at Wegmans when they were teenagers. One observer says, "When you're a 16-year- old kid, the last thing you want to do is wear a geeky shirt and work for a supermarket. But at Wegmans, it's a badge of honor. You are not a geeky cashier. You are part of the social fabric."

Employees at Wegmans are not selected based on intellectual ability or experience alone. "Just about everybody in the store has some genuine interest in food," states Jeff Burris, a store supervisor. Those employees who do not express this interest may not fit in and are sometimes not hired.

Questions

1. Would you characterize Wegmans' culture as strong or weak? Why? How is the strength of the culture at Wegmans likely to affect its employees, particularly new hires?

2. Wegmans attempts to maintain its core cultural values by hiring individuals who are passionate about the food industry and by staffing new stores partly with existing employees. What are some advantages and disadvantages of trying to impose a similar culture throughout different areas of a company?

3. What is the primary source of Wegmans' culture, and what are some ways that it has been able to sustain itself?

4. How might stories and rituals play a role in maintaining Wegmans' corporate culture?

Mergers Don't Always Lead to Culture Clashes

A lot of mergers lead to culture clashes and, ultimately, failure.[69] So in 2005, when banking giant Bank of America announced its $35-billion acquisition of credit card giant MBNA, many thought that in a few years, this merger would join the heap of those done in by cultural differences.

MBNA's culture was characterized by a free-wheeling, entrepreneurial spirit that was also quite secretive. MBNA employees also were accustomed to the high life. Their corporate headquarters in Wilmington, Delaware, could be described as lavish, and employees throughout the company enjoyed high salaries and generous perks—from the private golf course at its headquarters, to its fleet of corporate jets and private yachts.

Bank of America, in contrast, grew by thrift. It was a low-cost, no-nonsense operation. Unlike MBNA, it believed that size and smarts were more important than speed. It was an acquisition machine that some likened to *Star Trek's* relentless Borg collective.

In short, the cultures in the two companies were very, very different. Although these cultural differences seemed a recipe for disaster, it appears, judging from the reactions of Bank of America and MBNA employees, that the merger has worked. How can this be?

Bank of America had the foresight to know which MBNA practices to attempt to change, and which to keep in place. Especially critical was the bank's appreciation and respect for MBNA's culture. "On Day 1, I was directed that this was not like the ones you are used to," said Clifford Skelton, who had helped manage Bank of America's acquisition of FleetBoston Financial before moving on to MBNA.

To try to manage the cultural transition, executives of both companies began by comparing thousands of practices covering everything from hiring to call-centre operations. In many cases, Bank of America chose to keep MBNA's cultural practices in place. In other cases, the bank did impose its will on MBNA. For example, because MBNA's pay rates were well above market, many MBNA managers were forced to swallow a steep pay cut. Some MBNA employees have left, but most have remained.

In other cases, the cultures co-adapted. For example, MBNA's dress code was much more formal than the bank's business casual approach. In the end, a hybrid code was adopted, where business suits were expected in the credit card division's corporate offices and in front of clients, but business causal was the norm otherwise.

While most believe the merger has been successful, there are tensions. Some Bank of America managers see MBNA managers as arrogant and autocratic. Some MBNA managers see their Bank of America counterparts as bureaucratic.

What about those famous MBNA perks? As you might have guessed, most of those have gone away. All but one of the corporate jets is gone. The golf course was donated to the state of Delaware. Gone too are most of the works of art that hung in MBNA's corporate offices.

Questions

1. In what ways were the cultures of Bank of America and MBNA incompatible?

2. Why do you think their cultures appeared to mesh rather than clash?

3. Do you think culture is important to the success of a merger or acquisition? Why or why not?

4. How much of the smooth transition, if any, do you think comes from both companies glossing over real differences in an effort to make the merger work?

From **Concepts** to **Skills**

How to "Read" an Organization's Culture

The ability to read and assess an organization's culture can be a valuable skill.[70] If you are looking for a job, you will want to choose an employer whose culture is compatible with your values and in which you will feel comfortable. If you can accurately assess a prospective employer's culture before you make your decision, you may be able to save yourself a lot of grief and reduce the likelihood of making a poor choice. Similarly, you will undoubtedly have business transactions with numerous organizations during your professional career. You will be trying to sell a product or service, negotiate a contract, or arrange a joint venture, or you may merely be seeking out which individual in an organization controls certain decisions. The ability to assess another organization's culture can be a definite plus in successfully completing these pursuits.

For the sake of simplicity, we will approach the problem of reading an organization's culture from the point of view of a job applicant. We will assume you are interviewing for a job. Here is a list of things you can do to help learn about a potential employer's culture:

- Observe the physical surroundings. Pay attention to signs, pictures, style of dress, length of hair, degree of openness between offices, and office furnishings and arrangements.

- With whom did you meet? Just the person who would be your immediate manager? Or potential colleagues, managers from other departments, or senior executives? Based on what they revealed, to what degree do people other than the immediate manager have input into the hiring decision?

- How would you characterize the style of the people you met? Formal? Casual? Serious? Jovial?

- Does the organization have formal rules and regulations printed in a human resource policy manual? If so, how detailed are these policies?

- Ask questions of the people you meet. The most valid and reliable information tends to come from asking the same questions of many people (to see how closely their responses align) and by talking with boundary

spanners. *Boundary spanners* are employees whose work links them to the external environment and includes jobs such as human resource interviewer, salesperson, purchasing agent, labour negotiator, public relations specialist, and company lawyer.

Questions that will give you insights into organizational processes and practices might include the following:

- What is the background of the founders?

- What is the background of current senior managers? What are their functional specializations? Were they promoted from within or hired from outside?

- How does the organization integrate new employees? Is there an orientation program? Training? If so, could you describe these features?

- How does your manager define his or her job success? (Amount of profit? Serving customers? Meeting deadlines? Acquiring budget increases?)

- How would you define fairness in terms of reward allocations?

- Can you identify some people here who are on the "fast track"? What do you think has put them on the fast track?

- Can you identify someone who seems to be considered a deviant in the organization? How has the organization responded to this person?

- Can you describe a decision that someone made here that was well received?

- Can you describe a decision that did not work out well? What were the consequences for the decision maker?

- Could you describe a crisis or critical event that has occurred recently in the organization? How did top management respond? What was learned from this experience?

Practising Skills

After spending your first three years after college graduation as a freelance graphic designer, you are looking at pursuing a job as an account executive at a graphic design firm. You feel that the scope of assignments and potential for technical training far exceed what you would be able to do on your own, and you are looking to expand your skills and meet a brand-new set of challenges. However, you want to make sure you "fit" in to the organization where you are going to be spending more than eight hours every workday. What's the best way for you to find a place where you will be happy, and where your style and personality will be appreciated?

Reinforcing Skills

1. Choose two courses that you are taking this term, ideally in different faculties, and describe the culture of the classroom in each. What are the similarities and differences? What values about learning might you infer from your observations of culture?

2. Do some comparisons of the atmosphere or feeling you get from various organizations. Because of the number and wide variety that you will find, it will probably be easiest for you to do this exercise using restaurants, retail stores, or banks. Based on the atmosphere that you observe, what type of organizational culture do you think these organizations might have? If you can, interview three employees at each organization for their descriptions of their organization's culture.

3. Think about changes (major and minor) that you have dealt with over the past year. Perhaps these changes involved other people and perhaps they were personal. Did you resist the change? Did others resist the change? How did you overcome your resistance or the resistance of others to the change?

VIDEO CASE INCIDENT

CASE 10 Organizational Culture at TerraCycle

TerraCycle—a company co-founded by Canadian entrepreneurs Tom Szaky and Jon Beyer—makes a wide range of eco-friendly products from garbage. Szaky observes that the primary purpose of business has always been to make a profit. Early in the last century, some businesses engaged in some unreasonable activities—such as the use of child labour—in pursuit of profit. About 30 years ago, a new type of business emerged, one that was concerned about the environment. But it simply passed on the cost of being green to its customers. An even newer approach is called *eco-capitalism*, where the goal is to do the best thing for the environment *and* for society, and to do so while making more money than the big, traditional companies. In eco-capitalism, the goods drive the money instead of the money driving the goods.

When TerraCycle started out, it was financed on business plan contest winnings and the credit cards of its co-founders. Eventually, a few investors were found who were willing to put a large amount of money into the business. But Szaky felt that they wanted to move the company away from its eco-focus, and he was not willing to do that because it would not be consistent with the vision and culture that he wanted to establish at TerraCycle.

Albe Zakes is the company's director of public relations, and he says that TerraCycle is actually "making a difference." The company is not just riding the eco-friendly wave. It is making products that are useful and environmentally sound. Its culture is the new face of business. It is young, hip, eco-friendly, and socially responsible, and has a good relationship with the local community where it operates. Most of the workers are in their 20s, and the action is fast and furious. There is so much going on that there is no time to really organize. The culture is one of "let's get this job done and then move on to the next one."

The external walls of the company's factory—which are covered with graffiti—give a hint about what the company's culture is like inside. Zakes says that TerraCycle has the most colourful headquarters in the country. A "graffiti jam" is held every year, where up to 50 artists paint original graffiti on TerraCycle's external factory walls. It is a community event, and includes kids from different summer programs in the area. One advantage for TerraCycle is that the factory gets repainted every year.

Zakes says that the company is very aggressive and takes a lot of risks. It does not move slowly through research and development like a lot of big companies do. Rather, at TerraCycle, employees figure out what works and run as fast as possible with it. In that kind of culture, everyone must be very flexible and willing to change direction quickly. The work is very demanding, and people are given a lot of responsibility. Because everyone is on a first-name basis, they feel very close and can bond together to overcome challenges.

Questions

1. Describe the organizational culture at TerraCycle. How is it different from what you might find at a more traditional organization? How is it similar?

2. Is the way TerraCycle's culture developed consistent with what is proposed in Exhibit 10-3? Explain.

3. The walls at TerraCycle are covered in graffiti, the company holds graffiti jams, and now the company is selling graffiti-covered plant pots. Explain why graffiti is such a large part of the organization's culture.

4. Being socially responsible and eco-friendly are top priorities at TerraCycle. Explain how these values permeate the organization.

5. Each of the seven primary characteristics of culture can range from low to high. Rate each of the seven characteristics at TerraCycle. Explain your ratings.

Source: Based on "Organizational Culture at TerraCycle," *Organizational Behavior Video Library*, 2008. Copyrighted by Prentice-Hall.

Leadership

A major sporting equipment retailer wants to be as eco-friendly as possible. What kinds of leadership skills are needed to inspire and motivate employees to think about the environment?

1 What is the difference between a manager and a leader?

2 Are there specific traits, behaviours, and situations that affect how one leads?

3 How does a leader lead with vision?

4 Are there leadership roles for nonmanagers?

5 What are some of the contemporary issues in leadership?

Conventional wisdom suggests that visionary leaders are optimists.[1] Patagonia's founder, Yvon Chouinard, whose parents were French-Canadian, is living proof that that conventional wisdom isn't always right.

Patagonia is famous for its outdoor gear. But it is also famous for its eco-friendly ethic. Much of the credit for this balance goes to Chouinard, who has embraced the idea presented by the late environmentalist David Brower: "There is no business to be done on a dead planet." Chouinard is known for informality, favouring environmentalism, and a love of the outdoors.

Despite Chouinard's positive values, he is also a pessimist. He says, "I don't think we're going to be here 100 years from now as a society, or maybe even as a species." In another forum, he wrote, "Patagonia will never be completely socially responsible. It will never make a totally sustainable, nondamaging product."

Chouinard's business model may seem a little strange, but that's how his vision works. By portraying the future in its darkest terms, Patagonia builds the case for its way of doing business. If humans are on the verge of extinguishing themselves, then it becomes all the more important to buy from environmentally conscious companies.

In this chapter, we examine various studies on leadership to determine what makes an effective leader. First we consider the traits, behaviours, and situations that affect one's ability to lead, and then we consider inspirational leadership. As well, we look at how leadership is spread throughout an organization and how you might lead yourself, through self-management. Finally, we discuss contemporary issues in leadership.

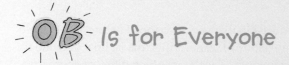 Is for Everyone

- Have you ever wondered if there was one right way to lead?
- Can anyone be a leader?
- How do you manage yourself?
- Do men and women get promoted differently?

 **Self-Assessment Library**

LEARNING ABOUT YOURSELF

- Leadership Style
- Least Preferred Co-worker
- Charisma
- Self-Management
- Ethical Leadership

Are Managers and Leaders the Same?

1   What is the difference between a manager and a leader?

Leadership and *management* are two terms that are often confused. What is the difference between them?

John Kotter of the Harvard Business School argues that "managers promote stability while leaders press for change and only organizations that embrace both sides of the contradiction can survive in turbulent times."[2]

McGill University professor Rabindra Kanungo notes there is a growing consensus emerging "among management scholars that the concept of 'leadership' must be distinguished from the concept of 'supervision/management.'"[3] Exhibit 11-1 illustrates Kanungo's distinctions between leadership and management. Leaders establish direction by developing a vision of the future; then they align people by communicating this vision and inspiring them to overcome hurdles. Managers implement the vision and strategy provided by leaders, coordinate and staff the organization, and handle day-to-day problems.

In our discussion of leadership, we will focus on two major tasks of those who lead in organizations: managing those around them to get the day-to-day tasks done, and inspiring others to do the extraordinary. It will become clear that successful leaders rely on a variety of interpersonal skills in order to encourage others to perform at their best. It will also become clear that, no matter the place in the hierarchy, from CEO to team leader, a variety of individuals can be called on to perform leadership roles.

Leadership as Supervision

Yvon Chouinard is a very different style of manager. He believes in the M.B.A. theory of management—"management by absence." He spends nearly half the year surfing or water skiing, because he does not believe that being a leader should require sacrificing one's lifestyle. He doesn't want to be in the office every day.

So what kind of employees do best under Chouinard's style of leadership? He explains: "our employees are so independent, we've been told by psychologists, that they would be considered unemployable in a typical company." He values employees who are independent thinkers, and who will question what they think are bad decisions.

Patagonia managers lead by example. There are no special parking places: "the best spots are reserved for fuel-efficient cars." Employees are able to inspect the financial records to see how the company is being run. The company runs on "flextime"—employees can choose their hours. Chouinard's philosophy is "let my people go surfing," which means that if the surf is good, employees can take some time out of the work day to go surfing. He trusts his employees to get their work done, even if they do take a surf break. Are Chouinard's views of employees and management unusual? How much supervision is needed if employees are guided by a vision?

2   Are there specific traits, behaviours, and situations that affect how one leads?

In this section, we discuss theories of leadership that were developed before 1980. These early theories focused on the supervisory nature of leadership—that is, how individuals managed the day-to-day functioning of employees. The theories took different approaches in understanding how best to lead in a supervisory capacity. The three general types of theories that emerged were (1) trait theories, which propose leaders have a particular set of traits that makes them different from nonleaders; (2) behavioural theories, which propose that particular behaviours make for better leaders; and (3) contingency theories, which propose the situation has an effect on leaders. When you think about these theories, remember that although they have been considered "theories of leadership," they rely on an older understanding of what "leadership" means, and they don't convey Kanungo's distinction between leadership and supervision.

trait theories of leadership
Theories that propose traits—personality, social, physical, or intellectual—differentiate leaders from nonleaders.

Trait Theories: Are Leaders Different from Others?

Have you ever wondered whether there is some fundamental personality difference that makes some people "born leaders"? **Trait theories of leadership** emerged in the

EXHIBIT 11-1   Distinguishing Leadership from Management

Management	Leadership
1. Engages in day-to-day caretaker activities: Maintains and allocates resources	Formulates long-term objectives for reforming the system: Plans strategy and tactics
2. Exhibits supervisory behaviour: Acts to make others maintain standard job behaviour	Exhibits leading behaviour: Acts to bring about change in others congruent with long-term objectives
3. Administers subsystems within organizations	Innovates for the entire organization
4. Asks how and when to engage in standard practice	Asks what and why to change standard practice
5. Acts within established culture of the organization	Creates vision and meaning for the organization
6. Uses transactional influence: Induces compliance in manifest behaviour using rewards, sanctions, and formal authority	Uses transformational influence: Induces change in values, attitudes, and behaviour using personal examples and expertise
7. Relies on control strategies to get things done by subordinates	Uses empowering strategies to make followers internalize values
8. Status quo supporter and stabilizer	Status quo challenger and change creator

Source: R. N. Kanungo, "Leadership in Organizations: Looking Ahead to the 21st Century," *Canadian Psychology* 39, no. 1–2 (1998), p. 77.

hope that if it were possible to identify the traits of leaders, it would be easier to select people to fill leadership roles. Being able to select good leaders is important because not all people know how to be good leaders, as *Focus on Research* shows.

FOCUS ON **RESEARCH**

Bad Bosses Everywhere

Doesn't leadership come naturally? Although much is expected of leaders, what is surprising is how rarely they seem to meet the most basic definitions of effectiveness.[4] A recent study of 700 employees revealed that many believe their supervisors don't give credit when it's due, gossip about them behind their backs, and don't keep their word. The situation is so bad that for many employees, the study's lead author says, "They don't leave their company, they leave their boss."

Key findings of the study are as follows:

- 39 percent said their supervisor failed to keep promises.
- 37 percent said their supervisor failed to give credit when due.
- 31 percent said their supervisor gave them the "silent treatment" in the past year.
- 27 percent said their supervisor made negative comments about them to other employees or managers.
- 24 percent said their supervisor invaded their privacy.
- 23 percent said their supervisor blames others to cover up mistakes or minimize embarrassment.

Why do companies promote such people into leadership positions? One reason may be the Peter Principle. When people are promoted into one job (say, as a supervisor or coach) based on how well they did another (say, salesperson or player), that assumes that the skills of one role are the same as the other. The only time such people stop being promoted is when they reach their level of incompetence. Judging from the results of this study, that level of leadership incompetence is reached all too often.

Trait theories of leadership differentiate leaders from nonleaders by focusing on personal qualities and characteristics. Individuals such as Pierre Trudeau, Barack Obama, South Africa's Nelson Mandela, Virgin Group CEO Richard Branson, and Apple co-founder Steve Jobs are recognized as leaders and described in terms such as *charismatic*, *enthusiastic*, and *courageous*. The search for personality, social, physical, or intellectual attributes that would describe leaders and differentiate them from nonleaders goes back to the earliest stages of leadership research.

Research efforts at isolating leadership traits resulted in a number of dead ends. For instance, a review in the late 1960s of 20 studies identified nearly 80 leadership traits, but only 5 of these traits were common to 4 or more of the investigations.[5] By the 1990s, after numerous studies and analyses, about the best thing that could be said was that most "leaders are not like other people," but the particular traits that were isolated varied a great deal from review to review.[6] It was a pretty confusing state of affairs.

A breakthrough, of sorts, came when researchers began organizing traits around the Big Five Personality Model (see Chapter 2).[7] What became clear was that most of the dozens of traits that emerged in various leadership reviews could be subsumed under one of the Big Five factors, and that this approach resulted in consistent and strong support for traits as predictors of leadership. For instance, ambition and energy—two common traits of leaders—are part of extraversion. Rather than focus on these two specific traits, it is better to think of them in terms of the more general trait of extraversion.

Comprehensive reviews of the leadership literature, when organized around the Big Five, have found that extraversion is the most important trait of effective leaders.[8] But results show that extraversion is more strongly related to leader emergence than to leader effectiveness. This is not totally surprising, since sociable and dominant people are more likely to assert themselves in group situations. While the assertive nature of extraverts is a positive, leaders need to make sure they are not too assertive—one study found that leaders who scored very high on assertiveness were less effective than those who were moderately high.[9]

Conscientiousness and openness to experience also showed strong and consistent relationships to leadership, but not as strong as extraversion. The traits of agreeableness and emotional stability don't appear to offer much help in predicting leadership. Overall, it does appear that the trait approach does have something to offer. Leaders who are extraverted (individuals who like being around people and are able to assert themselves), conscientious (individuals who are disciplined and keep commitments they make), and open (individuals who are creative and flexible) do seem to have an advantage when it comes to leadership, suggesting that good leaders do have key traits in common.

Based on the latest findings, we offer two conclusions. First, traits can predict leadership. Twenty years ago, the evidence suggested otherwise. But this was probably because of the lack of a valid framework for classifying and organizing traits. The Big Five Personality Model seems to have rectified that. Second, traits do a better job at predicting the emergence of leaders and the appearance of leadership than in actually distinguishing between *effective* and *ineffective* leaders.[10] The fact that an individual exhibits the traits and others consider that person to be a leader does not necessarily mean that the leader is successful at getting his or her group to achieve its goals.

This chapter's *Point/Counterpoint* on page 441 raises further issues on whether leaders are born or made. *Case Incident—The Kinder, Gentler Leader?* on page 445 looks at the trend toward leaders who have a sensitive and caring style.

Emotional Intelligence and Leadership

Recent studies are indicating that another trait that may indicate effective leadership is emotional intelligence (EI), which we discussed in Chapter 2. Advocates of EI argue that, without it, a person can have outstanding training, a highly analytical mind, a compelling vision, and an endless supply of terrific ideas, but still not make a great leader. This may be especially true as individuals move up in an organization.[11] But why is EI so critical to effective leadership? A core component of EI is empathy. Empathetic leaders can sense others' needs, listen to what followers say (and don't say), and are able to read the reactions of others. As one leader noted, "The caring part of empathy, especially for the people with whom you work, is what inspires people to stay with a leader when the going gets rough. The mere fact that someone cares is more often than not rewarded with loyalty."[12]

Despite these claims for its importance, the link between EI and leadership effectiveness is much less investigated than other traits. One reviewer noted, "Speculating about the practical utility of the EI construct might be premature." Despite such warnings, EI is being viewed as a panacea for many organizational malaises, with recent suggestions that EI is essential for leadership effectiveness."[13] But until more rigorous evidence accumulates, we cannot be confident about the connection.

Case Incident—The Kinder, Gentler Leader? looks at the trend toward leaders who have a more sensitive and caring style. *Case Incident—Moving from Colleague to Supervisor* on page 445 helps you think about the challenges one faces when moving from being a co-worker to taking on leadership responsibilities.

Behavioural Theories: Do Leaders Behave in Particular Ways?

The inability to strike "gold" in the trait "mines" led researchers to look at the behaviours that specific leaders exhibited. They wondered if there was something unique in the way that effective leaders behave. Trait theory, had it been successful, would have provided a basis for *selecting* the "right" people to assume formal positions in groups and organizations requiring leadership. In contrast, behavioural theories tried to identify critical behavioural determinants of leadership, in the hope that we could *train* people to be leaders.

The three most well-known **behavioural theories of leadership** are the Ohio State University studies, beginning in the late 1940s,[14] the University of Michigan studies conducted at about the same time, and Blake and Mouton's Leadership Grid, which reflects the behavioural definitions of both the Ohio and Michigan studies. All three approaches consider two main dimensions by which managers can be characterized: attention to production and attention to people.

The Ohio State Studies

In the Ohio State studies, these two dimensions are known as *initiating structure* and *consideration*. **Initiating structure** refers to the extent to which a leader is likely to define and structure his or her role and the roles of employees in order to attain goals; it includes behaviour that attempts to organize work, work relationships, and goals. **Consideration** is defined as the extent to which a leader is likely to have job relationships characterized by mutual trust, respect for employees' ideas, and regard for their feelings. A leader who is high in consideration shows concern for employees' comfort, well-being, status, and satisfaction.

Sally Jewell, CEO of Recreational Equipment, Inc. (REI), is an employee-oriented leader. During her tenure as CEO, Jewell has turned a struggling company into one with record sales. But she credits REI's success to the work of employees, stating that she does not believe in "hero CEOs." Jewell respects each employee's contribution to the company and includes in her leadership people who are very different from herself. Described as a leader high in consideration, she listens to employees' ideas and empowers them in performing their jobs.

behavioural theories of leadership Theories that propose that specific behaviours differentiate leaders from nonleaders.

initiating structure The extent to which a leader is likely to define and structure his or her role and the roles of employees in order to attain goals.

consideration The extent to which a leader is likely to have job relationships characterized by mutual trust, respect for employees' ideas, and regard for their feelings.

The Michigan Studies

Researchers at the University of Michigan, whose work is referred to as "the Michigan studies," also developed two dimensions of leadership behaviour that they labelled *employee oriented* and *production oriented*.[15] **Employee-oriented leaders** emphasize interpersonal relations. They take a personal interest in the needs of their subordinates and accept individual differences among members. **Production-oriented leaders**, in contrast, tend to emphasize the technical or task aspects of the job. They are mainly concerned with making sure the group accomplishes its tasks, and the group members are simply a means to that end.

The Leadership Grid

Blake and Mouton developed a graphic portrayal of a two-dimensional view of leadership style. They proposed a **Leadership Grid** (formerly called the *Managerial Grid*)[16] based on the styles of "concern for people" and "concern for production," which essentially represent the Ohio State dimensions of consideration and initiating structure or the Michigan dimensions of employee orientation and production orientation.

The grid, depicted in Exhibit 11-2, has 9 possible positions along each axis, creating 81 different positions in which the leader's style may fall, but emphasis has been placed on 5: impoverished management (1,1); authority-obedience management (9,1); middle-of-the-road management (5,5); country club management (1,9); and team management (9,9). The grid shows the dominating factors in a leader's thinking with respect to how to get results from people, without focusing on what the specific results are.

RESEARCH FINDINGS: Behavioural Theories of Leadership

While the results of the behavioural studies have been somewhat mixed,[17] a careful evaluation of the situations that leaders face provides some insights into when leaders should be production-oriented and when they should be people-oriented:[18]

- When subordinates experience a lot of pressure because of deadlines or unclear tasks, leaders who are people-oriented will increase employee satisfaction and performance.

- When the task is interesting or satisfying, there is less need for leaders to be people-oriented.

- When it's clear how to perform the task and what the goals are, leaders who are people-oriented will increase employee satisfaction, while those who are task-oriented will increase dissatisfaction.

- When people don't know what to do, or individuals don't have the knowledge or skills to do the job, it's more important for leaders to be production-oriented than people-oriented.

The followers of leaders who are high in people orientation are more satisfied with their jobs, more motivated, and also have more respect for their leaders. Leaders who are high in task orientation show higher levels of group and organizational productivity and receive more positive performance evaluations.

Contingency Theories: Does the Situation Matter?

It became increasingly clear to those studying leadership that predicting leadership success was more complex than simply isolating a few traits or preferable behaviours. The failure to obtain consistent results led researchers to focus on the situational factors that affect a leader's ability to act. The research pointed out that not all leaders can lead in every situation.[19] For instance, Apple brought Steve Jobs back as leader in 1996 despite having dismissed him 11 years earlier. It is unlikely that Jobs' leadership skills

---

employee-oriented leader A leader who emphasizes interpersonal relations.

production-oriented leader A leader who emphasizes the technical or task aspects of the job.

Leadership Grid A two-dimensional grid outlining 81 different leadership styles.

EXHIBIT 11-2   The Leadership Grid

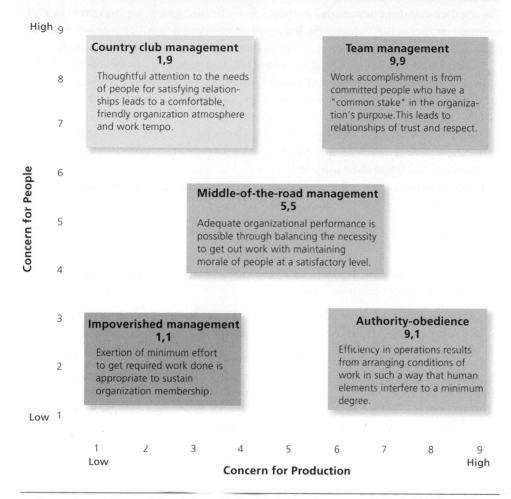

*Have you ever wondered if there was one **right** way to lead?*

changed that much during his absence, but the circumstances at Apple were quite different upon his return than when he left. The relationship between leadership style and effectiveness suggests that there is no one right style, but that style *depends* upon the situation the leader faces. There has been no shortage of studies attempting to isolate critical situational factors that affect leadership effectiveness. The volume of studies is illustrated by the number of moderating variables that researchers have identified in their discussions of **situational, or contingency, theories**. These variables include the degree of structure in the task being performed, the quality of leader-member relations; the leader's position power; the clarity of the employee's role; group norms; information availability; employee acceptance of leader's decisions; and employee maturity.[20]

We consider four situational theories below: the Fiedler contingency model, Hersey and Blanchard's Situational Leadership®, path-goal theory, and substitutes for leadership.

situational, or contingency, theories Theories that propose leadership effectiveness is dependent on the situation.

Fiedler Contingency Model

The first comprehensive contingency model for leadership was developed by Fred Fiedler.[21] The **Fiedler contingency model** proposes that effective group performance depends upon the proper match between the leader's style of interacting with his or her followers and the degree to which the situation allows the leader to control and influence.

Fiedler created the *least preferred co-worker (LPC)* questionnaire to determine whether individuals were primarily interested in good personal relations with co-workers, and thus *relationship-oriented*, or primarily interested in productivity, and thus *task-oriented*. Fiedler assumed that an individual's leadership style is fixed. Therefore, if a situation requires a task-oriented leader and the person in that leadership position is relationship-oriented, either the situation has to be modified or the leader must be removed and replaced for optimum effectiveness to be achieved.

Fiedler identified three contingency dimensions that together define the key situational factors for determining leader effectiveness:

- *Leader-member relations.* The degree of confidence, trust, and respect members have for their leader.

- *Task structure.* The degree to which job assignments are procedurized (that is, structured or unstructured).

- *Position power.* The degree of influence a leader has over power-based activities such as hiring, firing, discipline, promotions, and salary increases.

Fiedler stated that the better the leader-member relations, the more highly structured the job, and the stronger the position power, the more control the leader has. He suggested that task-oriented leaders perform best in situations of high and low control, while relationship-oriented leaders perform best in moderate control situations.[22] In a high control situation, a leader can "get away" with task orientation, because the relationships are good, and followers are easily influenced.[23] In a low control situation (which is characterized by poor relations, ill-defined task, and low influence), task orientation may be the only thing that makes it possible to get something done. In a moderate control situation, being relationship-oriented may smooth the way to getting things done.

Hersey and Blanchard's Situational Leadership Theory®

Paul Hersey and Ken Blanchard developed a leadership model that has gained a strong following among management development specialists.[24] This model—called **Situational Leadership® (SL)**—has been incorporated into the leadership system of more than 700 of the *Fortune* 1000 companies, and more than a million managers a year from a wide variety of organizations are being taught its basic elements.[25]

SL essentially views the leader-follower relationship as similar to that of a parent and child. Just as a parent needs to give up control as a child becomes more mature and responsible, so too should leaders. Hersey and Blanchard identify four specific leader behaviours—from highly directive to highly laissez-faire. The most effective behaviour depends on a follower's ability and motivation. This is illustrated in Exhibit 11-3. SL says that if a follower is *unable and unwilling* to do a task, the leader needs to give clear and specific directions (in other words, be highly directive). If a follower is *unable and willing*, the leader needs to display high task orientation to compensate for the follower's lack of ability, and high relationship orientation to get the follower to "buy into" the leader's desires (in other words, "sell" the task). If the follower is *able and unwilling*, the leader needs to use a supportive and participative style. Finally, if the employee is both *able and willing*, the leader does not need to do much (in other words, a laissez-faire approach will work).

Both the Fiedler contingency model and Hersey and Blanchard's SL have some intuitive appeal. Blanchard's work, for instance, is widely applied in the workplace. However, these approaches have received far less empirical support, and Fiedler's theory has been

---

Fiedler contingency model A leadership theory that proposes effective group performance depends on the proper match between the leader's style of interacting with his or her followers and the degree to which the situation gives the leader control and influence.

Situational Leadership® (SL) A leadership theory that focuses on the readiness of followers.

EXHIBIT 11-3   Hersey and Blanchard's Situational Leadership®

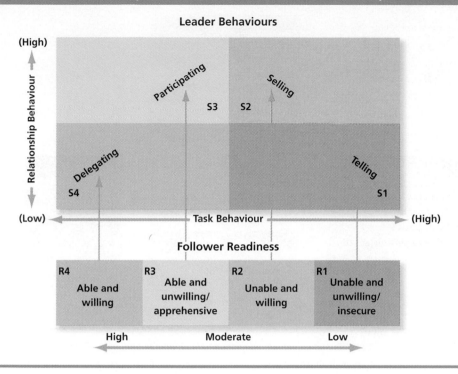

found to be more difficult to apply in the workplace than the next model we consider, path-goal theory.[26]

Path-Goal Theory

Currently, one of the most respected approaches to leadership is **path-goal theory**. Developed by University of Toronto professor Martin Evans in the late 1960s, it was subsequently expanded upon by Robert House (formerly at the University of Toronto, but now at the Wharton School of Business at the University of Pennsylvania). Path-goal theory is a contingency model of leadership that extracts key elements from the Ohio State leadership research on initiating structure and consideration, and from the expectancy theory of motivation.[27]

The essence of the theory is that it is the leader's job to assist followers in attaining their goals and to provide the necessary direction and/or support to ensure that their individual goals are compatible with the overall goals of the group or organization. The term *path-goal* derives from the belief that effective leaders both clarify the path, to help their followers achieve their work goals, and make the journey along the path easier by reducing roadblocks and pitfalls.

According to this theory, leaders should follow three guidelines to be effective:[28]

- *Determine the outcomes subordinates want.* These might include good pay, job security, interesting work, and autonomy to do one's job.

- *Reward individuals with their desired outcomes* when they perform well.

- *Let individuals know what they need to do to receive rewards* (that is, the path to the goal), remove any barriers that would prevent high performance, and express confidence that individuals have the ability to perform well.

Path-goal theory identifies four leadership behaviours that might be used in different situations to motivate individuals:

- The *directive leader* lets followers know what is expected of them, schedules work to be done, and gives specific guidance as to how to accomplish tasks.

path-goal theory A leadership theory that says it's the leader's job to assist followers in attaining their goals and to provide the necessary direction and/or support to ensure that their goals are compatible with the overall objectives of the group or organization.

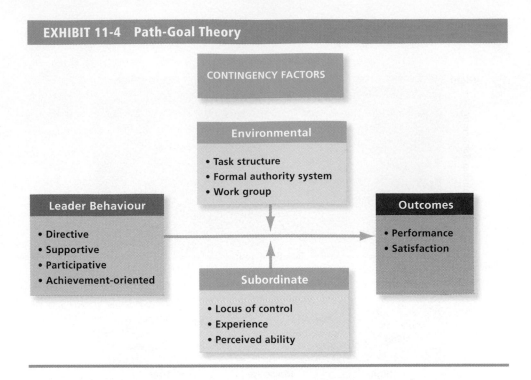

EXHIBIT 11-4   Path-Goal Theory

This closely parallels the Ohio State dimension of initiating structure. This behaviour is best used when individuals have difficulty doing tasks or the tasks are ambiguous. It would not be very helpful when used with individuals who are already highly motivated, have the skills and abilities to do the task, and understand the requirements of the task.

- The *supportive leader* is friendly and shows concern for the needs of followers. This is essentially synonymous with the Ohio State dimension of consideration. This behaviour is often recommended when individuals are under stress, or otherwise show that they need to be supported.

- The *participative leader* consults with followers and uses their suggestions before making a decision. This behaviour is most appropriate when individuals need to buy in to decisions.

- The *achievement-oriented leader* sets challenging goals and expects followers to perform at their highest level. This behaviour works well with individuals who like challenges and are highly motivated. It would be less effective with less capable individuals, or those who are highly stressed from overwork.

As Exhibit 11-4 illustrates, path-goal theory proposes two types of contingency variables that affect the leadership behaviour-outcome relationship: environmental variables that are outside the control of the employee and variables that are part of the personal characteristics of the employee. The theory proposes that employee performance and satisfaction are likely to be positively influenced when the leader compensates for what is lacking in either the employee or the work setting. However, the leader who spends time explaining tasks when those tasks are already clear or when the employee has the ability and experience to handle them without interference is likely to be ineffective because the employee will see such directive behaviour as redundant or even insulting.

RESEARCH FINDINGS: Path-Goal Theory

Due to the complexity of the theory, testing path-goal theory has not proven to be easy. A review of the evidence suggests mixed support. As the authors of this review commented, "These results suggest that either effective leadership does not rest in the removal of roadblocks and pitfalls to employee path instrumentalities as path-goal theories propose or that the nature of these hindrances is not in accord with the proposition of the theories."[29] Another review concluded that the lack of support was "shocking and disappointing."[30] These conclusions have been challenged by others who argue that adequate tests of the theory have yet to be conducted.[31] Thus, it is safe to say that the jury is still out regarding the validity of path-goal theory. Because it is so complex to test, that may remain the case for some time to come.

One question that arises from contingency theories is whether leaders can actually adjust their behaviour to various situations. As we know, individuals differ in their behavioural flexibility. Some people show considerable ability to adjust their behaviour to external, situational factors: They are adaptable. Others, however, exhibit high levels of consistency regardless of the situation. High self-monitors are generally able to adjust their leadership style to suit changing situations better than are low self-monitors.[32] Clearly, if an individual's leadership style range is very narrow and he or she cannot or will not adjust (that is, the person is a low self-monitor), that individual will only be successful in very specific situations suitable to his or her style.

Substitutes for Leadership

The previous three theories argue that leaders are needed, but that leaders should consider the situation in determining which style of leadership to adopt. However, numerous studies collectively demonstrate that, in many situations, leaders' actions are irrelevant. Certain individual, job, and organizational variables can act as *substitutes* for leadership or *neutralize* the leader's ability to influence his or her followers, as shown in Exhibit 11-5.[33]

If employees have appropriate experience, training, or "professional" orientation, or if employees are indifferent to organizational rewards, the effect of leadership can be

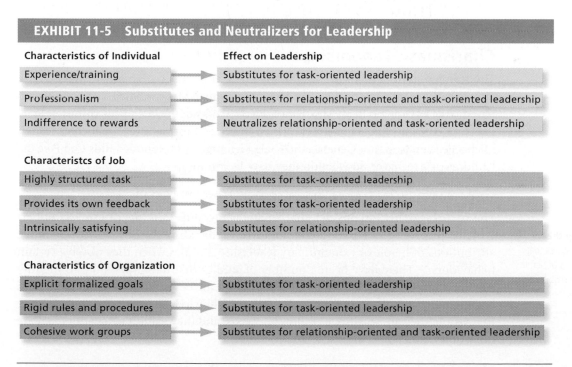

EXHIBIT 11-5   Substitutes and Neutralizers for Leadership

Characteristics of Individual	Effect on Leadership
Experience/training	Substitutes for task-oriented leadership
Professionalism	Substitutes for relationship-oriented and task-oriented leadership
Indifference to rewards	Neutralizes relationship-oriented and task-oriented leadership

Characteristcs of Job	
Highly structured task	Substitutes for task-oriented leadership
Provides its own feedback	Substitutes for task-oriented leadership
Intrinsically satisfying	Substitutes for relationship-oriented leadership

Characteristics of Organization	
Explicit formalized goals	Substitutes for task-oriented leadership
Rigid rules and procedures	Substitutes for task-oriented leadership
Cohesive work groups	Substitutes for relationship-oriented and task-oriented leadership

Source: Based on S. Kerr and J. M. Jermier, "Substitutes for Leadership: Their Meaning and Measurement," *Organizational Behavior and Human Performance*, December 1978, p. 378.

replaced or neutralized. Experience and training, for instance, can replace the need for a leader's support or ability to create structure and to reduce task ambiguity. Jobs that are inherently unambiguous and routine, provide their own feedback, or are intrinsically satisfying generally require less hands-on leadership. Organizational characteristics such as explicit formalized goals, rigid rules and procedures, and cohesive work groups can replace formal leadership.

Inspirational Leadership

Patagonia's mission statement, featured prominently on its website, is "Build the best product, do no unnecessary harm, use business to inspire and implement solutions to the environmental crisis." The company continues to grow, and Yvon Chouinard regularly declines offers to buy the firm ("I don't want some Wall Street greaseball running my company," he says). Patagonia receives 900 applications for every position it fills. Although Patagonia is not as large as some retailers, its use of environmentalism to its advantage has influenced other retailers—such as The Gap, Levi Strauss, and, most recently, Walmart—to follow in its footsteps. You would think all this would make Chouinard optimistic about the future. Not a chance. "I know everything's going to hell," he says.

Although he's uncharacteristic of leaders in some ways, Chouinard has the qualities of an inspirational leader—that is, he has a vision, sticks with it, and inspires followers to go beyond their own self-interests in pursuing it. What does it take for a person to lead with vision?

3 How does a leader lead with vision?

framing A way of using language to manage meaning.

The leadership theories we have discussed above ignore the importance of the leader as a communicator. **Framing** is a way of communicating to shape meaning. It's a way for leaders to influence how others see and understand events. It includes selecting and highlighting one or more aspects of a subject while excluding others. Framing is especially important to an aspect of leadership ignored in the traditional theories: the ability of the leader to inspire others to act beyond their immediate self-interests.

In this section, we present two contemporary leadership theories with a common theme. They view leaders as individuals who inspire followers through their words, ideas, and behaviours. These theories are charismatic leadership and transformational leadership.

Charismatic Leadership

The following individuals are frequently cited as being charismatic leaders: Frank Stronach of Aurora, Ontario-based Magna International; Mogens Smed, CEO of Calgary-based DIRTT (Doing It Right This Time); Pierre Trudeau, the late prime minister; René Lévesque, the late Quebec premier; Lucien Bouchard, former Bloc Québécois leader; Michaëlle Jean, Governor General; and Craig Kielburger, who founded Kids Can Free the Children as a teenager. So what do they have in common?

What Is Charismatic Leadership?

charismatic leadership theory A leadership theory that states that followers make attributions of heroic or extraordinary leadership abilities when they observe certain behaviours.

The first researcher to consider charismatic leadership in terms of OB was Robert House. According to House's **charismatic leadership theory**, followers make attributions of heroic or extraordinary leadership abilities when they observe certain behaviours.[34] There have been a number of studies that have attempted to identify the characteristics of the charismatic leader. One of the best reviews of the literature has documented four—they have a vision, they are willing to take personal risks to achieve that vision, they are sensitive to followers' needs, and they exhibit behaviours that are out of the ordinary.[35]

How Charismatic Leaders Influence Followers

How do charismatic leaders actually influence followers? The evidence suggests a four-step process.[36]

It begins by the leader articulating an appealing **vision**. A vision is a long-term strategy for how to attain a goal or goals. The vision provides a sense of continuity for followers by linking the present with a better future for the organization.

For example, at Apple, Steve Jobs championed the iPod, noting, "It's as Apple as anything Apple has ever done." The creation of the iPod achieved Apple's goal of offering groundbreaking and easy-to-use technology. The key properties of a vision seem to be inspirational possibilities that are value centred and realizable, with superior imagery and articulation.[37] Visions should be able to create possibilities that are inspirational and unique and that offer a new order that can produce organizational distinction. A vision is likely to fail if it does not offer a view of the future that is clearly and demonstrably better for the organization and its members. Desirable visions fit the times and circumstances and reflect the uniqueness of the organization. People in the organization must also believe that the vision is attainable. It should be perceived as challenging yet doable. Also, visions that are clearly articulated and have powerful imagery are more easily grasped and accepted.

A vision is incomplete unless it has an accompanying vision statement. A **vision statement** is a formal articulation of an organization's vision or mission. Charismatic leaders may use vision statements to "imprint" on followers an overarching goal and purpose. Once a vision and vision statement are established, the leader then communicates high performance expectations and expresses confidence that followers can attain them. This enhances follower self-esteem and self-confidence.

Next, the charismatic leader conveys, through words and actions, a new set of values and, by his or her behaviour, an example for followers to imitate. One study of Israeli bank employees showed, for example, that charismatic leaders were more effective because their employees personally identified with the leaders.[38]

Finally, the charismatic leader engages in emotion-inducing and often unconventional behaviour to demonstrate courage and convictions about the vision. There is an emotional contagion in charismatic leadership whereby followers "catch" the emotions their leader is conveying.[39]

What are examples of visions? The late Mary Kay Ash's vision of women as entrepreneurs selling products that improved their self-image guided her company, Mary Kay Cosmetics. Michael Dell created a vision of a business that sells and delivers a finished PC computer directly to a customer in less than a week.

RESEARCH FINDINGS: Charismatic Leadership

There is an increasing body of research that shows impressive correlations between charismatic leadership and high performance and satisfaction among followers.[40] People working for charismatic leaders are motivated to exert extra work effort and, because they like and respect their leader, express greater satisfaction. It also appears that organizations with charismatic CEOs are more profitable. And charismatic professors enjoy higher course evaluations.[41]

Charisma appears to be most successful when the follower's task has an ideological component or when the environment involves a high degree of stress and uncertainty.[42] This may explain why charismatic leaders tend to surface in politics, religion, wartime, or a business firm that is in its infancy or facing a life-threatening crisis.

Charismatic leadership may affect some followers more than others. Research suggests, for example, that people are especially receptive to charismatic leadership when they sense a crisis, when they are under stress, or when they fear for their lives. More generally, some peoples' personalities are especially susceptible to charismatic leadership.[43] Consider self-esteem. If a person lacks self-esteem and questions his or her self-worth, that person is more likely to absorb a leader's direction rather than establish his or her own way of leading or thinking.

vision A long-term strategy for attaining a goal or goals.

vision statement A formal articulation of an organization's vision or mission.

The inspiring vision of Apple's charismatic co-founder and CEO, Steve Jobs, is to make state-of-the-art technology easy for people to use. Through this vision, Jobs inspires, motivates, and leads employees to develop products such as Macintosh computers, iPod music players, and iPhones. "The iPhone is like having your life in your pocket," says Jobs; Apple's entry into the mobile phone market includes an iPod, a camera, an alarm clock, and Internet communication capabilities with an easy-to-use touch-screen design.

While the idea of charismatic leadership was developed based on North American observations, professors Dale Carl of the Faculty of Management at Ryerson University and Mansour Javidan at the University of Calgary also propose that charismatic leadership is expressed relatively similarly in a variety of countries, including Canada, Hungary, India, Turkey, Austria, Singapore, Sweden, and Venezuela.[44] This finding suggests that there may be some universal aspects of this style of leadership.

To learn more about how to be charismatic yourself, see the *Working with Others Exercise* on page 443.

The Dark Side of Charismatic Leadership

When organizations are in need of great change, charismatic leaders are often able to inspire their followers to meet the challenges of change. Be aware that a charismatic leader may become a liability to an organization once the crisis is over and the need for dramatic change subsides.[45] Why? Because then the charismatic leader's overwhelming self-confidence can be a liability. He or she is unable to listen to others, becomes uncomfortable when challenged by aggressive employees, and begins to hold an unjustifiable belief in his or her "rightness" on issues. Some would argue that Stephane Dion's behaviour after the Liberal party lost 19 seats in the 2008 federal election, first refusing to step down, and then trying to form a coalition government shortly thereafter, would fit this description.

Many have argued that the financial scandals and large losses experienced by investors in North America, including the ponzi scheme created by Bernie Madoff and the near bankruptcy of the Caisse de dépôt et placement du Québec because of the "audacious investment strategies" of Henri-Paul Rousseau, point to some of the dangers of charismatic leadership.[46]

Harvard Business School professor Rakesh Khurana argues that an inordinate number of today's chief executives have been "chosen for their ability to articulate messianic 'visions' for their companies; inspire employees to do whatever it takes to realize these grand designs; and imbue investors with faith in their own talents."[47] These traits, however, may have led to the corporate scandals that unfolded in recent years. Charismatic leadership, by its very nature, silences criticism. Thus, employees follow the lead of their visionary CEOs unquestioningly. Professor David Leighton, of the Richard Ivey School of Business at the University of Western Ontario, notes that even the boards of directors and auditors were reluctant to challenge these CEOs. He also suggests that Canada's "more balanced culture," which is less likely to turn CEOs into heroes, may help protect the country from some of the scandals that the United States has faced.[48]

A study of 29 companies that went from good to great (their cumulative stock returns were all at least three times better than the general stock market over 15 years) found that a key difference in successful charismatic leaders may be the *absence* of being ego-driven.[49] Although the leaders of these firms were fiercely ambitious and driven, their ambition was directed toward their company rather than themselves. They generated extraordinary results, but with little fanfare or hoopla. They took responsibility for mistakes and poor results but gave credit for successes to other people. They also prided themselves on developing strong leaders inside the firm who could direct the company to greater heights after they were gone. These individuals have been called **level 5 leaders** because they have four basic leadership qualities—individual capability, team skills, managerial competence, and the ability to stimulate others to high performance—plus a fifth quality: a paradoxical blend of personal humility and professional will. Level 5 leaders channel their ego needs away from themselves and into the goal of building a great company. So, while level 5 leaders are highly effective, they tend to be people you have never heard of and who get little notoriety in the business press. This study is important because it confirms that leaders don't necessarily need to be charismatic to be effective, especially where charisma is enmeshed with an outsized ego.

The current mood seems to be for CEOs with less vision, and more ethical and corporate responsibility. It seems clear that future research on charismatic leadership will need to provide greater insight into how this style relates to ethical and business behaviour.

level 5 leaders Leaders who are fiercely ambitious and driven, but their ambition is directed toward their company rather than themselves.

Transformational Leadership

A stream of research has focused on differentiating transformational leaders from transactional leaders.[50] Most of the leadership theories presented earlier in the chapter have concerned **transactional leaders**. These kinds of leaders guide or motivate their followers in the direction of established goals by clarifying role and task requirements. **Transformational leaders** inspire followers to transcend their own self-interests for the good of the organization, and are capable of having a profound and extraordinary effect on their followers. Andrea Jung at Avon, Richard Branson of the Virgin Group, and Jim McNerney of Boeing are all examples of transformational leaders. They pay attention to the concerns and developmental needs of individual followers; they change followers' awareness of issues by helping them to look at old problems in new ways; and they are able to excite, arouse, and inspire followers to put out extra effort to achieve group goals. Exhibit 11-6 on page 426 briefly identifies and defines the characteristics that differentiate these two types of leaders.

Transactional and transformational leadership should not be viewed as opposing approaches to getting things done.[51] Transformational and transactional leadership complement each other, but that doesn't mean they're equally important. Transformational leadership builds *on top of* transactional leadership and produces levels of follower effort and performance that go beyond what would occur with a transactional approach alone. But the reverse isn't true. So if you are a good transactional leader but do not have transformational qualities, you'll likely only be a mediocre leader. The best leaders are transactional *and* transformational.

transactional leaders Leaders who guide or motivate their followers in the direction of established goals by clarifying role and task requirements.

transformational leaders Leaders who inspire followers to transcend their own self-interests and who are capable of having a profound and extraordinary effect on followers.

EXHIBIT 11-6   Characteristics of Transactional and Transformational Leaders

Transactional Leader

Contingent reward: Contracts exchange of rewards for effort, promises rewards for good performance, recognizes accomplishments.

Management by exception (active): Watches and searches for deviations from rules and standards, takes corrective action.

Management by exception (passive): Intervenes only if standards are not met.

Laissez-faire: Abdicates responsibilities, avoids making decisions.

Transformational Leader

Idealized influence: Provides vision and sense of mission, instills pride, gains respect and trust.

Inspirational motivation: Communicates high expectations, uses symbols to focus efforts, expresses important purposes in simple ways.

Intellectual stimulation: Promotes intelligence, rationality, and careful problem solving.

Individualized consideration: Gives personal attention, treats each employee individually, coaches, advises.

Source: B. M. Bass, "From Transactional to Transformational Leadership: Learning to Share the Vision," *Organizational Dynamics*, Winter 1990, p. 22. Reprinted by permission of the publisher. American Management Association, New York. All rights reserved.

Full Range of Leadership Model

Exhibit 11-7 shows the full range of leadership model. Laissez-faire is the most passive and therefore the least effective of the leader behaviours. Leaders using this style are rarely viewed as effective. Management by exception—regardless of whether it is active or passive—is slightly better than laissez-faire, but it's still considered ineffective leadership. Leaders who practise management by exception leadership tend to be available only when there is a problem, which is often too late. Contingent reward leadership can be an effective style of leadership. However, leaders will not get their employees to go above and beyond the call of duty when practising this style of leadership.

Only with the four remaining leadership styles—which are all aspects of transformational leadership—are leaders able to motivate followers to perform above expectations and transcend their own self-interest for the sake of the organization. Using these transformational styles results in extra effort from employees, higher productivity, higher morale and satisfaction, higher organizational effectiveness, lower turnover, lower absenteeism, and greater organizational adaptability. Based on this model, leaders are generally most effective when they regularly use each of the four transformational behaviours.

How Transformational Leadership Works

In the past few years, a great deal of research has been conducted to explain how transformational leadership works. Transformational leaders are more effective because they themselves are more creative, but they are also more effective because they encourage those who follow them to be creative, too.[52]

Followers of transformational leaders are more likely to pursue ambitious goals, be familiar with and agree on the strategic goals of the organization, and believe that the goals they are pursuing are personally important.[53] Research has shown that vision explains part of the effect of transformational leadership. Indeed, one study found that vision was even more important than a charismatic (effusive, dynamic, lively) communication style in explaining the success of entrepreneurial firms.[54] Finally, transformational leadership also engenders commitment on the part of followers and instills in them a greater sense of trust in the leader.[55]

EXHIBIT 11-7   Full Range of Leadership Model

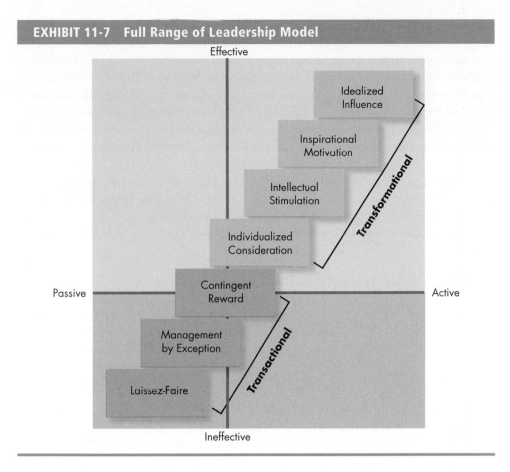

RESEARCH FINDINGS: Transformational Leadership

The evidence supporting the superiority of transformational leadership over transactional leadership is impressive. Transformational leadership has been supported in disparate occupations (for example, school principals, marine commanders, ministers, presidents of MBA associations, military cadets, union shop stewards, schoolteachers, sales reps) and at various job levels. One recent study of R & D firms found, for example, that teams led by project leaders who scored high on transformational leadership produced better-quality products as judged one year later and were more profitable five years later.[56] A review of 87 studies testing transformational leadership found that it was related to the motivation and satisfaction of followers and to the higher performance and perceived effectiveness of leaders.[57]

In summary, the overall evidence indicates that transformational leadership is more strongly correlated than transactional leadership with lower turnover rates, higher productivity, lower employee stress and burnout, and higher employee satisfaction.[58] Like charisma, it appears that transformational leadership can be learned. One study of Canadian bank managers found that those managers who underwent transformational leadership training had bank branches that performed significantly better than branches with managers who did not undergo training. Other studies show similar results.[59]

Transformational Leadership vs. Charismatic Leadership

There is some debate about whether transformational leadership and charismatic leadership are the same. The researcher most responsible for introducing charismatic leadership to OB, Robert House, considers them synonymous, calling the differences "modest" and "minor." McGill University professor Rabindra Kanungo agrees.[60] However, the individual who first researched transformational leadership, Bernard Bass, considers charisma to be part of transformational leadership, but argues that transformational leadership is broader than charisma, suggesting that charisma is, by itself, insufficient to "account for the transformational process."[61] Another researcher commented, "The purely charismatic [leader] may want followers to adopt the charismatic's world view and go no further; the transformational leader will attempt to instill in followers the ability to question not only established views but eventually those established by the leader."[62] Although many researchers believe that transformational leadership is broader than charismatic leadership, studies show that in reality a leader who scores high on transformational leadership is also likely to score high on charisma. Therefore, in practice, measures of charisma and transformational leadership may be roughly equivalent.

Contemporary Leadership Roles

People who are not in formal positions of leadership often wonder if there is any chance of being a leader without a formal role.[63] Patagonia helps its employees develop their leadership skills, particularly in the area of environmentalism. Each year, 40 of the company's employees can take a two-month internship with an environmental group, while still collecting their paycheque. Patagonia also gives training to individuals who want to participate in environmental protests by sponsoring civil disobedience workshops.

Chouinard believes his employees are well-suited for engaging in self-leadership. "Hire the people you trust, people who are passionate about their job, passionate about what they're doing. Just leave them alone, and they'll get the job done," he says. What are the different ways that people who are not officially in charge can also be effective leaders?

4 Are there leadership roles for nonmanagers?

Transformational leadership theory focuses on heroic leaders, leaders at the top echelons of the organization, and also on individuals rather than teams. However, the notion of "leader at the top" does not adequately reflect what is happening in some workplaces today, where there is less hierarchy and more connections, both inside and outside of the organization. There is a need for more "distributed leadership." In this form, leadership is "distributed across many players, both within and across organizations, up and down the hierarchy, wherever information, expertise, vision, and new ways of working together reside."[64]

Can anyone be a leader?

The following sections aim to explain how leadership can be spread throughout the organization through mentoring, self-leadership, team leadership, online leadership, and leading without authority. Even if you are not a manager or someone thinking about leadership in a corporate situation, this discussion offers important insights into how you can take on a leadership role in an organization.

Mentoring

mentor A senior employee who sponsors and supports a less-experienced employee.

Many leaders create mentoring relationships. A **mentor** is often a senior employee who sponsors and supports a less-experienced employee (a protégé). The mentoring role includes coaching, counselling, and sponsorship.[65] As a coach, mentors help develop their protégés' skills. As counsellors, mentors provide support and help bolster protégés' self-confidence. And as sponsors, mentors actively intervene on behalf of their protégés, lobby to get their protégés visible assignments, and politic to get their protégés rewards such as promotions and salary increases.

Successful mentors are good teachers. They can present ideas clearly, listen well, and empathize with the problems of their protégés. They also share experiences with their protégés, act as role models, share contacts, and provide guidance through the political maze of the organization. They provide advice on how to survive and get ahead in the organization, and act as a sounding board for ideas that protégés may be hesitant to share with their direct supervisors. Mentors vouch for their protégés, answer for them in the highest circles within the organization, and make appropriate introductions.

Some organizations have formal mentoring programs, in which mentors are officially assigned to new or high-potential employees. For instance, Montreal-based Bell Canada introduced Mentor Match in 2002 to bring together senior and junior employees. The mentors meet one-on-one for about an hour a month, to build a stronger understanding of leadership and organizational knowledge for the younger employees.[66] However, in contrast to Bell Canada's formal system, most organizations rely on informal mentoring—with senior managers personally selecting employees as protégés or junior employees asking senior employees to mentor them.

The most effective mentoring relationships exist outside the immediate boss-subordinate interface.[67] The boss-subordinate context has an inherent conflict of interest and tension, mostly attributable to managers' directly evaluating the performance of subordinates, that limits openness and meaningful communication.

Why would a leader want to be a mentor? There are personal benefits to the leader as well as benefits for the organization. The mentor-protégé relationship gives the mentor unfiltered access to the attitudes and feelings of lower-ranking employees. Protégés can be an excellent source of information on potential problems; they can provide early warning signals to upper managers because they short-circuit the formal channels. So the mentor-protégé relationship is a valuable communication channel that allows mentors to have news of problems before they become common knowledge to others in upper

Narayana Murtha (right in photo), one of the founders of Infosys Technologies in Bangalore, India, stepped down as CEO to serve the firm as chief mentor. In this role, Murtha shares his experiences, knowledge, and lessons learned while he built the company he started in 1981 and grew to 75 000 employees with sales of $3 billion. In mentoring Infosys's core management team, he wants to provide next-generation leadership for the firm. His goal is to build leadership qualities among Infosys employees by spending time at various corporate campuses and discussing issues that add value to the company. Murtha is shown here mentoring the new Infosys CEO, Nandan Nilekani.

management. In addition, in terms of leader self-interest, mentoring can provide personal satisfaction to senior executives. It gives them the opportunity to share with others the knowledge and experience that they have developed over many years.

From the organization's standpoint, mentoring provides a support system for high-potential employees. Where mentors exist, protégés are often more motivated, better grounded politically, and less likely to quit. A recent comprehensive review of the research, for instance, found that mentoring provided substantial benefits to protégés.[68] Specifically, mentored employees had higher compensation, a larger number of promotions, and were more satisfied with their careers than their nonmentored counterparts.

Are all employees in an organization equally likely to participate in a mentoring relationship? Unfortunately, the answer is no.[69] The evidence indicates that minorities and women are less likely to be chosen as protégés than are white males, and thus are less likely to accrue the benefits of mentorship. Mentors tend to select protégés who are similar to themselves on criteria such as background, education, gender, race, ethnicity, and religion. "People naturally move to mentor and can more easily communicate with those with whom they most closely identify."[70]

On a twist to the typical mentoring down idea, Procter & Gamble introduced a Mentoring Up program to help senior managers become more aware of what female managers can contribute to the organization. In its program, mid-level female managers mentor senior-level male executives. The program has led to fewer departures of female managers and has exposed women to top decision makers.[71]

You might assume that mentoring is important, but the research has been fairly disappointing. Two large-scale reviews suggest that the benefits are primarily psychological rather than tangible. Based on these reviews, it appears that the objective outcomes of mentoring, in terms of career success (compensation, job performance), are very small. One of these reviews concluded, "Though mentoring may not be properly labeled an utterly useless concept to careers, neither can it be argued to be as important as the main effects of other influences on career success such as ability and personality."[72] It may *feel* nice to have a mentor, but it does not appear that having a mentor, or even having a good mentor who provides both support and advice, is important to one's career.

Self-Leadership (or Self-Management)

A growing trend in organizations is the focus on self-leadership, or self-management.[73] (Recall our discussion of self-managed teams in Chapter 6.) With self-leadership, individuals and teams set goals, plan and implement tasks, evaluate performance, solve their own problems, and motivate themselves.

How do you manage yourself?

Several factors call for self-leadership: reduced levels of supervision; offices in the home; teamwork; and growth in service and professional employment where individuals are often required to make decisions on the spot. Following from our earlier discussion on substitutes for leadership, self-management can also be a substitute or neutralizer for leadership from others.

Despite the lack of studies of self-management techniques in organizational settings, self-management strategies have been shown to be successful in nonorganizational settings.[74] Those who practise self-management look for opportunities to be more effective in the workplace and improve their career success. Their behaviour is self-reinforced; that is, they provide their own sense of reward and feedback after carrying out their accomplishments. Moreover, self-reinforced behaviour is often maintained at a higher rate than behaviour that is externally regulated.[75] *OB in Action—Engaging in Self-Leadership* indicates ways in which you can practise effective self-leadership.

How do leaders create self-leaders? The following approaches have been suggested:[77]

- *Model self-leadership.* Practise self-observation, setting challenging personal goals, self-direction, and self-reinforcement. Then display these behaviours, and encourage others to rehearse and then produce them.

- *Encourage employees to create self-set goals.* Support employees in developing quantitative, specific goals; having such goals is the most important part of self-leadership.

- *Encourage the use of self-rewards to strengthen and increase desirable behaviours.* By contrast, limit self-punishment only to occasions when the employee has been dishonest or destructive.

- *Create positive thought patterns.* Encourage employees to use mental imagery and self-talk to further stimulate self-motivation.

- *Create a climate of self-leadership.* Redesign the work to increase the natural rewards of a job and focus on these naturally rewarding features of work to increase motivation.

- *Encourage self-criticism.* Encourage individuals to be critical of their own performance.

in ACTION

Engaging in Self-Leadership

To engage in effective self-leadership:[76]

→ **Think horizontally, not vertically.** Vertical relationships in the organization matter, but peers can become trusted colleagues and have a great impact on your work.

→ Focus on **influence, not control.** Work with your colleagues, not for them. Be collaborative and share credit.

→ **Create opportunities**, don't wait for them. Rather than look for the right time, be more action oriented.

The underlying assumptions behind self-leadership are that people are responsible, capable, and able to exercise initiative without the external constraints of bosses, rules, or regulations. Given the proper support, individuals can monitor and control their own behaviour. The *Learning About Yourself Exercise* on page 442 provides further examples of how to engage in self-leadership.

Learning About Yourself

1. Are You a Self-Manager?
(page 442)

Team Leadership

Leadership is increasingly taking place within a team context. As teams grow in popularity, the role of the leader in guiding team members takes on heightened importance.[78] Also, because of its more collaborative nature, the role of team leader is different from the traditional leadership role performed by first-line supervisors.

Many leaders are not equipped to handle the change to team leader. As one prominent consultant noted, "Even the most capable managers have trouble making the transition because all the command-and-control type things they were encouraged to do before are no longer appropriate. There's no reason to have any skill or sense of this."[79] This same consultant estimated that "probably 15 percent of managers are natural team leaders; another 15 percent could never lead a team because it runs counter to their personality. [They're unable to sublimate their dominating style for the good of the team.] Then there's that huge group in the middle: team leadership doesn't come naturally to them, but they can learn it."[80]

Effective team leaders need to build commitment and confidence, remove obstacles, create opportunities, and be part of the team.[81] They have to learn skills such as the patience to share information, the willingness to trust others, the ability to give up authority, and an understanding of when to intervene. New team leaders may try to retain too much control at a time when team members need more autonomy, or they may abandon their teams at times when the teams need support and help.[82]

Roles of Team Leaders

A study of 20 organizations that reorganized themselves around teams found certain common responsibilities that all leaders had to assume. These included coaching, facilitating, training, communicating, handling disciplinary problems, and reviewing team/individual performance.[83] Many of these responsibilities apply to managers in general. A more meaningful way to describe the team leader's job is to focus on two priorities: managing the team's external boundary and facilitating the team process.[84] We have divided these priorities into four specific roles that team leaders play:

- *Liaisons with external constituencies.* Outsiders include upper management, other internal teams, customers, and suppliers. The leader represents the team to other constituencies, secures needed resources, clarifies others' expectations of the team, gathers information from the outside, and shares this information with team members.

- *Troubleshooters.* When the team has problems and asks for assistance, team leaders sit in on meetings and try to help resolve the problems. This rarely relates to technical or operational issues because the team members typically know more about the tasks being done than does the team leader. The leader contributes by asking penetrating questions, by helping the team discuss problems, and by getting needed resources from external constituencies. For instance, when a team in an aerospace firm found itself short-handed, its team leader took responsibility for getting more staff. He presented the team's case to upper management and got the approval through the company's human resource department.

- *Conflict managers.* When disagreements surface, team leaders help process the conflict. What is the source of the conflict? Who is involved? What are the issues? What resolution options are available? What are the advantages and disadvantages of each? By getting team members to address questions such as these, the leader minimizes the disruptive aspects of intrateam conflicts.

- *Coaches.* They clarify expectations and roles, teach, offer support, cheerlead, and do whatever else is necessary to help team members improve their work performance.

Exhibit 11-8 offers a lighthearted look at what it means to be a team leader.

EXHIBIT 11-8

Source: DILBERT reprinted by permission of United Features Syndicate, Inc.

Online Leadership

How do you lead people who are physically separated from you and for whom interactions are basically reduced to written digital communications? This is a question that, to date, has received minimal attention from organizational behaviour researchers.[85] Leadership research has been directed almost exclusively to face-to-face and verbal situations. But we cannot ignore the reality that today's managers and their employees are increasingly being linked by networks rather than geographical proximity. Obvious examples include managers who regularly use email to communicate with their staff, managers overseeing virtual projects or teams, and managers whose telecommuting employees are linked to the office by a computer and modem.

If leadership is important for inspiring and motivating dispersed employees, we need to offer some guidance as to how leadership might function in this context. Keep in mind, however, that there is limited research on this topic. So our intention here is not to provide you with definitive guidelines for leading online. Rather, it's to introduce you to an increasingly important issue and to get you to think about how leadership changes when relationships are defined by network interactions.

In face-to-face communications, harsh *words* can be softened by nonverbal action. A smile and comforting gestures, for instance, can lessen the blow behind strong words like *disappointed*, *unsatisfactory*, *inadequate*, or *below expectations*. That nonverbal component does not exist with online interactions. The *structure* of words in a digital communication has the power to motivate or demotivate the receiver.

Leaders need to be sure the *tone* of their email correctly reflects the emotions they want to send. Is the message formal or informal? Does it match the verbal style of the sender? Does it convey the appropriate level of importance or urgency? The fact that many people's writing style is very different from their interpersonal style is certainly a potential problem.

Jane Howell at the Richard Ivey School of Business, University of Western Ontario, and one of her students, Kate Hall-Merenda, have considered the issues of leading from a distance.[86] They note that physical distance can create many potential problems, with team members feeling isolated, forgotten, and perhaps not cared about. It may result in lowered productivity. Their study of 109 business leaders and 371 followers in a large financial institution found that physical distance makes it more difficult to develop high-quality relationships.

Howell and Hall-Merenda suggest that some of the same characteristics of transformational leaders are appropriate for long-distance managing. In particular, they emphasize the need to articulate a compelling vision and to communicate that vision in an inspiring way. Encouraging employees to think about ways to strive toward that vision is another important task of the leader.

Online leaders confront unique challenges, the greatest of which appears to be developing and maintaining trust. Identification-based trust, for instance, is particularly difficult to achieve when there is a lack of intimacy and face-to-face interaction.[87] Online negotiations have also been found to be hindered because parties express lower levels of trust.[88] It's not clear whether it's even possible for employees to identify with or trust leaders with whom they only communicate electronically.[89]

This discussion leads us to the tentative conclusion that, for an increasing number of managers, good interpersonal skills may include the abilities to communicate support and leadership through written words on a computer screen and to read emotions in others' messages. In this "new world" of communications, writing skills are likely to become an extension of interpersonal skills.

Leading without Authority

What if your goal is to be a leader, even if you don't have the authority (or formal appointment) to be one? For instance, what if you wanted to convince the dean of your school to introduce new business courses that were more relevant, or you wanted to convince the president of the company where you work that she should start thinking about more environmentally friendly strategies in dealing with waste? How do you effectively lead in a student group, when everyone is a peer?

Leadership at the grassroots level in organizations does happen. Rosabeth Moss Kanter, in her book *The Change Masters*,[90] discusses examples of people who saw something in their workplace that needed changing and took the responsibility to do so upon themselves. Employees were more likely to do this when organizations permitted initiative at all levels of the organization, rather than making it a tool of senior executives only.

Leading without authority simply means exhibiting leadership behaviour even though you do not have a formal position or title that might encourage others "to obey." Neither Martin Luther King Jr. nor Nelson Mandela operated from a position of authority, yet each was able to inspire many to follow him in the quest for social justice. The workplace can be an opportunity for leading without authority as well. As Ronald Heifetz of Harvard's Kennedy School of Government notes, "Leadership means taking responsibility for hard problems beyond anyone's expectations."[91] It also means not waiting for the coach's call.[92]

What are the benefits of leading without authority? Heifetz has identified three:[93]

- *Latitude for creative deviance.* When a person does not have authority, and the trappings that go with authority, it's easier to raise harder questions and look for less traditional solutions.

- *Issue focus.* Leading without authority means that individuals can focus on a single issue, rather than be concerned with the myriad issues that those in authority face.

- *Front-line information.* Leading without authority means that an individual is closer to the detailed experiences of some of the stakeholders. Thus, more information is available to this kind of leader.

Not all organizations will support this type of leadership, and some have been known to actively suppress it. Still others will look aside, not encouraging, but not discouraging either. Nevertheless, you may want to reflect on the possibility of engaging in leadership behaviour because you see a need, rather than because you are required to act.

Contemporary Issues in Leadership

Yvon Chouinard believes in responsible leadership that promotes a better environment for the world.[94] He is not yet satisfied with the changes that Patagonia has made to create environmentally friendly clothing. "We have to dig deeper and try to make products that close the loop—clothing that can be recycled infinitely into similar or equal products, which is something we continue to strive for," he says.

Chouinard believes that doing the right thing for the environment is the right thing for company practice. "We've found that every time we've elected to do the right thing, even when it costs twice as much, it's turned out to be more profitable," he explains.

Chouinard believes that Patagonia will never be able to be a completely environmentally friendly company, no matter how hard it tries to do so. But he is pleased that other companies (Clif Bar, the Gap, and Levi Strauss) are now starting to follow Patagonia's lead. How does moral leadership relate to the company's bottom line?

5 What are some of the contemporary issues in leadership?

What is authentic leadership? Is there a moral dimension to leadership? Do men and women rely on different leadership styles, and if so, is one style inherently superior to the other? In this section, we briefly address these contemporary issues in leadership.

Authentic Leadership

Douglas R. Conant is not your typical CEO. His style is decidedly understated. When asked to reflect on the strong performance of Campbell Soup, he says, "We're hitting our stride a little bit more [than our peers]." He regularly admits mistakes and often says, "I can do better." Conant appears to be a good example of authentic leadership.[95]

Authentic leaders know who they are, know what they believe in and value, and act on those values and beliefs openly and candidly. Their followers would consider them to be ethical people. The primary quality, therefore, produced by authentic leadership is trust. How does authentic leadership build trust? Authentic leaders share information, encourage open communication, and stick to their ideals. The result: People come to have faith in authentic leaders.

Because the concept is so recent, there has not been a lot of research on authentic leadership. However, we believe it's a promising way to think about ethics and trust in leadership because it focuses on the moral aspects of being a leader. Transformational or charismatic leaders can have a vision and communicate it persuasively, but sometimes the vision is wrong (as in the case of Hitler), or the leader is more concerned with his own needs or pleasures, as in the case of business leaders Dennis Kozlowski (ex-CEO of Tyco International) and Jeffrey Skilling (ex-CEO of Enron).[96]

Moral Leadership

Only recently have ethicists and leadership researchers begun to consider the ethical implications in leadership.[97] Why now? One reason may be the growing general interest in ethics throughout the field of management. Another reason may be that ethical lapses by business leaders are never absent from the headlines.

During much of the 1990s, CEOs were viewed as heroes, and achieved star status in the media. They received personal credit as their companies' stock prices increased, and they were rewarded lavishly for improving company bottom lines. Meanwhile, perceptions of executives' integrity have dropped significantly since the 1990s.[98] CEOs are now less able to justify their wealthy pay packages, and some are reconsidering how much compensation is enough. Leaders are also being made to repay their companies if their compensation was unethically acquired.

Ethics relates to leadership in a number of ways. Transformational leaders, for instance, have been described by one authority as fostering moral virtue when they try to change the attitudes and behaviours of followers.[99] Charisma, too, has an ethical component. Unethical leaders are more likely to use their charisma to enhance power over followers, directed toward self-serving ends. Ethical leaders are considered to use their charisma in a socially constructive way to serve others.[100] There is also the issue of abuse of power by leaders—for example, when they give themselves large salaries and bonuses while also seeking to cut costs by laying off long-time employees. Because top executives set the moral tone for an organization, they need to set high ethical standards, demonstrate those standards through their own behaviour, and encourage and reward integrity in others.

Leadership effectiveness needs to address the *means* that a leader uses in trying to achieve goals, as well as the content of those goals. Recently, scholars have tried to integrate ethical and charismatic leadership by advancing the idea of **socialized charismatic leadership**—leadership that conveys values that are other-centred vs. self-centred by leaders who model ethical conduct.[101]

Leadership is not values-free. Before we judge any leader to be effective, we should consider both the means used by the leader to achieve goals and the moral content of those goals.

authentic leaders Leaders who know who they are, know what they believe in and value, and act on these values and beliefs openly and candidly. Their followers could consider them to be ethical people.

socialized charismatic leadership A leadership concept that states that leaders convey values that are other-centred vs. self-centred and who role model ethical conduct.

Bill Young created Toronto-based Social Capital Partners to help businesses hire the hard to employ: youths, single mothers, Aboriginal people, new immigrants, and those with disabilities or problems with substance abuse. His goal is to help people who are struggling get back into the economic mainstream.

George Cooke, CEO of Toronto-based Dominion of Canada General Insurance, believes in promoting women to senior positions. He is noteworthy for this; Dominion is well above the national average in the percentage of women who have made it to the executive ranks of Canada's top companies.

Professor James Clawson of the Darden Graduate School of Business, University of Virginia, suggests that there are four cornerstones to a "moral foundation of leadership":[102]

- *Truth telling.* Leaders who tell the truth as they see it allow for a mutual, fair exchange to occur.

- *Promise keeping.* Leaders need to be careful of the commitments they make, and then careful of keeping those commitments.

- *Fairness.* Leaders who are equitable ensure that followers get their fair share for their contributions to the organization.

- *Respect for the individual.* Leaders who tell the truth, keep promises, and are fair show respect for followers. Respect means treating people with dignity.

Moral leadership comes from within the individual, and in general means treating people well, and with respect. This chapter's *Ethical Dilemma Exercise* on page 444 raises some provocative issues about whether we should consider just the ends toward which a leader strives, or the means as well.

Gender and Leadership

How Many Women Make It to the Top?

Women make up 46.2 percent of the labour force in Canada,[103] but they hold only 32 percent of managerial roles, 14 percent of the senior management roles, and 6.7 percent of the highest corporate titles—CEO, chief financial officer, or chief operating officer.[104] They make up 57 percent of graduate degree holders and 51 percent of the Canadian population. Half of Canada's companies have no women in the senior ranks at all.[105] Commenting on the low numbers of women in leadership positions at top companies in 2004, Toronto-based Catalyst Canada president Susan Black suggests that "at the pace of change we are reporting . . . women's overall representation in Corporate Canada will not reach 25 percent until 2025. It will not reach parity until close to the end of the century."[106]

Despite women's lack of representation in large companies, they are highly involved in smaller companies. Industry Canada reports that in 2000, 45 percent of all small-to medium-sized enterprises had at least one female owner.[107] Moreover, women start almost half of all small businesses in Canada today and, among young people, women start almost 80 percent of small businesses.[108]

Promotion Similarities and Differences A study by the Center for Creative Leadership found that there were some differences, as well as many similarities, in the promotion processes for men and women. For instance, the men's supervisors mentioned in 75 percent of the cases that they felt comfortable with the candidates at an interpersonal level, and that is what led to their promotions. This factor was cited in only 23 percent of the cases where women were promoted. For women to be promoted, it was more important that they exhibit personal strength and a willingness to take risks and accept responsibility.[109]

Additional studies confirm that women and men are evaluated differently when in leadership positions. Deloitte found that its managers "rated men's lack of experience in any area as untested potential, while they often saw women with identical skills and career tracks as unprepared for promotion."[110] Debra Meyerson, a professor at Stanford University's School of Education, has done work on gender differences in organizations and finds that "for a woman, any slip-up is seen as evidence that you weren't up to the job, while men are more likely to be given the benefit of the doubt."[111]

> Do men and women get promoted differently?

Some research indicates that men and women view their workplaces differently. Linda Duxbury, a professor at the Sprott School of Business at Carleton University, found that 86 percent of men surveyed said that organizations actively communicate with employees, but only 65 percent of women agreed. Women were also less likely to state that their companies had established a policy of inclusion, with 44 percent of the women and 73 percent of the men agreeing with this statement.[112]

Similarities and Differences in Women's and Men's Leadership Styles

Do men and women lead differently? An extensive review of the literature suggests two conclusions.[113] First, the similarities between male and female leaders tend to outweigh the differences. Second, what differences there are seem to be that women fall back on a more democratic leadership style, while men feel more comfortable with a directive style.

The similarities among men and women leaders should not be completely surprising. Almost all the studies looking at this issue have treated managerial positions as synonymous with leadership roles. Both male and female managers have characteristics that set them apart from the general population. Just as people who choose careers in law enforcement or civil engineering have a lot in common, so do individuals who choose managerial careers. People with traits associated with leadership—such as intelligence, confidence, and sociability—are more

Emmie Wong Leung, founder and CEO of International Paper Industries (IPI) of North Vancouver, which collects, processes, and sells waste paper to offshore buyers, has been exporting to the United States, Hong Kong, Japan, China, the Philippines, India, and Indonesia for more than 20 years. She says: "I think an old-boys' network operates all over the world, but you can get them to accept you."

likely to be perceived as leaders and encouraged to pursue careers where they can exert leadership. This is true regardless of gender. Similarly, organizations tend to recruit and promote people who project leadership attributes into leadership positions. The result is that, regardless of gender, those who achieve formal leadership positions in organizations tend to be more alike than different.

Despite the previous conclusion, studies indicate some differences in the inherent leadership styles of women and men. A Conference Board of Canada study found that "women are particularly strong in managing interpersonal relationships and their approach is more consensual."[114] Other studies have shown that women tend to adopt a style of shared leadership. They encourage participation, share power and information, and attempt to enhance followers' self-worth. They prefer to lead through inclusion and rely on their charisma, expertise, contacts, and interpersonal skills to influence others. Men, on the other hand, are more likely to use a directive command-and-control style. They rely on the formal authority of their position for their influence base.

Given that men have historically held the great majority of leadership positions in organizations, it's tempting to assume that the differences noted between men and women would automatically work to favour men. They don't. In today's organizations, flexibility, teamwork, trust, and information sharing are replacing rigid structures, competitive individualism, control, and secrecy. The best leaders listen, motivate, and provide support to their people. Many women seem to do those things better than men.

Although it's interesting to see how men's and women's leadership styles differ, a more important question is whether they differ in effectiveness. Although some researchers have shown that men and women tend to be equally effective as leaders,[115] an increasing number of studies have shown that women executives, when rated by their peers, employees, and bosses, score higher than their male counterparts on a wide variety of measures, including getting extra effort from subordinates and overall effectiveness in leading. Subordinates also report more satisfaction with the leadership given by women.[116]

Although women seem to rate highly on those leadership skills needed to succeed in today's dynamic global environment, we don't want to fall into the same trap as the early leadership researchers who tried to find the "one best leadership style" for all situations. We know that there is no one best style for all situations. Instead, which leadership style is effective will depend on the situation. So even if men and women differ in their leadership styles, we should not assume that one is always preferable to the other.

Summary and Implications

1 **What is the difference between a manager and a leader?** Managers promote stability, while leaders press for change. Leaders provide vision and strategy; managers implement that vision and strategy, coordinate and staff the organization, and handle day-to-day problems.

2 **Are there specific traits, behaviours, and situations that affect how one leads?** Early leadership theories were concerned with supervision, and sought to find out if there were ways to identify leaders. Trait theories examined whether there were some traits that were universal among leaders. While there are some common traits, leaders are more different than similar in terms of traits. Emotional intelligence is one of the few traits that has been found to be extremely important for leadership success. Other research has tried to discover whether some behaviours create better leaders than others. The findings were mixed, suggesting that leaders need to be both task-oriented and people-oriented. The mixed findings led researchers to contingency theories that consider the effect of situations in which leadership is applied. This research tells us that leaders need to adjust their behaviours, depending on the situation and the needs of employees. Contingency theories were an important contribution to the study of leadership.

3 **How does a leader lead with vision?** The more recent approaches to leadership move away from the supervisory tasks of leaders and focus on vision-setting activities. These theories try to explain how certain leaders can achieve extraordinary levels of performance from their followers, and they stress symbolic and emotionally appealing leadership behaviours. These leaders, known as *charismatic* or *transformational leaders*, inspire followers to go beyond their own self-interests for the good of the organization.

4 **Are there leadership roles for nonmanagers?** There are several approaches to being a leader even if one does not have a formal position of leadership. Mentoring is one way to be an informal leader. Mentors sponsor and support less-experienced employees, coaching and counselling them about their jobs. With self-leadership, individuals and teams set goals, plan and implement tasks, evaluate performance, solve their own problems, and motivate themselves. The supervisor plays a much reduced role. A person can also act as an informal leader on a team. Providing leadership online to telecommuting and physically distant employees is another leadership role available to many people. Keeping online teams motivated can be a challenging role. Leading without authority means exhibiting leadership behaviour even though you do not have a formal position or title that might encourage others to obey.

5 **What are some of the contemporary issues in leadership?** One leadership challenge today is how to be an authentic leader. Authentic leaders know who they are, know what they believe in and value, and act on those values and beliefs openly and candidly. Leaders also face the demand to be moral in their leadership. Moral leadership comes from within the individual, and, in general, means treating people well and with respect. Another hot issue in leadership is the question of whether men and women rely on different leadership styles, and if that is the case, whether one style is inherently superior to the other. An extensive review of the literature suggests two conclusions.[117] First, the similarities between men and women tend to outweigh the differences. Second, what differences there are seem to be that women fall back on a more democratic leadership style, while men feel more comfortable with a directive style.

For Review

1. Trace the development of leadership research.

2. What traits predict leadership?

3. What is the Leadership Grid? Contrast its approach to leadership with the approaches of the Ohio State and Michigan studies.

4. What are the contingency variables in path-goal theory?

5. When might leaders be irrelevant?

6. Describe the strengths and weaknesses of a charismatic leader.

7. What are the differences between transactional and transformational leaders?

8. How do leaders create self-leaders?

9. What is moral leadership?

10. Why do you think effective female and male managers often exhibit similar traits and behaviours?

For Critical Thinking

1. Reconcile path-goal theory and substitutes for leadership.

2. What kind of activities could a full-time college or university student pursue that might lead to the perception that he or she is a charismatic leader? In pursuing those activities, what might the student do to enhance this perception of being charismatic?

3. Based on the low representation of women in upper management, to what extent do you think that organizations should actively promote women into the senior ranks of management?

4. Is there an ethical problem if leaders focus more on looking like a leader than actually being one? Discuss.

5. "Leaders make a real difference in an organization's performance." Build an argument in support of this statement. Then build an argument against this statement.

OB-for You

- It's easy to imagine that theories of leadership are more important to those who are leaders or who plan in the near future to become leaders. However, leadership opportunities occur throughout an organization. You have no doubt seen a student leader who did not necessarily have any formal authority be extremely successful.

- Leaders are not born, they learn how to lead by paying attention to the situation and what needs to be done.

- There is no one best way to lead. It is important to consider the situation and the needs of the people who will be led.

- Sometimes no leader is needed—the individuals in the group simply work well enough together that each takes turns at leadership without appointing a formal leader.

POINT

COUNTERPOINT

Leaders Are Born

In North America, people are socialized to believe they can be whoever they want to be—and that includes being a leader.[118] While that makes for a nice children's tale (think *The Little Engine That Could*—"I think I can, I think I can"), the world's affairs and people's lives are not always wrapped in pretty little packages, and this is one example. Being an effective leader has more to do with what you are born with than what you do with what you have.

That leaders are born, not made, is not a new idea. Victorian era historian Thomas Carlyle wrote, "History is nothing but the biography of a few great men." Although today we should modify this to include women, his point still rings true: Great leaders are what make teams, companies, and even countries great. Can anyone disagree that people like Lester Pearson and Pierre Trudeau were gifted political leaders? Or that Joan of Arc and George Patton were brilliant and courageous military leaders? Or that Henry Ford, Jack Welch, Steve Jobs, and Rupert Murdoch are gifted business leaders? As one reviewer of the literature put it, "Leaders are not like other people." These leaders are great leaders because they have the right stuff—stuff the rest of us don't have, or have in lesser quantities.

If you are not yet convinced, there is new evidence to support this position. A recent study of several hundred identical twins separated at birth found an amazing correlation in their ascendance into leadership roles. These twins were raised in totally different environments—some rich, some poor, some by educated parents, others by relatively uneducated parents, some in cities, others in small towns. But the researchers found that, despite their different environments, each pair of twins had striking similarities in terms of whether they became leaders.

Other research has found that shared environment—being raised in the same household, for example—has very little influence on leadership emergence. Despite what we might like to believe, the evidence is clear: A substantial part of leadership is a product of our genes. If we have the right stuff, we are destined to be effective leaders. If we have the wrong stuff, we are unlikely to excel in that role. Leadership cannot be for everyone, and we make a mistake in thinking that everyone is equally capable of being a good leader.

Leaders Are Made

Of course, personal qualities and characteristics matter to leadership, as they do to most other behaviours.[119] But the real key is what you do with what you have.

First, if great leadership were merely the possession of a few key traits—say, intelligence and personality—we could simply give people a test and select the most intelligent, extraverted, and conscientious people to be leaders. But that would be a disaster. It helps to have these traits, but leadership is much too complex to be reduced to a simple formula of traits. As smart as Steve Jobs is, there are smarter and more extraverted people out there—thousands of them. That is not the essence of what makes him, or political or military leaders, great. It is a combination of factors—upbringing, early business experiences, learning from failure, and driving ambition. Second, great leaders tell us that the key to their leadership success is not the characteristics they had at birth, but what they learned along the way.

Take Warren Buffett, who is admired not only for his investing prowess but also as a leader and boss. Being a great leader, according to Buffett, is a matter of acquiring the right habits. "The chains of habit are too light to be noticed until they are too heavy to be broken," he says. Buffett argues that characteristics or habits such as intelligence, trustworthiness, and integrity are the most important to leadership—and at least the latter two can be developed. He says, "You need integrity, intelligence, and energy to succeed. Integrity is totally a matter of choice—and it is habit-forming."

Finally, this focus on "great men and great women" is not very productive. Even if it were true that great leaders were born, it's a very impractical approach to leadership. People need to believe in something, and one of those things is that they can improve themselves. If we walked around thinking we were just some accumulation of genetic markers and our entire life was just a stage in which our genes played themselves out, who would want to live that way? People like the optimistic story of *The Little Engine That Could* because we have a choice to think positively (we can become good leaders) or negatively (leaders are predetermined), and it's better to be positive.

OB *AT WORK*

LEARNING ABOUT **YOURSELF** EXERCISE

Are You a Self-Manager?

To determine your self-management initiative, rate each of the following items, from 1 ("Never Do This") to 7 ("Always Do This").[120]

	Never Do This						Always Do This

Planning

1. I plan out my day before beginning to work.	1	2	3	4	5	6	7
2. I try to schedule my work in advance.	1	2	3	4	5	6	7
3. I plan my career carefully.	1	2	3	4	5	6	7
4. I come to work early to plan my day.	1	2	3	4	5	6	7
5. I use lists and agendas to structure my workday.	1	2	3	4	5	6	7
6. I set specific job goals on a regular basis.	1	2	3	4	5	6	7
7. I set daily goals for myself.	1	2	3	4	5	6	7
8. I try to manage my time.	1	2	3	4	5	6	7

Access management

1. I control the access subordinates have to me in order to get my work done.	1	2	3	4	5	6	7
2. I use a special place at work where I can work uninterrupted.	1	2	3	4	5	6	7
3. I hold my telephone calls when I need to get things done.	1	2	3	4	5	6	7

Catch-up activities

1. I come in early or stay late at work to prevent distractions from interfering with my work.	1	2	3	4	5	6	7
2. I take my work home with me to make sure it gets done.	1	2	3	4	5	6	7
3. I come in on my days off to catch up on my work.	1	2	3	4	5	6	7

Emotions management

1. I have learned to manage my aggressiveness with my subordinates.	1	2	3	4	5	6	7
2. My facial expression and conversational tone are important in dealing with subordinates.	1	2	3	4	5	6	7
3. It's important for me to maintain a "professional" manager-subordinate relationship.	1	2	3	4	5	6	7
4. I try to keep my emotions under control.	1	2	3	4	5	6	7

Scoring Key:

Higher scores mean a higher degree of self-management. For the overall scale, scores of 100 or higher represent high scores. For each area, the following represent high scores: planning, scores of 48 or higher; access management, scores of 18 or higher; catch-up activities, scores of 18 or higher; and emotions management, scores of 24 or higher.

More Learning About Yourself Exercises

Additional self-assessments relevant to this chapter appear on MyOBLab, (**www.pearsoned.ca/myoblab**).

II.B.1 What's My Leadership Style?
IV.E.5 What Is My LPC Score?
II.B.2 How Charismatic Am I?
IV.E.4 Am I an Ethical Leader?

When you complete the additional assessments, consider the following:

1. Am I surprised about my score?
2. Would my friends evaluate me similarly?

BREAKOUT **GROUP** EXERCISES

Form small groups to discuss the following topics, as assigned by your instructor:

1. Identify an example of someone you think of as a good leader (currently or in the past). What traits did he or she have? How did these traits differ from those in someone you identify as a bad leader?

2. Identify a situation when you were in a leadership position (in a group, in the workplace, within your family, etcetera). To what extent were you able to use a contingency approach to leadership? What made that easier or more difficult for you?

3. When you have worked in student groups, how frequently have leaders emerged in the groups? What difficulties occur when leaders are leading peers? Are there ways to overcome these difficulties?

WORKING WITH **OTHERS** EXERCISE

Being Charismatic

From Concepts to Skills on pages 446–447 indicates how to become charismatic. In this exercise, you will use that information to practise projecting charisma.[121]

a. The class should break into pairs.

b. Student A's task is to "lead" Student B through a new-student orientation to your college or university. The orientation should last about 10 to 15 minutes. Assume Student B is new to your college or university and is unfamiliar with the campus. Student A should attempt to project himself or herself as charismatic.

c. Roles now reverse and Student B's task is to "lead" Student A in a 10- to 15-minute program on how to study more effectively for college or university exams. Take a few minutes to think about what has worked well for you, and assume that Student A is a new student interested in improving his or her study habits. Again, Student B should attempt to project himself or herself as charismatic.

d. When both role plays are complete, each pair should assess how well it did in projecting charisma and how it might improve.

Do the Ends Justify the Means?

The power that comes from being a leader can be used for evil as well as for good.[122] When you assume the benefits of leadership, you also assume ethical burdens. But many highly successful leaders have relied on questionable tactics to achieve their ends. These include manipulation, verbal attacks, physical intimidation, lying, fear, and control.

Consider a few examples:

- Bill Clinton was viewed as a charismatic US president. Yet he lied when necessary and "managed" the truth.

- Former Prime Minister Jean Chrétien successfully led Canada through 10 years of economic change. Those close to him were committed and loyal followers. Yet concerns were raised that he may have been willing to quietly spend millions of dollars in sponsorship money to manage the Quebec situation.

- Apple CEO Steve Jobs received backdated stock options: He was allowed to purchase shares of Apple at prices well below their market price at the time he was given the options. In fact, the options were backdated so that he could buy the shares at the lowest possible price. Former Apple CFO Fred Anderson argues that he warned Jobs about the accounting problems produced by backdating, but says he (Anderson) is the one who took the fall.

Should leaders be judged solely on their end achievements? Or do the means they choose also reflect on their leadership qualities? Are employees, shareholders, and society too quick to excuse leaders who use questionable means if they are successful in achieving their goals? Is it impossible for leaders to be ethical and successful?

Moving from Colleague to Supervisor

Cheryl Kahn, Rob Carstons, and Linda McGee have something in common.[123] They all were promoted within their organizations into management positions. As well, each found the transition a challenge.

Kahn was promoted to director of catering for the Glazier Group of restaurants. With the promotion, she realized that things would never be the same again. No longer would she be able to participate in water-cooler gossip or shrug off an employee's chronic lateness. She says she found her new role to be daunting. "At first I was like a bulldozer knocking everyone over, and that was not well received. I was saying, 'It's my way or the highway.' And was forgetting that my friends were also in transition." She admits that this style alienated just about everyone with whom she worked.

Carstons, a technical manager at IBM, talks about the uncertainty he felt after being promoted to a manager from a junior programmer. "It was a little bit challenging to be suddenly giving directives to peers, when just the

day before you were one of them. You try to be careful not to offend anyone. It's strange walking into a room and the whole conversation changes. People don't want to be as open with you when you become the boss."

McGee is now president of Medex Insurance Services. She started as a customer-service representative with the company, then leapfrogged over colleagues in a series of promotions. Her fast rise created problems. Colleagues "would say, 'Oh, here comes the big cheese now.' God only knows what they talked about behind my back."

Questions

1. A lot of new managers err in selecting the right leadership style when they move into management. Why do you think this happens?

2. If new managers don't know what leadership style to use, what does this say about leadership and leadership training?

3. Which leadership theories, if any, could help new leaders deal with this transition?

4. Do you think it's easier or harder to be promoted internally into a formal leadership position than to come into it as an outsider? Explain.

The Kinder, Gentler Leader?

The stereotypical view of a CEO—tough-minded, dominant, and hyper-aggressive—may be giving way to a more sensitive image.[124] Nowhere is this shifting standard more apparent than at General Electric. There may be no CEO more revered for his leadership style than former CEO Jack Welch, a "tough guy," in his own words. Yet his hand-picked successor, Jeff Immelt, is remarkable for his very different leadership style. Whereas Welch was intense, brash, and directive, Immelt was described by *Financial Times* as "unshakably polite, self-deprecating and relaxed."

Of course, Immelt is only one leader, and his success at GE is hardly assured. But he is far from alone in the set of seemingly sensitive CEOs. Colgate-Palmolive CEO Reuben Mark says of his leadership credo, "I have made it my business to be sure that nothing important or creative at Colgate-Palmolive is perceived as my idea." In an interesting contrast to Chrysler CEO Bob Nardelli, Chrysler president Jim Press (formerly president of Toyota of America) embraces "servant leadership" and says one of his main functions is to "get out of the way" and support those who work with him.

A recent study of CEOs seems to suggest that this trend is spreading. The CEOs in its sample scored, on average, 12 points below average on tough-mindedness. Yes, that is below average. As one observer of the corporate world concludes, "The Jack Welch approach appears to be on the wane."

You might think a kinder, gentler approach works only for *Fortune* 500 CEOs, whose very job security might rely on glowing press coverage. In the United States, though, you don't get much farther from Wall Street than the Hanford, Washington, nuclear cleanup site, and there is evidence that the "nice" approach to leadership is taking

hold there, too. Jerry Long, VP of operations for CH2M HILL's cleanup of the Hanford site, argues that a central part of his job is "showing them you care."

Consider the meteoric rise of Barack Obama—all the way from state senator to president in just five years. While a student at Harvard Law School, Obama was famous attorney Laurence Tribe's research assistant. Tribe said of Obama, "I've known senators, presidents. I've never known anyone with what seems to me more raw political talent. He just seems to have the surest way of calmly reaching across what are impenetrable barriers to many people."

Although some have argued that Obama's presidential campaign represented an emphasis of style over substance, it may be that after years of acrimonious political wars, people considered the *how* as important as the *what*. It seems clear that part of Obama's incredible rise reflects people's desire for a kinder, gentler leader.

Questions

1. Do you think the kinder, gentler leader image is just a fad?

2. Do you think the kinder, gentler leadership approach works better in some situations than others? It is possible that Welch and Immelt are *both* effective leaders?

3. Do you think the leadership style of people like Immelt and Obama is a result of nature, nurture, or both? What factors can you think of to support your answer?

From **Concepts**
to **Skills**

Practising to Be Charismatic

In order to be charismatic in your leadership style, you need to engage in the following behaviours:[125]

1. *Project a powerful, confident, and dynamic presence.* This has both verbal and nonverbal components. Use a captivating and engaging voice tone. Convey confidence. Talk directly to people, maintain direct eye contact, and hold your body posture in a way that says you are sure of yourself. Speak clearly, avoid stammering, and avoid sprinkling your sentences with noncontent phrases such as "ahhh" and "you know."

2. *Articulate an overarching goal.* You need to share a vision for the future, develop an unconventional way of achieving the vision, and have the ability to communicate the vision to others.

   The vision is a clear statement of where you want to go and how you are going to get there. You need to persuade others that the achievement of this vision is in their self-interest.

   You need to look for fresh and radically different approaches to problems. The road to achieving your vision should be seen as novel, but also appropriate to the context.

   Charismatic individuals not only have a vision, but they are also able to get others to buy into it. The real power of Martin Luther King Jr. was not that he had a dream, but that he could articulate it in terms that made it accessible to millions.

3. *Communicate high performance expectations and confidence in others' ability to meet these expectations.* You need to demonstrate your confidence in people by stating ambitious goals for them individually and as a group. You then convey absolute belief that they will achieve their expectations.

4. *Be sensitive to the needs of followers.* Charismatic leaders get to know their followers individually. You need to understand their individual needs and develop intensely personal relationships with each. This is done through encouraging followers to express their points of view, being approachable, genuinely listening to and caring about followers' concerns, and asking questions so that followers can learn what is really important to them.

Practising Skills

You are a manufacturing manager in a large electronics plant.[126] The company's management is always searching for ways to increase efficiency. They recently installed new machines and set up a new simplified work system, but to the surprise of everyone—including you—the expected increase in production was not realized. In fact, production has begun to drop, quality has fallen off, and the number of employee resignations has risen.

You do not think that there is anything wrong with the machines. You have had reports from other companies that are using them, and they confirm your opinion. You have also had representatives from the firm that built the machines go over them, and they report that the machines are operating at peak efficiency.

You know that some aspect of the new work system must be responsible for the change, but you are getting no help from your immediate team members—four first-line supervisors who report to you and who are each in charge of a section—or your supply manager. The drop in production has been variously attributed to poor training of the operators, lack of an adequate system of financial incentives, and poor morale. All of the individuals involved have deep feelings about this issue. Your team does not agree with you or with one another.

This morning you received a phone call from your division manager. He had just received your production figures for the past six months and was calling to express his concern. He indicated that the problem was yours to solve in any way that you think best, but that he would like to know within a week what steps you plan to take.

You share your division manager's concern with the falling productivity and know that your employees are also concerned. Using your knowledge of leadership concepts, which leadership style would you choose? And why?

Reinforcing Skills

1. Think of a group or team to which you currently belong or of which you have been a part. What type of leadership style did the leader of this group appear to exhibit? Give some specific examples of the types of leadership behaviours he or she used. Evaluate the leadership style. Was it appropriate for the group? Why or why not? What would you have done differently? Why?

2. Observe two sports teams (either college/ university or professional—one that you consider successful and the other unsuccessful). What leadership styles appear to be used in these team situations? Give some specific examples of the types of leadership behaviours you observe. How would you evaluate the leadership style? Was it appropriate for the team? Why or why not? To what degree do you think leadership style influenced the team's outcomes?

CASE 11 Leadership at Kluster

Ben Kaufman is the CEO of Kluster, a web-based company that invites individuals and companies to send in ideas for new products. At age 17, Kaufman started his career as a web designer, but soon became bored with that. At 18, he came up with a new idea for a lanyard with integrated headphones to be used with the iPod, and that was the start of mophie, a company that makes a line of iPod accessories.

At Macworld 2007, Kaufman tried something new: a community-based decision-making process he calls "the illuminator project." At the show, he handed out sketch pads to attendees and invited them to design new products for mophie. Within three days, the company had three new products, and released them two months later. Although Kaufman considered that he was heading up a product development company, he eventually had to admit that all of his products were iPod accessories, and he did not want to be that limited. Kaufman sold the mophie brand in 2007 and launched Kluster.

Kluster gives consumers the opportunity to influence new products and marketing strategies using the approach established in the illuminator project. At Kluster, instead of a bunch of marketing people trying to figure out new products and how to market new products, consumers are invited to share their ideas and give feedback, which brings them into the product development cycle.

Andres Arango is the design coordinator at Kluster. He coordinates the activity of Kaufman and the top designers at the company. Arango says that Kaufman has weird charisma and vision. When Kaufman originally told Arango about the illuminator idea, Arango thought it was a little crazy. But he also thought the project was revolutionary, and that is why he joined the company.

Peter Wadsworth, an engineer at Kluster, says that Kaufman realizes that he is not a manager, and that is why Kaufman demoted himself to bring in a seasoned leader. The company needed good management in order to get venture capital and to make sales. Wadsworth says that Kaufman is confident, but Kaufman realized that other people just saw a teenage kid running amok with other people's money. Kaufman gets a lot of praise, but he does not have a big head about it. At the same time, he is not intimidated about meeting with celebrities or CEOs because he thinks everyone is equal.

Kaufman does not strive for consensus, and being popular is not a concern of his. He knows his limitations and skills. He will not tell someone else what to do with their skill set. His communication ability is not always the best, and he does not often praise employees for good work, but he does give them a lot of leeway to work on projects when he sees that they are doing a good job.

Kaufman does not hesitate when he makes decisions, and he is prepared to live with the consequences of his decisions. Wadsworth says he would not trust Kaufman to take care of his dog, but he does trust him to make good decisions on the big issues that affect the company.

Kaufman says that he closely supervises people in the company. He says he is a "madman." He wants to make sure that his employees are happy (or at least sort of happy). He does not know whether or not he is a good leader. He leaves that judgment to others.

Questions

1. What is the difference between leadership and management? Is Kaufman a leader? A manager? Both? Neither? Explain your reasoning.

2. Describe the leadership style of Ben Kaufman in terms of the behavioural theories of leadership described in this chapter. What are his leadership strengths and weaknesses?

3. Using a contingency theory of your choice, determine which style of leadership Ben Kaufman should be using.

4. What is the difference between transformational leaders and transactional leaders? What kind of leader is Kaufman? Explain your reasoning.

Source: Based on "Leadership at Kluster," Organizational Behavior Video Library, 2008. Copyrighted by Prentice-Hall.

Decision Making, Creativity, and Ethics

When word went out that food poisoning might be linked to a Maple Leaf Foods meat processing plant, the company's CEO had to make a decision. Did Michael McCain act fast enough to alert the public, and were his actions socially responsible?

1 Is there a right way to make decisions?

2 How do people actually make decisions?

3 How can knowledge management improve decision making?

4 What factors affect group decision making?

5 How can we get more creative decisions?

6 What is ethics, and how can it be used for better decision making?

7 What is corporate social responsibility?

On August 7, 2008, officials of Toronto-based Maple Leaf Foods were notified that there was a public health inquiry into some of its products.[1] On August 12, the Canadian Food Inspection Agency (CFIA) told the company it was launching a formal investigation into some products produced at its Toronto meat plant. Maple Leaf's distributors were told to take the questionable products off the market, but the public was not alerted to any potential problems.

It was not until four days later that the company's CEO, Michael McCain, was first notified that there was a problem, and by that time the CFIA had confirmed bacterial contamination in some Maple Leaf products. It took another week for Maple Leaf, through its CEO, to announce a massive product recall to the public.

McCain's decision about what to say to the public about the listeria contamination is just one example of the many decisions companies face every day. By acting quickly, he was praised for being honest with the public about what the company was doing to protect public health.

In this chapter, we describe how decisions in organizations are made, as well as how creativity is linked to decision making. We also look at the ethical and socially responsible aspects of decision making as part of our discussion. Decision making affects people at all levels of the organization, and it is engaged in by both individuals and groups. Therefore, we also consider the special characteristics of group decision making.

Dear Customers

All recalled Maple Leaf products have been removed from our Deli Counter.

For inquiries please call :
CFIA- 1-800-442-2342
Maple Leaf Consumer Foods- 1-800-568-5801

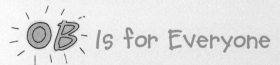

OB Is for Everyone

- Do people really consider every alternative when making a decision?
- Is it okay to use intuition when making decisions?
- Why is it that we sometimes make bad decisions?
- Why are some people more creative than others?
- Why do some people make more ethical decisions than others?

Self-Assessment Library

LEARNING ABOUT YOURSELF

- Decision-Making Style
- Creativity

How Should Decisions Be Made?

1   Is there a right way to
       make decisions?

decision The choice made from
two or more alternatives.

A **decision** is the choice made from two or more alternatives. Decision making occurs as a reaction to a problem or an opportunity. A *problem* is a discrepancy between some current state of affairs and some desired state, requiring consideration of alternative courses of action.[2] An *opportunity* occurs when something unplanned happens, giving rise to thoughts about new ways of proceeding.

Decision making happens at all levels of an organization. For instance, top managers determine their organization's goals, what products or services to offer, how best to finance operations, or where to locate a new high-tech research and development facility. Middle- and lower-level managers determine production schedules, select new employees, and decide how pay raises are to be allocated. Nonmanagerial employees also make decisions, such as whether to come to work on any given day, how much effort to put forward once at work, and whether to comply with a request made by the manager. In addition, an increasing number of organizations in recent years have been empowering their nonmanagerial employees with job-related decision-making authority that was historically reserved for managers alone. Thus, nonmanagerial employees may have the authority to make decisions about initiating some new project or solving certain customer-related problems without consulting their managers.

Knowing how to make decisions is an important part of everyday life. Below we consider various decision-making models that apply to both individual and group choices. (Later in the chapter, we discuss special aspects of group decision making.) We start with the *rational model*, which describes decision making in the ideal world, a situation that rarely exists. We then look at alternatives to the rational model, and how decisions actually get made.

rational Refers to choices that are
consistent and value-maximizing
within specified constraints.

rational decision-making model
A six-step decision-making model
that describes how individuals
should behave in order to maximize
some outcome.

The Rational Decision-Making Process

The **rational** decision maker makes consistent, value-maximizing choices within specified constraints.[3] These choices are made following a six-step **rational decision-making model**.[4] Moreover, specific assumptions underlie this model.

The Rational Model

The six steps in the rational decision-making model are presented in Exhibit 12-1.

First, the decision maker must *define the problem*. If you calculate your monthly expenses and find you are spending $50 more than your monthly earnings, you have defined a problem. Many poor decisions can be traced to the decision maker overlooking a problem or defining the wrong problem.

Once a decision maker has defined the problem, he or she needs to *identify the criteria* that will be important in solving the problem. In this step, the decision maker determines what is relevant in making the decision. This step brings the decision maker's interests, values, and similar personal preferences into the process. Identifying criteria is important because what one person thinks is relevant, another person may not. Also keep in mind that any factors not identified in this step are considered irrelevant to the decision maker.

To understand the types of criteria that might be used to make a decision, consider the many sponsorship requests that Toronto-based Canadian Imperial Bank of Commerce

**EXHIBIT 12-1   Steps in the Rational
Decision-Making Model**

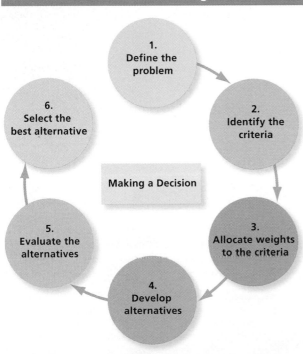

1. Define the problem
2. Identify the criteria
3. Allocate weights to the criteria
4. Develop alternatives
5. Evaluate the alternatives
6. Select the best alternative

Making a Decision

(CIBC) receives each year. In making a decision about whether or not to support a request, the bank considers the following criteria:[5]

- Strategic fit with CIBC's overall goals and objectives

- Ability to achieve marketing objectives for the youth customer segment

- Tangible and intangible benefits of the proposal, such as goodwill, reputation, and cost/potential revenue

- Organizational impact

- Business risks (if any)

If the sponsorship request does not meet these criteria, it is not funded.

The criteria identified are rarely all equal in importance. So the third step requires the decision maker to *allocate weights to the criteria* in order to give them the correct priority in the decision.

The fourth step requires the decision maker to *develop alternatives* that could succeed in resolving the problem. No attempt is made in this step to appraise these alternatives, only to list them.

Once the alternatives have been generated, the decision maker must critically *evaluate the alternatives*. The strengths and weaknesses of each alternative become evident as they are compared with the criteria and weights established in the second and third steps.

The final step in this model requires the decision maker to *select the best alternative*. This is done by evaluating each alternative against the weighted criteria and selecting the alternative with the highest total score.

Assumptions of the Model

The rational decision-making model we just described contains a number of assumptions.[6] Let's briefly outline those assumptions:

- *Problem clarity.* The problem is clear and unambiguous. The decision maker is assumed to have complete information regarding the decision situation.

- *Known options.* It's assumed the decision maker can identify all the relevant criteria and can list all the workable alternatives. Furthermore, the decision maker is aware of all the possible consequences of each alternative.

- *Clear preferences.* Rationality assumes that the criteria and alternatives can be ranked and weighted to reflect their importance.

- *Constant preferences.* It's assumed that the specific decision criteria are constant and that the weights assigned to them are stable over time.

- *No time or cost constraints.* The decision maker can obtain full information about criteria and alternatives because it's assumed that there are no time or cost constraints.

- *Maximum payoff.* The decision maker will choose the alternative that yields the highest perceived value.

Symantec CEO John Thompson made a decision in reaction to the problem of an explosion of Internet viruses. Thompson said, "About every 15 to 18 months, there's a new form of attack that makes old technologies less effective." So he decided to acquire 13 companies that specialize in products such as personal firewalls, intrusion detection, and early warning systems that protect everything from corporate intranets to consumer email inboxes.

How Do Individuals Actually Make Decisions?

When Michael McCain pondered what to say to the public about Maple Leaf's contaminated meat products, he carefully considered where to get advice.[7] "Going through the crisis, there are two advisers I've paid no attention to," he told reporters. "The first are the lawyers, and the second are the accountants. It's not about money or legal liability—this is about our being accountable for providing consumers with safe food."

McCain's actions suggest that he had genuine concern for public safety, and he apologized profusely to those who had been victims of the contamination. In putting consumers ahead of money and legal liability, he was seen to be doing the right thing for the public. When making a decision, how many different constituents should a CEO consider before taking action? Should shareholders have a say in the decision when public safety is at issue?

2 How do people actually make decisions?

Do decision makers actually follow the rational model? Do they carefully assess problems, identify all relevant criteria, use their creativity to identify all workable alternatives, and painstakingly evaluate every alternative to find an optimizing choice?

When decision makers are faced with a simple problem with few alternative courses of action, and when the cost of searching out and evaluating alternatives is low, the rational model provides a fairly accurate description of the decision process.[8] However, such situations are the exception. Most decisions in the real world don't follow the rational model. For instance, people are usually content to find an acceptable or reasonable solution to their problem rather than an optimizing one. As such, decision makers generally make limited use of their creativity. Choices tend to be confined to the problem symptom and to the current alternative. As one expert in decision making has concluded, "Most significant decisions are made by judgment, rather than by a defined prescriptive model."[9] What is more, people are remarkably unaware of making suboptimal decisions.[10]

In the following sections, we indicate areas where the reality of decision making conflicts with the rational model.[11] None of these ways of making decisions should be considered *irrational*; they are simply departures from the rational model that occur when information is unavailable or too costly to collect.

Bounded Rationality in Considering Alternatives

When you considered which university or college to attend, did you look at *every* workable alternative? Did you carefully identify all the criteria that were important in your decision? Did you evaluate each alternative against the criteria in order to find the optimum school? The answer to these questions is probably "no." But don't feel bad, because few people selected their educational institution this way.

Do people really consider every alternative when making a decision?

It's difficult for individuals to identify and consider every possible alternative available to them. Realistically speaking, people are limited by their ability to interpret, process, and act on information. This is called **bounded rationality**.[12]

Because of bounded rationality, individuals are not able to discover and consider every alternative for a decision. Instead, individuals identify a limited list of the most conspicuous choices. In most cases, the list will represent familiar criteria and previously tested solutions. Rather than carefully reviewing and evaluating each alternative in great detail, individuals will settle on an alternative that is "good enough"—one that meets an acceptable level of performance. The first alternative that meets the "good enough" criterion ends the search. So decision makers choose a final solution that **satisfices** rather than optimizes; that is, they seek a solution that is both satisfactory and sufficient. In practice this might mean that rather than interviewing 10 job candidates

bounded rationality Limitations on a person's ability to interpret, process, and act on information.

satisfice To provide a solution that is both satisfactory and sufficient.

for a position and then making a decision, a manager interviews one at a time until someone that is "good enough" is found—that is, the first job candidate encountered who meets the minimum criteria for the job. The federal government has proposed this rule for its own hiring, as *OB in the Workplace* shows.

IN THE WORKPLACE

Ottawa May Stop Hiring "Best-Qualified"

Is hiring the "best-qualified" person too much work? Executives and middle managers working in the federal government think so.[13] They argue that "being qualified and competent for a particular job should be enough" even though the person may not be the best possible candidate.

Civil servants asked for the rules on hiring to be loosened so that they could actually start hiring and filling positions rather than spending so much time finding the "best-qualified" person. They find those searches excruciating and exhausting. When managers follow the federal guidelines for hiring, it can take six months or more to fill a position.

Steve Hindle, former president of the Professional Institute of the Public Service of Canada, explained why hiring someone who is qualified is probably good enough: "If people are honest, what they want is someone who is qualified, but the idea of finding the best? Do we have the time, tools and money needed to find the very best? You want someone competent and good, and if they're the best, that's great."

Not everyone agrees that changing the rules for hiring is a good idea, however. The public sector unions worry that favouritism may become more common. But they do agree that the current system has too much red tape.

Intuition

Perhaps the least rational way of making decisions is to rely on intuition. **Intuitive decision making** is a nonconscious process created from distilled experience.[14] Its defining qualities are that it occurs outside conscious thought; it relies on holistic associations, or links between disparate pieces of information; it's fast; and it's affectively charged, meaning that it usually engages the emotions.[15]

intuitive decision making A subconscious process created out of a person's many experiences.

Is it okay to use intuition when making decisions?

Intuition is not rational, but that does not necessarily make it wrong. And intuition does not necessarily operate in opposition to rational analysis; rather, the two can complement each other. And intuition can be a powerful force in decision making. Research on chess playing provides an excellent illustration of how intuition works.[16]

Novice chess players and grand masters were shown an actual, but unfamiliar, chess game with about 25 pieces on the board. After 5 or 10 seconds, the pieces were removed, and each subject was asked to reconstruct the pieces by position. On average, the grand master could put 23 or 24 pieces in their correct squares, while the novice was able to replace only 6. Then the exercise was changed. This time, the pieces were placed randomly on the board. Again, the novice got only about 6 correct, but so did the grand master! The second exercise demonstrated that the grand master did not have a better memory than the novice. What the grand master *did* have was the ability, based on the experience of having played thousands of chess games, to recognize patterns and clusters of pieces that occur on chessboards in the course of games. Studies also show decisions in seconds, and exhibit only a moderately lower level of skill than when playing one game under tournament conditions, where decisions take half an hour or longer. The expert's experience allows him or her to recognize the pattern in a situation and draw on previously learned information associated with that pattern to arrive at a decision quickly. The result is that the intuitive decision maker can decide rapidly based on what appears to be very limited information.

As the example of the chess players shows, those who use intuition effectively often rely on their experiences to help guide and assess their intuitions. That is why many managers turn to intuition, as *Focus on Research* shows.

FOCUS ON **RESEARCH**

Many Managers Add Intuition to Data Analysis

Do senior managers use intuition in their decision making? A study of 60 experienced professionals holding high-level positions in major US organizations found that many of them used intuition to help them make workplace decisions.[17] Twelve percent said they always used it; 47 percent said they often used it. Only 10 percent said they rarely or seldom used intuition. More than 90 percent of managers said they were likely to use a mix of intuition and data analysis when making decisions.

When asked the types of decisions where they most often used intuition, 40 percent reported that they used it to make people-related decisions such as hiring, performance appraisal, harassment complaints, and safety issues. The managers said they also used intuition for quick or unexpected decisions so they could avoid delays. They also were more likely to rely on intuition in novel situations that had a lot of uncertainty.

The results from this study suggest that intuitive decisions are best applied when time is short; when policies, rules, and guidelines do not give clear-cut advice; when there is a great deal of uncertainty; and when quantitative analysis needs a check and balance.

For most of the twentieth century, experts believed that decision makers' use of intuition was irrational or ineffective. That is no longer the case.[18] There is growing recognition that rational analysis has been overemphasized and that, in certain instances, relying on intuition can improve decision making.[19] But while intuition can be invaluable in making good decisions, we cannot rely on it too much. Because it is so unquantifiable, it's hard to know when our hunches are right or wrong. The key is not to either abandon or rely solely on intuition, but to supplement it with evidence and good judgment.

Judgment Shortcuts

Why is it that we sometimes make bad decisions?

Decision makers engage in bounded rationality, but an accumulating body of research tells us that decision makers also allow systematic biases and errors to creep into their judgments.[20] These come from attempts to shortcut the decision process. To minimize effort and avoid difficult trade-offs, people tend to rely too heavily on experience, impulses, gut feelings, and convenient rules of thumb. In many instances, these shortcuts are helpful. However, they can lead to distortions of rationality, as *OB in the Street* shows.

IN THE STREET

Penalty Kick Decisions

Should you stand still or leap into action? This is the classic question facing a goalie in a faceoff against a midfielder for a penalty kick.[21] Ofer H. Azar, a lecturer in the School of Management at Ben-Gurion University in Israel, finds that goalies often make the wrong decision.

Why? The goalie tries to anticipate where the ball will go after the kick. There is only a split second to do anything after the kick, so anticipating and acting seem like a good decision.

Azar became interested in studying goalie behaviour after realizing that the "incentives are huge" for the goalie to get it right. "Goalkeepers face penalty kicks regularly, so they are not only high-motivated decision makers, but also very experienced ones," he explains. That said, 80 percent of penalty kicks score, so goalies are in a difficult situation at that instant when the kick goes off.

Azar's study found that goalies rarely stayed in the centre of the net as the ball was fired (just 6.3 percent of the time). But staying in the centre is actually the best strategy. Goalies halted penalty kicks when staying in the centre 33.3 percent of the time. They were successful only 14.2 percent of the time when they moved left and only 12.6 percent of the time when they moved right.

Azar argues that the results show that there is a "bias for action," explaining that goalies think they will feel worse if they do *nothing* and miss, than if they do *something* and miss. This bias then clouds their judgment, encouraging them to move to one side or the other, rather than just staying in the centre, where the odds are actually more in their favour.

In what follows, we discuss some of the most common judgment shortcuts to alert you to mistakes that are often made when making decisions.

Overconfidence Bias

It's been said that "no problem in judgment and decision making is more prevalent and more potentially catastrophic than overconfidence."[22]

When we are given factual questions and asked to judge the probability that our answers are correct, we tend to be far too optimistic. This is known as **overconfidence bias**. For instance, studies have found that, when people say they are 65 to 70 percent confident that they are right, they are actually correct only about 50 percent of the time.[23] And when they say they are 100 percent sure, they tend to be right about 70 to 85 percent of the time.[24]

From an organizational standpoint, one of the most interesting findings related to overconfidence is that those individuals whose intellectual and interpersonal abilities are *weakest* are most likely to overestimate their performance and ability.[25] So as managers and employees become more knowledgeable about an issue, they become less likely to display overconfidence.[26] Overconfidence is most likely to surface when organizational members are considering issues or problems that are outside their area of expertise.[27]

overconfidence bias Error in judgment that arises from being far too optimistic about one's own performance.

Anchoring Bias

The **anchoring bias** is a tendency to fixate on initial information and fail to adequately adjust for subsequent information.[28] The anchoring bias occurs because our mind appears to give a disproportionate amount of emphasis to the first information it receives.[29] Anchors are widely used by people in professions where persuasion skills

anchoring bias A tendency to fixate on initial information, from which one then fails to adequately adjust for subsequent information.

are important—such as advertising, management, politics, real estate, and law. For instance, in a mock jury trial, the plaintiff's attorney asked one set of jurors to make an award in the range of $15 million to $50 million. The plaintiff's attorney asked another set of jurors for an award in the range of $50 million to $150 million. Consistent with the anchoring bias, the median awards were $15 million and $50 million, respectively.[30]

Consider the role of anchoring in negotiations. Any time a negotiation takes place, so does anchoring. As soon as someone states a number, your ability to ignore that number has been compromised. For instance, when a prospective employer asks how much you were making in your prior job, your answer typically anchors the employer's offer. You may want to keep this in mind when you negotiate your salary, but remember to set the anchor only as high as you realistically can.

Confirmation Bias

confirmation bias The tendency to seek out information that reaffirms past choices and to discount information that contradicts past judgments.

The rational decision-making process assumes that we objectively gather information. But we don't. We *selectively* gather it. The **confirmation bias** represents a specific case of selective perception. We seek out information that reaffirms our past choices, and we discount information that contradicts them.[31] We also tend to accept at face value information that confirms our preconceived views, while we are critical and skeptical of information that challenges these views. Therefore, the information we gather is typically biased toward supporting views we already hold. This confirmation bias influences where we go to collect evidence because we tend to seek out sources most likely to tell us what we want to hear. It also leads us to give too much weight to supporting information and too little to contradictory information.

Availability Bias

availability bias The tendency for people to base their judgments on information that is readily available to them rather than complete data.

The **availability bias** is the tendency for people to base their judgments on information that is readily available to them rather than complete data. Events that evoke emotions, that are particularly vivid, or that have occurred more recently tend to be more available in our memory. As a result, we tend to overestimate unlikely events, such as airplane crashes, compared with more likely events, such as car crashes. The availability bias can also explain why managers, when doing annual performance appraisals, tend to give more weight to recent behaviours of an employee than to those of six or nine months ago.

Escalation of Commitment

escalation of commitment An increased commitment to a previous decision despite negative information.

Some decision makers escalate commitment to a failing course of action.[32] **Escalation of commitment** refers to staying with a decision even when there is clear evidence that it's wrong. For example, a friend had been dating a man for about four years. Although she admitted that things were not going too well in the relationship, she was determined to marry the man. When asked to explain this seemingly nonrational choice of action, she responded: "I have a lot invested in the relationship!"

Individuals escalate commitment to a failing course of action when they view themselves as responsible for the failure. That is, they "throw good money after bad" to demonstrate that their initial decision was not wrong and to avoid having to admit they made a mistake.[33] Many organizations have suffered large losses because a manager was determined to prove his or her original decision was right by continuing to commit resources to what was a lost cause from the beginning.

Randomness Error

Human beings have a lot of difficulty dealing with chance. Most of us like to believe we have some control over our world and our destiny. Although we undoubtedly can control a good part of our future through rational decision making, the truth is that the world will always contain random events. Our tendency to believe we can predict the outcome of random events is the **randomness error**.

Decision making becomes impaired when we try to create meaning out of random events. One of the most serious impairments occurs when we turn imaginary patterns into superstitions.[34] These can be completely contrived ("I never make important decisions on Friday the 13th") or evolve from a certain pattern of behaviour that has been reinforced previously (Tiger Woods often wears a red shirt during the final round of a golf tournament because he won many junior golf tournaments while wearing red shirts). Although many of us engage in some superstitious behaviour, it can be debilitating when it affects daily judgments or biases major decisions. At the extreme, some decision makers become controlled by their superstitions—making it nearly impossible for them to change routines or objectively process new information.

Winner's Curse

The **winner's curse** describes the tendency for the winning participants in a competitive auction to pay too much for the item won. Some buyers will underestimate the value of an item, and others will overestimate it, and the highest bidder (the winner) will be the one who overestimated the most. Therefore, unless the bidders dramatically undervalue, there is a good chance that the "winner" will pay too much.

Logic predicts that the winner's curse gets stronger as the number of bidders increases. The more bidders there are, the more likely that some of them have greatly overestimated the good's value. So, beware of auctions with an unexpectedly large number of bidders.

Hindsight Bias

The **hindsight bias** is the tendency to believe falsely, after the outcome of an event is actually known, that we could have accurately predicted that outcome.[35] When something happens and we have accurate feedback on the outcome, we seem to be pretty good at concluding that the outcome was relatively obvious. As Malcolm Gladwell, author of *Blink, Outliers,* and *The Tipping Point,* writes, "What is clear in hindsight is rarely clear before the fact. It's an obvious point, but one that nonetheless bears repeating."[36]

The hindsight bias reduces our ability to learn from the past. It permits us to think that we are better at making predictions than we really are, and can result in our being more confident about the accuracy of future decisions than we have a right to be. If, for instance, your actual predictive accuracy is only 40 percent, but you think it's 90 percent, you are likely to become falsely overconfident and less vigilant in questioning your predictive skills.

OB in Action—Reducing Biases and Errors in Decision Making provides you with some ideas for improving your decision making. To learn more about your decision-making style, refer to the *Learning About Yourself Exercise* on page 482.

Improving Decision Making through Knowledge Management

The process of organizing and distributing an organization's collective wisdom so the right information gets to the right people at the right time is called **knowledge**

OB in ACTION

Reducing Biases and Errors in Decision Making

→ **Focus on goals.** Clear goals make decision making easier and help you eliminate options that are inconsistent with your interests.

→ **Look for information that disconfirms** your **beliefs.** When we deliberately consider various ways we could be wrong, we challenge our tendencies to think we are smarter than we actually are.

→ **Don't create meaning** out of random events. Ask yourself if patterns can be meaningfully explained or whether they are merely coincidence. Don't attempt to create meaning out of coincidence.

→ **Increase** your **options.** The more alternatives you can generate, and the more diverse those alternatives, the greater your chance of finding an outstanding one.[37]

---

randomness error The tendency of individuals to believe that they can predict the outcome of random events.

winner's curse The tendency for the winning participants in an auction to pay too much for the item won.

hindsight bias The tendency to believe falsely, after an outcome of an event is actually known, that one could have accurately predicted that outcome.

knowledge management (KM) The process of organizing and distributing an organization's collective wisdom so that the right information gets to the right people at the right time.

Learning About Yourself

2. Decision-Making Style Questionnaire, **(page 482)**

---

3 How can knowledge management improve decision making?

management (KM).[38] When done properly, KM provides an organization with both a competitive edge and improved organizational performance because it makes its employees smarter.

A growing number of companies—including the Royal Bank of Canada, Cisco Systems, British Telecom, and Johnson & Johnson—have realized the value of KM. In fact, one survey found that 81 percent of the leading organizations in Europe and the United States say they have, or are at least considering adopting, some kind of KM system.[39]

KM is increasingly important today for at least three reasons:[40]

- Organizations that can quickly and efficiently tap into their employees' collective experience and wisdom are more likely to "outsmart" their competition.

- As Baby Boomers begin to leave the workforce, there is an increasing awareness that they represent a wealth of knowledge that will be lost if there are no attempts to capture it.

- A well-designed KM system reduces redundancy and makes the organization more efficient. For instance, when employees in a large organization undertake a new project, they need not start from scratch. They can access what previous employees have learned and avoid repeating previous mistakes.

How do organizations record the knowledge and expertise of their employees and make that information easily accessible? First, organizations need to develop *computer databases* of pertinent information that employees can readily access. This process includes identifying what knowledge matters to the organization.[41]

Second, organizations needs to create a *culture* that promotes, values, and rewards sharing knowledge. As we discussed in Chapter 8, information that is important and scarce can be a potent source of power. And people who hold that power are often reluctant to share it with others. KM will not work unless the culture supports information sharing.[42]

Finally, organizations need to develop *mechanisms* that allow employees who have built up valuable expertise and insights to share them with others.[43] *More* knowledge is not necessarily *better* knowledge. Information overload needs to be avoided by designing the system to capture only pertinent information and then organizing it so it can be quickly accessed by the people whom it can help. Royal Bank of Canada, for instance, created a KM system with customized email distribution lists carefully broken down by employees' specialty, title, and area of interest; set aside a dedicated site on the company's intranet that serves as a central information repository; and created separate in-house websites featuring "lessons learned" summaries, where employees with various expertise can share new information with others.[44]

4 What factors affect group decision making?

Group Decision Making

While a variety of decisions in both life and organizations are made at the individual level, the belief—characterized by juries—that two heads are better than one has long been accepted as a basic component of North American and many other countries' legal systems. This belief has expanded to the point that, today, many decisions in organizations are made by groups, teams, or committees. In this section, we will review group decision making and compare it with individual decision making.

Groups vs. the Individual

Decision-making groups may be widely used in organizations, but does that imply group decisions are preferable to those made by an individual alone? The answer to this question depends on a number of factors we consider below.[45] See Exhibit 12-2 for a summary of our major points.

EXHIBIT 12-2 Group vs. Individual Decision Making		
Criteria of Effectiveness	**Groups**	**Individuals**
More complete information	✔	
Diversity of views	✔	
Decision quality	✔	
Accuracy	✔	
Creativity	✔	
Degree of acceptance	✔	
Speed		✔
Efficiency		✔

Strengths of Group Decision Making

Groups generate *more complete information and knowledge*. By combining the resources of several individuals, groups bring more input into the decision process. Groups can bring an *increased diversity of views* to the decision process, and, thus, the opportunity to consider more approaches and alternatives. The evidence indicates that a group will almost always outperform even the best individual. So groups generate *higher-quality decisions*.[46] Group decisions also tend to be more *accurate*. If *creativity* is important, groups tend to be more creative in their decisions than individuals. Groups also lead to *increased acceptance of a solution*.[47] Many decisions fail after they are made because people don't accept them. Group members who participated in making a decision are likely to support the decision enthusiastically and encourage others to accept it.

Weaknesses of Group Decision Making

Despite the advantages noted, group decisions involve certain drawbacks. First, they are *time-consuming*. They typically take more time to reach a solution than would be the case if an individual were making the decision alone. Thus, group decisions are not always efficient. Second, there are *conformity pressures* in groups. The desire by group members to be accepted and considered an asset to the group can result in squashing any overt disagreement. Third, group discussion can be *dominated by one or a few members*. If this dominant coalition is composed of low- and medium-ability members, the group's overall effectiveness will suffer. Finally, group decisions suffer from *ambiguous responsibility*. In an individual decision, it's clear who is accountable for the final outcome. In a group decision, the responsibility of any single member is watered down.

Effectiveness and Efficiency

Whether groups are more effective than individuals depends on the criteria you use to define effectiveness. In terms of *accuracy*, group decisions are generally more accurate than the decisions of the average individual in a group, but they are less accurate than the judgments of the most accurate group member.[48] If decision effectiveness is defined in terms of *speed*, individuals are superior. If *creativity* is important, groups tend to be more effective than individuals. And if effectiveness means the degree of *acceptance* the final solution achieves, the nod again goes to the group.[49]

But effectiveness cannot be considered without also assessing efficiency. In terms of efficiency, groups almost always stack up as a poor second to the individual decision maker. With few exceptions, group decision making consumes more work hours than if an individual were to tackle the same problem alone. The exceptions tend to be the instances in which, to achieve comparable quantities of diverse input, the single decision maker must spend a great deal of time reviewing files and talking to people. Because groups can include members from diverse areas, the time spent searching for information can be reduced. However, as we noted, these advantages in efficiency tend to be the exception. Groups are generally less efficient than individuals. In deciding whether to use groups, then, consideration should be given to assessing whether increases in effectiveness are more than enough to offset the reductions in efficiency. This chapter's *Working with Others Exercise* on page 484 gives you an opportunity to assess the effectiveness and efficiency of group decision making vs. individual decision making.

Groupthink and Groupshift

Two by-products of group decision making have received a considerable amount of attention by OB researchers: groupthink and groupshift. As we will show, these two factors have the potential to affect the group's ability to appraise alternatives objectively and arrive at quality solutions.

Groupthink

Have you ever felt like speaking up in a meeting, classroom, or informal group, but decided against it? One reason may have been shyness. On the other hand, you may have been a victim of **groupthink**, a phenomenon in which group pressures for conformity prevent the group from critically appraising unusual, minority, or unpopular views. It describes a deterioration in an individual's mental efficiency, reality testing, and moral judgment as a result of group pressures.[50]

We have all seen the symptoms of the groupthink phenomenon:[51]

- *Illusion of invulnerability.* Group members become overconfident among themselves, allowing them to take extraordinary risks.

- *Assumption of morality.* Group members believe highly in the moral rightness of the group's objectives and do not feel the need to debate the ethics of their actions.

- *Rationalized resistance.* Group members rationalize any resistance to the assumptions they have made. No matter how strongly the evidence may contradict their basic assumptions, members behave so as to reinforce those assumptions continually.

- *Peer pressure.* Group members apply direct pressures on those who momentarily express doubts about any of the group's shared views or who question the validity of arguments supporting the alternative favoured by the majority.

- *Minimized doubts.* Those group members who have doubts or hold differing points of view seek to avoid deviating from what appears to be group consensus by keeping silent about misgivings and even minimizing to themselves the importance of their doubts.

- *Illusion of unanimity.* If someone does not speak, it's assumed that he or she is in full accord. In other words, abstention becomes viewed as a yes vote.

One place where groupthink has been shown to happen is among jurors, as *OB in the Street* shows.

OB IN THE STREET

Groupthink in an Enron Jury

Can pressure cause people to change their decision? Although most of us view Enron as the very symbol of corporate corruption, not every Enron employee behaved

groupthink A phenomenon in which group pressures for conformity prevent the group from critically appraising unusual, minority, or unpopular views.

unethically.[52] Twenty former Enron employees—most notably Ken Lay, Jeff Skilling, and Andrew Fastow—were either convicted of or pleaded guilty to fraudulent behaviour. The conviction of another Enron executive you have probably never heard of—former broadband finance chief Kevin Howard—provides a fascinating, and disturbing, glimpse into how juries use group pressure to reach decisions.

Howard's first trial ended in a hung jury. In the second trial, he was found guilty of conspiracy, fraud, and falsifying records. However, shortly after his conviction, two jurors and two alternate jurors said they were pressured by other jurors to reach a unanimous decision even though they believed Howard was innocent. Juror Ann Marie Campbell said, in a sworn statement, "There was just so much pressure to change my vote that I felt like we had to compromise and give in to the majority because I felt like there was no other choice." Campbell said that at one point a male juror tried to "grab her by the shoulders" to convince her, and another "banged his fist on the table during deliberations." Another jury member said, "There was an atmosphere of 'Let's fry them.'"

On appeal, a judge threw out Howard's conviction, based, in part, on the earlier judge's instruction to the convicting jury that pressured them to reach a unanimous decision. The Kevin Howard case shows how strong groupthink pressures can be, and the degree to which individuals can be pressured to give in to the majority.

Groupthink appears to be closely aligned with the conclusions Solomon Asch drew in his experiments with a lone dissenter, which we described in Chapter 6. Individuals who hold a position that is different from that of the dominant majority are under pressure to suppress, withhold, or modify their true feelings and beliefs. As members of a group, we find it more pleasant to be in agreement—to be a positive part of the group—than to be a disruptive force, even if disruption is necessary to improve the effectiveness of the group's decisions. This chapter's *Case Incident—The Dangers of Groupthink* on page 487 provides instances when groupthink proved to be harmful.

Do all groups suffer from groupthink? No. It seems to occur most often where there is a clear group identity, where members hold a positive image of their group, which they want to protect, and where the group perceives a collective threat to this positive image.[53] So groupthink is less a dissenter-suppression mechanism than a means for a group to protect its positive image.

What can managers do to minimize groupthink?[54]

- *Monitor group size.* People grow more intimidated and hesitant as group size increases, and, although there is no magic number that will eliminate group-think, individuals are likely to feel less personal responsibility when groups get larger than about 10.

- *Encourage group leaders to play an impartial role.* Leaders should actively seek input from all members and avoid expressing their own opinions, especially in the early stages of deliberation.

- *Appoint one group member to play the role of devil's advocate.* This member's role is to overtly challenge the majority position and offer divergent perspectives.

- *Stimulate active discussion of diverse alternatives to encourage dissenting views and more objective evaluations.*

While considerable anecdotal evidence indicates the negative implications of groupthink in organizational settings, not much actual empirical work has been conducted in organizations in this area.[55] In fact, researchers on groupthink have been criticized for suggesting that its effect is uniformly negative[56] and for overestimating the link between the decision-making process and its outcome.[57] A study of groupthink using 30 teams from five large corporations suggests that elements of groupthink may affect decision making differently. For instance, the illusion of invulnerability, assumption of morality, and illusion of unanimity were positively associated with team performance.[58] The most recent research suggests that we should be aware of groupthink conditions that lead to poor decisions, while realizing that not all groupthink symptoms harm decision making.

Groupshift

Research suggests that there are differences between the decisions groups make and the decisions that would be made by individual members within the group.[59] In some cases, group decisions are more conservative than individual decisions. More often, group decisions are riskier than individual decisions.[60] In either case, participants have engaged in **groupshift**, a phenomenon in which the initial positions of individual group members become exaggerated because of the interactions of the group.

What appears to happen in groups is that the discussion leads to a significant shift in the positions of members toward a more extreme position in the direction in which they were already leaning before the discussion. So conservative types become more cautious and more aggressive types assume more risk. The group discussion tends to exaggerate the initial position of the group.

Groupshift can be viewed as a special case of groupthink. The group's decision reflects the dominant decision-making norm that develops during the group's discussion. Whether the shift in the group's decision is toward greater caution or more risk depends on the dominant pre-discussion norm.

The greater shift toward risk has generated several explanations for the phenomenon.[61] It has been argued, for instance, that the discussion creates familiarity among the members. As they become more comfortable with each other, they also become bolder and more daring. Another argument is that our society values risk, that we admire individuals who are willing to take risks, and that group discussion motivates members to show that they are at least as willing as their peers to take risks. The most plausible explanation of the shift toward risk, however, seems to be that the group diffuses responsibility. Group decisions free any single member from accountability for the group's final choice. Greater risk can be taken because even if the decision fails, no one member can be held wholly responsible.

How should you use the findings on groupshift? You should recognize that group decisions exaggerate the initial position of the individual members, that the shift has been shown more often to be toward greater risk, and that whether a group will shift toward greater risk or caution is a function of the members' pre-discussion inclinations.

Group Decision-Making Techniques

Groups can use a variety of techniques to stimulate decision making. We outline four of them below.

Interacting Groups

The most common form of group decision making takes place in **interacting groups**. In these groups, members meet face to face and rely on both verbal and nonverbal interaction to communicate with each other. But as our discussion of groupthink demonstrated, interacting groups often censor themselves and pressure individual members toward conformity of opinion. *Brainstorming*, the *nominal group technique*, and *electronic meetings* have been proposed as ways to reduce many of the problems inherent in the traditional interacting group.

Brainstorming

Brainstorming is meant to overcome pressures for conformity in the interacting group that prevent the development of creative alternatives.[62] It achieves this by using an idea-

groupshift A phenomenon in which the initial positions of individual group members become exaggerated because of the interactions of the group.

interacting groups Typical groups, where members interact with each other face to face.

brainstorming An idea-generation process that specifically encourages any and all alternatives, while withholding any criticism of those alternatives.

generation process that specifically encourages any and all alternatives, while withholding any criticism of those alternatives.

In a typical brainstorming session, 6 to 12 people sit around a table. The group leader states the problem in a clear manner so that all participants understand it. Members then "free-wheel" as many alternatives as they can in a given period of time. No criticism is allowed, and all the alternatives are recorded for later discussion and analysis. With one idea stimulating others, and judgments of even the most bizarre suggestions withheld until later, group members are encouraged to "think the unusual."

A more recent variant of brainstorming is electronic brainstorming, which is done by people interacting on computers in order to generate ideas. For example, Calgary-based Jerilyn Wright & Associates uses electronic brainstorming to help clients design their workspaces through software that has been adapted for office-space design.[63]

Brainstorming may indeed generate ideas—but not in a very efficient manner. Research consistently shows that individuals working alone generate more ideas than a group in a brainstorming session. Why? One of the primary reasons is because of "production blocking." In other words, when people are generating ideas in a group, there are many people talking at once, which blocks the thought process and eventually impedes the sharing of ideas.[64] The following two techniques go further than brainstorming by offering methods that help groups arrive at a preferred solution.[65]

Nominal Group Technique

The **nominal group technique** restricts discussion or interpersonal communication during the decision-making process, hence the term *nominal* (which means "in name only"). Group members are all physically present, as in a traditional committee meeting, but members operate independently. Specifically, a problem is presented and then the following steps take place:

- Members meet as a group, but before any discussion takes place, each member independently writes down his or her ideas on the problem.

- After this silent period, each member presents one idea to the group. Group members take turns presenting a single idea until all ideas have been presented and recorded. No discussion takes place until all ideas have been recorded.

- The group then discusses the ideas for clarity and evaluates them.

- Each group member silently and independently ranks the ideas. The idea with the highest aggregate ranking determines the final decision.

The steps of the nominal group technique are illustrated in Exhibit 12-3. The chief advantage of the technique is that it permits the group to meet formally but does not restrict independent thinking, as does the interacting group. Research generally shows that nominal groups outperform brainstorming groups.[66]

nominal group technique
A group decision-making method in which individual members meet face to face to pool their judgments in a systematic but independent fashion.

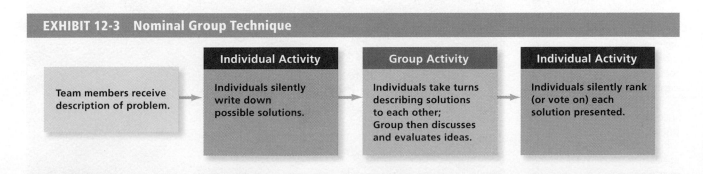

EXHIBIT 12-3   Nominal Group Technique

| Team members receive description of problem. | **Individual Activity**
Individuals silently write down possible solutions. | **Group Activity**
Individuals take turns describing solutions to each other; Group then discusses and evaluates ideas. | **Individual Activity**
Individuals silently rank (or vote on) each solution presented. |

Electronic Meetings

The most recent approach to group decision making blends the nominal group technique with sophisticated computer technology.[67] It's called the computer-assisted group, or **electronic meeting**. Up to 50 people sit around a horseshoe-shaped table, which is empty except for a series of computer terminals. Issues are presented to participants and they type their responses onto their computer monitors. Individual comments, as well as aggregate votes, are displayed on a projection screen in the room.

The major advantages of electronic meetings are anonymity, honesty, and speed. Participants can anonymously type any message they want, and it flashes on the screen for all to see at the push of a participant's keyboard. It also allows people to be brutally honest without penalty. And it's fast because chit-chat is eliminated, discussions don't digress, and many participants can "talk" at once without stepping on one another's toes. The future of group meetings undoubtedly will include extensive use of this technology. The early evidence, however, indicates that electronic meetings don't achieve most of their proposed benefits. Evaluations of numerous studies found that electronic meetings actually led to *decreased* group effectiveness, required *more* time to complete tasks, and resulted in *reduced* member satisfaction compared with face-to-face groups.[68] Nevertheless, current enthusiasm for computer-mediated communications suggests that this technology is here to stay and is likely to increase in popularity in the future.

Each of these four group decision techniques has its own strengths and weaknesses. The choice of one technique over another depends on what criteria you want to emphasize and the cost–benefit trade-off. For instance, as Exhibit 12-4 indicates, an interacting group is good for achieving commitment to a solution, brainstorming develops group cohesiveness, the nominal group technique is an inexpensive means for generating a large number of ideas, and electronic meetings minimize social pressures and conflicts.

Creativity in Organizational Decision Making

Although following the steps of the rational decision-making model will often improve decisions, a rational decision maker also needs **creativity**; that is, the ability to produce novel and useful ideas.[69] These are ideas that are different from what has been done before but that are appropriate to the problem or opportunity presented.

---

electronic meeting A meeting where members interact on computers, allowing for anonymity of comments and aggregation of votes.

5 How can we get more creative decisions?

creativity The ability to produce novel and useful ideas.

Unleashing the creative potential of employees is crucial to the continued success of video game maker Electronic Arts in developing innovative entertainment software. Designed to stimulate employees' creativity, EA's work environment is causal and fun, and employees are given the freedom to manage their own work time. To recharge their creativity, they can take a break from their projects and relax at a serenity pool, work out in a state-of-the-art fitness centre, play pool or table tennis in a games room, or play basketball, soccer, or beach volleyball in an outdoor recreation area.

EXHIBIT 12-4 Evaluating Group Effectiveness

Effectiveness Criteria	Type of Group			
	Interacting	Brainstorming	Nominal	Electronic
Number and quality of ideas	Low	Moderate	High	High
Social pressure	High	Low	Moderate	Low
Money costs	Low	Low	Low	High
Speed	Moderate	Moderate	Moderate	Moderate
Task orientation	Low	High	High	High
Potential for interpersonal conflict	High	Low	Moderate	Low
Commitment to solution	High	Not applicable	Moderate	Moderate
Development of group cohesiveness	High	High	Moderate	Low

Source: Based on J. K. Murnighan, "Group Decision Making: What Strategies Should You Use?" *Academy of Management Review*, February 1981, p. 61.

Why is creativity important to decision making? It allows the decision maker to more fully appraise and understand the problem, including seeing problems others cannot see. Such thinking is becoming more important.

Creative Potential

Most people have creative potential they can use when confronted with a decision-making problem. But to unleash that potential, they have to get out of the psychological ruts many of us fall into, and learn how to think about a problem in divergent ways.

People differ in their inherent creativity, and exceptional creativity is scarce. Albert Einstein, Marie Curie, Pablo Picasso, and Wolfgang Amadeus Mozart were individuals of exceptional creativity. In more recent times, Canadian artist Emily Carr, legendary Canadian concert pianist Glenn Gould, and Canadian author Margaret Atwood have been noted for the creative contributions they have made to their fields. But what about the typical individual? People who score high on openness to experience (see Chapter 2), for example, are more likely than others to be creative. Intelligent people also are more likely than others to be creative.[70] Other traits associated with creative people include independence, self-confidence, risk-taking, a positive core self-evaluation, tolerance for ambiguity, a low need for structure, and perseverance in the face of frustration.[71] A study of the lifetime creativity of 461 men and women found that fewer than 1 percent were exceptionally creative.[72] But 10 percent were highly creative and about 60 percent were somewhat creative. This suggests that most of us have creative potential; we just need to learn to unleash it.

From Concepts to Skills on pages 489–490 provides suggestions on how you can become more effective at solving problems creatively.

Three-Component Model of Creativity

Why are some people more creative than others?

Given that most people have the capacity to be at least somewhat creative, what can individuals and organizations do to stimulate employee creativity? The best answer to this question lies in the **three-component model of creativity**.[73] Based on an extensive body of research, this model proposes that individual creativity essentially requires expertise, creative-thinking skills, and intrinsic task motivation (see Exhibit 12-5 on page 468). Studies confirm that the higher the level of each of these three components, the higher the creativity.

three-component model of creativity The proposition that individual creativity requires expertise, creative-thinking skills, and intrinsic task motivation.

EXHIBIT 12-5   The Three Components of Creativity

Expertise

Creativity skills

Creativity

Task motivation

Source: Copyright © 1997, by The Regents of the University of California. Reprinted from *The California Management Review* 40, no. 1. By permission of The Regents.

Creativity and the bottom line can go hand in hand. In fact, at Vancouver-based Big House Communications, creativity rules. Big House develops communications, including websites, for other companies. It's known for giving clients several alternatives: traditional, wacky, and fun. The company must be doing something right. It's 20 years old, which makes it really old for its business.

Expertise is the foundation for all creative work. Film writer, producer, and director Quentin Tarantino spent his youth working in a video rental store, where he built up an encyclopedic knowledge of movies. The potential for creativity is enhanced when individuals have abilities, knowledge, proficiencies, and similar expertise in their field of endeavour. For example, you would not expect someone with a minimal knowledge of programming to be very creative as a software engineer.

The second component is *creative-thinking skills*. This encompasses personality characteristics associated with creativity, the ability to use analogies, and the talent to see the familiar in a different light.

Research suggests that we are more creative when we are in a good mood, so if we need to be creative, we should do things that make us happy, such as listening to music we enjoy, eating foods we like, watching funny movies, or socializing with others.[74]

Evidence also suggests that being around others who are creative can actually make us more inspired, especially if we are creatively "stuck."[75] One study found that "weak ties" to creative people—knowing creative people but not all that closely—facilitates creativity because the people are there as a resource if we need them, but they are not so close as to stunt our own independent thinking.[76]

The effective use of analogies allows decision makers to apply an idea from one context to another. One of the most famous examples in which analogy resulted in a creative breakthrough was Alexander Graham Bell's observation that it might be possible to apply the way the ear operates to his "talking box." He noticed that the bones in the ear are operated by a delicate, thin membrane. He wondered why, then, a thicker and stronger piece of membrane should not be able to move a piece of steel. From that analogy, the telephone was conceived.

Some people have developed their creative skills because they are able to see problems in a new way. They are able to make the strange familiar and the familiar strange.[77] For instance, most of us think of hens laying eggs. But how many of us have considered that a hen is only an egg's way of making another egg?

The final component in the three-component model of creativity is *intrinsic task motivation*. This is the desire to work on something because it's interesting, involving, exciting, satisfying, or personally challenging. This motivational component is what turns creativity *potential* into *actual* creative ideas. It determines the extent to which individuals fully engage their expertise and creative skills.

Creative people often love their work, to the point of seeming obsession. Our work environment can have a significant effect on intrinsic motivation. Stimulants that foster creativity include a culture that encourages the flow of ideas; fair and constructive judgment of ideas; rewards and recognition for creative work; sufficient financial, material, and information resources; freedom to decide what work is to be done and how to do it; a supervisor who communicates effectively, shows confidence in others, and supports the work group; and work group members who support and trust each other.[78]

Organizational Factors That Affect Creativity

Five organizational factors have been found to block your creativity at work:[79]

- *Expected evaluation.* Focusing on how your work is going to be evaluated.

- *Surveillance.* Being watched while you are working.

- *External motivators.* Focusing on external, tangible rewards.

- *Competition.* Facing win-lose situations with peers.

- *Constrained choice.* Being given limits on how you can do your work.

Canadian Tire built a better tent by giving people an environment that encouraged them to think creatively, as this *OB in the Workplace* shows.

OB IN THE WORKPLACE

Canadian Tire's "Innovation Room" Unleashes Creativity

Can playing with crayons help produce a better tent? Managers at Toronto-based Canadian Tire want better decisions than the kind that come from sitting around a boardroom table.[80] So they built an "innovation room" that is "a cross between a kindergarten classroom and a fantasy land."

To get new ideas for camping gear, they invited friends and family with an interest in camping to meet in the innovation room. The room has LEGO sets, crayons, a canoe, and a sundeck.

Managers were trying to create a new product—a tent with lighting—but were not sure how to develop a product that would sell. They left it to friends and family to get it right. By getting people together in the innovation room, where they could play and brainstorm, the idea emerged for a solar-lit tent. The tent is now a big seller.

"It's really about unlocking and unleashing creativity and getting people to just let loose and dream a little and have fun," says Glenn Butt, a senior vice-president at Canadian Tire. "It's a process that usually ends up with some very unique and different products and concepts."

What About Ethics in Decision Making?

When Michael McCain was first notified that some of Maple Leaf's meat products were being investigated for bacterial contamination, he did not immediately notify the public.[81] He did inform distributors to stop distributing the questionable products, but those packages already

> purchased could still be eaten by consumers. McCain faced a dilemma: at the time that he was notified of the problem, Maple Leaf products were only suspected of contamination, not found to be contaminated. What is the ethical thing to do in a situation like this?

6 What is ethics, and how can it be used for better decision making?

ethics The study of moral values or principles that guide our behaviour and inform us whether actions are right or wrong.

No contemporary discussion of decision making would be complete without the inclusion of ethics, because ethical considerations should be an important criterion in organizational decision making. **Ethics** is the study of moral values or principles that guide our behaviour and inform us whether actions are right or wrong. Ethical principles help us "do the right thing." In this section, we present four ways to ethically frame decisions and examine the factors that shape an individual's ethical decision-making behaviour. We also examine organizational responses to the demand for ethical behaviour, as well as consideration of ethical decisions when doing business in other cultures. To learn more about your approach to ethical decision making, see the *Ethical Dilemma Exercise* on page 486.

Four Ethical Decision Criteria

utilitarianism A decision focused on outcomes or consequences that emphasizes the greatest good for the greatest number.

An individual can use four criteria in making ethical choices.[82] The first is the *utilitarian* criterion, in which decisions are made solely on the basis of their outcomes or consequences. The goal of **utilitarianism** is to provide the greatest good for the greatest number. This view tends to dominate business decision making. It is consistent with goals such as efficiency, productivity, and high profits. By maximizing profits, for instance, business executives can argue that they are securing the greatest good for the greatest number—as they hand out dismissal notices to 15 percent of employees.

A second ethical criterion is to focus on *rights*. This criterion calls on individuals to make decisions consistent with fundamental liberties and privileges as set forth in documents such as the Canadian Charter of Rights and Freedoms. An emphasis on rights in decision making means respecting and protecting the basic rights of individuals, such as the rights to privacy, free speech, and due process. For instance, this criterion would be used to protect **whistle-blowers** when they report unethical or illegal practices by their organizations to the media or to government agencies on the grounds of their right to free speech.

whistle-blowers Individuals who report unethical practices by their employer to outsiders.

A third ethical criterion is *justice*. This criterion requires individuals to impose and enforce rules fairly and impartially so there is an equitable distribution of benefits and costs. Union members typically favour this view. It justifies paying people the same wage for a given job, regardless of performance differences, and it uses seniority as the primary determination in making layoff decisions. A focus on justice protects the interests of the underrepresented and less powerful, but it can encourage a sense of entitlement that reduces risk-taking, innovation, and productivity.

A fourth ethical criterion is *care*. The ethics of care can be stated as follows: "The morally correct action is the one that expresses care in protecting the special relationships that individuals have with each other."[83] Care as an ethical criterion came out of feminist literature[84] to address the idea that the male-dominated view of ethics was too impersonal and ignored the relationships among individuals.[85] The care criterion suggests that we should be aware of the needs, desires, and well-being of those to whom we are closely connected. Recent research does not suggest that men and women differ in their use of justice vs. care in making decisions.[86] However, this perspective does remind us of the difficulty of being impartial in all decisions.

Decision makers, particularly in for-profit organizations, tend to feel safe and comfortable when they use utilitarianism. Many questionable actions can be justified when framed as being in the best interests of "the organization" and stockholders. But many critics of business decision makers argue that this perspective should change because it can result in ignoring the rights of some individuals, particularly those with minority representation in the organization.[87] Increased concern in society about individual rights and social justice suggests the need for managers to develop ethical standards based on nonutilitarian criteria. Using nonutilitarian criteria presents a solid challenge to today's managers because making decisions using criteria such as individual rights and social justice involves far more ambiguities than using utilitarian criteria such as effects on efficiency and profits. This helps to explain why managers are increasingly criticized for their actions. Raising prices, selling products with questionable effects on consumer health, closing down inefficient plants, laying off large numbers of employees, moving production overseas to cut costs, and similar decisions can be justified in utilitarian terms. But that may no longer be the single criterion by which good decisions should be judged.

Factors That Influence Ethical Decision-Making Behaviour

What accounts for unethical behaviour in organizations? Is it immoral individuals or work environments that promote unethical activity? The answer is, *both!* The evidence indicates that ethical or unethical actions are largely a function of both the individual's characteristics and the environment in which he or she works.[88] The model in Exhibit 12-6 illustrates factors affecting ethical decision-making behaviour and emphasizes three factors: stage of moral development, locus of control, and the organizational environment.

Stages of Moral Development

Stages of moral development assess a person's capacity to judge what is morally right.[89] Research suggests that there are three levels of moral development, and each level has two stages.[90] The higher a person's moral development, the less dependent he or she is on outside influences and, hence, the more he or she will be predisposed to behave ethically. The first level is the preconventional level, the second is the conventional level, and the third, or highest, level is the principled level. These levels and their stages are described in Exhibit 12-7 on page 472.

Research indicates that people proceed through the stages one step at a time, though they do not necessarily reach the highest stage.[91] Most adults are at a mid-level of moral development—they are strongly influenced by peers and will follow an organization's rules and procedures. Those individuals who have progressed to the higher stages place increased value on the rights of others, regardless of the majority's opinion, and are likely to challenge organizational practices they personally believe are wrong. Those at the higher stages are most likely to make ethical decisions.

stages of moral development
The developmental stages that explain a person's capacity to judge what is morally right.

Why do some people make more ethical decisions than others?

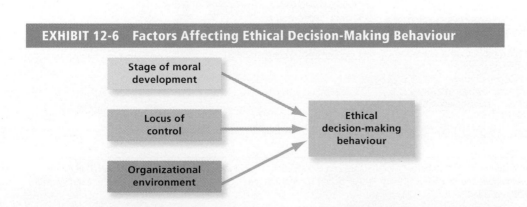

EXHIBIT 12-6   Factors Affecting Ethical Decision-Making Behaviour

Stewart Leibl, president of Perth's, a Winnipeg dry-cleaning chain, is a founding sponsor of the Koats for Kids program. The company's outlets are a drop-off point for no-longer-needed children's coats, which Perth's cleans free of charge before distributing them to children who have no winter coats. Leibl is going beyond the utilitarian criterion when he says, "We all have a responsibility to contribute to the society that we live in." He is also looking at social justice.

EXHIBIT 12-7   Stages of Moral Development

Principled

6. Following self-chosen ethical principles even if they violate the law.
5. Valuing rights of others and upholding absolute values and rights regardless of the majority's opinion.

Conventional

4. Maintaining conventional order by fulfilling obligations to which you have agreed.
3. Living up to what is expected by people close to you.

Preconventional

2. Following rules only when doing so is in your immediate interest.
1. Sticking to rules to avoid physical punishment.

Source: Based on L. Kohlberg, "Moral Stages and Moralization: The Cognitive-Developmental Approach," in *Moral Development and Behaviour: Theory, Research, and Social Issues*, ed. T. Lickona (New York: Holt, Rinehart and Winston, 1976), pp. 34–35.

Locus of Control

Research indicates that people with an external *locus of control* (that is, they believe their lives are controlled by outside forces, such as luck or chance) are less likely to take responsibility for the consequences of their behaviour and are more likely to rely on external influences to determine their behaviour. Those with an internal locus of control (they believe they are responsible for their destiny), on the other hand, are more likely to rely on their own internal standards of right or wrong to guide their behaviour.

Organizational Environment

The *organizational environment* refers to an employee's perception of organizational expectations. Does the organizational culture encourage and support ethical behaviour by rewarding it or discourage unethical behaviour by punishing it? Characteristics of an organizational environment that are likely to foster high ethical decision making include written codes of ethics; high moral behaviour by senior management; realistic performance expectations; performance appraisals that evaluate means as well as ends; visible recognition and promotions for individuals who display high moral behaviour; and visible punishment for those who act unethically.

In summary, people who lack a strong moral sense are much less likely to make unethical decisions if they are constrained by an organizational environment that frowns on such behaviours. Conversely, righteous individuals can be corrupted by an organizational environment that permits or encourages unethical practices. In the next section, we consider how to formulate an ethical decision.

Making Ethical Decisions

While there are no clear-cut ways to differentiate ethical from unethical decision making, there are some questions you should consider.

Exhibit 12-8 illustrates a decision tree to guide ethical decisions.[92] This tree is built on three of the ethical decision criteria—utilitarianism, rights, and justice—presented earlier. The first question you need to answer addresses self-interest vs. organizational goals.

The second question concerns the rights of other parties. If the decision violates the rights of someone else (the person's right to privacy, for instance), then the decision is unethical.

The final question that needs to be addressed relates to whether the decision conforms to standards of equity and justice. The department head who inflates the performance evaluation of a favoured employee and deflates the evaluation of a disfavoured employee—and then uses these evaluations to justify giving the former a big raise and nothing to the latter—has treated the disfavoured employee unfairly.

EXHIBIT 12-8   Is a Decision Ethical?

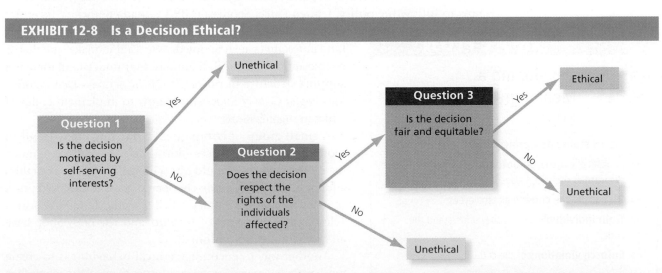

Unfortunately, the answers to the questions in Exhibit 12-8 are often argued in ways to make unethical decisions seem ethical. Powerful people, for example, can become very adept at explaining self-serving behaviours in terms of the organization's best interests. Similarly, they can persuasively argue that unfair actions are really fair and just. Our point is that immoral people can justify almost any behaviour. Those who are powerful, articulate, and persuasive are the most likely to be able to get away with unethical actions successfully. When faced with an ethical dilemma, try to answer the questions in Exhibit 12-8 truthfully.

Organizational Response to Demands for Ethical Behaviour

During the 1990s, an explosion in the demand for more ethics occurred in Canada and the United States. A second explosion occurred in 2002, after the Enron, WorldCom, and other accounting scandals. The lessons were still not learned, as evidenced by the large bonuses paid out to employees whose financial institutions were begging the US government to bail them out in 2009 because of heavy losses.

In Canada, more than 200 ethics specialists now offer services as in-house moral arbitrators, mediators, watchdogs, and listening posts.[93] Some work at Canada's largest corporations, including CIBC, Canada Post, Magna International, Royal Bank of Canada, Nortel Networks, and McDonald's Canada. These corporate ethics officers hear about issues such as colleagues making phone calls on company time, managers yelling at their employees, product researchers being asked to fake data to meet a deadline, or a company wanting to terminate a contract because the costs are higher than anticipated. Ethics professor Wayne Norman of the Université de Montréal believes that ethics officers are a positive trend, noting, "All sorts of studies show the companies that take ethics seriously tend to be more successful."[94]

Many corporations are also developing codes of ethics. For example, about 60 percent of Canada's 650 largest corporations have some sort of ethics code,[95] and nearly all of the companies in the *Fortune* 500 index have codes of ethics available on their websites.[96] Twenty percent of the top 300 Canadian organizations employ ethics specialists, compared with 30 percent of the *Fortune* 500 companies in the United States. Unlike the United States, however, Canada does not legally require companies to create an ethical culture. In the United States, when a company is sued for illegal practices, financial damages may be reduced considerably if the company has a fully functioning ethics program in place.

Having a corporate ethics policy is not enough; employees must be instructed in how to follow the policy. United Parcel Services (UPS) Canada launched its ethics training program in July 1999. As David Cole, vice-president of human resources at UPS, noted, "We want to make sure that as people approach ethical dilemmas, they understand there is a support structure in place."[97] *OB in Action—Developing a Meaningful Code of Ethics* shows how to implement codes of ethics in organizations.

A small group of companies is starting a new trend in monitoring ethical practices—hiring an ethics auditor in much the same way as they would hire a financial auditor. The ethics auditor is hired to "double-check an organization's perception of its own morals."[99] Vancity, Bell Canada, Tetra Pak, British Telecom, the University of Toronto, and The Body Shop have all brought in ethics auditors.

Another way to encourage ethical behaviour is to create mechanisms that encourage employees to speak up when they

OB in ACTION

Developing a Meaningful Code of Ethics

→ Clearly **state basic principles** and expectations.

→ Realistically **focus on potential ethical dilemmas** that employees face.

→ **Distribute** the **code** to all employees.

→ **Train individuals** so that they understand the code.

→ **Enforce violations** of the code.[98]

Paul Nielsen (shown with his wife, Dayle), owns Calgary-based DumpRunner Waste Systems, a specialty garbage and debris removal company. He encourages an ethical approach to dealing with both clients and employees. He notes that in Calgary, business is built on handshakes and being true to your word, and people are expected to act ethically. Ethical behaviour may be easier for Nielsen than for some others. He says he is guided by his passion for being in business, rather than a "quest for money."

see wrongdoing. Toronto-based BBDO Canada encourages "candour moments." Employees are empowered "to call each other on behaviour that goes against company values, even junior employees who want to be candid with managers," says the ad agency's president and CEO, Gerry Frascione.[100]

What About National Culture?

We have already shown that there are differences between Canada and the United States in the legal treatment of ethics violations and the creation of an ethical corporate culture. However, it's important to note that what is considered unethical in one country may not be viewed similarly in another country. The reason is that there are no global ethical standards. Contrasts between Asia and the West provide an illustration.[101] In Japan, people doing business together often exchange gifts, even expensive ones. This is part of Japanese tradition. When North American and European companies started doing business in Japan, most North American executives were not aware of the Japanese tradition of exchanging gifts and wondered whether this was a form of bribery. Most have come to accept this tradition now, and have even set different limits on gift giving in Japan than in other countries.[102]

In another example of the differences between Asia and North America, a manager of a large US company that operates in China caught an employee stealing. Following company policy, she fired the employee and turned him over to the local authorities for his act. Later she discovered, to her horror, that the former employee had been executed for the theft.[103] These examples indicate that standards for ethical behaviour and the consequences of particular acts are not universal. This presents a variety of problems for those doing business in other countries.

Companies operating branches in foreign countries are faced with tough decisions about how to conduct business under different ethical standards from those in Canada. For instance, Canadian companies must decide whether they want to operate in countries such as China, Burma, and Nigeria, which abuse human rights. Although the Canadian government permits investing in these countries, it also encourages companies to act ethically.

While ethical standards may seem ambiguous in the West, criteria defining right and wrong are actually much clearer in the West than in Asia and the Middle East. Few issues are black and white there; most are grey. John B. McWilliams, senior vice-president and general counsel for Calgary-based Canadian Occidental Petroleum (now known as Nexen), notes that requests for bribes are not necessarily direct: "Usually, they don't say, 'Give me X thousands of dollars and you've got the deal.' It's a lot more subtle than that."[104] Michael Davies, vice-president and general counsel for Toronto-based General Electric Canada, offers an example: "A payment [is] made to an administrative official to do the job that he's supposed to do. In other words, you pay a fellow over the counter $10 when you're in the airport in Saudi Arabia to get on the flight you're supposed to get on, because, otherwise, he's going to keep you there for two days."[105]

The need for global organizations to establish ethical principles for decision makers in all countries may be critical if high standards are to be upheld and if consistent practices are to be achieved. Having agreements among countries to police bribery may not be enough, however. The 34 countries of the OECD (Organisation for Economic Co-operation and Development) entered into an agreement to tackle corporate bribery in 1997. However, a study by Berlin-based Transparency International in 2008 found that 18 of the OECD countries are "doing little or nothing" to enforce the agreement. Canada, along with the United Kingdom and Japan, came under strong criticism. The three countries filed a total of four cases in 2007 and 2008, compared with a total of 245 cases filed by the United States, Germany, and France. "Canada is the only OECD country to bar its tax inspectors from reporting suspicions of foreign bribery to law enforcement authorities," Transparency International noted.[106]

Corporate Social Responsibility

When Maple Leaf Foods CEO Michael McCain realized that meat contamination that occurred in the company's Toronto meat processing plant had caused a number of deaths, he was faced with a possible public-relations disaster.[107] People might stop buying Maple Leaf products, perhaps forever. He chose to act in a socially responsible way. "The core principle here was to first do what's in the interest of public health, and second to be open and transparent in taking accountability," McCain said.

Many found McCain's willingness to taking responsibility for the food contamination a bit unusual, but reassuring, particularly when considering the massive bonuses many financial executives received in 2008, even though a number of financial institutions in the US faced collapse.

"His candour at a time when his contemporaries would have scurried behind spin doctors and legal eagles was a refreshing way to address a potentially devastating mistake. I actually trust the man!" said Peter Lapinskie of the *Daily Observer* in Pembroke, Ontario. "It's so rare to see a white-collar executive descend from the ivory tower, apologize and reach out to the public in such plain language," said Ruth Davenport of CJNI radio in Halifax. To what extent should companies be socially responsible?

7 What is corporate social responsibility?

corporate social responsibility
An organization's responsibility to consider the impact of its decisions on society.

Corporate social responsibility is defined as an organization's responsibility to consider the impact of its decisions on society. Thus, organizations may try to better society through such things as charitable contributions or providing better wages to employees working in offshore factories. Organizations may engage in these practices because they feel pressured by society to do so, or they may seek ways to improve society because they feel it is the right thing to do.

Eighty percent of Canadians feel that Ottawa should establish standards for corporate social responsibility, and require corporations to report on how they are meeting guidelines, according to a recent survey.[108] Many Canadian companies are feeling the pressure to act socially responsible as well. For example, a poll by Environics found that 9 out of 10 Canadian shareholders want environmental and social performance taken into account when companies are valued. In another survey, done by GlobeScan,

Mark Trang, an employee of Salesforce.com, teaches business basics to grade 5 students at an elementary school. Salesforce.com encourages every employee to donate 1 percent of his or her working time to the community. Through volunteer work, Salesforce.com gives employees the opportunity to experience the joy and satisfaction that comes from helping others. Employees give to the community by feeding the homeless,, tutoring kids, gardening in community parks, lending computer expertise to nonprofit organizations, and providing disaster relief.

71 percent of respondents believe that consumers can have an impact on whether companies behave responsibly.[109]

Not everyone agrees with the position of organizations that assume social responsibility. For example, economist Milton Friedman remarked in *Capitalism and Freedom* that "few trends could so thoroughly undermine the very foundations of our free society as the acceptance by corporate officials of a social responsibility other than to make as much money for their stockholders as possible."[110]

Joel Bakan, professor of law at the University of British Columbia, author of *The Corporation*,[111] and co-director of the documentary of the same name, is more critical of organizations than Friedman, though he finds that current laws support corporate behaviour that some might find troubling. Bakan suggests that today's corporations have many of the same characteristics as a psychopathic personality (for example, self-interested, lacking empathy, manipulative, and reckless in their disregard of others). Bakan notes that even though companies have a tendency to act psychopathically, this is not why they are fixated on profits. Rather, the only legal responsibility corporations have is to maximize organizational profits for stockholders. He suggests more laws and more restraints need to be put in place if corporations are to behave more socially responsibly, as current laws direct corporations to be responsible to their shareholders, and make little mention of responsibility toward other stakeholders.

A 2006 survey at 110 MBA programs in the United States and Canada conducted by Net Impact found that MBA students are very interested in the subject of corporate social responsibility. While students who were involved in Net Impact gave even more favourable responses, 81 percent of respondents not part of the club "believed business professionals should take into account social and environmental impacts when making decisions." Almost two-thirds of these respondents felt that corporate social responsibility should be part of core MBA classes, and 60 percent said "they would seek socially responsible employment."[112]

This chapter's *Case Incident—Syncrude Wants to Be a Good Neighbour* on page 488 describes a socially responsible approach to running a business located near an Aboriginal community. For more on the debate about social responsibility vs. concentrating on the bottom line, see this chapter's *Point/Counterpoint* on page 481.

Summary and Implications

1 **Is there a right way to make decisions?** The rational decision-making model describes the six steps individuals take to make decisions: (1) Define the problem, (2) identify the criteria, (3) allocate weights to the criteria, (4) develop alternatives, (5) evaluate the alternatives, and (6) select the best alternative. This is an idealized model, and not every decision thoroughly follows these steps.

2 **How do people actually make decisions?** Most decisions in the real world don't follow the rational model. For instance, people are usually content to find an acceptable or reasonable solution to their problem rather than an optimizing one. Thus, decision makers may rely on bounded rationality, satisficing, and intuition in making decisions. They may also rely on judgment shortcuts, such as overconfidence bias, anchoring bias, confirmation bias, availability bias, escalation of commitment, randomness error, winner's curse, and hindsight bias.

3 **How can knowledge management improve decision making?** Knowledge management makes employees smarter when it's carried out properly. By electronically storing information that employees have, organizations make it possible to share collective wisdom. As well, when new projects are started, individuals can see what others have done before them, to avoid going down unproductive paths.

4 **What factors affect group decision making?** Groups generate more complete information and knowledge, they offer increased diversity of views, they generate higher-quality decisions, and they lead to increased acceptance of a solution. However, group decisions are time-consuming. They also lead to conformity pressures, and the group discussion can be dominated by one or a few members. Finally, group decisions suffer from ambiguous responsibility, and the responsibility of any single member is watered down. Groups can suffer from groupthink and/or groupshift. Under groupthink, the group emphasizes agreement above everything else, often shutting down individuals who express any disagreement with the group's actions. In groupshift, the group takes a more extreme position (either more conservative or more risky) than individuals would take on their own.

5 **How can we get more creative decisions?** While there is some evidence that individuals vary in their ability to be creative, research shows that individuals are more creative when they have expertise in the task at hand, creative-thinking skills, and are motivated by intrinsic interest. Five organizational factors have been found to block your creativity at work: (1) *expected evaluation*—focusing on how work is going to be evaluated; (2) *surveillance*—being watched while working; (3) *external motivators*—focusing on external, tangible rewards; (4) *competition*—facing win-lose situations with peers; and (5) *constrained choice*—being given limits on how to do the work.

6   **What is ethics, and how can it be used for better decision making?** Ethics is the study of moral values or principles that guide our behaviour and inform us whether actions are right or wrong. Ethical principles help us "do the right thing." An individual can use four different criteria in making ethical choices. The first is the *utilitarian* criterion, in which decisions are made solely on the basis of their outcomes or consequences. The second ethical criterion is *rights*; this criterion focuses on respecting and protecting the basic rights of individuals. The third ethical criterion is *justice*; this criterion requires individuals to impose and enforce rules fairly and impartially so there is an equitable distribution of benefits and costs. The fourth ethical criterion is *care*; this criterion suggests that we should be aware of the needs, desires, and well-being of those to whom we are closely connected. There are advantages and disadvantages to each of these criteria.

7   **What is corporate social responsibility?** Corporate social responsibility is defined as an organization's responsibility to consider the impact of its decisions on society. Thus, organizations may try to better society through such things as charitable contributions or providing better wages to employees working in offshore factories. Organizations may engage in these practices because they feel pressured by society to do so, or they may seek ways to improve society because they feel it is the right thing to do.

For Review

1. What is the rational decision-making model? Under what conditions is it applicable?

2. Describe organizational factors that might constrain decision makers.

3. What role does intuition play in effective decision making?

4. Describe three judgment shortcuts.

5. What is groupthink? What is its effect on decision-making quality?

6. What is groupshift? What is its effect on decision-making quality?

7. Identify five organizational factors that block creativity at work.

8. Describe the four criteria that individuals can use in making ethical decisions.

9. Are unethical decisions more a function of the individual decision maker or the decision maker's work environment? Explain.

10. What is corporate social responsibility?

For Critical Thinking

1. "For the most part, individual decision making in organizations is an irrational process." Do you agree or disagree? Discuss.

2. What factors do you think differentiate good decision makers from poor ones? Relate your answer to the six-step rational decision-making model.

3. Have you ever increased your commitment to a failed course of action? If so, analyze the follow-up decision to increase your commitment and explain why you behaved as you did.

4. If group decisions are of consistently better quality than individual decisions, how did the phrase "a camel is a horse designed by a committee" become so popular and ingrained in our culture?

OB for You

- In some decision situations, consider following the rational decision-making model. Doing so will ensure that you review a wider variety of options before committing to a particular decision.

- Analyze the decision situation and be aware of your biases. We all bring biases to the decisions we make. Combine rational analysis with intuition. As you gain experience, you should feel increasingly confident in imposing your intuitive processes on top of your rational analysis.

- Use creativity-stimulation techniques. You can improve your overall decision-making effectiveness by searching for innovative solutions to problems. This can be as basic as telling yourself to think creatively and to look specifically for unique alternatives.

- When making decisions, think about their ethical implications. A quick way to do this is to ask yourself: Would I be embarrassed if this action were printed on the front page of the newspaper?

 **POINT**

 COUNTERPOINT

Organizations Should Just Stick to the Bottom Line

The major goals of organizations are and should be efficiency, productivity, and high profits. By maximizing profits, businesses ensure that they will survive and thus make it possible to provide employment. Doing so is in the best interests of the organization, employees, and stockholders. Moreover, it's up to individuals to show that they are concerned about the environment through their investment and purchasing activities, not for corporations to lead the way.

Let's examine some of the reasons why it's not economically feasible to place the entire burden of protecting the environment on the shoulders of big business.

Studies show that environmental regulations are too costly. The Conference Board of Canada suggested that environmental regulations cost Canadian companies $580 million to $600 million a year.[113] The Fraser Institute in Vancouver reported that all regulations, including those designed to protect the environment, cost Canadian industry $85 billion a year.[114] Environmental regulations can also be harmful to jobs. In British Columbia, the Forest Practices Code is said to have added $1 billion a year to harvesting costs and resulted in a number of job cuts.

While businesses are concerned with the high cost that results from environmental regulations, the general public are not completely supportive of protecting the environment either, particularly if it will inconvenience them.[115]

Companies would be better off sticking to the bottom line, and governments should stay away from imposing costly environmental regulations on business. Stringent environmental standards cause trade distortions, and governments rarely consider the cost of complying with regulations. Companies should be allowed to take their lead from shareholders and customers. If these constituencies want businesses to pay for environmental protection, they will indicate this by investing in firms that do so. Until they do, the cost of environmental legislation is simply too high.

Environmental Responsibility Is Part of the Bottom Line

Going green makes good economic sense. The studies reported in the *Point* argument tend to overstate the cost of environmental regulations.[116] They do not consider the benefits to society of those regulations.

A closer look at a few companies that have devoted efforts to being more environmentally friendly will illustrate the benefits of this approach. When Quaker Oats Canada started working toward a "greener" work environment, its Peterborough, Ontario, plant saved more than $1 million in three years through various environmental initiatives.[117]

As another example, Vale Inco (formerly Inco) spent $600 million to change the way it produces nickel at its Sudbury, Ontario, operations in order to be less devastating to the local environment. Its new smelting process is the most energy-efficient and environmentally friendly process in the world. Vale Inco continues to work to restore the appearance of Sudbury. Trees have grown back, the wildlife has returned, and the air is clean. Sudbury has even been listed as one of the 10 most desirable places to live in Canada. While Vale Inco invested a lot of money to change its production process, Doug Hamilton, controller at the company's Ontario division in Sudbury, says, "Our Sulphur Dioxide Abatement Program was an awesome undertaking. Not only did this investment allow us to capture 90 percent of the sulphur in the ore we mine, but the new processes save the company $90 million a year in production costs. That strikes me as a pretty smart investment."[118]

London, Ontario-based 3M Canada started a Pollution Prevention Pays (3P) program more than 30 years ago.[119] The program emphasizes stopping pollution at the source to avoid the expense and effort of cleaning it up or treating it after the fact. The recycling program at 3M Canada's tape plant in Perth, Ontario, reduced its waste by 96 percent and saved the company about $650 000 annually. The capital cost for the program was only $30 000.

The examples of Quaker Oats, Vale Inco, and 3M show that companies that are environmentally friendly have an advantage over their competitors. If organizations control their pollution costs better than their competitors, they will use their resources more efficiently and therefore increase profitability.

LEARNING ABOUT **YOURSELF** EXERCISE

Decision-Making Style Questionnaire

Circle the response that comes closest to how you usually feel or act. There are no right or wrong responses to any of these items.[120]

1. I am more careful about

   a. people's feelings   **b.** their rights

2. I usually get along better with

   a. imaginative people   **b.** realistic people

3. It's a higher compliment to be called

   a. a person of real feeling   **b.** a consistently reasonable person

4. In doing something with other people, it appeals more to me

   a. to do it in the accepted way   **b.** to invent a way of my own

5. I get more annoyed at

   a. fancy theories   **b.** people who do not like theories

6. It's higher praise to call someone

   a. a person of vision   **b.** a person of common sense

7. I more often let

   a. my heart rule my head   **b.** my head rule my heart

8. I think it's a worse fault

   a. to show too much warmth   **b.** to be unsympathetic

9. If I were a teacher, I would rather teach

   a. courses involving theory   **b.** factual courses

Which word in the following pairs appeals to you more? Circle a or b.

10. a. Compassion   **b.** Foresight

11. a. Justice   **b.** Mercy

12. a. Production   **b.** Design

13. a. Gentle   **b.** Firm

14. a. Uncritical   **b.** Critical

15. a. Literal   **b.** Figurative

16. a. Imaginative   **b.** Matter-of-fact

Scoring Key:

Mark each of your responses on the following scales. Then use the point value column to arrive at your score. For example, if you answered a to the first question, you would check 1a in the Feeling column. This response receives zero points when you add up the point value column. Instructions for classifying your scores are indicated following the scales.

Sensation	Point Value	Intuition	Point Value	Thinking	Point Value	Feeling	Point Value
2b _____	1	2a _____	2	1b _____	1	1a _____	0
4a _____	1	4b _____	1	3b _____	2	3a _____	1
5a _____	1	5b _____	1	7b _____	1	7a _____	1
6b _____	1	6a _____	0	8a _____	0	8b _____	1
9b _____	2	9a _____	2	10b _____	2	10a _____	1
12a _____	1	12b _____	0	11a _____	2	11b _____	1
15a _____	1	15b _____	1	13b _____	1	13a _____	1
16b _____	2	16a _____	0	14b _____	0	14a _____	1
Maximum Point Value	(10)		(7)		(9)		(7)

Circle *Intuition* if your Intuition score is equal to or greater than your Sensation score. Circle *Sensation* if your Sensation score is greater than your Intuition score. Circle *Feeling* if your Feeling score is greater than your Thinking score. Circle *Thinking* if your Thinking score is greater than your Feeling score.

A high score on *Intuition* indicates you see the world in holistic terms. You tend to be creative. A high score on *Sensation* indicates that you are realistic and see the world in terms of facts. A high score on *Feeling* means you make decisions based on gut feeling. A high score on *Thinking* indicates a highly logical and analytical approach to decision making.

More Learning About Yourself Exercises

Additional self-assessments relevant to this chapter appear at MyOBLab (**www.pearsoned.ca/myoblab**).

IV.A.2 Am I a Deliberate Decision Maker?

I.A.5 How Creative Am I?

When you complete the additional assessments, consider the following:

1. Am I surprised about my score?
2. Would my friends evaluate me similarly?

BREAKOUT **GROUP** EXERCISES

Form small groups to discuss the following topics, as assigned by your instructor:

1. Apply the rational decision-making model to deciding where your group might eat dinner this evening. How closely were you able to follow the rational model in making this decision?

2. The company that makes your favourite snack product has been accused of being weak in its social responsibility efforts. What impact will this have on your purchase of any more products from that company?

3. You have seen a classmate cheat on an exam or an assignment. Do you do something about this or ignore it?

WORKING WITH **OTHERS** EXERCISE

Wilderness Survival Exercise

You are a member of a hiking party. After reaching base camp on the first day, you decide to take a quick sunset hike by yourself. After a few exhilarating miles, you decide to return to camp. On your way back, you realize that you are lost. You have shouted for help, to no avail. It is now dark, and getting cold.

Your Task

Without communicating with anyone else in your group, read the following scenarios and choose the best answer. Keep track of your answers on a sheet of paper. You have 10 minutes to answer the 10 questions.

1. The first thing you decide to do is to build a fire. However, you have no matches, so you use the bow and drill method. What is the bow and drill method?

   a. A dry, soft stick is rubbed between one's hands against a board of supple green wood.

   b. A soft green stick is rubbed between one's hands against a hardwood board.

   c. A straight stick of wood is quickly rubbed back-and forth against a dead tree.

   d. Two sticks (one being the bow, the other the drill) are struck to create a spark.

2. It occurs to you that you can also use the fire as a distress signal. When signalling with fire, how do you form the international distress signal?

   a. 2 fires

   b. 4 fires in a square

   c. 4 fires in a cross

   d. 3 fires in a line

3. You are very thirsty. You go to a nearby stream and collect some water in the small metal cup you have in your backpack. How long should you boil the water?

   a. 15 minutes

   b. A few seconds

   c. 1 hour

   d. It depends on the altitude.

4. You are very hungry, so you decide to eat what appear to be edible berries. When performing the universal edibility test, what should you do?

   a. Do not eat for 2 hours before the test.

   b. If the plant stings your lip, confirm the sting by holding it under your tongue for 15 minutes.

   c. If nothing bad has happened 2 hours after digestion, eat half a cup of the plant and wait again.

   d. Separate the plant into its basic components and eat each component, one at a time.

5. Next, you decide to build a shelter for the evening. In selecting a site, what do you *not* have to consider?

   a. It must contain material to make the type of shelter you need.

   b. It must be free of insects, reptiles, and poisonous plants.

   c. It must be large enough and level enough for you to lie down comfortably.

   d. It must be on a hill so you can signal rescuers and keep an eye on your surroundings.

6. In the shelter that you built, you notice a spider. You heard from a fellow hiker that black widow spiders populate the area. How do you identify a black widow spider?

   a. Its head and abdomen are black; its thorax is red.

   b. It is attracted to light.

   c. It runs away from light.

   d. It is a dark spider with a red or orange marking on the female's abdomen.

7. After getting some sleep, you notice that the night sky has cleared, so you decide to try to find your way back to base camp. You believe you should travel north and can use the North Star for navigation. How do you locate the North Star?

   a. Hold your right hand up as far as you can and look between your index and middle fingers.

   b. Find Sirius and look 60 degrees above it and to the right.

   c. Look for the Big Dipper and follow the line created by its cup end.

   d. Follow the line of Orion's belt.

8. You come across a fast-moving stream. What is the best way to cross it?

   a. Find a spot downstream from a sandbar, where the water will be calmer.

   b. Build a bridge.

   c. Find a rocky area, as the water will be shallow and you will have hand- and footholds.

   d. Find a level stretch where it breaks into a few channels.

9. After walking for about an hour, you feel several spiders in your clothes. You don't feel any pain, but you know some spider bites are painless. Which of these spider bites is painless?

   a. Black widow

   b. Brown recluse

   c. Wolf spider

   d. Harvestman (daddy longlegs)

10. You decide to eat some insects. Which insects should you avoid?

    a. Adults that sting or bite

    b. Caterpillars and insects that have a pungent odour

    c. Hairy or brightly coloured ones

    d. All the above

Group Task

Break into groups of 5 or 6 people. Now imagine that your whole group is lost. Answer each question as a group, employing a consensus approach to reach each decision. Once the group comes to an agreement, write the decision down on the same sheet of paper that you used for your individual answers. You will have approximately 20 minutes for the group task.

WORKING WITH OTHERS EXERCISE (Continued)

Scoring Your Answers

Your instructor will provide you with the correct answers, which are based on expert judgments in these situations. Once you have received the answers, calculate (A) your individual score; (B) your group's score; (C) the average individual score in the group; and (D) the best individual score in the group. Write these down and consult with your group to ensure that these scores are accurate.

(A) Your individual score _____

(B) Your group's score _____

(C) Average individual score in group _____

(D) Best individual score in group _____

Discussion Questions

1. How did your group (B) perform relative to yourself (A)?

2. How did your group (B) perform relative to the average individual score in the group (C)?

3. How did your group (B) perform relative to the best individual score in the group (D)?

4. Compare your results with those of other groups. Did some groups do a better job of outperforming individuals than others?

5. What do these results tell you about the effectiveness of group decision making?

6. What can groups do to make group decision making more effective?

ETHICAL DILEMMA EXERCISE

Five Ethical Decisions: What Would You Do?

Assume that you are a middle manager in a company with about 1000 employees. How would you respond to each of the following situations?[121]

1. You are negotiating a contract with a potentially very large customer whose representative has hinted that you could almost certainly be assured of getting his business if you gave him and his wife an all-expenses-paid cruise to the Caribbean. You know the representative's employer would not approve of such a "payoff," but you have the discretion to authorize such an expenditure. What would you do?

2. You have the opportunity to steal $100 000 from your company with absolute certainty that you would not be detected or caught. Would you do it?

3. Your company policy on reimbursement for meals while travelling on company business is that you will be repaid for your out-of-pocket costs, which are not to exceed $50 a day. You don't need receipts for these expenses—the company will take your word. When travelling, you tend to eat at fast-food places and rarely spend in excess of $15 a day. Most of your colleagues submit reimbursement requests in the range of $40 to $45 a day regardless of what their actual expenses are. How much would you request for your meal reimbursements?

4. Assume that you are the manager at a gaming company, and you are responsible for hiring a group to outsource the production of a highly anticipated new game. Because your company is a giant in the industry, numerous companies are trying to get the

bid. One of them offers you some kickbacks if you give that firm the bid, but ultimately, it is up to your bosses to decide on the company. You don't mention the incentive, but you push upper management to give the bid to the company that offered you the kickback. Is withholding the truth as bad as lying? Why or why not?

5. You have discovered that one of your closest friends at work has stolen a large sum of money from the company. Would you do nothing? Go directly to an executive to report the incident before talking about it with the offender? Confront the individual before taking action? Make contact with the individual with the goal of persuading that person to return the money?

CASE INCIDENTS

The Dangers of Groupthink

Sometimes, the desire to maintain group harmony overrides the importance of making sound decisions. When that occurs, team members are said to engage in groupthink. Here are three examples:[122]

- A civilian worker at a large US Air Force base recalls a time that groupthink overcame her team's decision-making ability. She was a member of a process improvement team that an Air Force general had formed to develop a better way to handle the base's mail, which included important letters from high-ranking military individuals. The team was composed mostly of civilians, and it took almost a month to come up with a plan. The problem: The plan was not a process improvement. Recalls the civilian worker, "I was horrified. What used to be 8 step; now there were 19." The team had devised a new system that resulted in each piece of mail being read by several middle managers before reaching its intended recipient. The team's new plan slowed down the mail considerably, with an average delay of two weeks. Even though the team members all knew that the new system was worse than its predecessor, no one wanted to question the team's solidarity. The problems lasted for almost an entire year. It was not until the general who formed the team complained about the mail that the system was changed.

- Virginia Turezyn, managing director of Infinity Capital, states that during the dot-com boom of the late 1990s, she was a victim of groupthink. At first, Turezyn was skeptical about the stability of the boom. But after continually reading about start-ups turning into multimillion-dollar payoffs, she felt different. Turezyn decided to invest millions in several dot-coms, including I-drive, a company that provided electronic data storage. The problem was that I-drive was giving the storage away for free, and as a result, the company was losing money. Turezyn recalls one board meeting at I-drive where she spoke up to no avail. "We're spending way too much money," she screamed. The younger executives shook their heads and replied that if they charged for storage they would lose their customers. Says Turezyn, "I started to think, 'Maybe I'm just too old. Maybe I really don't get it.'" Unfortunately, Turezyn did get it. I-drive later filed for bankruptcy.

- Steve Blank, an entrepreneur, also fell victim to groupthink. Blank was a dot-com investor, and he participated on the advisory boards of several Internet start-ups. During meetings for one such start-up, a web photo finisher, Blank tried to persuade his fellow board members to change the business model to be more traditional. Recalls Blank, "I went to those meetings and started saying things like, 'Maybe you should spend that $10 million you just raised on acquiring a customer base rather than building a brand.' The CEO told me, 'Steve, you just don't get it—all the rules have changed.'" The team did not take Blank's advice, and Blank says that he lost hundreds of thousands of dollars on the deal.

According to Michael Useem, a professor at the University of Pennsylvania's Wharton College of Business, one of the main reasons that groupthink occurs is a lack of conflict. "A single devil's advocate or whistle-blower faces a really uphill struggle," he states. "But if you [the naysayer] have one ally, that is enormously strengthening."

Questions

1. What are some factors that led to groupthink in the cases described here? What can teams do to attempt to prevent groupthink from occurring?

2. How might differences in status among group members contribute to groupthink? For example, how might lower-status members react to a group's decision? Are lower-status members more or less likely to be dissenters? Why might higher-status group members be more effective dissenters?

3. Microsoft CEO Steve Ballmer says that he encourages dissent. Can such norms guard against the occurrence of groupthink? As a manager, how would you try to cultivate norms that prevent groupthink?

4. How might group characteristics such as size and cohesiveness affect groupthink?

Syncrude Wants to Be a Good Neighbour

Fort McMurray, Alberta-based Syncrude is "one of the largest employers of Aboriginal people in Canada."[123] The company, the largest producer of light sweet crude oil from oil sand, is strongly committed to working with the Aboriginal community. As Syncrude states in its 2007 Aboriginal Review, "As one of the largest employers of Aboriginal people in Canada, Syncrude is committed to providing successful and rewarding careers—whether it be in trades, sciences or business. Our goal is to create opportunities that enable Aboriginal people to fully participate in our operation, today and tomorrow."[124]

To make sure that members of the Aboriginal community are employable, Syncrude provides them with skill training before they are even considered for hiring. This makes it possible for Aboriginal people to compete for jobs in the oil sands industry on an equal footing with non-Aboriginal people. Nora Flett, Syncrude's Aboriginal affairs representative, explains that companies cannot just hire Aboriginal people directly without training, "because you don't just take someone from a small community, put them in a big corporation environment and expect that people will survive there, because that's quite a bit of a culture shock."

In addition to being sensitive to the employment needs of the Aboriginal community, Syncrude is committed to being a good neighbour in the community. The company gives preference to local suppliers to help the local population benefit economically from Syncrude's presence. Syncrude supports literacy programs for schools. As well, employment counsellors offer advice about the company, helping Aboriginal families learn about the company and what is expected of its employees.

Questions

1. What benefits do you think Syncrude might derive from being a good neighbour in Fort McMurray?

2. Should the company engage in practices that help the Aboriginal community, even if it means that the return to shareholders is not as large?

3. How does corporate social responsibility explain what Syncrude does?

From **Concepts** to **Skills**

Solving Problems Creatively

You can be more effective at solving problems creatively if you use the following 10 suggestions:[125]

1. *Think of yourself as creative.* Research shows that if you think you cannot be creative, you won't be. Believing in your ability to be creative is the first step in becoming more creative.

2. *Pay attention to your intuition.* Every individual has a subconscious mind that works well. Sometimes answers will come to you when you least expect them. Listen to that "inner voice." In fact, most creative people will keep a notepad near their bed and write down ideas when the thoughts come to them.

3. *Move away from your comfort zone.* Every individual has a comfort zone in which certainty exists. But creativity and the known often do not mix. To be creative, you need to move away from the status quo and focus your mind on something new.

4. *Determine what you want to do.* This includes such things as taking time to understand a problem before beginning to try to resolve it, getting all the facts in mind, and trying to identify the most important facts.

5. *Think outside the box.* Use analogies whenever possible (for example, could you approach your problem like a fish out of water and look at what the fish does to cope? Or can you use the things you have to do to find your way when it's foggy to help you solve your problem?). Use different problem-solving strategies, such as verbal, visual, mathematical, or theatrical. Look at your problem from a different perspective, or ask yourself what someone else, such as your grandmother, might do if faced with the same situation.

6. *Look for ways to do things better.* This may involve trying consciously to be original, not worrying about looking foolish, keeping an open mind, being alert to odd or puzzling facts, thinking of unconventional ways to use objects and the environment, discarding usual or habitual ways of doing things, and striving for objectivity by being as critical of your own ideas as you would be of someone else's.

7. *Find several right answers.* Being creative means continuing to look for other solutions even when you think you have solved the problem. A better, more creative solution just might be found.

8. *Believe in finding a workable solution.* Like believing in yourself, you also need to believe in your ideas. If you don't think you can find a solution, you probably won't.

9. *Brainstorm with others.* Creativity is not an isolated activity. Bouncing ideas off of others creates a synergistic effect.

10. *Turn creative ideas into action.* Coming up with creative ideas is only part of the process. Once the ideas are generated, they must be implemented. Keeping great ideas in your mind, or on papers that no one will read, does little to expand your creative abilities.

Practising Skills

Every time the phone rings, your stomach clenches and your palms start to sweat. And it's no wonder! As sales manager for Brinkers, a machine tool parts manufacturer, you are besieged by calls from customers who are upset about late deliveries. Your boss, Carter Hererra, acts as both production manager and scheduler. Every time your sales representatives negotiate a sale, it's up to Carter to determine whether production can actually meet the delivery date the customer specifies. And Carter invariably says, "No problem." The good thing about this is that you make a lot of initial sales. The bad news is that production hardly ever meets the shipment dates that Carter authorizes. And he does not seem to be all that concerned about the aftermath of late deliveries. He says: "Our customers know they're getting outstanding quality at a great price. Just let them try to match that anywhere. It can't be done. So even if they have to wait a couple of extra days or weeks, they're still getting the best deal they can." Somehow the customers do not see it that way. And they let you know about their unhappiness. Then it's up to you to try to soothe the relationship. You know this problem has to be taken care of, but what possible solutions are there? After all, how are you going to keep from making your manager angry or making the customers angry? Use your knowledge of creative problem-solving to come up with solutions.

Reinforcing Skills

1. Take 20 minutes to list as many words as you can using the letters in the word *brainstorm.* (There are at least 95.) If you run out of listings before time is up, it's OK to quit early. But try to be as creative as you can.

2. List on a piece of paper some common terms that apply to both water and finance. How many were you able to come up with?

VIDEO CASE INCIDENT

CASE 12 The "Feel-Better" Bracelet

CBC

Q-Ray advertisements say that its "Serious Performance Bracelet" is designed to help people play, work, and live better." The advertisements say that the $200 bracelet—which makes people feel better by balancing positive and negative forces—is ionized using a special secret process.

Golfers claim that the bracelet reduces their pain, so *Marketplace* went looking for answers at the golf course. Sandra Post, a champion golfer, is a paid spokesperson for the bracelet. When Wendy Mesley of *Marketplace* interviews her, Post emphasizes the jewellery aspect of the Q-Ray, not its pain-relief qualities. Mesley also interviews golfers Frank and Sam. Frank tells her that the bracelet has reduced his arthritis pain, but Sam (who also wears one of the bracelets) thinks the pain relief is mostly in peoples' heads.

Advertising that a product provides pain relief is a tricky business. Until 2006, people in Q-Ray ads said that the bracelet had cured their pain. But now they cannot say that because the US Federal Trade Commission ruled that such advertising is deceptive. There are no medical studies to back this claim.

Andrew Park is the man who brought the Q-Ray to North America, and his son Charles is marketing the product in Canada. Park says that 150 000 Q-Rays have been sold in Canada at a price of $200 each. In an interview with Mesley, Park claims that the company does not make pain-relief claims for the product in its advertisements. Mesley shows Park a hidden-camera film clip where he makes a pain-relief claim during the shooting of an infomercial. Park says that he believes that the product reduces pain, and that if a person believes the bracelet will relieve pain, it will. Mesley also plays a hidden camera clip showing retail salespeople telling customers that the Q-Ray reduces arthritic pain. Park says he cannot control what retailers tell their customers.

Marketplace asked Christopher Yip, an engineer at the University of Toronto, to test a Q-Ray bracelet to determine if it was ionized. Yip found that it did not hold an electrical charge and was therefore not ionized. When Park is confronted with this evidence, he says that he never claimed that the bracelet would hold an electrical charge. Rather, he simply says that the bracelet is ionized using an "exclusive ionization process." Hidden-camera video of retail salespeople shows them explaining ionization by saying things like "it picks up the iron in your blood and speeds up circulation" and "negative ions are collected in the ends of the bracelet." Retail salespeople say they are not sure what ionization is.

Mesley also shows Park a hidden-camera interview with the Q-Ray sales coordinator. The coordinator mentions several types of pain that Q-Ray bracelets relieve—migraine, carpal tunnel, and arthritis. Park says that he will have to meet with the sales coordinator and inform her that she cannot make these pain-relief claims.

Questions

1. What is ethics? How is the concept relevant for the Q-ray bracelet situation?

2. List and briefly describe the four criteria that a person might use when trying to make an ethical choice. Which criterion do you think Q-ray used in the marketing of its bracelet? Which criterion do you think should be used?

3. Do you think that individuals at Q-ray are behaving in an ethical or unethical way? Use Exhibit 12-8 to analyze the situation and help you make a decision. Do you see any problems with Exhibit 12-8? Explain.

4. What is social responsibility? Is Q-ray acting in a socially responsible fashion? Defend your answer.

Source: "Buyer Belief," *CBC Marketplace*, November 14, 2007.

Spirituality in the Workplace

Entrepreneur Robin Kirby (shown above) represents clothing manufacturers; she meets with retailers to sell them clothes produced by the factories she represents.[1] She also markets a line of her own clothing on The Shopping Channel.

Kirby is passionate about spiritual connections and the healing arts. "I'm a reiki master and I do crystal bowl healing. I'm known as 'the white witch' among my menswear clients." Kirby sometimes carries a deep crystal bowl and a rubber striker, which she uses to create tones that she says clear "difficult energies from the spaces she visits."

Kirby recently cleared the energy at a client's knitwear factory and showroom, after she arrived to find the staff and the client looking stressed out. She used prayers, meditations, and bowl-ringing to do this. The employees later told her that the workplace stayed calm for a week after she did her energy clearing, and they wanted her to come back and do it again.

What Is Spirituality?

In a study to determine what people mean by *spirituality*, the following elements were identified:[2]

- Not formal, structured, or organized

- Nondenominational, above and beyond denominations

- Broadly inclusive, embracing everyone; universal and timeless

- The ultimate source and provider of meaning and purpose in life

- The awe we feel in the presence of the transcendent

- The sacredness of everything, the ordinariness of everyday life

- The deep feeling of the interconnectedness of everything

- Inner peace and calm

- An inexhaustible source of faith and willpower

- The ultimate end in itself

In general, three streams of definitions have been identified. One stream defines *spirituality* in terms of a personal inner experience based on "interconnectedness."[3] A second stream focuses on "principles, virtues, ethics, values, emotions, wisdom, and intuition."[4] Organizations are then considered spiritual to the extent that they hold these values. Finally, a third stream considers spirituality as the link between one's "personal inner experience" and how this is modelled in "outer behaviours, principles, and practices."[5]

Comparing Spirituality and Religion

Spirituality and religion are not the same thing, although it's sometimes difficult to reach precise definitions of each term. One of the few empirical studies of spirituality in the workplace was conducted by Ian Mitroff and Elizabeth Denton.[6] Though the response rate to their mailed survey was low, they corroborated many of their findings through interviews with human resource managers and senior managers at other organizations. They discovered that individuals fall into four patterns in terms of how they view the relationship between religion and spirituality:

- *A person views both religion and spirituality positively.* This person sees religion and spirituality as synonymous, with spirituality developed through religious practices. About 30 percent of the participants fell into this category.

- *A person views religion positively but spirituality negatively.* This person focuses on the rituals and the practices of a particular religion. The emphasis is on salvation and being a member of a closely bound, shared community. About 2 percent of the participants fell into this category.

- *A person views religion negatively, but views spirituality positively.* This person sees religion as "organized, close-minded, and intolerant." Spirituality, by contrast, is viewed as "open-minded, tolerant, and universal," and intended to be a bonding force. About 60 percent of the participants fell into this category.

- *Finally, a person views both religion and spirituality negatively.* This person believes that "religion and spirituality have nothing to do with the modern, secular workplace." About 8 percent of the participants fell into this category.

These findings suggest that workplace spirituality is not about organized religious practices. It's not about God or theology. Workplace spirituality recognizes that people have an inner life that nourishes and is nourished by meaningful work that takes place in the context of community.[7] Organizations that promote a spiritual culture recognize that people have both a mind and a spirit, seek to find meaning and purpose in their work, and desire to connect with other human beings and be part of a community.

For instance, at Montreal-based Ouimet-Cordon Bleu Foods, a processed-foods company, CEO J. Robert Ouimet has installed meditation rooms in all of his factories. He took his idea from a conversation he had with Mother Teresa. "There is no talking or eating allowed—only silence. The idea is to give the workplace a feeling of serenity and a sense of higher purpose," he explains.[8] Ouimet wants his workplace to be not only a place where goods are produced, but also where employees find their lives enriched. He believes such practices as meditation rooms, prayers before meetings, and other "soulful initiatives" increase "not only human happiness and well-being, but company profitability as well."[9]

Another company that tries to encourage employees to look beyond themselves is New Hampshire-based Timberland, where boots symbolize what customers and employees are supposed to do: "Pull on your boots and make a difference."[10] The company pays its employees for up to 40 hours of volunteer work a year. It has also developed a plan for employees to apply for six-month paid sabbaticals if they want to give service to a nonprofit organization. Jeffrey B. Swartz, the company's president and CEO, believes that "doing well" and "doing good" help make this family-owned firm successful.

Why Spirituality Now?

Employees working for the District of North Vancouver take workshops to help them develop personal and professional effectiveness.[11] The workshops are led by Tanis Helliwell, a therapist in Vancouver, and are based on her book *Take Your Soul to Work*.[12] David Stuart, director of corporate services at the District of North Vancouver, read her book and decided that the municipality's 600 employees, be they ditch diggers or architects, would benefit from its practices.

Helliwell believes that employers should help their employees develop their whole person, rather than just the "9-to-5 person." "The more people look at what they need to do in order to develop their potential and find work that will encompass that, the more the employer is going to get in the workplace," she says.

Stuart says that the response to the workshops has been "spectacular." "Workers are expecting more from their employment situation. They need tools to give them a sense that they can in fact control what's happening in their lives and the changes happening around them and how they deal with them," he explains.

Workplace spirituality is a relatively new phenomenon. Historical models of management and organizational behaviour had no room for spirituality. The myth of rationality assumed that the well-run organization eliminated feelings. Similarly, concern about an employee's inner life had no role in the perfectly rational model. But just as we have now come to realize that the study of emotions improves our understanding of organizational behaviour, an awareness of spirituality can help us better understand employee behaviour in the twenty-first century.

The Sobey School of Business at Saint Mary's University in Halifax has taken the lead in Canada for trying to understand the implications of spirituality in the workplace. In fall 2004, the Sobey School of Business opened a centre devoted to teaching and studying spirituality in the workplace. The Centre for Spirituality in the Workplace is the first academic-based centre of its kind in Canada, though there are such centres in the United States and overseas.

"The centre is not devoted to religious dogma and theology," Allan Miciak, former dean of the Sobey School of Business, explains. Spirituality at work is about "creating better workplaces," he adds.[13]

Martin Rutte, co-author of *Chicken Soup for the Soul at Work*,[14] who spoke at a conference that marked the centre's opening, notes that "Over the past several years, there have been dramatic changes in the world of work, such as corporate downsizing, that have forced people to do more with less, and technologies that have replaced people." "These things have broken the feeling of security that came with work and changed people's attitudes about their jobs," he says.[15]

We summarize additional reasons why people are turning to spirituality in the inset *Reasons for the Growing Interest in Spirituality*.

Characteristics of a Spiritual Organization

Spiritual organizations are concerned with helping people develop and reach their full potential. This is analogous to Abraham Maslow's description of self-actualization that we discussed in relation to motivation in Chapter 4.

Reasons for the Growing Interest in Spirituality

- Spirituality acts as a counterbalance to the pressures and stress of a turbulent pace of life. Contemporary lifestyles—single-parent families, geographic mobility, the temporary nature of jobs, new technologies that create distance between people—underscore the lack of community many people feel and increase the need for involvement and connection.

- Formalized religion has not worked for many people, and they continue to look for anchors to replace lack of faith and to fill a growing feeling of emptiness.

- Job demands have made the workplace dominant in many people's lives, yet they continue to question the meaning of work.

- More people desire to integrate personal life values with their professional life.

- An increasing number of people are finding that the pursuit of more material acquisitions leaves them unfulfilled.

Similarly, organizations that are concerned with spirituality are more likely to directly address problems created by conflicts that occur in everyday life.

Sister Mangalam Lena, of the Franciscan Missionaries of Mary, started Ottawa-based Home-based Spiritual Care (HBSC) to help recovering patients in their homes. "[Traditional] home care provides nursing, counselling, and physiotherapy for the home-bound. But who cares for their spiritual needs in the home?" she asked.[16] This led to the start of her business. Lena believes that "people who are spiritually healthy are also physically healthier." She has convinced researchers at the University of Ottawa, including Dian Prud'homme Brisson, assistant director of the university's nursing program, to study the effects of such care.

New employees at Banff, Alberta-based High Country Inn might be surprised the first time they meet the inn's corporate chaplain, Lee-Ann Lavoie. She started working there in 2006, and sees her job as being to "offer care and support." "One thing I truly believe is that there is a spiritual side of life, and everyone has a spiritual side," Lavoie says. "Corporate chaplains open people up to that side at work."[17]

Canadian companies are starting to address the spiritual needs of employees. Scarborough, Ontario-based TELUS Mobility created prayer and meditation rooms for its employees, which led to it winning an award from the Association for Spirit at Work in 2002. TELUS's Transformation Workshop for call-centre employees have reduced turnover significantly. Edmonton-based CapitalCare, whose employees care for elderly and disabled adults, created a spirituality program emphasizing meditation for nurses and aides who work there.[18]

What differentiates spiritual organizations from their nonspiritual counterparts? Although research on this question is only preliminary, our review identified five cultural characteristics that tend to be evident in spiritual organizations.[19]

Strong Sense of Purpose

Spiritual organizations build their cultures around a meaningful purpose. While profits may be important, they are not necessarily the primary value of these organizations. People want to be inspired by a purpose that they believe is important and worthwhile. Nova Scotia-based Northwood, the largest nonprofit seniors' health care organization in Eastern Canada, offers full-time pastoral care in addition to the traditional services of a seniors facility. For Gael Page, who consults to Northwood, the emphasis on spirituality makes Northwood a better place to work. "There used to be a day when I was a nurse that you came to work and put your whole personal life aside, you'd pretend it didn't exist. It was very unnatural to be asked to do that. The whole workplace spirituality movement has changed all that. Workplace spirituality recognizes that we are all complex with many dimensions."[20]

Charlotte Kwon, owner and CEO of Vancouver-based Maiwa Handprints, pays the artisans from developing countries who provide textiles for her retail stores substantially more than what others pay them. She wants to protect craftspeople, so that they can continue to produce their artwork. She also notes that she does not need to pay minimum prices to survive: "I live okay. I don't need anything more."[21]

Focus on Individual Development

Spiritual organizations recognize the worth and value of people. They are not just providing jobs. They seek to create cultures in which employees can continually learn and grow. Recognizing the importance of people, they also try to provide employment security.

Trust and Openness

Spiritual organizations are characterized by mutual trust, honesty, and openness. Managers are not afraid to admit mistakes. They tend to be extremely upfront with their employees, customers, and suppliers. The president of Wetherill Associates, a highly successful American auto parts distribution firm, says, "We don't tell lies here, and everyone knows it. We are specific and honest about quality and suitability of the product for our customers' needs, even if we know they might not be able to detect any problem."[22]

FactBox

- 43% of Canadians believe the country is undergoing a "renaissance of spirituality."

- 39% of Canadians said religion was important to them, compared with 61 percent who said it was not.

- 43% of Canadians attended a religious service (not including weddings and funerals) in the previous six months.

- 60% of Americans say religious beliefs play a role in decision making at work.[23]

Employee Empowerment

The high-trust climate in spiritual organizations, when combined with the desire to promote employee learning and growth, leads to management empowering employees to make many work-related decisions. Managers in such organizations are comfortable delegating authority to individual employees and teams. They trust their employees to make thoughtful and conscientious decisions. Southwest Airlines exhibits these kinds of values when its employees—including flight attendants, customer-service representatives, and baggage handlers—are encouraged to take whatever action they deem necessary to meet customer needs or help fellow employees, even if it means breaking company policies.

Humanistic Work Practices

These practices embraced by spiritual organizations include flexible work schedules, group- and organization-based rewards, narrowing of pay and status differentials, guarantees of individual employee rights, employee empowerment, and job security. Hewlett-Packard, for instance, has handled temporary downturns through voluntary attrition and shortened workweeks (shared by all), and it has handled longer-term declines through early retirements and buyouts.

Toleration of Employee Expression

Finally, spiritual organizations don't stifle employee emotions. They allow people to be themselves—to express their moods and feelings without guilt or fear of reprimand. Employees at Southwest Airlines, for instance, are encouraged to express their sense of humour on the job, to act spontaneously, and to make their work fun.

At Ouimet-Cordon Bleu Foods, employees are encouraged to have annual one-on-one meetings with their managers where employees can express any and all frustrations without worrying that something negative will happen to them. When Ouimet first introduced this practice, employees were reluctant to voice their concerns. As Ouimet notes, "Over time, a sense of trust developed."[24] Ouimet's employees are also encouraged to engage in "gestures of reconciliation," where they apologize to one another when interpersonal conflicts arise. Ouimet says he sets the example by apologizing when he has "blown a gasket."

The inset *Organizational Models for Fostering Spirituality* describes models for spiritually based organizations.

Organizational Models for Fostering Spirituality

- **Religion-Based Organization:** The organization's practices are consistent with biblical teachings; there is an emphasis on prayer as a primary form of intrafirm communication; employees are expected to accept core Christian principles as guides to decision making.

- **Evolutionary Organization:** Spiritual openness is encouraged; the guiding texts are a mixture of Christian scriptures and philosophical works (Kant, Neibuhr, Buber); there is an emphasis on serving the customer, preserving the environment, and respecting stakeholders.

- **Recovering Organization:** The organization models itself after the 12-step program of Alcoholics Anonymous; spirituality is discussed in ways that are acceptable to the largest number of people. The 12-step program emphasizes confession (of failures), acceptance of God's will and guidance, and reliance on the help of others. This model is infrequently found in the business world.

- **Socially Responsible Organization:** Social concerns and values are part of everyday business activities; the organization emphasizes the expression of the individual's "whole person" and soul; customers, suppliers, and other stakeholders are expected to bond more readily to the firm; spirituality and soul are explicit core business principles.

- **Values-Based Organization:** The organization firmly rejects all notions of religious doctrine; it favours nonreligious and nonspiritual secular values or virtues (e.g., awareness, consciousness, dignity, honesty, openness, respect, integrity, and, above all, trust); values are guides for policy setting and decision making throughout the firm. The Golden Rule is the prime business principle.

- **Best-Practice Model:** The organization combines parts of all of the above models; it emphasizes values-based secular orientation; it adds an openly expressed spiritual dimension; it emphasizes the importance of "a higher power," periodic moral audits, and a broadly inclusive approach to stakeholders.[25]

Criticisms of Spirituality

Critics of organizations that embrace spiritual values have focused on three issues. First is the question of scientific foundation. What, really, is workplace spirituality? Is it just a new management buzzword? Second is the question of legitimacy. Specifically, do organizations have the right to impose spiritual values on their employees? Third is the question of economics: Are spirituality and profits compatible?

First, there is disagreement on how to conduct research on workplace spirituality.[26] Do the cultural characteristics just identified really separate spiritual organizations? What is a nonspiritual organization, anyway? Do employees of so-called spiritual organizations perceive that they work in spiritual organizations? Although there is some research suggesting support for workplace spirituality (as we discuss later), before the concept of spirituality gains full credence, the questions we have just posed need to be answered.

On the second question, clearly it is possible that an emphasis on spirituality may make some employees uneasy. Critics might argue that secular institutions, especially business firms, have no business imposing spiritual values on employees. This criticism is undoubtedly valid when spirituality is defined as bringing religion and God into the workplace.[27] However, the criticism seems less stinging when the goal is limited to helping employees find meaning in their work lives. If the concerns listed in the inset *Reasons for the Growing Interest in Spirituality* on page 494 truly characterize a growing segment of the workforce, maybe the time is right for more organizations to help

employees find meaning and purpose in their work and to use the workplace as a source of community.

The issue of whether spirituality and profits are compatible objectives is certainly relevant for managers and investors in business. However limited it may be, there is evidence that the two objectives may be very compatible. A research study by a major consulting firm found that companies that introduced spiritually based techniques improved productivity and significantly reduced turnover.[28] Another study found organizations that provide their employees with opportunities for spiritual development outperformed those that did not.[29] Other studies also report that spirituality in organizations was positively related to creativity, employee satisfaction, team performance, and organizational commitment.[30]

The cynic will say that all this caring stuff is in fact merely good public relations. Even so, the results at both Southwest Airlines and Ouimet-Cordon Bleu Foods suggest that a caring organization is good for the bottom line. Southwest Airlines is strongly committed to providing the lowest airfares, on-time service, and a pleasant experience for customers. Southwest employees have one of the lowest turnover rates in the airline industry, the company consistently has the lowest labour costs per miles flown of any major airline, and it has proven itself to be the most consistently profitable airline in the

United States.[31] Of Ouimet-Cordon Bleu Foods' 55 employees, 32 have been there for more than 20 years. Jacques Gingras, a production manager with the company, says Ouimet's practices really help the bottom line. "Obviously, people can't go to the silence rooms whenever they want, because we're running an assembly line. But they communicate well and respect one another. It makes the operation run more smoothly."[32]

Research Exercises

1. Look for data on the extent to which companies encourage spirituality in the workplace in Canada and the United States. Can you draw any inferences about whether there is a trend in this practice?

2. Identify three Canadian organizations or CEOs who have encouraged more openness toward spirituality in their organizations. What, if any, commonalities exist in these organizations?

Your Perspective

1. In this feature, we report on individuals' views on religion and spirituality. Do you see the two as linked or not linked?

2. What does spirituality mean to you?

Want to Know More?

Top executives at the Bank of Montreal read Ann Coombs' *The Living Workplace: Soul, Spirit and Success in the 21st Century* (Toronto: HarperCollins Canada, 2001), and were so impressed that they bought 800 copies, put the bank's logo on them, and started giving copies to their clients. Coombs is a Toronto-based corporate consultant, whose clients include Ford Canada, Campbell Soup Company, and TELUS.

Other books to consider include Joan Marques, Satinder Dhiman, and Richard King, *Spirituality in the Workplace: What It Is, Why It Matters, How to Make It Work for You* (Fawskin, CA: Personhood Press, 2007); and Gregory F. Augustine Pierce, *Spirituality at Work: 10 Ways to Balance Your Life on the Job* (Chicago, IL: Loyola Press, 2001).

Organizational Structure

What happens when an activity, such as filming a movie, needs to bring large groups of people together for a limited time? How do you design an organizational structure that will be flexible enough, yet ensure the work gets done?

1 What are the key elements of organizational structure?

2 How flexible can organizational structures be?

3 What are some examples of traditional organizational designs?

4 What do newer organizational structures look like?

5 Why do organizational structures differ?

*B*rollywood, the affectionate name given to the "Hollywood North" located in Vancouver because of the frequent need for umbrellas (brollies) in the city, is third behind Los Angeles and New York in the size of its movie industry.[1] It's big in every way imaginable: more than a billion dollars a year, about 230 productions a year, standard 60-hour weeks, substantial rewards. But, unlike the American cities or Toronto or Montreal, Brollywood has no major entertainment company or television network attached to it.

Vancouver's film industry represents a new and unique form of organization. Though there are a number of established production companies, the industry is also "made up of self-employed individuals, niche suppliers and production companies that start up and shut down in a matter of months." Companies don't just get things done in Vancouver's film industry; teams of free agents also do.

Brollywood's organizational structure is unusual, although more organizations are developing flexible structures and developing long- and short-term partnerships to get specific tasks done.

The theme of this chapter is that organizations have different structures, determined by specific forces, and that these structures have a bearing on employee attitudes and behaviour. Organizations need to think carefully about the best way to organize how people inside and outside the organization are connected to each other. These connections form the basis for organizational structure.

OB Is for Everyone

- What happens when a person performs the same task over and over again?
- What happens when you report to two bosses?
- Can an organization really have no boundaries?
- So what does *technology* mean?

Self-Assessment Library

LEARNING ABOUT YOURSELF

- Delegation
- Bureaucratic Orientation

What Is Organizational Structure?

1 What are the key elements of organizational structure?

organizational structure How job tasks are formally divided, grouped, and coordinated.

An **organizational structure** defines how job tasks are formally divided, grouped, and coordinated. The structure can represent a tall pyramid, or it can be relatively flat. For instance, Exhibit 13-1 shows a pyramidal organization with five layers (and some organizations have even more), while Exhibit 13-2 shows a flatter organization, with only three layers. The organizational structure can also be something intermediate between pyramid and flat. Among other things, the structure determines the reporting relationships of people. Thus, in a flat organization, if you have a problem, you can easily talk to the person at the top of the organization. In a pyramidal structure, you would talk to your manager, who might talk to his or her manager, who might talk to the manager above, until finally, if the message did actually reach the top of the organization, it might be very different from the original message you told your manager.

There are six key elements that managers need to address when they design their organization's structure: work specialization, departmentalization, chain of command, span of control, centralization and decentralization, and formalization.[2] Exhibit 13-3 presents all of these elements as answers to an important structural question. The following sections describe these six elements of structure. Organizations do change their structures from time to time, which is known as *restructuring*. Often this involves layoffs. Despite the profound impact restructuring has on employees, managers realize

EXHIBIT 13-1　Pyramidal Organizational Structure

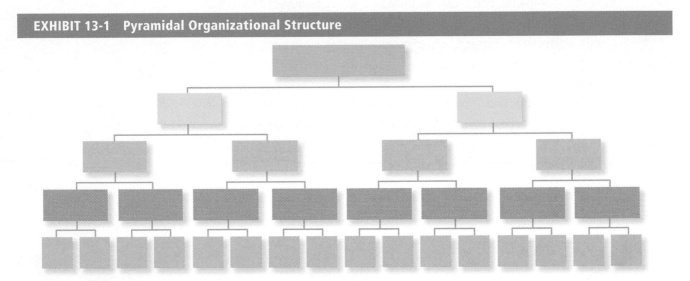

EXHIBIT 13-2　Flat Organizational Structure

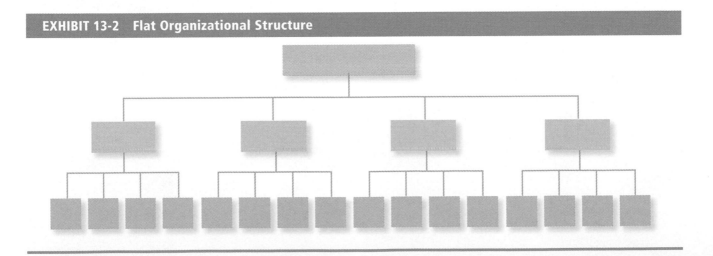

that in a dynamic and changing environment, inflexible organizations end up as bankruptcy statistics. This chapter's *Case Incident—Ajax University Needs a New Structure* on page 533 provides an opportunity for you to consider how to change an organizational structure in order to resolve some of the problems the organization faces.

Work Specialization

We use the term **work specialization**, or *division of labour*, to describe the degree to which tasks in the organization are subdivided into separate jobs.

What happens when a person performs the same task over and over again?

The essence of work specialization is that, rather than an entire job being completed by one individual, it's broken down into a number of steps, with each step being completed by a separate individual. In essence, individuals specialize in doing part of an activity rather than the entire activity.

Specialization can be efficient. Employee skills at performing a task improve through repetition. Less time is spent in changing tasks, in putting away tools and equipment from a prior step in the work process, and in preparing for another. It's easier and less costly to find and train workers to do specific and repetitive tasks. This is especially true of highly sophisticated and complex operations. For example, could Montreal-based Bombardier produce even one Canadian regional jet a year if one person had to build the entire plane alone? Not likely! Finally, work specialization increases efficiency and productivity by encouraging the creation of special inventions and machinery.

Specialization can lead to boredom, fatigue, stress, low productivity, poor quality, increased absenteeism, and high turnover, so it is not always the best way to organize employees. Giving employees a variety of activities to do, allowing them to do a whole and complete job, and putting them into teams with interchangeable skills can result in significantly higher output and increased employee satisfaction.

Organizations today exhibit a range of specialization. You will find, for example, high work specialization being used by McDonald's to make and sell hamburgers and fries efficiently, and by medical specialists in hospitals. On the other hand, companies such as Saturn have had success by broadening the scope of jobs and reducing specialization.

Individual Responses to Work Specialization

The evidence generally indicates that *work specialization* contributes to higher employee productivity but at the price of reduced job satisfaction. However, this statement ignores individual differences and the type of job tasks people do.

work specialization The degree to which tasks in the organization are subdivided into separate jobs.

EXHIBIT 13-3	Six Key Questions That Managers Need to Answer in Designing the Proper Organizational Structure	
The Key Question	**The Answer Is Provided By**
1. To what degree are tasks subdivided into separate jobs?	*Work specialization*
2. On what basis will jobs be grouped together?	*Departmentalization*
3. To whom do individuals and groups report?	*Chain of command*
4. How many individuals can a manager efficiently and effectively direct?	*Span of control*
5. Where does decision-making authority lie?	*Centralization and decentralization*
6. To what degree will there be rules and regulations to direct employees and managers?	*Formalization*

Work is specialized at the Russian factories that manufacture the wooden nesting dolls called matryoshkas. At this factory outside Moscow, individuals specialize in doing part of the doll production, from the craftsmen who carve the dolls to the painters who decorate them. Work specialization brings efficiency to doll production, as some 50 employees can make 100 matryoshkas every two days.

As we noted previously, productivity begins to suffer when the human diseconomies of doing repetitive and narrow tasks overtake the economies of specialization. As the workforce has become more highly educated and desirous of jobs that are intrinsically rewarding, the point where productivity begins to decline seems to be reached more quickly than in decades past.

However, some individuals want work that makes minimal intellectual demands and provides the security of routine. For these people, high work specialization is a source of job satisfaction.

Departmentalization

departmentalization The basis on which jobs are grouped together.

Once you have divided up jobs through work specialization, you need to group these jobs together so that common tasks can be coordinated. The basis on which jobs are grouped together is called **departmentalization**. One of the concerns related to departmental groups is that they can become *silos* within an organization. Often, departments start protecting their own turf and not interacting well with other departments, which can lead to a narrow vision with respect to organizational goals.

Functional Departmentalization

One of the most popular ways to group activities is by *functions* performed. For example, a manufacturing company might separate engineering, accounting, manufacturing, human resource, and purchasing specialists into common departments. Similarly, a hospital might have departments devoted to research, patient care, accounting, and so forth. The major advantage to functional groupings is obtaining efficiencies from putting people with common skills and orientations together into common units. Exhibit 13-4 illustrates how the City of Vancouver, in British Columbia, organizes its departments by function. Note that the chart reveals 10 main functions: community services, human resource services, engineering services, fire and rescue services, financial services, business

EXHIBIT 13-4   Departmentalization by Function

City of Vancouver

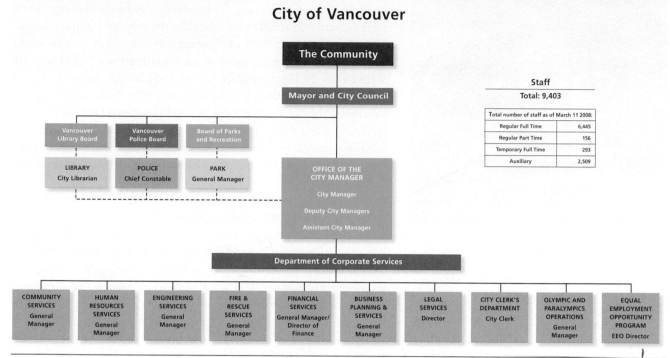

Staff

Total: 9,403

Total number of staff as of March 11 2008:	
Regular Full Time	6,445
Regular Part Time	156
Temporary Full Time	293
Auxiliary	2,509

Source: City Clerk's Department, City of Vancouver, "Organizational Chart," http://vancouver.ca/ctyclerk/orgcharts/109organization.pdf (accessed September 16, 2008). With permission.

planning and services, legal services, city clerk's department, Olympic and Paralympics operations, and equal employment opportunity program.

Product Departmentalization

Tasks can also be departmentalized by the type of *product* the organization produces. Estée Lauder, whose product lines include Clinique, Prescriptives, Origins, Canadian-created MAC Cosmetics, and Estée Lauder, operates each line as a distinct company. The major advantage to this type of grouping is increased accountability for product performance, since all activities related to a specific product line are under the direction of a single manager. If an organization's activities are service—rather than product—related, each service would be grouped autonomously. For instance, many of the big accounting firms now call themselves "professional services firms" to reflect the variety of services they offer, including tax, management consulting, auditing, and the like. Each of the different services is under the direction of a product or service manager.

Exhibit 13-5 illustrates Toronto-based Royal Bank of Canada's three distinct businesses, which are organized by product lines to make it easier to service very different customer needs.

EXHIBIT 13-5   Departmentalization by Product

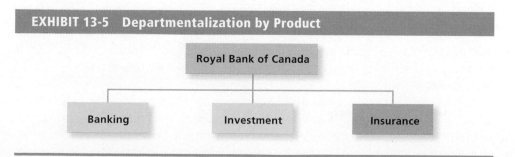

Until the mid-1990s, Montreal-based Hydro-Québec had been organized geographically, with each territory having its own business units responsible for production, transmission, and distribution, for a total of 40 business units. However, they decided that being organized functionally made more sense. Now they have only four divisions (Hydro-Québec Production, Hydro-Québec TransÉnergie, Hydro-Québec Distribution, and Hydro-Québec Équipement). They expect this change in structure will lead to greater growth in business both inside and outside Quebec.

Geographic Departmentalization

Another way to departmentalize is on the basis of geography, or territory. The sales function, for instance, may be divided regionally with departments for British Columbia, the Prairies, Central Canada, and Atlantic Canada. Each of these regions is, in effect, a department organized around geography. If an organization's customers are scattered over a large geographic area and have similar needs based on their location, then this form of departmentalization can be valuable. Exhibit 13-6 illustrates how Halifax-based Graybar Canada, an electrical and data/communication wholesale distributor, organizes itself by regional units: Harris & Roome Supply (which serves Atlantic Canada), Graybar Ontario, and Graybar West (which serves British Columbia to Manitoba).

Process Departmentalization

Some companies organize departments by the processing that occurs. For example, an aluminum tubing manufacturer might have the following departments: casting; press; tubing; finishing; and inspecting, packing, and shipping. This is an example of process departmentalization, because each department specializes in one specific phase in the production of aluminum tubing. Since each process requires different skills, this method offers a basis for the homogeneous categorizing of activities.

Process departmentalization can be used for processing customers, as well as products. For example, in some provinces, you may go through a series of steps handled by several departments before receiving your driver's licence: (1) validation by a motor vehicles division; (2) processing by the licensing department; and (3) payment collection by the treasury department.

Customer Departmentalization

Yet another way to departmentalize is on the basis of the particular type of customer the organization seeks to reach. The sales activities in an office supply firm, for instance, can be broken down into three departments to provide specialized service to different customer categories: service retail, wholesale, and government customers. A large law office can segment its staff on the basis of whether they service corporate or individual clients. The assumption underlying customer departmentalization is that customers of each department have a common set of problems and needs that can best be met by having specialists for each. Exhibit 13-7 illustrates how Dell Canada is divided into sales marketing units according to the type of customer serviced.

Organizational Variety in Departmentalization

Large organizations sometimes change their departmentalization to reflect new needs or emphases. In February 2002, Toronto-based TD Canada Trust announced that it

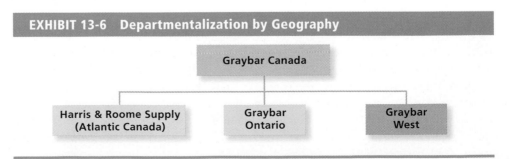

EXHIBIT 13-6   Departmentalization by Geography

Graybar Canada

Harris & Roome Supply (Atlantic Canada)   Graybar Ontario   Graybar West

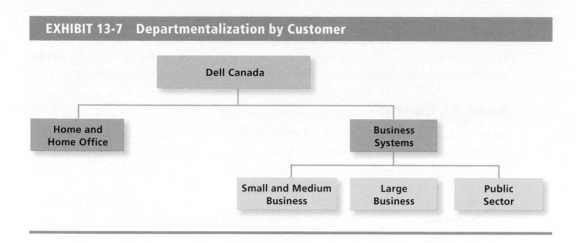

EXHIBIT 13-7   Departmentalization by Customer

would combine three of its businesses (private client services, discount brokerage, and financial planning) under the TD Waterhouse banner. The bank said that this move would help it better meet its customer needs. The former structure—with separate units for full-service, discount brokerage, and financial planning needs—was a product-oriented structure. Kathryn Del Greco, senior advisor at TD Waterhouse, explains why a comprehensive services strategy makes sense: Baby Boomers, who will be retiring in large numbers over the next 10 years, prefer to have all their investment needs (advice and service) offered within the same unit.[3] Large organizations often combine forms of departmentalization. For example, a major Japanese electronics firm organizes each of its divisions along functional lines and its manufacturing units around processes; it departmentalizes sales around seven geographic regions, and divides each sales region into four customer groupings. Two general trends in departmentalization seem to be gaining momentum. First, many organizations have given greater emphasis to customer departmentalization. Second, rigid, functional departmentalization is being increasingly complemented by teams that cross over traditional departmental lines. As we described in Chapter 6, as tasks have become more complex, and more diverse skills are needed to accomplish those tasks, management has turned to cross-functional teams.

Organizations may choose to go a step further than departmentalization and actually turn departments into divisions that are separate profit centres. For instance, within Estée Lauder's product-based departmentalization (discussed earlier), the Clinique, Prescriptives, Origins, MAC Cosmetics, and Estée Lauder product lines are each separate profit centres, responsible for setting their own strategic goals.

Chain of Command

The **chain of command** is the continuous line of authority that extends from upper organizational levels to the lowest level and clarifies who reports to whom. It helps employees answer questions such as, "Who do I go to if I have a problem?" and "To whom do I report?"

Twenty-five years ago, the chain-of-command concept was a basic cornerstone in the design of organizations. Today's workplace is substantially different.

Because managers have limited time and knowledge, they may choose to delegate some of their responsibilities to other employees. **Delegation** is the assignment of authority to another person to carry out specific duties, allowing the employee to make some of the decisions. Delegation is an important part of a manager's job, as it can ensure that the right people are part of the decision-making process. Through delegation, employees are being empowered to make decisions that previously were reserved for management. This chapter's *From Concepts to Skills* on pages 535–536 presents strategies to be a better delegator.

chain of command The continuous line of authority that extends from upper organizational levels to the lowest level and clarifies who reports to whom.

delegation Assignment of authority to another person to carry out specific duties, allowing the employee to make some of the decisions.

Self-managed and cross-functional teams, along with new structural designs that include multiple bosses, have decreased the relevance of the chain-of-command concept. There are, of course, still many organizations that find they can be most productive by enforcing the chain of command. There just seem to be fewer of them nowadays.

Span of Control

span of control The number of employees that report to a manager.

Span of control refers to the number of employees who report to a manager. This number will vary by organization, and by unit within an organization, and is determined by the number of employees a manager can efficiently and effectively direct. In an assembly-line factory, a manager may be able to direct numerous employees, because the work is well defined and controlled by machinery. A sales manager, by contrast, might have to give one-on-one supervision to individual sales reps, and, therefore, fewer would report to the sales manager. All things being equal, the wider or larger the span, the more efficient the organization. An example can illustrate the validity of this statement.

Assume that we have two organizations, both of which have approximately 4100 operative-level employees. As Exhibit 13-8 illustrates, if one has a uniform span of 4 and the other a span of 8, the wider span would have 2 fewer levels and approximately 800 fewer managers. If the average manager earned $56 000 a year, the wider span would save about $45 million a year in management salaries! Obviously, wider spans are more efficient in terms of cost. However, at some point, wider spans become less effective. That is, when the span becomes too large, employee performance suffers because managers no longer have the time to provide the necessary leadership and support.

Narrow or small spans have their advocates. By keeping the span of control to 5 or 6 employees, a manager can maintain close control.[4] But narrow spans have three major drawbacks. First, as already described, they are expensive because they add levels of management. Second, they make vertical communication in the organization more complex. The added levels of hierarchy slow down decision making and tend to isolate upper management. Third, narrow spans of control encourage overly tight supervision and discourage employee autonomy.

The trend in recent years has been toward wider spans of control, in part because of downsizing and the move to teamwork in some organizations.[5] Wider spans of control are also consistent with recent efforts by companies to reduce costs, cut overhead, speed up decision making, increase flexibility, get closer to customers, and empower

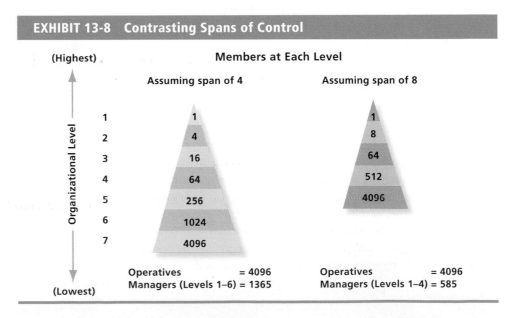

EXHIBIT 13-8   Contrasting Spans of Control

(Highest)

Members at Each Level

Organizational Level

Assuming span of 4

Level	Members
1	1
2	4
3	16
4	64
5	256
6	1024
7	4096

Operatives   = 4096
Managers (Levels 1–6) = 1365

Assuming span of 8

Level	Members
1	1
2	8
3	64
4	512
5	4096

Operatives   = 4096
Managers (Levels 1–4) = 585

(Lowest)

employees. However, to ensure that performance does not suffer because of these wider spans, organizations have been investing heavily in employee training. Managers recognize that they can handle a wider span when employees know their jobs inside and out or can turn to their co-workers when they have questions.

Individual Responses to Span of Control

A review of the research indicates that it's probably safe to say that there is no evidence to support a relationship between span of control and employee performance. While it is intuitively attractive to argue that large spans might lead to higher employee performance because they provide more distant supervision and more opportunity for personal initiative, the research fails to support this notion. At this point it's impossible to state that any particular span of control is best for producing high performance or high satisfaction among employees. The reason is, again, probably individual differences. That is, some people like to be left alone, while others prefer the security of a manager who is quickly available at all times. Consistent with several of the contingency theories of leadership discussed in Chapter 11, we would expect factors such as employees' experiences and abilities, and the degree of structure in their tasks, to explain when wide or narrow spans of control are likely to contribute to employees' performance and job satisfaction. However, there is some evidence to indicate that a manager's job satisfaction increases as the number of employees he or she supervises increases.

Centralization and Decentralization

Centralization refers to the degree to which decision making is concentrated at a single point in the organization. The concept includes only formal authority; that is, the rights inherent in one's position. Typically, it's said that if top management makes the organization's key decisions with little or no input from lower-level employees, then the organization is centralized. In contrast, the more that lower-level employees provide input or are actually given the discretion to make decisions, the more **decentralization** there is. As Dilbert points out in Exhibit 13-9 on page 510, however, some organizations do not seem able to decide upon an appropriate level of decentralization.

centralization The degree to which decision making is concentrated at a single point in the organization.

decentralization The degree to which decision making is distributed to lower-level employees.

An organization characterized by centralization is a much different structural animal from one that is decentralized. In a decentralized organization, action can be taken more quickly to solve problems, more people provide input into decisions, and employees are less likely to feel alienated from those who make the decisions that affect their work lives. Decentralized departments make it easier to address customer concerns as well.

Consistent with recent management efforts to make organizations more flexible and responsive, there has been a marked trend toward decentralizing decision making. The reason for decentralization in large companies is that lower-level managers are closer to "the action" and typically have more detailed knowledge about problems than do top managers. Big retailers such as The Bay and Sears Canada have given their store managers considerably more discretion in choosing what merchandise to stock. This allows those stores to compete more effectively against local merchants.

Individual Responses to Centralization

We find fairly strong evidence linking centralization and job satisfaction. In general, organizations that are less centralized have a greater amount of participative decision making. The evidence

When Surrey, BC, RCMP decentralized their offices, the results were positive. Merchants, local politicians, and police in Surrey say they are happy with the results. Some crime statistics have dropped, and the police feel that they are closer to the people they serve. The RCMP split their force into five units operating at regional stations, rather than out of one headquarters opposite Surrey's city hall. The advantage is that "regional offices can concentrate on the unique problems of the various areas."

EXHIBIT 13-9

Source: S. Adams, *Dogbert's Big Book of Business*, DILBERT reprinted by permission of United Feature Syndicate, Inc.

suggests that participative decision making is positively related to job satisfaction. But, again, individual differences surface. The decentralization-satisfaction relationship is strongest with employees who have low self-esteem. Because individuals with low self-esteem have less confidence in their abilities, they place a higher value on shared decision making, which means that they are not held solely responsible for decision outcomes.

Formalization

formalization The degree to which jobs within the organization are standardized.

Formalization refers to the degree to which jobs within the organization are standardized. If jobs are highly formalized, there are explicit job descriptions, lots of organizational rules, and clearly defined procedures covering work processes in organizations. Employees can be expected always to handle the same input in exactly the same way, resulting in a consistent and uniform output where there is high formalization. Where formalization is low, job behaviours are relatively nonprogrammed, and employees have a great deal of freedom to exercise discretion in their work. Because an individual's discretion on the job is inversely related to the amount of behaviour in that job that is preprogrammed by the organization, the greater the standardization, the less input the employee has into how his or her work is to be done. Standardization not only eliminates the possibility of employees engaging in alternative behaviours, but also removes the need for employees to consider alternatives.

The tasks of these women making cookies at a factory in South Korea are highly standardized. Individual differences influence how these employees respond to their high work specialization. For these women, specialization may be a source of job satisfaction because it provides the security of routine and gives them the chance to socialize on the job because they work closely with co-workers.

McDonald's is an example of a company where employee routines are highly formalized. Employees are instructed in such things as how to greet the customer (smile, be sincere, make eye contact), ask for and receive payment (state amount of order clearly and loudly, announce the amount of money the customer gives to the employee, count change out loud and efficiently), and thank the customer (give a sincere thank you, make eye contact, ask customer to come again). McDonald's includes this information in training and employee handbooks, and managers are given a checklist of these behaviours so that they can observe their employees to ensure that the proper procedures are followed.[6]

The degree of formalization can vary widely between organizations and within organizations. Certain jobs, for instance, are well known to have little formalization. University textbook sellers—the representatives of publishers who call on professors to inform them of their company's new publications—have a great deal of freedom in their jobs. They have no standard sales "spiel," and the extent of rules and procedures governing their behaviour may be little more than the requirement that they submit a weekly sales report and some suggestions on what to emphasize for the various new titles. At the other extreme, there are clerical and editorial positions in the same publishing houses where employees are required to "clock in" at their workstations by 8 a.m. or be docked a half-hour's pay and, once at that workstation, to follow a set of precise procedures dictated by management.

Mechanistic and Organic Organizations

Vancouver's film industry is known more for its service provision than for creating new works. Hollywood film producers come to Vancouver and rely on line producers who manage the financial and logistical details of productions. Line producer Warren Carr sees himself as a facilitator of foreign productions. If a Hollywood studio decides to film in Vancouver, people like Carr hire heads of departments, who then hire staff. He sets up short-term office and studio space. He then oversees the project, and the executive producers may never come up from Hollywood at all. In other words, Carr sets up a very flexible operation to help get the filming done. Is a flexible organization really more effective than a highly structured organization?

2 How flexible can organizational structures be?

mechanistic model A structure characterized by high specialization, rigid departmentalization, a clear chain of command, narrow spans of control, a limited information network, and centralization.

organic model A structure that is flat, uses cross-functional and cross-hierarchical teams, possesses a comprehensive information network, has wide spans of control, and has low formalization.

Learning About Yourself

1. Bureaucratic Orientation Test, **(page 530)**

In the previous section, we described six elements of organizational structure. If you think of these as design decisions that an owner or CEO makes about his or her organization, you begin to realize that a variety of organizational forms might emerge based on individual responses to each of the structural questions. Management in some firms may choose a highly formalized and centralized structure, while others might choose a structure that is looser and more amorphous. A variety of other designs exist somewhere between these two extremes.

Exhibit 13-10 presents two extreme models of organizational design. One extreme we will call the **mechanistic model**. It has high specialization, rigid departmentalization, a clear chain of command, narrow spans of control, a limited information network (mostly downward communication), and little participation by lower-level members in decision making. Historically, government bureaucracies have tended to operate at a more mechanistic level. At the other extreme is the **organic model**. This model is flat, uses cross-functional and cross-hierarchical teams, possesses a comprehensive information network (using lateral and upward communication, as well as downward), has wide spans of control, involves high participation in decision making, and has low formalization.[7] High-tech firms, particularly those in their early years, operate in a more organic fashion, with individuals collaborating on many of the tasks. You may want to explore how different structures affect performance in this chapter's *Working with Others Exercise* on page 531.

Individual Responses to Organizational Structure

As we review the different design possibilities of an organization, you might want to think about how organizational design would affect you. Your response to organizational design will be affected by factors such as your experience, personality, and the work task. For simplicity's sake, it might help to keep in mind that individuals with a high degree of bureaucratic orientation (see the *Learning About Yourself Exercise* on page 530) tend to place a heavy reliance on higher authority, prefer formalized and specific rules, and prefer formal relationships with others on the job. These people seem better suited to mechanistic structures. Individuals with a low degree of bureaucratic orientation would probably fit better in organic structures. Additionally, cultural background influences preference for structure. Thus, employees from high power distance countries, such as Malaysia, Guatemala, and the Philippines, will be much more accepting of

EXHIBIT 13-10   Mechanistic vs. Organic Models

The Mechanistic Model

The Organic Model

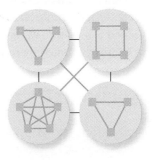

- High specialization
- Rigid departmentalization
- Clear chain of command
- Narrow spans of control
- Centralization
- High formalization

- Cross-functional teams
- Cross-hierarchical teams
- Free flow of information
- Wide spans of control
- Decentralization
- Low formalization

mechanistic structures than will employees who come from low power distance countries. So you need to consider cultural differences along with individual differences when making predictions on how structure will affect employee performance and satisfaction. These same factors should be considered if you are ever in the position to design a new organization; for instance, if you choose to become an entrepreneur. Musicians with the Edmonton Symphony Orchestra were unhappy enough with their organizational structure that they went on strike for a month in early 2002, as *OB in the Workplace* discusses.

Musicians Given More Control Over Decisions

Do symphony orchestra members care about their organizational structure? Musicians with the Edmonton Symphony Orchestra were so frustrated that their views on how the orchestra should be run were not being heard that they went on strike.[8] Decisions for the symphony orchestra were made by the Edmonton Symphony Society, which had 10 000 voting members, including subscribers, donors, musicians, and volunteers. The symphony also had a board of directors that made most management decisions without consulting with the members of the orchestra. The musicians argued that this structure gave too much control to outsiders, and no control to the musicians who had to perform.

During the dispute, the orchestra's then CEO, Elaine Calder, said that the musicians were asking for too much change in the structure of the Edmonton Symphony Orchestra. The musicians' request for seats on the board would "disenfranchise our entire community and give them complete control of our orchestra."

After a month-long strike, the musicians were granted more involvement in the running of the orchestra. Following the lead of both the Toronto and the Winnipeg orchestras, 2 musicians were to be added to the board (for a total of 3 positions out of 15), giving them more say in what performances would be held each year. With the strike over, Calder conceded some positive side to the changes. "Allowing musicians into the decision-making process will allow orchestras to use all their creativity. There's going to be a left-brain, right-brain aspect to that board and that can only help."

The success of including musician input in orchestra decisions was demonstrated in the hiring of William Eddins as the orchestra's music director in 2005 (his contract was renewed for two years in 2008). The musicians formed the bulk of the search committee, and were pleased with the way they had been consulted. Rhonda Taft, a double bass player, contrasted the old and new structures: "There's always been a board-administration-versus-musicians attitude. I may live to eat my words, but I think there's a very sincere attempt now to work more as a team."

The Edmonton Symphony Orchestra's structure is very different from many organizations in that the board—rather than an inside management team—makes many of the decisions. The conductor actually directs the musicians. Next we consider a variety of structures used by organizations.

Traditional Organizational Designs

With the mechanistic and organic models in mind, we now turn to describing some of the more common organizational designs found in use: the *simple structure*, the *bureaucracy*, and the *matrix structure*.

3 What are some examples of traditional organizational designs?

The Simple Structure

What do a small retail store, a start-up electronics firm run by a hard-driving entrepreneur, a new Planned Parenthood office, and an airline in the midst of a company-wide pilots' strike have in common? They probably all use the **simple structure**.

The simple structure is said to be characterized most by what it is *not* rather than by what it is. The simple structure is not elaborate.[9] It has a low degree of departmentalization, wide spans of control, authority centralized in a single person, and little formalization. The simple structure is a "flat" organization; it usually has only two or three vertical levels, a loose body of employees, and one individual in whom the decision-making authority is centralized.

The simple structure is most widely practised in small businesses in which the manager and the owner are one and the same, such as the local corner grocery store.

The strength of the simple structure lies in its simplicity. It's fast, flexible, and inexpensive to maintain, and accountability is clear. One major weakness is that it's difficult to maintain in anything other than small organizations. It becomes increasingly inadequate as an organization grows because its low formalization and high centralization tend to create information overload at the top. As size increases, decision making typically becomes slower and can eventually come to a standstill as the single executive tries to continue making all the decisions. This often proves to be the undoing of many small businesses. When an organization begins to employ 50 or 100 people, it's very difficult for the owner-manager to make all the choices. If the structure is not changed and made more elaborate, the firm often loses momentum and can eventually fail. The simple structure's other weakness is that it's risky—everything depends on one person. One serious illness can literally destroy the organization's information and decision-making centre.

The Family Business

Family businesses represent 70 percent of Canadian employment and more than 30 percent of the gross domestic product. Some of the most prominent family businesses in Canada over the past 50 years include the Seagram Company (the Bronfman family), Eaton's (the Eaton family), Birks (the Birk family), Irving Paper (the Irving family), Molson Breweries (the Molson family), and McCain Foods (the McCain family). Not all family businesses are as large as these, however, and many have relatively simple structures.

Family businesses have more complex dynamics than nonfamily businesses, because they face both family/personal relations and business/management relations. These companies generally have shareholders (family members and perhaps others), although the businesses may or may not be public companies listed on the stock exchange. Unlike nonfamily businesses, family businesses must manage the conflicts found within families, as well as the normal business issues that arise for any business. As John Davis of Harvard Business School notes, "In a family business, the business, the family, and the ownership group all need governance."

Good governance structures can help family businesses manage the conflicts that may arise. Good governance includes "a sense of direction, values to live by or work by, and well-understood and accepted policies that tell organization members how they should behave."[10]

One area in which governance can play a key role is in CEO succession. Family businesses need to figure out rules of succession for when the CEO retires, and also rules for who in the family gets to work in the business. Succession in family-owned businesses often does not work "because personal and emotional factors determine who the next leader will be," rather than suitability.[11] For instance, a father may want his first-born son to take over the business, even if one of the daughters might make a better CEO.

The issues become more complex when second- and third-generation family members become involved in the family business. *OB in the Street* shows the difficulties the McCain brothers had in deciding who would succeed them as head of McCain Foods and the fallout in their relationship as a consequence.

simple structure An organizational design characterized by a low degree of departmentalization, wide spans of control, authority centralized in a single person, and little formalization.

IN THE STREET

Brothers' Feud Leads to Breakup of Family

Does blood come before business? For 37 years, Wallace McCain and his older brother Harrison shared command of McCain Foods, the Florenceville, New Brunswick-based french fry empire they had built together.[12] In August 1993, however, that partnership came to an end, after the *Financial Post* profiled Wallace's son Michael, referring to him as "the leading candidate to become the potato king." Apparently, it was that reference to Michael as successor that started what the newspapers called "the feud of the century."

The public display of animosity came as somewhat of a surprise. The brothers started McCain Foods in 1956, and "one brother never made a decision without consulting the other." Their offices were linked by an unlocked door. They seemed suited to working together. Harrison was the outgoing salesperson. Wallace was quieter, the number cruncher who managed the books. The partnership worked. In the first year, sales were $152 678. Sales of McCain Foods products are still growing; while the core of the business remains french fries, nonfood subsidiaries include a large trucking division and a national courier company.

What brought these two brothers down was a conflict, which had simmered quietly for 20 years, over who would succeed the brothers to run the family business. Harrison convinced other family members that Wallace and his sons would not share the business with the other McCains. The dispute ended up in a New Brunswick arbitration court, where Wallace was ousted as co-CEO. Eighteen months after the *Financial Post* article appeared, Wallace left McCain Foods and moved to Toronto to become chair of Maple Leaf Foods. Meanwhile, Harrison fired his nephew Michael, and ordered the locks changed on his office door. Michael joined his father at Maple Leaf, where he is now president and CEO.

Harrison passed away in 2004, with no signs of a public reconciliation. However, Frank McKenna, the former premier of New Brunswick and friends with both McCain brothers, said that the relationship had improved prior to Harrison's death. "It's not commonly understood, but I think it's important now on Harrison's death to know that Wallace and Harrison had become very close," McKenna said.

So what makes family businesses unique? Founders of family business seek to "build businesses that are also family institutions."[13] As a result, there is added pressure on the business, which needs to balance business needs and family needs. Family businesses may have different goals than nonfamily businesses as well, emphasizing the importance of family values in maintaining and growing the business rather than wealth maximization.

The Bureaucracy

Standardization! That is the key concept underlying all bureaucracies. Take a look at the bank where you keep your chequing account, the department store where you buy your clothes, or the government offices that collect your taxes, enforce health regulations, or provide local fire protection. They all rely on standardized work processes for coordination and control.

A **bureaucracy** is characterized by highly routine operating tasks achieved through specialization, formalized rules and regulations, tasks that are grouped into functional departments, centralized authority, narrow spans of control, and decision making that follows the chain of command.

bureaucracy An organizational design with highly routine operating tasks achieved through specialization, formalized rules and regulations, tasks that are grouped into functional departments, centralized authority, narrow spans of control, and decision making that follows the chain of command.

Strengths of Bureaucracy

German sociologist Max Weber, writing in the early 1900s, described bureaucracy as an alternative to the traditional administrative form. In the traditional model, leaders could be quite arbitrary, with authority based on personal relations. There were no general rules, and no separation between the leader's "private" and "public" business. Bureaucracy solved some of the problems of leaders who took advantage of their situation.

The primary strength of the bureaucracy lies in its ability to perform standardized activities in a highly efficient manner. Putting together similar specialties in functional departments results in economies of scale, minimum duplication of staff and equipment, and employees who have the opportunity to talk "the same language" with their peers. Furthermore, bureaucracies can get by nicely with less talented—and, hence, less costly—middle- and lower-level managers. The pervasiveness of rules and regulations substitutes for managerial discretion. Standardized operations, coupled with high formalization, allow decision making to be centralized. There is little need, therefore, for innovative and experienced decision makers below the level of senior executives. In short, bureaucracy is an effective structure for ensuring consistent application of policies and practices and for ensuring accountability.

Weaknesses of Bureaucracy

Bureaucracy is not without its problems. One of its major weaknesses is that it can create subunit conflict. For instance, the production department believes that it has the most important role in the organization because nothing happens until something is produced. Meanwhile, the research and development department may believe that design provides added value to a product, while producing it is no big deal. At the same time, the marketing department views selling the product as the most important task in the organization. Finally, the accounting department sees itself in the central role of tallying up the results and making sure everything stays on budget. Thus, each department acts like a silo, focusing more on what it perceives as its own value and contribution to the organization. Each silo fails to understand that departments are really interdependent, with each having to perform well for the company as a whole to survive. The conflict that can happen among functional units means that sometimes functional unit goals can override the overall goals of the organization.

Bureaucracy can sometimes lead to power being concentrated in the hands of just a few people, with others expected to follow their orders unquestioningly. This chapter's *Ethical Dilemma Exercise* on page 533 illustrates what can happen when someone higher in the authority chain pressures someone below him or her to perform unethical tasks.

In thinking about the possible conflicts that can arise in a bureaucracy, you might want to refer to Chapter 8, which discussed the relationship of dependency to power. That chapter pointed out that importance, scarcity, and nonsubstitutability will all affect the degree of power an individual or unit has.

The other major weakness of a bureaucracy is something we have all experienced at one time or another when dealing with people who work in these organizations: obsessive concern with following the rules. When cases arise that don't precisely fit the rules, there is no room for modification. The bureaucracy is efficient only as long as employees confront problems that they have previously encountered and for which programmed decision rules have already been established. This chapter's *Case Incident—"I Detest Bureaucracy"* on page 534 lets you consider alternatives to bureaucracy and how you might feel about these alternatives. *OB Around the Globe* illustrates that multinationals should consider the country in which they will be located when choosing an organizational structure.

OB-AROUND THE GLOBE

Structural Considerations in Multinationals

Can the proper organizational structure vary by country? When bringing out a business innovation in any country, trudging through corporate bureaucracy can cause delays that result in a competitive disadvantage.[14] This is especially true in China, one of the world's fastest-growing economies. Successful multinational corporations operating in China are realizing that the optimal structure is decentralized, with a relatively high degree of managerial autonomy. Given that more than 1.3 billion people live in China, the opportunity for businesses is tremendous, and as a result, competition is increasing. To take advantage of this opportunity, companies must be able to respond to changes before their competitors.

For example, Tyson Foods gives its vice-president and head of the company's China operations, James Rice, the freedom to build the company's business overseas. While walking past a food vendor in Shanghai, Rice got the idea for cumin-flavoured chicken strips. Without the need to obtain approval from upper management, Rice and his team immediately developed the recipe, tested it, and, after receiving a 90 percent customer-approval rating, began selling the product within two months of coming up with the idea.

Other companies that have implemented more formalized, bureaucratic structures have fared less well. One manager of a consumer electronics company who wanted to reduce the package size of a product to lower its cost and attract lower-income Chinese customers had to send the idea to his boss. His boss, the vice-president of Asian operations, then sent the idea to the vice-president of international operations, who in turn sent the idea to upper management in the United States. Although the idea was approved, the process took five months, during which a competitor introduced a similarly packaged product.

So when it comes to innovating in a dynamic, fast-paced economy such as China, decentralization and autonomy can be major competitive advantages for multinational corporations. To gain this competitive advantage, companies like Tyson are empowering their overseas managers to make their own decisions.

The Matrix Structure

Another popular organizational design option is the **matrix structure**. You will find it being used in advertising agencies, aerospace firms, research and development laboratories, construction companies, hospitals, government agencies, universities, management consulting firms, and entertainment companies.[15] Ideally, the matrix combines the benefits of two forms of departmentalization—functional and product—without their drawbacks. Specifically, functional departmentalization groups similar specialists, which minimizes the number necessary, while it allows the pooling and sharing of specialized resources across products. Product departmentalization facilitates coordination among specialties to achieve on-time completion and meet budget targets. Furthermore, it provides clear responsibility for all activities related to a product, but with duplication of activities and costs.

The most obvious structural characteristic of the matrix is that it breaks the unity-of-command concept. Employees in the matrix have two bosses—their functional department managers and their product managers. Therefore, the matrix has a dual chain of command.

Exhibit 13-11 on page 518 shows the matrix structure used in a faculty of business administration. The academic departments of accounting, administrative studies, finance,

matrix structure An organizational design that combines functional and product departmentalization; it has a dual chain of command.

EXHIBIT 13-11   Matrix Structure for a Faculty of Business Administration

Academic departments \ Programs	Undergraduate	Master's	PhD	Research	Executive development	Community service
Accounting						
Administrative studies						
Finance						
Information and decision sciences						
Marketing						
Organizational behaviour						
Quantitative methods						

and so forth are functional units. Additionally, specific programs (that is, products) are overlaid on the functions. In this way, members in a matrix structure have a dual assignment—to their functional department, and to their product groups. For instance, a professor of accounting who is teaching an undergraduate course reports to the director of undergraduate programs, as well as to the chair of the accounting department.

Advantages of a Matrix Structure

The strength of the matrix lies in its ability to foster coordination when the organization carries out many complex and interdependent activities. As an organization becomes larger, its information-processing capacity can become overloaded. In a bureaucracy, complexity results in increased formalization. The direct and frequent contact between different specialties in the matrix can result in improved communication and more flexibility. Information permeates the organization and more quickly reaches those people who need to take account of it. Furthermore, the matrix reduces "bureaupathologies." The dual lines of authority reduce tendencies of departmental members to become so busy protecting their little worlds that the organization's overall goals become secondary.

The matrix offers another fundamental advantage: It facilitates the efficient allocation of specialists. When individuals with highly specialized skills are lodged in one functional department or product group, their talents are monopolized and underused. The matrix achieves the advantages of economies of scale by providing the organization with both the best resources and an effective way of ensuring their efficient deployment.

Disadvantages of a Matrix Structure

The major disadvantages of the matrix lie in the confusion it creates, its tendency to foster power struggles, and the stress it places on individuals.[16] For example, it's frequently unclear who reports to whom, and it's not unusual for product managers to fight over getting the best specialists assigned to their products. Confusion and ambiguity also create the seeds of power struggles. Bureaucracy reduces the potential for power grabs by defining the rules of the game. When those rules are "up for grabs," power struggles between functional and product managers result. For individuals who desire security and absence of ambiguity, this work climate can produce

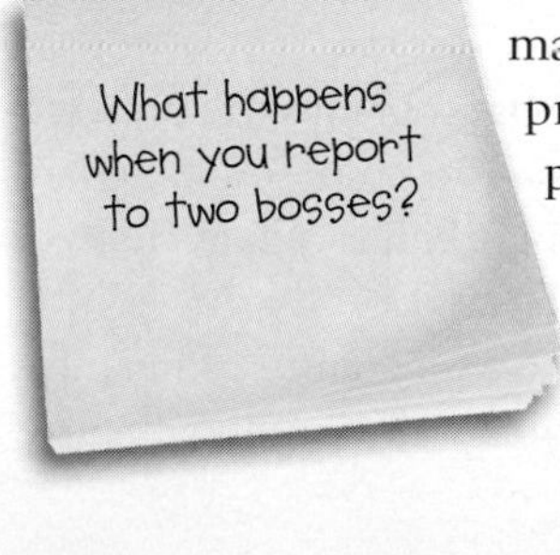

What happens when you report to two bosses?

stress. Reporting to more than one manager introduces role conflict, and unclear expectations introduce role ambiguity. The comfort of bureaucracy's predictability is absent, replaced by insecurity and stress.

New Design Options

Vancouver's film industry structure does not resemble the traditional corporate structure of large manufacturing organizations.[17] It needs to be flexible because its fortunes are affected by the strength of the Canadian dollar. When the dollar is weaker, more American studios work in Vancouver. The demand for flexiblity means that single-purpose companies may start up, do several million dollars in business, and close down in a matter of months. This flexibility reflects the creative nature of the movie business, and allows people to move from project to project rather fluidly. Most people expect that companies will only operate for three or four months.

This corporate "structure" means there are few permanent jobs, but many people in the industry have long, productive careers. David Murphy, who studied the industry for his PhD from the University of British Columbia, called the structure "a network model of industrial organization." Small companies and suppliers work together on a project, and when it's finished, move on to another project. Ironically, the strong union presence in Vancouver helps the industry thrive. "The unions run training programs for many jobs in the industry and refer qualified members to producers when needed," according to Professor Mark Thompson of the Sauder School of Business at UBC. Essentially, the unions provide a corporate structure. Can new forms of organization lead to better ways of getting things done?

Organizational theorists Jay Galbraith and Edward Lawler have argued that there is a "new logic of organizing" for organizations.[18] They suggest that new-style organizations are considerably more flexible than older-style organizations. Exhibit 13-12 compares characteristics of new-style and old-style organizations.

The new structural options for organizations involve breaking down boundaries in some fashion, either internally, externally, or a combination of the two. In this section,

4   What do newer organizational structures look like?

EXHIBIT 13-12 New-Style vs. Old-Style Organizations	
New	**Old**
Dynamic, learning	Stable
Information rich	Information is scarce
Global	Local
Small and large	Large
Product/customer oriented	Functional oriented
Skills oriented	Job oriented
Team oriented	Individual oriented
Involvement oriented	Command/control oriented
Lateral/networked	Hierarchical
Customer oriented	Job requirements oriented

Source: J. R. Galbraith and E. E. Lawler III, "Effective Organizations: Using the New Logic of Organizing," in *Organizing for the Future: The New Logic for Managing Complex Organizations*, ed. J. R. Galbraith, E. E. Lawler III, and associates (San Francisco: Jossey-Bass, 1993). Copyright © 1993 Jossey-Bass Inc. Publishers. Reprinted with permission of John Wiley & Sons, Inc.

we describe four such designs: the *team structure*, which modifies internal boundaries; the *modular* and *virtual organizations*, both of which modify external organizational boundaries; and the *boundaryless organization*, which attempts to break down both internal and external boundaries.[19]

The Team Structure

As described in Chapter 6, teams have become an extremely popular means around which to organize work activities. When management uses teams as its central coordination device, you have a **team structure**. The primary characteristics of the team structure are that it breaks down departmental barriers and decentralizes decision making to the level of the work team. Team structures also require employees to be generalists as well as specialists.[20]

In smaller companies, the team structure can define the entire organization. For instance, Toyota Canada's parts distribution centre in Toronto reorganized its workforce into work teams in 1995. Workers have a team-focused mission statement, and the staff are split into six work teams, each with its own leader. Among larger organizations, such as Xerox Canada and GM Canada, the team structure often complements what is typically a bureaucratic structure. This allows the organization to achieve the efficiency of bureaucracy's standardization while gaining the flexibility that teams provide.

The Modular Organization

Why do it all when sometimes someone else can do some of it better? That question captures the essence of the **modular organization**, which is typically a small core organization that outsources major business functions.[21]

Nike, Reebok, Liz Claiborne, Vancouver-based Mountain Equipment Co-op, and Dell Canada are just a few of the thousands of companies that have found that they can do hundreds of millions of dollars in business without owning manufacturing facilities. These organizations have created networks of relationships that allow them to contract out manufacturing, distribution, marketing, or any other business function where management believes that others can do it better or more cheaply. The modular organization, however, outsources many functions and concentrates on what it does best. For many Canadian firms, that means focusing on design or marketing rather than production.

Exhibit 13-13 shows a modular structure in which management outsources the marketing, sales, and service functions of the business. Top management directly oversees the activities that are done in-house and coordinates relationships with the other organizations that perform the marketing, sales, and service functions for the modular organization. Managers in modular structures spend some of their time coordinating and controlling external relations, typically by way of computer network links.

team structure The use of teams as the central device to coordinate work activities.

modular organization A small core organization that outsources major business functions.

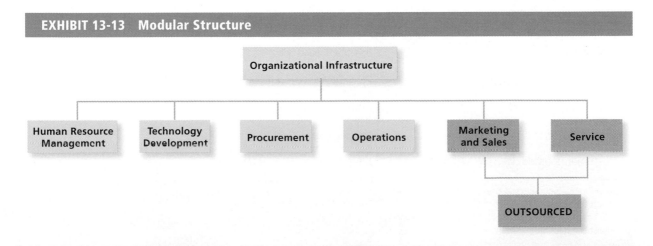

EXHIBIT 13-13   Modular Structure

There are several advantages to modular organizations. Organizations can devote their technical and managerial talent to their most critical activities. They can respond more quickly to environmental changes, and there is increased focus on customers and markets. The primary drawback to this structure is that it reduces management's control over key parts of its business. The organization is forced to rely on outsiders, which decreases operational control. Additionally, Nike and several other companies have come under attack for relying on low-paid, exploited labourers, many of whom are children, in less developed countries. These organizations are having to make decisions about the trade-offs between low-cost production strategies and criticisms from potential customers who are concerned about human rights.

The Virtual Organization

The **virtual organization** "is a continually evolving network of independent companies—suppliers, customers, even competitors—linked together to share skills, costs, and access to one another's markets."[22] In a virtual organization, units of different firms join together in an alliance to pursue common strategic objectives. While control in the modular structure remains with the core organization, in the virtual organization participants give up some of their control and act more interdependently. Virtual organizations may not have a central office, an organizational chart, or a hierarchy. Typically, the organizations come together to exploit specific opportunities or attain specific strategic objectives.

virtual organization A continually evolving network of independent companies—suppliers, customers, even competitors—linked together to share skills, costs, and access to one another's markets.

About one in nine Canadian companies engages in some sort of alliance. These alliances take many forms, ranging from precompetitive consortia to coproduction, cross-equity arrangements, and equity joint ventures with separate legal entities.[23] Exhibit 13-14 illustrates a virtual structure where the reference firm is responsible for technology development, and then works together with the alliance partners to complete the other functions. Another example of a virtual structure is Amazon.ca, which partners with Canada Post. Orders placed on Amazon.ca's website are fulfilled and shipped by Assured Logistics, which is part of Canada Post. Assured Logistics operates a Toronto-area warehouse that stores books, music, and movies so that they can be shipped when ordered, thus eliminating the need for Amazon to set up its own warehouse facility in Canada.

There are several advantages to virtual organizations. They allow organizations to share costs and skills, provide access to global markets, and increase market responsiveness. However, there are also distinct disadvantages. The boundaries between companies become blurred due to interdependence. In order to work together, companies must relinquish operational and strategic control. This form of organization also requires new managerial skills. Managers must build relations with other companies, negotiate "win-win" deals, find compatible partners in terms of values and goals, and then develop appropriate communication systems to keep everyone informed.[24]

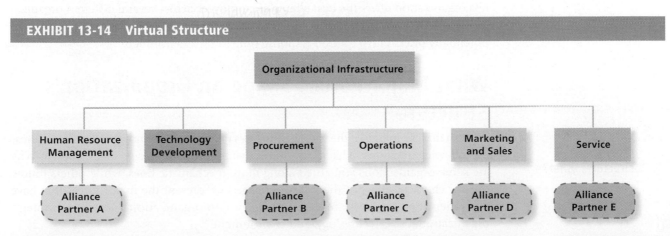

EXHIBIT 13-14   Virtual Structure

The Boundaryless Organization

boundaryless organization An organization that seeks to eliminate the chain of command, have limitless spans of control, and replace departments with empowered teams.

Both the modular organization and the virtual organization break down external boundaries of the organization without generally affecting the internal workings of each of the cooperating organizations. Some organizations, however, strive to break down both the internal and external boundaries. Former General Electric (GE) chairman Jack Welch coined the term **boundaryless organization** to describe his idea of what he wanted GE to become. The boundaryless organization seeks to eliminate the chain of command, have limitless spans of control, and replace departments with empowered teams. Because it relies so heavily on information technology, some have turned to calling this structure the *T-form* (or technology-based) organization.[25]

Can an organization really have no boundaries?

Although GE has not yet achieved this boundaryless state—and probably never will—it has made significant progress toward this end. So have other companies, such as Hewlett-Packard, AT&T, and Motorola. Let's explore what a boundaryless organization would look like and what some firms are doing to make it a reality.[26]

The boundaryless organization breaks down barriers internally by flattening the hierarchy, creating cross-hierarchical teams (which include top executives, middle managers, supervisors, and operative employees), and using participative decision-making practices and 360-degree performance appraisals (where peers and others above and below the employee evaluate his or her performance). The boundaryless organization also breaks down barriers to external constituencies (suppliers, customers, regulators, etcetera) and barriers created by geography. Globalization, strategic alliances, supplier-organization and customer-organization linkages, and telecommuting are all examples of practices that reduce external boundaries.

The one common technological thread that makes the boundaryless organization possible is networked computers. They allow people to communicate across intra-organizational and interorganizational boundaries.[27] Additionally, many large companies, including the City of Richmond (BC), Procter & Gamble Canada, FedEx, AT&T, and 3M, have intranets to help with internal communication. Interorganizational networks now make it possible for Walmart suppliers such as Procter & Gamble (P&G) to monitor inventory levels of laundry soap, because P&G's company computer system is networked to Walmart's system.

One of the drawbacks of boundaryless organizations is that they are difficult to manage. It's difficult to overcome the political and authority boundaries inherent in many organizations. It can also be time-consuming and difficult to manage the coordination necessary with so many different stakeholders. That said, the well-managed boundaryless organization offers the best talents of employees across several different organizations; enhances cooperation across functions, divisions, and external groups; and potentially offers much quicker response time to the environment.

What Major Forces Shape an Organization's Structure?

5 Why do organizational structures differ?

With an understanding of the various structures possible, we are now prepared to address the following questions: What are the forces that influence the design that is chosen? Why are some organizations structured along more mechanistic lines, while others follow organic characteristics? In the following pages, we present the major forces that have been identified as causes, or determinants, of an organization's structure: strategy, organizational size, technology, and environment.[28]

Strategy

An organization's structure is a means to help management achieve its objectives. Since objectives are derived from the organization's overall strategy, it's only logical that the structure should support the strategy.[29]

Most current strategy frameworks focus on three strategy dimensions—innovation, cost minimization, and imitation—and the structural design that works best with each.[30]

Innovation Strategy

To what degree does an organization introduce major new products or services? An **innovation strategy** does not mean a strategy merely for simple or cosmetic changes from previous offerings, but rather one for meaningful and unique innovations. Obviously, not all firms pursue innovation. This strategy may appropriately characterize 3M, but it certainly is not a strategy pursued by McDonald's.

innovation strategy A strategy that emphasizes the introduction of major new products and services.

Cost-Minimization Strategy

An organization that is pursuing a **cost-minimization strategy** tightly controls costs, refrains from incurring unnecessary innovation or marketing expenses, and cuts prices in selling a basic product. This would describe the strategy pursued by Walmart, as well as the sellers of generic grocery products.

cost-minimization strategy A strategy that emphasizes tight cost controls, avoidance of unnecessary innovation or marketing expenses, and price cutting.

Imitation Strategy

Organizations following an **imitation strategy** try to capitalize on the best of both of the previous strategies. They seek to minimize risk and maximize opportunity for profit. Their strategy is to move into new products or new markets only after viability has been proven by innovators. They take the successful ideas of innovators and copy them. Manufacturers of mass-marketed fashion goods that are "rip-offs" of designer styles follow the imitation strategy. This label also probably characterizes firms such as IBM and Caterpillar. They essentially follow their smaller and more innovative competitors with superior products, but only after their competitors have demonstrated that the market is there.

imitation strategy A strategy of moving into new products or new markets only after their viability has already been proven.

Exhibit 13-15 describes the structural option that best matches each strategy. Innovators need the flexibility of the organic structure, while cost minimizers seek the efficiency and stability of the mechanistic structure. Imitators combine the two structures. They use a mechanistic structure in order to maintain tight controls and low costs in their current activities, while at the same time they create organic subunits in which to pursue new undertakings.

Organizational Size

There is considerable evidence to support the idea that an organization's size significantly affects its structure.[31] For instance, large organizations—those typically employing 2000 or more people—tend to have more specialization, more departmentalization, more

EXHIBIT 13-15	The Strategy–Structure Relationship
Strategy	**Structural Option**
Innovation	*Organic:* A loose structure; low specialization, low formalization, decentralized
Cost minimization	*Mechanistic:* Tight control; extensive work specialization, high formalization, high centralization
Imitation	*Mechanistic and organic:* Mix of loose with tight properties; tight controls over current activities and looser controls for new undertakings

vertical levels, and more rules and regulations than do small organizations. However, the relationship is not linear. Rather, size affects structure at a decreasing rate. The impact of size becomes less important as an organization expands. Why is this? Essentially, once an organization has around 2000 employees, it's already fairly mechanistic. An additional 500 employees will not have much impact. On the other hand, adding 500 employees to an organization that has only 300 members is likely to result in a shift toward a more mechanistic structure.

This chapter's *Point/Counterpoint* on page 529 examines whether decreasing the number of employees through downsizing improves or hurts organizational performance.

Technology

technology The way in which an organization transfers its inputs into outputs.

The term **technology** refers to the way in which an organization transfers its inputs into outputs. Every organization has at least one technology for converting financial, human, and physical resources into products or services. The Ford Motor Company, for instance, predominantly uses an assembly-line process to make its products. On the other hand, universities may use a number of instruction technologies to develop coursework for students—the ever-popular formal lecture method, the case-analysis method, the experiential exercise method, the programmed learning method, and so forth. In this section, we show that organizational structures adapt to their technology.

So what does technology mean?

Variations in Technology

The common theme that differentiates technologies is their *degree of routineness*. By this we mean that technologies tend toward either routine or nonroutine activities. The former are characterized by automated and standardized operations, such as an assembly

The degree of routineness differentiates technologies. At Wallstrip.com, nonroutineness characterizes the customized work of employees, who create an entertaining daily web video show and accompanying blog about the stock market. The show relies heavily on the knowledge of specialists such as host Lindsay Campbell and writer/producer Adam Elend, who are shown here in the production studio, where they are getting ready to film an episode of their show.

line, where one might affix a car door to a car at set intervals. Nonroutine activities are customized. They include such varied operations as furniture restoring, custom shoe-making, and genetic research.

The Relationship between Technology and Structure

What relationship has been found between technology and structure? Although the relationship is not overwhelmingly strong, we find that routine tasks are associated with taller and more departmentalized structures. The relationship between technology and formalization, however, is stronger. Studies consistently show routineness to be associated with the presence of rule manuals, job descriptions, and other formalized documentation.

An interesting relationship has been found between technology and centralization. It seems logical that routine technologies would be associated with a centralized structure, whereas nonroutine technologies, which rely more heavily on the knowledge of specialists, would be characterized by delegated decision authority. This position has received some support. However, a more generalizable conclusion is that the technology-centralization relationship is moderated by the degree of formalization. Both formal regulations and centralized decision making are control mechanisms, and management can substitute one for the other. Routine technologies should be associated with centralized control if there is a minimum of rules and regulations. However, if formalization is high, routine technology can be accompanied by decentralization. So we would predict that routine technology would lead to centralization, but only if formalization is low.

Environment

An organization's **environment** is composed of those institutions or forces outside the organization that potentially affect the organization's performance. These typically include suppliers, customers, competitors, government regulatory agencies, public pressure groups, and the like.

Why should an organization's structure be affected by its environment? The answer is environmental uncertainty. Some organizations face relatively static environments—few forces in their environment are changing. There is, for example, no new competition, no new technological breakthroughs by current competitors, or little activity by public pressure groups to influence the organization. Other organizations face dynamic environments—rapidly changing government regulations affecting their business, new competitors, difficulties in acquiring raw materials, continually changing product preferences by customers, and so on. Static environments create significantly less uncertainty for managers than do dynamic ones. Since uncertainty is a threat to an organization's effectiveness, management will try to minimize it. One way to reduce environmental uncertainty is through adjustments in the organization's structure.[32]

Recent research has helped clarify what is meant by environmental uncertainty. It has been found that there are three key dimensions to any organization's environment: capacity, volatility, and complexity.[33]

Capacity

The *capacity* of an environment refers to the degree to which it can support growth. Rich and growing environments generate excess resources, which can buffer the organization in times of relative scarcity. Abundant capacity, for example, leaves room for an organization to make mistakes, while scarce capacity does not. In 2000, firms operating in the multimedia software business had relatively abundant environments, whereas in 2009, the same businesses faced relative scarcity.

Volatility

The degree of instability in an environment is captured in the *volatility* dimension. Where there is a high degree of unpredictable change, the environment is dynamic. This makes

environment Those institutions or forces outside the organization that potentially affect the organization's performance.

it difficult for management to predict accurately the probabilities associated with various decision alternatives. At the other extreme is a stable environment. Turmoil in the US financial markets in 2008 caught many by surprise and created a lot of instability. Canada's credit market faced significant tightening as a result, making it more difficult for corporations and individuals to borrow money. While the impact of the financial instability is not entirely clear at the time of this writing, many worry that the United States is heading into a recession. The US financial crisis was a valuable reminder to all organizations that they are operating in a global environment.

Complexity

Finally, the environment needs to be assessed in terms of *complexity*; that is, the degree of heterogeneity and concentration among environmental elements. Simple environments are homogeneous and concentrated. This might describe the tobacco industry, since there are relatively few players. It's easy for firms in this industry to keep a close eye on the competition. In contrast, environments characterized by heterogeneity and dispersion are called *complex*. This term sums up the current environment for firms competing in the cellular connection business. Every day, there seems to be another "new kid on the block" with whom current cellphone providers must deal.

Exhibit 13-16 summarizes our definition of the environment along its three dimensions. The arrows in this figure are meant to indicate movement toward higher uncertainty. Organizations that operate in environments characterized as scarce, dynamic, and complex face the greatest degree of uncertainty. Why? They have high unpredictability, little room for error, and a diverse set of elements in the environment to monitor constantly.

Given this three-dimensional definition of *environment*, we can offer some general conclusions. There is evidence that relates the degrees of environmental uncertainty to different structural arrangements. Specifically, the more scarce, dynamic, and complex the environment, the more organic a structure should be. The more abundant, stable, and simple the environment, the more mechanistic a structure should be.

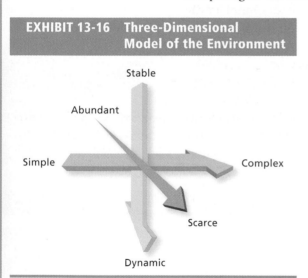

EXHIBIT 13-16   Three-Dimensional Model of the Environment

Summary and Implications

1   What are the key elements of organizational structure? An organizational structure defines how job tasks are formally divided, grouped, and coordinated. There are six key elements that managers need to address when they design their organization's structure: work specialization, departmentalization, chain of command, span of control, centralization and decentralization, and formalization. Organizations structured around high levels of formalization and specialization, strict adherence to the chain of command, limited delegation of authority, and narrow spans of control give employees little autonomy. Organizations that are structured around limited specialization, low formalization, wide spans of control, and low centralization and low formalization give employees greater autonomy.

2   How flexible can organizational structures be? For simplicity's sake, we can classify the extent to which organizations are flexible around one of two models: *mechanistic* or *organic*. A mechanistic organization has high specialization, rigid departmentalization, a clear chain of command, narrow spans of control, a limited information network (mostly downward communication), and little participation by lower-level members in decision making. Historically, government bureaucracies have tended to operate at a more mechanistic level. At the other extreme is the organic organization, which is flat, uses cross-functional and cross-hierarchical teams, possesses a comprehensive information network (using lateral and upward communication, as well as downward), has wide spans of control, involves high participation in decision making, and has low formalization. High-tech firms, particularly those in their early years, operate in a more organic fashion, with individuals collaborating on many of the tasks.

3 **What are some examples of traditional organizational designs?** Some of the more common organizational designs found in use are the *simple structure*, the *bureaucracy*, and the *matrix structure*. The simple structure has a low degree of departmentalization, wide spans of control, authority centralized in a single person, and little formalization. A bureaucracy is characterized by highly routine operating tasks achieved through specialization, formalized rules and regulations, tasks that are grouped into functional departments, centralized authority, narrow spans of control, and decision making that follows the chain of command. The most obvious structural characteristic of the matrix is that it breaks the unity-of-command concept. Employees in the matrix have two bosses—their functional department managers and their product managers. Therefore, the matrix has a dual chain of command.

4 **What do newer organizational structures look like?** The new structural options for organizations involve breaking down the boundaries in some fashion, either internally, externally, or a combination of the two. We have illustrated four such structural designs: the team structure, which modifies internal boundaries; the modular and virtual organizations, which modify external organizational boundaries; and the boundaryless organization, which attempts to break down both internal and external boundaries.

5 **Why do organizational structures differ?** Strategy, organizational size, technology, and environment determine the type of structure an organization will have.

For Review

1. Why isn't work specialization an unending source of increased productivity?

2. What are the different forms of departmentalization?

3. All things being equal, which is more efficient, a wide or narrow span of control? Why?

4. How does a family business differ from other organizational structures?

5. What is a matrix structure? When would management use it?

6. Contrast the virtual organization with the boundaryless organization.

7. What type of structure works best with an innovation strategy? A cost-minimization strategy? An imitation strategy?

8. Summarize the size-structure relationship.

9. Define and give an example of what is meant by the term *technology*.

10. Summarize the environment-structure relationship.

For Critical Thinking

1. How is the typical large corporation of today organized, in contrast with how that same organization was probably organized in the 1960s?

2. Do you think most employees prefer high formalization? Support your position.

3. If you were an employee in a matrix structure, what pluses do you think the structure would provide? What about minuses?

4. What could management do to make a bureaucracy more like a boundaryless organization?

5. What behavioural predictions would you make about people who worked in a "pure" boundaryless organization (if such a structure were ever to exist)?

 **for You**

- Think about the type of organizational structure that suits you best when you look for a job. You may prefer a structured workplace, like that of a mechanistic organization. Or you may prefer a much less structured workplace, like that of an organic organization.

- If you decide to start your own company, know the different structural considerations so that you can create an organization that meets your needs as both a business person and a person with additional interests.

- As a manager or as an entrepreneur, consider how much responsibility (centralization/decentralization) you want to take for yourself compared with how much you are willing to share with others in the organization.

POINT

COUNTERPOINT

Downsizing Improves Organizational Performance

There are not many leaders who like to downsize.[34] Doing so always means inflicting pain on employees and enduring attacks by politicians, labour groups, and the media. But if there is one thing we have learned in the past 20 years, it's that downsizing has been an indispensable factor in making companies more competitive.

In the 1970s and 1980s, most established companies in countries such as Canada were overstaffed. That made them vulnerable to foreign competition from companies with lower labour costs and a better ability to quickly adapt to new economic conditions and technologies. It's perhaps inevitable that companies do this; success breeds complacency, and, when business is good, companies tend to overstaff and become bloated. Like the patient with a heart condition, they find the remedy is often painful; but fail to address it, and the eventual harm may be much worse.

Nearly all major companies that were around in the 1970s have shrunk their workforces and streamlined their operations. Look at IBM. Once one of the largest employers in the world, it often touted its no-layoff policy. But in the 1980s and 1990s, it became quite clear that IBM was too big, too complex, and spread too thin. Today, IBM is profitable again, but only after it shed nearly 100 000 jobs. Here is what former IBM CEO Lou Gerstner said about the need to restructure the company:

> It got stuck because it fell victim to what I call the success syndrome. The more successful enterprises are, the more they try to replicate, duplicate, codify what makes us great. And suddenly they're inward thinking. They're thinking how can we continue to do what we've done in the past without understanding that what made them successful is to take risks, to change and to adapt and to be responsive. And so in a sense success breeds its own failure. And I think it's true of a lot of successful businesses.

Layoffs and restructuring are rarely the popular things to do. But without them, most organizations would not survive, much less remain competitive.

Downsizing Does Not Improve Long-Term Performance

Downsizing has become a sort of rite of passage for business leaders: You are not a real leader unless you have downsized a company.[35] However, to separate fact from myth, let's look at the evidence. Do companies that have downsized perform better as a result?

To study this, a research team looked at Standard & Poor's 500 (S&P 500) companies over 20 years. They asked whether reductions in employment at one period of time were associated with higher levels of financial performance at a later period in time.

What did they find? In analyzing 6418 occurrences of changes in employment among the S&P 500, they found that downsizing strategies did not result in improved long-term financial performance (as measured by industry-adjusted return on assets). It's important to remember that the results control for prior financial performance and reflect financial performance after the downsizing efforts occurred.

The authors of this study don't argue that downsizing is always a bad strategy. Rather, the upshot is that managers should not assume layoffs are a quick fix to what ails a company. In general, downsizing does not improve performance, so the key is to do it only when needed and to do it in the right way.

What are some ways organizations can do this? First, they should use downsizing only as a last resort. Second, and related, they should inform employees about the problem, and give them a chance to contribute alternative restructuring solutions. Third, organizations need to bend over backward to ensure that employees see the layoff process as fair, including making sure the layoff criteria are fair (and ideally result from employee involvement), advance notice is given, and job relocation assistance is provided. Finally, make sure downsizing is done to good effect—not just to cut costs, but to reallocate resources to where they can be most effective.

LEARNING ABOUT **YOURSELF** EXERCISE

Bureaucratic Orientation Test

For each statement, check the response (either "Mostly agree" or "Mostly disagree") that best represents your feelings.[36]

	Mostly Agree	Mostly Disagree
1. I value stability in my job.	_____	_____
2. I like a predictable organization.	_____	_____
3. The best job for me would be one in which the future is uncertain.	_____	_____
4. The federal government would be a nice place to work.	_____	_____
5. Rules, policies, and procedures tend to frustrate me.	_____	_____
6. I would enjoy working for a company that employs 85 000 people worldwide.	_____	_____
7. Being self-employed would involve more risk than I am willing to take.	_____	_____
8. Before accepting a job, I would like to see an exact job description.	_____	_____
9. I would prefer a job as a freelance house painter to one as a clerk for the Motor Vehicles Branch.	_____	_____
10. Seniority should be as important as performance in determining pay increases and promotion.	_____	_____
11. It would give me a feeling of pride to work for the largest and most successful company in its field.	_____	_____
12. Given a choice, I would prefer to make $70 000 per year as a vice-president in a small company than $85 000 as a staff specialist in a large company.	_____	_____
13. I would regard wearing an employee badge with a number on it as a degrading experience.	_____	_____
14. Parking spaces in a company lot should be assigned on the basis of job level.	_____	_____
15. If an accountant works for a large organization, he or she cannot be a true professional.	_____	_____
16. Before accepting a job (given a choice), I would want to make sure that the company had a very fine program of employee benefits.	_____	_____
17. A company will probably not be successful unless it establishes a clear set of rules and procedures.	_____	_____
18. Regular working hours and vacations are more important to me than finding thrills on the job.	_____	_____
19. You should respect people according to their rank.	_____	_____
20. Rules are meant to be broken.	_____	_____

Scoring Key:

Give yourself 1 point for each statement for which you responded in the bureaucratic direction:

Mostly agree: 1, 2, 4, 7, 8, 10, 11, 14, 16, 18, 19

Mostly disagree: 3, 5, 6, 9, 12, 13, 15, 17, 20

A very high score (15 or over) suggests that you would enjoy working in a bureaucracy. A very low score (5 or lower) suggests that you would be frustrated by working in a bureaucracy, especially a large one.

More Learning About Yourself Exercises

Additional self-assessments relevant to this chapter appear at MyOBLab (**www.pearsoned.ca/myoblab**).

III.A.2 How Willing Am I to Delegate?

IV.F.2 Do I Like Bureaucracy?

When you complete the additional assessments, consider the following:

1. Am I surprised about my score?
2. Would my friends evaluate me similarly?

BREAKOUT **GROUP** EXERCISES

Form small groups to discuss the following topics, as assigned by your instructor:

1. Describe the structure of an organization in which you worked. Was the structure appropriate for the tasks being done?

2. Have you ever worked in an organization with a structure that seemed inappropriate to the task? What would have improved the structure?

3. You are considering opening up a coffee bar with several of your friends. What kind of structure might you use? After the coffee bar becomes successful, you decide that expanding the number of branches might be a good idea. What changes to the structure might you make?

WORKING WITH OTHERS EXERCISE

Words-in-Sentences Company

Overview: You are a small company that

1. manufactures words; and

2. packages them into meaningful English-language sentences.[37]

Market research has established that sentences of at least 3 words but not more than 6 words are in demand. Therefore, packaging, distribution, and sales should be set up for **3- to 6-word sentences**.

Time: Approximately 30 minutes. (Note: A production run takes 10 minutes. While the game is more effective if 2 [or more] production runs are completed, even 1 production run will generate effective discussion about how organizational structure affects performance.)

Group Task: Your group must design and participate in running a W-I-S company. You will be competing with other companies in your industry. The success of your company will depend on (a) your objectives, (b) planning, (c) organizational structure, and (d) quality control. You should design your organization to be as efficient as possible during each 10-minute production run. After the first production run, you will have an opportunity to reorganize your company if you want.

Raw Materials: For each production run, you will be given a **"raw material phrase."** The letters found in the phrase serve as the raw materials available to produce new words in sentences. For example, if the raw material phrase is "organizational behaviour is fun," you could produce the words and sentence "Nat ran to a zoo." One way to think of your raw material phrase is to take all the letters appearing in the phrase and write them down as many times as they appear in the phrase. Thus, for the phrase "organizational behaviour is fun" you have: a-4; b-1; c-0; d-0; e-1; f-1; g-1; h-1; i-4; j-0; k-0; l-1; m-0; n-3; o-3; p-0; q-0; r-2; s-1; t-1; u-2; v-1; w-0; x-0; y-0; z-1, for a total of 28 raw material letters.

OB *AT WORK*

WORKING WITH OTHERS EXERCISE (Continued)

Production Standards:

There are several rules that have to be followed in producing "words-in-sentences." **If these rules are not followed, your output will not meet production specifications and will not pass quality-control inspection.**

1. A letter may appear only as often in a manufactured word as it appears in the raw material phrase; for example, "organizational behaviour is fun" has 1 letter *l* and 1 letter *e.* Thus "steal" is legitimate, but not "teller." It has too many *l*'s and *e*'s.

2. Raw material letters can be used again in different manufactured words.

3. A manufactured **word** may be used only **once** during a production run; once a word—for example, "the"—is used in a sentence, it is out of stock for the rest of the production run. No other sentence may use the word "the."

4. A new word may not be made by adding *s* to form the plural of an already used manufactured word.

5. Sentences must make grammatical and logical sense.

6. All words must be in the English language.

7. Names and places are acceptable.

8. Slang is not acceptable.

9. Writing must be legible. Any illegible sentence will be disqualified.

10. Only sentences that have a minimum of 3 words and a maximum of 6 words will be considered.

Directions:

Step 1

Production Run 1. The instructor will place a raw material phrase on the board or overhead. When the instructor announces, "Begin production," you are to manufacture as many words as possible and package them in sentences for delivery to the Quality Control Review Board. You will have 10 minutes.

Step 2

When the instructor announces, "Stop production," you will have 30 seconds to deliver your output to the Quality Control Review Board. Output received after 30 seconds does not meet the delivery schedule and will not be counted. You may use up to 2 sheets of paper, and each sheet of paper must identify your group.

Step 3

Your output should be delivered by your quality-control representative, who will work with the other representatives to evaluate the performance of each of the groups.

Measuring Performance: The output of your W-I-S company is measured by the total number of acceptable words that are packaged in sentences of 3 to 6 words only.

Quality Control: If any word in a sentence does not meet the standards set forth above, all the words in the sentence will be rejected. The Quality Control Review Board (composed of 1 member from each company) is the final arbiter of acceptability. In the event of a tie vote on the Review Board, a coin toss will determine the outcome.

Step 4

While the output is being evaluated, you should make plans for organizing the second production run.

Step 5

Production Run 2.

Step 6

The results are presented.

Step 7

Discussion.

Just Following Orders

In 1996, Betty Vinson took a job as a mid-level accountant for $50 000 a year with a small long-distance company in Jackson, Mississippi.[38] Within five years, that long-distance company had grown up to become telecom giant WorldCom.

Hard-working and diligent, within two years Ms. Vinson was promoted to a senior manager in WorldCom's corporate accounting division. In her new job, she helped compile quarterly results, along with 10 employees who reported to her. Soon after taking the new position, her bosses asked her to make false accounting entries. At first, she said "no." But continued pressure led her to finally cave in. Her decision to make the false entries came after the company's chief financial officer assured her that he would assume all responsibility.

Over the course of six quarters, Ms. Vinson made illegal entries to bolster WorldCom's profits at the request of her superiors. At the end of 18 months, she had helped falsify at least $3.7 billion in profits. Of course, the whole scheme unravelled in 2002, in what became the largest fraud case in corporate history.

Ms. Vinson pleaded guilty to two criminal counts of conspiracy and securities fraud, charges that carry a maximum sentence of 15 years in prison. In the summer of 2005, she was sentenced to five months in prison and five months of house arrest.

What would you have done had you been in Ms. Vinson's job? Is "just following orders" an acceptable excuse for breaking the law? If your livelihood is on the line, do you say "no" to a powerful boss? What can organizations do to lessen the chance that employees might capitulate to unethical pressures imposed by their boss?

Ajax University Needs a New Structure

Ajax University has recently been in the news for scandals within its athletics department.[39] The athletics department admits to doctoring athletes' transcripts so these athletes can gain admission or maintain eligibility; coaches have been charged with recruiting violations; and alumni have been found to be providing athletes with cars and illegal cash payments.

Despite widespread criticism of these practices, little seems to be done to implement changes to deal with these abuses. Why? There is a lot of money and prestige involved, and university administrators seem willing to look the other way so as not to upset the system.

Within the current structure of the university, the athletics department is responsible for all sports programs. The head of the department, the athletics director, reports to the president of the university, at least on paper. In practice, because the department brings so much money into the university, the athletics director is given free rein to do whatever he wants within his department. The separate and special status given to the athletics department makes abuse rather easy.

Gordon Gee, the chancellor at Vanderbilt University, in reflecting on the problems at Ajax University, believes that the problems are structural: "For too long, athletics has been segregated from the core mission of the university. As a result, we have created a culture, both on campus and nationally, that is disconnected from students, faculty and other constituents, where responsibility is diffused, the potential abuse considerable, and the costs—both financial and academic—unsustainable."

Ajax University needs a new organizational structure for its athletics department that would help eliminate much of the abuse that has happened. The department currently oversees 14 varsity sports, 37 club sports, and various intramural sports.

Varsity sports are elite programs; the significant amount of revenue they bring in not only covers the costs of all club and intramural sports, but also contributes to the general operating budget of the university. One of the problems facing varsity sports is how to recruit students who fit the profile of the university. Ajax athletes are typically admitted with a grade point average of 60 percent.

CASE INCIDENTS (Continued)

The overall student average for those admitted to Ajax is 70 percent.

Intramural sports provides opportunities to students, faculty, and staff to participate in sports on a league basis with post-secondary schools in the region. Rules for intramural sports are determined by representatives of league teams. Club sports provide a co-ed, competitive, recreational program for students, faculty, and staff. Students coordinate and administer the programs and find coaches to participate on a volunteer basis.

Questions

1. How would you classify Ajax University's structure with respect to the athletics department? Defend your choice.

2. Is Ajax University's problem one of poor leadership or inadequate structural design? Explain.

3. If you were a consultant advising Ajax University, what would you suggest to fix the problems noted?

"I Detest Bureaucracy"

Greg Strakosch, founder and CEO of interactive media company TechTarget, hates bureaucracy.[40] So he has created a workplace where his 600 employees are free to come and go as they please. There are no set policies mandating working hours or detailing sick, personal, or vacation days. Employees are free to take as much vacation as they want and to work the hours when they are most productive—even if it's between midnight and 4 a.m. And if you need a day off to take your kid to camp? No problem. Strakosch says ideas like setting a specific number of sick days "strike me as arbitrary and dumb." He trusts his employees to act responsibly.

Strakosch is quick to state that "this isn't a country club." A painstaking hiring process is designed to weed out all but the most autonomous. Managers set ambitious quarterly goals, and employees are given plenty of independence to achieve them. But there is little tolerance for failure. In the most recent 12 months, for instance, Strakosch had fired 7 percent of his workforce for underachieving.

And while hours are flexible, employees frequently put in at least 50 hours a week. In addition, regardless of hours worked, employees are required to remain accessible via email, cellphones, instant messaging, or laptops.

Strakosch's approach seems to be working. Started in 1999, sales in 2007 hit $95 million—up over 100 percent from 2004.

Questions

1. What type of organization is this?

2. Why does this type of structure work at TechTarget?

3. How transferable is this structure to other organizations?

4. Would you want to work at TechTarget? Why or why not?

Delegating Authority

Managers get things done through other people. Because there are limits to any manager's time and knowledge, effective managers need to understand how to delegate. *Delegation* is the assignment of authority to another person to carry out specific duties. It allows an employee to make decisions. Delegation should not be confused with participation. In participative decision making, there is a sharing of authority. In delegation, employees make decisions on their own.

A number of actions differentiate the effective delegator from the ineffective delegator. There are five behaviours that effective delegators will use:[41]

1. *Clarify the assignment.* The place to begin is to determine what is to be delegated and to whom. You need to identify the person most capable of doing the task, then determine if he or she has the time and motivation to do the job.

    Assuming you have a willing and able employee, it is your responsibility to provide clear information on what is being delegated, the results you expect, and any time or performance expectations you hold.

    Unless there is an overriding need to adhere to specific methods, you should delegate only the end results. That is, get agreement on what is to be done and the end results expected, but let the employee decide on the means.

2. *Specify the employee's range of discretion.* Every act of delegation comes with constraints. You are delegating authority to act, but not unlimited authority. What you are delegating is authority to act on certain issues and, on those issues, within certain parameters. You need to specify what those parameters are so employees know, in no uncertain terms, the range of their discretion.

3. *Allow the employee to participate.* One of the best sources for determining how much authority will be necessary to accomplish a task is the employee who will be held accountable for that task. If you allow employees to participate in determining what is delegated, how much authority is needed to get the job done, and the

standards by which they will be judged, you increase employee motivation, satisfaction, and accountability for performance.

4. *Inform others that delegation has occurred.* Delegation should not occur in a vacuum. Not only do you and the employee need to know specifically what has been delegated and how much authority has been granted, but anyone else who may be affected by the delegation act also needs to be informed.

5. *Establish feedback controls.* The establishment of controls to monitor the employee's progress increases the likelihood that important problems will be identified early and that the task will be completed on time and to the desired specifications. For instance, agree on a specific time for completion of the task, and then set progress dates when the employee will report back on how well he or she is doing and any major problems that have surfaced. This can be supplemented with periodic spot checks to ensure that authority guidelines are not being abused, organization policies are being followed, and proper procedures are being met.

Practising Skills

You are the director of research and development for a large pharmaceutical manufacturer. You have six people who report directly to you: Sue (your secretary), Dale (laboratory manager), Todd (quality standards manager), Linda (patent coordination manager), Ruben (market coordination manager), and Marjorie (senior projects manager). Dale is the most senior of the five managers and is generally acknowledged as the chief candidate to replace you if you are promoted or leave.

You have received your annual instructions from the CEO to develop next year's budget for your area. The task is relatively routine, but takes quite a bit of time. In the past, you have always done the annual budget yourself. But this year, because your workload is exceptionally heavy, you have decided to try something different. You are going to assign budget preparation to one of your subordinate managers.

The obvious choice is Dale. Dale has been with the company longest, is highly dependable, and, as your probable successor, is most likely to gain from the experience. The budget is due on your boss's desk in eight weeks. Last year it took you about 30 to 35 hours to complete. However, you have done a budget many times before. For a novice, it might take double that amount of time.

The budget process is generally straightforward. You start with last year's budget and modify it to reflect inflation and changes in departmental objectives. All the data that Dale will need are in your files, online, or can be obtained from your other managers.

You have just walked over to Dale's office and informed him of your decision. He seemed enthusiastic about doing the budget, but he also has a heavy workload. He told you, "I'm regularly coming in around 7 a.m. and it's unusual for me to leave before 7 p.m. For the past five weekends, I've even come in on Saturday mornings to get my work done. I can do my best to try to find time to do the budget." Specify exactly what you would say to Dale and the actions you would take if Dale agrees to do the budget.

Reinforcing Skills

1. When watching a video of a classic movie that has examples of "managers" delegating assignments, pay explicit attention to the incidence of delegation. Was delegating done effectively? What was good about the practice? How might it have been improved? Examples of movies with delegation examples include *The Godfather, The Firm, Star Trek, Nine-to-Five,* and *Working Girl*.

2. The next time you have to do a group project for a class, pay explicit attention to how tasks are delegated. Does someone assume a leadership role? If so, note how closely the delegation process is followed. Is delegation different in project or study groups than in typical work groups?

VIDEO CASE INCIDENT

CASE 13 The Next Level

CBC

Digital Extremes is a video game development company that is working hard to iron out the bugs in its new video game before the "drop dead" date. It has been fine-tuning the game for two months, and the company is under pressure from the publisher to deliver the finished product. Competition in the video game industry is intense, and it is a risky business.

The province of Quebec has been very aggressive in attracting video game companies by giving them subsidies. Quebec does this because it wants to be a major player in the video game industry. It's a big industry: US sales alone exceed $10 billion annually, and that is more than Hollywood box office receipts. Video games are not just for kids anymore.

Quebec's move to encourage the video game industry started quite a few years ago when the province decided on its long-term strategy. One of the companies it attracted was Ubisoft, which operates out of an abandoned textile mill building in Montreal. It makes video games like *Splinter Cell*, a commando-type game. Ubisoft received $50 million in grants from five different Quebec agencies.

Jean-Pierre Faucher, of Alliance NumeriQC, is active in trying to attract new video game companies to Quebec. At the agency's headquarters in Montreal, he talks with visiting game developers about how they can benefit by setting up shop in Quebec. He also travels to the places where new developments in video games are on display, such as the big Game Developers Conference in San Francisco. At the convention, Faucher's goal is to get Montreal on the map in the game industry. To do so, he tries to get invitations to parties that are sponsored by companies like Microsoft and Sony so that he can meet with industry experts.

Faucher is making progress, but Quebec still has a long way to go. Many non-Canadians don't see Montreal in their career future.

Canadian developers at the show are well aware of Quebec's strategy. One video game development firm owner from Ontario complains that as games become more complicated, costs soar, but Ontario does not grant subsidies to help with his business. Game development companies in BC also want their provincial government to provide subsidies so the industry remains viable in BC. Mike Wuetherick and Mark Bowman from Gekido Design Group say there is no support from the BC government, and they expect many BC companies to move to Quebec or to any place where it makes financial sense to operate (like, for example, Singapore).

Some Canadian provinces are following Quebec's lead. For example, John Eden from Technology PEI is trying to attract companies to that province. But most other Canadian provinces seem more interested in attracting filmmakers. Some are not attracted to video games because of their concern about the violence that is often central to the games. So they give subsidies for filmmakers, which is more glamorous anyway. Sonic the Hedgehog is no Brad Pitt.

Quebec continues to pursue its strategy. Another 1000 employees are going to be hired at Ubisoft, and it may become the biggest game development studio in the world.

Questions

1. What factors determine the degree of environmental uncertainty that an organization faces? Describe the video game industry using the three factors of environmental uncertainty.

2. What is the difference between creativity and innovation? Explain the importance of these two ideas for the video game development industry. (Review the relevant material in Chapters 12 and 14 before answering this question and the one that follows.)

3. How can managers encourage creativity and innovation?

Source: Based on "Video Gaming: The Next Level," *CBC Venture*, March 20, 2005, 942.

Organizational Change

All around it, competitors are looking for ways to beat it. How can Google continue to make the changes needed to stay ahead?

1 What are the forces for change?

2 How do organizations manage change?

3 Why do people and organizations resist change?

4 What are some of the contemporary issues in managing change?

Google is so well known for its search engine that the company's name is also used as a verb—people tell each other to "google" something to find out more about it. Google's search engine accounts for more than 60 percent of Internet searches, but this is just one part of the Google brand.[1] There is Google Earth, Gmail, and even a G1 mobile phone, to name just a few of the company's products.

Google is run by an ambitious CEO, Eric Schmidt, who was hired in 2001 to lead the company by the company's founders, Sergey Brin and Larry Page. There is no limit to what the three men believe Google can do. For instance, the company envisions digitizing all books, which has raised concerns among publishers and authors. Even Microsoft has been said to fear that Google is becoming too powerful.

So how does Google encourage innovation? Schmidt explains: "we try to encourage [innovation] with things like 20 percent time, and the small technology teams . . . , We also try to look for small companies that we can acquire. Because, often, it's small companies which have the great new ideas."

Google is just one of the many organizations that need to reinvent themselves often if they are to survive in a challenging business environment. Engaging in any kind of change in an organization is not easy. In this chapter, we examine the forces for change, managing change, and contemporary change issues.

OB Is for Everyone

- Are there positive approaches to change?
- How do you respond to change?
- What makes organizations resist change?

Self-Assessment Library

LEARNING ABOUT YOURSELF

- Tolerance for Change
- Stress

What Causes Change?

1   What are the forces for change?

A study of 309 human resource executives across a variety of industries found that *all* respondents were going through at least one of the following changes: mergers, acquisitions, divestitures, global competition, management and/or organizational structure.[2] A Statistics Canada Workplace and Employee Survey further identified types of changes that Canadian businesses went through recently: "integrating different functional areas; modifying the degree of centralisation; downsizing; relying more on temporary and/or part-time workers; re-engineering; increasing overtime hours; adopting flexible working hours; reducing the number of managerial levels; relying on job rotation and/or multi-skilling; implementing Total Quality Management; outsourcing; and collaborating more on interfirm research and development, production, or marketing."[3] The extent to which businesses undergo change varies by organizational size. More than 80 percent of companies that employed 100 or more people underwent at least one of these changes. Only 40 percent of the smaller companies underwent change.

Organizational change is not just confined to larger organizations; 18 percent of self-employed individuals also reported organizational change. The same study identified the following types of changes for the self-employed: engaging in "collaborative work, new inventory systems, introducing sub-contracting, new financial management techniques, computerisation of organisational practices, introduction of new corporate strategic orientation or redefining operating hours."[4]

What brings about change in organizations? Organizations face continuously changing environments. As a result, organizations must not only be aware of opportunities for change, but also consider how best to respond to them. They must also appoint people to help them manage organizational change efforts.

Forces for Change

As recently as the late 1990s, music retailers Virgin Records and Vancouver-based a&b sound were rapidly growing and profitable companies. Young people were flocking to their superstores because they offered a wide selection and competitive prices. But the market changed, and these chains and others like them suffered the consequences. Downloading, legal and otherwise, cut hard into CD sales, and growing competition from Indigo.com and Amazon.ca, as well as discounters such as Walmart and Costco, stole a sizable part of their market share.

More and more organizations today face a dynamic and changing environment. This, in turn, is requiring these organizations to adapt. "Change or die!" is the rallying cry among today's managers worldwide. Exhibit 14-1 summarizes six distinct forces that are acting as stimulants for change.

In a number of places in this textbook, we have discussed the changing *nature of the workforce*. For instance, almost every organization is having to adjust to a multicultural environment. Human resource policies and practices have to change to reflect the needs of an aging labour force. Many companies are having to spend large amounts of money on employee training to upgrade reading, math, computer, and other skills.

Technology is changing jobs and organizations. For instance, computers are commonplace in almost every organization, and cellphones and hand-held PDAs are now perceived as necessities by a large segment of the population. The music business, as a case in point, is now struggling to cope with the economic consequences of widespread online music sharing. For the longer term, recent breakthroughs in deciphering the human genetic code offer the potential for pharmaceutical companies to produce drugs designed for specific individuals, which creates serious ethical dilemmas for insurance companies as to who is insurable and who is not.

Beginning in the early 1970s, with the overnight quadrupling of world oil prices, *economic shocks* have continued to impose changes on organizations. In recent years,

EXHIBIT 14-1 Forces for Change	
Force	**Examples**
Nature of the workforce	More cultural diversity Aging population Many new entrants with inadequate skills
Technology	Faster, cheaper, and more mobile computers Online music sharing Deciphering of the human genetic code
Economic shocks	Rise and fall of dot-com stocks Record low interest rates 2007–2009 financial markets collapse
Competition	Global competitors Mergers and consolidations Growth of e-commerce
Social trends	Internet chat rooms Retirement of Baby Boomers Rise in discount and "big box" retailers
World politics	Iraq–US war Opening of markets in China Tsunamis and earthquakes worldwide

for instance, new dot-com businesses were created, turned tens of thousands of investors into overnight millionaires, and then crashed. Record low interest rates from 2004 to 2007 stimulated a rapid rise in home values, helped sustain consumer spending, and provided a spur to home builders and remodellers, furniture retailers, mortgage bankers, and other home-related businesses. Then, just as suddenly, the financial meltdown in 2008 eroded the average employee's retirement account considerably, forcing many employees to postpone their anticipated retirement date. Meanwhile, spending dropped, causing businesses that had been doing reasonably well a year earlier to suffer.

Competition is changing. In the global economy, competitors are as likely to come from across the ocean as from across town. Heightened competition also makes it necessary for established organizations to defend themselves against both traditional competitors who develop new products and services, and small, entrepreneurial firms with innovative offerings.

Social trends don't remain static. For instance, in contrast to just 15 years ago, people are meeting and sharing information in Internet chat rooms; Baby Boomers have begun to retire; and consumers are increasingly doing their shopping at discount warehouses and "big box" retailers such as The Home Depot and Future Shop.

Throughout this textbook, we have argued strongly for the importance of seeing organizational behaviour in a global context. Business schools have been preaching a global perspective since the early 1980s, but no one—not even the strongest proponents of globalization—could have imagined how *world politics* would change in recent years. We have seen the breakup of the Soviet Union; the opening up of China and Southeast Asia; the instability in the Middle East, India, and Pakistan; and, of course, the rise of Muslim fundamentalism. The unilateral invasion of Iraq by the United States has led to an expensive post-war rebuilding program and an increase in anti-American attitudes in much of the world.

Opportunities for Change

Organizations have many opportunities to engage in change. For instance, we noted the importance of motivating employees and discussed a variety of programs that could be used to motivate individuals for specific outcomes. We described job redesign as a way of motivating employees, and indicated that increasing factors such as autonomy and feedback generally increases job satisfaction. We looked at the greater emphasis on teamwork in organizations. We suggested that organizations are moving toward becoming more ethically and socially responsible. We discussed the leadership challenges of sharing power with employees. As well, we discussed reorganizing the workplace, noting how recent changes in organizational structure have, in some instances, led to flatter organizations and more interconnections with other organizations. We also noted that the culture of an organization is like the glue that holds the organization together, and that sometimes the entire culture of the organization needs to change for organizational change to be successful. Exhibit 14-2 summarizes the range of change targets available to organizations.

As we discussed the workplace in this textbook, and talked about possible change, we might have implied that change happens easily, perhaps overnight, and does not require careful thought or planning. This implication exists because we did not discuss how these changes actually happen in the workplace, what has to be done to achieve change, and how difficult change actually is. We wanted you to understand what changes were possible before we actually discussed how to carry them out.

Change Agents

change agents People who act as catalysts and assume the responsibility for managing change activities.

Who is responsible for managing change activities in an organization? The answer is change agents.[5] **Change agents** can be managers or nonmanagers, employees of the organization or outside consultants. A contemporary example of an internal change

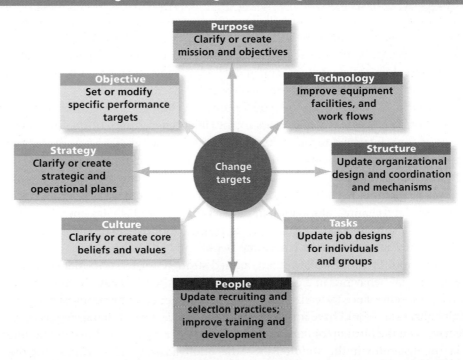

EXHIBIT 14-2   Organizational Targets for Change

Source: J. R. Schermerhorn Jr., J. G. Hunt, and R. N. Osborn, *Organizational Behavior*, 9th ed., 2005, p. 363, Figure 16.1. Copyright © 2005 John Wiley & Sons, Inc. Reprinted with permission of John Wiley & Sons, Inc.

agent is Lawrence Summers, president of Harvard University.[6] When he accepted the presidency in 2001, Summers aggressively sought to shake up the complacent institution by, among other things, leading the battle to reshape the undergraduate curriculum, proposing that the university be more directly engaged with problems in education and public health, and reorganizing to consolidate more power in the president's office. His change efforts generated tremendous resistance, particularly among Harvard faculty. Finally, in 2006, when Summers made comments suggesting that women were less able to excel in science than men, the Harvard faculty revolted, and in a few weeks, Summers was forced to resign. Despite Summers' support among students—a poll shortly before his resignation showed that students supported him by a 3:1 ratio—his efforts at change had ruffled one too many feathers. In 2007, he was replaced with Drew Gilpin Faust, Harvard's first female president, who promised to be less aggressive in instituting changes.[7]

In some instances, internal management will hire the services of outside consultants to provide advice and assistance with major change efforts. Because they are from the outside, these individuals can offer an objective perspective often unavailable to insiders. Outside consultants, however, are disadvantaged because they usually have an inadequate understanding of the organization's history, culture, operating procedures, and personnel. Outside consultants also may be prone to initiating more drastic changes—which can be a benefit or a disadvantage—because they don't have to live with the repercussions after the change is implemented. In contrast, internal staff specialists or managers, when acting as change agents, may be more thoughtful (and possibly more cautious) because they have to live with the consequences of their actions.

Fiat Group Automobiles hired an outsider as a change agent to return the ailing company to profitability. As Fiat's new CEO, Sergio Marchionne led a turnaround by changing a hierarchical, status-driven firm into a market-driven one. Marchionne reduced the layers of Fiat's management and fired 10 percent of its 20 000 white-collar employees. He improved relationships with union employees, reduced car-development time, and introduced new car designs. Marchionne is shown here with the redesigned version of the compact Fiat 500, which he hopes will be for the company what the iPod was for Apple.

Approaches to Managing Change

Now we turn to several approaches to managing change: Lewin's classic three-step model of the change process, Kotter's eight-step plan for implementing change, action research, and appreciative inquiry.

2 How do organizations manage change?

Lewin's Three-Step Model

To this point, we have discussed the kinds of changes organizations can make. Assuming that an organization has uncovered a need for change, how does it engage in the change process? Kurt Lewin argued that successful change in organizations should follow three steps, which are illustrated in Exhibit 14-3 on page 544: **unfreezing** the status quo, **moving** to a new state, and **refreezing** the new change to make it permanent.[8] The value of this model can be seen through the example of a large oil company whose management decided to reorganize its marketing function in Western Canada.

The oil company had three regional offices in the West, located in Winnipeg, Calgary, and Vancouver. The decision was made to consolidate the marketing divisions of the three regional offices into a single regional office in Calgary. The reorganization meant transferring more than 150 employees, eliminating some duplicate managerial positions, and instituting a new hierarchy of command. As you might guess, keeping such a big move secret was difficult. The rumours preceded the announcement by several months. The decision itself was made unilaterally. It came from the executive offices in Toronto. The people affected had no say whatsoever in the choice. For those in Vancouver or Winnipeg who disliked the decision and its consequences—the problems inherent in transferring to another city, pulling youngsters out of school, making new friends, having

unfreezing Change efforts to overcome the pressures of both individual resistance and group conformity.

moving Efforts to get employees involved in the change process.

refreezing Stabilizing a change intervention by balancing driving and restraining forces.

EXHIBIT 14–3 Lewin's Three-Step Change Model

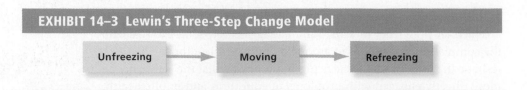

Unfreezing → Moving → Refreezing

new co-workers, undergoing the reassignment of responsibilities—the only recourse was to quit. The status quo was about to change.

The status quo can be considered to be an equilibrium state. To move from this equilibrium—to overcome the pressures of both individual resistance and group conformity—unfreezing is necessary. Exhibit 14-4 shows that unfreezing can occur in one of three ways. The **driving forces**, which direct behaviour away from the status quo, can be increased. The **restraining forces**, which hinder movement from the existing equilibrium, can be decreased. A third alternative is to *combine the first two approaches.* Companies that have been successful in the past are likely to encounter restraining forces because people question the need for change.[9] Similarly, research shows that companies with strong cultures excel at incremental change but are overcome by restraining forces against radical change.[10]

driving forces Forces that direct behaviour away from the status quo.

restraining forces Forces that hinder movement away from the status quo

EXHIBIT 14-4 Unfreezing the Status Quo

Desired state

Restraining forces

Status quo

Driving forces

Time ——→

The oil company's management expected employee resistance to the consolidation and outlined its alternatives. Management could use positive incentives to encourage employees to accept the change. The company could offer pay increases or liberal moving expenses to those who accepted the transfer. Management might offer low-cost mortgage funds to allow employees to buy new homes in Calgary. Of course, management might also consider unfreezing acceptance of the status quo by removing restraining forces. Employees could be counselled individually. Each employee's concerns and apprehensions could be heard and specifically clarified. Assuming that most of the fears are unjustified, the counsellor could assure the employees that there was nothing to fear and then demonstrate, through tangible evidence, that restraining forces are unwarranted. If resistance is extremely high, management may have to resort to both reducing resistance and increasing the attractiveness of the alternative if the unfreezing is to be successful.

Research on organizational change has shown that, to be effective, change has to happen quickly.[11] Organizations that build up to change do less well than those that get to and through the moving stage quickly.

Once the consolidation change has been implemented, if it is to be successful, the new situation must be refrozen so that it can be sustained over time. Unless this last step is taken, there is a high chance that the change will be short-lived and that employees will try to revert to the previous equilibrium state. The objective of refreezing, then, is to stabilize the new situation by balancing the driving and restraining forces.

How could the oil company's management refreeze its consolidation change? It could systematically replace temporary forces with permanent ones. For instance, management might impose a new bonus system tied to the specific changes desired. The formal rules and regulations governing behaviour of those affected by the change should also be revised to reinforce the new situation. Over time, of course, the work group's own norms will evolve to sustain the new equilibrium. But until that point is reached, management will have to rely on more formal mechanisms.

A key feature of Lewin's three-step model is its conception of change as an episodic activity. For a debate about whether change can continue to be implemented as an activity

EXHIBIT 14-5 Kotter's Eight-Step Plan for Implementing Change

1. Establish a sense of urgency by creating a compelling reason for why change is needed.

2. Form a coalition with enough power to lead the change.

3. Create a new vision to direct the change and strategies for achieving the vision.

4. Communicate the vision throughout the organization.

5. Empower others to act on the vision by removing barriers to change and encouraging risk-taking and creative problem-solving.

6. Plan for, create, and reward short-term "wins" that move the organization toward the new vision.

7. Consolidate improvements, reassess changes, and make necessary adjustments in the new programs.

8. Reinforce the changes by demonstrating the relationship between new behaviours and organizational success.

Source: Based on J. P. Kotter, *Leading Change* (Boston: Harvard Business School Press, 1996).

with a beginning, middle, and end, or whether the structure of twenty-first- century workplaces will require change to take place as an ongoing if not chaotic process, see this chapter's *Point/Counterpoint* on page 560.

Kotter's Eight-Step Plan for Implementing Change

John Kotter, professor of leadership at Harvard Business School, built on Lewin's three-step model to create a more detailed approach for implementing change.[12]

Kotter began by listing common failures that occur when managers try to initiate change. These include the inability to create a sense of urgency about the need for change; failure to create a coalition for managing the change process; the absence of a vision for change and to effectively communicate that vision; not removing obstacles that could impede the achievement of the vision; failure to provide short-term and achievable goals; the tendency to declare victory too soon; and not anchoring the changes in the organization's culture.

Kotter then established eight sequential steps to overcome these problems. These steps are listed in Exhibit 14-5, above.

Notice how Exhibit 14-5 builds on Lewin's model. Kotter's first four steps essentially represent the "unfreezing" stage. Steps 5 through 7 represent "moving." The final step works on "refreezing." Kotter's contribution lies in providing managers and change agents with a more detailed guide for successfully implementing change.

Action Research

Action research refers to a change process based on the systematic collection of data and then selection of a change action based on what the analyzed data indicate.[13] The importance of this approach is that it provides a scientific method for managing planned change.

The process of action research consists of five steps: diagnosis, analysis, feedback, action, and evaluation. The change agent, often an outside consultant in action research, begins by gathering information about problems, concerns, and needed changes from members of the organization. This *diagnosis* is analogous to the physician's search to find specifically what ails a patient. In action research, the change agent asks questions, interviews employees, reviews records, and listens to the concerns of employees.

Diagnosis is followed by *analysis*. What problems do people key in on? What patterns do these problems seem to take? The change agent organizes this information into primary concerns, problem areas, and possible actions.

action research A change process based on the systematic collection of data and then selection of a change action based on what the analyzed data indicate.

Action research includes extensive involvement of the change targets. That is, the people who will be involved in any change program must be actively involved in determining what the problem is and participating in creating the solution. So the third step—*feedback*—requires sharing with employees what has been found from steps one and two. The employees, with the help of the change agent, develop action plans for bringing about any needed change.

Now the *action* part of action research is set in motion. The employees and the change agent carry out the specific actions to correct the problems that have been identified.

The final step, consistent with the scientific underpinnings of action research, is *evaluation* of the action plan's effectiveness. Using the initial data gathered as a benchmark, any subsequent changes can be compared and evaluated.

Action research provides at least two specific benefits for an organization. First, it is problem-focused. The change agent objectively looks for problems, and the type of problem determines the type of change action. While this may seem intuitively obvious, a lot of change activities are not done this way. Rather, they are solution-centred. The change agent has a favourite solution—for example, implementing flextime, teams, or a process re-engineering program—and then seeks out problems that his or her solution fits. Second, because action research so heavily involves employees in the process, resistance to change is reduced. In fact, once employees have actively participated in the feedback stage, the change process typically takes on a momentum of its own. The employees and groups that have been involved become an internal source of sustained pressure to bring about the change.

Appreciative Inquiry

appreciative inquiry An approach to change that seeks to identify the unique qualities and special strengths of an organization, which can then be built on to improve performance.

Most organizational change approaches start from a negative perspective: The organization identifies problems that need solutions. **Appreciative inquiry** accentuates the positive.[14] Rather than looking for problems to fix, this approach seeks to identify the unique qualities and special strengths of an organization, which can then be built on to improve performance. That is, it focuses on an organization's successes rather than on its problems.

Are there positive approaches to change?

Advocates of appreciative inquiry argue that problem-solving approaches always ask people to look backward at yesterday's failures, to focus on shortcomings, and rarely result in new visions. Instead of creating a climate for positive change, action research and organizational development techniques such as survey feedback and process consultation end up placing blame and generating defensiveness. Proponents of appreciative inquiry claim it makes more sense to refine and enhance what the organization is already doing well. This allows the organization to change by playing to its strengths and competitive advantages.

The appreciate inquiry process (see Exhibit 14-6) essentially consists of four steps, or "Four *D*'s," often played out in a large-group meeting over a two- or three-day time period, and overseen by a trained change agent:

- *Discovery.* The idea is to find out what people think are the strengths of the organization. For instance, employees are asked to recount times they felt the organization worked best or when they specifically felt most satisfied with their jobs.

- *Dreaming.* The information from the discovery phase is used to speculate on possible futures for the organization. For instance, people are asked to envision the organization in five years and describe what is different.

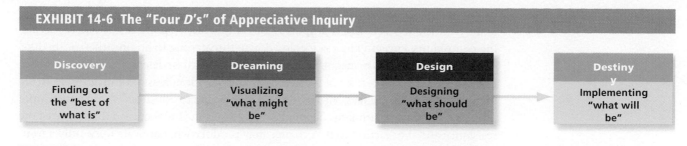

EXHIBIT 14-6 The "Four _D_'s" of Appreciative Inquiry

Discovery		Dreaming		Design		Destiny
Finding out the "best of what is"	→	Visualizing "what might be"	→	Designing "what should be"	→	Implementing "what will be"

Source: Based on D. L. Cooperrider and D. Whitney, _Collaborating for Change: Appreciative Inquiry_ (San Francisco: Berrett-Koehler, 2000).

- _Design._ Based on the dream articulation, participants focus on finding a common vision of how the organization will look, and agree on its unique qualities.

- _Destiny._ In this final step, participants discuss how the organization is going to fulfill its dream. This typically includes the writing of action plans and the development of implementation strategies.

Appreciate inquiry has proven to be an effective change strategy in organizations such as Toronto-based Orchestras Canada, Ajax, Ontario-based Nokia Canada, Burnaby, BC-based TELUS, Calgary-based EnCana, and Toronto-based CBC.

Nokia Canada employees consider the future, envision the perfect solutions to the future, and then identify what needs to happen to get to the future as envisioned. Of their appreciative inquiry work, general manager Nathalie Le Prohon says, "It's very unstructured, very open to innovation and imagination, and very powerful as a tool for developing new thought leadership, new ways to approach business problems."[15]

TELUS's Go East division in Calgary has used appreciative inquiry to increase positive ideas among customer-care employees. Barbara Armstrong, a senior manager, explains the positive impact of the process: "The fact that [front-line workers] are being heard completely changes the way they view things."[16]

The use of appreciative inquiry in organizations is relatively recent, and it has not yet been determined when it is most appropriately used for organizational change.[17] However, it does give us the opportunity of viewing change from a much more positive perspective.

Resistance to Change

One of the most well-documented findings from studies of individual and organizational behaviour is that organizations and their members resist change. One recent study showed that even when employees are shown data that suggests they need to change, they latch onto whatever data they can find that suggests they are okay and don't need to change. Our egos are fragile, and we often see change as threatening.[18]

In some ways, resistance to change is positive. It provides a degree of stability and predictability to behaviour. If there were not some resistance, organizational behaviour would take on the characteristics of chaotic randomness. Resistance to change can also be a source of functional conflict. For example, resistance to a reorganization plan or a change in a product line can stimulate a healthy debate over the merits of the idea and result in a better decision. But there is a definite downside to resistance to change. It hinders adaptation and progress.

Resistance to change does not necessarily surface in standardized ways. Resistance can be overt, implicit, immediate, or

3 Why do people and organizations resist change?

How do you respond to change?

deferred. It is easiest for management to deal with resistance when it is overt and immediate. For instance, a change is proposed, and employees respond immediately by voicing complaints, engaging in a work slowdown, threatening to go on strike, or the like. The greater challenge is managing resistance that is implicit or deferred. Implicit resistance efforts are more subtle—loss of loyalty to the organization, loss of motivation to work, increased errors or mistakes, increased absenteeism due to "sickness"—and hence more difficult to recognize. Similarly, deferred actions cloud the link between the source of the resistance and the reaction to it. A change may produce what appears to be only a minimal reaction at the time it is initiated, but then resistance surfaces weeks, months, or even years later. Or a single change that in and of itself might have little impact becomes "the straw that breaks the camel's back." Reactions to change can build up and then explode in some response that seems totally out of proportion to the change itself. The resistance, of course, has merely been deferred and stockpiled. What surfaces is a response to an accumulation of previous changes.

Let's look at the sources of resistance. For analytical purposes, we have categorized them by individual and organizational sources. In the real world, the sources often overlap.

Individual Resistance

Individual sources of resistance to change reside in basic human characteristics such as perceptions, personalities, and needs. This chapter's *Case Incident—GreyStar Art & Greetings Makes Technological Changes* on page 564 looks at an individual who resists change in the workplace. Exhibit 14-7 summarizes four reasons why individuals may resist change:[19]

- *Self-interest.* People worry that they will lose something of value if change happens. Thus, they look after their own self-interests rather than those of the total organization.

- *Misunderstanding and lack of trust.* People resist change when they don't understand the nature of the change and fear that the cost of change will outweigh any potential gains for them. This often occurs when they don't trust those initiating the change.

EXHIBIT 14-7 Sources of Individual Resistance to Change

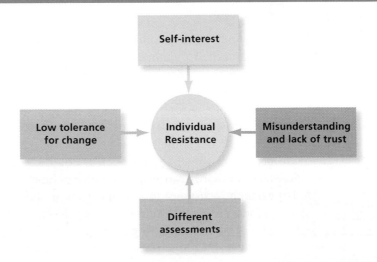

Source: Based on J. P. Kotter and L. A. Schlesinger, "Choosing Strategies for Change," *Harvard Business Review*, July–August 2008, pp. 107–109.

- *Different assessments.* People resist change when they see it differently than their managers do and think the costs outweigh the benefits, even for the organization. Managers may assume that employees have the same information that they do, but this is not always the case.

- *Low tolerance for change.* People resist change because they worry that they do not have the skills and behaviour required of the new situation. They may feel that they are being asked to do too much, too quickly.

In addition to the above, individuals sometimes worry that being asked to change may indicate that what they have been doing in the past was somehow wrong. Managers should not overlook the effects of peer pressure on an individual's response to change. As well, the manager's attitude (positive or negative) toward the change and his or her relationship with employees will affect an individual's response to change.

Cynicism

Employees often feel cynical about the change process, particularly if they have been through several rounds of "change," and nothing appears (to them) to have changed. One study identified sources of cynicism in the change process of a large unionized manufacturing plant.[20] The major elements contributing to the cynicism were as follows:

- Feeling uninformed about what was happening

- Lack of communication and respect from one's manager

- Lack of communication and respect from one's union representative

- Lack of opportunity for meaningful participation in decision making

The researchers also found that employees with negative personalities were more likely to be cynical about change. While organizations might not be able to change an individual's personality, they certainly have the ability to provide greater communication and respect, as well as opportunities to participate in decision making. The researchers found that cynicism about change led to such outcomes as lower commitment, less satisfaction, and reduced motivation to work hard. Exhibit 14 8 illustrates why some employees, particularly Dilbert, may have reason to feel cynical about organizational change. You can discover more about how comfortable you are with change by taking the test in this chapter's *Learning About Yourself Exercise* on page 561.

Learning About Yourself

1. Managing-in-a-Turbulent-World Tolerance Test, **(page 561)**

EXHIBIT 14-8

Source: Dilbert, by Scott Adams. August 3, 1996. DILBERT reprinted by permission of United Feature Syndicate, Inc.

Though most people and organizations resist change, at Advantech AMT, located in Dorval, Quebec, change is the norm. Françoise Binette, vice-president of finance, says that "managing change forms an intrinsic part of our corporate DNA, and it is this environment that has allowed us to consistently develop unique and innovative products."

Organizational Resistance

Organizations, by their very nature, are conservative.[21] They actively resist change. You don't have to look far to see evidence of this phenomenon. Government agencies want to continue doing what they have been doing for years, whether the need for their service changes or remains the same. Organized religions are deeply entrenched in their history. Attempts to change church doctrine require great persistence and patience. Educational institutions, which exist to open minds and challenge established ways of thinking, are themselves extremely resistant to change. Most school systems are using essentially the same teaching technologies today as they were 50 years ago. Similarly, most business firms appear highly resistant to change.

What makes organizations resist change?

In the study we mentioned at the outset of the chapter, half of the 309 human resource executives of Canadian firms surveyed rated their companies' ability to manage change as "fair."[22] One-third of them said that their ability to manage change was their weakest skill, and only 25 percent of the companies make a strong effort to train leaders in the change process. When organizations refuse to change with the times, they can face catastrophic results, as can be seen with the Big Three US automakers (Ford, Chrysler, and General Motors) who in late 2008 were begging for the US government to bail them out financially.

Six major sources of organizational resistance (shown in Exhibit 14-9) have been identified:[23]

- *Structural inertia.* Organizations have built-in mechanisms—such as their selection processes and formalized regulations—to produce stability. When an organization is confronted with change, this structural inertia acts as a counterbalance to sustain stability.

EXHIBIT 14-9 Sources of Organizational Resistance to Change

- Threat to established resource allocations
- Structural inertia
- Threat to established power relationships
- Organizational Resistance
- Limited focus of change
- Threat to expertise
- Group inertia

- *Limited focus of change.* Organizations are made up of a number of inter-dependent subsystems. One cannot be changed without affecting the others. So limited changes in subsystems tend to be nullified by the larger system.

- *Group inertia.* Even if individuals want to change their behaviour, group norms may act as a constraint.

- *Threat to expertise.* Changes in organizational patterns may threaten the expertise of specialized groups.

- *Threat to established power relationships.* Any redistribution of decision-making authority can threaten long-established power relationships within the organization.

- *Threat to established resource allocations.* Groups in the organization that control sizable resources often see change as a threat. They tend to be content with the way things are.

The *Working with Others Exercise* on page 563 asks you to identify how power relationships are affected by organizational change.

Overcoming Resistance to Change

Before we move on to ways to overcome resistance to change, it's important to note that not all change is good. Research has shown that sometimes an emphasis on making speedy decisions can lead to bad decisions. Sometimes the line between resisting needed change and falling into a "speed trap" is a fine one indeed. What is more, sometimes in the "fog of change," those who are initiating change fail to realize the full magnitude of the effects they are causing or to estimate their true costs to the organization. Thus, although the perspective generally taken is that rapid, transformational change is good, this is not always the case. Change agents need to carefully think through the full implications. The *Ethical Dilemma Exercise* on page 564 asks you to consider the stress that employees face after downsizing occurs in the workplace and when the pressure to take on more tasks increases.

Seven tactics can be used by change agents to deal with resistance to change.[24] Let's review them briefly.

- *Education and communication.* Resistance can be reduced through communicating with employees to help them see the logic of a change. Communication can reduce resistance on two levels. First, it fights the effects of misinformation and poor communication: If employees receive the full facts and get any misunderstandings cleared up, resistance should subside. Second, communication can be helpful in "selling" the need for change. Research shows that the way the need for change is sold matters—change is more likely when the necessity of changing is packaged properly.[25] A study of German companies revealed that changes are most effective when a company communicates its rationale, balancing various stakeholder (shareholders, employees, community, customers) interests, vs. a rationale based on shareholder interests only.[26]

- *Participation and involvement.* It's difficult for individuals to resist a change decision in which they participated. Before making a change, those opposed can be brought into the decision process. Assuming that the participants have the expertise to make a meaningful contribution, their involvement can reduce resistance, obtain commitment, and increase the quality of the change decision.

- *Building support and commitment.* Change agents can offer a range of supportive efforts to reduce resistance. When employees' fear and anxiety are high, employee counselling and therapy, new-skills training, or a short paid leave of absence may facilitate adjustment. Research on middle managers has shown that when managers or employees have low emotional commitment to change, they favour the status quo and resist it.[27] So building support with employees can also help them emotionally commit to the change rather than embrace the status quo.

- *Implementing changes fairly.* Try as managers might to have employees see change positively, most workers tend to react negatively. Most people simply don't like change. But one way organizations can minimize the negative impact of change, even when employees frame it as a negative, is to makes sure the change is implemented fairly. As we learned in Chapter 4, procedural fairness becomes especially important when employees perceive an outcome as negative, so when implementing changes, it's crucial that organizations bend over backwards to make sure employees see the reason for the change, and perceive that the changes are being implemented consistently and fairly.[28]

- *Manipulation and co-optation. Manipulation* refers to covert influence attempts. Twisting and distorting facts to make them appear more attractive, withholding undesirable information, and creating false rumours to get employees to accept a change are all examples of manipulation. *Co-optation,* on the other hand, is a form of both manipulation and participation. It seeks to "buy off" the leaders of a resistance group by giving them a key role in the change decision.

- *Selecting people who accept change.* Research suggests that the ability to easily accept and adapt to change is related to personality—some people simply have more positive attitudes about change than others.[29] It appears that people who adjust best to change are those who are open to experience, take a positive attitude toward change, are willing to take risks, and are flexible in their behavior. One study of managers in the United States, Europe, and Asia found that those with a positive self-concept and high risk tolerance coped better with organizational change. The study authors suggested that organizations could facilitate the change process by selecting people who score high on these characteristics. Another study found that selecting people based on a resistance-to-change scale worked well in eliminating those who tended to react emotionally to change or to be rigid.[30]

- *Explicit and implicit coercion.* Coercion is the application of direct threats or force upon the resisters. If the corporate management is determined to close a manufacturing plant should employees not acquiesce to a pay cut, then coercion would be the label attached to its change tactic. Other examples of coercion are threats of transfer, loss of promotions, negative performance evaluations, and a poor letter of recommendation.

Michael Adams, president of Environics Research Group in Toronto, has noted that Canadians may have become more resistant to change in recent years.[31] Between 1983 and the mid-1990s, Canadians increasingly reported that they "felt confident in their ability to cope with change." This trend has reversed in recent years. Half of Canadians aged 15 to 33 now "feel left behind and overwhelmed by the pace of life and the prevalence of technology." Those who feel left behind tend to be those who are not college- or university-educated, highly skilled, or adaptive.

This chapter's *Case Incident—GE's Work-Out* on page 565 looks at one organization's attempt to reduce resistance to change. *From Concepts to Skills* on pages 566–567 provides additional tips for carrying out organizational change.

The Politics of Change

No discussion of resistance to change would be complete without a brief mention of the politics of change. Because change invariably threatens the status quo, it inherently implies political activity.[32]

Politics suggests that the demand for change is more likely to come from employees who are new to the organization (and have less invested in the status quo) or managers who are slightly removed from the main power structure. Those managers who have spent their entire careers with a single organization and eventually achieve a senior position in the hierarchy are often major impediments to change. Change itself is a very real threat to their status and position. Yet they may be expected to implement changes to demonstrate that they are not merely caretakers. By trying to bring about change, they can symbolically convey to various constituencies—stockholders, suppliers, employees, customers—that they are on top of problems and adapting to a dynamic environment. Of course, as you might guess, when forced to introduce change, these long-time power holders tend to implement **first-order change** (change that is incremental and straightforward). Radical change is too threatening. This, incidentally, explains why boards of directors that recognize the need for the rapid introduction of **second-order change** (change that is multidimensional, multilevel, discontinuous, and radical) in their organizations frequently turn to outside candidates for new leadership.[33]

You may remember that we discussed politics in Chapter 8 and suggested ways to more effectively encourage people to go along with your ideas. That chapter also indicated how individuals acquire power, which provides further insight into the ability of some individuals to resist change.

first-order change Change that is incremental and straightforward.

second-order change Change that is multidimensional, multilevel, discontinuous, and radical.

Contemporary Change Issues for Today's Managers

In 2008, Google turned 10 years old.[34] Though the company was doing well after its first decade, growth was slowing at the same time that the economy was also facing a slowdown. Google knew it had to stay competitive if it expected users to keep using its search tools, so in 2008 the company made more than 350 improvements to the search engine. How does the company maintain such innovation?

Google's CEO Eric Schmidt recognizes that successful innovation requires time and thought. "Innovation is something that comes when you're not under the gun. So it's important that, even if you don't have balance in your life, you have some time for reflection," says Schmidt.[35] Thus, employees are encouraged to allocate 20 percent of work time to develop special projects of their own choosing, creating opportunities for many new products to be developed.

Can Schmidt continue to introduce more innovation to Google and also help the organization keep learning and adapting?

What can managers do to help their organizations become more innovative? How do managers create organizations that continually learn and adapt? Is managing change culture-bound? In this section, we briefly address these three contemporary change issues.

4 What are some of the contemporary issues in managing change?

Stimulating Innovation

How can an organization become more innovative? Although there is no guaranteed formula, certain characteristics surface again and again when researchers study innovative organizations. We have grouped them into structural, cultural, and human resource categories. Our message to change agents is that they should consider introducing these characteristics into their organization if they want to create an innovative climate. Before we look at these characteristics, however, let's clarify what we mean by innovation.

innovation A new idea applied to initiating or improving a product, process, or service.

Definition of Innovation

We said change refers to making things different. **Innovation** is a more specialized kind of change. Innovation is a new idea applied to initiating or improving a product, process, or service.[36] So all innovations involve change, but not all changes necessarily involve new ideas or lead to significant improvements. Innovations in organizations can range from small incremental improvements, such as Nabisco's extension of the Oreo product line to include double stuffs and chocolate-covered Oreos, up to radical breakthroughs, such as Toyota's battery-powered Prius. Keep in mind that while there are many product innovations, the concept of innovation also encompasses new production process technologies, new structures or administrative systems, and new plans or programs pertaining to organizational members.

Sources of Innovation

Structural variables have been the most studied potential source of innovation.[37] A comprehensive review of the structure-innovation relationship leads to the following conclusions:[38]

- *Organic structures positively influence innovation.* Because they are lower in vertical differentiation, formalization, and centralization, organic organizations facilitate the flexibility, adaptation, and cross-fertilization that make the adoption of innovations easier.

- *Long tenure in management is associated with innovation.* Managerial tenure apparently provides legitimacy and knowledge of how to accomplish tasks and obtain desired outcomes.

- *Innovation is nurtured when there are slack resources.* Having an abundance of resources allows an organization to afford to purchase innovations, bear the cost of instituting innovations, and absorb failures.

Respected as one of the world's most innovative companies, Starbucks turned a commodity product that was declining in sales and invented specialty coffees as a major new product category. Starbucks relies on its employees to share customer insights with managers and takes product development teams on inspirational field trips to view customer behaviour, local cultures, and fashion trends. Starbucks has extended its coffee shops from North American urban sites to locations throughout the world, including the shop shown here at a shopping centre in Ramadan, Dubai.

- *Interunit communication is high in innovative organizations.*[39] Innovative organizations are high users of committees, task forces, cross-functional teams, and other mechanisms that facilitate interaction across departmental lines.

Innovative organizations tend to have similar *cultures*. They encourage experimentation. They reward both successes and failures. They celebrate mistakes. Unfortunately, in too many organizations, people are rewarded for the absence of failures rather than for the presence of successes. Such cultures extinguish risk-taking and innovation. People will suggest and try new ideas only when they feel such behaviours exact no penalties. Managers in innovative organizations recognize that failures are a natural by-product of venturing into the unknown. 3M is known for its culture of innovation, as *OB in the Workplace* describes.

IN THE WORKPLACE

3M Is a Leader in Innovation

What does it take to be a leader in innovation? Many organizations strive to achieve the standard of innovation reached by 3M, the company responsible for the development of waterproof sandpaper, masking tape, and Post-it® notes.[40] 3M has developed a reputation for being able to stimulate innovation over a long period of time. It has a stated objective that 30 percent of its sales are to come from products less than four years old. In one recent year alone, 3M launched more than 200 new products.

The company encourages its employees to take risks—and rewards the failures, as well as the successes. 3M's management has the patience to see ideas through to successful products. It invests nearly 7 percent of company sales revenue (more than $1.4 billion a year) in research and development, yet management tells its R & D people that not everything will work. It also fosters a culture that allows people to defy their managers. For instance, each new employee and his or her manager take a one-day orientation class where, among other things, stories are told of victories won by employees despite the opposition of their boss.

All of 3M's scientists and managers are challenged to "keep current." Idea champions are created and encouraged by allowing scientists and engineers to spend up to 15 percent of their time on projects of their own choosing. And if a 3M scientist comes up with a new idea but finds resistance within the researcher's own division, he or she can apply for a $70 000 grant from an internal venture-capital fund to further develop the idea.

Within the *human resource* category, we find that innovative organizations actively promote the training and development of their members so that they keep current, offer high job security so employees don't fear getting fired for making mistakes, and encourage individuals to become champions of change. Once a new idea is developed, **idea champions** actively and enthusiastically promote the idea, build support for it, overcome resistance to it, and ensure that the idea is implemented.[41] The evidence indicates that champions have common personality characteristics: extremely high self-confidence, persistence, energy, and a tendency to take risks. Idea champions also display characteristics associated with transformational leadership. They inspire and energize others with their vision of the potential of an innovation and through their strong personal conviction in their mission. They are also good at gaining the commitment of others to support their mission. In addition, idea champions have jobs that provide considerable decision-making discretion. This autonomy helps them introduce and implement innovations in organizations.[42]

idea champions Individuals who actively and enthusiastically promote an idea, build support for it, overcome resistance to it, and ensure that the idea is implemented.

Creating a Learning Organization

The learning organization has recently developed a groundswell of interest from managers and organization theorists looking for new ways to successfully respond to a world of interdependence and change.[43] In this section, we describe what a learning organization looks like and methods for managing learning.

What Is a Learning Organization?

learning organization An organization that has developed the continuous capacity to adapt and change.

A **learning organization** is an organization that has developed the continuous capacity to adapt and change. Just as individuals learn, so too do organizations. "All organizations learn, whether they consciously choose to or not—it is a fundamental requirement for their sustained existence."[44] However, some organizations do it better than others. Canadian Tire is an example of a company that has worked hard to learn how to improve itself from year to year.

single-loop learning A process of correcting errors using past routines and present policies.

Most organizations engage in what has been called **single-loop learning**.[45] When errors are detected, the correction process relies on past routines and present policies. This type of learning has been likened to a thermostat, which, once set at 17°C, simply turns on and off to keep the room at the set temperature. It does not question whether the temperature should be set at 17°C. In contrast, learning organizations use **double-loop learning**. When an error is detected, it's corrected in ways that involve the modification of the organization's objectives, policies, and standard routines. Double-loop learning challenges deeply rooted assumptions and norms within an organization. In this way, it provides opportunities for radically different solutions to problems and dramatic jumps in improvement. To draw on the thermostat analogy, a thermostat using double-loop learning would try to determine whether the correct policy is 17°C, and whether changes might be necessitated by the change in season.

double-loop learning A process of correcting errors by modifying the organization's objectives, policies, and standard routines.

Exhibit 14-10 summarizes the five basic characteristics of a learning organization. It's an organization in which people put aside their old ways of thinking, learn to be open with each other, understand how their organization really works, form a plan or vision on which everyone can agree, and then work together to achieve that vision.[46]

Managing Learning

How do you change an organization to make it into a continual learner? What can managers do to make their firms learning organizations?

- *Establish a strategy.* Managers need to make their commitment to change, innovation, and continuous improvement explicit.

EXHIBIT 14-10 Characteristics of a Learning Organization

1. The organization has a shared vision that everyone agrees on.

2. People discard their old ways of thinking and the standard routines they use for solving problems or doing their jobs.

3. Members think of all organizational processes, activities, functions, and interactions with the environment as part of a system of interrelationships.

4. People openly communicate with each other (across vertical and horizontal boundaries) without fear of criticism or punishment.

5. People suppress their personal self-interest and fragmented departmental interests to work together to achieve the organization's shared vision.

Source: Based on P. M. Senge, *The Fifth Discipline* (New York: Doubleday, 1990).

- *Redesign the organization's structure.* The formal structure can be a serious impediment to learning. By flattening the structure, eliminating or combining departments, and increasing the use of cross-functional teams, interdependence is reinforced and boundaries between people are reduced.

- *Reshape the organization's culture.* Learning organizations are characterized by risk-taking, openness, and growth. Managers set the tone for the organization's culture both by what they say (strategy) and what they do (behaviour). Managers need to demonstrate by their actions that taking risks and admitting failures are desirable traits. That means rewarding people who take chances and make mistakes. Managers also need to encourage functional conflict. "The key to unlocking real openness at work," says one expert on learning organizations, "is to teach people to give up having to be in agreement. We think agreement is so important. Who cares? You have to bring paradoxes, conflicts, and dilemmas out in the open, so collectively we can be more intelligent than we can be individually."[47]

Managing Change: It's Culture-Bound

A number of change issues we have discussed in this chapter are culture-bound, meaning that they do not necessarily apply well cross-culturally. To illustrate, let's briefly look at five questions:

- *Do people believe change is possible?* Remember that cultures vary in terms of beliefs about their ability to control their environment. In cultures in which people believe that they can dominate their environment, individuals will take a proactive view of change. This, for example, would describe Canada and the United States. In many other countries, such as Iran and Saudi Arabia, people see themselves as subjugated to their environment and thus will tend to take a passive approach toward change.

- *If change is possible, how long will it take to bring it about?* A culture's time orientation can help us answer this question. Societies that focus on the long term, such as Japan, will demonstrate considerable patience while waiting for positive outcomes from change efforts. In societies with a short-term focus, such as Canada and the United States, people expect quick improvements and will seek change programs that promise fast results.

- *Is resistance to change greater in some cultures than in others?* Resistance to change will be influenced by a society's reliance on tradition. Italians, as an example, focus on the past, whereas Americans emphasize the present. Italians, therefore, should generally be more resistant to change efforts than their American counterparts.

- *Does culture influence how change efforts will be implemented?* Power distance can help with this issue. In the high power distance cultures of Mexico and Indonesia, change efforts will tend to be autocratically implemented by top management. In contrast, low power distance cultures value democratic methods. We would predict, therefore, a greater use of participation in countries such as Austria and Denmark.

- *Do successful idea champions do things differently in different cultures?* The evidence indicates that the answer is yes.[48] People in collectivist cultures, in contrast to individualistic cultures, prefer appeals for

Cross-functional support for innovation efforts appeals to people in collectivist cultures like Finland. Hannu Nieminen, head of Insight and Innovation of Nokia Design, leads a global team of more than 300 people representing 34 different nationalities in developing cellular phones for the Finland-based company. The team includes designers, psychologists, researchers, anthropologists, engineers, and technology specialists who are based in major cities around the world. They collaborate by blending macro trends with insights from local cultures in designing products that appeal to country-specific customer needs and tastes.

cross-functional support for innovation efforts; people in high power distance cultures prefer champions to work closely with those in authority to approve innovative activities before work is conducted on them; and the higher the uncertainty avoidance of a society, the more champions should work within the organization's rules and procedures to develop the innovation. These findings suggest that effective managers will alter their organization's championing strategies to reflect cultural values. So, for instance, while idea champions in Russia might succeed by ignoring budgetary limitations and working around confining procedures, idea champions in Greece, Portugal, and Uruguay or other cultures high in uncertainty avoidance will be more effective by closely following budgets and procedures.

Summary and Implications

1 **What are the forces for change?** The nature of the workforce, technology, economic shocks, competition, social trends, and world politics are all forces for change. Organizations have had to respond to these forces by making organizational changes, such as changing their reward structure, redesigning jobs, introducing teams, and meeting ethical challenges. To carry out change, organizations need to appoint *change agents*, individuals who manage change activities for the organization.

2 **How do organizations manage change?** Kurt Lewin argued that successful change in organizations should follow three steps: *unfreezing* the status quo, *moving* to a new state, and *refreezing* the new change to make it permanent. John Kotter built on Lewin's three-step model to create a more detailed eight-step plan for implementing change. Another approach to managing change is action research. *Action research* refers to a change process based on the systematic collection of data and then selection of a change action based on what the analyzed data indicate. Some organizations use appreciative inquiry to manage change. *Appreciative inquiry* seeks to identify the unique qualities and special strengths of an organization, which can then be built on to improve performance.

3 **Why do people and organizations resist change?** Individuals resist change because of basic human characteristics such as perceptions, personalities, and needs. Organizations resist change because they are conservative, and because change is difficult. The status quo is often preferred by those who feel they have the most to lose if change goes ahead.

4 **What are some of the contemporary issues in managing change?** Some of the contemporary issues include making organizations more innovative, creating learning organizations, and understanding the influence of culture on managing change.

OB AT WORK

For Review

1. "Resistance to change is an irrational response." Do you agree or disagree? Explain.

2. How does Lewin's three-step change model deal with resistance to change?

3. What is the difference between driving forces and restraining forces?

4. How does Kotter's eight-step plan for implementing change deal with resistance to change?

5. What are the factors that lead individuals to resist change?

6. What are the factors that lead organizations to resist change?

7. Why is participation considered such an effective technique for lessening resistance to change?

8. Why does change so frequently become a political issue in organizations?

9. In an organization that has a history of "following the leader," what changes can be made to foster innovation?

10. What does it mean to be a "learning organization"?

For Critical Thinking

1. How have changes in the workforce during the past 20 years affected organizational policies?

2. "Managing today is easier than at the start of the twentieth century, because the years of real change took place between Confederation and World War I." Do you agree or disagree? Discuss.

3. What is meant by the phrase "We live in an age of discontinuity"?

4. Are all managers change agents?

OB for You

- Not everyone is comfortable with change, but you should realize that change is a fact of life. It is difficult to avoid, and can result in negative consequences when it is avoided.

- If you need to change something in yourself, be aware of the importance of creating new systems to replace the old. Saying you want to be healthier, without specifying that you intend to go to the gym three times a week, or eat five servings of fruits and vegetables a day, means that change likely will not occur. It's important to specify goals and behaviours as part of change.

- Consider focusing on positive aspects of change, rather than negative ones. For instance, rather than noting that you did not study hard enough, acknowledge the effort you put into studying, and how that helped your performance, and then set positive goals as a result.

POINT

COUNTERPOINT

Organizations Are More Like Calm Waters

Organizational change is an episodic activity. That is, it starts at some point, proceeds through a series of steps, and culminates in some outcome that those involved hope is an improvement over the starting point. It has a beginning, a middle, and an end.

Lewin's three-step model represents a classic illustration of this perspective. Change is seen as a break in the organization's equilibrium. The status quo has been disturbed, and change is necessary to establish a new equilibrium state. The objective of refreezing is to stabilize the new situation by balancing the driving and restraining forces.

Some experts have argued that organizational change should be thought of as balancing a system made up of five interacting variables within the organization—people, tasks, technology, structure, and strategy. A change in any one variable has repercussions on one or more of the others. This perspective is episodic in that it treats organizational change as essentially an effort to sustain an equilibrium. A change in one variable begins a chain of events that, if properly managed, requires adjustments in the other variables to achieve a new state of equilibrium.

Another way to conceptualize the episodic view of looking at change is to think of managing change as analogous to captaining a ship. The organization is like a large ship travelling across the calm Mediterranean Sea to a specific port. The ship's captain has made this exact trip hundreds of times before with the same crew. Every once in a while, however, a storm will appear, and the crew has to respond. The captain will make the appropriate adjustments—that is, implement changes—and, having manoeuvred through the storm, will return to calm waters. Like this ship's voyage, managing an organization should be seen as a journey with a beginning and an end, and implementing change as a response to a break in the status quo that is needed only occasionally.

Organizations Are More Like Whitewater Rafting

The episodic approach may be the dominant paradigm for handling organizational change, but it has become obsolete. It applies to a world of certainty and predictability. The episodic approach was developed in the 1950s and 1960s, and it reflects the environment of those times. It treats change as the occasional disturbance in an otherwise peaceful world. However, this paradigm has little resemblance to today's environment of constant and chaotic change.[49]

If you want to understand what it's like to manage change in today's organizations, think of it as equivalent to permanent whitewater rafting.[50] The organization is not a large ship, but more akin to a 40-foot raft. Rather than sailing a calm sea, this raft must traverse a raging river made up of an uninterrupted flow of whitewater rapids. To make things worse, the raft has 10 paddlers who have never worked together or travelled the river before, much of the trip is in the dark, the river is dotted with unexpected turns and obstacles, the exact destination of the raft is not clear, and at irregular intervals the raft needs to pull to shore, where some new crew members are added and others leave. Change is a natural state and managing change is a continual process. That is, managers never get the luxury of escaping the whitewater rapids.

The stability and predictability characterized by the episodic perspective no longer captures the world we live in. Disruptions in the status quo are not occasional, temporary, and followed by a return to an equilibrium state. There is, in fact, no equilibrium state. Managers today face constant change, bordering on chaos. They are being forced to play a game they have never played before, governed by rules that are created as the game progresses.

Managing-in-a-Turbulent-World Tolerance Test

Listed below are some statements a 37-year-old manager made about his job at a large, successful corporation.[51] If your job had these characteristics, how would you react to them? After each statement are 5 letters, A to E. Circle the letter that best describes how you think you would react according to the following scale:

A I would enjoy this very much; it's completely acceptable.

B This would be enjoyable and acceptable most of the time.

C I would have no reaction to this feature one way or another, or it would be about equally enjoyable and unpleasant.

D This feature would be somewhat unpleasant for me.

E This feature would be very unpleasant for me.

1.	I regularly spend 30 to 40 percent of my time in meetings.	A	B	C	D	E
2.	A year and a half ago, my job did not exist, and I have been essentially inventing it as I go along.	A	B	C	D	E
3.	The responsibilities I either assume or am assigned consistently exceed the authority I have for discharging them.	A	B	C	D	E
4.	At any given moment in my job, I have on the average about a dozen phone calls to be returned.	A	B	C	D	E
5.	There seems to be very little relation in my job between the quality of my performance and my actual pay and fringe benefits.	A	B	C	D	E
6.	About 2 weeks a year of formal management training is needed in my job just to stay current.	A	B	C	D	E
7.	Because we have very effective employment equity in my company, and because it is thoroughly multinational, my job brings me into close working contact at a professional level with people of many races, ethnic groups, and nationalities and of both sexes.	A	B	C	D	E
8.	There is no objective way to measure my effectiveness.	A	B	C	D	E
9.	I report to 3 different bosses for different aspects of my job, and each has an equal say in my performance appraisal.	A	B	C	D	E
10.	On average, about a third of my time is spent dealing with unexpected emergencies that force all scheduled work to be postponed.	A	B	C	D	E
11.	When I must have a meeting of the people who report to me, it takes my secretary most of a day to find a time when we are all available, and even then, I have yet to have a meeting where everyone is present for the entire meeting.	A	B	C	D	E
12.	The university degree I earned in preparation for this type of work is now obsolete, and I probably should go back for another degree.	A	B	C	D	E
13.	My job requires that I absorb 100 to 200 pages per week of technical materials.	A	B	C	D	E
14.	I am out of town overnight at least 1 night per week.	A	B	C	D	E
15.	My department is so interdependent with several other departments in the company that all distinctions about which departments are responsible for which tasks are quite arbitrary.	A	B	C	D	E

LEARNING ABOUT **YOURSELF** EXERCISE (Continued)

16. I will probably get a promotion in about a year to a job in another division that has most of these same characteristics. A B C D E

17. During the period of my employment here, either the entire company or the division I worked in has been reorganized every year or so. A B C D E

18. Although there are several possible promotions I can see ahead of me, I have no real career path in an objective sense. A B C D E

19. Although there are several possible promotions I can see ahead of me, I think I have no realistic chance of reaching the top levels of the company. A B C D E

20. Although I have many ideas about how to make things work better, I have no direct influence on either the business policies or the personnel policies that govern my division. A B C D E

21. My company has recently put in an "assessment centre" where I and all other managers will be required to go through an extensive battery of psychological tests to assess our potential. A B C D E

22. My company is a defendant in an antitrust suit, and if the case comes to trial, I will probably have to testify about some decisions that were made a few years ago. A B C D E

23. Advanced computer and other electronic office technology are continually being introduced into my division, necessitating constant learning on my part. A B C D E

24. The computer terminal and screen I have in my office can be monitored in my bosses' offices without my knowledge. A B C D E

Scoring Key:

Score 4 points for each A, 3 for each B, 2 for each C, 1 for each D, and 0 for each E. Add up the points, divide by 24, and round to 1 decimal place.

While the results are not intended to be more than suggestive, the higher your score, the more comfortable you seem to be with change. The test's author suggests analyzing scores as if they were grade point averages. In this way, a 4.0 average is an A, a 2.0 is a C, and scores below 1.0 flunk.

Using replies from nearly 500 MBA students and young managers, the range of scores was found to be narrow—between 1.0 and 2.2. The average score was between 1.5 and 1.6—equivalent to a D+/C– grade! If these scores are generalizable to the work population, clearly people are not very tolerant of the kind of changes that come with a turbulent environment. However, this sample is now over a decade old. We should expect average scores today to be higher, as people have become more accustomed to living in a dynamic environment.

More Learning About Yourself Exercises

An additional self-assessment relevant to this chapter appears at MyOBLab (**www.pearsoned.ca/myoblab**).

III.C.2 How Stressful Is My Life?

When you complete the additional assessments, consider the following:

1. Am I surprised about my score?

2. Would my friends evaluate me similarly?

BREAKOUT **GROUP** EXERCISES

Form small groups to discuss the following topics, as assigned by your instructor:

1. Identify a local company that you think needs to undergo change. What factors suggest that change is necessary?

2. Have you ever tried to change the behaviour of someone you worked with (for instance, someone in one of your project groups)? How effective were you in getting change to occur? How would you explain this?

3. Identify a recent change that your college or university introduced, and its effects on the students. Did the students accept the change or fight it? How would you explain this?

WORKING WITH **OTHERS** EXERCISE

Power and the Changing Environment

Objectives

1. To describe the forces for change influencing power differentials in organizational and interpersonal relationships.

2. To understand the effect of technological, legal/political, economic, and social changes on the power of individuals within an organization.[52]

The Situation

Your organization manufactures golf carts and sells them to country clubs, golf courses, and consumers. Your team is faced with the task of assessing how environmental changes will affect individuals' organizational power. Read each of the five scenarios and then, for each, identify the 5 members in the organization whose power will increase most in light of the environmental condition(s).

Advertising expert (m)	Accountant–CGA (m)	Product designer (m)
Chief financial officer (f)	General manager (m)	In-house counsel (m)
Securities analyst (m)	Marketing manager (f)	Public relations expert (m)
Operations manager (f)	Computer programmer (f)	Human resource manager (f)
Corporate trainer (m)	Industrial engineer (m)	Chemist (m)

(m) = male   (f) = female

1. New computer-aided manufacturing technologies are being introduced in the workplace during the upcoming 2 to 18 months.

2. New federal emission standards are being legislated by the government.

3. Sales are way down; the industry appears to be shrinking.

4. The company is planning to go international in the next 12 to 18 months.

5. The Human Rights Commission is applying pressure to balance the male–female population in the organization's upper hierarchy by threatening to publicize the predominance of men in upper management.

WORKING WITH OTHERS EXERCISE (Continued)

The Procedure

1. Divide the class into teams of 3 to 4 students each.

2. Teams should read each scenario and identify the 5 members whose power will increase most in light of the external environmental condition described.

3. Teams should then address the question: Assuming that the 5 environmental changes are taking place at once, which 5 members of the organization will now have the most power?

4. After 20 to 30 minutes, representatives of each team will be selected to present and justify their conclusions to the entire class. Discussion will begin with scenario 1 and proceed through to scenario 5. Then the class will look at what might happen if all 5 environmental changes happened at once.

ETHICAL DILEMMA EXERCISE

Increasing Employee Productivity and Stress

Ellen West supervises a staff of 15 people handling back-office functions for a regional brokerage firm in Saskatoon. With company revenues down, Ellen's boss has put increasing pressure on her to improve her department's productivity.

The quickest way for Ellen to increase productivity in her department is to lay off two or three employees and fill the gap by asking the rest of the staff to work harder and put in more time on the job. Since all her employees are on salary, they are not paid for overtime. So if Ellen let three people go, and asked her remaining staff to each put in an additional 10 hours a week on the job, she could effectively handle the same workload with 20 percent fewer employees.

As Ellen considered this idea, she had mixed feelings. Reducing her staff and asking people to work more hours would please her boss and increase job security for those people remaining. On the other hand, she was fearful that she was taking advantage of a weak labour market. Her employees knew that jobs were scarce and would be hard put to find comparable positions elsewhere in the securities industry. The people laid off would have a tough time finding work. Moreover, she knew that her current staff was unlikely to openly complain about working longer hours for fear that they, too, would be let go. But was it fair to increase the department's productivity on the backs of already hard-working employees? Was it unethical to ask her employees to put in 10 hours more a week, for no additional money, because the current weak labour market worked to her advantage? If you were Ellen West, what would you do?

CASE INCIDENTS

GreyStar Art & Greetings Makes Technological Changes

Tammy Reinhold did not believe the rumours. Now that the rumours were confirmed, she was in denial. "I can't believe it," she said. "I've worked as a greeting-card artist here for 17 years. I love what I do. Now they tell me that I'm going to have to do all my work on a computer."

Tammy was not alone in her fear. The company's other two artists, Mike Tomaski and Maggie Lyall, were just as concerned. Each had graduated from art school near the top of his or her class. They came to work for GreyStar Art & Greetings right out of school—Mike in 1979, Tammy in 1986, and Maggie in 1991. They chose the company, which had been around for more than 50 years, because of its reputation as a good place to work. The company also had never had a layoff.

GreyStar Art & Greetings is a small maker of greeting cards and specialty wrapping paper. It has modest resources and modest ambitions. Management has always pursued progress slowly. Artists do much of their work by hand. Today, however, the company installed three high-powered Mac computers equipped with the latest graphics and photo-manipulation software.

Courtland Grey, the company's owner, called Tammy, Mike, and Maggie into his office this morning. He told them about the changes that were going to be made. Grey acknowledged that the three were going to have a lot to learn to be able to do all their work on computers. But he stressed that the changes would dramatically speed up the art-production and photo-layout processes, and eventually result in significant cost savings. He offered to send the three to a one-week course specifically designed to train artists in computer graphics. He also said he expected all of the company's art and photo operations to be completely digitalized within three months.

Tammy is not stupid. She has been following the trends in graphic art and knows that most work is being done on computers. She just thought, as did Mike and Maggie, that she might escape having to learn these programs. After all, GreyStar Art & Greetings is not Hallmark. But Tammy was wrong. Technology is coming to GreyStar Art & Greetings, and there is not much she can do about it. Other than complain or look for another job!

Questions

1. Explain Tammy's resistance.

2. Evaluate the way Courtland Grey handled this change.

3. What, if anything, would you have done differently if you had been Grey?

GE's Work-Out

General Electric (GE) established its Work-Out process in the early 1990s.[53] It continues to be a mainstay in GE's efforts to initiate change. In the interim years, the Work-Out process has also been adopted by such diverse organizations as General Motors, The Home Depot, and the World Bank.

The impetus for the Work-Out was the belief by GE's former CEO, Jack Welch, that the company's culture was too bureaucratic and slow to respond to change. He wanted to create a vehicle that would effectively engage and empower GE employees.

Essentially, Work-Out brings together employees and managers from many different functions and levels within an organization for an informal three-day meeting to discuss and solve problems that have been identified by employees or senior management. Set into small teams, people are encouraged to challenge prevailing assumptions about "the way we have always done things" and develop recommendations for significant improvements in organizational processes. The Work-Out teams then present their recommendations to a senior manager in a public gathering called a Town Meeting.

At the Town Meeting, the manager in charge oversees a discussion about the recommendation and then is required to make a yes-or-no decision on the spot. Only in unusual circumstances can a recommendation be tabled for further study. Recommendations that are accepted are assigned to managers who have volunteered to carry them out. Typically, a recommendation will move from inception to implementation in 90 days or less.

The logic behind the Work-Out is to identify problems, stimulate diverse input, and provide a mechanism for speedy decision and action.

Questions

1. What type of change process would you call this? Explain.

2. Why should it work?

3. What negative consequences do you think might result from this process?

From **Concepts**
to **Skills**

Carrying Out Organizational Change

In reviewing three US organizations that effectively underwent major changes (Sears, Roebuck & Company, Royal Dutch/Shell, and the US Army), three organizational change consultants used the US Army's After Action Review to summarize how an effective change process can be carried out in both business and the military.[54] The After Action Review is a nonhierarchical team debriefing to help participants understand performance. The consultants identified seven disciplines embedded in the After Action Review that help create effective change:

1. *Build an intricate understanding of the business.* Organizational members need to have the big picture revealed to them so they know why change is needed and what is happening in the industry. Let organizational members know what is expected of them as the change proceeds.

2. *Encourage uncompromising straight talk.* Communication cannot be based on hierarchy, but must allow everyone to contribute freely to the discussion.

3. *Manage from the future.* Rather than setting goals that are directed toward a specific future point in time (and thus encouraging everyone to stop when the goal is achieved), manage from the perspective of always looking toward the future and future needs.

4. *Harness setbacks.* When things do not go as planned, and there are setbacks, it's natural to blame yourself, others, or bad luck. Instead, teach everyone to view setbacks as learning opportunities and opportunities for improvement.

5. *Promote inventive accountability.* While employees know what the specific targets and goals are, they should also be encouraged in the change process to be inventive and take initiative when new opportunities arise.

6. *Understand the quid pro quo.* When organizations undergo change processes, employees are put under a lot of stress and strain. Organizations must ensure that employees are rewarded for their efforts. To build

appropriate commitment, organizations must develop four levels of incentives:

   a. Reward and recognition for effort

   b. Training and skill development that will make the employee marketable

   c. Meaningful work that provides intrinsic satisfaction

   d. Communication about where the organization is going and some say in the process for employees

7. *Create relentless discomfort with the status quo.* People are more willing to change when the current situation looks less attractive than the new situation.

These points indicate that effective change is a comprehensive process, requiring a lot of commitment from both the organization's leaders and its members.

Practising Skills

You are the nursing supervisor at a local hospital that employs both emergency room and floor nurses. Each of these teams of nurses tends to work almost exclusively with others doing the same job. In your professional reading, you have come across the concept of cross-training nursing teams and giving them more varied responsibilities, which in turn has been shown to improve patient care while lowering costs. You call the two team leaders, Sue and Scott, into your office to explain that you want the nursing teams to move to this approach. To your surprise, they are both opposed to the idea. Sue says she and the other emergency room nurses feel they are needed in the ER, where they fill the most vital role in the hospital. They work special hours when needed, do whatever tasks are required, and often work in difficult and stressful circumstances. They think the floor nurses have relatively easy jobs for the pay they receive. Scott, the leader of the floor nurse team, tells you that his group believes the ER nurses lack the special training and extra experience that the floor nurses bring to the hospital. The floor nurses claim they have the heaviest responsibilities and do the most exacting work. Because they have ongoing contact with patients and families, they believe they should not be called away from vital floor duties to help the ER nurses complete their tasks. What should you do about your idea to introduce more cross-training for the nursing teams?

Reinforcing Skills

1. Think about a change (major and minor) that you have dealt with over the last year. Perhaps the change involved other people, and perhaps it was personal. Did you resist the change? Did others resist the change? How did you overcome your resistance or the resistance of others to the change?

2. Interview a manager at three different organizations about a change he or she implemented. What was the manager's experience in implementing the change? How did the manager manage resistance to the change?

CASE 14 Change at TerraCycle

When Tom Szaky, a young Canadian entrepreneur, learned that worms eat garbage, he got an idea for a business. So he, along with Jon Beyer, started TerraCycle, a company whose first product was fertilizer made from worm droppings.

At present, the company produces various kinds of plant food (packaged in recycled plastic bottles), potting mix (packaged in recycled plastic milk jugs), cleaners, insect repellent, composters (made from old wine barrels), pots (made from crushed computer plastic or from recycled yogurt containers), and bird feeders (made from two-litre plastic bottles). The company will soon introduce a fire log made from waxed milk cartons. Szaky says that you have to do everything at once—product development, production, and sales. The company has orders from retailers for products that the company has not even figured out how to make.

Coming up with new ideas and product innovation ideas is a team effort at TerraCycle. You might think that getting garbage is easy, but it's not. You have to work through production, scientific, and legal issues as part of the innovation process. The company has a sourcing team that is responsible for finding the raw materials necessary to make the products. A legal team determines if it is legal to produce the products, and a finance team determines whether the product can be produced profitably. Most companies spend a lot of money and up to three years developing a new product. TerraCycle takes only about nine months from idea to store shelf.

Producing and selling eco-friendly plant food is a good thing, but what really motivates Szaky is his desire to change consumer products totally and to grow his company at a massive rate. He recognizes that the green movement is very strong, and he wants to capitalize on that by making a lot of new products from garbage. The timing is great for TerraCycle because large retailers are now looking to become more green, and they get good publicity when they buy products from companies that produce their products in a green way. Every company says they have a great product, but TerraCycle says, "We're going to reinvent the way to look at the product." It's an emotional decision, but then it has to translate into a good business decision. Szaky wants to change everything except the core idea of producing green products.

The stress levels in a company like TerraCycle can be high. Szaky recalls that when he did his first order for Walmart, in order to liquefy the worm droppings he bought a horse watering trough to produce the product (instead of a custom-made tank). He calls it "MacGuyvering your way around" (referring to the character in the 1990's television show). TerraCycle is supplying the world's biggest retailers with innovative products, and figuring things out as it goes along.

TerraCycle's assistant production manager, Milton Oppenheimer, came to the company because it produced innovative products that are eco-friendly. He says that things are hectic, but everything in production is working pretty well. He says that employees are open-minded and willing to try new things. Change is the only constant, and everyone has ideas. If employees find a shortcut, they let managers know. They take pride when they see the products on store shelves.

Szaky says that the company culture is the most important thing. If people see that their ideas are valued, they will come forward with a lot of new ideas. That drives new product development and innovation. If a new product idea fails, it's no big deal, he adds. "It's okay to fail. At least we tried."

Questions

1. Briefly describe the six specific forces that act as stimulants for change. Which of these forces are most important for TerraCycle? Which are least important? Explain your answer.

2. How is the notion of change reflected in the company's approach to product development and production? How does change shape TerraCycle's organizational culture?

3. A variety of "targets for change" are identified in Chapter 14. Which of these targets seem most important for TerraCycle? Explain.

4. Tom Szaky, CEO and founder of TerraCycle, says that the key to making product innovation successful at TerraCycle is the company's organizational culture. Explain how TerraCycle's organizational culture supports new product development.

5. Do you think that TerraCycle would benefit from a formal program of appreciative inquiry? Explain your reasoning.

Source: Based on "Change and Innovation at TerraCycle," *Organizational Behavior Video Library*, 2008. Copyrighted by Prentice-Hall.

Tech Depot

When Doug Aiken took over at Tech Depot, he replaced the man who had founded the company 23 years ago and had been its only CEO.[1] Aiken brought with him 30 years' experience working for a manufacturing company that prided itself on its strong "management culture," where managers were expected to measure all aspects of employee performance and give feedback continuously on whether employees were living up to expectations of their performance. That culture had done well for his previous employer, leading to years of innovation and high profits, even during economic downturns.

Three years later, however, Tech Depot's board of directors fired Aiken. The company was limping along with poor financial results, and employee turnover had reached a new high, increasing every year that Aiken was in charge. Employees showed little motivation to do a good job, they expressed little loyalty to the company, and productivity was at an all-time low. The board hired Meryl Francoli to replace Aiken and pick up the pieces. She wondered what she might do to turn the situation around.

Background

Tech Depot is the second-largest retailer of consumer electronics, personal computers, entertainment software, and major appliances in North America. In addition to its head office in the central United States, the company has 1400 stores across the United States and Canada, a website offering most of its products online, and a tech squad that provides 24-hour onsite computer help at homes and businesses.

In the 23 years that the company was run by its beloved founder, Andre Waters, it had grown to $35 billion in annual sales, making it one of the largest retailers in North America. Waters had encouraged a collaborative, supportive culture. The organizational structure was relatively flat, and managers were expected to be entrepreneurial and independent. Store managers were encouraged to do what they thought best, rather than rely on head office for specific directions. That spirit of entrepreneurialism was found in all employees, not just the managers.

When Aiken arrived, he could see plenty of evidence of the strong culture of the company. There were pictures of the company founder in every lunchroom, and hallways and washrooms were covered with motivating slogans on the walls. It was not uncommon for a group of associates to break out into the Tech Depot cheer at the start of the day, so loyal were they to their employer.

Bringing "Management Culture" to Tech Depot

Aiken was fine with the pictures, the slogans, and even the cheers the employees chanted. However, he was not happy with the collaborative, entrepreneurial culture. He believed this put too much power and authority into the hands of lower-level managers and employees, making it difficult for head office to "take charge." He was shocked to discover that employees thought of head office as "the store support center," and that each store was able to set its own targets, and order its own mix of products. Tech Depot was so decentralized that Aiken could not even send an email to all managers throughout North America at once.

Aiken understood the importance of organizational culture, and how culture could be used to mould employees to perform the way management wanted them to perform. He was eager to bring the "management culture" of his previous employer to Tech Depot. Aiken was certain that a disciplined approach where all aspects of the organization were constantly monitored and measured was what Tech Depot needed. He was convinced that loose structure and lack of centralization were the primary causes for the lack of sales growth in recent years.

The Changes Aiken immediately introduced inventory controls, standardized store displays, and

---

This case was written by Nancy Langton, Sauder School of Business, University of British Columbia. This case is a composite based on several different retail operations. © 2008, Nancy Langton.

hiring and performance measures. The new performance evaluation system focused on each employee's output, mainly emphasizing things that could be concretely measured, such as number of sales per hour in the store, or number of forms processed per hour in the online business. As one manager noted, "He measured everything: sales, coordination with other stores, number of employees per hour, the mix of full- and part-time staff, type of products sold by hour, everything. What he didn't seem to realize was that some of the important things that we should have been doing were not necessarily quantifiable."

To reduce the cost of paying benefits, Aiken cut the total number of employees and increased the share of part-time sales clerks from 20 percent to 50 percent. This was a significant change in strategy. When Aiken arrived at Tech Depot, almost 80 percent of store employees were full time, a strategy promoted by Waters, who believed that full-time employees deliver better service.

Aiken also introduced centralized purchasing so that he would have more power with suppliers. Previously the company had had nine buying offices. Suppliers could negotiate separate deals with each of the buying offices, with store managers ordering with local needs in mind. Aiken wanted to introduce national advertising to create a strong identity for customers, which meant that all stores needed to be more uniform in what they sold.

The Backlash   Managers recognized that "management culture" meant an attention to measurement. Once managers understood what was being measured, they started acting accordingly. For instance, managers were told to increase "inventory velocity" to get products out the door more quickly. Managers figured out that by ordering fewer products, the products went out the door more quickly, and thus their "inventory velocity" increased. For customers, however, it meant that they could not always find the products they wanted when they went to the store, because things were often sold out. They started complaining, or worse yet, shopping at the competition.

Managers also demanded more work out of fewer employees, as a way of increasing the productivity ratios of their units. In some units, employees felt pressured to work nights and weekends, sometimes not recording their hours (a violation of employment standards legislation, which requires overtime payments to employees who work in excess of a standard workweek).

Employees, who had been seen as collaborators and peers under Waters' leadership, were now being told what to do, how to do it, and when to do it. This made many of them unhappy, and some quit. Employee loyalty declined, and employees openly complained to each other and to their friends about the company.

Even some of the suppliers started to complain about the way Tech Depot operated. Suppliers no longer had the opportunity to work with local stores to solve problems. Instead, they were told by head office that they had to perform in particular ways, "or else."

The Results   During Aiken's first year, Tech Depot's results looked great. In his fourth quarter, there was a 35 percent increase in earnings, marking the fourth straight quarter of double-digit profit growth. He also opened 57 more stores. Stock prices were a bit lower over the year, however, and shareholders wanted even greater increases in sales and profits.

Two years later, Tech Depot's fortunes were not looking as bright. Fourth-quarter sales at established stores were down 10 percent, the second quarterly drop in a year. The company was losing ground to its main competitor, and turnover was approaching the highest rates in the industry.

The Board Hires A New CEO

Based on the results of Aiken's first three years, the board lost confidence in his "management culture." While they wanted someone who could be "just like" the founder, they realized that this would be an impossible set of shoes to fill. The board hired Meryl Francoli, who had been working in retail for 20 years, most recently for Tech Depot's chief rival. Francoli is friendly and outgoing, and is also known for achieving results.

Francoli's Initial Challenges

Francoli's first concern was to get the company back to the higher sales levels that the company had had under the first year of Aiken's leadership. She also wanted to reignite the commitment to the company that employees felt when they worked under Waters' leadership. She was concerned that turnover was making it difficult for employees to really work together as a team.

Francoli has been told that some of Tech Depot's younger (20-something) employees have quit, taking jobs elsewhere that permit them to schedule their work any way that they want. She knows from experience that younger employees like networks and connections more than they like cubicles. Meanwhile, her Baby Boomer employees are struggling because they are in the sandwich generation—trying to accommodate the needs of children and aging parents with their work schedules.

In talking with a small set of managers and employees, Francoli heard over and over that employees wanted more flextime, although managers were mixed on offering such an option. Flextime had first been introduced by Waters in his final two years at the helm. Under Aiken, flextime was discouraged, though it was still offered in some units, albeit reluctantly.

Francoli appreciates that employees need flexibility in their workday, but she does not believe that flextime is the answer to work-life balance because it is often limited in its approach. She notes that Tech Depot already has two flextime options: (1) employees can choose to work longer hours four days a week, in exchange for having Fridays off, or (2) employees can choose to be onsite between 10 a.m. and 3 p.m., scheduling their other three hours at their convenience as long as they add up to a total of eight continuous hours each day.

Managers feel the need to keep track of each employee's hours, making flextime an administrative nightmare for them. Employees who don't use flextime options resent those who do—suspecting that the flextime employees are not doing their fair share of work. Moreover, some managers have coped with flextime in pretty inflexible ways. One manager requests that employees keep note of whether they are in or out of the office, by marking a white board, and leaving contact numbers and estimated times of return every time they leave their cubicle. Another manager gives an award each week to the employee who was last to leave the most times during the previous week.

Output Matters Environment

In Francoli's previous position at the competition, she had proposed introducing an output matters environment (OME) to her CEO. She had been hired away by Tech Depot before she had had an opportunity to carry out the OME initiative, but she believed in it passionately.

Some of the elements of OME include no meetings unless absolutely required; no requirement that an employee be physically present at work at specific hours; performance evaluated on what is accomplished, not the number of hours worked; and performance appraisals conducted with data and evidence, "not perceptions or feelings about what someone has done."

OME involves 13 commandments, including the following:

- "No. 1: People at all levels stop doing any activity that is a waste of their time, the customer's time, or the company's money.

- No. 7: Nobody talks about how many hours they work.

- No. 9: It's O.K. to take a nap on a Tuesday afternoon, grocery shop on Wednesday morning, or catch a movie on Thursday afternoon."

Francoli believes that the OME initiative could be used to combat turnover, increase morale and productivity, and likely lead to high levels of innovation throughout the company. She also knows that it is not a "one size fits all" initiative. While the principles would be the same in every unit, the implementation would need to vary, depending on the specific needs and operations of the unit.

Francoli knows that she will encounter a lot of resistance in introducing OME. Some executives believe that her proposal is not much more than flextime in a new package. Others worry that OME will hurt interaction and idea sharing because there will be less face time at the office. Some employees worry whether they will be expected to work even more hours, making it impossible to separate work and personal time or to achieve work-life balance.

Francoli also knows that a number of her employees are very cynical toward change. With the arrival of yet another CEO in just over three years, employees are worried about what changes Francoli might want to introduce. About one-third of Tech Depot's employees talk longingly of the "wonderful founder" and what a kind and good person he was, and, by extension, what a mean, cold, heartless person Aiken was. These employees miss the more collaborative, family-like environment of the founder. About a third express more comfort with the measurement approach of Aiken, where expectations were spelled out, managers led, and employees followed. These employees and managers thrived under Aiken's "management culture," and were not really as comfortable under Waters' more touchy-feely style. The rest of the employees are not sure what kind of environment they prefer, but they don't want to be bounced around in yet more change experiments.

The Trial Units

Francoli knows that simply imposing OME at Tech Depot won't work. So she wants to begin a trial program where she can encourage managers and employees to try it out, and help them work out the problems. She hopes that a successful trial program will inspire other managers and employees to request trials for their own work groups. She has identified three units where she would like to introduce OME.

Rachel Abji, Extended Warranty Unit   Rachel Abji, manager of the extended warranty group, is desperate to try anything new. Her top-performing employees complain that their jobs are far too stressful, and they are threatening to quit. The employees feel they are always on, carrying their cellphones and checking their email numerous times during the day and night. Because of high customer demand, Abji expects her employees to work onsite. The employees are starting to resent that they have no personal life.

There are 27 people in her unit who handle the company's extended warranty services. Twenty of these employees work hourly, and they often complain about having to punch a time clock.

The overall tasks of the unit include entering data from all warranty cards, handling requests from customers for repair or replacement of defective products, negotiating with repair people to get products repaired, and shipping and receiving packages.

Members of the unit are responsible for entering the data from warranty cards that are returned by mail and checking the accuracy of warranty applications that are filled out by customers online. When customers contact the unit (via phone, fax, email, or mail) about a defective product, someone in the unit has to verify whether the product is still under warranty. If the product is still covered by warranty, arrangements are made for the customer to deliver the defective product to the closest store or mail it to the central warranty unit. If the product is delivered to a store, then someone at the store must send the product to the central warranty unit. Individuals in the unit unpack packages to inspect broken products. They then contact their network of repair people to have the product repaired, shipping the product to the appropriate repair person. Once repaired, the product is returned to the warranty unit, which then has to return the product to the customer. While there is generally no charge for repairs made under warranty, customers can elect to pay a service fee in order to have their product returned within 24 hours. Consequently, some weekend emergency staffing of the warranty office is necessary.

Bennet Omalu, Logistics

Bennet Omalu is the manager of one of the eight distribution centres within the logistics division. Logistics is a critical operation for Tech Depot because the division's employees handle every product that the retail stores and the online operation sell. Each distribution centre receives all of the products for its specific region, and then moves those products to the different stores within the region. When big sales days are planned (for instance, the Boxing Day sale), it is important that stores have enough product on the shelves to meet customer demand. Logistics plays a key role in making this happen.

The majority of the employees in Omalu's unit are logistics warehouse employees. These employees manage the receipt of all products that Tech Depot sells, loading and unloading packages from trucks, and helping to gather together deliveries for each store. All employees do some heavy lifting, and some employees drive forklift trucks. The distribution centre operates 24 hours a day seven days a week.

Some of Omalu's employees are logistics customer-service representatives. These employees are responsible for making sure that home deliveries are carried out effectively. The customer-service reps schedule deliveries with homeowners, trying to accommodate individual schedules. They provide customer support, set the delivery times, keep a database of delivery data, and follow up with customers who do not return calls about when to schedule a delivery. Because there are multiple customer-service reps coordinating deliveries to customers, they must work with each other to schedule efficient delivery routes and timings for the drivers. The reps are held responsible if drivers end up driving back and forth across town, or if the driver misses the two-hour delivery window that was promised to the customer. Logistics reps

also have to estimate the time that it will take to do the delivery—some products simply need to be dropped off, while other products need to be assembled at the customer's home. In addition to normal daytime hours, customer service reps often work evenings and weekends.

Omalu is a protégé of Aiken's. Thus, he is very "management" driven, wanting to micromanage his employees at every step. He loves working weekends, and thinks his employees should do the same. He seems unaware that his employees are stressed out and threatening to leave. He believes that face time, measured by the number of hours that individuals are at their desks, is the only valid way to make sure that employees get their work done. He is reluctant to introduce any "touchy-feely" elements, for fear he will lose control over his unit.

Francoli wants to introduce OME to Omalu's unit because of complaints she has been receiving from his employees. While she recognizes that Omalu will oppose such a change, she feels that there really is no alternative for this unit, because of its importance to store operations.

Chloé Wong, Store Manager

Francoli is particularly interested in introducing OME to the retail environment because the turnover rate in the retail stores is nearly 70 percent per year, a number far higher than the industry average. Employee morale is also low. Because of the nature of the work, retail stores will be Francoli's toughest challenge in introducing OME. However, Francoli believes that she cannot limit OME to units where it's easiest to implement. She is determined to find a way to make it work in the retail stores. Otherwise, she feels that retail employees will be resentful of employees in other parts of the organization who get to work under the OME principles.

Chloé Wong, the general manager of a store in Victoria, has expressed interest in having OME introduced in her store. As general manager, Wong is responsible for sales, operations, inventory management, and loss prevention for her store. She works with her employees to make sure that they offer exceptional customer service, and addresses customer issues when necessary. Wong is assisted by two assistant managers, whose job is to work closely with the customer-service reps. The assistant managers are responsible for maintaining high morale, providing feedback and coaching to sales associates, and providing them with sales goals and targets.

Customer-service reps focus on the customers, trying to find out what customers want, and then finding appropriate solutions. They engage in basic selling, ring in sales, answer customer inquiries, and handle special orders, returns, and exchanges. Wong's store is open from 9 a.m. to 8 p.m., seven days a week.

While Wong wants the opportunity to introduce OME to her store, she acknowledges that she will need a lot of support, direction, and encouragement to make the program work. Wong is highly respected by her employees, but has never introduced a major change to her employees before.

Early Response to OME

Francoli has informed all employees that changes are coming, although she has also told them that she will introduce the new OME program in just three units at first. She hopes the trials will minimize the disruption throughout the company, as well as provide time to work out any unexpected difficulties with introducing OME more widely.

Although she announced only yesterday which three units would be included in the OME trial, Francoli is already receiving complaints. Younger employees who are not part of the trial units are urging her to introduce the changes into more units more quickly so they can benefit right away. Some of them are even threatening to leave if she does not act quickly to get more units involved. Many of the Baby Boomers, who have worked for the company for 20 years or more, are resentful that work life is going to be easier for employees in their 20s and early 30s than it was for them when they were younger. Even though they appreciate an opportunity for more work-life balance, they resent having sacrificed much of their family life to help build the company. They believe younger employees should pay the same price. Thus, they are inclined to encourage Francoli to go more slowly in introducing OME.

Some employees are not sure that OME is a good idea at all. They are afraid that having more autonomy will also mean that there will be no clear guidelines about when work is supposed to start and stop. They are afraid that they will end up working 24 hours a day, and they don't know how to make sure that does not happen. Some managers have reminded Francoli that the store still needs to comply with employee standards legislation on overtime, meaning that most employees should not be working more than a 40-hour week or an 8-hour day.

Meanwhile, about one-third of her managers have said that they just don't believe what she is trying to do will work, and they won't support it, even if it does work in the trial units, because they believe that more rather than less control drives strong results.

The Decision

Francoli reviews the many concerns that her managers and employees have raised and wonders what she should do. How can she best introduce OME in each of the three "experimental" units so that it has the best chance to work? What should she do about all of the employees who are complaining that she is either moving too fast or not fast enough? And how quickly can OME become a way of life throughout the entire company?

Trouble at City Zoo

City Zoo has been an important visitor destination for generations of children.[2] Locally, provincially, and nationally, City Zoo has had a remarkable reputation for providing a high-quality environment for its animals while enabling children of all ages to learn about animals and see them in natural environments. The zoo operates with a dedicated staff, as well as a large number of volunteers. Over half of its revenues come from a special tax levy on city property owners, who vote on whether to renew the levy during city elections held every three years.

Despite its sterling reputation, the zoo went through a year of unpleasant publicity in 2005, after the board of directors dismissed head veterinarian Tim Bernardino. Newspaper reports of the dismissal suggested that Bernardino had been dismissed for speaking up about harm to some of the zoo's animals. The publicity forced zoo management to respond to many tough questions regarding its practices and operations regarding both animals and staff. City Council acted swiftly in the face of continued negative press coverage of the zoo, feeling a responsibility to the taxpayers. In order to answer all of the questions raised by the press, council created a special citizens' task force to review the zoo's finances and operations, including animal care.

It is February 2006, and Emma Breslin has just been hired by the board of directors to take over as executive director of the zoo. She is reviewing the many concerns raised by the task force and wondering how she might restore employees' and the public's confidence in the zoo. She will be meeting with the board in two weeks to present her recommendations for moving forward. The board has asked her to act quickly because city residents will vote on the next tax levy in just three months. A "no" vote would substantially reduce the zoo's revenues for the next several years. (Exhibit 1 outlines the revenues and expenses of the zoo for fiscal year 2005.)

Background

The City Zoological Gardens got its start in 1905, when Samantha Fraser donated a hedgehog to the city's Parks Board. Building on that first donation, the zoo has grown to be one of the most comprehensive zoological institutions in the country. The zoo's African Savannah recreates the look of Africa's plains and jungles. The Savannah houses the world-famous Hippoquarium, the first natural hippo habitat to be created in a zoo. The zoo includes exhibits for Siberian tigers, Asian sloth bears, and the endangered African wild dogs. The zoo has also renovated the Aviary and the Primate Forest. More recent improvements include a new parking lot and gift shop. The zoo is a top tourist attraction for the city, and the number of annual visitors to the zoo has nearly tripled from 1982 (364 000 visitors) to 2004 (more than 1 million visitors). In the past five years, the zoo has twice been ranked as one of the top 10 zoos in North America for children and families. It was also voted one of the top five zoos in North America in the "North America's Favorite Zoo" contest sponsored by Microsoft. The zoo's vision and mission statements (see Exhibit 2 on page 576) are widely credited with helping the zoo achieve these awards.

Until 1982, the zoo was run by the city. That year, ownership was transferred to the City Zoological Society, a private nonprofit organization. Because of its dedication, the society was able to introduce a number of improvements that the city had not been able to accomplish. The zoo has since doubled in size and now contributes significantly to the local economy. A recent study by a local university found that the zoo generates almost $8 in local economic activity for each tax dollar it receives.

The zoo employs 157 full-time staff members and more than 550 part-time and seasonal employees. There are also more than 300 volunteers who assist with programs, events, and community outreach. Donors and members provide financial support for animal conservation and educational programming.

The Ministry of Natural Resources Inquiry

The 2001 Inquiry In December 2000, Medusa, a female sloth bear mistakenly believed to be pregnant, was put into isolation, where it died. Zoo officials later admitted that they had misunderstood how to properly care for sloth bears. Tim French, the curator of Large Mammals at the time, made the decision to put the bear in isolation on his own, without reporting this to his supervisors. The bear's zookeeper, Melissa Fox, who reported to French, objected to his decision, but no one would listen to her, including acting head veterinarian Wynona Singh (who was in charge while Dr. Bernardino was away on research). Fox's daily notes, which she was required to file with her supervisor, described her worries about the bear. Fox finally became so upset with the bear's condition that she asked to be transferred to another part of the zoo. French resigned after the bear's death.

As a result of the investigation, the zoo was fined $1450 by the Ministry of Natural Resources for violating federal

This case was prepared by Nancy Langton, Sauder School of Business, University of British Columbia. This case is based on an actual set of events, although all names have been changed. © 2006, Nancy Langton.

EXHIBIT 1   City Zoo Revenues and Expenses, Fiscal Year 2005

Public Support

Property Tax Levy Receipts	$6 466 860
Grants	$174 780
Education Program Revenue	$344 110
Total Public Support	**$6 985 750**

Development Revenue

Membership	$3 903 420
Friends of the Zoo	$214 397
Annual Fundraising	$130 852
Corporate Support	$302 952
Development Events	$391 565
Total Development Revenue	**$4 943 186**

Earned Revenue

Admissions	$3 253 355
Advanced Sales	$337 908
Gross Revenue From Concessions and Gift Shop Operations	$7 153 483
Rides, Parking, and Tours	$1 560 727
Facility Rentals	$116 520
Total Earned Revenue	**$12 421 993**
Other Revenue	**$34 956**
Total Public Support and Revenue	**$24 385 885**

Expenses

Cost of Goods Sold	$2 448 164
Wages and Benefits	$13 900 524
Supplies, Maintenance, and Utilities	$4 387 642
Professional Services	$2 246 560
Other Expenses	$714 487
Conservation—Project Support	$45 093
Animal Purchases	$76 542
Special Exhibits	$293 630
Total Operating Expenses	**$24 112 642**
Excess (Deficit)	**$273 243**

animal welfare regulations. The zoo also agreed to create an animal reporting system so that employees could raise any concerns they had about animal welfare, although nothing ever resulted from this agreement.

The 2004 Inquiry   In February 2004, the Ministry of Natural Resources began an investigation of animal deaths that had occurred at the zoo over the past several years:

- Cupid, a hippopotamus, died in the summer of 2003 at the age of 49. While the veterinary staff raised some questionable circumstances concerning the death, zoo officials dismissed the animal's death as "old age."

- George, a 14-year-old giraffe, died in 2001 from tetanus three weeks after he was gored by a kudu when the two were put in an enclosure together.

- Medusa, the female sloth bear, died in December 2000.

EXHIBIT 2 City Zoo Vision and Mission Statements

Vision Statement
To be one of the world's outstanding zoological institutions.

Mission Statement
Our mission is to provide excellent animal management, educational programs, and scientific activities and to provide visitors with an enjoyable, educational, and family-oriented experience.

Objectives to achieve mission statement:

- Animal exhibits that reflect natural habitats

- Educational programs to help visitors understand the relationships of wildlife and the environment

- Refuges for rare and endangered species to protect and propagate them

- Scientific programs that contribute to greater understanding of animals and their habitats

- A clean, safe, and pleasant facility for visitors and employees

- A broad base of community support and involvement

- Operating on a sound business basis

Zoo officials were puzzled about why the Ministry of Natural Resources had decided to investigate these deaths. "Initially, my gut reaction was that the Ministry of Natural Resources was just stepping things up because of what had transpired at that other zoo," a zoo spokesperson said. The spokesperson was referring to several suspicious animal deaths, including an orangutan euthanized by mistake, at a large zoo in another part of the country.

As the Ministry of Natural Resources investigation progressed, however, many zoo staff became nervous about the way it was being conducted. Inspectors did not reveal the exact reason for their inspection, but they asked specific questions about the giraffe and the hippopotamus. The inspectors requested to speak to some employees, while refusing to speak with others. Zoo officials later said the surprise inspection was "unusual, unprecedented, and aggressive."

"As you can imagine, it was a very upsetting and confusing time. We've never had this kind of inspection, and the frustrating thing was they would not tell us what they were inspecting for," said William Lau, the zoo's executive director.

Before the Ministry of Natural Resources could issue a report, zoo officials decided to conduct their own internal investigation into the deaths of George, the giraffe, and Cupid, the hippopotamus. Officials were concerned that someone at the zoo had made a call to the Ministry of Natural Resources that led to the surprise inspection. Lau claimed that the investigation was not a "witch hunt," and

that officials were not trying to find out if anyone had acted as a whistle-blower. "We simply want to understand what the Ministry of Natural Resources is worried about," he said.

The Ministry of Natural Resources issued a report on its investigation the following month. In it, the inspectors noted that the zoo had ignored the warnings of Dr. Tim Bernardino, City Zoo's head veterinarian, about animal care. "From the review of numerous documents and interviews, it is clear that these veterinary recommendations from the attending veterinarian [Dr. Bernardino] have not been addressed in a reasonable time. The licensee [the City Zoo] has failed to provide the attending veterinarian with adequate authority to ensure the provision of adequate veterinary care," the report stated.

Zoo Management
Board of Directors

The board of directors oversees City Zoo's business affairs and strategic plan, but day-to-day operations are left in the hands of the executive director. There are 18 people on the board. Each board member serves a three-year term. The term can be renewed up to two times, if the board member is nominated by the Nominating Committee and approved by the board of directors. The board in recent years has been mostly hands-off, allowing the executive director a great deal of latitude in running the zoo.

Executive Director

The executive director is effectively the CEO of the zoo, carrying out the strategic plan of the board. William (Bill) Lau was appointed executive director in 1980, when the zoo was still run by the city. Under his leadership, the zoo expanded considerably, won numerous awards, and significantly increased its revenues.

Lau did a good job of raising the zoo's profile externally, particularly in leading fundraising efforts that brought numerous exotic animals to the zoo. He was not necessarily seen as a good internal leader, however. The board's Executive Management Committee reported at a March 13, 2002, board meeting that the zoo's work environment was characterized by numerous disagreements. The minutes of this meeting showed that the board discussed "'open warfare' between managers; backbiting and rude behaviour during meetings; and problems in managers' relationships with Mr. Lau." The minutes also reported that "Working with Bill is experienced by some as difficult, intimidating, or scary." Some staff had complained that Lau frequently yelled at staff and failed to acknowledge their value. "There is a fear of repercussion, and some people are afraid they will be . . . seen as stupid, belittled in meetings, [and] blamed and shamed in front of others," the minutes state.

Chief Operating Officer

The chief operating officer (COO) is second in command at the zoo, reporting to the executive director. The COO's responsibilities include most of the operational functions of the zoo: finance, human resources, maintenance and horticulture, interpretive services, and education. The Department of Veterinary Care was the only nonoperational function that also reported to the COO. All other animal-related departments, including the curators, reported to the executive director.

In early 2002, the zoo hired Robert (Bob) Stellenbosch to be the new COO. Unlike the COO he replaced, Stellenbosch had no animal care experience in his previous positions. Before coming to the zoo, he had been executive director of the National Funeral Directors Association for 14 years. Prior to that, he had been executive director of the Provincial Bankers Association. Nevertheless, veterinary care still fell under Stellenbosch's mandate, and the head veterinarian reported to him. Stellenbosch did not see this as a problem. As Stellenbosch pointed out, he often had to oversee "departments in areas I know very little about. The secret [is] having a strong line of communication with the people who report to you."

The zoo's executive director also did not see Stellenbosch's lack of animal care experience as a problem. "We were looking for anybody with a background that could run a zoo on a day-to-day basis. We didn't find anybody with an animal background who could do that. We chose Bob Stellenbosch because he was the best candidate," Lau said.

Caring for the Animals

Three sets of employees work closely with the animals: veterinarians, curators, and zookeepers.

The Veterinarians

Dr. Tim Bernardino Dr. Tim Bernardino, director of Animal Health and Nutrition at City Zoo, was the zoo's head veterinarian, and had been a zoo employee for 22 years. Eight full- and part-time employees in the Animal Health and Nutrition Department reported to him. Veterinarians are responsible for the health care program for the animals, and they also maintain all health records. Bernardino was also the "attending veterinarian" for the zoo, a position that carries with it the responsibility to communicate on a regular basis with the Ministry of Natural Resources. Part of this responsibility involved bringing questionable animal deaths to the attention of the Ministry of Natural Resources.

Bernardino was well respected by the international veterinarian community, and well-liked by the zookeepers. He was known to deeply care for all of the animals in the zoo, and kept up with the latest literature on the best ways to manage and display animals to maximize their comfort and well-being.

Bernardino's performance as head veterinarian was generally applauded by senior management. He had received glowing ratings in his annual performance reviews throughout his career. For instance, at the end of 2004, Bernardino received one of his best performance reviews ever. Robert Stellenbosch, his direct supervisor, wrote that Bernardino maintained "the highest quality of work!" He also wrote that "Tim is well respected throughout the zoo." Stellenbosch praised the veterinarian's technical skills, his dependability, and his tremendous work ethic.

There were occasional negative comments in his reviews, although these did not seem to weigh heavily in his overall evaluations. For instance, in his 2000 review, a former supervisor wrote, "Tim can be intense and inflexible, causing strained relations with fellow employees." Still, the supervisor noted that Bernardino "gets along reasonably well" with other zoo employees. In his 2004 review, the veterinarian was specifically asked to "focus more on people skills in the department and with curators." The review also noted that "Tim is strong in his beliefs, and sometimes needs to temper that once a final decision is made."

The negative performance appraisal comments were related to Bernardino's relationships with the curators and zookeepers. He was well respected by the zookeepers, and maintained good relations with them because their observations of the animals helped the animals stay healthy. However, some of the curators felt that Bernardino empowered the zookeepers too much, so that the zookeepers would sometimes go around their curators to make complaints about animal care. Bernardino worried that some of the zookeepers were disciplined by their curators when they spoke with him about their concerns regarding the animals. "People don't feel free to be open. Discussions don't happen. [There is] control of information, control of communications, control of decision making [by the curators]," he said.

Beth Else, curator of Conservation and Research, saw it differently. "I think he empowered the keepers to go around the supervisors and go to him when they didn't get the answer that they liked," she said, echoing comments of the other curators.

Despite his generally good reviews, Bernardino also felt that he was "alienated from the decision-making process . . . with the curatorial staff and with other administrators." He sometimes complained the curators were given more weight than the veterinary staff in decision making about the animals, even when the health of the animals was in question. He also felt that his role as attending veterinarian, where he was accountable to the Ministry of Natural Resources, was "not well defined or understood by those in the zoo community."

Bernardino's reviews took a turn for the worse after the Ministry of Natural Resources released the report of its 2004 surprise investigation. Just two months later, in May 2004, Stellenbosch gave Bernardino, in writing, what was termed a "verbal" reprimand about his performance. "We need to have team players, and you need to work through these issues in a more professional, less 'attacking' manner," the COO's warning stated. Bernardino was also told that he lacked "team attitude, professionalism, and judgment."

This warning was closely followed by the announcement that Bernardino would share the "attending veterinarian" position with two others: his subordinate, veterinarian Wynona Singh, and Mammals curator Randi Walker. Though Walker was also a veterinarian, she was not licensed to practise as one in the province. In August 2004, Bernardino was told that he would no longer serve as an "attending veterinarian," and that Singh would be the sole "attending veterinarian." At about the same time, Bernardino received a written reprimand, in which he was accused of "steadily undermining animal curator Dr. Walker, poor communication skills, and intimidating other employees."

Dr. Wynona Singh   Dr. Wynona Singh, who reported to Dr. Bernardino, had been a full-time veterinarian at the zoo since 1999. She first joined the zoo in 1989 as a part-time veterinarian. Singh was the veterinarian on call when the giraffe died in 2001 and the sloth bear died in 2000, although she was not implicated in either death.

Bernardino and Singh often butted heads. In his 2003 evaluation of her, Bernardino recommended that she receive no salary increase. In January 2004, Bernardino told the zoo's human resource director that "if she doesn't improve and we keep her, I'm out of here."

Bernardino was reflecting on a survey of her performance he had conducted with the veterinary and animal food staff. Only 29 percent of them gave her favourable ratings, while 61 percent noted that she had big communication problems. The zookeepers specifically complained that Singh did not relate well to them and was not always open to their concerns. This led Bernardino to tell her that she "had to continue to improve some management skills, including communication." Despite negative reviews from her immediate staff and subordinates, Singh received high marks from the curators and associate curators, who indicated their full and unambiguous support of her.

The Curators and Zookeepers

Curators make recommendations such as what animals to acquire, whether animals should be bred, and whether animals should be lent to other zoos for either breeding or display purposes. Curators are also responsible for the designing and planning of animal exhibits, including coming up with ideas for new exhibits that might be of interest to the public. Though curators are responsible for the overall well-being of the animals, they are certainly aware of the marketing and public relations functions of animal exhibits.

The general curator at a zoo oversees the entire animal collection and animal management, and is responsible for strategic collection planning. Zoos also have animal curators who manage a specific section of the animal collection. City Zoo had four area curators: curator of Fishes, curator of Reptiles, curator of Birds, and curator of Mammals. Some areas also had associate curators, such as the assistant curator of Large Mammals and the assistant curator of Small Mammals.

Senior zookeepers and zookeepers (also called *keepers*) report to the curators and work with individual animals, feeding them, handling them, keeping their cages clean, and looking after their welfare on a day-to-day basis. Keepers often work with the same animals for a number of years, so they can grow quite attached to their animals. Keepers can feel that they understand more about the welfare of their animals than the curators.

At City Zoo, there was significant tension between the curators and the keepers. The keepers complained that curators did not listen to their concerns, and curators complained that the keepers often went around them to share concerns about animals with Dr. Bernardino. The curators felt that the keepers should raise all concerns with them, rather than with the veterinarian.

Randi Walker   Randi Walker was curator of Mammals at the zoo. The Mammals department's 22 full-time employees (including 14 zookeepers) took care of the zoo's apes, great cats, bears, elephants, and all hoofed animals. This was the largest animal department at the zoo, and was twice the size of the next largest department, the Birds Department. All of the deaths investigated by the Ministry of Natural Resources had happened in Walker's unit.

The assistant curator of Large Mammals and the assistant curator of Small Mammals worked under Walker. The assistant curators were two of the most liked curators at the zoo. They had excellent animal care backgrounds, were very aware of the zoo's communication problems, and knew how to work effectively with the other employees. They were also respected by the zookeepers and other curators.

Although curators do not usually have veterinary training, Walker had completed her veterinary studies. However, she was not licensed to practise veterinary medicine in the province. Her background may have led to her difficult relationship with Bernardino. Sometimes she tried to second-guess him, and other times she attempted to overrule his decisions.

Walker was particularly uncomfortable with the relationship that Bernardino had with the Mammals zookeepers. She felt that his close relationship to them undermined her. "There are communication problems with mammal keepers and [Mammals curator Randi Walker]," one keeper said. "Some people can talk; other people, if they open their mouth, she jumps on them. That's the underlying thing why people talk to Dr. Tim."

Gorilla keeper Dale Petiniot noted that while she had no problem discussing issues with Walker, sometimes keepers needed to discuss issues with a neutral third party. "It's not always that we're justified, but sometimes you need to talk about things, and you don't have a next step, other than the vet," Ms. Petiniot said.

When zoo officials, responding to the Ministry of Natural Resources' surprise investigation, tried to investigate the death of George the giraffe, they quickly discovered that most employees in the Mammals Department would simply not talk about the event, saying that they feared retribution by Walker. Even though zoo officials offered immunity from any disciplinary action in exchange for clarification about what had happened, no one came forth to take responsibility for putting the two animals together. "Nobody claimed responsibility," Andy Yang, curator of Reptiles and head of the internal investigation, said.

The report of the internal investigation concluded, "The apparent failure of the mammal keeper staff to inform, discuss, and plan this introduction with the veterinary staff prior to any action was unacceptable and compromised the welfare of the giraffe." Yang's committee made a pointed observation regarding the Mammals Department: "There are significant communication problems in the Mammals Department that need attention. These communications problems have negatively affected animal welfare."

Xavier Tolson, a human resource consultant hired by the zoo at the end of 2004 to analyze workplace problems in the Mammals Department, reached many of the same conclusions. "I do not believe I have ever seen a department as dysfunctional as the Mammals Department" at City Zoo. He noted that there was a lot of conflict between the head curator and the zookeepers.

Tolson suggested that the keepers had a tendency to try to bully Walker into seeing their point of view about animal concerns.

Though most of her subordinates were quite critical of Walker's performance, managers at the most senior levels in the zoo were strongly supportive of her. She was always deferential to their views, and they felt she was right not to cave in to employee concerns.

The Biological Program Committee

In most zoos, the general curator oversees the work of the curators, zookeepers, and veterinarians and attempts to resolve any issue that might come up among the three groups. However, City Zoo had no general curator. When the zoo hired Robert Stellenbosch as COO in 2002, he was

unable to serve as general curator, a role his predecessor had filled, because he had no previous animal experience.

Shortly after Stellenbosch was hired, William Lau, the executive director, announced that the newly created Biological Program Committee (BPC) would perform the duties normally handled by the general curator. The committee consisted of the curators of Mammals, Birds, Reptiles, and Fishes, an animal behaviour specialist, and members of the zoo's veterinary staff. Only the four curators and the animal behaviour specialist had voting rights on the committee, however. The curators took turns chairing the monthly committee, rotating the position every few months. No one else was allowed to chair the committee.

Not everyone was happy with the new management committee meetings. Bernardino, who had had a very good relationship with the former general curator, felt that his authority was diminished because of the BPC structure. Bernardino also objected that he was not able to rotate into the role of committee chair. He complained that the curators did not pay enough attention to animal care issues. He also complained that the curators treated members of the veterinary staff who were on the committee like second-class citizens. After trying to get along with the new management structure for about six months, Bernardino took his concerns about the BPC to the executive director. Lau dismissed the veterinarian's concerns, suggesting that communication among committee members was good, except for some "troublemakers," which Bernardino took to be a reference to himself.

Beth Else, curator of Conservation and Research at the zoo, noticed a change in Bernardino's demeanour after the creation of the BPC. "It seemed in the past that Tim relied on gentle persuasion to bring people over to his way of thinking. In recent years, particularly in the past year, Tim has been more of a disruptive influence at the zoo," Else said. "I don't want to give the impression that I think Tim is malicious, because I don't," Else said. "Tim, in his own mind, thinks he is doing what is right."

Other employees must have agreed with Else that Bernardino was trying to do the right things at the zoo. On February 23, 2005, the zoo staff voted on nominees for "Outstanding Employee" of the year. Bernardino received the most votes.

Shockwaves at the Zoo
Head Veterinarian Fired

On February 28, 2005, City Zoo dismissed Bernardino from his $102 000-a-year position as head veterinarian. The executive director said that the dismissal had nothing to do with the 2004 Ministry of Natural Resources inspection, or with issues about animal care. "There is no question in my mind that he raised the level of animal care here at the zoo," Lau explained. "And while I do have a problem with the way Bernardino dealt with the Ministry of Natural Resources in the past, the termination was a result of our concerns over Dr. Bernardino's administrative and management skills that we had worked with him to address over the last several years."

Bernardino's dismissal created shockwaves both inside and outside of the zoo. The local newspaper contacted several well-known veterinarians throughout the country to find out what they could do about Bernardino. All of the contacted veterinarians spoke with great regard for the dismissed veterinarian. Reporters also uncovered previous performance reviews of Bernardino, which indicated that Bernardino had performed exceptionally in his work with the animals. Reporters concluded from their investigation that "The firing of Dr. Bernardino in late February was the culmination of a year-long struggle between him and zoo administrators beginning, it appears, with the veterinarian's frank comments last year during a routine animal care inspection by the Ministry of Natural Resources. Those comments led to an admonition by the Ministry of Natural Resources that the zoo failed to heed warnings about its animal care practices."

The intense press coverage prompted the city to start its own investigation of zoo administration. City Council felt an obligation to protect taxpayers' money, and recognized that public confidence in the zoo was at an all-time low because of all the negative publicity. Council appointed a 14-member citizens' task force in mid-March. The mandate of the task force was to review zoo finances and operations, including animal care, and to issue a report within 100 days.

As the task force was getting underway, more scandal struck the zoo. The local newspaper reported that Executive Director William Lau had traded in the Jeep he had been given at zoo expense for a luxury Volvo, also paid for by the zoo. Similarly, COO Robert Stellenbosch had traded in his Dodge. The two Volvos were costing taxpayers $700 per month.

Members of the public were outraged by this news, coming just two weeks after Bernardino's firing. One longstanding zoo member emailed the local newspaper that he was disgusted with zoo administrators: "The firing of the whistleblowing vet is enough to make one wonder if the chimpanzees could not do a better job of running the place. If anything would make me stop supporting the zoo, it is the attitude of the zoo director and [chief operating officer]. To rent Volvos for themselves, to be so wasteful with the dollars of the taxpayers, is tantamount to being part of the low-down reptile exhibit."

A Settlement and Resignations at the Top

After his dismissal, Bernardino approached the board of directors, requesting that they meet with him and give him back his job. The board was feeling under siege because of all the negative publicity. Bernardino's dismissal seemed to mobilize community sentiment toward the veterinarian, and against the zoo's senior management.

In an effort to quiet speculation by community members about zoo leadership, the board of directors made a settlement with Dr. Bernardino on May 1, 2005. The agreement reinstated him to his position of director of Animal Health and Nutrition of the zoo effective immediately, although he would serve in this role only as a "consultant," on an "as-needed basis." The agreement stated that Bernardino was not allowed to be on zoo grounds while performing his job, and could not enter the zoo as a private citizen for six months. The agreement prohibited him from discussing "his opinions as to the welfare of the animals at the Zoo, the circumstances of his termination or reinstatement of employment, his opinions regarding personnel at the Zoo, or any other matters pertaining to the Zoo" with anyone unless subpoenaed.

Bernardino's consulting position was to last for 18 months. He would be paid $105 000, plus health and retirement benefits, during that time. Under the settlement, he would also receive $42 815 in back pay, benefits, and attorney's fees. The board agreed to remove all negative evaluations that were added to his file in 2004. Bernardino agreed that he would not file claims of wrongful discharge or breach of contract against the zoo.

Two weeks after the settlement with Bernardino, the zoo board announced that Executive Director William Lau would retire immediately, after 25 years at the zoo. The board also announced that COO Robert Stellenbosch would resign once a new management team was in place.

The Findings of the Citizens' Task Force

The Citizens' Task Force presented its findings to City Council at a public meeting held on July 8, 2005. The task force divided its presentation into three parts: a discussion of the employee survey they had commissioned; a presentation of what they had learned about the politics of zookeeping; and a discussion of other observations about how the zoo operated.

Employee Survey   The Citizens' Task Force asked Maynard & Associates, a Toronto-based employee relations consulting firm, to determine employee morale. Exhibit 3 summarizes the results of the survey, including separate results for the Mammals Department. Maynard & Associates have collected baseline data as a result of their many employee surveys, and those data are also included.

On many dimensions, City Zoo employees were more critical than the average employee in Maynard's surveys. Zoo employees complained about the lack of effective leadership, poor communication, and the scarcity of teamwork. Only half of the employees said there was open and honest

EXHIBIT 3   Employee Attitude Survey of City Zoo, and Some Comparisons

Category	Question	Percentage of Employees Who Agree or Strongly Agree with Statement			
		City Zoo	Mammals Department	Other Zoos	Other Organizations
Pay	My compensation is satisfactory and fair compared with that of other employees who work here.	80	81	82	75
	My compensation is satisfactory and fair compared with what I would earn at similar companies.	81	81	82	74
Recognition	My supervisor recognizes and provides positive feedback for work well done.	63	57	68	72
Supervision	My supervisor treats me fairly.	43	43	63	63
	My supervisor helps me perform my work effectively.	41	39	70	70
Communication	I feel comfortable expressing my ideas to my supervisor and other leaders in the company.	41	35	71	73
	Leaders communicate pertinent information to employees.	51	48	55	74
Empowerment	I am free to make decisions that affect my work without consulting with my supervisor.	55	45	67	69
	My ideas are used when managers make decisions that affect the company.	49	41	65	70
Job Satisfaction	Overall, the company is a good place to work.	68	60	70	77
Management	The managers here are honest, fair, and ethical.	45	39	76	79
Participation	Managers seek employee input into the way work is done here.	53	45	68	77
Teamwork	Employees work together as a team here.	59	53	79	79
	Teamwork is encouraged here.	55	50	75	75
Training	I receive adequate job-related training to do my job.	85	83	81	76
	There are plenty of opportunities here to learn additional skills.	85	78	81	74
Work Demands	The workload is fair and reasonable.	75	74	73	79

communication at the zoo, and many employees noted that this lack of communication led to rumours and myths that spread throughout the zoo.

Employees said that they did not feel that they could talk freely to their supervisors about job-related problems, and they gave low marks to supervisors for resolving employee problems. Employees also gave low marks to supervisors for letting employees know what was expected of them. Supervisors were also criticized for not considering differing opinions, and a number of employees noted that they feared punishment if they expressed contrary opinions. Employees also expressed the expectation many employees placed on each other that "if you are not with us; you are against us," which created a lot of divisiveness across the zoo.

Despite the low morale uncovered by the survey, results indicated that employees loved working at the zoo, were fairly paid, and felt that they had been trained appropriately to do their jobs. However, they wanted to see an end to the political, communication, and leadership problems that dominated day-to-day work at the zoo.

The Politics of Zookeeping   Three members of the Citizens' Task Force were asked to discuss the events that had occurred at City Zoo with respected members of the zoo community throughout North America. Dr. Christopher Bondar, the associate veterinarian at the Central Canada Zoo, suggested that it was not surprising that there were tensions between zoo management and the veterinarians. "The zoo business in general, because people's emotions tend to run high about animals and their welfare and because it is a small community, tends to have a lot of politics," said Dr. Bondar, who added that he has not encountered such problems at his own zoo. It can be hard to understand all of the politics at zoos because "so many businesses are about paperwork or industry or goods that don't spawn the type of passion people have for living animals."

Members of the task force spoke with Dr. Philip Robinson, a former director of veterinary services at the San Diego Zoo and author of the book *Life at the Zoo: Behind the Scenes with the Animal Doctors*, and asked him about the relationship between curators and veterinarians. "The perception that [veterinarians] should stick to sick animals and leave the other issues to the other people on staff—traditionally, this is sort of a turf battle that has more to do with management style than anything that benefits the animals," he told them.

Other experts supported Dr. Robinson's position. They told the task force that it is crucial for veterinarians to interact with keepers to understand the needs of individual animals. "If the curator says to the keeper, 'You only tell me what's happening,' then the veterinarian is sort of between a rock and a hard place to know when the animal is on the road to a problem, or already is there and has the problem," said Randolph Stuart, the executive director of the Canadian Association of Zoo Veterinarians. "That's why most vets will keep a good rapport with keepers."

Experts in the area of zoo administration suggested that many zoo administrators don't appreciate the passion that veterinarians bring to their work. Veterinarians are chiefly concerned with animal welfare, while the zoo administration is also concerned with fundraising, providing an experience for zoo visitors, running successful gift shops and snack bars, and making sure parking lots are adequately designed for the visitor load.

Dr. Mark Cornwall, the director of animal health and attending veterinarian at the Maple Leaf Zoo, stressed the need for good communication among all zoo employees. The Maple Leaf Zoo was sued by an employee under whistleblower protection legislation. The employee was demoted and harassed after she complained to government officials about unsafe conditions at the zoo. "Everybody kind of learned something from that," said Dr. Cornwall. "Animal welfare comes first," he said. "Zoo veterinarians are really the ones who are in charge of that. Veterinarians tend to champion those causes because that is what they are expected to do. You have different perspectives and opinions on those things, but the key is to sit down with all the folks." He added, "Zoos are complicated organisms and organizations. Open communication can improve the situation, however."

Other Issues Raised by the Task Force   During its presentation, the Citizens' Task Force identified a number of other issues of concern, and they briefly reviewed these for council.

Organizational Culture   The task force found that lack of trust was a big issue among staff. They also found a "culture of fear" and noted that even though retaliation was often subtle, it was definitely there. In particular, keepers were afraid to admit actions or mistakes, even when immunity was offered. The task force expressed concern that many of the zookeepers were too focused on their own specific job duties and did not "see or support the 'big picture' of the zoo as both a wildlife conservation facility and a business."

Relationship among Curators, Veterinarians, and Zookeepers   Some curators were found to be good at managing animals but weak at managing people. The keepers complained that curators did not always respond in a timely manner to their proposals and suggestions for improving animal care. Veterinarians had some of the same complaints as the keepers—that curators did not always see the need to consult with veterinarians on animal management issues. The task force also noted that some keepers and curators held grudges that they might not be able to put behind them.

Curators complained that veterinarians undermined them through direct contact with the keepers. However, the task force noted that there was no defined communication path for keepers to raise concern with the veterinary staff. Moreover, experts throughout the zoo veterinary world stressed the importance of open communication between keepers and veterinarians so that vets can fulfill their obligations under the Fish and Wildlife Conservation Act.

The task force concluded that there was a lack of communication among keepers, veterinarians, and curators that led to questionable care standards for the animals. Because departments of the zoo did not work closely together, there was not a good system of checks and balances to maintain appropriate care.

The Biological Program Committee   The Citizens' Task Force was particularly critical of the BPC, suggesting that many of the zoo's problems resulted from the creation of the BPC. The BPC created a mutual admiration society for the curators, and allowed the curators to overlook the concerns of keepers and the veterinarian staff. The board also found that there was no real accountability for decisions because of the committee structure.

Organizational Structure   The task force raised a number of questions about the current structure of the zoo, noting that communication issues, lack of teamwork, and lack of coordination were all factors that resulted in animal deaths, and were likely related to the current structure. During their investigation, they had asked Lau whether all individuals directly involved with animal care had reported to him. He claimed they did, until a member of the task force, pointing to the organizational chart (see Exhibit 4 on page 584), noted that the veterinarians and veterinarian technicians reported to the COO.

"It was largely the size of the group, and the number of people reporting to different people. We were trying to divide the zoo up so that neither Bob nor I [had too many]," Lau explained. "Money being what it is, we didn't want another high-management position."

Employee Conduct   The task force found that there was a "lack of consistency, uniformity, accountability, and decisiveness in the enforcement of standards of conduct across departments," and that the Employee Relations Department was not good at enforcing standards of conduct. A number of employees complained that those who worked hard were often expected to compensate for employees who underperformed.

Employees are disciplined through a "five-step" process. An employee can be terminated if he or she receives five written infractions within a 12-month period. The task force found this process so burdensome that employees were almost never terminated. In fact, Jennifer Fisher, employee relations director, told the task force that "no animal keepers or other non-managerial employees had been fired in the past 20 years."

A New Executive Director Takes Over

Emma Breslin began her position as the new executive director last week, eight months after the resignation of the previous executive director.

Breslin's previous position was as executive director for the past 10 years at Maritimes Zoo, a smaller zoo with 51 employees, a general curator, and two contract veterinarians. Breslin had been hired by Maritimes Zoo to reunite a divided staff. She is known as a consensus leader, and at Maritimes Zoo she increased communication, improved supervisory skills, and taught employees to value each other's contributions to the successful operation of the zoo. Breslin was also successful in raising awareness among the community about why financial support from the public was so important to the zoo.

Breslin faces a large public relations problem as she begins her new job. She knows that much of the zoo's revenue is dependent upon public support. The next tax levy vote is three months from now. The zoo also raises significant revenue through the "Friends of the Zoo" program, an annual subscription program where people donate money to the zoo. She needs to restore community trust. At the same time, she needs to grow zoo attendance levels, which have fallen in the past six months, and develop a strategic plan for the zoo.

Breslin also faces a very divided and demoralized staff. She has reviewed what was written in the press and familiarized herself with the Citizens' Task Force review. She knows she needs to bring some peace and stability to employee relations. Her most difficult task will be to unite the staff. She needs to build staff morale and gain their trust. She wonders how she will accomplish these goals over the next year. The outline of what she intends to do over the next six months to get things back on track is to be presented to the board in two weeks.

EXHIBIT 4   Organizational Chart of City Zoo, January 2005

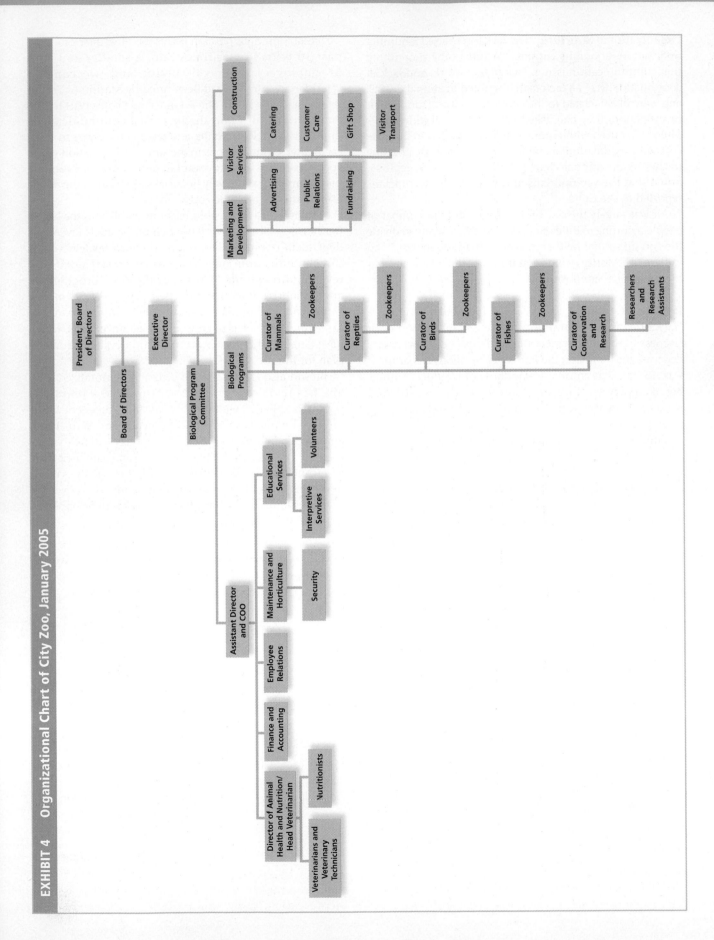

Arnold Schwarzenegger: Leader of California?

The governor of California, Arnold Schwarzenegger, or "Arnold" as the state's residents like to call him, is arguably playing the biggest role of his career. Elected in the October 2003 recall election that featured a hodgepodge of 135 candidates, including celebrities Gary Coleman, Larry Flint, and Mary "Mary Carey" Cook, Schwarzenegger replaced incumbent Gray Davis as the governor of the most populous state in the United States by raking in 48.1 percent of the popular vote. Californians, weary of Gray Davis's lack of progress, decided to put their trust in a man best known for his roles in action movies such as the *The Terminator* and *Total Recall.*

Schwarzenegger's ascent to the governor's seat is impressive when one considers his background. Born in the small town of Thal, Austria, on July 30, 1947, Schwarzenegger was the product of a modest and harsh upbringing. His parents strictly disciplined him—treatment that he says "would be called child abuse" today. Schwarzenegger explains, "My hair was pulled. I was hit with belts. So was the kid next door, and so was the kid next door. It was just the way it was. Many of the children I've seen were broken by their parents, which was the German–Austrian mentality. Break the will. They didn't want to create an individual . . . It was all about conforming. I was the one who did not conform and whose will could not be broken. Therefore I became a rebel. Every time I got hit, and every time someone said, 'You can't do this,' I said, 'This is not going to be for much longer, because I'm going to move out of here. I want to be rich. I want to be somebody.' "

Determined to leave Austria, Schwarzenegger began to search for a way out, a way to become "somebody." He found that way out through bodybuilding. As a child, he idolized bodybuilder Reg Park, a former Mr. Universe. Though his parents objected, Schwarzenegger pursued bodybuilding so vehemently that at one point he was able to bench-press 520 pounds (for comparison, physical fitness experts typically say that it is good to be able to bench press one's own body weight).

At age 19, Schwarzenegger was crowned Mr. Universe. He continued to win championships, and, in 1970, he even defeated his idol, Reg Park, for the Mr. Universe title. Schwarzenegger now says that bodybuilding was instrumental to his success as an actor and as a politician. "I know it from my bodybuilding—that I can see my goals very clearly . . . It takes the confidence to ignore critics and naysayers," he states.

Having accomplished his goal of becoming Mr. Universe, Schwarzenegger set his sights on the United States to pursue acting and moved there at age 21. Although he attended acting school, his odd last name and thick accent at first kept him from acquiring roles. He eventually landed a small role in the film *Hercules in New York* and continued to appear in other films such as *Stay Hungry* and *Pumping Iron*. In 1982, however, Schwarzenegger made his mark in the film *Conan the Barbarian*, which grossed more than US $100 million worldwide. His on-screen charisma, massive physique, and uniqueness compared to American actors made him a standout. Since moving to the United States, Schwarzenegger has made 33 movies and has become one of the most highly paid actors in the world. For *Terminator 3*, Schwarzenegger earned an astounding US $33 million—a record sum at the time.

After succeeding as a bodybuilder and an actor, Schwarzenegger began eyeing a bigger prize: the California governor's seat. During his acting career, Schwarzenegger had formed a strong network of powerful friends and advisors, including investor Warren Buffet, economist Milton Friedman, and Israeli Prime Minister Benjamin Netanyahu. As the recall election neared, Schwarzenegger consulted with his network of allies. Buffet told Schwarzenegger that California needed strong leadership, and Friedman gave him advice on how to improve California's dismal economy. All of this advice gave Schwarzenegger the vision he needed to propel himself to the rank of governor. Running as a moderate Republican, he sought to unite Democrats and Republicans, pass a balanced budget, reduce government spending, and resuscitate the business community. Once he accomplished these goals, Schwarzenegger would confidently state to the rest of the world that California was *back*. Schwarzenegger's vision came at a perfect time: Governor Davis witnessed the rise and fall of the tech boom. When the tech bubble burst, revenue plummeted. In 2001 and 2002, state revenue from income tax fell 27 percent, yet spending remained the same. Although Davis was not solely responsible for the resulting Californian debt, Californians were eager to place blame.

Hungry for someone to take the reins from Gray Davis and steer California away from its troubles, many Californians embraced Schwarzenegger as he campaigned across the state. His name recognition and charismatic personality made him a leading candidate. Schwarzenegger's style is vastly different from other politicians. His wit, honesty, and lack of concern for political correctness struck a chord with voters. (As he told one interviewer at *Fortune* magazine following the election, "I love smart women. I have no patience for bimbos.") It was perhaps this larger-than-life persona that led him to "terminate" Gray Davis in the recall election.

Following the election, Schwarzenegger immediately began making policy for California. Within only a few days of his swearing in, Schwarzenegger had a viable economic recovery plan. To the praise of the state's residents, he repealed the car-tax increase, which would have raised almost $4 billion in revenue but was hated by Californians. He continued his strong push for reform, passing propositions that made a US $15 billion bond offering possible and that paved the way for a balanced budget. In April 2004, he persuaded the state's legislature to pass a bill overhauling workers' compensation, a victory for businesses trying to reduce costs but a defeat for workers.

A testament to his approachable personality was the fact that he broke tradition by actually going from his office on the first floor to the upstairs offices of the legislators to meet with them. Schwarzenegger's chief of staff, Pat Clarey, can't remember the previous four governors doing that. All in all, the newly elected "governator," using his charisma and network of powerful friends, inched closer each day to his vision.

Even the Republican party took notice. Though more moderate than the Republican Party would like, Schwarzenegger knew that his popularity and charisma were an asset to the Republican convention during President George W. Bush's 2004 re-election campaign. While the Republican party convention organizers were debating whether to invite the moderate Schwarzenegger to speak, Schwarzenegger told the *New York Times*, "If they're smart, they'll have me obviously in prime time." Schwarzenegger got his wish. Two days after the interview, he was invited to speak during his requested time. Republican operatives weren't disappointed with quips such as "This is like winning an Oscar. As if I would know! Speaking of acting, one of my movies was called *True Lies*. And that's what the Democrats should have called their convention." Schwarzenegger's speech at the convention electrified the crowd, further solidifying his role as a charismatic leader.

Not everything has been rosy. One of his major goals was to pass a US $103 billion budget plan that he believed would be a tremendous step toward economic recovery. He set an optimistic timeline of passing the budget by June 30, 2004. Schwarzenegger worked tirelessly, negotiating budget reductions with state-affiliated organizations such as universities, prisons, and the teacher's union. However, negotiations began to fall apart when he made conflicting promises to the opposing parties on state and local budget linkages. Instead of victoriously passing his budget on time, the state legislature recessed for the July 4th weekend, leaving Schwarzenegger and his budget on hold.

Not to be dissuaded, Schwarzenegger began campaigning to the public to garner support for his budget. He even went so far as to call opponents "girlie men" at a public rally—an incident that infuriated his critics. Though eventually he was able to pass a revised version of his original budget, Schwarzenegger continued to attempt to fix California's financial crisis through various cost-cutting initiatives. He took on the California teachers' union, trying to persuade it to revamp entirely the way it hires, pays, and fires teachers. During this time, his approval rating fell to 55 percent. Though still high, his approval rating was down from a staggering 65 percent. Many of his ideas are abhorrent to the teachers' union. For example, Schwarzenegger wants to tie teachers' pay to test scores. Many teachers feel that this undermines their ability to teach what they think are important topics and will result in a narrow curriculum.

Some believe Arnold Schwarzenegger is a powerful politician, but he says that he really doesn't like the word power because it tends to have a negative connotation. Schwarzenegger says, "Power is basically influence. That's the way I see it. It's being able to have the influence to make changes to improve things." Schwarzenegger has a clear vision of how he wants to improve things; the question is not only whether he can create beneficial policies but also whether he has the ability and support to implement those policies. Although he realizes that his charisma helped him to become governor, Schwarzenegger also knows the importance of vision to a leader. As he puts it, "There is no one, and when I say no one, I mean no one, who will back me off my vision. I will go over burning coals for that."

Questions for Discussion

1. What words would you use to describe Arnold Schwarzenegger's personality? Do any of these fit into the Big Five taxonomy of personality? How might these personality traits influence Schwarzenegger's leadership skills? How might these traits have helped Schwarzenegger get to where he is now?

2. Based on the case, as governor of California, what types of power is Schwarzenegger likely to have? What types of influence tactics does Schwarzenegger appear to use?

3. How would you describe Schwarzenegger's leadership style using the leadership theories covered in this textbook? What details of the case lead you to these conclusions? Is Schwarzenegger's leadership style likely to be effective? Why or why not?

4. Applying concepts from goal-setting theory, explain how goals have influenced Schwarzenegger's progression to the governor's seat. What aspects of the case suggest that Schwarzenegger is committed to the goals that he has set for himself?

5. Are there any "dark sides" to Schwarzenegger's charisma and leadership skills? What might these be, and how might they affect his relationships with others and his ability to govern?

6. How might Schwarzenegger's personality and leadership style help or hinder his ability to effectively negotiate with other parties such as the teachers' union?

Sources: Based on B. Morris, A. Gil, P. Neering, and O. Ryan, "Arnold Power," *Fortune*, August 9, 2004, 77–87; and R. Grover and A. Bernstein, "Arnold Gets Strict with the Teachers," *Business Week*, May 2, 2005, 84–85.

What Customers Don't Know Won't Hurt Them, or Will It?

Sitting at her desk at the car rental shop where she worked, Elena couldn't believe what she was hearing. Gripping the phone tightly, Elena listened as the head manager of the company's legal department told her that a car that she had recently rented to a customer had blown a tire while the customer was driving on a nearby highway. Although the customer, Jim Reynolds, tried to maintain control of the vehicle, he crashed into another car, seriously injuring himself and the other driver. Apparently, the tire had noticeable structural damage that caused it to blow. Elena stared at her desk in shock as the legal department manager asked whether she was aware of the tire's condition before renting the car to Mr. Reynolds.

"I . . . I'm sorry, what did you say?" asked Elena.

"I asked whether you were aware that the tire was damaged before renting the car to Mr. Reynolds," repeated the manager.

Elena paused, thinking back to when she had rented the car to Mr. Reynolds. Unfortunately, she knew the answer to the manager's question, but she did not know whether she wanted to answer it. Her mind raced with worried thoughts about how she let herself get into this position, and then she remembered when her supervisor first told her to lie to a customer.

Elena had started working for the rental car company 2 years ago. Fresh out of college, she was intrigued by the possibilities of joining a company and moving up the ranks into management. She worked hard, sometimes putting in 50 or more hours a week. And she was good at her job, too. Customers would frequently tell her supervisor of Elena's great service and courtesy. Within no time, the supervisor began telling her that she was a strong candidate for management and would probably be running her own rental office within the next year.

Intrigued with becoming a manager, Elena began to work even harder. She was the first one at the office each morning and the last one to leave. Things were going well, until one particularly busy day, when the rental office had more business than it could handle. The office typically had a few vehicles left for walk-in customers, but on this day the lot was empty except for one SUV, which a couple had reserved for their vacation. The couple's reservation was for 1 P.M., and it was now 12 noon. Proactive as usual, Elena decided to go check the SUV to make sure it was ready for the couple. As she got up from her desk, the door to the rental office flew open, and a man rushed toward the counter.

"Do you have anything to rent?" he quickly asked. "I don't have a reservation, but I really need a car right now for the rest of the week."

Elena apologized and explained that the only vehicle they had at the moment was reserved, but that he could wait at the office until another car was returned. In fact, she said, they expected to have two vehicles returned around 3 P.M.

"That's not good enough," the man replied. "I need a car now."

"Again, I do apologize sir, but it wouldn't be fair to those with a reservation to rent the only car that is available," said Elena.

With a frown, the man turned to leave. As he did, Elena's supervisor, who had been listening to the conversation, chimed in. "So you really need a car, huh?" he asked the man.

The man whirled around. "Yes, I do."

"I'll rent it to you for $150 a day," said Elena's supervisor. One hundred and fifty dollars a day was much more than the rental company's usual fee.

The man paused for a moment and then said, "Fine, I'll take it."

As he left with the only vehicle left on the lot, a stunned Elena asked her supervisor why he had rented the SUV when he knew that it was reserved—and at such a high price.

"That guy would have paid anything, and he ended up paying twice as much as we would have gotten out of it," her supervisor said, laughing. "Look, if you're going to be a manager, you need to know how to make money. Always take the best deal you can get."

"Even if it means losing another customer?" Elena asked. "What are we going to tell the couple who had a reservation for that SUV?"

"*You're* going to tell them that it broke down unexpectedly and it's at the shop. If you want to be a manager, start acting like one."

Soon after, the couple with the reservation walked into the rental office. Elena didn't want to lie to them, but she also didn't want to jeopardize her chances of obtaining a management position. She also figured that the couple would be more understanding if she told them that the SUV had broken down than if she told them that she had rented it to another customer. So Elena followed her manager's advice and lied to the couple.

In the months that followed, Elena encountered several more instances where her supervisor asked her to lie to customers because her office had reserved too many vehicles. Pretty soon, it became second nature, as she found herself lying to customers without pressure from her supervisor. To date, however, her lies hadn't caused any serious harm to anyone, at least as far as she knew. That track record changed, however, the day Jim Reynolds rented a car from her.

The day was routine in that the rental office was very busy. There were only two vehicles on the lot—a compact car and a new luxury sedan. Mr. Reynolds had reserved the less expensive compact car. However, when checking the car over before Mr. Reynolds arrived, Elena noticed a large lump on the outside well of the passenger-side front tire. From her training, she knew that this lump could be dangerous. But Elena also knew that she would have to give Mr. Reynolds the luxury sedan for the same price as the compact car if she decided not to rent him the compact car. She thought about what her supervisor had told her and knew that he probably would be upset if she didn't get a high rate out of their new luxury sedan. Besides, she reasoned, the car will be fine and Mr. Reynolds would have it for only a day. So Elena went through the routine. With a smile and a handshake, she rented the compact car to Mr. Reynolds, who didn't notice the tire because it was on the passenger side, and Elena didn't walk Mr. Reynolds around the car—a routine practice at the rental company.

Fast-forward one day and Elena's world had completely changed. Now, Elena was on the phone with the manager of the company's legal department, wondering how she ever thought it would be safe to rent the car to Mr. Reynolds. She could admit that she knew about the tire and decided to rent the car anyway, or she could lie and say that the tire looked fine when she rented the car. If she told the truth, becoming a manager would probably be out of the question, at least for a long while. Anger welled up inside her. She had worked hard to get where she was. She regretted not having told her supervisor that she wasn't going to lie to customers, even if it meant getting a better rate. But that moment had passed. She could tell the legal department

manager that her supervisor had told her to lie to customers, but she knew that her manager would deny it. Either way, the options weren't too appealing.

"Hello? . . . hello?" asked the legal department manager.

Elena returned to the conversation. "Sorry, I lost you for a moment," she said. "Yeah . . . about Mr. Reynolds . . . "

Questions for Discussion

1. Using concepts from reinforcement theory, explain why Elena might be motivated to lie to customers. With reinforcement theory in mind, do you think that Elena will confess to the legal representative? Why or why not?

2. How might the rental office's climate influence Elena's behaviour? What factors contribute to the current climate? What steps could you take to improve the ethics at this office?

3. Do you blame Elena for her behaviour or do you attribute her behaviour to external factors? How do concepts from attribution theory fit in?

4. Consider Elena's personality. Would you predict that escalation of commitment will occur (and she will lie to the legal representative), or will she decide to come clean? Explain your answer.

5. Do you think Elena would make a good leader some day? Why or why not? What factors might this depend on?

6. What emotions might Elena be experiencing? How might Elena's emotions affect her decision to tell the legal department manager about the incident with Mr. Reynolds?

Are Five Heads Better Than One?

Evan, Conner, Alexis, Derek, and Judy had been team members for only one week, but they felt that they were already working well together. Upper management at their company, Advert, a medium-sized marketing firm, picked the five employees for a special project: the development of a commercial promoting the launch of a client's 60-inch plasma flat-screen television. The project was especially critical because the television company was one of Advert's most important clients, and the firm's revenues had been slipping lately due to a few poor ad campaigns. Needless to say, upper management at Advert wanted the team to hit a home run with the project.

Upper management didn't have any trouble picking the five employees. All were bright, talented individuals who came up with creative ideas. More important, reasoned the top managers, the employees were similar on a number of characteristics. Evan, Conner, Alexis, Derek, and Judy were around the same age, had worked for the company for about the same amount of time, and because they all tended to be sociable, friendly, and valued getting along with others, their personalities seemed to mesh as well.

To give the team creative room, management allowed them as much autonomy as possible. It gave the team the freedom to see the project through from start to finish—

coming up with their own ideas, hiring someone to film the commercial once the idea was in place, creating and maintaining a budget, and presenting the final commercial to the client. Advert's top managers had already met with and assured the client that it was in good hands with this team.

Excited to begin working, the team decided to meet in person to discuss ideas for the commercial. Conner, who was used to leading others in his previous work groups, took the head seat at the group's table. Immediately, he told the group his idea for the commercial.

"I've been thinking about this a lot since I was first told about the project," he said. "I know our client well, and I think they want us to do something out of the box—something that will grab people's attention."

Conner proceeded to explain his idea for the commercial, which centred on a college student "loser" trying to get a date. After one particularly attractive female turns him down, and she and her friends ridicule him, the student returns sullenly to his dorm, plunks down on an old sofa, and turns on his small, black-and-white "loser" television. But in the next shot, the student is setting up a 60-inch plasma television in his dorm room, door ajar. While he's doing this, the group of attractive females walks by. In the final shot, the student is in his dorm room watching his new television, with the group of attractive females around him.

Following his explanation, Conner leaned back in his seat and folded his arms across his chest. Grinning proudly, he asked, "Well, what do you think?"

Alexis was the first to speak up. "Um, I don't know." She paused. "I think it's a pretty good start." Hesitantly, she added, "The only thing that I worry about is that our client won't like it. They pride themselves on being more sophisticated than their competitors. To them, this television is both an electronics device and a work of art." But then Alexis quickly added, "But I don't know, maybe you're right that we need to do something different."

Conner, with a slight frown on his face, asked the other group members, "What do the rest of you think?"

Evan responded, "Yeah, I think it's a pretty good idea."

"Judy?" asked Conner.

"I agree. It has potential."

"Well, everyone else seems to agree with me. What do you think Derek?" Conner asked, with the other three members staring at Derek.

Derek paused for a moment. He had his own ideas as well, and because he had worked with the client, perhaps more than any of the other team members, he wasn't sure about Conner's idea. Derek had pictured a commercial that placed the television in a stylish, contemporary Manhattan apartment, with a couple in their 30s enjoying a classic movie, a bottle of red wine on the coffee table.

Feeling the heat from his teammates' gazes, reluctantly Derek said, "Yeah, that sounds good."

"Great, it's settled then," beamed Conner. "We'll have this commercial to them in no time if we stay at this pace."

So the team fleshed out the commercial over the next month. Everyone got along, and the feeling of camaraderie strengthened. Once on board with Conner's idea, the team members became more confident that they would be successful, so much so that they made the commercial even racier than the original idea. The attractive girls would be dressed provocatively, and instead of watching the television, the student and the girls would be laughing and drinking, with the television on in the background. There were a few hesitations here and there as members expressed other ideas, but each team member, enjoying the group's solidarity, decided that it would be better to keep the team in good spirits rather than risk losing the team's morale.

The team quickly decided on a company to shoot the commercial and approved the actors. In a short time, they had completed their commercial. The next step was to present the commercial to their client. Conner took it upon himself to alert management that the team was ready to present the commercial.

"Impressive. Your team is a month ahead of the deadline," said one of the top managers. "We have a lot riding on this, so I hope that it's good. I presume everything went well then?"

Conner nodded. "Yes, very well. No problems or disagreements at all. I think we worked really well together."

On the day of the presentation, the team waited anxiously in a meeting room for their client to arrive. Advert's top managers took their seats in the meeting room. Soon after, three of the client's managers, dressed in professional attire, walked into the meeting room and sat down quietly. After welcoming the clients to the presentation, Conner and his teammates began the presentation, with Conner leading the way. He explained that the idea had come to the team almost instantly, and that given that everyone thought it was a good idea, he was sure that their company would feel the same. Then he dimmed the lights, pressed play, and let the commercial run.

It did not take long for the team to realize that the commercial was not having the effect they had wanted on their clients or their managers. The clients exchanged several sideways glances with one another, and the managers shifted nervously in their seats. After what seemed like an eternity, the commercial ended and the lights came back on. An awkward silence filled the room. The clients began murmuring among themselves.

"That was, um, interesting," said one of the clients, finally.

Conner replied that he thought the idea was "out of the box," and that, therefore, audiences would easily remember it.

"Oh, they'll remember it all right," smirked one of the clients. She then turned to Advert's top managers and stated, "This is not at all what we were looking for. The commercial doesn't fit our needs and doesn't portray the image that we are trying to obtain. Given that you told us that we would be in good hands with this team, my colleagues and I fear that your company will not be able to meet our goals. We appreciate the time that this took, but we will likely employ another advertising firm to film our commercial." With that, she and her colleagues left the room.

After a thorough lecturing from Advert's top managers, the team was disbanded. One month later, Derek was at home watching television when a commercial came on. Classical music played in the background as the camera swept through a modern home. The camera slowly rose up behind a tan leather sofa seating a couple enjoying a bottle of wine and watching a new 60-inch plasma television. In the bottom corner of the screen, in small writing, was the name of one of Advert's competitors. Apparently, Advert's former clients got what they were looking for in the end, but from a competitor. Derek shook his head and vowed to speak up next time he had an idea.

Questions for Discussion

1. What factors contributed to the poor performance of the Advert team? As a manager, what could you have done to help the team perform better?

2. According to the case, the Advert team was given a relatively high degree of autonomy. How might this autonomy have contributed to the presence of groupthink?

3. Teams can be either homogeneous or heterogeneous. How would you characterize the Advert team, and how did this affect the team's creativity and performance?

4. What are some group decision-making techniques that could have helped reduce conformity pressures and groupthink among the Advert team?

5. What different forms of communication could have been employed to improve the sharing of ideas among the Advert team? How might this have affected its performance and satisfaction?

6. How would you describe Conner's leadership style? Why do you think his style wasn't effective? In what situations might Conner be an effective leader?

Walmart's World

Just how does Walmart, the world's largest retailer, maintain its corporate culture across all of its 4,000 stores? How does this giant, with sales a staggering $358 billion in fiscal year 2004, promote and preserve its image as a small-town store where the customer is king? Part of the answer lies in Walmart's legendary Saturday Morning Meeting.

The Saturday Meeting started with Walmart founder Sam Walton, who thought it unfair that he could take off on the weekends while his employees worked. So, in 1962, Sam Walton began arriving at his store, Walton's Five & Dime, in Bentonville, Arkansas, each Saturday between two and three in the morning. There, he would scrutinize the previous week's records to determine which merchandise was selling and which was not, as well as how sales were faring. However, Mr. Walton didn't stop there. When his store's "associates" (Walton called all his workers associates to emphasize that they were his colleagues as well as his employees) arrived, he would hold a quick morning meeting to openly share the store's information with them. He would also ask for their opinions on matters such as what items he should put on sale and how he should display certain products. Such meetings served not only to use the store's employees in multiple ways but also to convey to his employees that he valued their input and wanted them to learn the business.

Even as Walmart grew into a multibillion-dollar company, the Saturday Morning Meeting continued. Ever since, Walmart has held them at the home office in Bentonville. Each Saturday morning, some 600 managers, many of whom live in Bentonville and make weekly trips to their respective territories, pack the 400-seat auditorium, waiting for their fearless leader to arrive. First, it was Sam Walton. Then, it was CEO David Glass. Now, at 7:00 A.M. sharp, current CEO Lee Scott heads the meeting. As usual, Scott starts off the meeting by leading the crowd in a Walmart cheer: "Give me a W! Give me an A! Give me an L! . . . "

Though Saturday Morning Meeting topics typically include the company's financial performance, merchandising, and areas of improvement, the meeting is, above all else, a means to keep the company and its employees as close-knit as possible. Such solidarity is imperative to Walmart's strategy of quick market response. When new ideas or problems surface, managers are comfortable sharing them with others. Decisions are made quickly, and action is taken.

For example, while discussing merchandising mistakes during a meeting, Paul Busby, regional vice-president for the North-eastern United States, was concerned about a particular item that Walmart was not carrying. "I went into a Kmart near one of my stores to look around and found an item that made me wonder why we don't have it." With a Kmart bag next to him, Busby pulls out a poker table cover and chip set that Kmart is selling for $9.99. "We should really have this product because it's a much better value than ours."

In response to Busby's concern, Scott McCall, the divisional merchandise manager for toys, replied, "We've got a pretty nice poker set in our stores, but I'll check with our sources and get back to you."

A mere 10 minutes passed before McCall asked for the microphone again. With cheers from the crowd, McCall stated, "Paul, I just wanted you to know that I've arranged for those Kmart poker sets to be acquired and be on the trucks rolling out to all the stores next week." Examples such as this illustrate the trust that Sam Walton had in his staff to make decisions. Instead of going through layers of red tape, Walmart's managers can have their ideas implemented quickly. Of course, not all decisions are beneficial; however, those that are can result in immediate gains.

Such quick responses are difficult, if not impossible, for other large companies to execute. As former CEO David Glass explains, "The Saturday Morning Meeting was always a decision-making meeting to take corrective action, and the rule of thumb was that by noon we wanted all the corrections made in the stores." Glass clarifies, "Noon on Saturday." Glass further explains that since no other companies could even come close to the speed at which Walmart executes strategy and change, Walmart developed and sustains a competitive advantage. Walmart's vast distribution network and purchasing power allow it to move products efficiently and sell them at a low price. For example, following the devastation of hurricane Katrina, Walmart, rather than FEMA (Federal Emergency Management Agency), was one of the first organizations to distribute food and other goods to hurricane victims.

The Saturday Morning Meeting serves other purposes as well. Perhaps due to Walmart's culture of retail fanaticism and continuous improvement of efficiency, the culture of Walmart has been described as "neurotic." According to one Walmart insider, "Mechanisms like these meetings keep that neurotic tension alive even at this enormous scale."

In fact, the Saturday Morning Meeting is not the only meeting Walmart uses to maintain company culture. On Friday there is a merchandising meeting, where regional vice-presidents get together to discuss what products are selling well. And not all meetings are for managers. Consistent with Sam Walton's emphasis on employee involvement, every Walmart store has a 15-minute shift-change meeting three times a day. During these meetings, managers go over the store's performance numbers as well as ask their associates whether they have specific ideas that might improve sales. Managers send what they think are good ideas up to the regional vice-president, who then proposes the ideas at the Saturday-morning meeting. The Walmart greeter was one such idea, which a rank-and-file

employee suggested. The greeter helped to put a friendly face on what might be viewed as a large, impersonal organization. Such structure helps to ensure that Walmart's upper managers, who oftentimes are responsible for 100 or more stores, keep in touch with the daily happenings of their business.

One other aspect of Walmart's culture is its frugality, a characteristic of Sam Walton that has endured even through Walmart's tremendous growth and financial success. Walton began his strict focus on keeping costs low early on to gain an advantage over competitors such as Sears and Kmart. Walton was known to make executives sleep eight to a room on company trips. He himself drove a modest old pick-up truck and flew coach whenever he traveled. Amazingly, these characteristics have remained ingrained in Walmart's culture. The current CEO, Lee Scott, drives a Volkswagen Beetle and has also shared hotel rooms to reduce costs.

But maintaining Walmart's culture has not always been easy. In the late 1980s and early 1990s, attendance at the Saturday Morning Meetings grew tremendously, which made it impossible for everyone to speak. David Glass, CEO during that time, recalls complaints of boredom. So some of Walmart's suppliers (who often attend the Saturday Morning Meetings), eager to impress and ingratiate themselves with the top brass, began bringing in entertainers such as singer Garth Brooks and former football player Joe Montana. However, the meetings began to lose focus. As Glass recalls of the entertainment, "You had to be careful how you did that because it becomes more fun to do that than fix the problems." By the late 1990s, the company began inviting guests who had more educational value, such as Bill Clinton and CEOs Jack Welch and Warren Buffet. These speakers were able to share their success stories with Walmart's managers, giving them new ideas on how to conduct business and run the organization.

Perhaps the biggest obstacle to Walmart is the increased public scrutiny that comes with being the world's largest company. In the past, the company had more tolerance for employee mistakes. It would strongly reprimand an employee who made an offhand sexist remark, for example, but if the employee altered his or her behaviour, then the company let the employee stay. Today, however, Walmart adheres to a stricter policy. As Mr. Scott explains, Walmart is "not mean but less kind. Today, when you find somebody doing something wrong, you not only have to let them go, you have to document it so it is covered and people understand. That is a bit of a culture change. It's a company that operates in a different context than when Sam Walton was alive and when David Glass ran the company. Management cannot allow extraneous issues to bleed over. My role has to be, besides focusing on driving sales, to eliminate the constant barrage of negatives that causes people to wonder if Walmart will be allowed to grow."

Indeed, Walmart frequently finds itself in the news, though lately in stories that paint the company in a negative light. Controversies over Walmart's anti-union position, its hiring and promotion practices (such as outsourcing the cleaning of its US stores to illegal immigrants and working them seven days a week), and its treatment of employees (including accusations of discrimination and underpayment of employees) all make it increasingly difficult for Walmart to maintain the image of a friendly, affordable retailer that Sam Walton had in mind when he founded the company. On this topic, Scott says, "Over the last couple of years I've been spending much of the time talking about all the negative publicity we've been getting, not from the standpoint that we hate the press, but by asking our people what we are doing that allows people to perpetuate these kinds of negative discussions about Walmart."

If Walmart is to enjoy continued success, it will have to find solutions to the above problems and the negative publicity that results. Perhaps the company should go back to its Walton roots? Or maybe it should alter its culture and market position to match its growth. For a company that has over 4,000 stores operating in Canada, China, Europe, Korea, Mexico, South America, and the United States; 1.5 million employees; and over 100,000 different products for sale, sustaining or changing the company's culture is a tremendous challenge. Thus far, however, Walmart appears to be handling the challenge well.

Questions for Discussion

1. According to the textbook, there are seven primary characteristics that capture the essence of an organization's culture. How would you describe Walmart's culture using these seven characteristics?

2. Based on this case, would you characterize Walmart's culture as strong or weak? Why? How might Walmart's culture contribute to its long-term performance?

3. As an upper manager of Walmart, what steps could you take to either maintain or enhance the culture of Walmart?

4. What are some aspects of Walmart's culture that have persevered, but yet may be disadvantageous in today's economy?

5. How might Walmart's negative press affect employee morale, job satisfaction, and organizational commitment? As a manager, what steps would you take to improve employee attitudes?

6. Characterize Walmart's organizational structure. Is it mechanistic or organic? Does it have a high degree of centralization or decentralization? How might Walmart's structure affect its employees in terms of their productivity and job attitudes?

Sources: Based on D. Garbato, "Wal-Mart's Scott Concedes Size Impacts Corporate Culture," *Retail Merchandiser*, October 2004, p. 12; B. Schlender, "Wal-Mart's $288 Billion Meeting," *Fortune*, April 18, 2005, 90–99; and "Wal Around the World," *The Economist*, December 8, 2001, pp. 55–57.

Apple's Beethoven

Management guru Jim Collins calls him the "Beethoven of business," Wall Street loves him, and Bill Gates was once his nemesis. Who is this powerful man? It's Steve Jobs, co-founder and current chief executive officer of Apple Computer. But despite its trailblazing start, Apple has suffered in recent years, losing sales and market share to big companies such as IBM and Microsoft. The slide even caused many analysts to question whether Apple had anything innovative left to offer. But Jobs, in characteristic fashion, has once again cornered a market, thanks to a small device—with big musical power—called the iPod.

Although Apple competed with computer giant Microsoft during the early 1980s, it soon found itself on the fringes of the computer industry because its computer, the Mac, wasn't compatible with many software programs that businesses needed. Personal computers (PCs), along with Microsoft's Windows operating system, began to dominate, sending the Mac to niche markets. By 1986, Apple's board of directors forced Steve Jobs out of the company. By the late 1990s, even the most fanatic Apple users were turning to different products because of the Mac's compatibility issues and Microsoft's ever-increasing dominance. Apple's share in the computer industry continued to decline, bottoming out at a mere 2 percent in the mid-1990s.

Apple knew it had to improve its operating system, so it bought the computer company Next in 1997, which, as circumstances would have it, Jobs himself was running. Along with Next came Jobs, who eventually returned to the forefront of Apple. Jobs' plan was simple: Rather than focus on hardware, Apple should focus on software. Create the right software, he reasoned, and the hardware sales would follow.

So Jobs began making moves that at first seemed risky but in the end paid off. One of the first things he did was to partner with his former rival, Bill Gates. Gates agreed to supply Apple with its popular Office and Internet Explorer programs as well as buy $150 million of Apple stock. Though this deal was good for Microsoft, it was even better for Apple, whose future was now tied to the more successful Microsoft in that Microsoft now had an interest in maintaining Apple's survival. Apple was no longer a competitor in a strict sense.

Because developing software is a costly undertaking, Jobs tried to keep the company afloat by offering computer hardware, which was simply a means to get into the software business. He pushed the company's managers for innovative thinking, which led to the introduction of the iMac in 1998. The iMac immediately stood out from its competitors for its odd, colourful styling, but compatibility issues with some widely used programs still remained. Though the iMac was not the innovative success that Jobs had hoped for, it bought him time to continue developing software.

During this time, Apple developed a new operating system that Jobs thought would revolutionize the computer industry: Mac OS X. The system was based on the operating system Unix and was superior to Windows in several areas, including stability and security. Now that he had the operating system, Jobs needed exciting software to go along with it. Knowing that he already had a deal with Microsoft, Jobs headed to Adobe Systems to ask them to develop a video editing program for his new operating system. Jobs recalled, "They said flat-out no. We were shocked, because they had been a big supporter in the early days of the Mac. But we said, 'Okay, if nobody wants to help us, we're just going to have to do this ourselves.' "

Adobe's rejection may have been a blessing in disguise for Apple. Jobs quickened the pace on software development, and in less than a year released two video editing programs, one for professionals and one for consumers. The software helped keep the buzz alive for Apple's innovative reputation. Feeling confident, Jobs knew that Apple needed to develop more software applications if it were to thrive, but he still hadn't noticed a phenomenon taking place on the Internet: the birth of online music.

In 2000, music lovers the world over, particularly young adults and teenagers, were downloading MP3s (digital music files) by the thousands from what were then illegal online music services, Napster being the company most in the news at that time. Online music delivery was an exciting product for consumers in that they could easily pick and choose what songs to buy and create their own music libraries on their computers. It was also a controversial issue in that there was no way (yet) to compensate artists and their record companies for the sales.

But for Jobs, the opportunity to deliver music to online consumers in a legitimate, user-friendly way was right up his alley. "I felt like a dope," he said. "I thought we had missed it. We had to work hard to catch up." He set out to develop the best "customer experience" possible.

So Apple began to install CD-ROM burners as a standard feature on all of its computers, hoping that it hadn't missed an opportunity. The burners allowed users to save electronic files, such as digital music files, onto a CD. The addition of burners as a standard feature was a crucial first step in marketing digital music because it offered a way to play digital music on devices other than a computer.

But Apple still needed to offer software that allowed users to manage their digital music files. Microsoft already sold several computer programs of this sort. For Apple, developing software that could easily manage and navigate through thousands of songs and allow a user to call up a song on a whim was no easy task. Jobs didn't have the answer himself, but he found it in a company called SoundStep. Jeff Robbin, the founder of SoundStep, teamed with several engineers and developed the program iTunes in just over three months. Not only was iTunes Apple's answer to comparable Windows jukeboxes, but many consumers found it a superior program with great search and sorting capabilities.

Jobs then hit on his big, Apple-saving idea: Develop a small, portable device, like the Sony Walkman, that could hold a user's entire digital music library. Jobs turned to Robbin again. In November 2001—a mere nine months later—Robbin and his team had developed the iPod, which is basically a small, handheld computer the size of a deck of cards (now even smaller) with a simple interface for navigating through one's digital library and a set of earphones for easy listening. Music could be taken from a user's existing CD collection and "ripped" to the iPod via the user's computer, or online music file-sharing services could be used to download songs onto the iPod.

Though Jobs believed that the iPod would be a success, he kept at his goal of developing the best "customer experience" possible. Napster, as well as other online music file-sharing services, was in the midst of lawsuits, leaving the door open for legitimate, licensed services to emerge. By April 2003, Apple debuted its online iTunes Music store, allowing customers to legitimately buy songs for 99 cents that they could then download and store on their Mac computers and iPods. Major recording companies, such as Sony and Universal, agreed to sell their songs on iTunes, and the result was a tremendous success. As Eddy Cue, vice-president for applications at Apple recalled, "We had hoped to sell a million songs in the first six months, but we did that in the first six days." While the iTunes store was busy selling digital music, Robbin and his team developed a Windows version of the iTunes store, further broadening Apple's market.

To say that Apple has done well with the iPod is an understatement. By January 2005, the company had sold more than 10 million iPods and 250 million songs. As a result, its stock price hit a record high of almost $80 per share in February 2005.

Jobs credits Apple's success to maintaining its core values of innovation and a continuous focus on the consumer. "The great thing is that Apple's DNA hasn't changed. The place where Apple has been standing for the last two decades is exactly where computer technology and the consumer electronics markets are converging. So it's not like we're having to cross the river to go somewhere else; the other side of the river is coming to us." Jobs further stated, "At Apple we come at everything asking, 'How easy is this going to be for the user? How great is it going to be for the user?'"

Though it appears that Apple is on a roll, its competitors are beginning to catch up. Not only has Microsoft entered the online music market, but companies such as Walmart and Napster (Napster is now on legal footing) are trying to capture some of the market share. As of the latest look, Walmart was offering songs at 88 cents each, undercutting Apple's iTunes. Indeed, Apple's first-mover advantage will erode as competitors mimic Apple's product. Because they can copy Apple's online music store instead of creating it from scratch, start-up costs are lower for new entrants. What, then, will be the next move for Steve Jobs and Apple?

Questions for Discussion

1. Using the three-component model of creativity, describe what makes Steve Jobs, and by extension, Apple Computer, successful. Based on the case, which components does Jobs seem to possess in the highest degree? What aspects of the case led you to this conclusion?

2. What leadership theories are most applicable to Steve Jobs and why? How can these theories explain Jobs' recent successes?

3. Based on the case's description of Jobs, what can you infer about his personality? In other words, how would you describe his personality using terms from the book?

4. Are situational factors solely responsible for Apple's success, or is it due to the traits and leadership skills of Steve Jobs? If both contribute, which do you believe is more important and why?

5. Using Lewin's Three-Step Model of organizational change, explain Apple's development of and success with the iPod.

6. Would you characterize Apple as a learning organization? Why or why not? As a manager, what could you do to ensure that Apple continues to be innovative?

Source: Based on B. Schendler, "How Big Can Apple Get?" *Fortune*, February 21, 2005, 66–73.

GM and the UAW: A One-Sided Negotiation?

From 1947 through 1977, General Motors (GM) dominated the automobile industry, capturing an average of 45 percent of the US auto market. Of the "Big Three" North American automakers (GM, Ford, and Chrysler), GM ranked first in sales in every year during this time frame and ranked first in profits for 16 of the 20 years. Needless to say, GM sat comfortably atop the automobile industry.

Now, decades later, GM's share of the US automobile market is down to 25.4 percent, its lowest level since it competed with Henry Ford's Model T. Rumours of bankruptcy abound. In March of 2005, GM lowered its earnings forecast, which sent its stock price to its worst one-day fall since October 19, 1987, when the stock market crashed. Following this, GM announced that it had lost a

staggering 1 billion US dollars during its first quarter alone. Finally, adding insult to injury, GM disclosed that its sales were plummeting, and for this its stock earned Standard & Poor's grade of junk-bond status. The 2007–2009 financial crisis made GM's problems even worse. What once was the world's largest and most profitable auto manufacturer is now puttering along in the slow lane.

So who or what is responsible for GM's decline? Though there are numerous factors that are hurting the company, one major factor has been the United Auto Workers (UAW) union in the United States and its long relationship with GM over the years.

The relationship first took shape during the Depression, when demand for cars overall fell sharply and almost half of all autoworkers lost their jobs as a result. Those autoworkers that did keep their jobs received greatly reduced pay because the major auto companies could barely afford to stay in business. However, GM, through the leadership of Alfred Sloan, remained competitive and profitable. But working conditions paled in comparison to today's standards. It was not typical for companies, including GM, to provide benefits such as health insurance, and pension plans were unheard of.

All of this began to change for GM in 1936, when two major players in the UAW, Walter and Victor Reuther, staged a sit-down strike at one of GM's primary plants, Fisher Body Plant No. 1, in GM's hometown of Flint, Michigan. Though the governor at the time, Frank Murphy, instructed over 4000 guardsmen to maintain peace at the strike, he did not give them the authority to evict the strikers, forcing Sloan to negotiate with the UAW (though Sloan later stated that "we would not negotiate with the union while its agents forcibly held possession of our properties . . . we finally felt obliged to do so"). As a result of the strike, GM formally recognized the UAW as a legal organization in 1937. Shortly after, in 1941, Ford formally recognized the UAW, giving the union even greater power.

What followed was a relationship that endured over the years, giving the UAW and its members some of the best benefits in the country. Indeed, the UAW was a powerful negotiator. Victor Reuther, believing strongly that all workers should have health insurance, tried first to bargain with the federal government. After several failed attempts, he turned to Sloan at GM. Although Sloan initially viewed Reuther's request for health insurance and pension plans as "extravagant beyond reason," one of Reuther's proposals eventually persuaded him. Previously, GM and the UAW engaged in contract renegotiations each year, which made it difficult for GM's managers and workers to plan ahead because they were unsure what the costs would be for the following year. Reuther, capitalizing on this problem, offered to agree to longer contracts. As Sloan later stated, "Longer intervals gave the corporation more assurance that it could meet its long-range production schedules." What was the catch to the UAW's concession? In return for longer contracts, the UAW insisted that each and every contract be better for the UAW than the one before it. Sloan agreed to the terms of the negotiation, setting the stage for health insurance, pension plans, and other employee benefits.

During the economic boom following World War II, demand soared, leaving the auto industry rich with profit. As Reuther stated to the auto industry during these times, "It's a growing market—we have nothing to fight over." So, at first, contract renegotiations went smoothly and costs of employee benefits stayed at a minimum. But little by little, the UAW negotiated better benefits for its members. In 1943, GM allowed workers to purchase health insurance; however, GM did not incur any of the cost because workers put their money into a pool. Five years later, the union successfully negotiated two powerful benefits. The first, an "escalator clause," stipulated that GM give raises based on the cost of living. The second, the "improvement factor," rewarded workers for increasing efficiency. As a plant increased in efficiency, and lowered costs as a result, workers at the plant received raises. Then, in 1950, GM agreed to pay 50 percent of all its workers' health care premiums, including workers' families, and it also agreed to develop and pay for a pension plan. Three years later, GM extended these benefits to its retired workers.

Business was still booming in 1959, when the UAW persuaded GM to guarantee workers' wages—even for those workers the company had laid off. Thus, workers could be assured that they would receive no less than what GM had promised to pay them, even during economic hardship. The UAW continued to push GM to further sweeten its benefits—per their original deal—and in 1961, GM agreed to pay 100 percent of all health care premiums, again for workers and their families. Three years later, GM extended this benefit to its retirees.

GM's market share around that time peaked at 50.7 percent, but in 1966, the same year that Alfred Sloan died, a little-known company called Datsun exported a car to the United States, marking the entry of Japanese automakers in the US market. During this time, Japan's influence was minimal, and GM continued to agree to increase benefits to its workers. In 1970, for instance, the UAW persuaded GM to provide full retirement benefits after 30 years of service. In addition, GM agreed to extend health insurance benefits to cover mental and prenatal and postnatal conditions. As UAW negotiator Douglas Fraser recalls, "We had a lot of arguments over mental health. I don't believe we had any arguments over full premiums."

From GM's standpoint, the concessions it made over the years may be relatively minor when considered in isolation, but their cumulative impact is now taking its toll. As the company has lost market share to increased competition from both domestic and foreign producers, particularly Japanese producers, more and more workers have retired, leaving GM with huge expenses. GM anticipates health care costs to top $5.6 billion in 2005 alone, and it is estimated that GM's long-term health care liabilities are $77 billion. To fund its pension plans, GM has long-term liabilities of $89 billion—a tremendous amount when one considers that GM's revenues in 2004 were $193 billion.

And costs continue to soar as baby boomers retire in droves, leaving younger workers to support retirees and causing large discrepancies in the number of current and retired workers. GM now employs 150,000 people, yet it funds health care for 1.1 million people. And because of the ever-increasing benefits packages that the UAW negotiated with GM over the years, GM's health care plan is far better than what the average US company provides.

While average US citizens pay 32 percent of their medical costs, GM workers and members of the UAW pay only 7 percent. In fact, GM now spends more than double on health care what it spends on steel to produce its automobiles. As one former GM investor quipped, "When you invest in GM, you are not investing in a car company. You are investing in a money-management firm and an HMO."

All of these rising costs have caused GM considerable financial problems. Although some analysts suggest that GM should streamline operations, Thomas Kowaleski, a spokesperson for GM, said, regarding the enormous cost of benefits, "We cannot be profitable at 20 percent market share because legacy costs won't go away." Even closing a plant is no longer under GM's discretion—the UAW must approve it. To make matters worse, even if GM halts production at a given plant, it still has to pay its workers 95 percent of their regular wages, even though GM's wages are 60 percent more than the industry average.

All in all, GM may have negotiated itself into a stranglehold with the UAW. But there are two sides to consider. On the one hand, offering great employee benefits is a goal that all organizations should have, as workers should receive the best treatment possible and companies want to attract the best workers possible. On the other hand, if the UAW continues to press GM for improvements, and GM concedes, the company may no longer exist to provide those benefits.

Questions for Discussion

1. How would you characterize the type of conflict that exits between GM and the UAW using the various conflict-handling interventions described in Chapter 9?

2. Based on the case, would you conclude that GM and the UAW have engaged in distributive or integrative bargaining? Which type would be better for the two parties in the long term, and why?

3. What types of power does the UAW hold over GM? How has this power influenced its ability to negotiate with GM?

4. Based on the case, what decision-making errors with the union might have led GM to its current financial position? What can GM do to eliminate these errors in the future?

5. Although benefits such as a "guaranteed wage" likely are appealing to workers, how might such benefits affect employee motivation? How might they affect job satisfaction and organizational commitment? Could this be a case where management engages in the "folly of rewarding A, while hoping for B?"

6. As a manager of a large company such as GM that operates in a highly competitive environment, how would you attempt to strike an appropriate balance between employee treatment and company profitability?

Source: Based on R. Lowenstein, "What Went Wrong at GM," *Smart Money*, July 2005, 78–82.

A Question of Motivation

Alex and Stephanie have a few things in common. Both are university students, and both work full-time at a local supermarket to make ends meet and help pay for school. Though the pay isn't great, it's a steady job that allows them some flexibility, which helps when scheduling classes. Both students joined the supermarket two years ago, and, given their similar situations, became friends quickly.

Although Stephanie seems to enjoy her job, arriving and leaving work each day with a smile on her face, Alex often grumbles and complains about his work. Much of the time, Alex complains about his boss, Dan, who oversees the produce department. Stephanie works for Jonathan, a 10-year veteran who everyone generally admires for his friendly demeanour and relaxed management style.

Most employees want to work for Jonathan, as he often assigns his employees different duties each week so workers don't get bored. Stephanie, for instance, can be working at the checkout counter one week, stocking shelves the next, and the store's culinary centre the following week.

The culinary centre is a new service that the store is test-marketing. Employees show customers how to create exciting recipes from start to finish. It is Stephanie's favourite place in the store to work. She is also responsible for taking customers around the store to locate ingredients for a culinary centre recipe, many of the ingredients being some of the store's finest. And she enjoys allowing customers to sample what she cooks. So far, the culinary centre is a success, and many of the store's more expensive ingredients are becoming difficult to keep in stock. To help with this issue, Jonathan encourages his employees to notify him immediately when an item is running low and even empowers employees to reorder items from vendors. By doing this, Stephanie has quickly grasped how the supermarket operates.

Alex's supervisor, in contrast, prefers most of his employees to work in the same area each day—Alex is one of those employees. Dan believes that the best way to master a job is to do it over and over again. This means that Alex has to stock the same produce areas each day. As boxes of produce are delivered to the store's supply room, Alex unloads their contents onto the shelves. Alex also must constantly reorganize the produce already on the shelves to make it look as orderly as possible. Most of the time, though, he doesn't feel inclined to do either task.

After a particularly boring morning of restocking apples (the store had apples on sale that day), Alex met Stephanie for lunch in the break room. After sitting down, Alex reached into his lunchbox and pulled out an apple, a look of disgust on his face. "Ugh . . . If I have to look at another apple, I'm going to be sick."

"Bad day again?" asked Stephanie as Alex stuffed the apple back into his lunchbox.

"I stocked apples all morning—what do you think?" Alex retorted.

"Why don't you tell Dan you want to do something else?" Stephanie inquired. "I see that he lets Denise work in other areas." Stephanie leaned closer. "I've even heard that she gets paid more than you. Is that true?" she whispered.

"Apparently, she gets paid $2.00 more an hour, but I do the same things that she does. Oh, that's right. One thing I don't do is tell Dan what a cool shirt he has on or how awesome his car is. They're both pathetic if you ask me," frowned Alex.

"Two dollars more an hour, but she's been here for only 3 months!" Stephanie exclaimed. "And I know that you work just as hard as she does. No wonder you're so irritated all the time."

"I don't even care any more. What's the point? If I stock more apples, or something meaningless like that, what does it get me—another sticker that says 'good job'? Oooh, that's really great. Thanks a bunch Dan!" replied Alex, punctuating his last sentence with a sarcastic thumbs-up. "Anyway, enough about my day. How's yours going?"

"Pretty good, actually. Jonathan and I met earlier today, and we both set a goal for me to sell 10 bottles of truffle oil next week."

"Wow. That stuff is pretty expensive, isn't it?" asked Alex.

"Thirty-five dollars for four ounces," replied Stephanie. "It'll be tough, but I found a pretty good recipe that I'll be making for customers who stop by the culinary centre." She paused, then said, "I think I'll be able to do it. I've made quite a few similar recipes before, and even though this one is more difficult, it shouldn't be too bad. Besides, if I sell the oil Jonathan said that he'll give me a $75 bonus. So I'm definitely going to give it a shot. The nice thing is that I'll be able to do this on my own, without someone breathing down my neck."

"Well that's certainly more than I'll be making this week," said Alex. "This job is okay, but I'd probably leave if I could. It's too risky right now to just quit. If I can't find something, then I'll be in trouble when that next tuition bill comes around."

"Look on the bright side. At least you make more than Jean. She's been here for 7 years, still working in the deli," replied Stephanie.

"That's true," sighed Alex as he returned to his lunch. He looked up at the clock. They had been at lunch for a half hour already. Dan was quite the stickler about keeping lunch to a minimum. Although store policy allowed employees 45 minutes for lunch, Dan often pushed his employees to keep it to 30 minutes. As Alex quickened his chewing, Dan strolled into the break room and opened the refrigerator, his back to Alex and Stephanie.

Wheeling around with a soda in hand, Dan commented, "Bit of a long lunch, hey Alex?"

Alex could feel the blood rising to his face. "It's been exactly a half hour, and I'm almost finished," he said.

"Well, we're running low on apples again. So quit lying around and get back to work." Dan walked toward the door, stopped, and turned around. "I thought that university students were supposed to be smarter than this. At the very least I would hope that they could tell time." He added, "I guess the university must have glossed over your application." And with that, Dan left.

"What a jerk," said Stephanie after Dan was out of earshot.

"What else is new," said Alex. "I'd guess I'd better get back to work." Alex got up and returned what was left of his lunch to the refrigerator. When he opened the door, he noticed a sandwich labelled with a post-it note that read "Dan's." After glancing quickly to the door, he casually swept the sandwich onto the floor. Stephanie turned around at the sound.

"Oops," smirked Alex. He paused, staring down at the sandwich. "Five-second rule!" he said as he picked up the sandwich, being sure to smear the underside of it on the floor. After putting it neatly back on the shelf, Alex turned to Stephanie. "Well Steph, have a good one. I think maybe I'll take my time on those apples."

Questions for Discussion

1. How can expectancy theory be used to explain the differences in motivation between Alex and Stephanie? What specifics from the case apply to expectancy theory?

2. Alex states that he is underpaid for the work he does. What motivational theory does this apply to, and how would it explain Alex's behaviour?

3. Using concepts from organizational justice, explain why Alex knocks his boss's lunch to the floor. What should Alex's boss do to improve the fairness of his treatment?

4. Using emotional concepts from Chapter 2, explain why Alex retaliates toward his supervisor. Was his behaviour driven purely by emotion, or did cognition also play a role? How so?

5. Compare and contrast Alex and Stephanie in terms of each person's level of work stress. How might stress affect their attitudes and behaviours within their work environment?

6. Discuss Alex and Stephanie in terms of each person's job attitudes (for example, job satisfaction, organizational commitment). What factors might be responsible for any differences?

The Big Promotion

Devon and Isabella arrived outside their boss's office at the same time and took a seat. Both exchanged a cordial "hello," but they didn't say much else as they waited outside. Fidgeting nervously in their seats, the two knew that only one of them was going to receive what would be the biggest promotion of their careers.

Devon and Isabella worked for a large software company and each was responsible for managing one of the company's largest divisions. Both had been in their current position for years, hoping that a spot at the company's corporate headquarters would open up. That time had arrived a month earlier when one of the company's senior executives retired. Such positions did not open frequently, so Devon and Isabella knew that this was a tremendous opportunity.

For the past month, they had prepared for their meeting with the company's CEO, Paul McAllister. Although Paul already knew Devon and Isabella well, he wanted to meet with them at the same time to see how they handled the pressure of being interviewed in front of each other.

After waiting for what seemed like an eternity, Devon and Isabella looked up simultaneously as Paul opened the door to his office.

"Isabella. Devon. Good to see you. Come on in," said Paul.

Devon and Isabella entered Paul's office and took the chairs ready for them at the front of his desk.

Paul broke the silence by saying, "Well, you both know why you are here, so there's no need to waste time. I already know your resumes backwards and forwards, and I've gathered as much information as possible from those who know you best, so now it comes down to hearing it, 'straight from the horses' mouths.' I'm going to ask you both one question only, and it's the same question for both of you. Let me flip a coin to see who will respond first." He flipped the coin. "Devon, you're up."

Devon sat up with confidence, eyeing Paul.

Paul began. "To function effectively in an executive position requires strong leadership skills. Both of you have gained valuable experience as managers of your respective divisions, making decisions that have resulted in strong performances from those divisions. But you have also, as managers, followed directives that this corporate office has handed down. As an executive, this will change. You will no longer take directives—you will give them. In short, you will be responsible for guiding the future of this company, and its success will depend greatly on you. So my question to you both is: How do you plan to succeed as a leader if you are offered this position?"

"Well Paul," responded Devon, "That is an excellent question. I believe that, to be a successful leader, one must be able to exert influence. When you get down to it, that is what leadership is all about—the ability to influence others. I have demonstrated that I have this ability since I joined the ranks of management." Devon paused, collecting his thoughts. "It is my opinion that leadership boils down to what actions you take with your employees. For me, leadership is all about rewarding and punishing appropriately. I try to make my employees' jobs less complicated by stating exactly what they need to do, assigning particular tasks, setting appropriate goals, and ensuring that my subordinates have the resources they need."

Paul listened carefully as Devon continued. "Basically, I am an organizer. When employees accomplish a given task or goal, I reward them appropriately for their work. When employees fail to accomplish an assignment, an appropriate response from me is needed. If it is clear that the employee did not try to accomplish the task, then punishment is necessary, and this punishment could range from a verbal reprimand to termination, depending, of course, on the circumstances. If the employee did not have the necessary skills or resources to complete a task, then my job is to provide those skills and resources. By rewarding and punishing employees based on their performance, I am able not only to influence employee behaviour to match the goals of the organization but also to send a clear message as to what I expect."

Devon added, "I also want to note that a strong sense of fairness guides all of my decisions—I reward and punish justly. As a result, my employees are satisfied with their work and perform at high levels. So I will bring my ability to influence behaviour with me if I am offered this position, and in doing so will be able to shape the future of our company."

"Thank you, Devon," responded Paul. "Isabella, how would you answer this question?"

"Well, Paul," said Isabella, "I think you'll find that my perspective on leadership is different from Devon's. Although I certainly agree with Devon that giving clear guidance to employees, setting appropriate goals, and rewarding employees for accomplishing tasks is a fundamental leadership quality, I believe that it takes more than that to be a successful leader. You see, I do not believe that just anyone can be a leader. To be a leader requires a certain 'something' that not all people possess."

"And you believe that you possess that certain something?" interrupted Paul.

Isabella grinned. "I think you'll find that my record suggests that I do, in fact. You see, successful leadership is about motivating people beyond the formal requirements of their jobs. It is not enough in today's global economy to simply ensure that employees are completing their tasks. To survive, and moreover, grow, leaders must challenge employees to look ahead, to contribute ideas, and to make sacrifices for the good of the company. My job as a leader of this company is to create a vision of where we will be 5, 10, and 15 years from now. I see us creating new technologies, as well as merging existing technologies, to give our company the competitive advantage it needs to sustain growth in the long term. By sharing this vision with my employees, we will all be able to pursue the same goals."

Isabella continued, "I inspire my subordinates to see the company as their own, rather than as a means to a paycheque. I consider employee input and the different needs of each worker, and I challenge each and every one of them to think outside the box and develop innovative solutions to the problems facing us. The end result is, in my opinion, a highly motivated workforce with a common goal—to make sure our company is the industry leader."

Paul nodded, thinking about both answers. He had scrutinized each person's record carefully, and both were qualified for the job. However, the two candidates differed in important ways. Devon had built a strong reputation for being a traditional, straightforward leader, motivating his employees well, setting appropriate goals, and ensuring that employees accomplished tasks on time—even ahead of schedule. However, Devon was not known for developing the most creative solutions, and he lacked the vision that Paul knew was an important competency to have as an executive.

Isabella, in contrast, had built a reputation as being a visionary leader. Though her ideas were a bit unconventional at times, in many cases they were directly responsible for getting the company out of a jam. In addition, her magnetic personality made her a favourite among employees. However, Isabella often revealed a somewhat egotistical personality, and Paul was unsure whether this egoism would be amplified if she were in a more authoritative position.

Paul had to make a tough decision. He thought about his company's future. Things were relatively stable now, and business was good, but he knew that stability was not always certain.

"I would like to thank you both for coming today. You're making this a tough decision for me," said Paul. "I need to think about this a bit more, but I'll be getting back to you soon." He paused, then added, "You'll have my answer tomorrow morning."

Questions for Discussion

1. Using terms from the text, how would you describe Devon's leadership style? How would you describe Isabella's leadership style?

2. Whose leadership style do you believe would be more effective, Isabella's or Devon's? Why? What, if any, situational factors might their effectiveness depend on?

3. If you were Paul, who would you hire and why?

4. What are some potential downsides to each candidate's leadership style?

5. Whose employees do you think are likely to be more motivated, Devon's or Isabella's? Whose employees are likely to have higher job satisfaction, trust in leadership, and organizational commitment? Why?

6. Based on their leadership styles, in what type of organizational structure would Devon be most effective? What about Isabella? Why?

Chapter 1

1   E. Beaton, "Managing Growth: Rapid Recovery." *PROFIT*, June 2008, pp. 92–93.

2   T. Belford, "Strategy for the New Economy," *Financial Post (National Post)*, March 14, 2005, p. FP9.

3   C. R. Farquhar and J. A. Longair, *Creating High-Performance Organizations with People*, Report R164–96 (Ottawa: The Conference Board of Canada, 1996).

4   Cited in R. Alsop, "Playing Well with Others," *Wall Street Journal*, September 9, 2002.

5   See, for instance, C. Penttila, "Hiring Hardships," *Entrepreneur*, October 2002, pp. 34–35.

6   *The 2002 National Study of the Changing Workforce* (New York: Families and Work Institute, 2002).

7   I. S. Fulmer, B. Gerhart, and K. S. Scott, "Are the 100 Best Better? An Empirical Investigation of the Relationship between Being a 'Great Place to Work' and Firm Performance," *Personnel Psychology*, Winter 2003, pp. 965–993.

8   Based on E. Beaton, "Managing Growth: Rapid Recovery." *PROFIT*, June 2008, pp. 92–93.

9   T. A. Wright, R. Cropanzano, P. J. Denney, and G. L. Moline, "When a Happy Worker Is a Productive Worker: A Preliminary Examination of Three Models," *Canadian Journal of Behavioural Science* 34, no. 3 (July 2002), pp. 146–150.

10 Graham Lowe, *21st Century Job Quality: Achieving What Canadians Want*, Canadian Policy Research Networks, September 3, 2007, report # 48485.

11 B. Dumaine, "The New Non-Manager Managers," *Fortune*, February 22, 1993, pp. 80–84.

12 "Wanted: Teammates, Crew Members, and Cast Members: But No Employees," *Wall Street Journal*, April 30, 1996, p. A1.

13 M. Sashkin, "Participative Management Is an Ethical Imperative," *Organizational Dynamics*, Spring 1984, pp. 5–22.

14 See "What Self-Managing Teams Manage," *Training*, October 1995, p. 72.

15 S. Ross, "U.S. Managers Fail to Fit the Bill in New Workplace: Study," *Reuters News Agency*, November 19, 1999.

16 "Ask the Legends: Clive Beddoe," *PROFIT*, November 2007; C. Wells, "Secret to WestJet's Success Lies in Its People, Culture: Durfy," *Western Star*, May 16, 2007; "WestJet Tops List of Canada's 10 Most Admired Corporate Cultures," *CNW Group*, January 16, 2008, http://www.newswire.ca; and P. Verburg, "Prepare for Takeoff," *Canadian Business*, December 25, 2000, pp. 94–96+.

17 The Conference Board of Canada, *Employability Skills Profile*, 2000.

18 T. Belford, "Strategy for the New Economy," *Financial Post (National Post)*, March 14, 2005, p. FP9.

19 D. Nebenzahl, "People Skills Matter Most," *Gazette* (Montreal), September 20, 2004, p. B1.

20 See, for instance, R. R. Thomas Jr., "From Affirmative Action to Affirming Diversity," *Harvard Business Review*, March–April 1990, pp. 107–117; B. Mandrell and S. Kohler-Gray, "Management Development That Values Diversity," *Personnel*, March 1990, pp. 41–47; J. Dreyfuss, "Get Ready for the New Work Force," *Fortune*, April 23, 1990, pp. 165–181; and I. Wielawski, "Diversity Makes Both Dollars and Sense," *Los Angeles Times*, May 16, 1994, p. 11–3.

21 Based on K.-A. Riess, "SGI among Top 100 Diversity Employers," *StarPhoenix*, April 5, 2008, p. F12.

22 See, for instance, E. E. Kossek and S. A. Lobel, eds., *Managing Diversity* (Cambridge, MA: Blackwell, 1996); J. A. Segal, "Diversify for Dollars," *HR Magazine*, April 1997, pp. 134–140; and "Strength through Diversity for Bottom-Line Success," *Working Women*, March 1999, pp. 67–77.

23 "Study: Earnings of Temporary versus Permanent Employees," *The Daily*, January 26, 2005, http://www.statcan.ca/Daily/English/050126/d050126b.htm; and http://www40.statcan.ca/l01/cst01/labr66a.htm.

24 Statistics Canada, "Table 1: Labour Force Characteristics by Age and Sex," http://statcan.gc.ca/subjects-sujet/labour-travail/lfs-epa/+081205a1-eng.htm.

25 "Study: Earnings of Temporary versus Permanent Employees," *The Daily*, January 26, 2005, http://www.statcan.ca/Daily/English/050126/d050126b.htm.

26 D. W. Organ, *Organizational Citizenship Behavior: The Good Soldier Syndrome* (Lexington, MA: Lexington Books, 1988), p. 4.

27 M. G. Ehrhart and S. E. Naumann, "Organizational Citizenship Behavior in Work Groups: A Group Norms Approach," *Journal of Applied Psychology* 89, no. 6 (December 1, 2004), pp. 960–974.

28 "Corporate Culture," *Canadian HR Reporter* 17, no. 21 (December 6, 2004), pp. 7–11.

29 See, for example, P. M. Podsakoff and S. B. MacKenzie, "Organizational Citizenship Behavior and Sales Unit Effectiveness," *Journal of Marketing Research*, August 1994, pp. 351–363; P. M. Podsakoff, M. Ahearne, and S. B. MacKenzie, "Organizational Citizenship Behavior and the Quantity and Quality of Work Group Performance," *Journal of Applied Psychology*, April 1997, pp. 262–270;

L. A. Bettencourt, K. Gwinner, and M. L. Meuter, "A Comparison of Attitude, Personality, and Knowledge Predictors of Service-Oriented Organizational Citizenship Behaviors," *Journal of Applied Psychology* 86, 2001, pp. 29–41; and E. W. Morrison, "Organizational Citizenship Behavior as a Critical Link between HRM Practices and Service Quality," *Human Resource Management* 35, 1996, pp. 493–512.

30 J. Pfeffer, and J. F. Veiga, "Putting People First for Organizational Success," *Academy of Management Executive* 13, no. 2 (May 1999), pp. 37–48. See also L. Bassi and D. McMurrer, "How's Your Return on People?" *Harvard Business Review* 82, no. 3 (March 2004), p. 18.

31 M. A. Huselid, "The Impact of Human Resource Management Practices on Turnover, Productivity, and Corporate Financial Performance," *Academy of Management Journal* 38, 1995, p. 647.

32 L. Blimes, K. Wetzker, and P. Xhonneux, "Value in Human Resources," *Financial Times*, February 1997, p. 10.

33 See, for instance, V. S. Major, K. J. Klein, and M. G. Ehrhart, "Work Time, Work Interference with Family, and Psychological Distress," *Journal of Applied Psychology*, June 2002, pp. 427–436; D. Brady, "Rethinking the Rat Race," *BusinessWeek*, August 26, 2002, pp. 142–143; J. M. Brett and L. K. Stroh, "Working 61 Plus Hours a Week: Why Do Managers Do It?" *Journal of Applied Psychology*, February 2003, pp. 67–78.

34 Adapted from J. Pfeffer and J. F. Veiga, "Putting People First for Organizational Success," *Academy of Management Executive* 13, no. 2 (May 1999), pp. 37–48.

35 See, for instance, *The 2002 National Study of the Changing Workforce* (New York: Families and Work Institute, 2002).

36 Cited in S. Armour, "Workers Put Family First Despite Slow Economy, Jobless Fears."

37 S. Shellenbarger, "What Job Candidates Really Want to Know: Will I Have a Life?" *Wall Street Journal*, November 17, 1999, p. B1; and "U.S. Employers Polish Image to Woo a Demanding New Generation," *Manpower Argus*, February 2000, p. 2.

38 F. Luthans and C. M. Youssef, "Emerging *Positive Organizational Behavior*," *Journal of Management*, June 2007, pp. 321–349; and J. E. Dutton and S. Sonenshein, "Positive Organizational Scholarship," in *Encyclopedia of Positive Psychology*, ed. C. Cooper and J. Barling, (Thousand Oaks, CA: Sage, 2007).

39 L. M. Roberts, G. Spreitzer, J. Dutton, R. Quinn, E. Heaphy, and B. Barker, "How to Play to Your Strengths," *Harvard Business Review*, January 2005, pp. 1–6; and L. M. Roberts, J. E. Dutton, G. M. Spreitzer, E. D. Heaphy, and R. E. Quinn, "Composing the Reflected Best-Self Portrait: Becoming Extraordinary in Work Organizations," *Academy of Management Review* 30, no. 4 (2005), pp. 712–736.

40 M. Kaeter, "The Age of the Specialized Generalist," *Training*, December 1993, pp. 48–53; and N. Templin, "Auto Plants, Hiring Again, Are Demanding Higher-Skilled Labor," *Wall Street Journal*, March 11, 1994, p. A1.

41 J. Lee, "Family Business Has Nerves of Steel," *Vancouver Sun*, December 22, 1997, pp. D1, D3.

42 J. H. Eggers, "The Dynamics of Asian Business, Culture," *Globe and Mail*, March 13, 1998, p. C5.

43 The following examples are derived from M. P. Mangaliso, "Building Competitive Advantage from *Ubuntu*, Management Practices from South Africa," *Academy of Management Executive* 15, no. 3 (2001), pp. 23–33.

44 Based on E. Beaton, "Managing Growth: Rapid Recovery," *PROFIT*, June 2008, pp. 92–93.

45 M. Warner, "Organizational Behavior Revisited," *Human Relations*, October 1994, pp. 1151–1166.

46 Based on W. Chuang and B. Lee, "An Empirical Evaluation of the Overconfidence Hypothesis," *Journal of Banking and Finance*, September 2006, pp. 2489–2515; and A. R. Drake, J. Wong, and S. B. Salter, "Empowerment, Motivation, and Performance: Examining the Impact of Feedback and Incentives on Nonmanagement Employees," *Behavioral Research in Accounting* 19 (2007), pp. 71–89.

47 D. M. Rousseau and S. McCarthy, "Educating Managers from an Evidence-Based Perspective," *Academy of Management Learning & Education* 6, no. 1 (2007), pp. 84–101.

48 K. Holland, "Inside the Minds of Your Employees," *New Yorker*, January 28, 2007

49 J. Surowiecki, "The Fatal-Flaw Myth," *New Yorker*, July 31, 2006, p. 25.

50 Created based on material from R. E. Quinn, S. R. Faerman, M. P. Thompson, and M. R. McGrath, *Becoming a Master Manager: A Competency Framework* (New York: John Wiley & Sons, Inc. 1990), Chapter 1.

51 Based on M. J. Critelli, "Striking a Balance," *IndustryWeek*, November 20, 2000, pp. 26–36.

52 Based on K. H. Hammonds, "Handle with Care," *Fast Company*, August 2002, pp. 103–107.

53 Based on S. Boehle, "From Humble Roots," *Training*, October 2000, pp. 106–113.

54 R. E. Quinn, *Beyond Rational Management: Mastering the Paradoxes and Competing Demands of High Performance* (San Francisco: Jossey-Bass, 1991); R. E. Quinn, S. R. Faerman, M. P. Thompson, and M. R. McGrath, *Becoming a Master Manager: A Competency Framework* (New York: Wiley, 1990); K. Cameron and R. E. Quinn, *Diagnosing and Changing Organizational Culture: Based on the Competing Values Framework* (Reading, MA: Addison Wesley Longman, 1999).

55 R. E. Quinn, S. R. Faerman, M. P. Thompson, and M. R. McGrath, *Becoming a Master Manager: A Competency Framework* (New York: Wiley, 1990).

56 D. Maley, "Canada's Top Women CEOs," *Maclean's*, October 20, 1997, pp. 52 passim.

57 Written by Nancy Langton and Joy Begley, copyright 1999. (The events described are based on an actual situation, although the participants, as well as the centre, have been disguised.)

Chapter 2

1 Based on http://www.walmart.ca/wps-portal/storelocator/Canada-About_Walmart.jsp; "Wal-Mart Canada's Mario Pilozzi Awarded with Retail Industry's Highest Honour 'Distinguished Retailer of the Year,'" http://www.retailcouncil.org/news/media/press/2007/pr20070516.asp; and "Wal-Mart Canada Named One of Canada's Best Employers," http://www.newswire.ca/en/releases/archive/January2007/02/c2780.html.

2 T. Cole, "Who Loves Ya?" *Report on Business Magazine*, April 1999, pp. 44–60.

3 Based on S. Thomas, "COPE Council Delivers 'Stunning' Blow to Big Box Giant," *Vancouver Courier*, July 3, 2005, p. 13; and "Green Wal-Mart Should Be Given the Green Light," *Vancouver Sun*, June 13, 2005, p. A10.

4 H. H. Kelley, "Attribution in Social Interaction," in *Attribution: Perceiving the Causes of Behavior*, ed. E. Jones, D. Kanouse, H. Kelley, N. Nisbett, S. Valins, and B. Weiner (Morristown, NJ: General Learning Press, 1972).

5 See L. Ross, "The Intuitive Psychologist and His Shortcomings," in *Advances in Experimental Social Psychology*, 10, ed. L. Berkowitz (Orlando, FL: Academic Press, 1977), pp. 174–220; and A. G. Miller and T. Lawson, "The Effect of an Informational Option on the Fundamental Attribution Error," *Personality and Social Psychology Bulletin*, June 1989, pp. 194–204.

6 N. Epley and D. Dunning, "Feeling 'Holier Than Thou': Are Self-Serving Assessments Produced by Errors in Self- or Social Predictions?" *Journal of Personality and Social Psychology* 79, no. 6 (2000), pp. 861–875.

7 Focus on Diversity based on A. Kerr, "Illness Can Be a Workplace Handicap," *Globe and Mail*, July 15, 2002.

8 See K. R. Murphy and R. L. Anhalt, "Is Halo a Property of the Rater, the Ratees, or the Specific Behaviors Observed?" *Journal of Applied Psychology*, June 1992, pp. 494–500; K. R. Murphy, R. A. Jako, and R. L. Anhalt, "Nature and Consequences of Halo Error: A Critical Analysis," *Journal of Applied Psychology*, April 1993, pp. 218–225; P. Rosenzweig, *The Halo Effect* (New York: Free Press, 2007); and C. E. Naquin and R. O. Tynan, "The Team Halo Effect: Why Teams Are Not Blamed for Their Failures," *Journal of Applied Psychology*, April 2003, pp. 332–340.

9 S. E. Asch, "Forming Impressions of Personality," *Journal of Abnormal and Social Psychology*, July 1946, pp. 258–290.

10 See, for example, G. N. Powell, "The Good Manager: Business Students' Stereotypes of Japanese Managers Versus Stereotypes of American Managers," *Group & Organizational Management*, March 1992, pp. 44–56; W. C. K. Chiu, A. W. Chan, E. Snape, and T. Redman, "Age Stereotypes and Discriminatory Attitudes Towards Older Workers: An East–West Comparison," *Human Relations*, May 2001, pp. 629–661; C. Ostroff and L. E. Atwater, "Does Whom You Work with Matter? Effects of Referent Group Gender and Age Composition on Managers' Compensation," *Journal of Applied Psychology*, August 2003, pp. 725–740; and M. E. Heilman, A. S. Wallen, D. Fuchs, and M. M. Tamkins, "Penalties for Success: Reactions to Women Who Succeed at Male Gender-Typed Tasks," *Journal of Applied Psychology*, June 2004, pp. 416–427.

11 J. L. Eberhardt, P. G. Davies, V. J. Purdie-Vaughns, and S. L. Johnson, "Looking Deathworthy: Perceived Stereotypicality of Black Defendants Predicts Capital-Sentencing Outcomes," *Psychological Science* 17, no. 5 (2006), pp. 383–386.

12 "Wal-Mart Canada Named One of Canada's Best Employers," http://www.newswire.ca/en/releases/archive/January2007/02/c2780.html; "Wal-Mart Makes Green Pledge for All Its Stores; Not Just Hopping on a Bandwagon," *Province* (Vancouver), August 27, 2008, p. A35; and G. Scotton, "Shopping Boom Follows Wal-Mart," *Calgary Herald*, August 22, 2006, p. B1.

13 See, for example, E. C. Webster, *Decision Making in the Employment Interview* (Montreal: McGill University, Industrial Relations Centre, 1964).

14 See, for example, R. D. Bretz Jr., G. T. Milkovich, and W. Read, "The Current State of Performance Appraisal Research and Practice: Concerns, Directions, and Implications," *Journal of Management*, June 1992, pp. 323–324; and P. M. Swiercz, M. L. Icenogle, N. B. Bryan, and R. W. Renn, "Do Perceptions of Performance Appraisal Fairness Predict Employee Attitudes and Performance?" in *Proceedings of the Academy of Management*, ed. D. P. Moore (Atlanta: Academy of Management, 1993), pp. 304–308.

15 J. Schaubroeck and S. S. K. Lam, "How Similarity to Peers and Supervisor Influences Organizational Advancement in Different Cultures," *Academy of Management Journal* 45, no. 6 (2002), pp. 1120–1136.

16 K. A. Martin, A.R. Sinden, J. C. Fleming, "Inactivity May Be Hazardous to Your Image: The Effects of Exercise Participation on Impression Formation," *Journal of Sport & Exercise Psychology* 22, no. 4 (December 2000), pp. 283–291.

17 See, for example, D. Eden, *Pygmalion in Management* (Lexington, MA: Lexington Books, 1990); D. Eden, "Leadership and Expectations: Pygmalion Effects and Other Self-Fulfilling Prophecies," *Leadership Quarterly*, Winter 1992, pp. 271–305; D. B. McNatt, "Ancient Pygmalion Joins Contemporary Management: A Meta-Analysis of the Result," *Journal of Applied Psychology*, April 2000, pp. 314–322; and O. B. Davidson and D. Eden, "Remedial Self-Fulfilling Prophecy: Two Field Experiments to Prevent Golem Effects Among Disadvantaged Women," *Journal of Applied Psychology*, June 2000, pp. 386–398.

18 D. Eden and A. B. Shani, "Pygmalion Goes to Boot Camp: Expectancy, Leadership, and Trainee Performance," *Journal of Applied Psychology*, April 1982, pp. 194–199.

19 G. W. Allport, *Personality: A Psychological Interpretation* (New York: Holt, Rinehart and Winston, 1937), p. 48.

20 K. I. van der Zee, J. N. Zaal, and J. Piekstra, "Validation of the Multicultural Personality Questionnaire in the Context of Personnel Selection," *European Journal of Personality* 17 (2003), pp. S77–S100.

21 T. A. Judge, C. A. Higgins, C. J. Thoresen, and M. R. Barrick, "The Big Five Personality Traits, General Mental Ability, and Career Success Across the Life Span," *Personnel Psychology* 52, no. 3 (1999), pp. 621–652.

22 Reported in R. L. Hotz, "Genetics, Not Parenting, Key to Temperament, Studies Say," *Los Angeles Times*, February 20, 1994, p. A1.

23 See D. T. Lykken, T. J. Bouchard Jr., M. McGue, and A. Tellegen, "Heritability of Interests: A Twin Study," *Journal of Applied Psychology*, August 1993, pp. 649–661; R. D. Arvey and T. J. Bouchard Jr., "Genetics, Twins, and Organizational Behavior," in *Research in Organizational Behavior, vol. 16*, ed. B. M. Staw and L. L. Cummings (Greenwich, CT: JAI Press, 1994), pp. 65–66; D. Lykken and A. Tellegen, "Happiness Is a Stochastic Phenomenon," *Psychological Science*, May 1996, pp. 186–189; and W. Wright, *Born That Way: Genes, Behavior, Personality* (New York: Knopf, 1998).

24 S. Srivastava, O. P. John, and S. D. Gosling, "Development of Personality in Early and Middle Adulthood: Set Like Plaster or Persistent Change?" *Journal of Personality and Social Psychology*, May 2003, pp. 1041–1053.

25 See A. H. Buss, "Personality as Traits," *American Psychologist*, November 1989, pp. 1378–1388; and D. G. Winter, O. P. John, A. J. Stewart, E. C. Klohnen, and L. E. Duncan, "Traits and Motives: Toward an Integration of Two Traditions in Personality Research," *Psychological Review*, April 1998, pp. 230–250.

26 See, for instance, G. W. Allport and H. S. Odbert, "Trait Names, A Psycholexical Study," *Psychological Monographs* 47, no. 211 (1936); and R. B. Cattell, "Personality Pinned Down," *Psychology Today*, July 1973, pp. 40–46.

27 R. B. Kennedy and D. A. Kennedy, "Using the Myers-Briggs Type Indicator in Career Counseling," *Journal of Employment Counseling*, March 2004, pp. 38–44.

28 G. N. Landrum, *Profiles of Genius* (New York: Prometheus, 1993).

29 See, for instance, D. J. Pittenger, "Cautionary Comments Regarding the Myers-Briggs Type Indicator," *Consulting Psychology Journal: Practice and Research*, Summer 2005, pp. 210–221; L. Bess and R. J. Harvey, "Bimodal Score Distributions and the Myers-Briggs Type Indicator: Fact or Artifact?" *Journal of Personality Assessment*, February 2002, pp. 176–186; R. M. Capraro and M. M. Capraro, "Myers-Briggs Type Indicator Score Reliability Across Studies: A Meta-Analytic Reliability Generalization Study," *Educational and Psychological Measurement*, August 2002, pp. 590–602; and R. C. Arnau, B. A. Green, D. H. Rosen, D. H. Gleaves, and J. G. Melancon, "Are Jungian Preferences Really Categorical? An Empirical Investigation Using Taxometric Analysis," *Personality and Individual Differences*, January 2003, pp. 233–251.

30 See, for example, J. M. Digman, "Personality Structure: Emergence of the Five-Factor Model," in *Annual Review of Psychology, vol. 41*, ed. M. R. Rosenzweig and L. W. Porter (Palo Alto, CA: Annual Reviews, 1990), pp. 417–440; R. R. McCrae and O. P. John, "An Introduction to the Five-Factor Model and Its Applications," *Journal of Personality*, June 1992, pp. 175–215; L. R. Goldberg, "The Structure of Phenotypic Personality Traits," *American Psychologist*, January 1993, pp. 26–34; P. H. Raymark, M. J. Schmit, and R. M. Guion, "Identifying Potentially Useful Personality Constructs for Employee Selection," *Personnel Psychology*, Autumn 1997, pp. 723–736; O. Behling, "Employee Selection: Will Intelligence and Conscientiousness Do the Job?" *Academy of Management Executive* 12, 1998, pp. 77–86; D. B. Smith, P. J. Hanges, and M. W. Dickson, "Personnel Selection and the Five-Factor Model: Reexamining the Effects of Applicant's Frame of Reference," *Journal of Applied Psychology*, April 2001, pp. 304–315; and M. R. Barrick and M. K. Mount, "Yes, Personality Matters: Moving on to More Important Matters," *Human Performance* 18, no. 4 (2005), pp. 359–372.

31 See, for instance, M. R. Barrick and M. K. Mount, "The Big Five Personality Dimensions and Job Performance: A Meta-Analysis," *Personnel Psychology*, Spring 1991, pp. 1–26; G. M. Hurtz and J. J. Donovan, "Personality and Job Performance: The Big Five Revisited," *Journal of Applied Psychology*, December 2000, pp. 869–879; J. Hogan and B. Holland, "Using Theory to Evaluate Personality and Job-Performance Relations: A Socioanalytic Perspective," *Journal of Applied Psychology*, February 2003, pp. 100–112; and M. R. Barrick and M. K. Mount, "Select on Conscientiousness and Emotional Stability," in *Handbook of Principles of Organizational Behavior*, ed. E. A. Locke (Malden, MA: Blackwell, 2004), pp. 15–28.

32 M. K. Mount, M. R. Barrick, and J. P. Strauss, "Validity of Observer Ratings of the Big Five Personality Factors," *Journal of Applied Psychology*, April 1994, p. 272. Additionally confirmed by G. M. Hurtz and J. J. Donovan, "Personality and Job Performance: The Big Five Revisited," *Journal of Applied Psychology* 85, 2000, pp. 869–879; and M. R. Barrick, M. K. Mount, and T. A. Judge, "The FFM Personality Dimensions and Job Performance: Meta-Analysis of Meta-Analyses," *International Journal of Selection and Assessment* 9, 2001, pp. 9–30.

33 F. L. Schmidt and J. E. Hunter, "The Validity and Utility of Selection Methods in *Personnel Psychology*: Practical and Theoretical Implications of 85 Years of Research Findings," *Psychological Bulletin*, September 1998, p. 272.

34 M. Tamir and M. D. Robinson, "Knowing Good from Bad: The Paradox of Neuroticism, Negative Affect, and Evaluative Processing," *Journal of Personality and Social Psychology* 87, no. 6 (2004), pp. 913–925.

35 R. J. Foti and M. A. Hauenstein, "Pattern and Variable Approaches in Leadership Emergence and Effectiveness," *Journal of Applied Psychology*, March 2007, pp. 347–355.

36 L. I. Spirling and R. Persaud, "Extraversion as a Risk Factor," *Journal of the American Academy of Child & Adolescent Psychiatry* 42, no. 2 (2003), p. 130.

37 J. A. LePine, J. A. Colquitt, and A. Erez, "Adaptability to Changing Task Contexts: Effects of General Cognitive Ability, Conscientiousness, and Openness to Experience," *Personnel Psychology* 53, 2000, pp. 563–595.

38 B. Laursen, L. Pulkkinen, and R. Adams, "The Antecedents and Correlates of Agreeableness in Adulthood," *Developmental Psychology* 38, no. 4 (2002), pp. 591–603.

39 B. Barry and R. A. Friedman, "Bargainer Characteristics in Distributive and Integrative Negotiation," *Journal of Personality and Social Psychology*, February 1998, pp. 345–359.

40 T. Bogg and B. W. Roberts, "Conscientiousness and Health- Related Behaviors: A Meta-Analysis of the Leading Behavioral Contributors to Mortality," *Psychological Bulletin* 130, no. 6 (2004), pp. 887–919.

41 S. Lee and H. J. Klein, "Relationships between Conscientiousness, Self-Efficacy, Self-Deception, and Learning over Time," *Journal of Applied Psychology* 87, no. 6 (2002), pp. 1175–1182; G. J. Feist, "A Meta-Analysis of Personality in Scientific and Artistic Creativity," *Personality and Social Psychology Review* 2, no. 4 (1998), pp. 290–309.

42 T. A. Judge and J. E. Bono, "A Rose by Any Other Name... Are Self-Esteem, Generalized Self-Efficacy, Neuroticism, and Locus of Control Indicators of a Common Construct?" in *Personality Psychology in the Workplace*, ed. B. W. Roberts and R. Hogan (Washington, DC: American Psychological Association), pp. 93–118.

43 A. Erez and T. A. Judge, "Relationship of Core Self-Evaluations to Goal Setting, Motivation, and Performance," *Journal of Applied Psychology* 86, no. 6 (2001), pp. 1270–1279.

44 U. Malmendier and G. Tate, "CEO Overconfidence and Corporate Investment," *Journal of Finance* 60, no. 6 (December 2005), pp. 2661–2700.

45 R. Sandomir, "Star Struck," *New York Times*, January 12, 2007, pp. C10, C14.

46 R. G. Vleeming, "Machiavellianism: A Preliminary Review," *Psychological Reports*, February 1979, pp. 295–310.

47 R. Christie and F. L. Geis, Studies in Machiavellianism (New York: Academic Press, 1970), p. 312; and N. V. Ramanaiah, A. Byravan, and F. R. J. Detwiler, "Revised Neo Personality Inventory Profiles of Machiavellian and Non-Machiavellian People," Psychological Reports, October 1994, pp. 937–938.

48 R. Christie and F. L. Geis, *Studies in Machiavellianism* (New York: Academic Press, 1970).

49 C. Sedikides, E. A. Rudich, A. P. Gregg, M. Kumashiro, and C. Rusbult, "Are Normal Narcissists Psychologically Healthy?: Self-Esteem Matters," *Journal of Personality and Social Psychology* 87, no. 3 (2004), pp. 400–416, reviews some of the literature on narcissism.

50 P. T. Costa, and R. R. McCrae, "Domains and Factors: Hierarchical Personality Assessment Using the NEO Personality Inventory," *Journal of Personality Assessment* 64, 1995, pp. 21–50; and D. L. Paulhus, "Normal Narcissism: Two Minimalist Accounts," *Psychological Inquiry*, 12, 2001, pp. 228–230.

51 M. Maccoby, "Narcissistic Leaders: The Incredible Pros, the Inevitable Cons," *Harvard Business Review*, January–February 2000, pp. 69–77, http://www.maccoby.com/Articles/NarLeaders.shtml.

52 W. K. Campbell and C. A. Foster, "Narcissism and Commitment in Romantic Relationships: An Investment Model Analysis," *Personality and Social Psychology Bulletin* 28, no. 4 (2002), pp. 484–495.

53 T. A. Judge, J. A. LePine, and B. L. Rich, "The Narcissistic Personality: Relationship with Inflated Self-Ratings of Leadership and with Task and Contextual Performance," *Journal of Applied Psychology* 91, no. 4 (2006), pp. 762–776.

54 See M. Snyder, *Public Appearances/Private Realities: The Psychology of Self-Monitoring* (New York: W. H. Freeman, 1987).

55 See M. Snyder, *Public Appearances/Private Realities: The Psychology of Self-Monitoring* (New York: W. H. Freeman, 1987).

56 M. Kilduff and D. V. Day, "Do Chameleons Get Ahead? The Effects of Self-Monitoring on Managerial Careers," *Academy of Management Journal*, August 1994, pp. 1047–1060.

57 D. V. Day, D. J. Schleicher, A. L. Unckless, and N. J. Hiller, "Self-Monitoring Personality at Work: A Meta-Analytic Investigation of Construct Validity," *Journal of Applied Psychology*, April 2002, pp. 390–401.

58 R. N. Taylor and M. D. Dunnette, "Influence of Dogmatism, Risk-Taking Propensity, and Intelligence on Decision-Making Strategies for a Sample of Industrial Managers," *Journal of Applied Psychology*, August 1974, pp. 420–423.

59 I. L. Janis and L. Mann, *Decision Making: A Psychological Analysis of Conflict, Choice, and Commitment* (New York: Free Press, 1977); W. H. Stewart Jr. and L. Roth, "Risk Propensity Differences Between Entrepreneurs and Managers: A Meta-Analytic Review," *Journal of Applied Psychology*, February 2001, pp. 145–153; J. B. Miner and N. S. Raju, "Risk Propensity Differences between Managers and Entrepreneurs and between Low- and High-Growth Entrepreneurs: A Reply in a More Conservative Vein," *Journal of Applied Psychology* 89, no. 1 (2004), pp. 3–13; and W. H. Stewart Jr. and P. L. Roth, "Data Quality Affects Meta-Analytic Conclusions: A Response to Miner and Raju (2004) Concerning Entrepreneurial Risk Propensity," *Journal of Applied Psychology* 89, no. 1 (2004), pp. 14–21.

60 N. Kogan and M. A. Wallach, "Group Risk Taking as a Function of Members' Anxiety and Defensiveness," *Journal of Personality*, March 1967, pp. 50–63.

61 M. Friedman and R. H. Rosenman, *Type A Behavior and Your Heart* (New York: Knopf, 1974), p. 84.

62 M. Friedman and R. H. Rosenman, *Type A Behavior and Your Heart* (New York: Knopf, 1974), pp. 84–85.

63 K. A. Matthews, "Assessment of Type A Behavior, Anger, and Hostility in Epidemiological Studies of Cardiovascular Disease," in *Measuring Psychological Variables in Epidemiologic Studies of Cardiovascular Disease*, NIH Publication No. 85–2270, ed. A. M. Ostfield and E. D. Eaker (Washington, DC: US Department of Health and Human Services, 1985).

64 M. Friedman and R. H. Rosenman, *Type A Behavior and Your Heart* (New York: Knopf, 1974), p. 86.

65 D. C. Ganster, W. E. Sime, and B. T. Mayes, "Type A Behavior in the Work Setting: A Review and Some New Data," in *In Search of Coronary-Prone Behavior: Beyond Type A*, ed. A. W. Siegman and T. M. Dembroski (Hillsdale, NJ: Erlbaum, 1989), pp. 117–118; and B. K. Houston, "Cardiovascular and Neuroendocrine Reactivity, Global Type A, and Components of Type A," in *Type A Behavior Pattern: Research, Theory, and Intervention*, ed. B. K. Houston and C. R. Snyder (New York: Wiley, 1988), pp. 212–253.

66 A. Rozanski, J. A. Blumenthal, and J. Kaplan, "Impact of Psychological Factors on the Pathogenesis of Cardiovascular Disease and Implications for Therapy," *Circulation* 99, 1999, pp. 2192–2217; and J. Schaubroeck, D. C. Ganster, and B. E. Kemmerer, "Job Complexity, 'Type A' Behavior, and Cardiovascular Disorder," *Academy of Management Journal* 37, April 1994, pp. 426–439.

67 J. M. Crant, "Proactive Behavior in Organizations," *Journal of Management* 26, no. 3 (2000), p. 436.

68 S. E. Seibert, M. L. Kraimer, and J. M. Crant, "What Do Proactive People Do? A Longitudinal Model Linking Proactive Personality and Career Success," *Personnel Psychology*, Winter 2001, p. 850.

69 T. S. Bateman and J. M. Crant, "The Proactive Component of Organizational Behavior: A Measure and Correlates," *Journal of Organizational Behavior*, March 1993, pp. 103–118; A. L. Frohman, "Igniting Organizational Change from Below: The Power of Personal Initiative," *Organizational Dynamics*, Winter 1997, pp. 39–53; and J. M. Crant and T. S. Bateman, "Charismatic Leadership Viewed from Above: The Impact of Proactive Personality," *Journal of Organizational Behavior*, February 2000, pp. 63–75.

70 J. M. Crant, "Proactive Behavior in Organizations," *Journal of Management* 26, no. 3 (2000), p. 436.

71 See, for instance, R. C. Becherer, and J. G. Maurer, "The Proactive Personality Disposition and Entrepreneurial Behavior Among Small Company Presidents," *Journal of Small Business Management*, January 1999, pp. 28–36.

72 S. E. Seibert, J. M. Crant, and M. L. Kraimer, "Proactive Personality and Career Success," *Journal of Applied Psychology*, June 1999, pp. 416–427; and S. E. Seibert, M. L. Kraimer, and J. M. Crant, "What Do Proactive People Do? A Longitudinal Model Linking Proactive Personality and Career Success," *Personnel Psychology*, Winter 2001, p. 850.

73 Based on S. Thomas, "Wal-Mart Reluctant Star of Documentary," *Vancouver Courier*, November 13, 2005, p. 9.

74 See N. H. Frijda, "Moods, Emotion Episodes and Emotions," in *Handbook of Emotions*, ed. M. Lewis and J. M. Haviland (New York: Guilford Press, 1993), pp. 381–403.

75 H. M. Weiss and R. Cropanzano, "Affective Events Theory," in *Research in Organizational Behavior*, vol. 18, ed. B. M. Staw and L. L. Cummings (Greenwich, CT: JAI Press, 1996), pp. 17–19.

76 N. H. Frijda, "Moods, Emotion Episodes and Emotions," in *Handbook of Emotions*, ed. M. Lewis and J. M. Haviland (New York: Guilford Press, 1993), p. 381.

77 H. M. Weiss and R. Cropanzano, "Affective Events Theory," in *Research in Organizational Behavior*, vol. 18, ed. B. M. Staw and L. L. Cummings (Greenwich, CT: JAI Press, 1996), pp. 20–22.

78 See J. A. Morris and D. C. Feldman, "Managing Emotions in the Workplace," *Journal of Managerial Issues* 9, no. 3 (1997), pp. 257–274; S. Mann, *Hiding What We Feel, Faking What We Don't: Understanding the Role of Your Emotions at Work* (New York: HarperCollins, 1999); and S. M. Kruml and D. Geddes, "Catching Fire without Burning Out: Is There an Ideal Way to Perform Emotion Labor?" in *Emotions in the Workplace*, ed. N. M. Ashkansay, C. E. J. Hartel, and W. J. Zerbe (New York: Quorum Books, 2000), pp. 177–188.

79 Based on S. Treleaven "Cry, Baby; Demonstrating Fragility Could Work to Your Advantage," *National Post*, January 12, 2008, p. FW7; P. Kitchen, "Experts: Crying at Work on the Rise," *Newsday*, June 10, 2007; and S. Shellenbarger, "Read This and Weep," *Wall Street Journal*, April 26, 2007, p. D1.

80 P. Ekman, W. V. Friesen, and M. O'Sullivan, "Smiles When Lying," in *What the Face Reveals: Basic and Applied Studies of Spontaneous Expression Using the Facial Action Coding System (FACS)*, ed.

P. Ekman and E. L. Rosenberg (London: Oxford University Press, 1997), pp. 201–216.

81 A. Grandey, "Emotion Regulation in the Workplace: A New Way to Conceptualize Emotional Labor," *Journal of Occupational Health Psychology* 5, no. 1 (2000), pp. 95–110; and R. Cropanzano, D. E. Rupp, and Z. S. Byrne, "The Relationship of Emotional Exhaustion to Work Attitudes, Job Performance, and Organizational Citizenship Behavior," *Journal of Applied Psychology*, February 2003, pp. 160–169.

82 A. R. Hochschild, "Emotion Work, Feeling Rules, and Social Structure," *American Journal of Sociology*, November 1979, pp. 551–575; W.-C. Tsai, "Determinants and Consequences of Employee Displayed Positive Emotions," *Journal of Management* 27, no. 4 (2001), pp. 497–512; M. W. Kramer and J. A. Hess, "Communication Rules for the Display of Emotions in Organizational Settings," *Management Communication Quarterly*, August 2002, pp. 66–80; and J. M. Diefendorff and E. M. Richard, "Antecedents and Consequences of Emotional Display Rule Perceptions," *Journal of Applied Psychology*, April 2003, pp. 284–294.

83 B. M. DePaulo, "Nonverbal Behavior and Self-Presentation," *Psychological Bulletin*, March 1992, pp. 203–243.

84 C. S. Hunt, "Although I Might Be Laughing Loud and Hearty, Deep Inside I'm Blue: Individual Perceptions Regarding Feeling and Displaying Emotions at Work" (paper presented at the Academy of Management Conference, Cincinnati, August 1996), p. 3.

85 R. C. Solomon, "Back to Basics: On the Very Idea of 'Basic Emotions,'" *Journal for the Theory of Social Behaviour* 32, no. 2 (2002), pp. 115–144.

86 C. M. Brotheridge and R. T. Lee, "Development and Validation of the Emotional Labour Scale," *Journal of Occupational & Organizational Psychology* 76, no. 3 (September 2003), pp. 365–379.

87 A. A. Grandey, "When 'the Show Must Go On': Surface Acting and Deep Acting as Determinants of Emotional Exhaustion and Peer-Rated Service Delivery," *Academy of Management Journal*, February 2003, pp. 86–96; and A. A. Grandey, D. N. Dickter, and H. Sin, "The Customer Is Not Always Right: Customer Aggression and Emotion Regulation of Service Employees," *Journal of Organizational Behavior* 25, no. 3 (May 2004), pp. 397–418.

88 N. M. Ashkanasy and C. S. Daus, "Emotion in the Workplace: The New Challenge for Managers," *Academy of Management Executive* 16, no. 1 (2002), pp. 76–86.

89 This section is based on Daniel Goleman, *Emotional Intelligence* (New York: Bantam, 1995); J. D. Mayer and G. Geher, "Emotional Intelligence and the Identification of Emotion," *Intelligence*, March–April 1996, pp. 89–113; J. Stuller, "EQ: Edging Toward Respectability," *Training*, June 1997, pp. 43–48; R. K. Cooper, "Applying Emotional Intelligence in the Workplace," *Training & Development*, December 1997, pp. 31–38; "HR Pulse: Emotional Intelligence," *HR Magazine*, January 1998, p. 19; M. Davies, L. Stankov, and R. D. Roberts, "Emotional Intelligence: In Search of an Elusive Construct," *Journal of Personality and Social Psychology*, October 1998, pp. 989–1015; and D. Goleman, *Working with Emotional Intelligence* (New York: Bantam, 1999).

90   Based on D. R. Caruso, J. D. Mayer, and P. Salovey, "Emotional Intelligence and Emotional Leadership," in *Multiple Intelligences and Leadership*, ed. R. E. Riggio, S. E. Murphy, and F. J. Pirozzolo (Mahwah, NJ: Lawrence Erlbaum, 2002), p. 70.

91   This section is based on Daniel Goleman, *Emotional Intelligence* (New York: Bantam, 1995); P. Salovey and D. Grewal, "The Science of Emotional Intelligence," *Current Directions in Psychological Science* 14, no. 6 (2005), pp. 281–285; M. Davies, L. Stankov, and R. D. Roberts, "Emotional Intelligence: In Search of an Elusive Construct," *Journal of Personality and Social Psychology*, October 1998, pp. 989–1015; D. Geddes and R. R. Callister, "Crossing the Line(s): A Dual Threshold Model of Anger in Organizations," *Academy of Management Review* 32, no. 3 (2007), pp. 721–746; and J. Ciarrochi, J. P. Forgas, and J. D. Mayer, eds., *Emotional Intelligence in Everyday Life* (Philadelphia: Psychology Press, 2001).

92   F. I. Greenstein, *The Presidential Difference: Leadership Style from FDR to Clinton* (Princeton, NJ: Princeton University Press, 2001).

93   M. Maccoby, "To Win the Respect of Followers, Leaders Need Personality Intelligence," *Ivey Business Journal* 72, no. 3 (May–June 2008); J. Reid, "The Resilient Leader: Why EQ Matters," *Business Journal* 72, no. 3 (May–June 2008); and P. Wieand, J. Birchfield, and M. C. Johnson III, "The New Leadership Challenge: Removing the Emotional Barriers to Sustainable Performance in a Flat World," *Ivey Business Journal* 72, no. 4 (July–August 2008).

94   P. Wieand, J. Birchfield, and M. C. Johnson III, "The New Leadership Challenge: Removing the Emotional Barriers to Sustainable Performance in a Flat World," *Ivey Business Journal* 72, no. 4 (July–August 2008).

95   C. Cherniss, "The Business Case for Emotional Intelligence," *Consortium for Research on Emotional Intelligence in Organizations*, 1999, http://www.eiconsortium.org/research/business_case_for_ei.pdf.

96   K. S. Law, C. Wong, and L. J. Song, "The Construct and Criterion Validity of Emotional Intelligence and Its Potential Utility for Management Studies," *Journal of Applied Psychology* 89, no. 3 (2004), pp. 483–496.

97   H. A. Elfenbein and N. Ambady, "Predicting Workplace Outcomes from the Ability to Eavesdrop on Feelings," *Journal of Applied Psychology* 87, no. 5 (October 2002), pp. 963–971.

98   D. L. Van Rooy and C. Viswesvaran, "Emotional Intelligence: A Meta-Analytic Investigation of Predictive Validity and Nomological Net," *Journal of Vocational Behavior* 65, no. 1 (August 2004), pp. 71–95.

99   R. Bar-On, D. Tranel, N. L. Denburg, and A. Bechara, "Exploring the Neurological Substrate of Emotional and Social Intelligence," *Brain* 126, no. 8 (August 2003), pp. 1790–1800

100 E. A. Locke, "Why Emotional Intelligence Is an Invalid Concept," *Journal of Organizational Behavior* 26, no. 4 (June 2005), pp. 425–431.

101 J. M. Conte, "A Review and Critique of Emotional Intelligence Measures," *Journal of Organizational Behavior* 26, no. 4 (June 2005), pp. 433–440; and M. Davies, L. Stankov, and R. D. Roberts, "Emotional Intelligence: In Search of an Elusive Construct,"

Journal of Personality and Social Psychology 75, no. 4 (1998), pp. 989–1015.

102 T. Decker, "Is Emotional Intelligence a Viable Concept?" *Academy of Management Review* 28, no. 2 (April 2003), pp. 433–440; and M. Davies, L. Stankov, and R. D. Roberts, "Emotional Intelligence: In Search of an Elusive Construct," *Journal of Personality and Social Psychology* 75, no. 4 (1998), pp. 989–1015.

103 F. J. Landy, "Some Historical and Scientific Issues Related to Research on Emotional Intelligence," *Journal of Organizational Behavior* 26, no. 4 (June 2005), pp. 411–424.

104 S. L. Robinson and R. J. Bennett, "A Typology of Deviant Workplace Behaviors: A Multidimensional Scaling Study," *Academy of Management Journal*, April 1995, p. 556.

105 S. L. Robinson and R. J. Bennett, "A Typology of Deviant Workplace Behaviors: A Multidimensional Scaling Study," *Academy of Management Journal*, April 1995, pp. 555–572.

106 Based on A. G. Bedeian, "Workplace Envy," *Organizational Dynamics*, Spring 1995, p. 50.

107 A. G. Bedeian, "Workplace Envy," *Organizational Dynamics*, Spring 1995, p. 54.

108 K. Lee and N. J. Allen, "Organizational Citizenship Behavior and Workplace Deviance: The Role of Affect and Cognition," *Journal of Applied Psychology* 87, no. 1 (2002), pp. 131–142; and T. A. Judge, B. A. Scott, and R. Ilies, "Hostility, Job Attitudes, and Workplace Deviance: Test of a Multilevel Model," *Journal of Applied Psychology* 91, no. 1 (2006) 126–138.

109 Based on C. A. Bartela and R. Saavedra, "The Collective Construction of Work Group Moods," *Administrative Science Quarterly* 45, no. 2 (June 2000), pp. 197–231.

110 H. M. Weiss and R. Cropanzano, "Affective Events Theory: A Theoretical Discussion of the Structure, Causes and Consequences of Affective Experiences at Work," in *Research in Organizational Behavior*, vol. 18, ed. B. M. Staw and L. L. Cummings (Greenwich, CT: JAI Press, 1996), pp. 17–19.

111 J. Basch and C. D. Fisher, "Affective Events-Emotions Matrix: A Classification of Work Events and Associated Emotions," in *Emotions in the Workplace*, ed. N. M. Ashkanasy, C. E. J. Hartel, and W. J. Zerbe (Westport, CN: Quorum Books, 2000), pp. 36–48.

112 See, for example, H. M. Weiss and R. Cropanzano, "Affective Events Theory: A Theoretical Discussion of the Structure, Causes and Consequences of Affective Experiences at Work," in *Research in Organizational Behavior*, vol. 18, ed. B. M. Staw and L. L. Cummings (Greenwich, CT: JAI Press, 1996), pp. 17–19; and C. D. Fisher, "Antecedents and Consequences of Real-Time Affective Reactions at Work," *Motivation and Emotion*, March 2002, pp. 3–30.

113 Based on H. M. Weiss and R. Cropanzano, "Affective Events Theory: A Theoretical Discussion of the Structure, Causes and Consequences of Affective Experiences at Work," in *Research in Organizational Behavior*, vol. 18, ed. B. M. Staw and L. L. Cummings (Greenwich, CT: JAI Press, 1996), p. 42.

114 N. M. Ashkanasy, C. E. J. Hartel, and C. S. Daus, "Diversity and Emotion: The New Frontiers in Organizational Behavior Research," *Journal of Management* 28, no. 3 (2002), p. 324.

115 M. Eid and E. Diener, "Norms for Experiencing Emotions in Different Cultures: Inter- and International Differences," *Journal of Personality and Social Psychology* 81, no. 5 (2001), pp. 869–885.

116 S. Oishi, E. Diener, and C. Napa Scollon, "Cross-Situational Consistency of Affective Experiences Across Cultures," *Journal of Personality and Social Psychology* 86, no. 3 (2004), pp. 460–472.

117 Eid and Diener, "Norms for Experiencing Emotions in Different Cultures: Inter- and International Differences," *Journal of Personality and Social Psychology* 81, no. 5 (2001), pp. 869–885.

118 Eid and Diener, "Norms for Experiencing Emotions in Different Cultures: Inter- and International Differences," *Journal of Personality and Social Psychology* 81, no. 5 (2001), pp. 869–885.

119 B. E. Ashforth and R. H. Humphrey, "Emotion in the Workplace: A Reappraisal," *Human Relations*, February 1995, p. 104; B. Plasait, "Accueil des Touristes Dans les Grands Centres de Transit Paris," *Rapport du Bernard Plasait*, October 4, 2004, http://www.tourisme. gouv.fr/fr/navd/presse/dossiers/att00005767/dp_plasait.pdf; B. Mesquita, "Emotions in Collectivist and Individualist Contexts," *Journal of Personality and Social Psychology* 80, no. 1 (2001), pp. 68–74; and D. Rubin, "Grumpy German Shoppers Distrust the Wal-Mart Style," *Seattle Times*, December 30, 2001, p. A15.

120 H. A. Elfenbein and N. Ambady, "When Familiarity Breeds Accuracy: Cultural Exposure and Facial Emotional Recognition," *Journal of Personality and Social Psychology* 85, no. 2 (2003), pp. 276–290.

121 R. I. Levy, *Tahitians: Mind and Experience in the Society Islands* (Chicago: University of Chicago Press, 1973).

122 B. Mesquita and N. H. Frijda, "Cultural Variations in Emotions: A Review," *Psychological Bulletin*, September 1992, pp. 179–204; and B. Mesquita, "Emotions in Collectivist and Individualist Contexts," *Journal of Personality and Social Psychology*, January 2001, pp. 68–74.

123 D. Matsumoto, "Cross-Cultural Psychology in the 21st Century," http://teachpsych.org/resources/e-books/faces/script/index.htm.

124 H. M. Weiss and R. Cropanzano, "Affective Events Theory," in *Research in Organizational Behavior*, vol. 18, ed. B. M. Staw and L. L. Cummings (Greenwich, CT: JAI Press, 1996), p. 55.

125 H. Liao and A. Chuang, "A Multilevel Investigation of Factors Influencing Employee Service Performance and Customer Outcomes," *Academy of Management Journal* 47, no. 1 (2004), pp. 41–58.

126 D. J. Beal, J. P. Trougakos, H. M. Weiss, and S. G. Green, "Episodic Processes in Emotional Labor: Perceptions of Affective Delivery and Regulation Strategies," *Journal of Applied Psychology* 91, no. 5 (2006), pp. 1057–1065.

127 Cited in S. W. Floyd, J. Roos, F. Kellermanns, *Innovating Strategy Process* (Blackwell Publishing, 2005), p. 66.

128 D. Zapf and M. Holz, "On the Positive and Negative Effects of Emotion Work in Organizations," *European Journal of Work and Organizational Psychology* 15, no. 1 (2006), pp. 1–28.

129 D. Zapf, "Emotion Work and Psychological Well-Being: A Review of the Literature and Some Conceptual Considerations," *Human Resource Management Review* 12, no. 2 (2002), pp. 237–268.

130 J. E. Bono and M. A. Vey, "Toward Understanding Emotional Management at Work: A Quantitative Review of Emotional Labor Research," in *Emotions in Organizational Behavior*, ed. C. E. Härtel and W. J. Zerbe (Mahwah, NJ: Lawrence Erlbaum, 2005), pp. 213–233.

131 R. Christie and F. L. Geis, *Studies in Machiavellianism* (New York: Academic Press, 1970). Reprinted by permission.

132 R. D. Lennox and R. N. Wolfe, "Revision of the Self-Monitoring Scale," *Journal of Personality and Social Psychology*, June 1984, p. 1361. Copyright © 1984 by the American Psychological Association. Reprinted by permission.

133 Adapted from N. Kogan and M. A. Wallach, *Risk Taking: A Study in Cognition and Personality* (New York: Holt, Rinehart and Winston, 1964), pp. 256–261. Reprinted with permission of Wadsworth, a division of Thompson Learning: www.thompsonrights.com. Fax 800-730-2215.

134 Adapted from R. W. Bortner, "Short Rating Scale as a Potential Measure of Pattern A Behavior," *Journal of Chronic Diseases*, June 1969, pp. 87–91. With permission from Elsevier.

135 A. Fisher, "Success Secret: A High Emotional IQ," *Fortune*, October 26, 1998, p. 298. Reprinted with the permission of Time Warner Inc. Quiz copyright Daniel Goleman.

136 This dilemma is based on R. R. Hastings, "Survey: The Demographics of Tattoos and Piercings," *HR Week*, February 2007, http://www.shrm.org; and H. Wessel, "Taboo of Tattoos in the Workplace," *Orlando (Florida) Sentinel*, May 28, 2007, http://www. tmcnet.com/usubmit/2007/05/28/2666555.htm; S. O'Donnell, "Popularity of Piercing Pokes Holes in Traditional Workplace Standards," *Edmonton Journal*, March 12, 2006, p. A1; K. Dedyna, "Picture-Perfect Workers? TATTOOS: Inky Designs Gain Acceptance with Bosses, Clients," *Province* (Vancouver), August 28, 2005, p. A50.

137 Based on M. Blombert, "Cultivating a Career," *Gainesville (Florida) Sun*, May 9, 2005, p. D1.

138 Based on S. Shellenbarger, "Domino Effect: The Unintended Results of Telling Off Customer-Service Staff," *Wall Street Journal*, February 5, 2004, p. D1.

139 Based on V. P. Richmond, J. C. McCroskey, and S. K. Payne, *Nonverbal Behavior in Interpersonal Relations*, 2nd ed. (Englewood Cliffs, NJ: Prentice Hall, 1991), pp. 117–138; and L. A. King, "Ambivalence over Emotional Expression and Reading Emotions in Situations and Faces," *Journal of Personality and Social Psychology*, March 1998, pp. 753–762.

Chapter 3

1 Based on S. Klie, "Hail the New Chief," *Canadian HR Reporter*, July 14, 2008, p. 13.

2 M. Rokeach, *The Nature of Human Values* (New York: Free Press, 1973), p. 5.

3 See, for instance, B. Meglino and E. Ravlin, "Individual Values in Organizations," *Journal of Management* 24, no. 3 (1998), pp. 351–389.

4 M. Rokeach and S. J. Ball-Rokeach, "Stability and Change in American Value Priorities, 1968–1981," *American Psychologist,* May 1989, pp. 775–784.

5 M. Rokeach, *The Nature of Human Values* (New York: Free Press, 1973), p. 6.

6 J. M. Munson and B. Z. Posner, "The Factorial Validity of a Modified Rokeach Value Survey for Four Diverse Samples," *Educational and Psychological Measurement,* Winter 1980, pp. 1073–1079; and W. C. Frederick and J. Weber, "The Values of Corporate Managers and Their Critics: An Empirical Description and Normative Implications," in *Business Ethics: Research Issues and Empirical Studies,* ed. W. C. Frederick and L. E. Preston (Greenwich, CT: JAI Press, 1990), pp. 123–144.

7 W. C. Frederick and J. Weber, "The Values of Corporate Managers and Their Critics: An Empirical Description and Normative Implications," in *Business Ethics: Research Issues and Empirical Studies,* ed. W. C. Frederick and L. E. Preston (Greenwich, CT: JAI Press, 1990), pp. 123–144.

8 W. C. Frederick and J. Weber, "The Values of Corporate Managers and Their Critics: An Empirical Description and Normative Implications," in *Business Ethics: Research Issues and Empirical Studies,* ed. W. C. Frederick and L. E. Preston (Greenwich, CT: JAI Press, 1990), p. 132.

9 K. Hodgson, "Adapting Ethical Decisions to a Global Marketplace," *Management Review* 81, no. 5, May 1992, pp. 53–57. Reprinted by permission.

10 K. Hodgson, *A Rock and a Hard Place: How to Make Ethical Business Decisions When the Choices Are Tough* (New York: AMACOM, 1992), pp. 66–67.

11 *KPMG Code of Conduct,* http://www.kpmg.ca/en/about/documents/KPMGCodeofConduct.pdf.

12 G. Hofstede, *Culture's Consequences: International Differences in Work-Related Values* (Beverly Hills, CA: Sage, 1980); G. Hofstede, *Cultures and Organizations: Software of the Mind* (London: McGraw-Hill, 1991); G. Hofstede, "Cultural Constraints in Management Theories," *Academy of Management Executive* 7, no. 1 (1993), pp. 81–94; G. Hofstede and M. F. Peterson, "National Values and Organizational Practices," in *Handbook of Organizational Culture and Climate,* ed. N. M. Ashkanasy, C. M. Wilderom, and M. F. Peterson (Thousand Oaks, CA: Sage, 2000), pp. 401–416; and G. Hofstede, *Culture's Consequences: Comparing Values, Behaviors, Institutions, and Organizations Across Nations,* 2nd ed. (Thousand Oaks, CA: Sage, 2001). For criticism of this research, see B. McSweeney, "Hofstede's Model of National Cultural Differences and Their Consequences: A Triumph of Faith—A Failure of Analysis," *Human Relations* 55, no. 1 (2002), pp. 89–118.

13 G. Hofstede and M. H. Bond, "The Confucius Connection: From Cultural Roots to Economic Growth," *Organizational Dynamics,* Spring 1988, pp. 12–13.

14 M. H. Bond, "Reclaiming the Individual from Hofstede's Ecological Analysis—A 20-Year Odyssey: Comment on Oyserman et al. (2002)," *Psychological Bulletin* 128, no. 1 (2002), pp. 73–77; G. Hofstede, "The Pitfalls of Cross-National Survey Research: A Reply to the Article by Spector et al. on the Psychometric Properties of the Hofstede Values Survey Module 1994," *Applied Psychology: An International Review* 51, no. 1 (2002), pp. 170–178; and T. Fang, "A Critique of Hofstede's Fifth National Culture Dimension," *International Journal of Cross-Cultural Management* 3, no. 3 (2003), pp. 347–368.

15 The five usual criticisms and Hofstede's responses (in parentheses) are: 1. Surveys are not a suitable way to measure cultural differences (answer: they should not be the only way); 2. Nations are not the proper units for studying cultures (answer: they are usually the only kind of units available for comparison); 3. A study of the subsidiaries of one company cannot provide information about entire national cultures (answer: what was measured were differences among national cultures. Any set of functionally equivalent samples can supply information about such differences); 4. The IBM data are old and therefore obsolete (answer: the dimensions found are assumed to have century-old roots; they have been validated against all kinds of external measurements; recent replications show no loss of validity); 5. Four or five dimensions are not enough (answer: additional dimensions should be statistically independent of the dimensions defined earlier; they should be valid on the basis of correlations with external measures; candidates are welcome to apply). See A. Harzing and G. Hofstede, "Planned Change in Organizations: The Influence of National Culture," in *Research in the Sociology of Organizations, Cross Cultural Analysis of Organizations,* vol. 14, ed. P. A. Bamberger, M. Erez, and S. B. Bacharach (Greenwich, CT: JAI Press, 1996), pp. 297–340.

16 M. Javidan and R. J. House, "Cultural Acumen for the Global Manager: Lessons from Project GLOBE," *Organizational Dynamics* 29, no. 4 (2001), pp. 289–305; and R. J. House, P. J. Hanges, M. Javidan, and P. W. Dorfman, eds., *Leadership, Culture, and Organizations: The GLOBE Study of 62 Societies* (Thousand Oaks, CA: Sage, 2004).

17 P. C. Early, "Leading Cultural Research in the Future: A Matter of Paradigms and Taste," *Journal of International Business Studies,* September 2006, pp. 922–931; G. Hofstede, "What Did GLOBE Really Measure? Researchers' Minds versus Respondents' Minds," *Journal of International Business Studies,* September 2006, pp. 882–896; and M. Javidan, R. J. House, P. W. Dorfman, P. J. Hanges, and M. S. de Luque, "Conceptualizing and Measuring Cultures and Their Consequences: A Comparative Review of GLOBE's and Hofstede's Approaches," *Journal of International Business Studies,* September 2006, pp. 897–914.

18 B, Meglino, E. C. Ravlin, and C. L. Adkins, "A Work Values Approach to Corporate Culture: A Field Test of the Value Congruence Process and Its Relationship to Individual Outcomes," *Journal of Applied Psychology* 74, 1989, pp. 424–432.

19 B. Z. Posner, J. M. Kouzes, and W. H. Schmidt, "Shared Values Make a Difference: An Empirical Test of Corporate Culture," *Human Resource Management* 24, 1985, pp. 293–310; and A. L. Balazas, "Value Congruency: The Case of the 'Socially Responsible' Firm," *Journal of Business Research* 20, 1990, pp. 171–181.

20 C. A. O'Reilly, J. Chatman, and D. Caldwell: "People and Organizational Culture: A Q-Sort Approach to Assessing Person-Organizational Fit," *Academy of Management Journal* 34, 1991, pp. 487–516.

21 C. Enz and C. K. Schwenk, "Performance and Sharing of Organizational Values" (paper presented at the annual meeting of the Academy of Management, Washington, DC, 1989).

22 Material in this section based on the work of M. Adams, *Sex in the Snow* (Toronto: Penguin, 1997); and M. Adams, *Fire and Ice: The United States, Canada and the Myth of Converging Values* (Toronto: Penguin, 2003).

23 N. A. Hira, "You Raised Them, Now Manage Them," *Fortune*, May 28, 2007, pp. 38–46; R. R. Hastings, "Surveys Shed Light on Generation Y Career Goals," *SHRM Online*, March 2007, http://www.shrm.org; and S. Jayson, "The 'Millennials' Come of Age," *USA Today*, June 29, 2006, pp. 1D, 2D.

24 Statistics Canada, "Census of Population," *The Daily*, February 11, 2003.

25 Statistics Canada, "2006 Census: Immigration, Citizenship, Language, Mobility and Migration," *The Daily*, December 4, 2007.

26 Statistics Canada, "Immigration in Canada: A Portrait of the Foreign-born Population, 2006 Census: Immigrants in Metropolitan Areas," http://www12.statcan.ca/english/census06/analysis/immcit/city_life.cfm (accessed July 5, 2008).

27 K. Young, "Language: Allophones on the Rise," *National Post*, December 04, 2007.

28 K. Young, "Language: Allophones on the Rise," *National Post*, December 04, 2007.

29 Statistics Canada, "Ethnic Diversity Survey, 2002," *The Daily*, September 29, 2003.

30 The Pew Research Center for the People & the Press, *Views of a Changing World 2003* (Washington, DC: The Pew Research Center for the People & the Press, June 2003).

31 M. Adams, *Fire and Ice: The United States, Canada and the Myth of Converging Values* (Toronto: Penguin, 2003).

32 M. Adams, *Fire and Ice: The United States, Canada and the Myth of Converging Values* (Toronto: Penguin, 2003).

33 R. N. Kanungo and J. K. Bhatnagar, "Achievement Orientation and Occupational Values: A Comparative Study of Young French and English Canadians," *Canadian Journal of Behavioural Science* 12, 1978, pp. 384–392; M. W. McCarrey, S. Edwards, and R. Jones, "The Influence of Ethnolinguistic Group Membership, Sex and Position Level on Motivational Orientation of Canadian Anglophone and Francophone Employees," *Canadian Journal of Behavioural Science* 9, 1977, pp. 274–282; M. W. McCarrey, S. Edwards, and R. Jones, "Personal Values of Canadian Anglophone and Francophone Employees and Ethnolinguistic Group Membership, Sex and Position Level," *Journal of Psychology* 104, 1978, pp. 175–184; S. Richer and P. Laporte, "Culture, Cognition and English-French Competition," in *Readings in Social Psychology: Focus on Canada*, ed. D. Koulack and D. Perlman (Toronto: Wiley, 1973); and L. Shapiro and D. Perlman, "Value Differences Between English and French Canadian High School Students," *Canadian Ethnic Studies* 8, 1976, pp. 50–55.

34 R. N. Kanungo and J. K. Bhatnagar, "Achievement Orientation and Occupational Values: A Comparative Study of Young French and English Canadians," *Canadian Journal of Behavioural Science* 12, 1978, pp. 384–392.

35 V. Mann-Feder and V. Savicki, "Burnout in Anglophone and Francophone Child and Youth Workers in Canada: A Cross-Cultural Comparison," *Child & Youth Care Forum* 32, no. 6 (December 2003), p. 345.

36 R. N. Kanungo and J. K. Bhatnagar, "Achievement Orientation and Occupational Values: A Comparative Study of Young French and English Canadians," *Canadian Journal of Behavioural Science* 12, 1978, pp. 384–392.

37 V. Mann-Feder and V. Savicki, "Burnout in Anglophone and Francophone Child and Youth Workers in Canada: A Cross-Cultural Comparison," *Child & Youth Care Forum* 32, no. 6 (December 2003), pp. 337–354.

38 A. Stalikas, E. Casas, and A. D. Carson, "In the Shadow of the English: English and French Canadians Differ by Psychological Type," *Journal of Psychological Type* 38, 1996, pp. 4–12.

39 K. L. Gibson, S. J. Mckelvie, and A. F. De Man, "Personality and Culture: A Comparison of Francophones and Anglophones in Québec," *Journal of Social Psychology* 148, no. 2 (2008), pp. 133–165.

40 H. C. Jain, J. Normand, and R. N. Kanungo, "Job Motivation of Canadian Anglophone and Francophone Hospital Employees," *Canadian Journal of Behavioural Science*, April 1979, pp. 160–163; and R. N. Kanungo, G. J. Gorn, and H. J. Dauderis, "Motivational Orientation of Canadian Anglophone and Francophone Managers," *Canadian Journal of Behavioural Science*, April 1976, pp. 107–121.

41 M. Major, M. McCarrey, P. Mercier, and Y. Gasse, "Meanings of Work and Personal Values of Canadian Anglophone and Francophone Middle Managers," *Canadian Journal of Administrative Sciences*, September 1994, pp. 251–263.

42 G. Bouchard, F. Rocher, and G. Rocher, *Les Francophones Québécois* (Montreal: Bowne de Montréal, 1991).

43 K. L. Gibson, S. J. Mckelvie, and A. F. De Man, "Personality and Culture: A Comparison of Francophones and Anglophones in Québec," *Journal of Social Psychology* 148, no. 2 (2008), pp. 133–165.

44 A. Derfel, "Boy, Are We Stressed Out! Quebec Has Highest Rate of Work Absenteeism," *Gazette* (Montreal), May 29, 2003, http://www.canada.com/montreal/montrealgazette/story.asp?id=5D0D7AF8-DFCB-44D5-ABE4-DA4DACA11DEA (accessed May 29, 2003).

45 P. La Novara, "Culture Participation: Does Language Make a Difference?" *Focus on Culture* 13, no. 3, Catalogue no. 87-004-XIE (Ottawa: Statistics Canada, 2002).

46 J. Paulson, "First Nations Bank Launches First Branch with Sweetgrass Ceremony," *Canadian Press Newswire*, September 23, 1997.

47 L. Redpath and M. O. Nielsen, "A Comparison of Native Culture, Non-Native Culture and New Management Ideology," *Canadian Journal of Administrative Sciences* 14, no. 3 (1997), p. 327.

48 G. C. Anders and K. K. Anders, "Incompatible Goals in Unconventional Organizations: The Politics of Alaska Native Corporations," *Organization Studies* 7, 1986, pp. 213–233; G. Dacks, "Worker-Controlled Native Enterprises: A Vehicle for Community Development in Northern Canada?" *Canadian Journal of Native Studies* 3, 1983, pp. 289–310; and L. P. Dana, "Self-

Employment in the Canadian Sub-Arctic: An Exploratory Study," *Canadian Journal of Administrative Sciences* 13, 1996, pp. 65–77.

49 L. Redpath and M. O. Nielsen, "A Comparison of Native Culture, Non-Native Culture and New Management Ideology," *Canadian Journal of Administrative Sciences* 14, no. 3 (1997), p. 327.

50 R. B. Anderson, "The Business Economy of the First Nations in Saskatchewan: A Contingency Perspective," *Canadian Journal of Native Studies* 2, 1995, pp. 309–345.

51 D. C. Natcher and C. G. Hickey, "Putting the Community Back into Community-Based Resource Management: A Criteria and Indicators Approach to Sustainability," *Human Organization* 61, no. 4 (2002), pp. 350–363.

52 E. Struzik, "'Win-Win Scenario' Possible for Resource Industry, Aboriginals," *Edmonton Journal*, April 6, 2003, p. A12.

53 http://www.highlevelwoodlands.com.

54 Discussion based on L. Redpath and M. O. Nielsen, "A Comparison of Native Culture, Non-Native Culture and New Management Ideology," *Canadian Journal of Administrative Sciences* 14, no. 3 (1997), pp. 327–339.

55 Discussion based on L. Redpath and M. O. Nielsen, "A Comparison of Native Culture, Non-Native Culture and New Management Ideology," *Canadian Journal of Administrative Sciences* 14, no. 3 (1997), pp. 327–339.

56 D. Grigg and J. Newman, "Five Ways to Foster Bonds, Win Trust in Business," *Ottawa Citizen*, April 23, 2003, p. F12.

57 T. Chui, K. Tran, and J. Flanders, "Chinese Canadians: Enriching the Cultural Mosaic," *Canadian Social Trends*, no. 76, Spring 2005, pp. 26–34.

58 Statistics Canada, "Canada's Visible Minority Population in 2017," *The Daily*, March 22, 2005.

59 I. Y. M. Yeung and R. L. Tung, "Achieving Business Success in Confucian Societies: The Importance of Guanxi (Connections)," *Organizational Dynamics*, Special Report, 1998, pp. 72–83.

60 I. Y. M. Yeung and R. L. Tung, "Achieving Business Success in Confucian Societies: The Importance of Guanxi (Connections)," *Organizational Dynamics*, Special Report, 1998, p. 73.

61 Based on P. Krivel, "Culture of Openness Boosts Productivity; Accounting Firm Knows Welcoming Atmosphere Has a Positive Impact on the Bottom Line," *Toronto Star*, April 3, 2008, p. R5; S. Klie, "Hail the New Chief," *Canadian HR Reporter*, July 14, 2008, p. 13; and Lesley Young, "Diversity Drives KPMG to Top," *Canadian HR Reporter*, March 24, 2008, p. 15.

62 Based on C. Ricketts, "When in London, Do as the Californians Do," *Wall Street Journal*, January 23, 2007, p. B5.

63 G. Shaw, "Canada Lags World on Job Quality," *Vancouver Sun*, September 18, 2004, p. F5.

64 J. Barling, E. K. Kelloway, and R. D. Iverson, "High-Quality Work, Job Satisfaction, and Occupational Injuries," *Journal of Applied Psychology* 88, no. 2 (2003), pp. 276–283; and F. W. Bond and D. Bunce, "The Role of Acceptance and Job Control in Mental

Health, Job Satisfaction, and Work Performance," *Journal of Applied Psychology* 88, no. 6 (2003), pp. 1057–1067.

65 E. Diener, E. Sandvik, L. Seidlitz, and M. Diener, "The Relationship between Income and Subjective Well-Being: Relative or Absolute?" *Social Indicators Research* 28 (1993), pp. 195–223.

66 T. A. Judge and C. Hurst, "The Benefits and Possible Costs of Positive Core Self-Evaluations: A Review and Agenda for Future Research," in *Positive Organizational Behavior*, ed. D. Nelson & C. L. Cooper (London, UK: Sage Publications, 2007), pp. 159–174.

67 M. T. Iaffaldano and M. Muchinsky, "Job Satisfaction and Job Performance: A Meta-Analysis," *Psychological Bulletin*, March 1985, pp. 251–273.

68 T. A. Judge, C. J. Thoresen, J. E. Bono, and G. K. Patton, "The Job Satisfaction–Job Performance Relationship: A Qualitative and Quantitative Review," *Psychological Bulletin*, May 2001, pp. 376–407; and T. Judge, S. Parker, A. E. Colbert, D. Heller, and R. Ilies, "Job Satisfaction: A Cross-Cultural Review," in *Handbook of Industrial, Work, & Organizational Psychology*, vol. 2, ed. N. Anderson, D. S. Ones, H. K. Sinangil, and C. Viswesvaran (Thousand Oaks, CA: Sage, 2001), p. 41.

69 C. N. Greene, "The Satisfaction–Performance Controversy," *Business Horizons*, February 1972, pp. 31–41; E. E. Lawler III, *Motivation in Organizations* (Monterey, CA: Brooks/Cole, 1973); and M. M. Petty, G. W. McGee, and J. W. Cavender, "A Meta-Analysis of the Relationship between Individual Job Satisfaction and Individual Performance," *Academy of Management Review*, October 1984, pp. 712–721.

70 C. Ostroff, "The Relationship between Satisfaction, Attitudes, and Performance: An Organizational Level Analysis," *Journal of Applied Psychology*, December 1992, pp. 963–974; A. M. Ryan, M. J. Schmit, and R. Johnson, "Attitudes and Effectiveness: Examining Relations at an Organizational Level," *Personnel Psychology*, Winter 1996, pp. 853–882; and J. K. Harter, F. L. Schmidt, and T. L. Hayes, "Business-Unit Level Relationship between Employee Satisfaction, Employee Engagement, and Business Outcomes: A Meta-Analysis," *Journal of Applied Psychology*, April 2002, pp. 268–279.

71 D. W. Organ, *Organizational Citizenship Behavior: The Good Soldier Syndrome* (Lexington, MA: Lexington Books, 1988), p. 4.

72 D. W. Organ, *Organizational Citizenship Behavior: The Good Soldier Syndrome* (Lexington, MA: Lexington Books, 1988); C. A. Smith, D. W. Organ, and J. P. Near, "Organizational Citizenship Behavior: Its Nature and Antecedents," *Journal of Applied Psychology*, 1983, pp. 653–663.

73 J. Farh, C. Zhong, and D. W. Organ, "Organizational Citizenship Behavior in the People's Republic of China," *Academy of Management Proceedings*, 2000, pp. OB: D1–D6.

74 J. M. George and A. P. Brief, "Feeling Good-Doing Good: A Conceptual Analysis of the Mood at Work–Organizational Spontaneity Relationship," *Psychological Bulletin* 112, 2002, pp. 310–329; and S. Wagner and M. Rush, "Altruistic Organizational Citizenship Behavior: Context, Disposition and Age," *Journal of Social Psychology* 140, 2002, pp. 379–391.

75 P. E. Spector, *Job Satisfaction: Application, Assessment, Causes, and Consequences* (Thousand Oaks, CA: Sage, 1997), pp. 57–58.

76 P. M. Podsakoff, S. B. MacKenzie, J. B. Paine, and D. G. Bachrach, "Organizational Citizenship Behaviors: A Critical Review of the Theoretical and Empirical Literature and Suggestions for Future Research," *Journal of Management* 26, no. 3 (2000), pp. 513–563.

77 See T. S. Bateman and D. W. Organ, "Job Satisfaction and the Good Soldier: The Relationship between Affect and Employee 'Citizenship,'" *Academy of Management Journal*, December 1983, pp. 587–595; C. A. Smith, D. W. Organ, and J. P. Near, "Organizational Citizenship Behavior: Its Nature and Antecedents," *Journal of Applied Psychology*, October 1983, pp. 653–663; and A. P. Brief, *Attitudes in and Around Organizations* (Thousand Oaks, CA: Sage, 1998), pp. 44–45.

78 D. W. Organ and R. H. Moorman, "Fairness and Organizational Citizenship Behavior: What Are the Connections?" *Social Justice Research* 6, no. 1 (March 1993), pp. 5–18.

79 D. W. Organ and K. Ryan, "A Meta-Analytic Review of Attitudinal and Dispositional Predictors of Organizational Citizenship Behavior," *Personnel Psychology*, Winter 1995, p. 791.

80 J. Fahr, P. M. Podsakoff, and D. W. Organ, "Accounting for Organizational Citizenship Behavior: Leader Fairness and Task Scope Versus Satisfaction," *Journal of Management*, December 1990, pp. 705–722; R. H. Moorman, "Relationship between Organizational Justice and Organizational Citizenship Behaviors: Do Fairness Perceptions Influence Employee Citizenship?" *Journal of Applied Psychology*, December 1991, pp. 845–855; and M. A. Konovsky and D. W. Organ, "Dispositional and Contextual Determinants of Organizational Citizenship Behavior," *Journal of Organizational Behavior*, May 1996, pp. 253–266.

81 D. W. Organ, "Personality and Organizational Citizenship Behavior," *Journal of Management*, Summer 1994, p. 466.

82 See, for instance, E. Naumann and D. W. Jackson Jr., "One More Time: How Do You Satisfy Customers?" *Business Horizons*, May–June 1999, pp. 71–76; D. J. Koys, "The Effects of Employee Satisfaction, Organizational Citizenship Behavior, and Turnover on Organizational Effectiveness: A Unit-Level, Longitudinal Study," *Personnel Psychology*, Spring 2001, pp. 101–114; and J. Griffith, "Do Satisfied Employees Satisfy Customers? Support-Services Staff Morale and Satisfaction among Public School Administrators, Students, and Parents," *Journal of Applied Social Psychology*, August 2001, pp. 1627–1658.

83 M. J. Bitner, B. H. Booms, and L. A. Mohr, "Critical Service Encounters: The Employee's Viewpoint," *Journal of Marketing*, October 1994, pp. 95–106.

84 S. M. Puffer, "Prosocial Behavior, Noncompliant Behavior, and Work Performance among Commission Salespeople," *Journal of Applied Psychology*, November 1987, pp. 615–621; J. Hogan and R. Hogan, "How to Measure Employee Reliability," *Journal of Applied Psychology*, May 1989, pp. 273–279; and C. D. Fisher and E. A. Locke, "The New Look in Job Satisfaction Research and Theory," in *Job Satisfaction*, ed. C. J. Cranny, P. C. Smith, and E. F. Stone (New York: Lexington Books, 1992), pp. 165–194.

85 K. A. Hanisch, C. L. Hulin, and M. Roznowski, "The Importance of Individuals' Repertoires of Behaviors: The Scientific Appropriateness of Studying Multiple Behaviors and General Attitudes," *Journal of Organizational Behavior* 19, no. 5 (1998), pp. 463–480.

86 S. M. Puffer, "Prosocial Behavior, Noncompliant Behavior, and Work Performance among Commission Salespeople," *Journal of Applied Psychology*, November 1987, pp. 615–621; J. Hogan and R. Hogan, "How to Measure Employee Reliability," *Journal of Applied Psychology*, May 1989, pp. 273–279; and C. D. Fisher and E. A. Locke, "The New Look in Job Satisfaction Research and Theory," in *Job Satisfaction*, ed. C. J. Cranny, P. C. Smith, and E. F. Stone (New York: Lexington Books, 1992), pp. 165–194.

87 R. B. Freeman, "Job Satisfaction as an Economic Variable," *American Economic Review*, January 1978, pp. 135–141.

88 K. Holland, "Inside the Minds of Your Employees," *New York Times*, January 28, 2007, p. B1; "Study Sees Link between Morale and Stock Price," *Workforce Management*, February 27, 2006, p. 15; and "The Workplace as a Solar System," *New York Times* (October 28, 2006), p. B5.

89 G. J. Blau and K. R. Boal, "Conceptualizing How Job Involvement and Organizational Commitment Affect Turnover and Absenteeism," *Academy of Management Review*, April 1987, p. 290.

90 N. J. Allen and J. P. Meyer, "The Measurement and Antecedents of Affective, Continuance, and Normative Commitment to the Organization," *Journal of Occupational Psychology* 63, 1990, pp. 1–18; and J. P. Meyer, N. J. Allen, and C. A. Smith, "Commitment to Organizations and Occupations: Extension and Test of a Three-Component Conceptualization," *Journal of Applied Psychology* 78, 1993, pp. 538–551.

91 M. Riketta, "Attitudinal Organizational Commitment and Job Performance: A Meta-Analysis," *Journal of Organizational Behavior*, March 2002, pp. 257–266.

92 T. A. Wright and D. G. Bonett, "The Moderating Effects of Employee Tenure on the Relation between Organizational Commitment and Job Performance: A Meta-Analysis," *Journal of Applied Psychology*, December 2002, pp. 1183–1190.

93 See, for instance, W. Hom, R. Katerberg, and C. L. Hulin, "Comparative Examination of Three Approaches to the Prediction of Turnover," *Journal of Applied Psychology*, June 1979, pp. 280–290; H. Angle and J. Perry, "Organizational Commitment: Individual and Organizational Influence," *Work and Occupations*, May 1983, pp. 123–146; J. L. Pierce and R. B. Dunham, "Organizational Commitment: Pre-Employment Propensity and Initial Work Experiences," *Journal of Management*, Spring 1987, pp. 163–178; and T. Simons and Q. Roberson, "Why Managers Should Care About Fairness: The Effects of Aggregate Justice Perceptions on Organizational Outcomes," *Journal of Applied Psychology* 88, no. 3 (2003), pp. 432–443.

94 J. P. Meyer, S. V. Paumonen, I. R. Gellatly, R. D. Goffin, and D. N. Jackson, "Organizational Commitment and Job Performance: It's the Nature of the Commitment That Counts," *Journal of Applied Psychology* 74, 1989, pp. 152–156; L. M. Shore and S. J. Wayne, "Commitment and Employee Behavior: Comparison of Affective and Continuance Commitment with Perceived Organizational Support," *Journal of Applied Psychology* 78, 1993, pp. 774–780.

95 Corporate Leadership Council, "Driving Performance and Retention Through Employee Engagement," news release, September 2004.

96 J. R. Katzenback and J. A. Santamaria, "Firing up the Front Line," *Harvard Business Review*, May–June 1999, p. 109.

97 Based on Y. Cheng and M. S. Stockdale, "The Validity of the Three-Component Model of Organizational Commitment in a Chinese Context," *Journal of Vocational Behavior*, June 2003, pp. 465–489.

98 D. R. May, R. L. Gilson, and L. M. Harter, "The Psychological Conditions of Meaningfulness, Safety and Availability and the Engagement of the Human Spirit at Work," *Journal of Occupational and Organizational Psychology* 77, no. 1 (2004), pp. 11–37.

99 J. K. Harter, F. L. Schmidt, and T. L. Hayes, "Business-Unit-Level Relationship between Employee Satisfaction, Employee Engagement, and Business Outcomes: A Meta-Analysis," *Journal of Applied Psychology* 87, no. 2 (2002), pp. 268–279.

100 Lesley Young, "Diversity Drives KPMG to Top," *Canadian HR Reporter*, March 24, 2008, p. 15.

101 See http://www-03.ibm.com/employment/ca/en/diversity.html.

102 R. A. Roe and P. Ester, "Values and Work: Empirical Findings and Theoretical Perspective," *Applied Psychology: An International Review* 48, 1999, pp. 1–21.

103 M. Adams, *Sex in the Snow* (Toronto: Penguin, 1997), p. 102.

104 M. Adams, *Sex in the Snow* (Toronto: Penguin, 1997), p. 102.

105 Based on D. Calleja, "Equity or Else," *Canadian Business*, March 19, 2001, pp. 29–34.

106 P. C. Earley and E. Mosakowski, "Cultural Intelligence," *Harvard Business Review* 82, no. 10 (October 2004), pp. 139–146.

107 J. Sanchez-Burks, F. Lee, R. Nisbett, I. Choi, S. Zhao, and J. Koo, "Conversing Across Cultures: East-West Communication Styles in Work and Nonwork Contexts," *Journal of Personality and Social Psychology* 85, no. 2 (August 2003), pp. 363–372.

108 E. A. Locke, "The Nature and Causes of Job Satisfaction," in *Handbook of Industrial and Organizational Psychology*, ed. M. D. Dunnette (Chicago: Rand McNally, 1976), pp. 1319–1328.

109 See, for instance, R. D. Arvey, B. P. McCall, T. J. Bouchard Jr., and P. Taubman, "Genetic Influences on Job Satisfaction and Work Values," *Personality and Individual Differences*, July 1994, pp. 21–33; D. Lykken and A. Tellegen, "Happiness Is a Stochastic Phenomenon," *Psychological Science*, May 1996, pp. 186–189; D. Lykken and M. Csikszentmihalyi, "Happiness—Stuck with What You've Got?" *Psychologist*, September 2001, pp. 470–472; and "Double Take," *UNH Magazine*, Spring 2000, http://www.unhmagazine.unh.edu/sp00/twinsp00.html.

110 R. N. Lussier, *Human Relations in Organizations: A Skill Building Approach*, 2nd ed. (Homewood, IL: Richard D. Irwin, 1993). Reprinted by permission of the McGraw-Hill Companies, Inc.

111 This exercise is based on M. Allen, "Here Comes the Bribe," *Entrepreneur*, October 2000, p. 48.

112 Reconstructed, based on H. Sokoloff, "Firing of Teacher Upheld for His Opinions on Race," *National Post*, March 13, 2002, pp. A1, A11.

113 Based on M. Burke, "The Guru in the Vegetable Bin," *Forbes*, March 3, 2003, pp. 56–58.

OB on the Edge: Stress at Work

1 P. McGuire, "An Old Family Recipe for Success; Business Like His Father and Grandfather Before Him, Moosehead President Andrew Oland Has Managed to Remain Grounded," *Telegraph-Journal*, August 4, 2008, p. E2; and M. Dunne, "Demand for Wellness Programs Growing; Employment Workers Increasingly Seek Employers Who Offer Assistance, Conference Told," *Telegraph-Journal*, June 16, 2007, p. E1.

2 Paragraph based on D. Hansen, "Worker Who Felt 'Thrown Away' Wins," *Vancouver Sun*, August 16, 2006.

3 Statistics Canada, "Life Stress, by Sex, Household Population Aged 18 and Over, Canada, Provinces, Territories, Health Regions and Peer Groups, 2005," http://www.statcan.ca/english/freepub/82-221-XIE/2006001/tables/t004b.htm (accessed August 18, 2008).

4 Table compiled using data from Statistics Canada, "Life Stress, by Sex, Household Population Aged 18 and Over, Canada, Provinces, Territories, Health Regions and Peer Groups, 2005," http://www.statcan.ca/english/freepub/82-221-XIE/2006001/tables/t004b.htm (accessed August 18, 2008).

5 K. MacQueen, "Workplace Stress Costs Us Dearly, and Yet Nobody Knows What It Is or How to Deal with It," *Maclean's*, October 15, 2007.

6 K. MacQueen, "Workplace Stress Costs Us Dearly, and Yet Nobody Knows What It Is or How to Deal with It," *Maclean's*, October 15, 2007.

7 L. Duxbury and C. Higgins, "2001 National Work-Life Conflict Study," as reported in J. Campbell, "'Organizational Anorexia' Puts Stress on Employees," *Ottawa Citizen*, July 4, 2002.

8 K. Harding, "Balance Tops List of Job Desires," *Globe and Mail*, May 7, 2003, pp. C1, C6.

9 V. Galt, "Productivity Buckling under the Strain of Stress, CEOs Say," *Globe and Mail*, June 9, 2005, p. B1.

10 "Canadian Workers among Most Stressed," *Worklife Report* 14, no. 2 (2002), pp. 8–9.

11 N. Ayed, "Absenteeism Up Since 1993," *Canadian Press Newswire*, March 25, 1998.

12 N. Ayed, "Absenteeism Up Since 1993," *Canadian Press Newswire*, March 25, 1998.

13 Adapted from R. S. Schuler, "Definition and Conceptualization of Stress in Organizations," *Organizational Behavior and Human Performance*, April 1980, p. 189. For an updated review of definitions, see C. L. Cooper, P. J. Dewe, and M. P. O'Driscoll, *Organizational Stress: A Review and Critique of Theory, Research, and Applications* (Thousand Oaks, CA: Sage, 2002).

14 *Health* magazine as appearing in Centers for Disease Control and Prevention, US Department of Health and Human Services, "*Helicobacter pylori* and Peptic Ulcer Disease—Myths," http://www.cdc.gov/ulcer/myth.htm (accessed July 12, 2008).

15   See, for instance, M. A. Cavanaugh, W. R. Boswell, M. V. Roehling, and J. W. Boudreau, "An Empirical Examination of Self-Reported Work Stress among U.S. Managers," *Journal of Applied Psychology*, February 2000, pp. 65–74.

16   N. P. Podsakoff, J. A. LePine, and M. A. LePine, "Differential Challenge-Hindrance Stressor Relationships with Job Attitudes, Turnover Intentions, Turnover, and Withdrawal Behavior: A Meta-Analysis," *Journal of Applied Psychology* 92, no. 2 (2007), pp. 438–454; J. A. LePine, M. A. LePine, and C. L. Jackson, "Challenge and Hindrance Stress: Relationships with Exhaustion, Motivation to Learn, and Learning Performance," *Journal of Applied Psychology*, October 2004, pp. 883–891.

17   J. de Jonge and C. Dormann, "Stressors, Resources, and Strain at Work: A Longitudinal Test of the Triple-Match Principle," *Journal of Applied Psychology* 91, no. 5 (2006), pp. 1359–1374.

18   N. W. Van Yperen and O. Janssen, "Fatigued and Dissatisfied or Fatigued but Satisfied? Goal Orientations and Responses to High Job Demands," *Academy of Management Journal*, December 2002, pp. 1161–1171; and N. W. Van Yperen and M. Hagedoorn, "Do High Job Demands Increase Intrinsic Motivation or Fatigue or Both? The Role of Job Control and Job Social Support," *Academy of Management Journal*, June 2003, pp. 339–348; K. Daniels, N. Beesley, A. Cheyne, and V. Wimalasiri "Coping Processes Linking the Demands-Control-Support Model, Affect and Risky Decisions at Work," *Human Relations* 61, no. 6, (2008), pp. 845–874; and M. van den Tooren and J. de Jonge "Managing Job Stress in Nursing: What Kind of Resources Do We Need?" *Journal of Advanced Nursing* 63, no. 1 (2008), pp. 75–84.

19   This section is adapted from C. L. Cooper and R. Payne, *Stress at Work* (London: Wiley, 1978); S. Parasuraman and J. A. Alutto, "Sources and Outcomes of Stress in Organizational Settings: Toward the Development of a Structural Model," *Academy of Management Journal* 27, no. 2 (June 1984), pp. 330–350; and P. M. Hart and C. L. Cooper, "Occupational Stress: Toward a More Integrated Framework," in *Handbook of Industrial, Work and Organizational Psychology*, vol. 2, ed. N. Anderson, D. S. Ones, H. K. Sinangil, and C. Viswesvaran (London: Sage, 2001), pp. 93–114.

20   E. A. Rafferty and M. A. Griffin, "Perceptions of Organizational Change: A Stress and Coping Perspective," *Journal of Applied Psychology* 71, no. 5 (2007), pp. 1154–1162.

21   See, for example, M. L. Fox, D. J. Dwyer, and D. C. Ganster, "Effects of Stressful Job Demands and Control of Physiological and Attitudinal Outcomes in a Hospital Setting," *Academy of Management Journal*, April 1993, pp. 289–318.

22   G. W. Evans and D. Johnson, "Stress and Open-Office Noise," *Journal of Applied Psychology*, October 2000, pp. 779–783.

23   T. M. Glomb, J. D. Kammeyer-Mueller, and M. Rotundo, "Emotional Labor Demands and Compensating Wage Differentials," *Journal of Applied Psychology*, August 2004, pp. 700–714; and A. A. Grandey, "When 'The Show Must Go On': Surface Acting and Deep Acting as Determinants of Emotional Exhaustion and Peer-Rated Service Delivery," *Academy of Management Journal*, February 2003, pp. 86–96.

24   V. S. Major, K. J. Klein, and M. G. Ehrhart, "Work Time, Work Interference with Family, and Psychological Distress," *Journal of Applied Psychology*, June 2002, pp. 427–436; see also P. E. Spector, C. L. Cooper, S. Poelmans, T. D. Allen, M. O'Driscoll, J. I. Sanchez, O. L. Siu, P. Dewe, P. Hart, L. Lu, L. F. R. De Moraes, G. M. Ostrognay, K. Sparks, P. Wong, and S. Yu, "A Cross-National Comparative Study of Work-Family Stressors, Working Hours, and Well-Being: China and Latin America versus the Anglo World," *Personnel Psychology*, Spring 2004, pp. 119–142.

25   S. McKay, "The Work-Family Conundrum," *Financial Post Magazine*, December 1997, pp. 78–81; and A. Davis, "Respect Your Elders: Pressure on the Healthcare System Means Elderly Patients Aren't Staying in Hospitals as Long as They Used To," *Benefits Canada* 26, no. 8 (2002), p. 13.

26   L. T. Thomas and D. C. Ganster, "Impact of Family-Supportive Work Variables on Work-Family Conflict and Strain: A Control Perspective," *Journal of Applied Psychology* 80, 1995, pp. 6–15.

27   D. L. Nelson and C. Sutton, "Chronic Work Stress and Coping: A Longitudinal Study and Suggested New Directions," *Academy of Management Journal*, December 1990, pp. 859–869.

28   FactBox based on A. Picard, "The Working Wounded," *Globe and Mail*, June 22, 2008; S. McGovern, "No Rest for the Weary," *Gazette* (Montreal), August 19, 2003, p. B1; and D. McMurdy, "People Get Stress Relief Express-Style," *Financial Post (National Post)*, January 15, 2005, p. IN1.

29   H. Selye, *The Stress of Life* (New York: McGraw-Hill, 1976).

30   R. S. Schuler, "Definition and Conceptualization of Stress in Organizations," *Organizational Behavior and Human Performance*, April 1980, p. 191; and R. L. Kahn and P. Byosiere, "Stress in Organizations," *Organizational Behavior and Human Performance*, April 1980, pp. 604–610.

31   KPMG Canada, compensation letter, July 1998.

32   B. D. Steffy and J. W. Jones, "Workplace Stress and Indicators of Coronary-Disease Risk," *Academy of Management Journal* 31, 1988, p. 687.

33   C. L. Cooper and J. Marshall, "Occupational Sources of Stress: A Review of the Literature Relating to Coronary Heart Disease and Mental Ill Health," *Journal of Occupational Psychology* 49, no. 1 (1976), pp. 11–28.

34   J. R. Hackman and G. R. Oldham, "Development of the Job Diagnostic Survey," *Journal of Applied Psychology*, April 1975, pp. 159–170.

35   J. L. Xie and G. Johns, "Job Scope and Stress: Can Job Scope Be Too High?" *Academy of Management Journal*, October 1995, pp. 1288–1309.

36   S. J. Motowidlo, J. S. Packard, and M. R. Manning, "Occupational Stress: Its Causes and Consequences for Job Performance," *Journal of Applied Psychology*, November 1987, pp. 619–620.

37   See, for instance, R. C. Cummings, "Job Stress and the Buffering Effect of Supervisory Support," *Group & Organization Studies*, March 1990, pp. 92–104; M. R. Manning, C. N. Jackson, and M. R. Fusilier, "Occupational Stress, Social Support, and the Cost of Health Care," *Academy of Management Journal*, June 1996, pp. 738–750; and P. D. Bliese and T. W. Britt, "Social Support, Group Consensus and Stressor-Strain Relationships: Social Context Matters," *Journal of Organizational Behavior*, June 2001, pp. 425–436.

38   R. Williams, *The Trusting Heart: Great News About Type A Behavior* (New York: Times Books, 1989).

39   T. H. Macan, "Time Management: Test of a Process Model," *Journal of Applied Psychology*, June 1994, pp. 381–391.

40   See, for example, G. Lawrence-Ell, *The Invisible Clock: A Practical Revolution in Finding Time for Everyone and Everything* (Seaside Park, NJ: Kingsland Hall, 2002).

41   J. Kiely and G. Hodgson, "Stress in the Prison Service: The Benefits of Exercise Programs," *Human Relations*, June 1990, pp. 551–572.

42   E. J. Forbes and R. J. Pekala, "Psychophysiological Effects of Several Stress Management Techniques," *Psychological Reports*, February 1993, pp. 19–27; and G. Smith, "Meditation, the New Balm for Corporate Stress," *BusinessWeek*, May 10, 1993, pp. 86–87.

43   J. Lee, "How to Fight That Debilitating Stress in Your Workplace," *Vancouver Sun*, April 5, 1999, p. C3. Reprinted with permission.

44   H. Staseson, "Can Perk Help Massage Bottom Line? On-Site Therapeutic Sessions Are Used by an Increasingly Diverse Group of Employers Hoping to Improve Staff Performance," *Globe and Mail*, July 3, 2002, p. C1.

45   Health Canada, "Wellness Programs Offer Healthy Return, Study Finds," *Report Bulletin*, #224, October 2001, p. 1.

46   H. Staseson, "Can Perk Help Massage Bottom Line? On-Site Therapeutic Sessions Are Used by an Increasingly Diverse Group of Employers Hoping to Improve Staff Performance," *Globe and Mail*, July 3, 2002, p. C1.

47   B. Bouw, "Employers Embrace Wellness at Work: Fitness Programs Gaining Popularity as Companies Look to Boost Productivity with Healthier Staff," *Globe and Mail*, April 10, 2002, p. C1.

48   P. M. Wright, "Operationalization of Goal Difficulty as a Moderator of the Goal Difficulty-Performance Relationship," *Journal of Applied Psychology*, June 1990, pp. 227–234; E. A. Locke and G. P. Latham, "Building a Practically Useful Theory of Goal Setting and Task Motivation: A 35-Year Odyssey," *American Psychologist* 57, no. 9 (2002), pp. 705–717; K. L. Langeland, C. M. Johnson, and T. C. Mawhinney, "Improving Staff Performance in a Community Mental Health Setting: Job Analysis, Training, Goal Setting, Feedback, and Years of Data," *Journal of Organizational Behavior Management*, 1998, pp. 21–43.

49   S. Greengard, "It's About Time," *IndustryWeek*, February 7, 2000, pp. 47–50; and S. Nayyar, "Gimme a Break," *American Demographics*, June 2002, p. 6.

50   See, for instance, R. A. Wolfe, D. O. Ulrich, and D. F. Parker, "Employee Health Management Programs: Review, Critique, and Research Agenda," *Journal of Management*, Winter 1987, pp. 603–615; D. L. Gebhardt and C. E. Crump, "Employee Fitness and Wellness Programs in the Workplace," *American Psychologist*, February 1990, pp. 262–272; and C. E. Beadle, "And Let's Save 'Wellness.' It Works," *New York Times*, July 24, 1994, p. F9.

51   J. Lee, "How to Fight That Debilitating Stress in Your Workplace," *Vancouver Sun*, April 5, 1999, p. C3. Reprinted with permission.

Chapter 4

1   Opening vignette based on M. Beamish, "Lions Know Practice Makes Perfect," *Nanaimo Daily News*, August 23, 2005, p. B3; M. Sekeres, "Two Sides to Buono," *Kamloops Daily News*, September 8, 2005, p. A13; and J. Morris, "Still Feeling the Passion, Wally Buono Agrees to Contract Extension with Lions," *Canadian Press*, March 31, 2008.

2   See, for instance, T. R. Mitchell, "Matching Motivational Strategies with Organizational Contexts," in *Research in Organizational Behavior*, vol. 19, ed. L. L. Cummings and B. M. Staw (Greenwich, CT: JAI Press, 1997), pp. 60–62.

3   D. McGregor, *The Human Side of Enterprise* (New York: McGraw-Hill, 1960). For an updated analysis of Theory X and Theory Y constructs, see R. J. Summers and S. F. Cronshaw, "A Study of McGregor's Theory X, Theory Y and the Influence of Theory X, Theory Y Assumptions on Causal Attributions for Instances of Worker Poor Performance," in *Organizational Behavior*, ed. S. L. McShane, ASAC Conference Proceedings, vol. 9, part 5, Halifax, 1988, pp. 115–123.

4   K. W. Thomas, *Intrinsic Motivation at Work* (San Francisco: Berrett-Koehler, 2000); and K. W. Thomas, "Intrinsic Motivation and How It Works," *Training*, October 2000, pp. 130–135.

5   A. Kohn, *Punished by Rewards* (Boston: Houghton Mifflin, 1993).

6   Based on S. E. DeVoe and S. S. Iyengar, "Managers' Theories of Subordinates: A Cross-Cultural Examination of Manager Perceptions of Motivation and Appraisal of Performance," *Organizational Behavior and Human Decision Processes*, January 2004, pp. 47–61.

7   A. H. Maslow, *Motivation and Personality* (New York: Harper and Row, 1954).

8   K. Korman, J. H. Greenhaus, and I. J. Badin, "Personnel Attitudes and Motivation," in *Annual Review of Psychology*, ed. M. R. Rosenzweig and L. W. Porter (Palo Alto, CA: Annual Reviews, 1977), p. 178; and M. A. Wahba and L. G. Bridwell, "Maslow Reconsidered: A Review of Research on the Need Hierarchy Theory," *Organizational Behavior and Human Performance*, April 1976, pp. 212–240.

9   C. P. Alderfer, "An Empirical Test of a New Theory of Human Needs," *Organizational Behavior and Human Performance*, May 1969, pp. 142–175.

10   C. P. Schneider and C. P. Alderfer, "Three Studies of Measures of Need Satisfaction in Organizations," *Administrative Science Quarterly*, December 1973, pp. 489–505; and I. Borg and M. Braun, "Work Values in East and West Germany: Different Weights, but Identical Structures," *Journal of Organizational Behavior* 17, special issue (1996), pp. 541–555.

11   F. Herzberg, B. Mausner, and B. Snyderman, *The Motivation to Work* (New York: Wiley, 1959).

12   R. J. House and L. A. Wigdor, "Herzberg's Dual-Factor Theory of Job Satisfaction and Motivations: A Review of the Evidence and Criticism," *Personnel Psychology*, Winter 1967, pp. 369–389; D. P. Schwab and L. L. Cummings, "Theories of Performance and Satisfaction: A Review," *Industrial Relations*, October 1970, pp. 403–430; R. J. Caston and R. Braito, "A Specification Issue in Job Satisfaction Research," *Sociological Perspectives*, April 1985,

pp. 175–197; and J. Phillipchuk and J. Whittaker, "An Inquiry into the Continuing Relevance of Herzberg's Motivation Theory," *Engineering Management Journal* 8, no. 1 (1996), pp. 15–20.

13 R. J. House and L. A. Wigdor, "Herzberg's Dual-Factor Theory of Job Satisfaction and Motivations: A Review of the Evidence and Criticism," *Personnel Psychology*, Winter 1967, pp. 369–389; D. P. Schwab and L. L. Cummings, "Theories of Performance and Satisfaction: A Review," *Industrial Relations*, October 1970, pp. 403–430; and R. J. Caston and R. Braito, "A Specification Issue in Job Satisfaction Research," *Sociological Perspectives*, April 1985, pp. 175–197.

14 D. C. McClelland, *The Achieving Society* (New York: Van Nostrand Reinhold, 1961); J. W. Atkinson and J. O. Raynor, *Motivation and Achievement* (Washington, DC: Winston, 1974); D. C. McClelland, *Power: The Inner Experience* (New York: Irvington, 1975); and M. J. Stahl, *Managerial and Technical Motivation: Assessing Needs for Achievement, Power, and Affiliation* (New York: Praeger, 1986).

15 D. C. McClelland, *The Achieving Society* (New York: Van Nostrand Reinhold, 1961).

16 D. C. McClelland, *Power: The Inner Experience* (New York: Irvington, 1975); D. C. McClelland and D. H. Burnham, "Power Is the Great Motivator," *Harvard Business Review*, March–April 1976, pp. 100–110; and R. E. Boyatzis, "The Need for Close Relationships and the Manager's Job," in *Organizational Psychology: Readings on Human Behavior in Organizations*, 4th ed., ed. D. A. Kolb, I. M. Rubin, and J. M. McIntyre (Upper Saddle River, NJ: Prentice Hall, 1984), pp. 81–86.

17 D. G. Winter, "The Motivational Dimensions of Leadership: Power, Achievement, and Affiliation," in *Multiple Intelligences and Leadership*, ed. R. E. Riggio, S. E. Murphy, and F. J. Pirozzolo (Mahwah, NJ: Erlbaum, 2002), pp. 119–138.

18 Based on L. Ullrich, "Anything But Glamorous at 4 a.m.: No Security, Insane Hours, No Pension and Zero Benefits," *Province* (Vancouver), August 3, 2005, p. A40; and L. Little, "B.C. Lions Looking for a More Professional Effort," *Vancouver Sun*, June 15, 2008.

19 V. H. Vroom, *Work and Motivation* (New York: Wiley, 1964).

20 L. Ullrich. "Anything But Glamorous at 4 a.m.: No Security, Insane Hours, No Pension and Zero Benefits," *Province* (Vancouver), August 3, 2005, p. A40.

21 J. Choudhury, "The Motivational Impact of Sales Quotas on Effort," *Journal of Marketing Research*, February 1993, pp. 28–41; and C. C. Pinder, Work Motivation (Glenview, IL: Scott Foresman, 1984), Chapter 7.

22 Angus Reid Group, *Workplace 2000: Working Toward the Millennium*, Fall 1997, p. 14.

23 See http://www.radical.ca.

24 See, for example, H. G. Heneman III and D. P. Schwab, "Evaluation of Research on Expectancy Theory Prediction of Employee Performance," *Psychological Bulletin*, July 1972, pp. 1–9; T. R. Mitchell, "Expectancy Models of Job Satisfaction, Occupational Preference and Effort: A Theoretical, Methodological and Empirical Appraisal," *Psychological Bulletin*, November 1974, pp. 1053–1077; and L. Reinharth and M. A. Wahba, "Expectancy Theory as a Predictor of Work Motivation, Effort Expenditure,

and Job Performance," *Academy of Management Journal*, September 1975, pp. 502–537.

25 See, for example, L. W. Porter and E. E. Lawler III, Managerial Attitudes and Performance (Homewood, IL: Richard D. Irwin, 1968); D. F. Parker and L. Dyer, "Expectancy Theory as a within-Person Behavioral Choice Model: An Empirical Test of Some Conceptual and Methodological Refinements," *Organizational Behavior and Human Performance*, October 1976, pp. 97–117; H. J. Arnold, "A Test of the Multiplicative Hypothesis of Expectancy-Valence Theories of Work Motivation," *Academy of Management Journal*, April 1981, pp. 128–141; and W. Van Eerde and H. Thierry, "Vroom's Expectancy Models and Work-Related Criteria: A Meta-Analysis," *Journal of Applied Psychology*, October 1996, pp. 575–586.

26 P. C. Earley, *Face, Harmony, and Social Structure: An Analysis of Organizational Behavior Across Cultures* (New York: Oxford University Press, 1997); R. M. Steers and C. Sanchez-Runde, "Culture, Motivation, and Work Behavior," in *Handbook of Cross-Cultural Management*, ed. M. Gannon and K. Newman (London: Blackwell, 2001), pp. 190–215; and H. C. Triandis, "Motivation and Achievement in Collectivist and Individualistic Cultures," in *Advances in Motivation and Achievement*, vol. 9, ed. M. Maehr and P. Pintrich (Greenwich, CT: JAI Press, 1995), pp. 1–30.

27 J. Brown, "Quitters Never Win: The (Adverse) Incentive Effects of Competing with Superstars," University of California, Berkeley, unpublished paper, April 2008.

28 E. A. Locke, "Toward a Theory of Task Motivation and Incentives," *Organizational Behavior and Human Performance*, May 1968, pp. 157–189.

29 E. A. Locke, K. N. Shaw, L. M. Saari, and G. P. Latham, "Goal Setting and Task Performance: 1969–1980," *Psychological Bulletin*, July 1981, p. 126.

30 P. C. Earley, P. Wojnaroski, and W. Prest, "Task Planning and Energy Expended: Exploration of How Goals Influence Performance," *Journal of Applied Psychology*, February 1987, pp. 107–114.

31 "KEY Group Survey Finds Nearly Half of All Employees Have No Set Performance Goals," *IPMA-HR Bulletin*, March 10, 2006, p. 1; S. Hamm, "SAP Dangles a Big, Fat Carrot," *BusinessWeek*, May 22, 2006, pp. 67–68; and "P&G CEO Wields High Expectations but No Whip," *USA Today*, February 19, 2007, p. 3B.

32 See, for instance, S. J. Carroll and H. L. Tosi, *Management by Objectives: Applications and Research* (New York: Macmillan, 1973); and R. Rodgers and J. E. Hunter, "Impact of Management by Objectives on Organizational Productivity," *Journal of Applied Psychology*, April 1991, pp. 322–336.

33 E. A. Locke and G. P. Latham, *A Theory of Goal Setting and Task Performance* (Englewood Cliffs, NJ: Prentice Hall, 1980).

34 E. A. Locke, K. N. Shaw, L. M. Saari, and G. P. Latham, "Goal Setting and Task Performance," *Psychological Bulletin*, January 1981, pp. 125–152; and A. J. Mento, R. P. Steel, and R. J. Karren, "A Meta-Analytic Study of the Effects of Goal Setting on Task Performance: 1966–1984," *Organizational Behavior and Human Decision Processes*, February 1987, pp. 52–83.

35   R. E. Wood, A. J. Mento, and E. A. Locke, "Task Complexity as a Moderator of Goal Effects: A Meta-Analysis," *Journal of Applied Psychology*, August 1987, pp. 416–425.

36   P. M. Wright, "Operationalization of Goal Difficulty as a Moderator of the Goal Difficulty-Performance Relationship," *Journal of Applied Psychology*, June 1990, pp. 227–234; E. A. Locke and G. P. Latham, "Building a Practically Useful Theory of Goal Setting and Task Motivation: A 35-Year Odyssey," *American Psychologist* 57, no. 9 (2002), pp. 705–717.

37   P. M. Wright, J. R. Hollenbeck, S. Wolf, and G. C. McMahan, "The Effects of Varying Goal Difficulty Operationalizations on Goal Setting Outcomes and Processes," *Organizational Behavior and Human Decision Processes*, January 1995, pp. 28–43.

38   K. L. Langeland, C. M. Johnson, and T. C. Mawhinney, "Improving Staff Performance in a Community Mental Health Setting: Job Analysis, Training, Goal Setting, Feedback, and Years of Data," *Journal of Organizational Behavior Management*, 1998, pp. 21–43.

39   E. A. Locke and G. P. Latham, *A Theory of Goal Setting and Task Performance* (Englewood Cliffs, NJ: Prentice Hall, 1990).

40   J. J. Donovan and D. J. Radosevich, "The Moderating Role of Goal Commitment on the Goal Difficulty-Performance Relationship: A Meta-Analytic Review and Critical Reanalysis," *Journal of Applied Psychology*, April 1998, pp. 308–315.

41   P. M. Wright, J. M. George, S. R. Farnsworth, and G. C. McMahan, "Productivity and Extra-Role Behavior: The Effects of Goals and Incentives on Spontaneous Helping," *Journal of Applied Psychology*, October 1992, pp. 672–681.

42   S. W. Gilliland and R. S. Landis, "Quality and Quantity Goals in a Complex Decision Task: Strategies and Outcomes," *Journal of Applied Psychology*, October 1992, pp. 672–681.

43   C. Mainemelis, "When the Muse Takes It All: A Model for the Experience of Timelessness in Organizations," *Academy of Management Review* 26, no. 4 (2001), pp. 548–565.

44   Y. Fried, S. Melamed, and A. Ben-David, "The Joint Effects of Noise, Job Complexity, and Gender on Employee Sickness Absence: An Exploratory Study Across 21 Organizations—The Cordes Study," *Journal of Occupational and Organizational Psychology* 75, 2002, pp. 131–144; and R. L. Kahn and P. Byosiere, "Stress in Organizations," in *Handbook of Industrial and Organizational Psychology*, vol. 3, ed. M. D. Dunnette and L. M. Hough (Palo Alto, CA: Consulting Psychologists Press, 1992), pp. 571–650.

45   M. Csikszentmihalyi, *Flow: The Psychology of Optimal Experience* (New York: Harper and Row, 1990); C. Mainemelis, "When the Muse Takes It All: A Model for the Experience of Timelessness in Organizations," *Academy of Management Review* 26, no. 4 (2001), pp. 548–565.

46   A. Bandura, *Self-Efficacy: The Exercise of Control* (New York: Freeman, 1997).

47   A. D. Stajkovic and F. Luthans, "Self-Efficacy and Work-Related Performance: A Meta-Analysis," *Psychological Bulletin*, September 1998, pp. 240–261; and A. Bandura, "Cultivate Self-Efficacy for Personal and Organizational Effectiveness," in *Handbook of Principles of Organizational Behavior*, ed. E. Locke (Malden, MA: Blackwell, 2004), pp. 120–136.

48   A. Bandura and D. Cervone, "Differential Engagement in Self-Reactive Influences in Cognitively-Based Motivation," *Organizational Behavior and Human Decision Processes*, August 1986, pp. 92–113.

49   A. Bandura, *Self-Efficacy: The Exercise of Control* (New York: Freeman, 1997).

50   C. L. Holladay and M. A. Quiñones, "Practice Variability and Transfer of Training: The Role of Self-Efficacy Generality," *Journal of Applied Psychology* 88, no. 6 (2003), pp. 1094–1103.

51   R. C. Rist, "Student Social Class and Teacher Expectations: The Self-Fulfilling Prophecy in Ghetto Education," *Harvard Educational Review* 70, no. 3 (2000), pp. 266–301.

52   D. Eden, "Self-Fulfilling Prophecies in Organizations," in *Organizational Behavior: The State of the Science*, 2nd ed., ed. J. Greenberg (Mahwah, NJ: Erlbaum, 2003), pp. 91–122.

53   D. Eden, "Self-Fulfilling Prophecies in Organizations," in *Organizational Behavior: The State of the Science*, 2nd ed., ed. J. Greenberg (Mahwah, NJ: Erlbaum, 2003), pp. 91–122.

54   T. A. Judge, C. L. Jackson, J. C. Shaw, B. Scott, and B. L. Rich, "Self-Efficacy and Work-Related Performance: The Integral Role of Individual Differences," *Journal of Applied Psychology* 92, no. 1 (2007), pp. 107–127.

55   T. A. Judge, C. L. Jackson, J. C. Shaw, B. Scott, and B. L. Rich, "Self-Efficacy and Work-Related Performance: The Integral Role of Individual Differences," *Journal of Applied Psychology* 92, no. 1 (2007), pp. 107–127.

56   Based on L. Little, "Lions Lock up Clermont," *Times-Colonist*, September 12, 2007, p. D9; M. Beamish, "Simon's Work Day: Hair Cuts, Extensions," *Vancouver Sun*, May 26, 2006, p. G5; "B.C. Lions Sign Geroy Simon to Contract Extension through 2009," *Daily Townsman*, May 26, 2006, p. 7; "B.C. Lions Face 'Unbearable' Contract Pressures: Wally Buono's Challenge," *National Post*, April 26, 2006, p. S9; and S. Petersen, "Esks Re-Sign Tucker for Big 'Chunk of Change,'" *Edmonton Journal*, February 17, 2006, p. C8.

57   J. S. Adams, "Inequity in Social Exchanges," in *Advances in Experimental Social Psychology*, ed. L. Berkowitz (New York: Academic Press, 1965), pp. 267–300.

58   P. S. Goodman, "An Examination of Referents Used in the Evaluation of Pay," *Organizational Behavior and Human Performance*, October 1974, pp. 170–195; S. Ronen, "Equity Perception in Multiple Comparisons: A Field Study," *Human Relations*, April 1986, pp. 333–346; R. W. Scholl, E. A. Cooper, and J. F. McKenna, "Referent Selection in Determining Equity Perception: Differential Effects on Behavioral and Attitudinal Outcomes," *Personnel Psychology*, Spring 1987, pp. 113–127; T. P. Summers and A. S. DeNisi, "In Search of Adams' Other: Reexamination of Referents Used in the Evaluation of Pay," *Human Relations*, June 1990, pp. 497–511; S. Werner and N. P. Mero, "Fair or Foul? The Effects of External, Internal, and Employee Equity on Changes in Performance of Major League Baseball Players," *Human Relations*, October 1999, pp. 1291–1312; and R. W. Griffeth and S. Gaertner, "A Role for Equity Theory in the Turnover Process: An Empirical Test," *Journal of Applied Social Psychology*, May 2001, pp. 1017–1037.

59 C. T. Kulik and M. L. Ambrose, "Personal and Situational Determinants of Referent Choice," *Academy of Management Review*, April 1992, pp. 212–237.

60 "Women in the Workforce: Still a Long Way from Equality," *Canadian Labour Congress*, May 5, 2008, http://canadianlabour.ca/en/women-workforce-still-a-long-way-equality.

61 See, for example, E. Walster, G. W. Walster, and W. G. Scott, *Equity: Theory and Research* (Boston: Allyn and Bacon, 1978); and J. Greenberg, "Cognitive Reevaluation of Outcomes in Response to Underpayment Inequity," *Academy of Management Journal*, March 1989, pp. 174–184.

62 Based on V. Galt, "Low Pay Stresses Staff at Non-Profits: Study," *Globe and Mail*, January 10, 2003, p. B2.

63 P. S. Goodman and A. Friedman, "An Examination of Adams' Theory of Inequity," *Administrative Science Quarterly*, September 1971, pp. 271–288; R. P. Vecchio, "An Individual-Differences Interpretation of the Conflicting Predictions Generated by Equity Theory and Expectancy Theory," *Journal of Applied Psychology*, August 1981, pp. 470–481; J. Greenberg, "Approaching Equity and Avoiding Inequity in Groups and Organizations," in *Equity and Justice in Social Behavior*, ed. J. Greenberg and R. L. Cohen (New York: Academic Press, 1982), pp. 389–435; E. W. Miles, J. D. Hatfield, and R. C. Huseman, "The Equity Sensitive Construct: Potential Implications for Worker Performance," *Journal of Management*, December 1989, pp. 581–588; R. T. Mowday, "Equity Theory Predictions of Behavior in Organizations," in *Motivation and Work Behavior*, 5th ed., ed. R. Steers and L. W. Porter (New York: McGraw-Hill, 1991), pp. 111–131; and R. T. Mowday and K. A. Colwell, "Employee Reactions to Unfair Outcomes in the Workplace: The Contributions of Adams' Equity Theory to Understanding Work Motivation," in *Motivation and Work Behavior*, 7th ed., ed. L. W. Porter, G. A. Bigley, and R. M. Steers (Burr Ridge, IL: Irwin/McGraw-Hill, 2003), pp. 65–82.

64 See, for example, K. S. Sauley and A. G. Bedeian, "Equity Sensitivity: Construction of a Measure and Examination of Its Psychometric Properties," *Journal of Management* 26, no. 5 (2000), pp. 885–910; and M. N. Bing and S. M. Burroughs, "The Predictive and Interactive Effects of Equity Sensitivity in Teamwork-Oriented Organizations," *Journal of Organizational Behavior*, May 2001, pp. 271–290.

65 J. Greenberg and S. Ornstein, "High Status Job Title as Compensation for Underpayment: A Test of Equity Theory," *Journal of Applied Psychology*, May 1983, pp. 285–297; and J. Greenberg, "Equity and Workplace Status: A Field Experiment," *Journal of Applied Psychology*, November 1988, pp. 606–613.

66 P. S. Goodman, "Social Comparison Process in Organizations," in *New Directions in Organizational Behavior*, ed. B. M. Staw and G. R. Salancik (Chicago: St. Clair, 1977), pp. 97–132; and J. Greenberg, "A Taxonomy of Organizational Justice Theories," *Academy of Management Review*, January 1987, pp. 9–22.

67 See, for instance, J. Greenberg, *The Quest for Justice on the Job* (Thousand Oaks, CA: Sage, 1996); R. Cropanzano and J. Greenberg, "Progress in Organizational Justice: Tunneling through the Maze," in *International Review of Industrial and Organizational Psychology*, vol. 12, ed. C. L. Cooper and I. T. Robertson (New York: Wiley, 1997); J. A. Colquitt, D. E. Conlon, M. J. Wesson, C. O. L. H. Porter, and K. Y. Ng, "Justice at the Millennium: A Meta-Analytic Review of the 25 Years of Organizational Justice Research," *Journal of Applied Psychology*, June 2001, pp. 425–445; T. Simons and Q. Roberson, "Why Managers Should Care About Fairness: The Effects of Aggregate Justice Perceptions on Organizational Outcomes," *Journal of Applied Psychology*, June 2003, pp. 432–443; and G. P. Latham and C. C. Pinder, "Work Motivation Theory and Research at the Dawn of the Twenty-First Century," *Annual Review of Psychology* 56, 2005, pp. 485–516.

68 D. P. Skarlicki and R. Folger, "Retaliation in the Workplace: The Roles of Distributive, Procedural, and Interactional Justice," *Journal of Applied Psychology* 82, no. 3 (1997), pp. 434–443.

69 R. Cropanzano, C. A. Prehar, and P. Y. Chen, "Using Social Exchange Theory to Distinguish Procedural from Interactional Justice," *Group & Organization Management* 27, no. 3 (2002), pp. 324–351; and S. G. Roch and L. R. Shanock, "Organizational Justice in an Exchange Framework: Clarifying Organizational Justice Dimensions," *Journal of Management*, April 2006, pp. 299–322.

70 J. A. Colquitt, D. E. Conlon, M. J. Wesson, C. O. L. H. Porter, and K. Y. Ng, "Justice at the Millennium: A Meta-Analytic Review of the 25 Years of Organizational Justice Research," *Journal of Applied Psychology*, June 2001, pp. 425–445.

71 D. P. Skarlicki and R. Folger, "Retaliation in the Workplace: The Roles of Distributive, Procedural and Interactional Justice," *Journal of Applied Psychology* 82, no. 3 (1997), pp. 434–443.

72 R. de Charms, *Personal Causation: The Internal Affective Determinants of Behavior* (New York: Academic Press, 1968).

73 E. L. Deci, *Intrinsic Motivation* (New York: Plenum, 1975); R. D. Pritchard, K. M. Campbell, and D. J. Campbell, "Effects of Extrinsic Financial Rewards on Intrinsic Motivation," *Journal of Applied Psychology*, February 1977, pp. 9–15; E. L. Deci, G. Betly, J. Kahle, L. Abrams, and J. Porac, "When Trying to Win: Competition and Intrinsic Motivation," *Personality and Social Psychology Bulletin*, March 1981, pp. 79–83; and P. C. Jordan, "Effects of an Extrinsic Reward on Intrinsic Motivation: A Field Experiment," *Academy of Management Journal*, June 1986, pp. 405–412. See also J. M. Schrof, "Tarnished Trophies," *U.S. News & World Report*, October 25, 1993, pp. 52–59.

74 A. Kohn, *Punished by Rewards* (Boston: Houghton Mifflin, 1993).

75 W. E. Scott, "The Effects of Extrinsic Rewards on 'Intrinsic Motivation': A Critique," *Organizational Behavior and Human Performance*, February 1976, pp. 117–119; B. J. Calder and B. M. Staw, "Interaction of Intrinsic and Extrinsic Motivation: Some Methodological Notes," *Journal of Personality and Social Psychology*, January 1975, pp. 76–80; and K. B. Boal and L. L. Cummings, "Cognitive Evaluation Theory: An Experimental Test of Processes and Outcomes," *Organizational Behavior and Human Performance*, December 1981, pp. 289–310.

76 G. R. Salancik, "Interaction Effects of Performance and Money on Self-Perception of Intrinsic Motivation," *Organizational Behavior and Human Performance*, June 1975, pp. 339–351; and F. Luthans, M. Martinko, and T. Kess, "An Analysis of the Impact of Contingency Monetary Rewards on Intrinsic Motivation," *Proceedings of the Nineteenth Annual Midwest Academy of Management*, St. Louis, 1976, pp. 209–221.

77 E. L. Deci, R. Koestner, and R. M. Ryan, "A Meta-Analytic Review of Experiments Examining the Effects of Extrinsic Rewards on

Intrinsic Motivation," *Psychological Bulletin* 125, no. 6 (1999), pp. 627–668.

78   K. M. Sheldon, A. J. Elliot, and R. M. Ryan, "Self-Concordance and Subjective Well-being in Four Cultures," *Journal of Cross-Cultural Psychology* 35, no. 2 (2004), pp. 209–223.

79   J. E. Bono and T. A. Judge, "Self-Concordance at Work: Toward Understanding the Motivational Effects of Transformational Leaders," *Academy of Management Journal* 46, no. 5 (2003), pp. 554–571.

80   B. J. Calder and B. M. Staw, "Self-Perception of Intrinsic and Extrinsic Motivation," *Journal of Personality and Social Psychology*, April 1975, pp. 599–605; and J. Pfeffer, *The Human Equation: Building Profits by Putting People First* (Boston: Harvard Business School Press, 1998), p. 217.

81   B. M. Staw, "Motivation in Organizations: Toward Synthesis and Redirection," in *New Directions in Organizational Behavior*, ed. B. M. Staw and G. R. Salancik (Chicago: St. Clair, 1977), p. 76.

82   K. W. Thomas, E. Jansen, and W. G. Tymon Jr., "Navigating in the Realm of Theory: An Empowering View of Construct Development," in *Research in Organizational Change and Development*, vol. 10, ed. W. A. Pasmore and R. W. Woodman (Greenwich, CT: JAI Press, 1997), pp. 1–30.

83   Based on Lowell Ullrich. "Gassers a Reminder That Penalties Hurt the Whole Team," *Province* (Vancouver), September 6, 2005, p. A48.

84   R. Kreitner and A. Kinicki, *Organizational Behavior*, 6th ed. (New York: McGraw-Hill, 2004), p. 345. See also J. W. Donahoe, "The Unconventional Wisdom of B F Skinner: The Analysis-Interpretation Distinction," *Journal of the Experimental Analysis of Behavior*, September 1993, pp. 453–456.

85   B. F. Skinner, *Contingencies of Reinforcement* (East Norwalk, CT: Appleton-Century-Crofts, 1971).

86   F. Luthans and R. Kreitner, *Organizational Behavior Modification and Beyond*, 2nd ed. (Glenview, IL: Scott, Foresman, 1985); and A. D. Stajkovic and F. Luthans, "A Meta-Analysis of the Effects of Organizational Behavior Modification on Task Performance, 1975–95," *Academy of Management Journal*, October 1997, pp. 1122–1149.

87   This section based on C. Michaelson, "Meaningful Motivation for Work Motivation Theory," *Academy of Management Review* 30, no. 2 (2005), pp. 235–238; and R. M. Steers, R. T. Mowday, and D. L. Shapiro, "Response to Meaningful Motivation for Work Motivation Theory," *Academy of Management Review* 30, no. 2 (2005), p. 238.

88   C. Michaelson, "Meaningful Motivation for Work Motivation Theory," *Academy of Management Review* 30, no. 2 (2005), p. 237.

89   J. Zaslow, "Losing Well: How a Successful Man Deal with a Rare and Public Failure," *Wall Street Journal*, March 2, 2006, p. D1.

90   E. Biyalogorsky, W. Boulding, and R. Staelin, "Stuck in the Past: Why Managers Persist with New Product Failures," *Journal of Marketing*, April 2006, pp. 108–121.

91   Based on R. Steers and D. Braunstein, "A Behaviorally Based Measure of Manifest Needs in Work Settings," *Journal of Vocational Behavior*, October 1976, p. 254; and R. N. Lussier, *Human Relations in Organizations: A Skill Building Approach* (Homewood, IL: Richard D. Irwin, 1990), p. 120.

92   Adapted from an exercise developed by Larry Michaelson of the University of Oklahoma. With permission.

93   Based on C. Benedict, "The Bullying Boss," *New York Times*, June 22, 2004, p. F1.

94   "Quebecor Plays Hardball with Defiant Union: Vidéotron 'Ready to Listen': Aims to Sell Cable Installation Operations," *Financial Post (National Post)*, March 5, 2002, p. FP6; and S. Silcoff, "Quebecor and Union in Showdown over Costs," *Financial Post (National Post)*, February 28, 2002, p. FP3.

95   Based on S. P. Robbins and D. A. DeCenzo, *Fundamentals of Management*, 4th ed. (Upper Saddle River, NJ: Prentice Hall, 2004), p. 85.

Chapter 5

1   Opening vignette based on S. Baille-Ruder, "Sweet Devotion: How Chocolatier R.C. Purdy Developed the Perfect Recipe for a Superstar Workforce," *PROFIT*, December 2004, pp. 44–51; L. Pratt, "Management Tip from the Top," *National Post*, July 26, 2004. p. FP9; B. Constantineau, "Staff Discounts Can Make a Good Employer Great," *Vancouver Sun*, July 16, 2005, p. A1; Hewitt Associates, "Best Employers in Canada—2008 List," http://was7.hewitt.com/bestemployers/canada/the_list_2008.htm; and http://www.purdys.com/media_releases/Canada50BestEmployers2008.htm.

2   D. W. Krueger, "Money, Success, and Success Phobia," in *The Last Taboo: Money as a Symbol and Reality in Psychotherapy and Psychoanalysis*, ed. D. W. Krueger (New York: Brunner/Mazel, 1986), pp. 3–16.

3   T. R. Mitchell and A. E. Mickel, "The Meaning of Money: An Individual-Difference Perspective," *Academy of Management*, July 1999, pp. 568–578.

4   Information in this paragraph is based on D. Grigg and J. Newman, "Labour Researchers Define Job Satisfaction," *Vancouver Sun*, February 16, 2002, p. E2.

5   This paragraph is based on T. R. Mitchell and A. E. Mickel, "The Meaning of Money: An Individual-Difference Perspective," *Academy of Management*, July 1999, pp. 568–578. The reader may want to refer to the myriad of references cited in the article.

6   Based on S. Baille-Ruder, "Sweet Devotion: How Chocolatier R.C. Purdy Developed the Perfect Recipe for a Superstar Workforce," *PROFIT*, December 2004, pp. 44–51.

7   E. White, "Opportunity Knocks, and It Pays a Lot Better," *Wall Street Journal*, November 13, 2006, p. B3.

8   Based on J. R. Schuster and P. K. Zingheim, "The New Variable Pay: Key Design Issues," *Compensation & Benefits Review*, March–April 1993, p. 28; K. S. Abosch, "Variable Pay: Do We Have the Basics in Place?" *Compensation & Benefits Review*, July–August 1998, pp. 12–22; and K. M. Kuhn and M. D. Yockey, "Variable Pay as a Risky Choice: Determinants of the Relative Attractiveness of Incentive Plans," *Organizational Behavior and Human Decision Processes*, March 2003, pp. 323–341.

9   J. Ratner, "Dofasco Boss Took Home Biggest Pay," *National Post*, February 1, 2006, p. WK3.

10   Peter Brieger, "Variable Pay Packages Gain Favour: Signing Bonuses, Profit Sharing Taking Place of Salary Hikes," *Financial Post (National Post)*, September 13, 2002, p. FP5; and Hewitt Associates, "Calgary Salary Increases Reach New Heights, According to Hewitt," news release, September 6, 2007, http://www.hewittassociates.com/Intl/NA/en-CA/AboutHewitt/Newsroom/PressReleaseDetail.aspx?cid=4428 (accessed August 19, 2008).

11   C. Hallamore, "Merit Pay in Unionized Environments," *The Conference Board of Canada*, December 2005.

12   L. Wiener, "Paycheck Plus," *U.S. News & World Report*, February 24–March 3, 2003, p. 58.

13   Cited in "Pay Programs: Few Employees See the Pay-for-Performance Connection," *Compensation & Benefits Report*, June 2003, p. 1.

14   O. Bertin, "Is There Any Merit in Giving Merit Pay?" *Globe and Mail*, January 31, 2003, pp. C1, C7.

15   S. Baille-Ruder, "Sweet Devotion: How Chocolatier R.C. Purdy Developed the Perfect Recipe for a Superstar Workforce," *PROFIT*, December 2004, pp. 44–51.

16   M. Fein, "Work Measurement and Wage Incentives," *Industrial Engineering*, September 1973, pp. 49–51. For updated reviews of the effect of pay on performance, see G. D. Jenkins, Jr., N. Gupta, A. Mitra, and J. D. Shaw, "Are Financial Incentives Related to Performance? A Meta-Analytic Review of Empirical Research," *Journal of Applied Psychology*, October 1998, pp. 777–787; and S. L. Rynes, B. Gerhart, and L. Parks, "*Personnel Psychology*: Performance Evaluation and Pay for Performance," *Annual Review of Psychology* 56, no. 1 (2005), pp. 571–600.

17   E. Arita, "Teething Troubles Aside, Merit-Based Pay Catching On," *Japan Times*, April 23, 2004, http://search.japantimes.co.jp/cgi-bin/nb20040423a3.html.

18   E. White, "The Best vs. the Rest," *Wall Street Journal*, January 30, 2006, pp. B1, B3.

19   "Bonus Pay in Canada," *Manpower Argus*, September 1996, p. 5; E. White, "Employers Increasingly Favor Bonuses to Raises," *Wall Street Journal*, August 28, 2006, p. B3; and J. S. Lublin, "Boards Tie CEO Pay More Tightly to Performance," *Wall Street Journal*, February 21, 2006, pp. A1, A14..

20   Based on R. Curran, "Did Bonuses Help to Fuel Meltdown?" *Post.IE online*, September 21, 2008, http://www.sbpost.ie/post/pages/p/story.aspx-qqqt=NEWS???qqqm=nav-qqqid=36092-qqqx=1.asp; and V. Bajaj, A. R. Sorkin and M. J. de la Merced, "Goldman, Morgan to Become Bank Holding Companies," *New York Times*, September 21, 2008, http://dealbook.blogs.nytimes.com/2008/09/21/goldman-morgan-to-become-bank-holding-companies/index.html?hp.

21   G. E. Ledford Jr., "Paying for the Skills, Knowledge, and Competencies of Knowledge Workers," *Compensation & Benefits Review*, July–August 1995, pp. 55–62; B. Murray and B. Gerhart, "An Empirical Analysis of a Skill-Based Pay Program and Plant Performance Outcomes," *Academy of Management Journal*, February 1998, pp. 68–78; J. R. Thompson and C. W. LeHew, "Skill-Based Pay as an Organizational Innovation," *Review of Public Personnel Administration*, Winter 2000, pp. 20–40; and J. D. Shaw, N. Gupta, A. Mitra, and G. E. Ledford Jr., "Success and Survival of Skill-Based Pay Plans," *Journal of Management*, February 2005, pp. 28–49.

22   Based on D. Naylor, "In Pursuit of Level Playing Fields," *Globe and Mail*, March 9, 2002, p. S1; and T. Denison, "Formula for Success," August 13, 2004, http://www.collegecolours.com/columns/004.html.

23   See, for instance, S. C. Hanlon, D. G. Meyer, and R. R. Taylor, "Consequences of Gainsharing," *Group & Organization Management*, March 1994, pp. 87–111; J. G. Belcher Jr., "Gainsharing and Variable Pay: The State of the Art," *Compensation & Benefits Review*, May–June 1994, pp. 50–60; and T. M. Welbourne and L. R. Gomez Mejia, "Gainsharing: A Critical Review and a Future Research Agenda," *Journal of Management* 21, no. 3 (1995), pp. 559–609.

24   D. Beck, "Implementing a Gainsharing Plan: What Companies Need to Know," *Compensation & Benefits Review*, January–February 1992, p. 23.

25   W. Imberman, "Gainsharing Is a Concept Canadians Should Embrace," *Business in Vancouver*, March 20–26, 2001, p. 19.

26   T. M. Welbourne and L. R. Gomez-Mejia, "Gainsharing: A Critical Review and a Future Research Agenda," *Journal of Management* 21, no. 3 (1995), pp. 559–609.

27   M. Byfield, "IKEA's Boss Gives Away the Store for a Day," *Report Newsmagazine*, October 25, 1999, p. 47.

28   S. Baille-Ruder, "Sweet Devotion: How Chocolatier R.C. Purdy Developed the Perfect Recipe for a Superstar Workforce," *PROFIT*, December 2004, pp. 44–51.

29   M. Gooderham, "A Piece of the Pie as Motivational Tool," *Globe and Mail*, November 20, 2007, p. B8.

30   R. J. Long, "Patterns of Workplace Innovations in Canada," *Relations Industrielles* 44, no. 4 (1989), pp. 805–826; R. J. Long, "Motives for Profit Sharing: A Study of Canadian Chief Executive Officers," *Relations Industrielles* 52, no. 4 (1997), pp. 712–723; T. H. Wagar and R. J. Long, "Profit Sharing in Canada: Incidences and Predictors," *Proceedings of the Administrative Sciences Association of Canada* (Human Resources Division), 1995, pp. 97–105.

31   See K. M. Young, ed., *The Expanding Role of ESOPs in Public Companies* (New York: Quorum, 1990); J. L. Pierce and C. A. Furo, "Employee Ownership: Implications for Management," *Organizational Dynamics*, Winter 1990, pp. 32–43; J. Blasi and D. L. Druse, *The New Owners: The Mass Emergence of Employee Ownership in Public Companies and What It Means to American Business* (Champaign, IL: Harper Business, 1991); F. T. Adams and G. B. Hansen, *Putting Democracy to Work: A Practical Guide for Starting and Managing Worker-Owned Businesses* (San Francisco: Berrett-Koehler, 1993); and A. A. Buchko, "The Effects of Employee Ownership on Employee Attitudes: An Integrated Causal Model and Path Analysis," *Journal of Management Studies*, July 1993, pp. 633–656.

32   A. Toulin, "Lowly Staff Join Bosses in Receiving Stock Options," *National Post*, March 1, 2001, pp. C1, C12.

33 K. Vermond, "Worker as Shareholder: Is It Worth It?" *Globe and Mail*, March 29, 2008, p. B21.

34 A. A. Buchko, "The Effects of Employee Ownership on Employee Attitudes: An Integrated Causal Model and Path Analysis," *Journal of Management Studies*, July 1993, pp. 633–656.

35 K. Vermond, "Worker as Shareholder: Is It Worth It?" *Globe and Mail*, March 29, 2008, p. B21.

36 J. L. Pierce and C. A. Furo, "Employee Ownership: Implications for Management," *Organizational Dynamics*, Winter 1990, pp. 32–43; and S. Kaufman, "ESOPs' Appeal on the Increase," *Nation's Business*, June 1997, p. 43.

37 See data in D. Stamps, "A Piece of the Action," *Training*, March 1996, p. 66.

38 C. G. Hanson and W. D. Bell, *Profit Sharing and Profitability: How Profit Sharing Promotes Business Success* (London: Kogan Page, 1987); M. Magnan and S. St-Onge, "Profit Sharing and Firm Performance: A Comparative and Longitudinal Analysis" (paper presented at the 58th annual meeting of the Academy of Management, San Diego, CA, August 1998); and D. D'Art and T. Turner, "Profit Sharing, Firm Performance, and Union Influence in Selected European Countries," *Personnel Review* 33, no. 3 (2004), pp. 335–350.

39 T. M. Welbourne and L. R. Gomez-Mejia, "Gainsharing: A Critical Review and a Future Research Agenda," *Journal of Management* 21, no. 3 (1995), pp. 559–609.

40 C. B. Cadsby, F. Song, and F. Tapon, "Sorting and Incentive Effects of Pay for Performance: An Experimental Investigation," *Academy of Management Journal* 50, no. 2 (2007), pp. 387–405.

41 J. Pfeffer and N. Langton, "The Effects of Wage Dispersion on Satisfaction, Productivity, and Working Collaboratively: Evidence from College and University Faculty," *Administrative Science Quarterly* 38, no. 3 (1983), pp. 382–407.

42 "Risk and Reward: More Canadian Companies Are Experimenting with Variable Pay," *Maclean's*, January 8, 1996, pp. 26–27.

43 "Hope for Higher Pay: The Squeeze on Incomes Is Gradually Easing Up," *Maclean's*, November 25, 1996, pp. 100–101.

44 "Risk and Reward: More Canadian Companies Are Experimenting with Variable Pay," *Maclean's*, January 8, 1996, pp. 26–27.

45 Based on V. Galt, "No More Freebies for Hydro Staff: Arbitrator," *Globe and Mail*, February 16, 2002, p. B3.

46 B. E. Wright, "Work Motivation in the Public Sector," *Academy of Management Proceedings*, 2001, pp. PNP: D1–5.

47 B. E. Wright, "Work Motivation in the Public Sector," *Academy of Management Proceedings*, 2001, pp. PNP: D1–5.

48 S. Greenhouse, "Suits Say Wal-Mart Forces Workers to Toil Off the Clock," *New York Times*, June 25, 2002, http://www.nytimes.com/2002/06/25/national/25WALM.html?pagewanted=1 (accessed June 25, 2002).

49 See, for instance, M. W. Barringer and G. T. Milkovich, "A Theoretical Exploration of the Adoption and Design of Flexible Benefit Plans: A Case of Human Resource Innovation," *Academy of Management Review*, April 1998, pp. 305–324; D. Brown, "Everybody Loves Flex," *Canadian HR Reporter*, November 18, 2002, p. 1; J. Taggart, "Putting Flex Benefits Through Their Paces," *Canadian HR Reporter*, December 2, 2002, p. G3; and N. D. Cole and D. H. Flint, "Perceptions of Distributive and Procedural Justice in Employee Benefits: Flexible versus Traditional Benefit Plans," *Journal of Managerial Psychology* 19, no. 1 (2004), pp. 19–40.

50 D. A. DeCenzo and S. P. Robbins, *Human Resource Management*, 7th ed. (New York: Wiley, 2002), pp. 346–348.

51 Our definition of a formal recognition system is based on S. E. Markham, K. D. Scott, and G. H. McKee, "Recognizing Good Attendance: A Longitudinal, Quasi-Experimental Field Study," *Personnel Psychology*, Autumn 2002, p. 641.

52 D. Drickhamer, "Best Plant Winners: Nichols Foods Ltd.," *IndustryWeek*, October 1, 2001, pp. 17–19.

53 M. Littman, "Best Bosses Tell All," *Working Woman*, October 2000, p. 54.

54 Cited in S. Caudron, "The Top 20 Ways to Motivate Employees," *IndustryWeek*, April 3, 1995, pp. 15–16. See also B. Nelson, "Try Praise," *Inc.*, September 1996, p. 115.

55 S. Glasscock and K. Gram, *Workplace Recognition: Step-by-Step Examples of a Positive Reinforcement Strategy* (London: Brasseys, 1999).

56 Hewitt Associates, "Employers Willing to Pay for High Performance," news release, September 8, 2004, http://was4.hewitt.com/hewitt/resource/newsroom/pressrel/2004/09-08-04eng.htm (accessed October 9, 2004).

57 "Praise Beats Raise as Best Motivator, Survey Shows," *Vancouver Sun*, September 10, 1994.

58 J. A. Ross, "Japan: Does Money Motivate?" *Harvard Business Review*, September–October 1997. See also R. Bruce Money and John L. Graham, "Salesperson Performance, Pay, and Job Satisfaction: Tests of a Model Using Data Collected in the U.S. and Japan" (working paper, University of South Carolina, 1997).

59 Based on D. H. B. Welsh, F. Luthans, and S. M. Sommer, "Managing Russian Factory Workers: The Impact of U.S.-Based Behavioral and Participative Techniques," *Academy of Management Journal* 36, no. 1 (1993), pp. 58–79; S. K. Saha, "Managing Human Resources: China vs. the West," *Canadian Journal of Administrative Sciences* 10, no. 2 (1998), pp. 167–177; Chao C. Chen, "New Trends in Reward Allocation Preference: A Sino/U.S. Comparison," *Academy of Management Journal* 38, no. 2 (1995), pp. 408–492; N. Chowdhury, "Dell Cracks China," *Fortune*, June 21, 1999, pp. 120–124; and M. E. de Forest, "Thinking of a Plant in Mexico?" *Academy of Management Executive* 8, no. 1 (1994), pp. 33–40.

60 R. S. Schuler and N. Rogovsky, "Understanding Compensation Practice Variations Across Firms: The Impact of National Culture," *Journal of International Business Studies* 29, no. 1 (First Quarter 1998), pp. 159–177.

61 N. J. Adler, *International Dimensions of Organizational Behavior*, 4th ed. (Cincinnati, OH: South Western College, 2002), p. 174.

62 A. Kohn, *Punished by Rewards* (Boston: Houghton Mifflin, 1993).

63   W. G. Ouchi, *Theory Z* (New York: Avon Books, 1982); "Bosses' Pay," *Economist*, February 1, 1992, pp. 19–22; W. Edwards Deming, *Out of the Crisis* (Cambridge, MA: MIT Center for Advanced Engineering Study, 1986).

64   J. Pfeffer, *The Human Equation: Building Profits by Putting People First* (Boston: Harvard Business School Press, 1998).

65   G. Hofstede, "Motivation, Leadership, and Organization: Do American Theories Apply Abroad?" *Organizational Dynamics*, Summer 1980, p. 55.

66   J. K. Giacobbe-Miller, D. J. Miller, and V. I. Victorov, "A Comparison of Russian and U.S. Pay Allocation Decisions, Distributive Justice Judgments, and Productivity Under Different Payment Conditions," *Personnel Psychology*, Spring 1998, pp. 137–163.

67   S. L. Mueller and L. D. Clarke, "Political-Economic Context and Sensitivity to Equity: Differences Between the United States and the Transition Economies of Central and Eastern Europe," *Academy of Management Journal*, June 1998, pp. 319–329.

68   J. S. Lublin, "It's Shape-up Time for Performance Reviews," *Wall Street Journal*, October 3, 1994, p. B1.

69   Much of this section is based on H. H. Meyer, "A Solution to the Performance Appraisal Feedback Enigma," *Academy of Management Executive*, February 1991, pp. 68–76.

70   T. D. Schelhardt, "It's Time to Evaluate Your Work, and All Involved Are Groaning," *Wall Street Journal*, November 19, 1996, p. A1.

71   R. J. Burke, "Why Performance Appraisal Systems Fail," *Personnel Administration*, June 1972, pp. 32–40.

72   B. D. Cawley, L. M. Keeping, and P. E. Levy, "Participation in the Performance Appraisal Process and Employee Reactions: A Meta-Analytic Review of Field Investigations," *Journal of Applied Psychology*, August 1998, pp. 615–633; and P. E. Levy, and J. R. Williams, "The Social Context of Performance Appraisal: A Review and Framework for the Future," *Journal of Management* 30, no. 6 (2004), pp. 881–905.

73   List directly quoted from R. Kreitner and A. Kinicki, *Organizational Behavior*, 6th ed. (New York: McGraw-Hill/Irwin, 2004), p. 335 (emphasis added).

74   S. Kerr, "On the Folly of Rewarding A, While Hoping for B," *Academy of Management Executive* 9, no. 1 (1995), pp. 7–14.

75   "More on the Folly," *Academy of Management Executive* 9, no. 1 (1995), pp. 15–16.

76   Based on S. Baille-Ruder, "Sweet Devotion: How Chocolatier R.C. Purdy Developed the Perfect Recipe for a Superstar Workforce," *PROFIT*, December 2004, pp. 44–51; and M. Toneguzzi, "Desperate Employers Piling on the Perks," *Calgary Herald*, September 20, 2006, p. D1.

77   A. Kohn, *Punished by Rewards* (Boston: Houghton Mifflin, 1999), p. 181.

78   A. Kohn, *Punished by Rewards* (Boston: Houghton Mifflin, 1993), p. 181.

79   A. Kohn, *Punished by Rewards* (Boston: Houghton Mifflin, 1993), p. 186; see also Peter R. Scholtes, "An Elaboration of Deming's Teachings on Performance Appraisal," in *Performance Appraisal: Perspectives on a Quality Management Approach*, ed. Gary N. McLean, Susan R. Damme, and Richard A. Swanson (Alexandria, VA: American Society for Training and Development, 1990); H. H. Meyer, E. Kay, and J. R. P. French Jr., "Split Roles in Performance Appraisal," *Harvard Business Review*, 1965, excerpts reprinted in "HBR Retrospect," *Harvard Business Review*, January–February 1989, p. 26; W.-U. Meyer, M. Bachmann, U. Biermann, M. Hempelmann, F.-O. Ploeger, and H. Spiller, "The Informational Value of Evaluative Behavior: Influences of Praise and Blame on Perceptions of Ability," *Journal of Educational Psychology* 71, 1979, pp. 259–268; and A. Halachmi and M. Holzer, "Merit Pay, Performance Targeting, and Productivity," *Review of Public Personnel Administration* 7, 1987, pp. 80–91.

80   A. S. Blinder, "Introduction," in *Paying for Productivity: A Look at the Evidence*, ed. A. S. Blinder (Washington, DC: Brookings Institution, 1990).

81   A. Kohn, *Punished by Rewards* (Boston: Houghton Mifflin, 1999), p. 187.

82   D. Tjosvold, *Working Together to Get Things Done: Managing for Organizational Productivity* (Lexington, MA: Lexington Books, 1986); P. R. Scholtes, *The Team Handbook: How to Use Teams to Improve Quality* (Madison, WI: Joiner Associates, 1988); A. Kohn, *No Contest: The Case Against Competition*, rev. ed. (Boston: Houghton Mifflin, 1992).

83   E. L. Deci, "Applications of Research on the Effects of Rewards," in *The Hidden Costs of Rewards: New Perspectives on the Psychology of Human Motivation*, ed. M. R. Lepper and D. Green (Hillsdale, NJ: Erlbaum, 1978).

84   S. E. Perry, *San Francisco Scavengers: Dirty Work and the Pride of Ownership* (Berkeley: University of California Press, 1978).

85   A. Kohn, *Punished by Rewards* (Boston: Houghton Mifflin, 1999), p. 192.

86   T. H. Naylor, "Redefining Corporate Motivation, Swedish Style," *Christian Century*, May 30–June 6, 1990, pp. 566–570; R. A. Karasek, T. Thorell, J. E. Schwartz, P. L. Schnall, C. F. Pieper, and J. L. Michela, "Job Characteristics in Relation to the Prevalence of Myocardial Infarction in the US Health Examination Survey (HES) and the Health and Nutrition Examination Survey (HANES)," *American Journal of Public Health* 78, 1988, pp. 910–916; and D. P. Levin, "Toyota Plant in Kentucky Is Font of Ideas for the U.S.," *New York Times*, May 5, 1992, pp. A1, D8.

87   M. Bosquet, "The Prison Factory," reprinted from *Le Nouvel Observateur* in *Working Papers for a New Society*, Spring 1973, pp. 20–27; J. Holusha, "Grace Pastiak's 'Web of Inclusion,'" *New York Times*, May 5, 1991, pp. F1, F6; J. Simmons and W. Mares, *Working Together: Employee Participation in Action* (New York: New York University Press, 1985); D. I. Levine and L. D'Andrea Tyson, "Participation, Productivity, and the Firm's Environment," in *Paying for Productivity: A Look at the Evidence*, ed. A. S. Blinder (Washington, DC: Brookings Institution, 1990); and W. F. Whyte, "Worker Participation: International and Historical Perspectives," *Journal of Applied Behavioral Science* 19, 1983, pp. 395–407.

88   Based on S. Baille-Ruder, "Sweet Devotion: How Chocolatier R.C. Purdy Developed the Perfect Recipe for a Superstar Workforce," *PROFIT*, December 2004, pp. 44–51.

89   J. E. Rigdon, "Using Lateral Moves to Spur Employees," *Wall Street Journal*, May 26, 1992, p. B1.

90   S. Ross, "New Ideas Take 'Grunt' from Assembly Lines: Worker Participation Eliminates All-Too-Common Waste of 'Human Ingenuity,'" *Vancouver Sun*, September 1, 2001, p. E1.

91   N. Leckie, A. Léonard, J. Turcotte, and D. Wallace, *Employer and Employee Perspectives on Human Resource Practices*, 71–584–MIE no. 1 (Ottawa: Ministry of Industry, 2001).

92   See, for instance, data on job enlargement described in M. A. Campion and C. L. McClelland, "Follow-up and Extension of the Interdisciplinary Costs and Benefits of Enlarged Jobs," *Journal of Applied Psychology*, June 1993, pp. 339–351.

93   B. Livesey, "Glitch Doctor," *Report on Business Magazine*, November 1997, pp. 97–102.

94   W. Karl, "Bombardier Reaches Lofty Heights: The Challenge Now Is Maintaining Cruise Altitude," *Plant*, August 11, 1997, pp. 1, 12 ff.

95   J. R. Hackman and G. R. Oldham, "Motivation through the Design of Work: Test of a Theory," *Organizational Behavior and Human Performance*, August 1976, pp. 250–279.

96   J. R. Hackman and G. R. Oldham, *Work Redesign* (Reading, MA: Addison Wesley, 1980).

97   J. R. Hackman, "Work Design," in *Improving Life at Work*, ed. J. R. Hackman and J. L. Suttle (Santa Monica, CA: Goodyear, 1977), pp. 132–133.

98   J. R. Hackman, "Work Design," in *Improving Life at Work*, ed. J. R Hackman and J. L. Suttle (Santa Monica, CA: Goodyear, 1977), p. 129.

99   Based on X. Huang and E. Van De Vliert, "Where Intrinsic Job Satisfaction Fails to Work: National Moderators of Intrinsic Motivation," *Journal of Organizational Behavior* 24, no. 2 (2003), pp. 159–179.

100   D. A. Light, "Human Resources: Recruiting Generation 2001," *Harvard Business Review*, July–August 1998, pp. 13–16.

101   See "Job Characteristics Theory of Work Redesign," in *Theories of Organizational Behavior*, ed. J. B. Miner (Hinsdale, IL: Dryden Press, 1980), pp. 231–266; B. T. Loher, R. A. Noe, N. L. Moeller, and M. P. Fitzgerald, "A Meta-Analysis of the Relation of Job Characteristics to Job Satisfaction," *Journal of Applied Psychology*, May 1985, pp. 280–289; W. H. Glick, G. D. Jenkins, Jr., and N. Gupta, "Method versus Substance: How Strong Are Underlying Relationships between Job Characteristics and Attitudinal Outcomes?" *Academy of Management Journal*, September 1986, pp. 441–464; Y. Fried and G. R. Ferris, "The Validity of the Job Characteristics Model: A Review and Meta-Analysis," *Personnel Psychology*, Summer 1987, pp. 287–322; S. J. Zaccaro and E. F. Stone, "Incremental Validity of an Empirically Based Measure of Job Characteristics," *Journal of Applied Psychology*, May 1988, pp. 245–252; J. R. Rentsch and R. P. Steel, "Testing the Durability of Job Characteristics as Predictors of Absenteeism over a Six-Year Period," *Personnel Psychology*, Spring 1998, pp. 165–190; S. J. Behson, E. R. Eddy, and S. J. Lorenzet, "The Importance of the Critical Psychological States in the Job Characteristics Model: A Meta-Analytic and Structural Equations Modeling Examination," *Current Research in Social Psychology*, May 2000, pp. 170–189; and T. A. Judge, "Promote Job Satisfaction through Mental Challenge,"

in *Handbook of Principles of Organizational Behavior*, ed. E. A. Locke (Oxford, UK: Blackwell, 2000), pp. 75–89.

102   T. A. Judge, S. K. Parker, A. E. Colbert, D. Heller, and R. Ilies, "Job Satisfaction: A Cross-Cultural Review," in *Handbook of Industrial, Work and Organizational Psychology*, vol. 2, ed. N. Anderson and D S. Ones (Thousand Oaks, CA: Sage Publications, 2002), pp. 25–52.

103   C. A. O'Reilly and D. F. Caldwell, "Informational Influence as a Determinant of Perceived Task Characteristics and Job Satisfaction," *Journal of Applied Psychology*, April 1979, pp. 157–165; R. V. Montagno, "The Effects of Comparison [to] Others and Prior Experience on Responses to Task Design," *Academy of Management Journal*, June 1985, pp. 491–498; and P. C. Bottger and I. K.-H. Chew, "The Job Characteristics Model and Growth Satisfaction: Main Effects of Assimilation of Work Experience and Context Satisfaction," *Human Relations*, June 1986, pp. 575–594.

104   See, for example, J. R. Hackman and G. R. Oldham, *Work Redesign* (Reading, MA: Addison Wesley, 1980); J. B. Miner, *Theories of Organizational Behavior* (Hinsdale, IL: Dryden Press, 1980), pp. 231–266; R. W. Griffin, "Effects of Work Redesign on Employee Perceptions, Attitudes, and Behaviors: A Long-Term Investigation," *Academy of Management Journal*, June 1991, pp. 425–435; and J. L. Cotton, *Employee Involvement* (Newbury Park, CA: Sage, 1993), pp. 141–172.

105   F. Pomeroy, "Workplace Change: A Union Perspective," *Canadian Business Review* 22, no. 2 (1995), pp. 17–19.

106   M. Kane, "Flexwork Finds More Favour," *Vancouver Sun*, May 15, 1998, pp. F1, F2.

107   http://www.newswire.ca/en/releases/archive/August2008/14/c4289.html.

108   Statistics Canada, "Part-Time Work and Family-Friendly Practices," *The Daily*, June 26, 2003.

109   L. Rubis, "Fourth of Full-Timers Enjoy Flexible Hours," *HR Magazine*, June 1998, pp. 26–28.

110   See, for example, D. A. Ralston and M. F. Flanagan, "The Effect of Flextime on Absenteeism and Turnover for Male and Female Employees," *Journal of Vocational Behavior*, April 1985, pp. 206–217; D. A. Ralston, W. P. Anthony, and D. J. Gustafson, "Employees May Love Flextime, but What Does It Do to the Organization's Productivity?" *Journal of Applied Psychology*, May 1985, pp. 272–279; J. B. McGuire and J. R. Liro, "Flexible Work Schedules, Work Attitudes, and Perceptions of Productivity," *Public Personnel Management*, Spring 1986, pp. 65–73; P. Bernstein, "The Ultimate in Flextime: From Sweden, by Way of Volvo," *Personnel*, June 1988, pp. 70–74; and D. R. Dalton and D. J. Mesch, "The Impact of Flexible Scheduling on Employee Attendance and Turnover," *Administrative Science Quarterly*, June 1990, pp. 370–387.

111   D. Keevil, *The Flexible Workplace Study: Asking the Experts About Flexible Policies and Workplace Performance* (Halifax: Halifax YWCA in cooperation with Status of Women Canada, 1996).

112   L. Duxbury and G. Haines, "Predicting Alternative Work Arrangements from Salient Attitudes: A Study of Decision Makers in the Public Sector," *Journal of Business Research*, August 1991, pp. 83–97.

113 J. E. Fast and J. A. Frederick, "Working Arrangements and Time Stress," *Canadian Social Trends*, Winter 1996, pp. 14–19.

114 A. Sisco and R. Nelson, "From Vision to Venture: An Account of Five Successful Aboriginal Businesses," The Conference Board of Canada, May 2008.

115 K. Hanson, "Some Companies Go Beyond the Norm to Offer Services to Employees," *National Post*, October 8, 1999, p. C15.

116 S. Shellenbarger, "Two People, One Job: It Can Really Work," *Wall Street Journal*, December 7, 1994, p. B1.

117 "Telecommuting in Europe," *Manpower Argus*, April 1997, p. 9.

118 S. Shellenbarger, "Two People, One Job: It Can Really Work," *Wall Street Journal*, December 7, 1994, p. B1.

119 D. Hodges, "New Nunavut: Canada's Newest Territory Faces the Daunting Task of Creating a New Health Bureaucracy While Dealing with Traditional Recruitment Problems in the Arctic," *Medical Post*, November 13, 2001, p. 31.

120 See, for example, T. H. Davenport and K. Pearlson, "Two Cheers for the Virtual Office," *Sloan Management Review*, Summer 1998, pp. 61–65; E. J. Hill, B. C. Miller, S. P. Weiner, and J. Colihan, "Influences of the Virtual Office on Aspects of Work and Work/Life Balance," *Personnel Psychology*, Autumn 1998, pp. 667–683; and K. E. Pearlson and C. S. Saunders, "There's No Place Like Home: Managing Telecommuting Paradoxes," *Academy of Management Executive*, May 2001, pp. 117–128; and S. J. Wells, "Making Telecommuting Work," *HR Magazine*, October 2001, pp. 34–45.

121 "Canadian Studies on Telework," *InnoVisions Canada*, http://www.ivc.ca/studies/canada/(accessed September 22, 2008).

122 A. Joyce, "Telework a Productive Part of Many Companies," *Ottawa Citizen*, August 27, 2005, p. D12; and C. Said, "Work Is Where You Hang Your Coat," *National Post*, July 20, 2005, p. FP11.

123 J. Cote-O'Hara, "Sending Them Home to Work: Telecommuting," *Business Quarterly*, Spring, 1993, pp. 104–109.

124 N. Hulsman, "Farewell Corner Office," *BCBusiness Magazine*, June 1999, pp. 48–55.

125 R. Hearn, "First Banker in Space," *Canadian Business*, August 1997, p. 15.

126 Cited in R. W. Judy and C. D'Amico, *Workforce 2020* (Indianapolis, IL: Hudson Institute, 1997), p. 58.

127 P. Lima, "The Next Best Thing to Being There," *Globe and Mail*, April 26, 2006, p. 31.

128 L. Arnold, "Geographical, Organisational and Social Implications of Teleworking—Emphasis on the Social Perspectives" (paper presented at the 29th Annual Meeting of the Canadian Sociological and Anthropological Association, Calgary, June 1994); K. S. Devine, L. Taylor, and K. Haryett, "The Impact of Teleworking on Canadian Employment," in *Good Jobs, Bad Jobs, No Jobs: The Uncertain Future of Employment* in Canada, ed. A. Duffy, D. Glenday, and N. Pupo (Toronto : Harcourt Brace, 1997); C. A. Hamilton, "Telecommuting," *Personnel Journal*, April 1987, pp. 91–101; and I. U. Zeytinoglu, "Employment Conditions in Telework: An Experiment in Ontario," *Proceedings of the 30th Conference of the Canadian Industrial Relations Association*, 1992, pp. 281–293.

129 L. Arnold, "Geographical, Organisational and Social Implications of Teleworking—Emphasis on the Social Perspectives" (paper presented at the 29th Annual Meeting of the Canadian Sociological and Anthropological Association, Calgary, June 1994).

130 I. U. Zeytinoglu, "Employment Conditions in Telework: An Experiment in Ontario," *Proceedings of the 30th Conference of the Canadian Industrial Relations Association*, 1992, pp. 281–293; and K. S. Devine, L. Taylor, and K. Haryett, "The Impact of Teleworking on Canadian Employment," in *Good Jobs, Bad Jobs, No Jobs: The Uncertain Future of Employment in Canada*, ed. A. Duffy, D. Glenday, and N. Pupo (Toronto: Harcourt Brace, 1997).

131 I. U. Zeytinoglu, "Employment Conditions in Telework: An Experiment in Ontario," *Proceedings of the 30th Conference of the Canadian Industrial Relations Association*, 1992, pp. 281–293.

132 K. S. Devine, L. Taylor, and K. Haryett, "The Impact of Teleworking on Canadian Employment," in *Good Jobs, Bad Jobs, No Jobs: The Uncertain Future of Employment in Canada*, ed. A. Duffy, D. Glenday, and N. Pupo (Toronto: Harcourt Brace, 1997); and C. A. Hamilton, "Telecommuting," *Personnel Journal*, April 1987, pp. 91–101.

133 K. S. Devine, L. Taylor, and K. Haryett, "The Impact of Teleworking on Canadian Employment," in *Good Jobs, Bad Jobs, No Jobs: The Uncertain Future of Employment in Canada*, ed. A. Duffy, D. Glenday, and N. Pupo (Toronto: Harcourt Brace, 1997).

134 K. S. Devine, L. Taylor, and K. Haryett, "The Impact of Teleworking on Canadian Employment," in *Good Jobs, Bad Jobs, No Jobs: The Uncertain Future of Employment in Canada*, ed. A. Duffy, D. Glenday, and N. Pupo (Toronto: Harcourt Brace, 1997).

135 C. A. Hamilton, "Telecommuting," *Personnel Journal*, April 1987, pp. 91–101.

136 L. Arnold, "Geographical, Organisational and Social Implications of Teleworking—Emphasis on the Social Perspectives" (paper presented at the 29th Annual Meeting of the Canadian Sociological and Anthropological Association, Calgary, June 1994).

137 N. Hulsman, "Farewell Corner Office," *BCBusiness Magazine*, June 1999, pp. 48–55.

138 N. Nohria, B. Groysberg, and L.-E. Lee, "Employee Motivation: A Powerful New Model," *Harvard Business Review* 86, no. 7–8 (July–August 2008), pp. 78–84.

139 P. R. Lawrence and N. Nohria, *Driven: How Human Nature Shapes Our Choices* (San Francisco: Jossey-Bass, 2002).

140 T. R. Mitchell and A. E. Mickel, "The Meaning of Money: An Individual-Difference Perspective," *Academy of Management*, July 1999, pp. 568–578.

141 This paragraph is based on T. R. Mitchell and A. E. Mickel, "The Meaning of Money: An Individual-Difference Perspective," *Academy of Management*, July 1999, pp. 568–578. The reader may want to refer to the myriad of references cited in the article.

142 E. Beauchesne, "Pay Bonuses Improve Productivity, Study Shows," *Vancouver Sun*, September 13, 2002, p. D5.

143 K. O. Doyle, "Introduction: Money and the Behavioral Sciences," *American Behavioral Scientist*, July 1992, pp. 641–657.

144 S. Caudron, "Motivation? Money's Only No. 2," *IndustryWeek*, November 15, 1993, p. 33.

145 E. A. Locke, D. B. Feren, V. M. McCaleb, K. N. Shaw, and A. T. Denny, "The Relative Effectiveness of Four Methods of Motivating Employee Performance," in *Changes in Working Life*, ed. K. D. Duncan, M. M. Gruneberg, and D. Wallis (London: Wiley, 1980), pp. 363–383.

146 B. Filipczak, "Can't Buy Me Love," *Training*, January 1996, pp. 29–34.

147 http://www.watsonwyatt.com/canada-english/news/press. asp?ID=16418.

148 J. R. Hackman and G. R. Oldham, *Work Redesign* (Reading, MA: Addison-Wesley, 1980). Reprinted with permission.

149 This exercise is based on W. P. Ferris, "Enlivening the Job Characteristics Model," in *Proceedings of the 29th Annual Eastern Academy of Management Meeting*, ed. C. Harris and C. C. Lundberg (Baltimore, MD: May 1992), pp. 125–128.

150 E. Church, "Market Recovery Delivers Executive Payout Bonanza," *Globe and Mail*, May 4, 2005, pp. B1, B9; "Gimme Gimme: Greed, the Most Insidious of Sins, Has Once Again Embraced a Decade," *Financial Post*, September 28/30, 1996, pp. 24–25; and I. McGugan, "A Crapshoot Called Compensation," *Canadian Business*, July 1995, pp. 67–70.

151 H. Mackenzie, "The Great CEO Pay Race: Over Before It Begins," *Canadian Centre for Policy Alternatives*, December 2007.

152 This case is based on J. Sandberg, "Been Here 25 Years and All I Got Was This Lousy T-Shirt," *Wall Street Journal*, January 28, 2004, p. B1.

153 Based on T. Ogier, "Life as a Burger King," *Latin Trade*, December 2000, pp. 44–47.

154 J. R. Hackman, "Work Design," in *Improving Life at Work*, ed. J. R. Hackman and J. L. Suttle (Santa Monica, CA: Goodyear, 1977), pp. 132–133.

155 A. M. Grant, E. M. Campbell, G. Chen, K. Cottone, D. Lapedis, and K. Lee, "Impact and the Art of Motivation Maintenance: The Effects of Contact with Beneficiaries on Persistence Behavior," *Organizational Behavior and Human Decision Processes* 103 (2007), pp. 53–67.

Chapter 6

1 Based on "Emery 'Don't Take Responsibility' for Playoff Loss," *Province* (Vancouver), April 18, 2008, p. A62; and "Ducks Destroy Senators to Win Stanley Cup," *cbcsports.ca*, June 7, 2007, http://www.cbc.ca/sports/hockey/story/2007/06/06/nhl-senators-ducks.html.

2 J. R. Katzenback and D. K. Smith, *The Wisdom of Teams: Creating the High-Performance Organization* (New York: Harper Business, 1999), p. 45.

3 J. R. Katzenback and D. K. Smith, *The Wisdom of Teams: Creating the High-Performance Organization* (New York: Harper Business, 1999), p. 214.

4 See, for example, D. Tjosvold, *Team Organization: An Enduring Competitive Advantage* (Chichester, UK: Wiley, 1991); S. A. Mohrman, S. G. Cohen, and A. M. Mohrman Jr., *Designing Team-Based Organizations* (San Francisco: Jossey-Bass, 1995); P. MacMillan, *The Performance Factor: Unlocking the Secrets of Teamwork* (Nashville, TN: Broadman and Holman, 2001); and E. Salas, C. A. Bowers, and E. Edens, eds., *Improving Teamwork in Organizations: Applications of Resource Management Training* (Mahwah, NJ: Erlbaum, 2002).

5 J. H. Shonk, *Team-Based Organizations* (Homewood, IL: Business One Irwin, 1992); and M. A. Verespej, "When Workers Get New Roles," *IndustryWeek*, February 3, 1992, p. 11.

6 See, for example, C. C. Manz and H. P. Sims Jr., *Business without Bosses: How Self-Managing Teams Are Building High Performance Companies* (New York: Wiley, 1993); J. R. Barker, "Tightening the Iron Cage: Concertive Control in Self-Managing Teams," *Administrative Science Quarterly*, September 1993, pp. 408–437; and S. G. Cohen, G. E. Ledford Jr., and G. M. Spreitzer, "A Predictive Model of Self-Managing Work Team Effectiveness," *Human Relations*, May 1996, pp. 643–676.

7 R. I. Beekun, "Assessing the Effectiveness of Sociotechnical Interventions: Antidote or Fad?" *Human Relations*, October 1989, pp. 877–897.

8 S. G. Cohen, G. E. Ledford, and G. M. Spreitzer, "A Predictive Model of Self-Managing Work Team Effectiveness," *Human Relations*, May 1996, pp. 643–676.

9 S. Hirshorn, "Team-Work-Team," *OH & S Canada* 25, no. 1 (January–February 2005), pp. 32–36.

10 Statistics Canada, "Gender Pay Differentials: Impact of the Workplace, 1999," *The Daily*, June 19, 2002.

11 P. Booth, *Challenge and Change: Embracing the Team Concept*, Report 123–94 (Ottawa: The Conference Board of Canada, 1994); and S. Hirshorn, "Team-Work-Team," *OH & S Canada* 25, no. 1 (January–February 2005), pp. 32–36.

12 See, for instance, J. L. Cordery, W. S. Mueller, and L. M. Smith, "Attitudinal and Behavioral Effects of Autonomous Group Working: A Longitudinal Field Study," *Academy of Management Journal*, June 1991, pp. 464–476; R. A. Cook and J. L. Goff, "Coming of Age with Self-Managed Teams: Dealing with a Problem Employee," *Journal of Business and Psychology*, Spring 2002, pp. 485–496; and C. W. Langfred, "Too Much of a Good Thing? Negative Effects of High Trust and Individual Autonomy in Self-Managing Teams," *Academy of Management Journal*, June 2004, pp. 385–399.

13 J. Tutunjian, "Interview with Don Swann," *Canadian Grocer* 121, no. 10 (December 2007–January 2008), pp. 18–19.

14 G. Taninecz, "Team Players," *IndustryWeek*, July 15, 1996, pp. 28–32; D. R. Denison, S. L. Hart, and J. A. Kahn, "From Chimneys to Cross-Functional Teams: Developing and Validating a Diagnostic Model," *Academy of Management Journal*, August 1996, pp. 1005–1023; and A. R. Jassawalla, "Building Collaborative Cross-Functional New Product Teams," *Academy of Management Executive*, August 1999, pp. 50–63.

15 R. Lepine and K. Rawson, "Strategic Savings on the Right Track: How Canadian Pacific Railway Has Saved Millions of Dollars in

the Past Four Years through Strategic Sourcing," *CMA Management*, February 2003, pp. 20–23.

16   "Cross-Functional Obstacles," *Training*, May 1994, pp. 125–126.

17   P. Gwynne, "Skunk Works, 1990s-Style," *Research Technology Management*, July–August 1997, pp. 18–23.

18   See, for example, M. E. Warkentin, L. Sayeed, and R. Hightower, "Virtual Teams Versus Face-to-Face Teams: An Exploratory Study of a Web-Based Conference System," *Decision Sciences*, Fall 1997, pp. 975–993; A. M. Townsend, S. M. DeMarie, and A. R. Hendrickson, "Virtual Teams: Technology and the Workplace of the Future," *Academy of Management Executive*, August 1998, pp. 17–29; and D. Duarte and N. T. Snyder, *Mastering Virtual Teams: Strategies, Tools, and Techniques* (San Francisco: Jossey-Bass, 1999); M. L. Maznevski and K. M. Chudoba, "Bridging Space over Time: Global Virtual Team Dynamics and Effectiveness," *Organization Science*, September–October 2000, pp. 473–492; and J. Katzenbach and D. Smith, "Virtual Teaming," *Forbes*, May 21, 2001, pp. 48–51.

19   Based on S. L. Jarvenpaa, K. Knoll, and D. E. Leidner, "Is Anybody out There? Antecedents of Trust in Global Virtual Teams," *Journal of Management Information Systems*, Spring 1998, pp. 29–64.

20   C. Joinson, "Managing Virtual Teams," *HR Magazine*, June 2002, p. 71. Reprinted with the permission of *HR Magazine*, published by the Society for Human Resource Management, Alexandria, VA.

21   A. Malhotra, A. Majchrzak, and B. Rosen, "Leading Virtual Teams," *Academy of Management Perspectives*, February 2007, pp. 60–70; and J. M. Wilson, S. S. Straus, and B. McEvily, "All in Due Time: The Development of Trust in Computer- Mediated and Face-to-Face Teams," *Organizational Behavior and Human Decision Processes* 19 (2006), pp. 16–33.

22   B. L. Kirkman, B. Rosen, C. B. Gibson, P. E. Tesluk, S. O. McPherson, "Five Challenges to Virtual Team Success: Lessons From Sabre, Inc.," *Academy of Management Executive* 16, no. 3 (2002), pp. 67–79.

23   K. Warren, "A Team under Construction: The Senators, Much Like the Queensway, Are Undergoing Major Changes as Training Camp for the '08–09 Season Begins Today," *Ottawa Citizen*, September 17, 2008, p. B3.

24   Based on J. McIntosh, "On the Road to the 2010 Olympics," *Toronto Star*, February 10, 2008; M. Petrie, "Canada's Skeleton Crew Made Peace to Improve," *CanWest News Service*, February 21, 2005; and B. Graveland, "Pain Credits Team for Win," *Edmonton Journal*, February 22, 2005, p. D3.

25   See M. F. Peterson, P. B, Smith, A. Akande, S. Ayestaran, S. Bochner, V. Callan, N. Guk Cho, J. C. Jesuino, M. D'Amorim, P.-H. Francois, K. Hofmann, P. L. Koopman, K. Leung, T. K. Lim, and S. Mortaz, "Role Conflict, Ambiguity, and Overload: A 21-Nation Study," *Academy of Management Journal*, April 1995, pp. 429–452.

26   E. H. Schein, *Organizational Psychology*, 3rd ed. (Englewood Cliffs, NJ: Prentice Hall, 1980), p. 145.

27   For a recent review of the research on group norms, see J. R. Hackman, "Group Influences on Individuals in Organizations," in *Handbook of Industrial & Organizational Psychology*, vol. 3, 2nd ed., ed. M. D. Dunnette and L. M. Hough

(Palo Alto, CA: Consulting Psychologists Press, 1992), pp. 235–250.

28   Submitted by Don Miskiman, Chair and U-C Professor of Management, Malaspina University College, Nanaimo, BC. With permission.

29   D. C. Feldman, "The Development and Enforcement of Group Norms," *Academy of Management Journal*, January 1984, pp. 47–53; and K. L. Bettenhausen and J. K. Murnighan, "The Development of an Intragroup Norm and the Effects of Interpersonal and Structural Challenges," *Administrative Science Quarterly*, March 1991, pp. 20–35.

30   D. C. Feldman, "The Development and Enforcement of Group Norms," *Academy of Management Journal*, January 1984, pp. 47–53; and K. L. Bettenhausen and J. K. Murnighan, "The Development of an Intragroup Norm and the Effects of Interpersonal and Structural Challenges," *Administrative Science Quarterly*, March 1991, pp. 20–35.

31   C. A. Kiesler and S. B. Kiesler, *Conformity* (Reading, MA: Addison Wesley, 1969).

32   S. E. Asch, "Effects of Group Pressure upon the Modification and Distortion of Judgments," in *Groups, Leadership and Men*, ed. H. Guetzkow (Pittsburgh, PA: Carnegie Press, 1951), pp. 177–190; and S. E. Asch, "Studies of Independence and Conformity: A Minority of One Against a Unanimous Majority," *Psychological Monographs: General and Applied* 70, no. 9 (1956), pp. 1–70.

33   S. L. Robinson and A. M. O'Leary-Kelly, "Monkey See, Monkey Do: The Influence of Work Groups on the Antisocial Behavior of Employees," *Academy of Management Journal* 41, 1998, pp. 658–672.

34   J. M. George, "Personality, Affect and Behavior in Groups," *Journal of Applied Psychology* 78, 1993, pp. 798–804; and J. M. George and L. R. James, "Personality, Affect, and Behavior in Groups Revisited: Comment on Aggregation, Levels of Analysis, and a Recent Application of Within and Between Analysis," *Journal of Applied Psychology* 78, 1993, pp. 798–804.

35   K. Warren, "A Team under Construction: The Senators, Much Like the Queensway, Are Undergoing Major Changes as Training Camp for the '08–09 Season Begins Today," *Ottawa Citizen*, September 17, 2008, p. B3.

36   B. W. Tuckman, "Developmental Sequences in Small Groups," *Psychological Bulletin*, June 1965, pp. 384–399; B. W. Tuckman and M. C. Jensen, "Stages of Small-Group Development Revisited," *Group and Organizational Studies*, December 1977, pp. 419–427; and M. F. Maples, "Group Development: Extending Tuckman's Theory," *Journal for Specialists in Group Work*, Fall 1988, pp. 17–23.

37   J. F. George and L. M. Jessup, "Groups over Time: What Are We Really Studying?" *International Journal of Human-Computer Studies* 47, no. 3 (1997), pp. 497–511.

38   R. C. Ginnett, "The Airline Cockpit Crew," in *Groups That Work (and Those That Don't)*, ed. J. R. Hackman (San Francisco: Jossey-Bass, 1990).

39   C. J. G. Gersick, "Time and Transition in Work Teams: Toward a New Model of Group Development," *Academy of Management Journal*, March 1988, pp. 9–41; C. J. G. Gersick, "Marking Time:

Predictable Transitions in Task Groups," *Academy of Management Journal*, June 1989, pp. 274–309; E. Romanelli and M. L. Tushman, "Organizational Transformation as Punctuated Equilibrium: An Empirical Test," *Academy of Management Journal*, October 1994, pp. 1141–1166; B. M. Lichtenstein, "Evolution or Transformation: A Critique and Alternative to Punctuated Equilibrium," in *Academy of Management Best Paper Proceedings*, ed. D. P. Moore (National Academy of Management Conference, Vancouver, 1995), pp. 291–295; and A. Seers and S. Woodruff, "Temporal Pacing in Task Forces: Group Development or Deadline Pressure?" *Journal of Management* 23, no. 2 (1997), pp. 169–187.

40 C. J. G. Gersick, "Time and Transition in Work Teams: Toward a New Model of Group Development," *Academy of Management Journal*, March 1988, pp. 9–41; and M. J. Waller, J. M. Conte, C. B. Gibson, and M. A. Carpenter, "The Effect of Individual Perceptions of Deadlines on Team Performance," *Academy of Management Review*, October 2001, pp. 586–600.

41 C. J. G. Gersick, "Time and Transition in Work Teams: Toward a New Model of Group Development," *Academy of Management Journal*, March 1988, pp. 9–41 and C. J. G. Gersick, "Marking Time: Predictable Transitions in Task Groups," *Academy of Management Journal*, June 1989, pp. 274–309.

42 A. Chang, P. Bordia, and J. Duck, "Punctuated Equilibrium and Linear Progression: Toward a New Understanding of Group Development," *Academy of Management Journal* 46, no. 1 (2003), pp. 106–117.

43 K. L. Bettenhausen, "Five Years of Groups Research: What We Have Learned and What Needs to be Addressed," *Journal of Management* 17, 1991, pp. 345–381; and R. A. Guzzo and G. P. Shea, "Group Performance and Intergroup Relations in Organizations," in *Handbook of Industrial and Organizational Psychology*, vol. 3, 2nd ed., ed. M. D. Dunnette and L. M. Hough (Palo Alto, CA: Consulting Psychologists Press, 1992), pp. 269–313.

44 A. Chang, P. Bordia, and J. Duck, "Punctuated Equilibrium and Linear Progression: Toward a New Understanding of Group Development," *Academy of Management Journal* 46, no. 1 (2003), pp. 106–117; and S. G. S. Lim and J. K. Murnighan, "Phases, Deadlines, and the Bargaining Process," *Organizational Behavior and Human Decision Processes* 58, 1994, pp. 153–171.

45 K. Warren, "All-For-One, One-For-All; New Senators Coach Craig Hartsburg Says Stars and Role Players Alike Must All Buy into the Team-First Program," *Ottawa Citizen*, September 10, 2008, p. B1.

46 See, for instance, D. L. Gladstein, "Groups in Context: A Model of Task Group Effectiveness," *Administrative Science Quarterly*, December 1984, pp. 499–517; J. R. Hackman, "The Design of Work Teams," in *Handbook of Organizational Behavior*, ed. J. W. Lorsch (Englewood Cliffs, NJ: Prentice Hall, 1987), pp. 315–342; M. A. Campion, G. J. Medsker, and C. A. Higgs, "Relations between Work Group Characteristics and Effectiveness: Implications for Designing Effective Work Groups," *Personnel Psychology*, 1993; and R. A. Guzzo and M. W. Dickson, "Teams in Organizations: Recent Research on Performance and Effectiveness," in *Annual Review of Psychology*, vol. 47, ed. J. T. Spence, J. M. Darley, and D. J. Foss, 1996, pp. 307–338.

47 D. E. Hyatt and T. M. Ruddy, "An Examination of the Relationship between Work Group Characteristics and Performance: Once More into the Breech," *Personnel Psychology*, Autumn 1997, p. 555.

48 This model is based on M. A. Campion, E. M. Papper, and G. J. Medsker, "Relations between Work Team Characteristics and Effectiveness: A Replication and Extension," *Personnel Psychology*, Summer 1996, pp. 429–452; D. E. Hyatt and T. M. Ruddy, "An Examination of the Relationship between Work Group Characteristics and Performance: Once More into the Breech," *Personnel Psychology*, Autumn 1997, pp. 553–585; S. G. Cohen and D. E. Bailey, "What Makes Teams Work: Group Effectiveness Research from the Shop Floor to the Executive Suite," *Journal of Management* 23, no. 3 (1997), pp. 239–290; G. A. Neuman and J. Wright, "Team Effectiveness: Beyond Skills and Cognitive Ability," *Journal of Applied Psychology*, June 1999, pp. 376–389; and L. Thompson, *Making the Team* (Upper Saddle River, NJ: Prentice Hall, 2000), pp. 18–33.

49 See M. Mattson, T. V. Mumford, and G. S. Sintay, "Taking Teams to Task: A Normative Model for Designing or Recalibrating Work Teams" (paper presented at the National Academy of Management Conference, Chicago, August 1999); and G. L. Stewart and M. R. Barrick, "Team Structure and Performance: Assessing the Mediating Role of Intrateam Process and the Moderating Role of Task Type," *Academy of Management Journal*, April 2000, pp. 135–148.

50 Based on W. G. Dyer, R. H. Daines, and W. C. Giauque, *The Challenge of Management* (New York: Harcourt Brace Jovanovich, 1990), p. 343.

51 E. M. Stark, "Interdependence and Preference for Group Work: Main and Congruence Effects on the Satisfaction and Performance of Group Members," *Journal of Management* 26, no. 2 (2000), pp. 259–279; and J. W. Bishop, K. D. Scott, and S. M. Burroughs, "Support, Commitment, and Employee Outcomes in a Team Environment," *Journal of Management* 26, no. 6 (2000), pp. 1113–1132.

52 J. R. Hackman, *Leading Teams* (Boston: Harvard Business School Press, 2002).

53 P. Balkundi and D. A. Harrison, "Ties, Leaders, and Time in Teams: Strong Inference About Network Structure's Effects on Team Viability and Performance," *Academy of Management Journal* 49, no. 1 (2006), pp. 49–68; G. Chen, B. L. Kirkman, R. Kanfer, D. Allen, and B. Rosen, "A Multilevel Study of Leadership, Empowerment, and Performance in Teams," *Journal of Applied Psychology* 92, no. 2 (2007), pp. 331–346; L. A. DeChurch and M. A. Marks, "Leadership in Multiteam Systems," *Journal of Applied Psychology* 91, no. 2 (2006), pp. 311–329; A. Srivastava, K. M. Bartol, and E. A. Locke, "Empowering Leadership in Management Teams: Effects on Knowledge Sharing, Efficacy, and Performance," *Academy of Management Journal* 49, no. 6 (2006), pp. 1239–1251; and J. E. Mathieu, K. K. Gilson, and T. M. Ruddy, "Empowerment and Team Effectiveness: An Empirical Test of an Integrated Model," *Journal of Applied Psychology* 91, no. 1 (2006), pp. 97–108.

54 W. Immen, "The More Women in Groups, the Better," *Globe and Mail*, April 27, 2005, p. C3.

55 J. L. Berdahl and C. Anderson, "Men, Women, and Leadership Centralization in Groups over Time," *Group Dynamics: Theory, Research,* and Practice 9, no. 1 (2005), pp. 45–57.

56 R. I. Beekun, "Assessing the Effectiveness of Sociotechnical Interventions: Antidote or Fad?" *Human Relations*, October 1989, pp. 877–897.

57 S. G. Cohen, G. E. Ledford, and G. M. Spreitzer, "A Predictive Model of Self-Managing Work Team Effectiveness," *Human Relations*, May 1996, pp. 643–676.

58 D. R. Ilgen, J. R. Hollenbeck, M. Johnson, and D. Jundt, "Teams in Organizations: From Input-Process-Output Models to IMOI Models," *Annual Review of Psychology* 56, no. 1 (2005), pp. 517–543.

59 P. L. Schindler and C. C. Thomas, "The Structure of Interpersonal Trust in the Workplace," *Psychological Reports*, October 1993, pp. 563–573.

60 K. T. Dirks, "Trust in Leadership and Team Performance: Evidence from NCAA Basketball," *Journal of Applied Psychology*, December 2000, pp. 1004–1012; and M. Williams, "In Whom We Trust: Group Membership as an Affective Context for Trust Development," *Academy of Management Review*, July 2001, pp. 377–396.

61 "Relationship Building Breeds Success," *National Post*, August 11, 2008, p. FP7.

62 See S. T. Johnson, "Work Teams: What's Ahead in Work Design and Rewards Management," *Compensation & Benefits Review*, March–April 1993, pp. 35–41; and A. M. Saunier and E. J. Hawk, "Realizing the Potential of Teams through Team-Based Rewards," *Compensation & Benefits Review*, July–August 1994, pp. 24–33.

63 J. Pfeffer and N. Langton, "The Effect of Wage Dispersion on Satisfaction, Productivity, and Working Collaboratively: Evidence from College and University Faculty," *Administrative Science Quarterly* 38, 1993, pp. 382–407.

64 M. Bloom, "The Performance Effects of Pay Dispersion on Individuals and Organizations," *Academy of Management Journal* 42, 1999, pp. 25–40.

65 For a more detailed breakdown on team skills, see M. J. Stevens and M. A. Campion, "The Knowledge, Skill, and Ability Requirements for Teamwork: Implications for Human Resource Management," *Journal of Management*, Summer 1994, pp. 503–530.

66 S. T. Bell, "Deep-Level Composition Variables as Predictors of Team Performance: A Meta-Analysis," *Journal of Applied Psychology* 92, no. 3 (2007), pp. 595–615; and M. R. Barrick, G. L. Stewart, M. J. Neubert, and M. K. Mount, "Relating Member Ability and Personality to Work-Team Processes and Team Effectiveness," Journal of Applied Psychology, June 1998, pp. 377–391.

67 A. Ellis, J. R. Hollenbeck, D. R. Ilgen, C. O. Porter, B. West, and H. Moon, "Team Learning: Collectively Connecting the Dots," *Journal of Applied Psychology* 88, 2003, 821–835; C. O. L. H. Porter, J. R. Hollenbeck, and D. R. Ilgen, "Backing up Behaviors in Teams: The Role of Personality and Legitimacy of Need," *Journal of Applied Psychology* 88, no. 3 (June 2003), pp. 391–403; A. Colquitt, J. R. Hollenbeck, and D. R. Ilgen, "Computer-Assisted Communication and Team Decision-Making Performance: The Moderating Effect of Openness to Experience," *Journal of Applied Psychology* 87, no. 2 (April 2002), pp. 402–410; J. A. LePine, J. R. Hollenbeck, D. R. Ilgen, and J. Hedlund, "The Effects of Individual Differences on the Performance of Hierarchical Decision Making Teams: Much More Than G," *Journal of Applied Psychology* 82, 1997, pp. 803–811; C. L. Jackson and J. A. LePine, "Peer Responses to a Team's Weakest Link," *Journal of Applied Psychology* 88, no. 3 (2003), pp. 459–475; and J. A. LePine, "Team

Adaptation and Postchange Performance," *Journal of Applied Psychology* 88, no. 1 (2003), pp. 27–39.

68 M. R. Barrick, G. L. Stewart, M. J. Neubert, and M. K. Mount, "Relating Member Ability and Personality to Work-Team Processes and Team Effectiveness," *Journal of Applied Psychology* 83, no. 3 (1998), p. 388; and S. E. Humphrey, J. R. Hollenbeck, C. J. Meyer, and D. R. Ilgen, "Trait Configurations in Self-Managed Teams: A Conceptual Examination of the Use of Seeding for Maximizing and Minimizing Trait Variance in Teams," *Journal of Applied Psychology* 92, no. 3 (2007), pp. 885–892.

69 E. Sundstrom, K. P. Meuse, and D. Futrell, "Work Teams: Applications and Effectiveness," *American Psychologist*, February 1990, pp. 120–133.

70 See, for instance, M. Sashkin and K. J. Kiser, *Putting Total Quality Management to Work* (San Francisco: Berrett-Koehler, 1993); and J. R. Hackman and R. Wageman, "Total Quality Management: Empirical, Conceptual and Practical Issues," *Administrative Science Quarterly*, June 1995, pp. 309–342.

71 D. A. Harrison, K. H. Price, J. H. Gavin, and A. T. Florey, "Time, Teams, and Task Performance: Changing Effects of Surface- and Deep-Level Diversity on Group Functioning," *Academy of Management Journal* 45, no. 5 (2002), pp. 1029–1045; and J. S. Bunderson and K. M. Sutcliffe, "Comparing Alternative Conceptualizations of Functional Diversity in Management Teams: Process and Performance Effects," *Academy of Management Journal* 45, no. 5 (2002), pp. 875–893.

72 M. A. Neale, G. B. Northcraft, and K. A. Jehn, "Exploring Pandora's Box: The Impact of Diversity and Conflict on Work Group Performance," *Performance Improvement Quarterly* 12, no. 1 (1999), pp. 113–126.

73 R. J. Ely and D. A. Thomas, "Cultural Diversity at Work: The Effects of Diversity Perspectives on Work Group Processes and Outcomes," *Administrative Science Quarterly* 46, 2001, pp. 229–273; K. A. Jehn, G. B. Northcraft, and M. A. Neale, "Why Some Differences Make a Difference: A Field Study of Diversity, Conflict, and Performance in Workgroups." *Administrative Science Quarterly* 44, 1999, pp. 741–763; and W. E. Watson, K. Kumar, and L. K. Michaelsen, "Cultural Diversity's Impact on Interaction Process and Performance: Comparing Homogeneous and Diverse Task Groups." *Academy of Management Journal* 36, 1993, pp. 590–602.

74 For a review, see K. Y. Williams and C. A. O'Reilly, "Demography and Diversity in Organizations: A Review of 40 Years of Research," in *Research in Organizational Behavior*, vol. 20, ed. B. M. Staw and L. L. Cummings (Greenwich, CT: JAI Press, 1998), pp. 77–140.

75 E. Peterson, "Negotiation Teamwork: The Impact of Information Distribution and Accountability on Performance Depends on the Relationship Among Team Members," *Organizational Behavior and Human Decision Processes* 72, 1997, pp. 364–384.

76 J. Labianca, "The Ties That Blind," *Harvard Business Review* 82, no. 10 (October 2004), p. 19.

77 See, for instance, M. Sashkin and K. J. Kiser, *Putting Total Quality Management to Work* (San Francisco: Berrett-Koehler, 1993); and J. R. Hackman and R. Wageman, "Total Quality Management: Empirical, Conceptual and Practical Issues," *Administrative Science Quarterly*, June 1995, pp. 309–342.

78 J. S. Bunderson and K. M. Sutcliffe, "Comparing Alternative Conceptualizations of Functional Diversity in Management Teams:

Process and Performance Effects," *Academy of Management Journal* 45, no. 5 (2002), pp. 875–893, discusses some of the recent work in this area.

79   R. J. Ely and D. A. Thomas, "Cultural Diversity at Work: The Effects of Diversity Perspectives on Work Group Processes and Outcomes," *Administrative Science Quarterly* 46, 2001, pp. 229–273.

80   J. T. Polzer, L. P. Milton, and W. B. Swann Jr., "Capitalizing on Diversity: Interpersonal Congruence in Small Work Groups," *Administrative Science Quarterly* 47, no. 2 (2002), pp. 296–324.

81   *Focus on Diversity* based on B. L. Kelsey, "Increasing Minority Group Participation and Influence Using a Group Support System," *Canadian Journal of Administrative Sciences* 17, no. 1 (2000), pp. 63–75.

82   See D. R. Comer, "A Model of Social Loafing in Real Work Groups," *Human Relations*, June 1995, pp. 647–667.

83   W. Moede, "Die Richtlinien der Leistungs-Psychologie," *Industrielle Psychotechnik* 4, 1927, pp. 193–207. See also D. A. Kravitz and B. Martin, "Ringelmann Rediscovered: The Original Article," *Journal of Personality and Social Psychology*, May 1986, pp. 936–941.

84   See, for example, J. A. Shepperd, "Productivity Loss in Performance Groups: A Motivation Analysis," *Psychological Bulletin*, January 1993, pp. 67–81; and S. J. Karau and K. D. Williams, "Social Loafing: A Meta-Analytic Review and Theoretical Integration," *Journal of Personality and Social Psychology*, October 1993, pp. 681–706.

85   E. Sundstrom, K. P. Meuse, and D. Futrell, "Work Teams: Applications and Effectiveness," *American Psychologist*, February 1990, pp. 120–133.

86   D. E. Hyatt and T. M. Ruddy, "An Examination of the Relationship between Work Group Characteristics and Performance: Once More into the Breech," *Personnel Psychology*, Autumn 1997, p. 555; and J. D. Shaw, M. K. Duffy, and E. M. Stark, "Interdependence and Preference for Group Work: Main and Congruence Effects on the Satisfaction and Performance of Group Members," *Journal of Management* 26, no. 2 (2000), pp. 259–279.

87   R. Wageman, "Critical Success Factors for Creating Superb Self-Managing Teams," *Organizational Dynamics*, Summer 1997, p. 55.

88   M. A. Campion, E. M. Papper, and G. J. Medsker, "Relations between Work Team Characteristics and Effectiveness: A Replication and Extension," *Personnel Psychology*, Summer 1996, p. 430.

89   M. A. Campion, E. M. Papper, and G. J. Medsker, "Relations between Work Team Characteristics and Effectiveness: A Replication and Extension," *Personnel Psychology*, Summer 1996, p. 430.

90   K. Hess, *Creating the High-Performance Team* (New York: Wiley, 1987); J. R. Katzenbach and D. K. Smith, *The Wisdom of Teams* (Boston: Harvard Business School Press, 1993), pp. 43–64; and K. D. Scott and A. Townsend, "Teams: Why Some Succeed and Others Fail," *HR Magazine*, August 1994, pp. 62–67.

91   J. E. Mathieu and W. Schulze, "The Influence of Team Knowledge and Formal Plans on Episodic Team Process—Performance Relationships," *Academy of Management Journal* 49, no. 3 (2006), pp. 605–619.

92   A. Gurtner, F. Tschan, N. K. Semmer, and C. Nagele, "Getting Groups to Develop Good Strategies: Effects of Reflexivity Interventions on Team Process, Team Performance, and Shared Mental Models," *Organizational Behavior and Human Decision Processes* 102 (2007), pp. 127–142; M. C. Schippers, D. N. Den Hartog, and P. L. Koopman, "Reflexivity in Teams: A Measure and Correlates," *Applied Psychology: An International Review* 56, no. 2 (2007), pp. 189–211; and C. S. Burke, K. C. Stagl, E. Salas, L. Pierce, and D. Kendall, "Understanding Team Adaptation: A Conceptual Analysis and Model," *Journal of Applied Psychology* 91, no. 6 (2006), pp. 1189–1207.

93   E. Weldon and L. R. Weingart, "Group Goals and Group Performance," *British Journal of Social Psychology*, Spring 1993, pp. 307–334.

94   K. Tasa, S. Taggar, and G. H. Seijts, "The Development of Collective Efficacy in Teams: A Multilevel and Longitudinal Perspective," *Journal of Applied Psychology* 92, no. 1 (2007), pp. 17–27; C. B. Gibson, "The Efficacy Advantage: Factors Related to the Formation of Group Efficacy," *Journal of Applied Social Psychology*, October 2003, pp. 2153–2086; and D. I. Jung and J. J. Sosik, "Group Potency and Collective Efficacy: Examining Their Predictive Validity, Level of Analysis, and Effects of Performance Feedback on Future Group Performance," *Group & Organization Management*, September 2003, pp. 366–391.

95   For some of the controversy surrounding the definition of cohesion, see J. Keyton and J. Springston, "Redefining Cohesiveness in Groups," *Small Group Research*, May 1990, pp. 234–254.

96   C. R. Evans and K. L. Dion, "Group Cohesion and Performance: A Meta-Analysis," *Small Group Research*, May 1991, pp. 175–186; B. Mullen and C. Cooper, "The Relation between Group Cohesiveness and Performance: An Integration," *Psychological Bulletin*, March 1994, pp. 210–227; S. M. Gully, D. J. Devine, and D. J. Whitney, "A Meta-Analysis of Cohesion and Performance: Effects of Level of Analysis and Task Interdependence," *Small Group Research*, 1995, pp. 497–520; and P. M. Podsakoff, S. B. MacKenzie, and M. Ahearne, "Moderating Effects of Goal Acceptance on the Relationship between Group Cohesiveness and Productivity," *Journal of Applied Psychology*, December 1997, pp. 974–983.

97   A. Chang and P. Bordia, "A Multidimensional Approach to the Group Cohesion-Group Performance Relationship," *Small Group Research*, August 2001, pp. 379–405.

98   Paragraph based on R. Kreitner and A. Kinicki, *Organizational Behavior*, 6th ed. (New York: Irwin, 2004), pp. 459–461.

99   R. Kreitner and A. Kinicki, *Organizational Behavior*, 6th ed. (New York: Irwin, 2004), p. 460. Reprinted by permission of McGraw Hill Education.

100   Based on D. Man and S. S. K. Lam, "The Effects of Job Complexity and Autonomy on Cohesiveness in Collectivist and Individualistic Work Groups: A Cross- Cultural Analysis," *Journal of Organizational Behavior*, December 2003, pp. 979–1001.

101   A. P. J. Ellis, "System Breakdown: The Role of Mental Models and Transactive Memory on the Relationships between Acute Stress and Team Performance," *Academy of Management Journal* 49, no. 3 (2006), pp. 576–589.

102 S. W. J. Kozlowski and D. R. Ilgen, "Enhancing the Effectiveness of Work Groups and Teams," *Psychological Science in the Public Interest*, December 2006, pp. 77–124; and B. D. Edwards, E. A. Day, W. Arthur, Jr., and S. T. Bell, "Relationships among Team Ability Composition, Team Mental Models, and Team Performance," *Journal of Applied Psychology* 91, no. 3 (2006), pp. 727–736.

103 Based on K. M. Eisenhardt, J. L. Kahwajy, and L. J. Bourgeois III, "How Management Teams Can Have a Good Fight," *Harvard Business* Review, July–August 1997, p. 78.

104 K. M. Eisenhardt, J. L. Kahwajy, and L. J. Bourgeois III, "How Management Teams Can Have a Good Fight," *Harvard Business Review*, July–August 1997, p. 78.

105 K. M. Eisenhardt, J. L. Kahwajy, and L. J. Bourgeois III, "How Management Teams Can Have a Good Fight," *Harvard Business Review*, July–August 1997, p. 78.

106 K. Jehn, "A Multimethod Examination of the Benefits and Detriments of Intragroup Conflict," *Administrative Science Quarterly*, June 1995, pp. 256–282.

107 K. Hess, *Creating the High-Performance Team* (New York: Wiley, 1987).

108 D. Brown, "Innovative HR Ineffective in Manufacturing Firms," *Canadian HR Reporter*, April 7, 2003, pp. 1–2.

109 A. B. Drexler and R. Forrester, "Teamwork—Not Necessarily the Answer," *HR Magazine*, January 1998, pp. 55–58.

110 R. Forrester and A. B. Drexler, "A Model for Team-Based Organization Performance," *Academy of Management Executive*, August 1999, p. 47. See also S. A. Mohrman, with S. G. Cohen and A. M. Mohrman Jr., *Designing Team-Based Organizations* (San Francisco: Jossey-Bass, 1995); and J. H. Shonk, *Team Based Organizations* (Homewood, IL: Business One Irwin, 1992).

111 Based on N. Katz, "Sports Teams as a Model for Workplace Teams: Lessons and Liabilities," *Academy of Management Executive*, August 2001, pp. 56–67.

112 Based on N. Katz, "Sports Teams as a Model for Workplace Teams: Lessons and Liabilities," *Academy of Management Executive*, August 2001, pp. 56–67.

113 Adapted from D. A. Whetten and K. S. Cameron, *Developing Management Skills*, 3rd ed. © 1995, pp. 534–535. Adapted by permission of Pearson Education, Inc. Upper Saddle River, NJ.

114 This exercise is based on The Paper Tower Exercise: Experiencing Leadership and Group Dynamics, by Phillip L. Hunsaker and Johanna S. Hunsaker, unpublished manuscript. A brief description is included in "Exchange," *Organizational Behavior Teaching Journal* 4, no. 2 (1979), p. 49. Reprinted by permission of the authors. The materials list was suggested by Professor Sally Maitlis, Sauder School of Business, University of British Columbia.

115 This case is based on information in B. G. Chung and B. Schneider, "Serving Multiple Masters: Role Conflict Experienced by Service Employees," *Journal of Services Marketing* 16, 2002, pp. 70–88.

116 Based on C. Stapells, "Business Executives Bullish About Spa Time," *Toronto Star*, July 6, 2006, p. H3; C. Dahle, "How to Avoid a Rout at the Company Retreat," *New York Times*, October 31,

2004, p. 10; S. Max, "Seagate's Morale-athon," *BusinessWeek*, April 3, 2006, pp. 110–112; M. C. White, "Doing Good on Company Time," *New York Times*, May 8, 2007, p. C6; and N. H. Woodward, "Making the Most of Team Building," *HR Magazine*, September 2006, pp. 73–76.

117 S. P. Robbins and P. L. Hunsaker, *Training in Interpersonal Skills*, 2nd ed. (Upper Saddle River, NJ: Prentice Hall, 1996), pp. 168–184.

OB on the Edge: Trust

1 Vignette based on "Building Trust Since '31," *Windsor Star*, May 21, 2008, p. C11; "Come on Down," *Windsor Star*, September 20, 2007, p. D8; C. Vander Doelen, "Dodge's 'Aggressive' Theme Gets a Makeover," *Windsor Star*, September 18, 2007, p. B1; and http://www.reaumechev.com.

2 See, for example, K. T. Dirks and D. L. Ferrin, "Trust in Leadership: Meta-Analytic Findings and Implications for Research and Practice," *Journal of Applied Psychology*, August 2002, pp. 611–628; the special issue on trust in an organizational context, B. McEvily, V. Perrone, A. Zaheer, guest editors, *Organization Science*, January–February 2003; and R. Galford and A. S. Drapeau, *The Trusted Leader* (New York: Free Press, 2003).

3 F. K. Sonnenberg, "Trust Me, Trust Me Not," *IndustryWeek*, August 16, 1993, pp. 22–28; and L. T. Hosmer, "Trust: the Connecting Link between Organizational Theory and Philosophical Ethics," *Academy of Management Review*, April 1995, pp. 379–403.

4 T. Davis and M. J. Landa, "The Trust Deficit," *Worklife Report* 4, 1999, pp. 6–7.

5 T. Davis and M. J. Landa, "The Trust Deficit," *Worklife Report* 4, 1999, pp. 6–7.

6 D. J. McAllister, "Affect- and Cognition-Based Trust as Foundations for Interpersonal Cooperation in Organizations," *Academy of Management Journal*, February 1995, p. 25; R. C. Mayer, J. H. Davis, and F. D. Schoorman, "An Integrative Model of Organizational Trust," *Academy of Management Review* 20, 1995, pp. 709–734; and D. M. Rousseau, S. B. Sitkin, R. S. Burt, and C. Camerer, "Not So Different After All: A Cross-Discipline View of Trust," *Academy of Management Review*, July 1998, pp. 393–404.

7 J. K. Rempel, J. G. Holmes, and M. P. Zanna, "Trust in Close Relationships," *Journal of Personality and Social Psychology*, July 1985, p. 96.

8 M. Granovetter, "Economic Action and Social Structure: The Problem of Embeddedness," *American Journal of Sociology*, November 1985, p. 491.

9 J. B. Rotter, "Interpersonal Trust, Trustworthiness, and Gullibility," *American Psychologist*, January 1980, pp. 1–7.

10 J. D. Lewis and A. Weigert, "Trust as a Social Reality," *Social Forces*, June 1985, p. 970.

11 J. K. Rempel, J. G. Holmes, and M. P. Zanna, "Trust in Close Relationships," *Journal of Personality and Social Psychology*, July 1985, p. 96.

12 M. Granovetter, "Economic Action and Social Structure: The Problem of Embeddedness," *American Journal of Sociology*, November 1985, p. 491.

13   R. C. Mayer, J. H. Davis, and F. D. Schoorman, "An Integrative Model of Organizational Trust," *Academy of Management Review*, July 1995, p. 712.

14   C. Johnson-George and W. Swap, "Measurement of Specific Interpersonal Trust: Construction and Validation of a Scale to Assess Trust in a Specific Other," *Journal of Personality and Social Psychology*, September 1982, p. 1306.

15   P. L. Schindler and C. C. Thomas, "The Structure of Interpersonal Trust in the Workplace," *Psychological Reports*, October 1993, pp. 563–573.

16   Cited in D. Jones, "Do You Trust Your CEO?" *USA Today*, February 12, 2003, p. 7B.

17   J. K. Butler Jr. and R. S. Cantrell, "A Behavioral Decision Theory Approach to Modeling Dyadic Trust in Superiors and Subordinates," *Psychological Reports*, August 1984, pp. 19–28.

18   D. McGregor, *The Professional Manager* (New York: McGraw-Hill, 1967), p. 164.

19   B. Nanus, *The Leader's Edge: The Seven Keys to Leadership in a Turbulent World* (Chicago: Contemporary Books, 1989), p. 102.

20   Based on information in T. Simons, "The High Cost of Lost Trust," *Harvard Business Review*, September 2002, pp. 18–19.

21   K. T. Dirks and D. L. Ferrin, "Trust in Leadership: Meta-Analytic Findings and Implications for Organizational Research," *Journal of Applied Psychology* 87, 2002, pp. 611–628.

22   D. Shapiro, B. H. Sheppard, and L. Cheraskin, "Business on a Handshake," *Negotiation Journal*, October 1992, pp. 365–377; R. J. Lewicki, E. C. Tomlinson, and N. Gillespie, "Models of Interpersonal Trust Development: Theoretical Approaches, Empirical Evidence, and Future Directions," *Journal of Management*, December 2006, pp. 991–1022; and J. Child, "Trust—The Fundamental Bond in Global Collaboration," *Organizational Dynamics* 29, no. 4 (2001), pp. 274–288.

23   This section is based on D. E. Zand, *The Leadership Triad: Knowledge, Trust, and Power* (New York: Oxford University Press, 1997), pp. 122–134; and A. M. Zak, J. A. Gold, R. M. Ryckman, and E. Lenney, "Assessments of Trust in Intimate Relationships and the Self-Perception Process," *Journal of Social Psychology*, April 1998, pp. 217–228.

24   FactBox items cited in Z. Ezekiel, *Building Public Trust in Canadian Organizations: Preliminary Findings* (Ottawa: The Conference Board of Canada, May 2005), pp. 1–3.

25   M. E. Schweitzer, J. C. Hershey, and E. T. Bradlow, "Promises and Lies: Restoring Violated Trust," *Organizational Behavior and Human Decision Processes* 101 (2006), pp. 1–19.

26   L. Prusak and D. Cohen, "How to Invest in Social Capital," *Harvard Business Review*, June 2001, pp. 86–93.

27   L. Prusak and D. Cohen, "How to Invest in Social Capital," *Harvard Business Review*, June 2001, pp. 86–93.

28   Based on information in L. Prusak and D. Cohen, "How to Invest in Social Capital," *Harvard Business Review*, June 2001, p. 92.

29   K. T. Dirks, "Trust in Leadership and Team Performance: Evidence from NCAA Basketball," *Journal of Applied Psychology* 85, 2000, pp. 1004–1012.

30   Based on F. Bartolome, "Nobody Trusts the Boss Completely—Now What?" *Harvard Business Review*, March–April 1989, pp. 135–142; and P. Pascarella, "15 Ways to Win People's Trust," *IndustryWeek*, February 1, 1993, pp. 47–51.

31   Based on information in R. M. Kramer, "When Paranoia Makes Sense," *Harvard Business Review*, July 2002, p. 68.

32   C. W. Langfred, "Too Much of a Good Thing? Negative Effects of High Trust and Individual Autonomy in Self-Managing Teams," *Academy of Management Journal* 47, no. 3 (June 2004), pp. 385–399.

33   R. M. Kramer, "When Paranoia Makes Sense," *Harvard Business Review*, July 2002, pp. 62–69.

34   R. M. Kramer, "When Paranoia Makes Sense," *Harvard Business Review*, July 2002, p. 63.

Chapter 7

1   Based on B. Erskine, "Oil Sands: The Next Generation Sessions," submission to International Association of Business Communicators, http://www.iabc.com/awards/gq/WPMgt.htm.

2   See, for example, K. W. Thomas and W. H. Schmidt, "A Survey of Managerial Interests with Respect to Conflict," *Academy of Management Journal*, June 1976, p. 317.

3   L. Ramsay, "Communication Key to Workplace Happiness," *Financial Post*, December 6/8, 1997, p. 58.

4   See http://www.isrsurveys.com/default.asp (accessed March 14, 2002).

5   "Employers Cite Communication Skills, Honesty/Integrity as Key for Job Candidates," *IPMA-HR Bulletin*, March 23, 2007, p. 1.

6   D. K. Berlo, *The Process of Communication* (New York: Holt, Rinehart and Winston, 1960), p. 54.

7   J. C. McCroskey, J. A. Daly, and G. Sorenson, "Personality Correlates of Communication Apprehension," *Human Communication Research*, Spring 1976, pp. 376–380.

8   See R. L. Daft and R. H. Lengel, "Information Richness: A New Approach to Managerial Behavior and Organization Design," in *Research in Organizational Behavior*, vol. 6, ed. B. M. Staw and L. L. Cummings (Greenwich, CT: JAI Press, 1984), pp. 191–233; R. E. Rice and D. E. Shook, "Relationships of Job Categories and Organizational Levels to Use of Communication Channels, Including Electronic Mail: A Meta-Analysis and Extension," *Journal of Management Studies*, March 1990, pp. 195–229; R. E. Rice, "Task Analyzability, Use of New Media, and Effectiveness," *Organization Science*, November 1992, pp. 475–500; S. G. Straus and J. E. McGrath, "Does the Medium Matter? The Interaction of Task Type and Technology on Group Performance and Member Reaction," *Journal of Applied Psychology*, February 1994, pp. 87–97; J. Webster and L. K. Trevino, "Rational and Social Theories as Complementary Explanations of Communication Media Choices: Two Policy-Capturing Studies," *Academy of Management Journal*, December 1995, pp. 1544–1572.

9 I. Austen, "Telling Tales Out of School, on YouTube," *New York Times*, November 27, 2006; and D. Rogers, "Quebec Students Suspended for Posting Teacher's Outburst Online," *Ottawa Citizen*, November 25, 2006.

10 R. L. Daft, R. H. Lengel, and L. K. Trevino, "Message Equivocality, Media Selection, and Manager Performance: Implications for Information Systems," *MIS Quarterly*, September 1987, pp. 355–368.

11 "Virtual Pink Slips Start Coming Online," *Vancouver Sun*, July 3, 1999, p. D15.

12 Thanks are due to an anonymous reviewer for providing this elaboration.

13 Based on S. Klie, "Dawning of a New Day at Suncor," *Canadian HR Reporter*, October 22, 2007, p. 21.

14 M. Richtel, "Lost in E-mail, Tech Firms Face Self-Made Beast," *New York Times*, June 14, 2008.

15 S. I. Hayakawa, *Language in Thought and Action* (New York: Harcourt Brace Jovanovich, 1949), p. 292.

16 H. Weeks, "Taking the Stress Out of Stressful Conversations," *Harvard Business Review*, July–August 2001, pp. 112–119.

17 Based on S. Klie, "Dawning of a New Day at Suncor," *Canadian HR Reporter*, October 22, 2007, p. 21; and B. Erskine, "Oil Sands: The Next Generation Sessions," submission to International Association of Business Communicators, http://www.iabc.com/awards/gq/WPMgt.htm.

18 R. L. Simpson, "Vertical and Horizontal Communication in Formal Organizations," *Administrative Science Quarterly*, September 1959, pp. 188–196; and B. Harriman, "Up and Down the Communications Ladder," *Harvard Business Review*, September–October 1974, pp. 143–151.

19 P. Dvorak, "How Understanding the 'Why' of Decisions Matters," *Wall Street Journal* (March 19, 2007), p. B3.

20 E. Nichols, "Hyper-Speed Managers," *HR Magazine*, April 2007, pp. 107–110.

21 D. M. Saunders and J. D. Leck, "Formal Upward Communication Procedures: Organizational and Employee Perspectives," *Revue Canadienne des Sciences de l'Administration*, September 1993, pp. 255–268.

22 "Heard It through the Grapevine," *Forbes*, February 10, 1997, p. 22.

23 K. Davis cited in R. Rowan, "Where Did That Rumor Come From?" *Fortune*, August 13, 1979, p. 134.

24 L. Hirschhorn, "Managing Rumors," in *Cutting Back*, ed. L. Hirschhorn (San Francisco: Jossey-Bass, 1983), pp. 49–52.

25 R. L. Rosnow and G. A. Fine, *Rumor and Gossip: The Social Psychology of Hearsay* (New York: Elsevier, 1976).

26 This section is based on R. Kreitner and A. Kinicki, *Organizational Behavior*, 6th ed. (New York: McGraw-Hill, 2004), pp. 541–542.

27 H. B. Vickery III, "Tapping into the Employee Grapevine," *Association Management*, January 1984, pp. 59–60.

28 See, for instance, J. W. Newstrom, R. E. Monczka, and W. E. Reif, "Perceptions of the Grapevine: Its Value and Influence," *Journal of Business Communication*, Spring 1974, pp. 12–20; and S. J. Modic, "Grapevine Rated Most Believable," *IndustryWeek*, May 15, 1989, p. 14.

29 See, for instance, J. G. March and G. Sevon, "Gossip, Information and Decision Making," in *Decisions and Organizations*, ed. J. G. March (Oxford: Blackwell, 1988), pp. 429–442; M. Noon and R. Delbridge, "News from Behind My Hand: Gossip in Organizations," *Organization Studies* 14, no. 1 (1993), pp. 23–36; and N. DiFonzo, P. Bordia, and R. L. Rosnow, "Reining in Rumors," *Organizational Dynamics*, Summer 1994, pp. 47–62.

30 L. Hirschhorn, "Managing Rumors," in *Cutting Back*, ed. L. Hirschhorn (San Francisco: Jossey-Bass, 1983), pp. 54–56.

31 See, for instance, R. Hotch, "Communication Revolution," *Nation's Business*, May 1993, pp. 20–28; G. Brockhouse, "I Have Seen the Future," *Canadian Business*, August 1993, pp. 43–45; R. Hotch, "In Touch through Technology," *Nation's Business*, January 1994, pp. 33–35; and P. LaBarre, "The Other Network," *IndustryWeek*, September 19, 1994, pp. 33–36.

32 "Email Brings Costs and Fatigue," *Western News* (UWO), July 9, 2004, http://communications.uwo.ca/com/western_news/stories/email_brings_costs_and_fatigue_20040709432320/.

33 K. Macklem, "You've Got Too Much Mail," *Maclean's*, January 30, 2006, pp. 20–21.

34 "Overloaded Canadians Trash 42% of All E-Mails: Study," *Ottawa Citizen*, June 26, 2008, p. D5.

35 D. Brady, "*!#?@ the E-mail. Can We Talk?" *BusinessWeek*, December 4, 2006, p. 109.

36 E. Binney, "Is E-mail the New Pink Slip?" *HR Magazine*, November 2006, pp. 32–33; and R. L. Rundle, "Critical Case: How an Email Rant Jolted a Big HMO," *Wall Street Journal*, April 24, 2007, pp. A1, A16.

37 "Some Email Recipients Say 'Enough Already,'" *Gainesville* (Florida) *Sun*, June 3, 2007, p. 1G.

38 D. Goleman, "Flame First, Think Later: New Clues to E-mail Misbehavior," *New York Times*, February 20, 2007, p. D5; and E. Krell, "The Unintended Word," *HR Magazine*, August 2006, pp. 50–54.

39 R. Zeidner, "Keeping E-mail in Check," *HR Magazine*, June 2007, pp. 70–74; "E-mail May Be Hazardous to Your Career," *Fortune*, May 14, 2007, p. 24; "More Firms Fire Employees for E-mail Violations," *Gainesville* (Florida) *Sun*, June 6, 2006, p. B1.

40 Based on S. Proudfoot, "1 in 3 Workers Admit to Improper E-mail; Stories of Career-Killing Gaffes Leave Many Unfazed, Study Finds," *Edmonton Journal*, June 25, 2008, p. A1; E. Church, "Employers Read E-mail as Fair Game," *Globe and Mail*, April 14, 1998, p. B16; and J. Kay, "Someone Will Watch Over Me: Think Your Office E-mails Are Private? Think Again," *National Post Business*, January 2001, pp. 59–64.

41 E. Church, "Employers Read E-mail as Fair Game," *Globe and Mail*, April 14, 1998, p. B16.

42 Based on "At Many Companies, Hunt for Leakers Expands Arsenal of Monitoring Tactics," *Wall Street Journal*, September 11, 2006, pp. B1, B3; and B. J. Alge, G. A. Ballinger, S. Tangirala, and J. L. Oakley, "Information Privacy in Organizations: Empowering Creative and Extra-Role Performance," *Journal of Applied Psychology* 91, no. 1 (2006), pp. 221–232.

43 A. Harmon, "Appeal of Instant Messaging Extends into the Workplace," *New York Times*, March 11, 2003, p. A1.

44 Report released by the Canadian Wireless Telecommunications Association, as reported in P. Wilson, "Record Growth of Text Messaging Continues in Canada," *Vancouver Sun*, March 23, 2005, p. D2; and J. Bow, "Business Jumps on Text-Messaging Wave, *Business Edge*, April 5, 2007, p. 12.

45 J. Bow, "Business Jumps on Text-Messaging Wave, *Business Edge*, April 5, 2007, p. 12.

46 "Survey Finds Mixed Reviews on Checking E-mail During Meetings," *IPMA-HR Bulletin*, April 27, 2007, p. 1.

47 K. Gurchiek, "Shoddy Writing Can Trip Up Employees, Organizations," *SHRM Online*, April 27, 2006, pp. 1–2.

48 R. L. Birdwhistell, *Introduction to Kinesics* (Louisville, KY: University of Louisville Press, 1952).

49 J. Fast, *Body Language* (Philadelphia, PA: M. Evan, 1970), p. 7.

50 A. Mehrabian, *Nonverbal Communication* (Chicago: Aldine-Atherton, 1972).

51 N. M. Henley, "Body Politics Revisited: What Do We Know Today?" in *Gender, Power, and Communication in Human Relationships*, ed. P. J. Kalbfleisch and M. J. Cody (Hillsdale, NJ: Erlbaum, 1995), pp. 27–61.

52 E. T. Hall, *The Hidden Dimension*, 2nd ed. (Garden City, NY: Anchor Books/Doubleday, 1966).

53 This section largely based on C. G. Pinder and K. P. Harlos, "Silent Organizational Behavior" (paper presented at the Western Academy of Management Conference, March 2000); and P. Mornell, "The Sounds of Silence," *Inc.*, February 2001, pp. 117–118.

54 See D. Tannen, *You Just Don't Understand: Women and Men in Conversation* (New York: Ballantine Books, 1991); and D. Tannen, *Talking from 9 to 5* (New York: William Morrow, 1995).

55 D. Goldsmith and P. Fulfs, "You Just Don't Have the Evidence: An Analysis of Claims and Evidence in Deborah Tannen's *You Just Don't Understand*," in *Communications Yearbook*, vol. 22, ed. M. Roloff (Thousand Oaks, CA: Sage, 1999).

56 N. Langton "Differences in Communication Styles: Asking for a Raise," in *Organizational Behavior: Experiences and Cases*, 4th ed., ed. D. Marcic (St. Paul, MN: West Publishing, 1995).

57 See M. Munter, "Cross-Cultural Communication for Managers," *Business Horizons*, May–June 1993, pp. 75–76.

58 See E. T. Hall, *Beyond Culture* (Garden City, NY: Anchor Press/Doubleday, 1976); E. T. Hall, "How Cultures Collide," *Psychology Today*, July 1976, pp. 67–74; E. T. Hall and M. R. Hall, *Understanding Cultural Differences* (Yarmouth, ME: Intercultural Press, 1990); and R. E. Dulek, J. S. Fielden, and J. S. Hill, "International Communication: An Executive Primer," *Business Horizons*, January–February 1991, pp. 20–25.

59 N. Adler, *International Dimensions of Organizational Behavior*, 3rd ed. (Cincinnati, OH: South Western College, 1997), pp. 87–88.

60 S. A. Hellweg and S. L. Phillips, "Communication and Productivity in Organizations: A State-of-the-Art Review," in *Proceedings of the 40th Annual Academy of Management Conference*, Detroit, 1980, pp. 188–192.

61 Based on E. Jaffe, "The Science Behind Secrets," *APS Observer*, July 2006, pp. 20–22.

62 E. C. Glenn and E. A. Pood, "Listening Self-Inventory," *Supervisory Management*, January 1989, pp. 12–15. Reprinted by permission.

63 Cited in "Who's Lying Now?" *Training*, October 2000, p. 34.

64 Based on E. Wong, "Stinging Office E-Mail Lights 'Firestorm,'" *Globe and Mail*, April 9, 2001, p. M1; P. D. Broughton, "Boss's Angry Email Sends Shares Plunging," *Daily Telegraph of London*, April 6, 2001; and D. Stafford, "Shattering the Illusion of Respect," *Kansas City Star*, March 29, 2001, p. C1.

65 This case is based on N. J. Torres, "Playing Well with Others," *Entrepreneur*, February 2003, p. 30.

66 Based on S. P. Robbins and P. L. Hunsaker, *Training in Interpersonal Skills: TIPs for Managing People at Work*, 2nd ed. (Upper Saddle River, NJ: Prentice Hall, 1996), Chapter 3; and data in R. C. Huseman, J. M. Lahiff, and J. M. Penrose, *Business Communication: Strategies and Skills* (Chicago: Dryden Press, 1988), pp. 380, 425.

Chapter 8

1 Opening vignette based on R. Ouzounian, "Stratford's Fantastic Four," *thestar.com*, August 18, 2007 (accessed February 3, 2009); K. Taylor, "When Too Many Cooks Can Be Poison," *Globe and Mail*, March 29, 2008, p. R15; R. Ouzounian, "Similarities May Have Torn Stratford Trio Apart," *thestar.com*, March 25, 2008 (accessed February 3, 2009).

2 Based on B. M. Bass, *Bass & Stogdill's Handbook of Leadership*, 3rd ed. (New York: Free Press, 1990).

3 S. Prashad, "Fill Your Power Gap," *Globe and Mail*, July 23, 2003, p. C3.

4 J. R. P. French Jr. and B. Raven, "The Bases of Social Power," in *Studies in Social Power*, ed. D. Cartwright (Ann Arbor: University of Michigan, Institute for Social Research, 1959), pp. 150–167. For an update on French and Raven's work, see D. E. Frost and A. J. Stahelski, "The Systematic Measurement of French and Raven's Bases of Social Power in Workgroups," *Journal of Applied Social Psychology*, April 1988, pp. 375–389; T. R. Hinkin and C. A. Schriesheim, "Development and Application of New Scales to Measure the French and Raven (1959) Bases of Social Power," *Journal of Applied Psychology*, August 1989, pp. 561–567; and G. E. Littlepage, J. L. Van Hein, K. M. Cohen, and L. L. Janiec, "Evaluation and Comparison of Three Instruments Designed to Measure Organizational Power and Influence Tactics," *Journal of Applied Social Psychology*, January 16–31, 1993, pp. 107–125.

5   B. H. Raven, "Social Influence and Power," in *Current Studies in Social Psychology*, ed. I. D. Steiner and M. Fishbein (New York: Holt, Rinehart, Winston, 1965), pp. 371–382.

6   D. Kipnis, *The Powerholders* (Chicago: University of Chicago Press, 1976), pp. 77–78.

7   E. A. Ward, "Social Power Bases of Managers: Emergence of a New Factor," *Journal of Social Psychology*, February 2001, pp. 144–147.

8   S. Milgram, *Obedience to Authority* (New York: Harper and Row, 1974).

9   D. Hickson, C. Hinings, C. Lee, R. Schneck, and J. Pennings, "A Strategic Contingencies Theory of Intra-Organizational Power," *Administrative Science Quarterly* 16, 1971, pp. 216–229.

10   J. W. Dean Jr. and J. R. Evans, *Total Quality: Management, Organization, and Strategy* (Minneapolis-St. Paul, MN: West, 1994).

11   M. Folb, "Cause Celeb: From Deborah Cox to Maestro, Homegrown Talent Is Hocking Retail Fashion," *Marketing Magazine*, April 5, 1999, p. 13; and http://canada.roots.com.

12   G. Yukl, H. Kim, C. M. Falbe, "Antecedents of Influence Outcomes," *Journal of Applied Psychology* 81, no. 3 (June 1, 1996), pp. 309–317.

13   P. P. Carson, K. D. Carson, and C. W. Roe, "Social Power Bases: A Meta-Analytic Examination of Interrelationships and Outcomes," *Journal of Applied Social Psychology* 23, no. 14 (1993), pp. 1150–1169.

14   C. M. Falbe and G. Yukl, "Consequences for Managers of Using Single Tactics and Combinations of Tactics," *Academy of Management Journal* 35, 1992, pp. 638–652.

15   Cited in J. R. Carlson, D. S. Carlson, and L. L. Wadsworth, "The Relationship between Individual Power Moves and Group Agreement Type: An Examination and Model," *SAM Advanced Management Journal* 65, no. 4 (2000), pp. 44–51.

16   Vignette based on R. Ouzounian, "Resignations a Blow to Stratford," *thestar.com*, March 13, 2008 (accessed February 4, 2009); and R. Ouzounian, "Similarities May Have Torn Stratford Trio Apart," *thestar.com*, March 25, 2008 (accessed February 4, 2009).

17   R. E. Emerson, "Power Dependence Relations," *American Sociological Review* 27, 1962, pp. 31–41.

18   Thanks are due to an anonymous reviewer for supplying this insight.

19   H. Mintzberg, *Power in and Around Organizations* (Englewood Cliffs, NJ: Prentice Hall, 1983), p. 24.

20   See, for example, D. Kipnis, S. M. Schmidt, C. Swaffin-Smith, and I. Wilkinson, "Patterns of Managerial Influence: Shotgun Managers, Tacticians, and Bystanders," *Organizational Dynamics*, Winter 1984, pp. 58–67; T. Case, L. Dosier, G. Murkison, and B. Keys, "How Managers Influence Superiors: A Study of Upward Influence Tactics," *Leadership and Organization Development Journal* 9, no. 4 (1988), pp. 25–31; D. Kipnis and S. M. Schmidt, "Upward-Influence Styles: Relationship with Performance Evaluations, Salary, and Stress," *Administrative Science Quarterly*, December 1988, pp. 528–542; G. Yukl and C. M. Falbe, "Influence Tactics and Objectives in Upward, Downward, and Lateral Influence Attempts," *Journal of Applied Psychology*, April 1990, pp. 132–140; B. Keys and T. Case, "How to Become an Influential Manager," *Academy of Management Executive*, November 1990, pp. 38–51; D. A. Ralston, D. J. Gustafson, L. Mainiero, and D. Umstot, "Strategies of Upward Influence: A Cross-National Comparison of Hong Kong and American Managers," *Asia Pacific Journal of Management*, October 1993, pp. 157–175; G. Yukl, H. Kim, and C. M. Falbe, "Antecedents of Influence Outcomes," *Journal of Applied Psychology*, June 1996, pp. 309–317; K. E. Lauterbach and B. J. Weiner, "Dynamics of Upward Influence: How Male and Female Managers Get Their Way," *Leadership Quarterly*, Spring 1996, pp. 87–107; K. R. Xin and A. S. Tsui, "Different Strokes for Different Folks? Influence Tactics by Asian-American and Caucasian-American Managers," *Leadership Quarterly*, Spring 1996, pp. 109–132; and S. J. Wayne, R. C. Liden, I. K. Graf, and G. R. Ferris, "The Role of Upward Influence Tactics in Human Resource Decisions," *Personnel Psychology*, Winter 1997, pp. 979–1006.

21   This section adapted from G. Yukl, C. M. Falbe, and J. Y. Youn, "Patterns of Influence Behavior for Managers," *Group & Organization Studies* 18, no. 1 (March 1993), p. 7.

22   G. Yukl, *Leadership in Organizations*, 5th ed. (Upper Saddle River, NJ: Prentice Hall, 2002), pp. 141–174; G. R. Ferris, W. A. Hochwarter, C. Douglas, F. R. Blass, R. W. Kolodinksy, and D. C. Treadway, "Social Influence Processes in Organizations and Human Resource Systems," in *Research in Personnel and Human Resources Management*, vol. 21, ed. G. R. Ferris and J. J. Martocchio (Oxford, UK: JAI Press/Elsevier, 2003), pp. 65–127; and C. A. Higgins, T. A. Judge, and G. R. Ferris, "Influence Tactics and Work Outcomes: A Meta-Analysis," *Journal of Organizational Behavior*, March 2003, pp. 89–106.

23   C. M. Falbe and G. Yukl, "Consequences for Managers of Using Single Influence Tactics and Combinations of Tactics," *Academy of Management Journal*, July 1992, pp. 638–653.

24   G. Yukl, *Leadership in Organizations*, 5th ed. (Upper Saddle River, NJ: Prentice Hall, 2002), pp. 141–174.

25   G. Yukl, *Leadership in Organizations*, 5th ed. (Upper Saddle River, NJ: Prentice Hall, 2002), pp. 141–174.

26   C. M. Falbe and G. Yukl, "Consequences for Managers of Using Single Influence Tactics and Combinations of Tactics," *Academy of Management Journal*, July 1992, pp. 638–653.

27   G. R. Ferris, D. C. Treadway, P. L. Perrewé, R. L. Brouer, C. Douglas, and S. Lux, "Political Skill in Organizations," *Journal of Management*, June 2007, pp. 290–320; K. J. Harris, K. M. Kacmar, S. Zivnuska, and J. D. Shaw, "The Impact of Political Skill on Impression Management Effectiveness," *Journal of Applied Psychology* 92, no. 1 (2007), pp. 278–285; W. A. Hochwarter, G. R. Ferris, M. B. Gavin, P. L. Perrewé, A. T. Hall, and D. D. Frink, "Political Skill as Neutralizer of Felt Accountability–Job Tension Effects on Job Performance Ratings: A Longitudinal Investigation," *Organizational Behavior and Human Decision Processes* 102, 2007, pp. 226–239; D. C. Treadway, G. R. Ferris, A. B. Duke, G. L. Adams, and J. B. Tatcher, "The Moderating Role of Subordinate Political Skill on Supervisors' Impressions of Subordinate Ingratiation and Ratings of Subordinate Interpersonal Facilitation," *Journal of Applied Psychology* 92, no. 3 (2007), pp. 848–855.

28   Based on P. P. Fu, T. K. Peng, J. C. Kennedy, and G. Yukl, "A Comparison of Chinese Managers in Hong Kong, Taiwan, and Mainland China," *Organizational Dynamics*, February 2004, pp. 32–46.

29   Search of Business Source Premier and Canadian Newsstand articles conducted by the author, September 2005.

30   This is the definition given by R. Forrester, "Empowerment: Rejuvenating a Potent Idea," *Academy of Management Executive*, August 2000, pp. 67–80.

31   R. E. Quinn and G. M. Spreitzer, "The Road to Empowerment: Seven Questions Every Leader Should Consider," *Organizational Dynamics*, Autumn 1997, p. 38.

32   S. Wetlaufer, "Organizing for Empowerment: An Interview with AES's Roger Sant and Dennis Bakke," *Harvard Business Review*, January–February 1999, pp. 110–123.

33   C. Argyris, "Empowerment: The Emperor's New Clothes," *Harvard Business Review*, May–June 1998.

34   K. Kitagawa, *Empowering Employee–Learners with Essential Skills at Durabelt Inc.* (Ottawa: The Conference Board of Canada, March 2005).

35   J. Schaubroeck, J. R. Jones, and J. L. Xie, "Individual Differences in Utilizing Control to Cope with Job Demands: Effects on Susceptibility to Infectious Disease," *Journal of Applied Psychology* 86, no. 2 (2001), pp. 265–278.

36   Thanks are due to an anonymous reviewer for this insight.

37   R. C. Ford and M. D. Fottler, "Empowerment: A Matter of Degree," *Academy of Management Executive* 9, 1995, pp. 21–31.

38   Points are summarized from R. C. Ford and M. D. Fottler, "Empowerment: A Matter of Degree," *Academy of Management Executive* 9, 1995, pp. 23–25.

39   T. D. Wall, N. J. Kemp, P. R. Jackson, and W. W. Clegg, "Outcomes of Autonomous Work Groups: A Long-Term Field Experiment," *Academy of Management Journal* 29, 1986, pp. 280–304.

40   "Delta Promotes Empowerment," *Globe and Mail*, May 31, 1999, Advertising Supplement, p. C5.

41   G. M. Spreitzer, "Psychological Empowerment in the Workplace: Dimensions, Measurement, and Validation," *Academy of Management Journal* 38, 1995, pp. 1442–1465; G. M. Spreitzer, M. A. Kizilos, and S. W. Nason, "A Dimensional Analysis of the Relationship between Psychological Empowerment and Effectiveness, Satisfaction, and Strain," *Journal of Management* 23, 1997, pp. 679–704; and K. W. Thomas and W. G. Tymon, "Does Empowerment Always Work: Understanding the Role of Intrinsic Motivation and Personal Interpretation," *Journal of Management Systems* 6, 1994, pp. 39–54.

42   D. E. Hyatt and T. M. Ruddy, "An Examination of the Relationship between Work Group Characteristics and Performance: Once More into the Breech," *Personnel Psychology* 50, 1997, pp. 553–585; B. L. Kirkman and B. Rosen, "Beyond Self-Management: Antecedents and Consequences of Team Empowerment," *Academy of Management Journal* 42, 1999, pp. 58–74; P. E. Tesluck, D. J. Brass, and J. E. Mathieu, "An Examination of Empowerment Processes at Individual and Group Levels" (paper presented at the 11th annual conference of the Society of Industrial and Organizational Psychology, San Diego, 1996).

43   C. Robert, T. M. Probst, J. J. Martocchio, F. Drasgow, and J. J. Lawler, "Empowerment and Continuous Improvement in the United States, Mexico, Poland, and India: Predicting Fit on the Basis of the Dimensions of Power Distance and Individualism," *Journal of Applied Psychology* 85, 2000, pp. 643–658.

44   W. A. Randolph and M. Sashkin, "Can Organizational Empowerment Work in Multinational Settings?" *Academy of Management Executive*, February 2002, pp. 102–115.

45   T. Lee and C. M. Brotheridge, "When the Prey Becomes the Predator: Bullying as Predictor of Reciprocal Bullying, Coping, and Well-Being" (working paper, University of Regina, Regina, 2005).

46   "More and More Workplaces Have Bullies," *Leader-Post* (Regina), December 14, 2004, p. A1.

47   M. S. Hershcovis and J. Barling, "Comparing the Outcomes of Sexual Harassment and Workplace Aggression: A Meta-Analysis" (paper presented at the Seventh International Conference on Work, Stress and Health, Washington, DC, March 8, 2008).

48   Quebec Labour Standards, s. 81.18, *Psychological Harassment at Work*.

49   M. Bridge, "Female Firefighters Claim Harassment," *Vancouver Sun*, March 22, 2006, p. A1.

50   "Employers Underestimate Extent of Sexual Harassment, Report Says," *Vancouver Sun*, March 8, 2001, p. D6.

51   "Employers Underestimate Extent of Sexual Harassment, Report Says," *Vancouver Sun*, March 8, 2001, p. D6.

52   *Janzen v. Platy Enterprises Ltd.* [1989] 10 C.H.R.R. D/6205 SCC.

53   The following section is based on J. N. Cleveland and M. E. Kerst, "Sexual Harassment and Perceptions of Power: An Under-Articulated Relationship," *Journal of Vocational Behavior*, February 1993, pp. 49–67.

54   J. Goddu, "Sexual Harassment Complaints Rise Dramatically," *Canadian Press Newswire*, March 6, 1998.

55   K. Von Hoffmann, "Forbidden Fruit: Student-Faculty Relationships," *Yale Herald*, October 17, 2003, p. 1.

56   C. R. Willness, P. Steel, and K. Lee, "A Meta-Analysis of the Antecedents and Consequences of Workplace Sexual Harassment," *Personnel Psychology* 60, 2007, pp. 127–162.

57   S. A. Culbert and J. J. McDonough, *The Invisible War: Pursuing Self-Interest at Work* (New York: Wiley, 1980), p. 6.

58   H. Mintzberg, *Power in and Around Organizations* (Englewood Cliffs, NJ: Prentice Hall, 1983), p. 26.

59   T. Cole, "Who Loves Ya?" *Report on Business Magazine*, April 1999, p. 54.

60   D. Farrell and J. C. Petersen, "Patterns of Political Behavior in Organizations," *Academy of Management Review*, July 1982, p. 405. For a thoughtful analysis of the academic controversies under-

lying any definition of organizational politics, see A. Drory and T. Romm, "The Definition of Organizational Politics: A Review," *Human Relations*, November 1990, pp. 1133–1154.

61 J. Pfeffer, *Power in Organizations* (Marshfield, MA: Pittman, 1981).

62 G. R. Ferris, G. S. Russ, and P. M. Fandt, "Politics in Organizations," in *Impression Management in Organizations*, ed. R. A. Giacalone and P. Rosenfeld (Newbury Park, CA: Sage, 1989), pp. 143–170; and K. M. Kacmar, D. P. Bozeman, D. S. Carlson, and W. P. Anthony, "An Examination of the Perceptions of Organizational Politics Model: Replication and Extension," *Human Relations*, March 1999, pp. 383–416.

63 K. M. Kacmar and R. A. Baron, "Organizational Politics: The State of the Field, Links to Related Processes, and an Agenda for Future Research," in *Research in Personnel and Human Resources Management*, vol. 17, ed. G. R. Ferris (Greenwich, CT: JAI Press, 1999); and M. Valle and L. A. Witt, "The Moderating Effect of Teamwork Perceptions on the Organizational Politics-Job Satisfaction Relationship," *Journal of Social Psychology*, June 2001, pp. 379–388.

64 G. R. Ferris, D. D. Frink, M. C. Galang, J. Zhou, K. M. Kacmar, and J. L. Howard, "Perceptions of Organizational Politics: Prediction, Stress-Related Implications, and Outcomes," *Human Relations*, February 1996, pp. 233–266; K. M. Kacmar, D. P. Bozeman, D. S. Carlson, and W. P. Anthony, "An Examination of the Perceptions of Organizational Politics Model; Replication and Extension," *Human Relations*, March 1999, p. 388; and J. M. L. Poon, "Situational Antecedents and Outcomes of Organizational Politics Perceptions," *Journal of Managerial Psychology* 18, no. 2 (2003), pp. 138–155.

65 C. Kiewitz, W. A. Hochwarter, G. R. Ferris, and S. L. Castro, "The Role of Psychological Climate in Neutralizing the Effects of Organizational Politics on work Outcomes," *Journal of Applied Social Psychology*, June 2002, pp. 1189–1207; and J. M. L. Poon, "Situational Antecedents and Outcomes of Organizational Politics Perceptions," *Journal of Managerial Psychology* 18, no. 2 (2003), pp. 138–155.

66 K. M. Kacmar and R. A. Baron, "Organizational Politics: The State of the Field, Links to Related Processes, and an Agenda for Future Research," in *Research in Personnel and Human Resources Management*, vol. 17, ed. G. R. Ferris (Greenwich, CT: JAI Press, 1999); and M. Valle and L. A. Witt, "The Moderating Effect of Teamwork Perceptions on the Organizational Politics-Job Satisfaction Relationship," *Journal of Social Psychology*, June 2001, pp. 379–388.

67 R. W. Allen, D. L. Madison, L. W. Porter, P. A. Renwick, and B. T. Mayes, "Organizational Politics: Tactics and Characteristics of Its Actors," *California Management Review*, Fall 1979, pp. 77–83.

68 W. L. Gardner and M. J. Martinko, "Impression Management in Organizations," *Journal of Management*, June 1988, pp. 321–338; D. C. Gilmore and G. R. Ferris, "The Effects of Applicant Impression Management Tactics on Interviewer Judgments," *Journal of Management*, December 1989, pp. 557–564; M. R. Leary and R. M. Kowalski, "Impression Management: A Literature Review and Two-Component Model," *Psychological Bulletin*, January 1990, pp. 34–47; S. J. Wayne and K. M. Kacmar, "The Effects of Impression Management on the Performance Appraisal Process," *Organizational Behavior and Human Decision* Processes, February 1991, pp. 70–88; E. W. Morrison and R. J. Bies,

"Impression Management in the Feedback-Seeking Process: A Literature Review and Research Agenda," *Academy of Management Review*, July 1991, pp. 522–541; S. J. Wayne and R. C. Liden, "Effects of Impression Management on Performance Ratings: A Longitudinal Study," *Academy of Management Journal*, February 1995, pp. 232–260; and C. K. Stevens and A. L. Kristof, "Making the Right Impression: A Field Study of Applicant Impression Management during Job Interviews," *Journal of Applied Psychology*, October 1995, pp. 587–606.

69 M. R. Leary and R. M. Kowalski, "Impression Management: A Literature Review and Two-Component Model," *Psychological Bulletin*, January 1990, p. 40.

70 W. L. Gardner and M. J. Martinko, "Impression Management in Organizations," *Journal of Management*, June 1988, p. 333.

71 R. A. Baron, "Impression Management by Applicants during Employment Interviews: The 'Too Much of a Good Thing' Effect," in *The Employment Interview: Theory, Research, and Practice*, ed. R. W. Eder and G. R. Ferris (Newbury Park, CA: Sage, 1989), pp. 204–215.

72 A. P. J. Ellis, B. J. West, A. M. Ryan, and R. P. DeShon, "The Use of Impression Management Tactics in Structural Interviews: A Function of Question Type?" *Journal of Applied Psychology*, December 2002, pp. 1200–1208.

73 R. A. Baron, "Impression Management by Applicants during Employment Interviews: The 'Too Much of a Good Thing' Effect," in *The Employment Interview: Theory, Research, and Practice*, ed. R. W. Eder and G. R. Ferris (Newbury Park, CA: Sage, 1989); D. C. Gilmore and G. R. Ferris, "The Effects of Applicant Impression Management Tactics on Interviewer Judgments," *Journal of Management*, December 1989, pp. 557–564; C. K. Stevens and A. L. Kristof, "Making the Right Impression: A Field Study of Applicant Impression Management during Job Interviews," *Journal of Applied Psychology* 80, 1995, pp. 587–606; and L. A. McFarland, A. M. Ryan, and S. D. Kriska, "Impression Management Use and Effectiveness across Assessment Methods," *Journal of Management* 29, no. 5 (2003), pp. 641–661; and W.-C. Tsai, C.-C. Chen, and S.-F. Chiu, "Exploring Boundaries of the Effects of Applicant Impression Management Tactics in Job Interviews," *Journal of Management*, February 2005, pp. 108–125.

74 D. C. Gilmore and G. R. Ferris, "The Effects of Applicant Impression Management Tactics on Interviewer Judgments," *Journal of Management*, December 1989, pp. 557–564.

75 C. K. Stevens and A. L. Kristof, "Making the Right Impression: A Field Study of Applicant Impression Management during Job Interviews," *Journal of Applied Psychology* 80, 1995, pp. 587–606.

76 C. A. Higgins, T. A. Judge, and G. R. Ferris, "Influence Tactics and Work Outcomes: A Meta-Analysis," *Journal of Organizational Behavior*, March 2003, pp. 89–106.

77 C. A. Higgins, T. A. Judge, and G. R. Ferris, "Influence Tactics and Work Outcomes: A Meta-Analysis," *Journal of Organizational Behavior*, March 2003, pp. 89–106.

78 J. D. Westphal and I. Stern, "Flattery Will Get You Everywhere (Especially if You Are a Male Caucasian): How Ingratiation, Boardroom Behavior, and Demographic Minority Status Affect Additional Board Appointments of U.S. Companies," *Academy of Management Journal* 50, no. 2 (2007), pp. 267–288.

79   J. M. Maslyn and D. B. Fedor, "Perceptions of Politics: Does Measuring Different Foci Matter?" *Journal of Applied Psychology* 84, 1998, pp. 645–653; L. G. Nye and L. A. Witt, "Dimensionality and Construct Validity of the Perceptions of Organizational Politics Scale," *Educational and Psychological Measurement* 53, 1993, pp. 821–829.

80   G. R. Ferris, D. D. Frink, D. Bhawuk, J. Zhou, and D. C. Gilmore, "Reactions of Diverse Groups to Politics in the Workplace," *Journal of Management* 22, 1996, pp. 23–44; K. M. Kacmar, D. P. Bozeman, D. S. Carlson, and W. P. Anthony, "An Examination of the Perceptions of Organizational Politics Model: Replication and Extension," *Human Relations* 52, 1999, pp. 383–416.

81   T. P. Anderson, "Creating Measures of Dysfunctional Office and Organizational Politics: The DOOP and Short-Form DOOP Scales," *Psychology: A Journal of Human Behavior* 31, 1994, pp. 24–34.

82   G. R. Ferris, D. D. Frink, D. Bhawuk, J. Zhou, and D. C. Gilmore, "Reactions of Diverse Groups to Politics in the Workplace," *Journal of Management* 22, 1996, pp. 23–44; K. M. Kacmar, D. P. Bozeman, D. S. Carlson, and W. P. Anthony, "An Examination of the Perceptions of Organizational Politics Model: Replication and Extension," *Human Relations* 52, 1999, pp. 383–416.

83   K. M. Kacmar, D. P. Bozeman, D. S. Carlson, and W. P. Anthony, "An Examination of the Perceptions of Organizational Politics Model: Replication and Extension," *Human Relations* 52, 1999, pp. 383–416; J. M. Maslyn and D. B. Fedor, "Perceptions of Politics: Does Measuring Different Foci Matter?" *Journal of Applied Psychology* 84, 1998, pp. 645–653.

84   M. Warshaw, "The Good Guy's (and Gal's) Guide to Office Politics," *Fast Company*, April 1998, p. 156.

85   G. Yukl, C. M. Falbe, and J. Y. Youn, "Patterns of Influence Behavior for Managers," *Group & Organization Studies* 18, no. 1 (March 1993), p. 7.

86   J. F. Byrnes, "The Political Behavior Inventory." Reprinted by permission of Dr. Joseph F. Byrnes, Bentley College, Waltham, Massachusetts.

87   This exercise was inspired by one found in Judith R. Gordon, *Organizational Behavior*, 2nd ed. (Englewood Cliffs, NJ: Prentice Hall, 1992), pp. 499–502.

88   Based on C. Gasparino, "Out of School," *Newsweek*, January 17, 2005, pp. 38–39.

89   The identity of this organization and the people described are disguised for obvious reasons.

90   Based on J. Sandberg, "Sabotage 101: The Sinister Art of Backstabbing," *Wall Street Journal*, February 11, 2004, p. B1.

91   Based on S. P. Robbins and P. L. Hunsaker, *Training in Interpersonal Skills: Tips for Managing People at Work*, 2nd ed. (Upper Saddle River, NJ: Prentice Hall, 1996), pp. 131–134.

Chapter 9

1   Opening vignette based on "Students, Staff Return to Classes at York University," *cbcnews.ca*, February 2, 2009; J. Huber, "Four Arrested at York U Rally," *Windsor Star*, January 28, 2009, p. B1;

E. Church, "York University Braces For Strike," *Globe and Mail*, November 6, 2008, p. A4; and J. Gray, "York, Union No Closer To Deal," *Globe and Mail*, December 1, 2008, p. A8.

2   See, for instance, C. F. Fink, "Some Conceptual Difficulties in the Theory of Social Conflict," *Journal of Conflict Resolution*, December 1968, pp. 412–460. For an updated review of the conflict literature, see J. A. Wall Jr. and R. R. Callister, "Conflict and Its Management," *Journal of Management* 21, no. 3 (1995), pp. 515–558.

3   L. L. Putnam and M. S. Poole, "Conflict and Negotiation," in *Handbook of Organizational Communication: An Interdisciplinary Perspective*, ed. F. M. Jablin, L. L. Putnam, K. H. Roberts, and L. W. Porter (Newbury Park, CA: Sage, 1987), pp. 549–599.

4   K. W. Thomas, "Conflict and Negotiation Processes in Organizations," in *Handbook of Industrial and Organizational Psychology*, 2nd ed., vol. 3, ed. M. D. Dunnette and L. M. Hough (Palo Alto, CA: Consulting Psychologists Press, 1992), pp. 651–717.

5   K. Jehn, "A Multimethod Examination of the Benefits and Detriments of Intragroup Conflict," *Administrative Science Quarterly*, June 1995, pp. 256–282; K. A. Jehn, "A Qualitative Analysis of Conflict Types and Dimensions in Organizational Groups," *Administrative Science Quarterly*, September 1997, pp. 530–557; K. A. Jehn and E. A. Mannix, "The Dynamic Nature of Conflict: A Longitudinal Study of Intragroup Conflict and Group Performance," *Academy of Management Journal*, April 2001, pp. 238–251; C. K. W. De Dreu and A. E. M. Van Vianen, "Managing Relationship Conflict and the Effectiveness of Organizational Teams," *Journal of Organizational Behavior*, May 2001, pp. 309–328; and K. A. Jehn and C. Bendersky, "Intragroup Conflict in Organizations: A Contingency Perspective on the Conflict-Outcome Relationship," in *Research in Organizational Behavior*, vol. 25, ed. R. M. Kramer and B. M. Staw (Oxford, UK: Elsevier, 2003), pp. 199–210.

6   A. C. Amason, "Distinguishing the Effects of Functional and Dysfunctional Conflict on Strategic Decision Making: Resolving a Paradox for Top Management Teams," *Academy of Management Journal* 39, no. 1 (1996), pp. 123–148.

7   This section is based on S. P. Robbins, *Managing Organizational Conflict: A Nontraditional Approach* (Englewood Cliffs, NJ: Prentice Hall, 1974), pp. 31–55; and J. A. Wall Jr. and R. R. Callister, "Conflict and Its Management," *Journal of Management* 21, no. 3 (1995), pp. 517–523.

8   Based on A. Morgan, "York University Schedules Exams on Shabbat," *Canadian Jewish News*, April 11, 2002, p. 5.

9   Based on E. Church, "Striking York Staff Reject Offer," *Globe and Mail*, January 21, 2009, p. A1; and E. Church, "York University Braces For Strike," *Globe and Mail*, November 6, 2008, p. A46

10   D. Tjosvold, "Cooperative and Competitive Goal Approach to Conflict: Accomplishments and Challenges," *Applied Psychology: An International Review* 47, no. 3 (1998), pp. 285–342.

11   K. W. Thomas, "Conflict and Negotiation Processes in Organizations," in *Handbook of Industrial and Organizational Psychology*, 2nd ed., vol. 3, ed. M. D. Dunnette and L. M. Hough (Palo Alto, CA: Consulting Psychologists Press, 1992), pp. 651–717.

12 C. K. W. De Dreu, A. Evers, B. Beersma, E. S. Kluwer, and A. Nauta, "A Theory-Based Measure of Conflict Management Strategies in the Workplace," *Journal of Organizational Behavior* 22, no. 6 (September 2001), pp. 645–668. See also D. G. Pruitt and J. Rubin, *Social Conflict: Escalation, Stalemate and Settlement* (New York: Random House, 1986).

13 C. K. W. De Dreu, A. Evers, B. Beersma, E. S. Kluwer, and A. Nauta, "A Theory-Based Measure of Conflict Management Strategies in the Workplace," *Journal of Organizational Behavior* 22, no. 6 (September 2001), pp. 645–668.

14 R. A. Baron, "Personality and Organizational Conflict: Effects of the Type A Behavior Pattern and Self-Monitoring," *Organizational Behavior and Human Decision Processes*, October 1989, pp. 281–296; A. Drory and I. Ritov, "Effects of Work Experience and Opponent's Power on Conflict Management Styles," *International Journal of Conflict Management* 8, 1997, pp. 148–161; R. J. Sternberg and L. J. Soriano, "Styles of Conflict Resolution," *Journal of Personality and Social Psychology*, July 1984, pp. 115–126; and R. J. Volkema and T. J. Bergmann, "Conflict Styles as Indicators of Behavioral Patterns in Interpersonal Conflicts," *Journal of Social Psychology*, February 1995, pp. 5–15.

15 Based on K. W. Thomas, "Toward Multidimensional Values in Teaching: The Example of Conflict Behaviors," *Academy of Management Review*, July 1977, p. 487; and C. K. W. De Dreu, A. Evers, B. Beersma, E. S. Kluwer, and A. Nauta, "A Theory-Based Measure of Conflict Management Strategies in the Workplace," *Journal of Organizational Behavior* 22, no. 6 (September 2001), pp. 645–668.

16 These ideas are based on S. P. Robbins, *Managing Organizational Conflict: A Nontraditional Approach* (Upper Saddle River, NJ: Prentice Hall, 1974), pp. 59–89.

17 R. D. Ramsey, "Interpersonal Conflicts," *SuperVision* 66, no. 4 (April 2005), pp. 14–17.

18 R. D. Ramsey, "Interpersonal Conflicts," *SuperVision* 66, no. 4 (April 2005), pp. 14–17.

19 R. Kreitner and A. Kinicki, *Organizational Behavior*, 6th ed. (New York: McGraw-Hill, 2004), p. 492, Table 14-1. Reprinted by permission of McGraw Hill Education.

20 R. L. Tung, "American Expatriates Abroad: From Neophytes to Cosmopolitans," *Journal of World Business* 33, no. 2 (Summer 1998), pp. 125–144.

21 "Negotiating South of the Border," *Harvard Management Communication Letter* 2, no. 8 (August 1999), p. 12.

22 F. W. Swierczek, "Culture and Conflict in Joint Ventures in Asia," *International Journal of Project Management* 12, no. 1 (1994), pp. 39–47.

23 P. S. Kirkbride, S. Tang, and R. I. Westwood, "Chinese Conflict Preferences and Negotiation Behavior: Cultural and Psychological Influences," *Organization Studies* 12, no. 3 (1991), pp. 365–386; S. Tang, P. Kirkbride, "Development of Conflict Management Skills in Hong Kong: An Analysis of Some Cross-cultural Implications," *Management Education and Development* 17, no. 3 (1986), pp. 287–301; P. Trubisky, S. Ting-Toomey, and S. L. Lin, "The Influence of Individualism-Collectivism and Self-monitoring on Conflict Styles," *International Journal of Intercultural Relations* 15,

1991, pp. 65–84; and K. I. Ohbuchi and Y. Takahashi, "Cultural Styles of Conflict Management in Japanese and Americans: Passivity, Covertness, and Effectiveness of Strategies," *Journal of Applied Social Psychology* 24, 1994, pp. 1345–1366.

24 P. S. Kirkbride, S. Tang, and R. I. Westwood, "Chinese Conflict Preferences and Negotiation Behavior: Cultural and Psychological Influences," *Organization Studies* 12, 1991, pp. 365–386; and F. W. Swierczek, "Culture and Conflict in Joint Ventures in Asia," *International Journal of Project Management* 12, 1994, pp. 39–47.

25 C. L. Wang, X. Lin, A. K. K. Chan, and Y. Shi, "Conflict Handling Styles in International Joint Ventures: A Cross-cultural and Cross-national Comparison," *Management International Review* 45, no. 1 (2005), pp. 3–21.

26 M. A. Rahim, "A Measure of Styles of Handling Interpersonal Conflict," *Academy of Management Journal* 26, 1983, pp. 368–376; and C. H. Tinsley, "Model of Conflict Resolution in Japanese, German, and American Cultures," *Journal of Applied Psychology* 83, 1998, pp. 316–323.

27 R. T. Moran, J. Allen, R. Wichman, T. Ando, and M. Sasano, "Japan," in *Global Perspectives on Organizational Conflict*, ed. M. A. Rahim and A. A. Blum (Westport, CT: Praeger 1994), pp. 33–52.

28 D. C. Barnlund, *Communicative Styles of Japanese and Americans: Images and Realities* (Belmont, CA: Wadsworth 1989); and K. I. Ohbuchi and Y. Takahashi, "Cultural Styles of Conflict Management in Japanese and Americans: Passivity, Covertness, and Effectiveness of Strategies," *Journal of Applied Social Psychology* 24, 1994, pp. 1345–1366.

29 Z. Ma, "Chinese Conflict Management Styles and Negotiation Behaviours: An Empirical Test," *International Journal of Cross Cultural Management*, April 2007, pp. 101–119.

30 K. Leung, " Some Determinants of Reactions to Procedural Models for Conflict Resolution: A Cross-national Study," *Journal of Personality and Social Psychology* 53, 1987, pp. 898–908; K. Leung and E. A. Lind, "Procedure and Culture: Effects of Culture, Gender, and Investigator Status on Procedural Preferences," *Journal of Personality and Social Psychology* 50, 1986, pp. 1134–1140; M. W. Morris, K. Y. Williams, K. Leung, R. Larrick, M. T. Mendoza, D. Bhatnagar, J. Li, M. Kondo, J. Luo, and J. Hu, "Conflict Management Style: Accounting for Cross-national Differences," *Journal of International Business Studies* 29, 1998, pp. 729–747; and F. W. Swierczek, "Culture and Conflict in Joint Ventures in Asia," *International Journal of Project Management* 12, 1994, pp. 39–47.

31 J. S. Black and M. Mendenhall, "Resolving Conflicts with the Japanese: Mission Impossible?" *Sloan Management Review* 34, 1993, pp. 49–59.

32 B. Morrow and L. M. Bernardi, "Resolving Workplace Disputes," *Canadian Manager*, Spring 1999, p. 17.

33 Based on A. F. Westin and A. G. Feliu, *Resolving Employment Disputes without Litigation* (Washington, DC: Bureau of National Affairs, 1988); J. A. Wall Jr. and M. W. Blum, "Negotiations," *Journal of Management*, June 1991, pp. 283–287; and R. Kreitner and A. Kinicki, *Organizational Behavior*, 6th ed. (New York: McGraw-Hill, 2004), p. 502.

34   Based on P. Dvorak, "CEO and COO Try 'Marriage Counseling,'" *Wall Street Journal*, July 31, 2006, pp. B1, B3.

35   http://www.caut.ca/aufa/newsletter/0504/prescomm.htm.

36   A. Woods, "Season Down to Final Hours," *National Post*, February 11, 2005, pp. B8, B11.

37   C. Olsheski, "Resolving Disputes Has Just Become More Efficient," *Financial Post (National Post)*, August 16, 1999, p. D9.

38   B. Simon, "Work Ethic and the Magna Carta," *Financial Post Daily*, March 20, 1997, p. 14.

39   See, for instance, R. A. Cosier and C. R. Schwenk, "Agreement and Thinking Alike: Ingredients for Poor Decisions," *Academy of Management Executive*, February 1990, pp. 69–74; K. A. Jehn, "Enhancing Effectiveness: An Investigation of Advantages and Disadvantages of Value-Based Intragroup Conflict," *International Journal of Conflict Management*, July 1994, pp. 223–238; R. L. Priem, D. A. Harrison, and N. K. Muir, "Structured Conflict and Consensus Outcomes in Group Decision Making," *Journal of Management* 21, no. 4 (1995), pp. 691–710; and K. A. Jehn and E. A. Mannix, "The Dynamic Nature of Conflict: A Longitudinal Study of Intragroup Conflict and Group Performance," *Academy of Management Journal*, April 2001, pp. 238–251.

40   Based on D. Tjosvold, *Learning to Manage Conflict: Getting People to Work Together Productively* (New York: Lexington Books, 1993), pp. 12–13.

41   See J. A. Wall Jr. and R. R. Callister, "Conflict and Its Management," *Journal of Management* 21, no. 3 (1995), pp. 523–526 for evidence supporting the argument that conflict is almost uniformly dysfunctional.

42   R. L. Hoffman, "Homogeneity of Member Personality and Its Effect on Group Problem-Solving," *Journal of Abnormal and Social Psychology*, January 1959, pp. 27–32; and R. L. Hoffman and N. R. F. Maier, "Quality and Acceptance of Problem Solutions by Members of Homogeneous and Heterogeneous Groups," *Journal of Abnormal and Social Psychology*, March 1961, pp. 401–407.

43   J. Hall and M. S. Williams, "A Comparison of Decision-Making Performances in Established and Ad-Hoc Groups," *Journal of Personality and Social Psychology*, February 1966, p. 217.

44   R. E. Hill, "Interpersonal Compatibility and Work Group Performance Among Systems Analysts: An Empirical Study," *Proceedings of the Seventeenth Annual Midwest Academy of Management Conference*, Kent, OH, April 1974, pp. 97–110.

45   D. C. Pelz and F. Andrews, *Scientists in Organizations* (New York: Wiley, 1966).

46   J. A. Wall Jr., *Negotiation: Theory and Practice* (Glenview, IL: Scott, Foresman, 1985).

47   K. Harding, "A New Language, a New Deal," *Globe and Mail*, October 30, 2002, pp. C1, C10.

48   This model is based on R. J. Lewicki, "Bargaining and Negotiation," *Exchange: The Organizational Behavior Teaching Journal* 6, no. 2 (1981), pp. 39–40; and B. S. Moskal, "The Art of the Deal," *IndustryWeek*, January 18, 1993, p. 23.

49   J. C. Magee, A. D. Galinsky, and D. H. Gruenfeld, "Power, Propensity to Negotiate, and Moving First in Competitive Interactions," *Personality and Social Psychology Bulletin*, February 2007, pp. 200–212.

50   H. R. Bowles, L. Babcock, and L. Lei, "Social Incentives for Gender Differences in the Propensity to Initiative Negotiations: Sometimes It Does Hurt to Ask," *Organizational Behavior and Human Decision Processes* 103, 2007, pp. 84–103.

51   D. A. Moore, "Myopic Prediction, Self-Destructive Secrecy, and the Unexpected Benefits of Revealing Final Deadlines in Negotiation," *Organizational Behavior and Human Decision Processes*, July 2004, pp. 125–139.

52   J. R. Curhan, H. A. Elfenbein, and H. Xu, "What Do People Value When They Negotiate? Mapping the Domain of Subjective Value in Negotiation," *Journal of Personality and Social Psychology* 91, no. 3 (2007), pp. 493–512.

53   K. W. Thomas, "Conflict and Negotiation Processes in Organizations," in *Handbook of Industrial and Organizational Psychology*, 2nd ed., vol. 3, ed. M. D. Dunnette and L. M. Hough (Palo Alto, CA: Consulting Psychologists Press, 1992), pp. 651–717.

54   P. M. Morgan and R. S. Tindale, "Group vs. Individual Performance in Mixed-Motive Situations: Exploring an Inconsistency," *Organizational Behavior and Human Decision Processes*, January 2002, pp. 44–65.

55   C. E. Naquin, "The Agony of Opportunity in Negotiation: Number of Negotiable Issues, Counterfactual Thinking, and Feelings of Satisfaction," *Organizational Behavior and Human Decision Processes*, May 2003, pp. 97–107.

56   C. K. W. De Dreu, L. R. Weingart, and S. Kwon, "Influence of Social Motives on Integrative Negotiation: A Meta-Analytic Review and Test of Two Theories," *Journal of Personality and Social Psychology*, May 2000, pp. 889–905.

57   D, Malhotra and M. Bazerman, "Investigative Negotiation," *Harvard Business Review*, September 2007, pp. 72–78.

58   R. Fisher and W. Ury, *Getting to Yes: Negotiating Agreement without Giving In*, 2nd ed. (New York: Penguin, 1991).

59   M. H. Bazerman and M. A. Neale, *Negotiating Rationally* (New York: Free Press, 1992), pp. 67–68.

60   R. Fisher and W. Ury, *Getting to Yes; Negotiating Agreement without Giving In*, 2nd ed. (New York: Penguin, 1991).

61   R. Fisher and W. Ury, *Getting to Yes: Negotiating Agreement without Giving In*, 2nd ed. (New York: Penguin, 1991).

62   For a negative answer to this question, see C. Watson and L. R. Hoffman, "Managers as Negotiators: A Test of Power versus Gender as Predictors of Feelings, Behavior, and Outcomes," *Leadership Quarterly*, Spring 1996, pp. 63–85.

63   A. H. Eagley, S. J. Karau, and M. Makhijani, "Gender and the Effectiveness of Leaders: A Meta-Analysis," *Psychological Bulletin* 117, 1995, pp. 125–145.

64 A. F. Stuhlmacher and A. E. Walters, "Gender Differences in Negotiation Outcome: A Meta-Analysis," *Personnel Psychology* 52, 1992, pp. 653–677.

65 D. M. Kolb and G. G. Coolidge, "Her Place at the Table," *Journal of State Government* 64, no. 2 (April–June 1991), pp. 68–71.

66 "Women Must Be Ready to Negotiate for Equal Pay," *Financial Post*, October 5/7, 1996, p. 41.

67 "Women Must Be Ready to Negotiate for Equal Pay," *Financial Post*, October 5/7, 1996, p. 41.

68 "Women Must Be Ready to Negotiate for Equal Pay," *Financial Post*, October 5/7, 1996, p. 41.

69 "The Battle of the Sexes: Do Men and Women Really Have Different Negotiating Styles?" *CMA Management Accounting Magazine* 71, no. 1 (February 1997), p. 8.

70 C. C. Eckel and P. J. Grossman, "Are Women Less Selfish Than Men? Evidence from Dictator Experiments," *Economic Journal*, May 1998, pp. 726–735.

71 I. Ayres, "Further Evidence of Discrimination in New Car Negotiations and Estimates of Its Cause," *Michigan Law Review* 94, no. 1 (October 1995), pp. 109–147.

72 B. Gerhart and S. Rynes, "Determinants and Consequences of Salary Negotiations by Male and Female MBA Graduates," *Journal of Applied Psychology* 76, no. 2 (April 1991), pp. 256–262.

73 See N. J. Adler, *International Dimensions of Organizational Behavior*, 4th ed. (Cincinnati, OH: South Western, 2002), pp. 208–256; and W. L. Adair, T. Okumura, and J. M. Brett, "Negotiation Behavior When Cultures Collide: The United States and Japan," *Journal of Applied Psychology*, June 2001, pp. 371–385.

74 K. D. Schmidt, *Doing Business in France* (Menlo Park, CA: SRI International, 1987).

75 Y. Chen, E. A. Mannix, and T. Okumura, "The Importance of Who You Meet: Effects of Self—versus Other—Concerns among Negotiators in the United States, the People's Republic of China, and Japan," *Journal of Experimental Social Psychology*, January, 2003, pp. 1–15; Z. Ma, "Chinese Conflict Management Styles and Negotiation Behaviours: An Empirical Test," *International Journal of Cross Cultural Management*, April 2007, pp. 101–119.and S. Lubman, "Round and Round," *Wall Street Journal*, December 10, 1993, p. R3.

76 W. L. Adair, T. Okumura, and J. M. Brett, "Negotiation Behavior When Cultures Collide: The United States and Japan," *Journal of Applied Psychology*, June 2001, pp. 371–385; and W. L. Adair, L. Weingart, and J. Brett, "The Timing and Function of Offers in U.S. and Japanese Negotiations," *Journal of Applied Psychology* 92, no. 4 (2007), pp. 1056–1068.

77 Y. Chen, E. A. Mannix, and T. Okumura, "The Importance of Who You Meet: Effects of Self—versus Other—Concerns among Negotiators in the United States, the People's Republic of China, and Japan," *Journal of Experimental Social Psychology*, January, 2003, pp. 1–15; and J. W. Salacuse, "Ten Ways That Culture Affects Negotiating Style: Some Survey Results," *Negotiation Journal*, July 1998, pp. 221–240.

78 E. S. Glenn, D. Witmeyer, and K. A. Stevenson, "Cultural Styles of Persuasion," *Journal of Intercultural Relations*, Fall 1977, pp. 52–66.

79 J. Graham, "The Influence of Culture on Business Negotiations," *Journal of International Business Studies*, Spring 1985, pp. 81–96.

80 The points presented here were influenced by E. Van de Vliert, "Escalative Intervention in Small-Group Conflicts," *Journal of Applied Behavioral Science*, Winter 1985, pp. 19–36.

81 C. K. W. De Dreu, A. Evers, B. Beersma, E. S. Kluwer, and A. Nauta, "A Theory-Based Measure of Conflict Management Strategies in the Workplace," *Journal of Organizational Behavior* 22, no. 6 (September 2001), pp. 645–668. With permission.

82 Based on R. Cohen, "Bad Bidness," *New York Times Magazine*, September 2, 2006, p. 22; M. E. Schweitzer, "Deception in Negotiations," in *Wharton on Making Decisions*, ed. S. J. Hoch and H. C. Kunreuther (New York: Wiley, 2001), pp. 187–200; and M. Diener, "Fair Enough," *Entrepreneur*, January 2002, pp. 100–102.

83 Based on J. Carreyrou and J. S. Lublin, "How Bristol-Myers Fumbled Defense of $4 Billion Drug," *Wall Street Journal*, September 2, 2006, pp. A1, A7; S. Saul, "Marketers of Plavix Outfoxed on a Deal," *New York Times*, August 9, 2006; S. Saul, "Patent Trial Near, Bristol-Myers Counts on Resilience," *New York Times*, January 20, 2007; and S. Saul, "Drug Executive Is Indicted on Secret Deal," *New York Times*, April 24, 2008.

84 Based on D. Drickhamer, "Rolling On," *IndustryWeek*, December 1, 2002.

85 These suggestions are based on J. A. Wall Jr. and M. W. Blum, "Negotiations," *Journal of Management*, June 1991, pp. 278–282; and J. S. Pouliot, "Eight Steps to Success in Negotiating," *Nation's Business*, April 1999, pp. 40–42.

OB on the Edge:
The Toxic Workplace

1 L. M. Anderson and C. M. Pearson, "Tit for Tat? The Spiraling Effect of Incivility in the Workplace," *Academy of Management Review* 24, no. 3 (1999), p. 453.

2 The source of this quotation is N. Giarrusso, "An Issue of Job Satisfaction," unpublished undergraduate term paper, Concordia University, Montreal, 1990. It is cited in B. E. Ashforth, "Petty Tyranny in Organizations: A Preliminary Examination of Antecedents and Consequences," *Canadian Journal of Administrative Sciences* 14, no. 2 (1997), pp. 126–140.

3 P. Frost and S. Robinson, "The Toxic Handler: Organizational Hero—and Casualty," *Harvard Business Review*, July–August 1999, p. 101 (Reprint 99406).

4 L. M. Anderson and C. M. Pearson, "Tit for Tat? The Spiraling Effect of Incivility in the Workplace," *Academy of Management Review* 24, no. 3 (1999), pp. 452–471.

5 L. M. Anderson and C. M. Pearson, "Tit for Tat? The Spiraling Effect of Incivility in the Workplace," *Academy of Management Review* 24, no. 3 (1999), pp. 452–471. For further discussion of this, see R. A. Baron and J. H. Neuman, "Workplace Violence and Workplace Aggression: Evidence on Their Relative Frequency and Potential Causes," *Aggressive Behavior* 22, 1996, pp. 161–173; C. C. Chen and W. Eastman, "Towards a Civic Culture for Multicultural Organizations," *Journal of Applied Behavioral Science*

33, 1997, pp. 454–470; J. H. Neuman and R. A. Baron, "Aggression in the Workplace," in *Antisocial Behavior in Organizations*, ed. R. A. Giacalone and J. Greenberg (Thousand Oaks, CA: Sage, 1997), pp. 37–67.

6   L. M. Anderson and C. M. Pearson, "Tit for Tat? The Spiraling Effect of Incivility in the Workplace," *Academy of Management Review* 24, no. 3 (1999), pp. 452–471.

7   L. M. Anderson and C. M. Pearson, "Tit for Tat? The Spiraling Effect of Incivility in the Workplace," *Academy of Management Review* 24, no. 3 (1999), pp. 452–471.

8   R. Corelli, "Dishing Out Rudeness: Complaints Abound as Customers Are Ignored, Berated," *Maclean's*, January 11, 1999, p. 44.

9   R. Corelli, "Dishing Out Rudeness: Complaints Abound as Customers Are Ignored, Berated," *Maclean's*, January 11, 1999, p. 44.

10   See, for example, "The National Labour Survey," *The Canadian Initiative on Workplace Violence*, March 2000, www.workplaceviolence.ca/research/survey1.pdf (accessed September 26, 2005).

11   R. A. Baron and J. H. Neuman, "Workplace Violence and Workplace Aggression: Evidence on Their Relative Frequency and Potential Causes," *Aggressive Behavior* 22, 1996, pp. 161–173; K. Bjorkqvist, K. Osterman, and M. Hjelt-Back, "Aggression among University Employees," *Aggressive Behavior* 20, 1986, pp. 173–184; and H. J. Ehrlich and B. E. K. Larcom, *Ethnoviolence in the Workplace* (Baltimore, MD: Center for the Applied Study of Ethnoviolence, 1994).

12   J. Graydon, W. Kasta, and P. Khan, "Verbal and Physical Abuse of Nurses," *Canadian Journal of Nursing Administration*, November–December 1994, pp. 70–89.

13   C. M. Pearson and C. L. Porath, "Workplace Incivility: The Target's Eye View" (paper presented at the annual meetings of The Academy of Management, Chicago, August 10, 1999).

14   "Men More Likely to Be Rude in Workplace, Survey Shows," *Vancouver Sun*, August 16, 1999, p. B10.

15   R. Corelli, "Dishing Out Rudeness: Complaints Abound as Customers Are Ignored, Berated," *Maclean's*, January 11, 1999, p. 44.

16   R. Corelli, "Dishing Out Rudeness: Complaints Abound as Customers Are Ignored, Berated," *Maclean's*, January 11, 1999, p. 44.

17   R. A. Baron and J. H. Neuman, "Workplace Violence and Workplace Aggression: Evidence on Their Relative Frequency and Potential Causes," *Aggressive Behavior* 22, 1996, pp. 161–173; C. MacKinnon, *Only Words* (New York: Basic Books, 1994); J. Marks, "The American Uncivil Wars," *U.S. News & World Report*, April 22, 1996, pp. 66–72; and L. P. Spratlen, "Workplace Mistreatment: Its Relationship to Interpersonal Violence," *Journal of Psychosocial Nursing* 32, no. 12 (1994), pp. 5–6.

18   Information in this paragraph based on B. Branswell, "Death in Ottawa: The Capital Is Shocked by a Massacre That Leaves Five Dead," *Maclean's*, April 19, 1999, p. 18; "Four Employees Killed by Former Co-worker," *Occupational Health & Safety*, June 1999, pp. 14, 16; and "Preventing Workplace Violence," *Human Resources Advisor Newsletter*, Western Edition, May–June 1999, pp. 1–2.

19   W. M. Glenn, "An Employee's Survival Guide: An ILO Survey of Workplaces in 32 Countries Ranked Argentina the Most Violent, Followed by Romania, France and Then, Surprisingly, Canada," *Occupational Health & Safety*, April–May 2002, p. 28 passim.

20   D. Flavelle, "Managers Cited for Increase in 'Work Rage,'" *Vancouver Sun*, April 11, 2000, pp. D1, D11; and "Profile of Workplace Victimization Incidents," *Statistics Canada*, 2007, http://www.statcan.ca/english/research/85F0033MIE/2007013/findings/profile.htm.

21   E. Wulfhorst, "Desk Rage Spoils Workplace for Many Americans," *Reuters*, July 10, 2008, http://www.reuters.com/article/newsOne/idUSN0947145320080710.

22   S. James, "Long Hours Linked to Rising Toll from Stress," *Financial Post (National Post)*, August 6, 2003, p. FP12.

23   "Profile of Workplace Victimization Incidents," *Statistics Canada*, 2007, http://www.statcan.ca/english/research/85F0033MIE/2007013/findings/profile.htm.

24   W. M. Glenn, "An Employee's Survival Guide: An ILO Survey of Workplaces in 32 Countries Ranked Argentina the Most Violent, Followed by Romania, France and Then, Surprisingly, Canada," *Occupational Health & Safety*, April–May 2002, p. 28 passim.

25   Information for FactBox based on "Breeding Loyalty Pays for Employers," *Vancouver Sun*, April 22, 2000, p. D14; and P. Mackenzie, "Loyalty a Moving Target," *Toronto Star*, March 8, 2008, http://www.thestar.com/article/309355.

26   W. M. Glenn, "An Employee's Survival Guide: An ILO Survey of Workplaces in 32 Countries Ranked Argentina the Most Violent, Followed by Romania, France and Then, Surprisingly, Canada," *Occupational Health & Safety*, April–May 2002, p. 28 passim.

27   "A Quarter of Nova Scotia Teachers Who Responded to a Recent Survey Said They Faced Physical Violence at Work during the 2001–02 School Year," *Canadian Press Newswire*, February 14, 2003.

28   A. M. Webber, "Danger: Toxic Company," *Fast Company*, November 1998, pp. 152–157.

29   D. Flavelle, "Managers Cited for Increase in 'Work Rage,'" *Vancouver Sun*, April 11, 2000, pp. D1, D11; and G. Smith, *Work Rage* (Toronto: HarperCollins Canada, 2000).

30   "Work Rage," *BCBusiness Magazine*, January 2001, p. 23.

31   D. Flavelle, "Managers Cited for Increase in 'Work Rage,'" *Vancouver Sun*, April 11, 2000, pp. D1, D11.

32   D. E. Gibson and S. G. Barsade, "The Experience of Anger at Work: Lessons from the Chronically Angry" (paper presented at the annual meetings of the Academy of Management, Chicago, August 11, 1999).

33   H. Levinson, *Emotional Health in the World of Work* (Boston: South End Press, 1964); and E. Schein, *Organizational Psychology* (Englewood Cliffs, NJ: Prentice Hall, 1980).

34 E. W. Morrison and S. L. Robinson, "When Employees Feel Betrayed: A Model of How Psychological Contract Violation Develops," *Academy of Management Journal* 22, 1997, pp. 226–256; S. L. Robinson, "Trust and Breach of the Psychological Contract," *Administrative Science Quarterly* 41, 1996, pp. 574–599; and S. L. Robinson, M. S. Kraatz, and D. M. Rousseau, "Changing Obligations and the Psychological Contract: A Longitudinal Study," *Academy of Management Journal* 37, 1994, pp. 137–152.

35 T. R. Tyler and P. Dogoey, "Trust in Organizational Authorities: The Influence of Motive Attributions on Willingness to Accept Decisions," in *Trust in Organizations*, ed. R. M. Kramer and T. R. Tyler (Thousand Oaks, CA: Sage, 1996), pp. 246–260.

36 A. M. Webber, "Danger: Toxic Company," *Fast Company*, November 1998, pp. 152–157.

37 A. M. Webber, "Danger: Toxic Company," *Fast Company*, November 1998, pp. 152–157.

38 P. Frost, *Toxic Emotions at Work* (Cambridge, MA: Harvard Business School Press, 2003).

39 L. McClure, *Risky Business* (Binghamton, NY: Haworth Press, 1996).

40 "Men More Likely to Be Rude in Workplace, Survey Shows," *Vancouver Sun*, August 16, 1999, p. B10.

41 D. E. Gibson and S. G. Barsade, "The Experience of Anger at Work: Lessons from the Chronically Angry" (paper presented at the annual meetings of the Academy of Management, Chicago, August 11, 1999).

42 D. E. Gibson and S. G. Barsade, "The Experience of Anger at Work: Lessons from the Chronically Angry" (paper presented at the annual meetings of the Academy of Management, Chicago, August 11, 1999).

43 R. Corelli, "Dishing Out Rudeness: Complaints Abound as Customers Are Ignored, Berated," *Maclean's*, January 11, 1999, p. 44.

44 P. Frost and S. Robinson, "The Toxic Handler: Organizational Hero—and Casualty," *Harvard Business Review*, July–August 1999, p. 101 (Reprint 99406).

45 P. Frost and S. Robinson, "The Toxic Handler: Organizational Hero—and Casualty," *Harvard Business Review*, July–August 1999, p. 101 (Reprint 99406).

46 P. Frost and S. Robinson, "The Toxic Handler: Organizational Hero—and Casualty," *Harvard Business Review*, July–August 1999, p. 101 (Reprint 99406).

Chapter 10

1 Opening vignette based on M. Parker, "Identifying Enablers and Blockers of Cultural Transformation," *Canadian Business Online*, May 17, 2007 (accessed February 4, 2009); E. Lazarus, "Building the Perfect Franchise," *Profit*, February 2006, p. 48ff; M. Parker, "Why Can't Employers See The Paradox?" *Financial Post*, March 19, 2008, p. WK7.

2 "Organization Man: Henry Mintzberg Has Some Common Sense Observations About the Ways We Run Companies," *Financial Post*, November 22/24, 1997, pp. 14–16.

3 K. McArthur, "Air Canada Tells Employees to Crack a Smile More Often," *Globe and Mail*, March 14, 2002, pp. B1, B2.

4 K. McArthur, "Air Canada Tells Employees to Crack a Smile More Often," *Globe and Mail*, March 14, 2002, pp. B1, B2.

5 C. O'Reilly, "Corporations, Culture and Commitment: Motivation and Social Control in Organizations," *California Management Review* 31, no. 4 (1989), pp. 9–25.

6 E. Schein, "Coming to a New Awareness of Organizational Culture," *Sloan Management Review*, Winter 1984, pp. 3–16; E. Schein, *Organizational Culture and Leadership*, 2nd ed. (San Francisco, CA: Jossey-Bass, 1992); and E. Schein, "What Is Culture?" in *Reframing Organizational Culture*, ed. P. J. Frost, L. F. Moore, M. R. Louis, C. C. Lundberg, and J. Martin (Newbury Park, CA: Sage, 1991), pp. 243–253.

7 T. G. Stroup Jr., "Leadership and Organizational Culture: Actions Speak Louder Than Words," *Military Review* 76, no. 1 (January–February 1996), pp. 44–49; B. Moingeon and B. Ramanantsoa "Understanding Corporate Identity: The French School of Thought," *European Journal of Marketing* 31, no. 5/6 (1997), pp. 383–395; A. P. D. Van Luxemburg, J. M. Ulijn, and N. Amare, "The Contribution of Electronic Communication Media to the Design Process: Communicative and Cultural Implications," *IEEE Transactions on Professional Communication* 45, no. 4 (December 2002), pp. 250–264; L. D. McLean, "Organizational Culture's Influence on Creativity and Innovation: A Review of the Literature and Implications for Human Resource Development," *Advances in Developing Human Resources* 7, no. 2 (May 2005), pp. 226–246; and V. J. Friedman and A. B. Antal, "Negotiating Reality: A Theory of Action Approach to Intercultural Competence," *Management Learning* 36, no. 1 (2005), pp. 69–86.

8 See http://www.palliser.com/CompanyInfo.php (accessed September 8, 2008).

9 This seven-item description is based on C. A. O'Reilly III, J. Chatman, and D. F. Caldwell, "People and Organizational Culture: A Profile Comparison Approach to Assessing Person-Organization Fit," *Academy of Management Journal*, September 1991, pp. 487–516; and J. A. Chatman and K. A. Jehn, "Assessing the Relationship between Industry Characteristics and Organizational Culture: How Different Can You Be?" *Academy of Management Journal*, June 1994, pp. 522–553. For a description of other popular measures, see A. Xenikou and A. Furnham, "A Correlational and Factor Analytic Study of Four Questionnaire Measures of Organizational Culture," *Human Relations*, March 1996, pp. 349–371. For a review of cultural dimensions, see N. M. Ashkanasy, C. P. M. Wilderom, and M. F. Peterson, eds., *Handbook of Organizational Culture and Climate* (Thousand Oaks, CA: Sage, 2000), pp. 131–145.

10 See C. A. O'Reilly and J. A. Chatman, "Culture as Social Control: Corporations, Cultures, and Commitment," in *Research in Organizational Behavior*, vol. 18, ed. B. M. Staw and L. L. Cummings (Greenwich, CT: JAI Press, 1996), pp. 157–200.

11 T. E. Deal and A. A. Kennedy, "Culture: A New Look through Old Lenses," *Journal of Applied Behavioral Science*, November 1983, p. 501.

12 J. Case, "Corporate Culture," *Inc.*, November 1996, pp. 42–53.

13   T. Cole, "How to Stay Hired," *Report on Business Magazine*, March 1995, pp. 46–48.

14   R. McQueen, "Bad Boys Make Good," *Financial Post*, April 4, 1998, p. 6.

15   The view that there will be consistency among perceptions of organizational culture has been called the "integration" perspective. For a review of this perspective and conflicting approaches, see D. Meyerson and J. Martin, "Cultural Change: An Integration of Three Different Views," *Journal of Management Studies*, November 1987, pp. 623–647; and P. J. Frost, L. F. Moore, M. R. Louis, C. C. Lundberg, and J. Martin, eds., *Reframing Organizational Culture* (Newbury Park, CA: Sage, 1991).

16   See J. M. Jermier, J. W. Slocum Jr., L. W. Fry, and J. Gaines, "Organizational Subcultures in a Soft Bureaucracy: Resistance Behind the Myth and Facade of an Official Culture," *Organization Science*, May 1991, pp. 170–194; S. A. Sackmann, "Culture and Subcultures: An Analysis of Organizational Knowledge," *Administrative Science Quarterly*, March 1992, pp. 140–161; R. F. Zammuto, "Mapping Organizational Cultures and Subcultures: Looking Inside and Across Hospitals" (paper presented at the 1995 National Academy of Management Conference, Vancouver, BC, August 1995); and G. Hofstede, "Identifying Organizational Subcultures: An Empirical Approach," *Journal of Management Studies*, January 1998, pp. 1–12.

17   T. A. Timmerman, "Do Organizations Have Personalities?" (paper presented at the 1996 National Academy of Management Conference, Cincinnati, OH, August 1996).

18   S. Hamm, "No Letup—and No Apologies," *BusinessWeek*, October 26, 1998, pp. 58–64.

19   Based on "Rising on Three Pillars Strategy; 10 Most Admired Corporate Cultures," *Financial Post*, November 26, 2008, p. WK4; M. Parker, "Why Can't Employers See The Paradox?" *Financial Post*, March 19, 2008, p. WK7; M. Parker, "Identifying Enablers and Blockers of Cultural Transformation," *Canadian Business Online*, May 17, 2007 (accessed February 4, 2009).

20   See, for example, G. G. Gordon and N. DiTomaso, "Predicting Corporate Performance from Organizational Culture," *Journal of Management Studies*, November 1992, pp. 793–798; and J. B. Sorensen, "The Strength of Corporate Culture and the Reliability of Firm Performance," *Administrative Science Quarterly*, March 2002, pp. 70–91.

21   Y. Wiener, "Forms of Value Systems: A Focus on Organizational Effectiveness and Cultural Change and Maintenance," *Academy of Management Review*, October 1988, p. 536.

22   R. T. Mowday, L. W. Porter, and R. M. Steers, *Employee-Organization Linkages: The Psychology of Commitment, Absenteeism, and Turnover* (New York: Academic Press, 1982).

23   E. Ransdell, "The Nike Story? Just Tell It!" *Fast Company*, January–February 2000, pp. 44–46.

24   K. W. Smith, "A Brand-New Culture for the Merged Firm," *Mergers and Acquisitions* 35, no. 6 (June 2000), pp. 45–50.

25   D. M. Boje, "The Storytelling Organization: A Study of Story Performance in an Office-Supply Firm," *Administrative Science Quarterly*, March 1991, pp. 106–126; and C. H. Deutsch, "The Parables of Corporate Culture," *New York Times*, October 13, 1991, p. F25.

26   A. M. Pettigrew, "On Studying Organizational Cultures," *Administrative Science Quarterly*, December 1979, p. 576.

27   A. M. Pettigrew, "On Studying Organizational Cultures," *Administrative Science Quarterly*, December 1979, p. 576. See also K. Kamoche, "Rhetoric, Ritualism, and Totemism in Human Resource Management," *Human Relations*, April 1995, pp. 367–385.

28   V. Matthews, "Starting Every Day with a Shout and a Song," *Financial Times*, May 2, 2001, p. 11; and M. Gimein, "Sam Walton Made Us a Promise," *Fortune*, March 18, 2002, pp. 121–130.

29   A. Rafaeli and M. G. Pratt, "Tailored Meanings: On the Meaning and Impact of Organizational Dress," *Academy of Management Review*, January 1993, pp. 32–55.

30   Thanks to an anonymous reviewer for adding these.

31   M. Pendergast, *Uncommon Grounds: The History of Coffee and How It Transformed Our World* (New York: Basic Books, 1999), p. 369.

32   Thanks to a reviewer for this story.

33   Based on "Rising on Three Pillars Strategy; 10 Most Admired Corporate Cultures," *Financial Post*, November 26, 2008, p. WK4; and http://www.bostonpizza.com.

34   E. H. Schein, "The Role of the Founder in Creating Organizational Culture," *Organizational Dynamics*, Summer 1983, pp. 13–28.

35   E. H. Schein, "Leadership and Organizational Culture," in *The Leader of the Future*, ed. F. Hesselbein, M. Goldsmith, and R. Beckhard (San Francisco: Jossey-Bass, 1996), pp. 61–62.

36   See, for example, J. R. Harrison, and G. R. Carroll, "Keeping the Faith: A Model of Cultural Transmission in Formal Organizations," *Administrative Science Quarterly*, December 1991, pp. 552–582.

37   See B. Schneider, "The People Make the Place," *Personnel Psychology*, Autumn 1987, pp. 437–453; J. A. Chatman, "Matching People and Organizations: Selection and Socialization in Public Accounting Firms," *Administrative Science Quarterly*, September 1991, pp. 459–484; D. E. Bowen, G. E. Ledford Jr., and B. R. Nathan, "Hiring for the Organization, Not the Job," *Academy of Management Executive*, November 1991, pp. 35–51; B. Schneider, H. W. Goldstein, and D. B. Smith, "The ASA Framework: An Update," *Personnel Psychology*, Winter 1995, pp. 747–773; A. L. Kristof, "Person-Organization Fit: An Integrative Review of Its Conceptualizations, Measurement, and Implications," *Personnel Psychology*, Spring 1996, pp. 1–49; and J. Harris and J. Brannick, *Finding and Keeping Great Employees* (New York: AMACOM, 1999).

38   S. Fralic, "Even Playland's Interviews Are Fun for Job-Seekers," *Vancouver Sun*, Monday, July 14, 2008, http://www.canada.com/vancouversun/news/story.html?id=7ba15dd4-cbe8-4a09-a08c-cce86c73a694.

39   S. Fralic, "Even Playland's Interviews Are Fun for Job-Seekers," *Vancouver Sun*, Monday, July 14, 2008, http://www.canada.com/vancouversun/news/story.html?id=7ba15dd4-cbe8-4a09-a08c-cce86c73a694.

40 D. C. Hambrick and P. A. Mason, "Upper Echelons: The Organization as a Reflection of Its Top Managers," *Academy of Management Review*, April 1984, pp. 193–206; B. P. Niehoff, C. A. Enz, and R. A. Grover, "The Impact of Top-Management Actions on Employee Attitudes and Perceptions," *Group & Organization Studies*, September 1990, pp. 337–352; and H. M. Trice and J. M. Beyer, "Cultural Leadership in Organizations," *Organization Science*, May 1991, pp. 149–169.

41 J. S. Lublin, "Cheap Talk," *Wall Street Journal*, April 11, 2002, p. B14.

42 See, for instance, J. P. Wanous, *Organizational Entry*, 2nd ed. (New York: Addison Wesley, 1992); G. T. Chao, A. M. O'Leary-Kelly, S. Wolf, H. J. Klein, and P. D. Gardner, "Organizational Socialization: Its Content and Consequences," *Journal of Applied Psychology*, October 1994, pp. 730–743; B. E. Ashforth, A. M. Saks, and R. T. Lee, "Socialization and Newcomer Adjustment: The Role of Organizational Context," *Human Relations*, July 1998, pp. 897–926; D. A. Major, "Effective Newcomer Socialization into High-Performance Organizational Cultures," in *Handbook of Organizational Culture & Climate*, ed. N. M. Ashkanasy, C. P. M. Wilderom, and M. F. Peterson (Thousand Oaks, CA: Sage, 2000), pp. 355–368; and D. M. Cable and C. K. Parsons, "Socialization Tactics and Person-Organization Fit," *Personnel Psychology*, Spring 2001, pp. 1–23.

43 J. Impoco, "Basic Training, Sanyo Style," *U.S. News & World Report*, July 13, 1992, pp. 46–48.

44 B. Filipczak, "Trained by Starbucks," *Training*, June 1995, pp. 73–79; and S. Gruner, "Lasting Impressions," *Inc.*, July 1998, p. 126.

45 J. Van Maanen and E. H. Schein, "Career Development," in *Improving Life at Work*, ed. J. R. Hackman and J. L. Suttle (Santa Monica, CA: Goodyear, 1977), pp. 58–62.

46 D. C. Feldman, "The Multiple Socialization of Organization Members," *Academy of Management Review*, April 1981, p. 310.

47 J. Van Maanen and E. H. Schein, "Career Development," in *Improving Life at Work*, ed. J. R. Hackman and J. L. Suttle (Santa Monica, CA: Goodyear, 1977), p. 59.

48 T. Cole, "How to Stay Hired," *Report on Business Magazine*, March 1995, pp. 46–48.

49 J. E. Sheridan, "Organizational Culture and Employee Retention," *Academy of Management Journal*, December 1992, pp. 1036–1056.

50 See, for instance, D. Miller, "What Happens After Success: The Perils of Excellence," *Journal of Management Studies*, May 1994, pp. 11–38.

51 See C. Lindsay, "Paradoxes of Organizational Diversity: Living within the Paradoxes," in *Proceedings of the 50th Academy of Management Conference*, ed. L. R. Jauch and J. L. Wall (San Francisco, 1990), pp. 374–378; T. Cox Jr., *Cultural Diversity in Organizations: Theory, Research & Practice* (San Francisco: Berrett-Koehler, 1993), pp. 162–170; and L. Grensing-Pophal, "Hiring to Fit Your Corporate Culture," *HR Magazine*, August 1999, pp. 50–54.

52 A. F. Buono and J. L. Bowditch, *The Human Side of Mergers and Acquisitions: Managing Collisions Between People, Cultures, and Organizations* (San Francisco: Jossey-Bass, 1989); S. Cartwright and C. L. Cooper, "The Role of Culture Compatibility in Successful Organizational Marriages," *Academy of Management Executive*, May 1993, pp. 57–70; D. Carey and D. Ogden, "A Match Made in Heaven? Find Out Before You Merge," *Wall Street Journal*, November 30, 1998, p. A22; R. J. Grossman, "Irreconcilable Differences," *HR Magazine*, April 1999, pp. 42–48; J. Veiga, M. Lubatkin, R. Calori, and P. Very, "Measuring Organizational Culture Clashes: A Two-Nation Post-Hoc Analysis of a Cultural Compatibility Index," *Human Relations*, April 2000, pp. 539–557; and E. Krell, "Merging Corporate Cultures," *Training*, May 2001, pp. 68–78.

53 C. Isidore, "Daimler Pays to Dump Chrysler," *CNNMoney.com*, May 14, 2007, http://money.cnn.com/2007/05/14/news/companies/chrysler_sale/index.htm (accessed September 8, 2008); T. Watson, "In the Clutches of a Slowdown: Plant Closures Might Loom in DaimlerChrysler's Future as the Carmaker Tries to Correct Past Management Errors, a Misread of What Consumers Wanted to Drive off the Lot and a Clash of Cultures from Its Recent Merger," *Financial Post* (*National Post*), December 23, 2000, p. D7; T. Watson, "Zetsche Runs into Perfect Storm: Chrysler's Crisis," *Financial Post* (*National Post*), December 13, 2000, pp. C1, C4; M. Steen, "Chrysler to Improve: Schrempp: Shareholders Are Embittered by Steep Losses and Imprecise Earnings Forecasts: Better Operating Results," *Financial Post* (*National Post*), April 11, 2002, p. FP12; and "DaimlerChrysler Boss to Step Down," *BBC News World Edition*, July 28, 2005.

54 K. W. Smith, "A Brand-New Culture for the Merged Firm," *Mergers and Acquisitions* 35, no. 6 (June 2000), pp. 45–50.

55 Based on "Corporate Culture," *Canadian HR Reporter* 17, no. 21 (December 6, 2004), pp. 7–11; "Business Browser," *Edmonton Journal*, September 18, 2008, p. F2; S. Ladurantaye, "A Matter of Trust: These CEOs Fit the Bill," *Globe and Mail*, September 26, 2008, p. B15; and http://www.agrium.com/company_profile/our_business/index.jsp.

56 M. Raynaud and M. Teasdale, "Confusions & Acquisitions: Post-Merger Culture Shock and Some Remedies," *Communication World* 9, no. 6 (May–June 1992), pp. 44–45.

57 M. Raynaud and M. Teasdale, "Confusions & Acquisitions: Post-Merger Culture Shock and Some Remedies," *Communication World* 9, no. 6 (May–June 1992), pp. 44–45.

58 Vignette based on "Corporate Culture," *Canadian HR Reporter* 17, no. 21 (December 6, 2004), pp. 7–11; and P. Kuitenbrouwer, "Making Money, and Enjoying It: Dingwall at the Mint," *Financial Post* (*National Post*), December 29, 2004, p. FP1; and C. Clark, "Dingwall Severance in the Works," *Globe and Mail*, September 30, 2005, p. A5.

59 Based on http://www.bostonpizza.com; and "Rising on Three Pillars Strategy; 10 Most Admired Corporate Cultures," *Financial Post*, November 26, 2008, p. WK4.

60 M. L. Wald and J. Schwartz, "Shuttle Inquiry Uncovers Flaws in Communication," *New York Times*, August 4, 2003, http://www.nytimes.com.

61 J. P. Kotter, "Leading Changes: Why Transformation Efforts Fail," *Harvard Business Review*, March–April 1995, pp. 59–67; and J. P. Kotter, *Leading Change* (Boston: Harvard Business School Press, 1996).

62 See B. Victor and J. B. Cullen, "The Organizational Bases of Ethical Work Climates," *Administrative Science Quarterly*, March 1988, pp. 101–125; L. K. Trevino, "A Cultural Perspective on Changing and Developing Organizational Ethics," in *Research in Organizational Change and Development*, vol. 4, ed. W. A. Pasmore and R. W. Woodman (Greenwich, CT: JAI Press, 1990); M. W. Dickson, D. B. Smith, M. W. Grojean, and M. Ehrhart, "An Organizational Climate Regarding Ethics: The Outcome of Leader Values and the Practices That Reflect Them," *Leadership Quarterly*, Summer 2001, pp. 197–217; and R. L. Dufresne, "An Action Learning Perspective on Effective Implementation of Academic Honor Codes," *Group & Organization Management*, April 2004, pp. 201–218.

63   D. L. Nelson and C. L. Cooper, eds., *Positive Organizational Behavior* (London: Sage, 2007); K. S. Cameron, J. E. Dutton, and R. E. Quinn, eds., *Positive Organizational Scholarship: Foundations of a New Discipline* (San Francisco: Berrett-Koehler, 2003); and F. Luthans and C. M. Youssef, "Emerging Positive Organizational Behavior," *Journal of Management*, June 2007, pp. 321–349.

64   J. Robison, "Great Leadership Under Fire," *Gallup Leadership Journal*, March 8, 2007, pp. 1–3.

65   R. Wagner and J. K. Harter, 12: *The Elements of Great Managing* (New York: Gallup Press, 2006).

66   R. Wagner and J. K. Harter, "Performance Reviews without the Anxiety," *Gallup Leadership Journal*, July 12, 2007, pp. 1–4; and R. Wagner and J. K. Harter, 12: *The Elements of Great Managing* (New York: Gallup Press, 2006).

67   S. Fineman, "On Being Positive: Concerns and Counterpoints," *Academy of Management Review* 31, no. 2 (2006), pp. 270–291.

68   Based on E. Iwata, "Businesses Grow More Socially Conscious," *USA Today*, June 14, 2007, p. 3B; and M. Boyle and E. F. Kratz, "The Wegmans Way," *Fortune*, January 24, 2005, pp. 62–66.

69   Based on E. Dash, "A Clash of Cultures, Averted," *New York Times*, February 20, 2007, pp. B1, B3.

70   Ideas in this feature were influenced by A. L. Wilkins, "The Culture Audit: A Tool for Understanding Organizations," *Organizational Dynamics*, Autumn 1983, pp. 24–38; H. M. Trice and J. M. Beyer, *The Cultures of Work Organizations* (Englewood Cliffs, NJ: Prentice Hall, 1993), pp. 358–362; H. Lancaster, "To Avoid a Job Failure, Learn the Culture of a Company First," *Wall Street Journal*, July 14, 1998, p. B1; and M. Belliveau, "4 Ways to Read a Company," *Fast Company*, October 1998, p. 158.

Chapter 11

1   Opening and chapter vignettes based on "Endless Summer," *Fortune*, April 2, 2007, pp. 63–70; and Y. Chouinard, *Let My People Go Surfing*, (New York: Penguin Books, 2005).

2   J. P. Kotter, "What Leaders Really Do," *Harvard Business Review*, May–June 1990, pp. 103–111.

3   R. N. Kanungo, "Leadership in Organizations: Looking Ahead to the 21st Century," *Canadian Psychology* 39, no. 1–2 (1998), p. 77. For more evidence of this consensus, see N. Adler, *International Dimensions of Organizational Behavior*, 3rd ed. (Cincinnati, OH: South Western, 1997); R. J. House, "Leadership in the Twenty-First Century," in *The Changing Nature of Work*, ed. A. Howard (San Francisco: Jossey-Bass, 1995), pp. 411–450; R. N. Kanungo and M. Mendonca, *Ethical Dimensions of Leadership* (Thousand

Oaks, CA: Sage, 1996); A. Zaleznik, "The Leadership Gap," *Academy of Management Executive* 4, no. 1 (1990), pp. 7–22.

4   Based on D. Fost, "Survey Finds Many Workers Mistrust Bosses," *San Francisco Chronicle*, January 3, 2007, http://www.sfgate.com; and T. Weiss, "The Narcissistic CEO," *Forbes*, August 29, 2006, http://www.forbes.com.

5   J. G. Geier, "A Trait Approach to the Study of Leadership in Small Groups," *Journal of Communication*, December 1967, pp. 316–323.

6   S. A. Kirkpatrick and E. A. Locke, "Leadership: Do Traits Matter?" *Academy of Management Executive*, May 1991, pp. 48–60; and S. J. Zaccaro, R. J. Foti, and D. A. Kenny, "Self-Monitoring and Trait-Based Variance in Leadership: An Investigation of Leader Flexibility Across Multiple Group Situations," *Journal of Applied Psychology*, April 1991, pp. 308–315.

7   See T. A. Judge, J. E. Bono, R. Ilies, and M. Werner, "Personality and Leadership: A Review" (paper presented at the 15th Annual Conference of the Society for Industrial and Organizational Psychology, New Orleans, 2000); and T. A. Judge, J. E. Bono, R. Ilies, and M. W. Gerhardt, "Personality and Leadership: A Qualitative and Quantitative Review," *Journal of Applied Psychology*, August 2002, pp. 765–780.

8   T. A. Judge, J. E. Bono, R. Ilies, and M. Werner, "Personality and Leadership: A Review" (paper presented at the 15th Annual Conference of the Society for Industrial and Organizational Psychology, New Orleans, 2000).

9   D. R. Ames and F. J. Flynn, "What Breaks a Leader: The Curvilinear Relation between Assertiveness and Leadership," *Journal of Personality and Social Psychology* 92, no. 2 (2007), pp. 307–324.

10   T. A. Judge, J. E. Bono, R. Ilies, and M. Werner, "Personality and Leadership: A Review" (paper presented at the 15th Annual Conference of the Society for Industrial and Organizational Psychology, New Orleans, 2000); R. G. Lord, C. L. DeVader, and G. M. Alliger, "A Meta-Analysis of the Relation between Personality Traits and Leadership Perceptions: An Application of Validity Generalization Procedures," *Journal of Applied Psychology*, August 1986, pp. 402–410; and J. A. Smith and R. J. Foti, "A Pattern Approach to the Study of Leader Emergence," *Leadership Quarterly*, Summer 1998, pp. 147–160.

11   This section is based on D. Goleman, "What Makes a Leader?" *Harvard Business Review*, November–December 1998, pp. 93–102; J. M. George, "Emotions and Leadership: The Role of Emotional Intelligence," *Human Relations*, August 2000, pp. 1027–55; C. S. Wong and K. S. Law, "The Effects of Leader and Follower Emotional Intelligence on Performance and Attitude: An Exploratory Study," *Leadership Quarterly*, June 2002, pp. 243–274; and D. R. Caruso, and C. J. Wolfe, "Emotional Intelligence and Leadership Development" in *Leader Development for Transforming Organizations: Growing Leaders for Tomorrow*, ed. D. David and S. J. Zaccaro (Mahwah, NJ: Lawrence Erlbaum, 2004) pp. 237–263.

12   J. Champy, "The Hidden Qualities of Great Leaders," *Fast Company* November 2003, p. 135.

13   T. A. Judge, J. A. LePine, and B. L. Rich, "Loving Yourself Abundantly: Relationship of the Narcissistic Personality to Self- and Other Perceptions of Workplace Deviance, Leadership, and Task and Contextual Performance," *Journal of Applied Psychology* 91, no. 4 (2006), pp. 762–776.

14 R. M. Stogdill and A. E. Coons, eds., *Leader Behavior: Its Description and Measurement*, Research Monograph no. 88 (Columbus: Ohio State University, Bureau of Business Research, 1951). This research is updated in S. Kerr, C. A. Schriesheim, C. J. Murphy, and R. M. Stogdill, "Toward a Contingency Theory of Leadership Based upon the Consideration and Initiating Structure Literature," *Organizational Behavior and Human Performance*, August 1974, pp. 62–82; and C. A. Schriesheim, C. C. Cogliser, and L. L. Neider, "Is It 'Trustworthy'? A Multiple-Levels-of-Analysis Reexamination of an Ohio State Leadership Study, with Implications for Future Research," *Leadership Quarterly*, Summer 1995, pp. 111–145.

15 R. Kahn and D. Katz, "Leadership Practices in Relation to Productivity and Morale," in *Group Dynamics: Research and Theory*, 2nd ed., ed. D. Cartwright and A. Zander (Elmsford, NY: Row, Paterson, 1960).

16 R. R. Blake and J. S. Mouton, *The Managerial Grid* (Houston, TX: Gulf, 1964); R. R. Blake and A. A. McCanse, *Leadership Dilemmas—Grid Solutions* (Houston, TX: Gulf Publishing Company, 1991); R. R. Blake and J. S. Mouton, "Management by Grid Principles or Situationalism: Which?" *Group and Organization Studies* 7, 1982, pp. 207–210.

17 For a critical review, see A. K. Korman, "'Consideration,' 'Initiating Structure' and Organizational Criteria—A Review," *Personnel Psychology* 19, 1966, pp. 349–361. For a more supportive review, see S. Kerr and C. Schriesheim, "Consideration, Initiating Structure, and Organizational Criteria—An Update of Korman's 1966 Review," *Personnel Psychology* 27, 1974, pp. 555–568.

18 Based on G. Johns and A. M. Saks, *Organizational Behaviour*, 5th ed. (Toronto: Pearson Education Canada, 2001), p. 276.

19 A. J. Mayo and N. Nohria, "Zeitgeist Leadership," *Harvard Business Review* 83, no. 10 (2005), pp. 45–60.

20 See, for instance, P. M. Podsakoff, S. B. MacKenzie, M. Ahearne, and W. H. Bommer, "Searching for a Needle in a Haystack: Trying to Identify the Illusive Moderators of Leadership Behavior," *Journal of Management* 1, no. 3 (1995), pp. 422–470.

21 F. E. Fiedler, *A Theory of Leadership Effectiveness* (New York: McGraw-Hill, 1967).

22 Cited in R. J. House and R. N. Aditya, "The Social Scientific Study of Leadership: Quo Vadis?" *Journal of Management* 23, no. 3 (1997), p. 422.

23 G. Johns and A. M. Saks, *Organizational Behaviour*, 5th ed. (Toronto: Pearson Education Canada, 2001), pp. 278–279.

24 P. Hersey and K. H. Blanchard, "So You Want to Know Your Leadership Style?" *Training and Development Journal*, February 1974, pp. 1–15; and P. Hersey, K. H. Blanchard, and D. E. Johnson, *Management of Organizational Behavior: Leading Human Resources*, 8th ed. (Upper Saddle River, NJ: Prentice Hall, 2001).

25 Cited in C. F. Fernandez and R. P. Vecchio, "Situational Leadership Theory Revisited: A Test of an Across-Jobs Perspective," *Leadership Quarterly* 8, no. 1 (1997), p. 67. See also http://www.situational.com/leadership.htm.

26 For controversy surrounding the Fiedler LPC scale, see A. Bryman, "Leadership in Organizations," in *Handbook of Organization Studies*, ed. S. R. Clegg, C. Hardy, and W. R. Nord (London: Sage, 1996), pp. 279–280; A. Bryman, *Leadership and Organizations* (London: Routledge and Kegan Paul, 1986); and T. Peters and N. Austin, *A Passion for Excellence* (New York: Random House, 1985). For supportive evidence on the Fiedler model, see L. H. Peters, D. D. Hartke, and J. T. Pohlmann, "Fiedler's Contingency Theory of Leadership: An Application of the Meta-Analysis Procedures of Schmidt and Hunter," *Psychological Bulletin*, March 1985, pp. 274–285; C. A. Schriesheim, B. J. Tepper, and L. A. Tetrault, "Least Preferred Co-Worker Score, Situational Control, and Leadership Effectiveness: A Meta-Analysis of Contingency Model Performance Predictions," *Journal of Applied Psychology*, August 1994, pp. 561–573; and R. Ayman, M. M. Chemers, and F. Fiedler, "The Contingency Model of Leadership Effectiveness: Its Levels of Analysis," *Leadership Quarterly*, Summer 1995, pp. 147–167. For evidence that LPC scores are not stable, see, for instance, R. W. Rice, "Psychometric Properties of the Esteem for the Least Preferred Coworker (LPC) Scale," *Academy of Management Review*, January 1978, pp. 106–118; C. A. Schriesheim, B. D. Bannister, and W. H. Money, "Psychometric Properties of the LPC Scale: An Extension of Rice's Review," *Academy of Management Review*, April 1979, pp. 287–290; and J. K. Kennedy, J. M. Houston, M. A. Korgaard, and D. D. Gallo, "Construct Space of the Least Preferred Co-worker (LPC) Scale," *Educational & Psychological Measurement*, Fall 1987, pp. 807–814. For difficulty in applying Fiedler's model, see E. H. Schein, *Organizational Psychology*, 3rd ed. (Englewood Cliffs, NJ: Prentice Hall, 1980), pp. 116–117; and B. Kabanoff, "A Critique of Leader Match and Its Implications for Leadership Research," *Personnel Psychology*, Winter 1981, pp. 749–764. For evidence that Hersey and Blanchard's model has received little attention from researchers, see R. K. Hambleton and R. Gumpert, "The Validity of Hersey and Blanchard's Theory of Leader Effectiveness," *Group & Organization Studies*, June 1982, pp. 225–242; C. L. Graeff, "The Situational Leadership Theory: A Critical View," *Academy of Management Review*, April 1983, pp. 285–291; R. P. Vecchio, "Situational Leadership Theory: An Examination of a Prescriptive Theory," *Journal of Applied Psychology*, August 1987, pp. 444–451; J. R. Goodson, G. W. McGee, and J. F. Cashman, "Situational Leadership Theory: A Test of Leadership Prescriptions," *Group & Organization Studies*, December 1989, pp. 446–461; W. Blank, J. R. Weitzel, and S. G. Green, "A Test of the Situational Leadership Theory," *Personnel Psychology*, Autumn 1990, pp. 579–597; and W. R. Norris and R. P. Vecchio, "Situational Leadership Theory: A Replication," *Group & Organization Management*, September 1992, pp. 331–342. For evidence of partial support for the theory, see R. P. Vecchio, "Situational Leadership Theory: An Examination of a Prescriptive Theory," *Journal of Applied Psychology*, August 1987, pp. 444–451; and W. R. Norris and R. P. Vecchio, "Situational Leadership Theory: A Replication," *Group & Organization Management*, September 1992, pp. 331–342; and for evidence of no support for Hersey and Blanchard, see W. Blank, J. R. Weitzel, and S. G. Green, "A Test of the Situational Leadership Theory," *Personnel Psychology*, Autumn 1990, pp. 579–597.

27 M. G. Evans, "The Effects of Supervisory Behavior on the Path-Goal Relationship," *Organizational Behavior and Human Performance* 5, 1970, pp. 277–298; M. G. Evans, "Leadership and Motivation: A Core Concept," *Academy of Management Journal* 13, 1970, 91–102; R. J. House, "A Path-Goal Theory of Leader Effectiveness," *Administrative Science Quarterly*, September 1971, pp. 321–338; R. J. House and T. R. Mitchell, "Path-Goal Theory of Leadership," *Journal of Contemporary Business*, Autumn 1974, p. 86; M. G. Evans, "Leadership," in *Organizational Behavior*, ed. S. Kerr (Columbus, OH: Grid Publishing, 1979); R. J. House, "Retrospective Comment," in *The Great Writings in Management and Organizational Behavior*, 2nd ed., ed. L. E. Boone and D. D. Bowen (New York: Random House, 1987), pp. 354–364;

and M. G. Evans, *"Fuhrungstheorien, Weg-ziel-theorie,"* in *Handworterbuch Der Fuhrung*, 2nd ed., ed. A. Kieser, G. Reber, and R. Wunderer, trans. G. Reber (Stuttgart, Germany: Schaffer Poeschal Verlag, 1995), pp. 1075–1091.

28 G. R. Jones, J. M. George, C. W. L. Hill, and N. Langton, *Contemporary Management* (Toronto: McGraw-Hill Ryerson, 2002), p. 392.

29 J. C. Wofford and L. Z. Liska, "Path-Goal Theories of Leadership: A Meta-Analysis," *Journal of Management* 19, no. 4 (1993), pp. 857–876.

30 P. M. Podsakoff, S. B. MacKenzie, and M. Ahearne, "Searching for a Needle in a Haystack: Trying to Identify the Illusive Moderators of Leadership Behaviors," *Journal of Management* 21, 1995, pp. 423–470.

31 J. R. Villa, J. P. Howell, and P. W. Dorfman, "Problems with Detecting Moderators in Leadership Research Using Moderated Multiple Regression," *Leadership Quarterly* 14, 2003, pp. 3–23; C. A. Schriesheim, and L. Neider, "Path-Goal Leadership Theory: The Long and Winding Road," *Leadership Quarterly* 7, 1996, pp. 317–321; and M. G. Evans, "R. J. House's 'A Path-Goal Theory of Leader Effectiveness,'" *Leadership Quarterly* 7, 1996, pp. 305–309.

32 L. R. Anderson, "Toward a Two-Track Model of Leadership Training: Suggestions from Self-Monitoring Theory," *Small Group Research*, May 1990, pp. 147–167; G. H. Dobbins, W. S. Long, E. J. Dedrick, and T. C. Clemons, "The Role of Self-Monitoring and Gender on Leader Emergence: A Laboratory and Field Study," *Journal of Management*, September 1990, pp. 609–618; and S. J. Zaccaro, R. J. Foti, and D. A. Kenny, "Self-Monitoring and Trait-Based Variance in Leadership: An Investigation of Leader Flexibility Across Multiple Group Situations," *Journal of Applied Psychology*, April 1991, pp. 308–315.

33 S. Kerr and J. M. Jermier, "Substitutes for Leadership: Their Meaning and Measurement," *Organizational Behavior and Human Performance*, December 1978, pp. 375–403; J. P. Howell and P. W. Dorfman, "Substitutes for Leadership: Test of a Construct," *Academy of Management Journal*, December 1981, pp. 714–728; J. P. Howell, P. W. Dorfman, and S. Kerr, "Leadership and Substitutes for Leadership," *Journal of Applied Behavioral Science* 22, no. 1 (1986), pp. 29–46; J. P. Howell, D. E. Bowen, P. W. Dorfman, S. Kerr, and P. M. Podsakoff, "Substitutes for Leadership: Effective Alternatives to Ineffective Leadership," *Organizational Dynamics*, Summer 1990, pp. 21–38; P. M. Podsakoff, B. P. Niehoff, S. B. MacKenzie, and M. L. Williams, "Do Substitutes for Leadership Really Substitute for Leadership? An Empirical Examination of Kerr and Jermier's Situational Leadership Model," *Organizational Behavior and Human Decision Processes*, February 1993, pp. 1–44; P. M. Podsakoff and S. B. MacKenzie, "An Examination of Substitutes for Leadership within a Levels-of-Analysis Framework," *Leadership Quarterly*, Fall 1995, pp. 289–328; P. M. Podsakoff, S. B. MacKenzie, and W. H. Bommer, "Transformational Leader Behaviors and Substitutes for Leadership as Determinants of Employee Satisfaction, Commitment, Trust, and Organizational Citizenship Behaviors," *Journal of Management* 22, no. 2 (1996), pp. 259–298; P. M. Podsakoff, S. B. MacKenzie, and W. H. Bommer, "Meta-Analysis of the Relationships between Kerr and Jermier's Substitutes for Leadership and Employee Attitudes, Role Perceptions, and Performance," *Journal of Applied Psychology*, August 1996, pp. 380–399; and J. M. Jermier and S. Kerr, "'Substitutes for Leadership: Their Meaning and

Measurement'—Contextual Recollections and Current Observations," *Leadership Quarterly* 8, no. 2 (1997), pp. 95–101.

34 J. A. Conger and R. N. Kanungo, "Behavioral Dimensions of Charismatic Leadership," in *Charismatic Leadership*, ed. J. A. Conger and R. N. Kanungo (San Francisco: Jossey-Bass, 1988), p. 79.

35 J. A. Conger and R. N. Kanungo, *Charismatic Leadership in Organizations* (Thousand Oaks, CA: Sage, 1998); and R. Awamleh and W. L. Gardner, "Perceptions of Leader Charisma and Effectiveness: The Effects of Vision Content, Delivery, and Organizational Performance," *Leadership Quarterly*, Fall 1999, pp. 345–373.

36 B. Shamir, R. J. House, and M. B. Arthur, "The Motivational Effects of Charismatic Leadership: A Self-Concept Theory," *Organization Science*, November 1993, pp. 577–594.

37 P. C. Nutt and R. W. Backoff, "Crafting Vision," *Journal of Management Inquiry*, December 1997, p. 309.

38 R. Kark, B. Shamir, and G. Chen, "The Two Faces of Transformational Leadership: Empowerment and Dependency," *Journal of Applied Psychology* 88, no. 2 (2003), pp. 246–255.

39 P. D. Cherlunik, K. A. Donley, T. S. R. Wiewel, and S. R. Miller, "Charisma Is Contagious: The Effect of Leaders' Charisma on Observers' Affect," *Journal of Applied Social Psychology*, October 2001, pp. 2149–2159.

40 D. A. Waldman, B. M. Bass, and F. J. Yammarino, "Adding to Contingent-Reward Behavior: The Augmenting Effect of Charismatic Leadership," *Group & Organization Studies*, December 1990, pp. 381–394; and S. A. Kirkpatrick and E. A. Locke, "Direct and Indirect Effects of Three Core Charismatic Leadership Components on Performance and Attitudes," *Journal of Applied Psychology*, February 1996, pp. 36–51.

41 A. H. B. de Hoogh, D. N. den Hartog, P. L. Koopman, H. Thierry, P. T. van den Berg, and J. G. van der Weide, "Charismatic Leadership, Environmental Dynamism, and Performance," *European Journal of Work & Organizational Psychology*, December 2004, pp. 447–471; S. Harvey, M. Martin, and D. Stout, "Instructor's Transformational Leadership: University Student Attitudes and Ratings," *Psychological Reports*, April 2003, pp. 395–402; and D. A. Waldman, M. Javidan, and P. Varella, "Charismatic Leadership at the Strategic Level: A New Application of Upper Echelons Theory," *Leadership Quarterly*, June 2004, pp. 355–380.

42 R. J. House, "A 1976 Theory of Charismatic Leadership," in *Leadership: The Cutting Edge*, ed. J. G. Hunt and L. L. Larson (Carbondale, IL: Southern Illinois University Press, 1977), pp. 189–207; and Robert J. House and Ram N. Aditya, "The Social Scientific Study of Leadership," *Journal of Management* 23, no. 3 (1997), p. 441.

43 F. Cohen, S. Solomon, M. Maxfield, T. Pyszczynski, and J. Greenberg, "Fatal Attraction: The Effects of Mortality Salience on Evaluations of Charismatic, Task-Oriented, and Relationship-Oriented Leaders," *Psychological Science*, December 2004, pp. 846–851; and M. G. Ehrhart and K. J. Klein, "Predicting Followers' Preferences for Charismatic Leadership: The Influence of Follower Values and Personality," *Leadership Quarterly*, Summer 2001, pp. 153–179.

44 D. E. Carl and M. Javidan, "Universality of Charismatic Leadership: A Multi-Nation Study," *Academy of Management Proceedings*, 2001, pp. IM: B1–B6.

45 J. A. Conger, *The Charismatic Leader: Behind the Mystique of Exceptional Leadership* (San Francisco: Jossey-Bass, 1989); R. Hogan, R. Raskin, and D. Fazzini, "The Dark Side of Charisma," in *Measures of Leadership*, ed. K. E. Clark and M. B. Clark (West Orange, NJ: Leadership Library of America, 1990); D. Sankowsky, "The Charismatic Leader as Narcissist: Understanding the Abuse of Power," *Organizational Dynamics*, Spring 1995, pp. 57–71; and J. O'Connor, M. D. Mumford, T. C. Clifton, T. L. Gessner, and M. S. Connelly, "Charismatic Leaders and Destructiveness: An Historiometric Study," *Leadership Quarterly*, Winter 1995, pp. 529–555.

46 K. Yakabuski, "Henri-Paul Rousseau Was the King of Quebec's Pension Fund and His Returns the Envy of Many," *Globe and Mail*, January 31, 2009, p. B1.

47 Rakesh Khurana, "Toward More Rational CEO Succession," *Chief Executive*, April 2003, p. 16.

48 G. Pitts, "Scandals Part of Natural Cycles of Excess," *Globe and Mail*, June 28, 2002, pp. B1, B5.

49 J. Collins, "Level 5 Leadership: The Triumph of Humility and Fierce Resolve," *Harvard Business Review*, January 2001, pp. 67–76; J. Collins, "Good to Great," *Fast Company*, October 2001, pp. 90–104; J. Collins, "The Misguided Mix-up," *Executive Excellence*, December 2002, pp. 3–4; and H. L. Tosi, V. F. Misangyi, A. Fanelli, D. A. Waldman, and F. J. Yammarino, "CEO Charisma, Compensation, and Firm Performance" *The Leadership Quarterly* 15, 2004, pp. 405–420.

50 See, for instance, B. M. Bass, B. J. Avolio, D. I. Jung, and Y. Berson, "Predicting Unit Performance by Assessing Transformational and Transactional Leadership," *Journal of Applied Psychology*, April 2003, pp. 207–218; and T. A. Judge, and R. F. Piccolo, "Transformational and Transactional Leadership: A Meta-Analytic Test of Their Relative Validity," *Journal of Applied Psychology*, October 2004, pp. 755–768.

51 B. M. Bass, "Leadership: Good, Better, Best," *Organizational Dynamics*, Winter 1985, pp. 26–40; and J. Seltzer and B. M. Bass, "Transformational Leadership: Beyond Initiation and Consideration," *Journal of Management*, December 1990, pp. 693–703.

52 D. I. Jung, C. Chow, and A. Wu, "The Role of Transformational Leadership in Enhancing Organizational Innovation: Hypotheses and Some Preliminary Findings," *Leadership Quarterly*, August–October 2003, pp. 525–544; D. I. Jung, "Transformational and Transactional Leadership and Their Effects on Creativity in Groups," *Creativity Research Journal* 13, no. 2 (2001), pp. 185–195; and S. J. Shin and J. Zhou, "Transformational Leadership, Conservation, and Creativity: Evidence from Korea," *Academy of Management Journal*, December 2003, pp. 703–714.

53 J. E. Bono and T. A. Judge, "Self-Concordance at Work: Toward Understanding the Motivational Effects of Transformational Leaders," *Academy of Management Journal*, October 2003, pp. 554–571; Y. Berson and B. J. Avolio, "Transformational Leadership and the Dissemination of Organizational Goals: A Case Study of a Telecommunication Firm," *Leadership Quarterly*,

October 2004, pp. 625–646; and S. Shinn, "21st-Century Engineer," *BizEd*, January–February, 2005, pp. 18–23.

54 J. R. Baum, E. A. Locke, and S. A. Kirkpatrick, "A Longitudinal Study of the Relation of Vision and Vision Communication to Venture Growth in Entrepreneurial Firms," *Journal of Applied Psychology*, February 2000, pp. 43–54.

55 B. J. Avolio, W. Zhu, W. Koh, and P. Bhatia, "Transformational Leadership and Organizational Commitment: Mediating Role of Psychological Empowerment and Moderating Role of Structural Distance," *Journal of Organizational Behavior*, December 2004, pp. 951–968; and T. Dvir, Taly, N. Kass, and B. Shamir, "The Emotional Bond: Vision and Organizational Commitment Among High-Tech Employees," *Journal of Organizational Change Management* 17, no. 2 (2004), pp. 126–143.

56 R. T. Keller, "Transformational Leadership, Initiating Structure, and Substitutes for Leadership: A Longitudinal Study of Research and Development Project Team Performance," *Journal of Applied Psychology* 91, no. 1 (2006), pp. 202–210.

57 T. A. Judge, and R. F. Piccolo, "Transformational and Transactional Leadership: A Meta-Analytic Test of Their Relative Validity," *Journal of Applied Psychology*, October 2004, pp. 755–768.

58 H. Hetland, G. M. Sandal, and T. B. Johnsen, "Burnout in the Information Technology Sector: Does Leadership Matter?" *European Journal of Work and Organizational Psychology* 16, no. 1 (2007), pp. 58–75; and K. B. Lowe, K. G. Kroeck, and N. Sivasubramaniam, "Effectiveness Correlates of Transformational and Transactional Leadership: A Meta-Analytic Review of the MLQ Literature," *Leadership Quarterly*, Fall 1996, pp. 385–425.

59 See, for instance, J. Barling, T. Weber, and E. K. Kelloway, "Effects of Transformational Leadership Training on Attitudinal and Financial Outcomes: A Field Experiment," *Journal of Applied Psychology*, December 1996, pp. 827–832; and T. Dvir, D. Eden, and B. J. Avolio, "Impact of Transformational Leadership on Follower Development and Performance: A Field Experiment," *Academy of Management Journal*, August 2002, pp. 735–744.

60 R. N. Kanungo, "Leadership in Organizations: Looking Ahead to the 21st Century," *Canadian Psychology* 39, no. 1–2 (1998), p. 78.

61 R. J. House and P. M. Podsakoff, "Leadership Effectiveness: Past Perspectives and Future Directions for Research," in *Organizational Behavior: The State of the Science*, ed. J. Greenberg (Hillsdale, NJ: Erlbaum, 1994), pp. 45–82; and B. M. Bass, *Leadership and Performance Beyond Expectations* (New York: Free Press, 1985).

62 B. J. Avolio and B. M. Bass, "Transformational Leadership, Charisma and Beyond," working paper, School of management, State University of New York, Binghamton, 1985, p. 14.

63 S. Greenhouse, "Working Life (High and Low)," *New York Times*, April 20, 2008, pp. BU1, 4.

64 D. Ancona, E. Backman, and H. Bresman, "X-Teams: New Ways of Leading in a New World," *Ivey Business Journal* 72, no. 3 (May–June 2008), http://www.iveybusinessjournal.com/article.asp?intArticle_ID=755.

65 See, for example, L. J. Zachary, *The Mentor's Guide: Facilitating Effective Learning Relationships* (San Francisco: Jossey-Bass, 2000); M. Murray, *Beyond the Myths and Magic of Mentoring: How to Facilitate an Effective Mentoring Process*, rev. ed. (New York: Wiley,

2001); and F. Warner, "Inside Intel's Mentoring Movement," *Fast Company*, April 2002, pp. 116–120.

66   J. Cooney, *Mentoring: Finding a Perfect Match for People Development Briefing* (Ottawa: The Conference Board of Canada, June 2003).

67   J. A. Wilson and N. S. Elman, "Organizational Benefits of Mentoring," *Academy of Management Executive*, November 1990, p. 90; and J. Reingold, "Want to Grow as a Leader? Get a Mentor?" *Fast Company*, January 2001, pp. 58–60.

68   T. D. Allen, L. T. Eby, M. L. Poteet, E. Lentz, and L. Lima, "Career Benefits Associated with Mentoring for Protégés: A Meta-Analysis," *Journal of Applied Psychology*, February 2004, pp. 127–136.

69   See, for example, D. A. Thomas, "The Impact of Race on Managers' Experiences of Developmental Relationships: An Intra-Organizational Study," *Journal of Organizational Behavior*, November 1990, pp. 479–492; K. E. Kram and D. T. Hall, "Mentoring in a Context of Diversity and Turbulence," in *Managing Diversity*, ed. E. E. Kossek and S. A. Lobel (Cambridge, MA: Blackwell, 1996), pp. 108–36; M. N. Ruderman and M. W. Hughes-James, "Leadership Development Across Race and Gender," in *The Center for Creative Leadership Handbook of Leadership Development*, ed. C. D. McCauley, R. S. Moxley, and E. Van Velsor (San Francisco: Jossey-Bass, 1998), pp. 291–335; and B. R. Ragins and J. L. Cotton, "Mentor Functions and Outcomes: A Comparison of Men and Women in Formal and Informal Mentoring Relationships," *Journal of Applied Psychology*, August 1999, pp. 529–550.

70   J. A. Wilson and N. S. Elman, "Organizational Benefits of Mentoring," *Academy of Management Executive*, November 1990, p. 90.

71   D. Zielinski, "Mentoring Up," *Training* 37, no. 10 (October 2000), pp. 136–141.

72   T. D. Allen, L. T. Eby, M. L. Poteet, Mark L., E. Lentz, and L. Lizzette, "Career Benefits Associated with Mentoring for Protégés: A Meta-Analysis," *Journal of Applied Psychology*, February 2004, pp. 127–136; and J. D. Kammeyer-Mueller and T. A. Judge, "A Quantitative Review of the Mentoring Literature: Test of a Model," working paper, University of Florida, 2005.

73   C. C. Manz and H. P. Sims Jr., *The New SuperLeadership: Leading Others to Lead Themselves* (San Francisco: Berrett-Koehler Publishers, 2001).

74   A. Bandura, "Self-Reinforcement: Theoretical and Methodological Considerations," *Behaviorism* 4, 1976, pp. 135–155; P. W. Corrigan, C. J. Wallace, and M. L. Schade, "Learning Medication Self-Management Skills in Schizophrenia; Relationships with Cognitive Deficits and Psychiatric Symptom," *Behavior Therapy*, Winter, 1994, pp. 5–15; A. S. Bellack, "A Comparison of Self-Reinforcement and Self-Monitoring in a Weight Reduction Program," *Behavior Therapy* 7, 1976, pp. 68–75; T. A. Eckman, W. C. Wirshing, and S. R. Marder, "Technique for Training Schizophrenic Patients in Illness Self-Management: A Controlled Trial," *American Journal of Psychiatry* 149, 1992, pp. 1549–1555; J. J. Felixbrod and K. D. O'Leary, "Effect of Reinforcement on Children's Academic Behavior as a Function of Self-Determined and Externally Imposed Contingencies," *Journal of Applied Behavior Analysis* 6, 1973, pp. 141–150; A. J. Litrownik, L. R. Franzini, and D. Skenderian, "The Effects of Locus of Reinforcement Control on a Concept Identification

Task,"*Psychological Reports* 39, 1976, pp. 159–165; P. D. McGorry, "Psychoeducation in First-Episode Psychosis: A Therapeutic Process," *Psychiatry*, November, 1995, pp. 313–328; G. S. Parcel, P. R. Swank, and M. J. Mariotto, "Self-Management of Cystic Fibrosis: A Structural Model for Educational and Behavioral Variables," *Social Science and Medicine* 38, 1994, pp. 1307–1315; G. E. Speidel, "Motivating Effect of Contingent Self-Reward," *Journal of Experimental Psychology* 102, 1974, pp. 528–530.

75   D. B. Jeffrey, "A Comparison of the Effects of External Control and Self-Control on the Modification and Maintenance of Weight," *Journal of Abnormal Psychology* 83, 1974, pp. 404–410.

76   J. Kelly and S. Nadler, "Leading from Below," *Wall Street Journal*, March 3, 2007, pp. R4, R10.

77   C. C. Manz and H. P. Sims Jr., *The New SuperLeadership: Leading Others to Lead Themselves* (San Francisco: Berrett-Koehler, 2001).

78   See, for instance, J. H. Zenger, E. Musselwhite, K. Hurson, and C. Perrin, *Leading Teams: Mastering the New Role* (Homewood, IL: Business One Irwin, 1994); and M. Frohman, "Nothing Kills Teams Like Ill-Prepared Leaders," *IndustryWeek*, October 2, 1995, pp. 72–76.

79   See, for instance, M. Frohman, "Nothing Kills Teams Like Ill-Prepared Leaders," *IndustryWeek*, October 2, 1995, p. 93.

80   See, for instance, M. Frohman, "Nothing Kills Teams Like Ill-Prepared Leaders," *IndustryWeek*, October 2, 1995, p. 100.

81   J. R. Katzenbach, and D. K. Smith, *The Wisdom of Teams: Creating the High-Performance Organization* (Boston: Harvard Business School Press, 1993).

82   N. Steckler and N. Fondas, "Building Team Leader Effectiveness: A Diagnostic Tool," *Organizational Dynamics*, Winter 1995, p. 20.

83   R. S. Wellins, W. C. Byham, and G. R. Dixon, *Inside Teams* (San Francisco: Jossey-Bass, 1994), p. 318.

84   N. Steckler and N. Fondas, "Building Team Leader Effectiveness: A Diagnostic Tool," *Organizational Dynamics*, Winter 1995, p. 21.

85   B. J. Avolio, S. Kahai, and G. E. Dodge, "E-Leadership: Implications for Theory, Research, and Practice," *Leadership Quarterly*, Winter 2000, pp. 615–668; and B. J. Avolio and S. S. Kahai, "Adding the 'E' to E-Leadership: How It May Impact Your Leadership," *Organizational Dynamics* 31, no. 4 (2003), 325–338.

86   J. Howell and K. Hall-Merenda, "Leading from a Distance," in *Leadership: Achieving Exceptional Performance*, A Special Supplement Prepared by the Richard Ivey School of Business, *Globe and Mail*, May 15, 1998, pp. C1, C2.

87   S. J. Zaccaro and P. Bader, "E-Leadership and the Challenges of Leading E-Teams: Minimizing the Bad and Maximizing the Good," *Organizational Dynamics* 31, no. 4 (2003), pp. 381–385.

88   C. E. Naquin and G. D. Paulson, "Online Bargaining and Interpersonal Trust," *Journal of Applied Psychology*, February 2003, pp. 113–120.

89   B. Shamir, "Leadership in Boundaryless Organizations: Disposable or Indispensable?" *European Journal of Work and Organizational Psychology* 8, no. 1 (1999), pp. 49–71.

90   R. M. Kanter, *The Change Masters, Innovation and Entrepreneurship in the American Corporation* (New York: Simon and Schuster, 1983).

91   R. A. Heifetz, *Leadership without Easy Answers* (Cambridge, MA: Harvard University Press, 1996), p. 205.

92   R. A. Heifetz, *Leadership without Easy Answers* (Cambridge, MA: Harvard University Press, 1996), p. 205.

93   R. A. Heifetz, *Leadership without Easy Answers* (Cambridge, MA: Harvard University Press, 1996), p. 188.

94   S. Casey, "Patagonia: Blueprint for Green Business," *Fortune*, May 29, 2007; and Y. Chouinard, *Let My People Go Surfing*, (New York: Penguin Books, 2005).

95   A. Carter, "Lighting a Fire under Campbell," *BusinessWeek*, December 4, 2006, pp. 96–101.

96   R. Ilies, F. P. Morgeson, and J. D. Nahrgang, "Authentic Leadership and Eudaemonic Wellbeing: Understanding Leader-Follower Outcomes," *Leadership Quarterly* 16, 2005, pp. 373–394.

97   This section is based on E. P. Hollander, "Ethical Challenges in the Leader–Follower Relationship," *Business Ethics Quarterly*, January 1995, pp. 55–65; J. C. Rost, "Leadership: A Discussion About Ethics," *Business Ethics Quarterly*, January 1995, pp. 129–142; L. K. Treviño, M. Brown, and L. P. Hartman, "A Qualitative Investigation of Perceived Executive Ethical Leadership: Perceptions from Inside and Outside the Executive Suite," *Human Relations*, January 2003, pp. 5–37; and R. M. Fulmer, "The Challenge of Ethical Leadership," *Organizational Dynamics* 33, no. 3 (2004), pp. 307–317.

98   D. Leonhardt, "The Imperial Chief Executive Is Suddenly in the Cross Hairs," *New York Times*, June 24, 2002, www.nytimes.com (accessed June 24, 2002).

99   J. M. Burns, *Leadership* (New York: Harper and Row, 1978).

100 J. M. Howell and B. J. Avolio, "The Ethics of Charismatic Leadership: Submission or Liberation?" *Academy of Management Executive*, May 1992, pp. 43–55.

101 M. E. Brown and L. K. Treviño, "Socialized Charismatic Leadership, Values Congruence, and Deviance in Work Groups," *Journal of Applied Psychology* 91, no. 4 (2006), pp. 954–962.

102 J. G. Clawson, *Level Three Leadership* (Upper Saddle River, NJ: Prentice Hall, 1999), pp. 46–49.

103 B. Little, "It's True: Women Are Gaining Ground in Every Job Category," *Globe and Mail*, March 4, 2002, p. B8.

104 J. McFarland, "Women Still Find Slow Rise to Power Positions," *Globe and Mail*, March 13, 2003, pp. B1, B7.

105 R. McQueen, "Glitter Girls No More," *National Post Business*, March 2001, p. 68.

106 V. Galt, "Glass Ceiling Still Tough To Crack," *Globe and Mail*, May 4, 2005, pp. C1, C2.

107 L. Ramsay, "A League of Their Own," *Globe and Mail*, November 23, 2002, p. B11.

108 L. Ramsay, "A League of Their Own," *Globe and Mail*, November 23, 2002, p. B11.

109 Michelle Martinez, "Prepared for the Future: Training Women for Corporate Leadership," *HR Magazine*, April 1997, pp. 80–87.

110 M. McDonald, "They Love Me—Not: Once Hailed as Heroines, Female CEOs Now Face Harsh Critiques," *U.S. News & World Report*, June 24, 2002, http://www.usnews.com/usnews/issue/020624/biztech/24women.htm (accessed November 26, 2005).

111 M. McDonald, "They Love Me—Not: Once Hailed as Heroines, Female CEOs Now Face Harsh Critiques," *U.S. News & World Report*, June 24, 2002, http://www.usnews.com/usnews/issue/020624/biztech/24women.htm (accessed November 26, 2005).

112 J. Wells, "Stuck on the Ladder: Not Only Is the Glass Ceiling Still in Place, But Men and Women Have Very Different Views of the Problem," *Maclean's*, October 20, 1997, p. 60.

113 The material in this section is based on J. Cliff, N. Langton, and H. Aldrich, "Walking the Talk? Gendered Rhetoric Vs. Action in Small Firms," *Organizational Studies* 26, no. 1 (2005), pp. 63-91; J. Grant, "Women as Managers: What They Can Offer to Organizations," *Organizational Dynamics*, Winter 1988, pp. 56–63; S. Helgesen, *The Female Advantage: Women's Ways of Leadership* (New York: Doubleday, 1990); A. H. Eagly and B. T. Johnson, "Gender and Leadership Style: A Meta-Analysis," *Psychological Bulletin*, September 1990, pp. 233–256; A. H. Eagly and S. J. Karau, "Gender and the Emergence of Leaders: A Meta-Analysis," *Journal of Personality and Social Psychology*, May 1991, pp. 685–710; J. B. Rosener, "Ways Women Lead," *Harvard Business Review*, November–December 1990, pp. 119–125; "Debate: Ways Men and Women Lead," *Harvard Business Review*, January–February 1991, pp. 150–160; A. H. Eagly, M. G. Makhijani, and B. G. Klonsky, "Gender and the Evaluation of Leaders: A Meta-Analysis," *Psychological* Bulletin, January 1992, pp. 3–22; A. H. Eagly, S. J. Karau, and B. T. Johnson, "Gender and Leadership Style among School Principals: A Meta-Analysis," *Educational Administration Quarterly*, February 1992, pp. 76–102; L. R. Offermann and C. Beil, "Achievement Styles of Women Leaders and Their Peers," *Psychology of Women Quarterly*, March 1992, pp. 37–56; T. Melamed and N. Bozionelos, "Gender Differences in the Personality Features of British Managers," *Psychological Reports*, December 1992, pp. 979–986; G. N. Powell, *Women & Men in Management*, 2nd ed. (Thousand Oaks, CA: Sage, 1993); R. L. Kent and S. E. Moss, "Effects of Size and Gender Role on Leader Emergence," *Academy of Management Journal*, October 1994, pp. 1335–1346; C. Lee, "The Feminization of Management," *Training*, November 1994, pp. 25–31; H. Collingwood, "Women as Managers: Not Just Different, Better," *Working Woman*, November 1995, p. 14; and J. B. Rosener, *America's Competitive Secret: Women Managers* (New York: Oxford University Press, 1995).

114 B. Orser, *Creating High Performance Organizations: Leveraging Women's Leadership* (Ottawa: The Conference Board of Canada, 2000).

115 J. M. Norvilitis and H. M. Reid, "Evidence for an Association Between Gender-Role Identity and a Measure of Executive Function," *Psychological Reports*, February 2002, pp. 35–45; W. H. Decker and D. M. Rotondo, "Relationships among Gender, Type of Humor, and Perceived Leader Effectiveness," *Journal of Managerial Issues*, Winter 2001, pp. 450–465; H. Aguinis and S. K. R. Adams, "Social-Role versus Structural Models of Gender and Influence Use in Organizations: A Strong Inference Approach," *Group & Organization Management*, December 1998, pp. 414–446; and A. H. Eagly, S. J. Karau, and M. G. Makhijani,

"Gender and the Effectiveness of Leaders: A Meta-Analysis," *Psychological Bulletin* 117, 1995, pp. 125–145.

116   A. H. Eagly, M. C. Johannesen-Schmidt, and M. L. van Engen, "Transformational, Transactional, and Laissez-Faire Leadership Styles: A Meta-Analysis Comparing Women and Men," *Psychological Bulletin* 129, no. 4 (July 2003), pp. 569–591; K. M. Bartol, D. C. Martin, and J. A. Kromkowski, "Leadership and the Glass Ceiling: Gender and Ethnic Influences on Leader Behaviors at Middle and Executive Managerial Levels," *Journal of Leadership & Organizational Studies*, Winter 2003, pp. 8–19; and R. Sharpe, "As Leaders, Women Rule," *BusinessWeek*, November 20, 2000, pp. 74–84.

117   The material in this section is based on J. Grant, "Women as Managers: What They Can Offer to Organizations," *Organizational Dynamics*, Winter 1988, pp. 56–63; S. Helgesen, *The Female Advantage: Women's Ways of Leadership* (New York: Doubleday, 1990); A. H. Eagly and B. T. Johnson, "Gender and Leadership Style: A Meta-Analysis," *Psychological Bulletin*, September 1990, pp. 233–256; A. H. Eagly and S. J. Karau, "Gender and the Emergence of Leaders: A Meta-Analysis," *Journal of Personality and Social Psychology*, May 1991, pp. 685–710; J. B. Rosener, "Ways Women Lead," *Harvard Business Review*, November–December 1990, pp. 119–125; "Debate: Ways Men and Women Lead," *Harvard Business Review*, January–February 1991, pp. 150–160; A. H. Eagly, M. G. Makhijani, and B. G. Klonsky, "Gender and the Evaluation of Leaders: A Meta-Analysis," *Psychological Bulletin*, January 1992, pp. 3–22; A. H. Eagly, S. J. Karau, and B. T. Johnson, "Gender and Leadership Style among School Principals: A Meta-Analysis," *Educational Administration Quarterly*, February 1992, pp. 76–102; L. R. Offermann and C. Beil, "Achievement Styles of Women Leaders and Their Peers," *Psychology of Women Quarterly*, March 1992, pp. 37–56; T. Melamed and N. Bozionelos, "Gender Differences in the Personality Features of British Managers," *Psychological Reports*, December 1992, pp. 979–986; G. N. Powell, *Women & Men in Management*, 2nd ed. (Thousand Oaks, CA: Sage, 1993); R. L. Kent and S. E. Moss, "Effects of Size and Gender Role on Leader Emergence," *Academy of Management Journal*, October 1994, pp. 1335–1346; C. Lee, "The Feminization of Management," *Training*, November 1994, pp. 25–31; H. Collingwood, "Women as Managers: Not Just Different: Better," *Working Woman*, November 1995, p. 14; and J. B. Rosener, *America's Competitive Secret: Women Managers* (New York: Oxford University Press, 1995).

118   Based on R. D. Arvey, Z. Zhang, and B. J. Avolio, "Developmental and Genetic Determinants of Leadership Role Occupancy among Women," *Journal of Applied Psychology*, May 2007, pp. 693–706.

119   M. Pandya, "Warren Buffett on Investing and Leadership: I'm Wired for This Game," *Wharton Leadership Digest* 3, no. 7 (April 1999), http://leadership.wharton.upenn.edu/digest/04-99.shtml.

120   M. Castaneda, T. A. Kolenko, and R. J. Aldag, "Self-Management Perceptions and Practices: A Structural Equations Analysis," *Journal of Organizational Behavior* 20, 1999. Table 4, pp. 114–115. Copyright © John Wiley & Sons, Inc. Reproduced with permission.

121   This exercise is based on J. M. Howell and P. J. Frost, "A Laboratory Study of Charismatic Leadership," *Organizational Behavior and Human Decision Processes*, April 1989, pp. 243–269.

122   Based on C. E. Johnson, *Meeting the Ethical Challenges in Leadership* (Thousand Oaks, CA: Sage, 2001), pp. 4–5.

123   Based on D. Koeppel, "A Tough Transition: Friend to Supervisor," *New York Times*, March 16, 2003, p. BU-12.

124   Based on J. Hollon, "Leading Well Is Simple," *Workforce Management*, November 6, 2006, p. 50; A. Pomeroy, "CEOs Show Sensitive Side," *HR Magazine*, August 2006, p. 14; P. Bacon, Jr., "Barack Obama," *Time*, April 18, 2005, p. 60–61; J. Marquez, "Kindness Pays... Or Does It?" *Workforce Management*, June 25, 2007, pp. 40–41; and C. Woodyard, "Press: 'I Was in Love with Cars Every Second,'" *USA Today*, January 23, 2006, p. 5B.

125   Based on J. M. Howell and P. J. Frost, "A Laboratory Study of Charismatic Leadership," *Organizational Behavior and Human Decision Processes*, April 1989, pp. 243–269.

126   Based on V. H. Vroom, "A New Look at Managerial Decision Making," *Organizational Dynamics*, Spring 1973, pp. 66–80. With permission.

Chapter 12

1   Opening vignette based on G. Pitts, "The Testing of Michael McCain," *Report on Business Magazine*, November 2008, p. 60ff.

2   W. Pounds, "The Process of Problem Finding," *Industrial Management Review*, Fall 1969, pp. 1–19.

3   See H. A. Simon, "Rationality in Psychology and Economics," *Journal of Business*, October 1986, pp. 209–224; and A. Langley, "In Search of Rationality: The Purposes Behind the Use of Formal Analysis in Organizations," *Administrative Science Quarterly*, December 1989, pp. 598–631.

4   For a review of the rational model, see E. F. Harrison, *The Managerial Decision Making Process*, 5th ed. (Boston: Houghton Mifflin, 1999), pp. 75–102.

5   T. Barry, "Smart Cookies: Why CIBC Said Yes to the Girl Guides," *Marketing Magazine*, May 31, 1999, pp. 11, 14.

6   J. G. March, *A Primer on Decision Making* (New York: Free Press, 1994), pp. 2–7.

7   Based on G. Pitts, "The Testing of Michael McCain," *Report on Business Magazine*, November 2008, p. 60ff.

8   D. L. Rados, "Selection and Evaluation of Alternatives in Repetitive Decision Making," *Administrative Science Quarterly*, June 1972, pp. 196–206.

9   M. Bazerman, *Judgment in Managerial Decision Making*, 3rd ed. (New York: Wiley, 1994), p. 5.

10   J. E. Russo, K. A. Carlson, and M. G. Meloy, "Choosing an Inferior Alternative," *Psychological Science* 17, no. 10 (2006), pp. 899–904.

11   See, for instance, L. R. Beach, *The Psychology of Decision Making* (Thousand Oaks, CA: Sage, 1997).

12   See H. A. Simon, *Administrative Behavior*, 4th ed. (New York: Free Press, 1997); and M. Augier, "Simon Says: Bounded Rationality Matters," *Journal of Management Inquiry*, September 2001, pp. 268–275.

13   Based on K. May, "Ottawa May Stop Hiring Best Qualified," *National Post*, March 4, 2002, p. A4.

14 See T. Gilovich, D. Griffin, and D. Kahneman, *Heuristics and Biases: The Psychology of Intuitive Judgment* (New York: Cambridge University Press, 2002).

15 E. Dane and M. G. Pratt, "Exploring Intuition and Its Role in Managerial Decision Making," *Academy of Management Review* 32, no. 1 (2007), pp. 33–54.

16 As described in H. A. Simon, "Making Management Decisions: The Role of Intuition and Emotion," *Academy of Management Executive*, February 1987, pp. 59–60.

17 L. A. Burke and M. K. Miller, "Taking the Mystery Out of Intuitive Decision Making," *Academy of Management Executive*, November 1999, pp. 91–99.

18 See, for instance, L. A. Burke and M. K. Miller, "Taking the Mystery Out of Intuitive Decision Making," *Academy of Management Executive*, November 1999, pp. 91–99; N. Khatri and H. A. Ng, "The Role of Intuition in Strategic Decision Making," *Human Relations*, January 2000, pp. 57–86; J. A. Andersen, "Intuition in Managers: Are Intuitive Managers More Effective?" *Journal of Managerial Psychology* 15, no. 1–2 (2000), pp. 46–63; D. Myers, *Intuition: Its Powers and Perils* (New Haven, CT: Yale University Press, 2002); and L. Simpson, "Basic Instincts," *Training*, January 2003, pp. 56–59.

19 See, for instance, Burke and Miller, "Taking the Mystery Out of Intuitive Decision Making," pp. 91–99.

20 S. P. Robbins, *Decide & Conquer: Making Winning Decisions and Taking Control of Your Life* (Upper Saddle River, NJ: Financial Times/Prentice Hall, 2004), p. 13.

21 Based on P. Cohen, "Stand Still: Use Penalty-Kick Wisdom to Make Your Decisions," *National Post*, March 8, 2008, p. FW9.

22 S. Plous, *The Psychology of Judgment and Decision Making* (New York: McGraw-Hill, 1993), p. 217.

23 S. Lichtenstein and B. Fischhoff, "Do Those Who Know More Also Know More About How Much They Know?" *Organizational Behavior and Human Performance*, December 1977, pp. 159–183.

24 B. Fischhoff, P. Slovic, and S. Lichtenstein, "Knowing with Certainty: The Appropriateness of Extreme Confidence," *Journal of Experimental Psychology: Human Perception and Performance*, November 1977, pp. 552–564.

25 J. Kruger and D. Dunning, "Unskilled and Unaware of It: How Difficulties in Recognizing One's Own Incompetence Lead to Inflated Self-Assessments," *Journal of Personality and Social Psychology*, November 1999, pp. 1121–1134.

26 B. Fischhoff, P. Slovic, and S. Lichtenstein, "Knowing with Certainty: The Appropriateness of Extreme Confidence," *Journal of Experimental Psychology* 3 (1977), pp. 552–564.

27 J. Kruger and D. Dunning, "Unskilled and Unaware of It: How Difficulties in Recognizing One's Own Incompetence Lead to Inflated Self-Assessments," *Journal of Personality and Social Psychology*, November 1999, pp. 1121–1134.

28 See, for instance, A. Tversky and D. Kahneman, "Judgment Under Uncertainty: Heuristics and Biases," *Science*, September 1974, pp. 1124–1131.

29 J. S. Hammond, R. L. Keeney, and H. Raiffa, *Smart Choices* (Boston: HBS Press, 1999), p. 191.

30 R. Hastie, D. A. Schkade, and J. W. Payne, "Juror Judgments in Civil Cases: Effects of Plaintiff's Requests and Plaintiff's Identity on Punitive Damage Awards," *Law and Human Behavior*, August 1999, pp. 445–470.

31 See R. S. Nickerson, "Confirmation Bias: A Ubiquitous Phenomenon in Many Guises," *Review of General Psychology*, June 1998, pp. 175–220; and E. Jonas, S. Schultz-Hardt, D. Frey, and N. Thelen, "Confirmation Bias in Sequential Information Search After Preliminary Decisions," *Journal of Personality and Social Psychology*, April 2001, pp. 557–571.

32 See B. M. Staw, "The Escalation of Commitment to a Course of Action," *Academy of Management Review*, October 1981, pp. 577–587; and H. Moon, "Looking Forward and Looking Back: Integrating Completion and Sunk-Cost Effects within an Escalation-of-Commitment Progress Decision," *Journal of Applied Psychology*, February 2001, pp. 104–113.

33 K. F. E. Wong and J. Y. Y. Kwong, "The Role of Anticipated Regret in Escalation of Commitment," *Journal of Applied Psychology* 92, no. 2 (2007), pp. 545–554.

34 See, for instance, A. James and A. Wells, "Death Beliefs, Superstitious Beliefs and Health Anxiety," *British Journal of Clinical Psychology*, March 2002, pp. 43–53.

35 R. L. Guilbault, F. B. Bryant, J. H. Brockway, and E. J. Posavac, "A Meta-Analysis of Research on Hindsight Bias," *Basic and Applied Social Psychology*, September 2004, pp. 103–117; and L. Werth, F. Strack, and J. Foerster, "Certainty and Uncertainty: The Two Faces of the Hindsight Bias," *Organizational Behavior and Human Decision Processes*, March 2002, pp. 323–341.

36 M. Gladwell, "Connecting the Dots," *New Yorker*, March 10, 2003.

37 S. P. Robbins, *Decide & Conquer: Making Winning Decisions and Taking Control of Your Life* (Upper Saddle River, NJ: Financial Times/Prentice Hall, 2004), pp. 164–168.

38 See S. A. Mohrman, D. Finegold, and J. A. Klein, "Designing the Knowledge Enterprise: Beyond Programs and Tools," *Organizational Dynamics* 31, no. 2 (2002), pp. 134–150; and H. Dolezalek, "Collaborating in Cyberspace," *Training*, April 2003, pp. 32–37.

39 Cited in A. Cabrera and E. F. Cabrera, "Knowledge-Sharing Dilemmas," *Organization Studies* 5, 2002, p. 687.

40 B. Roberts, "Pick Employees' Brains," *HR Magazine*, February 2000, pp. 115–116; B. Fryer, "Get Smart," Inc., September 1999, p. 65; and D. Zielinski, "Have You Shared a Bright Idea Today?" *Training*, July 2000, p. 65.

41 B. Fryer, "Get Smart," *Inc.*, September 1999, p. 63.

42 E. Truch, "Managing Personal Knowledge: The Key to Tomorrow's Employability," *Journal of Change Management*, December 2001, pp. 102–105.

43 J. Gordon, "Intellectual Capital and You," *Training*, September 1999, p. 33.

44 D. Zielinski, "Have You Shared a Bright Idea Today?" *Training*, July 2000, pp. 65–67.

45 See N. R. F. Maier, "Assets and Liabilities in Group Problem Solving: The Need for an Integrative Function," *Psychological Review*, April 1967, pp. 239–249; G. W. Hill, "Group versus Individual Performance: Are N+1 Heads Better Than One?" *Psychological Bulletin*, May 1982, pp. 517–539; and A. E. Schwartz and J. Levin, "Better Group Decision Making," *Supervisory Management*, June 1990, p. 4.

46 See, for example, R. A. Cooke and J. A. Kernaghan, "Estimating the Difference between Group versus Individual Performance on Problem-Solving Tasks," *Group & Organization Studies*, September 1987, pp. 319–342; and L. K. Michaelsen, W. E. Watson, and R. H. Black, "A Realistic Test of Individual versus Group Consensus Decision Making," *Journal of Applied Psychology*, October 1989, pp. 834–839.

47 See, for example, W. C. Swap and Associates, *Group Decision Making* (Newbury Park, CA: Sage, 1984).

48 "Group Judgments," *Psychological Bulletin*, January 1997, pp. 149–167; and B. L. Bonner, S. D. Sillito, and M. R. Baumann, "Collective Estimation: Accuracy, Expertise, and Extroversion as Sources of Intra-Group Influence," *Organizational Behavior and Human Decision Processes* 103, 2007, pp. 121–133.

49 See, for example, W. C. Swap and Associates, *Group Decision Making* (Newbury Park, CA: Sage, 1984).

50 I. L. Janis, *Groupthink: Psychological Studies of Policy Decisions and Fiascoes*, 2nd ed. (Boston: Houghton Mifflin, 1982); W. Park, "A Review of Research on Groupthink," *Journal of Behavioral Decision Making*, July 1990, pp. 229–245; C. P. Neck and G. Moorhead, "Groupthink Remodeled: The Importance of Leadership, Time Pressure, and Methodical Decision Making Procedures," *Human Relations*, May 1995, pp. 537–558; and J. N. Choi and M. U. Kim, "The Organizational Application of Groupthink and Its Limits in Organizations," *Journal of Applied Psychology*, April 1999, pp. 297–306.

51 I. L. Janis, *Groupthink: Psychological Studies of Policy Decisions and Fiascoes*, 2nd ed. (Boston: Houghton Mifflin, 1982).

52 K. Hays, "Judge Dismisses Enron Convictions," *Houston (Texas) Chronicle*, February 1, 2007.

53 M. E. Turner and A. R. Pratkanis, "Mitigating Groupthink by Stimulating Constructive Conflict," in *Using Conflict in Organizations*, ed. C. De Dreu and E. Van de Vliert (London: Sage, 1997), pp. 53–71.

54 See N. R. F. Maier, *Principles of Human Relations* (New York: Wiley, 1952); C. R. Leana, "A Partial Test of Janis' Groupthink Model: Effects of Group Cohesiveness and Leader Behavior on Defective Decision Making," *Journal of Management*, Spring 1985, pp. 5–17; and J. K. Esser, "Testing the Groupthink Model: Effects of Promotional Leadership and Conformity Predisposition," *Social Behavior & Personality* 29, no. 1 (2001), pp. 31–41.

55 J. N. Choi and M. U. Kim, "The Organizational Application of Groupthink and Its Limitations in Organizations," *Journal of Applied Psychology* 84, 1999, pp. 297–306.

56 J. Longley and D. G. Pruitt, "Groupthink: A Critique of Janis' Theory," in *Review of Personality and Social Psychology*, ed. L. Wheeler (Newbury Park, CA: Sage, 1980), pp. 507–513; and J. A. Sniezek, "Groups Under Uncertainty: An Examination of Confidence in Group Decision Making," *Organizational Behavior & Human Decision Processes* 52, 1992, pp. 124–155.

57 C. McCauley, "The Nature of Social Influence in Groupthink: Compliance and Internalization," *Journal of Personality and Social Psychology* 57, 1989, pp. 250–260; P. E. Tetlock, R. S. Peterson, C. McGuire, S. Chang, and P. Feld, "Assessing Political Group Dynamics: A Test of the Groupthink Model," *Journal of Personality and Social Psychology* 63, 1992, pp. 781–796; S. Graham, "A Review of Attribution Theory in Achievement Contexts," *Educational Psychology Review* 3, 1991, pp. 5–39; and G. Moorhead and J. R. Montanari, "An Empirical Investigation of the Groupthink Phenomenon," *Human Relations* 39, 1986, pp. 399–410.

58 J. N. Choi and M. U. Kim, "The Organizational Application of Groupthink and Its Limitations in Organizations," *Journal of Applied Psychology* 84, 1999, pp. 297–306.

59 See D. J. Isenberg, "Group Polarization: A Critical Review and Meta-Analysis," *Journal of Personality and Social Psychology*, December 1986, pp. 1141–1151; J. L. Hale and F. J. Boster, "Comparing Effect Coded Models of Choice Shifts," *Communication Research Reports*, April 1988, pp. 180–186; and P. W. Paese, M. Bieser, and M. E. Tubbs, "Framing Effects and Choice Shifts in Group Decision Making," *Organizational Behavior & Human Decision Processes*, October 1993, pp. 149–165.

60 See, for example, N. Kogan and M. A. Wallach, "Risk Taking as a Function of the Situation, the Person, and the Group," in *New Directions in Psychology*, vol. 3 (New York: Holt, Rinehart and Winston, 1967); and M. A. Wallach, N. Kogan, and D. J. Bem, "Group Influence on Individual Risk Taking," *Journal of Abnormal and Social Psychology* 65, 1962, pp. 75–86.

61 R. D. Clark III, "Group-Induced Shift Toward Risk: A Critical Appraisal," *Psychological Bulletin*, October 1971, pp. 251–270.

62 A. F. Osborn, *Applied Imagination: Principles and Procedures of Creative Thinking* (New York: Scribner's, 1941). See also P. B. Paulus, M. T. Dzindolet, G. Poletes, and L. M. Camacho, "Perception of Performance in Group Brainstorming: The Illusion of Group Productivity," *Personality and Social Psychology Bulletin*, February 1993, pp. 78–89.

63 I. Edwards, "Office Intrigue: By Design, Consultants Have Workers Conspire to Create Business Environments Tailored to Getting the Job Done," *Financial Post Daily*, December 16, 1997, p. 25.

64 N. L. Kerr and R. S. Tindale, "Group Performance and Decision-Making," *Annual Review of Psychology* 55, 2004, pp. 623–655.

65 See A. L. Delbecq, A. H. Van deVen, and D. H. Gustafson, *Group Techniques for Program Planning: A Guide to Nominal and Delphi Processes* (Glenview, IL: Scott, Foresman, 1975); and P. B. Paulus and H.-C. Yang, "Idea Generation in Groups: A Basis for Creativity in Organizations," *Organizational Behavior and Human Decision Processing*, May 2000, pp. 76–87.

66 C. Faure, "Beyond Brainstorming: Effects of Different Group Procedures on Selection of Ideas and Satisfaction with the Process," *Journal of Creative Behavior* 38, 2004, pp. 13–34.

67 See, for instance, A. R. Dennis and J. S. Valacich, "Computer Brainstorms: More Heads Are Better Than One," *Journal of Applied Psychology*, August 1993, pp. 531–537; R. B. Gallupe and W. H. Cooper, "Brainstorming Electronically," *Sloan Management Review*, Fall 1993, pp. 27–36; and A. B. Hollingshead and

J. E. McGrath, "Computer-Assisted Groups: A Critical Review of the Empirical Research," in *Team Effectiveness and Decision Making in Organizations*, ed. R. A. Guzzo and E. Salas (San Francisco: Jossey-Bass, 1995), pp. 46–78.

68 B. B. Baltes, M. W. Dickson, M. P. Sherman, C. C. Bauer, and J. LaGanke, "Computer-Mediated Communication and Group Decision Making: A Meta-Analysis," *Organizational Behavior and Human Decision Processes*, January 2002, pp. 156–179.

69 T. M. Amabile, "A Model of Creativity and Innovation in Organizations," in *Research in Organizational Behavior*, vol. 10, ed. B. M. Staw and L. L. Cummings (Greenwich, CT: JAI Press, 1988), p. 126; and J. E. Perry-Smith and C. E. Shalley, "The Social Side of Creativity: A Static and Dynamic Social Network Perspective," *Academy of Management Review*, January 2003, pp. 89–106.

70 G. J. Feist and F. X. Barron, "Predicting Creativity from Early to Late Adulthood: Intellect, Potential, and Personality," *Journal of Research in Personality*, April 2003, pp. 62–88.

71 R. W. Woodman, J. E. Sawyer, and R. W. Griffin, "Toward a Theory of Organizational Creativity," *Academy of Management Review*, April 1993, p. 298; J. M. George and J. Zhou, "When Openness to Experience and Conscientiousness Are Related to Creative Behavior: An Interactional Approach," *Journal of Applied Psychology*, June 2001, pp. 513–524; and E. F. Rietzschel, C. K. W. de Dreu, and B. A. Nijstad, "Personal Need for Structure and Creative Performance: The Moderating Influence of Fear of Invalidity," *Personality and Social Psychology Bulletin*, June 2007, pp. 855–866.

72 Cited in C. G. Morris, *Psychology: An Introduction*, 9th ed. (Upper Saddle River, NJ: Prentice Hall, 1996), p. 344.

73 This section is based on T. M. Amabile, "Motivating Creativity in Organizations: On Doing What You Love and Loving What You Do," *California Management Review* 40, no. 1 (Fall 1997), pp. 39–58.

74 A. M. Isen, "Positive Affect," in *Handbook of Cognition and Emotion*, ed. T. Dalgleish and M. J. Power (New York: Wiley, 1999), pp. 521–539.

75 J. Zhou, "When the Presence of Creative Coworkers Is Related to Creativity: Role of Supervisor Close Monitoring, Developmental Feedback, and Creative Personality," *Journal of Applied Psychology* 88, no. 3 (June 2003), pp. 413–422.

76 J. E. Perry-Smith, "Social yet Creative: The Role of Social Relationships in Facilitating Individual Creativity," *Academy of Management Journal* 49, no. 1 (2006), pp. 85–101.

77 W. J. J. Gordon, *Synectics* (New York: Harper & Row, 1961).

78 See T. M. Amabile, *KEYS: Assessing the Climate for Creativity* (Greensboro, NC: Center for Creative Leadership, 1995); N. Madjar, G. R. Oldham, and M. G. Pratt, "There's No Place Like Home? The Contributions of Work and Nonwork Creativity Support to Employees' Creative Performance," *Academy of Management Journal*, August 2002, pp. 757–767; and C. E. Shalley, J. Zhou, and G. R. Oldham, "The Effects of Personal and Contextual Characteristics on Creativity: Where Should We Go from Here?" *Journal of Management*, November 2004, pp. 933–958.

79 Cited in T. Stevens, "Creativity Killers," *IndustryWeek*, January 23, 1995, p. 63.

80 M. Strauss, "Retailers Tap into War-Room Creativity of Employees," *Globe and Mail*, March 12, 2007, p. B1.

81 Based on G. Pitts, "The Testing of Michael McCain," *Report on Business Magazine*, November 2008, p. 60ff.

82 P. L. Schumann, "A Moral Principles Framework for Human Resource Management Ethics," *Human Resource Management Review* 11, Spring–Summer 2001, pp. 93–111; M. G. Velasquez, *Business Ethics*, 4th ed. (Upper Saddle River, NJ: Prentice Hall, 1998), Chapter 2; and G. F. Cavanagh, D. J. Moberg, and M. Valasquez, "The Ethics of Organizational Politics," *Academy of Management Journal*, June 1981, pp. 363–374.

83 P. L. Schumann, "A Moral Principles Framework for Human Resource Management Ethics," *Human Resource Management Review* 11, Spring–Summer 2001, pp. 93–111.

84 See, for instance, R. S. Dillon, "Care and Respect," in *Explorations in Feminist Ethics: Theory and Practice*, ed. E. Browning Cole and S. Coultrap-McQuin (Bloomington, IN: Indiana University Press, 1992), pp. 69–81; C. Gilligan, *In a Different Voice: Psychological Theory and Women's Development* (Cambridge, MA: Harvard University Press, 1982); and M. C. Raugust, "Feminist Ethics and Workplace Values," in *Explorations in Feminist Ethics: Theory and Practice*, ed. E. Browning Cole and S. Coultrap-McQuin (Bloomington, IN: Indiana University Press, 1992), pp. 69–81.

85 P. L. Schumann, "A Moral Principles Framework for Human Resource Management Ethics," *Human Resource Management Review* 11, Spring–Summer 2001, pp. 93–111.

86 S. Jaffee and J. Hyde, "Gender Differences in Moral Orientation: A Meta-Analysis," *Psychological Bulletin*, September 2000, pp. 703–726.

87 See, for example, T. Machan, ed., *Commerce and Morality* (Totowa, NJ: Rowman and Littlefield, 1988).

88 L. K. Trevino, "Ethical Decision Making in Organizations: A Person-Situation Interactionist Model," *Academy of Management Review*, July 1986, pp. 601–617; and L. K. Trevino and S. A. Youngblood, "Bad Apples in Bad Barrels: A Causal Analysis of Ethical Decision Making Behavior," *Journal of Applied Psychology*, August 1990, pp. 378–385.

89 See L. Kohlberg, *Essays in Moral Development: The Philosophy of Moral Development*, vol. 1 (New York: Harper and Row, 1981); L. Kohlberg, *Essays in Moral Development: The Psychology of Moral Development*, vol. 2 (New York: Harper and Row, 1984); and R. S. Snell, "Complementing Kohlberg: Mapping the Ethical Reasoning Used by Managers for Their Own Dilemma Cases," *Human Relations*, January 1996, pp. 23–49.

90 L. Kohlberg, *Essays in Moral Development: The Philosophy of Moral Development*, vol. 1 (New York: Harper and Row, 1981); L. Kohlberg, *Essays in Moral Development: The Philosophy of Moral Development*, vol. 2 (New York: Harper and Row, 1984); and R. S. Snell, "Complementing Kohlberg: Mapping the Ethical Reasoning Used by Managers for Their Own Dilemma Cases," *Human Relations*, January 1996, pp. 23–49.

91 J. Weber, "Managers' Moral Reasoning: Assessing Their Responses to Three Moral Dilemmas," *Human Relations*, July 1990,

pp. 687–702; and S. B. Knouse and R. A. Giacalone, "Ethical Decision-Making in Business: Behavioral Issues and Concerns," *Journal of Business Ethics*, May 1992, pp. 369–377.

92 This discussion is based on G. F. Cavanagh, D. J. Moberg, and M. Valasquez, "The Ethics of Organizational Politics," *Academy of Management Journal*, June 1981, pp. 363–374.

93 http://www.epac-apec.ca/cont-fra/documents/ EPACReprintMarch2008-ethikos.pdf.

94 D. Todd, "Business Responds to Ethics Explosion," *Vancouver Sun*, April 27, 1998, pp. A1, A7.

95 L. Bogomolny, "Good Housekeeping," *Canadian Business*, March 1, 2004, pp. 87–88; and L. Ramsay, "A Matter of Principle," *Financial Post (National Post)*, February 26, 1999, p. C18.

96 M. McCann, "Despite Costs, There Are Profits in Ethically Produced Products," *Telegraph-Journal*, May 30, 2008, p. B4.

97 G. Crone, "UPS Rolls Out Ethics Program," *Financial Post (National Post)*, May 26, 1999, p. C4.

98 Based on W. E. Stead, D. L. Worrell, and J. G. Stead, "An Integrative Model for Understanding and Managing Ethical Behavior in Business Organizations," *Journal of Business Ethics* 9, no. 3 (March 1990), pp. 233–242.

99 D. Todd, "Ethics Audit: Credit Union Reveals All," *Vancouver Sun*, October 19, 1998, p. A5.

100 "Corporate Culture," *Canadian HR Reporter* 17, no. 21 (December 6, 2004), pp. 7–11.

101 W. Chow Hou, "To Bribe or Not to Bribe?" Asia, *Inc.*, October 1996, p. 104; and T. Jackson, "Cultural Values and Management Ethics: A 10-Nation Study," *Human Relations*, October 2001, pp. 1267–1302.

102 T. Donaldson, "Values in Tension: Ethics Away From Home," *Harvard Business Review*, September–October 1996, pp. 48–62.

103 P. Digh, "Shades of Gray in the Global Marketplace," *HR Magazine*, April 1997, pp. 91–98.

104 A. Gillis, "How Can You Do Business in a Country Where Crooked Cops Will Kill You for a Song?" *Report on Business Magazine*, March 1998, p. 60.

105 A. Gillis, "How Can You Do Business in a Country Where Crooked Cops Will Kill You for a Song?" *Report on Business Magazine*, March 1998, p. 60.

106 N. Roland, "U.K., Japan and Canada Failing to Crack Down on Foreign Bribes, Says Watchdog Group," *Financial Week*, June 25, 2008, http://www.financialweek.com/apps/pbcs.dll/article?AID=/ 20080625/REG/814229098/1036.

107 Vignette based on G. Pitts, "The Testing of Michael Mccain," *Report on Business Magazine*, November 2008, p. 60ff; and K. Owram, "Maple Leaf Foods CEO Michael McCain Named Business Newsmaker of the Year," *Canadian Press*, January, 1, 2009.

108 "Many Canadian Businesses and Citizens Want to See Tougher Federal Rules Governing Corporate Responsibility and It's Time for the Government to Take Action, Says a Social Justice Coalition," *Canadian Press Newswire*, January 24, 2002.

109 Per 2003 Environics and 2004 GlobeScan polls, as reported in "Corporate Responsibility: An Implementation Guide for Canadian Business," http://www.ic.gc.ca/epic/site/csr-rse.nsf/ vwapj/CSR_mar2006.pdf/$FILE/CSR_mar2006.pdf.

110 M. Friedman, *Capitalism and Freedom* (Chicago: University of Chicago Press, 1962).

111 J. Bakan, *The Corporation* (Toronto: Big Picture Media Corporation, 2003).

112 http://www.greenbiz.com/news/2006/10/26/survey-shows-mba-students-believe-business-should-be-agent-social-change.

113 A. Howatson, *Lean Green: Benefits from a Streamlined Canadian Environmental Regulatory System* (Ottawa: The Conference Board of Canada, April 1996).

114 F. Mihlar, *Regulatory Overkill: The Cost of Regulation in Canada* (Vancouver: The Fraser Institute, September 1996).

115 R. Brunet, "To Survive and Thrive: Bled Dry by the NDP, BC Business Plots a New Course for the 21st Century," *British Columbia Report*, February 9, 1998, pp. 18–22.

116 G. Gallon, "Bunk Behind the Backlash: Highly Publicized Reports Exaggerate the Costs of Environmental Regulation," *Alternatives*, Fall 1997, pp. 14–15.

117 J. K. Grant, "Whatever Happened to Our Concern About the Environment?" *Canadian Speeches*, April 1997, pp. 37–42.

118 "The Business of Being Green," advertising supplement, *Canadian Business*, January 1996, pp. 41–56.

119 Minnesota Mining and Manufacturing Company (3M), *Pollution Prevention Pays: Moving toward Environmental Sustainability*, Brochure #78-6900-3343-2, St. Paul, MN, 1998; and J. K. Grant, "Whatever Happened to Our Concern About the Environment?" *Canadian Speeches*, April 1997, pp. 37–42.

120 Based on a personality scale developed by D. Hellriegel, J. Slocum, and R.W. Woodman, *Organizational Behavior*, 3rd ed. (St. Paul, MN: West Publishing, 1983), pp. 127–141, and reproduced in J. M. Ivancevich and M. T. Matteson, *Organizational Behavior and Management*, 2nd ed. (Homewood, IL: BPI/Irwin, 1990), pp. 538–539.

121 Several of these scenarios are based on D. R. Altany, "Torn Between Halo and Horns," *IndustryWeek*, March 15, 1993, pp. 15–20.

122 Based on C. Hawn, "Fear and Posing," *Forbes*, March 25, 2002, pp. 22–25; and J. Sandberg, "Some Ideas Are So Bad That Only Team Efforts Can Account for Them," *Wall Street Journal*, September 29, 2004, p. B1.

123 A. Kellogg, "Punch the Query 'Canada's Best Major Corporate Citizen' into Google on Your Computer and It's Likely the Image of Eric Newell Will Pop Up," *Calgary Herald*, November 30, 2003, p. C2; C. Petten, "Syncrude, Cameco Strike Gold with PAR," *Windspeaker*, March 2002, pp. B7–B8; http://www.syncrude.com/ community/aboriginal.html; http://www.syncrude.com/business/ business_04.html#4b; and http://www.syncrude.ca/users/folder. asp?FolderID=5641.

124 Syncrude Aboriginal Review 2007, http://www.syncrude.ca/users/folder.asp?FolderID=5641.

125 Based on J. Calano and J. Salzman, "Ten Ways to Fire Up Your Creativity," *Working Woman*, July 1989, p. 94; J. V. Anderson, "Mind Mapping: A Tool for Creative Thinking," *Business Horizons*, January–February 1993, pp. 42–46; M. Loeb, "Ten Commandments for Managing Creative People," *Fortune*, January 16, 1995, pp. 135–136; and M. Henricks, "Good Thinking," *Entrepreneur*, May 1996, pp. 70–73.

OB on the Edge:
Spirituality in the Workplace

1 Vignette based on J. Mawhinney, "Style with Heart and Soul; Spiritual Beliefs Guide Their Work," *Toronto Star*, September 1, 2005, p. E4.

2 I. I. Mitroff and E. A. Denton, "A Study of Spirituality in the Workplace," *Sloan Management Review*, Summer 1999, pp. 83–92.

3 I. I. Mitroff and E. A. Denton, "A Study of Spirituality in the Workplace," *Sloan Management Review*, Summer 1999, pp. 83–92.

4 W. J. Harrington, R. C. Preziosi, and D. J. Gooden, "Perceptions of Workplace Spirituality among Professionals and Executives," *Employee Responsibilities and Rights Journal* 13, no. 3 (2001), p. 156.

5 W. J. Harrington, R. C. Preziosi, and D. J. Gooden, "Perceptions of Workplace Spirituality among Professionals and Executives," *Employee Responsibilities and Rights Journal* 13, no. 3 (2001), p. 156.

6 Information in this section based on I. I. Mitroff and E. A. Denton, "A Study of Spirituality in the Workplace," *Sloan Management Review*, Summer 1999, pp. 83–92.

7 D. P. Ashmos and D. Duchon, "Spirituality at Work: A Conceptualization and Measure," *Journal of Management Inquiry*, June 2000, p. 139. For a comprehensive review of definitions of workplace spirituality, see R. A. Giacalone and C. L. Jurkiewicz, "Toward a Science of Workplace Spirituality," in *Handbook of Workplace Spirituality and Organizational Performance*, ed. R. A. Giacalone and C. L. Jurkiewicz (Armonk, NY: M. E. Sharpe, 2003), pp. 6–13.

8 P. Preville, "For God's Sake," *Canadian Business*, June 25–July 9, 1999, p. 58.

9 P. Preville, "For God's Sake," *Canadian Business*, June 25–July 9, 1999, p. 60.

10 A. Esposito, "Doing Well and Doing Good [Aaron Feuerstein Spirituality & Business Award]," *Financial Post (National Post)*, March 30, 2001, p. C2.

11 Example based on J. White, "Soul@Work: As We Begin a New Century, Do You Know How to Bring out the Best in Your Employees?" *Benefits Canada*, January 2000, p. 17.

12 T. Helliwell, *Take Your Soul to Work* (Toronto: Random House Canada, 1999).

13 L. Fowlie, "Spirituality Centre Is Canadian First," *National Post*, November 22, 2004, p. FP10.

14 J. Canfield, M. V. Hansen, M. Rutte, M. Rogerson, and T. Clauss, *Chicken Soup for the Soul at Work* (Deerfield Beach, FL: HCI, 1996).

15 L. Fowlie, "Spirituality Centre Is Canadian First," *National Post*, November 22, 2004, p. FP10.

16 B. Harvey, "Sister Mangalam Lena Believes Spiritual Care Is an Essential Part of Health Care, in and out of the Hospital," *Canadian Press Newswire*, April 10, 2001.

17 C. Silverman, "Spirituality Inc.," *Globe and Mail*, April 21, 2008, p. L3.

18 C. Silverman, "Spirituality Inc.," *Globe and Mail*, April 21, 2008, p. L3.

19 This section is based on I. I. Mitroff and E. A. Denton, *A Spiritual Audit of Corporate America: A Hard Look at Spirituality, Religion, and Values in the Workplace* (San Francisco: Jossey-Bass, 1999); J. Milliman, J. Ferguson, D. Trickett, and B. Condemi, "Spirit and Community at Southwest Airlines: An Investigation of a Spiritual Values-Based Model," *Journal of Organizational Change Management* 12, no. 3 (1999), pp. 221–233; E. H. Burack, "Spirituality in the Workplace," *Journal of Organizational Change Management* 12, no. 3 (1999), pp. 280–291; and F. Wagner-Marsh and J. Conley, "The Fourth Wave: The Spiritually-Based Firm," *Journal of Organizational Change Management* 12, no. 3 (1999), pp. 292–302.

20 M. McKee, "Northwood –Organizational Innovation on the Spirituality Front," *Newsletter for the Center for Spirituality and the Workplace* (St. Mary's University), June 2006.

21 A. Daniels, "Textile Importer Defends Artisans' Rights," *Vancouver Sun*, May 1, 2000, pp. C8, C10.

22 Cited in F. Wagner-Marsh and J. Conley, "The Fourth Wave: The Spiritually-Based Firm," *Journal of Organizational Change Management* 12, no. 3 (1999), p. 295.

23 FactBox based on R.W. Bibby, "Who Said God Is Dead?" *Globe & Mail*, March 17, 2006, p. A15; B. Bethune, "*Maclean's* Poll 2006: Praise the Lord and Call the Psychic," *Maclean's*, July 06, 2006, http://www.macleans.ca/article.jsp?content=20060701_129959_129959; "Question of the Week," *Maclean's*, April 19, 2004; and A. Useem, "Religion Is the New Diversity Push in the Workplace," *Leader Post* (Regina), April 28, 2007, p. G6.

24 M. Conlin, "Religion in the Workplace: The Growing Presence of Spirituality in Corporate America," *BusinessWeek*, November 1, 1999, pp. 151–158; and P. Paul, "A Holier Holiday Season," *American Demographics*, December 2001, pp. 41–45.

25 I. I. Mitroff and E. A. Denton, *A Spiritual Audit of Corporate America: A Hard Look at Spirituality, Religion, and Values in the Workplace* (San Francisco: Jossey-Bass, 1999).

26 M. C. McKee, "Workplace Spirituality," *Workplace Review*, November 2006, http://www.smu.ca/academic/sobey/workplacereview/nov2006/WorkplaceSpirituality.pdf.

27 M. Conlin, "Religion in the Workplace: The Growing Presence of Spirituality in Corporate America," *BusinessWeek*, November 1, 1999, pp. 151–158; and P. Paul, "A Holier Holiday Season," *American Demographics*, December 2001, pp. 41–45.

28 Cited in M. Conlin, "Religion in the Workplace: The Growing Presence of Spirituality in Corporate America," *BusinessWeek*, November 1, 1999, p. 153.

29 C. P. Neck and J. F. Milliman, "Thought Self-Leadership: Finding Spiritual Fulfillment in Organizational Life," *Journal of Managerial Psychology* 9, no. 8 (1994), p. 9.

30 D. W. McCormick, "Spirituality and Management," *Journal of Managerial Psychology* 9, no. 6 (1994), p. 5; E. Brandt, "Corporate Pioneers Explore Spiritual Peace," *HR Magazine* 41, no. 4 (1996), p. 82; P. Leigh, "The New Spirit at Work," *Training & Development* 51, no. 3 (1997), p. 26; P. H. Mirvis, "Soul Work in Organizations," *Organization Science* 8, no. 2 (1997), p. 193; and J. Millman, A. Czaplewski, and J. Ferguson, "An Exploratory Empirical Assessment of the Relationship between Spirituality and Employee Work Attitudes" (paper presented at the National Academy of Management Meeting, Washington, DC, August 2001).

31 Cited in J. Milliman, J. Ferguson, D. Trickett, and B. Condemi, "Spirit and Community at Southwest Airlines: An Investigation of a Spiritual Values-Based Model," *Journal of Organizational Change Management* 12, no. 3 (1999).

32 P. Preville, "For God's Sake," *Canadian Business*, June 25–July 9, 1999, p. 61.

Chapter 13

1 Opening vignette based on M. Cernetig, "20 Great Ideas That Were Born in B.C.," *Vancouver Sun*, March 1, 2008. p. A1; M. Cernetig, "'Brollywood' Must Get Creative Juices Flowing," *Vancouver Sun*, November 19, 2007, p. B1; and M. McCullough, "Virtual Tinseltown," *National Post Business*, June 2000, pp. 46–58.

2 See, for instance, R. L. Daft, *Organization Theory and Design*, 6th ed. (Cincinnati, OH: South Western College, 1998).

3 J. Chevreau, "Wealth Planning Comes of Age; Retiring Boomers Targeted with Holistic Approach," *National Post*, June 17, 2008, p. FP13.

4 See, for instance, L. Urwick, *The Elements of Administration* (New York: Harper and Row, 1944), pp. 52–53.

5 J. Child and R. G. McGrath, "Organizations Unfettered: Organizational Form in an Information-Intensive Economy," *Academy of Management Journal*, December 2001, pp. 1135–1148.

6 G. Morgan, *Images of Organization* (Newbury Park, CA: Sage, 1986), p. 21.

7 T. Burns and G. M. Stalker, *The Management of Innovation* (London: Tavistock, 1961); and J. A. Courtright, G. T. Fairhurst, and L. E. Rogers, "Interaction Patterns in Organic and Mechanistic Systems," *Academy of Management Journal*, December 1989, pp. 773–802.

8 Based on C. Gillis, "Musicians Launch Unexpected Strike," *National Post*, February 16, 2002, p. A5; B. Weber, "Edmonton Orchestra Deal Part of Trend to Give Musicians More Control," *Canadian Press Newswire*, March 21, 2002; and B. Rankin, "Successful Conductor Search Shows Symphony Rift Has Healed," *Edmonton Journal*, February 20, 2005, p. B1.

9 H. Mintzberg, *Structure in Fives: Designing Effective Organizations* (Englewood Cliffs, NJ: Prentice Hall, 1983), p. 157.

10 J. Davis, "Governing the Family-Run Business," *Harvard Business School Working Knowledge*, September 4, 2001.

11 D. Miller, L. Steier, and I. Le Breton-Miller, "Lost in Time: Intergenerational Succession, Change, and Failure in Family Business," *Journal of Business Venturing*, July 2003, pp. 513–531.

12 Based on P. Kuitenbrouwer, "Simmer . . . Then Raise to a Boil: A Family Stew Over Succession at the McCain Foods Empire Spills into the Courts [1993 review]," *Financial Post Daily*, 10, no. 205A, F 2 1998 anniversary ed., p. 22; P. Newman, "Tales from a Mellower Harrison McCain: Four Years After Winning a Bitter Feud with His Brother, Harrison Acknowledges That 'Strained' Family Relations Still Exist," *Maclean's*, January 19, 1998, p. 50; and "Harrison McCain: King of the Frozen French Fry," *Calgary Herald*, March 28, 2004, p. B6.

13 J. J. Chrisman, J. H. Chua, and L. P. Steier, "An Introduction to Theories of Family Business," *Journal of Business Venturing*, July 2003, pp. 441–448.

14 Based on C. Hymowitz, "Executives in China Need Both Autonomy and Fast Access to Boss," *Wall Street Journal*, May 10, 2005, p. B1.

15 K. Knight, "Matrix Organization: A Review," *Journal of Management Studies*, May 1976, pp. 111–130; and L. R. Burns and D. R. Wholey, "Adoption and Abandonment of Matrix Management Programs: Effects of Organizational Characteristics and Interorganizational Networks," *Academy of Management Journal*, February 1993, pp. 106–138.

16 See, for instance, S. M. Davis and P. R. Lawrence, "Problems of Matrix Organization," *Harvard Business Review*, May–June 1978, pp. 131–142.

17 Based on M. Andrews, "Film Industry Optimistic Amid Hopes That Dollar Stays Low," *Vancouver Sun*, October 31, 2008, p. H2; and M. McCullough, "Virtual Tinseltown," *National Post Business*, June 2000, pp. 46–58.

18 J. R. Galbraith and E. E. Lawler III, "Effective Organizations: Using the New Logic of Organizing," in *Organizing for the Future: The New Logic for Managing Complex Organizations*, ed. J. R. Galbraith, E. E. Lawler III, and Associates (San Francisco: Jossey-Bass, 1993).

19 G. G. Dess, A. M. A. Rasheed, K. J. McLaughlin, and R. Priem, "The New Corporate Architecture," *Academy of Management Executive*, August 1995, pp. 7–18; and C. Y. Baldwin and K. B. Clark, "Managing in an Age of Modularity," *Harvard Business Review*, September–October 1997, pp. 84–93.

20 M. Kaeter, "The Age of the Specialized Generalist," *Training*, December 1993, pp. 48–53.

21 See, for instance, E. A. Gargan, "'Virtual' Companies Leave the Manufacturing to Others," *New York Times*, July 17, 1994, p. F5; D. W. Cravens, S. H. Shipp, and K. S. Cravens, "Reforming the Traditional Organization: The Mandate for Developing Networks," *Business Horizons*, July–August 1994, pp. 19–27; R. T. King Jr., "The Virtual Company," *Wall Street Journal*, November 14, 1994, p. 85; R. E. Miles and C. C. Snow, "The New Network Firm: A Spherical Structure Built on Human Investment Philosophy," *Organizational Dynamics*, Spring 1995, pp. 5–18; G. G. Dess,

A. M. A. Rasheed, K. J. McLaughlin, and R. L. Priem, "The New Corporate Architecture," *Academy of Management Executive*, August 1995, pp. 7–20; D. Pescovitz, "The Company Where Everybody's a Temp," *New York Times Magazine*, June 11, 2000, pp. 94–96; W. F. Cascio, "Managing a Virtual Workplace," *Academy of Management Executive*, August 2000, pp. 81–90; and D. Lyons, "Smart and Smarter," Forbes, March 18, 2002, pp. 40–41.

22 G. G. Dess, A. M. A. Rasheed, K. J. McLaughlin, and R. Priem, "The New Corporate Architecture," *Academy of Management Executive*, August 1995, pp. 7–18.

23 "Why Do Canadian Companies Opt for Cooperative Ventures?" Micro: The Micro-Economic Research Bulletin 4, no. 2 (1997), pp. 3–5.

24 G. G. Dess, A. M. A. Rasheed, K. J. McLaughlin, and R. Priem, "The New Corporate Architecture," *Academy of Management Executive*, August 1995, p. 13. See also P. Lorange and J. Roos, "Why Some Strategic Alliances Succeed and Why Others Fail," *Journal of Business Strategy*, January–February 1991, pp. 25–30; and G. Slowinski, "The Human Touch in Strategic Alliances," *Mergers and Acquisitions*, July–August 1992, pp. 44–47.

25 H. C. Lucas Jr., *The T-Form Organization: Using Technology to Design Organizations for the 21st Century* (San Francisco: Jossey-Bass, 1996).

26 This section is based on D. D. Davis, "Form, Function and Strategy in Boundaryless Organizations," in *The Changing Nature of Work*, ed. A. Howard (San Francisco: Jossey-Bass, 1995), pp. 112–138; P. Roberts, "We Are One Company, No Matter Where We Are. Time and Space Are Irrelevant," *Fast Company*, April–May 1998, pp. 122–128; R. L. Cross, A. Yan, and M. R. Louis, "Boundary Activities in 'Boundaryless' Organizations: A Case Study of a Transformation to a Team-Based Structure," *Human Relations*, June 2000, pp. 841–868; and R. Ashkenas, D. Ulrich, T. Jick, and S. Kerr, *The Boundaryless Organization: Breaking the Chains of Organizational Structure*, rev. ed. (San Francisco: Jossey-Bass, 2002).

27 See J. Lipnack and J. Stamps, *The TeamNet Factor* (Essex Junction, VT: Oliver Wight Publications, 1993); J. R. Wilke, "Computer Links Erode Hierarchical Nature of Workplace Culture," *Wall Street Journal*, December 9, 1993, p. A1; T. A. Stewart, "Managing in a Wired Company," *Fortune*, July 11, 1994, pp. 44–56; and M. Hammer, *The Agenda* (New York: Crown Business, 2001).

28 This analysis is referred to as a contingency approach to organization design. See, for instance, J. M. Pennings, "Structural Contingency Theory: A Reappraisal," in *Research in Organizational Behavior*, vol. 14, ed. B. M. Staw and L. L. Cummings (Greenwich, CT: JAI Press, 1992), pp. 267–309.

29 The strategy-structure thesis was originally proposed in A. D. Chandler Jr., *Strategy and Structure: Chapters in the History of the Industrial Enterprise* (Cambridge, MA: MIT Press, 1962). For an updated analysis, see T. L. Amburgey and T. Dacin, "As the Left Foot Follows the Right? The Dynamics of Strategic and Structural Change," *Academy of Management Journal*, December 1994, pp. 1427–1452.

30 See R. E. Miles and C. C. Snow, *Organizational Strategy, Structure, and Process* (New York: McGraw-Hill, 1978); D. Miller, "The Structural and Environmental Correlates of Business Strategy," *Strategic Management Journal*, January–February 1987, pp. 55–76; D. C. Galunic and K. M. Eisenhardt, "Renewing the Strategy-Structure-Performance Paradigm," in *Research in Organizational Behavior*, vol. 16, ed. B. M. Staw and L. L. Cummings (Greenwich, CT: JAI Press, 1994), pp. 215–255; and I. C. Harris and T. W. Ruefli, "The Strategy/Structure Debate: An Examination of the Performance Implications," *Journal of Management Studies*, June 2000, pp. 587–603.

31 See, for instance, P. M. Blau and R. A. Schoenherr, *The Structure of Organizations* (New York: Basic Books, 1971); D. S. Pugh, "The Aston Program of Research: Retrospect and Prospect," in *Perspectives on Organization Design and Behavior*, ed. A. H. Van de Ven and W. F. Joyce (New York: Wiley, 1981), pp. 135–166; R. Z. Gooding and J. A. Wagner III, "A Meta-Analytic Review of the Relationship between Size and Performance: The Productivity and Efficiency of Organizations and Their Subunits," *Administrative Science Quarterly*, December 1985, pp. 462–481; and A. C. Bluedorn, "Pilgrim's Progress: Trends and Convergence in Research on Organizational Size and Environments," *Journal of Management*, Summer 1993, pp. 163–192.

32 See F. E. Emery and E. Trist, "The Causal Texture of Organizational Environments," *Human Relations*, February 1965, pp. 21–32; P. Lawrence and J. W. Lorsch, *Organization and Environment: Managing Differentiation and Integration* (Boston: Harvard Business School, Division of Research, 1967); M. Yasai-Ardekani, "Structural Adaptations to Environments," *Academy of Management Review*, January 1986, pp. 9–21; and A. C. Bluedorn, "Pilgrim's Progress: Trends and Convergence in Research on Organizational Size and Environments," *Journal of Management*, Summer 1993, pp. 163–192.

33 G. G. Dess and D. W. Beard, "Dimensions of Organizational Task Environments," *Administrative Science Quarterly*, March 1984, pp. 52–73; E. A. Gerloff, N. K. Muir, and W. D. Bodensteiner, "Three Components of Perceived Environmental Uncertainty: An Exploratory Analysis of the Effects of Aggregation," *Journal of Management*, December 1991, pp. 749–768; and O. Shenkar, N. Aranya, and T. Almor, "Construct Dimensions in the Contingency Model: An Analysis Comparing Metric and Non-Metric Multivariate Instruments," *Human Relations*, May 1995, pp. 559–580.

34 Based on "In Focus: Lou Gerstner," *CNN World Business*, July 2, 2004, http://www.cnn.com.

35 W. F. Cascio, "Strategies for Responsible Restructuring," *Academy of Management Executive* 19, no. 4 (2005), pp. 39–50.

36 Adapted from A. J. DuBrin, *Human Relations: A Job Oriented Approach*, 5th ed., 1992. Reprinted with permission of Prentice Hall, Inc., Upper Saddle River, NJ.

37 The source of this exercise is unknown.

38 Based on S. Pulliam, "A Staffer Ordered to Commit Fraud Balked, Then Caved," *Wall Street Journal*, June 23, 2003, p. A1; and E. McClam, "Ex-WorldCom Exec Gets 5-Month Term, House Arrest," *Clarion-Ledger*, August 5, 2005, http://www.clarionledger.com/apps/pbcs.dll/article?AID=/20050805/NEWS0108/50805011/1002/NEWS01 (accessed September 29, 2005).

39 Based on "Major Changes for Vanderbilt Athletics," *New York Times*, September 10, 2003, p. C19; M. Cass, "Vanderbilt Realigns Management," USA Today, September 10, 2003, p. 7C; and "Vanderbilt University Is Not Getting Rid of Sports," *Chronicle of Higher Education*, September 19, 2003, p. A35.

40   Based on P. J. Sauer, "Open-Door Management," *Inc.*, June 2003, p. 44; http://www.techtarget.com/html/ab_index.htm (accessed October 5, 2008) and http://www.techtarget.com/html/job_opps.htm (accessed October 5, 2008).

41   Based on S. P. Robbins and P. L. Hunsaker, *Training in Interpersonal Skills*, 3rd ed. (Upper Saddle River, NJ: Prentice Hall, 2003), pp. 95–98.

Chapter 14

1   Opening vignette based on J. Manyika, "Google's View on the Future of Business: An Interview with CEO Eric Schmidt," *The McKinsey Quarterly*, September 2008; and K. Auletta, "The Search Party," *The New Yorker*, January 14, 2008.

2   J. Lee, "Canadian Businesses Not Good at Adjusting, Survey Says," *Vancouver Sun*, December 14, 1998, pp. C1–2.

3   L. Earl, *An Overview of Organisational and Technological Change in the Private Sector, 1998–2000*, Catalogue no. 88F0006XIE no. 09 (Ottawa: Statistics Canada, June 2002), p. 13.

4   L. Earl, *An Overview of Organisational and Technological Change in the Private Sector, 1998–2000*, Catalogue no. 88F0006XIE no. 09 (Ottawa: Statistics Canada, June 2002), p. 13

5   See, for instance, K. H. Hammonds, "Practical Radicals," *Fast Company*, September 2000, pp. 162–174; and P. C. Judge, "Change Agents," *Fast Company*, November 2000, pp. 216–226.

6   J. Taub, "Harvard Radical," *New York Times Magazine*, August 24, 2003, pp. 28–45 ff.

7   A. Finder, P. D. Healy, and K. Zernike, "President of Harvard Resigns, Ending Stormy 5-Year Tenure," *New York Times*, February 22, 2006, pp. A1, A19.

8   K. Lewin, *Field Theory in Social Science* (New York: Harper and Row, 1951).

9   P. G. Audia, E. A. Locke, and K. G. Smith, "The Paradox of Success: An Archival and a Laboratory Study of Strategic Persistence Following Radical Environmental Change," *Academy of Management Journal*, October 2000, pp. 837–853.

10   J. B. Sorensen, "The Strength of Corporate Culture and the Reliability of Firm Performance," *Administrative Science Quarterly*, March 2002, pp. 70–91.

11   J. Amis, T. Slack, and C. R. Hinings, "The Pace, Sequence, and Linearity of Radical Change," *Academy of Management Journal*, February 2004, pp. 15–39; and E. Autio, H. J. Sapienza, and J. G. Almeida, "Effects of Age at Entry, Knowledge Intensity, and Imitability on International Growth," *Academy of Management Journal*, October 2000, pp. 909–924.

12   J. P. Kotter, "Leading Changes: Why Transformation Efforts Fail," *Harvard Business Review*, March–April 1995, pp. 59–67; and J. P. Kotter, *Leading Change* (Boston: Harvard Business School Press, 1996).

13   See, for example, A. B. Shani and W. A. Pasmore, "Organization Inquiry: Towards a New Model of the Action Research Process," in *Contemporary Organization Development: Current Thinking and Applications*, ed. D. D. Warrick (Glenview, IL: Scott, Foresman,

1985), pp. 438–448; and C. Eden and C. Huxham, "Action Research for the Study of Organizations," in *Handbook of Organization Studies*, ed. S. R. Clegg, C. Hardy, and W. R. Nord (London: Sage, 1996).

14   See, for example, G. R. Bushe, "Advances in Appreciative Inquiry as an Organization Development Intervention," *Organizational Development Journal*, Summer 1999, pp. 61–68; D. L. Cooperrider and D. Whitney, *Collaborating for Change: Appreciative Inquiry* (San Francisco: Berrett-Koehler, 2000); R. Fry, F. Barrett, J. Seiling, and D. Whitney, eds., *Appreciative Inquiry & Organizational Transformation: Reports from the Field* (Westport, CT: Quorum, 2002); J. K. Barge and C. Oliver, "Working with Appreciation in Managerial Practice," *Academy of Management Review*, January 2003, pp. 124–142; and D. van der Haar and D. M. Hosking, "Evaluating Appreciative Inquiry: A Relational Constructionist Perspective," *Human Relations*, August 2004, pp. 1017–1036.

15   R. Rabinovitch, "Training and Development," *Canadian HR Reporter* 17, no. 10 (May 17, 2004), pp. 7–10.

16   D. Sankey, "New Tool Solves Firms' Problems," *Calgary Herald*, July 12, 2003, p. CR1F.

17   G. R. Bushe, "Advances in Appreciative Inquiry as an Organization Development Intervention," *Organization Development Journal* 17, no. 2 (Summer 1999), pp. 61–68.

18   P. G. Audia and S. Brion, "Reluctant to Change: Self-Enhancing Responses to Diverging Performance Measures," *Organizational Behavior and Human Decision Processes* 102 (2007), pp. 255–269.

19   J. P. Kotter and L. A. Schlesinger, "Choosing Strategies for Change," *Harvard Business Review*, July–August 2008, pp. 130–139.

20   A. E. Reichers, J. P. Wanous, and J. T. Austin, "Understanding and Managing Cynicism About Organizational Change," *Academy of Management Executive* 11, 1997, pp. 48–59.

21   R. H. Hall, *Organizations: Structures, Processes, and Outcomes*, 4th ed. (Englewood Cliffs, NJ: Prentice Hall, 1987), p. 29.

22   J. Lee, "Canadian Businesses Not Good at Adjusting, Survey Says," *Vancouver Sun*, December 14, 1998, pp. C1, C2.

23   D. Katz and R. L. Kahn, *The Social Psychology of Organizations*, 2nd ed. (New York: Wiley, 1978), pp. 714–715.

24   J. P. Kotter and L. A. Schlesinger, "Choosing Strategies for Change," *Harvard Business Review*, March–April 1979, pp. 106–114.

25   J. E. Dutton, S. J. Ashford, R. M. O'Neill, and K. A. Lawrence, "Moves That Matter: Issue Selling and Organizational Change," *Academy of Management Journal*, August 2001, pp. 716–736.

26   P. C. Fiss and E. J. Zajac, "The Symbolic Management of Strategic Change: Sensegiving via Framing and Decoupling," *Academy of Management Journal* 49, no. 6 (2006), pp. 1173–1193.

27   Q. N. Huy, "Emotional Balancing of Organizational Continuity and Radical Change: The Contribution of Middle Managers," *Administrative Science Quarterly*, March 2002, pp. 31–69; D. M. Herold, D. B. Fedor, and S. D. Caldwell, "Beyond Change Management: A Multilevel Investigation of Contextual and Personal Influences on Employees' Commitment to Change," *Journal of Applied Psychology* 92, no. 4 (2007), pp. 942–951; and G. B. Cunningham, "The Relationships among Commitment to

Change, Coping with Change, and Turnover Intentions," *European Journal of Work and Organizational Psychology* 15, no. 1 (2006), pp. 29–45.

28   D. B. Fedor, S. Caldwell, and D. M. Herold, "The Effects of Organizational Changes on Employee Commitment: A Multilevel Investigation," *Personnel Psychology* 59, 2006, pp. 1–29.

29   S. Oreg, "Personality, Context, and Resistance to Organizational Change," *European Journal of Work and Organizational Psychology* 15, no. 1 (2006), pp. 73–101.

30   J. A. LePine, J. A. Colquitt, and A. Erez, "Adaptability to Changing Task Contexts: Effects of General Cognitive Ability, Conscientiousness, and Openness to Experience," *Personnel Psychology*, Fall, 2000, pp. 563–593; T. A. Judge, C. J. Thoresen, V. Pucik, and T. M. Welbourne, "Managerial Coping with Organizational Change: A Dispositional Perspective," *Journal of Applied Psychology*, February 1999, pp. 107–122; and S. Oreg, "Resistance to Change: Developing an Individual Differences Measure," *Journal of Applied Psychology*, August 2003, pp. 680–693.

31   Paragraph based on M. Johne, "Wanted: A Few Good Egocentric, Self-Serving Risk-Takers," *Globe and Mail*, May 27, 2002, p. C1.

32   See J. Pfeffer, *Managing with Power: Politics and Influence in Organizations* (Boston: Harvard Business School Press, 1992), pp. 7 and 318–320; and D. Knights and D. McCabe, "When 'Life Is but a Dream': Obliterating Politics through Business Process Reengineering?" *Human Relations*, June 1998, pp. 761–798.

33   See, for instance, W. Ocasio, "Political Dynamics and the Circulation of Power: CEO Succession in U.S. Industrial Corporations, 1960–1990," *Administrative Science Quarterly*, June 1994, pp. 285–312.

34   Vignette based on S. Shankland, "Google Keeps Its One-Trick Pony Healthy," *cnet.com*, January 22, 2009; and K. Auletta, "The Search Party," *The New Yorker*, January 14, 2008.

35   J. Manyika, "Google's View on the Future of Business: An Interview with CEO Eric Schmidt," *The McKinsey Quarterly*, September 2008.

36   See, for instance, A. Van de Ven, "Central Problems in the Management of Innovation," *Management Science* 32, 1986, 590–607; and R. M. Kanter, "When a Thousand Flowers Bloom: Structural, Collective and Social Conditions for Innovation in Organizations," in *Research in Organizational Behavior*, vol. 10, ed. B. M. Staw and L. L. Cummings (Greenwich, CT: JAI Press, 1988), pp. 169–211.

37   F. Damanpour, "Organizational Innovation: A Meta-Analysis of Effects of Determinants and Moderators," *Academy of Management Journal*, September 1991, p. 557.

38   F. Damanpour, "Organizational Innovation: A Meta-Analysis of Effects of Determinants and Moderators," *Academy of Management Journal*, September 1991, pp. 555–590.

39   See also P. R. Monge, M. D. Cozzens, and N. S. Contractor, "Communication and Motivational Predictors of the Dynamics of Organizational Innovation," *Organization Science*, May 1992, pp. 250–274.

40   Discussion of 3M is based on K. Labich, "The Innovators," *Fortune*, June 6, 1988, p. 49; R. Mitchell, "Masters of Innovation," *BusinessWeek*, April 10, 1989, p. 58; K. Kelly, "The Drought Is

Over at 3M," *BusinessWeek*, November 7, 1994, pp. 140–141; T. A. Stewart, "3M Fights Back," *Fortune*, February 5, 1996, pp. 94–99; and T. D. Schellhardt, "David in Goliath," *Wall Street Journal*, May 23, 1996, p. R14.

41   J. M. Howell and C. A. Higgins, "Champions of Change," *Business Quarterly*, Spring 1990, pp. 31–32; and D. L. Day, "Raising Radicals: Different Processes for Championing Innovative Corporate Ventures," *Organization Science*, May 1994, pp. 148–172.

42   J. M. Howell and C. A. Higgins, "Champions of Change," *Business Quarterly*, Spring 1990, pp. 31–32.

43   See, for example, the special edition on organizational learning in *Organizational Dynamics*, Autumn 1998; P. Senge, *The Dance of Change: The Challenges to Sustaining Momentum in Learning Organizations* (New York: Doubleday/Currency, 1999); A. M. Webber, "Will Companies Ever Learn?" *Fast Company*, October 2000, pp. 275–282; R. Snell, "Moral Foundations of the Learning Organization," *Human Relations*, March 2001, pp. 319–342; and M. M. Brown and J. L. Brudney, "Learning Organizations in the Public Sector? A Study of Police Agencies Employing Information and Technology to Advance Knowledge," *Public Administration Review*, January–February 2003, pp. 30–43.

44   D. H. Kim, "The Link between Individual and Organizational Learning," *Sloan Management Review*, Fall 1993, p. 37.

45   C. Argyris and D. A. Schon, *Organizational Learning* (Reading, MA: Addison-Wesley, 1978).

46   B. Dumaine, "Mr. Learning Organization," *Fortune*, October 17, 1994, p. 148.

47   B. Dumaine, "Mr. Learning Organization," *Fortune*, October 17, 1994, p. 154.

48   See S. Shane, S. Venkataraman, and I. MacMillan, "Cultural Differences in Innovation Championing Strategies," *Journal of Management* 21, no. 5 (1995), pp. 931–952.

49   For contrasting views on episodic and continuous change, see K. E. Weick and R. E. Quinn, "Organizational Change and Development," in *Annual Review of Psychology*, vol. 50, ed. J. T. Spence, J. M. Darley, and D. J. Foss (Palo Alto, CA: Annual Reviews, 1999), pp. 361–386.

50   This perspective is based on P. B. Vaill, *Managing as a Performing Art: New Ideas for a World of Chaotic Change* (San Francisco: Jossey-Bass, 1989).

51   P. B. Vaill, *Managing as a Performing Art: New Ideas for a World of Chaotic Change* (San Francisco: Jossey-Bass, 1989), pp. 8–9. Reproduced with permission of the publisher. All rights reserved.

52   Adapted from J. E. Barbuto Jr., "Power and the Changing Environment," *Journal of Management Education*, April 2000, pp. 288–296.

53   Based on D. Ulrich, S. Kerr, and R. Ashkenas, *The GE Work-Out* (New York: McGraw-Hill, 2002).

54   R. Pascale, M. Millemann, and L. Gioja, "Changing the Way We Change," *Harvard Business Review*, November–December 1997, pp. 127–139. The actual names of the points based on the After Action Review are taken from the article, although the summaries are provided by the authors of this textbook.

Cases

1   A. Bourdeau, "Retail Training Day," *Strategy*, November 2005, p. 16; M. Conlin, "Smashing the Clock," *BusinessWeek*, December 11, 2006, p. 60; R. J. Grossman, "Remodeling HR at Home Depot," *HR Magazine*, November 2008, pp. 67–72; P. J. Kiger, "Flexibility to the Fullest," *Workforce Management*, September 25, 2006, pp. 1–5; K. Lunau, "Justify Your Existence," *Gazette* (Montreal), November 18, 2006, p. B2; J. Thottam, "Reworking Work," *Time*, July 25, 2005, pp. 50–55; and "Best Buy: How to Break Out of Commodity Hell," *BusinessWeek*, March 27, 2006, p. 76.

2   "Zoo Mulls Qualities Sought in Next Director," *toledoblade.com*, September 9, 2005, http://toledoblade.com (accessed January 17, 2006); S. Eder, "Zoo Task Force Sets 100-Day Target for Submitting Investigation Report," *toledoblade.com*, March 25, 2005, http://toledoblade.com (accessed January 17, 2006); S. Eder, "Experience with Animals Lacking for Operations Chief," *toledoblade.com*, March 13, 2005, http:// toledoblade.com (accessed January 17, 2006); S. Eder, "Reichard Held in High Esteem by Fellow Zoo Veterinarians," *toledoblade.com*, March 9, 2005, http:// toledoblade.com (accessed January 17, 2006); M Greenwell, "Zoo Sees New Job As Way to Fix Problems," *toledoblade.com*, June 23, 2005, http://toledoblade.com (accessed January 17, 2006); J. Laidman, "Employee Relations Top Zoo Leaders' List," *toledoblade.com*, May 22, 2005, http://toledoblade.com (accessed January 17, 2006); J. Laidman, "Embattled Zoo Leaders Quit," *toledoblade.com*, May 5, 2005, http://toledoblade.com (accessed January 17, 2006); J. Laidman, "Clash of Philosophies, Loss of Animals Triggered Turmoil," *toledoblade.com*, March 13, 2005, http://toledoblade.com (accessed January 17, 2006); J. Laidman, "Fired Zoo Veterinarian's File Mostly Positive, with a Few Concerns," *toledoblade.com*, March 9, 2005, http://toledoblade. com (accessed January 17, 2006); J. Laidman, "Toledo Zoo Veterinarian Blames Firing on His Warnings to USDA," *toledoblade.com*, March 8, 2005, http://toledoblade.com (accessed January 17, 2006); J. Laidman, "Feds Probe 2 Animal Deaths at Toledo Zoo," *toledoblade.com*, February 24, 2004, http:// toledoblade.com (accessed January 17, 2006); J. Laidman and T. Vezner, "Staff Offers Criticism, Praise in Zoo Survey," *toledoblade.com*, May 27, 2005, http://toledoblade.com (accessed January 17, 2006); J. Laidman and T. Vezner, "Vet's Deal Isn't First to Silence Ex-Official," *toledoblade.com*, May 2, 2005, http:// toledoblade.com (accessed January 17, 2006); J. Laidman and T. Vezner, "Internal Battles Plunge Zoo into a Caldron of Discontent," *toledoblade.com*, March 20, 2005, http://toledoblade. com (accessed January 17, 2006); S. H. Staelin, "Zoo Board Tackles Challenges," *toledoblade.com*, April 16, 2005, http://toledoblade. com (accessed January 17, 2006); T. Vezner, "Zoo Names Chief Veterinarian, Ignoring Task Force's Proposal," *toledoblade.com*, December 17, 2005, http://toledoblade.com (accessed January 17, 2006); T. Vezner, "Consultant Hired to Oversee Zoo Administration," *toledoblade.com*, July 20, 2005, http://toledoblade. com (accessed January 17, 2006); T. Vezner, "Zoo's Ex-Vet on Hand for Report," *toledoblade.com*, July 9, 2005, http://toledoblade. com (accessed January 17, 2006); T. Vezner, "Zoo Task Force Report Demands Broad Changes," *toledoblade.com*, July 7, 2005, http://toledoblade.com (accessed January 17, 2006); T. Vezner and J. Laidman, "Flurry of Changes Leaves Workers Reeling," *toledoblade.com*, May 6, 2005, http://toledoblade.com (accessed January 17, 2006); T. Vezner, "Settlement Bars Zoo Vet from Speaking to Panel," *toledoblade.com*, May 1, 2005, http:// toledoblade.com (accessed January 17, 2006); T. Vezner, "Zoo Task Force's Questions for Dennler Hit Time Limit," *toledoblade.com*, April 1, 2005, http://toledoblade.com (accessed January 17, 2006); T. Vezner, "Inquiry in 2004 Disclosed Problems," *toledoblade.com*, March 27, 2005, http://toledoblade. com (accessed January 17, 2006); Lucas County Commissioners Special Citizens Task Force for the Zoo, Final Report, July 8, 2005, http://www.co.lucas.oh.us/ commissioners/Final_Report_Zoo_ Task_Force.pdf (accessed January 17, 2006); http://www. toledozoo.org (accessed January 17, 2006); and http://www. doctortim.org (accessed January 17, 2006).

GLOSSARY/SUBJECT INDEX

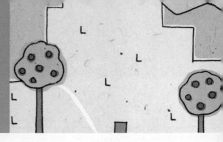

The page on which the key term is defined is printed in boldface.

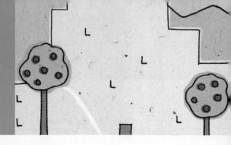

NAME AND ORGANIZATION INDEX

LIST OF CANADIAN COMPANIES

Prince Edward Island

Durabelt (Montague), 309

Quebec

Advantech AMT (Dorval), 550

Air Canada (Montreal), 5, 376

Alcoa-Aluminerie Lauralco (Deschambault),
 216

Bank of Montreal (Montreal), 55, 173, 197,
 498

Bell Canada (Montreal), 429

Bombardier (Montreal), 64, 189, 503

Clairol Canada (Montreal), 215

Entourage Technology Solutions (Montreal),
 165

Ericsson Canada (Montreal), 125

Hydro-Québec (Montreal), 175, 506

Molson Coors Brewing Company (Montreal),
 105, 173, 175, 514

National Bank Financial (Montreal), 95

National Bank of Canada (Montreal), 177

Ouimet-Cordon Bleu Foods (Montreal), 493,
 496, 497

Quebecor (Montreal), 165

SICO Paints (Longueil), 196

Vidéotron (Montreal), 250

Saskatchewan

First Nations Bank of Canada (Saskatoon), 95

Hitachi Canadian Industries (Saskatoon), 16

Saskatchewan Government Insurance (SGI)
 (Regina), 11

SaskCentral (Regina), 6

Other

Amazon.ca (headquartered in Seattle, WA),
 521

PHOTO CREDITS

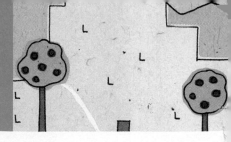